STRATEGIC MANAGEMENT

Kent Series in Management

Strategic Management: Concepts and Cases
Barnett/Wilsted

The Human Relations of Organizations
Berkman/Neider

Personnel: The Management of Human Resources, Fourth Edition
Crane

Business Research for Decision Making, Second Edition
Davis/Cosenza

Supervision: A Situational Approach
Kirkpatrick

Understanding Organizational Behavior, Second Edition
Klein/Ritti

Environment of International Business, Second Edition
Kolde

Applications in Personnel/Human Resource Management: Cases, Exercises, and Skill Builders
Nkomo/Fottler/McAfee

Introduction to Management, Second Edition
Plunkett/Attner

Personnel/Human Resource Management: Environments and Functions
Scarpello/Ledvinka

The Changing Environment of Business, Third Edition
Starling

Issues in Business and Society: Capitalism and Public Purpose
Starling/Baskin

Managing Effective Organizations: An Introduction
Steers/Ungson/Mowday

STRATEGIC MANAGEMENT
Concepts and Cases

John H. Barnett

University of New Hampshire

William D. Wilsted

University of Colorado

PWS-KENT PUBLISHING COMPANY
Boston

PWS–KENT
Publishing Company

Editor: Rolf Janke
Production Editor: Leslie Baker
Interior Designer: Outside Design
Cover Designer: Sally Bindari
Manufacturing Coordinator: Marcia A. Locke

© 1988 by PWS-KENT Publishing Company. All rights reserved. No part of
this book may be reproduced, stored in a retrieval system, or transcribed, in
any form or by any means, electronic, mechanical, photocopying, recording, or
otherwise, without the prior written permission of the publisher, PWS-KENT
Publishing Company, 20 Park Plaza, Boston, Massachusetts 02116.

PWS-KENT Publishing Company is a division of Wadsworth, Inc.

Printed in the United States of America
1 2 3 4 5 6 7 8 9 — 92 91 90 89 88

Library of Congress Cataloging-in-Publication Data

Barnett, John Hayes.
  Strategic management.

  Includes bibliographies and index.
  1. Strategic planning.   2. Strategic planning — Case
studies.   I. Wilsted, William D.   II. Title.
HD30.28.B368   1988   658.4′012   87–25734
ISBN 0-534-87176-3

for Vasilka and Karen

CONTENTS

Part I   **CONCEPTS IN STRATEGIC MANAGEMENT   1**

Chapter 1   **The Evolution of Strategic Management   3**

The Working Concept   3
Working Concept 1: Stages of Corporate Development   *4*
Stages of Corporate Development and Strategic Management   8
    Business Policy   8 / Strategic Planning   8 / Strategic Management   8
Working Concept 2: Levels of Strategy   *9*
Working Concept 3: Strategic Business Units   *11*
Strategy Research   14
Business History   14
Executive Comments   16
Key Terms   17
Bibliography   17

Chapter 2   **Strategic Management and the Strategic Manager   19**

Working Concept 4: The Strategic Manager   *19*
Working Concept 5: Military and Holistic Strategic Managers   *20*
Working Concept 6: Mintzberg's Roles and Styles   *23*
Strategic Management   24
    The Entrepreneurial Manager   24 / The Adaptive Manager   24 / The Planning
    Manager   25
Working Concept 7: Brunswik Lens and Perception   *25*
Strategy and the Strategist: A Summary   27
Strategy Research and the Strategic Manager   27
Executive Comments   29
Key Terms   29
Bibliography   29
Appendixes: A: Accounting for Nonaccountants   31 / B: Strategic Financial
Analysis   32 / C: University of New Hampshire Bookstore Case   34 / D: Bookstore Case
Analysis   45 / E: The Case Method   47

Chapter 3   **Defining Purpose   53**

Personal Values   54
Organizational Priorities   56

Working Concept 8: Mintzberg's Organizational Power *56*
Corporate Culture *58*
Social Goals *59*
Strategic Mission *61*
Working Concept 9: Strategic Analysis *61*
Levels of Strategy and Enterprise Mission *62*
Research and Mission *65*
Executive Comments *66*
Key Terms *66*
Bibliography *67*
Appendix: The Nonprofit and Stages of Development *68*

Chapter 4	**Determining Distinctive Competence** **71**

Resources Defined *71*
    Tangible Resources *71* / *Intangible Resources* *72*
Strengths and Weaknesses *73*
    Combining Related Symptoms *77* / *Product Life Cycle and Internal Factors* *80*
Working Concept 10: Product Life Cycle *78*
Defining Distinctive Competence *83*
    Market Needs and Comparative Advantage *83* / *Levels of Strategy* *85*
Significant Research *86*
Executive Comments *88*
Key Terms *88*
Bibliography *89*
Appendix: The Small Business *90*

Chapter 5	**Identifying Opportunities and Threats** **93**

External Environment Defined *93*
    Markets *93* / *Competition* *96* / *Technology* *96* / *Society* *97* /
    Government *97* / *The Changing External Environment* *99*
Strategic Analysis and Strategic Signals *101*
    Identifying Strategic Signals *101* / *Interpreting Strategic Signals* *101* / *Market
    Signals* *101* / *Competitive Signals* *106* / *Technology Signals* *108* / *Government
    Signals* *109* / *Social Signals* *113* / *Summarizing Strategic Signals — A Swiss
    Example* *116*
Working Concept 11: Customer Needs Analysis *103*
Working Concept 12: Porter's Determinants of Competition *106*
Working Concept 13: Technological Innovation *109*
Working Concept 14: Stakeholder Analysis *112*
Working Concept 15: The Precursor *115*
Strategy Research and the External Environment *118*
Executive Comments *122*
Key Terms *122*
Bibliography *122*
Appendix: The International Business Environment *124*

Chapter 6   **Formulating Strategy   136**

The Strategic Decision Process   136
Working Concept 16: The Strategic Decision Process   *137*
Decision Levels   139
    Functional Decisions   139   /   Business Decisions   139   /   Corporate
    Decisions   139
Working Concept 17: Levels of Strategy and the Decision Process   *140*
Strategic Management Tools   140
    Product Life Cycle   141   /   Porter's Determinants of Competition   141
Working Concept 18: Product Portfolios   *142*
Working Concept 19: Product Life Cycle–Competition Matrix   *144*
Working Concept 20: Directional Policy Matrix   *144*
Working Concept 21: Industry Analysis   *148*
Working Concept 22: Strategic Issue Analysis   *150*
Examples of Strategy Formulation   151
    Porter's Generic Strategies   151   /   Situational Strategy   152   /   Other
    Strategies   155
Evaluating Strategy   160
    Competitive Response Analysis   160   /   Risk   162   /   Synergy   163   /
    Consistency   164   /   Workability   164
An Overview of Strategy Formulation   164
Strategy Formulation Research   166
Executive Comments   169
Key Terms   169
Bibliography   170

Chapter 7   **Implementing Strategy   174**

No Right Answer   174
Implementation Defined   175
Implementation Illustrated   175
Structure and Systems Components   176
    Administrative Systems   176   /   Information Systems   177   /   Compensation and
    Measurement Systems   179
Selection Criteria   185
    Distinctive Competence   185   /   Congruence   186
Working Concept 23: Implementation Selection Model   *186*
Difficulties in Implementing Strategy   187
Implementation and Strategic Levels   188
An Implementation Illustration   188
    Corporate Strategy   189   /   Business Strategy   189   /   Functional Strategy   190
Strategy Implementation Research   190
Executive Comments   193
Key Terms   194
Bibliography   194
Appendix: Personal Strategy   197

Part II	**CASES IN STRATEGIC MANAGEMENT 205**	

Case 1   **Armbrusters at Blackstone   207**
Bill Armbruster reviews the results of the first two years of operating a restaurant in Blackstone, Virginia.

Case 2   **Magna International, Inc.   216**
Frank Stronach discusses his corporate culture of autonomy, employee ownership, and small-is-beautiful as he creates one of the largest corporations in North America.

Case 3   **American Skate Corporation   237**
An Ontario roller skate manufacturer considers whether or not to ride the roller skating boom into the American market by opening a plant in New England.

Case 4   **Mary Kay Cosmetics, Inc.   248**
Mary Kay, her son Richard, and other company strategists review the company's success and future growth opportunities.

Case 5   **The Grand Theatre Company   275**
The board of the non-profit Theatre London considers a proposal to hire Robin Phillips, who says of himself, "there is no better director."

Case 6   **The Nigel Thomas Center   287**
A new director of this non-profit agency tries to define the role of a director in strategic planning, board selection, performance measurement, staff operations, fund raising, and community relations.

Case 7   **Wall Drug Store, 1983   299**
The Hustead family continues strategic expansion of "the largest drugstore in the world — the only drugstore with a church in it" in Wall, South Dakota.

Case 8   **Dysys, Inc.   316**
The owners of a small computer-products-and-services company plan future strategy for their young, struggling venture.

Case 9   **Community National Bank of Crescent City   331**
Having recently purchased control of this Rocky Mountain bank, the president studies short-term objectives and the bank's long-term strategy.

Case 10   **Celestial Seasonings, Inc.   344**
The founder-president, having "made a million doing his own thing," analyzes the relationship among the three objectives of this Boulder, Colorado manufacturer of herb tea — financial reward, customer health, and growth.

Case 11   **C & C Yachts   361**
The North American yacht-designing-and-manufacturing enterprise studies the possibility of an expansion to Europe.

Case 12   **Apple Computer, Inc.   378**
The strategists of this entrepreneurial firm study new product opportunities and the plans and programs of competition.

Case 13 **Manville Corporation (1987) 394**

The plans for bankruptcy reorganization are reviewed against the backdrop of asbestosis lawsuits.

Case 14 **Barcelona Traction, Light and Power Company, Limited 411**

The international managers of this utility face a takeover threat from a Spaniard described as "a man possessed."

Case 15 **Polaroid and South Africa: The Management of Surprise 425**

A study team returns from South Africa to formulate strategy in the face of apartheid, employee "revolution," and the liberal philosophy of Polaroid's founder.

Case 16 **Bill Keane 439**

A multinational executive confronts a series of ethical challenges.

Case 17 **The Lincoln Electric Company, 1983**

Two decades after the death of the founder, the world's largest manufacturer of welding machines evaluates its incentive management plan in light of both employee comments and its strategic performance.

Case 18 **Federal Express Corporation 467**

Fred Smith and Federal Express management study their product portfolio, including the struggling Zapmail, in light of the evolving industry and competitive structure.

Case 19 **Nucor Corporation 495**

Nucor's chairman considers strategic alternatives for "the steel company that makes money."

Case 20 **VLSI Technology, Inc. 527**

The company formulates technology and competitive strategy in the fast-paced industry of computer chips.

Case 21 **New Hampshire Ball Bearings, Inc. 550**

The death-bed independence wishes of the company's founder ring in the ears of the founder's protégé as he considers a takeover offer from the company's fierce competitor, a Japanese firm that has very successfully invaded the U.S. ball bearing market.

Case 22 **Springfield Marine Bank 580**

The financial executive officer considers future strategy and structure in light of Illinois legislation allowing multibank holding companies.

Case 23 **Specialty Products Division — Continental Packaging Company 600**

Two general managers try to implement division strategies in an environment of significant corporate pressure.

Case 24 **American Express Company 627**

Executives pursue growth through a series of acquisitions and attendant implementation challenges.

Case 25 **Ashland Oil, Inc. 651**

The petroleum company's major acquisitions in the insurance and engineering services field are divested and new strategic plans that include strengthening finances and reducing costs in oil refining are begun.

Case 26   **The Alcoholic Beverage Industry   678**
*Consumer tastes, market segments, industry issues, company profiles, and wine, spirits,
and beer production and economics comprise this industry note.*

Case 27   **Heublein, Inc.   700**
*Heublein's president considers the acquisition of the Midwestern brewer Hamm's, as Heublein
continues to grow on the strength of its star product, Smirnoff vodka.*

Case 28   **The Ontario Wine Industry   728**
*The structure, products, competitors, and economics of the wine industry of Ontario provide
an environmental introduction to Inniskillin (Case 29 below).*

Case 29   **Inniskillin Wines Incorporated   747**
Strategic alternatives including selling and expanding face two young Ontario wine makers.

Case 30   **Coca-Cola Wine Spectrum   757**
*The Coca-Cola manager assigned to the newly formed wine division evaluates strategy and
the implementation of a comparison advertising campaign.*

Case 31   **Joseph E. Seagram & Sons, Limited   780**
*Charles Bronfman reviews Canadian performance in light of corporate culture and changes
in the American and Canadian markets.*

Case 32   **The Seagram Company Ltd.   814**
*A wine-division executive considers both personal future strategy and company plans in
light of Edgar Bronfman's acquisition of the Wine Spectrum from Coca-Cola and the wine
strategy planned by Mary Cunningham.*

Case 33   **Joseph Schlitz Brewing Company   837**
*The CEO plans strategy during the fierce Budweiser-Miller competition that has seen Schlitz,
once number one, slip to fourth place in the U.S.*

Case 34   **The Adolph Coors Company   872**
*The Budweiser-Miller competition affects the "Rocky Mountain mystique" and production-
based strategy of Coors and causes the Coors family to consider competing on a national
scale.*

Case 35   **Pabst Brewing Company   893**
*Hostile takeover battles, buying Olympia, trying to buy Schlitz, and being bought and sold
by Heileman leaves Pabst and its surviving strategist planning for an uncertain future.*

Case 36   **Patrick the Porter   908**
Resort-hotel management must decide on what to do with a heavy drinker.

Case 37   **Bill B.   912**
*A local A.A. representative reviews options in the face of shifting membership patterns,
dual addiction, and an increasing number of professional treatment centers.*

Index   925

PREFACE

This preface presents the rationale, structure, and content of Barnett and Wilsted's *Strategic Management*. This book is composed of text and cases that describe the art of strategic management and that allow you to apply your increasing skill at this art to a variety of specific examples of strategic management.

The text stresses both business examples of strategic management concepts and the findings and conclusions of strategic research. First, we cite many companies and quote numerous executives in our discussion of the art of strategy. Secondly, research and academic findings make up a part of each chapter.

In addition, models and theories of strategy comprise twenty-three working concepts. The text highlights these twenty-three working concepts, or tools of strategic management, including Porter's model of the determinants of competition, stages of development models, analytical matrices, and criteria for the selection of strategic implementation alternatives. Students can apply these working concepts to the cases.

Each chapter concludes with a description of current research efforts in, and corporate executives' comments about, topics included in the chapter.

The Chapters

The first chapter describes the evolution of strategic management, and introduces the working concept of the stages of corporate development as a dual foundation — supporting both the topic of strategic management, which evolves from strategic planning and the role of the general manager, and the concept of levels of strategy, functional (or department), business, and corporate.

The second chapter introduces the working concept of the strategic manager and the related strategic topics of managerial roles, responsibilities, and perceptions. Appendixes include financial tools for strategic analysis, a general approach to preparing cases, a sample case, and an illustrative analysis of that case.

The third chapter shows how the strategist defines purpose or mission. Personal values, organizational priorities, and social goals make up purpose, and these three components lead to a discussion of both the stages of development and levels of strategy and their relationship to purpose, organizational power, corporate culture, and social responsibility. An appendix shows how the nonprofit agency's mission differs from the for-profit enterprise, and how purpose evolves over stages of nonprofit development.

The fourth chapter addresses the problem of determining the distinctive competence of the enterprise. The text shows the relationship between this distinctive competence and (1) the firm's strengths and weaknesses, (2) the product life cycle, (3) market needs, (4) comparative advantage and competition, and (5) the levels of strategy. The appendix to Chapter four focuses on the small business.

The fifth chapter tells how the strategist must analyze the external environment to identify opportunities and threats in markets, competition, technology, government, and society. The text presents specific tools of analysis, including customer needs analysis, Porter's model of competition, the stages of technological innovation, stakeholders, and the precursor society. An appendix studies international business.

Chapter six discusses the formulation of strategy. The manager makes functional, business, and strategic corporate decisions based upon an understanding and utilization of topics such as preemptive competitive opportunities, product portfolio management and matrices analyses, generic and situational strategies including the new business, diversification, exit, and integration. Analysis of competitive response, risk, synergy, consistency, and workability help the strategist to evaluate strategy.

The seventh and final chapter presents a range of strategic implementation alternatives, such as organizational structure, information, compensation, and measurement systems. Distinctive competence and congruence help the manager select from among these alternatives, and the chapter shows how the manager implements strategy at the corporate, business, and functional levels. An appendix gives the student a chance to apply these strategic concepts to the student's personal strategy.

The Cases

The authors wrote twelve of the thirty-seven cases. Current significant managerial dilemmas such as disinvestment in South Africa, Japanese competition, and hostile takeovers combine with strategic management problems in these authored cases.

Contributed cases include some favorites — Heublein, Wall Drug, Manville, and Lincoln Electric — as well as those concerned with high-technology, small businesses, manufacturing and service industries, and a few nonprofit enterprises. Furthermore, the international business environment (including Canada, European markets, South Africa, and Spain) makes up a significant part of eleven cases.

Finally, ten cases cover issues in one industry over a twenty year period. This industry, alcoholic beverages, is experiencing significant changes. These changes, which are an important aspect of the cases, include the increasing popularity of wine, the decreasing market share for traditional "brown" whiskeys, anti-alcohol trends, and the marketing and competitive revolution in the beer industry. The student takes a look at the industry both over time and from different managerial perspectives — such as the production view of Coors, the "number one" view of Seagram, the marketing focus of Heublein, the survival perspective of Schlitz, and the takeover combatants at Pabst. Furthermore, cases that address the abuse of alcohol raise ethical and moral questions about the industry.

In many of the cases the focus is on personal values and in particular, on ethics. Ethics is central both to the text discussion of the executive householder and to many cases, most notably Manville, Polaroid and South Africa, Bill Keane, Patrick the Porter, and Bill B. (Alcoholics Anonymous).

Materials accompanying this text include the videotape program Strategic Insights to support some of the cases in this book and two data discs that contain five computer programs that utilize 1-2-3® from Lotus® to study specific strategic problems and to extract strategic information from a ten-year, industry-wide data base.

Acknowledgments First in our acknowledgments must be Carol Hebbard. Her smiling support in face of illegible notes and impossible deadlines as well as her knowledge of the ins and outs of courier, duplication, and parking systems are appreciated. In addition, we are fortunate to have benefited from the comments and criticisms of many excellent reviewers:

William E. Burr
University of Oregon

Robert W. Carney
Georgia Institute of Technology

Edward S. Dyl
University of Wyoming

David P. Gustafson
University of Missouri, St. Louis

Frederick C. Haas
Virginia Commonwealth University

William D. Kane, Jr.
Western Carolina University

Michael D. Lucas
Western Illinois University

Richard R. Merner
University of Delaware

Michael C. White
Louisiana State University

We would like to acknowledge the important case contributions of

Sexton Adams, North Texas State University; Larry Agranove, Wilfrid Laurier University; Larry Alexander, Virginia Polytechnic Institute and State University; John Barnett, University of New Hampshire; Edgar Barrett, Southern Methodist University; Paul Beamish, University of Western Ontario; Norman Berg, Harvard University; Robert Blunden, Dalhousie University; William Boulton, University of Georgia; William Davidson, University of Virginia; Philip Fisher, University of South Dakota; Jonathan Foster, London School of Economics; Joseph Fry, University of Western Ontario; Adelaide Griffin, Texas Woman's University; Frederick Haas, Virginia Commonwealth University; Charles Hinkle, University of Colorado; John Hogan, Sam Houston State University; Phyllis Holland, Georgia State University; Robert Johnson, University of South Dakota; Peter Killing, University of Western Ontario; Mark Kroll, University of Texas at Tyler; John Lymberopoulos, University of Colorado; Charles Meiburg, University of Virginia; Jeffrey Miner, Virginia Polytechnic Institute and State University; Robert Palmer, University of Massachusetts; Philip Rosson, Dalhousie University; Dean Schroeder, University of Massachusetts; Arthur Sharplin, McNeese State University; Neil Snyder, University of Virginia; Esther Stineman, Yale University; Charles Stubbart, University of Massachusetts; James Taylor, University of South Dakota; Robert Taylor, United States Air Force Academy; William Wilsted, University of Colorado.

We also want to thank the North American Case Research Association, at whose 1986 and 1987 meeting two of the text cases were reviewed.

Finally we would like to thank the editorial staff at PWS-KENT Publishing Co., ably led by Rolf Janke.

John Barnett
William Wilsted

PART I

CONCEPTS IN
STRATEGIC MANAGEMENT

THE EVOLUTION OF STRATEGIC MANAGEMENT

Management is the new technology that is making the American economy into an entrepreneurial economy.

Peter F. Drucker, *Innovation and Entrepreneurship*

Chapter 1 traces the evolution of strategic management and presents the plan of this book. It begins with Working Concept 1, "Stages of Corporate Development," a concept from the field of strategic management. Working Concept 1 relates the three stages of corporate development to the evolution of strategic management, from (1) business policy to (2) strategic planning to (3) strategic management. The chapter then presents a schematic of the strategic decision process, relating that process both to strategic management and to the plan of this book. This chapter then presents working concepts covering levels of strategy and the strategic business unit. As in all chapters, Chapter 1 contains insights into current research in strategic management; and "Executive Comments," quotes from today's top managers, chief executives, and a broad spectrum of observers.

THE WORKING CONCEPT

This text illustrates the topic of strategic management through a series of "Working Concepts," beginning with stages of corporate development and levels of strategy, and including industry and competitive analysis, organizational structure and power, and directional policy matrix. These Working Concepts can be used in the same way that a builder uses working drawings. Working drawings present detailed parts of the overall building project — a foundation, a door, or a roof. Similarly, these Working Concepts present in detail one aspect of the overall field of strategic management. The twenty-three Working Concepts in this book model the real world of strategic management; they are your tools for practicing strategic management, just as a builder's working drawings are tools aiding in the construction of a building.

These Working Concepts may deal with specific areas of the strategic decision, such as product ("Product Life Cycle," #10; "Product Portfolios," #18), competition ("Porter's Determinants of Competition," #12), the customer ("Customer Needs Analysis," #11), technology ("Technological Innovation," #13), or combinations of these areas ("Product Life Cycle — Competition Matrix," #19). Other Working Concepts describe specific aspects of strategic management ("Strategic Business Units," #3; "The Strategic Manager," #4; "Military and Holistic Strategic Managers," #5; "Mintzberg's Roles and Styles," #6; "Brunswik Lens and Perception," #7; and "Mintzberg's Organizational Power," #8).

Some Working Concepts are analytical tools ("Stages of Corporate Development," #1; "Levels of Strategy," #2; "Strategic Analysis," #9; "Stakeholder Analysis," #14; "The Precursor," #15; "Industry Analysis," #21; and "Strategic Issue Analysis," #22). Finally, some Working Concepts are decision-making models ("Strategic Decision Process," #16; "Levels of Strategy and Strategic Decision Process," #17; "Directional Policy Matrix," #20; and "Implementation Selection Model," #23).

WORKING CONCEPT 1

STAGES OF CORPORATE DEVELOPMENT

As business analysts — most especially Chandler, author of *Strategy and Structure: Chapters in the History of the American Industrial Enterprise* (1962) — looked at the business enterprise over many years, they identified a general pattern of development. This pattern, the *stages of corporate development,* became a part of the theory of business policy and corporate strategy, as described initially in the business policy course by Harvard Professors Christensen and Scott, and as elaborated by Slater (1970).

The most frequently encountered version of the model identifies three stages of corporate development: the entrepreneurial (Stage One), the functional management (Stage Two), and the decentralized (Stage Three) corporations.

STAGE ONE

The Stage One corporation is an entrepreneurial organization. One person dominates the firm; this entrepreneurial owner-manager performs a wide range of duties and participates in all aspects of the business.

The strategic purpose of the business is identical with the personal objective of the entrepreneur. The business centers on one or more of the entrepreneur's skills and interests, which frequently are technical engineering or inventive abilities.

The Stage One corporation often takes bold, aggressive actions. The entrepreneur thrives on challenge and is not afraid of risk.

STAGE TWO

If the Stage One corporation succeeds, sheer growth and success bring new problems. The growth of a business can prove too much for one entrepreneur-manager to handle. Semiautomated production facilities and several hundred employees create a complexity that never confronted the entrepreneur operating out of a garage in the backyard. Growing markets might call for new promotion, advertising, or packaging skills. Increasing paperwork can strain the

Stages of Corporate Development (continued)

simple administrative systems of an entrepreneurial company. The possible entrance of a competitor or government regulator can further add to the managerial burden.

The corporation responds with *functional specialization*, by assigning an executive to coordinate market, a second executive to control production, and other executives to handle the other business functions. Thus, the dominant characteristic of the Stage Two corporation is the management group, a team of specialized functional experts. The organization chart of the Stage One corporation, if indeed one exists, changes (see Figure 1.1).

STAGE THREE

The Stage One company relied on one entrepreneur until growth forced it to become a Stage Two corporation. The Stage Two corporation that seeks further growth, or seeks to diversify to reduce risk, is forced to rely on more than one product or market group. As it introduces further market groups or product groups, the firm responds by first a divisional, then a decentralized divisional, management (see Figure 1.2).

By using decentralized division, the decision maker — the decentralized division executive — is closest to the problem. Decentralized division executives have strategic information close at hand so that they can respond immediately to problems.

The Stage Three corporation, then, has a corporate headquarters with several or many operating divisions, each of which looks and acts like a Stage Two company.

SIGNIFICANCE

The stages of corporate development provide a way for the strategic manager to analyze (1) managerial abilities and (2) opportunities and threats.

As the corporation moves through the stages of corporate development, its essential managerial abilities change. The high-energy, technical skills of the entrepreneur are less important than the coordinative and integrative skills required of the Stage Two manager. The Stage Three manager at corporate headquarters must have greater planning and financial skills than the Stage One or Stage Two executive.

The managerial skills change because the

FIGURE 1.1
Stage One and
Stage Two firms

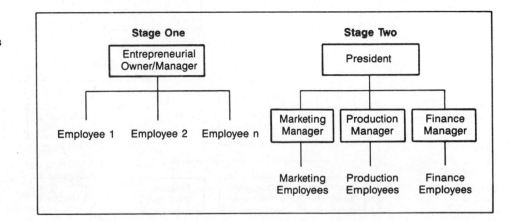

Stages of Corporate Development (continued)

opportunities and threats confronting the strategic manager change in the Stage One, Two, and Three corporations. The Stage One manager faces a series of operating crises — usually manufacturing, with occasional financial — and short-term survival problems. The entrepreneur often needs to delegate and even to decentralize decisions as the firm succeeds and grows.

The Stage Two manager, on the other hand, tries to provide organizational structures to handle longer-term problems. He or she replaces the "daily observation" measurement system of Stage One with formal reports and "responsibility" accounting systems designed to spotlight problems within each functional area.

The Stage Three strategic manager faces complex resource allocation decisions, coupled with an increasing breadth of investment opportunities. The operating and functional orientations of the Stage One and Stage Two managers, respectively, are replaced with a long-term profitability orientation, which means less reliance on personal performance and coordination and more reliance on institutional leadership, financial planning, external environment scanning, and increased research and development efforts. Outside stockholders, brought in to provide needed expansion capital, mean less managerial control. The Stage Three strategic manager must also guard against the dual internal threats of (1) an unresponsive, inflexible, risk-avoiding bureaucracy and (2) partial or less satisfying solutions within divisions, as divisional managers sacrifice long-term growth potential for short-term profits.

ILLUSTRATIONS

The experience of Peters and Waterman's "excellent" companies illustrates some of the problems incurred as a company evolves through the stages of corporate development. In their best-seller, *In Search of Excellence*, management consultants Peters and Waterman identified forty-three excellent companies. Two years later, in a cover story, *Business Week* (11/15/84) reported that at least fourteen of the forty-three companies had lost their luster. Waterman com-

FIGURE 1.2
Stage Three firm

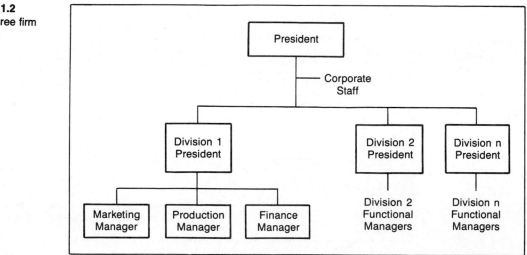

mented, "If you're big, you've got the seeds of your own destruction in there."

The banking industry offers dramatic examples of growth and decline, success and failure. Continental Illinois National Bank and Trust Company, which collapsed in 1984, was named one of the five best-managed companies by *Dun's Business Month* in 1981.

By the end of 1985, People Express Airlines had moved well past being the entrepreneurial, Stage One firm whose organization was the champion of "management humanists." Its initial (November 1980) public offering price was $8.50 a share. The price rose to its July 1983 high of almost fifty dollars and then fell to eight dollars one year later. The nonunion, "participatory management" People Express had acquired the multiunion, bureaucratic Frontier Airlines in a pursuit of growth and geographic coverage.

People Express president Donald Burr explained the Frontier purchase as a necessary response to competition, asserting that "leadership is not pandering to what people say they need. It's defining what . . . people need" (*Business Week*, 11/25/85, pp. 80, 91). Others may view such strategic and structural changes as inevitable consequences of the stages of corporate development.

CONCLUSION

The important, long-term strategic issues confronting a company can be highlighted by the model of the stages of corporate development. Chandler's major conclusion about the management of the business enterprise was that the structure of the organization — functional, divisional, decentralized, and so on — must be determined by the firm's strategy. Not only the operating problems centering around resistance to change, but the strategic problems of changing areas of managerial focus, are identified and resolved more easily through the stages of development model.

Galbraith and Kazanjian (1986) studied firms' implementing strategies, concluding that "only under competitive conditions does a mismatch between strategy and structure lead to ineffective performance." These researchers suggested that firms may proceed from the functional (Stage Two) form along three paths:

1. *Vertical integration*: If a firm pursues economies of scale (the low cost producer strategy) it probably will integrate vertically and maintain a centralized functional structure.
2. *Related diversification*: If a firm pursues internal growth through related diversification (market or product development), it might develop a multidivisional structure.
3. *Acquisition*: If a firm pursues growth by external acquisition, it probably will adapt a holding-company structure.

BIBLIOGRAPHY

Chandler, A. D., *Strategy and Structure: Chapters in the History of the American Industrial Enterprise* (Cambridge, MA: M.I.T. Press, 1962).

Galbraith, J. R., and R. K. Kazanjian, *Strategy Implementation: Structure, Systems, and Process*, 2nd ed. (St. Paul, MN: West Publishing, 1986).

Salter, M. S., "Stages of Corporate Development," *Journal of Business Policy* 1 (Spring 1970), pp. 23–27.

Thain, D. H., "Stages of Corporate Development," *The Business Quarterly* (London, Ontario: University of Western Ontario, Winter 1969), pp. 33–45.

STAGES OF CORPORATE DEVELOPMENT AND STRATEGIC MANAGEMENT

The model of the stages of corporate development shows the manager's task changing from an environment of (1) entrepreneurial decision making, including developing production and marketing systems; to (2) coordinating the efforts of functional managers toward a product-market objective; to (3) developing a strategic management system to allocate scarce resources among different divisions, businesses, and product markets in a way that maximizes growth and institutional objectives, such as social responsibility, while recognizing the differences in risk, competitive strengths, and opportunities that each division and business represents.

Business Policy

Just as the entrepreneur is the focal point of the successful Stage One firm, earlier writers in strategic management likewise focused their attention on the decision maker, referring to their field as *business policy*. These researchers studied the way chief executives make decisions. Cases were the dominant if not the sole method of instruction; business school teachers concentrated on the art and practice of decision making, often in an entrepreneurial role.

Strategic Planning

As researchers, tracing the stages of corporate development, moved on to the problems of coordinating functional managerial efforts and simultaneously deciding on desirable product markets, "business policy" became "strategic planning." *Strategic planning* is a process that represents part of strategic management. It is the process of analyzing the opportunities and threats in the marketplace, while building the strengths and correcting the weaknesses within the firm. Strategic planning also involves setting goals for specific product markets and for the firm.

Strategic Management

The strategist's job can be understood best from the perspective of the third stage of corporate development, that of the multidivisional, and often multinational, corporation. *Strategic management* deals with the same topics that concern the chief executive of the multinational, Stage Three corporation: creating the corporate portfolio of multiple businesses and product markets through (1) analyzing industry attractiveness, (2) analyzing each business unit's strategy, (3) formulating corporate strategy, and (4) implementing that strategy across multiple divisions and businesses.

At a very simplified level, the evolution of strategic management reads like this: business policy examined the decision maker; strategic planning studied the process the decision maker used; and what is now strategic management analyzes how to manage the entire process of planning, formulating, and allocating across time and among multiple businesses.

Just as the stages of corporate development make sense, since we would expect a successful business to evolve and grow, so also does the evolution of business policy to strategic planning to strategic management, since the strategic management field must evolve along with its subject, corporate management. The *process* underlying business policy, strategic planning, and strategic management is similarly very logical. This *strategic process* consists of reaching goals by using strengths to take advantage of the available opportunities.

Figure 1.3 summarizes the strategic process. The strategic manager (discussed further in Chapter 2) defines the mission of the enterprise — a mixture of personal values, organizational objectives, and social goals (to be discussed in Chapter 3). He or she next determines the enterprise's strengths that make up its distinctive competence (discussed in Chapter 4) and identifies opportunities — or threats — present in the markets, competition, technology, government, and society surrounding the enterprise (described in Chapter 5). The manager then formulates and evaluates a strategy (discussed in Chapter 6) which is implemented (see Chapter 7) by allocating resources; organizing; and measuring progress and performance.

This book introduces the field of strategic management in Chapter 1 and introduces the strategic manager in Chapter 2. The text then describes a step-by-step process for making strategic decisions.

Defining mission
Determining distinctive competence
Identifying opportunities and threats
Formulating and evaluating strategy
Implementing strategy

Working Concept 2 further illustrates the field of strategic management.

WORKING CONCEPT 2

LEVELS OF STRATEGY

As a firm evolves into a diversified company, strategic choices and decisions emerge that did not frequently confront — or often were not considered by — the entrepreneur. These decisions raise the following questions at the business level.

1. How are we to compete in this business?
2. What role will each function of this business perform?
3. How should each function be supported and/or developed?

At the corporate level, the president overseeing diversified divisions faces strategic decisions that include

1. What businesses should we be in?
2. What are the requirements for success in those businesses?

3. How can we provide these requirements to our organization and divisions?

The *corporate level* of strategy, then, considers multiple products, multiple industries, multiple markets, and multiple technologies. Corporate strategy determines what strategic objectives should be pursued and how individual businesses should be managed to achieve those objectives. Markets are viewed without borders, from a long-term perspective, such as two to five years. The portfolio or mix of businesses, and problems of generating and allocating resources to these businesses, are issues that confront the corporate strategist.

The *business level* of strategy considers how to use distinctive competency to compete in a specific business within a defined

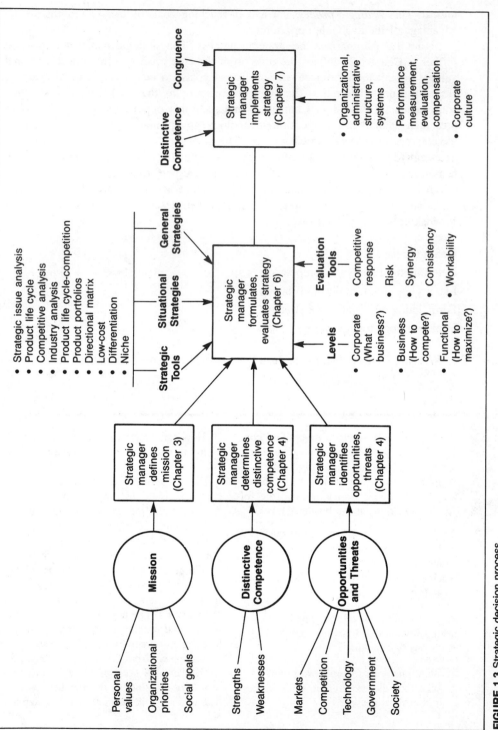

FIGURE 1.3 Strategic decision process

Levels of Strategy (continued)

product-market area. Business strategy determines where potential and profit lie within a firm's market; a typical time frame is six to twenty-four months.

The *functional level* of strategy addresses efficiency (quantity) and effectiveness (quality) decisions in maximizing the output of that functional unit, based upon inputs

provided by corporate- and business-level strategic decisions about resource allocation. The time perspective ranges from less than one month up to six months. Figure 1.4 presents a spectrum of the levels of strategy. Figure 1.5 further illustrates levels of strategy by incorporating strategic levels into the Stage Three firm of Figure 1.2.

We turn to the subject of the strategic business unit and its development in the world of business (principally by General Electric) in order to provide further illustration of the levels of strategy. The strategic business unit represents General Electric's response to the increasing complexities of its strategic management.

WORKING CONCEPT 3

STRATEGIC BUSINESS UNITS

Strategic business units (SBUs) are those individual parts of a business that interact with the external environment in such a distinctive and cohesive way that they can be viewed as independent strategic units. Generally, the distinctive and cohesive way the unit deals with the environment consists of a specific product-market segment — e.g., industrial power tools — although the grouping may center around customers or geographic areas. General Electric was a pioneer in identifying strategic business units and allowing the SBU to develop its own strategic plans.

The General Electric strategist offered a broad mix of products and services to international markets. Clearly, no single strategy would have been appropriate for G.E.'s multiple products and multiple markets. Thus, the firm turned to SBUs as the organizational solution to the need for multiple strategies.

G.E. AND DECENTRALIZATION

In 1950, General Electric's new president, Ralph Cordiner, examined several barriers

to the traditional corporate objectives of increasing profits and shareholder's return. G.E. was facing an increasingly competitive external environment, due in part to both a rapid business growth in response to post–World War II consumer demand and to rapid advances in technology propelled by an increase in research and development (R&D) and wartime technological advances. G.E. also was the target of frequent antitrust actions (thirteen cases between 1940 and 1950) brought about by the government. Another barrier to G.E.'s success was its extremely centralized internal environment, which produced (1) layers of bureaucracy and (2) a corporate culture of security, due in part to G.E.'s self-confidence based on its size and technology.

Cordiner formulated a strategy to bring decision making down to the levels in the organization in which market and technological changes impacted first. The company was too large, and the environment too complex, to be run as one giant corporation with a steadily growing staff. In Cordiner's view, bureaucracy was hiding, not highlighting, business environment change.

FIGURE 1.4
Levels of strategy

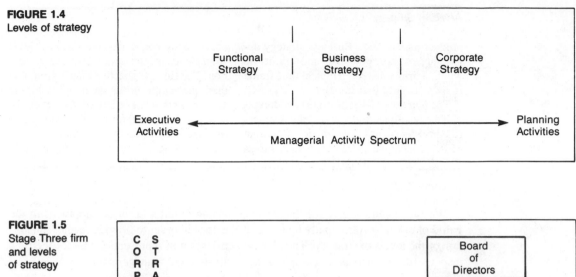

FIGURE 1.5
Stage Three firm
and levels
of strategy

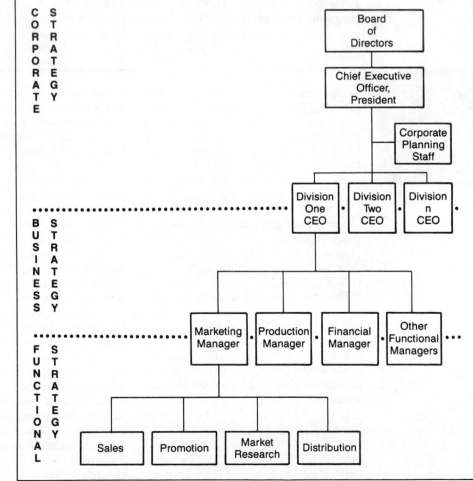

Strategic Business Units (continued)

To implement his strategy, Cordiner reorganized one highly centralized firm into twenty-seven autonomous divisions. Further, the twenty-seven divisions were made up of 110 companies; the head of each of the 110 companies was to act as the entrepreneur/boss of that business, setting budgets and approving all but major capital expenditures. This boss was to respond to competitive, technological, or antitrust problems.

DECENTRALIZATION REVERSED — THE G.E. SBU

General Electric became a decentralized company in the 1950s. During the 1960s, however, G.E. experienced profitless growth in which revenues increased but profits did not. G.E.'s 110 companies and twenty-seven divisions became 190 departments. These departments, organized into forty-six divisions and ten groups, did not generate enough profits to provide the heavy investment requirements of nuclear power, computers, and aerospace.

G.E. decided that the critical strategic objective for achieving its profitable growth purpose would be to add planning to its existing decentralized control system. During the 1970s, then, G.E. carried out the following implementation of its strategic objective.

1. Company operating units were reorganized into SBUs that had a unique business mission and unique competitors and that could plan for and implement long-term strategic plans. The 190 departments reported to and were part of forty SBUs.

2. The general manager of each SBU prepared an annual SBU strategic plan that was reviewed by sector executives. These SBU plans included environmental assessments; statement of objectives; strategy for

business and resource development; and a five-year, long-range forecast. Sectors were major business groupings determined by common markets, customers, products, or technology. Thus, the television and air-conditioning SBU managers forwarded their SBU plans to the Consumer Products and Services Sector executive vice president. Other sectors included Industrial Products and Components, Power Systems, and Technical Systems and Materials.

3. The sector executives reviewed and approved the SBU plans, then gathered them and forwarded the aggregated plan for review and approval to the Corporate Executive Office (CEO), which consisted of G.E.'s chairman and two vice chairmen. The aggregate SBU profit and investment needs were often below total planned profit and above total available investment funds. In this case, the CEO assigned higher profit targets and restricted investment amounts to the sectors for sector distribution to the SBUs.

4. The CEO also defined specific corporate planning challenges, such as productivity and general product-market targets for corporate and SBU growth. These target areas, called *arenas,* included such fields as energy, transportation and propulsion, and communication.

5. After finalizing its plans, each SBU developed an operating budget within the SBU plan guidelines. The approved budget then became the basis for monthly monitoring of current operating profit performance; profit responsibility was still decentralized down to the department level. This monthly monitoring included a series of financial statements that became less detailed at higher levels of the management hierarchy.

6. In addition to their financial goals, each G.E. manager developed a statement of nonfinancial objectives by which to be evaluated. These financial and nonfinancial

---

Strategic Business Units (continued)

objectives — in G.E. terms the *performance screen* — were reviewed with the manager's superior; together they assigned relative weights to each measure.

7. Performance evaluation sessions using the performance screen were held at least once a year. Further, the performance screens were used to rank managers for annual salary reviews, which also included substantial incentive compensation.

Thus, SBUs develop business opportunities in existing product markets; sectors develop new SBU opportunities within major industry groups; and the CEO develops new sector opportunities.

The Stage One, entrepreneurial company can be viewed as a single SBU; but the SBU is just one of many businesses within the Stage Three, divisionalized corporation. In the evolution of the corporation, the top executive moves from business policy to strategic planning and, finally, to strategic management.

STRATEGY RESEARCH

Each of the following chapters in this book will review research efforts in its subject area. In this introductory chapter, we will mention the work of Chandler, Andrews, and Ansoff, three researchers who shaped the strategic management field.

Alfred Chandler, in *Strategy and Structure* (1962), described in detail the strategic decisions made by General Motors; Sears, Roebuck; du Pont; and Standard Oil of New Jersey. Chandler not only analyzed the linkage between a firm's strategy and its environment, but he argued that a firm's structure should follow its strategy.

Kenneth Andrews was one of the main authors of the Harvard Business School text *Business Policy* (1965), and led the policy field toward suggesting what strategy should be, namely "objectives, purposes or goals and major . . . plans for achieving these goals, stated in such a way as to define what business the company is in or is to be in and the kind of company it is or is to be."

Igor Ansoff, in *Corporate Strategy* (1965), urged strategic managers to make decisions about growth and product markets based upon distinctive competence — one's competitive advantage — and synergy — the opportunity for 2 + 2 to achieve a sum greater than 4.

BUSINESS HISTORY

Research in business policy and strategy is hindered not only by the reluctance of managers to spell out decision factors and by the number and complexity of the variables involved in a strategic situation, but also by the difficulty of researching a company's strategy over time. Business histories often overcome this time restriction. The following text of a letter from C. F. Sise, the president of Bell Telephone of Canada, to F. G. Beach, the general manager of the Central Union Telephone Company of Chicago, written January 5, 1895, provides an example of the relevance of business history.

Dear Sir:

I beg to acknowledge receipt of yours of the 2nd instant, in reference to competition in the business.

It would hardly be possible, within the limits of a letter, to give you our experience in dealing with competition; but we may assume as the principal element in the matter, that there is no friendship in the business, and that if another Company can give as good service at a less rate, they will get your Subscribers. Of course you and I would naturally doubt the possibility of their giving as good service, but the Public is not so easily convinced.

I should recommend preparation for competition before it materializes, by making exclusive-franchise contracts with the Towns and Cities where you are operating, for say ten year terms. For this Franchise you can afford to give the City five per cent of your net receipts (in fact if these net receipts are to be figured by you, you could afford to give them ten per cent). We also make contracts with all Railroads, Telegraph Companies, and Electric Light Companies, whereby we interchange facilities; the Railroad for instance giving us free transportation and the exclusive right to enter their premises, in consideration of free telephone service on our part. Electric Light and Telegraph Companies are handled in practically the same manner; but they are important as they have pole rights which may be made available to your competitors.

We also take three year leases from our Subscribers (copy of one of which I enclose herewith), and of course a slight reduction is made to a Subscriber taking a three year lease. If the local rate were $50 I suppose we would take them at $45. They are very reluctant to break these leases, because if they do so before the expiration of the three years you have a claim for the full amount of the rental from the date of the lease. You will note that our rentals are payable every six months in advance.

It is far easier to stop competition in embryo than after it has got well started. Of course if the Public understands as it doubtless will, that competition means reduced rates, it will foster competition. For this reason your efforts should be devoted to opposing their franchises by securing to yourselves the exclusive rights in Cities and Towns, where possible to do so. The longer the opposition is deferred, the stronger you are getting, and the more difficult it will be to compete with you; and if the authorities can be convinced that you are giving a good service at a fair rate, they will be reluctant to allow competitors to come in for blackmailing purposes, and poling the streets of the City for that purpose. I attach great value to our relations with the Railways. Perhaps these are more important in Canada than in the United States, but in the smaller Towns in Canada no Merchant has any use for the telephone unless he can communicate with the Railway Station; and while doubtless efforts will be made through the Courts to compel the Railways to allow opposition Telephone Company's wires to be carried into their Stations, I have no doubt that such efforts can be defeated with the cooperation of the Railway Company. More than this I fear legislation compelling one Telephone Company to receive and transmit the messages of another, giving the opposition connection with your Exchange.

I shall be very glad to give you any other information, but you will of course understand that the subject is a very wide one, and efforts which are successful here may fail in your Territory. We are still constantly threatened with competition, but, with our City and Town contracts and the other alliances I have referred to, we do not give ourselves any uneasiness.

Yours truly,

C. F. Sise
President

This letter demonstrates how the history of business can provide a useful perspective for today's manager. Mr. Sise urges an entrepreneurial strategy: preparing for competition before it comes, and defending and seeking allies, such as the railroad (see Working Concept 5 in Chapter 2). How entrepreneurial is the telephone company executive today? Has today's executive the same view of ''the Public'' as President Sise?

EXECUTIVE COMMENTS

Finally, the comments of executives — and, occasionally, other observers of executive action — will appear at the end of each chapter to serve as real-world opinions against which to test the chapter's suggestions, prescriptions, and Working Concepts.

I know how not to make decisions. I know how to make decisions. Part of the secret of making decisions is to know which decisions not to make.
     Mario Cuomo, governor of New York, 9/30/84

The book [In Search of Excellence] *has been so popular that people have taken it as a formula for success rather than what it is intended to be. We were writing about the art, not the science, of management.*
     Robert M. Waterman, Jr., *Business Week*, 11/5/84

Our strategic planning process [at General Motors] *is straightforward. Instructions, in the form of sets of questions, are sent out each year to each division and are divided into categories that form a series of steps: (1) business definition, including market segments, (2) key success factors, (3) situation analysis of relative competitive strengths and weaknesses, and (4) strategy development* [systematically comparing] *individual strengths and weaknesses against each key success factor for each of the major competitors.*
     M. E. Naylor, General Motors executive

The brand of leadership we propose has a simple base of MBWA (Managing By Wandering Around). To ''wander,'' with customers and vendors and our own people, is to be in touch with the first vibrations of the new.
     Tom Peters and Nancy Austin, *A Passion for Excellence*

"Would you tell me, please, which way I ought to go from here?"
"That depends a good deal on where you want to get to," said the Cat.
"I don't care much where . . ." said Alice.
"Then it doesn't matter which way you go," said the Cat.
". . . so long as I get somewhere," *Alice added as an explanation.*
"Oh, you're sure to do that," said the Cat, "if only you walk long enough."

Lewis Carroll, *Alice's Adventures in Wonderland*

KEY TERMS

business policy (page 8)

business strategy (page 9)

corporate strategy (page 9)

functional strategy (page 12)

levels of strategy (page 9)

strategic business unit (SBU) (page 12)

strategic management (page 8)

strategic planning (page 8)

BIBLIOGRAPHY

Andrews, K. R., *The Concept of Corporate Strategy* (Homewood, Il: Richard D. Irwin, 1980).

Andrews, K. R., E. Learned, C. R. Christensen, and W. D. Guth, *Business Policy: Text and Cases* (Homewood, IL: Richard D. Irwin, 1965).

Ansoff, H. I., *Corporate Strategy: Business Policy for Growth and Expansion* (New York: McGraw-Hill, 1965).

Bower, J. L., "Business Policy in the 1980s," *Academy of Management Review*, 1982 (vol. 7, no. 4), pp. 630–638.

Chamberlain, N. W., *Enterprise and Environment: The Firm in Time and Place* (New York: McGraw-Hill, 1968).

Chandler, A. D., *Strategy and Structure: Chapters in the History of the American Industrial Enterprise* (Cambridge, MA: M.I.T. Press, 1962).

Cyert, R. M., and J. G. March, *A Behavioral Theory of the Firm* (Englewood Cliffs, NJ: Prentice-Hall, 1963).

Drucker, P. F., *Innovation and Entrepreneurship: Practice and Principles* (New York: Harper & Row, 1985).

Drucker, P. F., *Management: Tasks, Responsibilities, Practices* (New York: Harper & Row, 1974).

Evered, R., "So What Is Strategy," *Long Range Planning* 16 (June 1983), pp. 57–72.

Freeman, R., *Strategic Management — A Stakeholder Approach* (Boston: Pitman, 1984).

Hise, R., and S. McDaniel, "CEO's Views on Strategy," *Journal of Business Strategy* 4 (Winter 1984), pp. 79–86.

Kotter, J. P., *The General Managers* (New York: The Free Press, 1982).

Mintzberg, H., *The Nature of Managerial Work* (New York: Harper & Row, 1973).

Mintzberg, H., "Strategy-Making in Three Modes," *California Management Review* XVI (Winter 1973), pp. 44–53.

Naylor, M. E., "Regaining Your Competitive Edge," *Long Range Planning*, vol. 18, no. 1, pp. 30–35.

Peters, T. J., and R. H. Waterman, Jr., *In Search of Excellence: Lessons from America's Best-Run Companies* (New York: Harper & Row, 1982).

Schenkel, S., *Giving Away Success* (New York: McGraw-Hill, 1985).

Summer, C. E., and J. J. O'Connell, *The Managerial Mind* (Homewood, IL: Richard D. Irwin, 1971).

Sutton, C. J., *Economics and Corporate Strategy* (Cambridge, England: University of Cambridge Press, 1980).

Vancil, R. F., and P. Lorange, "Strategic Planning in Diversified Companies," *Harvard Business Review* (January–February 1975), pp. 81–90.

CHAPTER 2

STRATEGIC MANAGEMENT AND THE STRATEGIC MANAGER

If you really want to advise me, do it [during the game] on Saturday afternoon . . . [in] 25 seconds. Not on Monday. I know the right thing to do on Monday.

Alex Agase, former Purdue head coach (*Fortune*, 5/13/85)

This chapter will focus on the strategic manager, that executive who must make real-time (Saturday afternoon) decisions within the field of strategic management. We will discuss this strategic manager from both a military and a holistic perspective, and will consider the questions of managerial style — how decisions are made — and managerial perspective — how problems are perceived. Our first Working Concept examines an artificial being, the strategic manager.

WORKING CONCEPT 4

THE STRATEGIC MANAGER

No known firm has a position called "strategic manager." Nonetheless, the previous chapter's description of strategic management and the levels of strategy has shown that (1) managers at the operating, functional levels, such as research and development, or marketing; (2) divisional presidents at the product-market level; and (3) corporate executives at the multinational, multibusiness level (whether members of the board of directors, officers, or managers) all make strategic decisions that are both long term and of significance to the enterprise. Strategic decisions guide the enterprise in moving from its present position of products, markets, and technologies to its desired future position. Thus, the time perspective of the strategic manager is al-

ways the long term; moving from a present position in products or technologies to a future position is a long-term movement.

Thomas Urban, chief executive of America's biggest seed-corn supplier, Pioneer Hi-Bred International, spoke about strategy and long-term perspectives:

Quarter-to-quarter doesn't cut much around Pioneer. We have a hard time thinking about year-to-year changes. I'm not in the dress business; it takes us ten years to make a new product. If you want to know how good a job I'm doing, come see me in 1990. (Fortune, 10/28/85, p. 38)

This artificial being, the strategic manager with the long-term view, is used as a Working Concept in order to highlight

---

The Strategic Manager (continued)

the strategic management duties from other managerial activities of executives (Kotter, 1982). This Working Concept may even be used to point out situations in which no one was the strategic manager. For example, commenting on Coca-Cola's introduction of New Coke and its reissue of

Classic Coke four months later, Coca-Cola president Donald Keough said, "Some critics will say Coca-Cola made a marketing mistake. Some cynics will say that we planned the whole thing. The truth is we are not that dumb and we are not that smart."

The next Working Concept presents military and holistic versions of the strategic manager. The military version of the "general" stresses the authority and responsibility of the strategic manager. While researchers focus on the business enterprise, the strategic manager functions in the human arena; the holistic version of the "executive householder" stresses the interrelationship between the strategic manager as executive and human being. The strategic manager develops not just as a business executive, but grows in the emotional, mental, and psychological dimensions.

WORKING CONCEPT 5

MILITARY AND HOLISTIC STRATEGIC MANAGERS

THE GENERAL

Business texts often cite the military warrior origin of strategy, as evidenced also by the Random House Dictionary's definition of *strategy* as "generalship . . . the art . . . (of formulating) a series of maneuvers . . . for obtaining a specific goal."

Top Management Viewpoint

Three points should be made about this "generalship" definition. First, the viewpoint is that of the general, or, for our purposes, that of top management. Rather than being presented only with a financial problem or a limited marketing question, top management is presented with financial and marketing issues that affect the entire organization. These overall organizational issues must be considered from the point of view of the top executive, the *general (manager)*, who has authority — and re-

sponsibility — for the organization. The general manager must resolve conflicts between financial, marketing, and production goals, between the firm's perspective and functional interests.

The Art of Strategy

Second, the strategic process is an art. Accounting principles, mathematical models, and statistical formulae may provide answers for some business problems, but most often they cannot provide solutions for strategic issues. Analysis and mathematical techniques are extremely useful in determining the quantitative dimensions of problems — such as, how probable it is that competition will result in price cutting. However, these techniques can only provide measures to assist the top executive in making strategic decisions, which often must be based not only on hard facts and data, but also on judgment and intuition.

Military and Holistic Strategic Managers (continued)

For example, consider a military general, who has estimates of enemy troop strength, forecasts of weather conditions that might affect the battlefield, subordinates' assessments of the fighting potential of the troops, and dated descriptions and maps of the ground surfaces. With these data, which have varying degrees of reliability, the general must produce a battle strategy that will be based, at least in part, on personal judgment. In the business arena, the same principles apply; the principal organizer of General Motors, Will Durant, was "a man who would proceed on a course of action guided solely . . . by some intuitive flash of brilliance" (Sloan, 1941). Evered (1983) describes the link between military and corporate strategy. He asks "So What *Is* Strategy?" and answers in part by quoting von Clausewitz in *On War*, that "strategy forms the plan of the war, makes out the proposed course of the different campaigns which compose the war and regulates the battles to be fought in each."

In the mid-1980s, Canon, the Japanese manufacturer of office equipment, adopted a goal of direct competition with IBM in the international market of office automation products. *Business Week* (5/13/85, p. 98) quoted Canon's president, Ryuzaburo Kaku:

When you are climbing Mt. Fuji you can do it with wooden clogs, but when you are going to climb Mt. Everest, you have to be better prepared. [Business is becoming an age of] warring feudal lords. You look ahead for a time when there is a change in the marketplace. Then you move in.

Students initially may feel frustrated as they try to understand and practice the art of strategy, due to the fact that in strategy, as in any other art, there is no one right answer. Strategy can provide reasonable answers; an instructor's reluctance to provide *the* answer must be seen from this perspective. Instructors are interested primarily in students developing their own strategic decision-making capabilities.

Goals and Direction

Third, and finally, the general has a specific goal. When trying to decide between various strategic alternatives, a strategist is not without guidance. Which alternative is most likely to achieve the desired result? The general has some strategic objective in mind, whether it is capturing enemy personnel, resources, and territory; or creating a diversion so that another general may achieve a strategic objective.

What is the "battlefield" of the general (manager) in business? Business organizations compete in markets and in technologies; the battlefield is the external environment of the firm. The resources of the internal environment of the firm, including managers, employees, capital, equipment, and other tangible and intangible assets, are the organization's "troops." The job of the strategic manager, and the responsibility of the general, is to define and implement a timed sequence of movements that will reach the objective — to move through the competitive market process toward success. Commenting on its competition with Procter & Gamble, Colgate's CEO Reuben Mark said, "We're just starting to take the hill. Now we've got to work on getting more ammunition out to the troops" (*Business Week*, 11/11/85, p. 138).

Harrigan (1985) analyzed Mao Tse-Tung's principles of guerrilla warfare (consolidating resources in areas of relative strength — guerrilla bases — and attacking the enemy only with slack resources on the enemy's turf — guerrilla fronts). Harrigan showed how guerrilla warfare is an

Military and Holistic Strategic Managers (continued)

appropriate tactic for the weaker firm and/ or one with low market share. These firms engage "in skirmishes where market leaders cannot respond without shooting themselves in the foot." Guerrilla bases are "market niches where competitors are unlikely or unable to enter . . . . guerrilla fronts are . . . for drawing out opponents and wasting their resources . . . [guerrilla bases] will necessarily have to be defended with a *kamikazelike* devotion."

Acquisitions, and especially hostile takeovers, are a form of competitive warfare. The year 1985 saw mergers in oil, advertising, entertainment, and consumer goods. Phillip Morris bought General Foods and Procter & Gamble bought Richardson-Vicks. But the biggest merger in history, outside of the petroleum industry, was General Electric's $6.3 billion acquisition of RCA. The concept of generalship is apparent in G.E. chairman Jack Welch's explanation of the merger:

> *Being powerful domestically is an integral part of being powerful internationally. Every day we're meeting the Toshibas of the world, the Hitachis of the world. We have to get larger and more powerful to be able to compete or just give up and let the imports take over.* (Business Week, *12/30/85, p. 48*)

Burrough's successful $4.8 billion takeover of Sperry was called a tale of a "dogged pursuer and unwary prey . . . Sperry's management misjudged the determination of [Burrough's] Blumenthal . . . [and] had to rely on crisis management" (*Business Week*, 6/9/86, p. 29).

As opposed to the unidimensional model of the general, the holistic model that follows presents the strategic manager as a stage (the successful householder) on a path that moves from student to service and retirement.

THE EXECUTIVE HOUSEHOLDER

Some holistic philosophers divide human life into four phases of growth, of which the first is the student. The student learns from the instruction and example of the teacher. The second phase is the householder, in which the householder works and raises children, thus contributing to the economic well-being of the family. The third phase of life (service) involves a gradual deemphasis of the material world. The fourth stage (contemplative) is a retirement from life, in which one continues spiritual growth (Hopkins, 1971). These phases of life mark each person's growth and development within a lifetime. Of these four phases, great emphasis is placed on the householder phase; thus, Hopkins makes the following conclusion.

> *Householdership was the keystone . . . study was important, but preservation of the entire society depended on the householder. . . . Householdership was . . . highly valued as the base for all activities, and the productive and fruitful householder was given great honor by the students, teachers, priests and ascetics whom he supported.*
> *The householder did more than just support others, however. Householdership in the . . . system was not an alternative to a genuine religious life but an essential stage of personal spiritual development. (p. 77)*

The path of the householder is the foundation for further growth. By fulfilling the role of the householder, one understands and then grows beyond the pursuit of wealth and sensual pleasure. This world's material and sensual attractions are to be pursued and understood, not avoided.

In summary, the general model provides a model of how to be a good householder and of how to make a living. The householder model shows how to make a life.

The next Working Concept explores what managers do by elaborating on managerial roles and styles.

WORKING
CONCEPT **6**

MINTZBERG'S
ROLES AND
STYLES

MANAGERIAL ROLES

In a study of the nature of managerial work, Mintzberg (1973) described ten different managerial roles. First, among the *interpersonal* managerial roles, a manager performs (1) a leader role, exercising authority with the organization; (2) a liaison role, coordinating various functions and subordinates; and (3) a figurehead role, attending activities of a primarily ceremonial nature.

Second, within *informational* roles, a manager can be (4) a spokesperson, providing information about the organization to the outside world; (5) a disseminator, providing data within the organization; or (6) a monitor, receiving and collecting data.

Lastly, in *decision-making* managerial roles, the manager can be (7) a negotiator; (8) a disturbance handler; (9) a resource allocator, directing organizational effort toward specific activities; or (10) an innovator, introducing change.

STRATEGIST'S ROLES

Mintzberg's ten managerial roles include six roles of the strategic manager. Initially, the informational and decision-making roles are central to the activities of the strategic manager. The strategic manager is most concerned with receiving and collecting data (Role 6) about the internal strengths and external opportunities of the organization. The strategic manager then makes decisions that will become the organization's strategy. When these decisions require change, which they most frequently do, the strategic manager functions as a decision-making innovator (Role 10).

Implementing these strategic decisions encompasses four other managerial roles. As the strategic manager implements the formulated strategy, both leader (Role 1) and liaison (Role 2) roles will come into play. As details of the strategic plan are described to various organizational units, the strategic manager acts as an information disseminator (Role 5). In allocating specific resources, such as research monies for product development or capital funds for asset acquisitions, the strategic manager functions in a resource allocator, decision-making role (Role 9).

Depending on both the nature of the strategy and on the implementation tactics decided upon, the strategic manager could also serve as a disturbance handler and/or as a negotiator (Roles 7 and 8).

INTERNATIONAL ROLES

Do differences exist between strategic managers? Managers from different countries will, of course, have viewpoints shaped by their home countries' experiences. Three of the four business rules of British entrepreneur Richard Branson — (1) Keep overhead low; (2) Encourage entrepreneurship among employees; and (3) Never venture outside your core market — seem appropriate for many entrepreneurs. But Branson's fourth rule — (4) Avoid major capital investments — may make sense only in terms of the raging inflation experienced by Great Britain for two decades. Further, countries might basically differ in style (although resorting to generalizations may prove unwise). The American Management Association president, T. R. Horton, describes U.S. managers as being generally "impatient," and Japanese managers as having "enormous patience and enormous sense of detail." British managers "muddle through" and Russian managers "cover up" (*Dun's Business Month*, July 1985,

---

Mintzberg's Roles and Styles (continued)

pp. 69–70). Certainly there are greater differences between managers within a country, however, than between countries.

GENDER ROLES

National differences between managerial experiences and managerial style can be matched by differences in the experiences conditioning female and male strategic managers (Schenkel, 1985):

> *Only in the limited spheres of raising and educating children have women been allowed to control the behavior of others. We lack sufficient female role models for leadership in the larger world. As a result, when it comes to asserting authority,*

many of us have a gap in our concept of authority, our self-image and our behavioral repertoire.

These environmental differences between male and female managers are decreasing, in part due to the elimination of stereotypes. We need only to note that the strategic manager includes male and female managers, as the term *strategic manager* is used in this book. The strategic manager is androgynous, requiring both the Jungian characteristics of the masculine, *animus* archetype (action, linearity) as well as those of the feminine, *anima* archetype (creativity, nurturing).

STRATEGIC MANAGEMENT

How does the strategic manager perform these strategic managerial roles? There are as many strategic management systems as there are strategic managers. The strategic decision can involve so many complex variables and can be so situationally specific that to generalize about the detailed steps of strategic management is difficult, even with the benefit of hindsight.

The strategic manager's job can be better understood by looking at how that job is performed. Mintzberg (1973) describes three modes of strategic management: entrepreneurial, adaptive, and planning modes.

The Entrepreneurial Manager

The entrepreneurial strategic manager is a strong leader who takes bold, often risky actions in an active search for new opportunities. This manager operates in an economically risky environment and aggressively pursues growth.

The Adaptive Manager

As opposed to the dramatic leaps of the entrepreneur, the adaptive strategic manager reacts to existing problems rather than aggressively searching for new opportunities. The adaptive manager proceeds in halting, uneven steps, since the organization lacks clear goals for issues such as growth. The adaptive strategic manager often can be found in bureaucratic organizations. Lindblom (1959) commented that the adaptive manager ''is nevertheless a . . . problem solver who is wrestling bravely with a universe that he is wise enough to know is too big for him.'' While the entrepreneurial manager seeks the risky spectrum of the environment, the adaptive manager prefers an environment that is free of risk.

The Planning Manager

The planning strategic manager uses a systematic, and often formal, comprehensive analysis to foresee opportunities and anticipate problems. The planning manager is "proactive," versus the "reactive" adaptive manager; has a longer-term time frame for strategy making; and feels comfortable with or without risk.

The planning strategic manager, then, is one who systematically carries out a strategic planning process. Studies, such as those by Robinson (1982) or Karger and Malik (1975), have shown that companies that plan outperform nonplanners. Most strategic managers and business analysts believe that the planning strategic manager will make better strategic decisions than the nonplanner. Certainly that same belief underlies this text.

This chapter closes with the topic of managerial perceptions and the Working Concept of the Brunswick lens model. As a student of the strategic management process, your perspective, or "lens," will open to include more strategic data. Before describing the nature of those data, we will present this concept of perspective not only to provide deeper understanding of the strategic manager and strategic management, but also to encourage students to participate in the widening of their own lenses.

For example, appendices to this chapter review some accounting and financial tools and discuss the case method. As a student, you will need to understand the strategic concepts embedded in financial and accounting measures. Greater benefit also will be derived from in-class discussions of cases if you have come to a decision about the case before class. Experiential learning is the best — if not the only true — learning. If you learn through the class discussion about issues you did not see from your perspective, then you have learned about opening your perspective, or widening your own lens. This is only possible if you participate fully in the discussion and bring to the discussion a committed position and decision.

WORKING CONCEPT 7

BRUNSWIK LENS AND PERCEPTION

No strategist has a perfect view of the environment, and no strategist has perfect intuition. The strategic manager must (1) improve the quality of information received and (2) refine the accuracy of strategic judgments and managerial perceptions.

Figure 2.1 summarizes the process of managerial perception. This figure is derived from the framework of human judgment developed by the psychologist Egon Brunswik. Signals indicate the state of the environment (a market, technology, or competitor). These signals interact in much the same way as a competitor's advertising campaign interacts with customer demand and another firm's technology advance through an improved product. The strategic manager perceives these signals. Various strategic managers differ in (1) the accuracy of their perception and their degree of under- or overperception of the signal (i.e., the relative weight of each signal) and (2) the quality of their judgment, a combination of experience and information base, common sense, and intuition.

The perception of the general and the perception of the executive householder would clearly be different. The householder would add holistic concepts of growth, teaching, and mentoring to the general's attack/maneuver/retreat lenses. This lens model helps us stress the refinement of managerial perceptions and the improvement of information quality.

Brunswik Lens and Perception (continued)

FIGURE 2.1
Perceptions of the
strategic manager

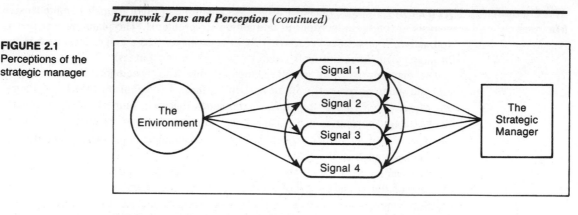

Refining managerial perceptions is part of the process of managerial development. The case methodology of the strategic management course tries to improve your strategic perceptions. As the student and strategic manager reassess their original assumptions, whether through a periodic review of conditions or through the process of class discussion, their ability to perceive strategic signals is refined.

The strategic manager improves the quality of the information received by

1. Recognizing the impossibility of perfect information.
2. Balancing the value of information and its cost.

3. Minimizing the danger of information overload by eliminating excess information through summarized feedback and exception reports, since every communication channel has a capacity limit.
4. Viewing the information system as evolutionary and flexible as opposed to formal and fixed.
5. Increasing, within cost constraints, the timeliness, format, and accuracy of reported data.

Figure 2.2 expands on the Brunswik lens model to include issues relating to improving the quality of information received and refining the accuracy of strategic judgments, decision, and managerial perceptions.

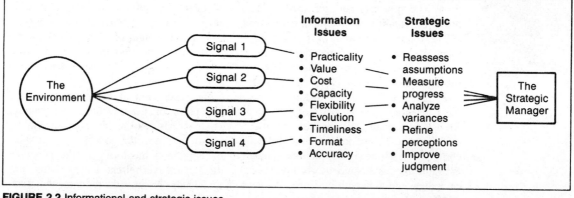

FIGURE 2.2 Informational and strategic issues

STRATEGY AND THE STRATEGIST: A SUMMARY

Before discussing research efforts, the most important messages of these first two chapters may be summarized as follows:

1. Successful firms grow in a discernible pattern.
2. Firms at different stages of growth require different managerial skills as they face changing yet predictable issues.
3. The required management skills change from entrepreneurial decision making to strategic planning to, lastly, strategic management.
4. The mature firm's specific strategic management skills include an understanding of functional strategy, business-level strategy, and corporate strategy.
5. Functional strategy addresses efficiency (quantity) and effectiveness (quality) decisions to maximize outputs, given a set of allocated resources.
6. Business-level strategy builds strengths into distinctive competence so that the firm may compete in a specific business within a defined product market.
7. Corporate strategy balances the corporate portfolio of existing business; analyzes industries, markets, and technologies for growth opportunities; and allocates resources among existing and potential new businesses to achieve overall corporate objectives.
8. Managers have many roles, but our focus is on the manager as strategic manager.
9. We may view the strategic manager either as a function — the general — or as a human being in a particular stage of personal development — the householder.
10. Strategic managers may have different styles — entrepreneurial, adaptive, or planning.
11. Strategic managers and students of management have viewpoints and capabilities limited by their lenses of perception.
12. This course of study seeks to open the lenses of perception.

STRATEGY RESEARCH
AND THE STRATEGIC MANAGER

Classical research efforts include those of Argenti, Chamberlain, Cyert and March, and Lindblom.

Argenti's *Systematic Corporate Planning* (1974) not only addressed the procedures of corporate strategy formulation, but also urged the strategic manager to ensure that the formulated strategy (1) took advantage of major opportunities and (2) defended against major threats. Further, Argenti encouraged the strategist to make contingency plans in the face of significant strategic threats.

Chamberlain's concept of ''counterpoint'' was presented in *Enterprise and Environment* (1968). While the operating supervisor tries to maintain equilibrium, the strategic manager must lead the firm through time (events) and space (markets) to deal with strategic changes in the environment. The strategist must deal with disequilibrium in the move from point to counterpoint.

Cyert and March presented a bargaining model that underlies the formulation of strategy in their book *A Behavioral Theory of the Firm* (1963). Organizational slack, conflicting objectives, sequential attention to functional goals, and personal aspirations result in adaptive, "satisficing" strategies.

Lindblom's message is similar to those of Cyert and March. Lindblom argued in "The Science of 'Muddling Through' " (1959) that the scientific management view of strategy formulation — the rational, comprehensive method of agreeing on purpose and selecting from alternatives based on purpose — was often ignored or inappropriate. Rather, he suggested that decision makers follow a successive limited comparison method in strategy formulation. This method involves achieving a consensus on means, not ends, and occurs especially in complex situations.

Current significant research efforts in strategy formulation include studies by the following authors.

Chaffee (1985) pointed out that definitions of strategy may be based on one or another of the following "three models of strategy."

1. *Linear*: "integrated decisions, actions, or plans that will set and achieve viable organization goals."
2. *Adaptive*: environmental assessment of internal and external conditions that leads to the organization adjusting to a viable match between opportunities and capabilities.
3. *Interpretive*: The organization attracts individuals in a social contract or a collection of cooperative agreements.

Chaffee concluded that the lack of consensus on a definition of strategy is due to its multidimensional and situational characteristics.

Ginter and Rucks studied wargame technology in 1984 and asked "Can business learn from wargames?" They concluded that wargaming was applicable to business as a strategic decision-making aid.

McGinnis (1984) studied strategic planning, and identified six traits that the organization must have if the strategic manager is to function: (1) intelligence, (2) organizational balance, (3) analysis, (4) innovation, (5) proactivity, and (6) risk taking. Central to "strategic success" is "the ability of the firm to integrate analysis and intuition."

Naylor studied the strategic process at General Motors (1985) and recommended implementation and planning that included the acronym STRATEGY: **S** (Stick to it), **T** (Think it through), **R** (Risk, responsibility, and reward), **A** (Awareness of self and competition), **T** (Talking to each other to communicate strategy), **E** (Evaluation of each step), **G** (Growing your people), and **Y** (Yes-I-Can winning attitude).

Stopford and Wells expanded on the stages of corporate development with their 1972 model, which included international divisions, based upon a study of U.S. firms expanding abroad.

EXECUTIVE COMMENTS

One of General Motor's most important characteristics [is] its effort to achieve open-minded communication and objective consideration of facts.

    Alfred P. Sloan, Jr., *My Years with General Motors*

Cruelties should be committed all at once, as in that way each separate one is less felt, and gives less offence; benefits, on the other hand, should be conferred one at a time, for in that way they will be more appreciated.

    Niccolò Machiavelli, *The Prince*

We've seen, all too clearly, how the actions of a few can hurt an entire company and all of its employees.

    J. Welch, in a letter to General Electric employees following G.E.'s guilty plea to fraud in a Minuteman missile project, 1985

An important thing to remember is that, in terms of building an organization that is big and successful, you are going to have to pay a big price, personally. And you won't realize that until you are far enough along and have already paid that price — so you'd better be willing to live with it. . . . You have to see your professional success as part of something larger — maybe that's a way of saying you have to have a philosophy of life. Achieving success, being right — that doesn't do anything for you. Mostly what it does is bring you a lot of problems.

    Fred Smith, founder of Federal Express, in *Inc.*, October 1980

KEY TERMS

adaptive manager (page 24)

entreprencurial manager (page 24)

managerial perceptions (page 25)

managerial roles (page 23)

planning manager (page 25)

strategic manager (page 19)

BIBLIOGRAPHY

Argenti, J., *Systematic Corporate Planning* (New York: Wiley, 1974).

Brunswik, E., *Perception and the Representative Design of Psychological Experiments* (Berkeley, CA: University of California Press, 1956).

Chaffee, E. E., "Three Models of Strategy," *Academy of Management Review* 10 (1985), pp. 89–98.

Chamberlain, N. W., *Enterprise and Environment: The Firm in Time and Space* (New York: McGraw-Hill, 1968).

Cyert, R. M., and J. G. March, *A Behavioral Theory of the Firm* (Englewood Cliffs, NJ: Prentice-Hall, 1963).

Evered, R., "So What Is Strategy?" *Long-Range Planning,* vol. 16, no. 3 (1983), pp. 57–72.

Ginter, P. M., and A. C. Rucks, "Can Business Learn from Wargames?" *Long-Range Planning* 17 (June 1984), pp. 123–128.

Hanna, R. G. C., "The Concept of Corporate Strategy in Multi-Industry Companies," D. B. A. dissertation, Harvard Business School, 1969.

Harrigan, K. R., *Strategic Flexibility: A Management Guide for Changing Times* (Lexington, MA: D. C. Heath, 1985).

Hopkins, T. J., *The Hindu Religious Tradition* (Encino, CA: Dickenson, 1971).

Jung, C. G., *Man and His Symbols* (London: Aldus Books, 1964).

Karger, D. W., and Z. A. Malik, "Long Range Planning and Organizational Performance," *Long Range Planning* (December 1975), pp. 60–64.

Kotter, J. P., *The General Managers* (New York: The Free Press, 1982).

Lindblom, C. E., "The Science of 'Muddling Through'," *Public Administration Review* (Spring 1959), pp. 79–88.

McGinnis, M. A., "The Key to Strategic Planning: Integrating Analysis and Intuition," *Sloan Management Review* (Fall 1984), pp. 45–52.

Mintzberg, H., *The Nature of Managerial Work* (New York: Harper & Row, 1973).

Mintzberg, H., "Strategy-Making in Three Modes," *California Management Review* XVI (Winter 1973), pp. 44–53.

Naylor, M. E., "Regaining Your Competitive Edge," *Long Range Planning* 18 (February 1985), pp. 30–35.

Organ, T. W., *The Hindu Quest for the Perfection of Man* (Athens, OH: Ohio University Press, 1970).

Robinson, R. B., Jr., "The Importance of Outsiders in Small Firm Strategic Planning," *Academy of Management Journal* (March 1982), pp. 80–93.

Schenkel, S., *Giving Away Success* (New York: McGraw-Hill, 1985).

Simon, H., "On the Concept of Organizational Goals," *Administrative Science Quarterly* (June 1964).

Sloan, A., Jr., *Adventures of the White Collarman* (New York: Doubleday, 1941).

Sloan, A., Jr., *My Years with General Motors* (Garden City, NY: Anchor Books, 1963).

Steiner, G., "Formal Strategic Planning in the U.S. Today," *Long Range Planning,* 16:3 (June 1983), pp. 12–18.

Stopford, J., and L. Wells, *Managing the Multinational Enterprise* (London: Longmans, 1972).

Weber, C. E., "Strategic Thinking — Dealing with Uncertainty," *Long Range Planning* 17 (October 1984), pp. 60–70.

Appendices: Appendices follow that serve as a checklist for further "refreshers" in either accounting or financial measures. The appendices also discuss case analysis, and present an example based upon the University of New Hampshire Bookstore.

APPENDIX A: ACCOUNTING FOR NONACCOUNTANTS

Jacques's Restaurant (*Chalet Le Hamberge*) at Ultra Excellence Ski Area has the following balance sheet as of the end of Year One.

Assets

Cash	$ 500
Accounts receivable	11,000
Food, wine inventory on hand	1,500
Furniture, equipment at original cost	5,000
Depreciation accumulated to date on furniture and equipment at 10-year life	(500)
	$17,500

Liabilities

Accounts payable to merchandise suppliers	$11,000

Equity

Investment by Jacques	$ 6,000
Earnings retained in the business	500
Total liabilities, equity	$17,500

Jacques's transactions during Year Two include the following checkbook totals.

Cash receipts		
Cash sales	$24,000	
Accounts receivable collected	$35,000	
Cash disbursed		
Payroll	$30,000	($20,000 to Jacques — $10,000 to part-time employees)
Rent (long-term lease)	$ 5,000	
Miscellaneous variable costs	$ 7,000	
Paid to merchandise suppliers for accounts payable	$15,000	

Note: Cash was paid for all expenses except food and wine. All food and wine for inventory was purchased on credit, and thus would be recorded as increases in inventory and accounts payable.

Additional information included a totaling of customer accounts receivable ledger cards at year end ($13,500 due to Jacques), a total of bills from food and wine supplier ($9,000 due from Jacques), and the checkbook balance of $2,500. Finally,

Jacques counted all the food and wine inventory on hand at the end of Year Two. It totaled $2,500 at invoice cost.

1. Prepare an income statement for Year Two and a balance sheet for the end of Year Two.
2. What is Jacques's
   (a) gross profit margin?
   (b) fixed costs?
   (c) break-even sales volume?
3. What do you estimate Year Three profits will be?
4. If Jacques should decide to sell, what price should he ask for the business?

APPENDIX B: STRATEGIC FINANCIAL ANALYSIS

The strategic manager must use the financial reports prepared by the organization's accountants as one source of strategic signals. Using financial reports aids both in analyzing one's own organization and in studying competitive businesses.

Two major kinds of strategic signals are contained in financial reports; namely, profitability signals and viability signals.

PROFITABILITY

Whether looking at a competitor or at our own company, we want to know how profitable the business is. The specific data and ratios that might contain strategic information include

 I. Total profits (What is the general picture?)
  1. Net profits in absolute terms
  2. Net profits as a percentage of sales
 II. Operating profits (How profitable are operations, disregarding financial and tax costs?)
  1. Operating profits (sales minus cost of sales and operating expenses) in absolute terms
  2. Operating profits as a percentage of sales
 III. Costs (What are the critical cost elements?)
  1. Cost of goods sold as a percentage of sales
   (a) materials
   (b) labor
   (c) overhead
  2. Selling costs as a percentage of sales
  3. Administrative costs as a percentage of sales
  4. Financial, interest costs as a percentage of sales
  5. Depreciation as a percentage of sales

6. Taxes as a percentage of sales
7. Research and development as a percentage of sales

Because the strategic manager is concerned with the long term, these profitability measures provide strategic significance if they are viewed over a number of periods, preferably at least three to five years. The strategic manager really is looking for positive and negative signals contained in the *trend* of these measures. The direction in which the measures are heading is of more strategic importance than a single measure.

The strategic manager must consider not only profitability trends within the company, but also competitor-to-competitor trends. The strategic manager can put quantitative measures on the relative strength of the company versus the competition, and can begin to predict competitive strategies. For example, lower profits probably indicate a lower chance of price competition; higher research costs probably indicate a higher chance of new product innovations. Profitability measures are always a potential source for strategic signals, and often they will contain essential data for strategic judgments and decisions.

VIABILITY MEASURES

Profits indicate how well a firm is performing; viability measures depict the strengths or weaknesses of the firm's resources. The specific data and ratios that might contain strategic information include

I. Return on investment (How satisfactory are the profits?)
  1. Operating and net profit as percentages of stockholder's equity
  2. Operating and net profit as percentages of total assets
II. Value added (How important is the function performed?)
  1. Sales minus costs paid outside the firm to suppliers
III. Sources of capital (Where are resources coming from?)
  1. Funds provided by net income and depreciation
  2. Changes in net working capital (current assets minus current liabilities)
  3. Changes in net "quick" assets (current assets minus inventories and minus current liabilities)
  4. Debt as a percentage of total capital (total liabilities and equity minus current liabilities)
  5. Equity as a percentage of total capital
  6. Inventory turnover (cost of goods sold divided by average inventory)
IV. Uses of capital (Where are resources being allocated?)
  1. Dividends as a percentage of earnings
  2. Dividends as a percentage of total funds used
  3. Plant and equipment expenditures as a percentage of total funds used
V. Stock prices (How does the stock market view the firm's prospects?)
  1. Stock market prices

2. Volume of stock traded
3. Price earnings ratio

As with profitability measures, these viability measures, describing how "healthy" a firm is, should be examined from both the long term and the competitor-to-competitor viewpoints. What measures point to problems, and what measures show a firm's relative strength in comparison to its competitors'?

Specific financial ratios measure specific abilities of a firm. Liquidity ratios measure a firm's ability to pay short-term debts. A common liquidity ratio is

$$\frac{\text{Current assets}}{\text{Current liabilities}} = \text{Current ratio}$$

Many liquidity ratios suggest a ratio of about 2 to 1. Leverage ratios measure long-term debt, as follows:

$$\frac{\text{Total debt}}{\text{Total assets}} = \text{Leverage ratio}$$

A leverage ratio greater than 0.5 may indicate a debt repayment risk and/or inadequate profits and stockholder investment.

Activity ratios measure turnover of inventory (sales ÷ inventory), accounts receivable (sales ÷ accounts receivable), and asset turnover (sales ÷ fixed assets). These activity ratios may indicate that management successfully or unsuccessfully employs resources.

Finally, not all measures will be strategic signals. Viability and profitability measures must be viewed as potential sources of strategic information, not as having any intrinsic value. There is no right or wrong debt ratio, inventory turnover, or price earnings multiple. The strategic manager uses these measures as a signal of strategic problems or advantages. Financial measures thus indicate an issue that will require further strategic analysis and conclusion. The next step for the strategic manager is to analyze those factors and characteristics that resulted in a favorable or unfavorable indicator. Financial data provide input for strategic decision making; they are not ends in themselves.

APPENDIX C: UNIVERSITY OF NEW HAMPSHIRE BOOKSTORE CASE

Dennis Bellucci and Dan Carr were student representatives on the University of New Hampshire special committee considering the leasing of the university-owned

Case prepared by John Barnett and Dennis Bellucci for classroom discussion purposes only. © 1985 by John Barnett.

and -operated bookstore. A conversation they had in mid-November 1983 went as follows:

DENNIS: *Well, Dan, how do we represent the student's viewpoint now? The committee meeting is in one hour, and we think student needs can best be met through university management of the bookstore. Yet, we know the way this committee has been changed, from "Should we lease the bookstore?" to "Should we lease the bookstore to Barnes & Noble or to another private company?" And it looks like today's meeting is going to be the final one where we give in to the university administrators and forget it.*

DAN: *It's totally frustrating. We've spent fifteen to twenty hours a week on this bookstore all fall, and for what? And who knows what is best for the university? One lesson I've learned is how you cannot accept either words or deeds at face value.*

DENNIS: *It's not as if we have a lot of choices on the committee. We can go along, abstain, or walk out and call the newspapers and tell them how the students have been railroaded again.*

Dennis sat back in his chair in the Student Senate office, and reviewed in his mind the events leading up to the forthcoming meeting and this decision.

THE UNIVERSITY

The University of New Hampshire (U.N.H.) was founded in 1866 as the first land-grant institution in the United States. Located in Durham, a small seacoast community about midway between Boston and Portland, Maine, U.N.H. today has ten thousand students enrolled in a wide range of undergraduate and graduate programs.

The University System of New Hampshire board of trustees oversees U.N.H. and two state colleges. Of the twenty-five trustees, eleven are appointed by the governor; six are elected by alumni; one, a student, is elected by the students of U.N.H., Keene State College, and Plymouth State College in rotation; and seven are ex officio. The ex officio members are the governor; the commissioner of education; the commissioner of agriculture; the chancellor of the university system; and the presidents of U.N.H., Plymouth State College, and Keene State College. A chart of the university administration appears in Exhibit 1.

Various classifications of organizations or enterprises exist within the university or college. The bookstores fall into what are known as auxiliary enterprises. These organizations by state law cannot be subsidized with monies appropriated for the university; they are essentially "stand-alone" enterprises, and should generate a surplus. Any surplus so generated remains within that enterprise in a reserve account; monies within this account can only be reused by that same enterprise, whether it be for renovations or extraordinary expenses, or to offset losses. The university administration is prohibited from moving monies from one auxiliary enterprise to another.

Conversely, other organizations that are not auxiliary enterprises within the univer-

EXHIBIT 1
Partial U.N.H.
organization chart
(1983)

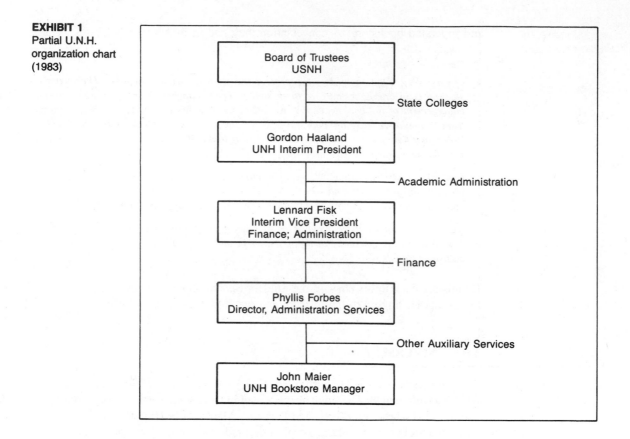

sity system — such as the library, the computer center, and athletic teams — are subsidized by appropriations. Monies generated by these activities can be moved by administration officials where needed.

Some university administrators view the auxiliary enterprises as services more than as profit centers, but feel that services such as the bookstore should not lose money. A well-stocked store, serving the needs of the students, faculty, and general public, was thought desirable.

GUBERNATORIAL REVIEW

In 1981, New Hampshire governor Hugh Gallen created a management review task force to analyze the operations of the state and find areas where the state could save money. One of the topics of the resultant report was an evaluation of the state's university system. The task force produced fourteen specific recommendations, one of which was to lease out the bookstore businesses at U.N.H. and Keene State College. The U.N.H. bookstore had shown a steady decline in income since

EXHIBIT 2
Management
Review
Commission
recommendations

Recommendations	Financial impact	Estimated amount
University System of New Hampshire		
Centralize all personnel services	Annual saving	$ 65,000
Consolidate information services	Annual saving	732,000
Terminate two positions on central Art Design and Graphics staff	Annual saving	35,000
Eliminate redundant physical plant activities	Annual saving	479,600
Identify and dispose of surplus property	One-time income	2,000,000
Eliminate the branch purchasing office at U.N.H.	Annual saving	38,400
Improve U.N.H. housekeeping services	Annual saving	455,000
Reduce inventory control staff at U.N.H. by one position	Annual saving	13,800
Raise fares for U.N.H. bus service	Annual income	253,800
Advance funding for U.N.H. steam system reconstruction by 12 months	One-time saving	1,000,000
Require adequate cost justification for U.N.H. research analyses	Annual saving	82,700
Designate all U.N.H. health services as limited auxiliary enterprises	Annual saving	290,000
Subcontract the bookstore operations at U.N.H. and Keene	Annual income	194,000
Develop housekeeping contracts for Plymouth	Annual saving	54,000

1980. Exhibit 2 presents excerpts from Governor Gallen's Review Commission Report.

THE UNIVERSITY BOOKSTORE

The University Bookstore spent most of its eighty-nine-year history as a monopoly. During the past decade, it grew at the rate of 10 percent a year and produced enough to cover its fixed expenses and allow it to at least break even or make a small profit of 1 or 2 percent. In the 1970s the bookstore built an image as a textbook and school-supply store; it stressed service and avoided competing with downtown merchants' soft lines or other products.

Problems started in 1981 when a private citizen, William Zucker, opened the Durham Book Exchange in a very advantageous downtown location. The Book Exchange broke the monopoly on textbooks held by the bookstore for years. The Book Exchange, through advertising its 5 percent discount of textbooks, succeeded in creating a desirable alternative to the high prices of the University Bookstore. The Book Exchange began to take some of the U.N.H. bookstore's business, resulting in an unanticipated decline in University Bookstore sales. From 1981 to 1984, the University Bookstore's sales declined, creating deficits. In fiscal year 1983 the bookstore suffered its greatest loss in its eighty-nine-year history, $75,000. Exhibit 3 presents a summary of the bookstore's results.

EXHIBIT 3 University Bookstore, summary of results, July–June fiscal year

	1978	1979	1980	1981	1982	1983
Revenues net of student discounts	$1,526,562	$1,723,754	$1,995,629	$2,167,325	$2,017,414	$2,054,393
Expenditures	$1,452,491	$1,662,439	$1,902,607	$2,145,039	$2,012,474	$2,158,149
Net from operations	$ 74,071	61,315	93,022	22,286	4,940	(103,756)
Inventory adjustment (see inventory investment, below*)	(46,554)	(32,498)	(161,660)	15,402	(39,140)	28,192
Building cost adjustment	—	26	—	—	—	—
Transfers to plant funds for capital additions	(75,000)	—	—	—	—	—
Net increase (decrease)	$ (47,483)	$ 28,843	$ (68,638)	$ 37,688	$ (34,200)	$ (75,564)
* Reserves invested in inventories	$ 202,727	$ 235,226	$ 396,887	$ 381,484	$ 420,624	$ 392,432

At approximately the same time the Book Exchange opened, the governor's management review task force began their analysis of the university system's financial situation. The task force recommended that the U.N.H. bookstore attain a 5.5 percent "net from operations" income by the end of fiscal year 1983. To help the bookstore achieve this goal, they also recommended that it become a "full-line" campus bookstore, incorporating the sale of books, art materials, office supplies, and other soft lines and souvenir merchandise customary to campus bookstores.

In the past an unwritten agreement had existed between the university and the Durham merchants that the University Bookstore not carry soft lines and no downtown merchant sell textbooks. After the entrance of the Durham Book Exchange, the trustees removed this restriction on the bookstore in October 1982. The University Bookstore then was given a nine-month deadline by which to increase the net income from operations from 1 to 2 percent to the 5.5 percent range. Failure to meet this goal would result in the Finance and Budget Committee's recommendation to develop specifications and solicitations for bids on the bookstore from outside companies.

MAIER'S STEPS

John Maier had worked for the University Bookstore since graduating from U.N.H. in 1972, and became its manager a few years before the 1981 management review.

Faced with financial and profit pressure, Maier, with the assistance of some U.N.H. business faculty, first undertook a study of revenue possibilities. He added higher margin soft lines, along with used books, the latter offering greater profit potential than the 20 percent margin allowed by textbook publishers. Finally, he also raised margins on nonbook items. The bookstore also turned to nonstudent markets, expanded its holdings of trade (i.e., nontextbook) publications, and dramatically increased advertising from $10,000 a year to $31,000 in an attempt to attract not only Durham, but seacoast New Hampshire customers as well.

Maier also directed his attention to cost control. He eliminated eight clerical personnel, five by attrition and three by termination. Exhibit 4 presents details of the July-to-June fiscal year's operating results. John Maier's nine-month deadline ended June 30, 1983 (the end of fiscal year 1983). The gubernatorial review had taken place in 1981 during the 1982 fiscal year (July 1 to June 30).

EXHIBIT 4 University Bookstore, selected operating data for the twelve months ending June 30

	1983		1982		1981	
	Percent	*Dollars*	*Percent*	*Dollars*	*Percent*	*Dollars*
Sales						
Textbooks	58	1,320,000	67	1,455,000	72	1,630,000
General books	15	355,000	11	240,000	7	160,000
Supplies	25	565,000	22	470,000	21	460,000
Clothing	2	55,000	–0–	–0–	–0–	–0–
Total sales	100	2,295,000	100	2,165,000	100	2,250,000
Computed gross profit						
Textbooks @ 20% (new 17%, used 33%)	43	265,000				
General books @ 30%	17	105,000				
Supplies @ 40%	36	225,000				
Clothing @ 50%	4	25,000				
	100	620,000				
Expenses						
Salaries, wages		390,000				
Student and sale discounts		170,000				
Supplies, office		55,000				
Advertising		30,000				
Accounting		10,000				
University interest, utilities, allocated costs		60,000				
		715,000				
Period profit (loss)		(75,000)		(35,000)		40,000

STUDENT INVOLVEMENT

Dennis Bellucci first became involved with the University Bookstore during the summer of 1983. Dennis, a member of the Class of 1985, had served as a representative from his dormitory to the Student Senate during his sophomore year. Representatives from the dormitories, fraternities, and commuters made up the elected senate.

Dennis was reelected to the senate for the 1983–1984 year. The student body president appointed Dennis to the seven-person executive board of the fifty-person Student Senate, as chairperson of Financial Affairs and Administration. This financial function led to his connection with the bookstore.

The Student Senate executive board routinely attended University System of New Hampshire board meetings as observers when the trustees were in Durham. The July 23, 1983, trustees meeting in Durham first made Dennis aware of the bookstore. Dennis later commented,

> *The board and President Haaland had been going along under the assumption that the bookstore would make its goal of 4.5 percent return. One of the trustees asked President Haaland if he thought the goal would be met. President Haaland said he thought so. John Maier, who was sitting with the public observers, stood up and said he didn't think the goal would be met. When asked further how the bookstore would do, John said he thought they would lose about $100,000. Jaws dropped. I felt especially embarrassed for the president.*

Later in the meeting the trustees directed that the situation be investigated further by U.N.H. administration.

Following the traditional decision-making format found at universities, Vice President Fisk put together a committee composed of Phyllis Forbes, the director of Administrative Services, John Maier, two faculty members, two administrators experienced both in purchasing and leased operations from other state colleges, and two student members, Dennis Bellucci and Dan Carr. The committee was called the Bookstore Bids and Specifications Committee. Dennis commented further:

> *Our committee met during the fall semester. Dan and I felt that the initial purpose of the committee was to see if the bookstore should be leased. We were also to prepare specifications to describe a minimum level of service an independent operator would have to provide, if a decision was made to lease.*
>
> *When I would report back to the Senate Executive Board, we would all discuss the question of the trend in student services. About three years ago the university had subcontracted out all the vending machines. Last year the student bus service was turned over to a private company that opened student buses to the public and changed student bus routes. Now there are rumors that the printing and rapid-copy service will be the next university activity to "go private and for-profit."*
>
> *As an example of how the university can get hurt, U.N.H. had to subsidize the private bus service with several hundred thousand dollars because the public demand expected*

by the private operator never materialized. But we were mostly concerned about the effect on the students of all this "for-profit" move.

Late in the summer Dennis and the executive board helped draft a resolution for the president. The resolution, one of the best forms of communication that the Student Senate has with the university, requires senate approval to be sent to the university president. The board decided that the resolution should be brief, and should ask for a delay in the bidding process until January 1, 1984, in order to see how the fall book rush went. *Book rush* is the time of the year when textbooks are sold at the beginning of classes; it is a peak revenue raising period for the bookstore. The resolution would represent a call to the university's attention that students were concerned with the bookstore matter.

The resolution addressed four central issues to be examined before leasing the bookstore. The first and most important issue was the bookstore's location. The present location was not near any major path running through campus and was too great a "psychological" distance from the center of campus; it was a ten-minute walk from the hub of campus activity, the Memorial Union Building. The resolution suggested that the Memorial Union Building would be a better location for the bookstore. A 1973 architectural study of U.N.H. also recommended a Memorial Union Building site for the bookstore. This proposed location would also provide a more direct position to compete with the downtown establishments.

The second resolution issue was that the views of faculty and students, as the main source of business and economic support to the university, should be considered before any action to be taken. Currently, the service was generally satisfactory to faculty; students were concerned mostly with the textbook service. Students will buy books at the location that provides texts at the lowest cost along with acceptable service levels.

Third, the Student Senate was concerned about products sold. For example, why were children's books included in the bookstore? John Maier noted that the faculty appreciated this children's book service and that they were the people most responsible for maintaining this service. Further, the bookstore's soft lines had the reputation of not being the best in the area. The senate felt that the bookstore should make a greater effort in this area, especially considering that these products had the highest margins.

Finally, the last area that the resolution examined was the Department of Administrative Services and the management of the bookstore. The Student Senate feared that the university would contract out too many vital services and would create future problems in controlling service levels and costs.

Dennis commented,

As students, it was felt that we really could accomplish something at the outset. We had the belief that deep down, we could prevent something from happening. The committee, as we viewed it, did not want to sell the bookstore and was searching for ideas to turn the slump around. The first thing that we picked up in committee was the constant reference to Barnes & Noble by the director of Administrative Services, Phyllis Forbes. It did not strike us as odd until the end of November.

The basic question among students concerned was, "Why would someone bid on an operation that was losing money? We felt that if there was money to be made, the university should make it."

CALL FOR BIDS AND REACTION

As fiscal year 1983 came to a close with a bookstore loss, and as the university trustees announced their decision to call for lease bids and proposals, bookstore employees and John Maier began talking to the press. This "media campaign" was not in full swing until the fall semester was under way in late 1983. The campaign centered on (1) "open" letters to the trustees from bookstore employees printed in the student newspaper and (2) bookstore employee interviews with a staff writer from the local daily newspaper, *Foster's Daily Democrat*. The three most active bookstore spokespeople were Roland Goodbody, Ted Whittemore, and Lauren Hill.

In November 1983 *Foster's Daily Democrat* reported:

The most recent recent letter was written by one of the bookstore's clerks. It is the second such letter from the bookstore in the past few months correcting [University trustee] Paul Holloway. . . . Holloway said he is tired of the letters from the bookstore and what is "getting to be a non-professional performance" on the part of bookstore employees. "If the management would spend more time managing and less time writing letters, they'd do a better job," he said.

Ted Whittemore, . . . one of the bookstore clerks active in the fight . . . noted that the bookstore workers are taking on the job of representing themselves to the public because they feel no one else will. (11/7/83)

Bookstore employee Lauren Hill . . . visited the trustee Finance and Budget Committee Wednesday. . . . The staff, he said, felt that the manager of the bookstore "had a personal feud with the competition, which we don't feel comfortable with." The staff felt the issue was much larger, that the atmosphere of an academic bookstore might be lost and in fact their jobs might be lost if trustees follow the route of contracting the management to a private operator.

Trustees seemed surprised that Hill made the comments directly to them, instead of pursuing the normal avenue of communication through bookstore manager John Maier.

Some praised his courage, but others said the matter shouldn't have been brought directly to them. Len Fisk, U.N.H. interim vice president of financial affairs, expressed having a "great deal of difficulty with the thought that the operating staff came directly to the trustees. It's a free country, but I sincerely hope you are on annual leave." (11/10/83)

Roland Goodbody sent a letter to all U.N.H. faculty pointing out the service objectives of the store and problems with leasing (see Exhibit 5, page 44–45).

Despite all these efforts, the committee agreed under pressure from Phyllis Forbes to solicit bids from eleven private companies, four of whom replied. The four formal bids received are summarized as follows:

1. *Barnes & Noble*: Would pay a fixed annual rent of $190,000 for the first three years and $215,000 for each of the last two years. In addition, renovations of $200,000 would be undertaken at the present bookstore location. Textbooks would be offered at a discount.

2. *Brennan College Services*: Would pay a fixed annual rent of $34,430 plus 2.48 percent of net sales. If sales were over $3 million, they would offer a 5.1 percent commission fee.

3. *Campus Services*: Would pay a fixed annual rent of $175,000 or 7.5 percent of net sales, whichever was higher. They also planned major renovations to maximize sales.

4. *College Stores*: Would pay a fixed annual rate of $50,000 plus a percentage of net sales, 3 percent on sales less than $4 million and 5 percent on sales over $4 million. They planned to discount supplies but not textbooks.

Dennis frankly admitted to himself that he was pretty tired of the bookstore issues. He eventually ignored repeated phone calls from John Maier, as Maier's direct (and indirect through the employees) press campaign became more of an annoyance than news. "If I never get another phone call from John Maier or his aides, Roland Goodbody or Ted Whittemore, I'll be happy," Dennis thought.

Maier himself had lost some credibility as the champion of the university-managed bookstore when it became known that several of the companies submitting bids for leasing the bookstore had contacted Maier about becoming their manager. Maier then resigned from the committee and was replaced by another bookstore employee.

Dennis and Don walked over to the committee meeting, talking about the change in Phyllis Forbes's questions from "Should we lease the bookstore?" to "Should we lease the bookstore to Barnes & Noble?" Despite constant rumors that the university and/or Maier would submit a bid for the university to continue running the bookstore, a bid had yet to materialize.

As Dennis reviewed his options of acquiescence, abstention, or adversarial accusation in the press, he was startled to see Vice President Fisk come to the meeting with Phyllis Forbes. "Looks like even a delay is going to be impossible," Dennis thought.

"The discussions of this committee today are to remain strictly confidential," Fisk began. "We are not here to decide if the bookstore is to be leased. President Haaland and I will decide on that and make recommendations to the trustees. What this committee should deal with, and the only thing it should deal with, is: If the bookstore is leased out, to whom should it be leased?"

24 October 1983

TO: All Department Chairpersons

FROM: UNH Bookstore Staff

RE: Impact on Faculty of Leasing of UNH Bookstore

We feel that the following information is of particular importance to you as faculty. We urge you to share it with others in your department and to support us in our effort to oppose the leasing of the bookstore.

A year ago, acting on GMR #153 (subcontracting the system bookstores), the Board of Trustees mandated that the UNH bookstore show a 5.5% profit margin, failing which bid specifications were to be prepared for possible contracting of operations in Fiscal 1984. In June the bookstore reported an operating deficit and so bid specifications were drawn up and sent out to prospective subcontractors earlier this month.

The bookstore leasing issue is therefore already at an advanced stage. Bidding will close on November 10, at which time a team of University administrators will review the bids and make appropriate recommendations. But this does not mean that the issue is closed. On November 9 the Trustee Finance and Budget Committee will meet to review the current financial status of the bookstore. If, as is expected, the figures indicate an upward trend toward achieving the mandated 5.5% profit margin, there is a chance that the Committee will recommend reconsidering the leasing question.

We believe, however, that the decision whether or not to lease the UNH bookstore should not rest on a simple comparison of profit margins, but should be based on an examination of all aspects of the issue. The Student Senate and some members of the faculty have already independently expressed their support for a more comprehensive approach. We urge you to examine the following information and voice your opinion on this issue.

1. *Service and Academic Resource.* The present UNH bookstore functions as a crucial educational resource for the institution and provides a high level of service. There is much evidence to suggest that many, and perhaps all, of these services will be drastically reduced or eliminated altogether under leased operations.

2. *Criteria Used.* The significance of this comparison lies in the fact that both the Governor's Management Review team and the Trustees specifically used the Plymouth store as the standard against which the UNH store was measured. According to one GMR member, the team simply abstracted Plymouth's financial arrangement and applied it to the UNH bookstore, having no reason to believe that such an application was inappropriate. This is where the 5.5% profit margin originated.

3. *Financial Viability.* For the five years prior to 1983 the UNH bookstore recorded a profit. This financial year has seen increased sales of 12% over last year and 33% more traffic in the store. Operating costs have also been cut by not moving Bookrush out of the store and by hiring work-study students in place of hourly staff. What this all indicates is that the bookstore is a financially viable operation which, given proper time for the recent changes to take effect, would demonstrate its capabilities.

4. *Other Options.* Rather than leasing the UNH bookstore to a private operator, it would be more fruitful for the institution to consider alternative profit-increasing options for the store. The possibility of relocating the store more centrally could be explored. Other considerations could include a student and staff operated co-op store, such as those at Dartmouth and the University of Connecticut, or a system-wide bookstore operation.

Please address your response to the Trustee Finance and Budget Committee, c/o Edward F. Smith, Dunlap Center, Lee, no later than October 31. *We apologize for the short notice, but hope that you will find time to respond to this.*

For the Bookstore Staff

Roland Goodbody

Roland Goodbody
Bookstore Clerk

APPENDIX D: BOOKSTORE CASE ANALYSIS

CASE OVERVIEW

Dennis Bellucci, student representative, is trying to decide what action he should take regarding the leasing of the U.N.H. bookstore to a private operator.

The bookstore has operated as a monopoly for almost a century. Now local competition has hit hard, and the former service strategy of the bookstore seems inappropriate to the store's critics, including some U.N.H. trustees and the recommendations of a gubernatorial "management review."

The bookstore has been given a deadline; instead of producing a profit, it has handed in a significant loss.

One of the issues that must be resolved is that of perspective. Should the case be analyzed from the point of view of Dennis Bellucci, the student representative? John Maier, the bookstore manager? A university administrator? Three levels of strategy present themselves. Dennis Bellucci might be thought of as representing the functional level: he is to express the student viewpoint. John Maier should have the business strategy perspective. How can he achieve success in his product market? The university administrators, President Haaland and Vice President Fisk, can represent the corporate strategy viewpoint. They seek to determine and implement a long-term direction for the university, of which the bookstore is only a small part.

This case, then, illustrates the Brunswik lens effect, for perception varies according to the role taken. This point is covered in the following section.

IDENTIFYING AND EVALUATING OPTIONS

In identifying his options, Dennis has three choices: (1) to give in to the university administration's wishes, (2) to abstain, or (3) to continue the fight to keep the bookstore within the university system.

Perspective is critical in evaluating the various options in the bookstore issue. Through John Maier's lens, the university has an ethical responsibility to its employees. A nine-month test does not seem adequate.

From the university's perspective, Barnes & Noble or other private operators are a source of "hard" dollars. The state's enterprise system sees to it that the university never gets any funds out of the owned bookstore; but lease payments would be available to the university administration if a private operator were installed.

From the students' perspective, the past has shown that the intangible feature of service is not as important as price. If Dennis Bellucci takes the long-term perspective of the strategic manager, under which option — lease or not lease — is the overall price level likely to remain the lowest? Will a Barnes & Noble lease lead to increased competition in the long run? Certainly in the short run, competition might increase; the Durham Book Exchange might not have the resources to compete effectively against a Barnes & Noble.

MAKING RECOMMENDATIONS AND IMPLEMENTING STRATEGY

It is presumably too late to save the University Bookstore, but one wonders if, in any event, the present management is capable of effective competition and profitable operation. Nonetheless, Dennis as strategic manager might try to establish a price-level monitoring system for student protection in the long term. Perhaps a price monitoring service for popular texts might be established with Boston universities and other nearby universities.

AFTERWORD

Over the Christmas recess, the university announced the decision to lease the bookstore to Barnes & Noble. John Maier then mailed a letter to all faculty announcing he would become the Barnes & Noble manager in May, and pledging the continuance of high levels of service. Barnes & Noble indicated they would review all employees

July 1. John Maier then left Barnes & Noble in July to become manager of the Phillips-Exeter Academy Bookstore in Exeter, New Hampshire.

APPENDIX E: THE CASE METHOD

The primary teaching method used in strategic management is the case method. Cases allow you to apply the art of the strategic process in real-life situations.

Two basic principles apply to case work. First, the cases are not designed to prepare you for a specific incident you may meet in your business career; they are simply vehicles that force you to practice systematic analysis and decision making. Second, there are no school solutions to the cases. Your job is to analyze the situation, define the major problem(s), decide on appropriate courses of action, and logically and rationally present and defend your recommendation. Recommendations to the cases may differ considerably, and many recommendations might be creditable alternatives. Your work will be evaluated in terms of how clearly, precisely, and logically you think the problems through and defend your recommendations.

The following outline provides a very broad, general checklist. In any specific case used in this course, only parts of this outlined analysis will be appropriate. Make sure you use this checklist only as a general reminder, not as a "cookbook" appropriate to every situation.

GENERAL APPROACH

Case analysis generally proceeds through the following seven stages or steps.

1. Sizing up the situation
2. Evaluating the present strategy
3. Identifying issues and options
4. Evaluating options
5. Making recommendations
6. Implementing strategy
7. Monitoring results

Sizing up the Situation

What is the enterprise doing at present? In what circumstances? With what results? As you answer these questions, you are getting a feel for the situation. You are obtaining the facts in a meaningful order and placing dimensions upon them.

1. Analyze the economics of the situation.
   1.1 Attributes of products and of the demand for them (the demand curve)
   1.2 Attributes of the technology, including the productive and distributive processes

1.3 The input mix, the cost mix, the unit (average) cost curve

1.4 The competitive situation both in the market for the inputs and in the market for the finished products

1.5 The price-cost-volume-profit relationships resulting from 1.1 through 1.4

2. Analyze opportunities and constraints, and strengths and weaknesses relative to them.

3. Identify the strategy of the enterprise, which refers to established company policy concerning

3.1 Mission, objectives, and goals

3.2 Strategy being employed

    3.2(1) to improve opportunities

    3.2(2) to overcome constraints

    3.2(3) to meet competition

    3.2(4) to gain access to markets, both as buyer and as seller, on favorable terms

3.3 Basic decisions concerning

    3.3(1) products and markets

    3.3(2) technology

    3.3(3) make-or-buy

    3.3(4) resource procurement

    3.3(5) location

    3.3(6) scale

    3.3(7) standards

From the outline you should derive insight into what the enterprise is trying to do — its "game plan" — and the circumstances in which this effort is being made. You will assemble and order the available facts, analyze them objectively, and withhold a decision until the size-up has been completed.

As you attempt to identify the strategy of an organization, you may study (1) its pronouncements as to its purpose, (2) its resource allocation, (3) its products and markets, and (4) its method of competition.

Pronouncements. Often you will come across a statement of strategy, such as "We want to be the General Motors of XYZ industry"; "We want constantly rising earnings"; or "We want to be on the cutting edge of technology." You should look for statements about what a company wants to be or what it wants to do.

Resource Allocation. Strategic pronouncements might be too general to be of help, or they might be contradictory or misleading. Assuming that the company has a logical procedure for allocating monies for capital expenditures, you may be able to deduce what the company's strategy is by where it spends its money. Unfortunately, a company might not have a logical procedure for capital budgeting. Certainly political and bureaucratic processes might outweigh strategic considerations, especially in a huge bureaucracy like the General Electric of 1950.

Products and Markets. What is the company selling and to whom? Reduce the product to its essential nature, if possible, in order to understand where the company's skills lie: Does a cruise line transport people or entertain them? Does a technical school train people or place them in jobs? The answer often varies, and you need analytical and judgmental tools to answer questions about the product.

The market may be described geographically, or as a customer or consumer group, or as one or more segments within customer groups. Again, use a very broad definition of markets; neat and tidy definitions may not work for many companies. What is Sears, Roebuck's market? Catalog and store customers? Financial consumers? Real estate purchasers and sellers?

Competitive Focus. The nature of a company's competitive thrust reveals a lot about a company's strategy. Does the company compete on the basis of price, quality, technology, and/or marketing skills? Is it a leader or a follower in product research? How important is service? A firm often competes on the basis of what it believes is the most significant resource in its internal environment.

Summary. To begin analyzing a company's strategy, identify critical aspects of the strategy by asking

What does the company say its strategy is?

How does the company spend its resources?

What does the company sell and to whom?

How does the company compete?

Analyzing the individual answers and the relationship of each answer to the sum of all four answers should move you beyond the identification of strategy to the more demanding evaluation of strategy.

Evaluating the Present Strategy

A company's game plan may or may not make sense or work well. Evaluate a game plan in terms of the following criteria.

1. Are the separate elements that make up the strategy consistent with each other and mutually supportive?
2. Is the strategy appropriate considering the surrounding circumstances (externalities) and the internal situation (resources, purpose)?
3. Are these policies and strategies likely to enable the enterprise to meet not only short-term goals but long-term objectives as well?
4. Have considerations of ethical and social responsibility been properly taken into account?
5. How satisfactory are the results?
6. Is the strategy practical and workable?
7. Does the strategy adequately consider risk?

Identifying Issues and Options

Against the background of the size-up and evaluation that you have made, what policy/strategy issues are most important? What are the alternatives to these issues — the realistic options open to the enterprise?

Try to distinguish between primary and secondary issues, the latter being either derived from and dependent upon the first, or of lesser importance. Concentrate on *one*, or, at most, *a few* primary issues. You will analyze more effectively by narrowing your field and sharpening your focus. Carefully and thoroughly considering a small number of important issues is far preferable to an extensive and, therefore, more superficial coverage. Cases often contain an "action" question which is only symptomatic of the real problem(s).

Evaluating Options

Develop the arguments for and against each option, including the option of making no change from the present course of action. Remember to consider *costs* and implications for *organization* and *personnel*. At a minimum, consider the following criteria for each option.

1. *Appropriateness*: Will the option allow us to achieve our objectives?
2. *Feasibility*: Do we have the resources — tangible and intangible — to achieve our objectives?
3. *Reality*: Do we want to go with this option? Will or does top management buy into it?
4. *Workability*: Can we gain corporate-wide organizational committment?

Making Recommen- dations

What would you recommend for change in the present strategy? And how should these recommendations be accomplished? Useful policy/strategy recommendations are specific, making explicit the *rate* of change and any scheduling or phasing being recommended; the additional resources, if any, to be procured; and any organizational and personnel changes involved.

Implementing Strategy

A proposed strategy is useless unless the organization commits to its adoption. When implementing a recommendation you must consider (at a minimum): *Who* will be in charge of its implementation? What *time* frame is involved in its implementation? Does the organization need to restructure, or is the present structure appropriate? Why? How will people be affected by its implementation? Will a new motivation or compensation system be necessary? How will you know if the plan is not working?

Monitoring Results

Timely and accurate information assists the strategic manager in determining if the proposed recommendations are working. The ongoing nature of the strategy process entails a constant monitoring and appraisal of results. Any variances must be quickly identified and corrected, so that operating remedies may be identified, evaluated, and implemented.

By following these seven steps to analyzing a case study, you will more quickly develop a logical approach to strategic problems. Nonetheless, since each case is unique, some aspects of some or even all of these steps may not be appropriate, given the nature of the case issues and alternatives.

INDUSTRY ANALYSIS

Since a company's success depends in part on the economics of its industry, you should look for information about the industry in general. Ideally, you would like to be able to answer the following four questions about the industry.

1. How does the general economy affect the industry?
2. How does the industry affect the economy?
3. What is the general trend of industry sales?
4. What are the characteristics of the industry?
   — number of companies
   — percentage share of industry sales
   — barriers to entry
   — capital versus labor intensity
   — value added
   — level of competition
   — method(s) of competition
   — rate of technological change
   — research and development expenditures
   — international factors
   — regulatory factors

Industry trends and industry characteristics will have important strategic implications. The strategic manager in a declining industry may be very reluctant to make major capital investments. The manager in an increasingly competitive industry may revise marketing promotion and pricing policies.

In addition, the performance of a specific company versus the performance of the industry as a whole can tell you a great deal about the success of a company's strategy and its strength relative to that of the industry.

CLASS PARTICIPATION

The primary role of the instructor is to facilitate discussion. Generally, the instructor will try to direct the discussion only when critical issues are being ignored or the discussion is not progressing. Occasionally the instructor may intervene in order to make sure your analysis is complete or to give you practice in defending your recommendations. These occasional interventions should be viewed as ultimately helpful, even if they may prove somewhat stressful. Since there is not one correct answer, the instructor will serve as a listener for reasonable suggestions and logical analyses.

Exhibit 1 includes some general guidelines for effective versus ineffective class participation.

EXHIBIT 1
Class participation factors

Positive Factors/Effective Participation

1. A complete analysis of one or more important case issues and problems
2. A well-reasoned conclusion following logically from a complete analysis
3. A reasonable recommendation for action while recognizing the consequences of that action
4. Constructive criticism of another student's comments
5. The integration of concepts and theories from other courses and/or from other cases
6. Effective communication

Negative Factors/Ineffective Participation

1. Repetition of case facts without analysis or conclusion
2. Irrelevant comments
3. Lack of participation
4. Poor communicative ability

CHAPTER 3

DEFINING PURPOSE

A man in Boston has dedicated
himself
to telling about injustice.
For three-thousand dollars he will
come to your town and tell you
about it.

William Stafford, "Things I Learned Last Week"

This chapter describes the three components of enterprise purpose: (1) personal values of managers, (2) organizational priorities, and (3) societal goals. The strategic manager analyzes these components and defines the enterprise purpose, or mission. The relative importance of each component depends upon the strategic manager's perspective.

In the long term, selling a product or service to a customer is the essence of mission. During some crises in the history of an enterprise, its mission can be stated very simply — *survival*. Corporations such as Lockheed, Chrysler, Continental Illinois National Bank and Trust, Braniff, American Motors, and Penn Central reached periods in their history during which their only motivation was to survive.

U.S. Steel chairman David Roderick issued survival orders based upon the concept that nothing is sacred. As *Business Week* reported (2/25/85, p. 50), Roderick

Closed 150 manufacturing sites.

Reduced capacity by 30 percent.

Eliminated 54 percent of administrative positions.

Dismissed one hundred thousand workers.

Sold $3 billion in assets.

Lee Iacocca commented on Chrysler's mission of survival in *Iacocca: An Autobiography*:

Everyone talks about "strategy," but all we knew was survival. Survival was simple. Close the plants that are hurting us most. . . . Fire the people who aren't absolutely necessary . . . two moves alone cut out $500 million in annual costs, but the firings were just tragic, and there's no way to pretend otherwise.

A popular assumption is that firms pursue growth. The pursuit of corporate growth was especially in evidence in the automobile industry in 1985. Both U.S. and West German automobile giants pursued high-tech growth by turning to the aerospace industry for major acquisitions. General Motors acquired Hughes Aircraft Company in a dramatic sealed-bid purchase, and Daimler-Benz purchased Germany's second-largest aerospace manufacturer, Dornier.

Leslie Wexner, founder and chairman of The Limited, the chain of women's clothing stores, talked about growth:

My vision of the business is always to have a large one. When I had two stores, ten stores seemed like a lot. [Now with 2,500 stores] . . . I'd like to believe that trees can grow to the sky. None have yet, but that doesn't mean it's impossible. (Fortune, 8/19/85, p. 154)

Although the pursuit of growth is necessary for survival in the face of increasing competition, the strategic manager must develop a perspective broader than the simplistic purposes of survival and growth. Figure 3.1 shows that the strategic manager views the enterprise purpose through a tri-focal lens. Defining purpose means identifying (1) personal values of managers, (2) organizational priorities, and (3) relevant social goals.

PERSONAL VALUES

Key managers have values that are personal, and thus are determined independently of the organization. The manager's personal values, held regardless of the organization, are the values of interest to the strategic manager. The personal values of top management may be the dominant, single driving force behind the entire enterprise. Edwin Land dominated Polaroid; Harold Geneen was the single force driving ITT;

FIGURE 3.1
Strategic managerial perspective

and Thomas Watson shaped IBM. Although one executive rarely dominates a large corporation (the preceding three being exceptions), little difference exists between the objectives of the small business and the personal values of its founder or leader.

In his autobiography, Lee Iacocca elaborated on personal values. At this stage in his life, money and "the good life" were important personal values:

> *I often ask myself why I didn't quit [Ford] at the end of 1975. Why did I accept the fate Henry [Ford] was dishing out? How could I let a guy take my destiny and pummel it?*
>
> *First, like anybody in a bad situation, I hoped things would get better. . . .*
>
> *I was also greedy. I enjoyed being president. . . . I was getting soft, seduced by the good life. And I found it almost impossible to walk away from an annual income of $970,000.*

Examples of personal values of key managers include (1) personal development and psychological/spiritual growth, (2) active parenting, (3) the acquisition of personal wealth, (4) prestige and recognition, (5) altruism, and (6) increase in the quality of life.

T. Roland Berner, the second of three chief executives at Western Union in four months, commented on personal values (in his case, active family and personal life) and work: "It was a tough job. The biggest Christmas present my family wanted was for me to become human again" (*Business Week*, 1/14/85, p. 36). The Limited's Leslie Wexner expressed another dimension (the drive to succeed) of personal values: "My biggest frustration is that I never feel I can work hard enough. I read *The Agony and the Ecstasy* three times and empathized with Michelangelo" (*Business Week*, 2/25/85, p. 78). And Sony's Morita forced the development of the Walkman cassette over strong opposition within Sony because he wanted music while he played golf!

W. L. Gore & Associates, Inc. in Delaware shows the influence that managers' personal values have on organizational priorities. Chairman Bill Gore, his wife and the company's secretary-treasurer, Genevieve, and other family members control the company stock with others who work at Gore. Gore's personal values, specifically his distaste for boss-employee relationships, has led to this worker-ownership of Gore. At Gore, workers are called *associates*, work units are led by group and area leaders, and plants are kept to the small size of two hundred workers. Although Gore has over thirty plants, employee productivity and morale are high.

The activities of corporate raiders put the spotlight on managers' personal values during the mid-1980s. Many speculate about a future stage of corporate development — Will professional managers be turning large, institutional (Stage Three) corporations over to institutional investors?

Raider Saul Steinberg made $32 million (plus $28 million in expenses) when Walt Disney bought his stock at a premium. Carl Icahn has made more than $100 million on takeover bids, while the "greenmail" (stock price premiums) profits of T. Boone Pickens and his partners have exceeded $800 million. British raider James Goldsmith asserted that raiders operate "for the public good, but that's not why I do it. I do it to make money" (*Business Week*, 3/4/85, p. 80).

Business Week's survey of executive salaries (5/6/85, p. 79) showed that arch-raider T. Boone Pickens received total compensation of $22,823,000 in 1984 from Mesa Petroleum; shareholders received only $14 million in dividends. Pickens's pay was equal to the total received by the chairs of Chrysler, Wang, Ford, IBM, Exxon, and Dun & Bradstreet combined. Pickens's primary target, oil companies, included some that responded to corporate raid threats and growth problems by getting rid of shareholders. Those that bought back their own stock included Phillips Petroleum (53 percent, after raids by Pickens and others), Atlantic Richfield (25 percent), Pennzoil (16 percent), Sun (13 percent), Exxon (12 percent), and Amoco (10 percent).

Among the questions raiders raise about mission and managers' personal values are:

1. If managers try to maximize shareholder returns, why do they pay "greenmail"?
2. Do raiders force managers to focus on short-term profits to keep stock prices up?
3. Do raiders assist in the efficient distribution of resources, correcting the mismanaged assets of the complacent, arrogant corporate giant?

ORGANIZATIONAL PRIORITIES

What are organizational priorities? How are they determined? How are they perpetuated?

While exceptional cases exist in which organizational priorities can be expressed simplistically as survival, growth, or profit maximization, the priorities of the organization reflect its economic, political, and social components. Thus there are economic priorities, such as a minimum level of profitability and return on investment, or the development of production and distribution systems. There are also political priorities, such as the development of a managerial budget negotiation system. And social priorities might include the provision of employment during times of high unemployment, and equal opportunity.

How do companies determine these priorities? Working Concept 8 on organizational power describes the mechanism for priority determination.

WORKING CONCEPT **8**

MINTZBERG'S ORGANIZATIONAL POWER

EXTERNAL SOURCES

Mintzberg's theory of organizational power and goals (1979) addresses organizational priorities from the perspective of power. Mintzberg first looks at those external sources of power—such as owners, unions, and the public—who directly influence the organization's priorities, through membership on the board of directors, employee labor contracts, social norms, or government regulation. These external power groups may be focused and gathered together by a dominant power; they may be divided; or they may be passive.

INTERNAL SOURCES

Mintzberg then looks at sources of internal power, including top management, middle line managers, operators, technical analysts, and support staff. He identifies four systems of influence through which organizational priorities are determined. The first is the personal control system dominated by the CEO and top management. Mintzberg's second system is the bureaucratic control system that replaces the top manager's power with a system of rules, policies, and procedures. The third is a political system which — because of ambiguities in formal goals, inclination to pursue one's personal values, group pressures, and political skills of people throughout the organization — consists of political power games. The games are played through (1) the decision-making process, (2) the provision of information and advice, and (3) the interpretation and implementation of policies. The fourth system is the ideology control system, in which dominant ideas — such as a religious doctrine or a social need — focus the organization.

Mintzberg concludes that internal power can then lead to (1) autocratic coalitions, (2) bureaucratic coalitions, (3) politicized coalitions, (4) ideologic coalitions, or (5) meritocratic coalitions. A meritocratic coalition is one in which a complex technology or professional service becomes the "best" or most meritorious coalition, and can then dominate priorities.

POWER CONFIGURATIONS

Mintzberg completes his model by grouping these external and internal power sources into six commonly encountered power configurations: (1) continuous chain, (2) closed system, (3) commander, (4) missionary, (5) professional, and (6) conflictive. One of these six power configurations determines the organization's priorities.

The continuous-chain power configuration couples a dominant external control force with clearly understood goals. The organization with this power configuration has "simple, mass-output systems" so that common goals can exist and power flows from the external controllers throughout the organization. Some examples of continuous-chain organizations are the stock exchange or, in the public sector, the post office.

One step removed from the continuous-chain organization is the closed-system power configuration typical of many widely held, divisionalized corporations. The closed system differs in that it has only a passive external power group, such as stockholders. It is more politicized and less autocratic or bureaucratic than its continuous-chain counterpart since it is not dominated by external power and does not have clear goals.

The commander, the third power configuration, is based upon an autocratic leadership. Commander power emerges in firms confronting extreme crisis, so that external and internal power groups surrender control to the leader for survival. Entrepreneurial firms also employ commander power configurations to determine priorities.

The fourth and fifth power configurations are the missionary and the professional, representative of the ideology and meritocracy groups respectively. Volunteer agencies and legal firms illustrate the missionary and the professional configurations.

Sixth and last is Mintzberg's conflictive power configuration, which may occur when any of the first five power configurations are under attack or experiencing internal dissension, such as separate but conflicting missions or a harsh conflict between two leaders. In these situations the organization's priorities are determined in a purely political way. Conflictive power organizations are usually short-term anomalies, since most organizations cannot survive continuous, prolonged conflict.

To review, priorities are determined by one of the following six power configurations: .

A *continuous chain* dominated by an external control force determining priorities
A *closed system* determining priorities through internal political and social means
A *commander*, in which a leader determines priorities
A *missionary*, in which the ideology defines the priorities
A *professional*, in which professional aims determine priorities
A *conflictive*, in which politics alone determine priorities

Once these priorities are determined, however, they must then be reinforced and perpetuated. Because organizational priorities are embodied in the corporate culture, their existence is ensured.

Mintzberg's power configurations also influence the personal values of key managers. Clearly, the manager's personal values interact with the priorities of the organization; the degree of the interaction and influence will depend on the degree to which the manager internalizes the organizational priorities. Internalizing and strengthening individual values and beliefs are subjective and dependent upon each specific circumstance. Nevertheless, it is recognized that, while the degree of interaction is an individual matter, it is a real phenomenon.

CORPORATE CULTURE

The shared values, beliefs, and traditions of an organization make up its corporate culture. The corporate culture is determined by the organization's priorities as defined by the commander, the external power control group, or another of Mintzberg's power configurations. Thus, organizational power determines organizational priorities, which then form the corporate culture, as Figure 3.2 depicts. The corporate

FIGURE 3.2
Power, priorities, and culture

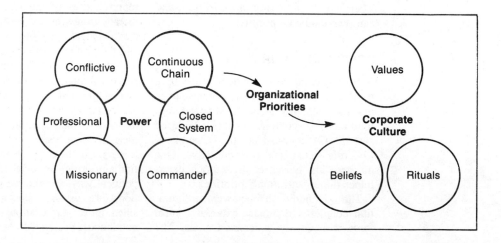

cultures applied to Mintzberg's six power configurations might include (1) accountability in the continuous-chain system, (2) productivity in the closed system, (3) loyalty in the commander system, (4) zeal in the missionary system, (5) objectivity in the professional system, and (6) competition in the conflictive system.

EXAMPLE: *Corporate Culture*

The effects of corporate culture can be seen in these observations about Heinz, Polaroid, Fluor, and St. Joe in 1985. Heinz's 1985 strategy (*Fortune*, 6/24/85, pp. 44–54) of becoming a low-cost producer resulted in a corporate culture of cost reduction. The result was referred to by the manufacturing vice president as a "culture [that] has been chip, chip, chip." Management and hourly employees formed cost-reduction suggestion teams, package size was reduced, and production was shifted offshore to Puerto Rico and Samoa.

Polaroid, whose Personnel Policy 251 guaranteed lifetime employment to those employees with ten years' experience, had to end the policy in 1985 in the face of a "civil service mentality," that is, a corporate culture requiring only the bare minimum from its employees. Polaroid needed to enter new industries, but lacked the talented, entrepreneurial executives necessary to accomplish the task.

"Incompatible corporate cultures" was one of the main reasons cited by *Business Week* in its analysis (6/3/85, pp. 92–93) of the failure of the merger of Fluor, an engineering and construction firm, with St. Joe, a mining company. St. Joe's managers, reflecting the company's corporate culture, were used to taking big risks. They had a streamlined overhead budget and freely exercised management initiative. Fluor, however, had a corporate culture that reflected its large, bureaucratic managerial structure. Their large overhead budget was evidenced in their fleet of helicopters and planes, and managers could expect a long wait in the decision-making process. The merger also failed because the deal was made in one week's time, while St. Joe was trying to escape from a Seagram takeover attempt. St. Joe's chairman described it as a time "so brief it was embarrassing."

An expert on corporate culture, Management Analysis Center's Howard Schwartz commented on the difficulty of "instant" changes in corporate culture: "You can't change culture by working on it directly. You must have some strategic ground to stand on, then build a vision of what a company wants to be before rubbing their noses in what they are" (*Fortune*, 10/17/83, p. 69). Schwartz and Davis (1981) stressed the importance of matching corporate culture and business strategy.

SOCIAL GOALS

The enterprise exists in a social environment that has goals. In a pluralistic society, such as in North America, different groups within society may have different goals. Some may consider personal liberty to be the ultimate social goal. For these libertarians, no social programs, including police procedures, must ever interfere with one's personal civil liberties. Others may feel that equality in all senses — especially economic equality — is the ultimate social goal. Egalitarians sacrifice elements of personal liberty in areas such as employment in order to achieve equality. Other alternative social goals are technological progress versus environmental integrity.

The enterprise in a pluralistic society thus finds itself with a spectrum of competing goals. Society also has a set of generally supported social goals (i.e., education; adequate, affordable health care; minority rights; religious freedom; and a strong military defense) which different individuals may be expected to prioritize in different ways.

Social goals, then, are ends that society views as important in themselves. Individual perceptions of the relative importance of these social ends differ significantly.

Social goals have greater impact as the enterprise becomes a more important member of society. An enterprise could grow more important because of its size, its goods and services, or a variety of other factors. As the enterprise increases its connections to society — and thus its social importance — through increasing product lines, growth in employment, or geographic expansion, it becomes more aware of its social responsibility.

Social responsibility may be defined as the obligation of the enterprise to act in accordance with social goals. Unfortunately, definition of social responsibility is deceptively simple, since it still raises some questions. First, how can an enterprise act in accordance with social goals if a pluralistic society does not agree on the priority of social goals? An enterprise may argue that a plant closing furthers the social goal of technological progress because an inefficient plant is no longer competitive. But what about the employees' loss of income, or the resulting increased welfare cost? It is relatively easy to agree on some acts of social *irresponsibility* (such as pollution), but it is not always easy to define social *responsibility*. To whom in society is the enterprise to be responsible? Shareholders? Unions? Communities? These groups have different priorities and different needs.

Second, even if it were possible to agree on the definition of socially responsible acts, measuring the specific impact of social responsibility on the decision process still would be difficult. One could always argue that a firm undertook a certain social program not for altruistic reasons but for sound business reasons, such as public relations and general advertising.

An individual's perspective on social responsibility depends on his or her view of the relationship between business and society. Does a business have the "right" to do business based upon property rights, or is a business "allowed" to do business and to make profits because society wants it to? The latter opinion seemed to be behind the aggressive stance that the Connecticut state banking commissioner took against E. F. Hutton. After the large investment banking firm was convicted in May 1985 of mail and wire fraud, which primarily centered on overdrawing accounts and transfering funds to take advantage of banking processing delays, or *float*, the banking commissioner, Brian Woolf, commented: "Integrity is at the core of this. To do business in Connecticut, Hutton has been given a license. That's a privilege and a trust, and they should be held to the highest standards'' (*Business Week*, 7/15/85, p. 33).

STRATEGIC MISSION

The strategic manager, understanding the three components of strategic mission — (1) personal values of key managers; (2) organizational priorities, embodied in the corporate culture; and (3) societal goals — now turns to the definition of *mission*, the first of three steps in the process of strategic analysis.

WORKING CONCEPT 9

STRATEGIC ANALYSIS

Defining strategic mission is the first of three analytical steps the strategic manager must complete in preparation for the formulation of strategy. The three preparation steps, as shown in Figure 3.3, consist of (1) defining mission; (2) analyzing the firm's strengths and weaknesses in order to determine its distinctive competence; and (3) identifying opportunities and threats in the external environment of the firm by means of product market, competition, and industry analysis.

FIGURE 3.3
Strategic analysis

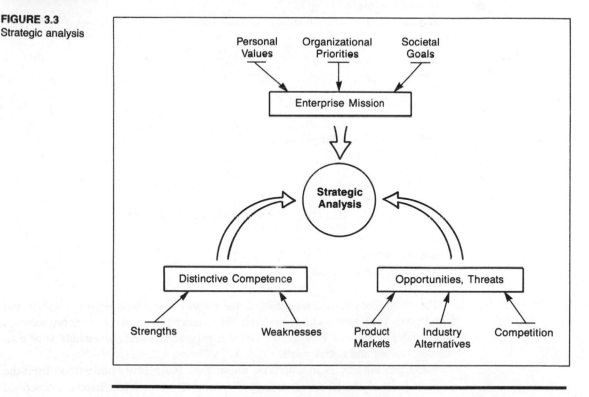

LEVELS OF STRATEGY
AND ENTERPRISE MISSION

Each enterprise naturally has organizational priorities that are specifically its own, although profitability is a common priority among all enterprises. The strategic manager prepares an explicit statement of these organizational priorities. Specific priorities depend upon the specific enterprise, but statements of organizational priorities encompass the following topics.

Earnings
    absolute amounts
    percentage increases
    minimum levels required for research, capital expenditures, dividends, etc.
Distinctive competency and competitive advantage
    present
    planned
Product and markets
    target markets
    innovation levels
    service levels
Growth
    sales
    assets
    earnings
    markets
    products
Responsibilities and obligations
    human resources
    political
    social
    ethical
    environmental
Legitimacy
    markets served
    social functions

The consistency between organizational priorities and both personal values and social goals must now to be considered. Experience has shown that inconsistencies may occur, as Table 3.1 suggests. You can expand this table to include your own personal values and social goals.

These inconsistencies in enterprise mission are more easily understood from the point of view of the levels of strategy. Working Concept 2 in Chapter 1 described the three levels of strategy. In the corporate level of strategy, the strategist seeks

TABLE 3.1
Possible
inconsistencies in
enterprise mission

Organizational priorities	versus	Personal values
Cost, including executive salary, minimization		Wealth accumulation
Hierarchical structure of formal organizations		Prestige
Dedicated, hardworking management		Parenting
Specialized functions		Personal development
Increase in public shareholders' wealth and fiduciary responsibilities		Top management's "taking private" a public company

Organizational priorities	versus	Social values
Minimizing labor costs		High employment
		Increasing living standards
Minimizing production costs		Job safety
		Environmental protection
Minimizing changeover costs		New products
Salary incentives		Economic equality

to achieve long-term objectives through managing the portfolio of new and existing product markets, technologies, industries, and opportunities. In the business level of strategy, the strategic manager seeks to compete in a defined business with a given product-market scope. In the functional level of strategy, the functional manager seeks to maximize output of a functional department. To define enterprise mission, the strategic manager must use the perspectives of both the three levels of strategy and the stages of corporate development, as depicted in Figure 3.4. The relative

FIGURE 3.4
Defining mission

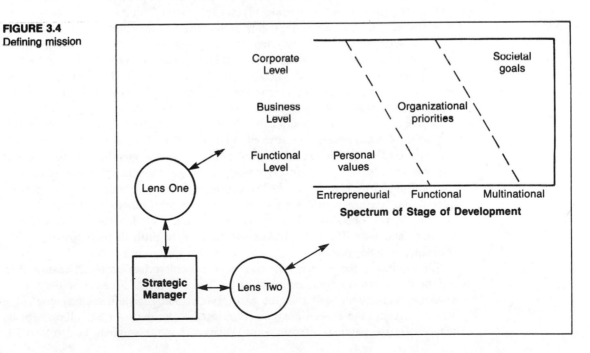

importance assigned to each component of mission — personal values of key managers, organizational priorities, and societal goals — will depend on the lens, or viewpoint, of the manager.

Long-term opportunities and long-term priorities are matched and managed at the corporate level of strategy. Thus the strategic manager carefully considers social responsibility and societal goals in both the analysis of opportunities — what social goals and trends will create what opportunities — and in the mixing and balancing of such long-term priorities as investment in human resources, capital appreciation, and asset growth.

Societal goals become somewhat less important, although always significant, at the business, and especially at the functional, levels. The functional-level manager, with a short-term perspective and a concern for maximizing outputs, must emphasize intradepartmental and functional cooperation, and thus give significant weight to the personal values of associates.

Similarly, the entrepreneurial manager attaches a great deal of importance to personal values of challenge and risk. In both the small business and the entrepreneurial enterprise, the personal values of the entrepreneur and the small-business owner will be reflected in the organization's priorities.

At the multinational, Stage Three level of development, however, societal goals are of increasing importance. Consider, for example, the attention the multinational manager must pay to a foreign host country's cultural values and goals, and especially to the host government. The relative strength and influence of the government and the multinational depend on the relative importance of each party's contributions. The multinational may contribute investment capital, products, technology, and potential exports that earn foreign currencies. The host country may be a source of scarce resources, new markets, and a low-cost labor supply. The multinational strategist must understand the relative contributions of the corporation and the host government, and especially the host country's societal goals. The strategist for the firm that contributes important technology has greater flexibility than the manager who desperately needs the low-cost labor of the host country.

Merck & Co.'s 1983 acquisition of Banyu Pharmaceutical of Tokyo led to difficulties when Merck misjudged its strength relative to that of the Japanese government. The increased cost of health care, given Japan's aging population, has been one of its government's major concerns. Accordingly, the government announced reductions on controlled drug prices. Merck-Banyu's drug prices were reduced by 12 percent overall, but the price of Banyu's best-seller, an oral antibiotic, was cut by 32 percent. Merck's head of Japanese operations said, "Well, what are we going to do? Cry about it? The environment has been more difficult than we expected" (*Fortune*, 3/18/85, p. 48).

Elf Aquitaine, the French state-controlled oil enterprise, acquired Texasgulf in one of the largest foreign takeovers in the United States. Because of the franc's weakness against the dollar in the early 1980s, and France's societal goal of a stable currency, the French government refused to let the over $1 billion debt be reduced by the payment of francs for dollars. Thus the original $1.3 billion Elf

Aquitaine debt cost the company the equivalent of over $3 billion a year as the franc fell almost one-third against the dollar in the mid-1980s.

The appendix to Chapter 5 discusses the international business perspective further. The relationship between societal and organizational goals and the evolution of strategic mission is illustrated by a nonprofit agency in an appendix to this chapter.

RESEARCH AND MISSION

Classic research studies of mission include those by Galbraith and Wood.

Galbraith, in *The New Industrial State* (1971), theorizes that managers (technocrats) have personal motives (e.g., wealth, status, and self-preservation) that are inconsistent with shareholder priorities. He believes that organizational priorities (the reduction of risk and uncertainty) become so important that they are translated into social goals (economic growth, elimination of downturns of the business cycle, high defense spending, and consumer expectations of constantly increasing standards of living). This transformation is achieved by the power of the corporation and big business.

Wood analyzed organizational priorities in *A Theory of Profits* (1975). Wood concluded that firms have priorities of sales — not profit — growth, since sales are generally something the manager can both influence and understand easily. This sales growth priority is also coupled with a minimum acceptable level of profits in absolute terms. Once this level seems reasonably assured — often through an annual budgeting process — the manager concentrates on sales. The minimum level of profits, furthermore, is determined by the level of investment needed to support dividends and sales growth.

Current research on mission, managerial values, and social responsibility include works of the following researchers.

Carroll and Hoy (1984), concluded that social policy and social responsibility had been a "residual factor" for too long. They urged the "need for incorporating social policy into strategic management process," and suggested steps to "integrate corporate social policy into strategic management."

Kirton (1984) evaluated managers by studying their missions. Kirton evaluated managers as the firm's internal resource (especially managerial capabilities with new initiatives) using an Adaption-Innovation Inventory; he concluded that "the change agent can be either an adaptor or an innovator."

Shrivastava and Grant (1985), in an empirical study of strategic processes, described four strategic decision making models that reflected varying degrees of importance of organizational priorities, personal values, and social goals. These strategic process models were (1) the managerial autocracy model, (2) the systemic bureaucracy model, (3) the adaptive planning model, and (4) the political expediency model.

EXECUTIVE COMMENTS

Go back ten years. Polaroid and Xerox could have been on everyone's list of the ten best-managed companies. How did they lose their way when they became multibillion-dollar corporations? When you start growing like that, you start adding middle management like crazy. . . . People in the middle have no understanding of the business. . . . To them, it's just a job. The corporation ends up with mediocre people that form a layer of concrete. We're trying to keep Apple as flat as possible.

Steven P. Jobs, founder of Apple Computer, in *Business Week* (11/26/84)

I firmly believe that [IBM or] any organization, in order to survive and achieve success, must have a sound set of beliefs on which it premises all its policies and actions. Next, I believe that the most important single factor in corporate success is faithful adherence to those beliefs.

T. J. Watson, Jr., IBM CEO, 1963

I don't know how you can run a company with a board of directors.

Richard Branson, British entrepreneur

We would never forsake those who kept this [United] airline going during the work stoppage. That is the word of this corporation, and it is worth something.

R. J. Ferris, United Airlines CEO, 1985

You've got to be stubborn. You've got to believe you're right. Most organizations are the shadow of one man. I've got about two hundred more patents to get out of my system before I kick the bucket.

Paul Taylor, American entrepreneur, 1985

A lot of people thought working at Polaroid was like having a government job. That just couldn't keep going on.

R. W. Young, Polaroid CEO, 1985

In Washington they sometimes *hit a man when he's down. In New York, they* always *hit a man when he's down.*

Harry S. Truman

If the arts, with all their power to accentuate and clarify, to explore and criticize, to teach and persuade, to stimulate and enhance, were left entirely reliant on government, not only would the pluralism of the arts be imperiled, but that of our social structure itself.

W. H. Krome George, Alcoa (Aluminum Company of America) CEO

KEY TERMS

corporate culture (page 58)
Mintzberg's theory (page 56)

organizational priorities (page 56)

personal values (page 54)

purpose, or mission (page 53)

social responsibility (page 60)

societal goals (page 59)

BIBLIOGRAPHY

Andrews, K. R., *The Concept of Corporate Strategy* (Homewood, IL: Richard D. Irwin, 1980), *cf* Chapters 4, 5.

Barnett, J. H., "Nonprofits and the Life Cycle," *Program Evaluation and Planning* (1987, in press).

Bell, D., *The Cultural Contradictions of Capitalism* (New York: Basic Books, 1976).

Capon, N., J. Farley, and J. Hulbert, "International Diffusion of Corporate and Strategic Planning Processes." *Columbia Journal of World Business* (Fall 1980), pp. 5–13.

Carper, W. B., and R. J. Litschert, "Strategic Power Relationships in Contemporary Profit and Nonprofit Hospitals," *Academy of Management Journal* 26 (June 1983), pp. 311–320.

Carroll, A. B., and F. Hoy, "Integrating Corporate Social Policy into Strategic Management," *Journal of Business Strategy* 4 (Winter 1984), pp. 48–57.

"Corporate Culture," *Business Week* (October 27, 1980), pp, 148–160.

Doz, Y. L., and C. K. Prahalad, "Headquarters Influence and Strategic Control in MNCs," *Sloan Management Review* 23 (Fall 1981), pp. 15–29.

Firstenberg, P. B., "Profit-Minded Management in the Nonprofit World," *Management Review* (July 1979), pp. 8–13.

Fitzpatrick, M., "The Definition and Assessment of Political Risk in International Business: A Review of the Literature," *Academy of Management Review* 8 (April 1983), pp. 249–254.

Galbraith, J. K., *The New Industrial State* (New York: New American Library, 1971).

Gupta, A., "Contingency Linkages Between Strategy and General Manager Characteristics: A Conceptual Examination," *Academy of Management Review* 9 (July 1984).

Hatten, M. L., "Strategic Management in Not-for-Profit Organizations," *Strategic Management Journal* (April-June 1982).

Hout, T., M. Porter, and E. Rudden, "How Global Companies Win Out," *Harvard Business Review* 60 (September-October 1982), pp. 98–108.

Iacocca, L., with W. Novak, *Iacocca: An Autobiography* (New York: Bantam Books, 1984).

Kimberly, J. R., "Initiation, Innovation, and Institutionalization in the Creation Process," in *The Organizational Life Cycle: Issues in the Creation, Transformation and Decline of Organizations,* J. R. Kimberly, R. H. Miles, and Associates, eds. (San Francisco: Jossey-Bass, 1980).

Kirton, M. J., "Adaptors and Innovators — Why New Initiatives Get Blocked," *Long Range Planning* 17 (April 1984), pp. 137–143.

Leibenstein, H., *Beyond Economic Man* (Cambridge, MA: Harvard University Press, 1980).

McKie, J. W., ed., *Social Responsibility and the Business Predicament* (Washington, DC: The Brookings Institution, 1974).

Mintzberg, H., "Organizational Power and Goals," in *Strategic Management,* D. E. Schendel and C. W. Hofer, eds. (Boston: Little, Brown, 1979), pp. 64–80.

Mitroff, I., and R. Mason, "Business Policy and Metaphysics: Some Philosophical Considerations," *Academy of Management Review* vol. 7, no. 3 (1982), pp. 361–371.

Newman, W. H., and H. W. Wallender, III, "Managing Not-for-Profit Enterprises," *Academy of Management Review* (January 1978), pp. 24–31.

Nutt, P. C., "A Strategic Planning Network for Non-Profit Organizations," *Strategic Management Journal* (January-March 1984).

Ouchi, W. G., "A Framework for Understanding Organizational Failure," in *The Organizational Life Cycle, op. cit.*

Ronstadt, R., and R. Kramer, "Getting the Most out of Innovation Abroad," *Harvard Business Review* 60 (March-April 1982), pp. 94–99.

Schwartz, H., and S. H. David, "Matching Corporate Culture and Business Strategy," *Organizational Dynamics* (Summer 1981), pp. 30–48.

Shanks, D. C., "Strategic Planning for Global Competition," *Journal of Business Strategy* 5 (Winter 1985), pp. 80–89.

Shrivastava, P., and J. H. Grant, "Empirically Derived Models of Strategic Decision-Making Processes," *Strategic Management Journal* 6 (April-June 1985), pp. 97–113.

Simon, H., "On the Concept of Organizational Goals," *Administrative Science Quarterly* (June 1964).

Stevens, J. M., and R. P. McGowan, "Managerial Strategies in Municipal Government Organizations," *Academy of Management Journal* 26 (September 1983), pp. 527–534.

Unterman, I., and R. M. Davis, "The Strategy Gap in Not-for-Profits," *Harvard Business Review* (May-June 1982), pp. 30–40.

Wood, A., *A Theory of Profits* (Cambridge, England: Cambridge University Press, 1975).

APPENDIX: THE NONPROFIT AND STAGES OF DEVELOPMENT

Barnett's analysis (1987) of 119 nonprofit agencies led to the identification of three stages of nonprofit development: (1) start-up, (2) professionalization, and (3) institutionalization.

START-UP

In the start-up stage, a small group of individuals perceives a need. Based upon this perceived need — or, in the case of the arts, a perceived area of artistic interest — a group experiments with alternative ways to service the need. Group members generally participate on a part-time basis; the group's board of directors is a working board, active in all areas of the agency. Service technology, or the method of providing service to clients, undergoes experimental changes during start-up as the technology is improved upon. Since the service technology is in the process of being developed, the group has informal, flexible operating procedures. Finally, the group's funding during start-up is limited, often based on one initial infusion of capital.

PROFESSIONALIZATION

The two principal characteristics of stage two in the nonprofit, professionalization, are the resolution of service experimentation and the creation of a professional service staff. The group, or agency, has agreed upon a way to service the perceived need that caused its start-up. A professional staff is now working full time to provide this service. With the service technology in place and the agency seeking funds, the board becomes less a working board and more a financial board. Though the agency is accumulating funds, it is doing so at an unreliable rate, with significant fluctuations.

INSTITUTIONALIZATION

Once the nonprofit agency reaches the third stage of development, institutionalization, it has a reliable, steady flow of revenues that provides at least an adequate base. The service technology is fully supported throughout the agency. The agency has standard operating procedures, an administration executive, and a formal organization structure. This administration executive, usually called the executive director, is often not a member of the professional staff. The administration executive performs or oversees grant writing and financing, so that the board's role evolves further from a financial role to an advisory and/or social one. By the institutionalization stage, an agency has developed an administrative group that is often separate from the group delivering the agency's service. Delegation, specialization, and the fine-tuning of administrative structure and systems have reduced the organizational stress and executive burnout that led to the turnovers in management of developing agencies. The institutionalization agency now builds its constituency and looks for additional revenue-generating activities based on its current capabilities, rather than responding to perceived areas of need.

Exhibit 1 summarizes this life-cycle model for nonprofit organizations. During start-up, the strategic manager's objective is experimentation, as the agency explores different ways to service a perceived need. During professionalization, the manager focuses all efforts on supporting the professional service resource. During institutionalization, after the professional service system is in place, the manager concentrates on the strategic objective of increasing agency legitimacy through expanding the agency's constituency.

The model suggests that the critical determining factor in the move to the institutionalization stage is legitimacy with the agency's constituency, or the degree of congruence between agency goals and the objectives of the society that is affected by the agency. An agency at this time must avoid the temptation to deviate from the norms of the society it serves. The agency whose goals are the same as society's goals will receive support, but "failure will occur . . . when the society deems the basic objective of the organization to be unworthy of continued support" (Ouchi, 1980). Exhibit 2 depicts the importance of legitimacy and goal congruence.

EXHIBIT 1 Nonprofit development stages

Factor	Start-up	Professionalization	Institutionalization
Strategic objective	Serve (altruistically) a perceived need	Strengthen and support the service vehicle	Increase legitimacy
Strategic time frame	Present	Medium term based upon service vehicle	Longer term based upon constituency
Service vehicle	Experimental	Focused	Formalized base for new revenue
Structure	Informal "zealots"	Functional hierarchy supporting professiona	Formal, joint professional service and administration
Critical issue to resolve for next stage	Select service vehicle	Align organizational and social goals	N/A
Board role	Working	Financial	Advisory/social
Staff makeup	Part-time volunteers	Full-time, paid professionals; new manager supplements founder	Separate administrative group and new executive director
Funding	One-shot "angels"	Variable amounts, increasing sources	Reliable "public" base
Causes of failure	Early burnout of founders	Staff fails to support chosen service vehicle, resists formal structure; organizational drift away from objective; staff burnout	Lack of legitimacy
Causes of success	The founders	Service provider commitment	Society-agency congruence

EXHIBIT 2
Toward institutional-
ization

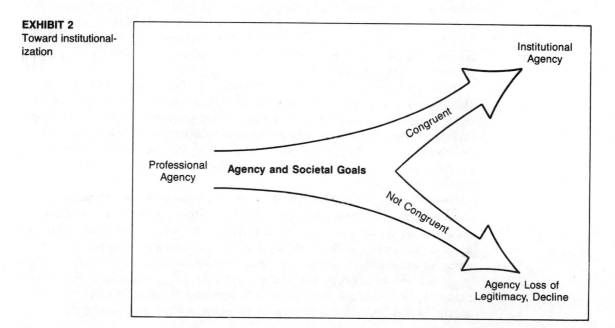

CHAPTER 4

DETERMINING DISTINCTIVE COMPETENCE

Opportunity without the organizational competence to capture it is an illusion.
A. A. Thompson, Jr. and A. J. Strickland, III, *Strategy Formulation and Implementation*

This chapter describes the second step in strategic analysis: how a firm's distinctive competence is determined. The strategic manager analyzes the firm's strengths and weaknesses, characteristics of the firm's resources, to determine distinctive competence. The importance of various competencies change depending on the stage of the product life cycle.

RESOURCES DEFINED

The resources of an organization are the tangible and intangible means by which it carries out its activities. The tangible resources of the organization include (1) people; (2) physical facilities and equipment; (3) product markets, including those bought from suppliers and those sold to customers; (4) distribution and communication systems to reach these supplier and customer product markets; and (5) financial assets. An organization's intangible assets might include (1) managerial processes and skills; (2) special relationships, such as marketplace reputation or banking connections; (3) other special skills and synergies, such as research capabilities; and (4) legal relationships, such as patents, licenses, or long-term contracts.

Tangible Resources

People Resources. The people who carry out the organization's goals include the management, administrative, and functional employees. People who serve as less obvious people resources are the shareholders and bankers and other creditors. The organization's part-time people resources include consultants in such areas as design, systems, and public relations, who are hired by the organization for a specific project or period of time.

Physical Facilities and Equipment. Production lines, assembly plants, research and development laboratories, computers, machine tools, warehouses, and transportation equipment are just a few examples of the many different kinds of facilities and equipment an organization can use. These can be catalogued by location (North American, European), by function (manufacturing equipment, office equipment), or by more subjective terms (fully utilized, inefficient). Finally, the organization can have different levels of investment in a facility or piece of equipment. Physical assets can be leased or owned, and fully owned equipment and facilities can be partially or fully depreciated.

Product Markets. Product groups include suppliers' products and products for customers. Suppliers' products are those goods and/or services purchased by the organization that will be resold directly after being produced, or that will be used in other functions (such as office supplies). Customers' products include all goods and/or services sold by the organization. Both suppliers' and customers' products are part of the organization's inventory at any one time.

Distribution and Communication Systems. An organization has one or more methods of distributing its products to its customers. A distribution system might be through wholly owned retail outlets and catalog locations at one end of the spectrum, or, at the other, more limited end, might only involve delivering items out the back door of the manufacturing facility to an independent trucking service.

The communication system for a product market also can range from the simple to the complex. The organization might communicate with its customers and suppliers using the regular mail service. Or, the organization might communicate through leased or owned computer terminals, transmission and telecommunication lines, and a host computer within the organization.

Financial Assets. The organization's financial resources include cash, and other resources that can be turned into cash. In the short term, government and other marketable securities represent resources that can be turned into cash to finance the organization's activities. Accounts receivable that can be factored and inventory that can be pledged represent other intermediate sources of cash. Land and buildings that can be mortgaged represent longer-term cash sources.

Intangible Resources

Managerial Processes and Skills. As well as being composed of resources that are tangible and can be described definitively, an organization also includes intangible resources, such as managerial procedures, processes, and skills. Nissan possesses special managerial skills for increasing employee productivity; Procter & Gamble is especially well known for its brand-management abilities; General Electric has a worldwide reputation for its managerial budgeting procedures. Whether these skills or processes encompass such diverse management functions as capital budgeting, employee development, or human resource management, they are as much a part of the internal working environment of the firm as distribution systems and assembly lines. The organization and its leaders specifically created these intangible resources.

Special Relationships. Caterpillar Tractor Company has been praised for its special relationship with its worldwide dealers; Dartmouth College has a very active alumni association; Joseph A. Seagram, Ltd., has developed a professional relationship with provincial liquor control boards across Canada. These are examples of special relationships that have been cultivated by top management. These relationships provide the specific means by which management operates, and thus they are resources — intangible, but real — of the organization.

Special Skills and Synergies. *Synergy* is an interaction between parts that increases the effectiveness of each part; in synergy, the whole is greater than the sum of the parts. (In other words, two plus two equals five.) An organization may have special skills such as synergy between research and customer service. Problems studied by a customer service manager, who reviews returned products or studies a major customer's special needs, might trigger solutions within a research technician's mind, who has been researching theoretical aspects related to the same product problem or to the same customer need. Similarly, two managers who previously had been working independently to develop new products might each individually improve the new product through the synergistic effect that information exchange, and the cross-pollinization of ideas, can produce.

Legal Relationships. An organization also might possess an intangible resource in the form of a process or product patent, or in some other long-term contractual relationship. For example, the world's major copper-mining firms often enter into long-term price and quantity (tonnage) contracts with major copper fabricators in order to produce a guaranteed satisfactory return for their mining efforts, even when world copper prices are depressed. These copper contracts often contain clauses for perpetual renewal, called "evergreen" clauses. These legal relationships are an integral part of the way the organization does business, and thus are an important part of the internal environment.

STRENGTHS AND WEAKNESSES

The strategic manager studies the resources of the organization to identify its strengths and weaknesses. The strategic manager asks, "Where are we strong, and where are we weak?" This is not an easy task. As Andrews (1980) points out, "Subjectivity, lack of confidence, and unwillingness to face reality may make it hard for organizations as well as for individuals to know themselves." The strategic manager's list of an organization's strengths and weaknesses cannot be prepared from a checklist of all possible strengths and weaknesses; in other words, strategy does not apply a "cookbook" approach. The definition of a "strength" or a "weakness" is partly a question of fact and partly a matter of judgment. You will develop your sense of strategic judgment as you analyze the cases in this course.

For example, having only enough cash in the bank to pay one or two days of daily operating expenses may mean one thing in a profitable, relatively debt-free, well-known company, and quite another in companies such as Continental Illinois National Bank in May 1984, or Public Service of New Hampshire during major construction problems at its Seabrook nuclear power plant. Henry (1980) examined other firms and how to evaluate a company's strengths and weaknesses; small-business strengths and weaknesses are discussed in the appendix to this chapter.

The job of the strategic manager is to use business judgment by objectively and professionally studying each component of the organization's internal, working environment. This text cannot provide a "cookbook" approach to identify the organization's strengths and weaknesses because each situation in the business world (and each case in this course) is unique. One purpose of this course is to help you develop your skills in applying strategic judgments to the analysis of an organization's internal environment. Thus, the following list presents only some — not all — examples of strengths and weaknesses.

1. *How strong (or weak) are managers?*
   knowledge of the firm's business
   knowledge of the industry and competition
   grasp of current problems
   anticipation of future problems
   development of solutions to current and future problems
   implementation of problem solutions
   cohesion
   executive development system
   age, experience of key managers
   quality of staff support groups
   relative difficulty of management task
   continuity/turnover
2. *How strong (or weak) are employees?*
   past, current, and future productivity
   morale and motivation
   extent of employee participation in decision making
   role and attitude of unions
   absenteeism and turnover
   employee training and development
   wage and salary systems
   relative contribution of employees/skill levels
3. *How strong are connections to shareholders? debt sources? consultants? others?*
   current and future needs
   number of alternative sources
   congruence of objectives
   role of board of directors
4. *How efficient is the equipment?*
   cost versus benefit
   cost-volume relationship

    flexibility
    machine alternatives
    obsolescence factors
    rate of technological advance
    reject/rework/downtime experience
    expansion capability
    maintenance
    degree of integration (continuous process versus job shop, batch systems)

5. *How effective are the facilities?*
    cost versus benefit
    cost-volume relationship
    location and its effect on cost and service
    capital intensity
    flexibility and resale potential
    expansion capability

6. *Other asset considerations*
    industrial engineering skills
    quality of production scheduling system
    financing arrangements
    tax consequences

7. *How strong (or weak) are customer ties?*
    nature of customer buying decision
    nature of customer needs
    market share
    stage of product life cycle
    breadth of product line
    basis of product appeal (price, service, multiple-purpose, reputation, financing, brand loyalty, technology, quality)
    market-research skills
    advertising skills
    packaging skills
    promotion skills
    sales force
    purchase follow-up
    product research and development abilities
    availability of substitutes
    number, concentration of customers

8. *How strong (or weak) are suppliers?*
    nature of buying decision
    nature of needs
    relative importance of suppliers
    availability of substitutes
    cost
    quality

service
reliability of inventory control system
number, concentration of suppliers

9. *How strong (or weak) are distribution and communication systems?*
coverage (local, regional, national, international)
cost
speed
reliability
capacity
impact on receiver
relative importance to receiver
flexibility
breadth
degree of firm's control

10. *How strong (or weak) are financial resources?*
financial requirements and needs
predictability of needs and requirements
seasonality
availability of financial resources
cost of financial resources
flexibility of financial arrangements
number of financial alternatives
tax consequences
relationship with financial community
exposure/risk (inflation, business cycle)
reliability of financial (cash management, capital budgeting) systems
percentage of requirements provided internally
present distribution/commitment of financial resources

11. *How strong (or weak) are managerial skills, processes, systems, and procedures?*
costs
response time
nature of skills
cost of improvements, managerial development
relationship between authority and responsibility
relative gap — what is versus what ought to be
availability of managerial alternatives
degree of integration of managerial systems
relative degree of bureaucracy, red tape

12. *How strong are special skills and relationships?*
nature of special skills, relationships
availability of alternatives
research and development

13. *What special legal resources does the firm possess?*
cost of legal relationships
duration

enforcement costs
flexibility
regulatory/governmental relationships

Combining Related Symptoms

In reviewing an organization's strengths and weaknesses, the strategic manager finds that each factor is really a manifestation or symptom of a larger or more common problem. Recognizing the core problem is important so that the strategic manager can deal with the real strength or weakness, not its manifestation. In other words, diagnosing the underlying illness is important so that the illness, not the symptoms, can be understood (and later, treated).

For example, you are the new owner of a manufacturing firm that produces precision electronic components that are modified frequently as customers' needs change. Your operating managers have put together the following partial list of weaknesses.

1. High level of customer complaints
2. High level of absenteeism in fabricating and assembly areas
3. Excessive level of rework in fabricating
4. Excessive overtime and high turnover in product and process engineering
5. High level of product returns

In reviewing these weaknesses, you see a common problem: Customer complaints are high, and product returns are high. You can deduce fairly safely that product quality is poor.

Next, you note that production is characterized by morale problems and poor quality (excessive fabricating rework). These morale and quality problems *in conjunction with* high overtime and turnover in the engineering department produce a further hypothesis. It seems likely that both the engineers studying the product, and those coming up with ways to fabricate the product — the process engineers — are overworked and are not performing at an acceptable level. You thus combine these five related symptoms into one strategic weakness, or "illness": The organization has insufficient engineering resources, which are manifested in poor manufacturing performance and unacceptable product quality.

Finding the opposite of the above five weaknesses — i.e., low instead of high levels of complaints and returns, rework, engineering overtime, and engineering employee turnover — would lead to the opposite conclusion: The organization has a strong engineering resource, as indicated by excellent manufacturing performance and outstanding product quality. In other words, you reach conclusions by combining related strengths and weaknesses.

Reviewing strengths and weaknesses is an exercise in fact finding. Combining strengths and weaknesses is an exercise in reaching conclusions. The skillful strategic manager, relying on a combination of experience and intuition, makes a strategic diagnosis based on the facts of the firm's resources. As you analyze the cases in this text, you will move from shuffling and regrouping strengths and weaknesses to understanding the significance of these strengths and weaknesses. You will move from the world of the business student to the world of the strategic manager.

Working Concept 10 shows how the product life cycle guides the strategic manager to those resources that are especially significant to the firm.

WORKING CONCEPT 10

PRODUCT LIFE CYCLE

Business and marketing research has shown that products go through a distinctive cycle and that different strengths are needed at different product life cycle stages. Although there are problems of definition (product brand versus company product versus industry product versus product group) and of interpretation (such as the number of phases of the cycle), Figure 4.1 presents one model of the life cycle. This figure is a simplified version of a typical life cycle of a successful product.

Some researchers conclude that the product life cycle is an important concept (Wasson, 1974; Levitt, 1965). Other researchers have found that the product life cycle is very difficult to apply with any precision (Dhalla and Yuspeh, 1976; Polli and Cook, 1969). Nonetheless, there is general agreement that the product life cycle is a model,

albeit an imperfect one, that has significant implications for the strategic manager. These include:

1. Product importance
2. Functional consequences
3. Profit and cash-flow expectations
4. Performance standard
5. Strategic emphasis

PRODUCT IMPORTANCE

An organization carries out its business by bringing products and services to the market; it succeeds or fails based upon how well and how profitably it provides those services. All strategic plans and contributions of researchers, engineers, marketers, producers, and financiers reach their ultimate expression in the product. Failure,

---

FIGURE 4.1
Product life cycle

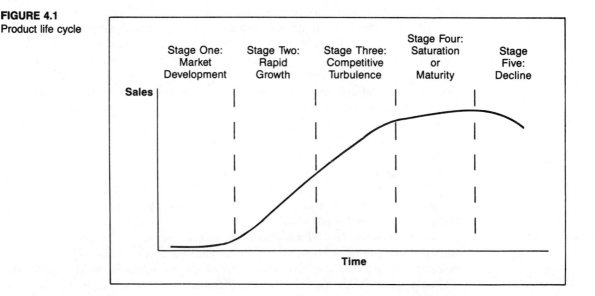

Product Life Cycle (continued)

survival, prosperity, and growth are all determined by the product's performance in the marketplace. Thus, the product life cycle is an appropriate lens for focusing management's attention on the product.

FUNCTIONAL CONSEQUENCES

The strategic manager, who has a high organizational level of authority and responsibility, must plan for and control the changing functional resources that are required as a product moves through the life cycle. During the market development stage, the developmental resources — managerial, tangible, and intangible — of product development, market research, and customer education are especially critical. The rapid growth stage of the life cycle requires increasing productive capacity and market skills to increase market share. As the company's rapid increase in sales, and then profits, attracts more competitors, the company will need the following resources: (1) advertising, customer service, selling, and promotional skills as it seeks to build market share and searches for volume; (2) industrial engineering skills to discover ways to lower costs in the production system; and (3) efficient distribution and communication systems, particularly the latter to provide feedback on competitive moves. During this stage of competitive turbulence the company changes its marketing emphasis from "Try our product" to "Prefer our brand."

Once in the saturation stage, the company emphasizes production efficiency. As margins decline throughout the industry, the company seeks a low-cost — if not lowest cost — position, possibly in combination with seeking a market niche through product differentiation. The company also tightens financial and accounting controls during the saturation stage.

The company further tightens its account-ing and financial control systems during the decline stage. The company tries to prune any and all unnecessary costs connected with the declining product, as the strategic manager takes resources from the declining product and allocates them to other uses.

PROFIT EXPECTATIONS

The strategic manager is, among other things, a resource allocator. The product life cycle is a tool to plan for the source and use of resources, since a product typically will (1) have its lowest (or nonexistent) profits during market development; (2) show profit levels that lag behind, but follow the growth patterns of, sales during the rapid growth and competitive turbulence stages; and (3) show profits that peak and decrease faster than sales during the maturity and decline stages of the cycle, as the marginal cost of each new sale becomes greater just as lower prices are enforced. Although sales changes are generally expected, the strategic manager must also plan for unit profit changes.

PERFORMANCE STANDARD

The simplified product life cycle pattern presented here is a stereotype that never will be followed by any one product. Nonetheless, any plan is better than none, and the predicted, stereotypical life cycle pattern is a standard against which actual performance can be analyzed. The strategic manager thus can use the product life cycle as a tool for evaluation. Further, the life cycle of the industry's group of products shows changes in the total market demand, while the life cycle of the company's product helps the strategic manager to evaluate the company's competitive strength.

STRATEGIC EMPHASIS

During the life cycle phases the strategic manager is concerned with different re-

Product Life Cycle *(continued)*

sources and emphasizes different steps in the strategic analysis process. The manager concentrates on purpose, goals, and values during the first stage of the product's life. At the second life cycle stage, internal resources — especially both the productive capacity to service rapid growth and the marketing skills to reach the first-time customer — are critical. These internal re-

sources become the foundation of the firm's distinctive competence. During the competitive-turbulence stage, the strategic manager concentrates on the external environment, especially the moves of competitors and their effect on market share. This changing strategic emphasis is summarized in Figure 4.2.

FIGURE 4.2 Life cycle and strategic emphasis

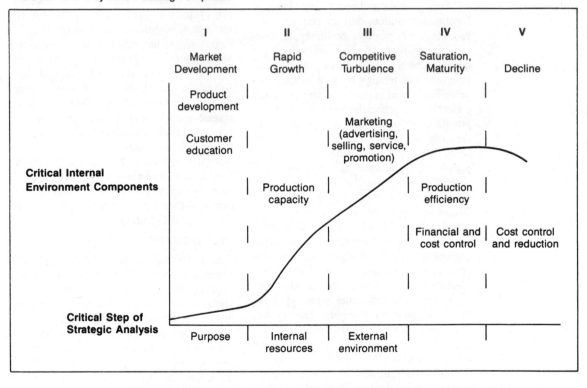

Product Life Cycle and Internal Factors

The product life cycle concept is a powerful tool for distinguishing between the important strengths and weaknesses of the internal environment and those that are less significant. Hofer (1975) concluded that "the most fundamental variable in determining an appropriate business strategy is the stage of the product life cycle."

Wasson (1974) has developed strategic objectives for the five phases of the product life cycle. These strategic objectives, and subsequent research in this important area of strategy, suggest that a number of factors are important at the five stages in the product life cycle, as shown in Table 4.1.

EXAMPLE: *Product Life Cycle Stages*

California Coolers, Schering-Plough, and AMF illustrate stages of the product life cycle. California Coolers grew at a fast rate typical of the growth stage of the cycle. Its owners, who began by making a bathtub mix of fruit punch and white wine, sold the company for $55 million in cash. Schering-Plough and AMF, however, faced problems of declining products. Schering-Plough's antibiotic Garamycin grew at a 17 percent rate for ten years, representing 25 percent of sales and 50 percent of profits (*Fortune*, 8/19/85, p. 50). Garamycin patents ran out in 1980, and Schering's profits from that year of $239 million dropped to $179 million in 1981. When AMF bet on an oil boom in 1981, its energy service business earned a high $63 million on operations for that year. By the 1983 oil bust, AMF's energy services had lost $24 million (*Business Week*, 8/12/85, p. 50).

EXAMPLE: *More on Product Life Cycles*

As MCI moved from growth to competitive turbulence with the long-distance telephone business, the strategic variable of cost became all-important. Earnings and stock prices dropped sharply from 1983 to 1984, as MCI paid higher connection charges to local telephone companies. Competitors keep pressure on revenues. *Busi-*

TABLE 4.1 Strategic life cycle factors	Product life cycle stage	Significant strengths or weaknesses

	1. Market development	1. Product introduction skills
		  a. ability to educate customer
		  b. ability to gain early use
		2. Product quality
		  a. fast correction of defects
		3. Customer education

	2. Rapid growth	1. Brand management skills 2. Distribution system 3. Productive capacity 4. Cash and human resources

	3. Competitive turbulence	1. Market development
		  a. dealer relationships
		  b. customer's perceptions/loyalties

	4. Saturation or maturity	1. Brand defense
		  a. communication and promotion system
		  b. distribution system
		2. Product improvement skills
		3. Cost advantages
		  a. production facilities, process

	5. Decline	1. Brand management in decline a. "harvest" strategy of cost minimization

ness Week (11/5/84, p. 40) reported the comment of Amy Newark, an industry analyst: "The unanswered question is who is the lowest-cost producer. Nobody knows for sure, except maybe AT&T, and they're not telling." Levi Strauss failed to see the consequences of competitive turbulence. Riding an annual growth of 15 percent in jeans sales, they spent little on local store promotions, had inflexible return policies, and refused to offer volume discounts. As blue jean wearers acquired more taste for fashions, retailers were fast to drop the Levi's line, since the company had "lost touch with its customers" (*Business Week*, 11/5/84, p. 79).

EXAMPLE: *Life Cycle Durations*

One fascinating variable within the product life cycle model is duration. How long does the product life cycle last? Selchow & Righter, the U.S. board game producer, presents an interesting example of the problem of the duration of a product life cycle. During 1984 the company sold over twenty million units of Trivial Pursuit, an amazing sales record when one considers that the company's Scrabble game has sold an annual average of three million units over its thirty-year life. (A rival game, Monopoly, sold by Parker Brothers, has sold an annual average of less than 1.5 million units over its fifty-year life.) As reported by *Business Week* (11/26/84, pp. 118, 122), Selchow & Righter are betting that the product life cycle of their game is of substantially longer duration than that of the hula hoops, pet rocks, and skateboards of other years. The company is ignoring new products and customers alike as it pushes itself to the breaking point to satisfy demand.

Capri Beachwear's filing for Chapter 11 bankruptcy in 1984 illustrates the danger of wrong product life cycle estimates. Although it had manufactured Colony beachwear almost since its founding in 1943, Capri diverted "most of its resources" (*Women's Wear Daily*, 8/9/84) in 1984 from the Colony label to Jane Fonda Workout Bodywear. Capri paid Fonda $162,500 in advance, and committed to annual payments of $650,000 in royalties to Fonda and $400,000 in Jane Fonda Workout Bodywear promotion and ads. Department store returns of $1 million out of $7 million worth of purchases, and Capri's overcutting of $1.5 million for expected orders, were direct symptoms of bankruptcy troubles stemming from the underlying illness of misjudged product life cycles. The company's $10.8 million in assets were mostly in inventory. Liabilities of $12.6 million included Century Factors ($8.3 million) and Jane Fonda herself ($157,800).

Compaq Computer's success is attributed to their completely IBM-PC–compatible line and to the professional business strategy and maturity of Compaq's executives. Compaq's chief executive, Rod Canion, spoke about the product life cycle and the resulting managerial skills:

> *I admire Steve Jobs and Steve Wozniak [founders of Apple Computer] . . . I don't think it takes anything away from them to then say that as markets begin maturing, those skills aren't what's important to compete. It's more business-oriented skills.* (Christian Science Monitor, 5/27/86, p. 25)

DEFINING DISTINCTIVE COMPETENCE

The strategic manager (1) identifies strengths and weaknesses of the firm's resources, (2) analyzes these strengths and weaknesses by related groups, and (3) determines the relative importance of these strengths and weaknesses based upon the stage of the product life cycle. The strategic manager then defines that important strength that (1) meets a market need and (2) gives the firm a comparative advantage over competition. That strength is the firm's *distinctive competence*. IBM's success in business computing is attributable to its strength in providing total service to businesses — services that included equipment, software, and maintenance. Subaru's success in automobiles is based on satisfying the American market's desire for quality (low maintenance) and reasonable prices. What is required for success in a marketplace? What strength is present in a firm's strategic resources that will satisfy this market requirement?

Secondly, what ability exists in a firm's strategic resources that gives it a comparative advantage? Distinctive competence comprises both market needs and competition. The strategist studies competitors' abilities and those of the firm. In what areas is a firm better than its competitor?

Sears has a comparative advantage over Montgomery Ward and J. C. Penney in its number of modern stores. The New York Yankees have a competitive advantage in higher salary scale, which allows the organization to attract skilled players. Mercedes-Benz and Cross pens have a competitive advantage in their perceived quality.

Market Needs and Comparative Advantage

Stevenson (1976) examined how firms define strengths and weaknesses, and found that executives (1) used past experience to find strengths but not weaknesses (90 percent versus 10 percent), (2) used judgment to find weaknesses but not strengths (80 percent versus 20 percent), and (3) used market and customer comparisons about twice as much to find strengths (67 percent) as to identify weaknesses (33 percent). He further elaborated:

> *The process of defining strengths and weaknesses should ideally require the manager to test his assumptions and to analyze the status quo in relationship to the requirements for future success given the competition and the changing environment. The analysis performed by managers is rarely so dispassionate. There is a great tendency toward inertia.*

The analysis of strengths and weaknesses *must* be coupled with market and competitive analyses to define distinctive competence. This chapter has presented the individual parts of the overall process of defining distinctive competence — identifying strengths and weaknesses, determining strategic importance, analyzing market needs, and studying comparative advantage versus competition — as discrete steps. In real-life situations, of course, these parts are not separate. Each time the strategist looks at a strength or a weakness, he or she also must consider the market and competition. South (1981) argued that competitive advantage is "the cornerstone of strategic thinking."

EXAMPLE: *Competitive Advantage*

Purolator Courier entered the air delivery business against the aggressive competition of Federal Express and the specialized competition of Emery, DHL Worldwide, and Airborne Express. Subsequently, Purolator's market share decreased by one-third, three chief Purolator executives moved in and out, and their stock fell from seventy dollars (1983) to twenty-two dollars (1985) per share. A competitor commented: "They made a tactical error by going into the air business. They had a marvelous ground operation in place" (*Business Week*, 8/12/85, p. 52).

Toys "R" Us, the toy discounter, pursued growth and profits in the mid-1980s by building on its distinctive competence — discount retailing — and its market base. Toys "R" Us, as *Fortune* reported (11/26/84, p. 135), opened children's clothing stores with a strategy based upon the discount prices, inventory control procedures, and volume purchasing strategy that had led to over $1 billion in toy sales.

Mayflower, predicting that high interest rates and business slowdowns would reduce household moving, turned to other segments of the transportation business — hauling computer equipment, delivering appliances, and operating school buses. They determined that transportation was their distinctive competence. Chief executive John Smith commented: "We'll look at any business that has to do with transportation. But I don't plan to take a fine company and wreck it by going into the fast-food business or running motels" (*Fortune*, 3/4/85, p. 60).

In Peters' and Waterman's study *In Search of Excellence*, two top executives commented on the importance of using your strengths and distinctive competence. Robert W. Johnson, Chairman of Johnson & Johnson, said, "Never acquire a business you don't know how to run." Edward G. Harness, C.E.O. of Procter & Gamble, commented: "This company has never left its base. We seek to be anything but a conglomerate."

EXAMPLE: *Distinctive Competence*

Few companies undergo such a dramatic change in their internal environment as did Arrow Electronics, a firm that specialized in distributing electronic components to industrial customers. The firm's strategy was to be an efficient distributor to all but the few major industrial users who were served directly by component manufacturers. During the 1970s Arrow grew from tenth to second in the electronics distribution industry, with sales exceeding $300 million.

In December 1980 Arrow held its annual budgeting sessions at a suburban conference center outside New York City. At midmorning on December 4, a fire at the conference center killed thirteen Arrow executives, including the forty-four-year-old chairman, one of the two executive vice presidents (aged forty-one), several department chiefs, the principal financial officers, and five sales executives.

The surviving executive vice president, John Waddell (then forty-three), who had skipped the meeting to wait at headquarters for announcements connected with a stock split, watched as the market price of the stock fell within thirty days to two-thirds of the price the day before the fire. Rumors of takeovers and competitors' moves, along with speculations about the fire's origins, flew through the organization. By the time the stock bottomed out, shares were trading below ten dollars from a high of twenty-six dollars per share, making the company even more vulnerable.

In what hindsight has proven was an excellent decision, Waddell, after viewing the decimated managerial resources; the concern of the financial markets; and the world of competitors, suppliers, and customers, concluded that the relationship with suppliers was Arrow's critical strategic resource. Waddell mounted an all-out campaign to reassure suppliers, such as Texas Instruments and the Silicon Valley manufacturers, that Arrow Electronics was not only here to stay but would continue its aggressive and successful growth. It took over six months to reassure suppliers; but four years after the fire earnings per share had advanced to twice the pre-fire level and sales grew to over $750 million. Waddell commented to *Fortune* (4/30/84, p. 98) that Arrow Electronics "represents the one truly creative opportunity in life that has come my way."

Levels of Strategy

During the early history of an entrepreneurial venture, the strategic concept of distinctive competence is relatively easy to understand and apply. The creator of a new product idea must have as a distinctive competence the ability to translate that invention or idea into a salable product. If the entrepreneur can subcontract production or license the product idea to an existing manufacturer, he or she may not need manufacturing skills. The entrepreneur may not need marketing skills if the product has great inherent market attractiveness. Financial resources could be managed by a venture capitalist who is willing to share profits with the entrepreneur. Nonetheless, the entrepreneur must possess the critical distinctive competence of managerial ability to overcome the barriers between the product and the marketplace. To the extent that these problems are primarily technical production problems (as they often are), the entrepreneur's distinctive competence must lie in the area of product engineering skills.

Similarly, distinctive competence is relatively easy to define at the functional level of strategy. As an organization evolves through the stages of corporate development and becomes more complex, the strategic concept of distinctive competence, while still easy to understand, becomes more and more difficult to apply.

The mature organization, because of its greater resources, has many more strategic opportunities than the young, entrepreneurial venture. The older organization, with its extensive line of products, services, and markets, faces many more threats than the entrepreneurial venture. National and international competitors, rapidly developing technologies and substitutes, and increasing governmental restraints may threaten the broad-based, diversified company; but these factors might be of little or no consequence to the small-product inventor. Multiple product life cycles are probable

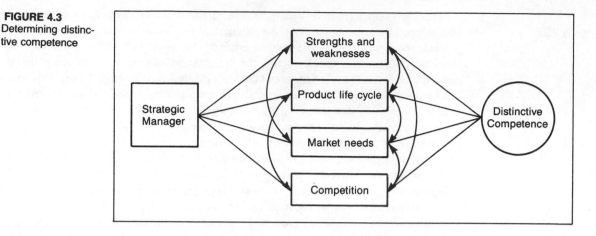

within each business division of the multiple division, multinational, Stage Three firm. Thus, at the corporate level of strategy, the strategic manager oversees scores, hundreds, or even thousands of distinctive competencies.

To summarize, distinctive competence consists of satisfying a market need while having a comparative advantage with competitors. Distinctive competence builds upon the firm's strengths — strengths that are of strategic significance based upon the stage of the product life cycle. Figure 4.3 summarizes this process. Determining distinctive competence is the second step — following defining purpose and preceding identifying strategic opportunities and threats — of the strategic analysis the manager must complete in order to formulate strategy.

SIGNIFICANT RESEARCH

Classic research studies in internal resources and competence include those of Ansoff, Schoeffler et al., and Stevenson.

Ansoff, in *Corporate Strategy* (1965), argues that the "common thread"— the common factor uniting a firm's products and markets — must be based on its competence profile. This competence profile is a list of the major skills and competences of the firm, and is used both for internal appraisal and for understanding the pattern of skills required in industries under review as possible diversification opportunities.

Schoeffler (1974) reported on the Profit Impact of Market Strategies (PIMS) study of over six hundred businesses. Those factors underlying distinctive competence and explaining profitability included (1) market share, (2) marketing expenditures, (3) research and development expenditures, (4) product quality, (5) investment levels, and (6) degree of diversification. Significantly profitable performance was linked primarily to high market share and high product quality. Thirty-six variables explained 77 percent of profitability variance.

Stevenson (1976) interviewed fifty executives in six companies to determine how they assess strengths and weaknesses. The organizational level and the area of responsibility of the responding executive significantly affected the category (financial, marketing, etc.) of strengths and weaknesses described. Further, past performance was most important in determining strengths; management theory and practice was most important in identifying weaknesses. Overall, Stevenson concluded that the process of defining strengths and weaknesses not only would improve the firm's strategy but also would serve as an instrument for managerial development.

Current studies include those by the following researchers.

Aaker and Mascarenhas (1974), describing "the need for strategic flexibility," pointed out that flexibility can come not only from diversification but also from internal resources, either through (1) "investment is underused resources" or (2) "reducing commitment of resources to a specialized use."

Hambrick and Lei (1985), to answer the question "How significant is the stage of the product life cycle?" studied ten variables, including product life cycle, as factors explaining strategy and performance. They found that the type of business (consumer or industrial) and the lack of frequency of customer purchase (once a year or less) were more important than product life cycle stage. They also studied other variables, such as technological change, degree of product differentiation, import levels, industry concentration, and instability of both demand and market share.

Lorange and Murphy (1983), researching the "concepts and practice" of "strategy and human resources," stressed the importance of human resources and strategic management.

Lucas and Turner (1982) studied the firm's information systems resource and degree of integration of the information processing function with the strategic process. They found that most firms have information systems that are concentrated on operational efficiency and are thus independent of strategy, with only a few systems supporting the strategy by producing data for standard, daily decisions. Nonetheless, the firm of the future will merge the information system into strategy formulation, especially by successfully answering the question "How can our information system provide us with technological and other trends to help us open new product markets?"

Rothschild (1984), a manager at General Electric, described the interplay between "surprise and the competitive advantage" and suggested that an "ideal" preemptive move should include (1) the possibility of rapidly occupying prime positions, (2) the difficulty of adversaries following your move, (3) the reduction of competitor's response rate, and (4) the ease of reversing the preemptive move if necessary.

Tyebjee, Bruno, and McIntyre (1983) studied the internal structure and marketing resources of rapidly growing high-tech companies. They concluded that these fast-growth companies passed through four stages of marketing for which a company must plan in advance: (1) entrepreneurial marketing (finding a market niche), (2) opportunistic marketing (penetrating the market), (3) responsive marketing (developing product markets), and (4) diversified marketing (developing new business).

Wheelwright and Hayes (1985) sought to answer the question "How does one carry out a policy of low-cost producer and other competitive strategies based upon production?" They provided some suggestions on "competing through manufacturing." They identified four stages of manufacturing strategy: (1) minimizing the negative potential of manufacturing by keeping it flexible and reactive; (2) achieving parity with competition primarily through capital investment; (3) providing support for the business strategy by systematically addressing long-term manufacturing developments and trends; and (4) providing a manufacturing base that is a competitive advantage with achieved capabilities in advance of needs. Wheelwright and Hayes cited examples at General Electric and IBM.

Williams (1984), constructed a generic matrix for "competitive strategy valuation," placing "relative competitive advantage" on one axis and "economic life in the market" on the other axis. He showed how profitability and cash flow per unit, capital investment, and managerial commitment varied within this matrix.

EXECUTIVE COMMENTS

[AMF] is an operating company, not a holding company. It's a different language. A financial man sees problems expressed in numbers and ratios, but the operations man is out there dealing with people.

J. W. Wolcott, former AMF executive, in *Business Week* (8/12/85) p. 50

[We at] Firestone would have had to invest another $150 [million] to $200 million to stay competitive in the plastics business, and if we had done that, we would have had to starve our other businesses. We are a company with extraordinary skills and strengths, but I don't think plastics was a well-advised battlefield for using those skills and strengths.

J. J. Nevin, Firestone CEO, in the *Wall Street Journal* (11/19/80), p. 37

If all you have is a hammer, everything looks like a nail.

Bernard Baruch, Wall Street investor and financier

[Our strategic] plan calls for Kaiser to identify its most promising businesses and to focus its resources on long-term development and profitability. Increased resources will be allocated to business lines where the company believes it has existing strengths, such as superior technology, low costs, or strong market positions.

C. Maier, Kaiser Chairman

KEY TERMS

comparative advantage (page 83)
competitive turbulence stage (page 78)

decline stage (page 78)

distinctive competence (page 83)

market development stage (page 78)

market needs (page 83)

maturity stage (page 78)

product life cycle (page 78)

strengths and weaknesses (page 73)

synergy (page 73)

BIBLIOGRAPHY

Aaker, D. A., and B. Mascarenhas, "The Need for Strategic Flexibility," *Journal of Business Strategy* 5 (Fall 1984), pp. 74–82.

Anderson, C., and C. Zeithaml, "Stage of the Product Life Cycle, Business Strategy, and Business Performance," *Academy of Management Journal* 27 (March 1984).

Andrews, K. R., *The Concept of Corporate Strategy* (Homewood, IL: Richard D. Irwin, 1980).

Ansoff, H. I., *Corporate Strategy: Business Policy for Growth and Expansion* (New York: McGraw-Hill, 1965).

Buchele, R. B., "How to Evaluate a Firm," *California Management Review* (Fall 1962), pp. 5–16.

Dhalla, N. K., and S. Yuspeh, "Forget the Product Life Cycle Concept," *Harvard Business Review* 54 (January-February 1976), pp. 102–112.

Drucker, P. F., *Management: Tasks, Responsibilities, Practices* (New York: Harper & Row, 1974).

Hambrick, D., "High Profit Strategies in Mature Capital Goods Industries: A Contingency Approach," *Academy of Management Journal* 26 (December 1983).

Hambrick, D., and D. Lei, "Toward an Empirical Prioritization of Contingency Variables for Business Strategy," *Academy of Management Journal* 28 (1985), pp. 763–788.

Hambrick, D., and S. Schecter, "Turnaround Strategies for Mature Industrial-Product Business Units," *Academy of Management Journal* 26 (June 1983), pp. 231–248.

Henry, H. W., "Appraising a Company's Strengths and Weaknesses," *Management Policy* (July-August 1980), pp. 31–36.

Hofer, C. W., "Toward a Contingency Theory of Business Strategy," *Academy of Management Journal* (December 1975), pp. 784–810.

Hussey, D. E., "The Corporate Appraisal: Assessing Company Strengths and Weaknesses," *Long Range Planning* (December 1968), pp. 19–25.

Levitt, T., "Exploit the Product Life Cycle," *Harvard Business Review* 43 (November-December 1965), pp. 81–94.

Lorange, P., and D. C. Murphy, "Strategy and Human Resources," *Human Resources Management* 22 (Spring-Summer 1983), pp. 111–135.

Lucas, H. C., Jr., and J. A. Turner, "A Corporate Strategy for the Control of Information Processing, *Sloan Management Review* 23 (Spring 1982), pp. 25–36.

Peters, T. J., and R. H. Waterman, Jr., *In Search of Excellence: Lessons from America's Best-Run Companies* (New York: Harper & Row, 1982).

Polli, R., and V. J. Cook, "Validity of the Product Life Cycle," *The Journal of Business* 42 (October 1969), pp. 385–400.

Rothschild, W. E., "Surprise and the Competitive Advantage," *Journal of Business Strategy* 4 (Winter 1984), pp. 10–18.

Schoeffler, S., R. D. Buzzell, and D. F. Heany, "Impact of Strategic Planning on Profit Performance," *Harvard Business Review* 54 (March-April 1974), pp. 137–145.

Salter, M. S., "Stages of Corporate Development," *Journal of Business Policy* 1 (Spring 1970), pp. 23–27.

South, S. E., "Competitive Advantage: The Cornerstone of Strategic Thinking," *Journal of Business Strategy* 1 (Spring 1981), pp. 15–25.

Stevenson, R. H., "Defining Corporate Strengths and Weaknesses," *Sloan Management Review* (Spring 1976), pp. 51–68.

Thompson, A. A., Jr., and A. J. Strickland, III, *Strategy Formulation and Implementation* (Dallas: Business Publications, 1980).

Tyebjee, T. T., A. V. Bruno, and S. M. McIntyre, "Growing Ventures Can Anticipate Marketing Stages," *Harvard Business Review* 61 (January-February 1983), pp. 62–66.

Wasson, C. R., *Dynamic Competitive Strategy and Product Life Cycle* (St. Charles, IL: Challenge Books, 1974).

Wheelwright, S. C., and R. H. Hayes, "Competing Through Manufacturing," *Harvard Business Review* 63 (January-February 1985), pp. 99–109.

Williams, J. R., "Competitive Strategy Valuation," *Journal of Business Strategy* 4 (Spring 1984), pp. 36–46.

APPENDIX: THE SMALL BUSINESS

SMALL BUSINESS CATEGORIES

We arbitrarily define a small business as any firm with less than twenty employees. Although they are insignificant in terms of assets, employment, investment, or profit when compared to U.S. multinational firms, small businesses represent over 90 percent of the businesses in the United States, according to the *Statistical Abstract of the United States*.

Two ways of categorizing these vast numbers of small businesses were suggested by both Susbauer and by Vesper in commentaries within Schendel and Hofer (1979).

Success Categories

Susbauer categorized small businesses into four groups in terms of increasing success. Least successful, but by far the most numerous, are the "survival firms," typically the "undercapitalized, undermanaged, limited-potential mom and pop stores." Next are the "attractive growth potential firms," which are small businesses on their way to success; in other words, intermediate-step firms such as high-tech companies on the verge of success.

Susbauer's third category is the "underachieving firm," the company that consciously or unconsciously does not achieve its potential. The final category is the "high success growth firm."

Economic Categories

Vesper, on the other hand, groups small businesses, based upon "the economic functions they perform," into nine categories:

1. Solo, self-employed entrepreneurs
2. Work-force builders (typically service companies)
3. Product innovators
4. Unutilized resource exploiters
5. Economy of scale exploiters
6. Pattern multipliers (franchise entrepreneurs such as Colonel Sanders)
7. Takeover artists
8. Capital aggregators (such as founders of small banks)
9. Speculators

SMALL BUSINESS ENVIRONMENT

The internal environment of the small business distinguishes it from other organizations. By definition, the small business has limited resources. Although limited financial resources are cited as the most important reason for the failure of small business, the small business strategic manager may also face limited (1) managerial talents, (2) productive capacity, (3) marketing options, and (4) information.

The small business strategist, then, has a narrowly defined distinctive competence, since the small firm usually does not possess many significant strengths. This limited distinctive competence means that the small business strategist confronts a higher risk than a strategist for a larger company. Higher risk may mean that the small business tries to avoid products at the competitive turbulence or mature stages of the product life cycle.

EXAMPLE: *Small Businesses*

EMF is a privately held service company that provides repair service for personal computers and minicomputers. Its sales goal for 1984 was $1 million. In the fall of 1984, EMF had an option to pursue the maintenance-agreement end of the repair market through retail distributors. In this field, EMF faced such competitors as TRW, RCA, Honeywell, and Arrow Electronics. If EMF decided to concentrate on start-up and foreign computer manufactuers, it would face such competitors as Sinclair and Acorn, who could not afford a national service organization. The latter group of manufacturers were clearly the preferable alternative; EMF did not possess a significant distinctive competence to use in competing against such mature, resourceful corporations as TRW and RCA.

Commenting on the move into biotechnology industry by du Pont and Monsanto, a manager at one of the two hundred small, start-up biotechnology businesses said, "It's becoming the waltz of the elephants, and the fleas are going to get squashed" (*Business Week*, 11/5/84, p. 137).

Although smaller businesses have significant advantages in the commitment of top executives, time flexibility, and lower fixed costs, Drucker (1974) concluded that the "typical small business has no strategy . . . it lives from problem to problem." While focusing on the present, the small business strategic manager also must anticipate the future investment and managerial needs caused by growth.

BIBLIOGRAPHY

Drucker, P. F., *Management* (New York: Harper & Row, 1974).

Susbauer, J. C., "Commentary," in *Strategic Management*, D. E. Schendel and C. W. Hofer, eds. (Boston: Little, Brown, 1979), pp. 327–332.

Vesper, K. H., in *Strategic Management*, op. cit., pp. 332–338.

CHAPTER 5

IDENTIFYING OPPORTUNITIES AND THREATS

Every enterprise must watch what is new in the environment, for this might eventually destroy it. . . . It is discouraging that most phonograph companies did not enter the radio field, wagon manufacturers did not enter the automobile business, and steam locomotive companies did not enter the diesel locomotive business.

P. Kotler, *Marketing Management: Analysis, Planning and Control*

This chapter will identify the components of the organization's external environment, describe a method for analyzing these external components, and show how this analytical method can be used by the strategic manager. An appendix to this chapter describes the special complexities of the international business environment.

EXTERNAL ENVIRONMENT DEFINED

The external environment of the firm consists of all outside factors that affect the firm. The impact may be direct, as in the short-term acts of a competitor, or indirect, as in long-term changes in social attitudes toward business. These factors may be grouped into five segments: (1) markets, (2) competition, (3) technology, (4) society, and (5) government. Each segment includes factors that have a direct and indirect effect on the organization.

Markets

The organization succeeds or fails based upon what happens in its markets. The markets in which the organization offers its products and services include customers and competitors.

As a company grows from a small, single-product firm to a complex, diversified multinational corporation, its markets grow in complexity. As complexity grows, the strategic manager's job of analyzing the marketplace becomes more difficult

How does a firm define its market? The answer to this question depends on the type of business. For example, a small family business may think of its market in terms of its product or service, such as being in the auto parts business or the television repair business. One company might see itself in a customer needs market, such as data processing, or in a technology market, such as aerospace. A large, diversified company might be active in many markets, or even in markets without definition or delineation — borderless markets with broad ranges of products and services. In Derek Abell's view (1980), a company can define its business by (1) who it sells to (customer group), (2) what it sells (customer needs), and (3) how the product or service is produced (technologies).

EXAMPLE: *TWA's Market*

Consider the example of Transworld Corporation. Trans World Airlines (TWA), formerly the major component of the Transworld Corporation, could define its market in definite terms. The market included the transportation of passengers and the provision of supporting services (i.e., baggage, freight, and in-flight items, including food and beverages). These transportation services operated between set cities and geographic regions, and were offered at prices easily defined by a few systems of fare regulation.

By early 1984, Transworld had sold its controlling interest in TWA stock; its markets included: (1) food service, ranging from over four hundred fast food outlets, including Hardee's, to a mammoth institutional service, Canteen Corporation; (2) real estate, via a national franchise of Century 21 real estate firms; (3) hotels, through its operation of approximately one hundred Hilton Hotels; and (4) personnel services, including Dunhill Personnel System. Transworld can now clearly define its markets as encompassing anyone who works, travels, eats, or sleeps. By the third quarter of 1984, Transworld had reported operating profits of $120 million on sales of $1.5 billion, with fast food outlets and Hilton Hotels contributing two-thirds of earnings.

The marketplace may be so complex as to seem limitless or without borders. Nonetheless, market may be defined within the following categories.

Customers
    industrial, consumer
    government, not-for-profit
Locations
    regional, national, international
Types of product
    goods or services
    stage of product life cycle
Nature of product
    household, technical
Nature of buying decision
    impulse, formalized analysis

Purchase decision factors
   price
   packaging
   service/maintenance
   availability
   convenience
   credit financing
   reputation
   others
Market structure
   competitive/commodity to regulated oligopoly/monopoly

The following list shows how the Transworld Corporation might define its current markets.

Customers
   Industrial/institutional customers sold to by Transworld's Canteen Corporation, Dunhill Personnel (employer)
   Consumer customers sold to by Transworld's Hardee's, Century 21, Hilton, Dunhill Personnel (employee)
Locations
   Regional (Hardee's [Southeast])
   National (Century 21, Dunhill Personnel)
   International (Hilton)
Product Type
   Goods (Hardee's, Canteen Corporation)
   Services (Century 21, Hilton, Dunhill Personnel)
Product Nature
   Household (Hardee's, Hilton, Canteen Corporation)
   Technical (Century 21, Dunhill Personnel)
Buying Decision
   Impulse (Hardee's)
   Formalized Analysis (Century 21)
Purchase Factors
   Price (Canteen Corporation)
   Service (Century 21)
   Others (Hilton)
Market Structure
   Competitive/commodity (Hardee's)
   Regulated oligopoly/monopoly TWA [former holding]

A definition of the external environment's market, then, can be presented as follows: The *market* is the present and potential *customers* in their range of *locations*, organized into economic *market structures*, who may decide to buy the firm's *product* — a buying *decision* that varies as to nature of the product and as to decision factors.

Competition

The firm's success or failure in the marketplace depends in part upon the strategic decisions of its competitors. *Competition*, then, consists of the present and potential alternative sources of a firm's goods and services. The breadth and variety of a firm's competitors depends on the extent of the firm's product offerings and market location. A strategic manager may face aggressive international competition or a few local competitors.

Competition may be direct, such as the computer offerings that AT&T presented to Digital Equipment Corporation's customers and others following the breakup of the Bell system. Competition can also be indirect, through product substitution. The North American beverage industry has made a clear shift away from distilled spirits (especially blends) toward table wines.

Technology

Scientific and engineering principles underlie all the product design and production knowledge found within an industry. Advances in production processes and product designs represent technological progress that will affect the organization to some degree. *Technology*, then, consists of the current scientific and engineering principles embodied in an organization's processes and products, and the expected advances in these production and design systems.

Communication and computers illustrate the force and potential of technological advance. With the technological breakthrough of fiberoptics, message capacities increased and operating costs decreased. Market and industry boundaries fell before the force of fiberoptic technology. The *Wall Street Journal* and *USA Today* transmitted their daily editions to Europe via satellite. Larger corporations (such as Kodak) that acquired their own communications systems in order to control costs found themselves with excess communication capacity, and so began to compete with AT&T by offering telephone services to others.

In the mid-1980s an estimated 9,000 robots worked in the United States, 12,500 in Europe, and 140,000 in Japan. Hitachi builds videocassette recorder chassis in one plant in Japan. After they installed eleven robots and fifty-two automatic assembly machines, their assembly time per chassis fell from twenty-four to three minutes; their number of workers dropped from 170 to 33.

The rate of technological change is determined primarily within a given business by economics, and within a given society by social values. An organization facing little competition in a structured market will have little incentive to make heavy investments in technological research and development. The manufacturer of microcomputers in the 1980s cannot expect economic survival without staying in the forefront of computer technology. Similarly, few advances in manufacturing technology can be expected of societies that value rural life most highly and stress the family agricultural unit as the foundation of society. Societies that value health and longevity, however, can be expected to pursue advances in medical technology.

Society

If markets seem difficult to define, society proves to be an even more elusive concept. *Society* can best be defined as the cultural values and expectations that surround the organization. These values and expectations are embodied in the population; they affect the organization directly through the attitudes of customers, employees, and others who deal with the organization. While many fast food operators began to despair at McDonald's industry dominance (40 percent of worldwide fast food hamburger sales and a history of constantly increasing quarterly earnings), others decided to follow the social trend of increasing attention to nutrition and personal health. Several national food retailers are hatching new outlets serving unbreaded chicken broiled without oil — a dish endorsed by medical groups.

One element of U.S. society, the labor union, today faces an unfavorable trend that has resulted from changing social values. A 1983 Gallup poll ranked labor officials second from the bottom in ethical behavior, only slightly more ethical than used car salespeople. A 1985 AFL-CIO report showed that 65 percent of nonunion workers thought union leaders forced members into certain contracts and actions. Union members are the lowest (19 percent) proportion of the work force in decades. The president of the Communication Workers of America, G. E. Watts, said, "What we're now saying to ourselves is that we should, we must adjust to a changing workplace. We've got to change some every day to keep up" (2/24/85).

Columbia University sociologist David Halle (1985) provides further insights into the worker in society. Halle's findings, which were based on a study of blue collar workers in northern New Jersey from 1974 to 1981, include:

Most workers get no deep satisfaction from religion or ethnicity.

Most workers believe they are wasting their lives in dull, repetitive jobs.

Most male workers get most enjoyment from drinking with male friends, fishing, hunting, and sports events.

Forty percent of workers are unhappily married.

Eight-three percent of workers believe big business runs the country.

Ninety-two percent of workers believe all politicians are corrupt.

As social values and expectations change and evolve, they create opportunities and threats for the strategic manager.

Government

Government is an administrative system for organizing human effort. The procedures of this administrative system are political. The government's scope of activities includes defense, the judiciary, the economic infrastructure (taxes, tariffs, and incentive programs), and regulation. The government is also the major domestic purchaser of goods and services, and the instrument of the critical fiscal and monetary policies that influence economic trends.

Government regulation of business changes and evolves as it reacts to perceived problems or abuses. Early regulation of business reacted to monopolies; the first regulation effort, the 1887 Interstate Commerce Commission, was established to control the monopolistic position of railroads. This industry-by-industry approach to regulation, built upon the principle of controlling or limiting monopolistic profits, changed with the administration of Franklin Roosevelt. Regulation changed further with the legislative acts regulating social problems in the mid-1960s and mid-1970s. These social problems or issues included equal employment opportunities, occupational safety, consumer protection, and environment.

Professor Manley Irwin of the University of New Hampshire warns of a new change in regulation as we enter the age of cold war technology: regulation by the Pentagon. Professor Irwin cites the following incidents as evidence of this Department of Defense regulation of business during the fall of 1984.

Harvard University report cites campus fear of federal control of research (December 1984).

Ericsson, Sweden's largest electronics company, cancels Eastern bloc sales under U.S. pressure (August 1984).

United States gets tough with Austria over high-tech leaks (November 1984).

United States investigates computer sales to Czechs by ASEA of Sweden (December 1984).

Austria toughens export controls in bid to preserve its access to U.S. technology (November 1984).

Digital Equipment Corporation to pay $1.1 million to settle U.S. export violations (September 1984).

ITT's German subsidiary cancels telephone exchange sale to Hungary (October 1984).

Belgium abandons nuclear plant contract in Libya (October 1984).

In summary, the strategic manager seeks answers to questions encompassing the market, competition, technology, government, and society, questions including:

Market
What present economic conditions influence my ability to profitably sell my goods and services in the marketplace?
What economic trends over the next one-, two-, and five-year periods do I anticipate?
What is the anticipated impact of these trends on my ability to sell my goods and services in the future?

Competition
What present competitive conditions influence my ability to profitably sell my goods and services in the marketplace?
What competitive trends in the one-, two-, and five-year time horizons do I anticipate?

What is the anticipated impact of these trends on my ability to sell my goods and services in the future?

Technology

What present technological conditions influence my ability to profitably sell my goods and services in the marketplace?

What technological trends in the one-, two-, and five-year time horizons do I anticipate?

What is the anticipated impact of these trends on my ability to sell my goods and services in the future?

Government/Society

What present regulatory/political/social conditions influence my ability to profitably sell my goods and services in the marketplace?

What regulatory/political/social trends in the one-, two-, and five-year horizons do I anticipate?

What is the anticipated impact of these trends on my ability to sell my goods and services in the future?

The Changing External Environment

The preceding list of questions focuses on change. To underscore the dynamic nature of the external environment, some basic social and cultural values will be examined from a historical viewpoint. What are the constant values of any society? Some of the fundamental concepts might be property rights, the role of the market and individual expectations, and the nature of the Deity. This brief review of these fundamental cultural concepts will provide a means for understanding change in the external environment.

Property Rights. What is the basis of the right to property? From the viewpoint of the historian and anthropologist, property rights have been built upon a changing foundation. Initially, as nomadic hunter-gatherers roamed the earth, rights to property were based upon the foundation of first occupancy. Further, these rights usually were collective or communal rights that were based upon tribal, not individual, ownership. Subsequent foundations for property rights included (1) superiority, such as the moral superiority supporting the divine right of monarchies; (2) labor, wherein an individual's labor on or toward something, such as agricultural land, determined ownership; (3) political liberty, wherein the ultimate goal of liberty required economic freedom, which in turn required the right to own property; and (4) utility, wherein the system of private property rights was enforced because it was the most effective system.

The Market and Individual Expectations. Some anthropological economists have hypothesized that the basic economic structure has changed from (1) reciprocal societies, in which individuals exchanged surplus, to (2) administered societies, in which a centralized, administrative (often either religious or military, or both) class redistributed surpluses for everyone, to (3) market societies, in which the flow of goods and services are determined by the market's demand and supply. Other social scientists have hypothesized that societal expectations have changed from simple survival to equality, liberty, education, and most recently (in developed societies) to increasing standards of living and individual development.

The Deity. Even such a basic concept as the nature of the Deity has changed. Early pantheistic views of the Deity in nature and all things moved to a period of goddess religions in which all the head deities were female, to a period of male principal deities. One might even argue that many persons currently view the Deity as a scientific principle, a "cosmic computer."

Business and Society. "Constants" in business change, just as cultures change, as witnessed by Coca-Cola's reformulating their 99-year-old Coke formula and Procter & Gamble's abandoning a 135-year-old trademark (thirteen stars and a "man" moon). *The Christian Science Monitor* (5/6/85, p. 31) reported on the Starch Advertisement Readership Service's study of basic interest in the United States; it included the following changes. (1) Religion, which ranked first among women and fifth among men as a basic interest in 1953, had disappeared entirely from the top ten list by 1983. (2) Women's first basic interest in 1983 in fashion and clothes, replacing religion; the first basic interest for men was business, replacing sports. (3) Health entered the top ten interests in 1983 (third for women and seventh for men) while gardening disappeared. (4) Travel became a new interest for women, while homemaking dropped from third in 1953 to eighth in 1983.

Change and Opportunity. The strategic manager identifies and seeks to direct the forces of change as a source of opportunity. Cultural changes thus can be seen as major opportunities.

Health Maintenance Organizations (HMOs) are an example of a mass market opportunity that resulted from significant cultural change. North Americans' increasing health consciousness represents a cultural change; the HMO responded by addressing concerns about rising hospitalization costs. HMOs charge monthly premiums just as do the traditional health insurers; however, their monthly fees are often lower, and small physician and medication fees are significantly lower. Blue Cross-Blue Shield of Massachusetts saw an increase in its HMO subscribers from 31,000 in 1981 to 200,000 in 1985. The director of the federal government's HMO office estimated that the more than fifteen million HMO members should double by 1989 (2/4/84).

Following in this same health trend, Riunite offered jogging gear with its faddish wines. Seagram, perhaps more logically, introduced a no-alcohol wine, St. Regis, in the mid-1980s.

EXAMPLE: *Change*

Strategic managers have found themselves in great difficulty when they have refused to recognize change. Howard Head clung steadfastly to a single product, the black metal ski, in the face of fiberglass technology and trends toward more fashionable, colorful skis. Fiberglass skis ended Howard Head's industry dominance. Sewall Avery of Montgomery Ward stood firmly committed to cost cutting, store consolidation, and cash-liquidity, expecting a post–World War II recession; Sears, Roebuck aggressively expanded after World War II to take advantage of pent-up demand and the move to suburbia. The effective strategic manager recognizes change as a fact of life. Montgomery Ward saved a lot of money, but Sears gained all the business.

STRATEGIC ANALYSIS AND STRATEGIC SIGNALS

The method used by the strategic manager to analyze the external environment consists of two steps: (1) identifying strategic signals and (2) interpreting strategic signals.

Identifying Strategic Signals

The job of the strategic manager is to identify those strategic signals which show that the environment is shifting in ways that will provide opportunities or will present threats to the firm. *Strategic signals* are early warning signs generated by the external environment that reveal both the nature and direction of external environmental change. As consumer tastes evolve, markets change. As societal values shift, social programs change. As competitors take actions in the marketplace, competitive pressures change. As one governmental leader succeeds another, governmental regulations change.

Interpreting Strategic Signals

After identifying early warning signals in the external environment, the strategic manager determines whether these signals are positive or negative. Positive signals (i.e., significant increases in the percentage of customers who are repeat customers after an initial trial purchase of a product) indicate opportunities for the firm in the external environment. Negative signals (i.e., continued decreases in a competitor's manufacturing costs) represent threats in the external environment.

Market Signals

The variety and number of strategic signals seem infinite. Nonetheless, the strategist must detect *and* interpret the signals. Business experience has shown the strategic manager can expect positive and negative signals of external environmental opportunities and threats relating to present products. Table 5.1 presents selected market signals. When the strategist turns away from existing products to look for new market opportunities, new signals become important. Of primary interest is the change in consumer tastes.

EXAMPLE: *Strategic Market Signals*

Experience in the steel container (tin can) packaging industry since World War II provides an illustration of some of these strategic market signals. Positive signals in the industry included (1) increase in total number of customers; (2) increase in

TABLE 5.1
Selected market strategic signals for existing products

Category	Positive	Negative
Customers		
total number	Increases	Decreases
per customer volume	Increases	Decreases
Location		
firm's geographic coverage	Increases	Decreases
industry geographic coverage	Expands	Contracts
Product type		
firm's product mix	Expands	Contracts
industry product mix	Expands	Contracts
Product, buying decision nature, factors		
firm's percentage contribution	Increases	Decreases
industry margins	Increase	Decrease
purchase frequency	Increases	Decreases
product substitutes	Decrease	Increase
Market structure		
price competition	Decreases	Increases
industry advertising	Decreases	Increases
barriers to entry	Increase	Decrease

per-customer volume; (3) geographic expansion; and (4) product mix expansion, including the introduction of aerosol cans. Nonetheless, the negative signals warned of what was really happening. Alcoa, Reynolds, and the other aluminum manufacturers were successfully introducing aluminum cans. Du Pont and others were developing plastic substitutes. Libby and other major customers were producing their own cans. The industry increased price competition as a result of these other negative factors. Thus, negative signals included (1) decrease in contribution and margins as the industry cut price to keep volume, (2) decrease in product mix, (3) increase in product substitutes, (4) increase in price competition, and (5) decrease in purchase frequency.

EXAMPLE: *Retailers and the Market*

Recognizing the market opportunity represented by the increasing numbers of professional women in the work force, Chicago retailer Carson Pirie Scott & Co. created a 40,000-square-foot "corporate level" that offered designer fashions, shoes, cosmetics, and accessories for the woman executive, along with a fashion consultant, shoe repair shop, restaurant, dry cleaners, and photocopy center.

Market signals or suggestions may appear from many sources. *Business Week* (4/22/85, p. 65) reported on entrepreneur Roy Raymond, who had established Victoria's Secret lingerie shops. At age thirty-seven, after the birth of his two children, Raymond formed My Child's Destiny, a chain of children's boutiques selling natural fiber clothes and nonviolent toys. The restrooms even provided free diapers! Working Concept 11 provides a tool for understanding markets; Figure 5.1 summarizes customer needs analysis.

WORKING CONCEPT 11

CUSTOMER NEEDS ANALYSIS

The strategic manager tries to determine what factors influence the customers' choice of one company's service or product over another's. These factors influencing customer choice make up the needs that the customer seeks to satisfy; they might include price, service, credit availability, durability and other measures of "quality," and location. Frequently, market research interviews will provide a number of these factors.

Through market research and market studies, the manager next determines the relative importance of these factors. These findings may range from imprecise "guesstimates" to numerical weights, depending on the data available. Clearly, some measure of importance is necessary; a 33-inch yardstick is better than no yardstick at all. The degree of precision will be determined by the specifics of the situation. By rating the firm's performance against competitors on each of these customer need factors, the manager can gain competitive insight.

The strategist then makes assumptions about the future likelihood of change, both as to customer need factors and as to their relative importance. The manager needs to determine how the purchase of tomorrow will differ from today's purchase. Manage-ment analyst Peter Drucker (1974) concluded,

It is the customer who determines what a business is. It is the customer alone whose willingness to pay for a good or for a service converts economic resources into wealth, things into goods. . . . What the customer thinks he is buying, what he considers value, is decisive — it determines what a business is, what it produces, and whether it will prosper. (p. 61)

The critical functional marketing questions — What market segments should we pursue? and How should we position our products? — can best, and perhaps only, be answered after customer needs are analyzed and understood. Differing needs create different market segments. The strategic manager can meet those needs through product positioning.

The president of Pepsi, Roger Enrico, commented on customer needs and product positioning as he compared Pepsi and Coke: "Coke . . . slapped their name on more and more kinds of products. Pepsi stands for something. . . . When people pick up Pepsi they know what they are getting. I don't think you can say that with the other product" (*Boston Globe*, 12/1/85, p. A-1).

FIGURE 5.1
Customer needs analysis

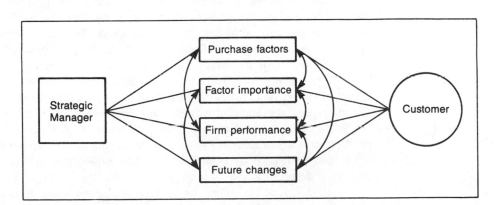

EXAMPLES: *Customer Needs*

Howard Head correctly attributed the success of his revolutionary metal ski to its responsiveness and turning ability that made skiing easier; he also stressed the importance of product longevity. Being an engineer, Head thought that people would want skis that would last a long time. However, he discounted fashion as a critical factor in the purchase decision, ignoring the striking cosmetics of the new fiberglass skis being introduced by Kneisl and other European manufacturers. Head also overlooked price as a measure of perceived quality. Inevitably, Head's market share dropped as other manufacturers positioned their skis at price points above Head skis.

The banking industry provides examples of the importance of understanding the customer. From 1980 to 1985 the Barnett Bank group climbed from number 3 to number 1 among the almost five hundred banks in Florida. The Barnett group's success in capturing the largest share of retired people's savings in this deposit-rich environment was attributed to its excellent customer services, based in turn on its knowledge of the factors that influence customer decisions. A Boston bank, on the other hand, was fined $500,000 for failing to report international cash transactions to the Internal Revenue Service between 1980 and 1984. Large cash transactions by alleged bosses of the New England crime syndicate were at the center of the unreported transactions. The bank asserted that it didn't know the "boss" family should be scrutinized, and didn't think to report the exchange of over $2.2 million in cash exchanged for certified checks by the "boss" family companies.

The Decision to Buy. Assessing market signals, then, is a process of (1) understanding the critical factors underlying the customer's buying decision and (2) identifying signals that will indicate strategic changes in a firm's relative position regarding these purchase factors.

EXAMPLES: *Purchase Decision*

The strategic importance of identifying the essence of the purchase decision can be seen in Beech-Nut's mid-1980s gain in the Gerber-dominated (70 percent) U.S. baby food market. Beech-Nut's biggest gain has been in its Stages baby foods, which are color-coded to four stages of infant development. Although Stages cost 10 to 30 percent more than their competition, *Fortune* reported that Stages had over 50 percent of the baby food business in some markets in 1984 (12/24/84, p. 56). Parents obviously had decided that Stages set Beech-Nut products apart from those of Gerber and Heinz, the other U.S. baby food producers. In the same issue, *Fortune* cited an example of misunderstanding the purchase decision when it reported on RCA's abandonment of video discs. Although RCA's video disc player sold at half the cost of competitors' video cassette machines, it could not record programs. This missing feature lay behind RCA's $500 million loss on "one of the decade's mangiest dogs."

In 1985 Coca-Cola turned its back on the secret Coke formula developed by John Pemberton in 1886. Coca-Cola was reacting to Pepsi's increasing market share;

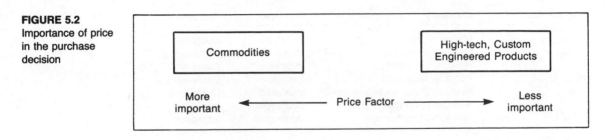

FIGURE 5.2
Importance of price
in the purchase
decision

the New Coke formula was sweeter, smoother, and closer to Pepsi's taste. Loyal Coke drinkers, however, didn't want a "better" Pepsi. The Coke "loyalist" purchasers raised such a ruckus — threatening class action lawsuits, moaning about Coke's "fixin' something that ain't broke," and flooding the company with protests — that the original Coke — now called Coca-Cola Classic — was brought back to life.

Price and the Decision to Buy. Figure 5.2 illustrates price as one aspect of the basic customer purchase decision. The simple illustration of price versus all other factors leads to the following questions.

1. As your products move toward the right, don't the following become more important distinctive competencies: (a) technical knowledge, (b) flexible production, and (c) customer relations?
2. As your products move toward the left, where price is more of a factor, don't the following become more important distinctive competencies: (a) production efficiencies, (b) administrative systems, and (c) economies of scale?

The simplicity of Figure 5.2 should not obscure the difficulty of determining the qualitative and psychological purchase factors, such as the emotional brand loyalty entirely unanticipated by those who withdrew the original Coke in April 1985, only to bring it back in July.

Quality and the Decision to Buy. Product quality is a second aspect of the customer purchase decision. Quality, of course, interacts with price; price is, to some, a measure of quality. The strategic manager must recognize the perception aspects of customer needs. If a customer needs quality, creating the perception of quality is a valid strategy. Don Burr, chairman of People Express, spoke about the opposite effect, the perception of a lack of quality: "Coffee stains on the flip-down trays mean [to the passengers] that we do our engine maintenance wrong" (*Fortune*, 5/13/85, p. 23).

EXAMPLES: *Customer Needs*

A firm's misunderstanding of customer needs and customers' interest in quality can lead to trouble in the marketplace. Procter & Gamble, *Business Week* reported (2/24/86, p. 36), "virtually created" the market for the disposable diaper by recognizing the customer need. A competitor, Kimberly-Clark, introduced a better, contoured

TABLE 5.2
Selected
competitive strategic
signals

Category	Positive	Negative
Market share	Increases	Decreases
Relative profitability	Increases	Decreases
Relative product quality	Increases	Decreases
Relative service levels	Increase	Decrease
Number of market segments	Increases	Decreases
Number of competitors	Decreases	Increases
Strength of competitors	Decreases	Increases

disposable diaper; Procter & Gamble "didn't realize that consumers would pay more for a better diaper." Their 75 percent market share declined rapidly, and Kimberly's Huggies became number 1 over P&G's Pampers.

Knowledge of the whole spectrum of her high fashion customer needs is central to Donna Karan's success. Chief designer for Anne Klein at age twenty-five, and now the head of a company that expects first year sales of $12 million, Karan's designs combine sophistication, sensuality, and convenience: "A working woman has no time to shop. I want quality. I want sophistication, and I want ease. Zip on, and get on with your life" (*Business Week*, 12/23/85, p. 56).

Competitive Signals

Although market research and analysis can help identify competitive strategic signals presented in Table 5.2, how can the manager analyze the strength of the competition? At the center of this dilemma is access to the competition's information. The strategic manager looks for signals of change in the relative strength between the organization and the competition. Possible measures of strength include price levels, store location, sales force, advertising budgets, R&D expenditures, inventory levels, financial resources, and management training programs. Several possible data sources contain information about these measures, such as salespeople, customers, market research, business periodicals, trade associations, and economic statistics. Porter's model of competitive activity, presented in Working Concept 12, helps the manager understand competition and its strategic signals.

WORKING CONCEPT 12

PORTER'S DETERMINANTS OF COMPETITION

Professor Michael Porter (1980) of the Harvard Business School has identified those factors that determine the level of competitive activity within an industry. These include (1) current level of competition, (2) relative power of suppliers and customers, (3) threat of entry from potential competitors, and (4) threat of substitute products. If customers are powerful, they may force price cutting within an industry. If substitute products or companies eager to enter an industry present strong threats, profits and prices within that industry will lower and competition will grow more intense.

Porter noted further that barriers to entry include (1) economies of scale; (2) product differentiation; (3) capital requirements; (4) cost disadvantages independent of size, such as a lack of experience; (5) access to distribution channels; and (6) government policy. These conditions change and they can be changed by the actions of those in the industry. Figure 5.3 summarizes Porter's concept. The strategic manager searches for signals about the likely future state of these five determinants of competition.

FIGURE 5.3
Porter's determi-
nants of competition

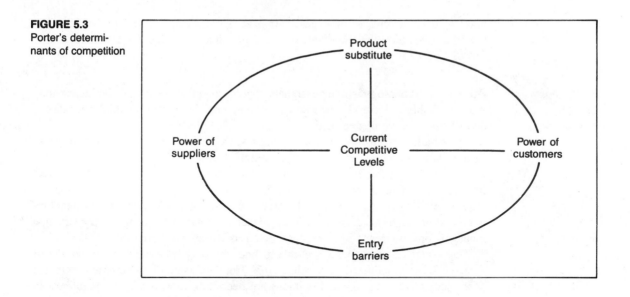

After understanding these factors that determine the level of competition, the strategist (1) positions the company in the best defensive posture, (2) influences competitive balance by strengthening the company, and (3) anticipates changes in the competitive balance and exploits these changes before competitors do. These three action plans all stem from identifying the company's crucial strengths and weaknesses.

EXAMPLES: *Competition*

Porter cited Dr. Pepper as an example of a company that strengthened its position by product differentiation, rather than by chasing after Pepsi and Coke. Polaroid, on the other hand, was vulnerable to attack (by Kodak) once its barrier to entry — its patents covering instant photography — expired.

Porter concluded that "the key to growth — even survival — is to stake out a position that is less vulnerable to attack [by competitors] . . . and less vulnerable to erosion from the direction of buyers, suppliers, and substitute goods."

In *Fortune* (4/29/85, pp. 153–166), Porter described how to attack the industry leader. Attacking the market leader requires (1) a competitive advantage in cost or in differentiation of the product, (2) an ability to counterbalance the leader's advantages, and (3) a barrier to retaliation that will keep the leader from a full-scale counterattack. Other competitive considerations include the stage of the economic cycle and the stage of maturity in the industry. More established industries, and industries within expansionary economic cycles, tend to be less competitive than younger industries and industries facing economic recessions. The greater the potential returns from economies of scale, the greater the competitive pressure.

Competition levels can also be affected by a change in top management. Jack Welch became chairman of General Electric in 1981; by 1985 he had purchased fifty businesses for G.E., including RCA. A saying circulated within G.E. that "if you put Jack in charge of a gas station at a corner with four gas stations, he wouldn't sleep until the other three guys had plywood over their windows" (*Business Week*, 12/30/85, p. 49).

Technology Signals

Additional technology strategic signals that frequently are more significant than those in Table 5.3 are (1) the rate of technological innovation within the industry and (2) the relative degree of risk.

The smaller organization with a smaller research budget usually views an increase in the pace of technology as a negative sign. Similarly, a firm's exposure to the risk of technological innovation increases directly as its technology and product line become more narrow. The body of scientific knowledge and technology is said to be doubling every decade. Further, the time lag between laboratory development and product introduction has been reduced dramatically. How can the strategic manager forecast trends in technology given its exponential growth?

The strategic manager may be able to find objective measures of the amount of research being conducted in specific areas from industry or government sources. More subjective measures and opinions are becoming more available as interest in futurism — reflected in popular literature such as studies of "megatrends" — accelerates.

Those studying specific technological trends must include an analysis of Japan's research efforts. The Japanese Ministry of International Trade and Industry (MITI) has organized and funded groups of researchers from different Japanese companies to work on R&D projects in target industries such as microelectronics, biotechnology, satellites, and artificial intelligence. After groups of leading engineers and scientists perfect technology, the individual companies convert the pilot technology, or laboratory efforts, to commercial operation and full-blown production.

The strategic manager can identify "precursor" research projects — such as solar energy, oil shale, and space shuttles — that provide leading indicators of the direction of technological change. Especially important are robotics and other automatic control systems within the manufacturing process. The strategic manager can also call on experts on technological trends who consult with organizations and industries. One such expert is Paolo Soleri of the Arcosanti project in Arizona. Soleri identifies technological trends of increasing (1) complexity, (2) miniaturization, and (3) duration. These technological trends will accelerate the pace of high technology, which Soleri sees as a necessity for the benefit of this limited planet.

TABLE 5.3
Selected technology strategic signals

Category	Positive	Negative
Level of research	Increases	Decreases
Share of industry research	Increases	Decreases
Research of suppliers	Increases	Decreases
Research of substitute suppliers	Decreases	Increases
Public/government research	Increases	Decreases

WORKING CONCEPT 13

TECHNO-LOGICAL INNOVATION

Technological innovation passes through three general phases: (1) research, (2) prototype testing, and (3) full-scale production.

RESEARCH

Research may consist of basic research, applied research, or a combination of both. Basic research concerns itself with general design concepts and scientific theories; but in applied research, these general design concepts and scientific theories are verified in a laboratory or some other controlled environment. In practice, it may be difficult to identify that point in technological innovation at which basic research becomes applied research.

PROTOTYPE TESTING

Prototype testing follows that phase of applied research that has verified the design or theory. It applies the design or theory in a full-scale trial, which may include commercial introduction. In other words, prototype testing takes place exclusively in the real world with real users and real customers, as opposed to applied research, which occurs in a controlled environment.

FULL-SCALE PRODUCTION

Full-scale production picks up where testing ends. The prototype tests have produced feedback on problems that need correcting or, in rare cases, on immediate acceptance in the marketplace. The project now goes into full production and is widely distributed to appropriate markets.

The strategic manager uses this model of technological innovation to track the progress of technological projects from the time they are possibilities — the research stage — to the time they become probable competitive threats. Harvey Brooks (1981) analyzed some of the forces that contribute to technological developments. His attempts to diagnose the trend of these forces follow:

1. *Economies of scale*: "There is some evidence that we may have come to the end of the road as far as the scale of individual technological embodiments are concerned."
2. *Centralization*: "The trend towards centralization in modern technology is less clear and less certain than is sometimes asserted" (Brooks cited as examples cable TV, transportation, and alternative energy sources).
3. *Standardization*: "Enterprises that transcend national boundaries" disseminate . . . standardization on a world scale.
4. *Labor versus energy and materials*: "Much more innovative effort in the future will be directed at saving resources and energy [versus the past emphasis on labor-saving]."

Brooks also considers (a) decreasing consumer sovereignty, in the face of the increasing complexity of products; and (b) environmental pollution.

Government Signals

Government strategic signals are limited as to their positivity or negativity (see Table 5.4) because that decision depends not only on one's personal philosophy about the role of government in business, but also upon specific circumstances. For example, Johnson & Johnson's strategic managers may have been opposed philosophically to government regulation of business. Nonetheless, after 1982, when seven people died from taking some Johnson & Johnson Tylenol capsules that had been criminally adulterated with cyanide, the company issued a call for federal

	Category	Positive	Negative
TABLE 5.4 Selected government strategic signals	Business/government communication	Increases	Decreases
	Quality of governmental executives regulating one company/industry	Increases	Decreases

government standards for tamper-proof packaging. Since Johnson & Johnson was an industry leader in profitability, the tamper-proof packaging standard meant cost increases for all companies in the industry. Johnson & Johnson ultimately had a relatively more profitable position than its competitors.

Government regulation of big business can create barriers of entry to potential competitors and weaken the relative strength of those competing with industry leaders. Also, regulation has created new industries. For example, legislation to improve water quality has created a large pollution control industry.

Government regulation was a benefit to Sprint, MCI, and other long-distance telephone companies. Before deregulation, these companies leased long-distance lines from AT&T at the Federal Communication Commission's discount rates of up to 70 percent, and then resold the lines to corporate and private telephone users. After the deregulation of AT&T, this discount rate disappeared; long-distance companies now have to compete with AT&T on equal terms.

Federal government insistence on the reduction of health care costs led to maximum allowances for medicare payments, resulting in a number of strategic responses. Private, for-profit hospital corporations turned to health insurance, clinics, and acquisitions for growth. Medical insurers such as Blue Cross of Michigan and hospitals such as Houston's Ben Toub pushed hard for generic drugs — cheaper but chemically equivalent versions of brand-name pharmaceuticals.

The critical issues now confronting the high-tech manufacturers venturing into laser applications in medicine are the responses of the government and doctors. On the regulation side, the Food and Drug Administration must first approve the use of lasers in each and every type of operation. On the professional side, the doctors performing the thirty million surgical operations each year must decide if they prefer the laser or the scalpel.

The Process of Government. Once a decision is reached on whether a certain government act is a positive or negative strategic signal, the strategic manager then must interpret the significance of the positive opportunity or negative threat in light of the governmental process. Figure 5.4 summarizes federal government action.

Government regulation (the output of the governmental process) may affect the firm in the following ways.

What can go in the product
How the product is made
Who makes the product

FIGURE 5.4
Governmental
process

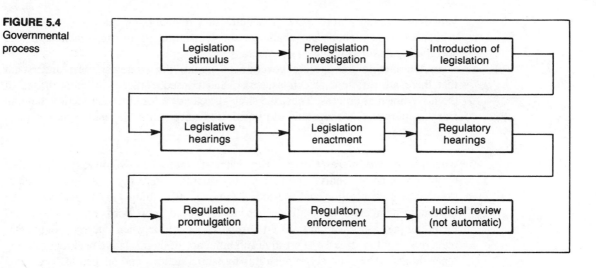

How much the product maker (and others) are paid

How the product is labeled

How the product is distributed

Who can (cannot) buy the product

How the product is priced

How the product is advertised

How the product purchase is financed

How financial results are reported

How financial results are taxed

How capital and debt are raised

How the work place is designed

How the firm affects the environment

How foreign competition affects the firm

Regardless of one's personal philosophy on regulation of business, one would conclude that the breadth of government regulation and the requirements for regulatory compliance are large. Some believe regulation is increasing.

As a specific government act moves from its stimulus stage through legislative hearings and into the regulatory stage — and possibly through the courts — the strategic manager must recognize that government reflects a process, not the desires of a "black box" or one specific interest group. An organization may choose to attempt to influence an important government act at the legislative phase by dealing with congressional representatives and their staff, or at the regulatory phase. The regulator's objectives may be substantially different from those of the legislator. Also, the actual impact of a government act on an organization can be influenced by the specific wording of the regulations (wherein the general legislative direction is converted into actual enforcement procedures and regulations). As a last resort, the organization may choose to challenge the legislation or its implementation (via specific regulations) in the court system.

In interpreting the specific government signal, the strategist must understand that there are different objectives, risks, and consequences at different stages of the governmental process. Thus, the strategist can develop different tactics, ranging from supportive and cooperative to hostile and adversarial, depending on the stage of the process.

Government and Interest Groups. The strategist examining government distinguishes between four components — politicians, bureaucrats, interest groups, and the media. Politicians seek election and reelection (among other things) by appealing to the maximum number of voters. Their appeals are based upon words and deeds, deeds including past assistance in transfering relative wealth between interest groups. Bureaucrats seek to increase the prestige and influence of their relative positions (among other things). They can accomplish this by taking actions and advocating programs that lead to more bureaucracy — more jobs and bigger budgets.

Interest groups naturally seek legislation in their own advantage. The larger the group, the less the per-member gain and the lower the per-member cost. Large groups tend to be relatively passive (except on significantly threatening issues). Small, concentrated interest groups often are most effective. An example is the lack of legislative results in Washington despite strong pockets of public support for gun control and prayer in the schools. With any one particular governmental issue, a strategic manager should assess not only an interest group's motivation (in connection with the issue), but should also consider how the issue affects the groups that are interested in the organization, including management, employees and unions, shareholders, creditors, suppliers, customers, competitors, communities, and governments. Are the interest groups allies, neutral observers, or adversaries?

The strategic manager also must recognize that public reality is what the media says it is. In the world of public reality, an event that is not covered by the media does not exist. In general, the more narrow, technical, or complex an issue, the less likely it is to exist as public reality.

The four components view of government can be extended, as in Working Concept 14.

WORKING CONCEPT 14

STAKEHOLDER ANALYSIS

Stakeholder analysis focuses on the various parties — ''stakeholders'' — who have a stake in the outcome of an issue. For example, in an issue involving passage of an act to reduce foreign competition in a domestic industry, the stakeholders would include the following, along with companies facing similar situations for whom this issue might become a precedent.

Companies in the domestic industry
    employees
    managers
    shareholders
    creditors
Suppliers
Customers
Foreign competitors

Stakeholder Analysis (continued)

Government employees
   diplomats
   economists
   trade and commerce
   congressional representative

Stakeholder analysis consists of (1) identifying the various stakeholders in an issue, (2) determining the cost-benefit impact on each stakeholder group from the alternative outcomes of the issue, (3) assessing the relative strength of each group, and (4) reaching conclusions as to the probable outcome.

MacMillan and Jones (1986) point out that the ideal is to manage all stakeholders over the long run, but that "few organizations have the resources required to manage all stakeholders during each and every strategic change." Therefore the firm must (1) identify stakeholders most affected by the strategic change, (2) develop political tactics to manage these stakeholders, or (3) modify the strategy if the stakeholder "cannot be managed." Understanding a policy's impact upon each stakeholder is essential, as is recognizing the different tactics required for internal versus external stakeholders. Competitors, for example, must be managed differently from employees or suppliers.

Chrysler's Lee Iacocca presented his view of the company's stakeholders in a speech in 1983, after Chrysler repaid the last of its government guaranteed loan:

What is often forgotten is the $2.2 billion that everybody else put up to keep the company together . . . all the guys who really had something at stake. So, our whole program was based on equality of sacrifice, because everybody offered up something — something important. First, we couldn't have made it without concessions from the members of the UAW. . . .

Next, our salary and management employees saw their numbers cut in half and those who stayed took cuts in pay and benefits. . . .

Next, our suppliers — all eleven thousand of them — rolled back prices, they bankrolled us by letting us pay them very slowly and even bought $75 million in debentures to provide us with capital. . . .

Next, our dealers really sacrificed — over 2,100 of them went out of business and the ones who survived lost lots of money for a couple of years running. But about four thousand of them are left — stronger than ever. . . .

Next, bankers helped save us during our darkest days, then supported our recapitalization program earlier this year. . . .

Then there were the state and local governments that helped us with loans and helped support our employees that were laid off. . . .

And then there is that unique institution, the Chrysler Guarantee Loan Board. . . .

Then there is one more big group [key members of the House and Senate], who had to stand up on the floor, and vote, and then convince the voters back home that they had done the right thing. . . .

And last, but maybe they should have been first, I want to thank the first one million people who bought our first million 'K' cars.

Social Signals Looking for strategic signals that indicate changes in social values and expectations (see Table 5.5) is similar to looking for technology signals — it includes few objective and many subjective measures. In addition to economic data that indicate society's affluence, statistical data on population demographics and life styles, and specialized social studies, there are statistical measures of societal attitudes such as those on consumer attitudes published by the University of Michigan Division of Consumer Research. Many strategic managers follow the economic predictions of modelers such as the University of Pennsylvania Wharton group (national predictions) and the MIT Forester/Club of Rome analysis (global predictions).

TABLE 5.5
Selected social
strategic signals

Category	Positive	Negative
Consumer confidence	Increases	Decreases
Attitude toward business	Supportive	Antagonistic
Economic indicators	Increase	Decrease

Future Schlock. One substantial problem confronting the strategic manager is the reliability of these social projections. *The Christian Science Monitor* (6/7/84, p. 23) contrasted the Carter administration's "Global 2000" report showing a "more crowded, more polluted, less stable ecologically" world in which "people will be poorer," with the Simon and Kahn report presented at the 1983 American Association for the Advancement of Science, which concluded that the "world in 2000 will be less crowded, less polluted, more stable ecologically" with life "less precarious economically." *The Christian Science Monitor* concluded, "Beware the prophets of doom, and many other 'futurologists,' for that matter. Their projections of where the world is headed are often more a statement of political bias than a sound extrapolation of available data."

Some consultants and futurism experts provide subjective predictions of social trends; unfortunately for the strategic manager, this information is often contradictory. The full spectrum of predictions ranges from the pessimistic view of economists such as Veblen and Galbraith about the unending pressure for conspicuous consumption, to the optimism of New Age social scientists such as Ferguson who envision business executives leading the way to an Aquarian age of spirituality and higher consciousness.

One social commentator, Arcosanti's Paolo Soleri, looked to technology for predictions about society. By focusing on the technological trends of increasing complexity, miniaturization, and duration, Soleri (1983) suggested that the consequences of these trends would be (1) containment of habitat; (2) increasing ecological health of the city; (3) urbanization of marginal lands to preserve agricultural resources; (4) decrease in segregation of the individual; and (5) corresponding increase in an individual's participation in society, and thus in self-image and self-identification.

Prediction, Wishful Thinking, and Ideologies. The difficult aspect of the strategic manager's interpretation of social signals is in distinguishing between false prediction and fact, between wishful thinking and long-term trends. For example, in the early stages of the 1984 U.S. presidential campaign many believed a national industrial policy was imminent (including candidate Walter Mondale, who cited industrial policy as key to the election). National planning, however, turned out to excite voters and politicians much less than it did academicians and political consultants.

Political events are especially difficult to cite as trends of real societal shifts, not only due to the so-called "silent majority" but also due to the role of emotion and ideologies. Ideologies and views on emotional issues often are held by society only temporarily, as a way of screening out distressing (but real) information and reducing complexities to more manageable terms. Nonetheless, as our overview of basic fundamental values showed, societal values are characterized by change. Today's social values and expectations will inevitably evolve and change.

Consider the evolution of military thinking between the end of World War II and today. When the Cold War between the Soviet Union and the United States began, the dominant technological trend was toward high-tech superweapons and state-of-the-art, computer-based communication and control systems. The dominant Western ideology was that a global, unified Communist threat existed. The strategic conclusion based on this technology and ideology was a nuclear arms buildup and a minimization of conventional war capability.

Social scientists and military planners suggest that this strategic conclusion may well be in error. The unified conspiracy ideology has been questioned by differences and armed conflicts *between* Communist nations. Further, battlefield experience in Korea, Vietnam, Lebanon, and Iran suggests that military achievements are made more difficult by the delays and loss of impact due to circular communications between the field, the Pentagon, and the White House.

The strategist must periodically review social values in a systematic way for evidence of change. Change becomes strategic opportunity. Major league baseball is an industry that demonstrates the danger in not foreseeing the consequences of change. After a series of legal decisions in the 1970s made baseball players free agents, owners paid increasingly higher salaries to get top players. Between 1976 and 1984 the average player's salary increased seven times, from $51,000 to $329,000, while revenues increased only three times. Thirty-seven players made over $1 million in 1985; TV revenues have not saved the clubs. Two-thirds of the teams lost money; the teams as a whole have lost money since 1978 (*Fortune*, 4/15/85, pp. 17–21).

WORKING CONCEPT 15

THE PRECURSOR

One method of predicting social change is through the precursor society. Sweden is often cited as a precursor society for the United States, because its values and expectations provide a good indication of what American society will be like despite the differences between the Swedish and American experiences. (See Figure 5.5 for an illustration of the precursor concept.) The validity of Sweden as an indicator has just been reaffirmed by the crackdown on drunken driving in the United States, which occurred some three to five years after the same legislation passed in Sweden. Social scientists now are analyzing social trends in Sweden that include (1) a large percentage (40 percent) of public housing; (2) a large percentage (70 percent) of working women, resulting in changing attitudes toward women, most notably a low level of physical abuse; (3) low hospitalization costs achieved through a system similar to American Health Maintenance Organizations; (4) fully paid child-care leave (six months) for either parent; (5) procedures for worker ownership of part of the equity of businesses; (6) equal pay for equal work not only between sexes in one company but among all companies for the same job, as Swedish unions argue for wage levels by job function; and (7) formal organization of economic interest groups across society, such as landlords' unions as well as tenants' unions.

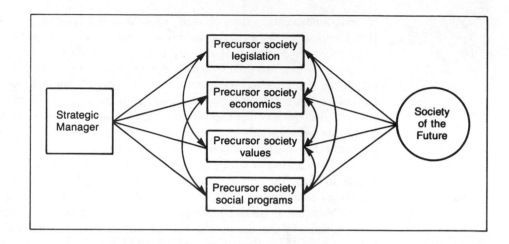

After completing an analysis of the external environment, the strategic manager prepares a summary of findings listing the positive signals that represent external opportunities and the negative signals that represent external threats. These forecasts represent only the beginning of the managerial process. Next comes strategic decision making and action; as the Noah Principle states, ''Predicting rain doesn't count; building arks does.''

Many observers of business (including the authors) have concluded that the more an organization engages in an analysis of the external environment, the more successful it will be. The more this analysis is a continuous process, the better it will be. Though this analysis (especially interpreting strategic signals and forecasting the consequences of those signals) is difficult and often lacks direction, the strategic manager knows what to look for, why to look for it, and what to do with the results. Perfect knowledge is impossible; the strategic manager seeks not to produce certainty but rather to reduce uncertainty.

Figure 5.6 shows the relationship between the firm and the external environment. One of the strategic manager's objectives is to move the firm to the right along this environment dependence spectrum. If the firm has sufficient resources and capabilities, the strategist may seek to shape and influence the environment, often through technology. On the other hand, a firm with limited resources and capability might have to adjust to the role of reacting to the environment.

**Summarizing
Strategic
Signals — A
Swiss Example**

In 1970 Hoffman-LaRoche, the Swiss pharmaceutical company, was the largest pharmaceutical manufacturer in the world. Its sales in 1970 were $840 million, compared with $670 million for Merck, the leading U.S. company. Hoffman-LaRoche had over thirty thousand employees, forty-two pharmaceutical plants, and two holding companies. F. Hoffman-LaRoche, a subsidiary in Basle, Switzerland, was responsible for Continental European, North African, and Middle Eastern business operations. SAPAC, a Canadian corporation headquartered in Uruguay, was responsible for

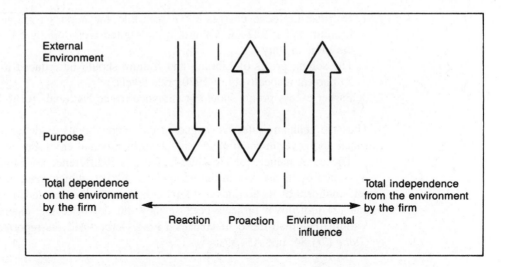

operations in all English-speaking countries, Asia, and South America. Two tranquilizers, Librium and Valium, represented almost three-fourths of company sales.

A summary of strategic signals regarding the firm's environment in 1970 might have included the following signals.

Positive Signals
    Expanding use (total customers; per customer)
    Strong competitive position (patent barriers to entry; little industry price competition; price small factor in purchase decision)
    Profitability (high margin products)
Negative Signals
    High technological risk (narrow product line)
    High level of regulation
    Adversarial social attitude (all health care costs; pharmaceutical industry)

Hoffman-LaRoche's strategic response to the external environment threats were effective with regard to technological risk. The company invested large sums in ongoing research in such areas as cancer and heart disease. Nonetheless, the company followed a less-than-effective strategy in the area of social values and government; its relatively passive strategies were inappropriate in view of emotional public attitudes about pharmaceuticals and in view of the highly regulated nature of the industry. Within a few years the company was under pressure to justify Librium and Valium prices in Australia, Canada, Germany, Holland, Sweden, and the United States. Further, the Monopolies Committee in England reported the following findings and recommendations to Parliament in 1973.

1. Hoffman-LaRoche charges £ 370 per kilo for imported active ingredients for Librium and £ 922 for Valium in the United Kingdom, yet £ 38 and £ 20 for the same in Italy.
2. The selling prices of Librium and Valium should be reduced to 40 percent and 25 percent respectively of 1970 price levels.
3. Earlier excess profits should be refunded to the National Health Service.

Thus the company effectively ignored the major threats evidenced by the negative social and government strategic signals in its external environment.

The consequences of Hoffman-LaRoche's indifference to public opinion were worsened by its success in the tranquilizer market, which made it (1) grow overly self-confident of its abilities and thus indifferent to the demands of the marketplace and (2) turn down projects because they did not offer the superstar potential of Valium. Hoffman-LaRoche chairman Fritz Gerber said, as reported by the *Boston Globe* (7/1/84, pp. A5–A7):

> *There was an arrogance with the success. LaRoche was taken by surprise and was not ready for it. This might have created some kind of over-built self-confidence. The company isolated itself, it became more conservative and probably quite litigious. . . .*
>
> *Once you have a best-seller that sells one million copies, a second book that sells ten thousand copies gets you no applause. Valium created a level of research expectation that was so high, we had a blank for new products.*

Between the mid-1970s and the mid-1980s, profits dropped from 16 percent to 4 percent, and the company fell from first to ninth place in total sales within the industry.

STRATEGY RESEARCH AND
THE EXTERNAL ENVIRONMENT

Classic research studies of the external environment include those of Aguilar, Chandler, Emery and Trist, Klein, Penrose, and Porter.

Aguilar, in *Scanning the Business Environment* (1967), analyzed the environmental study patterns of 137 managers in forty-one companies. He concluded that different kinds of scanning — indirect viewing, conditioned viewing, informal, and formal — were appropriate in specific situations. He discovered that firms made few environmental study efforts because managers relied primarily on oral and personal contacts for data (although this varied significantly according to firm size and organizational level). In reaction to this, Aguilar urged strategic managers to establish procedures to ensure the timely identification of environmental change.

Chandler analyzed the relationship between the external environment and strategy in *Strategy and Structure*: *Chapters in the History of the American Industrial Enterprise* (1962). Studying in depth the histories of Sears, du Pont, General Motors, and Standard Oil of New Jersey, Chandler suggested that change in demand in a firm's market was the principal stimulus for change. Strategy was primarily determined by market and population trends in these case studies, which dated from the 1920s and 1930s.

Emery and Trist (1965) studied "The Causal Texture of Organizational Environments." They identified four causal textures: (1) a placid (stable, unchanging), randomized (randomly distributed resources) environment, in which strategy should be to perform at top standard; (2) a placid, clustered (concentrated resources) environment, in which strategy should be based on location to gain access to concentrated resources; (3) a disturbed environment, in which competitive power is a key focus of strategy; and (4) a turbulent environment, which requires a dynamic strategy that includes constant monitoring of opportunities and threats and developing appropriate response.

Klein, in a dissertation at Columbia entitled "Incorporating Environmental Examination into the Corporate Strategic Planning Process," (1973) showed how the external environment affected an oil company through the following three factors.

Government
  regulation of oil industry
  legislation regarding safety, environment

Technology
  energy research
  pollution control
  advances in materials, electronics

Competition
  product strategy
  location strategy
  investment strategy

Penrose provided insight into strategic opportunities in the external environment by means of her discussion of interstices in *The Theory of the Growth of the Firm* (1968). She concluded that growth is possible because of *interstices*, or spaces, between product markets. Interstices are caused either because large firms do not or cannot exploit them, because managers seek not profit maximization but rather absolute dollar profit levels, which causes managerial inefficiency (managerial slack). Or, interstices are caused because of macroeconomic growth attributable to population increases, technology advances, and productivity improvements.

Porter asserted in *Competitive Strategy* (1980) that a firm's study of the external environment usually is centered on the acts of competitors. Profits and the level of competition within an industry are determined by (1) current competition, (2) relative power of suppliers, (3) relative power of customers, (4) threat of substitutes, and (5) threat of new firms. The strategist should analyze the current state of, and the likely future trend in, these five factors.

Additional research in the external environment includes studies by the following authors.

Aharoni (1966), in studying the foreign investments of thirty-eight U.S. companies, concluded that

1. A strong force is necessary to trigger an organization into a new path of studying the external environment.
2. Such external studies are designed and carried out in a step-by-step process, so that negative conclusions after each step will terminate the study.

Cooper, DeMuzzio, Hatten, Hicks, and Tock (1974) studied firms responding to new product technology, and found that

1. The first introduction of the new product was often made by a firm outside the industry.
2. The old firms tried, many unsuccessfully, to participate in both the old and new technologies.
3. Those old firms with small market share were particularly unsuccessful with the new technology.

Coplin and O'Leary (1985) studied eighty-two countries to assess the risk levels for international business. They rated the countries in terms of the probability of political and social turmoil (China and Japan, low; Jamaica and Poland, moderate; Iraq and South Africa; high) and assigned "grades" for financial risk, investment risk, and exporting risk.

Dess and Davis (1984) studied Porter's generic strategies, such as low-cost producer and market niche. They measured two factors — strategic group measurement and organizational performance — to test the predictive capabilities of these "generic strategies as determinants of strategic group membership and organizational performance."

Diffenbach (1983) listed seven advantages of "corporate environmental analysis in larger U.S. corporations," including

1. Increased management awareness of changes
2. Better strategic planning and decision making
3. Greater effectiveness in government matters
4. Better industry and market analyses
5. Better results in foreign businesses
6. Improvements in diversification and resource allocation
7. Better energy planning

Notwithstanding these advantages, environmental analysis still must overcome difficulties of interpretation, inaccuracy, misperception, and short-term orientation, as well as the complex environments of diversified companies.

Fahey and Narayanan (1986) distinguished between (1) the at-hand task environment (customers, suppliers), (2) the industry environment, and (3) the broad macroenvironment. These experts urged a four-step process: (1) identify general signals of change, (2) monitor specific trends and patterns, (3) forecast future changes, and (4) assess the organizational implications of these environmental changes. Each step should interact with another in a dynamic process.

Gold (1983) reviewed empirical and theoretical studies of technology in U.S. industries. Gold pointed out that strategists must recognize technology not just in production machinery, but in (1) technical personnel's expertise, (2) production system structure and operation, (3) change limits of product design and mix, (4) labor organization and skills, and (5) new capital goods.

Leemhuis (1985), Shell's manager of corporate planning, described the use of scenarios to develop strategies. Scenarios, or "descriptions of a possible future [of evolving] social, political, economic, and technical developments," were used to reduce uncertainty in Shell's strategic decision making. Leemhuis urged using scenarios as part of informal, flexible planning. This proposal contrasts with the formal planning found in large companies like Shell "with heavy reporting requirements and bureaucratic overloads."

Leidecker and Bruno (1984) studied critical success factors (CSFs) in environmental analysis. They concluded that the starting points for identifying critical factors should be (1) major business activity, (2) large dollar amounts involved, (3) major profit impact, and (4) major changes in performance.

McNamee (1984) studied three types of matrices to determine their effectiveness in displaying competitive analysis. McNamee concluded that strategic managers will be aided by matrix displays of competitive analysis in an approach "complementary to the Product Market Portfolio."

Steele (1983) listed four common strategic errors regarding technology. First, firms fail to accept "good enough" technology and seek only the best possible technology; cutting-edge technology doesn't necessarily lead to economic success. Second, some firms assume that the majority of innovations are successful; many are not. Third, firms overlook extensions of current technology and seek revolutionary advances rather than evolutionary, economically feasible ones. Finally, top management must direct and control the technology effort in order to have a productive scientific resource.

Stubbart (1982) researched formal environmental scanning systems in three empirical studies. Stubbart concluded that he was "reluctant to encourage top managers of diversified firms to establish corporate level environmental scanning units." He found that organizations concentrate on "industry analysis" and not on "general environmental scanning," and are thus too narrow in scope.

Utterback and Abernathy (1974) studied technological innovations and the stage of corporate development in 120 firms that witnessed 567 successful innovations. The researchers found that

1. Innovation as a strategy was most important to Stage I entrepreneurial firms.
2. Stage I entrepreneurial firms introduced "original" innovations; Stage III divisionalized firms innovated through imitations and adoptions from suppliers.

EXECUTIVE COMMENTS

The basic strategy for corporate survival is to anticipate the changing expectations of society, and serve them more effectively than competing institutions. This means that the corporation itself must change, consciously evolving into an institution adapted to the new environment.

R. H. Jones, chairman of General Electric, 11/25/74.

You can observe a lot by just watching.

Yogi Berra

KEY TERMS

competition (page 96)

government (page 97)

identification of strategic signals (page 101)

interpretation of strategic signals (page 101)

markets (page 93)

society (page 97)

strategic signals (page 101)

technology (page 96)

BIBLIOGRAPHY

Abell, D., *Defining the Business: The Starting Point of Strategic Planning* (Englewood Cliffs, NJ: Prentice-Hall, 1980).

Abernathy, W., K. Clark, and A. Kantrow. "The New Industrial Competition," *Harvard Business Review* (September-October 1981), pp. 168–181.

Aguilar, F. J., *Scanning the Business Environment* (New York: MacMillan, 1967).

Aharoni, Y., "The Foreign Investment Decision Process," Division of Research, Harvard Business School, 1966.

Becker, L. C., *Property Rights: Philosophic Foundations* (London: Routledge & Kegan Paul, 1977).

Boulton, W., et al., "Strategic Planning: Determining the Impact of Environmental Characteristics and Uncertainty," *Academy of Management Journal,* (September 1982).

Bright, J. R., "Evaluating Signals of Technological Change," *Harvard Business Review* (January-February 1970).

Brooks, H., "Technology, Evolution and Purpose," in A. Teich, ed., *Technology and Man's Future* (New York: St. Martin's Press, 1981).

Chandler, A. D., *Strategy and Structure: Chapters in the History of American Industrial Enterprise* (Cambridge, MA: MIT Press, 1962).

Cooper, A. C., E. DeMuzzio, K. Hatten, E. J. Hicks, and D. Tock, "Strategic Responses to Technological Threats," *Academy of Management Proceedings* (Boston, 1974).

Coplin, W., and M. O'Leary, "The 1985 Political Climate for International Business," *Planning Review* (May 1985), pp. 36–43.

Dess, G. G., and P. S. Davis, "Porter's (1980) Generic Strategies as Determinants of Strategic Group Membership and Organizational Performance," *Academy of Management Journal* 27 (September 1984), pp. 467–488.

Diffenbach, J., "Corporate Environmental Analysis in Large U.S. Corporations," *Long Range Planning* 16 (June 1983), pp. 107–116.

Drucker, P., *Management: Tasks, Responsibilities, and Practices* (New York: Harper & Row, 1974).

Edmunds, S., "The Role of Future Studies in Business Strategic Planning," *Journal of Business Strategy* (Fall 1982).

Emery, F., and E. Trist, "The Causal Textures of Organizational Environments," *Human Relations* (August 1965), pp. 124–151.

Fahey, L., and V. K. Narayanan, *Macroenvironmental Analysis for Strategic Management* (St. Paul, MN: West Publishing, 1986).

Ferguson, M., *The Aquarian Conspiracy: Personal and Social Transformation in the 1980s* (Los Angeles: J. P. Tarcher, 1980).

Galbraith, J. K., *The New Industrial State* (Boston: Houghton-Mifflin, 1967).

Gold, B., "Strengthening Managerial Approaches to Improving Technical Capabilities," *Strategic Management Journal* 4 (October-December 1983), pp. 209–220.

Halle, D., *America's Working Man* (Chicago: University of Chicago Press, 1985).

Hellbroner, R., "Does Capitalism Have a Future?" *New York Times Magazine* (August 15, 1982).

Kantrow, A., "The Strategy-Technology Connection," *Harvard Business Review* (July-August 1980), pp. 6–21.

Klein, H. E., *Incorporating Environmental Examination into the Corporate Strategic Planning Process*, Dissertations, Columbia University, 1973.

Klein, H., and R. Linneman, "The Use of Scenarios in Corporate Planning — Eight Case Histories," *Long Range Planning* 14 (October 1981).

Kotler, P., *Marketing Management: Analysis, Planning, and Control* (Englewood Cliffs, NJ: Prentice-Hall, 1980).

Lebell, D., and O. J. Krasler, "Selecting Environmental Forecasting Techniques for Business Planning Requirements," *Academy of Management Review* (July 1977).

Leemhuis, J. P., "Using Scenarios to Develop Strategies," *Long Range Planning* 18 (April 1985), pp. 30–37.

Leidecker, J. K., and A. V. Bruno, "Identifying and Using Critical Success Factors," *Long Range Planning* 17 (February 1984), pp. 23–32.

McCormick, R. E., and R. D. Tollison, *Politicians, Legislation and the Economy: An Inquiry into the Interest Group Theory of Government* (Boston: Martins-Nijhoff, 1981).

MacMillan, I. C., and P. E. Jones, *Strategy Formulation: Power and Politics*, 2nd ed. (St. Paul, MN: West Publishing, 1986).

McNamee, P., "Competitive Analysis Using Matrix Displays," *Long Range Planning* 17 (June 1984), pp. 98–114.

Meadows, D. H., et al., *The Limits to Growth: A Report for the Club of Rome's Project on the Predicament of Mankind* (New York: Universe Books, 1972).

Miles, R., *Coffin Nails and Corporate Strategies* (Englewood Cliffs, NJ: Prentice-Hall, 1982).

Moore, W. L., and M. L. Tushman, "Managing Innovation over the Product Life Cycle," in M. L. Tushman and W. L. Moore, eds., *Readings in the Management of Innovation* (Boston: Pitman, 1982).

Penrose, E., *The Theory of the Growth of the Firm* (Oxford, England: Blackwell, 1968).

Porter, M. E., *Competitive Strategy* (New York: Free Press, 1980).

Porter, M. E., "The Contributions of Industrial Organization to Strategic Management," *Academy of Management Review*, vol. 6, no. 4 (1981), pp. 609–620.

Porter, M. E., "How Competitive Forces Shape Strategy," *Harvard Business Review* (March-April 1979), pp. 137–145.

Soleri, P., "Excerpts from Arcosanti: An Urban Laboratory," *ReVision* (Fall 1983).

Steele, L., "Manager's Misconceptions About Technology," *Harvard Business Review* (November-December 1983), p. 133.

Stubbart, C., "Are Environmental Scanning Units Effective?" *Long Range Planning* 15 (June 1982), pp. 139–145.

Ulrich, D., and J. Barney, "Perspectives in Organization: Resource Dependence, Efficiency, and Population," *Academy of Management Review*, vol. 9, no. 3 (July 1984).

Utterback, J. M., and W. J. Abernathy, "A Test of a Conceptual Model Linking States in Firms' Process and Product Innovation," Harvard Business School Working Paper 74–23, Boston, 1974.

Veblen, T., *The Theory of the Leisure Class*: *An Economic Study of Institutions* (New York: Viking Press, 1899).

Wheelwright, S., and S. Makrodakis, *Forecasting Methods for Management* (New York: Wiley, 1980).

Zentner, R., "How to Evaluate the Present and Future Corporate Environment," *Journal of Business Strategy* (Spring 1981).

APPENDIX: THE INTERNATIONAL BUSINESS ENVIRONMENT

International businesses, or multinational firms, are those in which the strategist makes decisions and seeks opportunities from a worldwide viewpoint. What the U.S. multinational companies do explains what the U.S. business economy does. The multinational companies in the *Fortune* 500 account for approximately two-thirds of the output and employment and three-fourths of the profits of U.S. business.

The complexity of its external environment distinguishes the multinational corporation from other firms. In analyzing the external environment and looking for positive signals of strategic opportunities and negative signals of strategic threats, the multinational's strategic manager studies environments that may differ in important ways from those of the home country. These critical differences increase as the strategist moves further and further away from the North American, industrialized-nation experience into countries whose economic systems, infrastructures, and ethical and philosophical traditions are unfamiliar.

The multinational's strategic manager faces complexities that may include

Markets
    significantly earlier life cycle stages
    limited avenues of product promotion and advertising
    reduced consumer expectations (Western necessities versus Third World luxuries)

       lower service levels

       little or no consumer credit

       few distribution options

       less price flexibility

Competition

       new ways of competing due to different business ethics, practices

       limited competition

Technology

       lagging technical capabilities

       technology transfer pressures and opportunities

Government

       regional economic associations (i.e., European Economic Community)

       increased government role, often through unions

       currency controls and exposures

       international political situation

Society

       little data on trends

       different rates of change and growth

       different attitudes toward materialism

       great divergence of personal values of host country managers and organizational
          priorities

HOST COUNTRY POWER

The position of the host government is of special concern to the strategic manager. The relative strength and influence of the government and the multinational depend on the contributions of each. The multinational may contribute investment capital, potential exports that will earn currencies, products, and technology. The host country may be a source of scarce resources, new markets, and a labor supply. The multinational strategist must understand the relative contributions of the corporation and the host government.

The strategic trend of the relationship between the multinational and the host country favors the host country as more multinationals offer more technology and investment opportunities. The continuing labor cost gap between nations, the greater number of multinational companies and "superpowers," and the increasing scarcity of some resources (e.g., bauxite, uranium, and molybdenum) also boost the relative power of the host country.

Consider the significance of Japanese automobile manufacturers building manufacturing and assembly plants in Brazil or China rather than in the United States or Canada. The government of Brazil, facing high external debt and a dependency on imported oil, naturally will be more cooperative than the U.S. government that is faced with the protectionist demands of U.S. automobile producers.

As the host country power grows, the host country probably will reduce investment incentives, increase performance requirements, or both. Investment incentives include such acts as tax holidays, credit to subsidiary companies, and even outright cash grants. Frequently encountered performance requirements are local content (a percentage of the product must be produced within the host country), local equity (Mexico has required Mexican ownership of 51 percent of the equity of "foreign" corporations), export percentage requirements, and limits on local currency borrowings. Some of these performance requirements may be exactly what the multinational corporation would do anyway, such as local content requirements when the corporation is seeking scarce local resources.

MULTINATIONAL STRATEGY AND HOST COUNTRY POWER

The activities of Anaconda, ITT, and Kennecott in Chile illustrate the changing relationship of host country and the multinational.

Political Background

Chile, as did many other developing nations after World War II, experienced substantially growing economic nationalism during the 1950s and 1960s. A concurrent trend was an increase in social demands and expectations. With the social changes came the emergence of socialist and communist groups, who were met by the subsequent alliance of the liberals and conservatives.

The Communist party was outlawed in 1947, although the Communists had three elected cabinet ministers in the government in 1946. Communists were stricken from the electoral roles as the government in power moved toward the right, partially in order to obtain aid and development capital from the United States. During that period the Chilean conservatives held themselves out as the saviors of "Western Christian civilization"; the liberals, in announcing the outlawing of the Communist party and the expelling of the Communist ministers, said that those ministers "were instruments of a worldwide plan to deprive the United States of primary materials in the event of war."

In the 1958 election the conservative Alessandri received 32 percent of the vote, the radical Allende 29 percent, and the liberal Frei 21 percent. Frei threw his support to Alessandri, and in 1964 Frei, running as the combined conservative and liberal candidate, received 56 percent of the vote. In 1970, however, the radical Allende received 36 percent, higher than either the conservative Alessandri or the liberal (Christian Democrat) Tomic, Frei's successor. The final choice was then up to the Chilean Congress.

Exhibit 1 details some of the World Bank statistical estimates of Chile and selected neighboring "middle income developing nations."

The Copper Industry

The international copper industry is oligopolistic at the mining stage, and only slightly less so at the processing (smelting and refining) and fabricating stages. The major U.S. copper producers (Anaconda, Kennecott, and Phelps Dodge) account

EXHIBIT 1
World Bank
statistics

	Argentina	Chile	Peru	Venezuela
Population	25,700,000	10,500,000	15,800,000	12,500,000
Area (sq. kms.)	2,767,000	757,000	1,285,000	912,000
GNP per capita (U.S. $, mid-1970s)	$1,550	$1,050	$800	$2,570
GDP growth 1960–1970	4.2%	4.2%	5.4%	5.9%
Percentage GDP in industry 1960–1970	38%	38%	29%	22%
Population growth 1960–1970				
total	1.4	2.1	2.9	3.4
urban	2.3	3.7	4.3	4.9

for about 70 percent of domestic U.S. production. The other major global producers include the Roan-American Metals group, the Anglo-American group Union Miniere, and International Nickel.

There has been an increasing trend toward dilution of this oligopolistic concentration, due to new copper finds in Africa, Canada, and the South Pacific, and to backwards integration by the fabricators. Also, aluminum as a substitute for copper creates a constantly increasing threat to the industry.

Chilean copper has represented 15 to 20 percent of the total world copper production since World War II. In Chile, Anaconda operated the world's largest open-pit copper mine, Chuquicamata, which it purchased in 1923. Its annual output was over 200,000 metric tons. In Chile, Kennecott operated the world's largest underground copper mine, El Teniente, with an annual output of 150,000 metric tons. Kennecott had purchased El Teniente from the Guggenheims in 1915. Copper was and is an important resource to Chile. Kennecott and Anaconda copper production recently has represented between 7 and 20 percent of Chile's gross domestic product. Tax revenues paid by these two companies have represented between 10 and 40 percent of government expenditures; copper exports have represented between 30 and 80 percent of hard currency earnings. Exhibit 2 provides further measures of the relationship between Anaconda, Kennecott, and Chile.

The post–World War II Chilean government's position on copper mining has been that the foreign companies should (1) expand local employment and purchases, (2) refine more in Chile instead of the normal practice of refining in the United States, (3) develop more Chilean managers and copper technicians, and (4) raise prices. The government created a copper department in the 1950s (*Departmento del Cobre*), staffed with business, engineering, and legal personnel.

The push for higher prices often was resisted by the multinational companies, due to the system of "producer's prices." Producer's prices represented an attempt by copper miners and fabricators to remove uncertainty and fluctuation from copper prices. Basically, these producer prices were price and volume contracts between miners and fabricators; on the surface they were annual contracts, but they contained clauses (evergreen provisions) for perpetual renewal. The vast majority of copper tonnage was controlled by these contracts; only a small volume of copper moved

EXHIBIT 2
Anaconda and
Kennecott in Chile

	1945–1955	1955–1965	
Anaconda, Kennecott profits	$275,000,000	$465,000,000	
Chile direct taxes	$328,000,000	$909,000,000	
Investment			
Anaconda	$137,000,000	$212,000,000	
Kennecott	13,000,000	40,000,000	
total investment	$150,000,000	$252,000,000	
		Chile operation	Total global operations
Pretax income per sales $			
Anaconda		47¢	23¢
Kennecott		59¢	34¢
Return on assets			
Anaconda		11.5%	5%
Kennecott		29.5%	10.5%

Note: All amounts in U.S. dollars.

through the open markets of the New York Commodity Exchange and the London Metals Exchange. In essence, this system of producer prices meant that the miner would give up "windfall" profits in periods of higher demand in exchange for "normal" profits in periods of lower demand. To a Chilean government official, the producer price looked artificially low when the copper exchange markets enjoyed high prices in periods of increasing demand.

Chile felt especially exploited when the United States tried to freeze copper prices during the Korean War. Chile insisted that the frozen producer price arrangements be set aside and that Chilean copper be sold through open copper markets. Another U.S.-related historical event that resulted in increased economic nationalism within Chile was the Kennedy-inspired Alliance for Progress. Chilean conservatives responded most unfavorably to the Alliance's call for rapid advances in land reform.

By the mid-1960s Anaconda's Chilean mines produced one-half of total company production and about two-thirds of total company earnings. Anaconda's upper management had moved to the top along a path that included management responsibilities in Chile. For Kennecott, the reverse was true. El Teniente produced less than one-third of total production and less than one-eighth of total earnings.

Between 1930 and 1965, Anaconda had a net capital investment in Chile of approximately $100 million; Kennecott had a net capital disinvestment of $5 million. After World War II, Kennecott undertook no exploration or development projects; Anaconda opened two new mines and built a large plant.

Theodore Moran summarized the situation facing the copper companies, confronted by the slogan "El Cobre es Chileno," in his book *Copper in Chile: Multinational Corporations and the Politics of Dependence* (Princeton University Press, 1974):

Between 1945 and 1970 the Chileans closed in on the foreign-dominated copper industry in their country . . . [this period saw] the interaction of two systems — a system of multinational copper companies operating under unstable conditions of imperfect competition, and a system of domestic interest groups in Chile trying to respond to rising demands for national development and national welfare — both struggling to take advantage of each other and reduce each other to manageable proportions.

MULTINATIONALS AND STRATEGIC MANAGERS

ITT in Chile

Following a decade of growth through diversification and acquisition, ITT in 1970 was one of the biggest multinational corporations in the world. With worldwide sales of $7 billion, it was among the ten largest U.S. multinationals; like other U.S. firms, it faced the threat of expropriation by developing nations. In September 1970, ITT's chairman and chief executive officer, Harold S. Geneen, faced the threat of nationalization of ITT's Chilean telephone system by the government of Salvador Allende.

Geneen was born in England in 1910 to a Russian father, a director of tourist concerts, and an English mother, a light-opera singer. His parents emigrated to the United States; because of their early separation, Geneen spent his youth in boarding schools and camps. His father went bankrupt in the 1926 Florida land bust. Leaving school at age sixteen, Geneen worked at the stock exchange as a page, witnessing the great crash of 1929. While taking classes in accounting at New York University, he worked with the accounting firm of Lybrand, Ross and Montgomery. His special aptitude with figures led him to executive positions at Bell & Howell, Jones and Laughlin, and Raytheon. Twice married, most recently to his ex-secretary at Bell & Howell, Geneen is childless but, as one observer noted, "his life is his company." In ITT's 1967 Annual Report Geneen described management as "a philosophy of aggressive *anticipation* of goals and problems and of effective advanced counteractions to insure our attainment of final objectives."

Pessimistic about long-term international opportunities, Geneen undertook a series of acquisitions in the U.S., including Sheraton Hotels, Continental Banking, Avis, Levitt Homebuilders, and the Hartford Life Insurance Company. ITT's management system was based on careful review of business plans and budgetary controls. Internationally, the company developed governmental connections by various means; Latin American critics frequently accused ITT of bribery. ITT had 400,000 employees worldwide and 200,000 stockholders. In 1970 only three of the three thousand ITT executives were women.

In his book *Managing* Geneen describes a typical work day of ten to twelve hours, filled with staff meetings: "The only way I knew how to judge people at ITT was by the test of performance." In this atmosphere of applied pressure, insiders joked that one characteristic of ITT executives was insomnia. During a prolonged staff meeting, the overhead lights began to flicker. "Hal, even the lights are getting tired," one executive commented to Geneen. He replied, "Only the lesser lights."

By 1970 ITT had gained twenty-five years of experience in expropriation. Its subsidiary in Cuba was nationalized by Castro without compensation. Peron had compensated ITT for its Argentine subsidiary, nationalized in 1946. Peru's compensation of $18 million was tied to a reinvestment in Peru of $8 million, which was done through a Sheraton hotel in Lima. Brazil had paid ITT $20 million for the Brazilian operating company during the mid-1960s. By 1970, ITT operated telephone systems in Puerto Rico, Chile, and the Virgin Islands. ITT Chile employed six thousand workers and was valued by ITT at $150 million. The terms of the concession included payment to ITT in gold.

Anaconda in Chile

In 1969 Anaconda's stock had a market value of $1.4 billion. Its leadership had been through a series of three similar personalities — Clyde Weide, Charles Brincker-hoff, and Jay Parkinson. An industry observer commented that these three were "so bedazzled by the huge returns Chile yielded that they were blinded to the hazards of rising nationalism."

In 1969, a year in which 75 percent of Anaconda's profits were from Chile, Chairman Brinckerhoff said, "You can be absolutely certain that we have never considered for a moment that we couldn't live without the Chileans." Brinckerhoff's successor, Jay Parkinson, presented a company goal that he called "a five-hundred-year plan." Anaconda's managerial style was described by industry observers in *Forbes* (1/15/72) as

> a patrician stance and an attitude of affluence that is its corporate style of life . . . in true 19th century fashion, Anaconda runs its worldwide enterprises out of its richly paneled offices on the fringe of Wall Street, [complete with] male secretaries and uniformed attendants.

The Anaconda board of ten directors had four outside members, but "the real power was vested in an executive committee composed exclusively of company executives."

Anaconda faced the Chilean crisis from an almost colonialist, old-fashioned, narrow perspective. The leadership never thought of contingencies or change, but planned for a "constant" five hundred years.

Kennecott in Chile

Kennecott earned 11 percent of its 1969 profits from Chile. Its president was fifty-eight-year-old Frank Milliken, a tough-minded mining engineer. An industry spokesperson observed that Frank Milliken and Kennecott management "[do not] shy away from knockdown, drag-out fights with the government. Frank Milliken fought for years a federal order to divest Kennecott's wire and cable subsidiary . . . [Milliken] . . . recognized a full decade ago that the loss of the Chilean properties could only be postponed, not averted."

Kennecott's diversification activities had not been successful under Milliken. A 1950s excursion into South African gold resulted in a $36 million write-off in 1960; and a molybdenum mine in British Columbia was written off in 1970 for $23 million.

MULTINATIONAL STRATEGIES

The differences between the strategic managers Geneen, Parkinson, and Milliken and the relative economic power of Chile versus the companies naturally led to differences in company strategy. ITT's strategy was forceful and aggressive, if less than ethical. Anaconda was passive, or reactive, and relied on moral codes of conduct. These codes were inappropriate in the face of Chile's increased power, which grew due to Chile's increased technological knowledge and Anaconda's loss of power following its committed investment. Kennecott's strategy was active, tying Chile to a series of contracts that gave Kennecott 49 percent of a $300 million book value company versus 100 percent of a $70 million book value company. Kennecott made all the contractual relationships binding under New York law, and made allies of the U.S. government and Japanese and Italian interests.

ITT's Actions in Chile

In 1964 Frei, a Christian Democrat, was elected president of Chile. ITT had offered to provide campaign funds to Frei through CIA director John McCone. In 1965 McCone became a director of ITT, while continuing to serve as a secret consultant to the CIA.

In the September 1970 election, the Marxist-Socialist Salvador Allende received 36 percent of the vote, more than his rightist and Christian Democrat rivals, Alessandri and Tomic. Without an absolute majority, the choice of president was to be made by the Chilean congress seven weeks after the election. Geneen and others were convinced expropriation would follow an Allende victory.

As a congressional committee investigating multinationals in the 1970s disclosed, ITT and Geneen took the following steps prior to and after the election.

1. In July 1970 Geneen offered William Broe, the CIA's head of clandestine services for Latin America, "a substantial amount" for the campaign fund of the conservative Alessandri. This offer occurred at a meeting set up by McCone with his successor at the CIA, Richard Helms.

2. After the September 4th election, Geneen offered $1 million to create an anti-Allende coalition. This offer was transmitted by McCone to Helms and Henry Kissinger, who were to respond if the CIA decided to create such a coalition. McCone said he heard no more about such a plan.

3. Broe visited ITT's headquarters late in September with a plan to create economic instability in Chile through sabotage — delay of bank credit, withdrawal of technical help, and late shipments of goods and spare parts. ITT contacted a number of companies doing business with Chile from a list of companies provided by Broe, but Geneen concluded that the plan would fail because they could not trust the other companies.

4. After Allende's election by Congress on October 24, ITT applied persuasion and pressure on Secretary of State Rogers, Kissinger, and others in Washington to adopt an anti-Allende plan, later formalized into an eighteen-point program to see that Allende did not get through the next six months. The plan included economic pressure, fomenting discontent among the Chilean military, and encouraging support for the conservative right.

Copper Strategies

Anaconda, reasoning that it had been and was now a "good corporate citizen" of Chile, relied on continual lobbying with Chilean government officials, emphasizing its investment and development record. It also emphasized the inviolability of its corporate sovereignty.

Kennecott, having discovered that El Teniente's resources were much more vast than originally estimated in the early 1960s, negotiated the following deal with Frei's government in 1964.

1. Kennecott sold 51 percent interest in El Teniente, which had a book value in total of $70 million, to the Chilean government.
2. The purchase price was to be based on a doubling of book value and would total $80 million.
3. The newly composed El Teniente would modernize ($200 million of investment) and would almost double its capacity.
4. Modernization and expansion costs would be funded as follows:
    (a) $110,000,000 from the Export-Import Bank, partially "arranged" by Alliance for Progress officials.
    (b) The Chilean payment of $80 million, loaned back to the joint venture by Kennecott.
    (c) A Chilean government additional investment of $28 million.
    (d) The sale of future copper production to Japanese and European customers for $45 million.
5. The loan of $80 million (see point 4b) was guaranteed by the United States Agency for International Development (AID).
6. The loan of $110 million and the Chilean payment of $80 million (see points 2 and 4a) were to be guaranteed unconditionally by the Chilean state.
7. Collection rights on the Japanese and European contracts for $45 million (see point 4d) were sold to a Banca Comerciale Italiana consortium and to a Mitsui & Company consortium.
8. Kennecott would manage the joint venture for ten years for a fee.
9. The agreement was to be executed in, and made subject to the laws of, the State of New York.

As the 1970 Chilean election campaigns began organizing in the late 1960s, it was clear that Anaconda could expect increased political pressure. The leftist Allende, the centrist Tomic, and the rightist Alessandri — along with Cardinal Silva Henriquez and other Church leaders — were all advocating nationalization.

Anaconda refused to make a "Kennecott" deal with Chile, resisting any Chileanization or a Chilean 51 percent control with compensation. Anaconda instead asked to be fully nationalized with full compensation. In 1969, shortly before the end of Frei's term of office, an Anaconda nationalization-with-full-compensation plan was announced. Anaconda sold 51 percent of Chuquicamata and El Salvador mines to Chile for $197 million, to be paid in twenty-four payments over twelve years.

On July 16, 1971, in response to now-President Allende's legislative plans, the Chilean Congress passed a constitutional amendment nationalizing the Chilean subsidiaries of Anaconda and Kennecott. Compensation was offset in total by a deduction for "excessive profits" by the U.S. companies. The Chilean tribunal ruled Anaconda and Kennecott had made $774 million in excess profits since 1955. Theodore Moran: "A high Kennecott official in Santiago reflected: 'Nationalization was inevitable. It was only a question of time!' " An Anaconda legal adviser noted that the company was now on the receiving end.

Copper Aftermath   Despite Allende's pledge of "Ni un centavo!" the pressures on Chile from the United States, Europe, and Japan, plus Kennecott's legal acts including attachment writs against Chilean national aircraft landing in New York, resulted in Allende's government assuming and honoring all El Teniente's obligations except the ten-year management clause. Anaconda, on the other hand, was nationalized with no hope of compensation. The entire Anaconda top management was fired by the directors; the company, as Moran describes, tried to "do their best to forget about Chile."

While Kennecott collected $67 million from the U.S. government agency that insured the money lent by Kennecott to Chile, and while Kennecott seized shipments from El Teniente to Europe, Anaconda's chairman Parkinson (sixty-three), president John Hall (fifty-four), and senior vice president Charles Schwab (fifty-six) were swept out of office. A vice chairman of Chase Manhattan Bank, John Pace, was brought in as Anaconda president. Pace cut headquarters staff from 488 to 180, reduced total employment from 36,000 to 31,000, and eliminated 11 vice presidents.

Anaconda's 1969 stock market value of $1.4 billion dropped to $260 million in late 1971, a year that saw the company post a $357 million loss ($302 million of which was a write-off of its Chilean investment) — a loss of $15.30 per share against a stock price of $19.00. Shareholders also tried to "do their best to forget about Chile."

Chilean Lessons   Anaconda's limited perspective and ITT's manipulative managerial philosophy resulted in both firms' failure to note the strategic changes in the relative power of Chile vis-à-vis the multinational. Kennecott, on the other hand, took practical steps in recognizing the strategic shifts that occurred due to changes in power.

INTERNATIONAL BUSINESS LIFE CYCLE

Strategists react not only to power shifts but also to new international investing options, such as joint ventures, and to changes in international life cycles. Garland and Farmer (1986) described a product life cycle model for international business linking demand with strategic comparative advantage and highlighting the causative factors of firm level (versus national level) of competition.

Phase One   During the first stage of the product life cycle, the innovating firm produces and markets solely in the home market. At the moment when the products are introduced commercially, costs and prices are high. The innovating firm, however, typically benefits from real or perceived monopolistic advantages (if the product is sufficiently different from other existing products), and the initial buyers are relatively insensitive to price. If the product catches on, the market expands rapidly, eventually providing increasing economies of scale, lower unit costs, and further market expansion. This success encourages competitors, especially as production becomes more standardized. The market eventually becomes saturated and profits decline notably, for competitive reasons.

Phase Two   Vaster markets and greater economies of scale can be gained by exporting, however, and here begins phase two of the product life cycle. The assumption is that an imperfect market exists for knowledge and technology, and that the original advantage held by the innovator in the home market can be duplicated abroad. The U.S. producer typically has sought markets in Canada and Europe for two basic reasons: (1) they are large enough to be quite attractive; and (2) the demand patterns among industrialized countries are fairly similar, which precludes having to adapt the product substantially for the foreign market. Success in exporting to foreign markets prolongs the life of the product. Competitors eventually emerge — domestic firms in the targeted export market — but at first these competitors are noncompetitive due to normal start-up problems and to lack of economies of scale.

Phase Three   Eventually, foreign producers gain a substantial advantage by refining their production techniques and by gaining scales at least sufficient to cause a disadvantage to the original exporter, who has the added costs of distant transportation and communication. Cultural distance also becomes a factor, since foreign domestic companies are much more familiar with the market than foreign multinationals. Often, as in the case of the Japanese auto companies now investing in the United States, the foreign government will undertake protectionist actions in order to facilitate development or enhance the competitiveness of local producers. When these factors in aggregate become serious enough to affect exports adversely, phase three of the product life cycle emerges, in which the exporting firm shifts its strategy by locating production facilities abroad in the markets that have been served by exports up to this point. This pattern, until quite recently, has been dominated by U.S. multinational corporations, whose technological lead over the firms of war-devastated Europe and Japan was substantial for the two decades following World War II.

Phase Four   For those products that are particularly labor intensive and require mass manufacturing technologies, a final phase in the product life cycle allows the original, innovating firm to cease all production in the typically high-wage domestic market (and often also in the foreign markets that it first entered via exports and then production). Phase four also allows the firm to serve the home market through imports from those foreign subsidiaries located in low-wage areas abroad. These new production locations are typically in the most rapidly developing of the Third World countries such as Brazil or Singapore, where low labor costs are combined with sufficient infrastructure and generally excellent productivity levels.

These external complexities of evolving product life cycles and shifting host country power mean that the firm must commit extra resources to understand the environment. The multinational corporation must have a larger staff — especially in legal and financial areas — than the firm doing business in one location.

Some experts argue that the "global village" caused by worldwide communication creates a global market opportunity the strategist cannot ignore. Marketing expert Theodore Levitt commented in *Fortune*, "The new Republic of Technology homogenizes world tastes, wants, and possibilities into global market proportions, which allows for world-standardized products" (11/12/84, pp. 78, 80). Nonetheless, in the same issue of *Fortune*, Philip Kotler suggested, "There are only a very few products, if any, that you can safely standardize. I really think the whole global marketing craze is just a ploy by advertising agencies to get new business."

What is the likely trend of international strategic management? Garland and Farmer concluded that the "increasingly restrictive measures of host governments . . . and the substantially deteriorating foreign investment climate" mean two things for tomorrow's international strategist. First, the international strategic manager must "reappraise . . . overall strategy" because of the changed environment. Second, the manager will find it "more difficult . . . to globally integrate . . . functions and activities" in environments that "inevitably dictate suboptimizing behavior."

BIBLIOGRAPHY

Garland, J., and R. N. Farmer, *International Dimensions of Business Policy and Strategy* (Boston: PWS-KENT, 1986).

Geneen, H., and A. Moscow, *Managing* (Garden City, NY: Doubleday, 1984).

Moran, T., *Copper in Chile: Multinational Corporations and the Politics of Dependence* (Princeton, NJ: Princeton University Press, 1974).

Sampson, A., *The Sovereign State of ITT* (Briarcliff Manor, NY: Stein & Day, 1980).

CHAPTER 6

FORMULATING STRATEGY

Life can only be understood backwards, but it must be lived forward.
Søren Kierkegaard

There is no Model of Strategy and there is no strategy without a model.
Medicine Dog

Chapter 6 builds upon the twin foundations of (1) the three steps of strategic analysis — defining purpose, determining distinctive competence, and identifying opportunities and threats — and (2) the levels of strategic management — functional, business, and corporate. On this twin foundation, this chapter constructs the framework of the strategic decision process using the tools of strategic management, including product portfolio, industry, and competitive analysis. Next, this chapter illustrates strategy formulation by looking at examples of successful strategic alternatives in situations such as those of the new business, vertical integration, diversification, turnaround, and withdrawal. Finally, this chapter measures and evaluates the results of strategy formulation.

THE STRATEGIC DECISION PROCESS

Strategic decisions, or the formulation of strategy, consist of selecting those opportunities and threats indicated by strategic signals in the external environment (see Chapter 5) for which the enterprise has a distinctive competence (see Chapter 4). The distinctive competence is based upon using the enterprise purpose (see Chapter 3) as the selection criteria.

In commonsense terms, the strategic decision process consists of performing those alternative strategic acts that allow you to use your strengths to attain your purpose. Strategy formulation is thus a simple concept to describe, but a difficult one to apply. The factors that make this application difficult include the breadth and uncertainty of the external environment, the complexity of identifying distinctive competence, and the multiple and potentially conflicting forces that comprise enterprise purpose. It is easy to understand why only a small minority of firms and strategic managers are satisfied with their strategy formulation.

EXAMPLE: *Formulating Strategy*

Black & Decker, the manufacturer of power tools, saw a substantial external environment threat to its 50 percent share of the total world market for power tools. Its Japanese competitor, Makita Electric Works, in three years during the early 1980s had gained a share equal to Black & Decker's in industrial power tools, and was expected to introduce a line of consumer power tools. Makita had a cost advantage over Black & Decker and had competed primarily on price, to date. Further, Black & Decker felt that the power tool market had limited growth potential. Black & Decker also felt that international markets were growing increasingly similar.

Black & Decker's distinctive competence in the internal environment included its quality reputation. Its internal earning base was limited, however; the firm earned only $44 million on $1 billion in sales in 1983. In 1982 the firm lost $77 million.

Black & Decker formulated a strategy for achieving its purpose of growth and profitability through acquisition. In 1984 it acquired General Electric's worldwide small appliance business. Top management believed that the joint product lines of power tools and small appliances, both based on small motor technology, would provide the firm with sufficient revenues to fight competition. Black & Decker could increase sales by 50 percent just through the acquisition, which was made by issuing stock to G.E. and thus leaving cash flows free to fight competition through plant modernization.

Black & Decker also felt it could take advantage of the increasingly similar global markets by standardizing both its manufacturing and distribution worldwide for both power tools and small appliances. This strategy formulation was produced by a number of observations: (1) a perceived external environmental opportunity of worldwide market similarities, (2) a perceived threat of the competitor Makita, (3) an internal competence based on a reputation for quality, and (4) an enterprise purpose of growth.

It is important to recognize that neither Black & Decker in this example, nor the strategic manager in general, need evaluate *all* the strategic options and alternatives facing the enterprise. Each earlier step of strategic analysis has served as a filter for reducing the number of options and increasing the strategic manager's ability to make well-reasoned, subjective judgments.

WORKING CONCEPT 16

THE STRATEGIC DECISION PROCESS

The strategic decision process, illustrated in Figure 6.1, consists of the strategic manager (1) selecting those opportunities and threats in the external environment to which to respond based upon (2) the firm's distinctive competence and (3) enterprise purpose.

Strategic managers draw three conclusions from this process. First, the process makes sense; selecting opportunities for which you have competence in order to achieve your purpose means doing what you are good at in order to get what you want.

Second, processes are ongoing. The strategic process is dynamic: new opportunities arise; new competencies develop; new

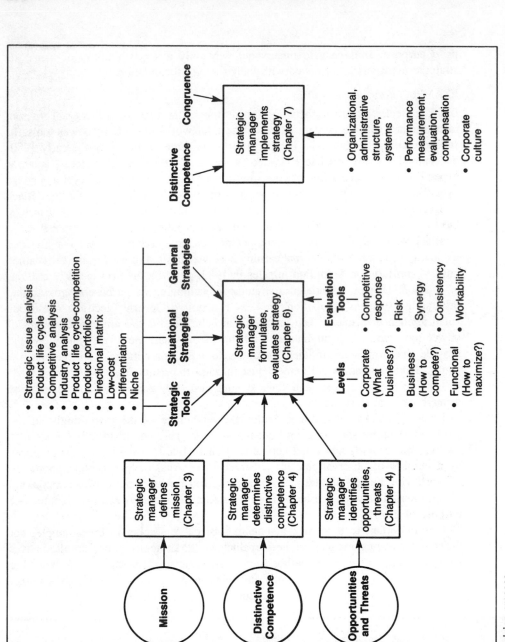

FIGURE 6.1 Strategic decision process

The Strategic Decision Process (continued)

strategies are formulated. Managers reassess performance and implemented strategies, and then they make changes. Performance assessment and evaluation provide new data to this dynamic process.

Finally, the process depends on all of its parts. Each step of the process must be undertaken, although identifying opportunities may require more resources than needed for defining purpose. Omitting strengths, threats, or social goals can result in a disastrous strategy.

DECISION LEVELS

Do the functional, business, and corporate strategists make decisions in the same way? Both commonsense and practical experience indicate that the answer is no. In general, functional managers pay particular attention to distinctive competence; business managers emphasize external opportunities and threats; and corporate managers focus on enterprise purpose.

Functional Decisions

A firm evaluates a functional manager by using a system that emphasizes such things as output, efficiency, and quality. These short-run measures can be affected most quickly by building on the firm's strengths and by correcting functional weaknesses such as production bottlenecks or ineffective marketing campaigns. The functional manager sees only a part of the whole picture; he or she concentrates on immediate results from a limited view of strengths and weaknesses, or distinctive competence.

Business Decisions

The business strategist has a broad view that encompasses all the functional areas of a business *and* the external environment, especially the marketplace. The business ultimately succeeds or fails based upon its reception in the market. Thus the business-level executive tends to rely on functional managers for short-term operating efficiency and effectiveness, and concentrates on the mid-term reaction of the market to both the firm's products and to competition.

Corporate Decisions

The corporate executive in the multinational, diversified corporation may know only the highlights of its short-term operating strengths and weaknesses. Corporate knowledge of business strategy includes awareness of the most important trends in the marketplace and of quantitative budgets, forecasts, and periodic financial results. The corporate executive cannot be expected to understand the details of the external environment of multiple international markets and multiple products. Rather, the corporate strategist seeks to maximize the attainment of long-term organizational priorities, such as maximizing shareholder wealth and developing managerial ability while exercising social responsibility through employment opportunities.

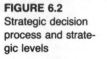

WORKING
CONCEPT **17**

LEVELS OF
STRATEGY AND
THE DECISION
PROCESS

Because of (1) emphasis on short-term results and (2) limited perspective, the functional manager concentrates on increasing those strengths and overcoming problems, or correcting those weaknesses, that underlie the distinctive competence. The business strategist relying on subordinates — functional managers and supervisors — studies the product market external environment. The corporate executive adjusts the long-term direction of the firm to achieve enterprise goals.

Many things affect the relative validity of these differences in managers: individual ability and initiative of the manager, complexity of technology, and breadth and depth of product lines, to name a few. For example, an ambitious, capable functional manager in a multinational, Stage Three corporation would have a long-term perspective that includes both social goals and a wide range of organizational priorities. Nonetheless, in most instances the levels of strategy affect the degree of emphasis within the strategic decision process. Thus, useful insight and practical guidelines can be gained from a model or Working Concept of this relationship, such as is suggested by Figure 6.2.

FIGURE 6.2
Strategic decision process and strategic levels

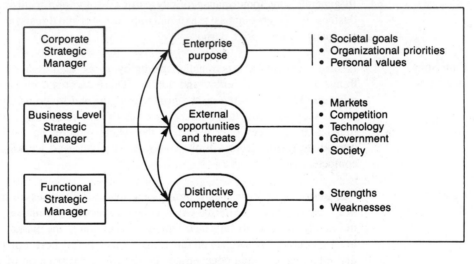

STRATEGIC MANAGEMENT TOOLS

When moving from functional strategy to corporate strategy, managers make strategic decisions that increasingly focus on external opportunities and enterprise purpose. Similarly, managers employ tools that range from the product life cycle (functional level) to product portfolios (business level) to industry and strategic issue analysis (corporate level). This general model for using strategic tools must not obscure the important fact that any one manager may indeed use any strategic tool, just as any one manager may focus on distinctive competence, external opportunities, or enterprise purpose.

The strategic manager can use one of seven methods or tools of strategic management. These methods include

1. Product life cycle
2. Porter's Determinants of Competition
3. Product portfolios
4. Product life cycle–competition matrix
5. Directional policy matrix
6. Industry analysis
7. Strategic issue analysis

Product Life Cycle

The functional manager uses the product life cycle to (1) focus attention on the all-important product market; (2) recognize the changing functional needs of promotion, production, and distribution; (3) forecast profits; and (4) measure performance. Working Concept 10 (Chapter 4) describes the product life cycle tool.

Porter's Determinants of Competition

The business-level manager uses Porter's model of the five determinants of competition for either (1) "positioning the company so that its capabilities provide the best defense against the competitive force" or (2) "influencing the balance of forces through competitive moves, thereby improving the company's position" (Porter 1979, p. 143). As Porter pointed out, Dr. Pepper chose to position itself against the Coke- and Pepsi-dominated industry by stressing its unique — if narrow — product line. Porter included marketing innovations that differentiate product and capital investments and that alter barriers to entry as ways the firm can influence the balance of competitive forces.

Porter (1979) also has shown how competition increases in an industry due to threats of new entrants or substitute products, or due to the economic power of customers and suppliers. These four forces affect the moves and countermoves — the fifth determinant of the levels of competition — of specific rival firms.

After analyzing competitive levels by Porter's methods, as described in Chapter 5, the strategic manager can choose specific strategic steps from among the preemptive opportunities presented in Table 6.1.

These preemptive moves primarily make up functional- and business-level strategies. Working Concept 12 (Chapter 5) describes Porter's model in detail.

TABLE 6.1
Preemptive opportunities

Critical competitive force à la Porter	Preemptive opportunity

Suppliers' power	1. Research new raw materials, components
	2. Secure access to supply
	   (a) long-term contracts
	   (b) production equipment link
	   (c) logistics domination

Buyers' power	1. Segment 2. Build brand loyalty 3. Secure key accounts 4. Link to customers by service, training 5. Dominate distribution logistics
Product substitution	1. Expand product scope 2. Introduce new products 3. Develop dominant design
New entrants	1. Expand capacity 2. Integrate vertically 3. Research production process
Competitor's moves, countermoves	1. Any and all of the above

WORKING CONCEPT 18

PRODUCT PORTFOLIOS

Product portfolio analysis, pioneered by the Boston Consulting Group (BCG), uses a matrix to examine products and markets, with market growth (business growth rate) as one axis and relative market share (relative competitive position) as the other. Figure 6.3 presents one version of this product analysis. Products with high relative market share in high-growth businesses are "stars"; those with low relative market share in low-growth businesses are "dogs." High market share assumes high profits through economies of scale. "Cash cows" are high market share products in low-growth businesses, and thus represent high profit. Cash cows are the stable earnings base that supports the firm. Uncertainty surrounds "question marks," those products with low share of high-growth businesses. The Boston Consulting Group's experience suggests that the organization should liquidate the dogs and use the cash resources generated by the cash cows to turn the most promising question marks into

FIGURE 6.3
BCG's product portfolio matrix

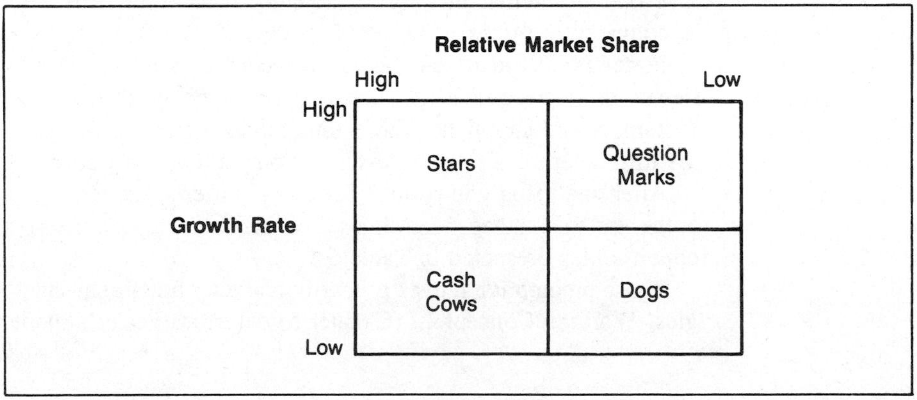

Product Portfolios (continued)

stars. The remainder of the question marks should be divested.

The market share assumptions underlying the product portfolio technique were supported by the PIMS research.

PIMS

The longitudinal data of over 1,700 businesses make up the PIMS (Profit Impact of Market Strategies) data base (Schoeffler et al., 1974). The findings reported in the "PIMS Newsletter" of the Strategic Planning Institute in Cambridge, Massachusetts, and in strategy literature include the impact of market share on profitability. Other important variables include investment intensity, a variable frequently ignored in strategic models (a product portfolio dog coupled with low investment could be a star in terms of return-on-investment); purchase frequency; product quality; research effort; capacity utilization; and relative price.

The PIMS data base is not without its limitations. First, the PIMS "businesses" are all portions of major diversified corporations. Thus, Stage One and Stage Two firms are not present. Secondly, businesses that perform better than average tend to stay in the PIMS data base; below-average firms tend to leave PIMS. Although PIMS has been in effect since 1970, only one hundred businesses have entered data for more than eight years. Less than six years' worth of data has been entered by 1,100 businesses, and less than four years' data has been entered by 200 businesses.

Further implications of the product portfolio, and the resulting strategies of "build, hold, and harvest," were discussed by Gupta and Govindarajan (1984). The limitations as well as the uses of portfolio analysis were described by Haspelslagh (1982) and Channon (1979).

PROBLEMS WITH PRODUCT PORTFOLIOS

Specific problems with product portfolios were discussed by Professor Day (1977) of the University of Toronto in his research paper "Diagnosing the Product Portfolio." First, the assumption that market share is a proxy for relative profit performance may not be true in many circumstances, such as when "one competitor has a significant technological advantage (resulting in a different cost reduction/experience curve)" or "profitability is highly sensitive to the rate of capacity utilization, regardless of size of plant." Day also points out that the pursuit of market share can be disastrous when financial resources are inadequate or when antitrust action results. Also, the definitional problems in product portfolios are substantial, as Day demonstrates by asking "what share of what market," raising segmentation, geographic, potential versus actual, and other measurement problems.

EXAMPLE: *Product Portfolios*

Gillette's strategy of diversification is an example of a portfolio management approach. Faced with declining sales in the early 1980s, Gillette sought new businesses to add growth to its stable, highly profitable (cash cow) razor blade core business. Gillette chairman C. M. Mocker told the *Boston Globe* (10/2/84, p. 53): "It's what we call an aggregation strategy. We can make minor investments in several companies in the field and as these companies develop we can take advantage of those that perform favorably and ignore those that do not."

Haspelslagh (1982) pointed out that one problem in the portfolio planning technique is "the difficulty of generating new internal growth opportunities." Wheelwright (1984) elaborated on this idea and warned that the "portfolio-based content approach . . . values management for cost reduc-

---

Product Portfolios (continued)

tion'' rather than for long-term technological competitive advantage.

Tom Peters and Nancy Austin, in *A Passion for Excellence,* argued that quality is the determining factor in portfolio planning, and that concentration on increasing market share by getting cost down might reduce quality and service.

The business-level strategist uses product portfolio analysis to study both the firm's and competitors' portfolios. In addition to suggesting how resources might be allocated among the firm's products, the analysis can show the strength of its competitive position. Competitive position is one dimension of the fourth strategic tool, the product life cycle–competition matrix.

WORKING CONCEPT 19

PRODUCT LIFE CYCLE– COMPETITION MATRIX

Charles W. Hofer (1977) developed conceptual constructs for formulating corporate and business strategies (also the name of his article). As Figure 6.4 shows, one of these constructs plotted the product life cycle with the relative strength of the firm's competitive position. Four products at various life cycle stages (Product 1 at development, Product 2 at growth, Product 3 at maturity, and Product 4 in decline) have different competitive positions. Products 2, 3, and 4 lack the competitive strength of Product 1. Hofer used circle size as an indication of total industry sales, and showed share of the market through a parenthesis inside the circle.

The life cycle focuses attention on the developing Product 1 and the growth Product 2; but market share (25 percent for Product 1 versus 7 percent for Product 2) and the stronger competitive position of Product 1 suggest that Product 1 should receive managerial attention and support. The product life cycle–competition matrix also leads to the conclusion that Product 3, because of its large market share, should be ''milked'' as a cash cow and its resulting funds used for Product 1. The company should minimize investment in Product 3 and should harvest and drop Product 4, it being weak competitively and with little market share. Perhaps Product 2 should also be neglected, unless its competitive position can be strengthened.

Competitive capabilities, or business strength, underlie the directional policy matrix, as well as the product life cycle–competition matrix.

WORKING CONCEPT 20

DIRECTIONAL POLICY MATRIX

The directional policy matrix extends the product portfolio matrix and makes it more qualitative. The result, as developed by companies such as General Electric and McKinsey & Company, is shown in Figure 6.5.

Will all strategic managers reach the same conclusions when they evaluate the product markets in the crosshatched area in Figure 6.5 between ''Invest'' and ''Divest''? Personal values and attitudes will lead one manager to invest based upon high firm strength, and another to invest based upon high industry attractiveness.

Risk can be added as another factor in the strategic manager's evaluation of the

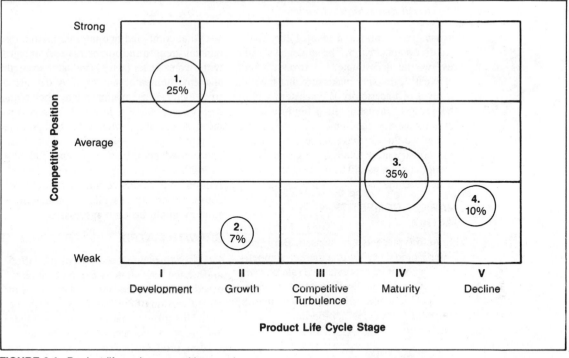

FIGURE 6.4 Product life cycle–competition matrix

Adapted from Hofer, C. W., "Conceptual Constructs for Formulating Corporate and Business Strategies (Boston: Harvard Case 9-378-754, p. 3).

FIGURE 6.5
Directional policy
matrix

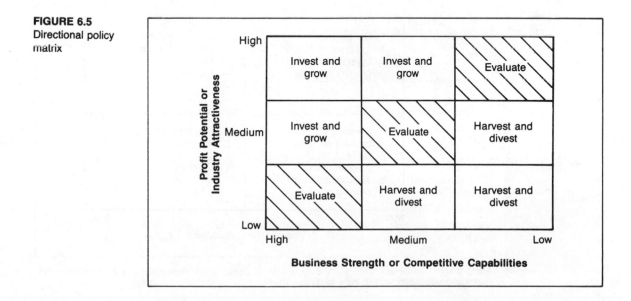

Directional Policy Matrix (continued)

crosshatched area, and also of the invest and divest conclusion. The strategist should review the "Evaluate," "Invest," and "Divest" groups to make sure that the risk or level of uncertainty is consistent within the groups. Investing in a high-industry-attractiveness, medium-business-strength option would not make sense if the medium-industry-attractiveness, high-business-strength option would be much more certain in its outcome.

MARKET-COMPETITION MATRIX

Figure 6.6 presents Christensen, Berg, and Salter's model (1976) of a market-competition matrix. It incorporates the rate of market growth and the firm's relative competitive position into a two-by-two matrix suggesting strategies appropriate for each matrix unit.

SPACE MATRIX

Rowe, Mason, and Dickel (1982) developed a matrix tool, known as a *space ma-*

trix, that combined two internal factors (financial strength and competitive advantage) with two external factors (industry strength and environmental stability). A defensive strategy might seem appropriate when competitive advantage is low and the environment is unstable, whereas a competitive strategy might be appropriate when competitive advantage is high and industry strength is significant. If financial strength is high, the defensive strategy might become conservative, while the competitive strategy might become aggressive.

GROWTH MATRIX

The growth matrix used by Ansoff (1965) to describe how strategy can be formulated based upon products and markets is a simplified version of the directional policy matrix. This growth matrix appears in Figure 6.7. A firm that concentrates on selling existing products to existing markets is following a *market penetration* strategy. If a firm sells existing products to new markets it is using a *market development* strategy;

FIGURE 6.6
Market-competition strategic choice matrix

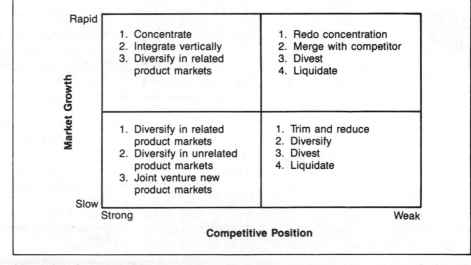

Adapted from Christensen, C. R., N. A. Berg, and M. S. Salter, *Policy Formulation and Administration*, 7th ed. (Homewood, IL: Richard D. Irwin, 1976), pp. 16–18.

Directional Policy Matrix (continued)

and if it sells new products to existing markets it is following a *product development* strategy. *Diversification* strategy involves selling new products to new markets. The four boxes in the matrix — or growth vector, as Ansoff calls it — in Figure 6.7 represent four possible sources of growth.

EXAMPLE: *Product Development*

The health care industry provides an illustration of the attractiveness of bringing new products to existing customers, or product development. The five major industry components — hospitals, nusing homes, home health care, health maintenance organizations (HMOs), and medical equipment — all saw the importance of expanding the products and services to their customers, so that the patient or customer could have "one-stop health shops." Individual companies tried expansion, joint ventures, horizontal integration, and acquisition in order to become the integrated health care company that would be the health care leader in the 1990s. Thus Hospital Corporation of America and Baxter Laboratories both pursued a merger with American Hospital Supply Corporation in 1985; and Whittaker bought an HMO, Health Plan of Virginia, to go with its newly purchased International Diagnostic Technology and General Medical (hospital supplies) subsidiaries.

Schering-Plough's strategy, as described in *Business Week* (8/20/84, p. 122), can be viewed as a balancing of market penetration with product development. As Schering-Plough's consumer businesses (Maybelline, Dr. Scholl, and St. Joseph aspirin) grew slowly but steadily, research funds of $170 million (about 10 percent of sales) were spent on biotechnology, chemical synthesis, and new drugs. While total employment fell by 3,000, the research staff grew by 30 percent to 1,400 during the 1983–1984 period.

In the mid-1980s, the new management at ITT turned away from the diversification strategy that had been pursued for twenty years and pursued a market development strategy. ITT entered a new market in the United States, telecommunications, based upon ITT's telecommunication systems already in place in Europe. As ITT brought its Modular System 12 products to the new U.S. market, the vice president of research said, "We've won every technical shoot-out we've entered" (*Business Week*, 10/22/84, p. 116).

EXIT STRATEGY

On the other side of Ansoff's growth matrix is divesting. Not all products reach stardom nor are all plans successful. The firm needs

FIGURE 6.7
Ansoff's growth matrix

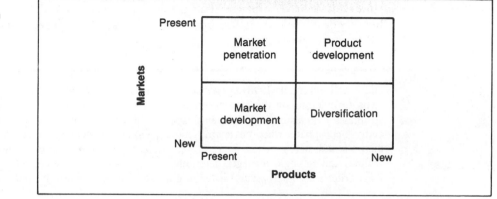

Directional Policy Matrix (continued)

an exit strategy for declining products and failed plans. An exit strategy formulates a way for the firm to divest a product and exit a market while minimizing adverse consequences such as customer relationships and closing costs. The U.S. farm equipment industry in the mid-1980s provides a good example of the necessity of following exit strategies, as companies such as International Harvester divest themselves of farm equipment businesses.

Many U.S. farmers, adversely affected by grain embargos, economic recessions, declining exports, a drop in debt capacity, and high interest rates, began to postpone or eliminate altogether their purchases of farm equipment. Tractors replaced every five to seven years during the 1970s were being held eight to ten years or longer during the 1980s.

The plant capacity expansion of J. I. Case, Deere, International Harvester, Ford, Allis-Chalmers, Massey Ferguson, and others resulted in overcapacity. By the 1980s the large (over 100 horsepower) tractor market had capacity for sixty thousand units and demand for thirty-five thousand. Japanese manufacturers dominated the small (under 40 horsepower) tractor business. Massey Ferguson turned to the Canadian

government for a massive refinancing. International Harvester, in an exit strategy move that many industry analysts expected to be repeated within the farm equipment industry, sold its farm equipment business to its competitor, J. I. Case.

The growth matrix helps the strategic manager to organize the alternative opportunities for which the firm has distinctive competences. Some opportunities are for market penetration (existing products, existing markets), others are for product development (new products, existing markets), and still others are for market development (existing products, new markets) — all of which build on the firm's experience with existing products or existing markets. If the strategic manager decides to pursue growth through diversification, then he or she can find no past experience — no "common thread," in Ansoff's terms — since the firm will be dealing in both new products and new markets. All other things being equal, diversification must offer greater opportunities than the three other options on the matrix, for diversification is the path of the greatest risk. The firm will accept this higher risk with diversification only in order to earn higher returns.

The business-level executive concentrates on the profit potential in the directional policy matrix; the corporate strategist is concerned with industry attractiveness. Industry analysis provides the corporate strategist with the tool necessary to determine industry attractiveness.

WORKING CONCEPT 21

INDUSTRY ANALYSIS

Hofer and Schendel (1978) suggested five steps to determining the attractiveness of an industry. Industry analysis seems especially appropriate when reviewing more than one industry.

First, the strategic manager determines what criteria are appropriate for judging a

particular industry. The strategist selects from among many options: (1) relative profitability; (2) level of government regulation; (3) competitive pressures; (4) product market size; (5) growth rates; and (6) the cost-volume-profit relationship, including capital, marketing, labor, and materials costs.

Industry Analysis (continued)

After selecting some appropriate criteria, the manager next assigns a weighting factor or priority ranking to each criterion. Then, he or she collects data about each criterion. As a fourth step, the manager analyzes the data and determines an appropriate measure for the criteria. This measure can be quantitative or subjective ("attractive, neutral, unattractive").

As a fifth and last step, the strategist compares the weighted ranking with the opinions of other managers and experts. This final step serves as a check against incomplete data or inappropriate criteria, which might be indicated by a big difference between the weighted ranking and expert opinion.

Porter (1980) adds a method of analyzing industries in his "strategic mapping" described in *Competitive Strategy: Techniques for Analyzing Industries and Competitors*. Figure 6.8 presents a strategic map with twin dimensions of distribution channels and quality/reputation. Various companies divide the total market into strategic groups, including electric saws

FIGURE 6.8
Strategic mapping: U.S. chain saw industry

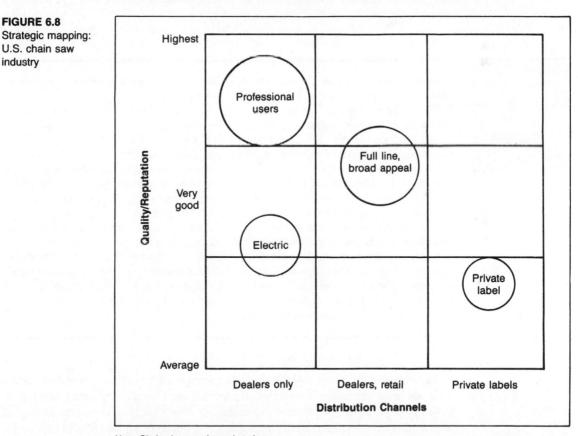

Note: Circle size equals market share.
Adapted from Porter, M.E., *Competitive Strategy: Techniques for Analyzing Industries and Competitors* (New York: Free Press, 1980), p. 153.

Industry Analysis (continued)

only (Skil), professional user manufacturers (Stihl), private labelers (Remington), and those competing in broad markets with full lines (McCulloch, Homelite).

Robinson and Pearce (1985), in a study of ninety-seven manufacturers in six industries, found five clusters of strategy that relate to Porter's strategy groups: (1) efficiency and service, (2) service/high-priced markets and brand/channel influence, (3) product innovation/development, (4) brand identification/channel influence and efficiency, and (5) no clear strategic orientation.

The corporate strategist uses industry analysis to determine which directions the firm will pursue to satisfy enterprise purpose. The executive may also face a specific strategic issue, such as the trend in energy price, social change, or the threat of entry into an industry. Strategic issue analysis provides a tool for studying a specific strategic issue.

WORKING CONCEPT 22

STRATEGIC ISSUE ANALYSIS

Strategic issue diagnosis (Dutton et al. 1983), or strategic issue analysis (King 1982), is the examination of an external environment strategic signal or group of related strategic signals. Strategic issues, although uncertain, are important topics that require analysis.

King (1982) presents one example of a strategic issue — Will a new company enter our industry? — and shows how to use strategic issue analysis to break the strategic issue down into its component parts in order to reach a conclusion. In the new entry example, King suggests considering the component parts of "economies of scale, product differentiation, capital requirements, cost advantages independent of size, access to distribution channels, and government policy."

King described ways of using strategic issue analysis to find the stimulus to action. When Dutton et al. researched strategic issue diagnosis, they emphasized that the strategist uses strategic issue diagnosis to stimulate the strategic process, so that these environmental signals become a part of proactive strategic management.

Strategic issues should be thought of as strategic signals, and strategic issue analysis as one term to describe the process of determining the positive or negative characteristics of strategic signals. Strategic issues thus become opportunities or threats.

In reviewing the seven tools of strategic management, we have found that certain tools are used primarily, although certainly not exclusively, by either functional, business-level, or corporate strategic managers. For example, corporate strategists may use Porter's determinants of competition to estimate future potential of industries. Figure 6.9 summarizes the tools and levels of strategy.

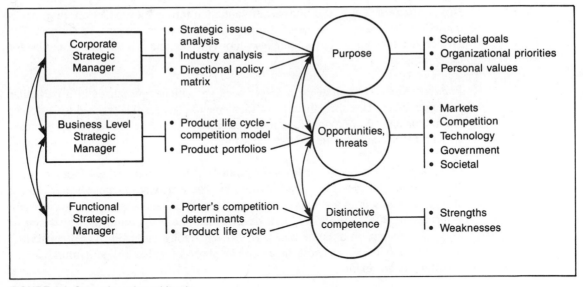

FIGURE 6.9 Strategic tools and levels

EXAMPLES OF STRATEGY FORMULATION

This next section of Chapter 6 gives examples of formulated strategy. These examples include Porter's broad, general (or generic) strategies and more specialized strategies for specific situations.

Porter's Generic Strategies

Harvard Business School professor Michael Porter (1980) identified three generic or basic categories of strategy: (1) low-cost producer, (2) differentiation, and (3) focused niche.

Low-Cost Producer. The business level strategist trying to be the lowest-cost producer considers such options as

Investing in plant and equipment
Riding the experience curve to economies of scale
Stringent cost control and minimization
Marginal contribution analysis and aggressive pricing to build volume

This general category of strategy seems appropriate for commodity products and high price elasticity markets.

Differentiation. A firm can pursue differentiation through a product offering that is unique to the market in terms of design, special features, quality, or service. The greater the breadth of buyer purchase motives, the greater the opportunities for differentiation.

Focused Niche. The strategic manager seeking a niche specializes in a particular product market. This specialization or focus may be geographic, related to customer groups, or related to product function. The smaller company with limited resources may find the focused niche strategy appealing.

Situational Strategy

Porter's generic strategies of low-cost producer, differentiation, and focused niche stem from his insights into ways to compete. Another way to categorize groups of strategies results from a situational perspective. Situational strategy categories stem from the particular stages of corporate development, i.e.; (1) starting the new business; (2) concentrating on a single business; (3) integrating vertically; (4) diversifying; or seeing a faltering business in a critical phase of either (5) turnaround or (6) divesting and/or exiting.

Starting the New Business. Hofer and Schendel (1978) emphasized two major strategic efforts each new business will have to make if it is to survive. First, the firm must acquire sufficient resources to support its growth from entrepreneur's idea up to profitable operating levels. The new firm's most critical resource is often financial. Second, the firm must prepare itself for a period of competition. It must develop strengths, and thus create the beginning — albeit a flexible and immature one — of a distinctive competence.

Concentrating on a Single Business. Successful single businesses have the common strategic characteristic of a strong distinctive competence. This distinctive competence may be focused on technology, as in the case of Polaroid, or on the customer, as in the example of McDonald's. It allows the firm to grow through market penetration or product development. Polaroid moved from instant black-and-white photography to ''35-millimeter quality'' color photographs. McDonald's became a global fast-food enterprise.

Integrating Vertically. Firms pursue backward and forward vertical integration strategies to ensure supply and distribution channels, and to try to capture the profit margins from suppliers and customers. Harrigan (1985) studied the linkage between corporate strategy and vertical integration in the make-or-buy decisions of 192 firms in sixteen industries. She found an explanation for the intra- and interindustry differences in their demand certainty. The more certainty existed, the more vertical integration; the less industry volatility, due to relatively higher concentration and exit barriers, the more firms turned to vertical integration. Harrigan pointed out that the chief executive officers must support synergy in integration: ''No synergy exists . . . unless executives consciously enforce policies causing SBUs to (1) communicate; (2) share inputs, outputs, R&D, or other useful attributes and capabilities; or (3) cooperate in some other useful manner.''

Diversifying. Firms diversify as they seek those growth and profit opportunities that are unavailable in single concentration or vertical integration strategies. A firm can diversify through internal research and development or corporate venturing (Burgelman 1985), through joint ventures, or through the acquisition of other firms. Benefits to diversifying include reduced risk (by broadening the base of activity) and greater rewards.

Strategic managers can pursue additional growth and profit opportunities in businesses related to their own through technology, products, or markets; or they can pursue opportunities in unrelated businesses. Sears diversified from retailing to insurance (through Allstate Insurance) and to real estate and financial services, but also built upon its retail customer market base in its diversification activities. ITT, on the other hand, diversified from the telephone and communications field into unrelated activities such as insurance, hotels (through Sheraton), and car rentals (through Avis).

The unrelated diversification strategy can be selected by those managers seeking not only greater growth and profit potential, but also those managers who believe the corporate management resources exist to supervise operating subsidiaries through financial portfolio management techniques and capital budgeting procedures. Few strategists try to manage unrelated subsidiaries at the business level; instead, they rely on financial controls at the corporate strategic level. Even fewer strategists succeed in operating unrelated businesses.

The critical strategic principle to remember in diversification, then, is that strategic implementation is just as difficult — if not more difficult — as strategy formulation. The diversified strategist must rely on key executives within the diversified, decentralized subsidiary. Strategic management succeeds or fails based upon the effectiveness of linking *planning* and *action*. Table 6.2 below summarizes managerial resources and diversification strategies.

Turnaround Strategies. The company facing financial pressures and profit squeezes selects a turnaround strategy. These strategies fall into general categories described by Hofer (1980), including (1) reducing and controlling costs, (2) increasing revenues, (3) withdrawing resources from profit drains and allocating resources to profit potentials, and (4) replacing strategic managers. A company can try one or more of

TABLE 6.2 Diversification strategies	Related diversification	Unrelated diversification
Managerial Resource	Operating company technology, product-market skills	Holding company financial control and capital budgeting
Diversification Method	Internal venturing and research, joint venture, merger	Acquisition

these strategies to turnaround a faltering business, but Hofer emphasizes that most successful turnarounds have included replacing top management. In 1985 Apple Computer relieved its founder, Steve Jobs, of most if not all of his strategic duties; other troubled computer companies like Wang, Data General, and Digital Equipment Corporation concentrated on employee layoffs.

Hall, in "Survival Strategies in a Hostile Environment" (1980), found a zero survival rate in eight industries. He concluded that turnaround efforts had arrived too late, since rivals were too strong and/or resources were too scarce for survival.

Caterpillar Tractor stressed cost reduction in its mid-1980s turnaround strategy. After losing more than $1 billion in three years, Caterpillar cut its work force by one-third, subcontracted production, and reduced manufacturing capacity so that costs were cut by 22 percent in 1985 (*Business Week*, 11/15/85, p. 41).

Divest and Exit. What does the strategic manager do with the "dog" business? Abell (1978) presented four options: (1) close the gap, (2) shift to selected market segments where a fit occurs, (3) cut back and milk the business, and (4) exit through liquidation or sale. Optimally, the failing business can be sold to some other firm that can produce a successful turnaround with its own capabilities and/or new synergies.

Harrigan (1982) analyzed firms in declining industries and marginal firms in nondeclining industries. Although these firms should be expected to divest and exit, the exit strategy was affected by

1. Economic exit barriers, such as losses on disposal of assets and expenses of unfunded pension obligations and other severance costs.
2. Noneconomic exit barriers, including fear of communicating a poor management image to customers and shareholders.

Harrigan concluded that exit barriers, especially asset disposal variables, were substantial. Firms pursuing a low-cost producer strategy built upon capital investment thus would encounter more exit and divesting difficulties than firms pursuing differentiation or focused niche strategies.

Exit strategies are those strategies that suggest when the firm should stop following growth and profit objectives. In other words, exit strategies are strategic plans for withdrawing from product markets. Such exit contingency plans are most effective if they include implementation guidelines. The strategic manager should not only propose carrying out a new venture that is expected to earn a return of, for example, 18 to 24 percent on investment, but should also plan that the firm withdraw from the new venture if returns of less than, for example, 12 percent are experienced. Finally, the manager should suggest alternative plans for withdrawal, such as liquidating, licensing, or selling the venture.

In January 1985, after trying diversification, General Mills was disillusioned. General Mills kept its Betty Crocker, Wheaties, and Gorton Seafood operations, but announced that its Izod and Parker Brothers subsidiaries were for sale. Commenting on General Mills's exit strategy, an industry observer noted in *Business Week*: "One thing the management group prides itself on is that they don't let the problem areas run for long" (2/11/85, p. 31).

Furchgott's, the Jacksonville, Florida, department store operator, saw its exit strategy collapse because of poor implementation. Furchgott's agreed in principle to sell its businesses to Stein Mart Inc., a discount department store. Nonetheless, Regency Square Mall, the operator of the premier mall where Furchgott's had a store, announced that it would not accept Stein Mart as a Regency Square operator. Furchgott's filed for Chapter 11 bankruptcy protection in January 1985 only hours after Stein Mart announced it was terminating acquisition negotiations.

Other Strategies   Other researchers have described variations on the basic low-cost producer, differentiation, or focused niche strategies for low market share businesses (Hammermesh et al., 1978); high market share businesses (Bloom and Kotler, 1975); global enterprises (Harrell and Kiefer, 1981); firms in stagnant (Porter 1976), unstable (Fredrickson and Mitchell, 1984), or decline industries (Harrigan 1984); and firms seeking growth (Kierulff 1981).

One path to growth is through the new venture division of the large, diversified company, such as General Electric. Burgelman (1985), in researching management of the new venture division, urged the large firms to "structure themselves for dealing for *more*, rather than less, autonomous behavior." Earlier (1983), Burgelman had presented a "process model of internal corporate venturing in the diversified major firm." Cooper (1978) noted that "an increasing number of corporations have developed new venture departments." These various strategies provide organized ways in which to view strategic options, as in Table 6.3. David (1986) has provided

TABLE 6.3 Strategic categories overview	**Categories**	**Context/Content**
	Porter's generic strategies	
	low cost producer	Commodity, economies of scale
	differentiation	Product uniqueness
	focused niche	Limited resources
	Situational strategy	
	new business	Build resources, strengths
	single business	Distinctive competence
	vertical integration	Certainty, little volatility
	diversification — related	Growth through operating management
	diversification — unrelated	Growth through portfolio management
	turnaround	Increase revenue, reduce cost, change allocations and management
	divest and exit	Sell, minimize exit barriers

additional guidelines for selecting integration, penetration, market and product development, diversification, and exit strategies.[*]

Forward Integration

When an organization's present distributors are especially expensive, or unreliable, or incapable of meeting the firm's distribution needs

When the availability of quality distributors is so limited as to offer a competitive advantage to those firms that integrate forward

When an organization competes in an industry that is growing and is expected to continue to grow markedly. This is a factor because forward integration reduces an organization's ability to diversify if its basic industry falters.

When an organization has both the capital and human resources needed to manage the new business of distributing its own products

When the advantages of stable production are particularly high. This is a consideration because an organization can increase the predictability of the demand for its output through forward integration.

When present distributors or retailers have high profit margins. This situation suggests that a company could profitably distribute its own products and price them more competitively by integrating forward.

Backward Integration

When an organization's present suppliers are especially expensive, or unreliable, or incapable of meeting the firm's needs for parts, components, assemblies, or raw materials

When the number of suppliers is few and the number of competitors is many

When an organization competes in an industry that is growing rapidly. This is a factor because integrative strategies (forward, backward, and horizontal) reduce an organization's ability to diversify in a declining industry.

When an organization has both the capital and human resources needed to manage the new business of supplying its own raw materials

When the advantages of stable prices are particularly important. This is a factor because an organization can stabilize the cost of its raw materials and the associated price of its products through backward integration.

When present suppliers have high profit margins, which suggests that the business of supplying products or services in the given industry is a worthwhile venture

When an organization needs to acquire a needed resource quickly

[*] List © Fred R. David, *Fundamentals of Strategic Management* (Columbus, OH: Merrill, 1986). Reproduced by permission. Adapted from David, F. R., "How Do We Choose Among Alternative Growth Strategies?" *Managerial Planning* 33, no. 4 (January-February 1985), pp. 14–17, 22.

Horizontal Integration

When an organization can gain monopolistic characteristics in a particular area or region without being challenged by the federal government for "tending substantially" to reduce competition

When an organization competes in a growing industry

When increased economies of scale provide major competitive advantages

When an organization has both the capital and human talent needed to successfully manage an expanded organization

When competitors falter due to a lack of managerial expertise or a need for an organization's particular resources. Note that horizontal integration is not appropriate if competitors are doing poorly because overall industry sales are declining.

Market Penetration

When current markets are not saturated with your particular product or service

When the usage rate of present customers can be increased significantly

When the market shares of major competitors have been declining while total industry sales have been increasing

When the correlation between dollar sales and dollar marketing expenditures has historically been high

When increased economies of scale provide major competitive advantages

Market Development

When new channels of distribution are available that are reliable, inexpensive, and of good quality

When an organization is very successful at what it does

When new untapped or unsaturated markets exist

When an organization has the needed capital and human resources to manage expanded operations

When an organization has excess production capacity

When an organization's basic industry is rapidly becoming global in scope

Product Development

When an organization has successful products that are in the maturity stage of the product life cycle. The idea here is to attract satisfied customers to try new (improved) products as a result of their positive experience with the organization's present products or services.

When an organization competes in an industry that is characterized by rapid technological developments

When major competitors offer better quality products at comparable prices

When an organization competes in a high-growth industry

When an organization has especially strong research and development capabilities

Concentric Diversification

When an organization competes in a no-growth or slow-growth industry

When adding new, related products significantly enhances the sales of current products

When new, related products can be offered at highly competitive prices

When new, related products have seasonal sales levels that counterbalance an organization's existing peaks and valleys

When an organization's products are currently in the decline stage of the product life cycle

When an organization has a strong management team

Conglomerate Diversification

When an organization's basic industry experiences declining annual sales and profits

When an organization has the capital and managerial talent needed to compete successfully in a new industry

When an organization has the opportunity to purchase an unrelated business that is an attractive investment opportunity

When financial synergy exists between the acquired and acquiring firm. Note that a key difference between concentric and conglomerate diversification is that the former should be based on some commonality in markets, products, or technology; whereas the latter should be based more on profit considerations.

When existing markets for an organization's present products are saturated

When antitrust action could be charged against an organization that has historically concentrated on a single industry

Horizontal Diversification

When revenues derived from an organization's current products or services would significantly increase by adding new, unrelated products

When an organization competes in a highly competitive and/or a no-growth industry, as indicated by low industry profit margins and returns

When an organization's present channels of distribution can be used to market the new products to current customers

When the new products have countercyclical sales patterns compared to an organization's present products

Joint Venture

When a privately owned organization forms a joint venture with a publicly owned organization. The advantages to being privately held include close ownership. The advantages to being publicly held include access to stock issuances as a source of capital. Sometimes the unique advantages of being privately and publicly held can be combined synergistically in a joint venture.

When a domestic organization forms a joint venture with a foreign company. Joint venture can provide a domestic company with the opportunity for obtaining local management in a foreign country, thereby reducing such risks as expropriation and harassment by host country officials.

When the distinctive competencies of two or more firms successfully complement each other

When a project is potentially very profitable, but requires overwhelming resources and risks (e.g., the Alaskan pipeline)

When two or more smaller firms have trouble competing with a large firm

When an organization needs to introduce a new technology quickly

Retrenchment

When an organization has a clearly distinctive competence, but has failed to meet its objectives and goals consistently over time

When an organization is one of the weakest competitors in a given industry

When an organization is plagued by inefficiency, low profitability, poor employee morale, and pressure from stockholders to improve performance

When an organization has failed to capitalize on external opportunities, minimize external threats, take advantage of internal strengths, and overcome internal weaknesses over time. That is, when the organization's strategic managers have failed (and possibly been replaced by more competent individuals).

When an organization has grown so large so quickly that major internal reorganization is needed

Divestiture

When an organization has pursued a failed retrenchment strategy to accomplish needed improvements

When a division, in order to be competitive, needs more resources than the company can provide

When a division is responsible for an organization's overall poor performance

When a division does not fit with the rest of an organization. This can result from radically different markets, customers, managers, employees, values, or needs.

When a large amount of cash is needed quickly and cannot reasonably be obtained from other sources

When government antitrust action threatens an organization

Liquidation

When an organization has pursued unsuccessful retrenchment and divestiture strategies

When an organization's only alternative is bankruptcy. Liquidation represents an orderly and planned means of obtaining the greatest possible cash for an organization's assets. A company can legally declare bankruptcy first and then liquidate various divisions to raise needed capital.

When the stockholders of a firm can minimize their losses by selling the organization's assets

EVALUATING STRATEGY

Although the strategic manager uses many tools and examples when formulating strategy, the strategic formulation process also requires subjective interpretation and judgment. Fortunately, the strategic manager can use five criteria to assess the results of the strategic formulation process: (1) competitive response analysis, (2) risk, (3) synergy, (4) consistency, and (5) workability. The manager should review the formulated strategy in terms of these criteria not just while the strategy is formulated, but at periodic future intervals. As David (1986) asserts, "success today is no guarantee for success tomorrow."

Competitive Response Analysis

First the strategic manager asks if the formulated strategy is appropriate in view of the firm's strengths and weaknesses versus those of *potential* competitors. In preparation, the manager has searched the environment for competitive threats. Now that the strategy is formulated — be it market development via globalization by Black & Decker, cementing existing supplier relationships by Arrow Electronics, divestiture and diversification by Trans World, or product development from a customer base by Sears — the manager must analyze not the present competitive threats but the future responses of competitors.

Competitors rarely do nothing in response to another firm's market and product development activities. The more competitors exist, the slower the total industry's growth, the lower the industry's profits, and the more standardized the industry's products — then the more likely it is a competitor will make significant responses to another's activities. The strategic manager must plan for competitors' responses.

The strategist selling in relatively competitive markets finds it useful to develop a series of countermoves, as contingency plans against a spectrum of possible competitive responses. In designing these countermoves, the manager assesses the strategy;

poor strategy formulation leaves the manager in situations with few, if any, options. More effective strategy gives the manager feasible countermove alternatives, allowing the manager to guide the firm into a flexible position, not into a dead end. Competitive response is comparable to a chess game. All plans, initial moves, and strategy must be based in part on the opponent's countermoves.

Competitive response analyses, then, consist of (1) anticipating competition's probable response to your strategic moves and (2) assessing your strategy according to the feasibility and quality of your available counterresponses to competition's moves. The more feasible a firm's counterresponses, the more effective the strategy formulated. The less threatening competition's response, the more effective the firm's formulated strategy.

EXAMPLES: *Competitive Response*

For a long time Anheuser-Busch, the leading U.S. brewer, was an industry follower. Perhaps its plodding Clydesdales were appropriate symbols for its slow and deliberate competitive responses. Anheuser-Busch waited four years to enter the national low-calorie beer market, during which time Miller's Lite beer became the second-best-selling beer after Budweiser. However, Anheuser-Busch's competitive response pattern changed 180 degrees after the Lite experience. In the summer of 1984, after only brief market tests, Anheuser-Busch's Clydesdales burst from the starting gate with the national introduction of the first low-alcohol beer, LA.

The St. Louis newspaper market has seen a series of strategic actions and competitive responses. After buying the conservative morning newspaper, the *St. Louis Globe-Democrat*, in early 1984, the new owner followed a market penetration strategy that built upon the paper's conservative reader base by including strongly conservative editorials. The competition, the more liberal *St. Louis Post-Dispatch*, which had only been the leader in its circulation race with the *Globe-Democrat* since 1982, switched from being an afternoon paper to a morning paper, thus more directly competing with the *Globe-Democrat*. Three months later the *Globe-Democrat* owners responded with a new afternoon paper, the *St. Louis Evening News*. Meanwhile, the *Post-Dispatch* added more stories to its paper and stepped up promotion efforts.

Sears, Roebuck was the big unknown in competitive response analysis in the credit card industry in 1985. Citicorp, with about ten million cardholders, was aggressively pursuing not only bank cards but its own Choice, Diners Club, and Carte Blanche cards. American Express was defending its share of fifteen million cardholders. But both Citicorp and American Express watched anxiously as Sears tested various forms of credit cards, and pondered its move from its base of sixty million Sears cardholders.

Two interesting aspects of competitive response analysis are the variables of experience and origin. How the industry responds the first time to a competitive move may be quite different from how it responds at subsequent times. And competitors can act differently based on who initiates competitive acts. For example, the 1982–1983 price cuts in the airline industry were started by the "old guard" companies, notably Pan Am. Most big airlines responded by across-the-board fare cuts, and for a time travelers could go just about anywhere for ninety-nine dollars. In the fare war of 1984, however, People Express and Braniff initiated the fare cuts. This time the big airlines, principally United and American, matched fare cuts on crucial routes, but raised fares on nondiscounted routes. Further, the big airlines placed significant limits on peak-hour discount seats.

Competitive response analysis is further complicated by companies' differing responses. During the early 1980s some tobacco companies (R. J. Reynolds, Brown & Williamson) cut cigarette prices. Liggett & Myers continued its commitment to "generic" cigarettes. Phillip Morris, on the other hand, pursued aggressive advertising and marketing tactics, experimenting with new, higher-capacity packages and other marketing innovations. The range of possible competitive responses, then, can make contingency strategies a necessity.

Risk

The strategic manager asks if the expected return from the formulated strategy is worth the risk. Although competition's countermoves represent one aspect of risk, the strategic manager must consider the following six other dimensions of risk, which represent measures of vulnerability.

Technological (How limited is our technological base?)

Product/market (How narrow is our product line and how few markets do we serve?)

Financial (How flexible is our financial structure and how many financial options do we have? What will be the short- and long-term effects on earnings?)

Managerial (Can management effectively carry out the strategy?)

Production (What percentage of capacity is committed to the formulated strategy?)

Environmental (Are there undesirable consequences for either society or government?)

The opposite of vulnerability and risk is opportunity. The strategic manager must be assured that the potential returns from the formulated strategy outweigh these risks.

EXAMPLES: *Risk and Timing*

One aspect of risk is timing. Generally, the sooner the firm takes strategic action, the greater the risk. Waiting for more information and more confirmation of environmental trends is generally less risky, but greater rewards often exist for those who take early advantage of environmental opportunities. Quinn (1980) saw "logical incrementalism" as one strategy for change. A cautious attitude can represent bad timing if technological progress and competitive response make waiting risky. Anheuser-Busch adopted a cautious attitude toward light beer and watched Miller's Lite capture an enviable share of the market. Having learned its lesson, Anheuser-Busch aggressively introduced its low-alcohol L.A. brand in 1984. IBM's view of the advisability of "being first" is seen in its delayed introduction of personal computers.

In the early 1970s Mars's Snickers became the number 1 candy bar, pushing out Hershey. Snickers plus M&Ms gave Mars half of the top 10 U.S. candy bars, with Hershey holding the other half of the top 10. An industry observer commented in *Fortune* on Hershey's sense of timing and competitive response: "It took the

Hershey people seven or eight years to realize that Mars was not going to go away. Then it took them another five years to get their act together'' (7/8/85, p. 53).

The proactive view of timing held by Leslie Wexner, head of The Limited, was described in *Fortune* by a division executive: "It'll be 11:30 at night, and we're figuring out how to market $1.99 panty hose, and suddenly Les is thinking five and ten years out, and encouraging everyone else to do the same'' (8/19/85, p. 157).

There are many aspects of risk. So far we have focused on the location and source of risk in the dimensions of risk, including (1) competition, (2) technology, (3) product market, (4) financial, (5) managerial, (6) production, and (7) environmental. Three other elements of risk are inherent in risk itself, just as important as the sources or timing of risk. Just as the strategic manager should not focus on only one measure of performance, so should the manager not assess and evaluate only one source or element of risk. The three elements of risk are

1. *Information*: Strategic risk originates from a lack of perfect information with which to make a strategic decision.
2. *Innovation*: Strategic risk or risk-taking means taking an innovative course of action. Risk, then, is built into entrepreneurship.
3. *Variability*: Risk means revenues and profits will vary. Strategies have a range of possible outcomes.

By examining these three elements of risk, the strategist will make conclusions about ways to reduce uncertainty and/or the necessity for contingency planning.

Synergy

In reviewing the selected strategy, the strategic manager looks for synergy. *Synergy* is the idea that the whole is greater than the sum of its parts, or that 2 + 2 equals more than 4. Synergy as it relates to strategy means that the formulated strategy results in an interaction of enterprise resources, producing total benefits greater than those that could be produced by the independent use of those resources.

Sears, Roebuck saw synergistic opportunities in the merger of its loyal customer base and convenient locations with financial and real estate services. Harlequin saw a combined benefit greater than the sum of each part in the addition of Western novels and science fiction to its production and distribution systems for romance literature. Synergy often is achieved by either applying distinctive competence to a related activity (market or product development within the growth matrix) or through using a few resources many times, resulting in efficiencies similar to those generated by economies of scale.

EXAMPLE: *Synergy*

Greyhound pursuit of synergy is reflected in its acquisitions. In February 1985 Greyhound announced its purchase of the consumer products of Purex Industries, products such as Purex bleach and Brillo soap pads. Greyhound already counted Parson's ammonia, Dial soap, and various antiperspirants among its consumer products. In the words of a Wall Street analyst, quoted in the *Christian Science Monitor*: "[The two groups] are both doing the same thing — their products are right next to each other on the shelf; they'll be able to combine their distribution systems. One plus one will make three, eventually'' (3/1/84, p. 11).

The absence of apparent opportunities for synergy suggests that the manager should rethink the strategic match for such opportunities, but it does not mean the formulated strategy is likely to be ineffective. Rather, the presence of apparent opportunities for synergy suggests that the strategy will be effective. Kitching (1967) showed how elusive synergy could be, and why mergers "miscarry."

Consistency

As a fourth quality check, the strategic manager asks if the formulated strategy is consistent with itself and with the organization's purpose and environments. Specifically, the test of consistency means assuring that the strategic path selected is appropriate for and consistent with (1) enterprise purpose, (2) the strengths and weaknesses of the internal environment, and (3) the opportunities and threats of the external environment.

Frohman and Bitondo (1981) studied the consistency between technology and strategy. They stressed the need for coordinating business strategy and technical planning. With the significant benefit of hindsight, inconsistencies in strategy formulation become apparent. Howard Head's refusal to expand his ski-making technology beyond metal skis to include fiberglass resulted in strategic risk inconsistent with the enterprise purpose of high growth. Harlequin's attempted transfer of its romance novel skills to science fiction novels proved inconsistent with the intellectual demands of the external environment's science fiction markets.

Workability

The strategist must determine if the strategy is workable and practical for the firm; in other words, if the strategy will succeed. The test of workability is a test of the likelihood that the strategic objectives will be achieved.

Examples of the unworkability of strategies abound. Aside from current examples, a list of unworkable strategies includes the World Football League, the League of Nations, the national dreams of world domination, and the domination of commodities by speculators. Paul et al. (1978) commented on workability in describing "the reality gap" in strategic planning. Linneman and Kennell (1977) pursued the practical and the workable in their "shirt-sleeve approach" to long-range plans.

AN OVERVIEW OF STRATEGY FORMULATION

To summarize the process of strategy formulation and to introduce the general topic of organizational structure discussed in Chapter 7, Figure 6.10 presents a schematic showing how (1) the levels of strategy interact and (2) the tools of strategic management fit within a strategic planning system or organizational structure. Subsets of this planning process include capital investment and operating budgets, which usually are planning cycles that follow strategic planning, although they may coincide with strategy formulation.

Figure 6.10 assumes a diversified, divisional firm. At earlier stages of corporate

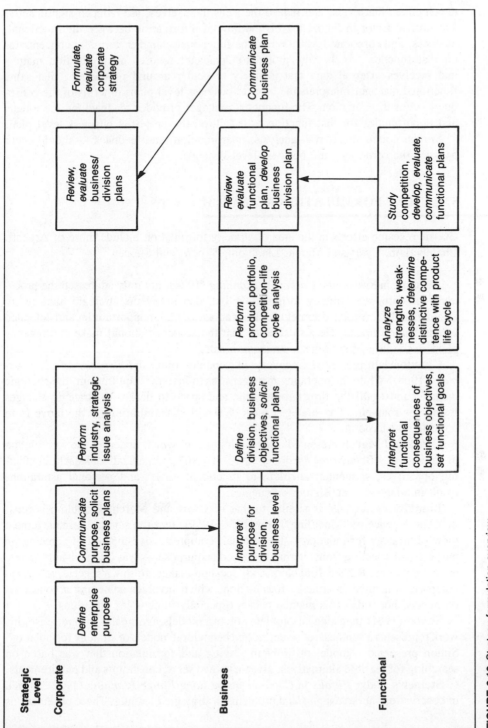

FIGURE 6.10 Strategy formulation overview

development the levels, and indeed the steps themselves, are reduced significantly. The critical factor in Figure 6.10 is the flow of information between the functional, business, and corporate levels. While the functional manager normally concentrates on that function, so that the production manager focuses on production matters and receives external data that is likely to center around production, that same functional manager interprets the broader business level plans in terms of the consequences for that function. The functional manager provides feedback on the threats and opportunities for that function as it follows the proposed business level plan.

Similar communication — analysis, interpretation, and feedback — should occur between the corporate- and business-level strategist.

STRATEGY FORMULATION RESEARCH

Classic research efforts in the area of strategy formulation include those of Argenti, Chamberlain, Cyert and March, Lindblom, Simon, and Steiner.

Argenti, in *Systematic Corporate Planning* (1974), not only addressed the procedures of corporate strategy formulation, but also urged the strategic manager to ensure that the formulated strategy took advantage of major opportunities and defended against major threats. He also stressed that the strategist should make contingency plans in the face of significant strategic threats.

Chamberlain presented his concept of ''counterpoint'' in *Enterprise and Environment* (1968). While the operating manager tries to maintain equilibrium, the strategic manager must pull the firm through time and space to deal with strategic changes in the environment. The strategist must deal with disequilibrium in the move from point to counterpoint.

Cyert and March presented a bargaining model which underlies the formulation of strategy in *A Behavioral Theory of the Firm* (1963). Organizational slack, conflicting objectives, sequential attention to functional goals, and personal aspirations result in adaptive, ''satisficing'' strategies.

Lindblom's message is similar to that of Cyert and March. Lindblom argued, in ''The Science of 'Muddling Through' '' (1959), that the scientific, management view of strategy formulation — the rational, comprehensive method of agreeing on purpose and selecting from alternatives based on purpose — was often not appropriate or was not done. Rather, Lindblom said, decision makers follow a successive limited comparison method in strategy formulation, which involves achieving a consensus on means, not ends. This method occurs especially in complex situations.

Simon (1964) investigated problem-solving models and goals. In one sense, his work represents a synthesis of scientific and behavioral models of strategy formulation. Simon presented a model of problem solving and formulation that was based on searching for feasible alternatives, given a known set of constraints and requirements.

Steiner's study, *Pitfalls in Comprehensive Long-Range Planning* (1972), is rich in observations about dangers and problems in strategic planning. These observations encompass organizational and procedural dangers, but also address strategy formulation itself, warning of (1) top management allowing focus on current operating problems to invalidate strategic decisions and (2) using intuition instead of the strategic decision process in strategy formulation.

Current significant research efforts in strategy formulation include works by the following authors.

Abbanat (1967), focusing on the strategies formulated by small companies competing against larger firms, reached two conclusions. (1) Small companies look for interstices; that is, for market gaps and untried products ignored by the larger companies. (2) Small companies compete by unconventional (customization, improved service) means, often attracting technicians who appreciate the environment of the small firm.

Chaffee (1985) pointed out that definitions of strategy may be based on one or another of three models of strategy:

1. *Linear*: Integrated decisions, actions, or plans that will set and achieve viable organization goals.
2. *Adaptive*: Environmental assessment of internal and external conditions that leads to the organization adjusting to a viable match between opportunities and capabilities.
3. *Interpretive*: The organization attracts individuals in a social contract or a collection of cooperative agreements.

Chaffee concluded that the lack of consensus on a definition of strategy is due to its multidimensional and situational characteristics.

Dutton, Fahey, and Narayanan (1983) researched SID (Strategic Issue Diagnosis) as both a planning trigger or stimulus and an implementation planning tool. These three researchers showed how SID can "mobilize behavioral and political forces toward action," presenting an input-process-output model of strategic issue diagnosis. Strategic issue diagnosis is a focused analysis of one strategic signal, or a group of interrelated signals.

Glueck (1976), building on Hofer's categories and a wealth of business articles from the 1930s to the 1970s, reclassified Hofer's twenty-eight challenges-responses into four broad strategies — growth, stability, retrenchment, and combination. Glueck found that trade (wholesale and retail) and consumer goods companies generally follow growth strategies; natural resources and construction companies generally follow stability strategies; and conglomerates generally follow retrenchment strategies. Glueck also discovered that most firms followed stability strategies in the thirties, growth strategies in the forties, combination strategies in the fifties, and retrenchment strategies in the sixties and seventies.

Gutmann's project (1964) analyzed fifty-three firms that had experienced high growth. Gutmann concluded that high-growth firms concentrate on a few product-market segments rather than covering many segments. Gutmann also observed that while half of the high-growth firms made acquisitions, they did not experience growth significantly greater than firms that did not follow the acquisition path.

Hanna (1969) studied three companies that each operated in several industries. He found that the multi-industry company strategies followed not only a corporate purpose but overall growth policies, financial policies, and organizational policies. He also noted that these companies paid more attention to these policies than to an analysis of existing products and markets.

Hofer categorized twenty-eight external challenges and threats and a matching set of strategic responses to these challenges. This initial effort reached general conclusions, and was further developed by Glueck. Part of Hofer's major contribution was his categories of challenges and responses, developed by studying four hundred challenges-responses contained in business articles over a twelve-year period.

King (1982) researched a methodology for integrating strategic issues analysis into the planning process, based upon a joint manager-analyst team approach. He recommended (1) identifying the strategic issue, (2) developing a formal statement of that issue, (3) developing a preliminary issue model, (4) critiquing and revising the model, (5) gathering data, and (6) using the model in the planning process.

Kitching (1967), in his study of sixty-nine of the mergers by twenty-two firms, reached two conclusions. (1) Acquisitions were most successful in instances of financial synergy; somewhat successful in marketing synergy instances; and least successful in cases of production and technology synergy. (2) Unsuccessful acquisitions resulted from the acquired company's top management's refusal to change strategies.

Rumelt, by examining 250 companies in 1949, 1959, and 1969, identified strategy types (single businesses, dominant-vertical firms, conglomerates, and so on) and five administrative structures (geographic, holding companies, product division, functional, and functional with subsidiaries). Rumelt reached two important conclusions. (1) Science firms used diversification to correct declining current businesses; nonscience firms did not. (2) Firms diversified to achieve EPS gains, but did not achieve real long-term improvements.

Schendel, Patten, and Riggs (1974) reached three conclusions after studying corporate turnarounds in fifty-four companies. (1) Overall strategy changes were necessary to reverse earnings declines. (2) Eighty-one percent of the turnaround companies changed management. (3) Marketing changes, plant additions, product and geographic diversifications, and efficiency programs were utilized more than divestiture in the successful turnaround strategies.

Weber (1984) asked, How does the strategic manager deal with uncertainty? To answer, Weber analyzed managerial uncertainty and found two kinds of ambiguity: uncertainty "about the gaps between what they want to achieve and what they have or expect to achieve" and uncertainty "about their steps to close the gaps." Weber advocated a dialectic process, "heuristics for achieving synthesis." Weber also proposed "challenging conditions with counterconditions" so that "new concepts or new data" emerge, resulting in a synthesis.

Wheelwright (1984) studied the difference between strategy using analytical concepts, as at Texas Instruments, and an incremental-value–based approach, as at Hewlett-Packard. Wheelwright commented on the differences in resulting strategy regarding the product life cycle, cost and pricing strategies, production plans, and portfolio balance. Wheelwright concluded that each firm must carefully select its strategy planning approach, since each approach has significant strengths and weaknesses.

EXECUTIVE COMMENTS

Strategy formulation is explicitly addressed within Searle at both the corporate and product line group levels. It is the intent of the process to stimulate congruence of strategy formulation efforts throughout the firm. In slightly different terms, we view formalized planning primarily as a managerial communications system and *process — and not as a separate functional exercise.*

R. C. Lancey, Searle executive (in Schendel & Hofer, 1979)

The really pressing problem [*at Gulf Oil is*] *"How do we know good strategy when we see it?"*

B. C. Ball, Jr., Gulf Oil executive (in Schendel & Hofer, 1979)

To use some of International Harvester's terminology, there are some key vulnerabilities . . . in strategic and policy research such as . . . the basic assumption of rationality. Many times business decisions are made or are impacted significantly by forces which objectively and according to competitive theory are not rational.

R. O. Aines, International Harvester executive (in Schendel & Hofer, 1979)

KEY TERMS

competitive analysis (pagc 160)

consistency (page 164)

directional policy matrix (page 144)

growth matrix (page 146)

industry analysis (page 148)

product portfolios (page 142)

risk (page 162)

strategic issues (page 150)

strategic levels (page 139)

strategy formulation (page 136)

synergy (page 163)

BIBLIOGRAPHY

Abbanat, R. F., "Strategies of Size," D.B.A. dissertation, Harvard Business School, 1967.

Abell, D. F., "Strategic Windows," *Journal of Marketing* (July 1978), pp. 21–26.

Ackoff, R., "On the Use of Models in Corporate Planning," *Strategic Management Journal* (October-December 1981).

Andrews, K. R., *The Concept of Corporate Strategy* (Homewood, IL: Richard D. Irwin, 1980).

Ansoff, H. I., *Corporate Strategy: An Analytical Approach to Business Policy for Growth and Expansion* (New York: McGraw-Hill, 1965).

Argenti, J., *Systematic Corporate Planning* (New York: Wiley, 1974).

Astely, W. G., "Toward an Appreciation of Collective Strategy," *Academy of Management Review* (July 1984).

"Black & Decker's Gamble on 'Globalization,'" *Fortune* (May 14, 1984), pp. 40–48.

Bloom, P., and P. Kotler, "Strategies for High Market Share Companies," *Harvard Business Review* 53 (November-December 1975), pp. 63–72.

Bower, J. L., *Managing the Resource Allocation Process: A Study of Corporate Planning and Investment* (Cambridge, MA: Division of Research, Graduate School of Business Administration, Harvard University, 1970).

Burgelman, R. A., "Managing the New Venture Division," *Strategic Management Journal* 6 (January-March 1985), pp. 39–54.

Chaffee, E. E., "Three Models of Strategy," *Academy of Management Review* 10 (1985), pp. 89–98.

Chamberlain, N. W., *Enterprise and Environment: The Firm in Time and Space* (New York: McGraw-Hill, 1968).

Chandler, A. D., Jr., *Strategy and Structure: Chapters in the History of the Industrial Enterprise* (Cambridge, MA: M.I.T. Press, 1962).

Channon, D. F., "Commentary," in D. E. Schendel and C. W. Hofer, eds., *Strategic Management* (Boston: Little, Brown, 1979), pp. 122–133.

Christensen, C. R., N. A. Berg, and M. S. Salter, *Policy Formulation and Administration*, 7th ed. (Homewood, IL: Richard D. Irwin, 1976).

Christopher, W., "Achievement Reporting — Controlling Performance Against Objectives," *Long Range Planning* 10 (October 1977), pp. 14–24.

Cooper, A. C., "Strategic Management: New Ventures and Small Business," in C. W. Hofer and D. E. Schendel, eds., *Strategy Formulation* (St. Paul, MN: West Publishing, 1978).

Cyert, R. M., and J. G. March, *A Behavioral Theory of the Firm* (Englewood Cliffs, NJ: Prentice-Hall, 1963).

David, F. R., *Fundamentals of Strategic Management* (Columbus, OH: Merrill, 1986).

Day, G. S., "Diagnosing the Product Portfolio," *Journal of Marketing* 41 (April 1977): pp. 29–38.

Dutton, V. E., L. Fahey, and V. K. Narayanan, "Toward Understanding Strategic Issue Diagnosis," *Strategic Management Journal* 4 (October-December 1983), pp. 307–323.

Fredrickson, J. W., and T. R. Mitchell, "Strategic Decision Processes: Comprehensiveness and Performance in an Industry with an Unstable Environment," *Academy of Management Journal* 27 (June 1984), pp. 399–423.

Frohman, A. L., and D. Bitondo, "Coordinating Business Strategy and Technical Planning," *Long Range Planning* 14 (December 1981), pp. 58–67.

Ginter, P. M., and A. C. Rucke, "Can Business Learn from Wargames?" *Long Range Planning* 17 (June 1984), pp. 123–128.

Glueck, W. F., *Business Policy, Strategy Formation, and Executive Action* (New York: McGraw-Hill, 1976).

Gupta, A. K., and V. Govindarajan, "Build, Hold, Harvest: Converting Strategic Intentions into Reality," *Journal of Business Strategy* 4 (March 1984), pp. 34–47.

Gutmann, P. M., "Strategies for Growth," *California Management Review* (Summer 1964), pp. 31–36.

Hall, W. K., "Survival Strategies in a Hostile Environment," *Harvard Business Review* 58 (September-October 1980), pp. 75–85.

Hammermesh, R. G., M. J. Anderson, Jr., and J. E. Harris, "Strategies for Low Market Share Businesses," *Harvard Business Review* 56 (May-June 1978), pp. 95–102.

Hanna, R. G. C., "The Concept of Corporate Strategy in Multi-Industry Companies," D. B. A. dissertation, Harvard Business School, 1969.

Harrell, G. D., and R. O. Kiefer, "Multinational Strategic Market Portfolios," *MSU Business Topics* (Winter 1981), pp. 5–15.

Harrigan, K. R., "The Effect of Exit Barriers Upon Strategic Flexibility," *Strategic Management Journal*, vol. 1 (1980), pp. 165–176.

Harrigan, K. R., "Exit Decisions in Mature Industries," *Academy of Management Journal* 25 (December 1982), pp. 707–732.

Harrigan, K. R., "Vertical Integration and Corporate Strategy," *Academy of Management Journal* 28 (June 1985), pp. 397–425.

Harrigan, K., and M. Porter, "End-Game Strategies for Declining Industries," *Harvard Business Review* 61 (July-August 1983).

Haspelslagh, P., "Portfolio Planning: Uses and Limits," *Harvard Business Review* 60 (January-February 1982), pp. 58–73.

Hedley, B., "Strategy and the Business Portfolio," *Long Range Planning* 10 (February 1977), pp. 9–15.

Henderson, B., "The Application and Misapplication of the Experience Curve," *Journal of Business Strategy* (Winter 1984).

Hofer, C. W., "Conceptual Constructs for Formulating Corporate and Business Strategies" (Boston: Harvard ICCH 9-378-754, 1977).

Hofer, C. W., "Some Preliminary Research on Patterns of Strategic Behavior," *Proceedings of the Business Policy and Planning Division of the Academy of Management*, Academy of Management, August 1973.

Hofer, C. W., "Toward a Contingency Theory of Business Strategy," *Academy of Management Journal* 18 (1975), pp. 789–810.

Hofer, C. W., "Turnaround Strategies," *Journal of Business Strategy* 1 (Summer 1980), pp. 19–31.

Hofer, C. W., and D. Schendel, *Strategy Formulation: Analytical Concepts* (St. Paul, MN: West Publishing, 1978).

Hussey, D. E., "Strategic Management: Lessons from Success and Failure," *Long Range Planning* 17 (February 1984), pp. 43–53.

Katz, R. L., *Management of the Total Enterprise* (Englewood Cliffs, NJ: Prentice-Hall, 1970).

Kierulff, H. W., "Finding the Best Acquisition Candidates," *Harvard Business Review* 59 (January-February 1981), pp. 66–68.

King, W. R., "Using Strategic Issue Analysis," *Long Range Planning* 15 (August 1982), pp. 45–49.

Kitching, J., "Why Do Mergers Miscarry?" *Harvard Business Review* 45 (November-December 1967), pp. 84–101.

Lindblom, C. E., "The Science of 'Muddling Through,'" *Public Administration Revew* (Spring 1959), pp. 79–88.

Linneman, R. E., and J. D. Kennell, "Shirt-Sleeve Approach to Long-Range Plans," *Harvard Business Review* 55 (March-April 1977), pp. 141–150.

McGinnis, M. A., "The Key to Strategic Planning: Integrating Analysis and Intuition," *Sloan Management Review* (Fall 1984), pp. 45–52.

MacMillan, I., "Preemptive Strategies," *Journal of Business Strategy* (Fall 1983).

Mintzberg, H., and J. A. Waters, "Tracking Strategy in an Entrepreneurial Firm," *Academy of Management Journal*, vol. 25, no. 3 (1982), pp. 465–499.

Paul, R. N., N. B. Donovan, and J. W. Taylor, "The Reality Gap in Strategic Planning," *Harvard Business Review* 56 (May-June 1978), pp. 124–130.

Peters, T., and N. Austin, *A Passion for Excellence* (New York: Random House, 1985).

Porter, M. E., *Competitive Strategy: Techniques for Analyzing Industries and Competitors* (New York: The Free Press, 1980).

Porter, M. E., "How Competitive Forces Shape Strategy," *Harvard Business Review* 57 (March-April 1979), pp. 137–145.

Porter, M. E., "Please Note Location of Nearest Exit: Exit Barriers and Planning," *California Management Review* 19 (Winter 1976), pp. 21–25.

Quinn, J. B., *Strategies for Change: Logical Incrementalism* (Homewood, IL: Richard D. Irwin, 1980).

Robinson, R. B., Jr., and J. A. Pearce, III, "The Structure of Generic Strategies and Their Impact on Business-Unit Performances," Academy of Management Proceedings 1985, pp. 35–39.

Robinson, S. J. Q., R. E. Hitchens, and D. P. Wade, "The Directional Policy Matrix: Tool for Strategic Planning," *Long Range Planning* 11 (June 1978), pp. 8–15.

Rothschild, W. E., "Surprise and the Competitive Advantage," *Journal of Business Strategy* 4 (Winter 1984), pp. 10–18.

Rowe, H., R. Mason, and K. Dickel, *Strategic Management and Business Policy* (Reading, MA: Addison-Wesley, 1982).

Rumelt, R., "Diversification Strategy and Profitability," *Strategic Management Journal* (October-December 1982).

Rumelt, R., *Strategy, Structure and Economic Performance* (Cambridge, MA: Harvard University Press, 1974).

Schendel, D. E., and C. W. Hofer, eds., *Strategic Management: A New View of Business Policy and Planning* (Boston: Little, Brown, 1979).

Schendel, D. E., R. Patten, and J. Riggs, "Corporate Turnaround Strategies," Academy of Management, Seattle, August 1974.

Schoeffler, S., R. D. Buzzell, and D. F. Heany, "Impact of Strategic Planning on Profit Performance," *Harvard Business Review* 54 (March-April 1974), pp. 137–145.

Scott, B. R., "Stages of Corporate Development" (Boston: Intercollegiate Case Clearing House, 9-371-294, 1971).

Seeger, J. A., "Reversing the Image of BCG's Growth/Share Matrix," *Society of Management Journal* (January-March 1984).

Simon, H. A., "On the Concept of Organizational Goals," *Administrative Sciences Quarterly* (June 1964), pp. 1–22.

Steiner, G., "Formal Strategic Planning in the U.S. Today," *Long Range Planning* 16 (June 1983), pp. 12–18.

Steiner, G., *Pitfalls in Comprehensive Long Range Planning* (Oxford, OH: Planning Executives Institute, 1972).

Taylor, B., "Strategic Planning — Which Style Do You Need?" *Long Range Planning* 17 (June 1984), pp. 51–62.

Thompson, J. D., *Organizations in Action* (New York: McGraw-Hill, 1967).

Weber, C. E., "Strategic Thinking — Dealing with Uncertainty," *Long Range Planning* 17 (October 1984), pp. 60–70.

Wheelwright, S. C., "Strategy Management and Strategic Planning Approaches," *Interfaces* 14:1 (January-February 1984), pp. 19–33.

Williams, J. R., "Technological Evolution and Competitive Response," *Strategic Management Journal* (January-March 1983).

Woo, C. Y., and A. Cooper, "The Surprising Case for Low Market Share," *Harvard Business Review* 60 (November-December 1982), pp. 106–113.

CHAPTER 7

IMPLEMENTING STRATEGY

Strategy formulation emphasizes the abilities to conceptualize, analyze, and judge. . . . Implementation depends upon the skills of working through others, instituting internal change, and guiding . . . activities. . . . Implementing strategy poses the tougher management challenge.

A. A. Thompson and A. J. Strickland, *Strategic Management*

This chapter defines the two components of implementation, namely, organization structure and motivation systems. It then presents two criteria for the implementation decision: distinctive competence and congruence.

The strategic manager implements strategy by selecting organizational structure, control, measurement, and reward systems from a range of alternatives. In addition to being a resource allocator (see Working Concept 6), the manager may need to serve as negotiator, disturbance handler, or innovator. The manager uses certain criteria to select specific implementation steps from the range alternatives, including (1) distinctive competence and the fit between strategy and structure and (2) congruence.

NO RIGHT ANSWER

This chapter reviews the wide range of structural, systematic, and procedural organizational alternatives that confront the strategic manager trying to implement strategy. The problem of choosing from among multiple alternatives is complicated further by variables connected with the new strategy, the current structure, and leadership style.

The type of strategy selected and the degree of change between the new and current strategy influence the choice of organizational alternatives. The organization's current state, and the types of organizational problems encountered by the strategic manager, affect the manager's choice. Implementation alternatives differ depending on whether the firm's leader is a visionary, an autocrat, a liaison/coordinator, a ''hands-on'' coparticipant, or a consensus builder. This vast range of interacting and important variables offers the strategic manager many different solutions. Each situation has several ''right answers.'' Emphasizing that simplicity is the key to good management, Peter Drucker concluded, ''The simplest organization structure that will do the job is the best one.''

IMPLEMENTATION DEFINED

The implementation of strategy occurs when the strategic manager selects a specific organizational structure and motivation system and allocates specific organizational resources to help create them. The manager selects these specific organizational resources and steps, which include managerial planning and control systems, administrative structure and hierarchies, and performance measurement and incentives, based upon strategic congruence and distinctive competence.

IMPLEMENTATION ILLUSTRATED

The strategic manager creates structures and systems that are supportive of and consistent with his or her formulated strategy. The basic requirement of the action and resource-allocation phase of strategy implementation is that action and allocation be determined by the formulated strategy. Strategy determines structure and its resulting systems, as Chandler (1962), Galbraith (1977), and others have asserted.

The strategic manager who pursues growth by developing a new product must create an organizational structure and supporting systems consistent with new product development. Aspects of such a consistent structure might include

Incentive systems for those sales personnel who contribute new product ideas

A strong product R&D staff supported by adequate budgets and a creative environment with minimal bureaucracy

Active scanning and analysis of customer needs and industry trends, including joint research projects with suppliers and customers

Because these motivation systems and information systems are a logical extension of the formulated strategy, they fully support that strategy. In the mid-1980s Peugeot acquisitions resulted in an inconsistent structure of duplicated production facilities — Peugeot, Citroen, and Talbot — which worked against the strategy of worldwide competition by preventing the achievement of economies of scale.

Table 7.1 suggests other structures and systems compatible with differing (market development and diversification) growth strategies. Because each strategic situation is different, however, these suggestions are general and tentative. They appear here to illustrate the process of implementation and resource allocation. A specific illustration of different organizational structures at different times (General Electric) was presented in Chapter 1 (pages 12–14).

Structure or system component	Formulated strategy	
	Market development	*Diversification*
Management structure	Centralized, at least in marketing and market research	Decentralized, to bring decision makers closer to opportunities
Compensation systems	Based on sales	Based on stock performance
Information systems	Highlight new markets and market shares	Show performance within the different product/ market groups, intergroup differences

TABLE 7.1
Organization systems and structures

STRUCTURE AND SYSTEMS COMPONENTS

What alternative organizational structures and motivations systems are available to the strategic manager? Table 7.1 suggests that they include management or administrative structure, information systems, and compensation systems. They also include performance measurement and nonmonetary aspects of organizational structure.

Administrative Systems

Administrative systems, or management structures, fit within a spectrum that has centralization on one end and decentralization on the other. The strategic manager selects certain alternatives based upon his or her formulated strategy. A centralized managerial structure is a well-defined, hierarchical reporting structure which reduces participation in strategic planning and decision making as one moves further down the management hierarchy. Such a structure might be appropriate for a company with limited products or markets, a developing company, or an organization that needs to respond quickly to threats.

As a firm decentralizes, more managers participate in strategic decision making as more decentralized divisions, and thus more divisional managers, are added to the firm. Diverse product markets require decentralized structures or else elaborate bureaucratic hierarchies, with their attendant problems of slow response time and high overhead. Nonetheless, the different divisions of decentralized companies duplicate such services as accounting and personnel. The decentralized strategic manager also may focus too much on the decentralized unit, never seeing the forest for the trees.

Two administrative systems, matrix organizations and strategic business units, were designed to have the breadth of the decentralized structure while achieving the fast response and strategic concentration of the centralized organization.

Matrix Organizations. A matrix organization is a two-tiered management structure that focuses on the manager. The strategic manager in the matrix organization has one responsibility to a product/market or project group, but that same strategic manager also has additional long-term responsibilities to a functional group. For example, a manager might be responsible for a personal computer product line while also planning for miniaturized printed circuits.

Matrix units help the manager to get the best of both worlds; that is, the special expertise and economies of scale of functional management with the new product innovation of product managers. However, Galbraith (1971) and Davis and Lawrence (1978) pointed out the problems of matrix organizations. Knight (1980) argued that the seven theoretical advantages of matrix organizations — (1) efficient use of resources, (2) flexibility in conditions of change and uncertainty, (3) technical excellence, (4) ability to balance conflicting objectives, (5) freedom of top management for long-range planning, (6) improving motivation and commitment, and (7) giving opportunities for personal development — must be weighed against four major problems — (1) controlling conflict, (2) achieving balance, (3) minimizing stress, and (4) incurring increased administrative and communication costs.

Strategic Business Units (SBUs). A strategic business unit is also a two-tiered management structure, but rather than focusing on the manager it revolves around groups of products and markets. All decentralized business components dealing with similar product markets are grouped together at the highest levels of the organization only, not at the level of the individual manager, into strategic business units. Individual management units and operating divisions dealing with ground weapons development or two-way military communication systems can be joined at the level of top management into a defense SBU. Hall (1978) described SBUs as "the hot new topic in the management of diversification." SBUs were covered in Working Concept 3 (pages 12–14).

Lawrence and Lorsch (1967) studied two aspects of administrative systems in depth: differentiation and integration. *Differentiation* is the degree of difference in attitudes and behavior of functional groups within the organization, including differences between managers as to goals, time frames, formality, and interpersonal relationships. *Integration* is the degree of collaboration and coordination among the functional groups and managers. A key factor in controlling organizational integration is in resolving conflicts effectively. The degrees of change, uncertainty, and stability in the external and internal environment determine the appropriateness and importance of differentiation and integration. Figure 7.1 presents some of the integration options against a spectrum of complexity and, presumably, expense.

Information Systems

An information system can fit into any number of categories, such as the extent and type of computerization, the relationship between the system and the organizational structure, or the costing and accounting techniques underlying the system. Strategists need to know whether the information system is primarily for one of three categories: (1) control, (2) planning, or (3) a combination of the two. Computerization, organization linkage, and costing methods are techniques used within these three important categories.

FIGURE 7.1
Integration
option spectrum

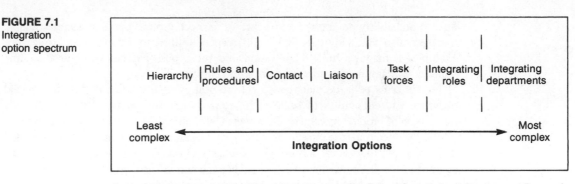

Source: Adapted from J. Galbraith and D. Nathanson, "The Role of Organizational Structure and Process in Strategy Implementation," in D. Schendel and C. Hofer, eds., *Strategic Management* (Boston: Little, Brown, 1979).

Control Systems. Control information systems measure and report current data from within the internal environment of the firm. Management reports might show the variance between standard costs and actual production costs; or they might report on the overhead costs of production and administrative departments. Control systems primarily function as the strategic manager's method of reviewing the efficiency of the internal environment. They are generally appropriate for formulated strategies of achieving lower costs to meet competition and/or to achieve growth, as lower production costs result in lower sales prices and thus higher volume. The marketplace is presumably stable for a firm using a control system; and the firm concentrates on production.

Planning Systems. Planning information systems are directed primarily toward the external environment; they are more concerned with estimating or detecting trends and problems than with measuring current performance data. Planning information systems might present reports showing simulations of what happens if a company takes actions 1, 2, or 3; if competitors take actions X, Y, or Z; and if the economic cycle is stagnant or experiencing slow growth. The planning reports might project various industry and economic data, including customers' and competitors' inventories and orders; or they might extrapolate foreign currency trends and the resulting currency exposures. Planning information systems are more appropriate for the strategic manager facing turbulent market conditions and complex environments.

Combination. This planning versus control dichotomy illustrates how the information system is determined by the manager's strategic objectives. In the vast majority of situations, the strategic manager utilizes a combination of planning and control reports, which emphasize current performance and project the consequences of this performance for the future. Managers use measurements of less than expected efficiency in order to stimulate corrective actions by management; they use projections of tomorrow's external environment in order to plan for modifications of today's operations. Thus, most information systems generally include both control and planning functions. The strategic manager knows which functions to stress based upon the formulated strategy and the selected strategic objectives. In reviewing the information systems during the implementation of strategy, the strategic manager asks two questions. (1) Is the control function of the information system consistent with and adequate for our formulated strategy? (Hobbs and Heany [1977] told how to "couple strategy to operating plans.") (2) Is the planning function of the information system consistent with and adequate for our formulated strategy? The strategic manager considers the present and future dimensions of both planning and control needs, encompassing both the internal and external environment.

Vancil (1973) explored what kind of management control a firm needs. Sihler (1971) gave pointers toward a better management control system. Christensen (1987) concluded,

> *It is virtually impossible to make meaningful generalizations about how proper standards might be set in particular companies. It can be said, however, that in any organization the overall strategy can be translated into more or less detailed future plans (the detail becoming less predictable as the time span grows longer), which permits comparison of actual with predicted performance.*

Compensation and Measurement Systems

After determining the appropriate administrative structure and the information content and flow within that structure, the strategist must turn to measuring and compensating for performance. Performance incentives include not only monetary items such as raises and bonuses, but less tangible compensation such as the physical work place and the firm's style and atmosphere (also called the *corporate culture*). Knowing the strategic objectives, the strategist decides what mix of the various performance, compensation, and intangible incentives will motivate the organization's employees. The spectrum of options includes the following incentives.

1. *Performance measurement unit*: The strategic manager might measure output and performance at the individual level at one end of the spectrum, or for the total organization only at the other end of the spectrum, or at intermediary stages such as production location or sales group.

2. *Performance measurement basis*: Measurement can be based on a long-term perspective or on the very short term. The measure itself can be quantitative or qualitative — the latter frequently stated in terms of tasks or objectives. Performance measurement will change from the personal, subjective criteria of the entrepreneur, to technical and cost criteria for functional managers, and to return and market criteria for diversified, decentralized managers.

3. *Performance and compensation linkage*: The extremes of the options range from compensation based completely on performance, as in an escalating commission plan, to compensation unrelated to any performance measure.

4. *Performance evaluation method*: The strategic manager has a range of options from a highly formalized, completely documented system of periodic peer and supervisory review, to an informal, catch-as-catch-can evaluation plan.

5. *Compensation*: Will compensation be limited to monetary rewards, or should it include a related plan of levels of office size and furnishings, praise, memberships, insurance benefits, vacation, travel allowances, stock options, and other nonmonetary benefits?

6. *Corporate culture*: Top management can create an atmosphere and operating style ranging from totally threatening and ruthless to totally supportive, nurturing, and forgiving. Leadership style can be based on persuasion or on commands. The organization form can be tight or loose (''mechanistic'' or ''organic'' [Burns and Stalker, 1961]). Some firms, such as Procter & Gamble, are known for their corporate culture and atmosphere of internal competition; others, such as the oft-cited Japanese enterprises, intentionally create a nonthreatening environment in which each person has long-term job security.

In extreme situations, such as the start-up or bankruptcy phases of a business, the strategic manager might choose extreme positions within these six preceding implementation options. Since relatively few extreme situations exist, most managers find themselves using a combination of options that center at about the middle of the option spectrum. They make their decisions based on the relative importance of the human resource factor in attaining strategic objectives, and upon the values of key managers.

Leontiades (1981) advised on how to choose the right manager to fit the strategy. Tichy et al. (1982) analyzed strategic human resource management. Christopher (1977) suggested ways to control performance against objectives that would result in ''achievement reporting.''

The strategic manager considers the total strategic situation; he or she does not rely merely on a few progress and performance measures. Financial managers might measure earnings growth, price multiples, and return statistics, but strategic managers view these as superficial symbols of environmental forces that must be analyzed and understood. Sales managers might study unit and dollar growth rates, but strategic managers assess the change in relative strength of competition and in market demand and technology.

Holistic Measures. Strategic evaluation of progress encompasses all aspects of the organization seen from the perspective of the chief executive. The strategic manager has a holistic perspective; he or she is concerned with the total system's progress, not with unidimensional measurement of one or a few parts of the whole. The following list presents holistic measures of strategic progress.

1. *Stage of completion*: How complete is the strategic activity that is being measured?
2. *Timing*: Is the activity on schedule?
3. *Resources*: Is the activity within budget?
4. *Modification*: Is the activity that is being measured achieving the strategic objective, or is some modification desirable?

Limited or unidimensional measures can result in undesirable behavior by those managers being measured. Managers might focus on short-term rather than strategic objectives; short-term measures such as quarterly profits do not measure strategic progress.

General Electric's multiple criteria for performance evaluation provides an example of an evaluation system that avoids the unidimensional or the suboptimizing measure. G.E.'s eight criteria include (1) balance between long-term and short-term objectives, (2) public responsibility, (3) productivity, (4) product leadership, (5) personnel development, and (6) employee attitudes — along with the more frequently encountered criteria of market position and profitability. The effective strategist recognizes not only the necessity for multiple measures of progress, but also the danger of short-term perspectives and the problem of means becoming ends.

Short-Term Perspective. Companies frequently assess performance and progress by measuring

Production
    capital/labor/material mix
    costs
    efficiency/output
    value added
Marketing
    sales growth
    market share
    margins
Finance
    stock price
    net profit
    earnings per share
    return ratios (assets, investment, equity, sales)
    liquidity
    leverage

The short-term perspective of these measures blurs their effectiveness as strategic evaluation tools. Strategy takes a long time to formulate and implement. Strategic frameworks are long term, but these measures are short term. The strategist studies trends in these measures, not the measures themselves.

A Long-Term Financial Measure. Many researchers have concluded that the stock exchange is an efficient capital market that incorporates economic data in an efficient way. From this conclusion, the strategist who works in a firm whose shares are traded on the stock exchange is provided with a measure of strategic performance, or relative earnings multiple (REM).

Securities sell on the stock exchange at an average multiple of earnings, called the *price-earnings ratio* or the *earnings multiple*. This earnings multiple is calculated by dividing current earnings per share into the stock price. A stock earning $2 per share and selling for $16 would have an earnings multiple of 8.

REM, the relative earnings multiple, compares the earnings multiple with the average stock market multiple, and quantifies this comparison by calculating a ratio of actual earnings multiple to the average earnings multiple.

$$\text{REM} = \frac{\text{Actual earnings multiple for stock}}{\text{Average stock market earnings multiple}}$$

If the stock market on average values shares at 8 times earnings, and our stock is trading at an earnings multiple of 10, our REM is 1.25 (10 ÷ 8). If our stock is trading at an earnings ratio of 6, our REM is 0.75 (6 ÷ 8).

The longer-term perspective of the stock exchange gives the strategic manager an outsider's evaluation of strategy that many believe is based upon an efficient capital market. REM can be even more insightful if the strategist uses as the denominator not the average stock market multiple, but averages for specific industries and companies, including competitors. REM should be calculated for a firm's competitors as well as for the firm itself; those REM trends should be studied by the strategist.

For example, on April 8, 1980, the Seagram Company sold its oil and gas subsidiary, Texas Pacific Oil, to Sun Company. Seagram had entered the oil and gas business in 1953; by 1979 oil and gas revenues were $190 million versus $2,363 million for spirits and wine, and oil and gas assets were $498 million versus $1,939 million for spirits and wine assets. Each 1979 dollar of oil and gas assets produced $0.38 of revenue, while each dollar of spirits and wine assets produced $1.22 of revenue for Seagram. Thus one could conclude that Seagram was more productive, and presumably more profitable, in its core business, spirits and wine. Further, this sale to Sun was for the equivalent of twelve dollars a barrel for oil in the ground, about three dollars a barrel more than the previous record payment by Shell for Belridge Petroleum in 1979.

Table 7.2 shows that Seagram's REM was greater than that of the Sun's, and that it increased relative to Sun's REM in the quarter of the sale and in the next quarter.

TABLE 7.2
Relative earnings multiple, Seagram and Sun

Quarter ending	Price earnings multiple		Standard & Poor's composite price earnings multiple	REM		Ratio Seagram to Sun's REM
	Sun	Seagram		Sun	Seagram	
December 1979	7	13	7.4	0.94	1.75	1.86
March 1980	6	13	6.7	0.90	1.94	2.17
June 1980[a]	6	14	7.6	0.79	1.84	2.33
September 1980	6	15	8.7	0.69	1.72	2.50

[a] Oil and gas sale in April 1980.

Means and Ends. The act of measuring performance can result in the organization focusing on the measure while excluding or ignoring the strategic ends. Thus a cost-reduction target that is the *means* to a competitive advantage might result in ABC firm treating cost reduction as an *end*. While ABC firm achieves cost reductions, XYZ company might introduce a product improvement that renders ABC's lower-cost product obsolete. Thus the means of cost reduction completely obscures the end of competitive advantage. The strategist, forewarned of the serious problems inherent in the substituting means for ends, monitors the evaluation system to ensure that means support, not replace, ends. Multiple measures are most helpful in this regard.

Verifying Assumptions. Measuring progress is only one part of strategic reporting and evaluation. Not only does the strategist need to know how well the firm is moving toward its objectives, but he or she also has to ensure that the original judgments made in formulating these objectives are still valid.

The strategic manager makes assumptions and judgments and reaches conclusions about both the internal and external environments based on perceptions of trends and opportunities. Strategic evaluation also includes reviewing these environments to ensure that these assumptions are still valid and that perceived trends are still in evidence. Most practitioners suggest that this review should be made as part of a recurring strategic planning cycle. Many firms utilize an annual planning cycle. Merchant (1982) studied and reported on planning cycles and on the control function of management.

In addition, it is recommended that new perspectives be added to this review effort by assigning strategic managers who did not participate in the original review. This strategic manager asks

1. What significant assumptions and judgments were reached about opportunities and threats in the external environment?
2. What conclusions were reached about strengths and weaknesses in the internal environment?
3. Are these assumptions, judgments, and conclusions still valid?

Contingency Planning. Recognizing the difficulty in accurately predicting strategic progress, many practitioners of strategy suggest that the original implementation plans, schedules, and budgets should be made on a contingency basis; the strategic manager should develop not one but several contingency plans. The importance of contingency planning is determined by the relative difficulty in predicting strategic progress. Contingency plans are also more appropriate over longer planning cycles. The harder it is to predict consumers' and competitors' moves, and the longer the term of the strategic plan, the more beneficial contingency planning will be.

Whether the strategic manager has one or a series of contingency implementation plans, it is clear that evaluating progress means redoing the strategy implementation phase of the strategic process. And verifying assumptions means redoing the strategy formulation phase of the strategic process. Thus, the strategic process is dynamic; the periodic evaluation of earlier strategic formulation and implementation sends messages that may restart the strategic process. Evaluation provides the feedback to the total system. Strategic feedback is the life force of the dynamic strategic process.

EXAMPLES: *Measurement*

AMF faltered when its strategic feedback collapsed. The oil boom that AMF counted on, which earned it operating revenues of $63 million in 1981, turned into an oil bust. In 1983 the energy services division lost $24 million. In an interview with *Business Week*, a former AMF manager said, ''The strategic planning was fine, but when the facts dictated that the thinking should change, it didn't.'' (8/12/85, p. 50).

One interesting variable in the strategic feedback and reporting system is the receptivity of the strategic manager. In reporting that Texas Instruments was ''Shot Full of Holes and Trying to Recover,'' *Business Week* (11/5/84, p. 82) explained that strategic feedback collapsed as the weight of ''the domineering styles of Chairman Mark Shepherd, Jr. and President J. Fred Bucy often intimidated product managers, who told them what they wanted to hear — not what was really going on. For example, neither learned of the home computer problems until the company was drowning in inventory.'' *Fortune* also commented on this phenomenon of strategic receptivity in ''No More Mickey Mouse at Disney'' (12/10/84, p. 57), describing Walt Disney's successor E. C. Walker as follows:

> *Subordinates feared Walker as a tyrant, quick to ridicule underlings in public and impervious to any point of view but his own. He made decisions according to what he thought Walt would have done. As a result the company steadily lost touch with modern taste, growing as hermetic as a religious sect or a communist cell. Executives clinched arguments by quoting Walt like Scripture or Marx, and the company eventually supplied a little book of the founder's sayings.*

Unfortunately, bad news often does not rise to the top. One task of the strategic manager is to ensure that the underlying spirit of the evaluation system is one that encourages the reporting of all news — bad and good. *Forbes* (3/26/84, p. 102) reported G.E. Chairman Welch's determination to tolerate mistakes and to report failures: ''To prove he means what he says, Welch has been loudly rewarding some near-misses. When a $20 million project was scrapped because of a change in the market, Welch promoted the manager and gave him a bonus.''

EXAMPLE: *Implementation and Corporate Culture*

A critical factor in the selection of these implementation options is not only the option itself but the degree of change between the proposed option and the existing implementation selection. Changing the system of performance measurement in an organization can produce shock waves; challenging or changing corporate culture can be especially difficult. *Fortune* reported on the difficulty in challenging corporate culture, especially in the case of Seiko, a firm with a corporate culture dating from 1881 (11/12/84, pp. 44–54). One grandson of Seiko founder Kintaro Hattori preferred to concentrate on the comfortable world of the watch industry. The other grandson, who preferred the challenges of high technology and computers, slowly tried to act as the general leading the firm into the diversification, high-tech battle, through internal ''prolonged combats of courtesies.''

Similarly, in describing the efforts of PPG's new chairman to cut costs, revitalize existing problem businesses, and expand the company, *Business Week* (11/12/84, p. 128) noted that ''his toughest job is ridding the company of its cautious culture. Traditionally, PPG has preferred studying moves rather than making them and penalizing risk-takers rather than rewarding them.''

One symptom of change in the corporate culture is executive turnover. Noting that twelve managers had left Hewlett-Packard in just six months, *Business Week* (11/5/84, p. 76) found the cause to be a change in marketing culture, from a ''technology-driven, engineering-oriented culture, in which decentralization and innovation were a religion and entrepreneurs were the gods.'' In the same issue, *Business Week* commented that eleven of thirty-four vice presidents had left Digital Equipment as the company sought to replace the ''rampant chaos'' of entrepreneurial individuals with a ''marketing-oriented, team spirit.''

SELECTION CRITERIA

Although many solutions exist to any implementation situation, two factors help the strategic manager choose among implementation alternatives. The first factor is distinctive competence, to ensure a fit between structure and strategy. The second factor is congruence.

Distinctive Competence

As shown in Figure 7.2, the strategic manager bases the formulated strategy on the firm's distinctive competence. Distinctive competence, as described in Chapter

FIGURE 7.2
Determinants of distinctive competence

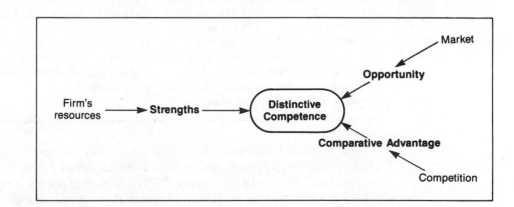

4, matches the firm's strength with both a market need, which represents an opportunity for the firm, and with a comparative advantage over competition, which represents a relative advantage of the firm compared to competition.

The manager selects implementation alternatives that will support and strengthen the distinctive competence and thus will ensure that structure fits strategy. The manager selects implementation alternatives that build upon the firm's strength, seize the market opportunity, and capitalize on the firm's comparative advantage. If a firm has a distinctive competence in high technology, for example (as is true in the U.S. large computer industry), it will select organization structures and control systems that encourage innovation and research. Its measurement and reward systems will provide incentives for engineering breakthroughs. This firm's corporate culture will include professionalism and a respect for science.

Congruence

Jay Galbraith (1977), building upon the major foundation of Lorsch and Morse (1974), showed that a firm needs congruence between (1) structure, (2) people, (3) rewards, and (4) information and decision processes in order to implement strategy successfully. Both Galbraith and Lorsch linked the degree of congruence to the level of the firm's performance.

The strategic manager considers the congruence or fit between each new implementation alternative being evaluated and those alternatives already selected. The law of congruence requires each alternative to be a part of the whole solution if it is to be successful. Galbraith (in Schendel and Hofer, 1979) argued, ''The firm should match its structure to its strategy, match all the components of the organization with one another, and match the strategy with the environment.''

WORKING CONCEPT **23**

IMPLEMEN-TATION SELECTION MODEL

In implementing strategy, the strategic manager selects from a spectrum of alternatives: administrative structure, information, measurement, and compensation systems (see Figure 7.3). The first criterion each alternative must satisfy is that it be consistent with the distinctive competence; in other words, that it supports or strengthens that distinctive competence. Secondly, each alternative must be consistent with the others; in other words, there must be a fit between, or congruence among, the alternatives.

This selection model underscores the fact that strategy is an art. The model proposes two criteria, both of which are subjective. Decision rules and operating policies may give an impression of scientific management, but the objective scientist must yield to the subjective artist — that is, the strategic manager.

Galbraith (in Schendel and Hofer, 1979) stressed that ''congruence among organizational structure, processes, and systems is the important factor, not fit with the environment.'' Nonetheless, Galbraith (1977) also pointed out that time complicates matters: congruence must be balanced between the short run and the long run. He

FIGURE 7.3
Implementa-
tion selection model

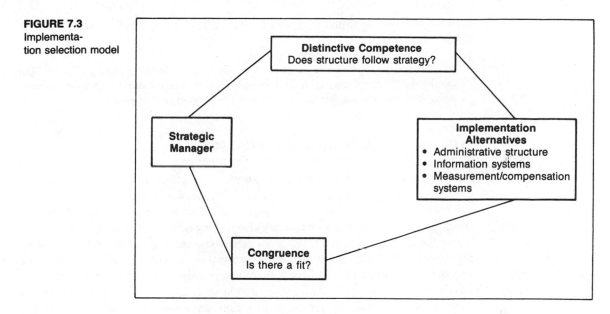

provided the illustration of excellent congruence in the Swiss watch industry, which was built to produce mechanical watches. This same strong short-run congruence, however, kept the Swiss manufacturers from switching to electronic watch technology.

Competition is also an important variable in congruence. Galbraith noted that the degree of congruence becomes increasingly important as the degree of competition increases. At the extreme, the monopolistic firm's performance may vary little with changes in congruence. Galbraith concluded, "Only under competitive conditions does a mismatch between strategy and structure lead to ineffective performance."

In summary, although many solutions exist to each implementation situation, the manager answers two questions: (1) Does this alternative support my distinctive competence? and (2) Is this alternative congruent with my structure, systems, and decision processes?

DIFFICULTIES IN
IMPLEMENTING STRATEGY

Implementing strategy and managing change is difficult at best. Not only do a multiplicity of solutions exist, but the strategic manager also confronts the natural resistance to change. Machiavelli warned the Prince that "there is nothing more difficult and dangerous, or more doubtful of success, than an attempt to introduce a new order of things . . . enemies [are] all those who derived advantages from the old order of things, while those who expect to be benefited by the new institutions will be but lukewarm defenders."

Business Week (8/19/85, p. 35) described the implementation difficulties that surrounded Beatrice, whose management ranks were "decimated" as it tried to recover from the "headstrong" James L. Dutt, who "systematically berated" executives:

> *"The longer you got with a guy like Dutt, the longer it takes to solve problems"* [*an analyst said*]. *The photos of Dutt that once hung in every Beatrice office are already being removed. But the imprint of his tenure won't be so easy to erase.*

IMPLEMENTATION AND STRATEGIC LEVELS

The implementation of strategy flows from and is determined by the formulation of strategy, which is in turn shaped by the opportunities and threats of the external environment, the distinctive competences of the internal environment, and purpose (mission). A well-implemented strategy also will include specific strategic objectives.

As the strategic manager determines objectives and implements strategy, he or she also will have reviewed the seven dimensions of managerial action that the management consultants McKinsey & Company call the *Seven S model*: Strategy, Structure, Systems, Skills, Staff, Style, and Shared values. In strategic implementation, the seven dimensions of managerial action are common to all levels of strategy. The corporate strategist might spend more time on strategy and structure, and the functional strategist more time on skills; still, the seven dimensions and the implementation activity are a critical part of levels of strategy. Since an ideal organization design and rules for matching structure to strategy do not exist, implementation offers a great deal of opportunity for creativity on the part of all strategic managers.

AN IMPLEMENTATION ILLUSTRATION

The issues confronting the university-owned bookstore were presented in Appendix C to Chapter 2. The decades-old monopoly of the University of New Hampshire (U.N.H.) bookstore had been ended by the competition for the student book market instituted by local stores.

The economics of the situation were that (1) the U.N.H. bookstore was an auxiliary enterprise under state law, which meant any surplus could only be reinvested in the specific enterprise, i.e., the bookstore and (2) the profit and cash flow, each averaging about $50,000, had changed to a loss of $75,000 and a cash drain of about $100,000. The bookstore manager, John Maier, had been trying to build business by offering more trade books and soft goods and by advertising to the general public. Some cost control measures had been taken, including eliminating eight clerical employees.

A gubernatorial efficiency commission had made many recommendations to the university, including leasing the bookstore to a private operator. The bookstore manager and staff responded through a public relations campaign directed at trustees, students, faculty, university administration, and the media, emphasizing the lack of service that leasing to an independent operator would mean.

The case analysis in Appendix D of Chapter 2 suggests that different levels of strategic perspective can be used in analyzing this case. From the corporate-level, the U.N.H. president felt that leasing for "real" dollars (i.e., dollars that can be used outside of the bookstore), was preferable to deficit operations, and to a bookstore staff that is vocal in the media. The "collegiality" objective of the university, however, should not conflict with any presidential actions.

From the point of view of the business level, John Maier needed to shift from a service objective to a profit objective, while maintaining or increasing support from within the university "family" of trustees, administration, faculty, and students. The administration's support was critical; the "captive" student market was also significant.

At a functional level within the bookstore, such as that of the employee in charge of soft goods, the functional strategy needed to support the store's profit objective. The functional employee would seek to increase efficiency and to generate new business.

The following text outlines specific steps that might serve to implement strategy.

Corporate Strategy

The corporate strategy (embodied by the U.N.H. president) might require conversion to an independent, private bookstore lease while maximizing consensus and minimizing resistance to "top down" management.

Administrative Structure. Delegate discussion and the generation of recommendations (but not final decisions) to an ad-hoc committee of trustees, faculty, students, and administration. Administration representatives should be well-respected, forceful individuals.

Information and Culture. Provide the committee with a brief but dramatic overview of the "big picture" — the university's commitment to education, along with its limited resources and alternative priorities (health care, residences, computer systems, and library). Create a culture that promotes university-wide perspective and the university family as a whole, not isolated (problem) areas such as the bookstore.

Procedures. Push for early resolution, with the decision announcement made when classes are not in session to minimize adverse reaction. Contribute a portion of the lease income to "Motherhood and Apple Pie" use, such as the acquisition of new library materials.

Business Strategy

The business strategy (embodied by the bookstore manager) might require support within the administration, not as controversial agent but as one trying to support education by means of service (special book orders and out-of-print services, streamlined semester start-up procedures, other university textbook lists for faculty), and, if possible, by pointing out problems at other leased locations for other schools. The business strategy will stress trying to "buy time" in order to reverse profitless operations, stressing the need for a longer-term view and the development of managerial abilities.

Administrative Structure. Streamlining the organization is necessary during this "survival" period; a hierarchy is essential to this process. A functional (soft goods versus school textbooks versus popular textbooks versus operations) structure must give way to efficiency and overlapping responsibilities.

Information and Culture. The trustees and administrators must not be viewed as "the enemy"; the manager must disseminate information down through the organization about administrative achievements regarding the main objective, education. All information from the bookstore to the outside, including the media, must come through the manager. The manager should stress the "big family" and "big picture" as part of the bookstore culture. Operating results should highlight the profit centers and problem centers.

Procedures. Rather than being a part of the problem by attacking the power structure, the manager should try to use the distinctive competence — the tie-in to the student body. Campaigns such as "Save the Bookstore" and "Show Your Loyalty" should stress patronizing the bookstore — rather than local competition — because "it's our store." A student committee might investigate making the store a student cooperative, especially if co-op fees can be directed to the university, not just to the bookstore.

Functional Strategy

The functional strategy (embodied by the soft goods manager) might require increasing efficiency through better resource utilization and decreased costs, postponing all nonessential expenditures, and generating new revenue.

Administrative Structure. Part-time and work-study students presumably will be less expensive to hire, although the functional manager then must make employee supervision and responsibility levels (approvals, controls) part of the structure.

Information and Culture. Operating statements should stress the areas of revenue and expense that the functional employee can influence and control. Competition between functions should be minimized, however, and cooperation stressed.

Procedures. Techniques to increase the number of purchases per visit should be developed, including traditional tactics such as loss leaders, suggestion selling, and merchandise layout to encourage impulse buying. Areas of major student purchases (music, fads, and games) should be offered. Pricing of identical items must be competitive.

STRATEGY IMPLEMENTATION RESEARCH

While Machiavelli and other political theorists have given advice and prescribed actions for implementing strategy, the classic research in implementation includes studies by the following authors.

Lorsch and Lawrence (1972), in *Organizational Planning* and elsewhere, studied the degree of specialization or differentiation within the organization's structure and systems. The greater the differentiation, the greater the need for integration by the strategic manager. Further, the degree of differentiation was caused by and followed from the degree of uncertainty in the environment. The more environmental uncertainty existed, the more the strategist would need differentiated structure and systems.

Other researchers include **Galbraith,** whose *Organization Design* (1977) continued Lorsch's work and stressed the importance of congruence. **Thompson** (1967) described organization's responses to domains that were either competitive — built on distinctive competence — or concentrated — gaining power from sources. **Burns and Stalker** (1961) identified "organic" structures appropriate for high rates of change, and "mechanistic" structures suitable for stable markets.

Current significant research projects in implementation include works by the following authors.

Alexander (1985), in surveying ninety-three firms, found that the ten most frequently encountered implementation problems were (1) more time to implement than allocated, (2) unanticipated major problems, (3) ineffective activity coordination, (4) attention distracted by competing or crisis activities, (5) insufficient employee capabilities, (6) inadequate training and instruction to lower levels, (7) uncontrollable external factors, (8) inadequate departmental manager leadership, (9) poorly defined implementation steps, and (10) inadequate monitor information system. Alexander urged that the good implementation idea be supported by detailed planning, adequate communication, sufficient resource support, and employee commitment to the idea.

Argyris (1982) described ways of changing managerial systems and styles from a "win/lose single-loop" model to a "win/win double-loop" model. These suggestions included switching from advocacy to inquiry and public testing, and switching from unilateral face-saving to learning situations. The consequences of such a switch would be more "effective problem solving" and less "self-dealing, error escalating processes."

Bower (1970), after studying strategy planning for three years in a large firm, made two conclusions. (1) Structure may determine strategy, in that the organization's structure (hierarchies, systems) determines what projects will be studied and how they will be studied. (2) Bargaining and persuasion are an important part of both project definition and project implementation.

Collier (1984) described eight strategic principles of implementation: (1) the chief executive officer commitment, (2) proper strategic management organization, (3) credible strategic plans, (4) functional action plans supporting the strategy, (5) realistic and goal-supporting resource allocations, (6) strategy-compatible organizational culture and manager psychology, (7) effective monitoring and early-warning system, and (8) rewards for operating managers for implementation success.

Heany and Vinson (1984) used the strategy-technology connection as a central part of their study of new product development. They concluded that the difficulty of linking business goals and technical goals was a major contributor to product innovation problems. Strategy formulation and implementation should improve communication and encourage initiative and responsibility so that the general manager and the new product staff can combine business and technical goals.

Hirschleim (1983), in researching information and control systems, concluded that the data base was a ''neglected corporate resource'' important to strategic planning. Hirschleim described ways in which strategic managers could use the data base.

Horovitz (1984), searching for new perspectives on strategic management, reported on an intellectual and a social process in strategy implementation and strategy formulation. The intellectual process of implementation is the ''fitted management design'' wherein organization structure and information and control systems are designed rationally. The social process of implementation is ''people activation,'' wherein the strategist gains commitment from others.

Huber and Power (1985) studied accuracy in strategic reports. They presented ''guidelines for increasing . . . accuracy'' in ''retrospective reports of strategic level managers.''

Jaeger and Baliga (1985) studied the Japanese experience with control systems and strategic adaptation. They analyzed the potential strategic costs and benefits of culture (Japanese) versus formal/bureaucratic (traditional American) control systems. They concluded that an ideal situation would be a ''swing back and forth as necessary between bureaucratic and cultural control systems.''

Kantrow (1980) stressed the importance of having the implementation structure encompass technology: ''Technology should be viewed as a central part of business thinking at all levels and not as a kind of a line phenomenon to be held at arm's length by all but R&D engineers.''

MacMillan and Jones (1984) studied ways of ''designing organizations to compete.'' They concluded that the strategic manager must answer seven questions to implement strategy:

1. What is the organization's strategy?
2. How will we know that the strategy has been accomplished?
3. How will the strategy affect competitors?
4. What major task groupings represent feasible design alternatives?
5. What linkages are necessary between groupings?
6. What support systems are needed?
7. What execution problems can be anticipated?

Mitroff and Kilmann (1975) showed how firms can recognize and take advantage of differing managerial perspectives on the ''ideal'' organization. They grouped managerial perspectives into four categories: (1) sensing-thinking, (2) sensing-feeling, (3) intuition-thinking, and (4) intuition-feeling.

Naylor (1985) studied the strategic process at General Motors and recommended implementation and planning with the acronym STRATEGY: S — Stick to it; T —

Think it through; R — Risk, responsibility, and reward; A — Awareness of self and competition; T — Talking to each other to communicate strategy; E — Evaluating each step; G — Growing your people; and Y — Yes-I-Can winning attitude.

Pearce (1983) studied financial measures of strategic performance, analyzing reporting orientation and reporting on "the relationship of internal versus external orientations to financial measures" of strategy.

Peters and Waterman (1982) identified forty-three "excellent" companies, and tried to evaluate the strategies that accounted for the excellence. Their "attributes" of excellent strategies included

1. Bias for action
2. Staying close to the customer
3. Autonomy and entrepreneurship
4. Simple form, lean staff
5. Stick to the knitting (staying with the distinctive competence)

Rockart and Scott Morton (1984), both M.I.T. researchers, stressed the need to consider information technology not only as a way of supporting business strategies but as a means of creating opportunities for new business strategy. Because data processing has become information technology — robotics, decision support systems, data bases, communications networks — technology should be driving management's processes. Information, after all, is power.

Rockart and Treacy (1982) focused on the CEO and information technology in their study of how "The CEO Goes On-Line."

Stopford and Wells expanded the stages of corporate development in their 1972 model, which included international divisions based upon a study of U.S. firms expanding abroad.

Vancil et al. studied strategic planning systems and performance for seventy-six companies from 1969 to 1972 (their series of planning studies was subsequently discontinued). Reports on this Formal Planning Systems Research Project at the Harvard Business School include "Setting Corporate Objectives" (Aguilar 1971) and "The Successful Use of Computer Models in Planning" (Hammond 1972).

EXECUTIVE COMMENTS

One of General Motor's most important characteristics [is] its effort to achieve open-minded communication and objective consideration of facts.

Alfred P. Sloan, Jr., *My Years with General Motors*

A good slogan can stop analysis for fifty years.

Wendell Wilkie

There isn't going to be any final analysis.

John DeLorean

KEY TERMS

administrative systems (page 176)

corporate culture (page 180)

differentiation and integration (page 177)

holistic measures (page 180)

implementation (page 175)

information systems (page 177)

matrix organizations (page 176)

performance evaluation and compensation (page 179)

strategic business units (SBUs) (page 177)

unidimensional measures (page 180)

BIBLIOGRAPHY

Alexander, L. D., "Successfully Implementing Strategy Decisions," *Long Range Planning* 18 (June 1985), pp. 91–97.

Argyris, C., "The Executive Mind and Double-Loop Learning," *Organizational Dynamics* (Autumn 1982), pp. 5–22.

Bariff, M. L., and J. R. Galbraith, "Interorganizational Power Considerations for Designing Information Systems," *Accounting, Organizations and Society* 3 (February 1978), pp. 15–27.

Bettis, R., and C. K. Prahalad, "The Visible and the Invisible Hand: Resource Allocation in the Industrial Sector," *Strategic Management Journal* (January–March 1983).

Blackburn, R. S., "Dimensions of Structure: A Review and Reappraisal," *Academy of Management Review*, vol. 7, no. 1 (1982), pp. 59–66.

Bourgeois, L. J., "Performance and Consensus," *Strategic Management Journal*, vol. 1 (July–September 1980), pp. 227–248.

Bower, J. L., *Managing the Resource Allocation Process*, Harvard Business School Research Division, 1970.

Branch, B., and B. Gale, "Linking Corporate Stock Price Performance to Strategy Formulation," *Journal of Business Strategy*, vol. 4, no. 1 (Summer 1983).

Brunswik, E., *Perception and the Representative Design of Psychological Experiments* (Berkeley, CA: University of California Press, 1956).

Burns, T., and G. M. Stalker, *The Management of Innovation* (London: Tavistock Publications, 1961).

Cameron, K., and D. Whetten, "Perceptions of Organizational Effectiveness and Organizational Life Cycles," *Administrative Science Quarterly* 26 (1981), pp. 525–544.

Caves, R. E., "Industrial Organization, Corporate Strategy, and Structure," *Journal of Economic Literature* (March 1980), pp. 64–92.

Chakravorthy, B., "Strategic Self-Renewal: A Planning Framework for Today," *Academy of Management Review* (July 1984).

Chandler, A. D., Jr., *Strategy and Structure* (Cambridge, MA: M.I.T. Press, 1962).

Christensen, C. R., et al., *Business Policy: Text and Cases* (Homewood, IL: Richard D. Irwin, 1987).

Christopher, W., "Achievement Reporting — Controlling Performance Against Objectives," *Long Range Planning* 10 (October 1977), pp. 14–24.

Collier, D., "How to Implement Strategic Plans," *Journal of Business Strategy* 4 (Winter 1984), pp. 92–96.

Daniels, J., B. Pitts, and M. Tretter, "Strategy and Structure of U.S. Multinationals: An Exploratory Study," *Academy of Management Journal* (June 1984).

Davis, S. M., and P. R. Lawrence, "Problems of Matrix Organizations," *Harvard Business Review* 56 (May–June 1978), pp. 131–142.

Drucker, P., *Management: Tasks, Responsibilities, and Practices* (New York: Harper & Row, 1974).

Dutton, J. E., L. Fahey, and V. K. Narayanan, "Toward Understanding Strategic Issue Diagnosis," *Strategic Management Journal* 4 (October–December 1983), pp. 307–323.

Galbraith, J. R., "Matrix Organizational Designs," *Business Horizons* 15 (February 1971), pp. 29–40.

Galbraith, J. R., *Organization Design* (Reading, MA: Addison-Wesley, 1977).

Galbraith, J. R., and D. Nathanson, *Strategy Implementation: The Role of Structure and Process* (St. Paul, MN: West Publishing, 1978).

Hall, W. K., "SBUs: Hot New Topic in the Management of Diversification," *Business Horizons* 21 (February 1978), pp. 17–25.

Heany, D. F., and W. D. Vinson, "A Fresh Look at New Product Development," *Journal of Business Strategy* (Fall 1984), pp. 21–31.

Herbert, T., "Strategy and Multinational Structure: An Interorganizational Relationships Perspective," *Academy of Management Review* (April 1984).

Hirschleim, R. A., "Data Base — A Neglected Corporate Resource?" *Long Range Planning* 16 (October 1983), pp. 79–88.

Hobbs, J., and D. Heany, "Coupling Strategy to Operating Plans," *Harvard Business Review* 55 (May–June 1977), pp. 119–126.

Horovitz, J., "New Perspectives in Strategic Management," *Journal of Business Strategy* 4 (Winter 1984), pp. 19–33.

Hrebiniak, L. G., and W. F. Joyce, *Implementing Strategy* (New York: MacMillan, 1984).

Huber, G. P., and D. J. Power, "Retrospective Reports of Strategic-Level Managers," *Strategic Management Journal* 6 (April–June 1985), pp. 171–180.

Jaeger, A. M., and B. R. Baliga, "Control Systems and Strategic Adaptation: Lessons from the Japanese Experience," *Strategic Management Journal* 6 (April–June 1985), pp. 115–134.

Jelinek, M., and M. C. Burstein, "The Production Administrative Structure: A Paradigm for Strategic Fit," *Academy of Management Review*, vol. 7, no. 2 (1982), pp. 242–252.

Kantrow, A. W., "The Strategy-Technology Connection," *Harvard Business Review* 58 (July–August 1980), pp. 6–21.

Kast, F., and J. Rosenzweig, *Organization and Management Systems and Contingency Approach* (New York: McGraw-Hill, 1979).

King, W. R., "Using Strategic Issue Analysis," *Long Range Planning* 15 (August 1982), pp. 45–49.

Knight, K., "Matrix Organization: A Review," in R. M. Miles, ed., *Resourcebook in Macro Organizational Behavior* (Glenview, IL: Scott, Foresman, 1980).

Lawrence, P. R., and J. W. Lorsch, *Organization and Environment* (Homewood, IL: Richard D. Irwin, 1967).

Leontiades, M., "Choosing the Right Manager to Fit the Strategy," *Journal of Business Strategy* 3 (Fall 1981), pp. 58–69.

Lorange, P., *Implementations of Strategic Planning* (Englewood Cliffs, NJ: Prentice-Hall, 1978).

Lorange, P., "Strategic Control," in Lamb, ed., *Latest Advances in Strategic Management* (Englewood Cliffs, NJ: Prentice-Hall, 1983).

Lorsch, J. W., and P. R. Lawrence, *Organizational Planning* (Homewood, IL: Richard D. Irwin, 1972).

Lorsch, J. W., and J. J. Morse, *Organizations and Their Members: A Contingency Approach* (New York: Harper & Row, 1974).

MacMillan, I. C., and P. E. Jones, "Designing Organizations to Compete," *Journal of Business Strategy* 4 (Spring 1984), pp. 11–26.

Merchant, K. A., "The Control Function of Management," *Sloan Management Review* 23 (Winter 1982), pp. 43–55.

Miles, R., and C. Snow, *Organizational Strategy, Structure and Process* (New York: McGraw-Hill, 1978).

Mintzberg, H., "Organization Design: Fashion or Fit?" *Harvard Business Review* 59:1 (January–February 1981), pp. 103–116.

Mintzberg, H., "Power and Organization Life Cycles," *Academy of Management Review* (April 1984).

Mitroff, I., and R. Kilmann, "Stories Managers Tell," *Management Review* (July 1975), pp. 18–28.

Naylor, M. E., "Regaining Your Competitive Edge," *Long Range Planning* 18 (February 1985), pp. 30–35.

Nutt, P. C., "Hybrid Planning Methods," *Academy of Management Review* 7:3 (July 1982), pp. 442–454.

Ouchi, W., "A Conceptual Framework for the Design of Organizational Control Mechanisms," *Management Science* 25:9 (September 1979), pp. 833–848.

Pascale, R. T., and A. G. Athos, *The Art of Japanese Management* (New York: Simon & Schuster, 1981).

Pearce, J. A., III, "The Relationship of Internal Versus External Orientations to Financial Measures of Strategic Performance," *Strategic Management Journal* 4 (October–December 1983), pp. 297–306.

Peters, T. J., and R. H. Waterman, Jr., *In Search of Excellence: Lessons from America's Best-Run Companies* (New York: Harper & Row, 1982).

Rockart, J. F., "Chief Executives Define Their Own Data Needs," *Harvard Business Review* 57 (March–April 1979), pp. 85–94.

Rockart, J. F., and M. S. Scott Morton, "Implications of Changes in Information Technology for Corporate Strategy," *Interfaces* 14 (January–February 1984), pp. 84–95.

Rockart, J. F., and M. E. Treacy, "The CEO Goes On-line," *Harvard Business Review* 60 (January–February 1982), pp. 82–88.

Rothschild, W. E., "How to Ensure the Continued Growth of Strategic Planning," *The Journal of Business Strategy*, vol. 1, no. 1 (Summer 1980).

Schoderbek, C., D. Schoderbek, and A. Kefalas, *Management Systems* (Dallas: Business Publications, 1980).

Sihler, W. H., "Toward Better Management Control Systems," *California Management Review* 14 (Winter 1971), pp. 33–39.

Sloan, Alfred P., Jr., *My Years with General Motors* (Garden City, NY: Doubleday, 1963).

Snow, C. C., and L. G. Hrebiniak, "Strategy, Distinctive Competence, and Organizational Performance," *Administrative Science Quarterly*, vol. 25 (June 1980), pp. 317–336.

Stopford, J., and L. Wells, *Managing the Multinational Enterprise* (London: Longmans, 1972).

Tichy, N. M., "Managing Change Strategically: The Technical, Political and Cultural Keys," *Organizational Dynamics* (Autumn 1982), pp. 59–80.

Tichy, N. M., C. J. Fombrum, and M. A. Devanna, "Strategic Human Resource Management," *Sloan Management Review* 23 (Winter 1982), pp. 47–61.

Tilles, S., "How to Evaluate Corporate Strategy," *Harvard Business Review* 41 (July–August 1963).

Vancil, R. F., "What Kind of Management Control Do We Need?" *Harvard Business Review* 51 (March–April 1973), pp. 75–86.

Vancil, R. F., et al., *Formal Planning Systems*, Division of Case Distribution, Harvard Business School, 1968, 1969, 1970, 1971.

APPENDIX: PERSONAL STRATEGY

But education is the hope of the world only in the sense that there is something better than bribery, lies, and violence for righting the world's wrongs. If this better thing is education, then education is not merely schooling. It is a lifelong discipline of the individual by himself.

Jacques Barzun, *Teacher in America*

Thus far you have studied strategy in terms of organizations. In this appendix you will be the strategic manager formulating a strategy for your personal life. You will study the external environment for personal opportunities and analyze your own strengths and weaknesses. To put things into a time period, this appendix is based on a five-year planning period for your personal life.

THE PERSONAL EXTERNAL ENVIRONMENT

Significant factors in your external environment include (1) markets, (2) competition, (3) technology, (4) society, and (5) government.

Markets

The market of most immediate concern to students is the employment market. In analyzing the employment market, you as the "organization's" strategic manager, must consider the various market segments. The reactive student will wait for the employment market to reveal opportunities through student placement announcements, employment advertisements, and family contacts. The proactive student, on the other hand, will examine the various employment segments, using some of the following categories.

Geography (cities versus towns, seacoasts versus mountains, heartland versus borders)

Function (accounting, marketing, production, finance, research, human resources, administration)

Responsibility level (entry, executive trainee, line or staff management)

Industry (high-tech, retail, service including financial or advertising, distribution, manufacturing, governmental, nonprofit including education)

Using a strategic point of view means that you study not only the existing characteristics of these employment segments, but also trends in these characteristics. What expectations do you have for these segments three and five years from now?

Finally, the student asks what purchase (employment) decision criteria are being used by employers in these segments. These criteria might include cost, appearance, education, work experience, references, availability, motivation, and personal interests.

Competition

What are the present and potential alternative sources for you as an employee? Your competition is not limited to other students; it includes inter- and intra-organization transfers, promotions, and reassignments. Depending on the function and industry, your present or future competition could include automation. And some futurists expect an increase in the amount of services subcontracted to independent organizations. Evidence of the rise of third-party service organizations can be seen in the number of third-party personal and small business computer maintenance organizations such as Xerox, Arrow Electronics, TRW, and Honeywell.

Technology

The personal strategist asks the following three questions.

1. What present technology underlies the different employment segments?
2. What is the expected future technology for these same segments?
3. What is the rate of technological change?

Just as in the business world, you probably will get more valuable assistance in answering these questions from knowledgeable experts rather than from statistics about past trends.

Society

The cultural values and expectations surrounding you can be described in terms of the expected and presumed amount of influence. These sources of influence include close friends; family members; and role models from school, work, or other experiences. As personal strategist, you will analyze the relationship between yourself — the strategist — and these values and influences.

Government

The student can be affected by governmental acts in many ways. You must analyze the present and future interactions between yourself and regional and federal governmental bodies, including

Military service
Source of financing
Employer
Regulator of employment
Influence in economy

For example, advanced study and graduate school may or may not be feasible for you, depending on the level of government support for higher education in terms of scholarships and loan guarantees. Administrative agencies of the government, including the Federal Trade Commission and the Agency for International Development (AID), employ graduates with business administration degrees. Most certainly, the level of employment demand concerns those responsible for influencing the economy through fiscal and monetary measures.

OPPORTUNITIES AND THREATS

After analyzing the external environment, the personal strategist next groups the identified positive and negative strategic signals into significant opportunities and threats. Opportunities might include such things as a major expansion by a local employer, a booming regional economy, or a national program of economic stimuli. Threats might encompass a population bulge in your age bracket, an increase in graduates with advanced degrees, or an increase in regional unemployment.

INTERNAL RESOURCES

Your resources include primarily intangible components, although you may have such tangible resources as investment capital or even production equipment. Your intangible resources include education, work experience, appearance, personality characteristics, and either personal or familial social and business contacts and relationships.

The personal strategist, recalling the earlier analysis of competition that comprised the assessment of the competitive factor in the external environment, prepares a strategic profile of personal strengths and weaknesses. Using this profile, the personal strategist next develops a distinctive competence.

What is it that distinguishes you from classmates and other competitors for employment positions? By answering this question you can determine your distinctive competence. Note that the concept of distinctive competence does not imply that you are the *only* one who has this or that strength or resource, just that it is an important strategic strength or resource. Keep in mind that your competitors also may share your strengths. Remember that strengths and resources include your planned future as well as existing present factors. Excellent communication skills might result in a future distinctive competence of high visibility and favorable attitudes with your employer and supervisors.

You also can use the life cycle model to suggest which strengths and weaknesses are especially critical. While desired strengths and competencies will vary from one employer to another, some strengths are particularly appropriate for various stages of your career. The ability to learn quickly can be presumed to be more important at earlier stages of your life than leadership capability, while the reverse may be true as your career progresses. Social relationships and verbal communication might be more important at intermediate stages of your career, while analytical skills might carry more importance early on in your business life.

PURPOSE

Just as the enterprise has a series of increasingly individualistic components of purpose, ranging from social goals to organizational priorities to personal values, the student also must review a spectrum of personal considerations. This spectrum includes physical, sensual, and material goals; mental and emotional values; and psychological and spiritual priorities.

The personal strategist must not only identify and define all the elements of personal purpose, but must recognize that

The spectrum is a mix of objectives and goals which may be competing or complementary.

Personal purpose is a guide to a general direction in life, but external environment factors and other circumstances can cause short-term courses of action that veer off from the desired target.

Changes do occur in either the relative weight assigned to various factors, or in the goals and priorities themselves.

Some priorities and goals are short term and others longer term. Some things, such as material rewards, may seem more important in one stage of life than in another. One relatively constant factor, responsibility to society, may be as difficult to define for an individual as it is to determine for the organization.

Clearly, determining and defining personal purpose is as subjective a task as is the definition of organizational purpose. Both tasks are limited and influenced by the internal and external environments. Put another way, some elements of purpose are adopted in response to other factors, and some elements are intrinsic.

STRATEGY FORMULATION

Personal strategy formulation, like its organizational counterpart, is easy to describe as a process yet difficult to perform. Simply put, the personal strategist uses personal purpose as the criterion for selecting opportunities for which he or she has a distinctive competence. In other words, what do you want to achieve? Which career opportunities, within the set of opportunities for which you have a present or a planned competence, will allow you to achieve your goals?

Many tools of the strategic manager, such as competitive response analysis, risk, synergy, and consistency assessment, also can help the personal strategist. Analyzing competitive response consists of considering people's future responses, which in turn depends on the nature of your competition. How competitive are (1) the current situation, (2) the power of suppliers and customers, (3) the threat of entry, and (4) the threat of substitutes? The personal strategist considers (1) the difficulty in obtaining a position, (2) the relative power of employee providers and of those offering employment, (3) the easiness of entry into a field, and (4) the employment alternatives and substitutes. This four-point review enables the strategist to determine the degree to which personal purpose must accommodate competitive realities. What compromises will your competition force you to make?

Risk assessment is an additional personal strategy tool. The spectrum ranges from high-security employment opportunities to high-risk positions. The decision about where to position yourself within that risk-security spectrum should be based upon your personal purpose.

Where does opportunity for synergy exist? What employment opportunity will provide you with a desired future competence, or will allow you to overcome a personal weakness while attaining other goals and objectives? How will your particular skills mesh with an employers' needs, products, or services so that the output of the whole is greater than the total output of the sum of each part?

The personal strategist asks if the formulated strategy is internally consistent — Is it free from internal contradictions and conflicts? — and if it is consistent with opportunities, personal purpose, and individual competence. Examples of possible conflicts and inconsistencies include

A job's travel requirement versus obligations to one's family

Learning objectives versus immediate income

Physical conditioning goals versus social entertaining job requirements

In formulating a strategy for the next five years, the personal strategist determines and then performs the specific steps required to carry out the formulated strategy. These specific steps and strategic objectives are the detailed plans to attain the formulated strategy. These plans should anticipate all major alternatives, provide decision criteria to use in making the choice between alternatives, and include schedules and timetables.

IMPLEMENTATION EXAMPLES

The personal strategist formulates a strategy of hard work in the investments field in order to become financially self-sufficient by age thirty-five, at which time the strategist might focus on such goals as raising a family and pursuing psychological growth. In implementing this plan, the strategist applies for a training program with most major securities brokers, and defines detailed contingency plans and criteria in the event (1) that no broker has a place in a training program; (2) that no broker offers a post-training position; and (3) that small regional brokers or banks must be sought out as employers.

In the final implementation phase of the strategic process, you must measure performance, asking (1) Am I progressing as planned? and (2) Are my original assumptions and conclusions still valid? Strategic evaluation is always subjective, so personal strategy evaluation is especially subjective. It is very difficult to measure subjective personal goals, such as the degree to which a job is challenging or whether or not you are happy. Nonetheless, the more advance planning you can do about how you will measure challenges or happiness, the more effective your evaluation will be.

Inherent resistance to change is a hindrance to accurate personal self-evaluation. Fear of the unknown and a lack of initiative may lull you into accepting lower and lower definitions and measures of such subjective things as challenges and happiness. Defining measures in advance provides one safeguard against lowering your standards.

You also need to step back and reassess the analysis of and conclusions about external opportunities, internal resources, and personal purpose. Have subsequent events supported or contradicted your judgments? Strategy is dynamic; periodically evaluating and updating your formulated strategy is an important aspect of the strategic process. You do know for certain that the external environment will change, and that your resources and personal objectives will grow and evolve.

OPTIONAL PERSONAL STRATEGY ASSIGNMENT

Write a paper applying the strategic process to the next five years of your life. Since the grade will be given based solely on your ability to apply the strategic process, and not upon the actual content of the strategy you determine, you may choose to make your paper as impersonal or as personal as you like. You can describe a fictitious person in your paper and make it nonpersonal. On the other hand, the paper may be a more worthwhile learning experience for you if you consider personal objectives.

It also might be easier for you to structure your paper beginning with objectives, so that you can then review a much more narrow external environment. If you start with the external environment, you may spend time on alternatives (graduate school, ski bum) that you may be able to eliminate through your personal objectives.

EXECUTIVE COMMENTS

I do not believe that I am going too far when I say that modern man, in contrast to his nineteenth-century brother, turns his attention to the psyche with very great expectations. . . . To me, the cause of the spiritual problem of today is to be found in the fascination which psychic life exerts upon modern man. If we are pessimists, we shall call it a sign of decadence; if we are optimistically inclined, we shall see in it the promise of a far-reaching spiritual change in the Western world.

    Carl Jung, *Modern Man in Search of a Soul*

And the Quality, the arete he has fought so hard for, has sacrificed for, has never betrayed, but in all that time has never once understood, now makes itself clear to him and his soul is at rest.

    Robert M. Pirsig, *Zen and the Art of Motorcycle Maintenance*

This, then, is held to be the duty of the man of wealth: First, to set an example of modest, unostentatious living, shunning display or extravagance; to provide moderately for the legitimate wants of those dependent upon him; and, after doing so to consider all surplus revenues which come to him simply as trust funds which he is called upon to administer . . . the man of wealth thus becoming the mere agent and trustee for his poorer brethren.

    Andrew Carnegie

In our era, the road to holiness necessarily passes through the world of action.

    Dag Hammarskjöld

The human race has had long experiences and a fine tradition in surviving adversity. But now we face a task for which we have little experience, the task of surviving prosperity.

    Alan Gregg of the Rockefeller Foundation

For a long time they looked at the river beneath them, saying nothing, and the river said nothing, too, for it felt very quiet and peaceful on this summer afternoon.
"Tigger is alright really," said piglet lazily.
"Of course he is," said Christopher Robin.
"Everybody is really," said Pooh. "That's what I think," said Pooh. "But I don't suppose I'm right," he said.
"Of course you are," said Christopher Robin.

    A. A. Milne, *Winnie-the-Pooh*

If A = success, then the formula is A = X + Y + Z. X is work, Y is play, Z is keep your mouth shut.

Albert Einstein

BIBLIOGRAPHY

Baba Ram Dass, *Be Here Now* (San Cristobal, NM: Lama Foundation, 1971).

Berne, E., *Games People Play* (New York: Grove Press, 1967).

Bolen, J. S., *Goddesses in Everywoman* (New York: Harper & Row, 1984).

de Chardin, Teilhard, *The Future of Man* (New York: Harper & Row, 1964).

Tillich, P., *The Courage To Be* (New Haven, CT: Yale University Press, 1952).

Wilber, K., *The Atman Project* (Wheaton, IL: Theosophical Publishing House, 1980).

PART II

CASES IN
STRATEGIC MANAGEMENT

ARMBRUSTERS AT BLACKSTONE

Mr. William (Bill) Armbruster, owner and manager of Armbrusters at Blackstone, and his wife Betty were having mixed emotions in the early spring of 1986 as they reviewed the financial results of fiscal 1985, their first full year of operations, in Blackstone, Virginia. (See Exhibit 1, 1985 Income Statement by Month; Exhibit 2, Balance Sheet, December 31, 1985; and Exhibit 3, Income Statement, December 31, 1985, 1984.) A total sales of $193,911.58 had resulted in a $5,302.22 net loss for the year. They could see some notable achievements and some things which they felt urgently needed improvement.

EARLY HISTORY

Bill Armbruster, age fifty-one, was in the restaurant business because he wanted to be. Early on during college days he had tried the business and liked it. Now, after a 26-year career in the Navy and being retired with the rank of captain, he was giving it a try. Betty, while not as drawn to the business as her husband, was nonetheless totally involved with it. She had been born in Blackstone and educated there. Although Bill's career had taken them to many places within and outside of the United States, they had agreed to return to Blackstone when he retired because that was where they wanted to be. They had had their eyes on the two houses now occupied by their doll museum and restaurant for several years prior to purchasing them.

Armbrusters had begun operation with an open house on October 10, 1984 in a building where a restaurant had previously failed to achieve a profitable volume of business. Despite this bad omen, the Armbrusters had had the courage to follow an unsuccessful operation because they believed they could avoid the problems it had encountered. One of these was the limited kitchen space which simply had not been adequate to prepare food in sufficient volume. Prior to opening, Bill had

EXHIBIT 1 Armbrusters at Blackstone, income statement, 1985 (by month)

	Month ended 1/31/85	Month ended 2/28/85	Month ended 3/31/85	Month ended 4/30/85	Month ended 5/31/85	Month ended 6/30/85	Month ended 7/31/85	Month ended 8/31/85	Month ended 9/30/85	Month ended 10/31/85	Month ended 11/30/85	Month ended 12/31/85
Sales												
Food	$7,628.67	$7,594.89	$ 9,940.29	$11,764.38	$15,270.38	$16,096.59	$18,719.93	$27,761.08	$14,571.06	$14,342.20	$14,464.73	$16,534.22
Liquor	480.25	329.25	631.25	474.25	1,029.25	917.25	1,358.85	2,079.00	835.75	528.75	678.80	1,371.00
Beer	66.75	31.00	99.50	61.50	119.00	206.75	194.50	194.75	194.75	80.25	109.50	63.50
Wine	303.00	326.75	612.75	419.36	588.03	580.50	703.75	1,429.25	386.00	432.25	490.25	532.25
Total	$8,478.67	$8,281.89	$11,283.78	$12,719.49	$17,006.29	$17,801.09	$20,977.03	$31,747.08	$15,987.56	$15,383.45	$15,744.28	$18,500.97
Food costs												
Food	$2,914.40	$3,101.70	$3,695.02	$5,075.42	$4,341.20	$5,426.75	$ 7,133.27	$ 8,129.65	$ 7,109.41	$ 5,307.55	$ 5,288.24	$ 6,117.02
Liquor	78.00	138.70	140.60	113.95	251.40	99.75	236.45	332.25	278.55	0.00	109.40	(103.85)
Beer	71.05	20.25	51.95	36.60	46.80	107.75	92.95	246.65	67.30	31.55	31.55	25.85
Wine	229.38	117.64	265.19	195.64	287.18	295.18	396.54	583.03	146.24	443.00	347.85	(367.00)
Total	$3,292.83	$3,378.29	$ 4,152.76	$ 5,421.61	$ 4,926.58	$ 5,929.43	$ 7,959.21	$ 9,291.58	$ 7,601.50	$ 5,782.10	$ 5,777.04	$ 5,672.02
Gross profit	$5,185.84	$4,903.60	$7,131.02	$ 7,297.88	$12,079.71	$11,871.66	$13,117.82	$22,455.50	$ 8,386.06	$ 9,601.35	$ 9,967.24	$12,828.95
Other expenses												
Salaries & wages	$2,604.28	$3,010.87	$ 4507.85	$ 3,522.46	$ 3,418.04	$ 3,880.41	$ 3,986.07	$ 8,589.91	$ 4,419.89	$ 4,192.53	$ 4,033.98	$12,996.79
Travel	0.00	0.00	0.00	0.00	0.00	0.00	0.00	0.00	0.00	0.00	0.00	1,544.00
Rent	67.55	67.55	135.10	67.55	67.55	67.55	67.55	67.55	67.55	94.49	67.55	67.55
Linen	222.84	191.16	224.71	293.27	237.25	240.52	287.26	235.99	231.08	412.30	241.95	304.21
Supplies	62.79	528.53	306.14	510.83	179.27	362.15	430.21	48.42	354.97	904.37	96.78	301.99
Utilities	766.67	585.81	1,126.08	546.40	711.21	643.15	453.53	675.16	742.31	768.00	506.84	562.34
Telephone	230.37	0.00	242.26	142.29	114.84	119.63	136.89	112.59	128.25	119.10	142.85	133.61
Taxes	864.23	702.32	330.10	1,286.12	1,037.04	615.74	2,234.42	700.00	815.00	3,395.72	1,645.28	(7,230.05)
Replacements	130.40	148.51	26.00	0.00	0.00	44.20	79.30	0.00	24.23	0.00	0.00	150.00
Repairs & maintenance	508.95	53.51	74.62	32.60	0.00	104.68	235.00	118.98	482.63	126.20	25.00	52.25
Advertising	190.40	15.00	30.00	118.22	175.56	10.00	0.00	0.00	116.00	140.40	75.00	232.71
Legal & professional	0.00	0.00	0.00	800.00	0.00	90.00	250.00	0.00	0.00	0.00	0.00	0.00
Dues & subscriptions	0.00	0.00	0.00	0.00	60.00	0.00	0.00	0.00	0.00	0.00	0.00	0.00
Interest	523.56	0.00	0.00	0.00	0.00	0.00	523.56	0.00	0.00	529.31	0.00	15,692.37
Employee discounts	1.88	7.95	24.47	17.54	17.33	9.39	11.99	18.33	11.03		3.00	4.25
Miscellaneous	319.16	90.10	(53.00)	0.00	0.00	111.00	58.05	137.27	(36.46)	67.52	17.00	473.68
Credits	57.81	20.02	33.04	51.72	35.19	237.56	49.01	116.92	308.29	(87.66)	99.38	220.06
Over/short	16.66	24.92	22.37	(7.60)	0.78	22.60	48.75	15.61	17.13	(0.72)	(48.41)	(14.11)
Wages—other	0.00	0.00	100.00	50.00	0.00	0.00	0.00	50.00	50.00	0.00	50.00	0.00
Insurance	0.00	0.00	600.00	1,200.00	0.00	1,076.00	0.00	0.00	0.00	0.00	0.00	1,593.00
Bank charges	71.38	46.47	121.69	76.75	154.34	5.39	94.94	143.47	287.74	188.90	104.40	151.85
Depreciation	0.00	0.00	0.00	0.00	0.00	0.00	0.00	0.00	0.00	0.00	0.00	14,500.00
Dining Club	0.00	0.00	0.00	0.00	0.00	0.00	12.30	25.70	65.64	35.12	24.75	24.65
Total	$6,638.93	$5,482.72	$ 7,851.43	$ 8,708.15	$ 6,208.40	$ 7,639.97	$ 8,958.83	$11,056.72	$ 8,102.47	$10,896.71	$ 7,085.37	$41,761.15
Total other income	0.00	0.00	0.00	23.72	0.00	133.12	0.00	283.59	0.00	0.00	47.30	57.26
Net operating income (loss)	($1,453.09)	($ 579.12)	($ 720.41)	($ 1,386.55)	$ 5,871.31	$ 4,364.81	$ 4,158.99	$11,398.78	$ 283.59	($ 1,295.36)	$ 2,929.17	($28,874.94)

EXHIBIT 2 Armbrusters at Blackstone, balance sheet, December 31, 1985

Assets			Liabilities and proprietor's capital	
Cash				
Bank	$ 8,723.00		Sales tax payable	$ 720.00
Register	128.00	$ 8,851.00		
Deposits		$ 1,203.00		
Inventory		1,990.00	Notes payable	$150,510.00
Property and equipment				
Building	$ 24,683.00		Proprietor's capital ($31,861.00)	
Building improvements	59,686.00			
Equipment	37,314.00			
Automobile (personal)	13,158.00			
	$134,841.00			
Less accumulated depreciation	(27,516.00)	107,325.00		
			Total liabilities and	
Total assets		$119,369.00	proprietor's capital	$119,369.00

a new, larger wing added to the building after having the old kitchen removed. The new kitchen was equipped with all of the cooking, baking, and crockery-handling equipment needed to support the volume of business they calculated was needed to provide an adequate cash flow. Well-cooked, consistent-quality meals were their prime consideration. Only fresh meats and vegetables cooked for the meal were served.

They anticipated two kinds of restaurant business. The primary customer would come to the restaurant for lunch or dinner, hopefully, on a repeat basis. Table seating from two to six persons were provided in four downstairs rooms. There would also be parties: birthday, retirement, christenings, holidays, and whatever else, served on the second floor, in a separate banquet room which provided tables for large groups. Betty Armbruster was optimistic that they could build both types of clientele because, as she explained, "There are lots of places to eat in Blackstone, but there is nowhere to dine." Armbrusters was to have the atmosphere and the menu that would qualify it as a place to *dine* rather than be just another place to eat.*

THE DOLL MUSEUM AND RESTAURANT BUILDINGS

In addition to the restaurant itself, there is a doll museum, housed in a separate building next door, run by Bill's mother, Mrs. Margaret Armbruster. Now eighty-two years old but still active and outgoing, she had been collecting dolls for several decades and had an outstanding collection. The doll museum, which had been

* See note at the bottom of p. 210.

EXHIBIT 3 Income statement, December 31, 1985, 1984

	For the year ended 12/31/85	Percent of total sales	Food cost %	For the 3 months ended 12/31/84	Percent of total sales	Food cost %
Sales						
Food	$174,688.04	90.09%		$31,598.84	90.02%	
Liquor	10,714.65	5.53%		2,111.23	6.01%	
Beer	1,704.75	0.88%		252.86	0.72%	
Wine	6,804.14	3.51%		1,139.94	3.25%	
	$193,911.58	100.01%		$35,102.87	100.00%	
Food costs	$ 63,639.63	32.82%	36.43%	$14,580.58	41.54%	46.14%
Food	1,675.20	0.86%	15.63%	1,180.14	3.36%	55.90%
Liquor	830.25	0.43%	48.70%	138.40	0.39%	54.73%
Beer	2,939.87	1.52%	43.21%	816.29	2.33%	71.61%
	$ 69,084.95	35.63%		$16,715.41	47.62%	
Gross profit	$124,826.63	64.38%		$18,387.46	52.38%	
Other income	$ 261.40	0.13%			0.00%	
Other expenses						
Salaries and Wages	$ 59,463.08	30.67%		$12,246.02	34.89%	
Depreciation	14,500.00	7.48%		8,141.00	23.19%	
Equipment Rental	905.09	0.47%		67.55	0.19%	
Linen	3,122.64	1.61%		975.25	2.78%	
Supplies	4,086.35	2.11%		1,567.14	4.46%	
Utilities	8,087.50	4.17%		1,014.34	2.89%	
Telephone	1,622.68	0.84%		366.08	1.04%	
Taxes	5,820.92	3.00%		806.25	2.30%	
Licenses	575.00	0.30%		540.00	1.54%	
Repairs & maintenance	1,814.42	0.94%		1,847.09	5.26%	
Insurance	4,469.00	2.30%		0.00	0.00%	
Advertising	1,291.45	0.67%		935.75	2.67%	
Travel	1,544.00	0.80%		865.00	2.46%	
Legal & professional	1,050.00	0.54%		544.55	1.55%	
Dues & subscriptions	150.00	0.08%		30.00	0.09%	
Interest	17,268.80	8.91%		7,718.17	21.99%	
Replacements	602.64	0.31%		0.00	0.00%	
Employee discounts	146.31	0.08%		29.59	0.08%	
Miscellaneous	1,149.32	0.59%		976.02	2.78%	
Credits	1,141.33	0.59%		247.61	0.71%	
Contributions	25.00	0.01%		0.00	0.00%	
Bank charges	1,447.34	0.75%		117.76	0.34%	
Over/short	107.98	0.06%		77.06	0.22%	
Total other expenses	130,390.85	67.28%		39,112.23	111.43%	
Net income (loss)	($ 5,302.82)	−2.77%		($20,724.77)	−59.05%	

The Blackstone Chamber of Commerce Business Directory for 1986–87 listed six restaurants: Armbrusters at Blackstone, Traditional Fine Southern Dining; Blackstone Restaurant, Try Blackstone's Favorite Eating Place; Brother's Pizza Restaurant, New York Style Italian Restaurant; Dairy Freeze, Fresh All-Beef Hamburger; Slaw's Restaurant, Restaurant & Sporting paraphernalia; and Sullivan's Restaurant and Tavern, Steaks, Seafood, and Mixed Drinks.

operating in Florida for several years, was transferred to Blackstone when the Armbrusters found that they could obtain the building adjacent to the restaurant to house it. This building required extensive renovation. The doll museum was opened in November 1983, about a year prior to the restaurant. People dining at Armbrusters are invited to visit the museum. A fee of $1.50 is charged to cover operating expenses, which include a carefully controlled climate. Conversely, people coming to the museum frequently dine at the restaurant. Thus, the two businesses complement each other.

The building housing the restaurant is a large, two-story colonial-revival–style brick structure with six massive white columns supporting the roof of the front porch. A former elegant residence, it provides an ideal setting for the restaurant. On the first floor, there is an entry foyer of heroic proportions. Four dining rooms open off the foyer. A bar (crafted from two massive pocket doors salvaged from a Victorian home now demolished) is located in one of these. The new kitchen is located to the rear. On the second floor is a large hall. The banquet room opens off to one side and the restrooms are to the rear. There is an apartment on this floor also.

In a separate, two-story frame building next door to the restaurant, the doll museum occupies all nine rooms on both floors and the entrance hallway and stairwell as well. The several thousand dolls, doll houses, carriages, and doll furniture plus a collection of antique items fill all of the available space to overflowing.

THE NEIGHBORHOOD

The two buildings are located on Church Street in Blackstone, Virginia. U.S. Highway 460 runs east-west in southern Virginia, connecting Richmond and Petersburg with Appomattox, Lynchburg, and Roanoke. Route 460 bypasses the town of Blackstone (population 3600), but a Business 460 runs through the town and Church Street is a residential part of that Business 460.

Bill and Betty believe they have a very suitable location in a desirable part of town. The street is called Church Street because there are two churches across the street from Armbrusters plus churches on the same side of the street one block away. The downtown section of Blackstone is a few blocks away, and there is a well-established traffic flow past the restaurant.

Armbrusters does not have a parking area for off-street parking. Street parking is adequate for casual traffic but is not sufficient for large parties. There is a paved parking lot located behind a church directly across the street from the restaurant which can be used except when services are being held.

Parking is one problem disturbing Bill and Betty, but there is another thing annoying them even more. The doll museum and the restaurant are two of three houses sharing a city block. There is a third house, which is now unoccupied. All three had once been elegant buildings. The two structures owned by the Armbrusters still are. The other privately owned house is not. It has deteriorated to the point of being an eyesore. It is owned by an elderly widow, a semirecluse, who is not having any maintenance done on it. The Armbrusters view it as a potential safety and health hazard. Town authorities have not taken action requiring maintenance of this property. Bill and Betty had once envisoned this house as a potential bed-and-breakfast facility which would complement both the restaurant and the museum (if it could be obtained before it deteriorates beyond restoration) or it could be torn down for a parking lot for the restaurant. They have not given up on the bed-and-breakfast idea although they cannot justify the added investment at this time. Its owner will neither sell it nor make any effort to maintain it. As Betty remarked, it had not even been painted in over 10 years. There is no question that it detracts from the atmosphere the Armbrusters are trying to create. If Bill is unable to buy the property, he'd like to see it cleaned and fixed up, or torn down.

OPERATING RESULTS

As the Armbrusters reviewed their first 3 months and their first full-year results, they noted several things. Breakeven had been briefly achieved in May 1985, but subsequent monthly cash receipts showed some very obvious variations and for the year they experienced a net loss. Bill noted that an important factor in their customer traffic is the officers and enlisted men and women of the National Guard training at Fort Pickett. The fort, which lies immediately adjacent to the town, hosts Guard units during much of the year by providing a place for training exercises. Officers and enlisted men and women of the units apparently find Armbrusters' atmosphere to their liking. It was military customers primarily who caused the 50 percent increase in sales in August 1985. However, since they had had only one year's results, Bill and Betty felt they would need at least one more year to see any strong patterns. Still, February had been so slow in 1985 they closed up for 2 weeks during February 1986. The restaurant was given a thorough cleaning and some deferred maintenance was done while they took a much-needed vacation.

THE CUSTOMER MIX

Another pattern they had observed was that while a loyal local patronage had developed, approximately 25–35 percent of their customer traffic was from out of town. Particularly on Saturdays and Sundays, out-of-town patrons were likely to outnumber locals. Helped by some favorable publicity in the Richmond press and the Virginia Automobile Association's newsletter, Armbrusters at Blackstone had begun to attract out-of-town customers almost immediately after it was opened. A Richmond reporter described Sunday dinner at Armbrusters as "dinner at Grandmother's house." People were coming from as far as 60 miles away. They came from Richmond, Petersburg, South Hill, Farmville, Crewe, Burkeville, and other towns. Many had become regulars. The original story in the Virginia Automobile Association's journal had accidentally placed the restaurant in Blacksburg instead of Blackstone. A correction in a subsequent issue gave it doubled publicity.

ADVERTISING

Bill described Armbrusters' advertising as primarily word-of-mouth. The guiding philosophy of treating diners as though they were houseguests resulted in first-time diners returning again. Quite frequently they brought guests; many first-time visitors said Armbrusters had been recommended by a friend.

Some advertising was done primarily in newspapers in Richmond and the principal towns in a 60-mile radius of Blackstone. Promotions consisted primarily of special menus, particularly on holidays or during town events in Blackstone.

Because the Armbrusters had been invited to place their advertising brochures in the Virginia Visitors' Welcome Centers near the state borders, they were also getting customers from out of state who were driving through Virginia. Bill noted that the personnel from the Automobile Club and also from the Visitors' Centers had personally "checked them out" by dining at Armbrusters before agreeing to recommend it and to encourage people to patronize the restaurant and the museum. He felt that that was entirely appropriate. Spurts in customer traffic were observed, some of which Bill felt could be the result of these favorable publicity events.

THE MENUS

The luncheon menu included Soup of the Day (bowl, $1.35; cup 75¢) or Brunswick stew with ham biscuits ($3.25). The main fare, served with vegetable and salad, included Our Special Quiche of the Day ($3.65), petit steak ($4.75), or chicken pie from an old Virginia recipe ($3.85). Croissants, other sandwiches, and desserts completed the luncheon offering.

Dinners included soup or juice appetizer, salad, entree, vegetables, and homemade rolls and muffins. They featured Chicken Old Virginia (chicken breast with Virginia country ham topped with white wine sauce for $7.75), Southside country pot roast ($6.75), sliced Surry County ham with redeye gravy ($7.25), southern fried chicken ($6.75), and broiled lamb chops ($11.95). Desserts included peanut pie and chocolate mousse pie, both with fresh whipped cream. The menu noted under beverages that wine and spirits are available.

SPECIAL EVENTS

Party bookings had risen steadily since their opening and offered substantial revenue. Certain organizations also provided profitable bar business in addition to their dinner bookings. The 1985 pre-Christmas party business had filled almost all available evenings. Because these events were preplanned and held on a separate floor, these bookings caused little disruption to the regular customer traffic. Additional personnel were always assigned to handle these large parties which gave the employees welcome added income. During the parties, designated cooks, waiters, and waitresses served the casual diners so they would not be neglected.

EMPLOYEE RELATIONS

Keeping a steady staff had been a continuing vexation to both Bill and Betty. Prior to opening, they had advertised the positions they planned to fill and selected what seemed like very suitable employees by picking carefully from a large number of applicants. All employees were hired as part-time help. Many of those hired first were still employed in early 1986, while others had lasted only a few days or weeks. All through the first year, there had been a constant process of replacing personnel who either had quit or been released for not meeting the standards the Armbrusters were trying to maintain. To keep a staff of sixteen for the first 12 months, they had hired a grand total of thirty-seven! As Bill observed, constantly training new employees was both disruptive and expensive. After a year and a half of operation, Armbrusters had acquired a sufficiently stable employee group to permit a smooth operation. They were now holding a list of potential employees, but were not actively seeking anyone to add to the staff.

SUMMARY

Despite these problems, they felt that all of their hard work and long hours had paid off. Income had risen steadily. Their debt was being promptly serviced. Much of the required additional improvements and maintenance had been done and all accounts payable had been handled promptly; the Armbrusters had established excellent credit standing with all of their suppliers. Not being dependent on the business because of income from other sources, they had not paid themselves any salaries. Net income was committed to helping the business grow.

The Armbrusters were hoping that customer traffic would grow enough to permit them to hire a manager for supervision of the day-to-day operations. This would given them an opportunity to begin doing some longer-range planning and to try to resolve some of their persistent problems instead of just living with quick fixes. They were well aware that their good start could be wasted if these problems were not resolved.

Approaching their second anniversary, Bill and Betty had some reasons to be optimistic. The restaurant had become well enough known throughout a 60-mile radius of Blackstone to have a regular, repeat clientele. There were forces in motion that could greatly increase the number of people visiting Blackstone, many of whom would be potential diners. One of these was an organized effort to have the city's business district, basically several blocks of one street, declared a historic area. Along with the request for historic designation, a restoration effort was underway to return the storefronts to something near their original, early 1900s appearance. Bill Armbruster was directly involved in both of these initiatives. Many out-of-town visitors to Armbrusters had remarked on the obvious historic value of some of the buildings and the desirability of preserving them.

The Armbrusters felt that as these efforts moved from planning to reality, restaurant traffic would increase along with that of the other businesses. They felt that if they could acquire the unoccupied third house on their block and make it into a bed-and-breakfast, an antiques sales outlet, or a combination of the two, the businesses would complement each other.

Despite his optimistic outlook, Bill Armbruster put his concerns into some pertinent questions:

The restaurant business was what I wanted to do, and Betty has been a good sport about going along with it. It's not her first choice by any means, although she was born and raised in Blackstone.

My son is also involved, he is doing the accounting statements for us. It's sort of a sideline for him, but he's been invaluable for us in terms of putting the numbers together and giving us a readout each month.

Further, Mother is involved through the doll museum. The best month has been July 1985 with almost 500 visitors. She now averages between 100 and 200 visitors per month.

What should we do now? We've made a substantial cash and time investment here. Including all the pre-opening arrangements, renovations and such, we've worked very hard here for over 2 years. What possibility is there that we will get a payoff for all of this? Can we hold out until it happens? When can we expect to be profitable, if we will be? What must we do now to make 1986 a profitable year? What about the future, say, 5 or 10 years from now?

MAGNA INTERNATIONAL, INC.

By mid-1986, annual sales of Magna International, Inc. were projected to top $1.0 billion for the first time. As Canada's largest manufacturer of automotive parts, Magna had just realized one of its corporate objectives of having an average of $100 of its auto parts built into every North American car.

Although company founder Frank Stronach and his management team continuously espoused a "small is beautiful" philosophy, their dreams for Magna were, by no means, small. Stronach stated in 1985 that he was intent on creating "one of the largest corporations in North America," and that he felt Magna could maintain 30 percent annual growth for many years. By 1986, it was also clear that Magna was committed to a strategy of increased internationalization of its operations. These goals clearly raised questions about the appropriateness of Magna's current operating philosophy and organization for the planned growth.

FRANK STRONACH AND MAGNA INTERNATIONAL

In 1985, Magna's flamboyant chairman and chief executive officer, Frank Stronach, was the highest-paid executive in Canada with a salary of $1.85 million. Many felt this was justified given Magna's almost unprecedented 30 percent annual growth in sales and profits over the past 15 years. Exhibit 1 provides statements from Magna's 1985 annual report detailing the company's financial performance.

The company, in its original form, was founded in 1957 by its controlling shareholder, chairman, and CEO Frank Stronach. By 1986 it employed more than 7,500 people in approximately sixty-five Canadian and five American plants and in one additional plant in West Germany. In 1984, 75 percent of sales were to U.S. customers. Magna's primary customers were the various operating divisions of Ford, General Motors, Chrysler, and AMC — the "Big Four" North American auto manufacturers. In fact, 95 percent of their products went into North American cars.

This case was written by Mr. William Webb under the direction of professor Paul W. Beamish, School of Business and Economics, Wilfrid Laurier University, as a basis for classroom discussion. Copyright © 1986 by Paul W. Beamish. Reprinted by permission.

EXHIBIT 1 10-year financial summary

	1985	1984	1983	1982	1981[a]	1980	1979	1978	1977	1976
Operations data										
Sales	$690,400	$493,559	$302,451	$226,534	$232,114	$183,456	$165,738	$128,189	$80,953	$55,010
Income from operations	69,430	57,124	25,473	9,055	12,054	9,249	15,924	12,899	8,185	5,734
Net income[d]	43,191	31,480	14,647	5,265	6,911	5,640	8,455	6,595	4,093	2,786
Extraordinary items						(1,922)	272	795		
Basic earnings per Class A and Class B share[b,c]	$ 2.00	$ 1.93	$ 1.10	$ 0.49	$ 0.64	$ 0.34	$ 0.89	$ 0.80	$ 0.48	$ 0.36
Fully diluted earnings per Class A and Class B share	$ 1.93	$ 1.85	$ 1.07	$ 0.44	$ 0.57	$ 0.33	$ 0.78	$ 0.68	$ 0.47	$ 0.32
Depreciation	24,322	15,044	11,267	9,325	9,188	6,154	4,506	3,349	2,210	1,416
Cash flow from operations	85,974	55,945	32,522	14,604	14,672	12,052	15,275	13,160	7,542	5,171
Dividends declared per Class A and Class B share[b,c]	$ 0.48	$ 0.31	$ 0.13[e]	$ 0.13	$ 0.18	$ 0.18	$ 0.14	$ 0.10	$ 0.06	$ 0.03
Financial position										
Working capital	64,121	79,804	48,291	31,792	30,792	28,223	19,174	15,351	7,412	4,925
Capital expenditures	222,878	110,239	29,806	17,434	21,052	23,630	23,085	16,231	8,584	3,456
Fixed assets (less accumulated depreciation)	357,371	179,817	87,388	70,553	74,074	62,629	47,089	30,269	19,387	8,940
Long-term debt	103,997	96,497	42,159	55,554	56,308	45,830	30,441	19,588	10,238	4,627
Equity relating to Class A and Class B shares	297,935	143,566	81,590	41,071	39,631	33,792	32,086	23,270	15,226	9,646
Equity per Class A and Class B share[b,c]	$ 12.44	$ 8.43	$ 5.59	$ 4.13	$ 3.84	$ 3.35	$ 3.18	$ 2.41	$ 1.68	$ 1.25

Note: Canadian dollars in thousands except per share figures.
[a] 1981 and prior figures include sales and income from Aerospace/Defence operations sold effective August 1, 1981.
[b] Adjusted for years prior to 1979 to give effect to the capital reorganization during 1979.
[c] 1983 and prior figures adjusted to give effect to the stock dividend issued June 1983.
[d] Before extraordinary items.
[e] In addition, stockholders received a special stock dividend issued June 1983.

The history of Magna was really the entrepreneurial life story of Frank Stronach, who emigrated to Canada from Austria in 1954. Trained as a tool and die maker, Stronach invested what little savings he had and opened up his own tool and die shop in a rented Toronto garage while still in his midtwenties. Business was good in the first 2 years and Stronach soon employed thirty people. When his foreman told him that he wanted to leave and start his own business, Stronach offered the man part-ownership in the business in order to keep him. The foreman stayed and set up the company's second tool and die shop. This was the first glimmer of what was to be part of Magna's future strategy for corporate growth — decentralization with equity participation by its employees.

Stronach summed up his feelings and reasons behind the philosophy: "If I lose a good person, I'm losing somebody who could be a competitor. I want those people in my camp. That's what business is all about — people management."

By 1969, Stronach owned eight plants that were run autonomously. In order to implement a plan to facilitate employee share ownership, he merged with the publicly traded Magna Electronics Corporation, substituting "International" for the word "Electronics" to reflect the company's broad range of products and greater ambitions.

For the next 15 years, Magna grew almost continuously at an annual rate of 30 percent or more and by 1985 was opening one new factory every 6 to 8 weeks to keep pace with demand. Its product lines had grown to over four thousand different components and assemblies, encompassing parts for nearly every section of the automobile. Exhibit 2 provides a list of product families manufactured by each of Magna's operating groups in 1984. Some products were manufactured to customer specifications while others were designed by Magna's staff and sold as original equipment based on their innovative designs.

THE MAGNA "SUCCESS FORMULA"

Magna consistently performed well in the cyclical auto parts industry whose performance followed the auto industry's traditional 4-year up-and-down cycle. One investment analyst commented that Magna had "the best growth record and highest returns on equity in the business." Appendix A provides a brief analysis of the auto parts industry and shows Magna's financial performance in comparison with three other major auto parts manufacturers.

Many explanations were offered for Magna's unequalled success. In the end, however, it seemed to boil down to the company's ability to manufacture the highest-quality product at the lowest possible cost.

Some observers, including Magna's management and, especially, Frank Stronach, attributed its success to Magna's unique "corporate culture" whose key elements were embodied in the company's "Corporate Constitution" published for the first time in Magna's 1984 annual report. The stated purpose of the Constitution was to "define the rights of employees and investors to participate in the Company's profits and growth and impose discipline on management." Stronach thought that Magna

EXHIBIT 2
Magna product
directory

CMT Group

Seat track mechanisms
Window winding regulators
Hand brake assemblies
Hood hinges
Door hinges

Door latches
Hood latches
Trunk latches
Clutch and brake pedal assemblies

Decorative Products Group

Front bumper and grille fascia
Rear bumper fascia
Rocker panels
Wheel house opening mouldings
Window channels
Weather strip channels
Headlamp retainers
Center hood mouldings

Windshield mouldings
Rear window mouldings
Drain trough mouldings
Exterior window mouldings
Tail light bezels
Rocker panel mouldings
Body size mouldings

MACI Group

Cooling fan motors
Heating fan motors
Windshield wiper motors
Immersible fuel pumps
Thermostatic air controllers
Magnetic capsule switches

Relay switches
Instrument clusters
Fuel control devices
Electronic tone and voice
   synthesized alarms
Electronic fluid level devices

Magna Manufacturing Group

Aluminum bumper reinforcements
Shock absorber towers
Rear cross members
Fuel tank straps
Sill plates
Scuff plates
Alternator fans
Motor mounts
Canister support brackets

Glove box doors
Seat belt anchors
Heat shields
Catalytic converters
Thermostat housings
Water pumps
Instrument panel supports
Headrests

Maple Group

Poly V crankshaft pulleys
Power steering pulleys
Alternator pulleys
Automatic Poly V belt tensioners
Water pump pulleys

Compressor pump pulleys
Two speed accessory drive system
Oil strainers
Oil pick-up tubes
Dip-stick tubes

might be the only company in the Western World with a corporate constitution that guaranteed employee rights and imposed discipline on management. Exhibit 3 shows the Magna Corporate Constitution. Appendix B provides some excerpts from the 1985 annual report that demonstrate the Constitution in practice at Magna.

Other critical components of the corporate culture included a commitment to keeping all Magna plants small with a maximum of one hundred employees each, an emphasis on research and development, and rewards for both management and workers through an attractive profit-sharing plan and a range of social benefits from day care for employees' children to a recently opened company-owned conservation and recreation area.

ORGANIZATION AND OPERATING STRUCTURE

Appendix C illustrates and describes Magna's unique operating structure of three levels of responsibility: the operating unit, group management (in charge of an operating group), and executive management.

EXHIBIT 3
Magna's corporate constitution

Board of directors: Magna believes that outside directors provide independent counsel and discipline. A majority of Magna's board of directors will be outsiders.

Employee equity and profit participation: Ten percent of Magna's profit before tax will be allocated to employees. These funds will be used for the purchase of Magna shares in trust for employees and for cash distributions to employees, recognizing both performance and length of service

Shareholder profit participation: Magna will distribute, on average, 20 percent of its annual net profit to its shareholders.

Management profit participation: In order to obtain a long-term contractual commitment from management, the company provides a compensation arrangement which, in addition to a base salary comparable to industry standards, allows for the distribution to corporate management of up to 6 percent of Magna's profit before tax.

Research and technology development: Magna will allocate 7 percent of its profit before tax for research and technology development to ensure the long-term viability of the Company.

Social responsibility: The company will contribute a maximum of 2 percent of its profit before tax to charitable, cultural, educational, and political institutions to support the basic fabric of society.

Minimum profit performance: Management has an obligation to produce a profit. If Magna does not generate a minimum after-tax return of 4 percent on share capital for two consecutive years, class A shareholders, voting as a class, will have the right to elect additional directors.

Major investments: In the event that more than 20 percent of Magna's equity is to be committed to a new unrelated business, class A and class B shareholders will have the right to approve such an investment with each class voting separately.

Constitutional amendments: Any change to Magna's corporate constitution will require the approval of the class A and class B shareholders with each class voting separately.

At the operating unit or individual factory level, maximum employment was kept to no more than one hundred workers because of Stronach's belief that management and employees should maintain close working relationships and that smaller units sparked individual initiative and a degree of entrepreneurialism. Stronach felt that a "family relationship" should exist among coworkers and management, with each person knowing the name of all fellow employees.

"Communication is very important. If you have a few thousand people under one roof, you need a hundred thousand rules. You lose the human touch. You create a faceless kind of management," said Stronach, adding that Magna's environment simply created "a damned good atmosphere to work in!"

Every Magna factory was unique in its own right, with its own product mandate, R&D department, marketing responsibilities, and production and profit objectives established by that unit's management team. Every employee had access to management and, since each earned shares in the company through a profit-sharing plan, they were likely to come forward with assembly-line suggestions to improve quality or cut costs — suggestions that could lead to promotion, more profits to share, and increased equity participation. The small scale of each unit's operations and Magna's emphasis on factory-floor technical skills (promoted by in-house technical education and upgrading programs) resulted in a high degree of flexibility and an ability to adapt quickly to changes in manufacturing operations.

Growth at the operating unit level, as for all levels of Magna, was somewhat "organic" in nature, rather than "planned" in the traditional sense. When a particular unit (factory) could no longer keep pace with demand and was running three shifts of one hundred people on a 24-hour schedule, the unit's general manager would be allowed to build a second factory. If more factories had to be built for a common product line, these might eventually form the basis of a new management group with the former general manager as group vice-president. As this suggests, Magna had a rather unusual and interesting method of delegating responsibility and controls between the executive management, group management, and the operating units. Magna's unit general managers were given 100 percent control, authority, and responsibility for their units, with the requirement that they clearly identify themselves as part of Magna International when communicating with suppliers or customers.

This high degree of decentralization did give rise to a number of trade-offs at the operating unit level. Magna realized higher transportation costs shipping from widely dispersed locations to the automotive assembly plants of the major manufacturers; however, significant quantities were still shipped such that discounts were not completely forgone.

Some diseconomies also arose from the lack of centralized purchasing of raw materials. Each unit dealt with its own suppliers but, frequently, general managers in the same operating group would cooperate to secure volume discounts when available.

Administrative costs were duplicated in some cases since each operating unit had its own personnel, accounting, and other departments, but management felt that, in general, the benefits of decentralization outweighed its costs.

At Magna, financial control was maintained by accountants at each of the Group offices and operating units. Each operating unit was required to submit a business plan for the year outlining the operating and capital budget to Group management. These plans were assessed by the Groups and submitted to corporate executive officers for final approval.

Once approved, the Groups and operating units set out independently in pursuit of their defined business goals. Performance was monitored monthly using uniform financial reports comparing actual operating results to budget and measuring capital spending against plan.

Although organic, growth was not indiscriminate at the factory level and was monitored by group management which worked within the broad corporate policy set by executive management. Executive management consisted of Frank Stronach and a handful of senior executives. Corporate headquarters were housed in a two-story office in a suburban Toronto business park and consisted of a lean, one-hundred-person staff.

Operating units were grouped geographically and by market under one of five group management teams which were destined to divide and form more groups as Magna expanded. Each group was responsible for specific technologies and product lines and had its own marketing, R&D, and planning responsibilities.

On average, each group management nucleus had ten to fifteen factories responsible to it. Magna's strategy was to keep these factories close together geographically, wherever possible, and, as the company grew sufficiently, to develop its own industrial parks.

In 1985, Magna consisted of five management groups: the CMT Group (Creative Mechanical Technologies), the Decorative Products Group, the MACI Group, the Magna Manufacturing Group, and the Maple Group. The products manufactured by each group in 1984 are found in Exhibit 2.

EQUITY PARTICIPATION

Frank Stronach maintained that employees had "a moral right to some of the profits they help generate. . . . If they get profit, and they put it into the company equity, there's a sort of discipline which helps the employee. We've got some people on machines who've got $30,000 sitting there. That's a lot of money for an average person."

In keeping with Stronach's belief, Magna had a type of deferred profit-sharing program for its employees to reward productivity and loyalty. Employees were awarded a point for every $1,000 they earned and a point for each year they stayed with the company. The more points they accumulated, the greater their share in the fund. Each year, 7 percent of profits before tax were transferred to an employee equity trust fund. Employees received quarterly statements of how many shares they owned and their value. If an employee left within 2 years, his or her shares reverted to other employees. After the third year with Magna, an employee owned a percentage which increased until the tenth year, when they became the employee property, even if he or she left. In Magna's earlier years, profit sharing was only available to middle management, but was expanded to cover all employees in 1978.

Magna's senior management team of about twenty executives enjoyed a separate profit-participation program for which 6 percent of before-tax profits were set aside. The result was some very generous bonuses in addition to their competitive salaries, but Frank Stronach had no qualms about this, stating that, "good management doesn't come cheap — I don't come cheap." The compensation received by Stronach and four other Magna executives placed them among the fifteen most highly paid managers in Canada in 1985.

Exclusive of the top executive, Magna's approximately 250 managers owned about $12\frac{1}{2}$ percent of the company. The over seven thousand workers held about the same equity position.

Although Magna's workers enjoyed equity participation, their hourly salaries were very low by industry standards — approximately $6 per hour in 1985. Some estimated that Magna, without a single union in any of its plants, therefore had an hourly wage burden about half the size of its unionized competitors — a substantial competitive advantage in an industry where cost control was a key success factor. Stronach maintained that increases in productivity were resulting in rising wages at Magna and that Magna would soon be catching up in terms of hourly wage rates, but low hourly wages and the lack of a union in any of its plants made Magna a favorite target of attacks by the United Auto Workers (UAW).

MAGNA AND THE UAW

Magna seemed to be an impregnable target for union organizers — a fact that some industry followers felt was vital to Magna's success. Stronach, himself, did not appear to harbor anti-union sentiments, stating: "Unions can be part of free enterprise because society needs checks and balances. . . . If you run a lousy ship, you deserve a union."

Regardless of the sincerity of these views, Stronach had the grudging respect of his UAW adversaries. Buzz Hargrove, administrative assistant to Canadian UAW leader Bob White, knew Frank Stronach personally and said, "I didn't agree with his ideology or his philosophy, but I thought he was a well-motivated, decent human being."

In one instance, in 1978, the UAW was granted automatic certification at one of Magna's Toronto plants because of management interference in the organizing drive. However, some union cards were burned; the UAW failed to negotiate a contract and was then voted out by the Magna employees. The negotiations stalled on the single issue of the now mandatory Rand formula (where all employees in the bargaining unit must pay union dues regardless of whether they choose to become union members), but in the UAW's opinion, this issue was irrelevant because Magna had really just chosen to dig in its heels.

Buzz Hargrove said:

Frank Stronach and I had lunch together one day and he told me that their strategy was essentially to find an issue that they knew we would not agree to that would force us to strike the plant in order to try to get an agreement and they would just let the thing sit. They wouldn't try to run the plant, or hire scabs, but to all intents and purposes the plant would remain closed as long as there was a picket line. Whether it took a year, or two, or three, or forever, it didn't matter. They were not going to have a union in their shop.

We have no alternative but to continue . . . and probably even step up . . . our efforts to organize Magna. We can't have a major segment of the automotive parts industry unorganized.

It was possible that the UAW would be aided in subsequent attempts to organize Magna by the company's ongoing strategy to cluster its five management groups and their related plants into industrial campuses. Frank Stronach, in a 1985 interview, admitted that he was concerned by the threat of renewed UAW action because "it's always a concern if someone would interfere with your environment, with your philosophies, with your basic framework." In an interview a year earlier, he had claimed:

I don't believe the UAW would really get out to organize us. They would if they heard complaints, or if the employees were unhappy. . . . We try to provide a better alternative. We say that if we had unions, we would lose individually because everything is then divided into group one, group two, group three. Such groups stop a person from voicing his opinion. This is the danger when one body or one group gets too strong; it's too structured and the individual gets lost. . . . Three or four years ago we had two people in labor relations. Now we have a department with ten people. We employ a labor lawyer, whose function is to make our managers understand that we insist on certain principles and standards. His job is not to squeeze employees but to educate managers.

CORPORATE STRATEGY

Magna had a clear set of corporate objectives and a strategy for achieving them. As Magna's success became well known, its senior executives, expecially Frank Stronach, were increasingly sought out for interviews. Features appeared repeatedly in newspapers and popular magazines, on television, and even in books, which described Magna's objectives and plans for realizing them.

The company's primary objective was to become the most diversified supplier of parts, components, and assemblies to the North American automotive industry and to steadily increase its dollar share of total industry sales from its 1985 level of one percent. Magna intended to accomplish this by increasing its average "penetration level" or the average dollar value of Magna parts that went into every North American automobile.

Over the period 1979 to 1985, Magna's penetration level had risen from $8.95 to $49.00, with a goal of $100 per vehicle by 1988. The company exceeded the $100 goal in the middle of its 1986 fiscal year.

Management consistently referred to a three-pronged strategy that it felt would allow Magna to sustain its remarkable growth and achieve its objectives: (1) continued increases in market share for existing Magna products, (2) introduction of new products and technologies to the marketplace, driven by ongoing in-house research and development and joint ventures with partners who were leaders in product design and manufacturing capabilities, and (3) manufacturing and marketing of modular assemblies using a variety of Magna parts and components. For example, instead of manufacturing cooling fans and radiators independently, Magna intended to market one complete unit which included a fan, radiator, and shrouds and could be bolted directly into a vehicle on an assembly line.

In addition to its diversification strategy of building ever greater numbers of parts and components, Magna simultaneously pursued an ongoing strategy of vertical integration. This was mainly in the form of backward integration, described by many as a key reason for Magna's success as it allowed the company to reduce costs and respond quickly and flexibly to design changes by its customers. Magna integrated vertically by undertaking its own tool and die making — the company's original business — and by developing and applying its in-house expertise in robotics and computer-aided design/computer-aided manufacturing (CAD/CAM) to equip Magna for the so-called factory of the future. There was even speculation that a Magna company, which had designed and built its own robotics system, might market the systems as another product in the future.

Magna's medium-term strategy was to geographically cluster its operating units and their plants into "industrial campuses," each with an infrastructure of company-supported social and recreational services, such as day care, medical, educational, and fitness centers. Each campus would consist of a cluster of ten to twenty small autonomous plants, with the related operating group's office and product development center located on the campus as well. The goal of this concept was to enhance the working environment for Magna employees. Stronach estimated that "50 cents spent on something like day care in our campuses will return $1.50 in increased productivity." Magna's first campus was begun in Newmarket, Ontario, in 1985 with three new plants and associated offices. Land for other campuses was quickly being assembled in anticipation of future growth. An announcement had also been made that Magna would begin construction of another ten to twenty factory industrial campus on a 26-acre parcel of land in Waterloo, Ontario, in 1986.

One strategy for dealing with the company's rapid growth was raised by Jim McAlpine, Magna's executive vice-president and chief financial officer, who suggested in a 1985 interview that Magna intended to spin off at least one of its operating units by selling or distributing shares to the public in 1986. Magna would retain at least 52 percent of the unit's shares, 20 percent would be given to the unit's employees, 5 percent would go to management, and the remainder would probably be distributed to the public through an equity issue or divided plan. Such a strategy would reinforce Magna's corporate philosophy of decentralization. McAlpine added that "a spin-off allows our management teams to continue to grow as managers. We hope it reduces the buildup of bureaucracy." It seemed that Magna

International's main role in the future might be that of a holding company or a birthplace for a number of new companies.

INTERNATIONAL ACTIVITIES

An increasingly important component of Magna's corporate strategy was the recognition of the emphasis on international activity within the automobile industry. By 1985, Magna's international activities, on a number of fronts, had been relatively modest, but had resulted in the development of relationships that management felt would position the company to take advantage of a variety of opportunities. The 1985 annual report stated: "With patience and persistence, we will be able to build successfully upon these relationships and establish Magna as a participant in the key automotive markets of the world."

Magna's international activities before 1986 had consisted primarily of joint ventures with foreign companies where Magna's goal was to acquire new technologies and knowledge of new products and processes. Magna sought joint ventures to build a technology base quickly. Frank Stronach said, "It's too time-consuming to do it on our own. . . . We don't want to reinvent the wheel constantly." Here is a list of some major joint ventures that Magna had been involved in up to 1986. In 1985, Magna was in thirteen active joint ventures.

Joint venture partner	Partner's nationality	Part produced
1. Philips Group	Dutch	Electronic components
2. Veglia SA	French	Instrument clusters for Renault
3. Chausson	French	Aluminum radiators for Renault
4. Webasto GmbH	West German	Sun roofs
5. Willibald Grammer	West German	Foam technology for seats
6. Brown, Boveri et Cie AG	Swiss	Power trains for electric vehicles

Typical joint ventures entered into by Magna were those with two French auto parts suppliers. With Veglia SA, a French producer of dashboard equipment, Magna set up Invotek Instruments of Toronto to manufacture instrument clusters for the Renault Alliance and Encore. In 1984 with Société Anonyme des Usines Chausson, a Renault subsidiary, Magna established Thermag Industries Inc. of Mississauga. The purpose was to produce aluminum radiators for Renaults built in North America by AMC, instead of shipping radiators from France. An $8 million plant was to be built with production to begin in 1986. Magna took a 60 percent interest in the venture, in order to gain access to technology and markets, while Chausson took the minority 40 percent interest and supplied its technology.

In July 1984, Magna signed a joint venture agreement with the Japanese parts manufacturer Niles Buhin Co. At that time Japanese manufacturers were beginning to try to increase their penetration of the lucrative North American market. Simultaneously, Magna began negotiating with four or five other Japanese companies for similar ventures that Frank Stronach felt could bring Magna hundreds of millions of dollars in revenues over the next few years.

Niles Buhin was an electronics components maker. Unlike many Japanese parts suppliers, it did not belong to a particular car-making group, although most of its business was with Nissan and Mitsubishi. At the time, Niles Buhin had annual sales of $150 million, while Magna's sales were $302 million.

Magna was again seeking access to advanced technology, primarily in electronics and light-weight materials, while Niles Buhin saw the venture as a good way to gain entry to a large and growing market far from its domestic bases. They were being encouraged to do so by the large Japanese car makers who wanted the parts makers to follow them to North America; but, because Japanese vehicle production would be insufficient to support them, the Japanese parts manufacturers required access to the big U.S. manufacturers as well. Some planned to try this on their own, but many saw joint ventures such as the one between Magna and Niles Buhin as a better alternative.

Japanese manufacturers were extemely sensitive about labor problems, but Magna's main selling point to the Japanese was its record of good labor relations. Management was of the opinion that the Japanese felt "quite comfortable" with Magna.

According to its 1985 annual report, in seeking additional joint ventures with the Japanese, Magna's primary targets were the Japanese vehicle manufacturers who had, or were planning to locate, production facilities in North America, as well as their suppliers, who were exploring opportunities to do business in North America. Magna's strategy was to demonstrate to the manufacturers that it could provide "world-class" products in terms of quality and value. With Japanese part suppliers, Magna sought to develop forms of cooperation in North America where both parties could contribute and prosper.

By 1985, Magna had licensed one of its products to Japanese parts suppliers for production and sale in Japan and had acquired licenses to manufacture and sell certain Japanese products in North America. The company was also in the midst of establishing a trading company with a Japanese parts supplier to coordinate the supply of certain products manufactured by Magna to one of the Japanese auto makers located in North America.

In 1985, a tooling and production facility had been established in West Germany to supply European OEMs. Contracts had also been signed to supply some North American components to two German automakers.

An agreement was signed late in the year to establish a joint venture in the People's Republic of China to manufacture components for the Chinese auto market.

As fiscal 1986 approached, it was increasingly clear that Magna International was stepping up the pace of its international activities with ambitious hopes for the future of these operations.

MAGNA'S FUTURE PROSPECTS

As fiscal 1986 came to a close, it was becoming increasingly evident that the company Frank Stronach had built up from a rented Toronto garage might be coming to a crossroads in its history. A number of issues required resolution.

It appeared certain that the company's strong growth would continue unabated for at least the next few years. However, one could not help but wonder if Magna's traditional success formula would be adequate to accommodate further phenomenal growth. Would continued growth and the spinning off of new companies make it easier for the UAW to finally unionize some of Magna's factories and what repercussions would such an event have on Magna as a whole?

There had been a trend for the North American auto makers to obtain 100 percent of their components in one place to ensure consistency. Certainly no company in Canada was better positioned than Magna to make the most of that trend. Yet would this trend continue?

Magna's increasing international activities seemed to be the next logical step in the company's uninterrupted growth, but concern existed about how this would fit into Magna's current organizational structure which emphasized geographic clustering and a commonality of product lines among related operating units. Would modifications or exceptions to the Magna formula have to be made to accommodate these relatively new activities which were growing rapidly in relative importance?

Stronach's dynamic, entrepreneurial personality and vision undoubtedly accounted for a considerable measure of Magna's success. How would this role change as Magna continued to grow and Stronach became a smaller part of Magna's operations? One person noted that Stronach had all the pieces in place so that any of his chief executives could manage the company quite well. Yet others asked what effect his retirement might have on the company.

Frank Stronach once called Magna International's Corporate Constitution "perhaps the most important chapter in western industrial society in many years . . . that I believe will have an enormous bearing in the future structure of corporations [and] law making." As the new fiscal year approached, one could not help wondering whether that document was well suited to guide Magna International and other corporations into the 1990s.

REFERENCES

Arnott, Sheila, "What Our Top Executives Are Earning." *Financial Post*, May 1986.

Avery, Nick, and Alison Burkett, "Comparison of the Auto-Parts Market 1981–1984." Wilfrid Laurier University MBA Report, November 27, 1985 (unpublished).

Barnes, Kenneth, and Everett Banning, *Money-Makers! The Secrets of Canada's Most Successful Entrepreneurs*. Toronto: McClelland & Stewart, Ltd., 1985.

"Everybody's Business" (Global Television Program), *Various Video Excerpts re: Magna International, Inc.*

Galt, Virginia, "Decentralizing, Worker Participation Plans Help Put Magna on the Road to Recovery." *Globe and Mail*, July 6, 1981, B1, B5.

Harrison, Douglas, "Franco-Canadian Economic Bonds Are Increasing." *Kitchener-Waterloo Record*, February 17, 1985, B9.

Hart, Matthew, "Frank As He'll Ever Be." *Financial Post Moneywise Magazine*, May 1986, 64–67.

Koch, Henry, "Magna Spinoffs to Spur Waterloo Growth: Carroll." *Kitchener-Waterloo Record*, January 23, 1985, B9.

Lilley, Wayne, "Small Is Beautiful." *Canadian Business*, 57 (6) (1984), 170–71.

"Magna Executive Optimistic About Firm's 1985 Showing." *Globe and Mail*, August 3, 1985, B5.

Magna International, Inc., *Annual Report 1984*, 1984.

Magna International, Inc., *Annual Report 1985*, 1985.

"Magna International, Inc." *Toronto Stock Exchange Review*, November 1984, 1–4.

Milner, Brian, "Magna, Japanese Firm Form Joint Venture." *Globe and Mail*, July 30, 1984, B1.

Partridge, John, "Small Is Beautiful to Magna Chief but He Still Aims to Be the Biggest." *Globe and Mail*, January 5, 1985, B1, B3.

Waddell, Christopher, "Magna Chairman Sells Shares but Remains Firmly in the Saddle." *Globe and Mail*, December 7, 1984, B1–B2.

Waddell, Christopher, "Magna Hopes to Be Supplier for GM's Saturn." *Globe and Mail*, April 19, 1985, B3.

Walker, Dean, "The Capitalist's Gospel According to Frank Stronach." *Executive*, May 1984, 46–49.

Wilson, Sharon E., "The Best of Both Worlds: How Large Corporations Can Benefit from Decentralized Manufacturing," Wilfrid Laurier University Report, August 1985 (unpublished).

APPENDIX A: MARKET OVERVIEW

The autoparts market can be divided into eight sections. Passenger car, light truck, medium and heavy truck, and off-highway vehicles give the four major sections and each of these can be broken into original equipment (O.E.) and aftermarket. A further subdivision could be made in aftermarket between the original equipment aftermarket and the third-party aftermarket. That subdivision is not considered here.

Most autoparts companies cover more than one segment, so companies can be competitors with some products and not others. Competitors also depend upon whether a company is in the original equipment market or aftermarket. Canadian aftermarket firms concentrate on the Canadian market because of the duty collectible in crossing the Canadian–U.S. border. Original equipment, on the other hand, is duty-free under the autopact, and therefore firms in both Canada and the United States compete for this business.

The business cycles for original equipment and the aftermarket tend to be counter-cyclical. When new vehicle sales are down, the sales of replacement parts tend to be up, thereby giving some protection to firms that are in both market segments. Major companies have the following characteristics:

Budd Canada	Passenger car	O.E. & aftermarket
	Light truck	O.E.
Hayes-Dana	Passenger car	O.E. & aftermarket
	Light truck	O.E. & aftermarket
	Medium and heavy truck	O.E. & aftermarket
	Off-highway vehicles	O.E. & aftermarket
Magna International	Passenger car	O.E. & aftermarket
	Light truck	O.E. & aftermarket
Long Manufacturing	Passenger car	O.E. & aftermarket
	Light truck	O.E. & aftermarket
	Medium and heavy truck	O.E. & aftermarket
	Off-highway vehicles	O.E.

INDUSTRY OVERVIEW FOR 1984

Sales of cars and light trucks again increased by 19 percent. The market for other trucks and off-highway vehicles did not improve.

Statistical process control and just-in-time delivery were taken up by the whole autoparts industry. The new threat to the autoparts industry was the statement from the manufacturers that the supplier base was to be cut 50 percent within 3 years to reduce their overhead in dealing with suppliers as well as to increase control.

BUDD CANADA IN 1984

Budd had a good year in 1984. Sales increased by 36 percent and net profits were $11.2 million compared to 1983's loss of $2.2 million.

This was due to several factors:

General administration expenses were kept under control, resulting in expenses as a percentage of sales of only 8 percent compared with their historical average of about 10 percent.

Cost of goods sold was reduced even lower than the 1980 level (81.2 percent compared with 84.9 percent in 1980). This was the result of fully utilizing the Kitchener plant because of the increased sales, as well as productivity gains made with the recent plant additions.

Budd not only showed a good profit in 1984, it also outperformed the market when we look at the net profits/net sales ratio. Return on investment ratios show it comparing favorable with the industry average.

The working capital management ratios show Budd comparing favorably with other companies. Aggressive management of accounts receivable shows a decrease from days receivable from 78 to 58 days.

Liquidity and solvency ratios show excellent positions.

HAYES-DANA IN 1984

1984 saw Hayes-Dana's sales increase by 31 percent, and profitability increase by 170 percent. The favorable profit picture comes from:

Improving the cost-of-goods-sold percentage by 3.5 percent of sales, resulting in a favorable variance of $11.9 million.

Depreciation expense was not at the 1983 levels, resulting in an additional favorable variance of $2.5 million. This and the increase in investment income were offset by increased operating expenses of a full one percent of sales, resulting in an unfavorable variance of $3.9 million.

Days receivable again continued to increase in a year where all other manufacturers studied managed to reduce their collection period. Inventory turnover improved, but still lagged behind the industry. These working capital items accounted for $24 million of the funds available. As well, plant additions of $9 million and an increase of investment in affiliates used the funds raised from increasing current loans and other liabilities and from increasing long-term debt.

The end-of-the-year inventory at Hayes-Dana was higher than in other companies. Cost of goods sold was improving, but was not at the level Budd had achieved.

The $9 million plant addition in 1984 should improve the operating expense ratio in coming years. It would be reasonable to assume that Hayes-Dana could achieve the 81 percent cost of goods sold level that Budd and others have achieved.

MAGNA IN 1984

Magna's sales increased 63 percent in 1984, and net profits more than doubled. Magna obtained more than its share of the improving market in 1984, when we see the other companies' sales increase somewhere from 30 to 40 percent. The very favorable net profit results can be explained by the management of operating expenses. Operating expenses as a percentage of sales dropped from 85.3 percent to 74.9 percent. This level of operating expense reduction was not achieved by any of the other three companies.

Accounts receivable management was excellent, reducing the days receivable from 68.8 days to 63.9 days, the lowest it had been since 1980. It still remained significantly higher, however, than at the other companies studied.

Inventory management resulted in a slight drop of inventory turns; the result was, however, well within the results obtained by the other companies studied.

Plant expenditures for the year totaled $107 million; this obviously had a good effect on the operating expense reduction already discussed. The plant expansion was funded by an increase in long-term debt of $54 million and a stock offering which raised an additional $35 million.

At year end 1984, Magna was in a favorable liquidity and solvency position relative to the other companies studied.

LONG MANUFACTURING IN 1984

Long's sales increased to $49.5 million, up 39 percent from 1983. Return on equity at 41 percent was the best of the companies studied.

Long was driving down debt. The success was shown by the long-term debt to total assets ratio dropping to the low of the group of companies studied as well as the common stock equity to total assets ratio rising to a more usual level of 26 percent. This was achieved by paying off $6 million of the $7 million long-term debt and an additional $1.1 million of current debt.

The current ratio remained at 1.1 and the quick ratio dropped slightly to 0.5. Accounts receivable were brought down to 35 days and inventory turns rose again, up to 9.3; both were better than the other three companies showed.

APPENDIX B: EXCERPTS FROM 1985 ANNUAL REPORT (CORPORATE CONSTITUTION IN PRACTICE)

Magna's continued growth is based upon our unique corporate culture which allows the Company to make a better product for a better price.

Our culture recognizes that it takes three ingredients to be successful in business, namely: management, employees, and capital. Furthermore it requires that each of these ingredients has a right to share in the profits that it helps to generate. This foremost principle and other operating principles are enshrined in Magna's Corporate Constitution.

We in management continuously search for ways to stimulate employees to achieve greater productivity. In recent years this has been partially accomplished through the introduction of new technology. At Magna we continue to emphasize the human capital as we introduce technology in a manner that does not result in the displacement of employees. We are focusing on productivity improvements through new technology as a means of continuing to upgrade wages for production employees in the years ahead while maintaining our competitive position in the marketplace.

Management's primary responsibility is to demonstrate to employees that we care for their well-being, particularly with regard to wages, environment, safety in the workplace, fairness and equal opportunity for advancement. We are committed to these principles and intend to strengthen further our Human Resources department to make sure that our standards are maintained. A structure like this can only function through total openness. It is an education process. In our view the employees must fully understand the competitive factors facing the company as well as the facts surrounding our financial structure. I like to see employees reading the financial section of the papers in the morning realizing that they are shareholders of Magna. In fact, at this stage, our manufacturing and office employees own more than $30 million of Magna stock.

Members of management are also large shareholders in the Company. The value of their shares amounts to approximately $30 million and accordingly they have an interest in protecting the value of their investments. It is important for a healthy, growing company to have a strong equity base in relation to debt but we are sensitive to the effect of equity dilution on our ability to maintain investor confidence. Accordingly, we try to balance issues of new equity with growth in earnings per share.

Sales growth translates into the need for new production facilities. As a result, Magna's investment in land and buildings continues to increase. Management utilizes Magna's job creation capability to obtain favorable terms when purchasing land. We also seek joint venture partners to assist in the development of those lands. Our objective is to minimize Magna's capital outlay for land so as not to divert capital from our automotive components manufacturing activities.

QUALITY ASSURANCE

Quality is stressed throughout Magna — our success has been built on it — our future depends on it. We continue to train employees at all levels in matters relating to quality including the use of sophisticated measuring devices and statistical process control techniques. As a result of efforts in the area of quality, our operating units received many quality awards from our customers. Magna is dedicated to supplying automotive components and systems which are "world class" in quality and value.

HUMAN RESOURCES

Magna's greatest asset is its motivated work force. We continuously strive to provide a positive, safe and fair environment for all employees.

With this in mind we continue to expand our Human Resources departments at the Group and Corporate offices and sponsor seminars which stress the importance of good communications between management and employees. Wherever possible productivity gains are recognized with improved wages and expenditures to improve the working environment.

During the year we introduced *Magna People*, a bimonthly newsletter about Magna and its people. Simeon Park, which opened officially in June 1984, saw the introduction of many employee-organized functions, both winter and summer. The allocation to our Employee Equity Participation and Profit Sharing Program amounted to $8.3 million in 1985 compared to $6.4 million last year.

OTHER EMPLOYEE PROGRAMS

We provide a number of other programs for our employees including the following:

1. *Simeon Park*: Magna has developed a recreational park on 100 acres of natural countryside just north of Toronto. This park, available to all Magna employees and their families, features a 23-acre lake, sports and recreation facilities including children's playgrounds, tennis and volleyball courts, soccer fields, a baseball diamond, barbecue pits and picnic areas, nature trails, fishing docks and a large swimming pool.

The park is readily accessible to the majority of Magna's employees. During 1985 it was used extensively for company picnics, competitive team sports and casual family outings.

2. *Industrial Campus Concept*: To provide employees with an improved work environment, Magna is developing an industrial campus which will consist of a cluster of ten to twenty small autonomous plants together with the related group office and product development center supported by social and recreational facilities such as day care, a medical office, educational and sporting facilities.

In 1985 three new plants went into production in our first campus being developed in Newmarket, Ontario. A new group administration office and product development center associated with these plants also opened during the year. Two additional plants were under construction at year end. Land for other campuses is being assembled in preparation for our future growth.

3. *Technical Training Center*: Consistent with our commitment to high quality in-house technical strength, Magna opened its first Technical Training Center in the fall of 1984. The school is equipped with modern classroom and shop facilities and the latest in machinery and equipment.

On completion of their training, apprentices will work in a Magna operating unit to complete the requirements for trade qualification.

The purpose of the center is to help fulfill Magna's demand for skilled tool and die makers and other technical trades. These students will also receive training in management practices.

4. *Continuing Education*: Magna encourages all employees continually to improve their skills and education. For this reason, we offer in-house training and education in areas of communication, safety, quality control, microcomputer applications and management skills.

SOCIAL RESPONSIBILITY

Magna believes it has a responsibility to support the basic fabric of society. We fulfill this obligation by giving financial assistance and contributing our time to programs and projects in the areas of health and welfare, youth, the advancement of art and culture, education, and in support of the political process. Examples of the programs we support include:

1. *University Teaching and Research Support*: Magna currently provides financial support to four universities for teaching and research concerning entrepreneurship and fair enterprise.

2. *Student Sponsorship*: Each year Magna sponsors a number of outstanding students to attend the GMI Engineering and Management Institute in Michigan. GMI is a private university offering degrees in engineering and industrial administration.

Sponsorship guarantees students financial support and planned work assignments in Magna plants as well as the offer of a full-time position with Magna upon graduation.

APPENDIX C: OPERATING STRUCTURE

OPERATING UNIT

Each operating unit is directed by a general manager and an assistant general manager who have complete authority and responsibility for the operation of their unit within broad guidelines established by Executive Group Management. These decentralized units generally employ approximately one hundred people, thus giving the management teams close contact with staff and immediate control of all matters affecting personnel, product quality, efficiency, and profitability of the unit.

GROUP MANAGEMENT

The operating units are grouped — geographically and by markets — under the direction of a group management team which is accountable to Executive Management. A group vice-president is responsible for all areas of activity in his group and is supported by marketing, financial, and human resources executives.

Each group has its own sales team which maintains the day-to-day contact with the customers, the group office, and the operating units.

The group financial staff monitors all financial activities including capital spending and operating results. Each group has its own quality control and human resources personnel which review the operating unit's performance and serve as a resource to the units.

Group Management also oversees research and technology development conducted for their group.

EXECUTIVE MANAGEMENT

Executive Management is responsible for establishing policies consistent with the company's philosophy as developed by the board of directors.

Strategic planning is a priority of Executive Management. This involves the

FIGURE 1
Magna operating
structure

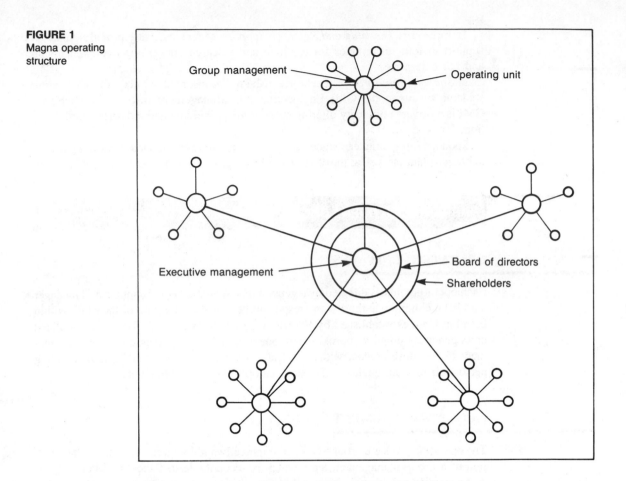

identification of specific products and technologies that Magna must develop in
order to meet the challenges of an evolving marketplace. It also includes the establishment of management teams capable of implementing Magna's marketing, quality,
human resources, and financial goals and objectives. As part of its responsibilities,
Executive Management secures and allocates financial resources and, together with
Group Management, monitors the performance of the operating units.

The corporate office serves as a resource to the groups and operating units in
the acquisition of capital equipment, raw materials, and services. This system allows
the groups and operating units to benefit from Magna's corporate buying power
when it is to their advantage. However, responsibility for product quality and delivery
rests with each operating unit and, accordingly, the units make purchases from
whatever source best meets their individual requirements.

AMERICAN SKATE CORPORATION

INTRODUCTION

In August 1979, Mr. Alan Adams (general manager of American Skate Corporation) and Mr. C. Herbert Charlton (president of American Skate's Canadian parent, Dominion Skate, and, incidentally, Mr. Adam's father-in-law) were reviewing the $2,000,000 financial package put together during the summer of 1979 for the opening of a roller skate plant in Berlin, New Hampshire. The New Hampshire plant was viewed by both men as a critical element in the Canadian parent's plan for a major United States expansion to take advantage of the tremendous roller skating boom in North America. Nonetheless, Alan Adams and Herb Charlton wanted to reconsider all the relevant aspects of the plan before making a final decision to proceed with the Berlin plant. The proposed package involved a $1,650,000 long-term debt from various U.S. and New Hampshire development groups, a lease-purchase agreement totaling $500,000 for a 44,000-square-foot plant capable of initially adding 20 percent (and, within a year, 200 percent) to Dominion's production capacity. All of the debt issued to the subsidiary American Skate was to be guaranteed by both Dominion Skate, which owned all of American Skate's stock, and by Herb Charlton personally.

"Alan, I don't mind going out on the limb if the deal is a good one," Herb told his son-in-law, "but I want you to help me doublecheck this New Hampshire project in all its aspects. I know I've called the shots pretty much so far, but this will be your baby."

The following paragraphs describe the roller skate industry, the backgrounds of both Dominion and American Skate and their top managements, and the financial package put together during spring and summer of 1979.

This case was prepared by John Barnett, University of New Hampshire, with Jonathan Foster, London School of Economics, for classroom discussion only. It is not intended to illustrate effective or ineffective handling of an administrative situation. © 1984 by J. Barnett. Reprinted by permission.

THE ROLLER SKATING INDUSTRY

Roller skates were first introduced in Holland during the eighteenth century, but consisted of wooden spools strung on a wooden frame, which was in turn nailed onto the bottom of wooden shoes. These skates were difficult to turn, but this problem was overcome by an American inventor, James Leonard Plympton of New York. In 1863 Mr. Plympton put four independent wooden wheels on a shoe, making the skate easier to turn. This original pair of Plympton's skates is now housed in the National Museum of Roller Skating in Lincoln, Nebraska, along with pictures of the first roller skating arena, which Mr. Plympton opened in New York a few years later.

The modern roller skate consists of the boot, a base plate, wheels, ball bearings, and the toe stop. The manufacturing process of a complete roller skate includes the following steps: (1) using sets of dies to cut the various parts of the boot from leather or other boot material; (2) machine stitching the various parts of the boot, including adding "counters" of reinforcing material in the heel and adding eyelets; (3) stitching the boot together around a mold of a foot, called a "last"; (4) buffing or "roughing" the leather so that it will accept glue; (5) using a combination of glue and staples and a series of machine steps to complete the toe and heel; (6) removing the last; (7) attaching the base plate; (8) securing the wheels and toe stops to the base plate; and (9) inspecting and packing.

Very few manufacturers performed all these steps. Many bought the finished boot from others, and attached the base plate, wheels, and toe stop. The manufacturers sold completed skates to sporting goods retailers, distributors, wholesalers, chain stores and roller skating rinks.

The stimulus for growth in the roller skating industry came from skateboard technology. During the skateboard craze in the mid-1970s, wide polyurethane wheels and precision bearings were perfected that allowed for a quiet ride on pavement. Further, the polyurethane wheels were much more absorbent than earlier metal or hard rubber wheels. As the roller skate manufacturers adopted these wheels and bearings in the late 1970s, the roller skate explosion began as skates moved out of rinks and into the streets and parks.

The roller skating industry just prior to the 1978–79 explosion consisted of a few privately held companies of which Dominion Skate was the only fully integrated major manufacturer. *Time* reported that total industry sales were about a million pair of skates per year.[1] The major firms included Roller Derby Skate, Chicago Roller Skate, Dominion Skate, and Sure-Grip International; total dollar sales for the industry were estimated by the casewriters as $25 to $30 million. Roller Derby Skate of Litchfield, Illinois, *Business Week* observed, "dominated U.S. roller skate manufacturing with aggressive pricing of its low-end models."[2]

---

[1] *Time*, August 6, 1979, p. 66.

[2] *Business Week*, August 27, 1979, p. 120.

The roller skate explosion had North American and international repercussions. Exhibit 1 shows *Business Week*'s estimate of 1979 sales by the U.S. leaders. Keith Parker, the marketing vice-president of Nash Manufacturing, described how his company, a major skateboard manufacturer, converted to roller skates in a 60-day period in the fall of 1978. Producing eight thousand pairs a day by the summer of 1979, Mr. Parker commented:

> *The key to our success is that we've expanded much quicker than others. But demand has to hold for another year if we're going to make much profit. . . . The skate business is in such an uproar that we could ship a million pairs tomorrow and still have back orders.*[4]

New U.S. manufacturers joined the industry, including Nash and Mattel, the $500 million toy manufacturer that invested over $1 million to begin producing roller skates in March 1979. Further, foreign manufacturers expanded into the North American market. Imports rose from $2 million in 1978 to $30 million in 1979, led by Taiwanese imports. Over ninety factories produced skates in Taiwan, and that nation soon had 85 percent of the U.S. imported market.[5]

The top-of-the-line, premium-priced skates continued to be manufactured in the United States. While children's and low-priced skates might retail from $20 to $50, with adult prices averaging $60, the well-regarded competition skates produced by the Dayton-based Snyder Skate Company were selling from $110 to $175 a pair. Snyder reports 1979 sales up 30 percent from 1978.

EXHIBIT 1
Estimated 1979
skate sales

Company	Estimated 1979 sales[a]
Roller Derby Skate (Illinois)	$ 50–60
Nash Manufacturing (Texas)	25
Sure-Grip International/RC Sports (California)	$ 20–25
Chicago Roller Skate (Illinois)	15–20
Mattel (California)	7–10
Total top five U.S. companies	$117–140
Estimated total U.S. sales	$200

[a] In millions of dollars
Source: *Business Week*[3]

[3] *Business Week*, op. cit.

[4] *Business Week*, op. cit.

[5] *Wall Street Journal*, April 6, 1981, p. 25.

Articles on roller skating appeared in almost every major periodical during 1979, including *Changing Times*, *Saturday Evening Post*, *Popular Mechanics*, *People*, *McCall's*, *Redbook*, and *Glamour*. Skates were endorsed by O. J. Simpson and were worn by Linda Ronstadt on a phonograph album cover. The number of roller skating rinks doubled to over six thousand during the 1970–78 period — five hundred new rinks were being added in 1979 — and roller disco became a major leisure activity.

Bill Butler, the "godfather of roller disco," looked forward to the opening in the fall of 1979 of his chic New York nightspot, the Roller Ballroom. Butler, who had skated for thirty-eight of his forty-five years, had a perspective on skating including a "whole philosophy of life" based on the sport. Nonetheless, *Popular Mechanics* commented:

> *New products come on the market so fast nowadays that even the Godfather of Roller Disco has trouble keeping up. Consider, for example, the two cycle, 1.2 h.p. engine that Motoboard International of Sunnyvale, California, suggests you slip on the back of your skate. For $289 you can zip down the highway at 40 m.p.h. with the wind blowing through your hair and your whole life passing before your eyes.* [6]

Sports Illustrated devoted several pages to a guide to buying skates in its October 15, 1979 issue; it specifically recommended Reidell and Oberhamer tops for boots ($40 to $90 retail), Chicago or Sure-Grip for the plates and wheels ($20 to $100 retail), and Snyder as the top of the line, with custom skates as high as $400 a pair. Butler commented that his ideal choice was a plate by Snyder, a Reidell boot, and Krypto wheels.

Positive signs for the roller skating industry included a Gallup Sports Poll in early 1979 showing roller skating fifth in popularity among teenagers, ahead of both tennis and skiing, and following basketball, baseball, swimming, and bowling. Both the Girl Scouts and Boy Scouts gave merit badges for roller skating proficiency.

Fifty percent of the U.S. teenage market would represent about 25 million pairs of skates. The total for North American skaters was estimated at between 30 and 40 million individuals, most of whom skated at rinks where rental skates were available. Chicago Roller Skate was particularly aggressive in skating rink sales.

Many commentators were optimistic. A vice-president of Herman's World of Sporting Goods reported a 400 percent increase in skate sales during the first half of 1979 at its ninety stores, noting that "the only thing that is slowing growth is product availability." [7] Mattel's Louis Miraula stated:

> *The universe of potential skaters is enormous. Because of the new wheel, people discovered roller-skating was an outdoor sport, à la jogging, but a lot more fun. The growth of*

[6] *Popular Mechanics*, vol. 151, June 1979.

[7] *Business Week*, op. cit.

this industry has a fad quality right now, but there is still that hard-core business that is not going to change substantially.[8]

The optimistic manufacturers predicted $400 million in annual skate sales would be achieved by the early 1980s.

Somewhat more cautious views were expressed by Chicago Skate, which had concentrated on rink sales. Said Joseph Sheuelson, Chicago Skate's vice-president of sales: "An idiot could make money in today's market. I'm walking on tiptoe, trying to gauge whether this is just another fad or has several years of life."[9] Roller Derby's national sales manager, Kenneth Neidl, said, "The demand is tremendous, but we don't know exactly where it is going. In many ways, what is happening is as new to us as to anybody, although we're the leader in the business."[10] Dennis Lane, international marketing director for Sure-Grip/RC Sports, was also cautious: "This is an extremely fast-growing industry, paralleling the sustained demand for bicycles that began 10 years ago. Most manufacturers are now living in a fairy-tale world where demand exceeds supply. In such an atmosphere, those that don't keep their heads could get hurt very badly."[11] A more negative view was expressed by financial analyst Harold Vogel: "By its very definition, the 'in thing' gets stale after a while. When everyone who is interested in roller skates has a couple of pairs, that's going to be it." Brunswick Corp., the national sporting goods company, sold its small skate division. A skateboard manufacturer, whose 1979 sales were one-fifth of 1978's, said he couldn't tell if "roller skates might be like skateboards — here today, gone tomorrow."

DOMINION AND AMERICAN SKATE

Dominion Skate's Early Years

Herb Charlton had gone to work for his uncle, owner of Dunn's Skate, Ltd., when he was very young. By the time his uncle died in 1946, Herb, then thirty-two, had substantial experience in all aspects of roller skate manufacture. Not wishing to continue working for his aunt, Herb left Dunn's and began Dominion Skate in the basement of his house in Ontario. Within a few years, Dominion with its three employees overflowed Herb's basement and garage, and it moved into a vacant school a few doors from the house. In 1958 an older plant facility in Mississauga, a short drive from Herb's house, was leased, giving Dominion a 3,000-square-foot, two-story building. Additions were made to this plant in 1962, 1970, and 1972. A second plant was leased 15 miles away in Toronto in 1973, as was an

[8] *Business Week*, op. cit.

[9] *Business Week*, op. cit.

[10] *Business Week*, op. cit.

[11] *Business Week*, op. cit.

assembly plant in Mississauga in January 1979. By August 1979, Dominion employed 120 people at three rented locations:

Location	Year opened	Activity	Square feet
Mississauga	1958	Manufacturing, assembly	20,000
Toronto	1973	Manufacturing, assembly	20,000
Mississauga	1979	Assembly	10,000

Each plant had a salaried plant manager who had worked with Herb for some time. Herb Charlton's policy of no layoffs and competitive wages resulted in a hard-working labor force which also had a low turnover rate.

Management

Herb Charlton, sixty-five years old in 1979, is president and chief financial officer of Dominion Skate and president of American Skate. While Herb made all important decisions, he was assisted by his son Paul (age thirty-three, director of plant engineering), his daughter Naomi (age thirty-one, office manager), and his son-in-law, Alan Adams (age thirty-seven, production manager and, more recently, general manager of the American subsidiary, American Skate Corporation).

Like Herb Charlton, Alan had dropped out of school and had held several positions as a factory worker and as a printer's apprentice. In 1958, Alan, then seventeen, went to work for Dominion Skate at the suggestion of Herb's daughter, whom Alan was then dating and subsequently married.

Dominion sold roller skates, ice skates, and children's double-runner bob skates through a distributor to a small group of retail accounts throughout Canada, ice skates helping to offset the seasonality of roller skates. Paul and Alan would occasionally call on these retail accounts; Herb would infrequently show customers around the Ontario plants. Dominion had a reputation for a high-quality, medium-priced skate. Dominion had kept pace with industry technology, and its advertisements referred to its "space age skates" with models called "All American Dream" and "Inertia."

U.S. sales were handled by a marketing firm, King R. Lee and Associates, of Santa Ana, California. King Lee in turn called on ten specialty distributors in the United States. These distributors bought from Lee and from others.

Operations were financed by small working capital loans from local banks, by advances from Herb Charlton, and by trade credit.

Total production capacity was about 285,000 pairs a year. This capacity was based upon one-shift operations. Alan Adams noted that Herb Charlton did not like to have more than one shift.

> I guess it was partially due to his wanting to be on top of things. Herb relied on personal inspection rather than formal production control systems. This philosophy of personal control extended to stock ownership as well. I had asked him about my owning some stock, so that I could have some security, but even after twenty-plus years of working for him, I never got any stock.

Financial Results

Exhibits 2, 3, and 4 present balance sheets, income statements, and related financial statistics for the years 1976, 1977, and 1978 and the 6 months ending June 1979.

The Financial Package

Berlin, New Hampshire, was considered as a site for U.S. expansion because a Canadian supplier had recently expanded into New Hampshire and had told Mr. Charlton that he "got a good deal" in New Hampshire. Northern New Hampshire was less than a day's drive from Toronto and less than half a day's drive from Montreal, where Dominion's Canadian distributor was located. Finally, Berlin development groups had actively pursued Dominion once its expansion interests were known.

EXHIBIT 2 Dominion Skate balance sheets

	1979 (June 30)	1978 (December 31)	1977 (December 31)	1976 (December 31)
Assets				
Current assets				
Cash, certificates of deposit	$ 109,100	$ 239,700	$173,800	$ 22,400
Accounts receivable	1,081,300	682,600	464,000	286,300
Net inventory	486,000	461,700	218,300	211,500
Total current assets	$1,676,400	$1,384,000	$856,100	$520,200
Fixed assets — net				
Machinery, equipment	$ 93,100	$ 103,400	$ 78,100	$ 50,400
Vehicles, leasehold improvements	23,400	26,700	13,300	4,400
Total fixed assets	$ 116,500	$ 130,100	$ 91,400	$ 54,800
Other assets				
Goodwill	$ 15,000	$ 15,000	$ 15,000	$ 15,000
Land deposits	211,200	211,200	—	—
Total other assets	$ 226,200	$ 226,200	$ 15,000	$ 15,000
Total assets	$2,019,100	$1,740,300	$962,500	$590,000
Liabilities				
Accounts payable, accruals	$ 636,800	$ 706,100	$497,400	$257,600
Taxes payable	173,700	170,200	38,600	12,200
Bank loan	–0–	50,000	–0–	95,000
Shareholder advances	246,600	219,900	101,200	54,800
Total liabilities	$1,057,100	$1,146,200	$637,200	$419,600
Equity				
Preferred stock	$ 100	$ 100	$ 100	$ 100
Retained earnings	961,900	594,000	325,200	170,300
Total equity	$ 962,000	$ 594,100	$325,300	$170,400
Total liabilities, equity	$2,019,100	$1,740,300	$962,500	$590,000

Note: Figures are in Canadian dollars.

EXHIBIT 3
Dominion Skate
income statement

	Six months ending June 30, 1979	Twelve months ending		
		December 31, 1978	December 31, 1977	December 31, 1976
Sales	$2,655,800	$4,267,100	$3,182,600	$1,518,600
Less: cost of sales	1,581,900	2,540,500	2,099,900	889,200
Gross profit	$1,073,900	$1,725,600	$1,082,700	$ 629,400
Operating expenses				
Administrative payroll, sales commissions	$ 410,500	$ 811,800	$ 649,800	$ 445,800
Supplies, freight	65,500	137,500	69,300	51,300
Advertising	1,100	10,600	3,400	2,400
Insurance	12,200	15,800	9,700	6,800
Professional fees	1,800	2,200	1,200	900
Office expenses	4,500	10,500	6,700	4,600
Repairs	3,300	2,700	2,100	500
Rent	34,300	52,800	42,000	33,800
Telephone, utilities	13,400	20,000	15,400	11,100
Travel	1,300	1,300	500	200
Vehicle	2,400	2,200	4,100	2,800
Miscellaneous[a]	27,500	54,400	30,200	16,400
Depreciation	13,600	34,400	24,800	15,000
Bad debt	12,700	21,500	1,000	(5,300)
Total operating expenses	$ 604,100	$1,177,700	$ 860,200	$ 586,300
Operating profit	$ 469,800	$ 547,900	$ 222,500	$ 43,100
Interest expense	$ 5,900	$ 5,100	$ 9,200	$ 6,800
Taxes	180,500	189,300	58,500	17,400
Total	$ 186,400	$ 194,400	$ 67,700	$ 24,200
Profit after tax	$ 283,400	$ 353,500	$ 154,800	$ 18,900

Note: Figures are in Canadian dollars.
[a] Donations to Baptist Church, 1978, 1979 at annual rate of $22,000. Pensions at annual rate of $11,000 (1978), $15,000 (1979). Balance is discounts.

EXHIBIT 4
Dominion Skate
selected financial
statistics

	1979	1978	1977	1976
Solvency				
Debt/equity	1.1	1.9	2.0	2.5
Times interest earned	47	70	17	3
Liquidity				
Net working capital	$619,300	$237,800	$218,900	$100,600
Current ratio	1.6	1.2	1.3	1.2
Funds management				
Day's sales in receivables	74	58	53	68
Day's cost goods in payables	72	101	87	107
Inventory turnover	3.3	7.5	9.8	
Profitability				
Return on sales	11%	8%	5%	1%
Return on assets	14%	20%	16%	3%
Return on equity	29%	60%	48%	11%

The financial plan put together as of August 1979 included: (1) a working capital loan of $1,150,000 from the U.S. Economic Development Administration (EDA), (2) a loan of $100,000 from a New Hampshire venture capital group, (3) a loan of $400,000 from the Berlin (New Hampshire) Economic Development Council (BEDCO), and (4) a lease purchase agreement with the Berlin Industrial Development and Park Authority (BIDPA).

Berlin, New Hampshire, about 175 miles north of Boston, had a serious unemployment problem among its population of thirteen thousand. The Converse Rubber Company, a manufacturer of athletic shoes, had closed in early 1979, laying off four hundred. The only significant employers in Berlin were the James River Paper Company, employing 1,200 to 1,500, and Bass Shoe, employing 250 to 350. Thus BEDCO and BIDPA were anxiously encouraging American Skate to locate in Berlin. BEDCO, directed by a board of business and labor officials and city government representatives, usually lent $5,000 for every job created by a new employer. BEDCO offered American Skate $400,000 at 6 percent annual interest, due in quarterly installments of $10,000, provided that American match its $400,000 with equity.

BIDPA, the developer/administrator of a small industrial park, had a board of directors similar to BEDCO. BIDPA had already built a 44,000-square-foot building, which was vacant and incurring interest charges. BIDPA offered American a 22-year lease purchase agreement totaling $500,000, with gradually increasing monthly payments. Real estate taxes were waived.

In addition to the Berlin debt, a New Hampshire venture capital group offered a $100,000 loan at prime (then about 12 percent) plus one percent. The state of New Hampshire was of course attractive to Charlton and Adams as it had no personal state income, sales, or use taxes and was replacing inventory and similar taxes with a flat tax on businesses of 8 percent of net profits.

The EDA, a branch of the U.S. Department of Commerce, offered a 10½ percent $1,150,000 loan, payable over 7 years, with gradually increasing monthly payments. Thus, pressure for economic support expressed itself not only from local and state groups, but at the federal level as well.

Equipment for the Berlin plant location was available to American Skate for $130,000 from Tiera Footwear of Dover, New Hampshire, which was in liquidation. Tiera's equipment would be sufficient for U.S. needs.

In trying to determine sales and costs, Herb Charlton and Alan Adams asked King Lee for an estimate of the potential total skate orders from the ten U.S. distributors for all skate manufacturers. This estimate, totaling 586,500 pairs a year, is reproduced in Exhibit 5. Lee was unsure what percentage of these total orders American Skate might expect to receive.

Dominion Skate estimated its own Canadian sales potential as 312,000 pairs a year, as opposed to its production capacity of 286,000 pairs a year. Dominion estimated that the total North American industry sales for all manufacturers would climb from the pre-1979 level of $30 million to over $200 million in the early 1980s, falling to $100 million by 1984.

The Berlin plant would initially produce at an annual level of 65,000 pairs, and within one year could be producing as many as 520,000 pairs on a two-shift basis. Initial employment of one hundred should rise to three hundred in 2 years, if the company's predictions were accurate.

The differential cost of producing a pair of skates as estimated by the company is shown in Exhibit 6. This cost is for an average pair, and it would be equally valid for Ontario and New Hampshire production. New Hampshire administrative salaries would be about $200,000 a year, half of which would be the general manager's salary; other overhead costs might total an additional $100,000.

EXHIBIT 5
Estimated total skate orders by Lee's ten distributors for all skates of all manufacturers

Firm	Annual volume in pairs
Gordon & Smith, San Diego, Calif.	93,500
L. Cohen, Los Angeles, Calif.	20,500
Smoothill, San Rafael, Calif.	65,000
West Coast Cycle, Culver City, Calif.	156,000
Bike Factory, Bellevue, Wash.	31,000
Donel Distributors, Garland, Tex.	31,000
Southeastern Sales, Florence, Ala.	15,500
Tuflex, Ft. Lauderdale, Fla.	78,000
A.W.H. Sales, Evanston, Ill.	65,000
Lubins, Watertown, Mass.	31,000
Total	586,500

EXHIBIT 6

American Skate cost estimates for average pair of skates

Selling Price		$12.95
Materials		
Boot	$2.85	
Plate	.77	
Wheels	1.28	
Bearings	1.04	
Toe stop	.14	
Hardware	.35	
Axle	.20	
Box	.19	
Other	.16	
Total materials		6.98
Labor		.75
Selling commission		1.56
Total		$ 9.29
Gross profit		$ 3.66

Summary

Both Herb Charlton and Alan Adams believed that the financial package available to them at the time could not be modified further. At a meeting to reach a decision on the Berlin plant, the following dialogue occurred:

ADAMS: *In addition to liens on all the equipment, you will have to personally guarantee all these loans. But how can you beat $400,000 at 6 percent and $1,500,000 at 1½ percent below prime?*

CHARLTON: *Alan, I believe in growth. Every two or three years we've leased new space or bought new equipment. That cycle means 1979 is a year for more growth. Still, it will be your project to live with. What do you think?*

MARY KAY COSMETICS, INC.

BACKGROUND OF THE COMPANY

A proliferation of products and a change of patterns that might dazzle a square dance caller have characterized the cosmetics industry in the late 1970s and the 1980s. Witness Eli Lilly's purchase of Elizabeth Arden, Squibb's acquisition of Lanvin-Charles of Ritz, Pfizer's take-over of Coty, Norton Simon's of Max Factor, Colgate-Palmolive's of Helena Rubenstein, not to mention British-American Tobacco's gobbling up Germaine Monteil.

Accompanying the change of corporate identities there has been a distinct shift in management styles as practiced in cosmetics concerns. The "flair and flamboyance" of the old school cosmetics moguls — the Revsons, Rubensteins, and Ardens of the industry — has been replaced by a new breed of management types. Charisma has given way to pragmatism. The new styles are diverse, however — as urbane, cool, and international as ITT-trained Revlon's chief executive, the Frenchman Michel Bergerac, or as fundamentalist, *nouveaux riches*, and Texas-grown as Mary Kay Ash, founder and driving force behind Mary Kay Cosmetics, Inc., whose pink Cadillac incentive plan for sales agents and skyrocketing corporate profits have made Mary Kay a legend in the highly competitive American cosmetics business.

In 1963 Mary Kay Ash, a much decorated veteran of in-home sales (Child Psychology Bookshelf, Stanley Home Products, World Gift) founded Mary Kay Cosmetics, Inc., on $5,000 for product formulas, containers, and secondhand office equipment and on the belief that women could be sold on using a proven skin care regimen through an educational approach. Mary Kay Ash's expertise in the area of human motivation and in direct sales combined with son Richard Rogers's wizardry in finance and marketing catapulted the company from its humble Dallas beginnings to a major national cosmetics corporation. Exhibit 1 charts this growth pattern. By August 1976 Mary Kay Cosmetics was listed on the New York Stock Exchange.

Case prepared by Charles L. Hinkle, University of Colorado, and Esther F. Stineman, Yale University. © 1984 Prentice-Hall, Inc. Reprinted by permission.

EXHIBIT 1
Mary Kay growth,
1971–1981

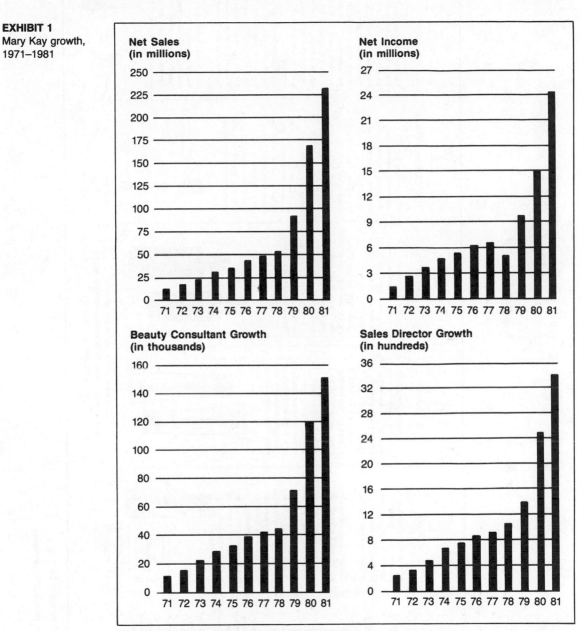

Net Sales
(in millions)

Net Income
(in millions)

Beauty Consultant Growth
(in thousands)

Sales Director Growth
(in hundreds)

Source: Mary Kay Cosmetics, Inc., *1981 Annual Report*, p. 20.

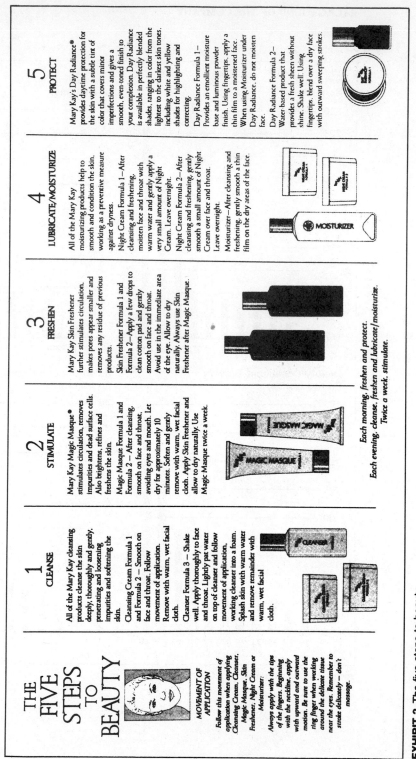

THE FIVE STEPS TO BEAUTY

MOVEMENT OF APPLICATION

Follow this movement of application when applying Cleansing Cream, Cleanser, Magic Masque, Skin Freshener, Night Cream or Moisturizer:

Always apply with the tips of the fingers. Beginning with the neckline, apply with upward and outward motion. Be sure to use the ring finger when working around the delicate tissue near the eyes. Remember to stroke delicately — don't massage.

1 CLEANSE

All of the Mary Kay cleansing products cleanse the skin deeply, thoroughly and gently, penetrating and loosening impurities and softening the skin.

Cleansing Cream Formula 1 and Formula 2 — Smooth on face and throat. Follow movement of application. Remove with warm, wet facial cloth.

Cleanser Formula 3 — Shake well. Apply thoroughly to face and throat. Lightly pat water on top of cleanser and follow movement of application, working cleanser into a foam. Splash skin with warm water and remove remainder with warm, wet facial cloth.

2 STIMULATE

Mary Kay Magic Masque® stimulates circulation, removes impurities and dead surface cells. Also brightens, refines and freshens the skin.

Magic Masque Formula 1 and Formula 2 — After cleansing, smooth on face and throat, avoiding eyes and mouth. Let dry for approximately 10 minutes. Soften and gently remove with warm, wet facial cloth. Apply Skin Freshener and allow to dry naturally. Use Magic Masque twice a week.

3 FRESHEN

Mary Kay Skin Freshener further stimulates circulation, makes pores appear smaller and removes any residue of previous products.

Skin Freshener Formula 1 and Formula 2 — Apply a few drops to clean cotton pad and gently smooth on face and throat. Avoid use in the immediate area of the eye. Allow to dry naturally. Always use Skin Freshener after Magic Masque.

4 LUBRICATE/MOISTURIZE

All of the Mary Kay moisturizing products help to smooth and condition the skin, working as a preventive measure against dryness.

Night Cream Formula 1 — After cleansing and freshening, moisten face and throat with warm water and gently apply a very small amount of Night Cream. Leave overnight.

Night Cream Formula 2 — After cleansing and freshening, gently smooth a small amount of Night Cream over face and throat. Leave overnight.

Moisturizer — After cleansing and freshening, gently smooth a thin film on the dry areas of the face.

5 PROTECT

Mary Kay's Day Radiance® provides daytime protection for the skin with a subtle tint of color that covers minor imperfections and gives a smooth, even-toned finish to your complexion. Day Radiance is available in perfectly blended shades, ranging in color from the lightest to the darkest skin tones, including white and yellow shades for highlighting and correcting.

Day Radiance Formula 1 — Provides an emollient moisture base and luminous powder finish. Using fingertips, apply a thin film to a moistened face. When using Moisturizer under Day Radiance, do not moisten face.

Day Radiance Formula 2 — Water based product that provides a fresh sheen without shine. Shake well. Using fingertips, blend over a dry face with outward sweeping strokes.

Each morning, cleanse, freshen and protect.
Each evening, cleanse, freshen and lubricate/moisturize.
Twice a week, stimulate.

EXHIBIT 2 The five steps to beauty

Source: Mary Kay, Inc. promotional literature.

250

Mary Kay Cosmetics consists of "a scientifically formulated line of skin products" that is presented to the user programmatically during home beauty shows with emphasis on Mary Kay's Five Steps to Beauty (Exhibit 2). Over 50 percent of the company's sales are derived from the basic skin care line. Skin, body, and hair care products in addition to cosmetics, toiletries, and fragrances compose the remainder of the relatively small Mary Kay line (Exhibit 3).

The company uses self-employed women billed as Beauty Consultants to introduce the products to customers in the home where customers sample the products and are instructed in their use. This deceptively simple format has resulted in dramatic growth in the company's sales and sales force since the beginning, when Mary Kay Cosmetics had only nine consultants. By 1981 net sales were $235.3 million, and about 150,000 consultants were selling the products (and, one presumes, faithfully using them). Exhibit 4 analyzes the productivity of the Mary Kay sales people. Major distribution centers in the United States assure rapid delivery of the products to the consultants who are able to provide the customers with their products without delay at the beauty show. Thus, there should never be a gap between ordering and receiving the product as there is in Avon's distribution method.

An oft-quoted management truism in the cosmetics industry is Michel Bergerac's conclusion that "every management mistake ends up in inventory." Mary Kay has addressed this concern and has avoided the pitfall through its unique distribution and operations systems. Charged with the task of instantaneously providing each consultant with the inventory she requires at the moment she requires it, Mary Kay has developed five domestic regional distribution centers, located in Atlanta; Chicago; Los Angeles; Piscataway, New Jersey; and the corporate warehouse in Dallas. Dallas is mission control for the company, where the products are manufactured and the orders received. The Marketing Department has instant access via computer to individual and unit sales. Manufacturing uses the data bank at Dallas to control inventory by forecasting and planning products' runs. On the microlevel, directors of sales units are only a toll-free call away from comprehensive information about the performance of their unit or of specific individuals.

EXHIBIT 3
Analysis of sales by products,
1977–1981

	1977	1978	1979	1980	1981
Skin care products for women	48%	50%	49%	52%	49%
Skin care products for men	2	1	1	2	1
Makeup items	21	21	26	22	26
Toiletry items for women	13	12	10	10	10
Toiletry items for men	2	3	2	2	2
Hair care	4	3	2	2	2
Accessories	10	10	10	10	10
Total	100%	100%	100%	100%	100%

Source: Mary Kay, Inc., *1981 Annual Report*, p. 21.

EXHIBIT 4
Mary Kay Cosmetics
sales analysis,
1970–1982E

Year	Sales (000)	Number of beauty consultants and sales directors at year end	Avg. no. of beauty consultants and sales directors	Sales beauty consultant and sales director (productivity)	Year-to-year increases in productivity
1982E	$346,000	190,000	175,000	$1,980.0	3.4%
1981E	242,000	150,000	140,072	1,915.0	9.0
1980	166,938	120,145	94,982	1,757.6	11.5
1979	91,400	69,820	57,989	1,576.2	26.9
1978	53,746	46,158	43,282	1,241.7	0.7
1977	47,856	40,407	38,818	1,232.8	−3.4
1976	44,871	37,229	35,176	1,275.6	13.3
1975	34,947	33,123	31,042	1,125.8	−6.0
1974	30,215	28,961	25,234	1,197.4	1.4
1973	22,199	21,508	18,805	1,180.5	−3.1
1972	17,232	16,103	14,142	1,218.5	1.5
1971	12,367	12,181	10,299	1,200.7	7.2
1970	8,091	8,418	7,224	1,120.0	−6.3
Average annual growth					
1975–1980	36.7%	29.4%	25.1%	9.3%	
1970–1975	34.0	31.5	33.9	0.1	

Source: Mary Kay, Inc. data.

In 1978 Mary Kay Cosmetics formed a sister company in Toronto that has evolved into one of Canada's largest cosmetic enterprises. As of 1971 and 1980, respectively, separate operations were launched in Australia and Argentina. The Argentine Mary Kay undertaking has run into difficulties because of international problems. During May 1982, in the midst of the dispute between Argentina and Britain over the Falkland Islands with sky-high inflation in Argentina, Mary Kay was forced to write off $1.5 million there in a reassessment of the value of the company's marketing unit in Argentina.

MARY KAY ASH'S PERSONAL STORY

Mary Kay Ash's personal story is a rags-to-riches success saga in the great American tradition, and it mirrors the stories of many of the company's beauty consultants. In her autobiography, the best selling *Mary Kay*, "the success story of America's most dynamic businesswoman," published by Harper & Row in 1981, Mary Kay tells of her life. In the company literature, this simple story is told and retold, and the lesson of self-discipline is underscored (Exhibit 5). Mary Kay Ash received the Horatio Alger Award from Dr. Norman Vincent Peale in 1978, and the company refers to Mrs. Ash's story as "a Horatio Alger Story."

EXHIBIT 5
Mary Kay — A
Horatio Alger story

A Childhood Filled with Challenge

From a small Texas town to national prominence was not an easy journey. Mary Kay's success can largely be attributed to the discipline and independence she learned in her childhood.

The youngest of four children, she was born in the small town of Hot Wells, Texas, where her parents owned a hotel. When her father's health deteriorated and he became an invalid, the family moved to Houston so Mary Kay's mother could find work.

While her mother worked 14-hour days managing a restaurant, seventeen-year-old Mary Kay stayed home cleaning, cooking, and caring for her father.

Throughout those early years, Mary Kay's mother strongly influenced her daughter by encouraging her to excel in everything she did and told her over and over again, "You can do it." Whether in school or at home, Mary Kay wanted to be the best. Another lasting influence on her life has been her Christian faith. Her sincere convictions enabled her to express her love and affection toward those around her, and her faith has also been the cornerstone of her business success. Her basic philosophies are "God first, family second, career third," and the Golden Rule.

Young Adulthood

After finishing high school, Mary Kay married and had three children. Her husband was soon called away for World War II active duty, leaving Mary Kay with mounting financial problems. She worked as a secretary at a Baptist Church to help support the overwhelming cost of raising three children.

A postwar divorce left Mary Kay the lone support of her young family. With the same determination that brought her through her earlier years, Mary Kay became a dealer for Stanley Home Products, a direct sales party plan company. This job enabled her to earn a living and still spend time with her children.

After three weeks of work and average sales of only $7 worth of products per party, Mary Kay attended a sales convention. She sat in the back row and decided that she would one day be crowned "Queen of Sales." Upon sharing her goal with the president of the company, Frank Stanley Beveredge, he replied, "Somehow, I think you will."

Mary Kay triumphantly won the crown the following year and eventually moved to Dallas where she continued her 13-year career with Stanley Home Products. But this was only the beginning of Mary Kay's rise to success.

Later, upon joining World Gift, a company that sold decorative accessories, she quickly became National Training Director. In 1962, though, she experienced a personal ordeal that threatened her health and her career. She suffered from a rare form of paralysis on one side of her face, but after surgery and several months of hospitalization, she recovered completely.

The Company Begins

Upon her recovery and after her retirement from World Gift, Mary Kay remarried and began to think about starting her own direct sales company. She planned to run the sales division, while her husband acted as administrator. One month prior to the launching of the company, her husband had a heart attack and died. Mary Kay's three children joined their mother in the early days of the new venture. Today, Richard Rogers, her youngest son, is the president of Mary Kay Cosmetics, Inc.

Source: Mary Kay, Inc. promotional literature, 1981.

THE BEAUTY CONSULTANT
AND THE BEAUTY SHOW

The lifeblood of the Mary Kay organization is the beauty consultant and director force who have generated Mary Kay's phenomenal sales and following. Independent beauty consultants, who buy their own sample case and products, are organized into sales units led by a sales director. Mary Kay Ash believes the cash system has assured the health of the company. "At Mary Kay, our consultants and directors pay in advance for their merchandise with a cashier's check or money order — no personal checks."

> *It's impossible for a Consultant to run up a debt with the company. Therefore, we have few accounts receivable. We don't have the expense of collecting bad debts, and we pass the savings on in the form of higher commissions. This way, everyone benefits. Most financial people just marvel at it — it's unheard of for a company of our size.*[1]

Richard Rogers sums up the distribution plan this way: "Each Mary Kay consultant is an independent contractor. They are not employees of the company. Mary Kay serves as a wholesale house — freight in, freight out. The consultant buys directly from the company at wholesale prices and sells at retail prices. The difference is her profit."

Although the beauty consultant is in business for herself — the point is stressed in the corporate literature that "she is not by herself." The director is available as a consultant and teacher to the beauty consultant to help her successfully present the all-important beauty show. An effective director, according to the company, can handle in embryo the problems of poor consultant performance and thus control turnover in the ranks.

Because the beauty consultant is not a cosmetologist, federal and state laws prohibit her from applying cosmetics to the faces of the five or six participants at each show. Rather, her task is to assist each woman who attends the session, usually held at the home of a voluntary hostess, to determine her skin type and to answer questions about the five steps of beauty process. "This is an effective teaching method. We don't sell — we teach!" emphasizes Mary Kay. "Polite persuasion" is the Mary Kay euphemism for selling. The hard sell is avoided, according to the literature.

In its *1981 Annual Report*, Mary Kay Cosmetics, Inc., shared with readers the philosophy of the beauty show.

> *The Beauty Show is our primary marketplace. Its importance cannot be overstated. Here the Consultant has undivided attention as she presents the entire line. She has ample time to give each guest personal attention. The customer learns valuable tips on skin care and grooming and, because she receives her order at the Show, puts the lessons into practice immediately.*

[1] Mary Kay Ash, *Mary Kay* (New York: Harper & Row, 1981), p. 29.

During the course of the two-hour beauty show, the consultant demonstrates, presents, persuades, collects, and delivers. (Exhibit 6 is the price list for Mary Kay products demonstrated in the beauty show.) In addition to the sales activities implicit in the show, a consultant may recruit other consultants and arrange bookings for future shows at the demonstration. The person who agrees to host a show at her home "earns" Mary Kay products. Often if the consultant notes a potential customer's reluctance to purchase because of the cost, she may suggest that the woman earn products by hosting.

To become a consultant, a woman submits a signed beauty consultant agreement with a cashier's check or money order to Mary Kay Cosmetics. The pink beauty showcase is then shipped immediately to her from Dallas. Before she is a full-fledged consultant, a recruit must attend three beauty shows with an experienced consultant, book five beauty shows for her first week's activity, and attend training classes conducted by a director in her area. Because each Mary Kay show provides yet another opportunity to recruit beauty consultants into the company, to book future shows, and to establish reorder business, Mary Kay puts a premium on running a smooth and professional show. Mary Kay consultants are expected to present a well-groomed, Mary Kay–cosmeticized image and to dress in a manner consistent with Mary Kay Ash's personal philosophy of feminine attractiveness.

Mary Kay annual reports feature attractive models representing the consultants on their appointed rounds, dressed in tailored suits, tastefully manicured, coiffured, and made up, usually wearing soft, pastel blouses and Mary Kay jewelry (golden bumblebees and Mary Kay pins are sought-after prizes in the company). The ideal image of the consultant is that of the "dressed-for-success" career woman.

EXHIBIT 6 1982 Mary Kay price list

ITEM	PRICE	✔
Complete Collection (as shown)	$71.00	
Basic Skin Care	39.00	
CLEANSE		
Cleansing Cream Formula 1, 4 oz.	6.50	
Cleansing Cream Formula 2, 4 oz.	6.50	
Cleanser Formula 3, 3.75 oz.	6.50	
STIMULATE		
Magic Masque Formula 1, 3 oz.	7.50	
Magic Masque Formula 2, 3 oz.	7.50	
FRESHEN		
Skin Freshener Formula 1, 5.75 oz.	7.50	
Skin Freshener Formula 2, 5.75 oz.	7.50	
LUBRICATE/MOISTURIZE		
Night Cream Formula 1, 4 oz.	12.00	
Night Cream Formula 2, 4 oz.	12.00	
Moisturizer, 2.8 oz.	12.00	
PROTECT		
Day Radiance Formula 1, .5 oz.	5.50	
Day Radiance Formula 2, 1 oz.	5.50	
☐ Ivory Beige ☐ Toasted Tan ☐ Light Beige ☐ Cinnamon ☐ Medium Beige ☐ Chestnut ☐ Warm Beige ☐ Coffee ☐ Suntan Beige ☐ White ☐ Suntan ☐ Yellow ☐ Honey Tan		
GLAMOUR COLLECTION		
Blush Rouge	4.00	
Eyeliner ☐ Black ☐ Brown	5.00	

ITEM	PRICE	✔
Eyebrow Pencil ☐ Black ☐ Brown ☐ Auburn ☐ Charcoal ☐ Light Brown ☐ Blonde	$ 3.00	
Mascara ☐ Black ☐ Brown	5.50	
Lip and Eye Palette (Complete with 2 brushes)	14.50	
Lip Palette (Complete with lip brush)	12.50	
Eye Palette (Complete with eye brush)	12.50	
Retractable Lip or Eye Brush	2.00	
Lip or Eye Palette Refill	4.00	
Great Fashion Lip Color Shade Selections: ☐ Pinks ☐ Plums ☐ Russets ☐ Reds ☐ Corals ☐ Spices		
Great Fashion Eye Shadow Shade Selections: ☐ Blues ☐ Greens ☐ Browns ☐ Plums		
Blusher ☐ Soft Pink/Soft Peach ☐ Tawny Rose/Tawny Amber ☐ Cinnamon/Mahogany	8.50	
Lip Liner Pencils ☐ Raisin/Ripe Cherry	6.50	
Lip Gloss	4.50	
SPECIALIZED SKIN CARE		
Moisturizer, 2.8 oz.	12.00	
Facial/Under Makeup Sun Screen, 2.7 oz.	7.00	
Hand Cream, 2.8 oz.	5.50	

ITEM	PRICE	✔
BODY CARE		
Cleansing Gel, 8 oz.	$ 7.00	
Buffing Cream, 6 oz.	7.50	
Moisturizing Lotion, 8 oz.	6.50	
Sun Screening Lotion, 6 oz.	8.50	
BASIC HAIR CARE		
Shampoo for Normal/Dry Hair, 8 oz.	4.50	
Shampoo for Oily Hair, 8 oz.	4.50	
Protein Conditioner, 8 oz.	6.00	
Intense Conditioner, 3 oz.	7.00	
Non-Aerosol Hair Spray, 8 oz.	4.50	
FRAGRANCE BOUTIQUE		
Avenir Spray Cologne, 2 oz.	15.00	
Intrigue Spray Cologne, 1.75 oz.	10.00	
Facets Spray Cologne, 2 oz.	11.00	
Facets Cologne, 1 oz.	6.50	
Angelfire Spray Cologne, 1.75 oz.	12.00	
Exquisite Body Lotion, 8 oz.	6.50	
MEN'S PRODUCTS		
Mr. K Skin Care System	34.50	
Cleanser, 2.7 oz.	4.50	
Mask, 2.6 oz.	6.50	
Toner, 2.6 oz.	4.50	
Moisture Balm, 2.5 oz.	12.00	
Sun Screen, 2.7 oz.	7.00	
Mr. K Cologne, 3.75 oz.	9.50	
Mr. K Lotion, 3.4 oz.	4.50	
ReVeur After Shave Cologne, 3.75 oz.	10.00	

Source: Mary Kay, Inc., price list for beauty consultants.

A career woman should dress in a businesslike manner. Personally, I'm opposed to wearing pants on the job. In fact, that's a company policy at Mary Kay (except in the manufacturing area). After all, we are in the business of helping women look more feminine and beautiful, so we feel very strongly that our Beauty Consultants should dress accordingly. We suggest they always wear dresses to Shows, rather than pants, and we emphasize well-groomed hair and nails. After all, can you imagine a woman with her hair up in curlers, wearing jeans, calling herself a Beauty Consultant — and trying to tell other women what they should be doing to look good? We're really selling femininity, so our dress code has to be ultra-feminine.[2]

MOTIVATION — MARY KAY STYLE

Within the honeycomb of the sales unit — the basic organizational entity in Mary Kay, though it is not included in the company organization chart — the consultant receives weekly sales training and encouragement, sings Mary Kay booster songs, and applauds the successes of others. Personal vignettes are as legitimate in this revival-style gathering as is instruction in specific sales techniques. The professionalization program at Mary Kay also includes regional workshops, Jamborees (conducted by national sales directors), leaders' conferences, and seminars. "The Seminar" is the "multimillion-dollar extravaganza" staged each year at the Dallas Convention Center where thousands of Mary Kay consultants and directors converge for inspiration, entertainment, and education — Mary Kay style. It is in this immense convention forum that Mary Kay leaders are recognized publicly, where they share their own sagas of success with the audience. Here the Cadillacs, mink coats, diamond bumblebees, and other coveted Mary Kay status symbols are meted out to the deserving ones; and here women aspire to these material rewards by goal-setting activities for the coming year. Seminar classes, conducted by successful Mary Kay directors, teach the intricacies of sales technique, bookkeeping, leadership, customer service, and other skills necessary for Mary Kay entrepreneurship. In 1980 the special effects staff for the seminar arranged for the pink Buicks and Cadillacs to "float" phantomlike through mist onstage via a remote control process much to the delight of the assembled. Seminar showmanship has proven effective in creating the Mary Kay myths.

The company believes that tangible symbols of success motivate the Mary Kay women and serve to fuel the belief "that if they work hard enough — if they give of themselves — that they will be successful, personally and professionally." Vacation trips, prizes, contests, photographs of Mary Kay with members of the sales force, and constant praise are among the motivators the company has used with great success. In 1980, 311 sales directors earned more than $30,000; 98 earned more than $50,000. Almost 500 are designated as "Cadillac-status" directors. The highest-paid Mary Kay saleswomen are the national sales directors, a group of

[2] Ibid., p. 10.

more than 39 women who began as consultants. They average more than $150,000 annually. Mary Kay Cosmetics gives a great deal of publicity to these star earners, for example, Helen McVoy who started back in the humbler days of the company and now earns $300,000 a year.

EARNINGS

A consultant is in business for herself and therefore her earnings are determined by her sales at retail. She purchases products from the company at a discount (up to 50 percent) from retail and her gross profit is the difference between her purchase price and the retail selling price that she herself determines.

In 1981 Mary Kay Cosmetics raised prices 16 percent and simultaneously upped the commission thresholds to increase productivity on a sustained basis. If the consultant wants to qualify for a 50 percent discount, she must order $1,000 of products at the suggested retail price. Previously an $800 order qualified her for a 50 percent discount. Selling $800 of merchandise currently entitles her to $360. Price hikes and the revised commission thresholds allow the consultant to increase her earnings if she manages to maintain her customer base. But there is no time to rest on her laurels, because the Mary Kay system is geared toward the sales woman who aggressively builds her business.

While it is relatively easy to become a Mary Kay consultant, the company demands considerably more of those women who wish to qualify as sales directors. The labor of the sales director is sweetened by the possibility of substantially increased financial rewards over the consultant status, however. Like the consultant, the sales director is self-employed. As the resident advisor for her unit, she supplies her people with inspiration, positive suggestions for improving sales performance, and business advice of all kinds. A carefully orchestrated program for the directors and a rigorous screening process that admits only those women who have met stringent performance standards in terms of volume sales and number of recruits assures that the directors will be an experienced, aggressive sales group. In 1982 the company numbered 3,500 directors. The director-in-qualification travels to Dallas (at her own expense, as is the case of travel arrangements for the entire Mary Kay sales force) to receive training in management of a sales unit.

The directors' commissions were revised upward in 1981 along with the consultants'. To receive the pink Cadillac ("those little pink jars mean little pink cars"), the director must maintain a wholesale volume of $12,000 per month. Under the previous commission scheme, the director earned 12 percent if her unit volume topped $6,000. After the revision, her unit needed to "politely persuade" customers to buy from $8,000 to $12,000 to receive 12 percent. Although the director currently gets only 11 percent on unit volume between $5,000 and $8,000, a 13 percent commission is now possible for the director on volume over $12,000. The director must maintain the momentum of her unit if she is to succeed. Simply put, success for consultants spells success for directors, and vice versa.

GROWTH OF THE COMPANY

Inside and outside of Mary Kay, declining recruitment of consultants was expected in the early 1980s, and the 50 percent growth rate experienced up until 1980 was considered unsustainable. Anxiety that the company might reach an early saturation point due to its rapid growth has proved to be groundless, however, with 180,000 consultants projected by December 1982.

Cosmetics, along with beer and cigarettes, have generally been earmarked "recession-proof." Yet cosmetics unit sales in late 1981 and 1982 for Mary Kay and other companies did falter as disposable incomes declined in recessionary environment. During this period Mary Kay Ash's autobiography went on sale. Her promotional tour to major U.S. cities to discuss her life, career, and company on television and radio provided unprecedented visibility for the Mary Kay message and gave recruitment a shot in the arm. The company spent an estimated $450,000 in television and other advertisements during this period (Exhibit 7).

THE MARY KAY PHILOSOPHY

At Mary Kay, attention to the family unit is central to company ideology. Mary Kay Ash often states the formula, "God first, family second, career third." Since most Mary Kay consultants have families, the organization realizes that enlisting family cooperation makes for happier, more successful Mary Kay salespersons. A husband who is unfavorably disposed to his wife's Mary Kay career, "who gets upset when she comes home an hour late from an evening beauty show" may be "disastrous" to the business. So Mary Kay consultants are urged early on to enlist the cooperation of husbands with tact and caring. At the seminar in Dallas each year, husbands participate in workshops led by experienced Mary Kay husbands designed to imbue them with "that Mary Kay enthusiasm" at best or at least to help them handle issues that sometimes arise in a Mary Kay household: ego crises that occur when a wife brings in more income than her spouse, household crises when a woman may not be on hand to perform all the "wifely" functions to which the family has become accustomed, readjustment problems for the family when the wife and mother may be away from home attending Mary Kay functions. To cheer those husbands left at home when wives are in Dallas, training to be directors, letters are dispatched to them from Mary Kay headquarters thanking them for the support they are giving to their wives' careers.

If you are a working woman, getting your husband involved is so important! It's always been my observation that people will support that which they help to create. When a woman goes to work, she must not only sell her husband on her career, but if she's wise, she'll find ways to get him involved. Once he's involved, she'll get his support. One area where many of our Beauty Consultants have gotten their husbands involved is in the bookkeeping and record-keeping that goes with any business. Many sales-oriented

EXHIBIT 7
Advertising for the
Mary Kay
autobiography

"YOU'VE GONE PRETTY FAR FOR A WOMAN." THEY SHOULDN'T HAVE TOLD ME THAT.

"I had been a success in my field for more than 25 years. A promotion to a top executive position was long overdue. Instead, I was passed over again and again. Has that happened to you?

"Well, my response was to create an opportunity that would reward women for what they were really worth!

"My dream was to offer women not only a wonderful new Skin Care Program, but also an opportunity to prove how far we can go."

Today Mary Kay Cosmetics has more than 120,000 Beauty Consultants on three continents and our sales are in the hundreds of millions of dollars!

Now the Mary Kay story is available in a book.

It is a personal business history of a dream that happened when all the skeptics said it would fail.

"If you have ever been told you can't do something,

Yes, there really is a Mary Kay.
Portrait by Francesco Scavullo, June 1981.

my story will prove you can. I urge you to read it right away, and I hope it will open some closed doors and closed minds in your life."

It's available at your local bookstore. Or ask your Beauty Consultant how you can get a copy. If you don't have a Consultant, look in the Yellow Pages under Cosmetics/Retail. Or call toll-free (800) 527-6270.

women don't especially like record keeping, so they welcome their husband's help in this area, and it's been our experience that most husbands enjoy keeping their wives' records.[3]

To assist the woman in rendering to the family the time that is theirs, and to Mary Kay Cosmetics its fair share, Mary Kay Ash advocates good time management. Since she has found that getting up at five in the morning gives her an additional workday each week, she urges consultants and directors to join her Five O'Clock Club: a routine of rising early each morning, using the early hours to dress, apply makeup, do household chores, and prepare to begin Mary Kay business-related activities by 8:30 A.M. The ideal consultant will stop for a half-hour lunch and stay with business until five in the evening. In the best of all possible Mary Kay worlds, a woman will earn enough to allow her to delegate many household duties to a housekeeper, the better to perform her sales duties. Getting organized, however, is key to the success of the woman who cannot afford a housekeeper:

I know many women do manage to wear all those hats, but it can certainly take its toll. In order to be effective in their careers and still be good wives and mothers, they must be organized. As a general rule, I have found that getting organized is one of the biggest problems working women have. And if a woman is trying to wear a great many hats and she isn't organized, she's operating under a tremendous handicap.[4]

A unique feature of the company is the flexibility built in for working mothers. Inherent in the company philosophy is the notion that women working as a team can cover for each other in case of family emergency. The beauty show will go on, but perhaps another consultant will carry on when a woman needs to care for a sick child or spouse, a procedure called "the dovetail system."

The Mary Kay organization becomes an extended family for its sales force, a bountiful maternal figure dispensing prizes of minks, diamonds, and Cadillacs to dutiful daughters. The nonhierarchical family atmosphere of the company promotes high morale, according to Mary Kay and upper-level staffers.

The personal touch — be it serving cookies mixed up by Mary Kay Ash with her own hands at company functions or sending Christmas, birthday, anniversary cards and condolence messages — underscores the familial concept of the organization and builds company loyalty. The allegiance of the sales force to the company, personified in Mary Kay Ash, surfaces in every aspect of the consultant's training. In problem solving, consultants are asked to think what Mary Kay herself "would do in your situation," much as if Mary Kay Ash were an exemplary, albeit absent, mother. Adopting Mary Kay Ash's personal routine as their own in many cases, consultants and directors are attached to Mary Kay by an umbilical cord of personal habit and life-style. Many of the sales force display photographs of Mary Kay in their workspaces at home.

[3] Ibid., p. 72.

[4] Ibid., pp. 169–170.

SKIN CARE PRODUCTS AND MARY KAY

Mary Kay Cosmetics in 1963 had hit upon an idea whose time had come with its introduction of skin care products, now the staple of almost every major cosmetics house. The basic five-step skin care process includes cleansing, stimulating, freshening, moisturizing, and protecting the skin. The company suggests that the basic set not be broken as it is the centerpiece of the Mary Kay concept, that is, to teach people how to care for their skin.

> *The best reason to start a new company is that* there is a need for what you have to offer, *or that you're better than what is being offered. When we began, no cosmetic company was actually teaching skin care. All of them were just selling rouge or lipstick or new eye colors. No company was teaching women how to care for their skin. So we came into a market where there was a real need — and we filled it. Oddly enough, it's still true today that women are not knowledgeable about skin care, despite all the information on television, in magazines, and in newspapers. They buy a product here, there, and everywhere, but they don't have a coordinated program. We fill a void by helping women understand how to take care of their skin. So, if you want to start a successful business, you must offer something different or something better than what is available.*[5]

In what is being called a "cosmetic revolution" by some, major cosmetics firms in the 1980s are taking scientific approaches to beauty. While the promise of cosmetics before the 1980s was one of glamor, the present appeal is made to the customer's consciousness that the scientific result of good skin care is healthy, younger-looking, cleaner skin. Advertising stresses the chemical properties of collagen, linoleic acid, and many more ingredients. Consumers are presumed, in such high-tech ads, to be conscientious about skin care and conversant with its sophisticated vocabulary replete with such terms as *cell renewal, exfoliation,* and *hydration.*

This scientific approach began in the 1960s when Dr. Erno Lazlo introduced his pathbreaking line of skin care products to an enthusiastic public. Worship at the altars of Revlon's Eterna 27 and Clinique also began in the 1960s and has continued into the 1980s.

Scientific research in the 1950s set the stage for the cosmetic revolution. Although Mary Kay Cosmetics maintains that the original recipe for its skin preparations emanated from a hide tanner in Texas.

From the 1950s to the 1970s, soluble collagen became available to cosmetic chemists at that time seeking a protein to be used in products to treat dry, flaking, aging skin.[6] Marketing research had demonstrated (and continues to reveal) that approximately 90 percent of American women perceive their most serious skin problem to be dry skin.

---

[5] Ibid., p. 120.

[6] See R. D. Todd and L. I. Biol, "Soluble Collagen: New Protein for Cosmetics," *Drug and Cosmetic Industry*, Vol. 117 (October 1975), pp. 50–52.

According to scientist Bernard Idson of Hoffman-La Roche, when it was understood that it is not oil but water that causes skin to be soft and flexible, cosmetic marketing shifted emphasis from total emolliency to the moisturizing qualities of various products. Idson and other researchers found that a water level of less than 10 percent in an individual's skin results in dried keratin, which causes lowered skin elasticity, a characteristic of sun-damaged, chapped, and aged skin.[7]

With over half its sales in the skin care area, Mary Kay finds itself in the 1980s heavily invested in the fastest-growing product category in cosmetics. Industry analysts project continued growth for skin care products, estimating in optimistic moments the general moisturizer market to number 100 million persons.

PSYCHOGRAPHICS, DEMOGRAPHICS, AND MARY KAY

Psychographic market segmentation stretches beyond the more traditional demographic and socioeconomic descriptors used to predict consumer behavior. Product psychographics are bound up with product promises, price-value perception, and the overall image of the product. Because of this relational posture, psychographic market segmentation is particularly applicable to the behavior of the cosmetics purchaser, who according to an old aphorism, is buying not only a product but hope. In a way, however, proponents of the scientific approach to marketing skin care are placing bets on a consumer's responding to demonstrations of empirical results and moving away from purchasing merely out of *hopes* that the product will deliver.

The past decade has seen a tremendous consumer responsiveness to computerized and education-oriented beauty programs (Clinique) and carefully orchestrated, scientific-based programs to control "age zones" (Charles of Ritz). According to those in the testing area at Ritz, their test methodology for the product Age-Zone Controller used 100 subjects and, according to Eileen Kregan, Director of Consumer Education for Charles of Ritz (1982), "consisted of making silicone skin replicas of the subject's outer eye area on the first, seventh, and fourteenth days of the test. To measure line reduction, light was passed through the positive skin replicas and a transparency was made. Direct measurements were then made of the transparencies to determine what changes occurred in the length and number of age lines over a 14-day period." Advertising for the product will reflect the scientific findings.

Mary Kay relies much more heavily on the educational than on the high-tech approach with its customers. *Quality control* is a term that surfaces more often at Mary Kay than specific scientific terminology and vocabulary. The company envisions customers as interested more in the process of using the product than its specific theoretical underpinnings.

---

[7] See Bernard Idson, "Dry Skin Moisturizing and Emolliency," *Drug and Cosmetic Industry* Vol. 117 (October 1975), pp. 43–45.

The demographic trends as projected by U.S. Census figures indicate that Mary Kay will continue to find an increasing number of women customers in the 25- to 44-year age group, a group Mary Kay has already targeted as one vitally interested in skin care. Projections call for the 63 million persons in the 25- to 44-year age group in 1980 to increase to 80 million in 1990. Although the teenage and early-twenties market is dwindling, this should not be problematic for Mary Kay since its products presently do not get high visibility among this group due to the beauty show method of sales.

Mary Kay Cosmetics sees many positive signals in the 1980 Census data (Exhibit 8). Constructing ''the woman of the '80s,'' the company profiled a woman ''in her mid-30s'':

Her husband has a good job, but they could use extra income. They have one child.

She has completed some college and would like to return, part-time, for more. She is highly inclined to a job or career — both from economic necessity and from a desire to experience something new and to test her abilities.

The woman of the '80s has a new awareness of political affairs but, at the same time, is keenly aware of improving herself, physically, intellectually and professionally.

She wants to live life on her terms. She is interested in acquiring things and achieving goals, but above these she places experience. She is not content to be a spectator. While she may admire the looks and figure of a fashion model, she would rather be one.

Even though she enjoys her homelife, she seeks to expand her world by finding a part-time job or full-time career. This new world makes her more aware of her appearance. She works hard to stay fit; she is nutrition-conscious; she cares deeply about how she looks — her wardrobe, her skin, and her grooming.

To the ends of feeling and looking good, she has educated herself in the accoutrements

EXHIBIT 8
U.S. population projections by age group (both sexes)

Age group	1970	1975	1980	1985	1990	Compound % increase (decrease)			
						1975 vs. 1970	1980 vs. 1975	1985 vs. 1980	1990 vs. 1985
15–19	19.3	21.0	20.6	18.0	16.8	1.7%	(0.4)%	(2.7)%	(1.4)%
20–24	17.2	19.2	20.9	20.5	18.0	2.3	1.7	(0.5)	(2.6)
25–29	13.7	16.9	18.9	20.6	20.2	4.3	2.3	1.7	(0.4)
30–34	11.6	14.0	17.2	19.3	20.9	3.8	4.2	2.3	1.6
35–39	11.2	11.6	14.0	17.3	19.3	0.6	3.8	4.9	2.2
40–44	12.0	11.2	11.7	14.1	17.3	(1.3)	0.9	3.8	4.1
45–49	12.1	11.8	11.0	11.5	13.9	(0.7)	(1.4)	0.9	3.8
50–54	11.2	12.0	11.7	10.9	11.4	1.4	1.4	(1.4)	0.9
55–59	10.0	10.5	11.4	11.1	10.4	1.0	1.7	(0.5)	(1.3)
60–64	8.7	9.2	9.8	10.6	10.4	1.1	1.3	1.6	(0.4)

Note: Figures in millions.
Source: U.S. Department of Commerce, Bureau of Census, 1970, 1980, Series P-25, *Population Estimates and Projections.*

of fitness and appearance. She is more conscious than her mother's generation about matters of sophistication, taste in clothing and cosmetic fashions.

She eagerly searches for products and services that satisfy her powerful sense of self and her need for self-improvement. She is a customer in the market for what Mary Kay has always offered. And now, more than ever, she is willing to try both our products and our career opportunity.

The inevitable meeting of Mary Kay and the woman of the '80s usually takes place at a Mary Kay beauty show.[8]

As Mary Kay Cosmetics looks to the 1990s, it sees a population in which 60 percent of all women will be working. Women working outside the home have clearly demonstrated that they spend more on cosmetics than do their counterparts in the home. One-third of all households will be composed of single persons, people who have discretionary income to spend on their own needs. Mary Kay sees great opportunities to convert a "middle-aged" population to skin care products. On another level, there will be a large middle-aged working female population from which to recruit the corps of Mary Kay consultants. That the number of women entering the labor force is tapering off (in 1980, 50 percent of the female population between ages 18 and 65 were working) does not appear to be of major concern to the company.

MARK KAY AND
THE FOOD AND DRUG ADMINISTRATION

Inquiries made to the Food and Drug Administration (FDA) regarding the claims made by cosmetics companies for their products is a major escalating problem at the agency, which is receiving less funding than it says it needs to investigate. The FDA sustains the burden of proof in establishing that the claims made by cosmetics companies are misleading to the consumer. Although cosmetics companies, including Mary Kay, express concern about a climate of increased regulation, the FDA complains that "we are not in any position to challenge the cosmetics industry. It is a $12 billion industry being regulated by a handful of people at the FDA."

Until the 1970s, the government took a strong stance with regard to the regulation of cosmetics formulations. Consumer activism across the board in the 1970s resulted in more stringent regulation of the industry. The use of dyes, hexachlorophene, and mercury in cosmetics and toiletries sparked debates and engendered legislation on the appropriate labeling of cosmetics. Major regulatory requirements imposed on manufacturers included

Responsibility for the safety of the cosmetic being marketed

Responsibility for required testing to determine toxicity, irritation, and/or sensitivity to the product

---

[8] *1980 Annual Report*, p. 5.

Compliance should the FDA insist on further discretionary testing by an FDA-appointed, independent organization to verify the safety of ingredients

Mandatory labeling of cosmetic packages or containers with specific ingredients in order of predominance, although flavor and fragrance need only be indicated by the words "flavor" and "fragrance"

A waiting period of 20 days before the release of the new product after notification of the FDA

Reports of increased regulation hover over the industry, but the fact is, according to the *1982 U.S. Industrial Outlook*, that less than 1 percent of the FDA's budget goes toward regulation of the cosmetics industry. The FDA depends on voluntary programs for the reporting of product formulas and adverse effects, for example, the Cosmetic Ingredient Review (CIR), a screening and warning process to alert the industry to possible harmful effects of cosmetic ingredients.

Mary Kay's reaction to regulation has resulted in expansion of its laboratories, acquisition of capital equipment to support skin science, and development of contacts in the scientific fields of dermatology and skin science. "Regulatory agencies are responding to increased scientific information, ensuring a more complex environment in the '80s for our entire industry," the company reported to stockholders in 1981.

OF TOILETRIES AND COSMETICS

Increasingly the distinction drawn between toiletries and cosmetics is becoming a matter of semantics. Because they are higher priced, cosmetics theoretically are geared to the individual whereas toiletries at a lower unit price are targeted to the mass market. The mode of distribution of cosmetics — through department stores and drugstores on a franchise or semifranchise basis or through direct sales — differs from that of toiletries, which are found in mass marketing outlets. This distinction is beginning to blur as cosmetic houses begin limitedly to place lower-priced lines in grocery stores and discount houses, although it is doubtful that toothpaste will appear in department stores. More utilitarian in nature, toiletries, including shampoos, toothpastes, and deodorants because of their proletarian nature, occupy a more competitive marketing niche, one in which higher promotional advertising expenditures are the rule. Lipsticks, fragrance products, eye makeup, face makeup, and the treatment lines — the mainstays of cosmetics — tend to engender a strong brand-name loyalty if the product delivers, even though it may be less advertised than a toiletry. A satisfied Mary Kay customer, for instance, often will use no other brand of cosmetic, although she may use several brands of toothpaste. Mary Kay and other cosmetic companies are making strong bids to sell toiletries as cosmetics, especially in the hair care line, by marketing a cluster of such products as a hair care program with much the same educational approach found successful for the skin care line (Exhibit 9).

EXHIBIT 9 Total U.S. cosmetic and toiletry trends, 1970–1980

Year	Sales manufacturing prices (millions)	Price increase (decrease)	Real sales (increase)	U.S. female population (millions)	Cosmetic and toiletry sales per woman[a] (mfg. prices)	Real cosmetic use index[b] (per capita)
1980	$3,950	n/a	n/a	113.6	$29.55	1.33
1979	3,653			112.7	27.55	1.36
1978	3,317			111.8	25.18	1.32
1977	3,040			110.9	23.29	1.20
1976	2,816			110.1	21.71	1.25
1975	2,476			109.2	19.27	1.19
1974	2,275			108.5	17.84	1.16
1973	2,110			107.7	16.62	1.15
1972	1,980			106.9	15.74	1.10
1971	1,875			106.0	15.06	1.04
1970	1,735			104.9	14.08	1.00
% Increase (decrease)						
1980–1979	8.1%	10.1%	(2.1)%	0.8%	7.3%	(2.8)%
1979–1978	10.1	6.0	4.1	0.8	9.4	3.4
1978–1977	9.1	4.0	5.1	0.8	8.1	4.1
1977–1976	8.0	4.0	4.0	0.7	7.3	3.3
1976–1975	13.7	7.2	6.5	0.8	12.7	5.5
1975–1974	8.8	4.6	4.2	0.6	8.0	3.4
1974–1973	7.8	6.4	1.4	0.7	7.3	0.9
1973–1972	6.7	0.0	6.7	0.8	5.6	5.6
1972–1971	5.4	(0.8)	6.2	0.9	4.5	5.1
1971–1970	8.1	2.5	5.6	1.0	6.9	4.4
Compound growth						
1980 vs. 1970	9%			1%	8%	3%
1980 vs. 1975	10			1	9	3
1975 vs. 1970	7			1	6	3

Note: From sources believed reliable. Excludes toothpaste and other categories in which Mary Kay does not compete.
[a] Assumes 85% of U.S. cosmetics and toiletry industry sales of products Mary Kay sells are used by women.
[b] Cosmetic and toiletry sales per woman minus price increases, indexed to 1970.

A common property to both cosmetics and toiletries is their appeal to the psyche of the user. No one would argue with the idea that people buy these products with the expectation that they will look and feel better after using them.

Analysts have concluded that one problem in capturing the potentially vast market for men's cosmetics is in breaking down the image that it is normal for a man to buy toiletries but somehow "abnormal" for him to purchase cosmetics. In recent years men appear to have been convinced that colognes are acceptable masculine cosmetic items. Mary Kay and other firms believe that growth in the men's cosmetic market will be slow and will probably begin with a skin care line accompanied by an educational process of some sort.

MARY KAY COSMETICS AND THE FUTURE

Returning to the familial theme at the end of her autobiography, Mary Kay reflects on the possibility of her retirement — if and when she can no longer present the glamorous, ageless public persona that people recognize through photographs such as the one taken by celebrity photographer Francesco Scavullo for the cover of her book. In passing she remarks that her mother's skin, even at age 87 "looked wonderful."

Looking toward the long term, Mary Kay Cosmetics purchased 176 acres of land in Dallas in June 1981 to pursue a major four-year expansion program to encompass production, distribution, and administrative facilities. Construction was set to start in October 1982 on the first of several manufacturing and distribution facilities.

> *We're also so fortunate to have as president my son, Richard, who has filled in for me on many occasions and won the hearts of our people. He, one day, will not only fill his job as chief executive but mine as well, as motivator of our people.*[9]

Appendix A portrays the management team at Mary Kay Cosmetics.

The development strategy to see the company through a lengthier expansion period will call for construction as needed to support sales, to be financed from retained earnings. The leased 300,000-square-foot manufacturing facility allows Mary Kay Cosmetics to support $400 million in sales volume. The $12 million site development project, underway in 1982, was capitalized and also financed by internal cash flow and limited bank borrowing — a conservative fiscal strategy consistent with Mary Kay Ash's personal philosophy of paying cash rather than incurring heavy, long-term debts.

Richard Rogers has publicly set the goal of $500 million in annual sales by 1990, emphasizing that 35 percent of the Mary Kay business is repeat sales to faithful customers. "As we grow, we're bringing our customer base forward," he states. His plan for growth reflects the guarded optimism of industry analysts. They predict that beauty products will rebound in the 1980s as the economy limps toward recovery. Most companies are placing their chips on moisturizing products, although many will continue diversification strategies, for example, Chesebrough-Ponds, a leader in the moisturizing business with Vaseline Intensive Care Lotion, but also a leader in spaghetti sauce, children's clothing, and casual footwear with the Ragu, Health-tex, and G. H. Bass brands. Meanwhile, Avon, Mary Kay's most look-alike competitor, continues to diversify. In 1982 Avon began peddling magazine subscriptions along with its vast cosmetic and costume jewelry lines. In a surprising 1979 move, Avon picked up Tiffany and Company, the preeminent jewelry concern.

[9] Ash, *Mary Kay,* p. 205.

Mary Kay intends to ride the moisturizing and skin care wave. Its Basic Skin Care Program will remain the staple product line. While other cosmetic companies (Avon and Bonne Bell, to name just two) are sponsoring women's running, bowling, and tennis competitions, Mary Kay Cosmetics will channel its energies into support of women working — for Mary Kay. An Avon piece of advertising copy reads, ''At Avon, sports, health and beauty go naturally together.'' Mary Kay, however, will continue to endorse a work and beauty ethic.

Introduced in 1982, the four-step Body Care Program seemed the next logical step for Mary Kay Cosmetics, a continuation of the company's appeal to the 25- to 44-year-old segment. Other major product constellations for the 1980s include Specialized Skin Care products (sun screen and hand cream), the Glamour Collection (cosmetics), and the Beauty Boutique, an array of bath and after-bath products. In keeping with the programmatic presentation pioneered in the Skin Care System, the company has developed a Basic Hair Care System, including shampoos, conditioner, and hair spray. Mary Kay Cosmetics hopes to nurture the presently minuscule market for the Mr. K. line of men's skin care products.

> I've talked about how important it is for women to look good, but I think men care just as much about their appearance. However, unfortunately, often you'll see a man dressed in beautiful clothes, with good-looking shoes, an expensive briefcase, well-groomed hair, and manicured nails — but whose face could look so much better with a little help! A woman wouldn't look complete without her face made up. So why shouldn't a man do the same thing?[10]

As the company feels its way through the 1980s, it will accentuate quality control aspects ensured by a vigilant R&D policy. John Beasley, vice president of manufacturing, addressed this major concern in an interview, which appears as Appendix B. Also, see Appendix C, an excerpt from *U.S. Industrial Outlook*.

Because of the style of life that Mary Kay is selling along with the product — that of the independent, well-compensated, career-woman beauty consultant — the company has not been altogether successful in translating the Mary Kay concept into other, non-English–speaking, more patriarchal cultures. Mary Kay Cosmetics internally appears sanguine that ''the philosophy of Mary Kay Cosmetics has proven well suited for women everywhere,'' but this remains a debatable area in places like Japan.

Mary Kay Ash has stated on many occasions that Mary Kay Cosmetics is ''in the business of helping women create better self-images so that they will feel better about themselves.'' Whether she is invoking Ralph Waldo Emerson's ''Nothing great was ever achieved without enthusiasm'' or leading her devoted consultants and directors in a chorus of ''That Mary Kay Enthusiasm,'' Mary Kay Ash, genius of direct sales motivation, thinks and dreams enthusiasm: ''My own dream,'' she states in her autobiography, ''is that Mary Kay Cosmetics will someday become the largest and best skin care company in the world.''

[10] Ibid., pp. 130–131.

APPENDIX A: MARY KAY MANAGEMENT TEAM, 1982

Mary Kay Ash, Chairman of the Board

Richard Rogers, President. Co-founder of Mary Kay Cosmetics, Inc. Served as General Manager, Vice President. 1968 ''Marketing Man of the Year'' Award from North Texas Chapter of the American Marketing Association.

Gerald M. Allen, Vice President, Administration. Responsible for planning, organizing, and directing the delivery of administrative services to the beauty consultant and supervising a staff of sales promotion directors. Supervises company security, communications and word processing, sales administration and compensation programs. B.B.A., Arlington State College.

J. Eugene (Gene) Stubbs, Vice President, Finance, and Treasurer. Responsible for financial planning and accountable for company's financial assets and profitability objectives. Directs the treasury, controllership, and internal audit functions. Also responsible for all financial reporting. M.B.A., University of Texas; C.P.A.; B.B.A., Texas A & M University.

Richard C. Bartlett, Vice President, Marketing. Responsible for planning and implementing marketing strategy including incentive programs, education and development of consultants, special events and meetings, public relations, and market-related research. B.S., University of Florida.

Monty C. Barber, Vice President, Secretary, and General Counsel. Responsible for supervising activities prescribed by law and the company regulations, establishing legal policies, advising and rendering opinions, supervises the public affairs program. As corporate secretary, attends to administrative matters for the board, shareholder relations, consumer relations, and coordinates all contribution requests. J.D., University of Texas; B.B.A., University of Texas.

John Beasley, Group Vice President, Manufacturing. Responsible for planning, organizing, and evaluating all manufacturing decisions. Directs the development of the product line and ensures the quality of the products. B.A., Georgia Tech, Industrial Engineering National Merit Scholarship.

Phil Bostley, Vice President, Operations. Responsible for planning, directing, and coordinating the distribution of all Mary Kay cosmetics and sales aids through regional distribution centers. Also responsible for directing the forecasting of product mix, the maintenance of inventory levels and coordinating the company's data processing group. B.A., Penn State University, math and science.

Myra O. Barker, Ph.D., Vice President, Research and Product Development. Responsible for planning and directing skin technology, process technology, and product development. Directs regulatory and medical affairs and ensures product safety. Ph.D., Tulane University, biochemistry; B.S., University of Texas, chemistry.

Bruce C. Rudy, Ph.D., Vice President, Quality Assurance. Responsible for the procedures that assure the quality of raw materials in the product line. Controls the finished products certifying that they meet cosmetic, FDA and company standards. Plans and directs quality audits of all phases of product development, research, manufacture, and distribution. B.S., E. Stroudsburg State College; M.S., Clemson University; M.B.A., Columbia University; Ph.D., University of Georgia.

Pat Howard, Vice President, Manufacturing Operations. Responsible for manufacturing material control including purchasing, warehousing, production, planning, and international manufacturing. B.S., St. Mary's University; M.S., Texas A & M University.

Jack Dingler, Vice President, Controller. Responsible for all operating financial functions of the company, including expenditure review, to ensure the continuation of the company's sound financial position. B.B.A., University of Texas at Arlington, accounting; C.P.A.

William H. Randall, Director, Marketing Services. Responsible for marketing research, incentive program, visual communications, marketing publications, communications, and creative efforts. M.B.A., Harvard; B.A., Rutgers, economics.

Dean Meadors, Director, Public Relations. Responsible for all public relations activity. M.S., University of Illinois, advertising; B.S., University of Illinois, journalism.

Netta Jackson, Director, Product Service. Responsible for the marketing rationale for product development. Ensures that the company remains competitive in price and positioning. Active in sales force training. B.S.B.A., University of Arkansas, marketing.

Michael C. Lunceford, Director, Public Affairs. Responsible for monitoring of local, state, and federal laws and regulations; community liaison with emphasis on corporate philanthropy. Master's program, Southern Methodist University, business administration; M.S., Southern Methodist University, public administration; B.B.A., East Texas State University, business administration, finance/economics.

APPENDIX B: AN INTERVIEW WITH JOHN BEASLEY

The following is an interview with John Beasley, Vice President, Manufacturing Group for Mary Kay Cosmetics, Inc. Mr. Beasley has been with Mary Kay since September 1975 and is currently responsible for planning, organizing, and evaluating all U.S. and international manufacturing decisions. A major portion of his responsibility is quality assurance. The interview was conducted in May 1982 at Mary Kay's corporate headquarters in Dallas.

Q: How does the quality of Mary Kay products compare with others on the market?

A: We direct our research and development and all our efforts toward producing the finest products we can produce. We know what other companies are producing. We understand all major competitive concepts, formulas, and approaches. But our focus is on producing the best product for the Mary Kay system. You see, we have a different orientation from most cosmetic companies. We can't just produce a product for a particular market segment. Our skin care products are used in a teaching system, so we are systems oriented. Our products work together, they're modular, and there's a synergism between them.

Q: Wasn't Mary Kay a pioneer in teaching skin care?

A: Mary Kay, as a specialist in skin care, has set trends for the only product segment of the market that's really growing. In 1963, we began marketing a five-step program of skin care. In 1976, we started teaching the scientific basis of skin care to and through our beauty consultants who today number over 150,000. Now every major cosmetic company in the country is talking about the scientific basis of skin care.

Q: How did the new Body Care System happen?

A: We've always had products aimed at body skin. The idea evolved from what we had learned about facial skin care. Body skin is different from facial skin, yet there are functional needs that need to be addressed in a complementary way. Body care was a natural extension from the Mary Kay tradition of scientific skin care.

Our Body Care products have been formulated according to the same high standards we use in skin care. We've tested them and used them ourselves. We've come up with a very, very high-quality system for an economical price.

Q: What standards do you use internally for making product decisions?

A: We came up with four factors that have to be included in every decision that is made from every level. Since we are a participative management organization, everybody has to know what the rules are, exactly what is important. The first thing that has to be considered in every decision is quality . . . the impact on product quality. The second is service. Service to the beauty consultant and consumer.

The third thing that everybody has to take into account is the flexibility of the decision. What range does it work in? The fourth is the actual cost of the decision: total cost of capital investment, impact on cost of goods, and cash flow.

We teach all management and some hourly people to use the four criteria. I will not look at any proposal that doesn't address these four things — and the first thing I see has to be quality. Richard Rogers [president of Mary Kay] uses the saying "If it's worth doing, do it right." That is the kind of quality statement that underlines everything we do all day long. That's the way the company was founded.

Q: You mentioned you are a "participative management organization." How does this work at Mary Kay?

A: You cannot get quality by having only one part of your company responsible for quality. The assumption that the better traditional organizations have made is that if you want to get something accomplished, you have to focus on it through a special part of your organization.

Our assumption here is much different. Everybody is in charge of quality. The Research and Development Department is in charge of quality. The Marketing Department is in charge of quality. The Material Control Department is in charge of quality.

The actual "Quality Assurance" function serves as a measuring device. The quality audit measures how well we are matching our stated quality standards. These specifications are set in a type of committee process that starts in research and development and get approved right up through the CEO in final form. From there our job is to expand them backward, through all the maze of processing, all the way back to vendor level. It's very much like the idea behind the Japanese quality circles when you get everybody involved in focusing on quality. For example, in 1976 we gave everybody in the hourly (nonexempt) group an across-the-board pay increase, explaining that we were adding the quality inspection responsibility to their job. We said, "Part of your job is to make sure we always produce Mary Kay quality."

Q: How did they respond to this?

A: Many of them consider quality to be the predominant part of their job. The people in the plant don't simply report a problem; they are actually the ones doing the rejecting. And most of them are very tough. They see things that you and I won't see because they have developed a whole different set of skills out there. We normally produce on only one shift, we hire special people, we evaluate them and reward them. Mary Kay was always, from the very beginning, attracted to people who are quality conscious. If you look around, you see a very consistent type of person in dress and quality standards. When new people come in from other companies, and we've had to do a good bit of recruiting because we've grown so fast, they usually come from companies that were more interested in cost as the first factor. Even top executives don't understand that quality is the first criterion. So we create a whole culture that reinforces our standards.

Q: How many of the products Mary Kay sells are made in your own facilities?

A: We manufacture probably 99 percent of the products in house; and 100 percent is quality inspected here. The same quality standards apply internationally. In general, if they don't pass the same quality standards that we use here in the United States, they don't go to the consumer.

Q: How does your sales force respond to this?

A: The sales force is very, very conscious of the quality aspect. Sometimes there has been some disappointment when we've said, "We're sorry, we can't sell this product because it's not Mary Kay quality." But it's very important to the sales force that they be very proud of the products and systems they teach . . . and sell.

Q: What are your long-term goals for Mary Kay?

A: We want to be the finest teaching-oriented skin care company in the world with sales of $500 million by 1990. That's our corporate objective. It has been stated in our annual report, and everybody around here can quote it.

Q: How do you begin to meet that goal?

A: Research and development is the leading edge. Since 1975, Research and Development has grown from 1 Ph.D. and a technician to a staff of 47. We recruited Dr. Myra Barker to be our vice president of research and development. We go after the top 10 percent of the people in the country who have the skills that we're looking for and personal integrity. They don't come necessarily from the cosmetic industry. Many have come from the drug industry because we see cosmetics, especially skin care products, more like drugs than traditional glamor products.

In addition, the Research and Development Department is in the forefront in developing new technology. We have a group that has been formed to do nothing but research how the skin relates to the rest of the body and how it relates to its environment. A very large part of the research and development budget, for example, is aimed at research all over the world. We're funding a research dermatologist in Wales who is doing research into skin attribute measurement. We have grants in England. When you came in, I was signing a purchase order that goes for a research grant to Southwestern Medical School.

Q: What types of tests are you doing?

A: There are many levels of testing and two major issues: one is safety, one is efficacy. We don't take risks with the consumer. Our products must meet acceptable levels in terms of oral toxicity . . . sensitization . . . irritation. We are having to stretch current technology in establishing some new standards in the industry in the area of comedogenicity, the interaction of the new product, the environment, and the skin-causing comedones (acne).

We screen raw materials at the vendor level. If you get something that's 99 percent pure, it means it's 1 percent impure. In our business we're interested in the 1 percent impure. We made substantial investments in computerized instrumentation so that we can screen raw materials routinely for impurities.

Efficacy testing is also something that is fairly new. Cosmetic products used to be a coverup, but now we're producing skin care products that are functional. We need to measure how a product actually performs, but we're having to develop the technology.

Q: As vice president in charge of manufacturing, how do you challenge your departments?

A: We have no negatives in terms of product quality, number one. We can't afford any big savings in quality. We have to be consistently above the line in terms of the impact on the consumer. Consistently positive! Then what we try to do is to raise that line to the top of the industry. We establish a consistent quality level, and then we figure out how to make that better. That's our drive, our constant challenge. The quality standard has never, ever been stagnant. We always strive to be the best we can be.

APPENDIX C: SUMMARY OF COSMETICS PROSPECTS FOR 1982 AND BEYOND

Moderately priced products are expected to sell best, especially hair, skin, nail, and eye care products.

Fragrances will become more popular, especially among men, in the 1980s.

Source: *1982 U.S. Industrial Outlook.*

Ethnic cosmetic sales are expected to pick up.

Up to 45 percent of males in the population will use cosmetics by 1986.

Sun-screen agents that reportedly protect skin from damaging ultraviolet rays will be added to many skin care products to prevent premature aging, wrinkling, or cancer of the skin.

An estimated 65 percent of all cosmetics are purchased on impulse, although during recessionary periods consumers are most cost conscious.

The industry's principal target group of teenagers and young women is shrinking, although the "baby boom" generation is aging and is likely to spend money for beauty aids.

Among the present 20- to 35-year-old age group, there is a much larger lower-income sector.

Rising costs of raw materials and the high cost of research are the scourge of the cosmetics industry.

New products are essential for greater sales, yet new product introductions lag because of the decrease in research and development.

The skin care market, including moisturizers, sun-care creams, lotions, scrubs and cleansers, collagen and elastin protein rejuvenating agents, is growing and reached $2.5 billion in 1981 because of increased concern among consumers over aging skin, personal cleanliness, and the damaging effects of ultraviolet rays.

Hypoallergenic and fragrance-free products have been demonstrated to be most successful in the skin care market.

The hair preparations market increased to $2.2 billion in 1981 due to consumer interest in healthy looking hair and frequent shampoos by both men and women. Women frequently use cream rinse and hair conditioning products, although an untapped male market exists for such products. Hair spray remains popular with older women.

Industry shipments of cosmetics, toiletries, and fragrances were valued at $9.9 billion in 1981, only a 0.6 percent increase from 1980, as opposed to a 2.6 percent average annual increase from 1972 through 1981.

THE GRAND THEATRE COMPANY

"There is no better director than me. Some may be as good, but none better."[1]

In December 1982, the board of directors of Theatre London (see Exhibit 1) were considering a proposal to hire Robin Phillips as artistic director, to replace Bernard Hopkins. The hiring decision was complicated by Phillips's ambitious plans for the theater, which included a change from a subscription theater to repertory, an increase in budget from $1.9 million to $4.5 million, and even changing the organization's name. The board had to act quickly as plans had to be made, and actors hired, for the next season.

THEATER IN ONTARIO

Theater is big business. In Toronto alone (including cabaret, dinner theater, and opera) some 3.5 million people attended 120 productions in 1982, in twenty-eight locations. There are twenty-four nonprofit professional theaters in Toronto, and eighteen in the rest of Ontario.

Most theater organizations are nonprofit (with rare exceptions such as Ed Mirvish's Royal Alexandra) and are subsidized by local, provincial, and federal grants. Thus theaters compete for funds with charitable, educational, and health care organizations. As shown in Exhibit 2, a third of revenue typically comes from government sources and half of this comes from The Canada Council. Another 10 percent comes from individual and corporate donors, and the balance from the box office. Because of

[1] Robin Phillips, quoted in the Toronto *Globe and Mail*, Dec. 31, 1983, p. E1.

This case was prepared by Dr. Larry M. Agranove with the assistance of Dr. J. Peter Killing from published sources and interviews with numerous people in theater, government, and arts organizations. It was prepared as a basis for class discussion rather than to illustrate correct or incorrect handling of an administrative situation. Copyright © 1986 by Wilfrid Laurier University. Reprinted by permission.

EXHIBIT 1
Grand Theatre
Company board of
directors, December
1982

J. Noreen De Shane (president).	President of a stationery firm
Peter J. Ashby.	Partner, major consulting firm
W. C. P. Baldwin, Jr.	President, linen supply firm
Bob Beccarea.	Alderman and civic representative
Art Ender.	Life insurance representative
Ed Escaf.	Hotel and restaurant owner
Dr. John Girvin.	Surgeon
Stephanie Goble.	Representative of London Labour Council
Elaine Hagarty.	Former alderman, active in arts community
Barbara Ivey.	Active board member of various theater groups
Alan G. Leyland.	Entrepreneur
John F. McGarry.	Partner, major law firm
C. Agnew Meek.	Corporate marketing executive
Robert Mepham.	Insurance company executive
Elizabeth Murray.	Board member of theater groups and Ontario Arts Council
John H. Porter.	Vice-president and partner, major accounting firm
Peter Schwartz.	Partner, major law firm
Dr. Tom F. Siess.	University professor
Dr. Shiel Warma.	Surgeon

EXHIBIT 2 Major arts organizations in Canada

Arts organizations	Total revenue 1982–1983	Box office and earnings	Government grants	Private donations	Accumulated surplus (deficit), end of 1982–1983
1. Stratford Festival	$12,314,300	$9,678,285	$1,405,939	$1,230,076	(1,731,492)
2. Toronto Symphony	9,480,503	6,020,112	1,893,100	1,567,291	(149,391)
3. National Ballet	7,271,616	3,233,810	2,943,856	1,093,950	(675,096)
4. Orchestre Symphonique de Montreal	7,071,886	4,048,749	2,164,350	858,787	(857,662)
5. Canadian Opera Company	5,969,077	2,668,698	2,029,100	1,271,279	(290,168)
6. Vancouver Symphony	5,189,041	2,488,690	1,784,315	916,036	(818,951)
7. Shaw Festival	4,801,700	3,848,200	586,000	367,500	(45,167)
8. Royal Winnipeg Ballet	4,021,263	1,884,339	1,611,463	525,461	343,639
9. Centre Stage	3,483,020	1,923,312	1,316,000	243,708	(212,108)
10. Citadel Theatre	3,541,911	2,097,096	1,117,733	327,082	(177,821)
.					
.					
.					
18. Grand Theatre	1,990,707	1,277,625	390,000	323,082	0[a]

[a] Reduced by Wintario Challenge Fund.
Source: Council for Business and the Arts in Canada.

the pressing need for box office revenues, most theater companies sell subscriptions of five or so plays from October to May.

In 1982–1983, audience size was 570,000 for the Stratford Festival, the largest arts organization in Canada, and 268,000 for the Shaw Festival, the second largest theater company. According to a Stratford audience study, audiences break down into: (1) committed theater goers (27 percent) who see a number of plays each year and who tend to be older and more educated and live in Ontario, (2) casual theater goers (53 percent) who attend a theater every year or two to see plays of particular interest, and (3) first-timers (20 percent). The challenge for these theaters is to develop these first-timers to be the audience of the future.

Theater audiences tend to be well educated, with most having university education and slightly over 50 percent having attended a graduate or professional school. Those aged thirty-six through fifty make up 35 percent of the Stratford audience, and the twenty-one–thirty-five and fifty-one–sixty-four age groups each make up 25 percent. Visitors from the United States account for 35 percent of box office receipts at the Stratford Festival, Toronto residents account for 25 percent, and the remaining 40 percent come from elsewhere in Ontario. Twice as many women attend as men. It is understood that Shaw's market is similar, with slightly fewer coming from the United States.

A recent study showed that, while 42 percent of Ontario residents attended live plays and musicals in 1974, this grew to 55 percent by 1984.[2] Some 24 percent of the Ontario population are "frequent attenders" (at least six times a year). They come from all age groups, but many are "singles," and many are university educated and affluent. In fact, while only 63 percent of Ontarians without a high school education attended live theater, 94 percent with university degrees have attended live theater.

There is some price sensitivity: 73 percent said they would attend more often if tickets were less expensive. However, 77 percent (which included young adults and lower-middle-income families) said they would accept a tax increase of up to $25 to support the arts.

THE ORGANIZATION OF A THEATER COMPANY

The Board of Directors

The Board of Directors is fiscally and legally responsible for the theater. They may determine the theater's artistic objectives and then delegate the fulfilling of these objectives to the artistic director. However, any artistic plan has financial objectives, and the board's responsibility is essentially financial. Artistic directors generally demand, and are generally granted, a great deal of autonomy in such matters as programming and casting; to a large extent the board "bets" on the

[2] Special Committee for the Arts, *Report to the Honourable Susan Fish, The Minister of Citizenship and Culture, Province of Ontario,* Spring 1984.

artistic director's ability to put on a season of theater, subject to his accountability in meeting budgets and providing an appropriate level of quality.

Board members are typically expected to assist in fund raising and to set an example by contributing generously themselves.

Board members often have business backgrounds. As a result, they may be — and are certainly often perceived to be — insensitive to the unique needs of an artistic organization. Artistic boards often include lawyers and accountants, who are often recruited to serve a specific function, but who tend to remain on long enough to achieve positions of power.

Busy business people serve on boards for a number of reasons. They may perceive their serving as a civic responsibility. Others may see it as an opportunity to wield power at a board level, something they are not allowed to do in their own organizations. Membership on a board allows people to widen their social and business contacts; this can be important to professionals who are limited in their freedom to advertise. One common motivation for business people to join arts boards is the opportunity to mingle with luminaries in the arts. Here is one view of their performance:

> *It has often been charged that many a hard-headed businessman loses his business sense on entering a meeting of an arts board. Lacking a profit motive to guide the affairs of the organization, businessmen who serve on arts boards sometimes feel unsure of themselves and their expertise. Compounding this problem is the inclination on the part of arts organizations to consider themselves a breed apart, outside the realm of normal business practice. But whether a company manufactures widgets or mounts exhibitions, the basic business concerns remain the same: strategic planning, good marketing, adequate financing, and competent management are essential to any enterprise.*[3]

Theater Management

In addition to the artistic director, there is usually a general manager who is responsible for the business affairs of the organization. Since artistic directors strive for maximum quality, which is expensive, and since business managers have to find and account for the money to run the theater, conflicts often occur. Not surprisingly, boards often side with the business manager because of their similarities of culture and values. Typically both artistic director and general manager report directly to the board.

MOUNTING A PRODUCTION

The theater company selects "products" to suit its objectives and audiences. For example, a theater might select a playbill of classics or children's plays. A regional theater might select a Canadian play (to satisfy government grant-giving agencies),

---

[3] "Developing Effective Arts Boards," undated publication of The Council for Business and the Arts in Canada, pp. 28–29.

a classic (to satisfy the artistic aspirations of the artistic director), a resounding hit from Broadway or England (to help sell the series), and one or more plays that have been successful elsewhere.

Each production requires a producer (who may be the artistic director) to act as the "entrepreneur" to put the show together. The producer acquires the rights to the play, if it is not in the public domain, for a fee of 7 to 10 percent of the box office revenue, and also retains a director, who may be on staff or who may be a freelance director retained for the run of the play. In the latter case, minimum scale would be $6,174.80 for a run of 3 weeks of rehearsal and 3 to 4 weeks of performance.

Casting is done, beginning with the major parts, on the basis of a uniform contract, which sets out fees (minimum of $416.27 per week for a major company), starting date, billing, working time, and "perks" (e.g., dressing room, accommodation).

Finally, a stage manager is contracted, as are designers for sets, costumes, and lighting. It is essential, of course, that all these people work well together.

This describes the typical "stock," or subscription, company. However, Stratford and Shaw operate as "repertory" companies, hiring a group of actors for one or more seasons, and allocating roles among the members of the company. Repertory companies typically sell tickets for individual plays, while subscription companies sell their series at the beginning of the season, with few single-ticket sales.

Lead times are considerable. In Stratford, for example, plays that open in May are firmly cast by the previous December, and the entire session is planned by March, when rehearsals begin.

THEATRE LONDON

Background

The Grand Opera House was opened in London on September 9, 1901, by Ambrose J. Small, a Toronto theatrical entrepreneur and frustrated producer. It quickly became the showcase of Small's theatrical chain, opening with such attractions as the Russian Symphony Orchestra, and later offering such performers as Barry Fitzgerald, Bela Lugosi, Clifton Webb, Sidney Poitier, and Hume Cronyn. Small sold his theater chain in 1919, deposited a million dollars in his bank, and disappeared. There has been no explanation to this day; however, Small's ghost is said to haunt the Grand.

Famous Players bought the theater in 1924, tore out the second balcony, and converted the theater to a cinema. They sold to The London Little Theatre for a token amount in 1945, and the building housed an amateur community theater until the spring 1971. The theater employed professional business management and a professional artistic director, but the actors were all amateurs. Some of London's leading citizens acted in plays, and some even displayed a high level of competence. The theater was prominent in the social life of the city and attracted one of the largest subscription sales in North America, both as a percentage of available seats and in absolute terms. It also achieved a reputation for a very high level of quality, given that it was essentially an amateur theater. Articles about the theater appeared in such magazines as *Life*.

However, there was some concern in the theater that the level of quality was as high as it was going to get as a company of amateurs and that the community deserved, and was ready to support, a professional theater. Another local organization, the London Symphony, had engaged a conductor with an international reputation, and it was changing from an amateur to a professional orchestra. An association was formed to work toward providing London with a major art gallery. Although strong objections were raised against the proposal for a professional theater (particularly because of the increased financial burden, the risk, and the denial to many of the theater's supporters of an opportunity to participate in their hobby of acting), London Little Theatre changed to Theatre London in 1971 under artistic director Heinar Piller. The progressives were vindicated, as theatergoers in the London area were treated to a decade of artistically and financially successful theater.

Piller was succeeded, at the end of the 1975 season, by William Hutt, who had achieved great success as an actor at Stratford, and was well known to Londoners. He served from 1976 to 1978. Bernard Hopkins arrived in 1979, and was artistic director until May 1983.

The Grand was attractively and authentically renovated at a cost of $5.5 million, reopening in fall 1978, after being closed for a full season. (The company had a reduced season during that time, in small, rented accommodations.) During the renovation, seating capacity was reduced from 1,100 to 845.

Theatre London ran successful stock seasons from 1979 to 1982. The 1981–1982 season was particularly successful, operating at 85 percent of capacity. Eighty percent of its tickets were sold through subscription to some 13,431 subscribers. Financial statements are shown in Exhibits 3 and 4.

THE LONDON ENVIRONMENT

London was founded at the forks of the Thames River in 1793 by Governor Simcoe with the intention of making it the capital of Upper Canada. Instead, it became the cultural and commercial center of southwestern Ontario. Located on three railroad lines and on Highway 401 serving the Quebec–Windsor corridor, London also has a major airport served by two airlines. London is 2 hours away from Detroit and Toronto; however, it is in a major snow belt. London is a major retail center, with the second highest per capita retail capacity in North America. It serves as a trading area for almost a million people, although its own population is only 259,000. (See Exhibit 5.) There are four hotels near the core area and motels in outlying areas. Many interesting restaurants had opened with a great deal of excess capacity; a few restaurants closed or changed hands.

There is little heavy industry in London, but there is a major university, a community college, a teacher's college, and two small church-affiliated colleges. Four major hospitals serve a wide area and provide teaching facilities for the university

EXHIBIT 3 Theatre London, condensed 5-year operating results

Revenue	June 30, 1979	June 30, 1980	June 30, 1981	June 30, 1982	June 30, 1983 (estimate)
Productions					
Ticket sales	$ 551,650	$ 585,938	$ 620,313	$ 664,058	$1,100,000
Sponsored programs	26,000	25,000	26,500	9,000	9,000
Program advertising	17,283	17,270	19,652	24,241	24,000
	594,933	628,208	666,465	697,299	1,133,000
Grants					
Canada Council	145,000	163,000	173,000	185,000	210,000
Ontario Arts Council	145,000	152,000	160,000	170,000	180,000
Wintario	89,254	—	—	—	—
City of London	12,500	—	—	—	—
Cultural Initiative Program	—	—	25,000	—	—
	391,754	315,000	358,000	355,000	390,000
Other					
Operating fund drive	41,222	27,462	182,559	183,188	160,000
Special projects	36,811	36,525	43,881	41,281	65,000
Interest	34,553	50,608	62,128	86,106	80,000
Concessions	33,500	75,073	69,581	62,065	78,000
Theater school	8,720	17,687	19,481	—	—
Box office commissions	3,319	3,721	651	6,142	3,000
Theater rental & misc.	3,170	—	—	4,704	2,000
	161,295	211,076	378,281	383,486	388,000
Total revenue	$1,147,982	$1,154,284	$1,402,946	$1,435,785	$1,911,000
Expenses					
Public relations	179,880	128,502	139,907	177,267	270,000
Administration	91,973	115,798	162,723	167,749	330,000
Production overhead	190,911	237,606	282,270	339,474	350,000
Productions	466,906	414,644	416,440	421,151	780,000
Front of house, box office, and					
concessions	75,563	123,910	107,617	126,673	140,000
Facility operation	131,445	139,215	152,153	142,061	140,000
Theater school	9,742	20,832	34,804		
Total expenses (see Salaries and Supplies, below)	1,146,420	1,180,507	1,295,914	1,374,375	2,010,000
Excess of revenue over expense	1,562	(26,223)	107,032	61,410	(99,000)
	$1,147,982	$1,154,284	$1,402,946	$1,435,785	$1,911,000
Salaries, fees, and benefits	$ 658,507	$ 754,109	$ 791,954	$ 823,260	$1,000,000[a]
Supplies and expenses	487,913	426,398	503,960	551,115	911,000
	$1,146,420	$1,180,507	$1,295,914	$1,374,375	$1,911,000

[a] In addition, development costs for the establishment of a repertory company in the 1983–1984 season could be incurred which could be largely offset by federal and provincial grants.

EXHIBIT 4 Theatre London, condensed balance sheets

	June 30, 1979	June 30, 1980	June 30, 1981	June 30, 1982
Assets				
Current assets				
Cash and term deposits	$351,010	$372,868	$325,631	$316,939
Accounts receivable	3,908	13,957	35,208	10,916
Inventory	7,463	7,146	6,050	
Prepaid expenses	20,257	32,788	46,938	72,471
	$382,638	$426,759	$413,827	$400,326
Liabilities and Surplus				
Current liabilities				
Bank loan		$ 25,000		
Accounts payable	$ 26,253	24,041	$ 30,112	$ 67,198
Advance ticket sale	280,431	324,524	319,843	302,983
Advance grants	1,060		15,201	14,805
Payable to Theatre London Foundation		4,523		15,340
	307,744	378,088	365,156	400,326
Surplus	74,894	48,671	48,671[a]	
	$382,638	$426,759	$413,827	$400,326

[a] In addition, there was equity of $453,080 from the Wintario Challenge Fund Program in 1981 and $807,289 in 1982. Under the terms of the program, Wintario would match $2 for every eligible contributed dollar raised (during the 3-year period ending June 30, 1983) in excess of 5.9 percent of the current year's operating expenses. All these matching contributions were placed in a separate investment fund for at least 5 years, although interest earned on the fund could be used for current operations.

medical school and dental school. In addition to being a retail center, London is the home of major financial institutions and agribusiness firms as well as a major brewery.

London is also a major cultural center. In addition to Theatre London, London has a professional symphony orchestra and a couple of significant choral groups. The university has an active program of theater and music, and the community is a center for visual artists. There are various commercial art galleries, an art gallery connected with the university, and a major public art gallery located in the city center. There are several museums, including a unique children's museum and a museum of Indian archaeology. The latter two attract visitors from a wide area.

THE GRAND THEATRE COMPANY

In late 1981, a decade after the company had become professional, concern was again raised in the Theatre that the level of quality had stagnated, and the Theatre would have to move in new directions. Bernard Hopkins was a superb actor and a

EXHIBIT 5 Grand Theatre Company, disposable income by census metropolitan area, 1983

	Income rating		Per capita personal disposable income	
	Index	Rank	Dollars	Rank
Toronto	117	6	$12,693	7
Montreal	103	11	11,212	14
Vancouver	118	5	12,793	6
Ottawa-Hull	118	5	12,796	5
Edmonton	126	4	13,668	4
Calgary	132	1	14,324	1
Winnipeg	111	8	11,997	9
Quebec	98	14	10,623	18
Hamilton	112	7	12,114	8
St. Catharines	103	11	11,223	13
Kitchener	101	13	10,974	16
London	106	10	11,462	11
Halifax	101	13	10,923	17
Windsor	107	9	11,602	10
Regina	130	2	14,056	2
Saskatoon	129	3	14,021	3
Oshawa	106	10	11,450	12
Thunder Bay	102	12	11,089	15
Canada	100		10,851	

Note: This list shows all eighteen census metropolitan areas in which the principal city had a population of at least 100,000 in the 1981 Census.

London-centered seven-county market area data

	Population, June 1, 1983 (thousands)	10-year growth rate	Households, June 1, 1983 (thousands)	Wage earner average income, 1981	Per capita disposable income, 1983	Per capita retail sales, 1983
Seven counties	838.5	5.7%	293.7	$14,522	$10,669	$4,238
Canada	24,886.6	12.0	8,335.0	$15,141	$10,851	$4,153

Source: *Canadian Markets*, 1984, and 1981 income tax returns.

competent artistic director. He had directed a few plays, rather than have to pay for a freelance director, with some success. However, some members of the board believed that he had taken the Theatre as far as he was able, and there was no initiative on either side to extend Hopkins's contract beyond its expiration in May 1983.

A planning committee, under one of the board members, addressed the issue of continuing the growth in quality. They conducted a number of retreats and interviewed experts in professional theater as well as officers of the Canada Council and Ontario Arts Council. During the course of the investigation, they interviewed Robin Phillips.

Phillips had been artistic director at the Stratford Festival and was well known to Barbara Ivey (who served on both the Stratford and Theatre London boards) and to other Theatre London directors. He also had directed, with considerable artistic success, two productions for Theatre London: *The Lady of the Camellias* and *Long Day's Journey Into Night*.

Robin Phillips

Robin Phillips is a highly talented artistic director and a person of incredible charm. (In *all* of the interviews conducted by the casewriter, words such as *charm*, *charisma*, and *talent* abounded.) Actress Martha Henry said, "Once you've worked with Robin, it's almost impossible to work for anyone else."

He came to Canada from England in 1974 to plan the 1975 Stratford season, although he would not direct any specific plays until 1976. His tenure at Stratford has been described as successful but stormy. When he was contracting to direct a production for the Canadian Opera Company in 1976, he said he would not renew his Stratford contract unless he had more evidence of support for his ambition to make Stratford the focus of Canadian theater, with film and television productions as well as live theater. He received a 5-year contract to run from November 1, 1976; the contract could be terminated with 4 months notice.

There was a series of resignations from, and returns to, Stratford starting in July 1978, until Phillips's departure in 1981. In addition to his Stratford activities, Phillips was involved with theater in Calgary, New York, Toronto's Harbourfront, and Vancouver. He also filmed *The Wars*, a novel by Timothy Findley. It was generally understood that he was seeking a theater in Toronto to serve as a base for his stage, film, and television ambitions. However, none was available.

The Phillips Plan

Robin Phillips had a plan for Theatre London, and he would only come if he had a budget to fulfill his plan and complete artistic autonomy. His plan called for raising Theatre London from eighteenth place in Canadian theater to third and changing its name to "The Grand Theatre Company."

The plan required a budget of $4.5 million, up from $1.9 million. This included $400,000 of capital cost to improve the Grand's facilities. Box office and concessions would provide 73 percent of the budget, 18 percent would come from donations, 5 percent from the Canada Council, and 4 percent from the Ontario Arts Council. Revenue projections were based on playing to 80 percent of capacity; this was considered feasible because Phillips had surpassed that performance at Stratford, and Theatre London had been operating at 85 percent. The Theatre requested a permanent tax exemption from the City of London; the deputy mayor described this request as "cavalier."

Three of the stage productions would be adapted for television and filmed by Primedia Productions of Toronto. This would provide some $100,000 of additional revenue for each production as well as audience exposure.

Robin Phillips strongly favored a repertory company over a subscription policy. He believed, and often stated, that subscriptions denied audiences a choice, and audiences must learn to discriminate. A change had to be made to make the theater different, special, and exciting. A repertory company would provide a company of salaried actors who could not be lured away during the season and who would be attracted by steady employment.

Another advantage of the repertory concept is the flexibility afforded patrons who may choose the dates they see a play and their seat locations. In a subscription series, patrons are restricted to the same seat location on the same night for each performance. In repertory theater, several productions are typically run simultaneously.

The Playbill

Phillips proposed to offer these plays on the main stage (in addition to a children's program in a small, secondary theater):

Godspell by John-Michael Tebelak. A rousing rock musical with audience appeal, especially for younger audiences

The Doctor's Dilemma by George Bernard Shaw. An established, classical hit

Waiting for the Parade by John Murrell. A Canadian play, with an all-female cast, showing what women did while their men were fighting World War II

Timon of Athens by William Shakespeare. A little-performed, little-known Shakespearean play, ignored by Stratford

The Club by Eve Merriam. A musical spoof of men's clubs, with a female cast playing the part of men

Arsenic and Old Lace by Joseph Kesselring. A well-known classic comedy of American theater

The Prisoner of Zenda adapted by Warren Graves. A comedy of political intrigue and romance, set in a mythical Eastern European kingdom

Hamlet by William Shakespeare. One of his best-known plays

Dear Antoine by Jean Anouilh. A comedy by a leading contemporary French playwright

Casting for these plays would not be a problem, as leading actors from Canada, the United States, and England were eager to work with Phillips.

Pricing

Since the plan envisioned a box office yield of $3.2 million, up from the $1.2 million planned for the 1982–1983 season, revenue would have to be increased in two ways. The number of productions would be increased, with nine productions in the season instead of the previous six. There would be a record 399 performances, instead of the 230 performances in the 1982–1983 season. Thus the plan projected an audience of 217,000, compared with the 137,000 planned for the 1982–1983 season. In addition, prices would be increased.

A subscriber in the 1982–1983 season could see five plays for $55 on weekends or $45 on weekdays. This pricing schedule was proposed for the 1983–1984 repertory season:

	Price	
Number of seats	Weekdays	Weekends
178	$20.00	$22.50
245	$14.50	$15.50
422	$10.50	$12.50

Promotion

Since the Theatre would require an expanded audience from a wider area, the plan envisioned a program of investment spending in major area newspapers: the *Toronto Star* and *Globe and Mail*, the *Kitchener-Waterloo Record*, and the *Detroit Free Press* as well as the *London Free Press*. The advertising would be directed at a first-time audience.

Group sales would be stressed, particularly to schools. Hotel-restaurant-transportation-theater ticket packages were projected. However, data on expenditures was not available.

THE DECISION

The directors were impressed by the charm and reputation of Robin Phillips. The proposal to hire Phillips — and to accept his plan — was supported by board members who had sound business backgrounds and who had worked in theater for some years. They had a comfortable, modern theater with a recently acquired computer to issue tickets. They had a proven record in selling tickets, as did Robin Phillips.

On the other hand, if Phillips were hired, his artistic strengths might not be matched administratively. There was an administrative director (who had been there for only two years) and a chief accountant, but no controller. And Stratford, Canada's leading theater, was less than an hour's drive down the road. Would this be an audience-builder or a competitive threat?

THE NIGEL THOMAS CENTER

INTRODUCTION

John Bell, who had joined the board of directors of the Nigel Thomas Center in May 1986, reviewed the Center's planning process and wondered what action, if any, he should take in light of (1) the challenges facing the Center and (2) the planning process.

The Nigel Thomas Center was located in a rural area of Southern California. After joining the board in May 1986, John had attended a board planning retreat, led by a consultant and sponsored by a grant from a regional foundation fund, over the weekend of June 6–7, 1986. The consultant said she would prepare a written summary of the planning meeting to be distributed prior to the regular board meeting, but instead "Notes from the Board Retreat," consisting of typed replications of flip-chart worksheets completed during the weekend retreat, were distributed at the regular board meeting. These "Notes" are summarized in Exhibit 1.

The president, Rosemary Kelly, explained that the consultant who facilitated the board planning retreat would not be able to provide a formal report until August, due to vacation plans and other scheduling difficulties.

John thought that his response to the board planning retreat should not only be based upon the strategic planning process at the Center and upon his position as a new member of the board, but also should be influenced by the historical development of the Nigel Thomas Center and by the current problems facing the Center.

Case prepared by John Barnett, University of New Hampshire, formerly visiting faculty, California State University. This case is for classroom discussion purposes only and is not intended to illustrate either effective or ineffective handling of an administrative situation. Names have been disguised. © 1987 by John Barnett. Reprinted by permission.

EXHIBIT 1
Consultant's notes
from the board re-
treat

I. Goals identified prior to the meeting
  1. To define the board's role, the director's role, and the staff's roles
  2. To establish a planning mechanism for revamping the management structure, includ-
     ing budget projections, adding staff, and identifying revenue sources
  3. To bring the new members on board by "team building"
II. Mission
  1. Provides community services with strong family orientation
  2. Coordinates networking with other agencies
  3. Provides "normalizing" program for early intervention (birth to three years old)
  4. Extends services to three-to-six–year-olds, day care, and alternatives to what the
     school system provides
  5. Be a training site for other programs throughout the state
  6. To do follow-up on a regular basis
III. Key issues
  Board role
  Funding
  Program development
  Community relations
  Management structure

HISTORICAL BACKGROUND

Mary and Robert Thomas, whose only child, Nigel, was born in 1971 with a metabolic disorder, founded the Center in 1973, initially as a means for parents with special needs children to see that their children had the companionship of other children. It also provided a place where parents could get some emotional support from each other. The Center, then called the Southern California Children's Center, hired a teacher who, working with volunteers, expanded the Center's services to include not only companionship, but special education programs. The Center then had one teacher, seven children, and a budget of $9,000. As enrollment grew, Mary Thomas and two other mothers wrote a successful grant application to fund more services.

When Nigel died at age four-and-a-half, the Center was renamed the Nigel Thomas Center. As an example of the emotional support activities and events at the Center, the Thomases established the practice of bringing a birthday cake to the Center on Nigel's birthday in the years following his death.

By 1980, the school had an enrollment of twenty-five preschool children and had a staff, primarily employed on a part-time basis, of special educators and counselors plus occupational, physical, and speech therapists. Funding for the program was renegotiated annually from a variety of sources in an informal way.

Three significant events in the Center's history included (1) the late 1970s passage of a law which lowered the age of special education skills coverage from six to three years, (2) the expanded state support during the period 1984–1987 under a court order for infant services (birth to three years), and (3) the 1985 assumption of the responsibilities of the California Children's Rehabilitation Center for infant services.

STATE COVERAGE

During its early history the Center served children from ages three to six. At age six, children often received special services from the local school districts. During the late 1970s the state extended the responsibilities of the local school districts to include ages three to six. In response, the Center initiated in 1980 an infant-toddler program and an early intervention program. Early intervention, the philosophy of which will be discussed, essentially means the attempted minimization of developmental problems by addressing these problems as early in life as possible.

In May 1982 the local school districts decided that they themselves would provide specialized preschool services (for children age three to six), rather than pay an agency such as the Center to provide these services. The Center suddenly had a reduced enrollment of eight infants, but still served the birth-to-three population by means of early intervention. Additional funds were secured so that twenty children were served by January 1983. Growth continued and stabilized at thirty-five to forty children by 1984.

STATE SUPPORT

In 1984 a California court ordered that the provisions of a state act, which established that every developmentally impaired client has a right to adequate and humane rehabilitation and treatment, meant that the state must provide certain monies to the Center and like institutions. These monies were to be paid by the State Department of Health and Welfare. This court order provided for specific dollar funding from 1984 through 1987.

This state support was critical to the Center, as Exhibit 2 shows.

THE SECOND LOCATION

In August 1985, the California Children's Rehabilitation Center's (CCRC) board of directors ended its program of providing rehabilitation services to special needs children from birth to three years of age. The State Division of Mental Health, on the basis of the Center's excellent reputation, and because of its relative proximity (about 30 minutes by car), asked the Center to assume responsibility for the twenty-five CCRC children. Executive director Sally Miller, the staff, and the directors recognized the substantial difficulties of fulfilling the state's request. Nonetheless, the Center felt that they must respond to a need, and they entered into a contract

EXHIBIT 2
Financial
statements
summary for years
ended June 30

	1986	1985	1984	1983
Revenues				
State Division of Mental Health	$153,300	$75,200	$41,700	$17,400
Federal grants–Title XX	–0–	–0–	5,200	21,600
Fundraising, grants, miscellaneous	10,700	14,500[a]	18,000	8,500
Parents' fees	6,300	2,300	4,000	1,000
United Way	17,000	4,300	–0–	–0–
Total revenues	$187,300	$96,300	$68,900	$48,500
Expenses				
Salaries	$141,100	$62,000	$44,100	$31,600
Rent, insurance	26,100	11,100	10,100	6,300
Consultants, professional fees	2,500	2,500	1,500	1,800
Office, operating costs	17,600[b]	19,700	13,200	7,500
Total expenses	$187,300	$95,300	$68,900	$47,200
Increase (decrease)	$ –0–	$ 1,000	$ –0–	$ 1,300

[a] Insurance	$ 6,500
Restricted gifts	5,500
Bureau of Handicapped Children	2,000
Miscellaneous	500
Total	$14,500
[b] Memberships, meetings	$5,200
Capital equipment	4,600
Telephone, printing, postage	3,900
Other	3,900
Total	$17,600

to provide early intervention services, using the former CCRC facilities, but providing existing and newly hired staff.

The CCRC expansion caused serious problems with both Nigel Thomas and CCRC parents and, especially, with the Center's staff.

As staff support was transferred to CCRC, service levels were reduced at Nigel Thomas. Parents of children in the program noticed the drop in service, while newly applying parents began to face a waiting list of two or more months. Further, CCRC parents faced (1) a change in service philosophy, as they were asked to assume more responsibility for the rehabilitation process; (2) a change in the service staff as Nigel Thomas extended an employment offer to only one of the CCRC staff; and (3) for many parents, a lowering in the appraisal of the child's ability, as the Center's staff applied more detailed and objective tests of the degree of the developmental problem.

Finally, the Center's staff not only had to deal on a daily basis with the parent problems, but they also faced the problem of working in two locations. Administrative coordination support was limited, in addition, as the executive director took an 11-week maternity leave during the first part of 1986.

Specific examples of problems caused by operating in two locations were discussed by the executive director:

> *The most serious problem is our inability to carry out the team concept, whereby a group of professionals specializing in speech, physical, and developmental therapies can work together with a child. Scheduling problems make it very difficult to get a team together.*
>
> *Secondly, it is very difficult for the program coordinator or myself to provide supervision and training. While the staff all wants to learn from each other's special knowledge, and while we as supervisors should be ensuring that the staff is developing to its potential, it is most difficult with split staff and two locations.*

ORGANIZATION AND STAFFING

The Center's organization is outlined in Exhibit 3.

Both the executive director and the program coordinator have Masters of Education degrees, and both have been active in special training and education programs for

EXHIBIT 3 Organization chart, June 1986

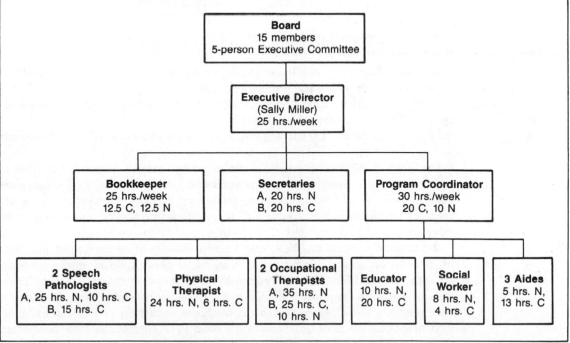

N = Nigel Thomas.
C = California Children's Rehabilitation Center.

over 10 years. They are well respected by professionals in the state and nationally. Their salaries totaled about $25,000 per annum.

Board member profiles are included in Appendix A. These board members were active in the area, primarily in business. John Bell had been recruited by a neighbor, a former member who also recruited two other new board members. This neighbor talked about the satisfaction from working with the children, but John was later convinced that this had been a recruiting technique and that the board–client interaction would be nonexistent.

Further, John felt that there were a range of interests represented on the board, from the Thomases, who were extremely interested in the fund-raising concert and in selected other Center activities, to those who had had children enrolled at the Center in the past (there were no current parents on the board), to interested business professionals and/or area residents. Thus the board was quite mixed in perspective and interest, and there seemed to be little if any social interaction between board members except at meetings.

The Thomases had an obvious interest in the Center and were forceful in presenting their views on subjects of importance to them, whether it be hourly wages for secretaries or the decorator for the concert. The Thomases' circle of acquaintances and friends included many who had made contributions to the Center.

THE SERVICE PHILOSOPHY

The service philosophy, as it has evolved over the years, stressed early intervention, along with normalization and parental responsibility.

Early intervention means to give children special attention as early on in life as possible in one or more of the following six areas: (1) motor development, (2) cognitive development, (3) learning ability, (4) social interaction, (5) communication skills, and (6) self-sufficiency. The principle underlying early intervention is that the severity of the disability will be minimized by early diagnosis and treatment. Further, secondary handicaps, such as antisocial behavior caused by frustration or sibling rejection, will be prevented or minimized by early intervention. Since all areas of development are interrelated, delay in one area may lead to delays in other areas.

Normalization means that the Center strives to make both the learning environment of, and the opportunities available to, the special needs child as similar to other children's as possible. Parental responsibility in this case means that the Center sees the parents as the primary teachers of the special needs child. Thus, the Center's staff generally holds therapy sessions in the home so that the parents can learn the techniques that are most beneficial to the child. The parents can then incorporate these techniques into daily routines.

THE SERVICE PROCEDURE

Children are referred to the Center by family physicians and pediatricians, by the parents, and occasionally by others. Initially, the child goes through a developmental assessment by a team of Center specialists who observe the child's gross motor, fine motor, cognitive, communication, self-help, feeding, social, and emotional skills.

Next, an individual service plan is designed with specific goals and objectives. Progress toward meeting this service plan's goals is the basis of formal quarterly reports to the parents and medical specialists and health professionals involved with the child. Individual and/or group sessions are available to help parents learn specific educational and therapeutic materials and adaptive equipment pertinent to their child's needs.

The children who enter the program may be (1) born with a handicap, (2) born with a medical problem that may cause a developmental delay, (3) born prematurely and thus at risk for developmental problems, or (4) lagging behind their peers in one or more developmental aspects.

Disabilities displayed by the forty Nigel Thomas children and twenty-five CCRC children in the program included hearing loss, visual impairments, cerebral palsy, muscular dystrophy, mental retardation, and delays in language and motor skills.

There is a natural resistance to the philosophy of early intervention. This is the resistance on the part of the parents to recognize that a developmental problem may exist. Other resistance to the Center's program may come from the physician or pediatrician. This may include the less likely resistance to the concept of early intervention or the more likely disagreement with methods and procedures. One function of the typed quarterly progress report was overcoming physician or pediatrician resistance to the Center. The Center of course knew by the referral levels which doctors were supporters of the Center.

THE CURRENT SITUATION

In June 1986 the Nigel Thomas Center faced three problems: (1) staff and morale, (2) the building, and (3) planning.

Staff and Morale The Center's operating and morale problems — caused in part by the expansion of service to CCRC, the subsequent difficulty in recruiting new staff, and, less importantly, the temporary absence of the executive director — were also due to inherent staff burnout (a common complaint in human service agencies) and to staff–board communication problems.

The board was composed predominantly of business and public administrators, so members sometimes were not familiar with the body of theory and the resulting methodology which are the foundation of the early intervention philosophy. Further, some board members were not familiar with the details of the daily operating problems of the staff.

As an example, the board's building committee vetoed a request by the staff for a parent's room in the proposed new building, a room the staff thought was important. The board, for its part, was concerned about building costs, although the original purpose of the Center was for the support of parents as well as the development of children.

The amount of board participation in the Center's functions varied. Some board members tended to get very involved in limited areas of the Center's operation, such as staff hiring or the annual fund-raising concert. This concert was a major regional social event of the late summer. Tickets were $70 a couple. The Thomases spent a lot of time on this fund-raising concert, although most board members viewed the concert as an obligation, not as a social event. Few staff members could afford tickets.

The staff, for its part, was often unaware of or uninterested in some of the financial constraints that resulted in operating policies handed down by the board, although the executive director, who attended all board and executive committee meetings, attempted to put these policies in perspective when time permitted.

The staff was also frustrated by not having enough time to talk about difficult cases or to attend seminars and workshops. Limited supervision was also a concern, especially to the new staff. Finally, as the Center grew, more internal support and more formal procedures were needed. Referrals were continuing to increase at Nigel Thomas, although CCRC referrals were limited, especially since they were not being actively sought by the Center, given the existing stress.

Funding and reporting changes also placed new demands on the Center's staff. For example, in April 1985 the state funding agency established a regional office to oversee the Center and other agencies. New standards and regulations led to unforeseen paperwork and negotiations, demands that were difficult for the staff to appreciate, since the staff was focused on service delivery.

Administrative problems were aggravated by the announcement at the June regular board meeting that the executive director, Sally Miller, had resigned effective July 31.

The Building   In response to the problem of operating at two locations, and also in recognition of the difficulty of a tenant position — the Center having relocated five times in the past 13 years — the board authorized a building project. A local architect volunteered to develop a design concept, and board members hired a consultant, the ex-manager of a local chamber of commerce, at a fee of $2,000 per month, to help the board raise funds for a building and find a permanent site. By June 1986 over $100,000 had been pledged of a total need estimated to be $300,000, less $100,000 to be raised by a mortgage. A schedule recognized as most ambitious called for an August 1986 ground breaking.

Planning Late in 1985 board president Kelly, having received a regional foundation mailing, wrote an application for $6,700 for board planning and a management systems improvement involving planning sessions and management consultant services for a 6-month period. The grant application, after giving a history of the Center, mentioned six management issues to be addressed: (1) inadequate time to plan for such a dramatic change in program and budget size, (2) concern by staff and board members about the resource drain on the Nigel Thomas program, (3) the need to develop community resources and community relations in a new program area, (4) the increase in enrollment beyond current capacity as a result of heightened community awareness of available services, (5) lack of board representation from the CCRC area, and (6) the efficient management of two sites by one administrative staff.

In line with the regional foundation's staff opinion that the budgeted $5,550 of consultants' fees could be reduced, the foundation awarded $3,500 for management systems and $1,500 for board planning at its December 1985 meeting.

During April 1986, the consultant selected by the board interviewed some members of the board and staff. She presented a report of findings in May 1986. This report is summarized in Exhibit 4.

On June 6 and 7, the board planning retreat was held at a conference center with the consultant as discussion leader or facilitator. Board attendees included the five executive committee members, John Bell, and three other board members for a part of the session. While initial plans envisioned a joint board–staff meeting, the president asked Sally Miller, who also attended, to explain to the staff that the May meeting and planning retreat were only for the board. Notable absences at the session included the Thomases.

After the board resisted the consultant's initial efforts to have each member prepare a psychological self-profile, it became clear that the consultant's view and board members' views of the meeting were quite different. Primarily made up of businesspersons, the board proposed a restructuring of the planning session to actually make plans. The session then turned to a definition of long-term mission, key issues facing the Center including the role of the board, and the development of plans to carry out that long-term mission.

The 2 days of planning was summarized in the "Notes from the Board Retreat" presented to the board at its meeting in June 1986. It seemed to John Bell that the 2-day planning session could be divided into five parts or phases. During the first part the consultant presented (1) goals that she had identified for the meeting, including "team building" and (2) the definition of a team.

During the second part, the board members presented three specific problems that they wanted to work on: (1) the future mission of the Center, (2) the key issues facing the Center, and (3) a definition of the board's role in the future.

During the third part, the discussion centered on (1) the future mission, with most of the contribution being made by the executive director; (2) the issues facing the Center, with general discussion; and (3) the board's role, with most of the contribution being made by the executive committee members of the board, who

EXHIBIT 4
Consultant's pre-
retreat findings

Environment

The catchment area the Center serves houses a large percentage of culturally and economically disadvantaged families. At this writing, more requests for services are made than
can be comfortably or easily handled through the current intake procedures.

Output of Services and Products

Chiefly, the services provided through the Nigel Thomas Center are and have always
been highly regarded by families, staff, and the community in general. The primary
complaints of the staff are (1) the paperwork necessary to thoroughly track each child
(much of which is required by the state for statistical and financial purposes) and (2)
inadequate time to keep up with it. The professional staff's concern is also that programming suffers from lack of coordination of all staff involved in a case, their ideal being
to make themselves into a transdisciplinary team.

Overall, communications between staff and board, between the two facilities, and among
staff is reported as being poor, with many examples cited of misinterpretation of statements made or actions taken. This is not at all surprising since communication takes
time (which is in short commodity) and the tendency during rapid change is to retrench
and streamline and to look for a convenient scapegoat on whom to blame the turmoil.

Relationships

As in all organizations, subgroups are a part of the Nigel Thomas culture. These subgroups
exist among staff and board, but with only limited overlap. Groupings seem to be made
along old/new, social, and/or business lines. This increases the strain on open communications.

Conflict is not always openly or constructively addressed or made use of. There appear
to be undercurrents of hostility or anger about an unspecified condition. Rather than
dealing directly and enthusiastically with conflicts, members seem to either burn out
and/or withdraw. This is a direct result of lack of trust and team-connectedness.

generally expressed a desire to minimize their participation in operating matters,
matters that had taken up a lot of their time during the past year.

In the fourth phase, participants suggested ways of structuring the organization
to carry out the identified goals and to deal with the recognized issues.

In the fifth and final part of the meeting, the participants sought to make specific
task assignments and to reaffirm commitments in order to maintain an organizational
momentum begun at the board retreat. It was commonly felt that recent board
meetings had not achieved an effective level of commitment, momentum, and strategic
direction.

CONCLUSION

In resolving the question of what would be an appropriate course of action to
pursue in the future, John Bell believed that he should try to answer several questions
in his own mind:

1. What were the consequences of having a board that did not include any "operating" officer, such as the executive director? This total separation of board versus staff, while perhaps typical of nonprofit agencies, was clearly abnormal based upon the experience of for-profit organizations.

2. How should a new director act? This question should be answered only after considering what the board should do and how it should work. How it should work would be influenced by the personalities involved. Rosemary Kelly, the president, appeared to be quite shy. Her manner was quiet and businesslike, yet most reserved. Other board members did not seem to be very well acquainted.

3. How should directors be selected and motivated? Various directors seem to represent (1) professional and/or functional skills, (2) other child or social welfare groups, (3) regional areas, or (4) leaders of financial or social interests. How could one keep this diverse group's enthusiasm and altruism at a high level? How should new directors be selected?

4. What should be the relationships between the board and staff, board and parents, and board and children?

John remembered that one new board member had commented to him, "The people on this board don't seem to like each other." He also recalled telling president Rosemary Kelly that he had been disturbed about the board selection process after running into the neighbor who had recruited him for the job. They had talked about some board problems, including the fact that the executive director had just resigned and that the board seemed to subdivide itself into specialized committees with mandatory meetings, while no one studied the big picture. For example, the program development committee has held meetings to discuss new service programs without any revenue or cost discussions. John had learned quite by accident that the building committee was anxiously awaiting the recommendations of the program development committee that would "show us how to pay for the building with new money-making programs." John's neighbor listened and replied: "If I had told you the truth in the beginning, you never would have gone on the board." Rosemary said in return that if John or other directors were concerned about planning, they should come to her with their concerns: "I can't be calling the board all the time to ask 'How's it going?'"

APPENDIX A: BOARD OF DIRECTORS, OFFICERS, AND DIRECTORS, 1986–1987

The abbreviation "(1)" indicates a member of the executive committee. The abbreviation "(2)" indicates a new member as of June 1986.

OFFICERS

President: Rosemary Kelly (1). A former Nigel Thomas Center parent, Rosemary works in fund-raising and development. She is serving her second term as president of the Nigel Thomas Center.

Vice-president: Peter Davidson (1), (2). A captain in the U.S. Navy, Peter is public works officer at the Naval Shipyard and has been a naval officer for 25 years.

Treasurer: Beverly Atwood (1). Treasurer of the investment counseling firm of Markson & Associates, Inc., Beverly is also a registered securities representative.

DIRECTORS

John Bell (2). A professor of business, John also regularly consults to industry and nonprofit organizations.

Gloria Hall. Gloria is a member of the American Society of Interior Designers and has owned an interior design business since moving to California in 1984.

Jane Chandler (2). Jane has 15 years of experience in the medical field, having worked in several hospitals in varying administrative capacities. Her most recent position was with a real estate development firm.

Samuel Heap (1). Sam is a psychotherapist and holds two professional degrees.

Lois Dennison (2). Before passing the bar exam and joining a law firm, Lois was a pediatric nurse for 5 years.

Denise Wilson (2). Denise is parent-child coordinator for the Community Health Services and has a Bachelor of Science in nursing.

Robert and Mary Thomas. The Nigel Thomas Center is named after their son who died at an early age of a metabolic disorder. Both Bob and Mary have been involved with preschool special education since that time. Currently, Bob is a licensed real estate broker.

Sarah Gladstone (1). Sarah has been involved in the insurance industry for 10 years and presently is employed as a property and casualty agent.

Nancy Harris. Director of special education for California school administrative District 9, Nancy has been involved in education for many years.

Lance Kingman (2). Lance is vice president of the Valley Insurance Agency and has 12 years of experience in the insurance field.

Louis and Kathy Baker. Very involved with local youth, the Bakers are themselves the parents of a special needs child. Louis is currently a physical education teacher and coach, while Kathy's job experience includes working with a CPA and an orthodontist.

WALL DRUG STORE, 1983

The Wall Drug Store is a complex of retail shops located on the main street of Wall, South Dakota, population 770, owned and managed by the Hustead family of Wall. It includes a drug store, a soda fountain, two jewelry stores, two clothing stores, a restaurant with four dining rooms, a western art gallery, a bookstore and shops selling rocks and fossils, camping and backpacking equipment, saddles and boots as well as several souvenir shops. In 1983, a major expansion was underway which would add five more shops and a chapel. "The decision, as when you first wrote the case in 1974,[1] is are we going ahead with our building program or not? That hasn't changed," announced Bill Hustead as he talked about his plans for Wall Drug. The tourist season was just beginning on June 1. The Spring had been cool and wet, and sales for the year to June 1 were down considerably from the previous year. Bill continued,

> *We are still going ahead with building program. The building program is not necessarily to make more money, but mainly it is to enlarge and enhance the store, so that it makes more of an impression on the traveling public. The church, the art gallery, the apothecary shop — we naturally feel these things will pay their way and make money, but the good part is, when the signs go down, we will have a place that people just won't miss. The place is so crazy, so different — it's the largest drugstore in the world, it may get in the Guiness Book of Records as the only drugstore with a church in it. People and writers will have a lot to talk about. We will continue to seek publicity. We will advertise in crazy places, we will have packets for writers and we will try to seek national and international publicity.*

[1] Professors James D. Taylor and Robert L. Johnson are co-authors of "Wall Drug Store," a case written in 1974.

This case was prepared by Professors James D. Taylor, Robert L. Johnson, and Philip C. Fisher of the University of South Dakota as the basis of class discussion. Reprinted by permission.

WALL DRUG HISTORY

Ted Hustead graduated from the University of Nebraska with a degree in pharmacy in 1929 at the age of 27. In December of 1931, Ted and his wife Dorothy bought the drug store in Wall, South Dakota, for $2,500. Dorothy and Ted and their four-year-old son Bill moved into living quarters in the back twenty feet of the store. Business was not good (the first month's receipts were $350) and prospects in Wall did not seem bright. Wall, South Dakota, in 1931 is described in the following selection from a book about the Wall Drug Store.

> Wall, then: a huddle of poor wooden buildings, many unpainted, housing some 300 desperate souls; a 19th century depot and wooden water tank; dirt (or mud) streets; few trees; a stop on the railroad, it wasn't even that on the highway. U.S. 16 and 14 went right on by, as did the tourists speeding between the Badlands and the Black Hills. There was nothing in Wall to stop for.[2]

Neither the drugstore nor the town of Wall prospered until Dorothy Hustead conceived the idea of placing a sign promising free ice water to anyone who would stop at their store. The sign read "Get a soda/Get a beer/Turn next corner/Just as near/To Highway 16 and 14/Free ice water/Wall Drug." Ted put the sign up and cars were turning off the highway to go to the drugstore before he got back. This turning point in the history of Wall Drug took place on a blazing hot Sunday afternoon in the summer of 1936.

The value of the signs was apparent and Ted began putting them up all along the highways leading to Wall. One sign read "Slow down the old hack/Wall Drug Corner/Just across the railroad track." The attention-catching signs were a boom to the Wall Drug and the town of Wall prospered too. In an article in *Good Housekeeping* in 1951, the Husteads' signs were called "the most ingenious and irresistable system of signs ever derived."[3]

Just after World War II, a friend traveling across Europe for the Red Cross got the idea of putting up Wall Drug signs overseas. The idea caught on and soon South Dakota servicemen who were familiar with the signs back home began to carry small Wall Drug signs all over the world. Many wrote the store requesting signs. One sign appeared in Paris, proclaiming "Wall Drug Store 4,278 miles (6,951 kilometers)." Wall Drug signs have appeared in many places including the North and South Pole areas, the 38th parallel in Korea and on Vietnam jungle trails. The Husteads sent more than 200 signs to servicemen requesting them from Vietnam. These signs led to news stories and publicity which further increased the reputation of the store.

[2] Jennings, Dana Close; *Free Ice Water: The Story of Wall Drug* (Aberdeen, South Dakota: North Plains Press, 1969), p. 26.

[3] Ibid., p. 42.

EXHIBIT 1 Wall Drug then and now

By 1958, there were about 3,000 signs displayed along highways in all 50 states, and two men and a truck were permanently assigned to service signs. Volunteers continue to put up signs. The store gives away 14,000 6-by-8-inch signs and 3,000 8-by-22-inch signs a year to people who request them. On the walls of the dining rooms at Wall Drug are displayed pictures from people who have placed signs in unusual places and photographed them for the Husteads.

The signs attracted attention and shortly after World War II articles about Ted Hustead and Wall Drug began appearing in newspapers and magazines. In August, 1950, *Redbook Magazine* carried a story which was later condensed in October's *Readers Digest*. Since then, the number of newspapers and magazines carrying feature stories or referring to Wall Drug has increased greatly. In June of 1983, Wall Drug store files contained 543 clippings of stories about the store. The number by 10-year periods was as follows:[4]

1941–1950	19 articles
1951–1960	41
1961–1970	137
1971–1980	260
1981 through April 1983	59

The store and its sales have grown steadily since 1936. From 1931 until 1941 the store was in a rented building on the west side of Wall's Main Street. In 1941, the Husteads bought an old lodge hall in Wasta, S.D. (15 miles west of Wall) and moved it to a lot on the east side of the street in Wall. The building, which had been used as a gymnasium in Wasta, became the core around which the current store is built.

Tourist travel greatly increased after World War II and the signs brought so many people into Wall Drug that the Husteads claim they were embarrassed because the facilities were not large enough to service them. The store did not even have modern restrooms. Sales during this period grew to $200,000 annually.

In 1951, Bill Hustead, now a pharmacy graduate of South Dakota State University at Brookings, joined his parents in the store.

In 1953, Wall Drug was expanded into a former store room to the south. This became the Western Clothing Room. In 1954, they built an outside store on the south of the Western Clothing Room. This was accompanied by a 30% increase in business. In 1956, a self-service cafe was added on the north side of the store. In the early 1950s sales were in the $300,000 per year range and by the early 1960s had climbed to $500,000. (A map of the store with the dates of expansion are shown in Exhibit 2.)

---

[4] Twenty-seven clippings were undated.

EXHIBIT 2 Map of Wall Drug

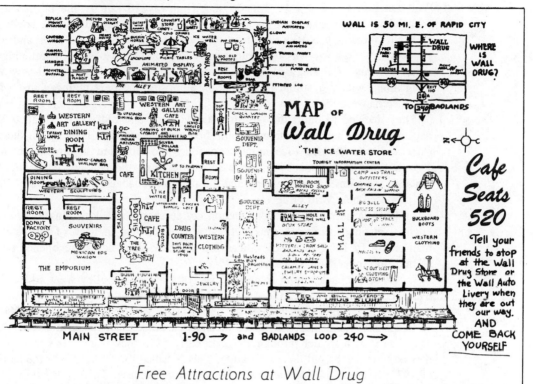

Free Attractions at Wall Drug

THE ORCHESTRAS

The Cowboy Orchestra and Chuckwagon Quartet (life-size and animated) sing and play in the store every half hour and sometimes more often during the season (mid-May to October 1st).

IN THE BACK YARD

We have a large replica of Mt. Rushmore, a bucking horse, a giant Jackalope replica, a six-foot rabbit (stuffed), a mounted buffalo, a covered wagon and the Ice Water Well . . . all for picture taking purposes during the busy season which is usually from May to the first of October. The 1908 Hupmobile, with a driver and his girl friend (life-size and animated), are also in the Back Yard.

WALL DRUG MALL

Walk down the main street of Wall Drug's typical western town. These buildings are all constructed of a collection of native timber and old brick. The street is made from Cheyenne River rock.

WESTERN ART GALLERY CAFE AND DINING ROOM

Wall Drug has 179 original oil paintings, some in the dining rooms and the rest in other parts of the store. The Western Art Gallery Cafe is paneled in American Black Walnut and has life-size carvings of Butch Cassidy and the Sundance Kid, which is made from a 187-year-old cedar tree. Please note also the Silver Dollar Bar and the collection of Arikara Indian artifacts. In the Western Art Gallery Dining Room is a collection of Tiffany-type lamp shades (hand leaded glass) and 600 cattle brands, taken from the 1889 and 1970 South Dakota registered brands books. In a third dining room, the Cowboy Art Dining Room is a display of Tony Chytka's original sculptures, a tiffany-type ceiling and brass bedstead booths.

ICE FOR JUGS . . . FREE

FREE ICE WATER!

CAFE   **COFFEE**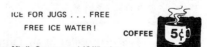

FREE COFFEE and DONUTS — For Hunters, Skiers, Honeymooners, Missile Crewmen and 18 Wheelers

In the early 1960s, Ted and his son Bill began seriously thinking of moving Wall Drug to the highway. The original Highway 16 ran by the north side of Wall, about two blocks from the store. It was later moved to run by the south side of Wall, about two blocks also from the drugstore. In the late 1950s and early 1960s a new highway was built running by the south side of Wall paralleling the other highway. Ted and Bill Hustead were considering building an all-new Wall Drug along with a gasoline filling station alongside the new highway just where the interchange by Wall was located.

They decided to build the gasoline station first, and did so. It is called Wall Auto Livery. When the station was finished, they decided to hold up on the new store and then decided to continue expanding the old store in downtown Wall. This was a fortunate decision, since soon after that, the new interstate highway replaced the former new highway and the new interchange ran through the site of the proposed new Wall Drug.

In 1963, a new fireproof construction coffee shop was added. In 1964, a new kitchen, again of fireproof construction, was added just in back of the cafe and main store. In 1964 and 1965 offices and the new pharmacy were opened on the second floor over the kitchen.

In 1968, the back dining room and backyard across the alley were added. This was followed in 1971 with the Art Gallery Dining Room.

By the late 1960s and early 1970s, annual sales volume went to $1,000,000.

In 1971 the Husteads bought the theater that bordered their store on the south. They ran it as a theater through 1972. In early 1973 they began construction of a new addition in the old theater location. This is called the "Mall." By the summer of 1973 the north part of the Mall was open for business. The south side was not ready yet. That year the Wall Drug grossed $1,600,000 which was an increase of about 20% over 1972. Bill believes the increase was due to their new Mall addition.

The development of the Mall represents a distinct change in the development of Wall Drug. All previous development had been financed out of retained earnings or short-term loans. In effect, each addition was paid for as it was built or added.

THE MALL

The owners of Wall Drug broke with their previous method of expansion when they built the Mall by borrowing approximately $250,000 for 10 years to finance the Mall and part of 20 large new signs which stand 660 feet from the interstate highway.

During the last half of the 1960s and early 1970s Bill Hustead had thought about and planned the concept of the Mall. The Mall was designed as a town within a large room. The main strolling mall was designed as a main street with each store or shop designed as a two-story frontier Western building. The Mall is thus like a re-created Western town. Inside the stores various woods are used in building and paneling. Such woods, as pine from Custer, South Dakota, American black walnut, gumwood, hackberry, cedar, maple, and oak are among the various woods used. The store fronts are recreations of building fronts found in old photos of Western towns in the 1880s. Many photos, paintings, and prints line the walls. These shops stock products that are more expensive than the souvenir merchandise found in most other parts of the store. The shops are more like Western boutiques.

The northern part of the Mall was open for business shortly after July 10, 1973. In the fall of 1973, Bill was uncertain as to whether or not to open the south side. The Husteads perceived a threat to the tourist business in the 1974 season. They agonized over whether to finish the Mall and order the normal amount of inventory, or to hold up the Mall and order conservatively. Among the conditions that seemed to threaten tourism were rising gasoline prices, periodic gasoline shortages in parts of the country, and trouble with American Indian Movement (AIM) at Wounded Knee and on the Pine Ridge Reservation. The more long-term threat to the businesses that depend on tourists, especially Wall Drug, was the highway beautification laws of the 1960s that threatened the removal of roadside advertising signs.

Bill finally decided in the winter of 1973 to prepare for a full tourist season, therefore had the Mall finished and ordered a full inventory for the 1974 season.

The decisions the Husteads confronted in the fall and winter of 1973 marked the first time they had seriously considered any retrenchment in their 27 years of growth.

In May and June, the opening of the 1974 tourist season, there were nine shops in the Mall. Bill estimated in the winter of 1974 that the year would be a record breaker of $2 million. June, July and August sales were up 15 to 20%. September business was up 20 to 30%, October was up 40%, and November was a record setter for that month.

Bill gave the following reasons for the 1974 season:

1. Many other businesses bought light, Wall Drug bought heavy. Therefore, while others ran short, Wall Drug had merchandise towards the end of the summer.
2. Expensive items sold well in spite of the recession scare of the late 1974 period. Bill indicated that articles in Eastern merchandising journals indicated luxury items were doing well all over. Wall Drug had to reorder even into the fall on hot items, such as books, jewelry, and Western clothes.
3. Wall Drug had more goods and space than it ever had before, and each person was buying more.
4. There were more hunters than ever before in the fall. Signs on the highway advertising free donuts and coffee for hunters brought many in and they bought heavy.
5. Although visitations to Mt. Rushmore were down in the summer of 1974, Wall Drug sales were up. Why? Bill speculates that more people from South Dakota and bordering states took shorter trips this year, and thus went to the Black Hills. These people had likely been in the Black Hills before and had seen Mt. Rushmore on their first trip. However, these people like to pay another visit to Wall Drug to eat, see what has been added and to shop.

In the fall of 1974, Wall Drug invested in more large signs to set 660 feet back from the interstate. By 1976, they had 29 of these signs. These were the only legal type signs that they could put up along the interstate, but by the spring of 1976, the language of the Highway Beautification Act was changed to put these signs outside the law also. Their signs (smaller ones) in neighboring states have been removed.

In 1975 and 1976, expansion continued with the addition of the Emporium, more dining area, and more rest rooms at the north end of the store. (See map of Wall Drug.)

In 1978, the location of the Wall post office at the south end of the store beyond the Mall which had previously been purchased, furnished expansion for the western clothing stores, boots and harness shop.

Currently, in 1983, there is further expansion under construction east of the Mall to the alley. The new area will feature a chapel modeled after a church built by Trappist Monks in Dubuque, Iowa in 1850. Also featured will be a replica of the original Wall Drug Store, which will be called Hustead's Apothecary and will serve as the Drug Store Museum. The store will sell Caswell-Massey products from the store of that name in New York which is the oldest drug store in the U.S. Other shops will be a western art gallery, a poster shop and western gift shop, an iron and pottery shop, and Hustead's Family Picture Gallery. The shops will be modeled after famous old western establishments. There will also be a new set of restrooms. In effect, the new addition will be an extension of the Mall.

STORE OPERATION

Wall is a small town of 770 people as of 1980. The economic base of the town is primarily built around the Wall Drug and is dependent on tourist business.

Wall is situated right on the edge of the Badlands and 52 miles east of Rapid City. For miles in either direction, people in autos have been teased and tantalized by Wall Drug signs. Many have heard of the place through stories in the press, or have heard their parents or friends speak of the Wall Drug. In the summer of 1963, in a traffic count made on the highway going by Wall, 46% were eastbound and 54% were westbound. Of the eastbound traffic, 43% turned off at Wall. Of the westbound traffic, 44% turned off at Wall.

When people arrive at Wall (those westbound usually after driving 40 miles or more through the Badlands) they are greeted by the large Wall Drug sign on the interchange and an 80-foot-high, 50-ton statue of a dinosaur. The business district of Wall is two blocks long and is about three blocks to five blocks from the interchange. The town has eleven motels and a number of gasoline filling stations.

Cars from many states line the street in front of and several blocks on either side of the drugstore. Tabulation of state licenses from autos and campers parked in front of Wall Drug, June 1, 1983, at 12:00 noon are summarized as follows:

South Dakota (not local county)	20%
South Dakota, local county	22%
Balance of states and Canada	58%

Wall Drug is more than a store. It is a place of amusement, family entertainment, a gallery of the West, a gallery of South Dakota history, and a place that reflects the heritage of the West. Nostalgia addicts find Wall Drug particularly interesting. Children delight in the animated life-size cowboys singing, tableau of an Indian camp, a stuffed bucking horse, six-foot rabbit, a stuffed buffalo, old slot machines that pay out a souvenir coin for 25¢, statues of cowboys, dancehall girls and other characters of the old West, a coin-operated quick-draw game, and souvenirs by the roomful which make up part of the attractions.

The food is inexpensive and good, and although as many as 10,000 people might stream through on a typical day, the place is air conditioned and comfortable. The dining rooms are decorated with beautiful wood paneling, paintings of Western art are displayed, and Western music plays. One can dine on buffalo burgers, roast beef or steak, 5¢ coffee or select wine, and beer from the rustic, but beautiful, American walnut bar.

About one-fourth of the sales in Wall Drug is food, plus about 5% to 10% for beverages and soda fountain. (This varies with the weather.) About 10% to 15% is jewelry, 15% clothing and hats, 35% to 40% for souvenirs, and 5% to 10% for drugs, drug sundries and prescriptions.

The store is manned by a crew of 201 people, 76 of which are college girls and 25 are college boys who work there in the summer. Student help is housed in homes that have been bought and made into dormitory apartments. There is a modern swimming pool for their use, also. The clerks are trained to be courteous, informed and pleasant.

Orders for the following summer season begin being placed in the preceding fall. Orders begin arriving in December, but most arrive in January, February, March and April. Many large souvenir companies post-date their invoices until July and August. Each year brings new offerings from souvenir companies and other suppliers. Much of the purchasing is done by Bill, who admits he relies on trusted salespeople of their suppliers who advise him on purchasing. Many of these companies have supplied Wall Drug for 30 years or so. Wall Drug generally buys directly from the producers or importers including photo supplies and clothing.

Years ago, much of what Wall Drug bought and sold was imported or made in the eastern part of the country. In recent years, much of the merchandise is being made regionally and locally. Indian reservations now have small production firms and individuals who make handicraft which is sold through Wall Drug. Examples of such firms are Sioux Pottery, Badlands Pottery, Sioux Moccasin, and Milk Camp Industries.

The Husteads rely a great deal on the department managers for buying assistance. The manager of the jewelry, for instance, will determine on the basis of last year's orders and her experience with customer reaction and demand, how much to order for the next season. All ordering is centered through Bill.

HIGHWAY BEAUTIFICATION AND PROMOTION

In the year 1965, Congress passed the Highway Beautification Act, which was designed to reduce the number of roadside signs. Anticipating the removal of the many Wall Drug advertising signs, Bill Hustead invested in new signs that were allowed under that legislation. These signs were to be placed no closer than 660 feet away from the road. To be read, these signs must be larger than the older signs, and cost close to $9,000 each. Now even these large signs are included in the laws for regulation or removal.

There has been slow compliance with this legislation by many states including South Dakota, since many states in less populated areas have many tourist attractions, and find road signs the only practical way to advertise these attractions. Since President Reagan has been in office, there has been little enforcement of the sign legislation since there has been less money available for federal enforcement. There is new legislation being proposed by the Federal Highway Administration of the Department of Transportation as of 1983 that could have an impact on Wall Drug and other tourist dependent establishments.

Bill and Ted also decided that they must gain as much visibility and notoriety as possible, and to help achieve this, they began using advertising in unusual places. In the 1960s, Wall Drug began taking small ads in unlikely media such as the *International Herald Tribune,* and *The Village Voice,* in New York City's Greenwich Village, advertising 5¢ coffee and 49¢ breakfast as well as animal health remedies. This brought telephone calls and some letters of inquiry. It also brought an article in the *Voice* and probably attracted the attention of other media. In January 31, 1971, (Sunday) *The New York Times* carried an article about Wall Drug. This article may have led to Bill Hustead's appearance on Garry Moore's television program "To Tell the Truth." In the year 1979, there were 75 articles in newspapers and magazines about Wall Drug. In August 31, 1981, edition of *Time,* a full page article in the American Scene featured the store and the Husteads. Also, in 1981, Wall Drug was featured on NBC television's "Today Show" and Atlanta Cable "Winners."

For awhile, the Wall Drug was advertised in the London city buses and subways, Paris Metro (subway) in the English language, and on the dock in Amsterdam where people board sight-seeing canal boats.

FINANCES

Exhibits 3 and 4 present summary income statements and balance sheets from 1973 through 1982. The Wall Auto Livery was consolidated into Wall Drug Store, Inc.,

EXHIBIT 3 Income statements, Wall Drug

	1982	1981	1980	1979	1978	1977	1976	1975	1974	1973
Sales	$4,733	$4,821	$3,970	$3,552	$4,125	$3,777	$3,464	$2,679	$1,991	$1,607
Cost of sales	2,644	2,676	2,230	2,072	2,228	2,098	1,879	1,484	1,100	806
Gross profit	2,089	2,145	1,740	1,480	1,897	1,679	1,586	1,195	891	801
G&A expense	1,802	1,857	1,473	1,433	1,578	1,453	1,312	1,000	754	691
Income from operations	287	288	267	47	319	226	274	195	137	110
Other income (expenses)	36	81	43	(8)	35	23	2	3	(8)	(10)
Income before tax	323	369	310	39	354	249	276	198	129	100
Tax	120	144	125	6	148	94	111	80	54	41
Net income	$ 203	$ 224	$ 185	$ 33	$ 206	$ 155	$ 165	$ 118	$ 75	$ 59

Note: Figures in thousands.

EXHIBIT 4 Balance sheets on December 31

	1982	1981	1980	1979	1978	1977	1976	1975	1974	1973
Cash and short term investments	$ 240	$ 282	$ 449	$ 11	$ 82	$ 65	$ 51	$ 93	$ 145	$ 74
Inventories	631	547	369	403	338	276	249	248	174	144
Other current assets	60	57	53	99	51	58	50	32	26	26
Total current assets	$ 931	$ 886	$ 871	$ 513	$ 471	$ 399	$ 350	$ 373	$ 345	$ 244
Property, equipment	2907	2591	2380	2297	2230	1960	1739	1484	1234	1130
Accumulated depreciation	(1355)	(1254)	(1147)	(1030)	(906)	(790)	(674)	(576)	(496)	(428)
Other assets	24	25	27	53	55	33	29	31	34	34
Total assets	$2507	$2248	$2131	$1833	$1850	$1602	$1444	$1312	$1117	$ 980
Current maturities of long-term debt	$ 43	$ 40	$ 46	$ 8	$ 11	$ 5	$ 8	$ 7	$ 21	$ 20
Notes payable	0	0	0	68	20	0	0	5	70	20
Accounts payable	56	58	63	47	43	64	36	42	31	23
Accruals, other current liab.	252	244	310	124	232	167	178	193	136	110
Total current liab.	$ 351	$ 342	$ 419	$ 247	$ 306	$ 236	$ 222	$ 247	$ 258	$ 173
Long-term debt	191	149	179	238	133	130	133	136	222	244
Deferred tax	7	1								
Stockholder's equity	1958	1756	1533	1348	1411	1236	1089	929	637	563
Total liab., equity	$2507	$2248	$2131	$1833	$1850	$1602	$1444	$1312	$1117	$ 980

Note: Figures in thousands.

EXHIBIT 5 Percent of sales statements

	1982	1981	1980	1979	1978	1977	1976	1975	1974	1973
Sales	100.0	100.0	100.0	100.0	100.0	100.0	100.0	100.0	100.0	100.0
Cost of sales	55.9	55.5	56.2	58.3	54.0	55.6	54.2	55.4	55.2	50.2
Gross profit	44.1	44.5	43.8	41.7	46.0	44.4	45.8	44.6	44.8	49.8
G&A expense	38.1	38.5	37.1	40.3	38.3	38.4	37.9	37.3	37.9	43.0
Income from operations	6.0	6.0	6.7	1.3	7.7	6.0	7.9	7.3	6.9	6.8
Other income (expenses)	.8	1.7	1.1	(.2)	.9	.6	.1	.1	(.4)	(.6)
Income before tax	6.8	7.7	7.8	1.1	8.6	6.6	8.0	7.4	6.5	6.2
Tax	2.5	3.0	3.1	.2	3.6	2.5	3.2	3.0	2.7	2.5
Net income	4.3	4.7	4.7	.9	5.0	4.1	4.8	4.4	3.8	3.7

in May 1975. Had this transition occurred prior to 1973, sales for 1973, 1974 and 1975 would have been about $192,000, $248,000 and $52,000 larger, and net profit would have been about $19,000 larger in 1973, and $21,000 larger in 1974, with a negligible effect in 1975. The value of the acquired net assets was about $180,000.

The company's growth and expansion has been financed primarily by retained earnings, temporarily supplemented at times with short-term borrowings. A major exception was a $250,000, ten year installment loan in 1973 used to help finance

EXHIBIT 6 Components of rate of return on equity

	1982	1981	1980	1979	1978	1977	1976	1975	1974	1973
$\dfrac{\text{Gross profit}}{\text{Sales}}$	.441	.445	.438	.417	.460	.444	.458	.446	.448	.498
$\dfrac{\text{Income from operations}}{\text{Gross profit}}$	.137	.134	.153	.032	.168	.135	.163	.163	.154	.137
$\dfrac{\text{Sales}}{\text{Assets}}$	1.89	2.14	1.86	1.94	2.23	2.36	2.40	2.04	1.78	1.64
$\dfrac{\text{Income from operations}}{\text{Assets}}$	.114	.128	.125	.026	.172	.141	.190	.148	.123	.112
$\dfrac{\text{Net income}}{\text{Income from operations}}$	.707	.778	.698	.702	.646	.686	.602	.605	.547	.536
$\dfrac{\text{Assets}}{\text{Equity}}$	1.28	1.28	1.39	1.36	1.31	1.30	1.33	1.41	1.75	1.74
$\dfrac{\text{Net income}}{\text{Equity}}$	.103	.128	.121	.025	.146	.126	.152	.126	.118	.105

the mall and some large signs located 660 feet from the highway. In 1975, this loan was prepaid through 1980. At the end of 1982, only $34,500 remained to be paid on this loan. Other long-term debt at the end of 1982 includes installment contracts for the purchase of real estate and a stock redemption agreement (occurring in 1979) for the purchase by the company of some Class B, non-voting stock. As indicated on the December 31, 1982 balance sheet, current maturities of long-term debt were $43,436. Of this amount, $34,496 is the final payment on the 1973 loan due in 1983.

Both the growth and the volatility of the business should be apparent from the income statements presented in Exhibit 3. Exhibit 5 presents the income statements as a percentage of sales. Exhibit 6 is an analysis of the rate of return on equity broken into the component parts using the format:

$$\frac{\text{sales}}{\text{assets}} \times \frac{\text{gross profit}}{\text{sales}} \times \frac{\text{operating income}}{\text{gross profit}} \times \frac{\text{net income}}{\text{operating income}} \times \frac{\text{assets}}{\text{equity}} = \frac{\text{net income}}{\text{equity}}$$

Between 1973 and 1982, prices, as measured by the Consumer Price Index, increased by about 115%. Percentage increases in some balance sheet and income accounts for Wall Drug over this period are:

Sales	163%
Total G. + A. expense	145
Net income	159
Total assets	115
Equity	169

These percentages are based on combining Wall Auto Livery with Wall Drug in 1973 as if the merger occurring in 1975 had taken place.

Given below are percentage changes in some of the general and administrative expenses from 1976 through 1982:

Total G. + A.	37%
Utilities	137
Officers' salaries	2
Other salaries	42
Depreciation	5
Advertising	116
Profit sharing contribution	49

The items mentioned accounted for 77% of total general and administrative expenses in 1982 and 76% in 1976. These same items as percentages of sales were:

	1982	1976
Utilities	1.7%	1.0%
Officers' salaries	2.9	3.8
Other salaries	18.5	17.7
Depreciation	2.3	2.9
Advertising	2.1	1.3
Profit sharing contributions	2.0	1.8

Depreciation methods on various assets vary from straight line to 200% declining balance and over lives of from 15 to 40 years for buildings and improvements to 5 to 10 years for equipment, furniture and fixtures. Although not evaluated or recognized on the financial statements, it is likely that some assets, such as the western art and the silver dollar bar, have appreciated.

STORE MANAGEMENT

Recruiting and training the seasonal work force is a major task at Wall Drug. College students are recruited through college placement services. Training is of short duration but quite intense. Summer employees are tested on their knowledge of store operations and their ability to give information about the area to tourists. Bill Hustead commented:

> *"I really think that there isn't anything more difficult than running a business with 20 to 30 employees in the winter and then moving into a business with 180 to 200 employees, and you have to house a hundred of them and you have to supervise them, and train them. This lasts through June, July and August, then the next year you start all over. It's kind of exciting and fun for the first 25 years but after 30 years you begin to think its a tough racket."*

The store had a permanent nucleus of 20 to 30 employees. While the business could operate with fewer employees during the winter, the Husteads believed that they needed the experienced employees to give stability to the operations in the summer. Permanent employees with seniority could get as much as six weeks paid vacation. Commenting on this policy Bill said:

> *"We probably go through the winter with more employees than we really need, but we give them time off in the winter because a seasonal business is so demanding. When the Fourth of July comes, you're working, when Memorial Day comes, you're working; when all those summer fun times come, you're working six days a week and it's quite a sacrifice. So, we try to be very generous with our paid vacations."*

Dependence on seasonal tourists for the major portion of Wall Drug's business has inherent risks, and uncertainty over the future of the roadside signs, which

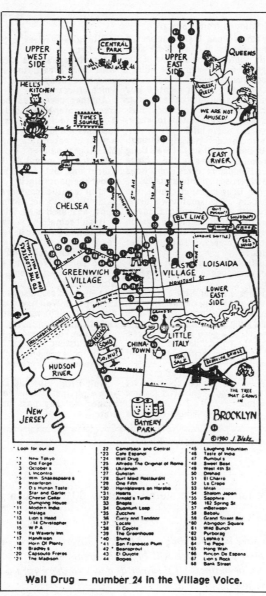

Wall Drug ads mystify New Yorkers

By RUTH·HAMEL
Argus Leader Staff

SoDak is a long way from SoHo, where west can mean New Jersey and Wall Drug could reasonably be thought to exist near Wall Street.

But, as usual, mere distance has not deterred Wall Drug owner Bill Hustead from advertising his business. Off and on for the past 20 years, Hustead has bought advertising space in the Village Voice, a New York City weekly based in Greenwich Village.

In every recent issue, a Wall Drug advertisement can be spotted between the columns devoted to Manhattan's vegetarian lunchspots and sushi bars. The small box may advertise petrified wood clocks one week, flying jackalopes on another and free ice water on another.

The tiny advertisements do not tell Voice readers where Wall Drug is, nor that it is more than a subway jaunt away for any New Yorker who might want to shop around for a petrified wood clock on a Saturday afternoon.

And the Voice's accompanying Manhattan map that shows where various restaurants are located denotes Wall Drug with a small arrow that simply points west from New York's Hell's Kitchen.

All of which adds to the Wall Drug mystique.

"We do get inquiries from time to time," Katherine Rogers, Village Voice restaurant sales coordinator, said. " 'What is that?' We give them the address."

Once told where Wall Drug is, people respond with the same question, she said: " 'Why?' "

But the baffling ads work. Over the
*WALL DRUG
Continued on page 2A

Wall Drug — number 24 in the Village Voice.

Look for our ad	22 Camelback and Central	45 Laughing Mountain
1 New Tokyo	23 Cate Espanol	46 Taste of India
2 Old Forge	24 Wall Drug	47 Rumbul's
3 October's	25 Alfredo The Original of Rome	48 Sweet Basil
4 L Incontro	26 Ukranean	49 West 4th St
5 Wm Shakespeare's	27 Gulston	50 Ditshad
6 Intertreron	28 Surf Maid Restaurant	51 El Charro
7 D s Human Taste	29 One Fifth	52 La Creps
8 Star and Garter	30 Hornblowers on Horatio	53 Mitali
9 Cheese Cellar	31 Hearts	54 Shalom Japan
10 Dumpling House	32 Arnold s Turtle	55 Sapphire
11 Modern India	33 Shapla	56 162 Spring St
12 Malaga	34 Quantum Leap	57 inBetween
13 Lion s Head	35 Zucchini	58 Babalu
14 14 Christopher	36 Curry and Tandoor	59 Grand Street Bar
15 W P A	37 Locale	60 Abingdon Square
16 Ye Waverly Inn	38 El Coyote	61 Wild Bunch
17 Manhkwan	39 The Greenhouse	62 Purborag
18 Horn Of Plenty	40 Shima	63 Leshko s
19 Bradley s	41 San Francisco Plum	64 Tio Pepe
20 Capsouto Freres	42 Beansprout	65 Hong Wah
21 The Madison	43 El Quijote	66 Rincon De Espana
	44 Bogos	67 Lion s Rock
		68 Bank Street

EXHIBIT 7
(continued)

Continued from page 1A

July 4th weekend, Wall Drug served five busloads of New York-area youth, some of whom knew of the drugstore from reading the Village Voice, Hustead said.

"One time, late at night, a guy from Massachusetts called" after spotting one of the Voice ads, Hustead said. "He wanted to know, 'What is a horse hitch?'."

New Yorkers passing through South Dakota will stop at Wall Drug to read the copies of the Village Voice Hustead receives every week and advertises on Interstate-90.

(Wall Drug signs, of course, are legendary. The small-town drugstore with the multi-national advertising campaign has placed signs in Amsterdam, London and along the French Riviera, among other places.)

Hustead's account with the Village Voice began about 20 years ago.

Always a fan of New York City, the drugstore owner was sitting in a Greenwich Village coffeehouse reading the paper when "I thought it might be a good move to advertise in the Voice," he said. "I knew that a lot of writers take that paper."

So Hustead placed an ad that emphasized the reasonable price of Wall Drug food compared to New York food.

Eventually, the Village Voice ads led to a Newsweek article about Wall Drug.

Ms. Rogers said a recent ad for Wall Drug's rattlesnake bite kits prompted many calls to the Village Voice offices.

Another recent ad boasting of free ice water hit a chord when New York was in a drought and its restaurants would only give customers a glass of water if they asked for it, Ms. Rogers said.

Hustead is proud of the Village Voice ads but has reservations about the paper itself.

"I'm a little conservative," he said. "I feel it's not as wholesome a paper as it used to be. The language ... it isn't something you want to lay around and let your 10-year-old girl read."

On a given week, Wall Drug may share Voice advertising space with naughty bakeries and naughtier film houses. And the newspaper that Hustead said used to resemble the paper in Wall now contains articles that might make some South Dakota jaws drop.

But the Voice association has allowed Hustead to meet interesting people between his forays to New York and New Yorkers' forays to Wall.

Wall Drug, Hustead says, "is a stop that those New Yorkers will make" as they pass through the state.

Source: *Sioux Falls Argus Leader*, July 8, 1981, p. 1.

have brought customers to the store for nearly 50 years, is a grave concern to the Husteads.

We will try to have ideas to modify our outdoor advertising program to adapt to changes in the law which we are sure will be forthcoming. If they are drastic changes, they could put us out of business. If they nail it down so there isn't a sign on the interstate, that will do the job.

Asked about diversification as a hedge against this risk, Bill replied,

We will try to diversify within our own community. By that I mean probably on our highway location in and around our Auto Livery. We have several hundred acres there (in sight of the interstate), and a motel and a modified drug store would be our last straw if we were wiped out in town.

The Husteads hoped to be able to create a fund to provide self-insurance for their dormitory houses. This fund would then also provide some measure of security from business risks as well.

Although over 80, Ted Hustead is still active in the management of the store, involved in everything from physical inspections of the premises to acting jointly with Bill in making policy decisions. Ted can frequently be seen on the grounds picking up litter. Dorothy, Ted's wife, comes to the store every day, summer and winter, helps with the banking and spends from two to six hours each day on various chores. Bill's son Rick, 33, joined the store in 1980 and now shares in the management. Rick has a Master's Degree in guidance and counseling and spent four years as a guidance counselor and teacher in high school. Rick also spent two years in the real estate business and one year in the fast food business before returning to Wall. During his school years, Rick spent ten seasons working in Wall Drug. His wife, Kathy, is a pharmacist and also works in the store.

Bill Hustead expressed his continuous concern with the future of Wall Drug in light of future action concerning roadside sign advertising. Can the store expansion continue; should diversification be attempted in the community; should diversification into areas not affected by the tourist be considered? Will Wall Drug be able to continue to gain publicity as they have in the past to keep people aware of their "attraction" characteristics? The costs of doing business are rising, such as the increase in utilities, which is sizeable. How can they plan for a bad year or two given the increasing uncertainty in tourist industry? With these thoughts in mind, the 1983 tourist season at Wall Drug was underway.

CASE 8

DYSYS INC.

As spring began to show itself in April 1984, Peter Gregson and Ted Mussett were wondering about the future direction of Dysys Inc., a two-year-old company in which they each had a 50 percent shareholding. The company, while profitable, was not performing at the level desired, and the co-owners were concerned about this situation.

THE CURRENT SITUATION

By 1984 Dysys had a number of market offerings. It acted as a dealer for a computerized restaurant information system and for a line of microcomputers and peripheral devices. Dysys also produced custom computer hardware and software in response to individual orders from customers. It provided consulting assistance to microcomputer users in the local area and, finally, was developing two products that it felt would have relatively wide application. These were the Production Information Network and the Brick. (Financial data are presented in Exhibit 1.)

In 1984 Dysys employed seven individuals, although only four of these were full-timers. The firm's management was: Peter Gregson — the founder of the business and president; Ted Mussett — vice president and general manager; and Chris Zinck — chief technologist and systems engineer.

The four full-time persons were Ted Mussett, Chris Zinck, Tom Cooper, and David Lane. David was an engineering technologist, hired to complete one of the R&D projects. Tom was a customer service representative trainee and looked after sales of the restaurant system and computer supplies. Ted was nominally in charge of marketing but found that he was involved in every facet of the company's operations

This case was prepared by Professors Philip Rosson and Robert Blunden of Dalhousie University. The authors gratefully acknowledge the financial support of the Department of Regional Industrial Expansion, Small Business Secretariat in the development of the case. Some of the case information was collected by MBA students Tom Boudreau, Mellany Hellstern, Alan McGee, Douglas Munn, and Roberta Thomson. Copyright © 1985 by Philip Rosson and Robert Blunden. Reprinted by permission.

EXHIBIT 1
Financial data (eight
months, 1983–1984,
by business activity)

Activity	Revenue	Percent of total	Cost of goods sold	Percent margin
Remanco Restaurant Information System	$ 30,000	18.5%	n.b.a.	?
Computer systems (Chameleon, peripherals, software)	67,000	41.4	$51,375	23%
Computer supplies	9,300	5.7	8,300	11
System maintenance	8,500	5.3	3,800	55
Custom products (the Brick, Bar Code Reader, etc.)	24,600	15.2	13,197	46
Custom software	8,400	5.2	n.b.a.	?
Industrial Research Assistance Program grant	14,000	8.7	n.a.	n.a.
Total	$161,800			

Notes: 1. Remanco revenues are commissions earned by company.
     2. n.b.a. = No breakdown available.
     3. n.a. = Not applicable.
     4. Total salaries for the period were $45,000.
     5. Total overhead for the period (including salaries) was $75,000.

from project scheduling to payables and receivables. Chris had become the firm's production man and was also involved in price quotes. (See Exhibit 2 for an organization chart.)

Matt Silver was employed part-time on a contract basis in his capacity as a business systems analyst. Fay Pape acted as a consultant, working on implementation and training in restaurants that adopted the computerized information systems. Peter Gregson was the final part-timer. Although president of the company, Peter had many "irons in the fire." He had a part-time teaching position at the Technical University of Nova Scotia as well as being a Ph.D. student at the same institution. When Peter was around, he got involved with all kinds of activities, such as contacting customers, dreaming up new product ideas, and constructing hardware.

DYSYS HISTORY

When Peter Gregson founded Dysys, he was 30 years old. He was an electrical engineer by training, with a diploma in engineering (St. Mary's University, Halifax), and bachelor and master degrees in electrical engineering (Technical University of Nova Scotia) earned between 1969 and 1977. Following schooling, Peter worked in a local electronics firm and as a scientist at a government research establishment. During the school and employee period, Peter had run his own small businesses on the side. He found moonlighting enjoyable because it provided him with an extra challenge as well as additional income.

EXHIBIT 2
Organization chart

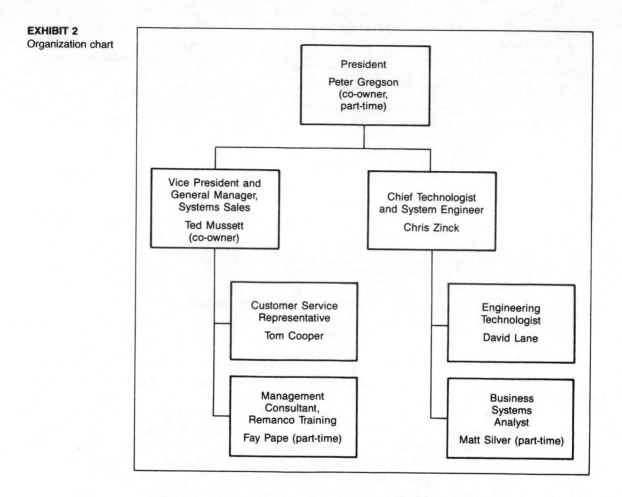

In 1977 he had formed his most serious business venture, along with a partner. This company, called Micronet Limited, grew quickly, from sales of $10,000 in its first year to almost $1 million in 1980–81. The principal product the company developed was an automatic meter reader for use in an experiment into electrical consumption patterns conducted by the Nova Scotia Power Corporation. Other products revolved around the use of microprocessors to control energy. Peter joined the company full-time as vice president of R&D in 1980, but Micronet found it hard to sustain sales, so that by the end of 1981, a cash infusion was needed. This was secured from a venture capital company in Boston. One of the agreements worked out by this firm and his partner was that Peter should no longer be an equal shareholder.

Angered by this decision, Peter decided to sell most of his shares and to leave the company six months later. In the meantime, with his adrenaline pumping hard, he strode off to the office of the Registry of Joint Stock Companies in Halifax, Nova Scotia, determined to register a new company. On the way, he decided on the name Dysys — a contraction of dynamic systems. This reflected his skill and experience designing microprocessors for dynamic situations. Once the company was registered, his thoughts turned to the matter of what exactly the company would do. Peter considered this during his last months with Micronet. One very real constraint was finance. With no capital behind him, there was considerable pressure to produce an immediate cash flow. Apart from anything else, there would be a mortgage payment due on his home a month after he left Micronet. This would be the first hurdle to be surmounted.

Given this situation, Peter realized that he had no time for any development work. Any computer-based product that he sold had to be built and ready to go. His first few days in business (in May 1982) involved a furious round of telephone calls to both potential customers and dealers. Eventually, a likely customer was located at the Technical University of Nova Scotia (TUNS). With this customer in mind, he decided to buy a system with his credit card. Since he was able to collect the price of the system from TUNS quickly, Peter used the 45-day credit period (from the purchase) to provide initial financing for his firm.

Next, a research contract was entered into with the provincially owned Nova Scotia Research Foundation, and some modems (a peripheral device that lets the computer transmit or receive information over a telephone line) were sold to Dalhousie University, both in Halifax. He also lined up a part-time teaching position at TUNS. Business developed over the ensuing months. However, things did not move as quickly as expected — for whereas Peter felt he could acquire a year's worth of income in about 7 months, it ended up taking 18 months.

Ted Mussett (whom Peter had known for about 10 years) joined Dysys as an equal partner with Peter in July 1982. Ted was a biologist by training who, since graduating from Dalhousie University in 1977, had taken further courses in mathematics, statistics, computer science, accounting, and data processing. Ted had also worked for the ill-fated Micronet as a representative responsible for sales of a computerized restaurant management system. He brought this line of products across to Dysys when Micronet went out of business in the summer of 1982.

In April 1983 Chris Zinck joined the company. Chris had earned bachelor degrees in computer science (Dalhousie, 1981) and in engineering (TUNS, 1983). In his last three years as a student, Chris had worked with local computing firms during summer vacations, developing his software skills in a business context. Chris's name was recommended to Peter and Ted when they were looking for an additional staff member, and he joined Dysys on a summer student employment grant. Chris originally worked at developing an interface between the restaurant information system and a liquor dispensing system. Later he was kept on to work on the Production Information Network (PIN), a plant automation project Dysys was developing for small- and medium-sized manufacturers.

THE DYSYS MISSION

In establishing Dysys, Peter Gregson was cognizant of the huge potential for any competent firm in the computer field. Initially Peter realized that he had to run his business so that his family's bills might be paid. With time, however, he saw a viable role for a company that acted in a technically sophisticated *consulting* capacity and as a *designer* and *manufacturer* of innovative microelectric products.

In the consulting capacity, Peter's experience told him that small- and medium-sized local businesses needed advice on the computer hardware and software best suited to their own particular applications and requirements. At the same time, Peter wanted to continue development of the PIN, which he had initiated while at Micronet, as well as other industrial control devices.

DYSYS ACTIVITIES IN 1984

By the spring of 1984 Dysys was operating in a number of different areas. Dysys acted as a dealer for the Remanco Restaurant Information System, for Seequa's Chameleon line of microcomputers, and for various computer peripheral devices.

Dealer Business   *The Remanco Restaurant Information System.* Remanco Systems Inc. was a Canadian company headquartered in Toronto that developed a computer-based management tool for the restaurant industry. The company was founded by a restauranteur looking for a solution to improving the productivity of his operation with technology. Established in 1977, it made its first volume shipments in 1981. In 1983 it expected to sell about 1,500 systems, 65 percent in the United States, 15 percent in Canada, and 20 percent in other world markets.

The Remanco system covered three areas of restaurant operation: service, payment, and management. Users of the system talked about it as bringing the restaurant into the 1980s. A typical system included a microprocessor, a terminal with keyboard, and two disk drives located near the kitchen or another central place, plus an array of terminal/printers or printers with preset menu instructions scattered around the serving stations. One adopter describes the system as follows:

> The server's terminal relays a clearly printed order to the kitchen or the bar, so there's no misunderstanding there. And at the end the guest is given a clear, complete, legible bill. It puts the finishing touch to the gracious service, the elegant presentation of the food.
>
> For the servers, the terminal unclutters their minds, frees them from pencils and paper, gives them a calmer, unruffled approach to serving guests. In the kitchen, orders are placed in sequence, clearly, and the chefs don't feel harassed. The system cuts down on the confusion all round.
>
> For reports and data gathering, we use information on what has been ordered to help us establish trends and demands. We like to satisfy our guests — who tend to be discriminating about their food — so we change the menu every three months or so.

With the data we can get from the Remanco system, we can take popular offerings and let our chefs create new and imaginative things from them.

The comprehensive record of all sales helps us exercise tight cash control and also speeds up the process of determining our food and liquor costs — and inventory — on a daily basis. [See Appendix A.]

Dysys was the agent for this system in Nova Scotia, receiving a 21 percent commission on sales and fees for installation, training, and implementation. It had sold the Remanco system to a number of restaurants in Halifax, including The Henry House, Le Bistro, and Clipper II. These were fine-quality restaurants, which seated 100 diners or more and had their own definable "ambience." The price of a typical Remanco system was in the order of $25,000 plus service contract fees. However, price could vary from $20,000 to $200,000 depending on the number of terminals required.

Systems like the Remanco were felt to be too costly for small establishments, owner-operated businesses, and beverage rooms with limited food offerings. Since the Halifax market was restricted to about 20 more sales, Dysys management was planning to move outside the metropolitan area, hoping to secure orders from other eating establishments. As well, they expected to capitalize on a verbal agreement with Remanco giving them the line for the Maritime provinces of New Brunswick, Nova Scotia, and Prince Edward Island. However, the company could not even entertain such expansion with its present staffing and commitments.

In the opinion of the Dysys personnel, the Remanco system was the best currently available. It was a simple, proven system and competitive with competing offerings such as NCR, Sweda, and Data General. Competition in the local market was provided by five manufacturers.

The Chameleon Line of Microcomputers. Microcomputers were a phenomenal growth industry in the early 1980s. As well as the computers themselves, computer peripherals (such as printers), software, and publications all experienced large sales increases. Numerous entries were made by companies hoping to achieve their financial dreams. In the Halifax area alone — which lagged behind other parts of the country — there were more than 50 computer consultants, distributors, dealers, and franchise stores. There was also a small number of hardware and software producers.

By 1983 it was estimated that more than 150 computer manufacturers were competing in the microcomputer market. Two companies — Apple Computer, Inc., and Tandy Corporation (with its Radio Shack brand and retail stores) — had made much of the early running and in 1981 were the leading and second companies, respectively. Then in August 1981 IBM launched its Personal Computer (PC) and within two years developed a 26 percent share of the critical United States market.

The success of the PC meant that IBM was unable to fill all its orders quickly. In fact, it was reported that demand for PCs was six times in excess of IBM's building capacity.[1] This situation spawned an entirely new industry — the production

[1] "Personal Computers: And the Winner Is IBM," *Business Week*, October 3, 1983, p. 78.

of IBM-compatible computers by companies such as Eagle, Corona, and Compaq. These firms and others were able to produce PC clones because IBM had published the computer's technical specifications, showing how the machine was built and how it operated. This decision — an unusual one for IBM — had been consciously taken in 1981 so that other manufacturers could write applications software and make additional products for the PC. IBM management considered this a vital component in a strategy to quickly establish a strong presence in microcomputers.

Whether a long-term future existed for IBM-compatible computers was not certain. Some analysts felt that once IBM was able to make up the production shortfall of 1982 and 1983, problems would exist for the PC clones. Others, however, saw a good future for these firms, predicting that United States retail sales of IBM-compatible computers would hit $7 billion (equal to estimated IBM PC sales) in 1988.[2]

In view of the apparent opportunities in microcomputers in December 1983, Dysys management was able — at Matt Silver's suggestion — to secure the Atlantic Provinces dealership for the Chameleon microcomputer line manufactured by the Seequa Computer Corporation of Annapolis, Maryland. Seequa was a privately owned corporation that had been in existence since 1979. Growth had recently forced the company to move to larger premises and expand its work force. An IBM or Apple dealership would have been preferred, but both companies were already well represented in the Halifax/Dartmouth area. Given this situation, Dysys considered the Chameleon to be the next-best choice, for Seequa claimed real benefits for its computer. Its advertising noted that

> *The Chameleon by Seequa does everything an IBM PC does, for about $2,000 less than an IBM.*
>
> *The Chameleon lets you run popular IBM software like Lotus 1-2-3 and Wordstar. It has a full 83-key keyboard just like an IBM, disk drives like an IBM, and a bright 80 × 25 character screen just like an IBM.*
>
> *But it's not just the Chameleon's similarities to the IBM that should interest you. Its advantages should, too.*
>
> *The Chameleon also has an 8-bit microprocessor that lets you run any of the thousands of CPM-80 programs available. It comes complete with two of the best programs around, Perfect Writer and Perfect Calc. It's portable, and you can plug it in and start computing the moment you unwrap it.*
>
> *So if you've been interested in an IBM personal computer, now you know where you can get one for $2,650. Wherever they sell Chameleons.*

An independent review in a leading computer magazine found the Chameleon Plus to be reliable (running most IBM software) and to offer more features and a lower price than its IBM equivalent. Some drawbacks noted included: faults with casing and latch, the unavailability of certain software supposed to be included in the basic price of the machine, and the 28-pound weight of the computer. On this latter point, however, the Chameleon fared no worse than other "portables."

---

[2] "IBM's Personal Computer Spawns an Industry," *Business Week*, August 15, 1983, p. 88.

Dysys saw three market segments which offered potential for the Chameleon product line: (1) business, (2) students, and (3) personal usage. They operated on a mark-up of about 25 percent and offered a service contract to adopters in return for a fee of $300 each year. Dysys also handled repairs — either in-house or through return to the manufacturer. Seequa extended Dysys 15 days' credit.

In addition to the Chameleon computers, a line of computer peripherals was also carried so that Dysys could offer customers a complete range from which to buy.

Custom Hardware and Software Business

Several pieces of custom hardware and software had been developed by Dysys. One recent development was the Bar Code Reader — others are highlighted in Exhibit 3.

The Bar Code Reader. It was believed that many applications existed for this piece of applied technology, although Dysys had only filled one contract to date. This was at the Dalhousie University athletic complex, where two bar code readers were part of an entrance and security system. Users of the facility slid their ID card through the slot on top of the reader. If the bar code shown on the ID card was "cleared" by the main-frame university computer (to which the reader was connected), a green light shone and the turnstile would permit entry.

Other bar code reader system applications were envisaged in manufacturing, where the ID card would be replaced by a work ticket, material control card, or voucher. Such applications included: employee timekeeping, inventory and shipping control, and security. It was also planned to use the Bar Code Reader in PIN.

The other hardware developments Dysys was involved with could be customized but had general application and so were believed to have wide sales potential.

EXHIBIT 3
Dysys's custom hardware and software projects

Among the projects Dysys has completed are:

Hardware

1. Bar Code Reader.
2. Emergency Intercom Controller — a contract with the Victoria General Hospital in Halifax. This device, designed by Peter Gregson, included a computer board which was set in an intercom. By activating one switch, such as a buzzer in a bathroom, a number of stations could be contacted simultaneously, including a base station (nurses) and the appropriate emergency unit.
3. Eye Movement System — two units sold, one each to McMaster University Medical School (Hamilton) and Dalhousie University Medical School. Developed by Peter prior to founding of Dysys, the system was used for studying the motion of eyes in humans and animals.

Software

1. Membership systems for Maritime Commercial Travellers Association and Halifax Board of Trade.
2. Accounting system for Halifax Board of Trade.

The Brick. This was a fully functional, single-board computer that had been developed for in-house use at Dysys. It had been in Peter Gregson's mind for a couple of years, and he had used a three-week break between projects at the end of the summer in 1983 to push it along. The key element of the Brick was the board's design which permitted a great deal of flexibility in use. All parts of the Brick would be bought-in, assembly involving the soldering of off-the-shelf chips to the Dysys-designed boards. It was anticipated that a Brick could be assembled in about 45 minutes. The Brick was to be an integral part of the PIN, but other applications were envisaged.

This cleverly designed computer would sell for between $300 and $600, depending on the precise features demanded by the customer. Some $200 had recently been spent to produce photos and a specification sheet for promotion purposes. Copies of each had been sent to a number of publications requesting that the Brick be described in their new product sections. These included such magazines as *Byte* (computers) and *Industrial Engineering*. It was hoped that a good level of interest would result from this initiative.

The Production Information Network. PIN was the brainchild of Peter Gregson, and he had begun to work on this project back in his Micronet days. A PIN prototype had been installed by Crossley Karastan — a carpet manufacturer located in Truro, Nova Scotia. Details of this installation had generated a lot of excitement at a production show in Toronto in 1981, but Micronet never followed up on the enquiries made.

Peter and Chris talked about factory productivity as follows:

In these days of increasing labour costs and reduced selling prices, manufacturers must make their profits from increased automation and plant optimization. Tools that assist them to do this are necessary. Only the largest corporations are able to finance complete automation, and as a result there are an enormous number of firms that are still labour intensive or at least require significant amounts of labour to run the production line.

The needs of the smaller firm have only recently started to attract the attention of system suppliers. A 1983 report in Fortune *magazine described the market as "new and relatively naive . . . a little mystery and a lot of promises go a long way." At Dysys we have a tool for the smaller producer concerned about productivity.*

Dysys had in mind a system that would allow manufacturers to exert control over the production line as well as to collect information on production. Production control might include: (1) tracking, controlling, and providing alarms on small changes in process parameters such as temperatures and pressures, thereby reducing waste of materials, and (2) tracking work in process to anticipate bottlenecks and raw materials shortages. Production information collected might be: (1) machine down-time data including reasons, so as to improve plant productivity, and (2) data on line for materials resource planning systems. It was estimated that a manufacturer could recover 3 to 5 percent of gross sales if these and other tasks were performed.

EXHIBIT 4
The production information network

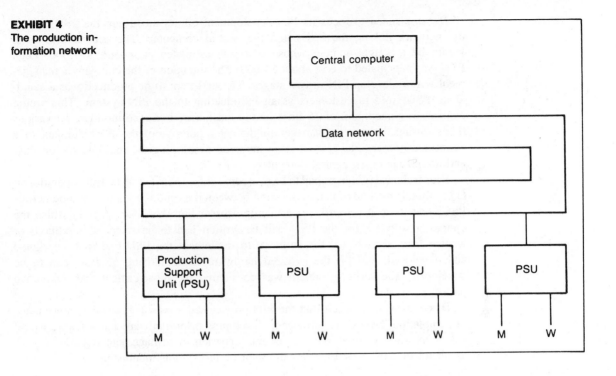

This would be achieved as shown in Exhibit 4. The three main components of the system were the *production support units* (PSU), connected through a *data network* to a *central computer*. The PSUs would be installed on key machines and at other workstations, providing some control capability, and have an operator interface to assist the worker at the station. Summary data and alarm conditions would be passed to the central computer for further processing.

Peter and Chris continued:

> *When completed the PIN will be a general purpose, flexible, low-cost means to obtain detailed and up-to-date information on every major aspect of a factory's operation. It allows management to improve quality, productivity, and profitability by keeping them informed about the factory now instead of a week from now.*

Development of PIN and the Brick

Although Dysys management anticipated that the PIN and Brick would contribute significantly to future revenue, both projects had slipped behind schedule in recent months. Chris Zinck headed up the research and development on PIN, but with the need for business to sustain Dysys operations, he found himself working on a variety of projects. As a result, PIN deadlines had been hard to meet. This was not a significant problem at this stage as no other company offered a similar production information system.

Dysys planned to focus its PIN development efforts mostly on the PSU and on the network linking the PSUs and the central computer. The central computers would be a bought-in item whose cost was estimated at around $75,000. Each PSU was anticipated to cost about $3,000. The intention of the company's management was to develop PIN in two stages. The first item to be produced was a stand-alone PSU, sold to customers as an introduction to the PIN system. This would connect to a maximum of 16 lines on the machinery it was to monitor. At various times during the day, a manager might get reports from the PSU dumped to a connected printer. The second stage involved developing the multiple-station PSU and its linkage to the central computer.

Four technical problems had to be overcome before PIN would be fully operational: (1) a suitable method of communicating between the central computer and numerous PSUs had to be developed; (2) a microprocessor high-level language in which the operating software for the PSU will be written had to be selected, modified, or written from scratch; (3) the software to implement the PSU had to be designed and developed; and (4) the required hardware to implement the PSU had to be developed. The second problem was considered the most critical and innovative part of the system.

Dysys management felt that the PIN project had a reasonably successful chance of completion. Dysys's experience in developing prior hardware and software would aid them with the PIN. Because of this experience, management regarded Dysys as ahead of most companies in the area of production monitoring at the present time.

Some 40 companies in the metropolitan Halifax area were thought to be potential customers. At some stage Dysys would have to line up one company for test purposes. Crossley Karastan was the obvious candidate — having had four years of useful life from the previous prototype, but Peter's main contact there was no longer with the firm.

If the Dysys development worked out, the market for the system could be very large. The management of Dysys occasionally speculated how the PIN would be marketed. For the most part, however, their attention was focused on solving the technical problems the system faced and in keeping the firm's "head above water." In part, work on the PIN was financed by a $30,000 grant from the National Research Council under its Industrial Research Assistance Program. A second payment in the same amount was expected in September 1984. By the spring of 1984 Dysys was about six months behind the schedule they had in mind for the PIN. As one component of the PIN, the Brick was also experiencing some slippage in development.

THE DYSYS MANAGEMENT

Peter Gregson was regarded by other member of the Dysys organization as something of a visionary. He was quite eager to take on any technically interesting job for one customer if it had the potential for later, broader sales. Although devoted to the development of the PIN, he was favourably disposed to considering other innovative product areas as long as these offered the possibility of long-run profitability.

Ted Mussett was generally considered to be strong in the areas of consulting with small- and medium-sized businesses on the applicability of microprocessors and associated software to office applications and in marketing the products for which Dysys held dealerships. Where Ted felt he could use more expertise, however, was in the custom end of the business, for he felt ill-equipped to prepare price quotations and to schedule work involving in-house development of hardware or software. This problem had shown itself when a Board of Trade contract took longer than expected and, consequently, ran over budget.

Because of this sort of difficulty, Chris Zinck was consulted prior to many projects being accepted. In fact, Chris ended up working in a number of areas which made it hard to push the PIN project ahead quickly. Chris partly covered for Peter Gregson's absence from the firm. He shared many of Peter's characteristics, being technically competent and liking involvement in new and interesting projects.

One idea the management team was toying with was the recruitment of a technical salesperson to compensate for Ted's lack of experience in bidding on and developing technical proposals. Such an appointment would also help Ted by freeing up some time for general administration. Dysys had no office personnel, so it was Ted who looked after payables, receivables, payroll, paper flow, and telephone reception. This meant that he spent a lot of time dealing with office concerns when he felt his skills were in the selling function.

THE FUTURE

Peter, Ted, and Chris were all a little concerned about the future of Dysys. The need to generate cash flows to ensure survival had pulled the firm in some directions that were not initially planned. Furthermore, due to project conflicts, some of the areas where the company believed it had a real edge had not been developed as quickly as they might. Although neither of the two co-owners had invested much money in the firm, both were anxious to see it succeed. Ted enjoyed being his own boss and was prepared to settle for a "reasonable" income to ensure the firm's survival and future prosperity. Peter continued to enjoy having his own company.

Working capital requirements had increased quite a bit recently with the adoption of the Chameleon line. Considerable inventory had to be carried, and Dysys acquired a bank loan of $10,000 for this purpose in January 1984. Management hoped to limit future bank financing to that needed to cover purchase orders on a short-term basis. However, they were beginning to recognize that more substantial funding might be necessary. Both of the owners were really against the idea of increased debt. Having been "burned" with Micronet, Peter was hesitant to become too financially exposed with Dysys. As well, the newness of Dysys and its lack of really tangible assets did not predispose bankers too favourably to the firm.

EXHIBIT 5
Project
assessments

	Assessment	
	Dysys	*Customer*
Remanco Restaurant Information System:		
A number of installations for a Halifax restaurant owner	Good	Good
Clipper II (Autobar — see below)	Fair	Good
Computer systems:		
The predecessor to Chameleon	Poor	Fair
Chameleon	Good	Good
Custom hardware and software:		
Shipboard Rules of Road Training Device	Good	Good
Two consulting projects carried out by Peter Gregson	Good(2)	Good(1)/Fair(1)
Maritime Commercial Travellers Association	Poor	Good
Autobar — development of automatic liquor dispenser to tie into Remanco system	Poor	Poor
Bar Code Reader	Poor	Poor
The Brick	Good	Good
Eye Movement system	Poor	Good
Production Support Unit	Good	Not completed
Board of Trade/Emergency Intercom Controller	Poor	Not completed

Projects Dysys had undertaken to date were assessed by Peter Gregson, Ted Mussett, Chris Zinck, Tom Cooper, and David Lane. Assessments were made of each project's financial return to Dysys as well as the project's success as perceived by the customer.

However, further capitalization appeared necessary if the dealer activities, development of the PIN and the Brick, and custom work were all to go ahead. More government money was one option. Although not to be overlooked, government funding had certain associated drawbacks. First, they required extensive record keeping and the generation of considerable paperwork — all expensive activities. Second, too much reliance on government could also lead to insularity from the rigorous competition of the marketplace. All things considered, the Dysys management team had to decide what to do — both in the near future as well as in the longer term. To aid them in their deliberations, the four full-timers and Peter Gregson had come up with an assessment of the various projects Dysys had been involved in since its formation in 1982 (see Exhibit 5).

APPENDIX A: REMANCO RESTAURANT INFORMATION SYSTEM — BENEFITS AND COMPETITION

A. *Service Benefits*:

1. Increase in server efficiency eliminating trips to bar and kitchen.
2. Reduces overhead by eliminating prenumbered guest checks
    No purchase cost.
    No distribution cost.
    No auditing cost.
    No storage cost.
3. Increase kitchen efficiency:
    Orders in sequence.
    Orders readable.
    No errors.
4. Out-of-stock items displayed immediately.

RESULT: Improved customer service, larger sections, higher table turns, reduced labour cost . . . higher profit.

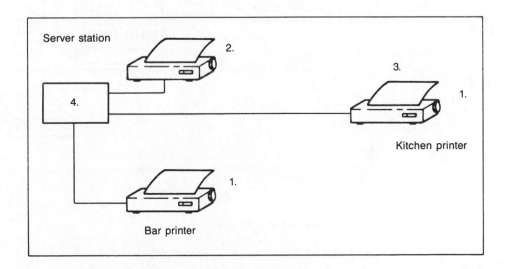

B. *Payment Benefits*:

1. All information regarding a guest check is available at any terminal.
2. All transaction data recorded.

3. Permits server payment with security through accountability.
4. Front desk posting in hotel.

RESULT: Quick and simple function requiring *no* cashier leading to:

Labour savings.

Greater control of cash.

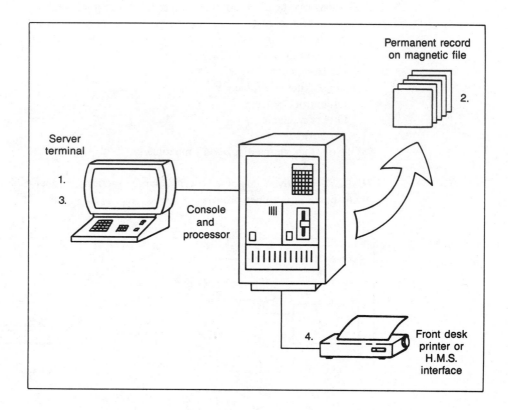

C. Management Benefits:

1. All voids and adjustments:
     Reported concisely.
     Accounted for by reason, guest check, and server/manager.
2. Organizes and reports by category, sales of each item:
     Per shift.
     Per day.
     Per week, per month, quarterly, yearly.

3. Automatically updates perpetual inventory daily. Receipts and other adjustments are easily accepted by system. Daily ordering needs printed.
4. Logs all employees' time (serving and kitchen staff) enabling daily labour cost reporting as percent of sales:
   Group.
   Category.
   Individually.

D. Dysys Competition — As Viewed by Dysys Management:

Data Terminal System: Comparable benefits to Remanco, limited market penetration due to restricted marketing efforts.

NCR: Similar benefits to Remanco; servicing not satisfactory in Halifax.

Sweda: Limited report generating and storage capabilities but popular with buyers not requiring advanced management benefits; expanding product offerings; good local reputation.

Micro Systems and Victor: Limited capabilities in current systems but potential to expand offerings; presently not a serious competitor to Remanco.

COMMUNITY NATIONAL BANK OF CRESCENT CITY

Mr. George Atlas, president of Community National Bank, is currently reviewing the short-term objectives of the bank in 1987 in order to assure himself that they are appropriate at this time. He is particularly concerned that the pursuit of these objectives continues to strengthen a position that was precarious, at best, when he took over control of the strategic elements in order to achieve the combination of financial growth and stability which he feels to be necessary goals of Community National Bank.

The Community National Bank of Crescent City is a locally owned and managed commercial bank. As such, it provides such services to its customers as demand deposit accounts, savings accounts, mortgage loans, commercial and consumer loans, and issuance of traveler's checks, MasterCard and BankAmericard. The bank was formed in 1969 with the primary stockholder being Mr. Roger Overstreet, the current chairman of the board of directors. Mr. Overstreet, a long-time area rancher and businessman, is currently serving as a county commissioner. The initial capitalization of the bank was $400,000 on 20,000 shares of common stock authorized and issued.

Crescent City is a Rocky Mountain town of some 180,000 people with an equal number of people living in a 30-mile radius of the core area. Light industry, tourism, and construction form the economic bases of the area. Crescent City has experienced tremendous growth in the past two decades. One of the nation's largest metropolitan areas is just 30 minutes from Crescent City, with several arterial highways providing easy access. Since 1978, Crescent City has enjoyed a significant surge in the area of high technology. The addition of two industrial parks in the west end of town in the early eighties has been able to accommodate a number of small firms which serve, primarily, as major suppliers to three large computer companies. Crescent City has long been recognized as a research and development center, and it is the site of a major university.

This case was originally prepared by Professor William D. Wilsted of the University of Colorado and Robert L. Taylor of the United States Air Force Academy. It was revised in 1987 by Professors P. John Lymberopoulos and William D. Wilsted, both of the University of Colorado. The case should be used as a basis for class discussion rather than to illustrate either effective or ineffective handling of an administrative situation. Reprinted by permission.

Ranked by size of deposits, Community National Bank is the seventh largest of twenty banks in the Crescent City area. In most areas Community National's services are comparable, and in some cases favorable, to those of the other banks in the city. Areas of competitive advantage are the banking hours (although two area banks provide 24-hour teller service) and charges for business accounts. Areas in which Community National is falling behind its competition are extended trust services (although a larger and more comprehensive trust department is planned in the future) and special packages (such as checking and 24-hour teller machines). The real competitive edge for Community National is its customer service. Since it is a small, locally owned, independent bank, its services are personalized with the needs of the customer given great importance. The quality of service can be identified as one of the prime reasons for past deposit growth. The deposit balances of customers are small in size, averaging $1,100, and are characteristic of suburban banks. The customers of competitors are basically the same, with the exception of the downtown core banks, which attract the large industrial and commercial accounts. Community National is located outside of the downtown core of Crescent City.

The major competition comes from the five largest banks in Crescent City. Ranked by size, they are First National Bank, Mountain National Bank, City National Bank, Consolidated Bank, and West Bank. Exhibit 1 shows that the top three banks together control 52.8 percent of the bank deposits while Community National currently holds 3.4 percent. The West Bank, with 3.7 percent of the market, is not only Community National's closest competitor in terms of deposits, but is also the closest competitor due to its geographic location. Competition is keen since there are twelve other established banks in the metropolitan area. Also, new banks are being formed, with the Home State Bank having opened in April 1981, and a new bank in the downtown area opening for business in the summer of 1988.

RECENT HISTORY OF THE BANK

The period of the late 1970s and early 1980s represented tremendous economic and population growth for Crescent City. The performance of the Community Bank in terms of deposit growth and income growth, however, lagged behind the local economy. This was due, primarily, to the conservative nature of the bank president and major stockholder, Mr. Overstreet, as well as the lack of experienced, professional bank management. The bank's customers have historically been small depositors and borrowers, with commercial accounts coming primarily from small businesses, ranchers, and farmers.

The Crescent City area gas tap moratorium (which restricted construction in the area) and the double-digit inflation and interest rates that characterized the national economy during 1972–1974 resulted in major problems for the Community National Bank. The bank was already suffering annual loan losses substantially in excess of net income, and the weak local and national economy resulted in increased loan losses and cash flow problems. In spite of the subsequent recovery, Community

EXHIBIT 1
Total deposits at six
selected banks

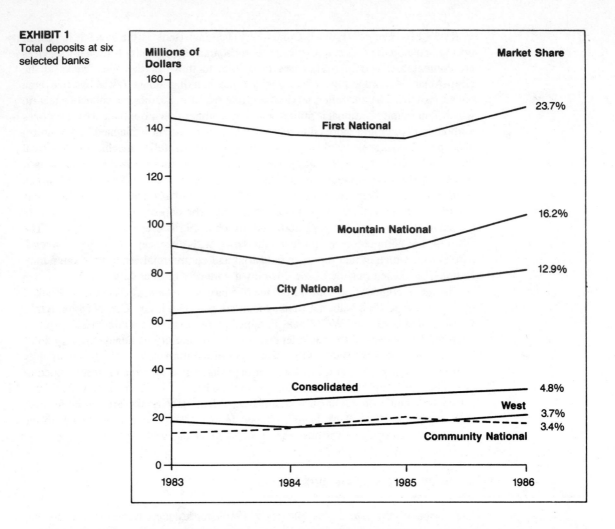

National continued to be plagued by these problems and considerable uncertainty. The problems were of such significance that the bank was being closely scrutinized by the bank examiners due to its delinquent loans and cash problems.

George Atlas took control of Community National Bank in 1984. This transaction resulted in an increase in the total capital of the bank of $350,000. The board members who joined Atlas in the acquisition are all real-estate–oriented businessmen who have been his long-term customers and support his business philosophy and his concept of the role of the bank and its operations.

Mr. Atlas was originally employed by the First National Bank where, as a mortgage loan officer, he built his department into one of the largest mortgage-loan–servicing organizations in the nation. In 1970, Atlas was elected president of First National, the largest financial institution in the city and the lead bank of the third largest bank holding company in the state. During this period of time, First National and the holding company continued to expand their emphasis on construction lending and mortgage lending with activities in all markets in the state.

First National was also strongly affected by the economic problems resulting from the local construction moratorium plus the inflation and interest rates. The loan losses and delinquencies that resulted caused the holding company to alter its emphasis and policies relative to real estate lending. Atlas became uncomfortable with the holding company structure and he also disagreed with the new policies regarding mortgage lending and the best method for dealing with delinquent loans, especially delinquent construction loans. He resigned from First National.

While Atlas desired to remain in banking, he preferred to be involved in a position that would avoid the holding company structure. He examined several of the small, local banks as possible investments. Negotiations with Mr. Overstreet concerning Community National Bank ensued. With the financial assistance of several members of the current board of directors of the bank (who made substantial investments in the common stock), Atlas acquired controlling interest.

CHANGES UNDER MR. ATLAS

Since gaining control of the bank, Mr. Atlas has initiated several strategic and managerial changes in the bank. His primary focus has been in the following areas:

1. A remodeling of the bank facilities to give them a fresh, new appearance.
2. Staff additions at managerial levels to improve operations and attract customers. (New officers include the head of commercial loans, the head of mortgage loans, and personnel administrator.)
3. Significant expansion of the drive-in facilities.
4. A marketing program — designed to bring the bank into the public eye — which emphasized the local, independent operation of the institution.
5. Implementation of a viable, functioning mortgage loan department to develop new business.
6. A renewed effort to resolve delinquent loans and limit loan losses through a combination of improved managerial controls and a movement away from questionable farm, ranch, and small commercial loans.

These changes have resulted in an improved bank image and in a solid growth in deposits as Mr. Atlas has succeeded in attracting several of his old customers to Community National Bank.

More specifically, Mr. Atlas's policies have resulted in a steady growth in profitability (see Exhibit 2) as well as a steady improvement in the bank's liquidity position (see Exhibit 3). While the bank's capitalization is still relatively thin when compared to the three larger banks in the area (see Exhibit 3), as Community matures and accumulates equity capital, its capital structure should fall more into line with that

EXHIBIT 2
Return on assets at
six selected banks

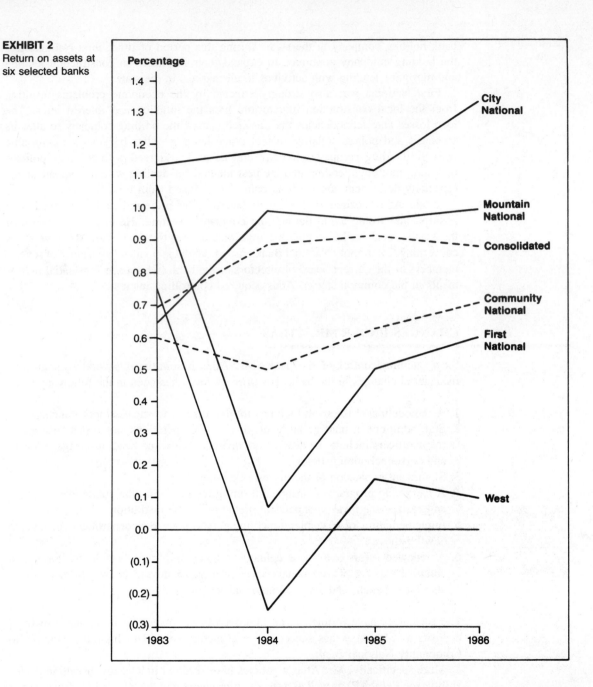

EXHIBIT 3
Capital ratios

	Community National — 5-year trend				
	1982	*1983*	*1984*	*1985*	*1986*
Average equity/average loans	5.5	7.4	8.3	10.2	10.1
Average equity/average deposits	4.0	4.7	5.7	6.5	6.5
Average equity/average risk assets	4.2	5.0	6.0	6.6	6.3
Average loans/average deposits	73.0	63.7	67.8	63.3	64.4

	Community National and 3 other banks			
	City National	*Mountain National*	*First National*	*Community National*
Average equity/average loans	15.6	15.0	14.6	10.1
Average equity/average deposits	8.9	8.0	9.0	6.5
Average loans/average deposits	57.0	53.3	61.6	64.4

of the other banks. The 3-year period after Mr. Atlas's takeover saw an 81 percent increase in net income. This was accomplished mostly by the great drop in loan losses relative to the size of the loan portfolio.

Also during this period, the mix of the loan portfolio was altered considerably. (See Exhibit 4.) The primary emphasis was placed on commercial loans, while

EXHIBIT 4
Loan mix

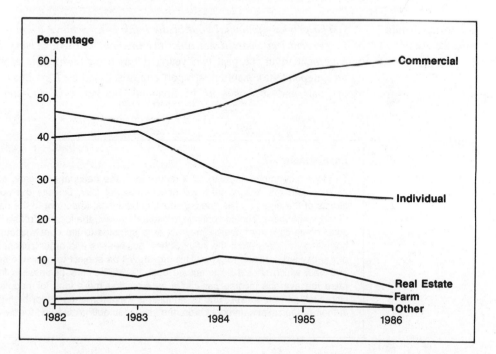

loans to individuals were reduced to the present 27.7 percent. This resulted in an increase in the percentage return on average loans from 9.6 to 11.3 percent. This rise in interest and fee income plus the drop in loan losses has turned what was a dangerously unprofitable loan portfolio when Mr. Atlas assumed control into a very lucrative investment.

In summary, Mr. Atlas's financial policies have resulted in an increase in profitability which has brightened the liquidity position of Community National considerably. This strong growth in size and profits is grounded on a stronger base of equity capital, a shift in emphasis toward commercial and real estate lending, and the implementation of controls to improve the yield on investments.

ORGANIZATIONAL MISSION

The overall mission of Community National Bank is to provide high-quality banking services to its customers at reasonable prices, to generate a satisfactory return on stockholder investment which will allow the bank to grow, to create a work environment for employees that challenges their energy and ingenuity and values them as individual contributors, and to be a responsible citizen within the community and aid in civic betterment.

Each of these guiding principles is supported by various long-range goals and a corresponding set of objectives in each of four areas — financial, market, product or service, and personnel.

Financial Goals and Strategy

1. *The primary financial goal of the bank is to achieve a long-term growth rate of 15 percent per year in net after tax income.* Growth is very important to top management; over the past two years, it has been high. This growth is supported by an independent consultant's report commissioned by Mr. Atlas. (See Exhibit 5.) Most goals and strategies in the financial, market, product, and personnel areas

EXHIBIT 5
Consultant's report

Environment

The local economy is not simply a reflection of the national economy, although general inflation and the energy crisis will affect Crescent City. Despite the possible negative effects of the energy crisis, the construction business, important to the bank as a source of mortgage loans, should continue to expand. In fact, the location of the Rocky Mountain solar research center nearby may act as a stimulus to the construction of solar-heated homes in the state. With the influx of new businesses and organizations, the population of the city will continue to grow. This growth will be subject to available supplies of water and gas, which should be adequate until 1990. The new businesses in town will also raise the average income per capita by providing more jobs for people already in the city, such as housewives, and by bringing in trained managers for high-paying positions in their organizations. In conclusion, the economic outlook is good for the next five years.

support the achievement of this growth rate. Other financial goals for the bank can be related back to this growth objective. In the past, the strategy of the bank has been to utilize retained earnings to finance growth. In the future, long-term debt will be used to increase capital and allow for continued expansion. The specific objectives for the coming year are:

Increase deposits to $25,000,000.00 and
Reach a return on total assets of 1.25 percent.

Daily earnings reports are used by managers to monitor the bank's progress in achieving its growth goals.

2. *Maintain a strong, well-balanced financial position to ensure the safety of shareholder and depositor funds.* Specific objectives are:

Loan-to-deposit ratio of 68 to 72 percent
Liquidity ratio of 20 percent

3. *Minimize losses from loan delinquency.* For 1988, the specific objectives are:

2.5 percent delinquency rate for the commercial loan department.
2 percent or lower delinquency rate for the installment loan department.

The bank's strategy for minimizing loan losses is to assign full responsibility to the individual loan officers for their loans. Detailed loan policy and procedures are prescribed, to be followed by the loan officers in making and approving loans. The bank encourages and requires careful follow-up on loans that have been made.

Market Goals and Strategy

The competitive edge of Community National lies in its independence from a holding company. The importance of this independence in attracting customers is primarily the image that it creates. Local control of the bank by owners and officers allows it to provide better service to residents of the area and to tailor its services more quickly to the changing local environment. Community National's market goals for next year are:

1. *Expand the mortgage loan market from the county to the state.* In order to accomplish this goal, the department must expand its ability to place conventional loans with other financial institutions, such as large insurance companies.

2. *Increase market penetration of banking services in the county.* Community National's strategy for growth in banking (nonmortgage) services is to confine activities to the Rocky Mountain area and the county, relying on community growth and on attracting customers from other financial institutions. Unlike many smaller banks, Community National's management would welcome branch banking in the state and does not fear competition from the larger holding companies. Competition will also become more intense as the distinctions between banks, savings and loans, credit unions, and other institutions are lessened and the services offered by each become more uniform. Employees are an important source of feedback to management on customers' response. Customer surveys have been used in the past to determine reaction to current services and to obtain suggestions for improvements and new services. A summary of the most recent survey is found in the Appendix.

3. *Maintain a favorable image within the community and develop contacts with potential customers.* The bank encourages involvement by all staff members in community, civic, and social activities. Much of the officers' time is spent developing and maintaining good customer relations. Personal service results in repeat business, attraction of customers to other bank services, and the establishment of additional contacts through satisfied customers.

Service Goals and Strategy

The ultimate service goal of Community National is to become a full service bank. Mr. Atlas wants to expand the MasterCard and BankAmericard departments. An expanded trust department will be required for the bank to increase its deposits above $30 million. Other services such as 24-hour automatic teller service will be added as they are required and as their implementation becomes possible. The bank is preparing to exploit the opportunity of electronic funds transfer and would welcome the ability to expand services and grow through branch banking.

To accommodate the growth of existing services and to make room for new ones, the bank will expand its physical size within the next year. A key part of market strategy is location, which is currently being investigated. Alternatives are to expand the existing building, to build on an adjacent site, and to move to a new location.

Quality of service is one of the few ways that banks can distinguish themselves from each other. The strategy to ensure provision of quality service is to provide training and the proper tools and equipment to employees for them to do their jobs. In some instances, job rotation has been used to broaden employees' knowledge and improve morale. The importance of high-quality, friendly service is frequently emphasized to all employees.

Personnel Goals and Strategy

A goal of the bank is to develop a staff with expertise and experience in the various banking activities to increase the value of its personnel. This will improve the quality of service offered and will allow management to promote from within, thereby increasing future opportunities for advancement by employees. The top management organization is portrayed in Exhibit 6. In the past, management talent has been brought in from other banks to strengthen departmental expertise. In the future, the bank plans to develop its own managers.

To develop an experienced, knowledgeable, promotable staff, the bank makes available many training programs and technical courses to its employees. Many of these are taught by industry, government, or educational institutions and some are taught by personnel within the bank itself. Job rotation is another method used for

EXHIBIT 6   Organization chart

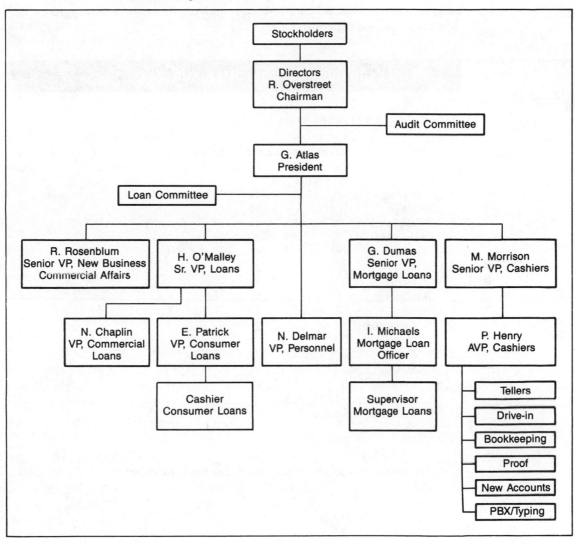

employees to learn new tasks and gain experience. Annual performance appraisals and merit pay reviews are used to keep employees informed of their progress and to reward them for performance.

APPENDIX: RESULTS OF CUSTOMER SURVEY

Total Return: 1,177 out of 4,000

1. Which of our services do you presently use?

Checking	1,154
Savings	592
Home loans	29
Auto loans	109
Boat loans	3
Trust	22
Personal	139
Safety box	236
Other	
Commercial	22
Motorcycle	2
Farm	3
Signature	2
Christmas Club	10
IRA	2
Certificate of Account	4
SBA loan	1

2. What new service would you like to see the bank offer?

Guaranteed check card	750
Overdraft banking privileges	382
24-hour automated teller machine	358
Trust department	79
Other	
Telecommunications transfer	14
Free checks, no balance	3
No service charge, $200 balance	2
Checking with interest	3

3. What services are important on Saturday mornings?

Check cashing and deposits	1,014
Making change	119
Opening new accounts	39
Purchase of traveler's/cashier's checks	207
Safe deposit box	169
Other	
Money orders	1
Savings withdrawal	1

4. What banking hours are most convenient for you?

8:30 A.M.–4:30 P.M.	367
9:00 A.M.–3:00 P.M.	40
9:00 A.M.–4:00 P.M.	38
9:00 A.M.–4:30 P.M.	218
Other	
9:00 A.M.–6:00 P.M.	80
7:30 A.M.–6:00 P.M.	105
24 hours a day	5
Sat. 8:30 A.M.–4:30 P.M.	9
Sat. 8:00 A.M.–12:00 noon	6

CASE 10

CELESTIAL SEASONINGS, INC.

STATEMENT OF PHILOSOPHY

Celestial Seasonings is a consumer packaged goods company committed to marketing internally manufactured, health-oriented, high-quality products to the consumer and sold via health food and mass market outlets. Our job is to serve consumers by filling voids in the marketplace with quality products that consumers want. Our mission is to solve major health problems according to our corporate definition. Our objective: a healthy, nourished, disease-free, exercised public.

Under the name Celestial Seasonings, the product line and style of magic is set for the future. We sell high-quality products with the most beautiful packaging possible. Each package is sprinkled with bits of wisdom and is designed to give consumers an added bonus . . . Lighthearted Philosophy.

For stockholders our objective is a minimum sales growth of 27 percent compounded annually with a minimum of 27 percent growth in earnings. Celestial offers shareholders the opportunity to reap financial reward while getting people healthy.

For our employees, our objective is to build a strong and stable company with dynamic opportunity for upward mobility through loyalty, pursuit of excellence, hard work, and quality. This company is dedicated to mutual reward systems based on the achievement of worthwhile and aggressive goals. We remain loyal to the continual search and practice of advanced management systems that build working bridges between exempt and nonexempt employees, believing that a united, fully utilized work force can accomplish far-reaching objectives with work satisfaction and mutual reward for all. Our philosophy encourages creative, productive, possibility thinking throughout the organization.

In summary, the foundation of Celestial Seasonings is based on serving health needs through good products and expressed in a beautiful form. Our profit will increase 100-fold by dedicating our total efforts to these ends, which in turn will make this world a better place for our children and our children's children.[1]

---

[1] Source: Corporate files.

Case prepared by Charles L. Hinkle, University of Colorado, and Esther F. Stineman, Yale University. © 1984 by Prentice-Hall, Inc. Reprinted by permission.

344

BOULDER, COLORADO, 1982

Boulder, Colorado, is a sleepy but fashionable town located north of Denver on the Front Range of the Rocky Mountains. During the early 1970s, hippies trudged through its streets lugging worn backpacks and sleeping bags, many of them living from hand to mouth supporting themselves by panhandling or selling "dope" to university students around The Hill area of town. Today, Boulder presents a more affluent face to visitors. The hippies have either left town or have cashed in their patched jeans for snappier, more socially acceptable though casual attire — Chemise La Coste shirts and L. L. Bean chinos, for example. Many have joined the ranks of the young professionals and zip around the town in foreign-made cars, said to be better than domestic models for mountain driving.

Jogging and bicycling are popular Boulder pastimes. Former marathon Olympic star Frank Shorter is now a local businessman selling chic running shorts and shoes in his own shop on the Mall, which marks the center of town. Most of the youthful, health-conscious people in town are glad not to have a ragtag population marring their peaceful local scenes of outdoor cafés and trendy businesses done up in natural cedar or red brick façades. Casualness seems to be a fetish.

CELESTIAL SEASONINGS BACKGROUND

In this idyllic setting Mr. Mo Siegel, president and co-founder of Celestial Seasonings, Inc., reigns over his herb tea kingdom, an empire that includes among its all-natural products such innovative no-caffeine offerings as Red Zinger, Mandarin Orange Spice, and Cinnamon Rose herb teas, graphically tricked out in flamboyant fantasy packaging (see Exhibit 1). Celestial competes in its own small market, the $75-million-a-year herb tea share of all tea sales, with other counterculturally costumed competitors — Select, San Francisco Herbs, Lipton, and the rest. The purchaser of Siegel's tantalizingly titled teas buys not only a beverage to sustain body but messages from such unlikely and diverse sources as Abraham Lincoln and Sophia Loren to sustain the soul. "Please write, we like to respond. We are interested in your suggestions, ideas, queries, quotations, and short essays for use on the packages," invites a box-top bit of prose. Mo Siegel, himself an inveterate collector of quotations, includes pithy morsels of wit and wisdom in business correspondence. Under the cable and Telex information on a recent Siegel letter, the reader is treated to some Goethe: "Whatever liberates our spirit without giving us self-control is disastrous."

Mr. Siegel sits at mission control site between a portrait of Lincoln on one wall and the Iced Delight bear on the other. He has little reason to meditate on disasters these days with his closely held Celestial Seasonings now dominating the domestic herbal tea market with annual earnings of more than $1 million. Sales to foreign markets have leapt to 6 percent of Celestial's total current annual sales. Still a dwarf in the overall $825 million black tea market, Celestial at $23 million a year

EXHIBIT 1
Description of se-
lected products

CELESTIAL SEASONINGS

AMERICA'S #1 SELLING HERB TEA

SLEEPYTIME®: Our No. 1 Selling Herb Tea — The perfect before bedtime drink. A great non-caffeinated tea with chamomile, spearmint leaves and lemon grass with seven other herbs. Helps you relax and wind down from a hectic day. Designed to round off the day's rough edges. Its sweet flowered flavor can be enjoyed by young and old.

MANDARIN ORANGE SPICE: One of our most popular teas. The delicious flavor of imported natural mandarin oranges makes this tea drinkable any time of day. We captured a tangy citrus flavor with just the right spice bouquet by combining orange peels, hibiscus flowers, rosehips, blackberry leaves and a touch of sweet cloves, a flavor you will also enjoy iced.

CINNAMON ROSE™: A bright, refreshing tea that combines the sweet explosion of cinnamon with the naturally round flavors of rosehips, orange peels, blackberry leaves and sweet cloves. A uniquely flavored herbal blend that is excellent both hot or cold.

COUNTRY APPLE™: The luscious apple flavor unfolds with every sip. The aroma of Country Apple Herb Tea will take you back to breezy afternoons in a country orchard. Truly an apple adventure, combining rosehips and hibiscus flowers for a bit of tartness, chamomile and chicory for smoothness and body, plus cinnamon and nutmeg for just the right touch of spice.

ALMOND SUNSET™: Our newest tea, a romantic blend of herbs with the soothing natural flavor of almonds. A delicate blend of rich roasted carob, barley and chicory root; spiced with cinnamon, sunny orange peel and a hint of anise seed. A taste for almond lovers of all ages.

RED ZINGER®: A Celestial tradition, imitated often but never equalled. The deep ruby red color, the tangy citrus flavor, the powerful bolt of flavor. All these combine to make Red Zinger a unique herbal soft drink enjoyed by young and old alike. Red Zinger is an indescribale brew that can only be appreciated by tasting it.

Soothing teas for a nervous world.®

in sales has stunned the big tea marketers by making steady inroads into major supermarket chains, gourmet and health stores, and into foreign markets during the late 1970s and early 1980s.

Tea giants such as Thomas J. Lipton, until as recently as 1980, tended to discount Celestial's entrepreneurs as amateurs playing flower-child games in a tough marketplace. Now Lipton and others look at Celestial, a company that has experienced a high growth rate, as a feisty wunderkind to emulate and contend with. Lipton in 1982 began marketing herb teas packaged in rainbow colors at prices close to Celestial's — about 5½ cents a bag, although Lipton packaged its herbals in packs of 16, while Celestial preferred the 24-teabag format.

The compelling Mr. Siegel was the subject of wide-ranging publicity.[2] He popped up regularly on television programs such as "Merv Griffin" and "Donahue," and business magazines took turns publishing a colorful sketch of the president who was given to quotable remarks as he ruminated aloud. "We have an obligation to make the shelves astonishing! to keep magic alive," he said when asked about Celestial Seasonings' devotion to creative packaging. "We must continue to create beautiful, outstanding-quality packaging with truthful writings." Later he told the casewriters upon entering the elegant Celestial board room, "We want Louvre quality in our artwork," and "If Walt Disney could do it better, we aren't interested" (Exhibit 2).

Some of the press that Siegel received suggested that the success realized for Celestial "just sort of happened." In fact, Mo Siegel is a very ambitious person, addicted to reading management books, Drucker one of his favorites. "I like big rather than small," he admitted to us with a gleam in his eye. Then he explained how he recruited outside of Celestial to professionalize management, hiring a regional manager from Lipton and a plant manager from General Mills. Along the way he recruited a vice president of PepsiCo for his marketing team and brought in a chief engineer from Pepperidge Farm. Celestial's head tea brand manager was recruited from Quaker Oats, another from Vaseline Intensive Care, and still another from Samsonite. Clearly, Siegel sought marketing expertise for the company from proven training camps. He followed marketing stories of large companies as if they were detective novels: "Tylenol is bright," and "Johnson & Johnson is as good as P and G." And his strategy was pragmatic: "We don't have the time or the money to test in the same way as Quaker."

His objectives for the company were specific and hardhitting. In 1981, which was "the first year for our real-live-moving-growing marketing department," Siegel decided that any product line not reaching $10 million in sales in five years should be discontinued. Other objectives included the achievement of a 30 percent increase

---

[2] See Eric Morgenthaler, "From Hippies to $16 Million a Year, *The Wall Street Journal*, May 6, 1981; "What's Brewing at Celestial," *Money*, January 1981; Margaret Thoren, "It Wasn't the Bankers' Cup of Tea. . .," *The Christian Science Monitor*, April 21, 1981; and Barth David Schwartz, "How to Make a Million Doing Your Own Thing," *Fortune*, June 4, 1979, among others.

EXHIBIT 2
Celestial Seasonings graphics

An ancient tea for the tensions of a modern world.

"For 2,000 years my ancestors have sipped ginseng tea when they wanted to relax.

"So I have followed carefully their wise advice, combing the steppes of Siberia and the vast reaches of China to find the rarest and best ginseng. And from it, I've made one of the most relaxing herb teas in the world: Emperor's Choice.

"Of course, an emperor's taste requires a delicious tea, too.

"So I combined the best cinnamon, licorice root, rosehips and other herbs and spices. And created a flavor to please the most discerning royal palate.

"And I made my tea without caffeine. Or anything artificial.

"Try Emperor's Choice. You'll see why my ancestors said: 'A few sips of this delicious tea everyday can help chase the woes of the world away.'"

—The Emperor

Available in your favorite health or natural food store.

CELESTIAL SEASONINGS HERB TEAS

NO CAFFEINE
WITH GINSENG

24 TEA BAGS

EMPEROR'S CHOICE™

Naturally caffeine free.
For your good health.

of tea sales in standard units; a broadening of grocery volume from 35 percent to 55 percent on at least four items; and the expansion of tea section placements from 15 percent to 30 percent on Sleepytime, Mandarin Orange Spice, Cinnamon Rose, Country Apple, Iced Delight, Red Zinger, Almond Sunset, Emperor's Choice, Peppermint, and the variety-pack four flavors.

Siegel believed that Celestial should continue expanding trial tastings among nonusers and increase the frequency of consumption among users from one to two cups each day. Since Colorado was Celestial's most active market area, Siegel's 1981 goals stated that the company needed "to determine upside volume potential outside of Colorado." Finally, and perhaps most important since Siegel claimed he was not interested in being a "food company" but was interested in preventive health care, Celestial targeted an improvement in its position in health food stores through a carefully orchestrated shelf management program in 1981 and 1982.

Siegel is not particularly modest about what he thinks are Celestial's most successful characteristics. At the top of the list he counts the distinctive and unique aspects of Celestial, including quality, packaging, products, names, and writings. In the "tricky herb industry," because of the adverse publicity about herbs and regulatory difficulties, he believes that he has accomplished no small feat in achieving the "highest quality standards in the herb industry." Because health products, not food, is the area in which he is interested, Siegel believes Celestial's success to be inextricably tied to its provision of a "real alternative to other caffeinated hot beverages." That the company has embraced a "wide variety of flavors and product concepts" he believes is all to the good. The lead products in Celestial have a strong consumer positioning and best of all — from Mo Siegel's perspective of the health-focused "corporateur" as he terms himself — Celestial's products remain all natural and health oriented. Exhibit 3 summarizes Celestial's strengths, weaknesses, and strategies for the 1980s as seen by top management.

Not that everything is coming up rosehips, however. Celestial has experienced its share of problems. A brief and abortive romance with a product called Salad Snacks failed to meet quality control standards. Juice products, despite great corporate hopes, could not make a go of it.

Observed Siegel:

The caution is that we deal with limited resources, both people and finances, and we cannot effectively execute against multiple priorities especially when the objectives are not compatible with our central corporate mission. The key is maximum sales effectiveness. An example of the dilution of resources was the introduction of BreakAway during the major drive for Iced Delight — no one's fault — and penetrating a new channel of distribution — placing Salad Snacks in produce departments — without adequate development of our basic business. Launching VITA during the key prewinter sales drive on Herb Tea would have been a similar mistake.

Mo Siegel hardly underestimates the importance of marketing. One of his trump suits has been a strategy of strong and consistent marketing to the health foods market segment. As markets drift away from hot caffeinated products, there Celestial

EXHIBIT 3
Strengths, weaknesses, and strategies of Celestial Seasonings

Strengths

Growth via health consciousness
Strong consumer loyalty
Financial stability and excellent gross margins
Distinctive packaging
Readily acceptable flavor varieties
Significantly higher brand awareness than the competition
Professional management
Vertical integration: from raw product to finished teabag

Weaknesses

Extensive product line
Premium product line
No line pricing
24-teabag count
Compressed timetables

Strategies for the 1980s. Continue to take the leadership position in

Unique packaging
Inventing blended herb teas
Offering the largest selection of blended teas
Offering special packs
Ability to sample
Offering the best quality herb teas
Marketing solution teas, for example, Sleepytime

will be. The sweet dream of high coffee prices has always kept spirits high at the tea factory, and the strong growth of health food stores has been a trend that fueled the Celestial team's marketing enthusiasm. With increasing professionalization of the team, however, no one is naïve enough to think that people can rest on their tea leaves and achieve continuing growth. Rather, the annual building of new distribution channels is seen as a perennial strategic topic as are plans to develop a wider product mix (Exhibit 4). Always Celestial is striving to improve its professional approach to sales and marketing.

MARKETERS AND MARKETING AT CELESTIAL

Keith Brenner, a pleasant, self-assured Canadian — some might say slightly arrogant — became vice president of marketing at Celestial in 1980. Before that, marketing at Celestial had been strictly an in-house, family affair. Brenner, who owned his own beverage manufacturing company in Canada, met Mo Siegel at a food show. He worked with Celestial first as a consultant, assisting the company in its attempt to enter the natural beverage market, an effort that flopped. Although Brenner

EXHIBIT 4 Advertising for a new (1982) product

Delicious to the core.

Before you decide on your favorite Celestial Seasonings Herb Tea, try this one.

Country Apple Herb Tea is a delicious blend of apples, rosehips and cinnamon enhanced by hibiscus flowers and chamomile, with absolutely no caffeine.

The flavor of Country Apple unfolds with each sip, as the aroma of orchards takes you back to breezy afternoons in the country and all your fondest memories.

Try our new Country Apple Herb Tea. Then pick your Celestial favorite.

hoped to work in general management, he was asked by Siegel to head the marketing function of the organization. He has not put aside his preference to get into general management where he could be involved in finance and production as well as marketing.

Besides his stint as a beverage manufacturer Brenner acquired an impressive set of credentials from his work with Pepsi Cola in Canada and with General Foods. Like Siegel, he attained success early. At 32 he was a vice president and general manager for Pepsi Cola, globetrotting for a three-year period to Pepsi operations in South Africa and the Philippines as well as serving in Canada. He cited as his major reason for joining Siegel and Celestial "the opportunity to impact a healthy growing concern instead of attempting to climb the ladder in a vast corporation."

Both Brenner and Siegel believe in the Celestial mystique: "Our goal is to manufacture only healthful, nutritional products — nothing artificial." At Brenner's urging, Celestial planned to abandon its sole caffeine product, Morning Thunder: "Since Celestial Seasonings' customers are a segment based upon their penchant for natural food products, a clean bill of health with customers will be strengthened by severing ties with caffeine."

As for his marketing efforts, Brenner terms Celestial "an alternative kind of company which has achieved success without hammering people with incessant advertising. We tell a simple story in a colorful way, only the truth, not embellished with a lot of hoopla."

Brenner professes a belief that "Celestial's success was a major reason why Lipton decided to enter the herb tea market. Instead of thinking that such competition works to Celestial's detriment, we credit the Lipton move to raising overall public awareness of products such as ours. In fact, the Lipton competition creates a bigger market for everyone." Brenner is sanguine about growth possibilities for Celestial even though teas was a low-growth category, according to the marketing vice president, 1 percent annual growth, the same as the population growth rate:

Any extra we get has to come out of somebody else's business, but there is a trend by large stores to stock more nutritional foods . . . health foods and the like . . . which is good for us. This will help us reach our target of 25 percent annual growth, compounded, but only through 1985, I believe, with our present product line. This means that to continue meeting our objective we must develop new ideas — beyond herbal teas.

Brenner's overall strategy for growth in 1982 was succinct:

First, we widen our grocery distribution base with tea section placement. This has been difficult, but it gets easier as we get stronger. Second, we go after consumer awareness and trial through the use of Sunday supplement coupons, trial packages, and displays. Last, we move more strongly into the iced tea market, which is three times larger than that for hot tea.

Regarding trips into the marketplace, Brenner has confessed, "I do get into the field occasionally, but not enough." Like Siegel, he is emphatic that one distribution channel cannot be sacrificed to another. "We had 100 percent distribution in the health food outlets, so we moved into the supermarkets. But we are not neglecting our health food outlets."

LIFE AT THE TEA FACTORY

The music of James Taylor wafted through the tea factory on a typical day in 1982 as Italian-made machinery moved the teas 24 hours a day on a computerized schedule. This new equipment made it possible to pack the major Celestial blends into horizontal boxes, found by market testing to lure the purchaser more effectively than vertical packages. Employees in production appeared to be blissfully engaged in their tasks. The cafeteria awaited them at some point in their shift, with a meal of natural foods — soup, salad, granola cookies, and a selection from the company's herb tea line. Mo Siegel, who frequently dresses in shorts and a sports shirt for the office, and rides his bicycle to work, stresses quality of the workplace.

If it is possible to tell something about a person or an organization by surveying the reading material that is strewn about, perhaps the following survey of books and magazines in the Celestial Seasonings' employee waiting room offers some insights: Pierre Teilhard de Chardin's *Man's Place in Nature*; M. Scott Myer's *Every Employee a Manager: More Meaningful Work Through Job Enrichment*; works by Drucker and Toffler; and copies of the periodicals *New Health*, *New Age*, *Prevention*, *Runner*, *New West*, *Runner's World*, and *Processed Prepared Foods*.

In one section of the main plant, Marelynn W. Zipser, Ph.D., a food technologist and the mother of Mandarin Orange Spice, Cinnamon Rose, Iced Delight, and BreakAway, presides over herbs and test tubes in a pristine but cheery testing laboratory. As manager of new product development, Zipser reports directly to Brenner. "I take the concept and turn it into reality," she explained. Among her research and development tasks, Dr. Zipser conducts taste panels — mainly among women's groups and employees — to test the latest reactions to Celestial's expanding product lines. Quality and taste of the tea are as important to Celestial as other major points of difference with their competition: packaging style and graphics, the number of teabags per box, premium pricing, and channels of distribution. Thus, Celestial taste tests against Select, Alvita, Golden Harvest, Health Valley, Traditionals, San Francisco Herbs, Worthington, Horizon, and other regional and local brands in the health food market as well as Bigelow, Lipton, and Magic Mountain in the grocery market.

Systematic product development grew out of Mo Siegel's demands for specific types of products that he and Brenner instructed Zipser and her group to conjure up in the laboratory. "Conservative planning plus optimistic action plus intelligent work equals success" is a favorite Siegel maxim, which seems eminently practicable in the laboratory part of the tea factory.

HISTORY OF CELESTIAL

In the beginning were the herbs. Siegel, his wife Peggy, and sidekick Wyck Hay pioneered the operation by gathering Colorado mountain herbs with other friends "for fun" and selling them to local health food stores. These were the early days of health food awareness of the late 1960s and early 1970s, and Siegel and Hay's philosophy then was to provide a pleasant living for themselves and a congenial group of Boulder comrades by selling a product that was good for people. "One of the things we found in Europe is that people who live to 100 drink a lot of herb tea and eat herbs continually," Siegel states.

The company's appellation, derived from the fanciful nickname of a female friend who participated in the early days of Celestial's movement into what some have termed "cosmic capitalism," suggests the tone and tempo of those early times. Celestial began as a relatively tranquil cottage business in which Siegel, Peggy, and friends patiently stuffed the heady concoctions of orange peel, wild cherry bark, rosehips, hibiscus flowers, lemon grass, and peppermint into hand-sewn, hand-stamped muslin bags with solicitous instructions to buyers as to the particulars of brewing and steeping, along with a reminder to them that a bit of honey would enhance flavor. This early, successful blend, entitled Red Zinger, propelled Celestial out of the cottage and into a corporate setting. In 1982 Celestial required six buildings to house its manufacturing, warehousing of herbs and spices from 35 countries, and other functions.

From the outset, Celestial espoused causes and amplified these from its boxes — reminding customers about a foundation needing support to protect vanishing species of flowers, sometimes warning about world hunger, and promoting save the whales or other conservational causes. Celestial saw itself as having an instructive, positivistic mission, perhaps as important as its more pedestrian, grocery-focused one. "Happiness is the only thing we can give without having" and other messages of its kind became inherent aspects of Celestial's packaging concepts. But such aphorisms were more to Celestial than a way of selling tea. Siegel's enterprise was a mission (see Appendix for a brief biography).

With lots of help from his friends, Siegel organized a corporate structure based on communitarian concerns and centered on quality-of-life issues: concern with providing employees enough time for family and leisure, flexitime, pleasant working conditions, and many more. As the alternative to business that they were, the merry band was not quite able to do away with a hierarchical structure, and they developed a seven-person board of directors, most of them major stockholders, to hold down the fort. Living was easy then with only a few blends in their tea portfolio, and only 50 or so stockholders in the entire corporation.

MOVING INTO THE 1980s

Red Zinger was ultimately joined by some 40 other herbals, including a new tea in 1982, Almond Sunset: "a wonderfully romantic blend of herbs with the soothing natural flavor of almonds. A delicate blend of lovely things like rich roasted carob, barley and chickory root; spiced with cinnamon, sunny orange peel and a hint of anise seed. . . . Almond Sunset will remind you of holiday cookies baking in the oven of a farmhouse kitchen." Introduction of new products was carefully considered; Celestial's marketing and advertising budget was expected to be $5 million in 1982.

Seeking to market Celestial more aggressively, Siegel recognized the "be big or bust" paradigm that has ruled decision making at the larger beverage companies and the expansion imperative that was its corollary. New products, including body care preparations and vitamins, loom large in Siegel's mind as he looks toward

EXHIBIT 5
Annual changes in
dollar sales, fiscal
1973–1982

Fiscal year	Dollar sales	
	Amount	Increase
1973	$ 70	—
1974	293	+320%
1975	1,316	+350
1976	2,930	+125
1977	5,636	+ 92
1978	8,887	+ 58
1979	10,524	+ 18
1980	11,557	+ 10
1981	16,662	+ 44
1982	23,327	+ 40

Note: Net sales in thousands of dollars.
Source: Celestial Seasonings records.

product expansion and toward a goal of 27 percent compounded annual growth (Exhibit 5) with anticipated sales of $50 million by the mid-1980s.

As time went on Celestial people gave less attention to the fun-and-games enterprises of more carefree years, for instance, the world-famous Red Zinger bicycle races, a promotional activity the company sponsored from 1975 to 1980 because "Mo Siegel is into bikes." The races underscored a long-time Siegel belief that if more people rode bikes as their only transportation, the world would be a better place. "Celestial Seasonings is dedicated to improving the quality of life on this planet, having a major concern in environmental life," he wrote in literature promoting the Red Zinger Bicycle Classic. In 1980, however, it became an issue of bicycle races or teas for Celestial, just as it became an issue of hiring executives with sophisticated managerial expertise versus possible corporate extinction. Case in point: in the summer of 1980 the company came close to being swallowed by General Mills due to one disgruntled, major stockholder's wish to rid himself of $1 million worth of Celestial's stock. Siegel saved the day by borrowing money to purchase the stock himself.

In hiring heavyweight marketing types like Keith Brenner to draft a new marketing strategy, the main component being to move the herbal teas out of the less trafficked, specialty sections of grocery stores into the mainline beverage sections, Mo Siegel underscored his ambition to be big rather than small. Siegel and Brenner shared a perception that "the 35- to 50-year-old market remains to be captured if Celestial is to be truly successful." See Exhibit 6 for estimated herbal tea market shares from 1978 to 1980.

There were significant changes in Celestial's corporate culture once new management began to join the firm. Several members of the original cadre left the company presumably because of the new style of life at the tea factory. Although Siegel continued promoting quality of work life, his corporateurial mind was on priority

EXHIBIT 6
Market share (in $), estimated U.S. herbal tea market

	1978	1979	1980
Celestial Seasonings	38%	33%	30%
Magic Mountain	5	12	11
Lipton	—	—	8
Bigelow	—	4	8
G.N.C.	4	4	4
Other	53	47	39

Source: Company records.

markets for Celestial and criteria for selecting such markets. He reread his Drucker and listened to his cassette tape course on strategic planning. And he repeated to himself a six-word formula: "Concentrate on preventive health care foods." If such foods were curative in nature, so much the better.

A LOOK TO THE FUTURE

To keep the team spirit alive, Mo Siegel retreats frequently with his top staff members to discuss possible new directions for Celestial Seasonings. "We must operate in a basically unfriendly environment as retailers become more self-assured as to their position in relation to manufacturers." In the periodic strategic planning sessions in scenic and secluded Colorado resort areas, top managers at Celestial concentrate in 2½-hour segments on such tough-to-analyze questions as, What business are we in? What business should we be in? What is our company philosophy? Is our philosophy changing and if so in what ways? Who are our customers and how are

EXHIBIT 7
Organizational structure

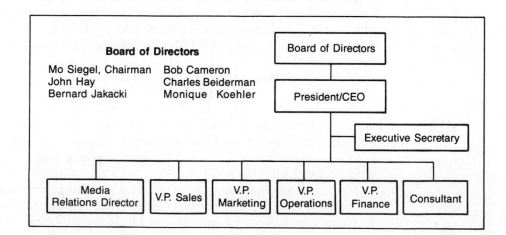

Board of Directors

Mo Siegel, Chairman   Bob Cameron
John Hay   Charles Beiderman
Bernard Jakacki   Monique Koehler

Board of Directors

President/CEO

Executive Secretary

Media Relations Director | V.P. Sales | V.P. Marketing | V.P. Operations | V.P. Finance | Consultant segments changing? What are Celestial's strengths and weaknesses? What threats and opportunities face us over the next several years? Is caffeine compatible with Celestial? What are our criteria for business development ?

Underlying the retreats' agendas was Siegel's own ambition for the company: "To be a billion dollars in sales at the turn of the century."

Exhibit 7 depicts Celestial Seasonings' organizational structure; Exhibit 8, from Celestial's press kit, summarizes some of Mo's reflections for successful living.

EXHIBIT 8
Mo's ideas for suc-
cessful living

On Successful Living

Ideas: The best ideas are the ones that fill a need. If people want to make money, start with an idea that fills a need for someone else. Do something useful!

Goals: I'm a believer in goal-setting. If you know what you want, it's pretty hard to lose.

Failures: I've had plenty. You've got to learn to accept them. You're going to fail sometimes. Don't be afraid of it.

Hard work: Be persistent. Work hard, but use your intelligence.

Hiring: Never hire anyone else unless they're smarter than you are in the area in which they're going to be working for you.

Marketing: What does the public think of it? Is it good for other people?

Believing: You could do something you don't believe in, but it really takes the fun out of it. I've had some hard times along the way, and if I didn't believe in the product, I would have sold the company a long time ago.

Health: People are tired of paying doctors, and they want to stay healthy. I see people around the country getting more interested in prevention.

Incentives: If we want the labor force to work well, why not let them own part of it?

Labor: Create a condition in which the work force feels better about their lives. What is good for labor should be good for management and vice versa.

Faith: There is only one place to have faith and that is in God. The disappointments that are hardest to bear are those that never come. Faith in an active life is a positive attitude.

Mo's Steps to Successful Living

1. Do something worthwhile for someone else.
2. Have faith, maintain a positive attitude.
3. Learn the art of setting goals, what you want.
4. It isn't enough to work hard, you must work SMART!
5. Do not be afraid to fail.
6. Don't take yourself too seriously.
7. Stay healthy.
8. Believe in and be dedicated to quality.
9. Do not be afraid to take a risk.
10. Family love and support maintain stability and help you keep priorities in perspective.

Source: Company's 1982 press kit.

APPENDIX: MR. SIEGEL'S RÉSUMÉ AND MISSION

CELESTIAL SEASONINGS ®

Cable: CELESEAS BLDR
TWX: 910-940-3448

1780 55th Street
Boulder, Colorado 80301 U.S.A.
(303) 449-3779

MO SIEGEL
630 Spruce Street
Boulder, Colorado 80302
(303) 447-9599

Business Address: 1780 - 55th Street
                 Boulder, Colorado 80301
                 (303) 449-3779

EDUCATIONAL HISTORY

1967
and on-going   Attended parochial schools; attended numerous
                      college courses; completed numerous professional
                      CEO and executive seminars and courses.

On-going   Independent Study - I am a devoted and perpetual
                      student of the health sciences, business management,
                      religion, philosophy, and government. I am
                      currently engaged in authoring a series of programs
                      for political reform in the United States which
                      began with the publication of the essay "Fire in
                      the American People".

1979   Travel Study - I sponsored a three-week, 5,000
                      mile study-tour of health and nutrition through
                      the Soviet Union with special focus on "The Garden
                      of the Centenarians" in the Trans-Caucasian
                      Republic of Azerbaijan and Georgia, home of the
                      "long dwellers."

1980   Travel Study - I completed a three week interior
                      study tour of China, involving the study of food
                      production and Chinese herbal science.

                      Other travels include North America, Central
                      America, South America, Europe, Middle East,
                      and Asia.

EMPLOYMENT HISTORY

1968 to
1970   Owner, health food store; first mate, commercial
                      fishing vessel, Key West, Fla.; harmonica playing
                      sandwich board advertiser; carrot juicer salesman.

1970 to present	Founder, President and Chairman of the Board, Celestial Seasonings Herb Tea Company, Boulder Colorado.

My responsibilities at Celestial Seasonings include planning, organizing and directing the over-all growth and development of the company; providing executive management to the divisions of Operations, Marketing, Sales, Human Resources, and Finance.

My principal goals have been to ensure the achievement of all corporate objectives and the fulfillment of all responsibilities to employees, shareholders, and customers by directing all executive decisions affecting the current and long-range operations of the company.

PERSPECTIVE ON CELESTIAL SEASONINGS

In 1971 Celestial Seasonings sold a grand total of 10,000 hand-sewn tea bags, containing hand-picked Rocky Mountain herbs, to a small group of health food stores.

Celestial now imports herbs from 35 countries for use in blends which are milled at the Boulder plant at a rate of over 4 million pounds per year . . .

In 1982 Celestial will manufacture and serve 700 million tea bags and the fiscal year sales will exceed twenty-five million dollars . . .

Celestial Seasonings Herb Teas are available in more than 35,000 retail outlets throughout the world including 60% of all U.S. supermarkets and foreign distribution in Canada, Australia, New Zealand, and Great Britain.

PROFESSIONAL ACCOMPLISHMENTS

Founder of America's finest International Class stage bicycle race; formerly the Red Zinger Bicycle Classic, now the Coors Classic.

Podium Speaker at the Democratic National Convention 1980; served on the Rules Committee of the Democratic National Party, 1980.

Keynote Speaker for numerous professional, religious, and civic organizational activities.

Guest appearances on ABC-TV's "Success, It Can Be Yours,
PM Magazine, Donahue, Donahue on Today, HBO's "Money Matters",
Merv Griffin, Mike Douglas, Dinah Shore, Sandy Freeman, USam,
700 Club, Cable Health Network.

Featured in People Magazine, Sports Illustrated, Wall Street
Journal, Fortune Magazine, Money Magazine, BusinessWeek
Magazine, New York Times, Los Angeles Times, San Francisco
Chronicle, Boston Globe, Chicago Sun-Times, Christian
Science Monitor, Washington Post, Denver Post, Rocky Mountain
News, Seattle Times, Minneapolis Tribune, In-Flight Magazines,
US Magazine, San Jose Mercury News, Seattle Post Intelligencer.

CHARACTER SKETCHES

Abiding concern...The health and fitness of the American
people. Political reform.

Personal Heroes...Jesus, Abraham Lincoln, Walt Disney, Thomas J.
Watson (founder of IBM), Dr. Kenneth Cooper (founder of the
Aerobics Institute), Eddie Merckx (six-time Tour de France
champion).

Quote..."I want Celestial Seasonings to enter the 21st
century as one of America's leading corporations."

Favorite tea bag homily..."Angels can fly because they
take themselves lightly."

Quote..."Where we go in the hereafter, depends on what
we go after here."

Dream...of the day when the typical American employee
enjoys the dignity and the equity he has earned and
deserves.

Hoped for epitaph..."Mo Siegel was a good father."

Explanation of insatiable appetite for social and
business advance...Because I don't believe that when
St. Peter asks me, "Mo, what have you done with your
life?", that it will be sufficient to reply, "Well,
I cornered the herb tea market."

Quote..."I want to help change the course of American
business, I want to help make all forms of Art more
available to the American People, and I want to get
the word out on health and fitness."

C & C YACHTS LIMITED

"I'm effectively taking over the position of marketing vice-president for the next three months so that Moray Edwards can devote himself totally to studying our situation in Europe. I want to see a plan to resolve our problems there." George Cuthbertson, president of C & C Yachts, was concerned about the company's budgeted loss of over $10,000 per month for 1976 on its European operations, an estimate that he personally felt was about half the real cost of being in Europe as it did not include management time. In Cuthbertson's words, the status quo was "no longer acceptable — the company has to either make a larger commitment in Europe or abandon the market altogether. We cannot remain as we are at present."

THE COMPANY

C & C Yachts Limited, although only 6 years old in September 1975, was the largest yacht builder in Canada and one of the half-dozen largest fibreglass sailboat manufacturers in the world. Although still small ($13 million sales), the firm's success was very visible; the yachting and popular press was always ready to report major race results, and C & C's early history was studded with race-winning boats. The firm's most important victory was that of *Red Jacket* in 1967. This boat was designed by Cuthbertson and Cassian Limited of Port Credit, and was built by Bruckmann Manufacturing of Oakville, two of the four firms that joined in 1969 to form C & C Yachts Limited. *Maclean's Magazine* commented:

Each year, the first race to grab the attention of the industry, and of the fans with the sort of scratch actually to buy one of these craft, is the Southern Ocean Racing Conference. This is where all the previous months' drawing-board sweating over prismatic coefficients, wetted surfaces, ratios of sail plans, and overlap either pays off or flops in a horrible way. The SORC is the ultimate tropical test tank for designers, sailors, owners, riggers, and sailmakers. For the pros.

Case prepared by J. Peter Killing. Case material of the Western School of Business Administration is prepared as a basis for classroom discussion. Copyright © 1976 by The University of Western Ontario, revised 1980. Reprinted by permission.

You cannot win the SORC without beating anywhere from sixty to ninety of the costliest, best-designed, best-sailed offshore-racing yachts in North America. And that is exactly what Red Jacket *did. She's the only boat from outside the United States ever to win the SORC.*

Looking back on this period from the vantage point of 1975, Cuthbertson explained the importance of the firm's racing successes.

In this business, small size is no barrier to recognition. There are simply too many magazines and journals concerned with the sailing industry, and they're all looking for fine photographs and dramatic stories about winning races. If you win something that's major, you can be a household name in the North American yachting community on about one month's notice. That happened to us. We were doing some pretty good designs in the mid sixties and we got them to some pretty good builders and some pretty good sailors and we started knocking off the top events on the continent. Instant household name.

In 1969, Cuthbertson and Cassian Limited merged with three of these "pretty-good builders" to form C & C Yachts Ltd. The smallest of the three firms was Bruckmann Manufacturing Limited of Oakville, Ontario, a builder of custom yachts, among them *Red Jacket* and *Manitou.* The latter, built in 1968 (another well-known Cuthbertson and Cassian design), won the Canada's cup in 1969. This firm had 20 employees and annual sales of about $500,000 at the time of the merger. The second merger partner, Belleville Marine Yards, built three Cuthbertson and Cassian designs ranging in length from 31 to 40 feet at the time of the merger. This firm's 55 employees built 57 yachts in 1968–1969, 45 of which were sold in the United States through the company's dealer network. The other merging firm, Hinterhoeller Ltd. of Niagara-on-the-Lake, was approximately the same size as Belleville Marine, with annual sales over $1 million and 57 employees. This firm produced two Cuthbertson and Cassian designs, as well as three by George Hinterhoeller, the company's owner. In 1968–1969, approximately 60 percent of the firm's output of 190 yachts was sold in the U.S. market. It was believed that C & C Yachts Ltd. would be the only firm in North America capable of designing and producing both "production" boats, built to a standard design and price, and "custom" boats, built on a standard hull (generally larger than those of the production boats), but with interior, deck layout, and sailplan to customers' specifications. Production boats would be built on assembly lines at Niagara and Belleville, custom boats on a one-off basis at Bruckmann's plant in Oakville.

The creation of C & C Yachts did not have a major effect on the operations of its four subsidiaries. Cuthbertson still presided over the design office in Port Credit, Bruckmann produced very expensive custom boats to C & C designs in Oakville, and Hinterhoeller and Belleville continued to produce higher-volume, lower-priced yachts. The new president of C & C Yachts, Ian Morch, formerly head of Belleville Marine, tried to centralize control of the company, but with little success. Twice he brought proposals to more closely coordinate the activities of the firms to the board of directors (presided over by Cuthbertson), and twice he was defeated. Finally, he gained some success, but still over the opposition of Cuthbertson, who strongly believed that the subsidiaries should be autonomously operating units. The decision was made at this time to expand the Niagara plant so that it would be the major production-boat manufacturing facility, and to not expand Belleville further.

In 1971, the board of directors (primarily "inside" directors) faced its first major crisis. Belleville Marine had been losing money ever since the formation of C & C Yachts and Morch had not been able to turn it around. In late 1971, the Belleville operations were shut down and Morch was fired. The Belleville assets were sold back to him, although they were no longer used for boat building. Morch subsequently sold the majority of his shares in C & C to Credit Foncier, and this firm placed a man on C & C's board.

The company was now without a president and none of the three remaining principals was eager for the job. George Hinterhoeller accepted the position on an interim basis, pending recruitment of an acceptable candidate.

The board could not find a new president acceptable to a majority of its members. Hinterhoeller was, at heart, a boat builder, not an executive, and within less than a year he wanted to leave the presidency and go back to his division. He was much happier on the shop floor and wanted to get back in touch with building boats. In Cuthbertson's view, the company was "frankly in trouble" and in need of strong leadership. Cuthbertson finally decided that he was the only one with a "snowball's chance of turning the company around." He decided to take over the presidency on the condition that Hinterhoeller would allow Bob Forsey to run the production-boat division.

Bob Forsey, an R.I.A., had started with Hinterhoeller Ltd. in 1969 as the cost accountant charged with introducing costing programs and production-planning methods. After a little arm twisting by Cuthbertson, Hinterhoeller returned to Niagara as a manager in charge of special projects, primarily refinements in the boat-building process. Cuthbertson explained the rationale behind the change:

> The Niagara plant had to grow out of being a hobby shop, a cottage industry, into a properly managed business. It wasn't going to achieve that transition, it wouldn't grow, and I certainly was not interested in assuming the presidency of a stagnating, declining company.

Cuthbertson's growth goals soon became evident. In May 1974, he presented a major plan to the board of directors outlining a proposal for the growth and development of the company over the following 3 years. This plan called for an increase in sales to $35 million by 1976–1977 (from a 1973 level of $9 million) through the construction of plants in the southern United States and in Europe. The plan called for an investment of $4.6 million over the 3-year period, financed largely by earnings, mortgages on the new plants, and a $1.5 million increase in bank credit for working capital. The board rejected Cuthbertson's proposal. In spite of this, the document accurately predicted the company's strategic moves — in 1975, a manufacturing plant was opened in the United States, and in early 1976, a decision

EXHIBIT 1 Financial summary

	1970	1971	1972	1973	1974	1975
Income statement						
Sales	3,894	5,175	6,951	9,071	11,753	12,966
Gross profit	771	1,058	1,521	1,775	2,472	2,591
Selling and administrative						
expenses	618	757	792	849	1,131	1,769
Interest	N/A	N/A	N/A	N/A	126	160
Earnings before tax	152	300	729	927	1,162	661
Earnings after tax	69	192	412	533	657	378
Dividends	—	—	—	76	95	114
Balance sheet						
Total assets	4,678	5,280	5,983	7,174	8,294	10,218
Goodwill	2,493	2,493	2,493	2,493	2,493	2,493
Working capital	676	797	959	803	1,203	1,270
Long-term debt	18	351	338	236	133	1,548
Equity	3,903	4,095	4,507	4,964	5,526	5,790
Performance measures						
Gross profit/sales	20%	20%	22%	20%	21%	20%
Net earnings/sales	2%	4%	6%	6%	6%	3%
Net earnings/equity	2%	5%	9%	11%	12%	7%
Earnings per share	7¢	20¢	43¢	56¢	69¢	40¢

Note: Figures in thousands of dollars.
N/A = not available.

had to be made on whether or not a manufacturing facility should be established in Europe.

Under Cuthbertson's direction, the firm maintained its early growth rate until the 1975 fiscal year, when after-tax earnings declined from $656,000 to $378,000. Summarized data are presented in Exhibit 1 and major shareholdings are identified in Exhibit 2. Cuthbertson commented on the 1975 earnings' decline:

1975 was a recession year in the United States and Canada, and we had to spend more on marketing to keep our sales up. As you can see, our selling and administrative expenses increased from 10 percent of sales in 1974 to 13 percent in 1975. This was quite intentional.

The other reason selling and administrative expenses increased is that we are slightly overstaffed at the top. Deliberately and knowingly, I've built up overhead higher than it really should be and it shows in the expenses. Our history has always been to underanticipate, understaff, and underplan. The Niagara plant is a prime example. We realize now that when it was built, it was grossly inadequate. It has been through expansion upon expansion upon expansion. It is less than an ideally efficient plant because nobody could see that it would ever approach 50,000 square feet, let alone its present 96,000. We thought too small.

The earnings drop is only a technical disappointment because we have used the recession year to increase our market share and to build the Rhode Island plant.

EXHIBIT 2
Major shareholders'
percentage of stock
held, 1976

G. H. Cuthbertson[a]	10.6%
E. K. L. Bruckmann[a]	15.8
M. C. Edwards[a]	0.1
G. Cassian[b]	6.3
G. Brinsmead[b]	6.8
I. Morch[c]	5.3
R. Sale[d]	1.1
Caisse de Depot, P. Q.[e]	5.3
Trucina Investments[e]	9.5
Credit Foncier	10.0
Other minority shareholders (820 plus)	29.2
	100.0

[a] Officer and director.
[b] Employee.
[c] Former officer.
[d] Director.
[e] Implicit shareholders, estimated holdings.

THE EVOLVING ORGANIZATION

In an interview in late 1975, Cuthbertson spoke of the organizational changes made since he had assumed the presidency:

The first year I was in this job, I took satisfaction from the fact that I hadn't lost anybody. The second year, I took satisfaction from the fact that the half-dozen or so major changes I had made seemed to be working out. Even looking back from 1975, I don't see one change that gives me any regrets. I include myself taking over as president, when I say that. I've also kept the place operating in the black. Not personally, of course, but my job has to be making sure that the place is staffed appropriately and then let people do their own thing. If it's not being done right, then I have a problem which I have to work on. There have been some very major changes, such as Hinterhoeller allowing Forsey to take over the production division. More recently, Forsey has moved up to vice-president of manufacturing, which gives him authority over all our manufacturing operations and that includes the new plant in Rhode Island, plus most particularly the custom division where today we are in much the same position as we used to be in Niagara.

Exhibit 3 presents the organization chart as of early 1976. The position of vice-president of finance was a new one, created for Michael Carter who was hired in the summer of 1975. Cuthbertson indicated that he was very pleased with Carter's performance and the decision to create a new vice-presidency:

He is doing a terrific job. I myself didn't understand the amount of upgrading it is possible to achieve. Everything comes down to a financial question, sooner or later.

EXHIBIT 3 Corporate organization

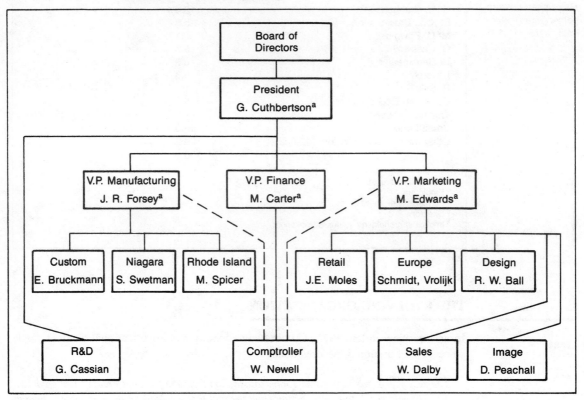

[a] Member of the Executive Committee.

For instance, a decision to build a few boats for stock will involve Forsey, who will consult Edwards on color. However, if the decision is to build twenty boats for stock, Carter will be consulted as well. That's finance.

Other recent changes reflected in Exhibit 3 were to have Wes Dalby, the sales manager for production boats, report to Edwards rather than to Forsey, and to split Cassian off from the design division to report directly to Cuthbertson on a number of research and development projects. Accountants in each of the divisions reported to Wayne Newell through their own vice-presidents, and Newell in turn reported to Carter. Cuthbertson explained the rationale for the six divisions reporting to Edwards and Forsey:

We now have six division managers reporting to two vice-presidents, Edwards and Forsey. Design, Ontario retail, and Europe report to Edwards; the manufacturing plants to Forsey. We operate divisionally because our divisions are very dissimilar. For example, the production division and custom division both have the job of building boats, but they are very different by virtue of one's being assembly-line production, the other, a series of one-

offs. They're two different kinds of businesses. The retail division is simply a retail store, selling Lasers, Boston Whalers, and new and used yachts, with a host of different problems from a boat-building concern. Finally, we have an architect's office (design) that has nothing in common in a business sense with either a boat builder or a retail store.

Another organizational innovation for the firm was the creation of the executive committee, consisting of Cuthbertson, Carter, Edwards, and Forsey. Cuthbertson explained its rationale and method of operation:

This committee formalizes consultations which took place anyway, but simply makes the process more convenient. Each of us knows we will be meeting every second Tuesday. The agenda is circulated in advance. I would say that the most important decisions in the company are made in that committee. For instance, Moray Edwards will bring his recommendations on Europe to us for consideration and a decision on what to present to the board.

DIVISIONS

The following sections describe the major activities of each of the company's divisions.

Production Boats

In 1976, the production-boat line consisted of six models ranging in length from 24 feet to 38 feet and in price from $9,500 to $46,900. All of the boats were of fixed-keel design, built from fiberglass, and had sleeping accommodations for 4 to 8 people, depending on the size of the boat. The newest model, C & C 24, was a major departure for C & C in terms of its simplicity and very low price (under $10,000).

The Niagara plant was one of the largest establishments of its type in the world. The backbone of the company, it could produce 580 boats per year with a value of over $10 million. The six boat models were built on a series of production lines, each with a number of stations at which standard operations were performed. While not nearly so automated as an automobile plant, there were economies to be gained by producing one model per line, although production could be shifted where necessary for altering the mix of output. The work force of two hundred had been unionized in 1974. Wages paid at the Niagara plant were the highest in the North American boat-building industry.

The major concern of division management was to institute more formal, accurate, and consistent measures and controls. The division saw itself as producing a high-quality product in which the critical production variables were the integrity of the building process, material selection, time spent in production, and quality checks. Formal systems to monitor such variables were not in place, however, and the division had to rely, to some extent, on the craftsmanship of its workers. In recent years, the division's rudimentary accounting, cost and inventory control, and production-scheduling procedures were increasingly inadequate. Forsey hoped to make improvements in these areas, moving the division more positively from the craft to the assembly-line stage of development. Steve Swetman, general manager of the Niagara plant, commented on the level of sophistication in his plant:

Maybe by line balancing and flow diagrams we could produce more throughput on our four lines. Maybe with industrial engineering we could determine how best to use and combine our resources, labor and materials; how best to estimate production overs and production costs. This is an area of weakness in the company. The traditional steps set by historical practice and applied by the foremen and supervisors may bear little relevance to an activity that has moved from the craft to the assembly-line stage of development. The reality is that current methods have been developed by people who wanted to build a good boat and the strength of the organization has been in people knowing their product, what it should look like when it is finished, and knowing how well it should be built.

A chance conversation in early 1976 revealed that at least one model produced at Niagara required 10 percent fewer labor hours to build than a competitor's equivalent product.

Getting the maximum output from its production-boat facilities was important, not only to division management, but also to the company as a whole. In spite of almost continuous plant expansion in the early 1970s, the firm could not keep up with demand for its production boats. During the 1972–1974 period, the division was constantly in a sold-out position, with backlogs of 3 to 6 months common. In the summer of 1973, the company's own retail outlet in Oakville stood empty. There were no boats to show prospective customers and the available production was rationed to dealers. A variety of reasons were offered for the product line's success, including the racing reputation of C & C's boats, its expanded dealer system, the growing concern with pollution and ecology, and the high quality of the C & C product. Cuthbertson commented on the role of C & C's racing successes in selling boats:

We believe the vast majority (say 85 percent) of our production-boat customers are not serious racing people. They race, if at all, casually on Wednesday night at the local yacht club. Very few aspire to entering the southern ocean-racing circuit or the world championships. They love to read about it and they're influenced by it; but if they race at all, they only do it with the family aboard and a bottle of beer in their hands. But that's okay. If they're sailing a boat designed by us and one of our boats won the southern circuit last year, in their minds they could do it too. They like to be associated with success, even though their C & C production boat may be very different from the boat in the southern series.

Moray Edwards, vice-president of marketing, added further information on the C & C production-boat customer:

Although not many of our customers are full-time racers, they certainly aren't novice sailors either. Our production boats are very expensive, priced at the very top of each size range and we very seldom attract the first-time buyer. Usually, a sailor will begin *with a less expensive boat and once he becomes hooked on sailing and can recognize quality in a sailboat, will trade up to one of ours. We can charge the highest prices because of the extremely high quality of our boats. Of course, once he begins to buy C & C, we hope to trade him up to bigger boats. With our new "24" priced at under $10,000, we hope to shift our position somewhat and pick up the first-time buyer.*

Edwards indicated that he felt the dealer network had played a key role in the growth of the production division. When C & C Yachts was formed in 1969, the subsidiary companies had fifteen U.S. dealers and sold in Canada directly from their plants. In 1970, the U.S. network was increased to twenty-three, and five Canadian dealers were established, along with a company-owned retail outlet in Oakville. In 1971, nine more U.S. dealers wre added, largely in the Southeast and West Coast areas, in the hope that the longer sailing season in these areas would offset C & C's very seasonal sales pattern. The number of dealers did not increase greatly after 1972, averaging about forty in total, although a gradual upgrading did take place. Dealers received a margin between 15 and 20 percent of retail price, and purchased boats F.O.B. Niagara. Most of the company's sales were made in the United States, although the proportion had decreased from 75 percent in 1971 to just over 50 percent in 1975.

The company knew little in a quantitative sense about its competition or customers. Edwards commented:

Certainly we know our own sales breakdown, but other than some very general data on total market size, we really have no idea of the market or potential market for any given boat in any given area. This includes the new 24-foot boat. Even the general data from Statistics Canada is so out of date by the time it's issued that it's virtually useless. Our lack of knowledge in this area is becoming increasingly bothersome to us.

Statistics Canada data suggested that the Canadian sailboat market in 1972 was $17.5 million, having grown from a very small base in 1961 at an annual rate of 39 percent per year. Cabin boats were stated to make up 80 percent (by value) of the market. Many industry personnel were highly skeptical of these data, but they agreed that the market had grown quickly, particularly in the late 1960s and early 1970s. Data on the U.S. market were equally soft, but suggested that the market there tripled in size between 1966 and 1972. If Statistics Canada data were accurate, C & C's market share in Canada in 1972 was 37 percent. This figure seemed too low to most observers.

C & C would not obtain much information on its major competitors in the United States, as they were either private or divisions of larger firms. Bangor Punta owned Ranger Yachts and Jensen Marine. Whittaker Corporation owned Columbia Yachts. Grumman Allied Industries owned Pearson Yachts. It was believed that many of these firms were approximately the same size as C & C. None were significantly larger.

In 1975, the Niagara production-boat operation earned $1 million before tax on sales of $8.6 million. In spite of Niagara's profitability, several factors led C & C executives to conclude that further growth in plant capacity should be in the United States. Manufacturing costs were likely to be cheaper in that country, as Canadian wage rates were very high, and the Canadian dollar, at $1.04 U.S., was widely predicted to be on its way to $1.10 U.S. In addition, the Niagara plant could not be expanded because of the physical size of its site, and there was not enough labor available for a second shift. Any boat built by C & C in the United States would have to be sold there, as the duty on U.S. boats entering Canada was 17½ percent or 25 percent depending on length. The duty on Canadian boats entering the U.S. market was only 2 percent or 5 percent, and this discrepancy had U.S. boat builders upset. A Washington lobby had been formed to urge legislation to raise the U.S. duty or to put pressure on the Canadians to lower their duty. This was another reason C & C felt it would be prudent to have a plant in the United States.

In 1975, C & C decided to build a production-boat facility in Rhode Island. The Rhode Island location was chosen largely because the state was willing to supply financing for land, plant, equipment, and start-up costs; a total of $1.7 million at 9 percent interest, which was 4–5 percent lower than funds available elsewhere. It was expected that C & C would need to provide working capital of $200,000 in the first year, which would rise to $400,000 by the end of the second year. Bond repayments to Rhode Island would begin in 1976–1977 at an annual rate of approximately $100,000 per year. The first boat produced in the new plant (in early 1976) was the C & C 24. The Rhode Island plant was budgeted to break even in 6 months and to earn an $80,000 profit by the end of its first full year of operation.

Custom Boats

All of C & C's custom boats were produced in the Oakville plant, under the direction of Eric Bruckmann. Typically, custom boats were more than 40 feet long, with interiors and deck layouts designed to customers' specifications. The custom boats produced by C & C had amassed an impressive list of racing victories over the years. Recently, however, the C & C custom boats had fared less well in major events, losing the Canada's Cup challenge in the summer of 1975, faring poorly in the Admiral's Cup, and not doing well in any class of the 1976 Southern Ocean Racing Conference. In many cases, these failures could be ascribed to poor sailing or a lack of organization ability on the part of the boat owner rather than the design or quality of the boat. Free publicity did not, however, disappear. In 1976, Air Canada's *En Route* magazine carried an article featuring C & C Yachts, in particular the company's custom-built 61- and 66-foot yachts sailed on the French and Italian Rivieras by such prominent Europeans as Herbert von Karajon, conductor of the Berlin Philharmonic. These large boats, selling for up to $250,000, were built during 1972 and 1973, during what the company called the "big-boat" boom, which ended as the economy declined in 1974 and 1975.

The custom division consisted of 35 skilled and semiskilled workers, with an administrative staff of four. This work force in the Oakville plant was capable of working on 5 boats at the same time, giving an annual capacity of approximately

25 boats. Orders were scheduled as received. This demanded flexibility of the work force, as they might be working on a 42-footer one week and a 60-footer the next. The labor force was not unionized and each worker considered himself a craftsman by profession. The highest paid and highest skilled were the woodworkers who produced the superb teak interiors on C & C's custom boats. Over 60 percent of the labor force was comprised of immigrant workers who had boat-building experience in their native countries.

There seemed to be two types of custom-boat buyers. The largest group was believed to be the very serious racers, who bought C & C custom boats to campaign in the major races of North America. The second group was the very wealthy, who wanted the prestige of a C & C custom boat and were willing to pay for the extra workmanship in a custom boat. Sales were made directly to the customer with design and production coordination handled by a custom-boat sales manager. As with production boats, approximately 50 percent of sales were outside Canada. The major difficulty with custom-boat sales was that it tended to be a boom or bust business. There were not many customers for such boats and the personal decisions of a small number of individuals in a given year could have significant consequences.

The major problem for the custom division in 1975 was poor profitability. In 1974, the division earned $45,000 (before tax) on sales of $1.65 million. In 1975, the profit turned to a loss of $67,000 on sales of $1.4 million. Cost of goods sold rose from 79 percent of sales in 1974 to 87.5 percent in 1975. According to Cuthbertson, part of the problem was poor control:

> *When Bruckmann brought his business into this company in 1969, it was the most profitable of the four. Now he's losing money. You'll hear the argument that the custom division should be subsidized because it's so valuable for company image. While there is some truth in that, it's not a justification for existence.*
>
> *A couple of weeks ago, Eric quoted a customer on a quarter-million-dollar job. His quote worked out to $10 per pound. That's incredibly high. When I heard about it, I called him and said, "But Eric, the customer will never go for it! How can you quote so high?" Well, Eric believes he is building the best in the market and that means all-teak interiors with eight coats of hand-rubbed varnish. I reply that the public won't pay for it and Eric states that that's his level of quality and that's the way he builds his boats. Now what should I do? That's Eric's plant and always has been. He's very independent. Those craftsmen are probably as loyal to him as to C & C, if not more so.*

Design

C & C's design office, consisting of seven designers and three support staff, was thought one of the largest in-house design offices in the industry. Other yacht builders had a tendency to use the services of outside design firms, such as Sparkman and Stevens in New York. C & C relied strictly on its own design group which produced designs for both custom and production boats. Typically, a custom boat involved a greater time commitment by the design office, as extensive liaison with the customer was often required. Design work for custom boats often found its way into subsequent production boats. Several of C & C's most successful production boats had hull shapes that could be traced directly to race-winning custom boats.

Cuthbertson believed the design office had not suffered since he left it to become president of the company:

> *The quality of work coming out of that office today is first class. I firmly believe they are doing better work now than they would if I were still in charge of that office. What you're seeing is the effect of recent education and new, bright engineering minds. I came out of engineering 25 years ago. That's prehistoric in terms of the technology the designers are dealing with today.*

Looking to the future of the design division, Cuthbertson noted two things. The first was that the design office was currently in the process of designing a "pure" cruising boat, the first boat ever created by C & C without the racing circuit in mind. Second, he thought that Rob Ball's position as head of design would be shortly elevated to a vice-presidency, "to more accurately reflect the importance of design in this company, and to help us hang on to Rob, whom the competition would dearly love to hire away from us." It was also expected that the amount of work done by the design office for outside customers (noncompeting boats) would increase from the 1975 level of $100,000.

Retail

The retail division of C & C was essentially a company-owned C & C dealer located in Oakville. He sold new C & C yachts, as well as other noncompeting lines of boats and used boats. Sales in 1975 were $3.5 million, earning $63,000. The margin on new C & C boats was 15 percent, similar to that obtained by any other dealership. The major expense in the operation was the $108,000 paid in commissions. Total value of new C & C boats sold in 1975 was $2.25 million. Plans for the future included opening a second store, in Chicago.

C & C in Europe

C & C's European sales office was run by two young Germans, Michael Schmidt and Rolf Vrolijk. Schmidt, aged twenty-six, explained their concerns when Cuthbertson recruited them for their present positions:

> *Cuthbertson telephoned Rolf and me in December 1974 to see if we wanted to take over C & C's operations in Europe. That was quite a question! We had learned during the 6 months that we worked for Godfrey (the previous C & C manager) in England that the company had lost close to $300,000 in Europe in the previous 2 years. Only four boats had been sold. Four! We knew that there were four 39-footers that had been exported from Canada more than a year ago still waiting to be sold. Not only that, but Godfrey had set up a contract with OY Baltic in Finland to supply us with six 46-foot boats built to C & C design — one a month for 6 months — to which we were committed. He had sold the first one, but the onus would be on us to sell the rest.*
>
> *We also tried to assess C & C's chances of making it in Europe in the long run. We were very impressed with their boats, which are top quality, and with their North American operations. Europe is a tough, fragmented market for boats and two of C & C's U.S.*

competitors had just given up on trying to establish plants here. One firm, Ranger Yachts, went ahead with a plant in Italy. In some countries here — such as Italy, France, and Switzerland — there is a lot of money around and a market for big boats. In others, we could only sell small boats. But the economics of exporting small boats (under 35 feet) from North America do not make sense because the transportation cost is such a high proportion of the boats' value. Also, C & C has never tried to sell boats less than 39 feet long in Europe, and this limits the available market. On the positive side, the competition in Europe is mostly small, family-owned companies and in my view these are very poorly managed. Many will collapse, giving C & C and one or two good European firms an opportunity. Overall, we felt C & C had a fighting chance to make it in Europe.

Both Rolf and I are as involved with this company as if we owned it. I've been home two weekends since accepting the job. We've got results though. In January, we sold a boat at the Paris boat show, and with Moray Edwards's help, established a new French dealer. We only want six dealers for Europe; one in each of France, Belgium, north Germany, south Germany, Italy, and Denmark. We are not interested in sailors as dealers. We're looking for businessmen. Through a very good Italian dealer now in place, we sold all five of the 46-footers supplied by Baltic.

Results for C & C Europe for the year ending June 30 were a loss of $130,000 on sales of $1.1 million. However, the performance of the company had improved dramatically in the latter half of 1975, after Schmidt and Vrolijk took over, operating at very close to breakeven. Looking to the future, Schmidt forecasted sales of $2.5 million, but was not sure about profits. He felt that a new, larger office was needed, a full-time C & C employee should be hired to monitor the operations of the Baltic plant, and an accountant was needed. Even more expensive was the campaign he envisaged to get C & C's name known in Europe. "The quality of the boats is fine, and the design is good, but we are still unknown in Europe. We need to win some races over here and to spend a lot on advertising." Marketing costs for the 1974–1975 year were $100,000. Schmidt was in favor of sending a "factory team" to the world championships in a "33," a crew consisting of himself and Rolf and several of their friends who were top sailors. C & C in Canada frowned on this practice, arguing that if such a crew lost, it would be a disaster, leading potential customers to think, "if those guys couldn't make that boat win, I'm certainly not going to buy one," and even if it won, the credit would go to the sailors, not the boat. In Schmidt's view, the publicity of a win would be so valuable that they should take the risk.

Schmidt thought that C & C Europe should have four lines of boats for sale in 3 or 4 years, and total sales of between $4 and $5 million. He believed only the highest-quality yachts should be offered at each length the firm decided to sell.

THE DECISION

Moray Edwards, charged by Cuthbertson with recommending a plan of action in Europe, voiced his concerns and outlined the options he felt the company faced:

Michael Schmidt has done wonders with our sales in Europe, but we're still not making money. One of the reasons for this is that there are too many profit margins. By the time Baltic makes a profit, and our dealers take their margin, there's not much left for us. Our gross margin last year was less than 12 percent. Baltic, by the way, is definitely not for sale although I feel at times we own them anyway. We are their only customer, and we have over $500,000 tied up in advances to them. However, the Finnish government is involved with the firm and it's clear we will not be given the chance to buy it. Baltic itself is not in the best of financial health. Michael has looked for an alternate builder and found one good possibility in Sweden. However, I don't know if we want another contract builder.

We've made a huge investment in Europe to get a marketing network established and the only real justification for spending that much money is that we're going to build our boats in Europe. There is even less market data there than in North America, which means we would be going in partially blind. However, we've done that before, most recently in Rhode Island. We certainly know the yachting market as well as anyone.

The options facing us in Europe are no secret. In fact, I've got a feasibility study right here [see Appendix for excerpt] prepared a couple of years ago which lays them out. We tried using licensees in the early 1970s, and that did not work out. We are now subcontracting and that, as you can see, has its problems. The only options left are to build our own plant, take over an existing company, or leave Europe altogether. The economics of the most recent area under consideration, Kiel, Germany, are as follows:

Capital Investment Required		Supplied by:	
Land	$ 80,000	Government grant	$214,000
Plant	600,000	Government mortgage	526,000
Machinery, equipment, tooling	200,000	C & C equity	140,000
	$880,000		$880,000

Plant capacity: $3 million. Sales are expected to reach this level by 1979.

Breakeven: The operation would be expected to begin generating profits by late 1978.

Working capital: Approximately $500,000 needed.

Return: Projected at 20 percent return on investment on a discounted-cash-flow basis.

Grant: The $214,000 grant from the German government had to be repaid if C & C closed the operation within 5 years.

APPENDIX: MAY 1974 FEASIBILITY STUDY

This appendix presents a report on the feasibility of C & C Yachts establishing itself as a major supplier of production yachts to the European market.

MARKET REVIEW

The area is considerably different in concept and content from North America. Obvious differences stem from the language and cultural variances experienced between Northern Europe (Scandinavia) and the Mediterranean area (southern France and Italy).

Over the past 5 to 6 years, a marked change has occurred in European yachting. The general level of affluence enjoyed by Europeans has increased dramatically and more disposable income is available for leisure; in all spheres of leisure-time pursuits, the past years have been ones of rapid growth.

The boat-building industry during this period has also changed in a radical way. Prior to 1965, production-boat builders of sailing yachts between 25 and 35 feet were almost unknown. Boats were produced by large companies such as Camper and Nicholson's on a custom basis, or by small local boat builders working mostly in wood. Glass fiber construction was still regarded as a new and untried technique and the industry had little or no integration over the European market. Starting from 1967 onward, particularly in France and England, production builders emerged producing series-constructed boats and the industry started to create volume production as it is understood in North America. This intensification of output made it necessary to market the boats over a much wider area in order to support the requirements of volume production.

The industry has developed now to the point where there are several major manufacturers involved in series production of boats between 25 feet and 35 feet, whose methods of construction, styling, and approach to the production process are in no way inferior to North American techniques. Most notable is the company Michel Dufour S.A., which is the European leader in this field with a gross sales volume of $10 million. Other companies exist, notably in France and Germany. In spite of the emergence of these larger companies, there are still many small, disorganized, traditional builders operating in local market areas in an extremely inefficient manner. The larger builders have organized their distribution patterns and created markets throughout the area. It is untrue to say that the market is anywhere near saturated by these builders since the percentage share held by the smaller builders is still considerable. The population of Europe is about the same as that of North America. However, the number of boats, in very rough terms, is one-tenth of that in North America. Hence, with increasing congestion on the roads and increasing disillusionment with conventional forms of recreation due to population pressure, there is an active interest by the public in moving into the sport of sailing. European governments are aware of these changes and are creating facilities to enable increasing numbers of yachtsmen to berth their boats in well-equipped marinas around the coastline. Generally, the market has the requisites for growth, i.e., increasing affluence, added motivation to find a more attractive form of leisure away from crowded roads and holiday resorts, plus the increasing availability of facilities designed exclusively for water sports.

HISTORICAL REVIEW —
C & C YACHTS' PRESENCE IN EUROPE

C & C Yachts has so far been represented by the use of licensees. These companies have not proven successful in acquiring major market shares. Currently, both licensees operate under renegotiated contracts which ensure that C & C Yachts has complete freedom to develop its own image and product line without interference from its licensees. The problems encountered with these two licensees may be considered typical of any negotiations that would be held with licensees in Europe. If a company is large enough to be successful and has the necessary capital and resources to aggressively attack the European market, it will almost certainly wish to purchase an exclusive design, whereas a smaller company without the required resources is tempted to enter into a licencing arrangement in order to try to use the brand name of the designer to achieve success and restrict the investment to promote the image of the boats.

POSSIBLE MEANS OF OPERATION WITHIN EUROPE

Means may be summarized as follows:

1. Licensing of designs
2. Subcontracting of designs for ultimate marketing by C & C Yachts
3. Takeover of an existing company
4. Erection of own manufacturing facilities

The conclusions reached on these four possibilities are briefly summarized as follows:

1. *Licencing of designs.* The revenue earned from licensees is small, and because the licensee is carrying out his own marketing, creation of image and identity is subject to very limited controls. If licensees are allowed to use C & C's image and brand name, damage to the overall acceptability of C & C Yachts in Europe can easily result. The use of licenced designs to achieve a maximum penetration of the market is not practical in terms of direct benefits in image and earnings to C & C Yachts.

2. *Subcontracted capacity.* This has the attraction of requiring relatively little capital investment for start-up. Experience has shown that other companies operating in this manner have experienced great difficulties in ensuring adequate quality-control standards and maintaining pricing parity with competitors. Quality control is hard to supervise unless constant presence is maintained by the purchaser. This adds to the overhead and is difficult to put into practice. Pricing parity is a problem since double profits have to be allowed for. The boat producer requires his normal margins and, in order for C & C Yachts to market the boats at an adequate return, it is essential to add on a further percentage for marketing. This double profit tends to be higher than that which would be taken by a company building and marketing its own boats. It is extremely difficult to find capable companies who are in a position to offer subcontract facilities at the required degree of efficiency and capacity to satisfy a marketing program for Europe.

3. *Takeover of an existing company.* The European market is divided among a small number of reasonably efficient, larger manufacturers and a large number of small, more efficient builders. If a takeover attempt is considered for one of the larger manufacturers, the asset value of that company will be relatively high. Because C & C Yachts is not interested in the acquisition of existing designs by other architects and the associated tooling, the asset value inherent in these — and also the goodwill factor associated with the products — will be of no value. Consequently, the price demanded for the company would be completely out of proportion to its value.

As for taking over a small company, in general these are located on sites of small dimensions which would not permit the necessary expansion. The only benefit to be obtained from purchasing one of these companies would be in the form of an existing work force (small in number). The assets of the company, in terms of tooling and designs, would be quite worthless and, because the site on which the factory is located would also be inadequate, a high price would again be paid for a small work force. It was concluded, after studying several companies, that the takeover approach to acquire capacity was really an impractical way of approaching the problem.

4. *Erection of a C & C manufacturing facility in Europe.* This approach would allow the development of a facility based on the best techniques available, operating in a plant that could be custom-built to use these methods. Providing that the criteria of adequate labor availability can be guaranteed, such an approach would give the best chance of success in developing a C & C presence in a major way in Europe.

CONCLUSIONS

The optimum approach would be to erect a facility wholly owned and operated by C & C Yachts and to establish in this facility a manufacturing unit capable of progressive development to meet the demands of the European market. All the other solutions considered produced lower returns and a less secure position for C & C Yachts in the European market.

APPLE COMPUTER INC.

HELLO, I'M YOUR INFORMATIVE AND INEXPENSIVE ELECTRONIC COMPANION. LINK YOUR MIND WITH MY MICROPROCESSOR AND LET US MAKE TIMELY DECISIONS TOGETHER.[1]

MAKE BREAD WITH AN APPLE. EVEN IF YOUR COMPANY HAS A BIG COMPUTER SYSTEM, YOU COULD PROBABLY DO YOUR JOB BETTERFASTERSMARTER WITH AN APPLE . . . SITTING ON YOUR DESK.[2]

MY NAME IS REVEREND APPLE. . . . GROOM, WHAT'S YOUR NAME?[3]

Apple Computer Inc. hasn't given its blessing to the computer marriages, but a spokesperson has said, "It's good to have divinity on your side." Reputedly the world's first ordained computer, the Apple II's human co-pastor in a California church used his electronic helper "to get people interested in marriage, the church, and God," offering the programmed ceremony free along with marriage counseling by a warm-blooded being for the lucky couple.

Personal computer-craze cartoons abound. For example, a boy stares incredulously at a book, a gift just handed to him by someone who looks suspiciously like a harried mother, and asks how it can be full of information since it doesn't even have a display screen.[4] Another lists on a house-for-sale sign features that include 9 rooms, 3 baths, and 2 computer terminals.[5] The third example, a cover cartoon,

---

[1] Opening conversational gambit on an Apple II.

[2] Excerpt from fall 1981 Apple Computer Inc. advertisement.

[3] Marilyn Chase, "Do You Take This Input to Be Your Lawfully Wedded Interface?" *The Wall Street Journal*, July 28, 1981, p. 29.

[4] *The Wall Street Journal*, n.d.

[5] *The New Yorker*, July 26, 1982, p. 33.

Case prepared by Charles L. Hinkle, University of Colorado, and Esther F. Stineman, Yale University. © 1984 by Prentice-Hall, Inc. Reprinted by permission.

portrays a psychoanalyst fingering a lap-held keyboard and asking the couch occupant to tell him when the urge first struck to buy a home computer.[6]

CORPORATE BACKGROUND

Widely acknowledged as the leader in the personal computer arena, Apple Computer Inc. was founded in 1976 by 21-year-old Steve Jobs, whose private goal was to make computer capability widely accessible — not unlike Henry Ford's desire to provide automobiles for the masses, and by Steve Wozniak, both college dropout design engineers.

> *Basically, Steve Wozniak and I invented the Apple because we wanted a personal computer. Not only couldn't we afford the computers that were on the market, those computers were impractical for us to use. We needed a Volkswagen. . . . After we launched the Apple in 1976, all our friends wanted one.*[7]

Jobs likened the Apple offspring's contribution to human efficiency to the IBM Selectric typewriter, the calculator, the Xerox copying machine, and advanced telephone systems.

The youthful entrepreneurs used $1,300 from the sale of a Volkswagen to assemble their first prototype. Both Steves wanted to avoid a threatening name, one smacking of high technology, and Jobs was a fruitarian, so the corporate name "Apple" sounded appropriate. The unspoken corporate motto might well have been, "Don't trust any computer you can't lift."

After meeting in the garage of a mutual friend, Jobs and Wozniak's friendship evolved into the partnership that became Apple Computer Inc., primarily by the happenstance of assembling computers for friends, not realizing that they were on to something that could be a leading-edge effort in making computers available to the masses. Before forming the company, Wozniak worked as a technician at Hewlett-Packard and Jobs was employed developing video games at Atari. Apple II was designed for the most part by fall 1976, using 4K dynamic random access memories (RAMs), which no other firm used at the time. As Jobs put it, "Going out with a product based on dynamic memories was untried; fortunately, we didn't know how risky it was." According to the chairman, Commodore saw the Apple II and immediately made overtures to acquire the fledgling firm, which would have transformed Apple II to Commodore I. The partners wanted reliable manufacturers who could build a total package for them, so they visited familiar haunts. "Atari couldn't get involved because of a heavy commitment, quite correctly, to developing their games, and Hewlett-Packard, which was working on the HP-85 at that time, was dubious

---

[6] *Forbes*, August 2, 1982, front outside cover.

[7] Fall 1981, corporate advertisement.

of our abilities, I'm convinced, because we didn't have electrical engineering or computer science degrees.''

ADVENT OF PERSONAL COMPUTING

What is a personal computer (PC)? It is an extension of the microprocessor, a computer on a chip, developed by Intel Corp. in the early 1970s and in those earlier years bought principally by hobbyists. Unlike their predecessors, units of the 1980s became total systems, including input keyboards, video readout monitors, and software found at laboratory benches, in manufacturing plants, on executive side tables, and in schools and private dwellings.

The PC industry grew from nothing in 1975 to an estimated $1.5 billion plus in 1981 and was forecasted by industry specialists to continue an annual growth of from 40 to 50 percent through the mid-1980s. Stock prices of such firms as Apple, Tandy, and Commodore soared. Apple went on the market at $22 a share in 1980, and traded over the counter at $25 in August 1981, or roughly 100 times earnings, definitely a glamour stock. In November 1982, prices hovered in the area of $30, having risen from $11 earlier in the year.

Apple's first units, small, simple, and relatively inexpensive, were designed for consumer use, not for business and scientific applications, but after add-on small-disk memory was introduced in 1978, many software authors started developing Apple programs for business. One, a general-purpose financial analysis program, is credited with giving Apple a year's lead time over competitors, making it the top banana in the business PC bunch.

According to various sources at the company's Cupertino, California, headquarters, independent software vendors were thought to spend a large proportion, possibly more than half, of their time on Apple software. The April 1982 issue of *BYTE* had no fewer than 11 pages of ads from companies promoting products to boost Apple II's performance. Rather than a hardware race, software technology was seen as the desirable focus to help buyers increase the usefulness of their machines.

As research and development proceeded rapidly, Apple III was announced in May 1980, finally making a full-fledged debut in March 1981. Initially technical problems had led to customer complaints that were covered by a policy of outright exchange. Both software and hardware came in for varied and widespread criticism as users bombarded Apple management with queries and grievances. It was rumored that the new units were about to be replaced by improved hardware and operating systems, but management denied this, predicting a 10-year life span for Apple III.

Operating mostly in leased facilities, manufacturing operations consisted of purchase, assembly, and test of materials and components used in Apple products. Facilities were located in Dallas; Cupertino, San Jose, and Los Angeles, California; County Cork, Ireland; and Singapore.

Purchases of personal computers for home use were at first disappointing; still, leading producers continued to emphasize these markets while consumer analysts warned that sales to these segments would not be sensational until the hardware and software were designed to serve the needs of household users. Home computers can be entertaining and educational and might even prove useful as information and transaction devices. One writer, whose personal computer was an Apple II, described dialing into a central network to view an airline schedule and suggested numerous other potential dimensions of what he called "home computer bulletin boards," speculating that students would have access to information comparable to the complete Library of Congress and that mail would be instantaneous.[8]

As electronic hobbyists' purchases dwindled in the late 1970s and early 1980s, manufacturers started eyeing the 80 million U.S. households, stressing fun and educational aspects. Predictions were that one of every four American homes would have a computer by the late 1980s. Planners spoke of two or three in every home and one atop every businessperson's desk. Speedups in automation, including PCs, were to affect directly the jobs of some 9 million managers and 14 million professionals in American industry.[9] Small computers were expected to be information processing building blocks in this changing structure.

CULTIVATING EDUCATIONAL MARKETS

In 1979, Apple helped to create the nonprofit Foundation for the Advancement of Computer-Aided Education with the goal of furthering efforts of software authors. In 1980, Atari and Texas Instruments sponsored software writing contests. About this time, Tandy launched collaborative efforts with textbook publishers to enrich educational software. Most microprocessor makers hoped that expanded use in schools would stimulate computer sales in the home market. Educators claimed that poor software, frustrated users, and attempts at electronic humor in response to users' errors were insulting deterrents to students, although youngsters were said to approach the keyboard enthusiastically and to become comfortable quickly when exposed to computers.

Far below expectations, 1980 shipments of 50,000 microcomputers to schools were predicted by many to rise to some 250,000 units annually over a five-year period. Sales to schools in 1981 were estimated at $150 million. The shrinking cost of computer power was credited with the sudden popularity of school computers. C. Gregory Smith, director of educational marketing at Apple, expressed conviction

[8] Neil Shapiro, "Now Your Home Computer Can Call Other Computers on the Telephone," *Popular Mechanics*, February 1981, p. 130.

[9] "The Speedup in Automation," Special Report in *Business Week*, August 3, 1981, pp. 58–67.

that not only were schools sold on computers but they also were more likely than business buyers to make repeat purchases. That computer literacy would become a survival skill equal in importance to reading, writing, and arithmetic was not in doubt in the Apple hierarchy.

Engineering and business students at many colleges and universities opted for their own computers — individual units either owned or leased — partly because of the difficulties encountered gaining access to the institution's central devices. Several schools began leasing computers and telephone modems so students could have remote access to the larger processors on campus. Some colleges — for example, Stevens Institute of Technology in Hoboken, New Jersey — required that a student studying science, systems analysis, management, and other computer-intensive courses in 1982 own a microprocessor. Quite apart from relieving demand for the institution's scarce terminals, schools taking this approach expected it to encourage students to become more familiar with and dependent upon computers, to treat them as an integral part of their intellectual support systems.

Donating an Apple II computer to some 83,000 public elementary and secondary schools in the United States seems a laudable and easily attainable goal, one that could be accomplished simply by management fiat. Not so, however, particularly when the would-be contributor posed a condition: boosting the ceiling on the annual amount of such a donation to 30 percent of its taxable income from 10 percent, the existing maximum. Without success Apple lobbied for a change permitting it to "further the cause of computer literacy in the nation's public schools," an attempt rejected by the House Ways and Means Committee.

New hope came in September 1982, as the House passed part of a temporary tax break giving the proposed program a boost.[10] The legislation (323 for and 62 against) would permit computer manufacturers to donate computers to public schools and to receive the favorable tax treatment reserved for donations of scientific equipment to universities. Congressional tax analysts estimated the tax break to be worth about $36 million in fiscal years 1982 and 1983 for Apple or for any others who wished to make such contributions. The Senate was yet to consider a similar bill. Apple executives thought the bill would stimulate computer education and, in turn, the computer industry; Treasury Department spokespersons opposed the idea on grounds that tax law should not be used to form social policy.

TOP-LEVEL ORGANIZATIONAL CHANGES

In early 1981, Apple Computer Inc. restructured its management team, naming former vice president of marketing, then chairman, A. C. Markkula, Jr., 39 years

---

[10] "Apple Clears Hurdle on Its Plan to Send Computers to Class," *The Wall Street Journal*, September 23, 1982, p. 31.

old, to the post of president and chief executive officer to concentrate on day-to-day operations of the company; Markkula was succeeded in the chairmanship by former Vice Chairman Jobs. Michael Scott, age 38, shifted from the position of president/CEO to the role of vice chairman, in charge of long-range business growth planning, and in 1982 left the company.

Self-taught computer engineer Stephen Wozniak programmed himself out of the Apple family portrait when he decided to seek gratification beyond the corporate agenda. Following an airplane wreck and a five-week loss of memory, he took a leave of absence from the company and enrolled at the University of California-Berkeley, under an assumed name, to take undergraduate computer science courses he had dropped out of for lack of interest 11 years previously.[11] The wizard — "Woz" to his friends — promoted a new-kind-of-unity rock concert at which 200,000 Californians and others showed up to hear music and relate to a philosophy pushing "us" instead of "me." At 32, with an estate thought to be over $50 million, Wozniak was said to be out approximately $3 million unless subsequent film and album revenues would cover his expenditures.[12]

FINANCIAL HIGHLIGHTS

As unemployment hovered around 10.4 percent in October 1982, and many industries were in the doldrums, the microcomputer marketers enjoyed continued increases in sales and profits. "One reason," CEO Markkula pointed out, "is that a recession prompts many companies to invest in products that will boost productivity. That perspective has helped our sales not just here but also in Europe and England." Apple estimated that its profits rose 70 percent on sales gains of 80 percent in the fourth quarter ending in September. For its fiscal year, earnings were up more than 50 percent on a revenue increase of almost 75 percent. Exhibit 1 provides a review of selected financial statistics.

Cash flow was consistently healthy at Apple, partly because the company encouraged its 1,400 North American and 1,600 international dealers and distributors to pay in full for shipments within two weeks, while Apple generally took up to six weeks to pay its own suppliers.

Markkula was pleased with the company's financial shape, pointing to return on equity of 28 percent, return on assets of 20 percent, and return on investment of 33 percent. The balance sheet at the end of fiscal 1982 also revealed about $150 million in cash and equivalents and negligible debt, stellar performance from a company in existence only five years. There was talk around the company of breaking into the *Fortune* 500 list.

[11] Paul Ciotti, "California Magazine," in the *Denver Post*, August 1, 1982, p. D-1.

[12] Rom Morganthau, David R. Friendly, and William Cook, "A Wizard called 'Woz,'" *Newsweek*, September 20, 1982, p. 69.

EXHIBIT 1
Selected Apple
financial statistics,
fiscal years
September 30,
1977–1982

	1977	1978	1979	1980	1981	1982
Net sales	$0.8	$7.9	$48	$117	$335	$583
R&D expenses	NA	0.6	4	7	21	38
Marketing expenses	NA	1.3	4	12	46	32
Net income	0.4	0.8	5	12	39	61

Figures in millions, rounded.
NA—Not available
Notes: Net sales increases were not greatly affected by price changes.
Net income in 1981 was increased principally by improved gross margins and higher interest income, partially offset by increased marketing (increased advertising and other promotion costs and expansion of the distribution system) and general and administrative expenses (resulting mainly from foreign exchange losses, which were included in G&A expenses in 1981). Interest income in 1981 of $11.7 million was over 10 times the previous year's, resulting from investment in short-term securities of the proceeds from Apple's common stock offering in December 1980.
Apple paid no cash dividends, choosing to reinvest earnings to finance growth.
During the first quarter, a one-time, after-tax charge of $700,000 was accrued for an extra week's vacation awarded to employees as the company exceeded $100 million in quarterly sales for the first time.
A common stock issue of 2,600,000 shares was subscribed in 1981. Apple's 13 officers and directors own approximately 25 million of the company's almost 58 million common shares outstanding. Jobs has over 7.5 million, Markkula over 7 million, and Wozniak over 4 million, the three totaling almost a third of all shares.

FACING THE COMPETITION

Digital Equipment Corporation

After a winter of discontent that saw IBM storm down the field and a surge by Tandy and Commodore, 1982 was the season for Digital's challenge in the personal computer wars. Months earlier the company had moved into office automation. The acknowledged leader in superminicomputers — machines offering the performance of larger mainframe systems for a mini's price — presumably was counting on a strong position in information processing at major companies to give it a needed competitive edge. Digital bought advertisements in a few trade magazines in early summer and ran announcement-type ads in selected business periodicals. Observers concluded that this campaign was intended to reach the company's existing markets, not to cultivate awareness and interest in the much wider market already penetrated by the microprocessor pioneers, and believed that Digital looked to the new line as an aid to sustain its high growth rate. However, insiders expected that the company would concentrate on sales to professionals and small businesses in an attempt to gain a share of the crowded $2.5 billion microcomputer markets. Meanwhile, by 1982 Digital had had three years of experience operating its chain of retail stores, computer shops intended to eliminate computer fear, to communicate benefits information in a friendly atmosphere, and to be flexible in how its systems were presented to the public. The overall goal was to keep prospects from being intimidated.

Osborne Computer Corporation

Fall 1982 brought an advertising headline "the best holiday offer your career ever had," showing a picture of the unit followed by "The Osborne Personal Business Computer. $1795. dBASE II Data Base Software. Free." Most of the body copy promoted available software packages. The pre-Christmas theme (the free offer was to end December 24) announced "the best buy in a personal computer just got better."

Commodore International

An enviable stock performance record reflected this company's second-generation system's success. Entering the market in 1976 by purchasing MOS Technology to get a supply of calculator chips, CI benefited serendipitously from the acquired firm's research and development in microprocessor technology. The principal result of that development was named PET (personal electronic transactor) and was merchandised primarily in Europe simply because there was less competition there than in the United States. Calling themselves "the American Japanese," Commodore's strategy became that of offering a processor that could emulate those made by others, offering it at a price under $1,000, compared with prices of four times that for competitors' models. The rallying cry from Commodore was "A real computer for the price of a toy," while insisting that this computer went beyond games to teach computing skills to users. "The Commodore 64. Only $595. What nobody else can give you at twice the price," showing a picture of a user's hands, a keyboard, and color graphics, covered one side of a two-page advertisement. The opposite page showed how favorably Commodore 64 compared with Apple II ($1,530), IBM ($1,565), TRS-80 III ($999), and Atari 800 ($899). Commodore was apparently "coming home" to make its mark against entrenched microprocessor makers.

Tandy Corporation

Industry sources estimated that Tandy's 25 percent of the PC market in 1981 had declined to 24 percent in 1982. Tandy distributed through its chain of about 8,000 Radio Shack outlets, 200 of which sold only personal computers. Its TRS-80 and Apple were the most common stand-alone computers used by managers. Tandy widely advertised low prices ranging from $250 for a hand-held computer to a $10,000 system for small businesses. Science and science-fiction author Isaac Asimov was spokesman for Radio Shack's TRS-80, announcing in 1982 a price of $399.95 for the color computer. A 1981 survey reported that businesses typically spent about $9,460 for a computer system, while hobbyists' outlays averaged $1,574.[13] Factors delaying proliferation of executive desk-top computers reportedly included lack of communication software and physical design as well as resistance from entrenched data processing departments in the larger firms.[14]

---

[13] Small Business section, *The Wall Street Journal*, July 6, 1981, p. 17.

[14] "Microcomputers Invade the Executive Suite," *Computer Decisions*, February 1981, p. 70.

Texas Instruments

Lessons learned in selling hand-held calculators were apparently being used by Texas Instruments in slashing the price of its entry in the home computer field. The offer was a $100 rebate to customers buying the 99-4A computer. The predecessor 99-4 system came on the market in 1979 at about $1,000, the 4A was introduced in 1981 at $525, and the 1982 list price was pegged at $299.50. Comedian Bill Cosby was spokesman for TI's home computer.

Sinclair and Timex

"Under $200," advertised Sinclair Research Ltd. for its ZX80, describing it as a complete and powerful full-function computer that matched or surpassed other computers costing "many times more." The 1981 brochures proclaimed, "You simply take it out of the box, connect it to your TV, and turn it on. . . . With the manual in your hand, you'll be running programs in an hour. Within a week, you'll be writing complex programs with confidence." The company announced a 30-day moneyback guarantee and a 90-day limited warranty along with its national service-by-mail facility. After Timex acquired the computer maker, Timex Sinclair's 1000 became an update of the ZX series and was called "the first ready-to-go personal computer for under $100" (actually $99.95), aimed at the consumer market. Should the machine become available where Timex watches were distributed, 100,000 retail outlets might display and sell the ZX 1000. Some analysts recommended that the leaders should carefully observe the progress of this efficient and low-priced product, claiming it could well provide a substantial impetus for the personal computers revolution. The assumption was that introducing neophytes to computers with low-priced units could provide a reservoir of demand for trading up to units such as those made by Apple.

IBM

In all its years of successful EDP product introductions, IBM avoided growing slovenly or complacent, even though the giant firm was not always the undisputed leader in new products. With its large war chest of R&D and promotional funds and an eye for where much of the present, and probably a considerable portion of the future, seemed to lie, the company's riposte in microprocessors made its mark in this burgeoning field, eliminating the downside risk of ignoring the opportunities and sharing in the upside potential after parrying opponents' lunges. IBM personal computers were distributed through 150 ComputerLand stores and at Sears Business Systems Centers, as well as at IBM product centers that sold and serviced the system. October 1982 demand for its systems exceeded supply, as the company announced anticipated output of 15,000 machines each month. While prophets of gloom heralded IBM's entry as a severe blow to competitive hardware precursors, many observers considered it yet another good omen for the booming business of software, an industry based on writing those coded sets of instructions that provide maps for computers to follow in processing data. As with all other entrants, IBM's success in PC markets would depend heavily on availability of software to drive the systems. With an estimated 5,000-plus software producers in the United States alone, competition was strong, and after details of IBM's configuration became available, conversion work in software supply houses became a major priority.

In an amicable mood, an Apple ad campaign in 1981 forthrightly greeted the newcomer:

Welcome, IBM. Seriously . . . to the most exciting and important marketplace since the computer revolution began 35 years ago. . . . When we invented the first personal computer system, we estimated that over 140 million people worldwide could justify the purchase of one, if only they understood its benefits. Next year alone, we project that well over one million will come to that understanding. . . . We look forward to responsible competition in the massive effort to distribute this American technology to the world. . . . what we are doing is increasing social capital by enhancing individual productivity. Welcome to the task.

Using mass media to address the general public about its personal computer, IBM's fall 1982 advertisements pushed such product features as nonglare screen (easy on the eyes), 80 characters a line (with upper- and lower-case letters for a quick and easy read), flexibility of moving components about (the keyboard could be placed on one's lap and the user could rest his or her feet on the desk or elsewhere), and user memory expandable up to 256K, with 40K of permanent memory. Friendliness to users was claimed; BASIC language and high-resolution color graphics on the user's own TV set were mentioned as IBM invited shoppers to look around and compare theirs with others. The action imperative asked readers and viewers to visit an authorized IBM Personal Computer dealer, promising an address, along with other information, at an 800 number. And the competitive price was mentioned: "The quality, power and performance of the IBM Personal Computer are what you'd expect from IBM. The price isn't."[15] One headline announced: "30 years of computer experience: $1,565 and up."

On television, IBM employed a "humanizing" approach to hawking its machines by claiming they "are warm and friendly and okay to touch." The Chaplin-like figure attempting to understand a computer's intricacies, and finally emerging triumphant, presumably was meant to persuade the reluctant that microprocessing could be conquered.

Meanwhile, Dick Cavett was acting as spokesman for Apple, and Tandy planned to show some at-home, family sorts of applications for its machines during the 1982 fall football broadcasts, but the NFL strike altered those intentions. All three producers pushed utilitarian simplicity.

Hewlett-Packard

HP announced its desk-top model, designed to compete with the IBM Personal Computer and Apple III, in late winter 1982. This producer of precision electronics, with annual sales of over $4 billion, fired promotional salvos headlining HP-87

---

[15] Early in 1982, IBM announced standardizing its typewriter line, cutting prices on some models and offering volume discounts for the first time. In late 1982, American Express Company sent a special mailer to cardholders announcing availability of the Selectric III, through American Express, at the going price, equal payments over 20 months, and no interest charges.

maximum memory of 544K, analytic software including the CP/M module, and the read-only-memory-based operating system that put built-in BASIC to work for the user. "We're building power, friendliness and reliability . . ." announced the body copy, with the tag line, "It's very good at what you do." HP's program library offered only two games in contrast to the dozens provided by competitive producers. One of HP's advertisements used the headline: "The personal computer comes of age." Perhaps the idea was old or useless by this time, but Apple ran no promotion welcoming Hewlett-Packard to the field of front-runners. Moving rapidly, in late summer, the company unveiled HP-75, its 26-ounce, battery-operated machine set to retail at $995. HP sources indicated the easily portable unit was intended to provide a transition between pocket calculators and desk-top computers.

Xerox

A formidable entry was Xerox, going for a total system configuration by promoting integrated office automation products — including a microcomputer doubling as low-cost word processor — and threatening to vie for the anticipated largesse ready to be harvested in homes across the land.

Other competitors were expected to emerge, particularly since the capital gains tax, which was cut to 40 percent (from 50 percent) in 1978, favored high-technology entrepreneurs ready, with this added incentive, to start new businesses in the data processing field.

MARKET SHARES AND DISTRIBUTION

Based on several sources, it was estimated in mid-1982 that personal computer sales were shared as follows: Apple and Tandy/Radio Shack combined dominating almost half the market, with the market shares of 24 percent each; next came Commodore at 9 percent; Nippon Electric Company with 6 percent; Hewlett-Packard and IBM at 5 percent each; Osborne accounting for 3 percent, and others, including Xerox, Digital Equipment, Texas Instruments, and perhaps 20 smaller producers sharing the remainder.

Estimates varied widely, but it was conjectured that stores were the channel of distribution for about 60 percent of desk-top computers purchased in 1982, while mail order accounted for 15 to 20 percent and direct sales 10 to 15 percent, the remainder being sold by other means.

Except for Tandy and Texas Instruments' units, personal computers were available at computer stores; and Texas Instruments sold through department stores and catalogs. Struggling for display space was a way of life, and marketing became extremely vital to PC sales. Such firms as Sears reportedly planned to carry no more than four brands in 1983, all chosen according to what seems logical for the most customers. The chain's 26 business retail centers stocked IBM, Osborne, and Vector Graphics systems in 1982. A Sears manager rejected the idea that this limited array hindered customers' choices: "Most suppliers are merely assemblers of components by other firms that provide the same components for many manufacturers, so it is difficult when you look inside the case to tell them all apart.'' MOS Technology, Zilog, Inc., and Intel Corporation were the leading processor designers.

Apple's retail dealers were asked by the company, in November 1981, to sign an amended dealer contract to prohibit telephone and mail-order sales of its products under penalty of losing dealership status. The rationale was simple: success depends on customer satisfaction, which, in turn, depends on dealers providing support services to users. Although some mail-order firms were discounting prices, Apple management said that this was not the issue, maintaining that its effort to eliminate mail-order sales was legal and in line with the company's philosophy of adequately serving customers' postpurchase needs. Filing a suit to block the company from enforcing the new policy, a group of mail-order distributors accused Apple of bowing to pressure from full-service dealers by attempting to fix prices and restrain trade.

A long-standing central buying agreement with a Minneapolis-based retail chain was renewed for 1983. Team Central, entering its sixth year of association with Apple, is a franchiser of approximately 90 retail stores that sell general consumer products in medium-sized and smaller markets nationwide.[16]

''We're happy the negotiations are complete and look forward to another strong selling year with the Team organization,'' announced Gene Carter, Apple vice president of sales. ''Team provides Apple with an important presence in secondary and tertiary markets.''

Gary Thorne, Team executive vice president of sales and marketing, said his company's strategy in 1983 would be to emphasize personal computer sales through its franchisees. ''The pervasiveness of personal computers and Team's importance in the markets we serve make the Apple line an exciting part of our sales thrust in the coming year.''

Earlier in the year, Apple ended a similar agreement with ComputerLand Corp., to help achieve geographic control of new franchisees.

APPLE'S DIRECT ATTACK

In February 1982 Apple's offensive included this campaign: ''NOW THAT YOU'VE SEEN THEIR FIRST GENERATION, TAKE A LOOK AT OUR THIRD,'' making the comparison shown in Exhibit 2. Highlights of claims for the Apple III are shown in Exhibit 3.

Promoting its third generation, Apple announced: ''The only thing we didn't build into the Apple III is obsolescence.'' The new product was available at over 1,000 dealers in the United States and Canada, all offering technical support.

In contrast to some Apple advertisements that were hard-hitting and directly confrontational, others were somewhat whimsical, appealing to specific market segments. Consider these headlines: ''Grow Corn with an Apple,'' targeted to the agribusiness segment, pushing its more than 1,000 full-service dealers as the contact

[16] Based on corporate press release, August 12, 1982.

EXHIBIT 2   Apple's features compared with selected competitors'

	Xerox 820	Hewlett-Packard 125, model 10	IBM Personal Computer	Apple III
Standard memory	64K	64K	64K	128K
Maximum memory when fully configured[a]	64K	64K	192K	256K
Expandability	No expansion slots	No expansion slots	No extra expansion slots in fully configured[a] 192K system	4 extra expansion slots in fully configured[a] 256K system
Diskette storage (per drive)	92K	256K	160K	140K
Mass storage (per drive)	—	1.16 megabyte floppy disk	—	5 megabyte hard disk
Display graphics capability	High resolution, B/W	High resolution, B/W	High resolution, B/W or 4-color (color requires additional card)	High resolution, B/W or 16-color
Software available	Word processing SuperCalc®	Word processing VisiCalc® 125	Word processing VisiCalc®	Prod processing VisiCalc® III
	—	Business graphics	—	Business graphics
	—	Data base management	—	Data base management
	Communications	Communications	Communications	Communications
	—	—	—	Apple II software library
	CP/M® library	CP/M® library	CP/M® 86 programs	CP/M® library (Spring 1982)

Note: Based on manufacturer's information available as of December 1981.
[a] "Fully configured" means that the system includes, at a minimum, monitor, printer, two disk drives, and RS-232 communicator.

point for farmers desiring to aid their decision making; "E. F. Hutton simplifies life with Apples," attempted to persuade life insurance agents to have an Apple to help ensure their futures; "Make bread with an Apple," a third-party testimony about Apple's role at Pepperidge Farm; "Baked Apple," described how a fire-damaged Apple, "*mirabile dictu*," still worked when brought into one of the nearly 1,000 Apple dealers with complete service centers, where everything would be "well done"; and a fourth quarter 1982 ad listed 1,100 Apple-compatible computer programs.

> *Consumer awareness and brand recognition are prerequisites to long-term success in a marketplace of intensifying competition. Apple has been known for its marketing emphasis, with a resultant identity that we consider memorable and strong. Awareness of Apple, according to market surveys, rose from approximately 10 percent at the beginning of 1981 to nearly 80 percent at year-end.[17]*

[17] *1981 Annual Report*, p. 3.

EXHIBIT 3
Claims for Apple III,
1982

Dollar for dollar, the most powerful personal computer.
Up to 256K of usable internal memory.
New software packages exclusively for the Apple III, including VisiCalc III.
Apple Writer III software — professional word processing capability — for less than the
price of most word processors.
Apple business graphics — plots, graphs, bars or pie charts in 16 high-resolution colors
or 16 gray scales.
Mail list manager lets you store nearly 1,000 names on one disk.
Access III communications software: access to mainframe computers.
Apple III can run thousands of Apple II programs . . . soon . . . thousands of CP/M
programs. More available software than any other personal computer.
ProFile, a new hard-disk option. With this addition, Apple III can store over 1,200 pages
of text (5 million bytes of information). Enables you to handle problems once reserved
for big computers.

Apple also launched Apple Expo — a dealer trade seminar, trade show, and public exposition — in major U.S. cities and created extensive merchandising aids and dealer training programs.

> [Apple's] marketing emphasis in the past two years has been on the business, professional and managerial segment, which today accounts for approximately 40 percent of revenues. . . . Ultimately, the greatest demand for personal computers will come from a broader spectrum.[18]

Apple supported the advertising campaigns of retail dealers with reimbursements of up to 3 percent of their dollar purchases from the company for actual advertising expenses incurred and provided there was compliance with standards set by Apple. At its own expense, Apple provided demonstration models, brochures, and point-of-sale posters and conducted sales seminars to assist dealers. Corporate expenditures for product advertising accelerated from $573,000 in 1978, to $2 million in 1979, $4.5 million in 1980, $6.4 million in 1981, and an estimated $26 million in 1982. Internal estimates were, as Apple continued fending off those who would challenge its industry leadership, that advertising expenditures would remain in the interval of 4 to 5 percent of sales.

SUMMER OF 1982 LEGAL ISSUES[19]

Imitators of good ideas seemed to come out of the woodwork as Apple's executives lost count of look-alikes. In July 1982 the company filed a number of lawsuits overseas, notably in Taiwan, Hong Kong, and New Zealand, in an ongoing effort

[18] Ibid., p. 3.

[19] Based primarily on corporate memoranda, July–August 1982.

to stop the manufacture and export of bogus Apple II personal computers. Investigations continued in Japan, Singapore, and Australia.

In Taipei, Taiwan, Apple brought a civil action under Taiwan's copyright laws against Sunrise Computer, maker of the "Apolo II" computer, an Apple copy.[20] As a first step in this action in accordance with Taiwanese law, Apple seized as evidence several Apolo computers during a surprise raid on a Sunrise facility in Taipei. Apple planned to press similar charges against another Taiwanese manufacturer. The government of Taiwan, according to the company, was collaborating with Apple to help prevent export of Apple II copies.

In Hong Kong, Apple filed a civil action under local patent laws against a small manufacturer selling Apple II copies, a number of which were seized as evidence in a surprise raid similar to the one in Taiwan. Sales and purchase records of the company were also seized. Because its patents and copyrights were enforceable in Hong Kong, Apple expected to halt all manufacturing and selling of copies there.

In New Zealand, Apple obtained an injunction against Orbit Electronics, which was passing off "Orange" computers from an unknown Taiwanese manufacturer as Apple II computers.

Apple registered its trademarks and copyrights with U.S. Customs authorities and expected that bogus Apple products would be confiscated by the U.S. government at the port of entry. On August 19, Apple announced that the U.S. Customs Service had begun detaining and seizing imitations of the Apple II personal computer. "All copies seized will be destroyed," a company spokesperson reported. "The imitations originated in Taiwan and Hong Kong. The company will take whatever action is necessary to prevent unlawful reproductions of its products from being imported and sold in the United States and abroad."

On August 16, 1982, Apple reported asking the U.S. District Court of eastern Pennsylvania in Philadelphia to reconsider its denial made on August 2 of a preliminary injunction in Apple's lawsuit against Franklin Computer Corporation.

On the same day as the district court denial, the Third Circuit Court of Appeals in Philadelphia issued its opinion in the *Williams Electronics, Inc.* v. *Artic International, Inc.* case involving similar issues. The circuit court, Apple believes, decided some of the key issues that the district judge in the Apple case felt were open questions. Specifically, the circuit court found that U.S. copyright statutes cover object code stored in a computer's read-only-memory (ROM) components.

On May 13, Apple sued Franklin for "patent infringement, copyright infringement, unfair competition, and misappropriation," charging Franklin with copying Apple's diskette- and ROM-form computer programs. Apple sought preliminary and permanent injunctions against the manufacture or sale of Franklin products. A company

---

[20] During a trip to the Orient, the casewriters were made aware of Taiwanese-assembled microprocessors closely resembling Apple II selling at prices below U.S. $300, and in the shadow of a major Hong Kong shopping complex, counterfeit computers very much like Apple II regularly sold at 60 percent less than local retail for the U.S.-made counterpart and could be bargained down on slow days.

report claimed, ''Copying the programs enabled Franklin to produce a computer known as the ACE 100 which can run programs available for the Apple II personal computer.''

TOWARD NEW HORIZONS

Chairman Stephen Jobs summarized his view of the corporate mission: ''Apple is dedicated to making the personal computer not only indispensable, but understandable.'' Indications are that the company that invented the personal computer, specializing in nothing else, had just about mastered the delicate balance of technology and customer need in its stated intent to bring ''computer power to all the people.'' Like IBM, Apple has been characterized by restlessness, change, and an absence of complacency, as management spanned the gap between the conflicting aphorisms ''haste makes waste'' and ''those who hesitate are lost.''

Speaking with schoolchildren, operating as part of management's information systems, performing as factory servomechanism controllers, translating foreign languages for tourists, playing ''Dungeons and Dragons,'' handling bank-at-home and in-home shopping transactions — the list of potential applications seems endless. In the words of Chairman Jobs, ''There are 140 million people in the world who could justify buying a personal computer, if they could only see the benefits to be derived from it.''

As the year ended, President and Chief Executive Officer Mike Markkula and his staff were grappling with such crucial issues as product distribution, long-term product strategy, dealer relations, software development, pricing and promotional strategies, and a variety of issues that ordinarily confront rapidly growing organizations.

MANVILLE CORPORATION (1987)

Perhaps no other mineral is so woven into the fabric of American life as is asbestos. Impervious to heat and fibrous — it is the only mineral that can be woven into cloth — asbestos is spun into fireproof clothing and theater curtains, as well as into such household items as noncombustible drapes, rugs, pot holders, and ironing-board covers. Mixed into slurry, asbestos is sprayed onto girders and walls to provide new buildings with fireproof insulation. It is used in floor tiles, roofing felts, and in most plasterboards and wallboards. Asbestos is also an ingredient of plaster and stucco and of many paints and putties. This "mineral of a thousand uses" — an obsolete nickname: the present count stands at around 3,000 uses — is probably present in some form or other in every home, school, office building, and factory in this country. Used in brake linings and clutch facings, in mufflers and gaskets, in sealants and caulking, and extensively used in ships, asbestos is also a component of every modern vehicle, including space ships.

This was written by columnist Bruce Porter in 1973, just as the dangers of breathing asbestos dust were becoming widely recognized by those outside the asbestos industry. From about the turn of the century, Johns-Manville Corporation (renamed Manville Corporation in 1981) had been the world's leading asbestos company, involved in mining and sale of the raw fibers as well as development, manufacture, and marketing of intermediate and finished asbestos products. This distinction made Manville target of a trickle of asbestos health lawsuits in the 1920s and early thirties which would become a flood by the 1980s.

Late on the evening of August 25, 1982, the Manville board of directors, after a briefing on bankruptcy reorganization and upon the recommendation of three senior outside directors who had been studying the issue, voted to file a petition for protection from creditors under Chapter 11 of the U.S. Bankruptcy Code. The petition had already been prepared and was filed the next day. It would be more than 4 years before a plan to emerge from court protection would be offered for approval by creditors and stockholders.

This case was prepared by Arthur Sharplin, distinguished professor of management, McNeese State University, Lake Charles, LA. © 1986 by Arthur D. Sharplin. Reprinted by permission.

COMPANY BACKGROUND

Until the seventies, Manville was a successful company by the usual standards. Incorporated in 1901, the company had seen consistent growth in sales and profits. Dividends had been paid every year except for the war years of 1915–1916 and the depths of the Depression in 1933–1934. The company had been one of the "Dow-Jones Industrial Thirty" for many years.

In the decades before 1970, Manville's sales had grown somewhat slower than the Gross National Product. But the company had benefited from relatively low fixed costs, due to a largely depleted and depreciated capital base and the total absence of long-term debt in the capital structure. With low operating and financial leverage, the firm had been able to adapt to sales downturns in 1957, 1960, 1967, and 1970 and still earn profits in each of those years. By 1970, Manville had nearly $800 million in book value net worth garnered almost entirely from the mining, manufacture, and sale of asbestos products, for which it held a dominant market position.

During the 1960s, a number of the senior officials who had been with the company since the 1930s died or retired. Compared to the 1966 board of directors, the 1970 board had a majority of new members. In 1970, departing from a tradition of promoting from within, the board of directors installed an outsider, psychologist Richard Goodwin, as president. Goodwin immediately set about changing the company's image. He arranged to move the corporate headquarters from its old Madison Avenue brick building to Denver, purchasing the 10,000-acre Ken Caryl Ranch and planning a luxurious "world headquarters," the first phase of which was to cost $60 million.

Goodwin led the company through more than twenty small acquisitions — in lighting systems, golf carts, irrigation sprinklers, and other products. In the process, Manville's long-term debt went from zero to $196 million and fixed costs increased severalfold. A short, steep recession in 1975 cut Manville's profits in half, back to 1970 levels. U.S. asbestos sales had begun a rapid decline, which was to accelerate and total more than 50 percent in just 5 years. And Manville was suffering reverses in its fight against asbestos tort lawsuits, as will be discussed.

In what *Fortune* called "The Shootout at the J. M. Corral," Goodwin was removed in September 1976 and John A. McKinney, Manville's legal/public affairs chief — who had joined the company before 1950 — took over as chief executive. McKinney divested many of the Goodwin acquisitions and turned his attention to what he called "aggressive defense" of the asbestos lawsuits and the search for a "substantial acquisition." He also made plans for a $200 million expansion in the company's fiberglass operations. In his 1977 "Presidents Review," McKinney wrote, "we do not expect asbestos fiber to dominate J-M earnings to the extent it has in the past." (In 1976, asbestos fiber alone — not including manufactured asbestos products — provided about half of Manville's operating profit, though it constituted only about one-eighth of sales.)

After Ideal Basic Industries, a major producer of potash and portland cement, spurned a Manville buyout initiative, the company began a takeover battle with Texas Eastern Corporation for Olinkraft Corporation, a wood products company concentrating in paperboard and paper. Olinkraft's main assets were about 600,000 acres of prime southern timberland and several paper mills.

Manville won the battle and closed the deal in the last half of 1978. The purchase price was $595 million, half paid in cash and half represented by a new issue of preferred stock. That price was 2.24 times Olinkraft's book value and over twice its recent market value. While the Olinkraft merger was being negotiated, Manville common stock declined in value to $22, a total drop of over $225 million. Olinkraft's shares rose to approximate the purchase price of $65 a share. In conformity with purchase-method accounting, Olinkraft's assets were placed on Manville's books at the purchase price, creating over $300 million in new net worth.

Manville's sales and common stock earnings reached peaks of $2.92 billion and $144 million (expressed in constant 1981 dollars), respectively, in 1978. But both would fall steadily afterward, to $1.64 billion and a $101 million *loss* in 1982.

In 1981, management reorganized the company, separating the asbestos operations into incorporated divisions. Also, the executives surrendered their stock options for "special incentive units," which were soon to become valueless, and signed "special termination agreements," providing for large severance settlements after any "change in control" of the company. The company also reaffirmed its commitment to indemnify its executives and directors against the asbestos lawsuits.

Although Manville was able to defer the asbestos health costs (they totaled only $12 million in 1981) and extract more than $100 million in cash flows from the Olinkraft assets, the situation in early 1982 was worsening. Company debt had been downgraded. Coopers and Lybrand, the company's accounting firm, had qualified its opinion on Manville's financial reports. Manville's insurance carriers had stopped paying asbestos settlements and providing defense against the asbestos lawsuits. At the same time, the number and size of the asbestos health judgments were skyrocketing (although the large awards were all stayed by appeals). Suits frequently named Manville officials in their personal capacities. And after 1980, many juries awarded punitive damages, sometimes over $1,000,000 per claimant, in addition to compensatory damages.

The five highest-paid executives of Manville in 1982 had all been with the company since 1952 or earlier. The 1982 board of directors had the same membership as the 1976 board and was mostly unchanged since the 1960s. One of the five long-tenured executives left just before the Chapter 11 filing and others would leave afterwards, generally with severance pay and pensions. For example, on August 1, 1986, John A. McKinney retired with $1.3 million in severance pay and retirement pay exceeding $300,000 per year. His salary had increased from $408,750 to $638,005 per year while Manville was in Chapter 11.

Financial summaries are shown in Exhibit 1 (1978–June 1982) and Exhibit 2 (1982–1985).

EXHIBIT 1 Manville Corporation financial summaries, before August 26, 1982

Income statements, 1978–82 (millions)

	1982 (6 mos.)	1981	1980	1979	1978
Sales	$949	$2,186	$2,267	$2,276	$1,649
Cost of sales	784	1,731	1,771	1,747	1,190
Selling, G&A exp.	143	271	263	239	193
R&D and eng. exp.	16	34	35	31	33
Operating income	6	151	197	259	232
Other income, net	1	35	26	21	28
Interest expense	35	73	65	62	22
Income before inc. taxes	(28)	112	157	218	238
Income taxes	2	53	77	103	116
Net income	(25)	60	81	115	122
Div. on preferred stock	12	25	25	24	0
Net income for C.S.	$ (37)	$ 35	$ 55	$ 91	$ 122

Revenues and income from operations by business segment, 1976–1981 (millions)

	1981	1980	1979	1978	1977	1976
Revenues						
Fiberglass products	$ 625	$ 610	$ 573	$ 514	$ 407	$ 358
Forest products	555	508	497	0	0	0
Nonfiberglass insulation	258	279	268	231	195	159
Roofing products	209	250	273	254	204	171
Pipe products & systems	199	220	305	303	274	218
Asbestos fiber	138	159	168	157	161	155
Industrial & spec. prod.	320	341	309	291	301	309
Corporate revenues, net	12	9	11	20	12	(22)
Intersegment sales	(95)	(84)	(106)	(94)	(74)	(56)
Total	$2,221	$2,292	$2,297	$1,677	$1,480	$1,291
Income from operations						
Fiberglass products	$ 90	$ 91	$ 96	$ 107	$ 82	$ 60
Forest products	39	37	50	0	0	0
Nonfiberglass insulation	20	27	27	35	28	18
Roofing products	(17)	9	14	23	14	8
Pipe products & systems	0	(5)	18	26	24	(3)
Asbestos fiber	37	35	56	55	60	60
Industrial & spec. prod.	50	55	43	36	25	19
Corporate expense, net	(23)	(38)	(23)	(23)	(24)	(49)
Eliminations & adjustments	3	11	(2)	1	3	2
Total	$ 198	$ 223	$ 280	$ 260	$ 212	$ 116

EXHIBIT 1 (continued)

EXHIBIT 1 (continued)

Balance sheets (millions)

	June 30, 1982	1981	1980	1979	1978
		December 31			
Assets					
Cash	$ 10	$ 14	$ 20	$ 19	$ 28
Marketable securities	17	12	12	10	38
Accounts & notes receivable	348	327	350	362	328
Inventories	182	211	217	229	219
Prepaid expenses	19	19	20	31	32
Total current assets	$ 576	$ 583	$ 619	$ 650	$ 645
Property, plant & equipment					
Land & land improvements		119	118	114	99
Buildings		363	357	352	321
Machinery & equipment		1,202	1,204	1,161	1,043
		$1,685	$1,679	$1,627	$1,462
Less: accum. depr. & depl.		(525)	(484)	(430)	(374)
		$1,160	$1,195	$1,197	$1,088
Timber & timberland, net		406	407	368	372
	$1,523	$1,566	$1,602	$1,565	$1,460
Other assets	148	149	117	110	113
	$2,247	$2,298	$2,338	$2,324	$2,217
Liabilities					
Short-term debt		$ 29	$ 22	$ 32	$ 23
Accounts payable	$ 191	120	126	143	114
Employee comp. & benefits		77	80	54	45
Income taxes		30	22	51	84
Other liabilities	149	58	61	50	63
Total current liab.	$ 340	$ 316	$ 310	$ 329	$ 329
Long-term debt	499	508	519	532	543
Other noncurrent liab.	93	86	75	73	60
Deferred income taxes	186	185	211	195	150
	$1,116	$1,095	$1,116	$1,129	$1,083
Stockholders' equity					
Preferred stock	$ 301	$ 301	$ 300	$ 299	$ 299
Common stock	60	59	58	208	197
Capital in excess of par	178	174	164	0	0
Retained earnings	642	695	705	692	643
Cum. currency transl. adj.	(47)	(22)	0	0	0
Less: cost of treas. stock	(3)	(3)	(4)	(4)	(6)
	$1,131	$1,203	$1,222	$1,196	$1,134
Total	$2,247	$2,298	$2,338	$2,324	$2,217

Note: Totals may not check, due to rounding.

EXHIBIT 2 Manville Corporation financial summaries, after August 26, 1982

Income statements, 1982–1985 (millions)

	1985	1984	1983	1982
Sales	$1,880	$1,814	$1,729	$1,772
Other income, net	62	59	61	34
	1,942	1,873	1,791	1,806
Cost of sales	1,473	1,400	1,370	1,391
Selling, G&A expenses	246	238	224	222
R&D and eng. exp.	35	36	35	28
Operating income	188	200	161	163
Gain on disp. of assets	151	0	(3)	110
Asbestos health costs	52	26	20	16
Interest expense	23	21	26	52
Chapter 11 costs	9	17	18	2
Income from cont. oper.	(47)	135	100	(56)
Income taxes	(1)	58	40	35
Net income from cont. opers.	45	77	60	88
Net income from discont. oper.	0	0	7	10
Net income	$ 45	$ 77	$ 67	$ 98

Revenues and income from operations by business segment (millions)

	1985	1984	1983	1982
Revenues				
Fiberglass products	$ 803	$ 781	$ 718	$ 609
Forest products	459	451	415	436
Specialty products	674	645	683	829
Corporate revenues, net	43	38	36	15
Intersegment sales	(37)	(42)	(61)	(82)
Total	$1,942	$1,873	$1,791	$1,806
Income from operations				
Fiberglass products	$ 106	$ 115	$ 97	$ 75
Forest products	43	63	52	48
Specialty products	33	28	19	51
Corporate expense, net	(1)	(6)	(6)	(18)
Eliminations & adjustments	7	0	0	7
	$ 188	$ 200	$ 161	$ 164

EXHIBIT 2 (continued)

EXHIBIT 2 (continued)

Balance sheets (millions)

		Decem	ber 31	
	1985	1984	1983	1982
Assets				
Cash	$ 7	$ 9	$ 19	$ 11
Marketable securities, at cost	314	276	240	206
Accounts and notes receivable	314	285	277	310
Inventories	153	164	141	152
Prepaid expenses	29	17	22	17
Total current assets	817	752	700	696
Property, plant & equipment				
Land and land improvements	95	96	97	108
Buildings	299	308	303	332
Machinery & equipment	1,160	1,121	1,036	1,090
Less: accum. depr. & depl.	538	513	472	547
	1,017	1,013	984	983
Timber & timberland, net	385	392	395	402
	1,402	1,405	1,379	1,385
Other assets	174	182	174	154
	$2,393	$2,339	$2,253	$2,236
Liabilities				
Short-term debt	$ 26	$ 20	$ 94	$ 12
Accounts payable	84	102	65	86
Accr. employee comp. & benefits	94	81	14	63
Income taxes	12	18	9	32
Other accr. liabilities	69	35	26	29
Total current liab.	286	256	209	221
Long-term debt	92	84	713	736
Liab. subj. to Chap. 11 proceedings	578	574	5	12
Other noncurrent liab.	115	67	61	60
Deferred income taxes	144	162	136	140
	1,214	1,142	1,122	1,170
Stockholders' Equity				
Preferred stock	$ 301	$ 301	$ 301	$ 301
Common stock	60	60	60	60
Capital in excess of par	178	178	178	178
Retained earnings	667	713	635	568
Cum. currency transl. adj.	(26)	(53)	(41)	(39)
Cost of treas. stock	(2)	(2)	(2)	(2)
	878	896	831	765
Total	$2,393	$2,339	$2,253	$2,236

Note: Totals may not check, due to rounding.

THE ASBESTOS TORT LAWSUITS

Beginning in the 1920s a steadily increasing number of lawsuits were filed on behalf of Manville employees who had fallen ill or died from breathing asbestos dust (made up of microscopic fibers released as the product is mined or otherwise handled — or through normal deterioration as asbestos-containing buildings and machines vibrate and as asbestos tiles, roof coverings, brake linings, water pipes, and so forth are eroded or abraded). By 1982 there was litigation pending against the company on behalf of over 16,000 persons, who generally claimed that their injuries (mostly asbestosis[1]) had resulted from Manville's suppression and manipulation of research and publicity about asbestos dangers. An average of 425 cases were filed each month in the first half of 1982 and the company's projections were for over 32,000 new cases by the year 2001. Appendix A provides a chronology of selected events related to the asbestos lawsuits.

THE BANKRUPTCY REORGANIZATION

Manville Corporation and its twenty main subsidiaries filed petitions for reorganization under Chapter 11 of the U. S. Bankruptcy code on August 26, 1982. (Appendix B provides a description of bankruptcy reorganization.) The company would later cite management's stated desire to "obtain prompt and equitable payment" of all allowed claims and to "create and preserve values to the extent possible" for the equity holders as reasons for the filings. Manville's two Canadian divisions, which owned the world's largest asbestos mine and some asbestos manufacturing facilities, emerged from reorganization in 1983 and Manville sold the common stock of those divisions to a group headed by the divisions' managers. Under the sale agreement, Manville will continue to share the profits of these divisions. Also, the Forest Products Division emerged from reorganization in 1984, paying all its creditors essentially the full value of their claims. That division remained a subsidiary of Manville Corporation.

On May 23, 1986, Manville submitted its "Second Amended and Restated Plan of Reorganization" for the remaining divisions. The plan had the support of the legal representative the court had appointed to represent future asbestos victims and each of the claimant committees except the one representing equity holders.

---

[1] Ingested asbestos causes mechanical injury to moving tissue, especially the lungs. The microscopic fibers are impervious to body fluids and oxygen and are almost impossible to filter out of air. The constant motion of the lungs causes tissue to be penetrated and cut by the fibers. This leads to progressive and irreversible scarring, thickening, and calcification of the lungs and their linings, a condition called asbestosis. A rare and always fatal cancer, mesothelioma, is strongly connected with asbestos exposure as are increased incidence and severity of many other respiratory ailments. The first outward symptoms of asbestos disease typically appear 10 to 30 years after exposure begins. But early damage is easily detectable by X-rays and some cancers and respiratory deficiencies show up after only a year or two.

Ballots were mailed to unsecured creditors (including asbestos claimants) and equity holders in September 1986 and confirmation hearings were scheduled to begin in December that year. Appendix C summarizes the Manville reorganization plan.

Based on a liquidation analysis performed by Morgan Stanley and Company, Manville estimated that liquidation would provide 47 to 69 percent recovery for asbestos claims (including property damage claims) and unsecured creditor claims. Manville estimated that execution of the plan would provide 99 to 100 percent recovery for these claims.

APPENDIX A: SELECTED EVENTS CONCERNING ASBESTOS AND HEALTH

1898: Manville founder and inventor of uses for asbestos, Henry Ward Johns, dies of "dust phthisis pneumonitis," later known as asbestosis.

1929: Manville defends early lawsuits for asbestos deaths. The company claims employees assumed the risks of employment, knew or should have known the dangers, and were contributorily negligent. Legal documents in these cases bear signatures of senior Manville officials who would remain with the company until the 1960s.

1930: Dr. A. J. Lanza of Metropolitan Life Insurance Company (Manville's insurer) begins a 4-year study on the "Effects of Inhalation of Asbestos Dust upon the Lungs of Asbestos Workers."

1933: Based on interim results of his study, Dr. Lanza suggests Manville engage an outside consultant to do dust counts at company plants. A decision is made to train an insider to do this rather than bring in someone from outside the company.

1934: Asbestosis considered for classification as a disease for workmen's compensation purposes. Manville's chief attorney writes to the company:

> In particular we have urged that asbestosis should not at the present time be included in the list of compensation diseases, for the reason that it is only within a comparatively recent time that asbestosis has been recognized by the medical and scientific professions as a disease — in fact one of our principal defenses in actions against the company on the common law theory of negligence has been that the scientific and medical knowledge has been insufficient until a very recent period to place on the owners of plants or factories the burden or duty of taking special precautions against the possible onset of the disease in their employees.

After reviewing a draft of Dr. Lanza's report, Manville vice-president and corporate secretary Vandiver Brown writes Dr. Lanza requesting changes. His letter states:

> All we ask is that all of the favorable aspects of the survey be included and that none of the unfavorable be unintentionally pictured in darker terms than the circumstances justify. I feel confident that we can depend upon you and Dr. McConnel to give us this 'break.'

1935: Brown writes another industry executive, Sumner Simpson, "I quite agree that our interests are best served by having asbestosis receive the minimum of publicity.'' He is commenting on Simpson's response to a letter by Anne Rossiter (editor of the industry journal *Asbestos*) in which she has written:

> *You may recall that we have written you on several occasions concerning the publishing of information, or discussion of, asbestosis. . . . Always you have requested that for obvious reasons, we publish nothing, and, naturally your wishes have been respected.*

1936: Messrs. Brown and Simpson convince nine other asbestos companies to provide a total of $417 per month for the industry's own 3-year study of the effects of asbestos dust on guinea pigs and rabbits by Dr. LeRoy U. Gardner. Simpson writes Gardner, ''we could determine from time to time after the findings were made, whether we wish any publication or not.'' In a separate letter, Brown states, ''the manuscript of your study will be submitted to us for approval prior to publication.'' Gardner will tell the companies of ''significant changes in guinea pigs' lungs within a period of one year'' and ''fibrosis'' produced by long fibers and ''chronic inflammation'' caused by short fibers. He makes several requests for additional funding but dies in 1946 without reporting final results.

1940: Lawsuits have increased in number through the 1930s, but Manville continues to successfully defend or settle them, using the same defenses as in the 1920s but adding a statute-of-limitations defense, made possible by the long latency period of asbestos diseases. The companies continue to be able to prevent significant publicity about asbestos and health. World War II will bring spiraling sales and profits, as thousands of tons of asbestos are used in building war machines, mainly ships — resulting in exposure of tens of thousands of shipyard workers and seamen, thousands of whom die of asbestos diseases decades later.

1947: A study by the Industrial Hygiene Foundation of America finds that from 3 to 20 percent of asbestos plant workers already have asbestosis and a Manville plant employing three hundred is producing ''5 or 6 cases annually that the physician believes show early changes due to asbestos.''

1950: Dr. Kenneth W. Smith, Manville chief physician, has given superiors his report that of 708 workers he studied, only 4 were free of asbestos disease. Concerning the more serious cases, he has written:

> *The fibrosis of this disease is irreversible and permanent so that eventually compensation will be paid to each of these men but as long as the man is not disabled it is felt that he should not be told of his condition so that he can live and work in peace and the company can benefit from his many years of experience.*

1952: John A. McKinney, Fred L. Pundsack, Chester E. Shepperly, Monroe Harris, and Chester J. Sulewski (who later are Manville's top five officers as it prepares to seek bankruptcy court protection in 1982) have all joined the company in various capacities.

1953: Dr. Smith tries to convince senior Manville managers to authorize caution labeling for asbestos. In a 1976 deposition, he will characterize their responses: ''We recognize the potential hazard that you mentioned, the suggested use of a caution label. We will discuss it among ourselves and make a decision.'' Asked why he was overruled, Smith will say, "application of a caution label identifying a product as hazardous would cut out sales."

1956: The board of governors of the Asbestos Textile Institute (made up of Manville and other asbestos companies) meets to discuss the increasing publicity about asbestos and cancer and agrees that "every effort should be made to disassociate this relationship until such a time that there is sufficient and authoritative information to substantiate such to be a fact."

1957: The Asbestos Textile Institute rejects a proposal by the Industrial Health Foundation that asbestos companies fund a study on asbestos and cancer. Institute minutes report, "There is a feeling among certain members that such an investigation would stir up a hornet's nest and put the whole industry under suspicion."

1959: An increasing number of articles connecting asbestos with various diseases has appeared in scholarly medical journals over the past few years.

1963: Dr. I. J. Selikoff, of Mount Sinai Medical Center in New York, reads a report of his study of asbestos workers before the American Medical Association meeting. Like the earlier research, the Selikoff study implicates asbestos ingestion as the causal factor in many thousands of deaths and injuries. Selikoff will soon estimate that at least 100,000 more Americans will die of asbestos diseases this century. The study and the articles, news stories, and academic papers that follow focus public attention on the asbestos and health issue. An estimated one hundred articles on asbestos-related diseases appear in 1964 alone.

1964: For the first time, Manville agrees to place caution labels on asbestos products. The labels say, "Inhalation of asbestos in excessive quantities over long periods of time may be harmful" and suggests that users avoid breathing the dust and wear masks if "adequate ventilation control is not possible." The consistent position of Manville managers regarding their failure to warn users earlier is restated in 1986:

> During the periods of alleged injurious exposure, medical and scientific authorities, government officials and companies supplying products containing asbestos fiber believed that the dust levels for asbestos recommended by the United States Public Health Service did not constitute a hazard to the health of workers handling asbestos-containing insulation products. Accordingly, the company has maintained that there was no basis for product warnings or special hazard controls until the 1964 publication of results of scientific studies linking pulmonary disease in asbestos insulation workers with asbestos exposure. (emphasis added)

1970: The senior managers and directors from the 1930s have retired, most within the past few years. Compared to the 1966 board of directors, the 1970 board has a majority of new members. The five managers who joined the company in the late 1940s and early 1950s and who will lead Manville into Chapter 11 reorganization are in senior positions now — McKinney and Pundsack are vice-presidents. However, outsider Richard Goodwin is installed as president.

1973: Manville and other asbestos companies lose their last appeal in the case of Clarence Borel, who died of mesothelioma and asbestosis before the decision.

In reviewing the case, the U. S. Court of Appeals writes what many considered a scorching indictment of Manville and the other defendants. The court concludes:

> *By the mid-1930s the hazard of asbestos as a pneumoconiotic dust was universally accepted. . . . Indeed the evidence tended to establish that the defendants gave no instructions or warnings at all. . . . The unpalatable facts are that in the twenties and thirties the hazards of working with asbestos were recognized.*

Concerning the caution labels, which came after Borel's exposure, the decision states:

> *None of the so-called 'cautions' intimated the gravity of the risk: the danger of a fatal illness caused by asbestosis and mesothelioma or other cancers. . . . The admonition that a worker should "avoid breathing the dust" is black humor: there was no way for insulation workers to avoid breathing asbestos dust.*

1976: Psychologist Richard Goodwin is asked to resign as president and lawyer/public affairs specialist John A. McKinney takes over. McKinney is shortly elevated to chairman of the board and Fred Pundsack becomes president. Asbestos use is dropping rapidly and Goodwin has increased long-term debt from zero to $196 million by buying companies in other fields. But asbestos is still so profitable that the fiber alone — not including manufactured asbestos products — produces 51 percent of Manville's operating profit while constituting only about 12 percent of sales.

1977: A mass of papers from asbestos company files, variously called the "Sumner Simpson Papers" and the "Raybestos-Manhattan Correspondence" is accidentally discovered by plaintiff attorneys and presented in a New Jersey asbestos lawsuit. The papers include the letters from the 1930s mentioned earlier. In admitting the new evidence in another trial, a South Carolina judge will soon write:

> *The Raybestos-Manhattan correspondence reveals written evidence that Raybestos-Manhattan and Johns-Manville exercised an editorial prerogative over the publication of the first study of the asbestos industry which they sponsored in 1935. It further reflects a conscious effort by the industry to downplay, or arguably suppress, the dissemination of information to employees and the public for fear of the promotion of lawsuits.*

1978: The stream of asbestos lawsuits has become a flood. Armed with the Raybestos-Manhattan Correspondence, asbestos victims are seeking huge amounts, often including punitive damages. The Manville executives choose not to mention the lawsuits in the 1977 annual report, but the Securities and Exchange Commission report on Form 10K reveals that there are now 623 asbestos lawsuits for amounts totaling at least $2.79 billion. This year alone, the number of suits doubles. Many court decisions are going against Manville, although the company is able to delay paying in most cases by appealing decisions, requesting new trials, and other legal tactics.

1979: Asbestos use declines another 35 percent this year alone. This is compounded by a recession in construction lasting through 1982. Manville's sales and earnings, buoyed by the Olinkraft acquisition to $2.92 billion and $144 million, respectively, start a steady decline leading to sales of only $1.64 billion in 1982 and a $100 million annual-rate loss for the first half of that year. (These figures are in constant 1981 dollars.)

1981: No significant changes in senior managers or directors have occurred since 1976. The directors decide to reorganize the company, segregating the asbestos-related elements into separately incorporated divisions. Special termination agreements, commonly called "golden parachutes," are approved for all the top executives. Actual asbestos health costs have never been a significant expense and this year total only $12 million, less than one-half of one percent of sales. But Manville is now losing many cases — and, shown the Raybestos-Manhattan Correspondence and other new evidence, juries frequently award hundreds of thousands of dollars in punitive damages. Manville's insurers are refusing to pay, or even to provide defense against, the asbestos lawsuits. Many of the recent lawsuits name the directors and officers personally — but the recently restated corporate bylaws promise that the company will indemnify them.

1982: Manville continues to forestall payments to asbestos claimants through repeated appeals and other legal tactics. But the company's operations are increasingly unprofitable and major losses are reported for both the first and second quarters. The asbestos judgments increase in number and magnitude. A consulting firm hired by Manville reports that 40,000 additional lawsuits will cost the company $1.9 billion by the year 2001. Upon the recommendation of McKinney and three outside directors, the board of directors approves the Chapter 11 filing on the evening of August 25 and the necessary papers are filed in the U. S. Bankruptcy Court for the Southern District of New York the next day. All the asbestos lawsuits and all efforts to collect previously won judgments are stopped. Within a few days the company is awash in cash, as accounts receivable flow-in and $615 million in debt is stayed. An estimated 2,000 of the 16,500 present asbestos claimants will die during the years Manville is negotiating its reorganization plan, and, with few exceptions, none of the 16,500 will be paid. In support of Manville's decision to reorganize under bankruptcy law, First Boston Corporation and Morgan Stanley and Company prepare secret reports estimating the "going concern value" of the company's assets at slightly above their $1.8 billion liquidation value.

APPENDIX B: HOW CHAPTER 11 WORKS

Chapter 11 of the U. S. Bankruptcy Code is based upon the assumption that a business is worth more as a going concern than in liquidation. If this is true, stockholders and creditors may get more out of a troubled company by allowing it to continue operating than by shutting it down. Additional benefits of keeping the company operating are that employees keep their jobs and the community keeps the tax base and economic and social activity related to the firm.

To assure maintenance of the company's value and equitable distribution of claims on that value, a U. S. bankruptcy judge assumes oversight of any firm that desires to "reorganize" under Chapter 11. Insolvency is not a prerequisite. A committee of unsecured creditors and one made up of stockholders are appointed to assist management and the court in arriving at an equitable plan. Other committees or advocates may be established to represent interests that diverge from those of shareholders and unsecured creditors.

In negotiations with the committees, company executives prepare a formal reorganization plan and submit it to creditor and stockholder groups for approval. One hundred eighty days is allowed for this, but the period is routinely extended. If all impaired classes of claimants approve the plan, the court may confirm it and place it into effect. "Impaired" claimants are those whose legal, equitable, or contractual rights are modified by the plan, except by curing defaults and reinstating maturity or providing for cash payment. The plan may also be confirmed if the judge holds that it treats nonapproving impaired classes equally with respect to other classes of equal rank and that allowed claims of nonapproving classes will be fully satisfied under the plan before more junior classes receive any distribution at all.

While the plan is being negotiated, approved, and confirmed, all prefiling claims are stayed. Executory contracts may be unilaterally canceled by the debtor and mortgaged assets may be abandoned to mortgagees. Management operates the company in the "ordinary course of business" and is protected against direct control or removal by stockholders. Major assets, including whole divisions, may be divested with court approval.

Ideally, the plan will provide that the value of the going concern that emerges from reorganization will be allocated first to the administrative costs of the proceeding and then to the claimant classes in order of their "absolute priority in liquidation." This suggests that prefiling claims on the debtor estate will be satisfied in this sequence: (1) secured debt (up to the value of respective collateral as of the filing date), (2) unsecured debt, and (3) equity claims in order of preference (e.g., preferred, then common). However, plans commonly depart from this "fair and equitable" standard in order to get the support of junior claimant classes. Also, the "value" claimants receive may be in the form of cash, securities, or other real or personal property.

Provision is made to pay postfiling claims as they come due. To insure that the reorganized firm is viable, prefiling claims not provided for in the plan are discharged.

APPENDIX C: SELECTED PROVISIONS OF THE MANVILLE REORGANIZATION PLAN

Class 1 claims (unpaid administrative expenses totaling about $26 million, most administrative costs being paid as accrued) will be paid in full upon consummation.

Class 2 claims (secured debts) will be reinstated, with interest, and $13.4 million in arrearages will be paid in cash.

Class 3 claims (over $80 billion in property damage claims — due to the need to remove asbestos from existing buildings — most of which were filed after 1982) will be paid as they are "liquidated" from the PD Trust (set up to pay the property damage claims). The PD Trust will be initially funded with $125 million in cash and any insurance proceeds in excess of the $615 million committed to fund the trust for asbestos health claims ("the Trust"). Any future funding for the PD Trust will come from the excess of that needed by the Trust to pay asbestos health claims.

Class 4 claims (existing asbestos health claims, totaling over $30.5 billion, and claims for contribution and indemnity by Manville's asbestos company codefendants) will be paid from the Trust as they are liquidated and approved by the "Claims Resolution Facility," to be controlled by a panel of trustees approved by the bankruptcy court. (None of the initial trustees has been affiliated with Manville Corporation.) The Trust will also be responsible for defending asbestos lawsuits brought against it, Manville, past and present Manville executives and directors, and certain insurance companies. Future asbestos health claims are not classified, but they will also be paid from the Trust as liquidated. The Trust will be funded with the following assets:

1. All rights under Settlement Agreements Manville has or will execute with its insurers by the Consummation Date (30 days after an order of the bankruptcy court confirming the plan becomes final and unappealable). Manville reported the "face value" of these agreements to be $505 million as of May 23, 1986. Payment of the agreed amounts by the Settling Insurers is contingent upon a number of conditions, among them approval of the agreements by the bankruptcy court (none had been approved when Manville filed its plan) and a final and unappealable court order barring future asbestos claims against the insurers.

2. $150 million in cash and accounts receivable.

3. A $50 million unsecured Manville Corporation note, promising payment with interest in two equal installments in the third and fourth years after the Consummation Date.

4. A Manville Corporation unsecured bond requiring payments of $75 million a year, without interest, from the fourth through the twenty-fifth year after the Consummation Date, subject to deferral after the thirteenth year if the Trust is adequately funded in accordance with specified standards.

5. A Manville Corporation unsecured bond requiring payment of $75 million in the twenty-sixth and twenty-seventh years after the Consummation Date, subject to deferral if the Trust is adequately funded in accordance with specified standards.

6. Certain interest on amounts set aside to fund the Trust if consummation occurs later than July 1987.

7. If needed by the Trust in accordance with specified standards and starting in the fifth year after consummation, up to 20 percent of Manville's profits and 20 percent of proceeds from the federal government. (Manville claims government should pay part of the asbestos costs mainly because many of the claims resulted from work on navy ships.)

8. One-half of Manville's common stock at consummation. For four years after consummation the Trust must vote this stock for management's nominees for director-ships unless Manville allows certain events to occur that might prejudice the Trust. With certain exceptions, this stock cannot be transferred by the Trust for years after consummation. The company has the right of first refusal on any sale of common stock by the Trust that would result in the buyer holding more than 15 percent of Manville's outstanding common stock.

9. New convertible preferred stock which would give the Trust 80 percent of the firm's common equity if converted on the Consummation Date. (Convertibility is restricted.)

Class 5 claims (about $20 million in miscellaneous claims on behalf of employees, users of defective roofing and siding products, and so forth) will be paid in full as liquidated, requiring payment of about $1 million in cash upon consummation.

Class 6 claims (unsecured claims not to exceed $472.5 million and not included in other classes) will be paid as follows:

1. Paid in cash if under $10,000 or if holder is willing to reduce claim to $10,000.

2. Paid pro rata share of $247.5 million less amounts paid in compliance with (1), just above.

3. Issued "Class 6 Note" for remaining principal amount of claim. Class 6 Notes will be four and one-half year, unsecured obligations of Manville Corporation drawing 12 percent interest and requiring biannual payments after consummation of at least $33.75 million each. They may be redeemed by Manville at any time and may be accelerated under certain conditions.

4. Paid cash for certain interest and investment income which will accrue if consummation does not occur by July 1, 1987.

5. Issued "Class 6 Interest Debentures," Series B preference stock, common stock, and common stock warrants for interest accrued from August 26, 1982 (the date of Manville's Chapter 11 petition) to the Consummation Date.

Class 7 claimants (preferred stock holders) will receive for each preferred share a share of new "Series B preference stock" which will pay cumulative dividends of $2.70 per share beginning 6 years after consummation (if certain conditions are met) and about 1.94 shares of common stock.

Class 8 claimants (common stock holders) will receive their pro rata share of 8.3 percent of common shares outstanding at consummation, subject to further dilution down to about 3 percent.

Class 9 claimants (certain purchasers of Manville common stock who have sued the company and certain of its officers and directors in federal court) will receive payment to the extent of certain insurance proceeds.

Among the "conditions precedent" to consummation of the plan are final and unappealable court orders establishing the following:

1. Any future asbestos health claims against Manville, the Settling Insurers, or the Canadian subsidiaries divested in 1983 are prohibited.

2. Allowed Class 6 claims (unsecured claims not elsewhere classified) will never exceed $472.5 million.

3. No punitive damages will be allowed for Class 3 or Class 4 claims (asbestos property damage and asbestos health claims) except for previously issued final judgments respecting liquidated asbestos health claims.

4. All transfers of property to the trusts by Manville are "legal, valid and effective transfers," vest "good title to such property free and clear of all encumbrances, debts, obligations, liabilities, and claims other than asbestos claims as contemplated by the Plan," are not "fraudulent," and "do not, except as contemplated by the Plan, subject the Trusts to any liability."

5. Certain agreements with the Settling Insurers are approved.

After consummation of the plan, Manville's fifteen-person board of directors will consist of eight preconsummation directors and seven new directors. Two of the new directors will be chosen from persons suggested by representatives of the asbestos health claimants, three from a list of candidates approved by Manville and representatives of the asbestos health claimants, one from a list approved by Manville and the Unsecured Creditors' Committee, and another selected by the board of directors in consultation with claimant committees.

The eight preconsummation directors include six outside directors. The years they joined the Manville board are as follows: three in 1969, one in 1972, one in 1976, and the last in 1982. The outside director who joined in 1982 did so when his firm was hired as Manville's Chapter 11 law firm. The two inside directors are Manville's senior inside lawyer, G. Earl Parker, and the president, W. Thomas Stephens. The chairman of the board will be George C. Dillon, who has been a director of Manville since 1969.

The new directors include the chief executive of a regional discount store chain, the chief financial officer of a national department store chain, a professor of finance, a management consultant, a lawyer, and a financial consultant.

BARCELONA TRACTION, LIGHT AND POWER COMPANY, LIMITED

THE DIRECTOR'S MEETING, YEAR-END, 1947

At the close of calendar year 1947, Dannie Heineman, Henri Speciael, and the other directors of Barcelona Traction, Light and Power Company were reviewing the history of the company's relations with Sr. Juan March in order to determine what steps should be taken with regard to its Spanish operations and what moves might be expected from Sr. March. One director noted:

> *They say in Spain Juan March is Spain's greatest capitalist, but he reminds me more of a nineteenth century robber baron. He has nerve and patience, and is highly skilled, if that's an appropriate word, at bribery. He is always accompanied by Bernardo, his bodyguard, and there are many rumors about his role in smuggling, wartime espionage, and even assassinations.*
>
> *A few times we've had to take actions, such as getting currency out of Spain during World War II at the request of the British government, that might not look totally ethical. We've avoided some Spanish taxes, and we've paid "commissions" to minimize competition, but "robber barons" we're not. We've always fought for our shareholders.*
>
> *March has been trying to get control of us since 1940, and now he's buying up all our pound sterling bonds. We can't make payments in sterling because Franco, March's friend, won't let us convert pesetas into sterling. March helped Franco during the Civil War, but this is a new era. Spain needs the West. And March knows this. So why is he buying our bonds?*
>
> *Possession, even majority possession, of bonds doesn't give control, except if a firm is bankrupt. And we're anything but bankrupt. We've got $15,000,000 in pesetas in Spain.*
>
> *What's Sr. "Robber Baron" up to, anyway?*

Case prepared by John Barnett primarily from material included in two "Annals of Finance" articles appearing in *The New Yorker* (May 21 and May 28, 1979) by John Brooks. This case was written as the basis for class discussion and is not intended to illustrate either effective or ineffective handling of an administrative situation. Mr. Brooks included this material in the chapter entitled "Spanish Privateer" in his book *The Games Players* (New York: Times Books, 1981). © 1987 by John Barnett. Reprinted by permission.

The following pages describe the background of the company and the overtures made by Sr. March, beginning in 1940 and continuing until the present.

BARCELONA TRACTION LTD.

Barcelona Traction, Light and Power Company, Ltd., was organized by an American engineer with mainly British backing. The American, Fred Pearson, had previously been responsible for hydroelectric plants in Mexico and Brazil. Fred Pearson and Carlos Montanes, the principals who planned Barcelona Traction, first viewed the hydroelectric project from the Catalan peak of Tibidabo, the place according to Spanish legend where Satan tempted Christ. The firm was incorporated in 1911 in the Canadian province of Ontario because of favorable tax laws granted there to hydroelectric utilities. The company developed the tremendous hydroelectric potential of the mountainous Catalan region west of the city of Barcelona. The company maintained its corporate offices in Toronto, while its two principal Spanish operating subsidiaries were Ebro Irrigation and Power Company, Ltd., and Barcelona Electric Company. By 1946, Barcelona Traction's Spanish subsidiaries were generating 15 percent of Spain's total electricity.

In 1911 and 1915, Barcelona Traction sold two issues of sterling bonds due 50 years later. The bonds were nominally issued in Great Britain, but were sold internationally. These bonds were Prior Lien indentures which would be superior to all other obligations in bankruptcy. Holders of the sterling bonds were entitled to receive all interest and eventual principal repayment in pound sterling. To meet this indenture requirement, Barcelona Traction's management expected to exchange the pesetas earned from its subsidiaries in Spain for pound sterling purchased from Spain's Institute of Foreign Exchange.

In 1923 Barcelona Traction's ownership changed hands when 75 percent of its 2 million common shares were purchased by the large Belgian holding company SIDRO (Société Internationale d'Energie Hydro Electrique), led by Alfred Lowenstein. The following year, SIDRO, faced with financial difficulty, sold controlling interest in SIDRO's shares to another Belgian holding company, SOFINA (Société Financière de Transport et d'Entreprises Industrielles). SIDRO's stock was enough to give SOFINA control of Barcelona Traction. Consequently, by the midtwenties, Barcelona Traction had assumed quite a complex international structure. It operated solely in Spain through subsidiaries, was incorporated and domiciled in Toronto for tax purposes, was financed by British and Spanish debentures, but was wholly owned by SIDRO and, ultimately, SOFINA of Belgium. By 1947, 90 percent of the shareholders were Belgian nationals. Only a few shareholders were Canadian. Exhibit 1 illustrates this structure.

This international structure did not go unnoticed in the Spanish Cortes (parliament) where many felt key Spanish industries ought to be Spanish-owned. During its history, Barcelona Traction has been accused of avoiding Spanish taxes and other "vices" of the multinational firm. Sir Wardock, a British attorney working for the

EXHIBIT 1
Corporate structure

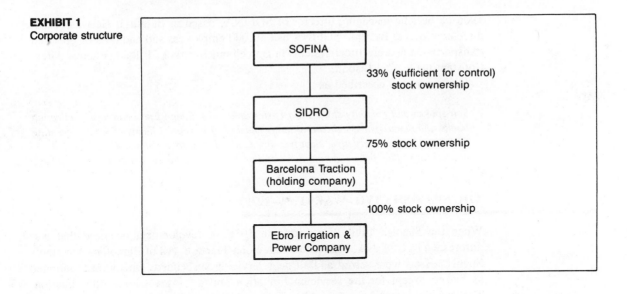

Spanish government, comments that the company's history repeatedly shows traces of "the cloven hoof."[1] During World War II, for example, funds were taken out of Spain to "safer" countries.

The real economic consequences of "safe-currency" maneuvers and tax-minimization steps are known only to those with inside knowledge. Barcelona had used commissions, bribes, and other means to try to control its competition, but "commissions" are the normal course of business affairs in Spain.

Fred Pearson was lost in May 1915, while en route to Britain aboard the Lusitania, which was sunk by a German submarine.

Alfred Lowenstein, the Belgian financier who acquired Barcelona Traction in 1923, reportedly fell out of his private plane while crossing the English Channel in 1928, apparently unnoticed by his pilot, mechanic, two stenographers, and valet, all of whom were aboard the plane, in "one of the strangest fatalities in the history of commercial aviation."[2]

DANNIE HEINEMAN

SOFINA's managing director was D. N. Heineman. Born in North Carolina in 1872, Dannie N. Heineman and his mother moved to Germany after his father's death in 1880. He graduated from the University of Hanover with a degree in electrical engineering and took a job with a General Electric affiliate in Berlin. In

---

[1] John Brooks, "Annals of Finance," *New Yorker*, May 21 and 29, 1979.

[2] John Brooks, op. cit.

1905 he became managing director of SOFINA, based in Belgium. He was one of three employees. By 1940 SOFINA had 40,000 employees and had built or operated transportation and electrical systems in Barcelona, Bangkok, Bilbao, Buenos Aires, Constantinople, and Lisbon.

Heineman was described as

> *Soft-spoken and publicity shy . . . a businessman in the high European style, collecting books and manuscripts, cultivating the friendship of European heads of state, operating SOFINA along conservative, debt-free lines, and liking to discuss politics, writing, or music in his office before getting down to business . . . actually uninterested in money.*

THE SPANISH CIVIL WAR (1936–1939)

When the Spanish Civil War started in 1936, a development occurred that was unforeseen by SOFINA, SIDRO, or Barcelona Traction. All of Barcelona Traction's Spanish assets were seized and all debt servicing suspended. Operations continued as before except for the servicing limitation and a "fuzzy" asset title situation. The seizure was by the Republican government, which held parts of Catalonia throughout the war. Upon Franco's victory over the Republic, the company was returned to its owners.

Franco, a rightist military leader, rose against the Spanish Republic (1931–1939), which had come into being after the dictator de Rivera (1923–1930). England initially supported Franco and later maintained a neutral stance. Outside intervention prolonged this extremely bitter civil war, as eventually Germany and Italy supported Franco, while the Soviet Union plus some independent liberal groups such as the Abraham Lincoln brigade supported the Republic. The Republic fell shortly after the end of Soviet assistance, which followed the nonaggression pact between Germany and Russia.

In the *Twenty-Second Annual Report*, which covered the period January 1, 1936–December 31, 1940, Ebro President Fraser Lawton described the Civil War period:

> *On 18 July 1936 fighting began in Barcelona. . . . Confusion reigned and foreigners of many nationalities were pressed by their consulates to leave the country: consequently we lost a number of our foreign employees but most of the chiefs of departments and of the other more responsible employees remained.*
>
> *Early in September 1936 an open conflict arose between the workers' committee and myself on account of my refusal to sign cheques for normal payments so long as the committee retained in their possession funds of the company exceeding a million pesetas and continued to seize all collections. They were able to circumvent my refusal, however, as the "Red" Government's interventor instructed the banks to accept his and the committees' signatures and to ignore mine.*
>
> *At this period we were instructed to leave the country.*
>
> *Many of us were taken off by the British naval ships, and others got away by road.*
>
> *In April 1938, the forces under General Franco advanced sufficiently to liberate some of the more important hydraulic plants which were taken over at once by our engineers.*

The directors' report continued:

> *July 18, 1936 to January 26, 1939 was the period during which the Workers' Committee had assumed complete control of the enterprises under the authority of the "Red" Government. The results of the trading for such period are unknown.*
>
> *The funds belonging to the Ebro Company in the hands of Bankers in Spain at the outbreak of the Civil War in July 1936 amounted to approximately pts. 36,700,000. At the 26th of January 1939, the date when the Nationalist forces occupied Barcelona, the above amount had increased to 54,128,000. The Ebro Company has now obtained through the proper authorities a restitution of the greater portion of such funds . . . [although none to date of the] gold coin equal to 10,898,000 . . . removed by the authority of the "Red" Government.*

The financial consequences of the Spanish Civil War were described in the *Twenty-Second Annual Report* (1936–1940) and *Twenty-Third Annual Report* (1941):

> *[During this] period . . . the Workers' Committee had assumed complete control of the enterprises under the authority of the "Red" Government. . . . It is necessary to appropriate $17,618,000 from the Earned Surplus account to cover the losses of the Spanish subsidiaries for the period . . . due to physical damages . . . during the Civil War. All surplus reserves and revenues balances have been absorbed, leaving a net deficit of $3,494,900.* (Twenty-Second Annual Report)

The Steam Plants suffered considerable damage during the Civil War.

	Normal capacity (kw)	Present effective capacity
Calle Mata	27,000	10,000
San Adrian	27,000	
Figols	10,000	
Tortosa	750	750
Calle Carreras	2,700	
	67,450	10,750

Repairs are being continued. (Twenty-Third Annual Report)

After Franco's victory came the reestablishment of a relatively stable operating environment. Assets were returned to Barcelona Traction, although profits had fallen badly. However, management were still frustrated with their inability to have the ban on their debt serving lifted. In 1940, the Franco government finally permitted the resumption of servicing on the peseta bonds, but refused to lift the foreign exchange restrictions which effectively curtailed the resumption of servicing on the sterling debentures. Barcelona Traction's plea to government officials to sell them the pound sterling foreign exchange came to no avail.

A Canadian publication, *The Financial Post's* "Survey of Corporate Securities," included these comments:

> *Steady improvement in the position and outlook for Barcelona has been evident since the reorganization of 1924, when readjustments in capitalization were achieved. Captain Alfred Lowenstein, the spectacular Belgian financier, is on the Board of Directors of this Company and there have been reports that he and his associates now control the enterprise. . . . Investment is more promising than it has been since the war.*
>
> *The Company has fourteen hydroelectric power plants, two steam power plants, forty-two miles of railway lines, and many miles of transmission lines. (1927)*

> *It is probably that control of this Company now rests in Britain and Continental Europe. . . . The outlook . . . continues favorable under the present excellent management. (1929)*

> *The outlook for this Company remains promising. (1930)*

> *Future progress is dependent upon the political stability attained by the country. (1931)*

FINANCIAL HIGHLIGHTS

Exhibit 2 presents selected data on the company.

From 1942 to 1946 the company continued its profitable operations, as the table shows:

	1942	1943	1944	1945	1946
Revenue (000's)	$4,234	$4,542	$4,574	$3,973	$3,854
Less:					
Bond interest	1,413	1,363	1,363	1,359	1,294
Contingency reserve	400	400	400		
Miscellaneous					186
Net profit (000's) and surplus	$2,421	$2,779	$2,811	$2,614	$2,374
Stock price, Toronto					
Stock Exchange: High	NA	NA	NA	5	2
Low	NA	NA	NA	5	6

Exhibit 3 presents balance sheets before the Spanish Civil War (1931) and afterwards (1941).

In 1947 the board of directors included: from Toronto, E. Allan Graydon (vice-president, secretary); from New York, J. B. Alley, J. D. Duncan, D. N. Heineman, and C. K. Wilmers; from Brussels, Henri Speciael (president), Baron Raoul Richard, and Viscount A. Van de Vyvere; from Barcelona, Marques de Foronda, F. F. Lawton, Domingo Sert, and William Menschaert; and, from London, R. O. McMurtry.

EXHIBIT 2 Selected operating and miscellaneous data, 1920–1932

	1920	1921	1922	1923	1924	1925	1926	1927	1928	1929	1930	1931	1932
Gross revenue	1,998	2,065	2,575	2,727	2,999	3,678	4,030	4,603	4,812	4,832	4,596	3,228	2,943
Less:													
Interest	1,989	2,061	2,212	2,366	2,419	2,234	2,049	2,054	1,918	1,728	1,638	1,568	1,400
General expense	188	160	142	154	163	149	197	162	134	150	197	151	183
Reorganization expense			198	183	342	47				49	49	49	49
Other	52												
Net profits	(232)	(156)	23	21	74	1,248	1,783	2,548	2,760	2,905	2,715	1,460	1,310
Stock price													
High	$9\frac{1}{8}$	$5\frac{7}{8}$	$15\frac{7}{8}$	22	23	30	$40\frac{1}{2}$	$68\frac{1}{8}$	78	65	30	24	$10\frac{1}{4}$
Low	$3\frac{1}{4}$	$3\frac{1}{4}$	$3\frac{1}{4}$	$12\frac{1}{2}$	$12\frac{7}{8}$	$18\frac{1}{4}$	26	$33\frac{1}{2}$	56	$47\frac{1}{2}$	21	$8\frac{1}{2}$	$10\frac{1}{4}$
Common dividends								287	143	143	1,942	899	
Fixed assets	NA	NA	NA	111,479	113,721	112,553	103,945	104,851	106,677	108,216	113,624	116,712	115,166

Note: NA = not available. Figures in thousands of Canadian dollars.
Source: *Financial Post*, "Survey of Corporate Securities" (1927, 1928, 1931, 1932, 1933).

EXHIBIT 3
Selected balance
sheet data, 1931,
1941

	1931	1941
Assets		
Current assets	$ 4,900	$ 14,913[b]
Long-term investments	724	2,094
Fixed assets[a]	116,172	114,072
Total assets	$121,796	$131,089
Liabilities		
Current liabilities	$ 5,423	$ 9,090
Unpaid interest, dividends		11,640
Long-term debt	70,887	64,751[c]
Total liabilities	$ 76,310	$ 85,481
Capital		
Common stock	$ 39,566	$ 39,566[d]
Sinking fund and special steam-generation reserve		7,475
Reserves and earned surplus	5,920	(1,433)[e]
Total capital	$ 45,486	$ 45,608
Total liabilities and capital	$121,796	$131,089

Note: Figures in thousands of Canadian dollars.
[a] Annual depreciation expense approximately $ 2,000,000
[b] Includes cash in bank of $11,716,317.
[c] £5,000,000 authorized, issued £3,000,000
   consolidated 6½ % prior lien bonds @ $4.86   14,600,000
   £1,677,300 5½ % first mortgage bonds @ 4.86   8,162,860
   6% 45-year peseta bonds
   Pts. 61,895,500 @ Pts. 5.8   11,953,364
   Funded debts of subsidiaries   30,035,202
                          64,751,426

[d] Authorized 2,500,000 issued 1,798,854 no par shares
[e] Beginning balance (deficit) plus   ($ 3,494,909)
   Reduction in reserve for deficits of Spanish subsidiaries   756,101
   Income from subsidiaries 1941   2,862,249
     less: bond interest 1941
              6½ % prior lien bonds   (776,607) unpaid
              5½ % first mortgage bonds   (233,098) unpaid
              6% 45-year bonds   (403,076) paid
   Administration expense 1941   (143,776)
   1941 net results   1,305,692
   Ending balance $ 1,433,116

JUAN ALBERT MARCH ORDINAS

Juan March was born October 4, 1880, near Palma on the island of Majorca in
the Mediterranean. He was the son of a pig farmer and never went to school. He
nurtured his sense for business and dealing while working as a longshoreman around
Palma harbor. In 1900, March went to Spanish Morocco and acquired a failing
tobacco plantation for a few thousand dollars. He turned it around and began to

buy out other landowners. Soon he started his own shipping company, Compania Transmediteranea, which eventually controlled Spanish passenger and freight traffic on the Mediterranean. The ships, a later parliamentary commission charged, were used to smuggle March's tobacco into Spain.

Eventually, in 1917, King Alfonso (1903–1923) awarded March the country's tobacco import monopoly. According to evidence, the king did so because March had been importing so much contraband tobacco into Spain that this was the only way that the king could collect some of the taxes due. March's smuggling was so effective that legally sold tobacco taxes had fallen from tens of millions of dollars to less than $50,000 in 1916. Even then March continued large-scale tobacco smuggling, cheating his own company as well as customs. In the first and second world wars he profited heavily by selling to both sides, supplying British ships at Gibraltar and German submarines.[3]

After World War I, March went to Madrid and became a leading Monarchist. He was influential in the government of dictator General Miguel Primo de Rivera and obtained the tobacco monopoly for Spanish Morocco. The monopoly for Spain was then held by a company controlled by a combination of interests.

In 1923, de Rivera ordered March arrested on charges of selling guns to the rebellious Arabs in Morocco. He escaped over the Pyrenees disguised as a priest and lived in exile in Geneva. During this period his agents bought up shares in the Spanish tobacco manufacturing monopoly Compania Anrendeteria de Tebacos. When March had acquired the controlling interest, he returned to Spain, made his peace with the government, and began building his empire. He founded a chain of banks (Banco March) in Madrid, cornered the rich Catalonia potash deposits, extended his shipping line, and invested in petroleum, newspapers, agriculture, minerals, and textiles. It was during this period that he became interested in utilities when he realized how tremendously profitable they were for the risk.

March "is cynical, free spending, boastful and conceited in his business affairs but above all else, dedicated to augmenting his wealth and influence by whatever means necessary."[4]

As owner of two Madrid newspapers, March entered politics as a conservative Monarchist in 1923. March's tenure with the Spanish Cortes began when he was elected as a representative of his home island of Majorca. He won his first election victory after throwing an islandwide fiesta for all citizens of the island on the eve of the election, when he donated a large sum of money to the island's school system. Upon election, March said, "The best way to relieve myself of troublesome government officials was to become part of the government."[5] In the Cortes, March made himself many influential friends in the legal system as well as the government. To those who supported him, he lent money to finance election campaigns as well

[3] John Brooks, op. cit.

[4] John Brooks, op. cit.

[5] John Brooks, op. cit.

as for private purposes. These favors "are never forgotten by March. He expects favourable treatment in his business interests as repayment."[6]

March's political life was not without strife, however. In 1932, he was ousted from the Cortes and jailed on charges of bribery in acquiring the Moroccan tobacco monopoly. During the 18 months he spent in jail, awaiting a trial which was never held, he ran his affairs from his well-furnished cell where he maintained two full-time servants and his own chef. He bitterly attacked the ruling Republican government through his newspapers. In November 1933, he was reelected while still in jail. Later that month, he escaped to Gibraltar. A few weeks later, he was able to return to Spain after a formal government apology and acquittal from all bribery charges in early 1934. March then became involved in the plot to overthrow the Republic and reportedly chartered the plane that flew Generalissimo Franco, in political exile in the Canary Islands, to Spanish Morocco to lead the Spanish revolutionaries in 1936. March became Franco's leading bankroller, loaning huge sums to the insurgents.

The current Spanish minister of industry and commerce, Juan Antonio Suances, at the end of the Civil War said of March: "Europe, the West, and — why not say it! — Christianity are in that fabulous man's debt for the support he gave at certain crucial moments. His support was the sole decisive factor in Spain's triumph over Communism."[7] Certainly March's contributions were crucial early in the war when Franco had no other sources to draw upon, Hitler and Mussolini having not yet offered their assistance.

After the Civil War, March was rewarded. The national tobacco monopoly was returned to him and, in 1938, his London office, J. March & Co., became the clearinghouse for almost all government trade between Britain and Spain. He also arranged barter deals for Franco with Hitler and Mussolini to bolster the Spanish economy.

March's character was eloquently summed up during the course of his expulsion from the Cortes in 1932 on bribery charges. The minister of finance described March to his colleagues in this way:

> *March is an extraordinary case, a businessman ordinarily given to careful speech rather than political rhetoric. March is not an enemy of the Republic any more than he is a friend of the Republic. . . . March was neither friend nor enemy of the Directory; March is neither friend nor enemy of anyone; March is March. . . . March is an exceptional man and to judge by his intelligence and perspicacity it's perhaps necessary to go back to the Middle Ages. . . . March is one of those men in search of his own destiny; seeking to realize his will, who considers as enemies only those who crimped or attempted to halt the course of that will. . . . This is a man possessed; he believes himself master of all truth.*[8]

[6] John Brooks, op. cit.

[7] John Brooks, op. cit.

[8] John Brooks, op. cit.

March was described as "a small man of sickly aspect, slightly stooped, who played dominoes enthusiastically."[9]

CURRENCY RESTRICTIONS, STERLING BONDS, AND THE PLAN OF COMPROMISE

By 1947, the company still had not been able to take any money out of Spain and, consequently, had not been able to make a single interest payment on its sterling debentures for 11 years. Government officials steadfastly maintained the position that Spain continued to suffer a critical foreign exchange shortage and could not afford to sell any sterling regardless of indenture obligations. The only exception to the postrevolution exchange restrictions that Franco's regime permitted was proof that foreign currency was used to repay debts arising from the importation of foreign capital leading to a net benefit to the Spanish economy. Over the preceding decade, the value of the sterling bonds had plummeted. In 1946 and 1947, they were selling at a deep discount on all British and European trading desks.

In an attempt to expedite a repayment agreement that would satisfy both the Spanish controls and the creditors' demands for interest payments, SOFINA-SIDRO directors worked out an agreement between the British holders and the Spanish and British governments which became known as the Plan of Compromise. The directors of SOFINA-SIDRO asked certain subsidiaries operating outside Spain to raise £3.5 million or $14 million in order to repay a substantial portion of the bond interest in arrears. The balance still owed was to be made up in common stock of Barcelona Traction. Specifically, the holders of the £2,684,900 outstanding 6½ percent prior lien bonds would get £100 for each £100 bond, plus 134,245 shares of stock (5 shares for each £100 bond). The holders of the £1,561,920 outstanding 5½ percent first mortgage bonds would receive £45 for each £100 bond, plus 78,146 shares of Barcelona stock (5 shares for each £100 bond). Under this compromise agreement, the bondholders would get their money out, the Spanish Institute of Foreign Exchange would not deplete its reserves, and thus the apparent basis for their objection to resumed servicing was eliminated. The plan was approved in 1945 by a majority of bondholders in London and the Supreme Court of Ontario, Barcelona Traction's home province. Exhibit 4 summarizes the Plan of Compromise.

However, the plan was jeopardized through a series of diplomatic decisions and eventually fell through in December 1945 when the Spanish government suddenly withdrew its approval (presumably because of March's influence). Most people connected with the plan were confused as to what had happened since Spain was trying to bolster trade with Britain and Belgium after the end of World War II. Both the management and directors of SOFINA foresaw difficult times ahead if they could not pay off the bonds expediently or resume servicing.

[9] John Brooks, op. cit.

EXHIBIT 4
Highlights of the
Plan of Compromise

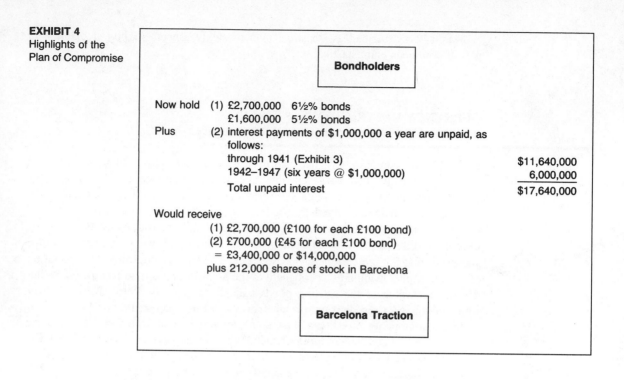

Bondholders

Now hold (1) £2,700,000   6½% bonds
          £1,600,000   5½% bonds
Plus   (2) interest payments of $1,000,000 a year are unpaid, as
          follows:
          through 1941 (Exhibit 3) $11,640,000
          1942–1947 (six years @ $1,000,000)   6,000,000
          Total unpaid interest $17,640,000

Would receive
          (1) £2,700,000 (£100 for each £100 bond)
          (2) £700,000 (£45 for each £100 bond)
          = £3,400,000 or $14,000,000
          plus 212,000 shares of stock in Barcelona

Barcelona Traction

JUAN MARCH AND BARCELONA TRACTION

Juan March had been making overtures that he wished to gain control of Barcelona Traction since 1940, the year that servicing on the peseta bonds had resumed. In October 1940, Carlos Montanes offered on behalf of "a solid European financial group" (assumed to be Sr. March) to buy Barcelona Traction for £1,700,000 (about $7,000,000) and warned of the presence of German troops a few miles from the Catalonian border. The Barcelona Traction directors, then in New York as refugees from occupied Belgium, refused the offer.

In 1944, March met with Heineman in Spain. March said he was buying up the company's bonds and that he wanted control of the company both "as an investment and for personal prestige."[10] Heineman rebuffed March, stating that Barcelona Traction shares were not for sale. It was at this 1944 meeting that March first indicated that he had been buying up the company's sterling bonds. In fact, the company knew March had been purchasing as many of the deep discount debentures as he could find on the markets. He was offering holders a premium above their listed price to induce these creditors to sell. Few refused.[11]

[10] John Brooks, op. cit.

[11] John Brooks, op. cit.

At the same time as he purchased bonds, March had been actively campaigning through various government officials to have the Plan of Compromise defeated. By the end of 1946, once news of the rejection was public knowledge, March had managed to purchase nearly £2 million (at face value) of the debentures, though, because of their deeply discounted price, his costs were only a fraction of the figure. This total was enough to give him a controlling majority of the bonds issued, though few people understood his motives for purchasing them. Meanwhile, Juan March was personally thanking loyal government supporters for their valuable roles exercised in defeating the Plan of Compromise.

THE DIRECTORS MEET

Though March had given them notice of his intentions to gain control of Barcelona Traction, the Barcelona directors remained confused as to why March continued to purchase the sterling debentures. To be absolutely sure of Barcelona Traction's financial position, Heineman asked that it be thoroughly reviewed. When the report was given at the board meeting, any uncertainty concerning Barcelona Traction's solvency was removed, as profitability and cash flow were better than in any previous year.

The company's lawyers assured the directors that they stood on firm ground. Only a small fraction of Barcelona's shares were publicly traded. Further, any pressure that March could put on the firm by means of the sterling bonds could be turned against the Spanish government, the attorneys reasoned, since the Spanish government was preventing the payment of the sterling obligation. The board was told:

> *Corporate profits from Ebro alone grew 23 percent last year. The company has enough cash and liquid assets in Spanish banks to pay off instantly all its obligations. I believe the auditors said we have $24.5 million in Spain. Our problem is what next to expect from, and what next to do about, Sr. Juan March.*

March's reputation and persistence left all in the boardroom with a lingering feeling of doubt and uncertainty. His past exploits were all too well known in the boardrooms of European businesses. Nobody felt completely at ease when he made his presence known.

Though March had managed to purchase a controlling share of the sterling debentures, he still did not own any of the outstanding common stock of Barcelona Traction. Barcelona's directors had been concerned with the turn of affairs since early 1946, when it became obvious that March was the majority owner of the bonds and, thus, their major creditor. At the end of 1947, however, they had no intention of ever selling any of Barcelona Traction's common stock and certainly never to Juan March.

To open the topic of Juan March, Dannie Heineman reported on his meeting with March in Switzerland in November. He commented:

I asked March if he would sell his bonds and at what price. March said his price was immediate control of the company. I thereupon ended the negotiation, whereupon March said he would need to take further action based upon his duties . . . with regard to the higher interests of the Spanish nation.

You directors know now as much as I do about March. What should we do?

POLAROID AND SOUTH AFRICA: THE MANAGEMENT OF SURPRISE

During 1970 and 1971, Robert Palmer, director of community relations for the Polaroid Corporation, was a witness to and participant in a series of escalating events centering around Polaroid's activities in South Africa. This case presents those events as they occurred and as they were perceived by Polaroid's senior management.

A group of senior managers was assigned the initial responsibility of (1) analyzing and responding to these events on a day-to-day basis and (2) determining the longer-term strategic position of the company. These senior managers in 1971 principally included Robert Palmer, Thomas Wyman (vice-president, sales), and Peter Wensberg (vice-president, advertising), oftentimes working with other Polaroid executives. For the purposes of case narrative, events that happened to this Polaroid group will be described as if they happened to Robert Palmer. In reality, they may have happened to others in the group, although they were immediately brought to Mr. Palmer's attention.

Before these events are described as they happened, background data on the Polaroid Corporation is presented.

COMPANY BACKGROUND

Polaroid Corporation's founder, Edwin H. Land, was, in 1970, chairman of the board, president, director of research, and principal (30 percent) stockholder. Just as the Polaroid Corporation was totally built around Edwin Land, Land was totally involved in the process of "sensing a significant human need in our field and delivering the final product. . . . We're not here to make profits. We're here to make innovation."

Case prepared by John Barnett, University of New Hampshire, with Robert Palmer, University of Massachusetts. © 1985 by John Barnett. This case has been prepared for classroom discussion purposes only and is not intended to illustrate either effective or ineffective handling of an administrative situation. Reprinted by permission.

In 1928, Land left his studies at Harvard to work on reducing light glare by diffusion through the polarization of light. Nine years later he had perfected this polarization and started the Polaroid Corporation in Boston to sell polarizers to the automobile industry. When this tactic failed, Land built up the business of Polaroid nonglare sunglasses, which was a success.

During World War II, Land began developing a system of instant photography; the first Polaroid Land camera was introduced in the marketplace in November 1947. Between 1947 and 1970, instant photography product offerings expanded to include color, automatic exposure, and low-price models.

Land wrote to Polaroid employees in August 1970:

> This is no ordinary company that we have built together. . . . It is the proud pioneer that set out to teach the world how people should work together . . . Polaroid is on its way to lead the world — perhaps even to save it — by this interplay between science, technology, and real people.

EXHIBIT 1
Financial statements for Polaroid and domestic subsidiaries, 1969–1970

	1970	1969
Net assets		
Current assets		
Cash	$ 6,118	$ 8,478
Marketable securities	195,363	200,682
Receivables, less allowance of $670 ($675 in 1969)	103,987	100,203
Inventories	39,899	47,595
Prepaid expenses	2,781	1,453
Total current assets	$348,148	$358,411
Current liabilities		
Payables and accruals	31,291	44,044
Federal and state income taxes	15,824	16,503
Total current liabilities	47,115	60,547
Working capital	301,033	297,864
Property, plant, and equipment, at cost		
Land	2,742	2,577
Buildings	69,064	56,124
Machinery and equipment	112,360	97,484
Construction in progress	63,192	32,082
	247,358	188,267
Less accumulated depreciation	74,909	63,197
Net property, plant, and equipment	$172,449	$125,070
Other assets		
Investments in and advances to unconsolidated foreign subsidiaries, at cost	1,163	959
Patents and trademarks (at nominal value of $1)	—	—
Total net assets	$474,645	$423,893

EXHIBIT 1
(continued)

Ownership of net assets
Capital and retained earnings
Common stock, $1 par value, authorized 36,000,000 shares,
  issued: 1970 — 32,831,950 shares; 1969 — 32,838,200

shares	$ 32,832	$ 32,828
Additional paid-in capital	119,843	119,725
Retained earnings	321,970	271,340
Total ownership of net assets	$474,645	$423,893

Income

Net sales and royalty income	$426,534	$454,582
Other income, principally interest and dividends	17,751	11,027
Total net sales and other income	444,285	465,609
Cost of sales	207,266	222,451
Selling, research, engineering, distribution, and administrative expenses	123,445	112,226
Total costs	330,711	334,677
Earnings before taxes	113,574	130,932
Federal and state income taxes	52,438	67,811
Net earnings	61,136	63,121
Retained earnings at beginning of year	271,340	218,631
	332,476	281,752
Less cash dividends paid	10,506	10,412
Retained earnings at end of year	$321,970	$271,340

Note: Figures in thousands of dollars.

Sales in 1970 were $426,500,000 for Polaroid and its domestic subsidiaries and $88,800,000 for its 100-percent-owned unconsolidated foreign subsidiaries. Net earnings were $61,100,000. Polaroid had marketing subsidiaries in thirteen countries and manufacturing subsidiaries in Scotland and the Netherlands. The company held 1,100 American patents, most of them (955) in the field of instant photography. Financial data is contained in Exhibit 1.

CORPORATE CITIZENSHIP

Polaroid was described by the *Boston Globe* (November 1, 1970) as:

> *An enlightened company that takes pride in its national reputation for humanism. . . .*
> *Its program in black hiring is a matter of record and far ahead of most companies in the nation.*
> *About 9 percent of the company's employees are black . . . of the 2,383 hired (in 1969), 523, or 22 percent were black.*

Also in 1969 30 percent of the company's black employees completed company courses. Additionally, there is Inner City, a wholly owned Polaroid subsidiary in Roxbury which opened in 1968 to help unemployed and underemployed people develop work records to help them get and hold permanent jobs in industry.

Inner City had 125 graduates by 1970, of whom 82 percent remained in their permanent positions.

The 1970 annual report described Polaroid's participation in more than one hundred urban problem projects in 1970 and detailed its efforts in pollution control.

October 7, 1970   Robert Palmer, out of town on a business trip, was called by his office in Cambridge on October 6, 1970, with the message that two black Polaroid employees, Kenneth Williams and Caroline Hunter, were to hold a protest the next day at corporate headquarters. Palmer thought: "No problem. Williams has been protesting regularly" and did not ask what the protest was about, an omission he was to regret. In a few days Williams and Hunter became the Polaroid Revolutionary Workers Movement.

Caroline Hunter was a laboratory technician at Polaroid. She graduated from Xavier University in New Orleans in 1968, majoring in chemistry.

Williams began employment at Polaroid as a janitor in 1965 and was shifted to a quality control function that involved his taking pictures with Polaroid film. He was thought of as a capable photographer, and a brochure of his Polaroid photographs was distributed with the 1968 Polaroid annual report. Eventually, questions about control of his photographic assignments led to his being reassigned to community relations activities.

The sun-filled midday afternoon of October 7, 1970 witnessed Williams, public address system in hand, yelling in street language about Polaroid's enslavement of black South Africans. The invited press frantically recorded the event for the evening television news and morning newspapers, reporting that "hundreds protest Polaroid's racist South African oppression." The "hundreds" consisted of Hunter and Williams, the press, and hundreds of Polaroid employees who were enjoying the demonstration and eating brown bag lunches in the warm afternoon air.

Exhibit 2 shows the population of South Africa, estimates from *South Africa: Official Yearbook of the Republic of South Africa*. According to the same official publication, in 1969–1971, the national life expectancy for males was 59.3 for Asians, 51.2 for blacks, 48.8 for coloureds, and 64.5 for whites. Blacks are not citizens and do not vote. Whites are divided approximately 60 percent Afrikaner, 40 percent English.

Confronted essentially with integration or segregation, since 1948 the South African electorate has chosen the latter, known as *apartheid* or "separateness." Social segregation between whites and blacks means that separate facilities are provided for the different racial groups, intermarriage is prohibited, separate residential areas

EXHIBIT 2 South Africa population estimates

Year	Total Total	Total % Incr.	Asians Total	Asians % Incr.	Blacks Total	Blacks % Incr.	Coloureds (mixed) Total	Coloureds (mixed) % Incr.	Whites Total	Whites % Incr.
1951	12,671,000		367,000		8,560,000		1,103,000		2,642,000	
1960	15,994,000	2.5	447,000	3.0	10,928,000	2.3	1,509,000	2.7	3,080,000	1.7
1970	21,794,000	3.3	630,000	2.9	15,340,000	3.4	2,051,000	3.1	3,773,000	2.1

are demarcated, population registration on a racial basis is compulsory, and urban blacks are being resettled in their traditional tribal areas.[1]

Compulsory population registration means one thing for whites and another for blacks. Instead of the simple, driver's-license-type card for whites, blacks carry a multiple-page book with an identification photograph, police records of the passbook holder and all relatives, plus rules as to where the holder is allowed to live, work, and to be.

Week One

The Polaroid Revolutionary Workers Movement's (PRWM) demands were three: (1) get out of South Africa, (2) state the company position on apartheid, and (3) turn over all South African profits to black liberation groups in South Africa.

That evening and all that week the lights burned late at Polaroid headquarters. The discussion encompassed (1) the discrepancy between the PRWM charges and Polaroid's corporate citizenship efforts, (2) outrage at the personal abuse of Dr. Land, and (3) methods to contain what the Polaroid executives in their now emotional state felt was "the enemy," the PRWM.

In trying to decide what to do, some asked, "What happens if we do nothing and say nothing?" The answer was that the interest of the press is finite, and General Motors and/or other corporations will be next.

Others said, "Let's find out what, if anything, we're doing in South Africa." And Dr. Land quietly said, "Well, the issues have been raised, we've got to deal with them in the open and honestly."

The morning after the protest, Robert Palmer issued a statement that the company condemned apartheid, that Polaroid would not negotiate in the streets, and that the company would determine its business interests, if any, in South Africa and report its findings.

That day and evening everyone at corporate headquarters was involved in determining what if anything Polaroid was doing in South Africa. No one knew. The company

[1] This prohibition on interracial marriage ended in June 1985.

policy was to set up subsidiary distributorships in all countries in which Polaroid had approximately a million dollars in sales, but there was no such subsidiary in South Africa. Marketing executives said there was no involvement in South Africa and "don't worry about it." Nevertheless, a marketing representative was sent on a plane to South Africa "to find out what we're doing" and to report back on any potential problems. Meanwhile, top executives from Polaroid had to accept staff responses ranging from "we're not sure" to the question "are we there?"

Two days later the marketing representative reported that "There was no problem. We aren't really in South Africa at all, since we have no direct sales and only sell our products through an independent distributor there."

Polaroid had no investment whatsoever in this distributor, Frank and Hirsch. Accordingly, Robert Palmer issued a second press release stating that Polaroid had no involvement, although an independent wholesale distributor handled Polaroid cameras and sunglasses.

In early October 1970, all eight thousand Polaroid employees received an internal "memorandum of legal matters" from Polaroid's legal department stating:

> Polaroid has not sold its I.D. equipment to the government of South Africa for use in the apartheid program. . . . All sales of the I.D.-2 system to the South African distributor have been carefully traced to verify the use of which our equipment has been put. . . . [Our distributor] is unique in South Africa in its adoption of full equal employment practices for blacks.

This incorrect and inaccurate memo was fuel to the smoldering fire of the Polaroid Revolutionary Workers Movement.

For example, Polaroid's assertion that Frank and Hirsch stood "unique in South Africa" for "full equal employment practices for blacks" assumed a wage policy illegal under South African law.

Helmut Hirsch commented to *The Star* (Johannesburg) on November 21, 1970: "I do not know where they could have obtained such a statement. We are governed by the laws of the country. Would they allow the existence of such a policy? It is not possible."

More importantly, Polaroid's equipment was being used in the passbook program. Any black who paid a slightly higher passbook fee was photographed using Polaroid equipment and received the passbook immediately. About 10 percent of the blacks chose the Polaroid photograph alternative.

Williams and the PRWM then issued a denunciation of Polaroid's "cover-up" and asserted that Polaroid equipment was being used in the oppressive passbook system. The passbook was an integral part of apartheid. The details of the passbook system were generally unknown to most Polaroid executives.

By this time, as the first week drew to a close, Polaroid felt it was in a "lose-lose" situation. Land announced that there was to be a formal review and that a committee should be established to examine the situation. Consensus, not executive action, was to be the desired outcome of the process.

In response to an announcement in the Polaroid internal newsletter, fifteen employees indicated their interest in serving on a committee to review the South Africa–Polaroid connection. The committee held its first meeting on October 28, 1970. Dr. Land told the members that other companies and the world were watching Polaroid.

The Trip   The ad hoc Polaroid committee reviewing Polaroid's connection to South Africa included blacks and whites, males and females, and many levels within the company ranging from corporate vice-president to hourly worker. It decided to send a four-person delegation (two blacks, two whites) to South Africa. This delegation was to report its findings and recommendations to the committee of fifteen.

The idea for the South Africa trip became a fully supported and desired event after one black hourly Polaroid worker told the other committee members, who were asking him what should be done: "Look: For two hundred years you've told me what I've needed and never asked me. Now you're asking me to do the same thing for those blacks, and I won't. We should go ask them."

Polaroid delegations actually made a number of trips ranging from several to ten days each to South Africa. For purposes of this case, no distinction will be made between events occurring on one or another trip. The perceptions and impressions of the delegations are given next. It will be necessary to identify some individuals only in general terms, as the delegation met unofficially, often in somewhat clandestine situations, with individuals whose identity will not be revealed. Bob Palmer commented on the mood of the delegation of four as they prepared to leave for South Africa:

> *The group was apprehensive and had a lot of uncertainty about the trip, even though privately three of the four were leaning toward withdrawal of any Polaroid activities and/or products, with only one person undecided as to the best course of action. We were anxious about the glare of the klieg lights and the scrutiny of the media. We were also alarmed at the visa-issuing procedures within the South African embassy, which led to the impression that the embassy knew the names of the four delegates shortly after they were selected by the committee of fifteen at Polaroid's headquarters in Cambridge.*
>
> *This alarm continued after we landed in South Africa. Each day it became clearer that our "guides" had observing/reporting responsibilities as well as tourism duties within South Africa.*
>
> *The other immediate impression we got was of the scale of life, even during our first 24 hours of perfunctory meetings, chiefly with Helmut Hirsch, the director of our independent distributor, Frank and Hirsch. Helmut, who was a Jewish refugee from Hitler's Germany, lived, as did the majority of whites, in a style we think of as reserved for Hollywood — pools, polo fields, and multiple servants and bedrooms.*

During the trip, the delegation never met officially with any representative of the South African government, although they made known their willingness to do so. They did meet with (1) a non-Afrikaner white observer of the Afrikaner phenomenon, (2) an Afrikaner business leader and other business leaders, (3) a banned black in the antiapartheid movement, and (4) Helmut Hirsch and employees (both black and white) of the distributorship. They also received, in both South Africa and the United States, letters from American businessmen, church leaders, and Polaroid shareholders.

Comments of a White, Non-Afrikaner

The historical roots of the Afrikaner and the Afrikaner version of Calvinism are as critical to your understanding of the Afrikaner or Boer as is the legend of the cowboy and the Hollywood version of John Wayne and Burt Reynolds to an understanding of the American trucker.

First, the Afrikaners, descendants of the Dutch settlers who came to South Africa in 1652, determined to be masters of their own fate and left the now English-dominated Capetown and coastal cities during the Great Trek beginning in 1836. They suffered massacre by the Zulus and, later, continued domination by the expansionary British, led by Cecil Rhodes.

One tactic protected the Afrikaner on the Trek, the laager *or circle of wagons. The worst thing an Afrikaner could do would be to leave the circle.*

Second, the Calvinism of the South Africa Dutch Reformed Church stresses Calvin's notion of an "elect," along with fundamentalism. Thus, in the Afrikaner view, the Afrikaner is God's elite who has a constant, unchanging, and comprehensive guide to life in the Bible. Any turning away from the Afrikaner way, any hint of compromise or negotiation, would be not only leaving the circle of wagons unguarded and unprotected, but would be turning away from God. How can the Right compromise with the Wrong? The Volk, *the Afrikaner people, cannot do wrong and cannot compromise the right.*

Finally, the Afrikaners, although defeated by the English in the Boer War of 1899–1902, regained political control of the Union of South Africa because of their larger numbers, organization, and shared belief in their own destiny to rule South Africa. Immediately after World War II, during which time the Afrikaner sympathized with Germany, the Afrikaner's power, through the parliamentary control of the Boer Nationalist Party, was totally solidified.

The British, though with overwhelming control of industry, particularly mining, were nonetheless politically ineffectual against the Afrikaner, who, though only a supervisor in the English mine — or, more likely, a shopkeeper — was nevertheless politically all powerful.

The all-powerful Afrikaner thus implemented apartheid, the complete separation of the races, especially between 1948 and 1954. The swart gevaar *or black menace was pushed away, as the Afrikaner tried to resettle blacks onto "homelands" in much the same way as you Yanks tried to force the redman onto reservations. About 15 percent of the land is now assigned to the blacks, 75 percent of the population.*

The Afrikaner, by the way, feels that Americans should be sympathetic to apartheid, since it is not all that different from your own segregation policies of a few years ago.

In any event, the Afrikaner sees himself pushing back the blacks just as he did during the Great Trek. The economic motive is just as strong, since the Afrikaner is caught beneath the economic, but not political, dominance of the English. The Afrikaner must protect himself from being replaced by the obviously less-expensive black laborer. Thus the Afrikaner has created a larger bureaucracy and military structure where he can be employed. The Afrikaner has also ensured himself of supervisory positions by laws prohibiting blacks from any supervisory work or training.

Blacks' education is limited, but exists since the whites — English and Afrikaner alike — need the cheap labor and minimal literacy. Total separation of races is economically impossible, but only black males can come into the working areas, and only with the passbook. They return to their families in the "homelands" perhaps one month a year.

The black's mobility is totally restricted by means of the passbook, which says what areas, if any, the holder is allowed in, at what hours, and so on, and contains details of all arrests of the holder or of the holder's relatives.

"Waar's jou' pass', jong?" "Where's your pass, boy?" This phrase is the phrase of the control system, and results in 160,000 to 175,000 arrests per year, or about one black every three minutes on the average.

Modern apartheid is based on fear. This fear is substantiated by some black leaders' belief that real change will only occur when minority exploitation is replaced by majority rule.

Comments of an Afrikaner Businessman

America must protect itself. You will be under increasing pressure from Japanese and other competition. You cannot afford to antagonize host country governments. You cannot afford to withdraw from a tremendous market, for your competition will just take your place.

And, on the humanitarian side, the blacks will only suffer by any anti–South Africa acts. Under apartheid we are trying to raise all living standards. Who knows what will happen 50 years from now when everyone here enjoys higher standards of living. But it will take time. You must remember that in your history you exterminated the indigenous populace. We are trying to raise them up, along with the Boer and all in South Africa.

Most assuredly, growth will lead to social change. As Anglo-American's Oppenheimer — by the way, an opposition Progressive Party member — often says, "Economic growth won't destroy apartheid, but will create the social, cultural, political, and industrial pressures for making changes." And this change will be evolutionary, not revolutionary.

Comments of a Black Actively Resisting Apartheid

If apartheid continues, we said in the 1950s, the situation will escalate to disastrous consequences. There is no alternative to the Freedom Charter of 1955, endorsing a nonracial democratic society.

Today we say disinvestment and withdrawal will not bring escalation. Escalation is taking place now, and disinvestment will end it in the longer term by bringing matters to a head. By not withdrawing, you justify the present system and you support apartheid.

The slave will not suffer. The slave will sacrifice.

Comments of Helmut Hirsch. In discussing the possibility of Polaroid trying to make a contribution toward more equality, or less inequality, such as black training programs within the Frank and Hirsch distributorship, Mr. Hirsch said: "If you want to do it, please issue me an order and then I can justify my action by saying, 'Polaroid made me do it.' I have over one hundred products that I distribute, but Polaroid is important to me. It means 15 percent of my business."

GENERAL SUMMARY OF BLACK VIEWS

The group met with about 120 blacks. There were three things generally consistent at each of those 120 meetings.

First, as to location, no black would speak freely and openly if any other person were present, including a family member such as a brother or sister. The only free discussions were held walking through the open streets with the black and the Polaroid employee talking rapidly in low voices.

Second, the blacks assured Polaroid that "revolution is our decision, not yours."

Finally, there was general agreement that the company could make some advances for blacks in South Africa working within Frank & Hirsch. Wage disparities could be decreased between blacks and whites, and blacks could be trained for positions of more responsibility. A black department could be created so that it could have a black supervisor. (It was illegal for blacks to supervise whites.) Medical help could be made available within the company. Further, direct grants might be made to black education programs.

Two Zulu Chiefs The late Zulu chief Albert Lutuli said: "The economic boycott of South Africa will entail undoubted hardship for Africans. We do not doubt that. But if it is a method which shortens the day of blood, the suffering to us will be a price we are willing to pay."

The current Zulu chief Gatsha Buthelezi argued that:

Those who advocate trade sanctions and economic withdrawal to help my people and punish the whites in South Africa may be killing us with kindness. What we need is not disengagement, but full foreign participation in South Africa's overall economic development to create more jobs, higher wages, and better training opportunities. I am no apologist for apartheid, but a realist who knows that a job may make the difference between living and starving for many black families in South Africa.

Outside Experts Bob Palmer wrote about his experience with outside advice during this fact-finding period:

While there seems to be almost no interest on the part of employees, I can't believe the number of calls from outside people. I've heard from every possible viewpoint, all conflicting and all assuring me that they are objective experts.

The largest group of calls are from banned, black South Africans who urge total withdrawal. Clearly the downfall of the present government is the only way they can ever go back to their native land.

Others urge withdrawal "as the only moral thing to do," but can't explain the morality of Polaroid condemning a foreign government's policy.

All these "experts" have convinced me that I don't as yet have enough information to understand what this is really about.

Excerpts from comments by two "experts" follow.

"Expert One"

Can you be in South Africa and still have a soul? Does a company have a soul? Can a company have a moral obligation?

Ultimately, the question will be answered based upon your conclusion about the role of a non–South African company. Can such an outside company help to create real progress, or is the outside company a partner, albeit an unwilling partner, in a system that fosters apartheid? Is doing nothing actually siding with the status quo? Is external investment a significant factor in the maintenance of apartheid?

"Expert Two"

You have to be very careful about the facts. For example, some quote public opinion surveys among the blacks, but don't tell you that it is illegal in South Africa under security laws for anyone to publicly advocate divestment or disinvestment.

But we know some facts. These include economic facts such as:

1. Total foreign investment is dominated by Britain, which accounts for 60 percent of South African foreign investment. Twenty-five percent of South Africa's top one hundred companies are British. Britain dominates the mining industry, and invests 10 percent of its overseas investments in South Africa.

2. American companies control numerically few, but strategically significant, industries, including automobiles and trucks (about 50 percent American-controlled, now converting to a 65 percent local-products government regulation), energy (oil), and computers.

3. About half of Fortune's 500 companies have South African offices, and others are involved through licenses and distributors. On the average, South Africa represents one percent (sales) and more than one percent in profits.

4. Between 1946 and 1955, average annual foreign investment was £70,000,000, and between 1956 and 1969, £71,500,000. Overseas capital, 23 percent of total capital investment in the post–World War II period, is now about 11 percent. South African gross domestic product is about £7,000,000,000, currently increasing at about 9 percent per year.

5. The white-to-black wage ratio in 1966 in mining was 17.6 to 1, in manufacturing 5.1 to 1. In 1971 the ratio was 20.3 in mining and 5.7 in manufacturing.

6. Poverty datum line (PDL) figures from the University of Port Elizabeth are R90.00 for a family of six in Johannesburg, with a minimum effective level (MEL) of PDL + 50 percent. Polaroid's distributor's average salaries are R84 for blacks. Frank and Hirsch's minimum wage in Soweto, the South African township outside of Johannesburg where the distributorship was located, was below the Soweto PDL. Frank and Hirsch employs 155 Africans and their sunglass manufacturing subsidiary another 14.

7. American companies employ 100,000 nonwhites. Polaroid's Tom Wyman described the company's acts as "a teaspoon in the ocean."

8. South Africa has 50 percent of the world's known gold; 75 percent of platinum, chrome and vanadium; 20 percent of industrial diamonds; 78 percent of all manganese; and 18 percent of the Western World's uranium.

The Church   Church leaders were unanimous in urging withdrawal on moral grounds. During the fall and winter Bob Palmer received many phone calls and letters urging withdrawal.

The Church Ecumenical Committee which visited South Africa in 1971 stated:

Most of us believe that American corporations should totally disengage from southern Africa; that the presence of American corporations in which we are shareholders undergirds the system of racism, colonialism, and apartheid which prevails in southern Africa. . . . Even progressive employment on the part of American companies will not bring the basic changes in society that we support because of our Christian commitment to freedom, justice, and self-determination.

In a conversation with one church leader, Bob Palmer was informed that the churchman would be leading a delegation to the April 1971 stockholders meeting. The churchman requested that Bob send him all information relating to Polaroid's history and investments in South Africa. Bob replied:

We are an $800 million institution that has been in South Africa since 1938. You are a $2 billion institution, the Anglican church, that has been in South Africa for centuries. Would you please send me information about your history and investments in South Africa, and maybe we can learn something from each other.

The churchman hung up.

EXHIBIT 3
PRWM circular

UNWANTED

EDWIN LAND, Pres. & Chair., Polaroid Corp.

Crimes: Complicity in apartheid (the South African racist system which means murder, starvation, and imprisonment of blacks); complicity in grand larceny — the theft of South Africa from its people; espionage; unfair labor practices.

Polaroid's ID-2 system, which produces instant identification cards with photographs, is used in the manufacture of pass books which must be carried by South African blacks. The pass books are a key tool of control for the white minority in South Africa: with the pass book system the blacks may be kept from entering the 87% of all South African land reserved for whites, prevented from holding any kind of meetings, and hounded into submission.

Land has not only ignored the demands of the Polaroid Workers Revolutionary Movement that Polaroid disengage from doing business in South Africa, but has fired PWRM leaders.

Land is not a gangster limited to one branch of crime. As the head of the Intelligence Committee of the Foreign Intelligence Advisory Board under Kennedy, Land is credited with developing the cameras for the CIA's U-2 spy planes.

THIS MAN HAS BEEN CHOSEN ONE OF BOSTON'S TEN LEAST WANTED MEN. THESE ANNOUNCEMENTS WILL BE PUBLISHED AND THE LIST EXPANDED AND REVISED FROM TIME TO TIME IN A CONTINUING EFFORT TO WARN PEOPLE AGAINST THE DANGEROUS CRIMINALS IN OUR MIDST.

**Other
Comments**

As part of fact-finding, Bob Palmer reviewed comments from American business. The commentary from American business was mixed. Some firms were noncommittal. Most asked how to handle black employee pressure. A few were highly critical of Polaroid's meddling in "a high-stake poker game with ten-cent chips."

Bob also reviewed material being distributed by the PRWM. (See Exhibits 3 and 4.)

Ken Williams had resigned from Polaroid, spilling a red substance on the desk of the Polaroid receptionist at corporate headquarters and announcing "I will no longer accept blood money." Caroline Hunter was warned several times about issuing proboycott statements; she was finally dismissed in early 1971. Williams and Hunter were later to testify before a United Nations subcommittee about South Africa and foreign business investment.

EXHIBIT 4
PRWM press release

Polaroid Workers Revolutionary Movement

November 2, 1970

Brothers and Sisters:

The Polaroid Revolutionary Workers Movement is a group of black workers in Cambridge, Massachusetts, who have come together to act and protest against the sale of Polaroid products in South Africa.

We see the South African apartheid system as the symbol of the many "inhumanities" in the United States. We cannot begin to deal with racism in Polaroid or in the U.S. until Polaroid and the U.S. cease to uphold and support apartheid. Black people in South Africa are enslaved and dehumanized in order to insure the security of apartheid and the capitalists' margin of profit. The United States and its corporate society have made explicit its intentions of profits at any human expense.

We demand that we no longer be used as tools to enslave our brothers and to insure corporate profits.

On October 8, the Movement presented Polaroid Corp. with the following demands:

1. That Polaroid announce a policy of complete disengagement from South Africa. We believe that all American companies doing business there reinforce that racist system.
2. That Polaroid announce its position on apartheid publically, in the U.S. and South Africa.
3. That Polaroid contribute profits earned in South Africa to the recognized African liberation movements.

Polaroid has refused to meet with the PRWM or recognize the demands.

On October 27, the PRWM called for a worldwide boycott of Polaroid products by all right-on thinking people until Polaroid discontinues all sales in South Africa. We are building a coalition of right-on thinking people to press the demands that Polaroid and all American business discontinue support of the South African racist government.

IMMEDIATE ACTION AND YOUR SUPPORT IS NECESSARY. POWER TO THE PEOPLE.

THE DECISION

It was now time to make a recommendation. What should Polaroid do about the PRWM and Polaroid's activities in South Africa? How should the decision be announced and implemented? What reaction might Polaroid expect? What reaction might the committee expect from Polaroid? Bob Palmer thought: "The facts are easy to discern. It's the truth that is elusive."

BILL KEANE

Bill Keane faced three issues in managerial and personal ethics during his assignment as managing director and chairman of Szabo Diamond Company, S.A. Before describing the incidents and issues of these three ethical decisions, Bill and Szabo Diamond are described.

BILL KEANE

Bill was born in New York, in March 1950. His parents both worked in the business his father owned, and the family was upper middle class. Bill attended Lawrenceville School and studied government at Williams College. Following military service in the Army Signal Corps, from 1970 to 1972, Bill completed his studies at Williams. He became active in mountain climbing, an activity he still pursues.

Bill entered the M.B.A. program at Stanford University, graduating in 1976. His initial job was with an international consulting firm. One of his first assignments was with Lyon, Churchman and Associates, West Coast importers of diamonds. After 9 months of this consulting effort, Bill joined the diamond operations of Lyon, Churchman and Associates in Los Angeles. He also was married during this period.

The wholesale distribution of diamonds is significantly controlled by DeBeers. The digging, processing, and exporting of diamonds is somewhat more open, although increasingly less so as one moves toward the wholesale customer through the DeBeers distribution system. Nonetheless, occasional opportunities arise, and Bill found himself undertaking various assignments in Brazil, Zaire, Australia, and Indonesia.

Case prepared by John Barnett. The case is intended for classroom discussion purposes only. All events are real, although names, dates, and locations have been disguised. © 1987 by John Barnett. Reprinted by permission.

SZABO

In early 1981, Bill became the managing director and chairman of Szabo Diamonds. Szabo, on the northeast coast of South America, became a sovereign state within the British Commonwealth on May 11, 1968, and became a republic in 1978. Its capital, Luna, then had a population of 280,000 and the country a population of 3,200,000.

Diamonds were first discovered in Szabo in the early 1930s by prospectors from the Consolidated Minerals Trust (CMT). CMT subsequently formed Szabo Trust (ST) Limited in the mid-1930s and ST negotiated a series of agreements with the government in which ST paid the government a percentage of net profits and a mineral rent in exchange for a monopoly in the mining and exportation of diamonds. The Universal Diamond Corporation (UNDICO) participated in diamond exporting and, in various ways, in CMT and ST. UNDICO sorted, graded, and marketed diamonds.

One way for the outsider to enter the diamond industry is as a diamond processor. A local Szabo processing company offered several things. First, to the outsider, it might be the only means of entry into the diamond fraternity, although one would also have to ensure a source of supply by making CMT/ST and the government of Szabo partners. Second, the processing stage would be a further means of controlling smuggling, a rampant problem throughout many stages of the diamond business. Toward this end, the Szabo government should clearly be made a partner.

Thus, Szabo Diamonds, S.A. — a partnership of international interests and the Szabo government with Lyon, Churchman and Associates (LCA) as the managing partner — opened and operated a diamond-processing factory in Szabo as a foothold toward securing a portion of the overall exportation of diamonds or other natural resource development projects.

LCA made the Szabo government an interest-free long-term loan, which the Szabo government used to acquire a majority interest in Szabo Diamonds, S.A. Factory operations and all managerial decisions were controlled by LCA for a fee. Bill oversaw all the financial controls of Szabo Diamond. He stayed out of day-to-day factory operations, which were supervised by an English factory manager.

DECISION ONE — MARCH 1981

Bill's first ethical decision came in his early weeks in Szabo. Part of his duties included calling on all the government ministers connected with mining and exporting. LCA made contributions to schools and hospitals, which could be the reason for a visit to a minister or to the premier. Friendship with the ministers, partially based on mutual favors, was most helpful in both the short and long terms. LCA wanted Bill to have considerable influence with the government of Szabo.

During his second visit to a particularly important government minister, after polite conversation about Bill's new home, tennis, and the weather, the minister said: "I have a large, 60-carat yellow diamond. On one of your trips, would you be interested in taking this out of the country for me for a fee?"

DECISION TWO — MAY 1982

In New York, Szabo Diamond Company had hired an excellent manager, Manuel Ramon, a native of Szabo. He was the number two manager in Szabo, reporting directly to Bill Keane, who was most impressed with Manuel Ramon's ability. Bill and Manuel Ramon came to Szabo together in 1981 after both had undertaken international assignments for LCA. As typically was done by companies hiring expatriate managers, Szabo Diamond leased a local residence for use by Bill Keane and another for use by Manuel Ramon.

The political situation in Szabo was active. Occasionally, a group of politicians in and/or out of the government would put together a leadership alternative and would try to convince some of the army and others to help them overturn the existing government. While the current premier had kept control for almost a decade, there nevertheless were ongoing coalitions and plans for a coup d'état surfacing every 2 or 3 years.

A year after Bill got to Szabo, rumors of a plot to overthrow the premier began to circulate in Luna. In January 1982, Manuel Ramon's brother, Jose, who had been living outside Szabo while undertaking an assignment for the World Health Organization, returned to Szabo and to Luna. As often was done with the extended families within Szabo, Jose and his family moved into the house occupied by Manuel Ramon and rented by Szabo Diamond Company.

Jose had been a leader of the opposition to the premier, although he had never been directly proven to be a conspirator. A few of his associates had been, and they were subsequently tried and hanged for treason. Jose was widely respected and well known throughout Szabo. From Jose's return in January until May 1982, the rumors of his involvement in a plot to overthrow the premier were an increasing topic of conversation among close groups and trusted individuals. Further, the house occupied by Manuel Ramon, and now by Jose, was increasingly the site of evening meetings which were presumably political.

Bill knew Manuel Ramon was important to him, to Szabo Diamond, and LCA, and that he was close to Jose. Accordingly, he was most disturbed when the minister of internal affairs, who was very close to the premier, said to Bill during his visit to the Government House:

We, the Government of Szabo, are the majority shareholders in Szabo Diamond Company, which you manage. We are most disturbed to see our investment being used to pay rent for a house inhabited by an enemy of this government. Our house is being used for meetings plotting against us. The house is too close to a military installation. What are you going to do to correct this unacceptable condition?

DECISION THREE — DECEMBER 1983

Just before Christmas 1983, Bill was compelled to participate in a smuggling investigation being conducted by a witch doctor or shaman.

The diamond factory procedure involved the Szaboan workers, of whom there were about 115, coming to a glass-enclosed area called the bench. There the worker would receive a packet of diamonds of a specified grade, never larger than one carat, to be either cut along a mark (sawed), rounded (girdled), or polished. The worker and one of the European administrators (the English manager, his English assistant, or a Dutchman also supervising operations) would count the number of diamonds (usually six to eight), agree on a total, and the Szaboan would perform the necessary step, returning the diamonds for checking.

General labor problems arose because the workers specialized as polishers, sawyers, or girdlers, and they were paid on a piecework basis. This piecework rate meant that they were relatively well paid by Szabo standards. There were frequent times, however, when the various stages of the process would become uneven. That is, there would be no girdled stones to be polished or no cut stones to be girdled, because workers in one group were slow or had been absent due to personal or tribal reasons. The workers resented these frequent shutdowns of one or more sections of the production process.

A more specific labor problem was when a difference arose between what the bench said a worker should have and what the worker said. Differences could arise because of (1) bench error; (2) worker error, such as a diamond actually flying out of the polisher as the worker failed to control the gem and the machine; (3) smuggling; and (4) substitution, in which an inferior stone is brought into the factory and exchanged for a superior stone.

Just before Christmas the number of differences increased. The workers were unhappy about being suspected of stealing. One day the Szaboan head of the labor union came to Bill with a request that a tribal shaman investigate the matter.

Bill, who had seen shamans perform various rituals in Szabo, including healing and exorcism, agreed to the use of the shaman. Bill reasoned that such an investigation might reduce the workers' dissatisfaction and the "differences," and that it would also show some respect for tribal customs and procedures.

Thus, shortly before the end of the next work day the shaman arrived. All European and Szaboan employees participated in the investigation, led by Bill. Bill had anticipated that this shaman would follow the practice Bill had seen other shamans use, namely, going amongst the employees with a "magic" stick or broom that would only strike the guilty. This investigation, however, consisted of a different procedure, which was described to everyone beforehand by the shaman. Bill and then every other employee lined up single file, walked up to a pot full of palm oil placed over a stove. The oil was heated to a rolling boil. Then a large rock was dropped to the bottom of the pot. Each person was to pick up the stone, lift it out of the boiling oil, and put it back in the pot. The shaman assured everyone that only the guilty persons would be burned.

Bill went first, picked up the stone, and replaced it in the boiling oil. He felt nothing. Only two persons were burned, one Szaboan and the Dutchman (they both wore bandages for several weeks). Bill was certain that some out-of-the-ordinary phenomenon occurred, and he wondered what to do. He commented:

I was and am totally convinced that there's something behind all of this. The boiling oil wasn't even hot to my touch, nor to over one hundred other people's touch. While I don't go to church, and we have not had our three children baptized, I still consider myself a Christian. I've always believed in some power, and this experience probably showed some aspect of that power.

THE LINCOLN ELECTRIC COMPANY, 1983

INTRODUCTION

The Lincoln Electric Company is the world's largest manufacturer of welding machines and electrodes. Lincoln employs 2400 workers in two U.S. factories near Cleveland and approximately 600 in three factories located in other countries. This does not include the field sales force of more than 200 persons. It has been estimated that Lincoln's market share (for arc-welding equipment and supplies) is more than 40 percent.

The Lincoln incentive management plan has been well known for many years. Many college management texts make reference to the Lincoln plan as a model for achieving high worker productivity. Certainly, Lincoln has been a successful company according to the usual measures of success.

James F. Lincoln died in 1965 and there was some concern, even among employees, that the Lincoln system would fall into disarray, that profits would decline, and that year-end bonuses might be discontinued. Quite the contrary, eighteen years after Lincoln's death, the company appears stronger than ever. Each year, except the recession year 1982, has seen higher profits and bonuses. Employee morale and productivity remain high. Employee turnover is almost nonexistent except for retirements. Lincoln's market share is stable. Consistently high dividends continue on Lincoln's stock.

A HISTORICAL SKETCH

In 1895, after being "frozen out" of the depression-ravaged Elliott-Lincoln Company, a maker of Lincoln-designed electric motors, John C. Lincoln took out his second patent and began to manufacture his improved motor. He opened his new business,

The research and written case information were presented at a Case Research Symposium and were evaluated by the North American Case Research Association's Editorial Board. This case was prepared by Arthur D. Sharplin of McNeese University, Lake Charles, LA, as a basis for class discussion. © 1983 by Arthur D. Sharplin. Reprinted by permission.

unincorporated, with $200 he had earned redesigning a motor for young Herbert Henry Dow, who later founded the Dow Chemical Company.

Started during an economic depression and cursed by a major fire after only one year in business, Lincoln's company grew, but hardly prospered, through its first quarter century. In 1906, John C. Lincoln incorporated his company and moved from his one-room, fourth-floor factory to a new three-story building he erected in east Cleveland. In his new factory, he expanded his work force to 30 and sales grew to over $50,000 a year. John Lincoln preferred being an engineer and inventor rather than a manager, though, and it was to be left to another Lincoln to manage the company through its years of success.

In 1907, after a bout with typhoid fever forced him from Ohio State University in his senior year, James F. Lincoln, John's younger brother, joined the fledgling company. In 1914 he became the active head of the firm, with the titles of General Manager and Vice President. John Lincoln, while he remained President of the company for some years, became more involved in other business ventures and in his work as an inventor.

One of James Lincoln's early actions as head of the firm was to ask the employees to elect representatives to a committee which would advise him on company operations. The Advisory Board has met with the chief executive officer twice monthly since that time. This was only the first of a series of innovative personnel policies which have, over the years, distinguished Lincoln Electric from its contemporaries.

The first year the Advisory Board was in existence, working hours were reduced from 55 per week, then standard, to 50 hours a week. In 1915, the company gave each employee a paid-up life insurance policy. A welding school, which continues today, was begun in 1917. In 1918, an employee bonus plan was attempted. It was not continued, but the idea was to resurface and become the backbone of the Lincoln Management System.

The Lincoln Electric Employees' Association was formed in 1919 to provide health benefits and social activities. This organization continues today and has assumed several additional functions over the years. In 1923, a piecework pay system was in effect, employees got two-week paid vacations each year, and wages were adjusted for changes in the Consumer Price Index. Approximately 30 percent of Lincoln's stock was set aside for key employees in 1914 when James F. Lincoln became General Manager and a stock purchase plan for all employees was begun in 1925.

The Board of Directors voted to start a suggestion system in 1929. The program is still in effect, but cash awards, a part of the early program, were discontinued several years ago. Now, suggestions are rewarded by additional "points," which affect year-end bonuses.

The legendary Lincoln bonus plan was proposed by the Advisory Board and accepted on a trial basis by James Lincoln in 1934. The first annual bonus amounted to about 25 percent of wages. There has been a bonus every year since then. The bonus plan has been a cornerstone of the Lincoln Management System and recent bonuses have approximated annual wages.

By 1944, Lincoln employees enjoyed a pension plan, a policy of promotion from within, and continuous employment. Base pay rates were determined by formal job evaluation and a merit rating system was in effect.

In the prologue of James F. Lincoln's last book, Charles G. Herbruck writes regarding the foregoing personnel innovations,

> *They were not to buy good behavior. They were not efforts to increase profits. They were not antidotes to labor difficulties. They did not constitute a "do-gooder" program. They were expressions of mutual respect for each person's importance to the job to be done. All of these reflect the leadership of James Lincoln, under whom they were nurtured and propagated* (Lincoln, 1961, p. 11).

By the start of World War II, Lincoln Electric was the world's largest manufacturer of arc-welding products. Sales of about $4,000,000 in 1934 had grown to $24,000,000 by 1941. Productivity per employee more than doubled during the same period.

During the War, Lincoln Electric prospered as never before. Despite challenges to Lincoln's profitability by the Navy's Price Review Board and to the tax deductibility of employee bonuses by the Internal Revenue Service, the company increased its profits and paid huge bonuses.

Certainly since 1935 and probably for several years before that, Lincoln productivity has been well above the average for similar companies. Lincoln claims levels of productivity more than twice those for other manufacturers from 1945 onward. Information available from outside sources tends to support these claims.

COMPANY PHILOSOPHY

James F. Lincoln was the son of a Congregational minister, and Christian principles were at the center of his business philosophy. The confidence that he had in the efficacy of Christ's teachings is illustrated by the following remark taken from one of his books:

> *The Christian ethic should control our acts. If it did control our acts, the savings in cost of distribution would be tremendous. Advertising would be a contact of the expert consultant with the customer, in order to give the customer the best product available when all of the customer's needs are considered. Competition then would be in improving the quality of products and increasing efficiency in producing and distributing them; not in deception, as is now too customary. Pricing would reflect efficiency of production; it would not be a selling dodge that the customer may well be sorry he accepted. It would be proper for all concerned and rewarding for the ability used in producing the product.*[1]

There is no indication that Lincoln attempted to evangelize his employees or customers — or the general public for that matter. The current Board chairman,

---

[1] James F. Lincoln, *A New Approach to Industrial Economics* (New York: The Devin Adair Co., 1961), p. 64.

Mr. Irrgang, and the President, Mr. Willis, do not even mention the Christian gospel in their recent speeches and interviews. The company motto, "The actual is limited, the possible is immense," is prominently displayed, but there is no display of religious slogans, and there is no company chapel.

Attitude Toward the Customer

James Lincoln saw the customer's needs as the *raison d'être* for every company. "When any company has achieved success so that it is attractive as an investment," he wrote, "all money usually needed for expansion is supplied by the customer in retained earnings. It is obvious that the customer's interests, not the stockholder's, should come first."[2] In 1947 he said, "Care should be taken . . . not to rivet attention on profit. Between 'How much do I get?' and 'How do I make this better, cheaper, more useful?' the difference is fundamental and decisive."[3] Mr. Willis still ranks the customer as Lincoln's most important constituency. This is reflected in Lincoln's policy to "at all times price on the basis of cost and at all times keep pressure on our cost. . . ."[4] Lincoln's goal, often stated, is "to build a better and better product at a lower and lower price."[5] "It is obvious," James Lincoln said, "that the customer's interests should be the first goal of industry."[6]

Attitude Toward Stockholders

Stockholders are given last priority at Lincoln. This is a continuation of James Lincoln's philosophy: "The last group to be considered is the stockholders who own stock because they think it will be more profitable than investing money in any other way."[7] Concerning division of the largess produced by incentive management, Lincoln writes, "The absentee stockholder also will get his share, even if undeserved, out of the greatly increased profit that the efficiency produces."[8]

Attitude Toward Unionism

There **has** never been a serious effort to organize Lincoln employees. While James Lincoln criticized the labor movement for "selfishly attempting to better its position at the expense of the people it must serve,"[9] he still had kind words for union members. He excused abuses of union power as "the natural reactions of human beings to the abuses to which management has subjected them."[10] Lincoln's idea of the correct relationship between workers and managers is shown by this comment:

[2] Ibid., p. 119.

[3] "You Can't Tell What a Man Can Do — Until He Has the Chance," *Reader's Digest*, January 1947, p. 94.

[4] George E. Willis's letter to author of 7 September 1978.

[5] Lincoln, 1961, p. 47.

[6] Ibid., p. 117.

[7] Ibid., p. 38.

[8] Ibid., p. 122.

[9] Ibid., p. 18.

[10] Ibid., p. 76.

"Labor and management are properly not warring camps; they are parts of one organization in which they must and should cooperate fully and happily."[11]

Beliefs and Assumptions About Employees

If fulfilling customer needs is the desired goal of business, then employee performance and productivity are the means by which this goal can best be achieved. It is the Lincoln attitude toward employees, reflected in the following quotations, which is credited by many with creating the record of success the company has experienced:

> *The greatest fear of the worker, which is the same as the greatest fear of the industrialist in operating a company, is the lack of income. . . . The industrial manager is very conscious of his company's need of uninterrupted income. He is completely oblivious, evidently, of the fact that the worker has the same need.[12]*

> *He is just as eager as any manager is to be part of a team that is properly organized and working for the advancement of our economy. . . . He has no desire to make profits for those who do not hold up their end in production, as is true of absentee stockholders and inactive people in the company.[13]*

> *If money is to be used as an incentive, the program must provide that what is paid to the worker is what he has earned. The earnings of each must be in accordance with accomplishment.[14]*

> *Status is of great importance in all human relationships. The greatest incentive that money has, usually, is that it is a symbol of success. . . . The resulting status is the real incentive. . . . Money alone can be an incentive to the miser only.[15]*

> *There must be complete honesty and understanding between the hourly worker and management if high efficiency is to be obtained.[16]*

LINCOLN'S BUSINESS

Arc-welding has been the standard joining method in the shipbuilding industry for decades. It is the predominant way of joining steel in the construction industry. Most industrial plants have their own welding shops for maintenance and construction. Manufacturers of tractors and all kinds of heavy equipment use arc-welding extensively in the manufacturing process. Many hobbyists have their own welding machines and use them for making metal items such as patio furniture and barbeque pits. The popularity of welded sculpture as an art form is growing.

[11] Ibid., p. 72.

[12] Ibid., p. 36.

[13] Ibid., p. 75.

[14] Ibid., p. 98.

[15] Ibid., p. 92.

[16] Ibid., p. 39.

While advances in welding technology have been frequent, arc-welding products, in the main, have hardly changed except for Lincoln's Innershield process. This process, utilizing a self-shielded, flux cored electrode, has established new cost saving opportunities for construction and equipment fabrication. The most popular Lincoln electrode, the Fleetweld 5P, has been virtually the same since the 1930s. The most popular engine-driven welder in the world, the Lincoln SA-200, has been a gray-colored assembly including a four-cylinder continental "Red Seal" engine and a 200 ampere direct-current generator with two current-control knobs for at least three decades. A 1980 model SA-200 even weighs almost the same as the 1950 model, and it certainly is little changed in appearance.

Lincoln and its competitors now market a wide range of general purpose and specialty electrodes for welding mild steel, aluminum, cast iron, and stainless and special steels. Most of these electrodes are designed to meet the standards of the American Welding Society, a trade association. They are thus essentially the same as to size and composition from one manufacturer to another. Every electrode manufacturer has a limited number of unique products, but these typically constitute only a small percentage of total sales.

Lincoln's research and development expenditures have recently been less than one and one-half percent of sales. There is evidence that others spend several times as much as a percentage of sales.

Lincoln's share of the arc-welding products market appears to have been about 40 percent for many years, and the welding products market has grown somewhat faster than the level of industry in general. The market is highly price-competitive, with variations in prices of standard products normally amounting to only a percent or two. Lincoln's products are sold directly by its engineering-oriented sales force and indirectly through its distributor organization. Advertising expenditures amount to less than one-fourth of one percent of sales, one-third as much as a major Lincoln competitor with whom the casewriter checked.

The other major welding process, flame-welding, has not been competitive with arc-welding since the 1930s. However, plasma-arc-welding, a relatively new process which uses a conducting stream of super heated gas (plasma) to confine the welding current to a small area, has made some inroads, especially in metal tubing manufacturing, in recent years. Major advances in technology which will produce an alternative superior to arc-welding within the next decade or so appear unlikely. Also, it seems likely that changes in the machines and techniques used in arc-welding will be evolutionary rather than revolutionary.

Products

The company is primarily engaged in the manufacture and sale of arc-welding products — electric welding machines and metal electrodes. Lincoln also produces electric motors ranging from one-half horsepower to 200 horsepower. Motors constitute about eight to ten percent of total sales.

The electric welding machines, some consisting of a transformer or motor and generator arrangement powered by commercial electricity and others consisting of an internal combustion engine and generator, are designed to produce from 30 to

1000 amperes of electrical power. This electrical current is used to melt a consumable metal electrode with the molten metal being transferred in a super hot spray to the metal joint being welded. Very high temperatures and hot sparks are produced, and operators usually must wear special eye and face protection and leather gloves, often along with leather aprons and sleeves.

Welding electrodes are of two basic types: (1) Coated "stick" electrodes, usually fourteen inches long and smaller than a pencil in diameter, which are held in a special insulated holder by the operator, who must manipulate the electrode in order to maintain a proper arc-width and pattern of deposition of the metal being transferred. Stick electrodes are packaged in six- to fifty-pound boxes. (2) Coiled wire, ranging in diameter from 0.035″ to 0.219″, which is designed to be fed continuously to the welding arc through a "gun" held by the operator or positioned by automatic positioning equipment. The wire is packaged in coils, reels, and drums weighing from fourteen to 1000 pounds.

MANUFACTURING OPERATIONS

Plant Locations

The main plant is in Euclid, Ohio, a suburb on Cleveland's east side. The layout of this plant is shown in Exhibit 1. There are no warehouses. Materials flow from the half-mile long dock on the north side of the plant through the production lines to a very limited storage and loading area on the south side. Materials used on each work station are stored as close as possible to the work station. The administration offices, near the center of the factory, are entirely functional. Not even the President's office is carpeted. A corridor below the main level provides access to the factory floor from the main entrance near the center of the plant.

A new plant, just opened in Mentor, Ohio, houses some of the electrode production operations, which were moved from the main plant. The main plant is currently being enlarged by 100,000 square feet and several innovative changes are being made in the manufacturing layout.

Manufacturing Processes

The electrode manufacturing process is highly capital intensive. Metal rods purchased from steel producers are drawn or extruded down to smaller diameters, cut to length and coated with pressed-powder "flux" for stick electrodes or plated with copper (for conductivity) and spun into coils or spools for wire. Some of Lincoln's wire, called "Inner-shield," is hollow and filled with a material similar to that used to coat stick electrodes. Lincoln is highly secretive about its electrode production processes, and the casewriter was not given access to the details of those processes.

Welding machines and electric motors are made on a series of assembly lines. Gasoline and diesel engines are purchased partially assembled but practically all other components are made from basic industrial products, e.g., steel bars and sheets and bar copper conductor wire, in the Lincoln factory.

Individual components, such as gasoline tanks for engine-driven welders and steel shafts for motors and generators, are made by numerous small "factories

EXHIBIT 1 Factory layout

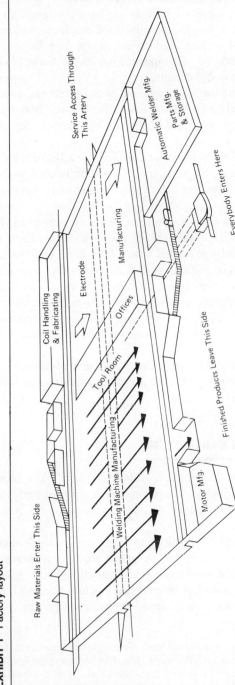

Raw Materials Enter This Side

Coil Handling & Fabricating

Electrode

Manufacturing

Service Access Through This Artery

Automatic Welder Mfg.

Parts Mfg. & Storage

Everybody Enters Here

Tool Room

Offices

Welding Machine Manufacturing

Finished Products Leave This Side

Motor Mfg.

within a factory.'' The shaft for a certain generator, for example, is made from a raw steel bar by one operator who uses five large machines, all running continuously. A saw cuts the bar to length, a digital lathe machines different sections to varying diameters, a special milling machine cuts a slot for a keyway, and so forth, until a finished shaft is produced. The operator moves the shafts from machine to machine and makes necessary adjustments.

Another operator punches, shapes and paints sheetmetal cowling parts. One assembles steel liminations onto a rotor shaft, then winds, insulates and tests the rotors. Finished components are moved by crane operators to the nearby assembly lines.

Worker Performance and Attitudes

Exceptional worker performance at Lincoln is a matter of record. The typical Lincoln employee earns about twice as much as other factory workers in the Cleveland area. Yet the labor cost per sales dollar at Lincoln, currently 23.5 cents, is well below industry averages.

Sales per Lincoln factory employee currently exceed $157,000. An observer at the factory quickly sees why this figure is so high. Each worker is proceeding busily and thoughtfully about his task. There is no idle chatter. Most workers take no coffee breaks. Many operate several machines and make a substantial component unaided. The supervisors, some with as many as 100 subordinates, are busy with planning and recordkeeping duties and hardly glance at the people they supervise. The manufacturing procedures appear efficient — no unnecessary steps, no wasted motions, no wasted materials. Finished components move smoothly to subsequent work stations.

Worker turnover at Lincoln is practically nonexistent except for retirements and departures by new employees. The appendix includes summaries of interviews with Lincoln employees.

ORGANIZATION STRUCTURE

Lincoln has never had a formal organization chart.[17] The object of this policy is to insure maximum flexibility. An open door policy is practiced throughout the company, and personnel are encouraged to take problems to the persons most capable of resolving them.

Perhaps because of the quality and enthusiasm of the Lincoln workforce, routine supervision is almost nonexistent. A typical production foreman, for example, supervises as many as 100 workers, a span-of-control which does not allow more than infrequent worker-supervisor interaction. Position titles and traditional flows of authority do imply something of an organizational structure, however. For example,

---

[17] Once, Harvard Business School researchers prepared an organization chart reflecting the below-mentioned implied relationships. The chart became available within the Lincoln organization, and present Lincoln management feels that it had a disruptive effect. Therefore, the casewriter was asked not to include any kind of organizational chart in this report.

the Vice-President, Sales, and the Vice-President, Electrode Division, report to the President, as do various staff assistants such as the Personnel Director and the Director of Purchasing. Using such implied relationships, it has been determined that production workers have two or, at most, three levels of supervision between themselves and the President.

PERSONNEL POLICIES

Recruitment and Selection

Every job opening at Lincoln is advertised internally on company bulletin boards and any employee can apply for any job so advertised. External hiring is done only for entry level positions. Selection for these jobs is done on the basis of personal interviews — there is no aptitude or psychological testing. Not even a high school diploma is required except for engineering and sales positions, which are filled by graduate engineers. A committee consisting of vice presidents and superintendents interviews candidates initially cleared by the Personnel Department. Final selection is made by the supervisor who has a job opening. Out of over 3500 applicants interviewed by the Personnel Department during a recent period fewer than 300 were hired.

Job Security

In 1958 Lincoln formalized its lifetime employment policy, which had already been in effect for many years. There have been no layoffs at Lincoln since World War II. Since 1958, every Lincoln worker with over one year's longevity has been guaranteed at least 30 hours per week, 49 weeks per year.

The policy has never been so severely tested as during the 1981–83 recession. As a manufacturer of capital goods, Lincoln's business is highly cyclical. In previous recessions Lincoln has been able to avoid major sales declines. Nineteen eighty-two sales, however, were about one-third below those of 1981. Few companies could withstand such a sales decline and remain profitable. Yet, Lincoln not only earned profits, but no employee has been laid off, the usual year-end incentive bonuses were paid (averaging $15,600 per worker for 1982), and common shareholders continue to receive about the normal dividend (around $8 per share).

Performance Evaluations

Each supervisor formally evaluates his subordinates twice a year using the cards shown in Exhibit 2. The employee performance criteria, "quality," "dependability," "ideas and cooperation," and "output," are considered to be independent of each other. Marks on the cards are converted to numerical scores which are forced to average 100 for each evaluating supervisor. Individual merit rating scores normally range from 80 to 110. Any score over 110 requires a special letter to top management. These scores (over 110) are not considered in computing the required 100 point average for each evaluating supervisor. Suggestions for improvements often result in recommendations for exceptionally high performance scores. Supervisors discuss individual performance marks with the employees concerned. Each warranty claim on a Lincoln product is traced to the individual employee whose work caused the

EXHIBIT 2
Performance
appraisal cards

────────── Increasing Quality ──────────▶

This card rates the QUALITY of the work you do.

It also reflects your success in eliminating errors and in reducing scrap and waste.

Quality

This rating has been done jointly by your department head and the Inspection Department in the shop and with other department heads in the office and engineering.

────────── Increasing Dependability ──────────▶

This card rates how well your supervisors have been able to depend upon you to do things that have been expected of you without supervision.

It also rates your ability to supervise yourself including your work safety performance, your orderliness, care of equipment and the effective use you make of your skills.

Dependability

This rating has been done by your department head.

────────── Increasing Ideas & Cooperation ──────────▶

This card rates your Cooperation, Ideas and Initiative.

New ideas and new methods are important to your company in our continuing effort to reduce costs, increase output, improve quality, work safely and improve our relationship with our customers. This card credits you for your ideas and initiative used to help in this direction.

It also rates your cooperation — how you work with others as a team. Such factors as your attitude towards supervision, co-workers, and the company, your efforts to share your expert knowledge with others, and your cooperation in installing new methods smoothly, are considered here.

Ideas & Cooperation

This rating has been done jointly by your department head and the Times Study Department in the shop and with other department heads in the office and engineering.

────────── Increasing Output ──────────▶

This card rates HOW MUCH PRODUCTIVE WORK you actually turn out.

It also reflects your willingness not to hold back and recognizes your attendance record.

Output

This rating has been done jointly by your department head and the Production Control department in the shop and with other department heads in the office and engineering.

454

defect. The employee's performance score may be reduced by one point, or the worker may be required to repay the cost of servicing the warranty claim by working without pay.

Compensation

Basic wage levels for jobs at Lincoln are determined by a wage survey of similar jobs in the Cleveland area. These rates are adjusted quarterly in accordance with changes in the Cleveland Area Consumer Price Index. Insofar as possible, base wage rates are translated into piece rates. Practically all production workers and many others — for example, some forklift operators — are paid by piece rate. Once established, piece rates are never changed unless a substantive change in the way a job is done results from a source other than the worker doing the job. In December of each year, a portion of annual profits is distributed to employees as bonuses. Incentive bonuses since 1934 have averaged about the same as annual wages and somewhat more than after-tax profits. The average bonus for 1981 was about $21,000. Individual bonuses are exactly proportional to merit-rating scores. For example, assume incentive bonuses for the company total 110 percent of wages paid. A person whose performance score is 95 will receive a bonus of 1.045 (1.10 × 0.95) times annual wages.

Work Assignment

Management has authority to transfer workers and to switch between overtime and short time as required. Supervisors have undisputed authority to assign specific parts to individual workmen, who may have their own preferences due to variations in piece rates.

Employee Participation in Decision Making

When a manager speaks of participative management, he usually thinks of a relaxed, nonauthoritarian atmosphere. This is not the case at Lincoln. Formal authority is quite strong. "We're very authoritarian around here," says Mr. Willis. James F. Lincoln placed a good deal of stress on protecting management's authority. "Management in all successful departments of industry must have complete power," he said, ". . . Management is the coach who must be obeyed. The men, however, are the players who alone can win the game."[18] Despite this attitude, there are several ways in which employees participate in management at Lincoln.

Richard Sabo, Manager of Public Relations, relates job-enlargement to participation. "The most important participative technique that we use is giving more responsibility to employees." Mr. Sabo says, "We give a high school graduate more responsibility than other companies give their foremen." Lincoln puts limits on the degree of participation which is allowed, however. In Mr. Sabo's words,

> When you use "participation," put quotes around it. Because we believe that each person should participate only in those decisions he is most knowledgeable about. I don't think production employees should control the decisions of Bill Irrgang. They don't know as much as he does about the decisions he is involved in.

[18] Lincoln, *Incentive Management* (Cleveland, OH: The Lincoln Electric Company, 1951), p. 228.

The Advisory Board, elected by the workers, meets with the Chairman and the President every two weeks to discuss ways of improving operations. This board has been in existence since 1914 and has contributed to many innovations. The incentive bonuses, for example, were first recommended by this committee. Every Lincoln employee has access to Advisory Board members, and answers to all Advisory Board suggestions are promised by the following meeting. Both Mr. Irrgang and Mr. Willis are quick to point out, though, that the Advisory Board only recommends actions. "They do not have direct authority," Mr. Irrgang says, "and when they bring up something that management thinks is not to the benefit of the company, it will be rejected."[19]

A suggestion program was instituted in 1929. At first, employees were awarded one-half of the first year's savings attributable to their suggestions. Now, however, the value of suggestions is reflected in performance evaluation scores, which determine individual incentive bonus amounts.

Training and Education

Production workers are given a short period of on-the-job training and then placed on a piecework pay system. Lincoln does not pay for off-site education. The idea behind this latter policy is that everyone cannot take advantage of such a program, and it is unfair to expend company funds for an advantage to which there is unequal access. Sales personnel are given on-the-job training in the plant followed by a period of work and training at one of the regional sales offices.

Fringe Benefits and Executive Perquisites

A medical plan and a company-paid retirement program have been in effect for many years. A plant cafeteria, operated on a break-even basis, serves meals at about sixty percent of usual costs. An employee association, to which the company does not contribute, provides disability insurance and social and athletic activities. An employee stock ownership program, instituted in about 1925, and regular stock purchases have resulted in employee ownership of about fifty percent of Lincoln's stock.

As to executive perquisites, there are none — crowded, austere offices, no executive washrooms or lunchrooms, and no reserved parking spaces. Even the company President pays for his own meals and eats in the cafeteria.

FINANCIAL POLICIES

James F. Lincoln felt strongly that financing for company growth should come from within the company — through initial cash investment by the founders, through retention of earnings, and through stock purchases by those who work in the business. He saw the following advantages of this approach:[20]

[19] Incentive Management in Action, *Assembly Engineering*, March 1967, p. 18.

[20] Lincoln, 1961, pp. 220–228.

1. Ownership of stock by employees strengthens team spirit. "If they are mutually anxious to make it succeed, the future of the company is bright."
2. Ownership of stock provides individual incentive because employees feel that they will benefit from company profitability.
3. "Ownership is educational." Owners-employees "will know how profits are made and lost; how success is won and lost. . . . There are few socialists in the list of stockholders of the nation's industries."
4. "Capital available from within controls expansion." Unwarranted expansion will not occur, Lincoln believed, under his financing plan.
5. "The greatest advantage would be the development of the individual worker. Under the incentive of ownership, he would become a greater man."
6. "Stock ownership is one of the steps that can be taken that will make the worker feel that there is less of a gulf between him and the boss. . . . Stock ownership will help the worker to recognize his responsibility in the game and the importance of victory."

Lincoln Electric Company uses a minimum of debt in its capital structure. There is no borrowing at all, with the debt being limited to current payables. Even the new $20 million plant in Mentor, Ohio, was financed totally from earnings.

The unusual pricing policy at Lincoln is succinctly stated by President Willis: "at all times price on the basis of cost and at all times keep pressure on our cost." This policy resulted in Lincoln's price for the most popular welding electrode then in use going from 16 cents a pound in 1929 to 4.7 cents in 1938. More recently, the SA-200 Welder, Lincoln's largest selling portable machine, decreased in price from 1958 through 1965. According to Dr. C. Jackson Grayson of the American Productivity Center in Houston, Texas, Lincoln's prices in general have increased only one-fifth as fast as the Consumer Price Index since 1934. This has resulted in a welding products market in which Lincoln is the undisputed price leader for the products it manufactures. Not even the major Japanese manufacturers, such as Nippon Steel for welding electrodes and Asaka Transformer for welding machines, have been able to penetrate this market.

Huge cash balances are accumulated each year preparatory to paying the year-end bonuses. The bonuses totaled $55,718,000 for 1981 and about $41,000,000 for 1982. This money is invested in short-term U.S. government securities until needed. Financial statements are shown in Exhibits 3 and 4.

HOW WELL DOES LINCOLN SERVE ITS PUBLIC?

Lincoln Electric differs from most other companies in the importance it assigns to each of the groups it serves. Mr. Willis identifies these groups, in the order of priority Lincoln ascribes to them, as (1) customers, (2) employees, and (3) stockholders.

Certainly Lincoln customers have fared well over the years. Lincoln prices for

EXHIBIT 3 Summary of balance sheet information

	1977	1978	1979	1980	1981	1982
Assets						
Cash	$ 2,203	$ 1,588	$ 2,261	$ 1,307	$ 3,603	$ 1,318
Govt. securities & certificates of deposit	24,375	28,807	38,408	46,503	62,671	72,485
Notes & accounts receivable	34,093	38,786	41,598	42,424	41,521	26,239
Inventories (life basis)	28,449	35,916	37,640	35,533	45,541	38,157
Deferred taxes & prepayments	2,275	1,729	1,437	2,749	3,658	4,635
	$ 91,395	$106,826	$121,344	$128,516	$156,994	$142,834
Other intangible assets	14,172	19,420	19,164	19,723	21,424	22,116
Investments in foreign subs.	4,696	4,976	4,986	4,695	4,695	7,696
	$ 18,868	$ 24,396	$ 24,150	$ 24,418	$ 26,119	$ 29,812
Property, plant, equipment						
Land and buildings (net)	23,137	22,622	22,496	23,895	25,624	24,255
Machinery, tools and equipment (net)	17,035	18,458	21,250	25,339	27,104	26,949
	$ 40,172	$ 41,080	$ 43,746	$ 49,234	$ 52,728	$ 51,204
Total assets	$150,435	$172,302	$189,240	$202,168	$235,841	$223,850
Liabilities						
Accounts payable	$ 9,891	$ 14,330	$ 16,590	$ 15,608	$ 14,868	$ 11,936
Accrued wages	839	882	917	1,504	4,940	3,633
Taxes, including income taxes	8,057	9,116	9,620	5,622	14,755	5,233
Dividends payable	4,327	5,730	5,889	5,800	7,070	6,957
	$ 23,114	$ 30,058	$ 33,016	$ 28,534	$ 41,633	$ 27,759
Deferred taxes and other long-term liabilities	—	—	—	$ 3,807	$ 4,557	$ 5,870
Shareholders' equity						
Common stock	4,479	286	280	276	272	268
Additional paid-in capital		4,216	4,143	2,641	501	1,862
Retained earnings	122,842	137,742	151,801	166,910	188,878	188,091
	$127,321	$142,244	$156,224	$169,827	$189,651	$190,221
Total liabilities & shareholders' equity	$150,435	$172,302	$189,240	$202,168	$235,841	$223,850

Note: figures in thousands of dollars.

welding machines and welding electrodes are acknowledged to be the lowest in the marketplace. Lincoln quality has consistently been so high that Lincoln "Fleetweld" electrodes and Lincoln SA-200 welders have been the standard in the pipeline and refinery construction industry, where price is hardly a criterion, for decades. The cost of field failures for Lincoln products was an amazing four one-hundreths of one percent in 1979. A Lincoln distributor in Monroe, Louisiana, says that he

EXHIBIT 4 Summary of income statement information

	1977	1978	1979	1980	1981	1982
Income						
Net sales	$276,947	$329,652	$373,789	$387,374	$450,387	$310,862
Other income	5,768	7,931	11,397	13,817	18,454	18,049
	$282,715	$337,583	$385,186	$401,191	$468,841	$328,911
Costs and expense						
Cost of products sold	$175,733	$210,208	$244,376	$260,671	$293,332	$212,674
General and administrative expense	23,821	28,126	33,699	37,753	42,656	37,128
Year-end incentive bonus	29,263	39,547	44,068	43,249	55,718	36,870
Payroll taxes on bonuses[a]	—	—	1,349[a]	1,251	1,544	1,847
Pension expense	4,062	5,881	6,131	6,810	6,874	5,888
	$232,879	$283,762	$329,623	$349,734	$400,124	$294,407
Income before taxes	$ 49,836	$ 53,821	$ 55,563	$ 51,457	$ 68,717	$ 34,504
Provision for taxes						
Federal	25,936	22,700	22,400	20,300	27,400	13,227
State and local	—	3,573	3,165	3,072	3,885	2,497
	25,936	26,273	25,565	23,372	31,285	$ 15,724
Net Income	$ 23,900	$ 27,548	$ 29,998	$ 28,085	$ 37,432	$ 18,780
Eligible employees (for bonus)	2,431	2,533	2,611	2,637	2,684	2,634

[a] Payroll tax expense paid by The Lincoln Electric Company relating to year-end incentive bonus were distributed to Cost of Products Sold, Selling, Administrative and General Expenses prior to Year 1979.

has sold several hundred of the popular AC-225 welders, and, though the machine is warranted for one year, he has never handled a warranty claim.

Perhaps best-served of all Lincoln constituencies have been the employees. Not the least of their benefits, of course, are the year-end bonuses, which effectively double an already average compensation level. The foregoing description of the personnel program and the comments in the Appendix further illustrate the desirability of a Lincoln job.

While stockholders were relegated to an inferior status by James F. Lincoln, they have done very well indeed. Recent dividends have exceeded $7 a share and earnings per share have exceeded $20. In January 1980, the price of restricted stock committed by Lincoln to employees was $117 a share. By February 4, 1983, the stated value, at which Lincoln will repurchase the stock if tendered, was $166. A check with the New York office of Merrill, Lynch, Pierce, Fenner and Smith on February 4, 1983 revealed an estimated price on Lincoln stock of $240 a share, with none being offered for sale. Technically, this price applies only to the unrestricted stock owned by the Lincoln family, a few other major holders, and employees who have purchased it on the open market, but it gives some idea of the value of Lincoln stock in general. The risk associated with Lincoln stock, a major determinant of stock value, is minimal because of the absence of debt in Lincoln's capital structure, because of an extremely stable earnings record, and because of Lincoln's practice of purchasing the restricted stock whenever employees offer it for sale.

A CONCLUDING COMMENT

It is easy to believe that the reason for Lincoln's success is the excellent attitude of Lincoln employees and their willingness to work harder, faster, and more intelligently than other industrial workers. However, Mr. Richard Sabo, Manager of Publicity and Educational Services at Lincoln, suggests that appropriate credit be given to Lincoln executives, whom he credits with carrying out the following policies:

1. Management has limited research, development and manufacturing to a standard product line designed to meet the major needs of the welding industry.
2. New products must be reviewed by manufacturing and all production costs verified before being approved by management.
3. Purchasing is challenged to not only procure materials at the lowest cost, but also to work closely with engineering and manufacturing to assure that the latest innovations are implemented.
4. Manufacturing supervision and all personnel are held accountable for reduction of scrap, energy conservation, and maintenance of product quality.
5. Production control, material handling, and methods engineering are closely supervised by top management.
6. Material and finished goods inventory control, accurate cost accounting and attention to sales cost, credit, and other financial areas have constantly reduced overhead and led to excellent profitability.
7. Management has made cost reduction a way of life at Lincoln, and definite programs are established in many areas, including traffic and shipping, where tremendous savings can result.
8. Management has established a sales department that is technically trained to reduce customer welding costs. This sales technique and other real customer services have eliminated nonessential frills and resulted in long-term benefits to all concerned.
9. Management has encouraged education, technical publishing, and long range programs that have resulted in industry growth, thereby assuring market potential for the Lincoln Electric Company.

APPENDIX: EMPLOYEE INTERVIEWS

During the late summer of 1980, the author conducted numerous interviews with Lincoln employees. Typical questions and answers from those interviews are presented below. In order to maintain each employee's personal privacy, the names used for the interviewees are fictitious.

PART I

Interview with Betty Stewart, a 52-year-old high school graduate who had been with Lincoln thirteen years and who was working as a cost accounting clerk at the time of the interview.

Q: What jobs have you held here besides the one you have now?

A: I worked in payroll for a while, and then this job came open and I took it.

Q: How much money did you make last year, including your bonus?

A: I would say roughly around $20,000, but I was off for back surgery for a while.

Q: You weren't paid while you were off for back surgery?

A: No.

Q: Did the Employees Association help out?

A: Yes. The company doesn't furnish that, though. We pay $6 a month into the Employees Association. I think my check from them was $105.00 a week.

Q: How was your performance rating last year?

A: It was around 100 points, but I lost some points for attendance with my back problem.

Q: How did you get your job at Lincoln?

A: I was bored silly where I was working, and I had heard that Lincoln kept their people busy. So I applied and got the job the next day.

Q: Do you think you make more money than similar workers in Cleveland?

A: I know I do.

Q: What have you done with your money?

A: We have purchased a better home. Also, my son is going to the University of Chicago, which costs $10,000 a year. I buy the Lincoln stock which is offered each year, and I have a little bit of gold.

Q: Have you ever visited with any of the senior executives, like Mr. Willis or Mr. Irrgang?

A: I have known Mr. Willis for a long time.

Q: Does he call you by name?

A: Yes. In fact he was very instrumental in my going to the doctor that I am going to with my back. He knows the director of the clinic.

Q: Do you know Mr. Irrgang?

A: I know him to speak to him, and he always speaks, always. But I have known Mr. Willis for a good many years. When I did Plant Two accounting I did not understand how the plant operated. Of course you are not allowed in Plant Two, because that's the Electrode Division. I told my boss about the problem one day and the next thing I knew Mr. Willis came by and said, "Come on, Betty, we're going to Plant Two." He spent an hour and a half showing me the plant.

Q: Do you think Lincoln employees produce more than those in other companies?

A: I think with the incentive program the way that it is, if you want to work and achieve, then you will do it. If you don't want to work and achieve, you will not do it no matter where you are. Just because you are merit rated and have a bonus, if you really don't want to work hard, then you're not going to. You will accept your ninety points or ninety-two or eighty-five because, even with that, you make more money than people on the outside.

Q: Do you think Lincoln employees will ever join a union?

A: I don't know why they would.

Q: What is the most important advantage of working for Lincoln Electric?

A: You have an incentive, and you can push and get something for pushing. That's not true in a lot of companies.

Q: So you say that money is a very major advantage?

A: Money is a major advantage, but it's not just the money. It's the fact that having the incentive, you do wish to work a little harder. I'm sure that there are a lot of men here who, if they worked some other place, would not work as hard as they do here. Not that they are overworked — I don't mean that — but I'm sure they wouldn't push.

Q: Is there anything that you would like to add?

A: I do like working here. I am better off being pushed mentally. In another company if you pushed too hard you would feel a little bit of pressure, and someone might say, "Hey, slow down; don't try so hard." But here you are encouraged, not discouraged.

PART II

Interview with Ed Sanderson, 23-year-old high school graduate who had been with Lincoln four years and who was a machine operator in the Electrode Division at the time of the interview.

Q: How did you happen to get this job?

A: My wife was pregnant, and I was making three bucks an hour and one day I came here and applied. That was it. I kept calling to let them know I was still interested.

Q: Roughly what were your earnings last year including your bonus?

A: $37,000.00

Q: What have you done with your money since you have been here?

A: Well, we've lived pretty well and we bought a condominium.

Q: Have you paid for the condominium?

A: No, but I could.

Q: Have you bought your Lincoln stock this year?

A: No, I haven't bought any Lincoln stock yet.

Q: Do you get the feeling that the executives here are pretty well thought of?

A: I think they are. To get where they are today, they had to really work.

Q: Wouldn't that be true anywhere?

A: I think more so here because seniority really doesn't mean anything. If you work with a guy who has twenty years here, and you have two months and you're doing a better job, you will get advanced before he will.

Q: Are you paid on a piece rate basis?

A: My gang does. There are nine of us who make the bare electrode, and the whole group gets paid based on how much electrode we make.

Q: Do you think you work harder than workers in other factories in the Cleveland area?

A: Yes, I would say I probably work harder.

Q: Do you think it hurts anybody?

A: No, a little hard work never hurts anybody.

Q: If you could choose, do you think you would be as happy earning a little less money and being able to slow down a little?

A: No, it doesn't bother me. If it bothered me, I wouldn't do it.

Q: What would you say is the biggest disadvantage of working at Lincoln, as opposed to working somewhere else?

A: Probably having to work shift work.

Q: Why do you think Lincoln employees produce more than workers in other plants?

A: That's the way the company is set up. The more you put out, the more you're going to make.

Q: Do you think it's the piece rate and bonus together?

A: I don't think people would work here if they didn't know that they would be rewarded at the end of the year.

Q: Do you think Lincoln employees will ever join a union?

A: No.

Q: What are the major advantages of working for Lincoln?

A: Money.

Q: Are there any other advantages?

A: Yes, we don't have a union shop. I don't think I could work in a union shop.

Q: Do you think you are a career man with Lincoln at this time?

A: Yes.

PART III

Interview with Roger Lewis, 23-year-old Purdue graduate in mechanical engineering who had been in the Lincoln sales program for fifteen months and who was working in the Cleveland sales office at the time of the interview.

Q: How did you get your job at Lincoln?

A: I saw that Lincoln was interviewing on campus at Purdue, and I went by. I later came to Cleveland for a plant tour and was offered a job.

Q: Do you know any of the senior executives? Would they know you by name?

A: Yes, I know all of them — Mr. Irrgang, Mr. Willis, Mr. Manross.

Q: Do you think Lincoln salesmen work harder than those in other companies?

A: Yes. I don't think there are many salesmen for other companies who are putting in fifty to sixty-hour weeks. Everybody here works harder. You can go out in the plant, or you can go upstairs, and there's nobody sitting around.

Q: Do you see any real disadvantage of working at Lincoln?

A: I don't know if it's a disadvantage but Lincoln is a spartan company, a very thrifty company. I like that. The sales offices are functional, not fancy.

Q: Why do you think Lincoln employees have such high productivity?

A: Piecework has a lot to do with it. Lincoln is smaller than many plants, too; you can stand in one place and see the materials come in one side and the product go out the other. You feel a part of the company. The chance to get ahead is important, too. They have a strict policy of promoting from within, so you know you have a chance. I think in a lot of other places you may not get as fair a shake as you do here. The sales offices are on a smaller scale, too. I like that. I tell someone that we have two people in the Baltimore office, and they say, "You've got to be kidding." It's smaller and more personal. Pay is the most important thing. I have heard that this is the highest paying factory in the world.

PART IV

Interview with Jimmy Roberts, a 47-year-old high school graduate, who had been with Lincoln 17 years and who was working as a multiple-drill press operator at the time of the interview.

Q: What jobs have you had at Lincoln?

A: I started out cleaning the men's locker room in 1963. After about a year I got a job in the flux department, where we make the coating for welding rods. I worked there for seven or eight years and then got my present job.

Q: Do you make one particular part?

A: No, there are a variety of parts I make — at least twenty-five.

Q: Each one has a different piece rate attached to it?

A: Yes.

Q: Are some piece rates better than others?

A: Yes.

Q: How do you determine which ones you are going to do?

A: You don't. Your supervisor assigns them.

Q: How much money did you make last year?

A: $47,000.

Q: Have you ever received any kind of award or citation?

A: No.

Q: Was your rating ever over 110?

A: Yes. For the past five years, probably, I made over 110 points.

Q: Is there any attempt to let others know . . . ?

A: The kind of points I get? No.

Q: Do you know what they are making?

A: No. There are some who might not be too happy with their points and they might make it known. The majority, though, do not make it a point of telling other employees.

Q: Would you be just as happy earning a little less money and working a little slower?

A: I don't think I would — not at this point. I have done piecework all these years, and the fast pace doesn't really bother me.

Q: Why do you think Lincoln productivity is so high?

A: The incentive thing — the bonus distribution. I think that would be the main reason. The pay check you get every two weeks is important too.

Q: Do you think Lincoln employees would ever join a union?

A: I don't think so. I have never heard anyone mention it.

Q: What is the most important advantage of working here?

A: Amount of money you make. I don't think I could make this type of money anywhere else, especially with only a high school education.

Q: As a black person, do you feel that Lincoln discriminates in any way against blacks?

A: No. I don't think any more so than any other job. Naturally, there is a certain amount of discrimination, regardless of where you are.

PART V

Interview with Joe Trahan, 58-year-old high school graduate who had been with Lincoln 39 years and who was employed as a working supervisor in the tool room at the time of the interview.

Q: Roughly what was your pay last year?

A: Over $50,000; salary, bonus, stock dividends.

Q: How much was your bonus?

A: About $23,000.

Q: Have you ever gotten a special award of any kind?

A: Not really.

Q: What have you done with your money?

A: My house is paid for — and my two cars. I also have some bonds and the Lincoln stock.

Q: What do you think of the executives at Lincoln?

A: They're really top notch.

Q: What is the major disadvantage of working at Lincoln Electric?

A: I don't know of any disadvantage at all.

Q: Do you think you produce more than most people in similar jobs with other companies?

A: I do believe that.

Q: Why is that? Why do you believe that?

A: We are on the incentive system. Everything we do, we try to improve to make a better product with a minimum of outlay. We try to improve the bonus.

Q: Would you be just as happy making a little less money and not working quite so hard?

A: I don't think so.

Q: You know that Lincoln productivity is higher than that at most other plants. Why is that?

A: Money.

Q: Do you think Lincoln employees would ever join a union?

A: I don't think they would ever consider it.

Q: What is the most important advantage of working at Lincoln?

A: Compensation.

Q: Tell me something about Mr. James Lincoln, who died in 1965.

A: You are talking about Jimmy Sr. He always strolled through the shop in his shirt sleeves. Big fellow. Always looked distinguished. Gray hair. Friendly sort of guy. I was a member of the advisory board one year. He was there each time.

Q: Did he strike you as really caring?

A: I think he always cared for people.

Q: Did you get any sensation of a religious nature from him?

A: No, not really.

Q: And religion is not part of the program now?

A: No.

Q: Do you think Mr. Lincoln was a very intelligent man, or was he just a nice guy?

A: I would say he was pretty well educated. A great talker — always right off the top of his head. He knew what he was talking about all the time.

Q: When were bonuses for beneficial suggestions done away with?

A: About fifteen years ago.

Q: Did that hurt very much?

A: I don't think so, because suggestions are still rewarded through the merit rating system.

Q: Is there anything you would like to add?

A: It's a good place to work. The union kind of ties other places down. At other places, electricians only do electrical work, carpenters only do carpenter work. At Lincoln Electric we all pitch in and do whatever needs to be done.

Q: So a major advantage is not having a union?

A: That's right.

FEDERAL EXPRESS CORPORATION

Federal Express proved the virtue of persistence with the right product in a growing market. In 1985 the company held a $1.2 billion share of the $3 billion overnight delivery industry which it had originally created. Most, if not all, of the credit went to the founder, chairman, and chief executive officer of Memphis-based Federal Express, Frederick W. Smith.[1] He had taken an idea originally developed in a college term paper, for which he was awarded a "C," and gone on to change the way America does business. In the process he added a new cliché to the language, "when it absolutely, positively has to be there overnight."[2]

In 1985 Fred Smith reviewed the history of the company and its current mix of products and services. Mr. Smith especially focused his attention on its new electronic mail service, ZapMail. The following paragraphs describe the company and the express delivery industry, including Federal Express's principal competitors.

INDUSTRY

Within the aerospace and air transport industry, Federal Express became a leader in only a few short years.[3] While its main competitors had been around for two decades, satisfied with the traditional air freight forwarding market share they occupied, Federal took the market by storm and "changed the rules of the game."[4]

Federal Express laid claim to being the founder of the small-package/document express market. This sector experienced phenomenal growth in the late 1970s and early 1980s, constantly expanding into areas of new services and extended service areas.

Markets for all classes of cargo movement grew in 1984, from heavyweight to documents and letters. Those firms involved in cargo movement included all-cargo

This case was prepared by R. J. Balhorn, Beverly Bowen, Jane Shouse, Steve Spencer, and Carey Spriggs under the supervision of Professor Sexton Adams, North Texas State University, and Professor Adelaide Griffin, Texas Woman's University. Reprinted by permission.

air carriers, traditional air freight forwarders, passenger airlines, ground transportation companies, and air couriers. Although air freight movement in general experienced a profitable year in 1984, the small-package express shipping sector continued its 5-year annual growth rate of 20 percent.[5]

Competitors directly involved in the small-package/document express market included Federal Express, Emery Air Freight, Purolator, UPS, and the United States Postal Service. Through 1983 and 1984, price and service innovations abounded as participants struggled to gain a competitive edge.[6] This sector of the air cargo industry was characterized by price wars, constant cost-cutting strategies, and innovative marketing plans. Most competitors felt an urgency to earmark large capital investments for future expansion in order to keep in the running for the growing market.[7]

Regulatory authority for participants in this industry was under the Federal Aviation Act of 1958, the Civil Aeronautics Board (CAB), and the Federal Aviation Administration (FAA). When the CAB was in existence, its authority related to the economic aspects of air transportation. The FAA's regulatory authority, however, related primarily to the safety aspects of air transportation, including aircraft standards and maintenance. Ground transportation services were exempt from regulation by the Interstate Commerce Commission, but because of the use of radio and communication equipment in ground and air units, Federal Express operations were subject to regulation by the Federal Communications Act of 1934. Finally, Federal Express, as of May 1984, was in compliance with all regulations of the Environmental Protection Agency with regard to smoke emissions.[8]

HISTORY

Fred Smith obtained his revolutionary idea for his firm — an air cargo firm that specialized in door-to-door overnight delivery, using its own planes — in the 1960s while majoring in economics and political science at Yale. He had a close acquaintance with aviation: he'd earned a pilot's license at age fifteen and pursued his flying hobby while a student at Yale. During this same period, such companies as IBM and Xerox were already flying material out of airports not far from Yale's Connecticut campus.[9]

Smith spelled it all out in an overdue economics paper. To cut cost and time, packages from all over the country would be flown to a central point, there to be sorted, redistributed, and flown out again to their destinations. The flying would be late at night when air lanes were comparatively empty. Airports used would be in sizeable cities; trucks would carry packages to their final destinations, whether in those cities or in smaller communities. Equipment and documents from anywhere in the United States could be delivered anywhere else in the United States the next day.[10]

Smith was thinking not only of parts and contracts, but also of canceled checks. His concept, he thought, could be sold to the Federal Reserve to cut down on the float, the period between receipt of a check and collection of funds. A general commercial delivery system could be built on that basis. When the time came to create his company years later, his ambition to serve the Federal Reserve and his desire for an impressive name with a broad geographic connotation led him to the name "Federal Express." The Fed turned down his contract bid, but it now has its own check-delivery system, which Smith said was patterned after his operations.[11]

After college, Smith served two tours of duty in Vietnam, first as a platoon leader and then as a reconnaissance pilot. Upon returning home, he decided to give his air express idea a try. Starting with $4 million which he had inherited, he chose Memphis as a home base. A company study showed that Memphis was near the center of business shipping in the continental United States, and it was only closed an average of 10 hours per year due to adverse weather conditions. The airport offered long runways, a large abandoned ramp, and a pair of inexpensive World War II hangars.[12]

Of course, $4 million was not much for starting a company that needed an entire fleet of planes. Smith had to have more funds. He went to New York and Chicago and brought Wall Streeters to Memphis. His knowledge of the air freight field impressed investors, and at the end of the year he had managed to raise a whopping $72 million in loans and equity investment.

Then Federal Express, which had been marking time operating a charter service, got down to its present business. It began transporting packages of under 70 pounds in April 1973, serving thirteen airports. The first night's package total was eighteen. Volume picked up rapidly, and service was extended. Federal Express was an overnight success, but not for long. OPEC's inflation of fuel prices sent costs up faster than revenues were growing, and by mid-1974, the company was losing more than $1 million per month.[13]

Smith went back to his disappointed investors for more money to keep the company growing until revenues could catch up with expenses. Bankruptcy was a real possibility. After being turned down many times, Smith was able to raise $11 million, enough to get Federal Express over the hump. Federal Express, which lost $27 million in its first 2 years, went $3.6 million into the black in 1976 on $75 million in revenues. It has remained on the upswing ever since.[14]

Federal's short-term goals included increased surface productivity, telecommunications, and international expansion. Federal Express also considered the tempting possibility of going into the passenger business. All of Federal's big jets were easily convertible between freight container pallets and passenger seats, and the utilization of these jets averaged only 4.7 hours out of every 24. Nevertheless, the return on investment from carrying passengers would have been far below that from carrying small packages, and the chance of planes being delayed and out of position for the nightly race to deliver packages on schedule was too great. "Nothing," said Smith, "can be allowed to impair our primary business."[15]

MANAGEMENT/PERSONNEL

Fred Smith — Entrepreneur

Fred Smith was a man of integrity whose charisma enabled him to motivate investors and employees to believe in his dream. His drive was mainly attributed to the scars that he carried from his military service — feelings so strong that Smith himself stated that Federal Express was a creature of Vietnam, and he would not have had the same perspective if not for his experiences there.[16]

As a true entrepreneur, Smith never threw in the towel. When the Arab oil embargo in 1974 forced fuel costs sky high, Smith ran to investors, courting them for more money. When outdated CAB regulations made it impossible for Federal to expand into the larger aircraft which it needed, Smith went to Washington and lobbied for deregulation of the airlines. When the Postal Service relaxed its regulations against private delivery of extremely urgent mail, Smith jumped at the opportunity and began testing the overnight letter service.[17]

Smith did all this with style. To win support from prominent Capitol Hill figures, he wined and dined them. To win the confidence of investors, he was always prepared with thorough market and economic analyses to support his ideas.[18] Unfortunately, by the late 1970s, Federal Express had grown too large for the wheeler-dealer, entrepreneurial approach to running an organization. But Smith believed that some principles remained the same between managing a $1.2 billion operation and a $1.2 million operation:

> One of the biggest principles is that you've got to take action. Most large organizations reach a static point. They cannot take any action, because there are all types of barriers to doing so. There are institutionalized barriers that weren't there when the company was considerably smaller. What changes is your knowledge and your appreciation of how to deal with those institutional barriers, to eliminate them or use them to your advantage. . . . There are myriad number of changes that have to take place in the management style for the company to continue growing.[19]

Corporate Giants

Smith's colleagues had the same "fighter pilot attitude" toward Federal Express. They were all former pilots and entrepreneurs. Although most thought his idea very strange, each one had the "right stuff" needed to make Federal Express fly.[20] From day one, the comradery and loyalty exhibited by employees of Federal Express was strong, strong enough to hold Federal together and transform it from an "entrepreneurial crusade" (us against them) to a respected corporate strength. (See Exhibit 1 for organizational chart.)

The year 1979, however, brought much change to Federal's ranks. President Art Bass, one of the initial crusaders, decided to leave and, like a wave, took five vice-presidents with him, all but one of whom had been with Federal from the start. The reason for their departure was shocking to some but easily understood by Smith. Federal had matured, and Bass and his colleagues felt they lacked the ability to adapt their entrepreneurial perspectives to managing a mature operation. Smith replaced his elite few with managers who were more comfortable with the traditional corporate organization, but he maintained associations with Bass and

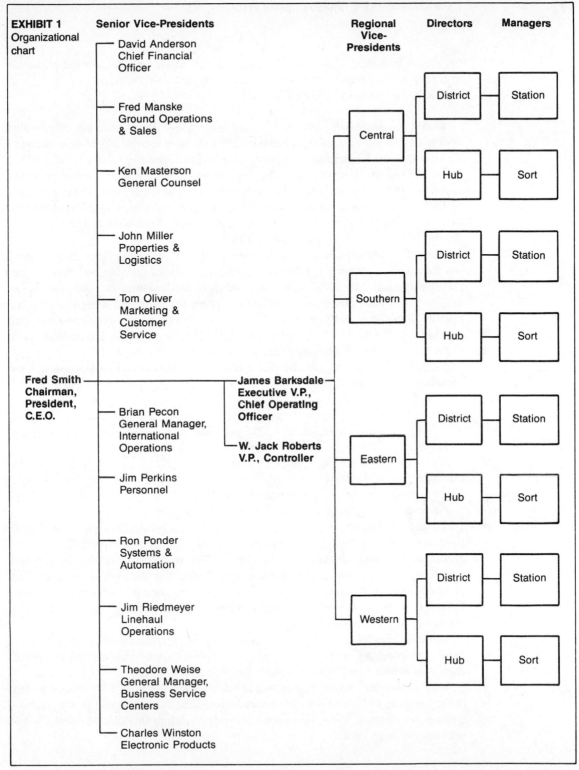

EXHIBIT 1
Organizational chart

Senior Vice-Presidents

David Anderson
Chief Financial
Officer

Fred Manske
Ground Operations
& Sales

Ken Masterson
General Counsel

John Miller
Properties &
Logistics

Tom Oliver
Marketing &
Customer
Service

Fred Smith
Chairman,
President,
C.E.O.

Brian Pecon
General Manager,
International
Operations

Jim Perkins
Personnel

Ron Ponder
Systems &
Automation

Jim Riedmeyer
Linehaul
Operations

Theodore Weise
General Manager,
Business Service
Centers

Charles Winston
Electronic Products

James Barksdale
Executive V.P.,
Chief Operating
Officer

W. Jack Roberts
V.P., Controller

Regional Vice-Presidents

Central

Southern

Eastern

Western

Directors

District

Hub

District

Hub

District

Hub

District

Hub

Managers

Station

Sort

Station

Sort

Station

Sort

Station

Sort

Source: Federal Express 1984 Annual Report. J. C. Camillus, "Federal Express Corporation," in W. F. Glueck and L. R. Jauch, eds., *Business Policy and Strategic Management* (New York: McGraw-Hill, 1984).

471

the others in a think-tank type of arrangement.[21] Their only responsibility, as far as Smith was concerned, was to think about the future of Federal.

The key executives in 1985 included:

James L. Barksdale, executive vice-president and chief operating officer. Jim Barksdale joined the company in February 1979 as senior vice-president–data systems. He was appointed executive vice-president and chief operating officer in May 1983. From 1973 until his employment by the company, he had held various positions with Cook Industries, Inc., including corporate vice-president. He served as president of ISD, Inc., a data processing subsidiary, the assets of which were purchased by Cook in 1978, and president of its subsidiary, Cook, Treadwell & Harry, Inc., a general insurance agency and brokerage firm.

David C. Anderson, senior vice-president and chief financial officer. Dave Anderson joined the company in 1976 as vice-president–controller. He was named vice president–treasurer in 1979, senior vice-president and treasurer in 1980, and senior vice-president and chief financial officer in September 1983. For more than 4 years prior to joining Federal Express, he was employed in various accounting and financial positions at Trans World Airlines, including director of general accounting and director of cost and disbursement accounting.

Fred A. Manske, Jr., senior vice-president–ground operations and sales. Fred Manske joined Federal Express in April 1978 as vice-president of the central region. From 1968 to 1978, he was employed by Eastern Airlines in various management positions including manager of airport services, manager of reservations, director of training, and executive assistant to the president. He assumed his present position in September 1980.

Kenneth R. Masterson, senior vice-president and general counsel. Ken Masterson was a partner in the Memphis law firm of Thomason, Crawford and Hendrix prior to his appointment as vice president–legal in January 1980. Ken was elected senior vice-president and general counsel in 1981.

Thomas R. Oliver, senior vice-president–electronic products. Tom Oliver joined Federal Express in 1978 as vice-president–marketing and was elected senior vice-president–marketing and customer service in 1980. In August 1985, he moved into his present position which is responsible for leading the ZapMail product into the profit column for the company. For more than 5 years prior to joining the company, Tom was a senior vice-president and director of Thomas Cook, Inc., a retail and wholesale travel company.

James A. Perkins, senior vice-president and chief personnel officer. Jim Perkins joined the company in 1974 and was employed in various training and personnel capacities before being elected senior vice-president in 1979.

Ron J. Ponder, senior vice-president–information systems. Ron Ponder joined the company in 1977 as director of operations research. He was named vice president–advanced projects in 1980, vice-president–systems design in 1982, and senior vice-president in June 1983.

James R. Riedmeyer, senior vice-president–linehaul operations. Jim Riedmeyer joined the company in 1974 as senior vice-president–maintenance and engineering and then was appointed senior vice-president–linehaul operations in 1983.

Theodore L. Weise, senior vice-president–central support services. Ted Weise joined the company during its formative stages in Little Rock in 1972. He came from General Dynamics Corp., where he was a flight test engineer on the F-111 series fighter/bomber aircraft. He became a vice-president–special projects and advanced planning in 1977 and became vice-president of operations planning in 1978. He was named senior vice-president of that division in 1979. In March 1985, he assumed his present position.

W. Jack Roberts, vice-president and controller. Jack Roberts joined Federal Express in 1977. He served as manager of general accounting and director of accounting until his appointment as vice-president and controller in June 1979.

Federal's Backbone

Dedication to professional, faultless service enabled Federal to "get it there overnight." From the beginning Federal was a people organization. With an employee force of over 24,000, management felt a strong responsibility to provide an array of training programs to support the image it wanted to portray.[22] For example, training for the ZapMail service when it was first introduced included courses for over 18,000 employees.[23] In addition to a thorough training program, Federal boasted of an active file of 45,000 applicants for positions ranging from pilot to courier and made the claim that this was an indication of the attractiveness of company policy and benefits.[24] One generous benefit offered by Federal was paying the tuition in full for college students working at the hub in Memphis.

These policies further supported Federal's commitment to maintaining the image of professionalism and stability.

When the company hired an employee, it was viewed as a long-term investment. To minimize the necessity to furlough any employee, Federal utilized the scheduling of part-time employees which permitted operations to expand or contract according to traffic levels.[25] Smith, though, was exceedingly canny about labor. By employing part-time college students who would come and go as their education progressed, Federal set up a buffer between its operations and the entrance of unions to the hub.[26] This approach also allowed Federal to keep its labor costs low, lower than any other company in the industry.[27]

Recruiting

Because of Federal's reputation of being a leader in the industry, it was never difficult to find qualified people to uphold that image. Unfortunately, the old tactics used to fill Federal's ranks did not work when it came time for Federal to staff its ZapMail operation in 1984. The ZapMail operation required high-tech professionals who could go out to a client and sell them on the new, revolutionary service, but the ads Federal was running were not attracting this type of candidate. Federal had to target advertising to a new, young professional crowd who were looking for career opportunities on the leading edge of technology.[28]

Hundreds of qualified candidates were recruited, all because Federal targeted its advertising to a specific audience. But not only did Federal change its recruiting approach, it also restructured its compensation plan for the ZapMail sales force. ZapMail salespeople received lower base salaries with commissions based solely on the number of machines installed in offices. Federal's management felt that this would help make ZapMail grow at a faster rate.[29]

OPERATIONS

Federal Express provided an overnight door-to-door express delivery service for high-priority packages and documents. In essence, two industries were merged together to accomplish this: aviation and pickup/delivery trucking service. Federal Express services were available Monday through Saturday between 145 airports in the United States, Canada, Puerto Rico, Europe, and Asia. Approximately 90 percent of the U.S. population was serviced through an intricate ground/air network, Smith's brainchild, the hub-and-spoke system.

Hub and Spoke   The service operation that made Federal Express unique in its field was its central sorting facility located in Memphis. The key factor was that every package and letter transmitted by Federal passed through the center in Memphis, where it was sorted and dispatched to the points of delivery across the country and world.

The operations at the hub had been fine-tuned for maximum efficiency. The central sorting process occurred in the middle of the night under "time bomb" pressure.[30] An executive gazing out over the bustling hub said, "If they decide to sit down for an hour, we're dead."[31] All during the day packages had been collected in sorting facilities and local offices in three hundred cities. Once transported to the local airports, the packages were flown to Memphis, where all planes arrived about midnight. The planes were directly unloaded into a giant warehouse of elaborate conveyor belts where they were frantically sorted and loaded back into the planes headed for their intended destinations. By 3 A.M. the planes were ready to depart for sorting facilities located at the local airports, where couriers would then transport packages to local offices and then on to the receiver — and all of this happened overnight!

Contact with couriers was maintained through the use of digitally assisted dispatch systems (DADS). The system was installed in over 70 percent of Federal's vehicles and enabled the company to leave dispatch information in couriers' vans even when unoccupied. In late 1984, hand-held DADS units were introduced to help eliminate duplicated routes, retraced steps, and other inefficiencies.[32] This prototype microprocessor maintained constant data and voice contact between the courier and dispatcher even if the courier was on the upper floor of an office building, as foot couriers often were.

COSMOS, Federal Express's computer network for dispatch entry and tracking, used a satellite and telephone network to locate a customer's shipment at any time as it passed through six electronic gates during transit. Each parcel was bar-coded so that movement could be monitored and recorded every step of the journey. Thus, the whereabouts of a package, not just the paperwork, could be recalled at an instant.[33]

Facilities

Federal Express leased its facilities at the hub from the Memphis-Shelby County Airport Authority. These facilities consisted of a central sorting facility, aircraft hangars, flight training and fuel facilities, warehouse space, and a portion of the administrative offices.[34] Off-airport facilities in Memphis, also leased, consisted of Federal Express headquarters, PartsBank operations, and other administrative offices.[35]

City station operations were located in three hundred cities throughout the United States, Canada, Puerto Rico, Europe, and the Far East. These stations were leased for 5- to 10-year periods. In 1984, a station and service center expansion program was begun which included the construction of Business Service Centers and the installation of unstaffed Overnight Delivery Counters to supplement the city stations and to provide improved access to services in high-density areas.[36]

Equipment and Vehicles

Federal operated almost ten thousand delivery vehicles with approximately two thousand of these leased. Other vehicles owned by Federal mainly included ground-support equipment, cargo loaders, transports, and aircraft tugs.[37] As of July 31, 1984, Federal owned fifty-eight aircraft and an inventory of spare engines and parts for each type. The company was committed to purchase eleven additional aircraft to be delivered in 1985 through 1987.[38] Deposits and payments made according to these agreements were:

$ 98,700,000 in the remainder of 1985
$169,800,000 in the remainder of 1986
$105,800,000 in the remainder of 1987

PRODUCT LINES

On a domestic level, Federal Express offered three basic services, Priority One, ZapMail, and Standard Air, a one- to two-day package and document delivery service. Additionally, Federal provided special handling for dangerous goods and restricted articles, an air cargo charter service, and an inventory parts shipment service. Through the use of expanded direct service and exclusive agents, Federal Express could also deliver documents and custom-cleared packages internationally to areas in Canada, Puerto Rico, Western Europe, the Far East, and Australia.[39]

Priority One

Priority One, an overnight door-to-door delivery of business goods, absolutely, positively guaranteed a 10:30 A.M. next-morning delivery. In either the sender's packaging or that of Federal Express, time-sensitive letters, boxes, and tubes up to

150 pounds in weight, 62 inches in length, or 120 inches in length and girth combined could be shipped to almost any location in the contiguous states.[40] Couriers were utilized for pickup and delivery or customers could bring packages and documents to self-service centers or Federal Express Business Service Centers. Permitting face-to-face customer contact, these staffed, storefront facilities were located in high-traffic, high-density areas. Over three hundred of the centers were planned to be in place by the end of fiscal 1985.[41]

Rates for overnight letters were $11 if delivered to a drop-off location by the sender and $14 if picked up by a courier. Courier-Pak boxes and tubes were subject to a 5-pound or $34 minimum charge, while Courier-Pak envelopes were priced at a 2-pound or $25 minimum. Schedules indicating price per pound then applied for parcels over the minimum weight. Discounts of up to 40 percent were offered to qualified shippers.[42]

Standard Air

Standard Air gave the same array of service features offered under Priority One, only packages were scheduled for delivery no later than the second business day after pickup. At approximately one-half the Priority One rates, Standard Air was promoted as, "when it has to be there, but doesn't have to be there overnight."[43] Many packages arrived the next business day, making this one- to two-day service an economical alternative for time-pressured shippers.

Charter/ PartsBank

Beyond delivering packages, Federal offered two unique services to serve the larger distribution needs of American business. The first, Air Cargo Charter, allowed the charter of McDonnell DC-10s, Boeing 727s, or Dassault Falcons on either a one-time or contractual basis. Subject to availability, aircraft could be chartered 24 hours a day, 7 days a week. The second, PartsBank, arose from the need for the speedy handling of critical inventories. Combining a parts warehouse system with an overnight airline, PartsBank allowed companies to place time-sensitive inventory such as computer parts, medical supplies, and electronic components in Federal's Memphis PartsBank warehouse. A toll-free telephone call to PartsBank could have the item shipped immediately.[44]

ZapMail

Zapmail was conceived approximately 7 years before its 1984 introduction as an answer to electronic mail. (See Exhibits 2, 3, and 4.) It evolved into a major product because of indications of strong demand.[45] Users called requesting the service, and within an hour a courier arrived to pick up the document. The courier then delivered the document to the nearest input station where the document was inserted into a scanner, digitized, and sent over the Federal Express network to the receiving station. There it was printed and delivered to the recipient by courier. Total elapsed time from initial call to delivery time was 2 hours. If the sender took the document himself to a manned Federal Express facility, ZapMail delivery was accomplished in one hour. In contrast to electronic mail, ZapMail was an electronically transmitted document rather than just a message. As a result, charts, contracts, invoices, and artwork could be reproduced into high-resolution copies.

EXHIBIT 2
ZapMail press release

For Immediate Release

Federal Express Corporation has launched the major phase of its ZapMail electronic transmission service, installing ZapMail equipment in customers' offices. It is the first single-source paper communications system that reaches almost everybody in America with the best quality, most convenient, and most economical facsimile service ever seen.

Installation of the specially designed equipment not only enables customers to establish intracompany networks, but also to avail themselves of the entire Federal Express ZapMail network, putting them within hours of the majority of the nation's business population.

Cost to customers for a "ZapMailer" on their premises is minimal. There are neither equipment leasing fees nor telephone bills because the units are directly linked to Federal Express's own communications network. Charges are based solely on a per-page basis (subject to a minimum charge), with discounts available based on length of time of service agreements and quantities of terminals installed. (See attached price list.)

The ZapMailer scans, sends, and prints high-quality copies of documents on plain bond paper. The documents are reproduced at either another ZapMail unit in the recipient company or at a Federal Express office with delivery by a courier to the recipient. The document is transmitted over Federal Express's own vast, packet-switched network which is already handling more than 40,000 pages a day of the highest-quality facsimile ever available. ZapMail has eight times more resolution per square inch than standard Group 3 facsimile, the highest industry standard up to this point.

Federal Express markets and services ZapMail equipment through its own sales and service network.

The ZapMail unit can also be used as a local convenience copier.

Federal Express views the ZapMailer as a natural replacement for facsimile systems and telex terminals and as a complement for its overnight document delivery services.

–30–

Source: Federal Express Corporation.

Original documents would either be forwarded to the recipient or returned to the sender by 10:30 A.M. the next business day.[46]

ZapMail charges were $25 for the first twenty pages and $1 per page after twenty pages. If sent from a Service Center, the cost was reduced by $5.[47] For a leasing fee of approximately $200 per month, a frequent user could have a ZapMail terminal placed in his office with no installation or maintenance fees.[48]

Although much had been staked on the success of ZapMail, initial results had been disappointing. Several marketing and operational problems had hindered the initial launch of the project, but optimism remained high for the long term.

From an operational standpoint, there had at first been a delay, later resolved, in the installation of dedicated long-distance lines by AT&T. More recently, in the second stage of the project, that of placing on-premise terminals (ZapMailers) with volume users, a one-month delay resulted from awaiting installation of the software required for simultaneous transmission of documents to multiple destinations. Thus the targeted goal of three thousand ZapMailers in place by the end of May 1985

EXHIBIT 3
ZapMailer pricing,
February 1985

Term	Minimum	Quantity	Page price	Delivery charge
1 year	$200	1–9 units	.95	$10.00
2 years	$200	1–9 units	.90	$10.00
3 years	$200	1–9 units	.85	$10.00
1 year	$125	10–50 units	.90	$10.00
		51–100 units	.85	$10.00
		101+ units	.80	$10.00
2 years	$100	10–50 units	.85	$10.00
		51–100 units	.80	$10.00
		101+ units	.75	$10.00
3 years	$ 75	10–50 units	.80	$10.00
		51–100 units	.75	$10.00
		101+ units	.70	$10.00

Local copy charge is 25¢ per page.
Transmissions, local copies, and delivery/pickup services apply to attaining monthly minimums.
No drop-off or hold-at-location charges.

1. All orders must be installed within 12 months of order date to guarantee quantity pricing.
2. On a quarterly basis, subject to item # 1, Federal Express will extend additional discounts to customers that have moved into a higher discount range based on the combination of open orders and installations the customer has achieved on a rolling year-to-date basis.
3. For billing purposes, these discounts will be applied to all customer installations 30 days after the close of the quarter.
4. This price list is part of your service agreement.
5. Above monthly minimum charge is applicable for Dial-Up circuit only.
6. Prices are subject to change prior to actual order.

Source: Federal Express Corporation.

was in doubt. As of the end of January 1985, over seven hundred orders for the machines had been placed.[49]

On the marketing front, management noted it had been perhaps overly optmistic in relying on its market research indicating a pent-up need for the new service. ZapMail shipments were averaging about 3,200 per day, far below the 20,090 to 30,000 needed to reach the initial projected breakeven level 12 to 18 months after start-up.[50] It had become clear that the marketing approach that had been effective for small packages was not working in the same-day market. Part of the problem rested in consumer education. As with its overnight express service, Federal needed to get potential customers to understand exactly what was being offered and how

EXHIBIT 4
ZapMailer service agreement/pricing summary

Term	Number of terminals	Monthly rental per terminal	Transmitted price per page	Copier price per page
1 Year	1	$525	.25	.10
1 Year	2–15	$500	.25	.10
1 Year	16+	$475	.25	.10

Additionally
1. Pickup/delivery charge of $10 will apply to documents picked up or delivered by Federal Express that are billed to your ZapMailer account.
2. Drop-off or hold-at-location charge of $5 will apply to documents dropped off or held for pickup at Federal Express locations that are billed to your ZapMailer account.
3. All orders must be installed within 4 months of order date to guarantee quantity pricing.
4. Prices are subject to change prior to actual order.
5. Move charges: within the same building — $250.
   to another building — $250 plus freight.
6. The above pricing is applicable to domestic services only.

Source: Federal Express Corporation.

to use it. The company had overestimated the ease with which its customer base could be educated about the benefits of ZapMail and set about rectifying the problem.

Stressing how the new service should be used as a part of the business routine rather than merely in emergencies, Federal began pumping an additional $10 million into its planned advertising budget.[51] Anticipating difficulty in convincing prospects of the necessity for on-premise ZapMailers, Federal equipped its sales force with preprogrammed Radio Shack calculators. These were to be utilized in running a comparison of the prospect's current communications systems cost (based on estimated activity levels) with that of a comparable ZapMailer system.[52] Federal targeted the following industries as having the highest potential, at least initially, for ZapMailer installations:

Legal
Accounting
Consulting
Retail
Insurance
Banking
Manufacturing
Advertising
Commercial and financial printing
Government[53]

In spite of its initial difficulties, ZapMail was highly regarded by analysts in the investment community who felt it would become an unqualified success once the glitches involved with any new product were resolved. Further, Federal's management indicated that possible future enhancements to ZapMailers might include the ability to communicate with word processors and personal computers.[54] Speculation was that Federal intended to be a major player in the office of the future through the use of ZapMailers. By connecting word processors and personal computers to the ZapMail network, Federal could leverage its ability to capture office document traffic once the software was developed to do so.

Executive Vice-President and Chief Operating Officer Jim Barksdale described the evolution of ZapMail at a press conference on January 31, 1985:

> *About 3 years ago . . . we had a series of meetings in which we looked toward the future, trying to picture the business world of the late 1980s, the 1990s, and the twenty-first century. Would Federal Express, we asked ourselves, continue its meteoric growth as the needs of the commercial world changed? Those were months of soul-searching.*
>
> *As we looked out over the next several years, we saw a threat to what had become such a comfortable leadership position: the increasing reliance on computer technology in every facet of business, and the world becoming gradually wired together electronically.*
>
> *In the face of these fundamental, sweeping changes, we knew we had to make major adjustments in our corporate strategy or see our leadership position gradually erode. While we could have taken the safe course and continued with business as usual, that would have been counter to everything we have come to symbolize in our brief but exciting corporate history.*
>
> *We decided to take an aggressive approach. . . . What people really wanted when they used Federal Express was delivery as soon as possible. They settled for overnight because that was the best thing going. . . .*
>
> *We quickly established a few ground rules for what a Federal Express same-day service would have to include. We knew it would have to be of the highest quality since Federal Express built its reputation on a first-class service. We didn't want to enter this market with a ''me-too'' product. We also knew it would have to build on the essential strengths that Federal Express had already established: a vast telecommunications network, the largest fleet of vehicles and aircraft in the transportation industry, and a proven record of marketing expertise. More than that, the final product would have to capitalize on our most important resource, the army of highly motivated Federal Express employees that covered this continent with friendly smiles and helpful attitudes every working day.*
>
> *The final result of this effort in rethinking our corporate strategy is now well known . . . Zapmail. Zapmail builds solidly on our strong foundation; it plays to our strengths. It prepares us for entry into the next century by turning back the hand of the delivery clock once again.*

International Operations

Federal Express also delivered Courier-Pak envelopes and packages up to 70 pounds to many international locations. Because of distance and time differences in the areas served, time of day of delivery varied. For those areas they did not serve, Federal Express offered a Worldwide Referral Service to arrange delivery to additional locations.[55]

In an effort to expand outside North America, in fiscal 1984, Federal acquired Gelco Express International, a worldwide, on-board courier service with offices in London, Amsterdam, Paris, Brussels, Hong Kong, Tokyo, and Singapore. In 1985, the Gelco operation was to be absorbed into the system with the Federal Express name and identity.[56]

At home, Federal was preparing for international service by opening an international customer service department with multilingual representatives. An added effort by Federal was made to give special attention to customs and cultures of the international markets.[57] But critics abroad said that running a domestic service in the United States was entirely different from operating an international one because it required a different expertise, and a common market approach could not be taken. Competition was growing in the international market as well as the U.S. market, so analysts felt that Federal could have problems promoting itself in Europe with only the experience of a small European courier to depend on for guidance.[58]

MARKETING/ADVERTISING

The image of Federal Express was one of an innovator. Smith and his colleagues had created a demand for small-package express delivery and then cleverly set out to satisfy that demand. Smith, in analyzing Federal Express, stated that Federal was selling time and that people who save time in their daily routines and functions are more effective.[59] Once the message was heard, the public immediately altered their perspective from "get it there as soon as possible" to "get it there overnight."

Smith spared nothing to get the message across. Federal Express needed dramatic advertising to reach an indifferent world that needed to know about Federal Express.[60] Tom Oliver, senior vice-president of marketing and customer service, said, "At the outset the advertising was oriented toward explaining the network system . . . focusing on the difference in Federal's system from their competitors"; however, people could not understand how this strange combination of airplanes, hubs, and couriers could keep the boss from yelling.[61] The public just wanted to trust that Federal would do what it claimed to do, no matter how they did it.

After much effort, Federal did get the message across and won award after award for clever spots. In recalling the "motor-mouth" businessman, the pitch was "Federal Express. When it absolutely, positively has to be there overnight"; a man was uprooting a phone booth as the announcer said, "Federal Express is so easy to use, all you have to do is pick up the phone." It was easy to appreciate the humor, and that was what Oliver wanted.[62]

But not everyone felt that Federal's humorous ads were of benefit to the company objective. Competitors and advertisers alike felt that Federal ads often offended the little guy, and, although attention-getters, the ads left no message as to what Federal really offered.[63] Unaffected by criticisms hurled at its campaigns, Federal believed that another factor, price, was not as important as dramatizing the problem people have getting fast, sure, easy delivery. Cost of delivery was important to people only after they were sure it was going to get to the destination when they wanted it to.[64]

Federal's marketing plan for ZapMail also came under fire by industry analysts. The original ZapMail marketing plan was ill conceived: no one really understood what ZapMail was.[65] But, with the newly recruited sales force for ZapMail and new leasing plans as an alternative to purchase of the machines, analysts still believed that ZapMail would evolve into a necessary tool for business activities.

COMPETITION

Federal Express Corporation was a major competitor in the time-sensitive package-delivery or courier industry. It faced stiff competition from such firms as Purolator Courier Corporation, Emery Air Freight Corporation, United Parcel Service, and the U.S. Postal Service.

Purolator Courier Corporation

Purolator said its packages were "overnight not overpriced," and the company mandated that each package be delivered the next business day or on some other time-sensitive schedule. Most packages weighed less than 5 pounds, and each was picked up and delivered door-to-door, either on call or on a scheduled basis.[66]

The company in 1984 had two major products that were designed to make its door-to-door courier services easier and more economical. Customers could send 2 ounches (up to ten pages) of important documents anywhere in the continental United States at a very low price with the PuroLetter. The PuroPak could handle as much as 2 pounds of documents for delivery across town or across the country, and the customer was automatically billed at the lowest applicable rate. Very low rates applied up to 300 miles or between certain pairs of cities, and a competitive rate was applied for longer distances. A related product, PuroPak Box, offered a very low rate for one- to 6-pound shipments.[67]

Purolator operated an air network with its central hub located in Columbus, Ohio, to enable the movement of shipments over longer distances for next-day delivery. However, major volume constraints and operating inefficiencies were being experienced at the Columbus facility. To alleviate this problem and in anticipation of future growth needs, Purolator had a continuing program to upgrade terminal facilities. A major new air hub facility was under construction in Indianapolis, Indiana, and upon its completion in 1986 would have a capacity of 125,000 packages per night.[68]

Purolator Courier, Ltd., the company's Canadian subsidiary, offered courier services to over six thousand cities and towns in the ten provinces of Canada. Partly because of sluggish growth in the Canadian economy, operating results of this subsidiary had been mediocre. Management had concentrated on improving operating efficiency and modestly expanding its terminal facilities.[69]

The management of Purolator Courier Corporation saw the company as "the most economical national supplier of overnight package delivery." Purolator planned to aggressively exploit this position by capitalizing on its large fleet of airplanes and ground-delivery vehicles, all supported by an aggressive advertising campaign. As the U.S. and Canadian economies continued to improve, management expected Purolator to continue its record growth.[70] For a comparison of Purolator, Federal Express, and their competitors, see Exhibits 5 and 6.[71]

Emery Air Freight

Emery was one of the largest domestic air cargo carriers and was a major competitor in the international field as well. The company maintained 165 offices, 53 of which were outside the United States in twenty-seven different countries and territories. In another forty-two countries, agents acted on the company's behalf.[72]

Emery could provide overnight door-to-door delivery of any size, any weight package or shipment to over 56,000 cities and towns in North America. The company also had 24- to 72-hour door-to-door service to various cities around the world. Emery offered a variety of overnight delivery services including, Same Day, A.M., P.M., Day 2, and the 5-ounce Emery Urgent Letter.[73]

According to management, Emery's goal was to have "the lowest-cost, highest-quality, worldwide transportation system." In order to achieve this goal, Emery had spent large sums for expansion of existing facilities and the modernization of existing aircraft as well as the acquisition of new aircraft. In addition, the company had made major capital investments in state-of-the-art technology to foster its future business growth. For example, a $20 million expansion of its "superhub" terminal facility in Dayton, Ohio, was begun in March 1984 and was completed at year's end. This expansion increased the company's handling capacity to almost 2 million

EXHIBIT 5
Sales revenues of Federal Express and selected competitors, 1983

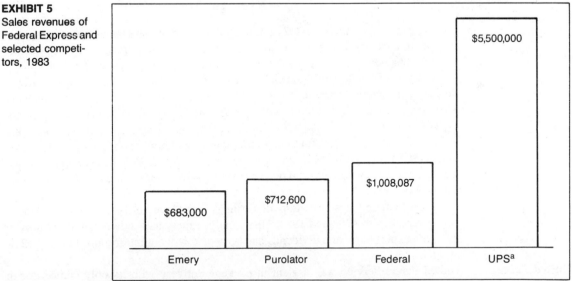

Note: Figures are in thousands of dollars.
[a] Estimated sales revenue as no actual figure is available.

EXHIBIT 6
In-service aircraft and vehicles: Federal Express and selected competitors, 1983

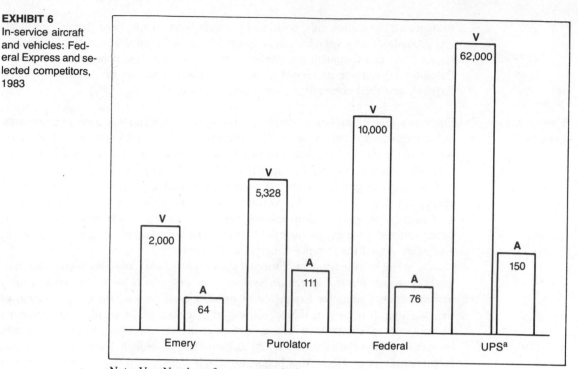

Note: V = Number of revenue-producing vehicles in service.
    A = Number of aircraft in service.
[a] U.P.S. also makes extensive use of commercial airlines to ship its parcels.

pounds per night, up from 1.7 million pounds. A major capital improvement at the Dayton facility in 1983 was the installation of an automated envelope-sorting system capable of handling 10,000 Emery Urgent letters or envelopes per hour.[74]

Emery had maintained a special "heavyweight" niche in the package delivery business. Its unique ability to deliver heavy air cargo the next day gave the company a competitive edge during the recent economic recovery. Approximately 45 percent of the company's 70-pound traffic had a next-morning delivery requirement. This ability was particularly useful to large customers that often required cargo transportation services for shipments of any size, weight, or shape. This heavyweight service was restricted to customers who purchased over $1 million of air cargo transportation services per year.[75]

Emery suffered a sharp drop in earnings per share in 1982 but had made a strong recovery in 1983 and 1984. Historically, Emery had shown consistent growth in earnings per share, and dividends had been paid without interruption since 1952.[76]

United Parcel Service

United Parcel Service was a giant in package delivery with its only competitor in terms of volume being the U.S. Postal Service. No other company could match its basic claim that it could deliver a package in 2 days anywhere in the continental

United States if the customer was willing to pay the price. UPS had long had a reputation for dependability, productivity, and efficiency which was admired by customers and envied by competitors.

Building upon the success of its basic business, UPS late in 1982 entered the overnight package delivery market. Any UPS customer currently served by daily pickups could make use of this overnight delivery service. Rates were usually 50 percent lower than those charged by Federal Express.[77]

UPS occupied a very strong position in the transportation industry. It was the largest single private shipper on most railroads, owned a large fleet of airplanes, and also shipped packages on other airlines. In addition, it owned a huge fleet of delivery trucks. (See Exhibit 6.) Its drivers were unionized and called on some 600,000 offices, factories, and stores each day.[78]

Financially, UPS was solid, with earnings that had more than quadrupled from $76.1 million in 1978 to $331.9 million in 1982. During this same period, revenues doubled, going from $2.8 billion in 1978 to $5.2 billion in 1982. Very few companies in any industry could match this earnings and productivity record.[79]

U.S. Postal Service

The U.S. Postal Service had been a competitor in the overnight package delivery business for a number of years. With its Express Mail next-day service, the postal service could ship packages weighing up to 70 pounds and guarantee delivery to the addressee the next day. To make use of this service, customers simply took their packages and letters to the Express Mail window at the post office. Shipments were delivered to the addressee by 3:00 P.M. the following day. The addressee also had the option of picking up the package personally as early as 10:00 A.M. of the next business day. All shipments were guaranteed to arrive on time, and if they did not, the customer could obtain a full refund. According to Postal Service statistics, 95 percent of all shipments did arrive on time.[80]

The U.S. Postal Service also offered package pickup from the customer's place of business, but only on a planned, regularly scheduled basis. A single, flat charge was made per pickup, regardless of the number of packages or letters the customer might be sending.

The Express Mail Service could ship packages and letters to almost any major metropolitan area in the United States. Express Mail Service was also available on an international basis, serving major cities in the United Kingdom, Australia, Brazil, Japan, Belgium, France, and the Netherlands, as well as Hong Kong.[81]

FINANCIAL

Federal Express was not a financial success overnight. It took 4 years and $70 million in venture capital before their first profitable period in late 1975. The company nearly went bankrupt several times during that 4-year drought because the venture capital market was in a profound depression of its own.

In 1975, new capital was $10 million (versus $3 billion in 1983), and the initial

EXHIBIT 7
Consolidated
financial highlights
for years ended
May 31

	1984	1983	1982
Operating results			
Express service revenues	$1,436,305	$1,008,087	$803,915
Operating income	165,208	150,737	119,466
Income before income taxes	152,260	150,216	131,080
Net income	115,430	88,933	78,385
Earnings per share	$2.52	$2.03	$1.85
Average shares outstanding	45,448	43,316	41,788
Stock price range	$27.75–$48.50	$21.13–$43.00	$21.07–$35.63
Financial position			
Working capital	$ 72,226	$ 89,878	$ 79,669
Property and equipment, net	1,112,639	596,392	457,572
Long-term debt	435,158	247,424	223,856
Common stockholders' investment	717,721	503,794	350,319
Other operating data			
Average daily package volume	263,385	166,428	125,881
Average pounds per package	5.5	5.8	6.5
Average revenue per pound	$3.80	$4.02	$3.81
Aircraft fleet at end of year:			
McDonnell DC-10-10s	6	6	4
McDonnell DC-10-30s	4	0	0
Boeing 727-100s	35	38	31
Boeing 727-200s	12	0	0
Dassault Falcons[a]	0	32	32
Average number of full-time			
equivalent employees during year	18,368	12,507	10,092

Note: Figures in millions of dollars, except per share and other data.
[a] As of May 31, 1984, the company removed its Dassault Falcons from scheduled operations. Ten of the aircraft had been disposed of at that date, and, as of July 31, 1984, twelve were under contract for sale. The company is evaluating plans for the ultimate disposition of the remaining fleet.

offering in 1974–1975 raised only $32 million (against $5.5 billion in 1984). Federal Express was constantly asking banks, corporations, and venture capitalists for new loans and equity participations. Ultimately, the company survived as over a dozen equity groups participated in three major rounds of financing. In his desperate search for money, Smith had to give up virtually all his equity in his company. (He eventually recaptured a substantial portion in later refinancings.)

Throughout the bad times, however, Smith earned the undying loyalty of those who worked for him. ''He was a fantastic motivator of people,'' said Charles Tucker Morse, the company's first general counsel. ''I have not worked since in a situation so intense and so free of politics.''[82]

Financial results for fiscal 1984 were gratifying, despite the considerable expense incurred to improve existing service and to introduce a new electronic document transmission product. Revenues increased by 42 percent to $1.4 billion. Net income totaled $115 million or $2.52 per share, gains of 30 percent and 24 percent, respectively, over $89 million or $2.03 per share in fiscal 1983. (See Exhibits 7 and 8.)[83]

Other extraordinary expenses during 1984 were incurred to expand the network geographically and to add Business Service Centers in high-density, downtown areas. Also, increasing customer use of volume discounts and the relatively rapid growth of the lower-priced Overnight Letter and Standard Air Services resulted in a decline in the yield, or average revenue, per package. This trend exceeded the impressive decrease in operating costs per package achieved during the fiscal year.

Management expected the trend in declining yields to reverse because of three policy changes the company made during fiscal 1984 which produced higher than average yields. The first change was increasing the per package weight limit from 70 to 150 pounds. The second change was introducing a Saturday pick-up for Monday morning delivery service. The third and most important change was charging by the pound rather than the package for multiple-package shipments. Management hoped the third policy change would enable the company to enter the high-revenue, air freight market for the first time.[84]

EXHIBIT 8
Consolidated
statement of income

	1982	1983	1984
Express service revenues	$803,915	$1,008,087	$1,436,305
Operating expenses			
Salaries and employee benefits	320,345	419,644	622,675
Depreciation and amortization	56,353	77,421	111,956
Fuel and oil	69,282	71,262	93,520
Equipment and facilities rental	46,116	59,115	89,775
Maintenance and repairs	38,795	44,083	59,482
Advertising	25,302	34,558	39,345
Other	128,256	151,267	254,344
Total	684,449	857,350	1,271,097
Operating income	119,466	150,737	165,208
Other income (expenses)			
Interest expense	(15,933)	(23,451)	(36,350)
Interest capitalized	2,852	5,831	11,851
Interest income	11,994	9,679	13,166
Gain on aircraft sales	7,318	4,224	2,463
Other	5,383	3,196	(4,078)
Total	11,614	(521)	(12,948)
Income before income taxes	131,080	150,216	152,260
Provision for income taxes	52,695	61,283	36,830
Net income	$78,385	$88,933	$115,430
Earnings per share	$1.85	$2.03	$2.52
Average shares outstanding	41,788	43,316	45,488

Note: Figures in thousands of dollars.

EXHIBIT 9
Consolidated
balance sheet for
fiscal year ended
May 31

	1983	1984
Assets		
Cash	$ 204	$ 2,190
Short-term investments	105,233	35,500
Net receivables	124,841	207,256
Inventories	16,203	39,725
Prepayments, etc.	18,690	43,465
Total current assets	$ 265,171	$ 328,136
Property, plant, and equipment	817,650	1,427,281
Accumulated depreciation and amortization	(221,258)	(314,642)
Net property, plant, and equipment	596,392	1,112,639
Construction funds in escrow	47,839	32,168
Equipment deposits and other	82,315	52,862
Total assets	$ 991,717	$1,525,805
Liabilities and equity		
Current debt maturity	$ 12,171	$ 22,001
Notes payable	15,912	0
Accounts payable	59,047	129,960
Accrued liabilities	88,163	103,949
Total current liabilities	$ 175,293	$ 255,910
Long-term debt	247,424	435,158
Deferred income tax	59,094	112,439
Total liabilities	$ 481,811	$ 803,507
Preferred stock	6,112	4,577
Common stock	2,197	4,639
Paid-in-surplus	222,782	321,768
Retained earnings	278,815	391,314
Total equity	$ 509,906	$ 722,298
Total liabilities and equity	$ 991,717	$1,525,805

Note: Figures in thousands of dollars.

Federal Express had a fiscal 1984 current ratio of 1.28:1 which declined from 1.5:1 in fiscal 1983. One of the reasons for this decline was the 1984 implementation of ZapMail. The company had been relatively conservative with its financial policies in order to maintain large credit agreements with banks and other lenders. They had not paid any dividends on common stock throughout their incorporated history and maintained minimum levels of working capital and certain financial ratios. Their stock price showed consistent growth and split three times since the company went public in 1978. As of May 31, 1984, there were 46,386,287 shares of common stock. The 1983 and 1984 balance sheets are compared in Exhibit 9.[85]

The company was determined to grow and expand service geographically, as evidenced by the large increases in capital expenditures during the 3 years prior to 1985. (See Exhibit 10.) The bulk of these expenditures were for additional aircraft plus additions and improvements to ZapMail equipment. The source of these capital

EXHIBIT 10
Capital expenditures

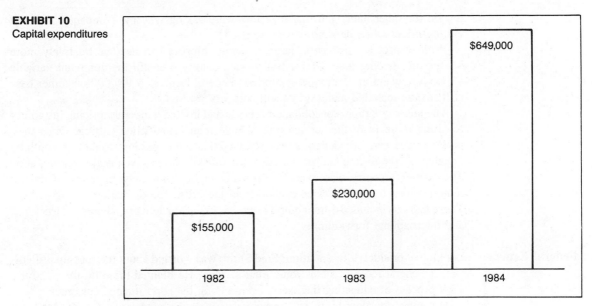

$649,000

$230,000

$155,000

1982   1983   1984

Note: Figures in thousands of dollars.

funds had been internally generated money, proceeds from loan agreements, tax-exempt bond issues, and equity offerings. Their commitment to growth had a significant effect on the company's cash and working capital, which, as of May 31, 1984, had suffered declines of 64 percent and 20 percent, respectively, from the previous year.

LEGAL

Federal's only threat for liability due to litigation involved their ZapMail product. Federal was sued in November 1984 by Zap Legislative Courier Service of Albany, New York, for alleged trademark infringement over the use of the name ZapMail. A judge ruled the company could seek unspecified monetary and punitive damages from Federal Express. As of May 1985, a trial date had not been set.[86]

OUTLOOK

Industry   Andrew B. Kim, a stock analyst for F. Eberstadt & Co., Inc., predicted that from a stock market standpoint, investors perceived that the profit margin squeeze would intensify as downward pressures on prices increased, especially if a downturn in the economy materialized. Kim also felt that the rapid increase in demand for the services of the air express and freight industry had been partly due to price reduction, but on the other hand, felt that investors were asking why the companies were all cutting prices when demand was so strong.[87]

With respect to customers, large frequent shippers had become relatively more sensitive to pricing than before. But service quality was still the dominant variable for both frequent and infrequent shippers. Federal Express's 400,000-customer base at that time included many infrequent shippers.[88]

The industry's rapid consolidation process had invited temporary pricing instability resulting more from the service mix change than actual price cutting. Once their product lines were broadened, it was expected that future pricing would be essentially dictated by the differential in the cost structure of six or seven major participants. The barrier to entry was expected to grow higher, not only in terms of capital requirements, but also service capability in the full range of markets being served. These markets included 4-hour courier service, extended delivery, short-haul trucking, and international forwarding.

Federal Express

Looking at product differentiation, Fred Smith was worried about the start-up difficulties of Federal Express's electronic mail service. He blamed these on the painfully slow process of educating the users, even among the sophisticated customers.[89]

However, the possibility still remained that predicted demand for ZapMail did not actually exist. Start-up losses already dramatically exceeded projections, and volume was significantly below expectations. Considering the enormous capital investment involved in the project, Federal was determined to make ZapMail a success and was placing a large stake of the company's future on the service. Viewing the enormity of the challenge and the complexity of the logistical problems, historical experience suggested that such a revolutionary new service would need both time and effective marketing to generate volume.

ZapMail and Federal Express Services

Fred Smith discussed ZapMail at length in a January 31, 1985, press conference:

With the ZapMail product, we have begun an odyssey which I think will do nothing less than change the way people do business forever. . . .

A recurring theme over the last several years has been heard from our customers who ship documents. They have told us unequivocally and clearly that they want a system to move exact copies over long distances on an instantaneous basis. Since its inception, the ZapMail project has been aimed towards the point in time when we could begin offering our customers machines for their offices which would let them achieve this type of instantaneous communication. Our development of a pickup and delivery service with ZapMail in July was a deliberate step to establish Federal Express's credentials in the same-day document transmission business. To date we have been disappointed with the rate of growth of this particular service.

I believe one of the reasons our initial ZapMail Service has not grown at the rate we expected is that our marketing message was not specified enough about the service. . . . We modified our approach in November and succeeded in increasing our volume growth substantially. We will be increasing these efforts even further in February.

I must also point out, however, that the level of user satisfaction among those who

*have tried ZapMail has been exceedingly high, and these customers have told us they
are very interested in achieving even faster and easier-to-use same-day transmission capabilities. . . .*

*I personally believe there is another message coming through loud and clear from
our customers. And that is, if anything, we have underestimated the rapidity with which
this demand for same-day transmission services is accelerating. . . .*

*What an entrepreneurial company like Federal Express must continue to do is to
listen to its customers and make changes accordingly. This ability to recognize the signals*

EXHIBIT 11 Quarterly product line statistics

	1984				1985		
	First quarter (June–Aug.)	Second quarter (Sept.–Nov.)	Third quarter (Dec.–Feb.)	Fourth quarter (Mar.–May)	First quarter (June–Aug.)	Second quarter (Sept.–Nov.)	Third quarter (Dec.–Feb.)
Total packages (thousands)							
Priority One and Courier- Pak	8,469	9,093	9,828	10,689	11,295	12,319	13,180
Standard Air	1,921	2,448	3,089	3,678	4,092	4,487	4,990
Overnight letter	3,126	3,919	4,993	6,173	6,832	7,522	8,513
ZapMail	—	—	—	—	28	112	168
Total	13,516	15,460	17,910	20,540	22,247	24,440	26,851
Yields							
Priority One and Courier- Pak	$28.58	$28.64	$28.08	$27.40	$27.05	$26.96	$25.98
Standard Air	14.49	14.25	13.56	13.30	13.09	13.97	13.23
Overnight letter	10.77	10.66	10.58	10.52	10.44	10.91	11.02
ZapMail	—	—	—	—	26.12	30.50	25.19
Composite[a]	22.46	21.81	20.70	19.80	19.38	19.65	18.86
Percentage of revenues							
Priority One and Courier- Pak	78.7%	76.4%	73.5%	70.9%	69.6%	68.5%	66.7%
Standard Air	9.1	10.2	11.2	11.8	12.2	12.9	12.8
Overnight letter	11.0	12.3	14.1	15.7	16.2	16.9	18.3
ZapMail	—	—	—	—	.2	.7	.8
Other	1.2	1.1	1.2	1.6	1.8	1.0	1.4
	100.0%	100.0%	100.0%	100.0%	100.0%	100.0%	100.0%
Operating weekdays	65	63	63	65	65	63	62
Pounds/package	5.6	5.7	5.5	5.4	5.5	5.8	5.5
Revenue/pound	$ 4.02	$ 3.80	$ 3.78	$ 3.66	$ 3.50	$ 3.40	$ 3.43
[a] Composite yields excluding ZapMail	$22.46	$21.81	$20.70	$19.80	$19.36	$19.60	$18.82
Composite costs excluding ZapMail	19.56	18.90	18.37	17.60	17.30	17.50	17.08
ZapMail revenues (thousands)					$90	$3,400	$4,110
ZapMail operating costs (thousands)					$30,000	$33,000	$35,500

being sent by the marketplace and then respond to them is what entrepreneurship is all about. We are listening to what our customers are telling us about ZapMail and we are responding to them with modifications that we feel will make ZapMail easier to use, more competitive, and more in line with what our customers most need and want for communicating intracompany and intercompany.

I would like to emphasize Federal Express's commitment to ZapMail. We believe this market is huge. No one can name the clear market leader for same-day document transmission services because there is no clear leader. We intend to attain an unequivocal leadership position in this market and then to build on that lead.

ZapMail was becoming increasingly important to Federal Express, and might reach $175,000,000 in investment (or about 7.5 percent of total assets) in a year. In preparation for Mr. Smith's review of company services, product line statistics for the most recent quarters had been collected. These statistics are summarized in Exhibit 11.

Fred Smith pondered the future of ZapMail:

How do you start a whole new communications system like this, where you need a machine at both ends? It's like the early telephone system. The most remarkable salesperson in history was the first telephone salesman. You had this fantastic instrument to talk to people, but unless everyone else had one, it wasn't worth much.[90]

REFERENCES

1. Linden, Eugene, "Frederick W. Smith of Federal Express: He Didn't Get There Over Night," *Inc.*, April 1984, p. 89.
2. Ibid.
3. Standard & Poors *Industry Surveys*, December 6, 1984, p. A36.
4. Colvin, Geoffrey, "Federal Express Dives into Air Mail," *Fortune*, June 15, 1981, pp. 106–8.
5. *Industry Surveys*, p. A36.
6. Ibid.
7. Ibid.
8. *Federal Express 10K*, May 31, 1984.
9. Altman, Henry, "A Business Visionary Who Really Delivered," *Nation's Business*, November 1981, p. 50.
10. Ibid.
11. Ibid.
12. Colvin, "Federal Express Dives," p. 107.
13. Altman, "Business," p. 54.
14. Ibid.
15. *Business Week*, "Federal Express Rides the Small Package Boom," March 31, 1980, p. 111.
16. "Creativity with Bill Moyers: Fred Smith and the Federal Express," *PBS Video*, 1981.
17. "The Memphis Connection," *Marketing & Media Decisions*, May 1982, p. 62.

18. Ibid., p. 63.
19. Hafner, Katie, "Fred Smith: The Entrepreneur Redux," *Inc.*, June 1984, p. 40.
20. Ibid.
21. Colvin, "Federal Express Dives," p. 107.
22. *Federal Express 1984 Annual Report*, p. 13.
23. Ibid.
24. *Federal Express 1982 Annual Report*, p. 14.
25. Ibid.
26. Colvin, "Federal Express Dives," p. 107.
27. Ibid., p. 108.
28. Stoops, Rick, "How Federal Express Recruited for a New High-Tech Image," *Personnel Journal*, August 1984, p. 16.
29. "Federal Express Readdresses ZapMail," *Sales and Marketing Management*, March 11, 1985, p. 26.
30. Ibid.
31. Colvin, "Federal Express Dives," p. 107.
32. Ibid., pp. 6, 7.
33. Ibid., p. 9.
34. *Federal Express 10K*, May 31, 1984, p. 9.
35. Ibid., p. 10.
36. Ibid., p. 10.
37. Ibid., p. 9.
38. Ibid., p. 10.
39. *Federal Express Corporation 1984 Annual Report*, p. 1.
40. *Federal Express Service Guide*, October 1, 1984, p. 19.
41. *Federal Express 1984 Annual Report*, p. 10.
42. *Service Guide*, p. 19.
43. Ibid., p. 23.
44. Ibid., p. 27.
45. *Air Freight Progress Report*, Morgan Stanley Investment Research, New York, January 21, 1985, p. 1.
46. *Service Guide*, p. 17.
47. *Air Freight Progress Report*, p. 1.
48. *Research, Federal Express*, Morgan Keegan & Company, Inc., November 28, 1983, p. 4.
49. *Air Freight*, January 21, 1985, p. 1.
50. Ibid.
51. Ibid.
52. *Research, Federal Express*, Morgan Keegan & Company, Inc., February 14, 1985, p. 4.
53. Ibid.
54. Ibid., pp. 3, 4.
55. *Service Guide*, p. 162.
56. *Federal Express 1984 Annual Report*, pp. 14, 15.
57. Ibid., p. 14.
58. Milmo, Sean, "British Air Couriers Welcome U.S. Entrant," *Business Marketing*, April 1984, p. 9.
59. Ibid.

60. Ibid.

61. "The Memphis Connection," p. 62.

62. Ibid., p. 128.

63. Seiden, Hank, "The Delivery Doesn't Fly," *Advertising Age*, October 31, 1983, p. M66.

64. "The Memphis Connection," p. 62.

65. "Federal Express Readdresses ZapMail," p. 26.

66. Ibid.

67. *Purolator Courier Corporation 1982 Annual Report*, Introduction.

68. *Standard & Poors N.Y.S.E. Stock Reports*, 1984, p. 1885.

69. *Purolator Courier Corporation 1982 Annual Report*, p. 10.

70. Ibid., p. 8.

71. *Standard & Poors N.Y.S.E. Stock Reports*, p. 1885.

72. Ibid., p. 827.

73. *Emery Air Freight 1983 Annual Report*, Introduction.

74. Ibid., p. 3.

75. Ibid., p. 13.

76. *Standard & Poors N.Y.S.E. Stock Reports*, p. 827.

77. "Behind the UPS Mystique: Puritanism and Productivity," *Business Week*, June 6, 1983, p. 66.

78. Ibid.

79. Ibid.

80. "Express Mail Next Day Service," *U.S. Postal Service Pamphlet Notice # 43*, July 1977, p. 2.

81. Ibid., p. 6.

82. Linden, p. 89.

83. *Federal Express 1984 Annual Report*.

84. Ibid.

85. *Standard & Poors Industry Report*, 1984, p. 2551.

86. *Wall Street Journal*, December 28, 1984, p. 33.

87. "Research Notes," F. Eberstadt & Co., Inc., May 3, 1984.

88. Ibid., p. 2.

89. Ibid.

90. "Federal Express's Fred Smith," *Inc.*, October 1986, p. 42.

NUCOR CORPORATION

It's the closest thing to a perfect company in the steel industry.
> Daniel Roling, analyst for Merrill Lynch

With earnings growth over the past decade averaging better than 23 percent per year, Nucor prospered in the steel industry while giant companies barely survived. Few "high-tech" companies could match Nucor's record. But in 1986, Nucor was moving into an era where the easy pickings were over. One securities analyst believed that Nucor would not be able to find alluring new opportunities, stating: "Their rapid growth of the last 10 years is simply not repeatable."

BACKGROUND

Nuclear Corporation

Nuclear Corporation of America was formed by a merger of Nuclear Consultants, Inc., and parts of REO Motors in 1955. Between 1955 and 1964 various managements tried (unsuccessfully) by way of acquisitions and divestitures to make a profit. One of the acquisitions was Vulcraft, a steel joist manufacturer. By 1965 Nuclear Corporation was losing $2 million on sales of $22 million. A new group got control of the company in 1965 and installed Vulcraft general manager Ken Iverson (who headed the only profitable division) as president. "I got the job by default," Iverson said.

Entry into Steel Industry

Iverson decided that Vulcraft — a manufacturer of steel joists for buildings — ought to make its own steel. His goal was to match the prices of imported steel: "We had some vision that if we were successful, we could expand and create another business by selling steel in the general marketplace." In 1968 Nucor built its first steel mill in Darlington, South Carolina. By 1985 Nucor operated four steel mills, six joist plants, two cold finishing plants, three steel deck plants, and a grinding ball plant throughout the south, southwest, and west. About 65 percent of Nucor's

Prepared by Professors Charles I. Stubbart and Dean Schroeder, the University of Massachusetts-Amherst. © 1986 by Stubbart and Schroeder. Reprinted by permission.

steel was sold in open markets, while 35 percent went to Vulcraft and other Nucor products. Until the recession of 1982–83 sales and earnings grew at an astonishing clip. Even during the recession Nucor managed to eke out a profit while other integrated steel companies lost billions.

STEEL INDUSTRY CONDITIONS, 1985

Industry Participants

Companies competing in the U.S. steel industry in 1985 were of several distinct types: integrated U.S. companies, foreign manufacturers, minimills, and specialty steel producers. The large integrated domestic companies (e.g., U.S. Steel) got their start at the turn of the century. Integrated companies held about 45 to 55 percent of the market. Specialty steel producers manufactured relatively low volumes

EXHIBIT 1
U.S. raw steel production, finished steel shipments, and steel imports, 1956–1984

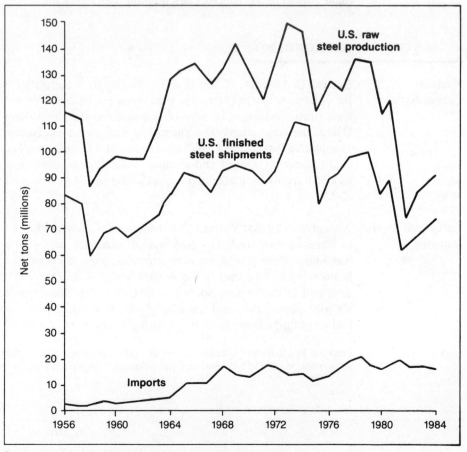

Source: American Iron and Steel Institute, *Annual Statistical Reports.*

of steel with varying degrees of hardness, purity, and strength. Imports of steel into the United States accounted for about 20 to 25 percent of domestic sales. (Imports probably held a larger share, taking into account the steel in imported automobiles and other products.) Minimills, which transformed scrap metal into steel using electric furnaces, had a market share of about 20 to 25 percent of the domestic market.

Recent History

Since the early 1960s the integrated steel industry had suffered a painful decline. The stagnation of the early 1960s gave way to faster growth (and rising imports) in the late 1960s. During 1965–74 steel demand was strong, and industry officials expected major growth after 1974. But they were wrong. Steel production in the United States had fallen from its 1974 level, and many analysts believed that the 1974 levels would never be reached again (Exhibit 1). Much of this decline was traceable to the long-term trends toward smaller, lighter cars; the inroads of competing materials (such as aluminum and plastics); a shift in emphasis away from smokestack industries to service industries; and greater use of imported steel in U.S. products.

Between 1960 and 1985 foreign competitors and domestic minimills invested heavily in building all-new facilities with the latest technology. Major integrated companies invested in older, more familiar technologies to try to spruce up existing plants and correct gross inefficiencies. Facing weak demand, having less efficient facilities, and with the U.S. dollar appreciating in value, the biggest domestic integrated companies suffered huge losses in the late 1970s and early 1980s (Exhibits 2 and 3).

EXHIBIT 2
Production capacity of largest U.S. integrated steel companies, 1984

Firm	Raw steel capacity
1. U.S. Steel	26.2
2. LTV	19.1
3. Bethlehem	18.0
4. Inland	9.4
5. Armco	6.8
6. National	5.6
7. Wheeling-Pittsburgh	4.5
8. Weirton	4.0
9. Ford Motor Co. (Rouge Steel)	3.6
10. McLouth	2.0
11. CF&I	2.0 (partially closed)
12. Interlake	1.4
13. Sharon	1.0
14. California	2.1 (closed)
Total	105.7

Note: Figures in millions of tons per year.
Source: Company reports; Oppenheimer & Co., Metal Bulletin, *Iron and Steel Works of the World,* 8th edition.

EXHIBIT 3 U.S. domestic steel industry, 1972–1984

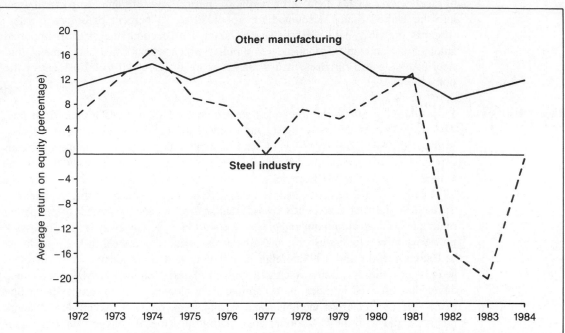

Source: *Forbes*, May 1986.

Other problems also contributed to the rapid slide. The steelworkers union was able to negotiate large wage increases in 1968 and 1971, and union work rules hampered steel company efforts to increase productivity in their plants. Only in 1983 did the steelworkers union reluctantly agree to wage concessions and work rule modifications under the pressure of plant closings.

Investments

Expecting major increases in demand for 1975–85, integrated companies made large investments in ore mines and iron pelletizing facilities. An important share of their investment dollars went into meeting environmental regulations. Integrated companies' financial calculations persuaded them to stick with modifications of existing plants instead of building new "greenfield" (environmentally proper) plants. As a result, not one all-new integrated steel plant had been built for over 20 years in the United States. Given the high cost of capital, the complex environmental constraints, weak demand, and intense foreign/domestic competition, it was unlikely that any new integrated plants would be built in the United States in the foreseeable future.

Imports and Protection

The steel strike of 1959 provided the first opportunity for foreign steel firms to make inroads into the U.S. market. By the 1980s — despite several attempts to limit imports via voluntary restraints and trigger pricing (a minimum pricing rule) —

the integrated companies found themselves with 140 million tons of excess capacity, much of it in old inefficient plants. They had no choice but to face the music and close many plants and sell unproductive assets — a protracted and painful process for the companies, the steelworkers, and many local communities. Within one four-year period steelmakers wrote off $4.4 billion in assets and took $7 billion in losses. Steel companies, steelworkers, and endangered communities struggled mightily to persuade a Reagan administration and the Congress to limit steel imports. A reluctant Reagan administration agreed to negotiate "voluntary" restraints in 1985. Even so, to the integrated companies, the "rust bowl" communities, and to over 200,000 permanently laid off steelworkers, it seemed that too little had been done too late.

Foreign steel imports in 1985 accounted for about 25 percent of the U.S. market in spite of the Reagan administration's negotiating bilateral voluntary restraints with foreign governments. These restraint agreements aimed at limiting imports to about 21 percent of the market. Sentiment was growing in Congress to stem the tidal wave of foreign imports in the face of a $130 billion trade deficit during 1985. Ken Iverson, Nucor's CEO, steadfastly argued against protecting the domestic steel industry:

> We've had this "temporary" relief for a long time. We had a voluntary quota system in the early 1970s. We had trigger prices in the late 1970s. And what happened during these periods? As soon as prices began to rise so that steel companies would begin to be profitable, they stopped modernizing. It's only under intense competitive pressure — both internally from minimills and externally from the Japanese and the Koreans — that the big steel companies have been forced to modernize. . . . In 1980 the industry still had rolling mills dating from the Civil War. . . . Out of all this turmoil will come a lot of things which are beneficial: more of an orientation toward technology, greater productivity, certainly a lot of changes in management structure.

Future Prospects

Speculating about 1986, steel producers expected another year like 1985: declining tonnage, stable prices, slightly declining import shares, and overall profitability near zero for the industry. Their forecasts hinged on a GNP growth of approximately 3 percent. Industry analysts foresaw that a reduction in imports (traced to the falling value of the U.S. dollar) would offset an expected decline in steel consumption. Demand for steel in machinery, railroad equipment, farm equipment, and other capital items was falling. Analysts were also uncertain about the 1986 demand for autos. Some estimates placed 1986 domestic steel shipments in the range of 70 to 75 million tons (not counting imports). The prospect of labor negotiations beginning in the second half of 1986 represented a major uncertainty for steel producers and customers.

But there was a bright side too. Steel companies entered the year determined to extract concessions from the United Steelworkers Union. Companies had eliminated most of their grossly inefficient facilities. Prices were edging up. Capacity utilization approached 70 percent, compared to a low of 48 percent in 1982 (Exhibit 4). A weakening dollar made imports less attractive.

EXHIBIT 4

U.S. steelmaking capacity utilization, 1975–1985

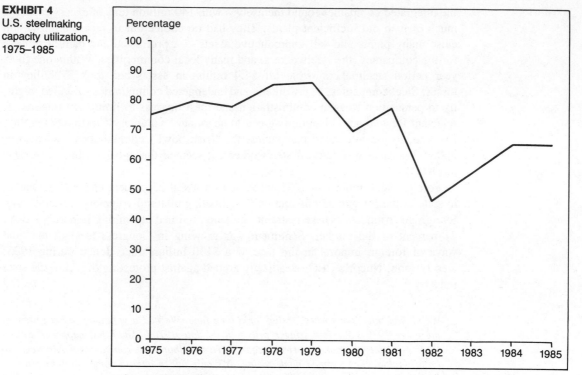

Source: AISI statistics.

Analysts estimated that worldwide demand had stabilized. From 1979 to 1985 steel output in the industrial nations dropped precipitously from 442 million tons to 331 million tons. Capacity had been cut back 28 million tons in Europe, 23 million tons in the United States, and 17 million tons in Japan. One U.S. steel producer predicted that an additional 20 million tons in U.S. capacity would have to go. Exhibit 5 offers some industry projections for steel. A steel executive summed up a grim situation and his skepticism about a future that U.S. steel companies felt helpless about: "You light a candle at every altar."

STEEL MINIMILLS: AN INDUSTRY WITHIN AN INDUSTRY

Nucor is best known for its steel minimill business. Nucor operated four steel minimills in South Carolina, Nebraska, Texas, and Utah, with a total capacity of about 2 million tons. That made Nucor the eighth largest steel company in the United States.

The United States had about 50 minimills. As U.S. Steel, Bethlehem, Republic,

EXHIBIT 5
Steel industry
projections

	1980	1985	1990	2000
Import share of U.S. market (percent)	17.0	24.0	28.0	32.0
Domestic shipments (millions of tons)	83.9	76.0	73.1	71.4– 78.2
Imports (millions of tons)	17.2	24.0	28.4	33.6– 36.8
Total shipments (millions of tons)	86.7	77.0	74.1	72.4– 79.2
Minimill shipments (millions of tons)	12.0	14.4	20.5	29.0
Minimill capacity (millions of tons)	16.0	22.0	27.0	35.0
Minimill productivity (work hours per ton)	4.0	2.8	2.2	1.5
Integrated shipments (millions of tons)	74.7	62.6	53.6	43.4– 50.2
Integrated raw steel production (millions of tons)	102.3	82.3	67.8	49.9– 57.7
Integrated capacity (millions of tons)	138.4	108.3	80.0	55.4– 64.1
Integrated productivity (work hours per ton)	9.5	7.2	6.0	4.5
Capacity utilization rate (percent)	75.3	76.0	85.0	90.0
Total employment (in thousands)	401.6	247.9	195.0	129.6–141.7

Source: Barnett, *Minimills.*

National, and LTV surrendered market share and lost billions, new entrants into the domestic market such as North Star, Nucor, Co-Steel, Florida Steel, and others prospered — and even displaced imports. Contrary to typical relationships between scale and efficiency, minimills manufactured high-quality steel inexpensively, with plants of 200,000 to 1 million tons of annual electric-furnace capacity; integrated plants producing 2 million to 10 million tons using open-hearth and basic oxygen furnace equipment were the high-cost producers.

Technology

The electric-furnace technology of minimills was first developed by Northwestern Steel and Wire in the 1930s. Exhibit 6 shows a comparison of the two processes, integrated versus minimill; the comparative simplicity of minimills is apparent. First, minimills use electric arc furnaces compared to integrated plants that use open-hearth (about 10 percent) or basic oxygen furnaces (about 90 percent). They simply charge scrap into an electric arc furnace to produce molten steel, then continuously cast the molten metal into semifinish shapes. Continuous casters eliminated reheating and increased the yield from molten metal to finished product. Unlike integrated mills, minimills were expressly designed for rebuilding and technical updating. Many integrated plants used obsolete ingot-casting technologies.

EXHIBIT 6
Comparative steel
production

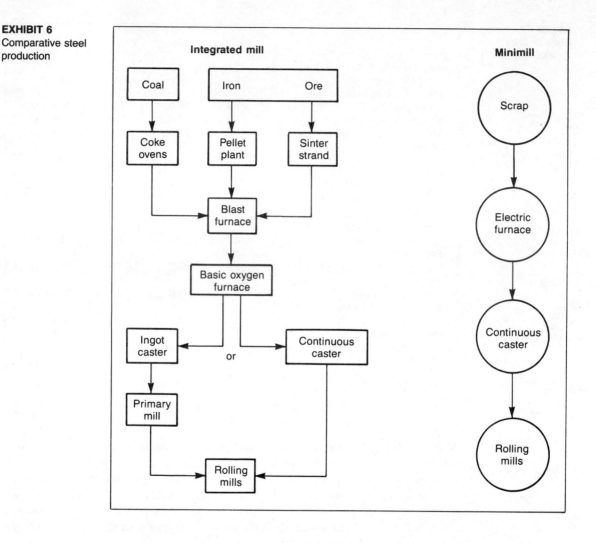

**Product
Specialization**

Early on, minimills fashioned small specialized steel products like reinforcing rods for use in concrete work, rather than making huge beams, slabs, or sheets. Product specialization increased their efficiency. Steel slabs were still predominantly the private preserve of the integrated companies. But, as time passed, minimill companies expanded their product lines. Exhibit 7 compares minimill product lines to integrated mill product lines. Nucor in 1985 produced cold-finished bars and was devoting a major innovative effort to the challenge of adapting minimill technology to sheet steel production. If Nucor could perfect this new technology, the company would be able to challenge integrated companies on their "home ground," the flat-rolled steel used in automobiles, appliances, and roofing.

EXHIBIT 7
Product categories
of integrated mills
and minimills

Integrated products	Minimill production?
Slabs	
Hot rolled sheets	No
Cold rolled sheets	No
Coated sheets	No
Plates	Yes
Welded pipe and tube	Limited
Blooms and Billets	
Wire rods	Yes
Bars	Yes
Reinforcing bars	Yes
Small structural shapes	Yes
Large structural shapes	Limited
Rails	No
Seamless tube	Yes
Axles	No

Location

Only by the 1960s did minimills become a force within the industry. Their strategy was to utilize only electric furnaces and to locate their plants in regions near customer markets and scrap supplies but more distant from integrated plants (steel being expensive to ship). During the 1970s minimills grew explosively, capturing significant market shares (Exhibit 8).

Input Costs

Scrap steel was the principal raw material input for minimill production. While the cost of iron ore had constantly risen (as rich high-quality sources in the United States ran out), scrap remained plentiful. Over the last 10 years scrap prices had declined relative to iron ore prices.

Workforce Flexibility

Another important advantage of minimills was their workforce flexibility. Most minimills employed nonunion workers. Union attempts to organize minimills had met with little success. Although nonunion minimill wages were not always lower than union wages, their worker productivity was always much higher, primarily because of the flexibility and latitude management had in organizing work. Without union work rule restrictions, management could introduce labor-saving technology and link earnings to productivity.

Productivity

Electric furnace technology, workforce flexibility, and constant efforts to operate facilities more efficiently added up to a significant cost advantage (that translated into a price advantage) for minimills. The advantage in 1985 was about $100 per ton ($375 for integrated firms versus $275 for minimills). Much of the advantage stemmed from the fact that output per worker at minimills ran about double the

EXHIBIT 8   U.S. steel production by process, 1975–1985

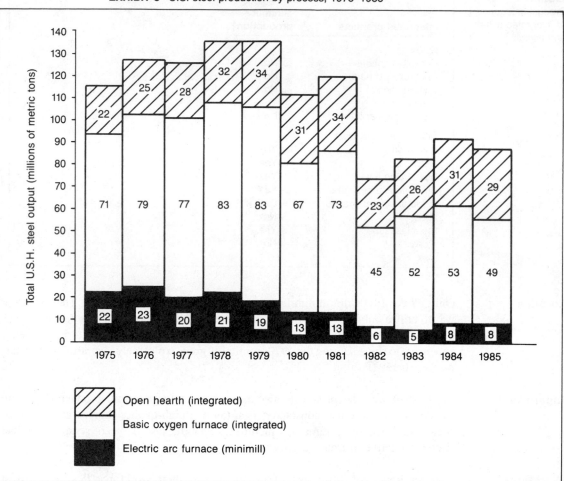

Source: AISI statistics.

350 tons per employee at integrated companies. Because minimill wages were comparable (some lower but not much) to workers' earnings in the unionized plants of bigger, integrated producers, minimills had about half the labor costs per ton of integrated companies.

Developmental Sequence   Minimills did not win their market niche overnight. Some minimills failed. While minimills had advantages in low-cost labor and low-cost scrap, they faced scale disadvantages and began with an untested technology and no customer base. The initial market penetration successes came in low-grade steel products. Then, as they learned and made operating improvements, they moved gradually and selectively to challenge integrated mills and imports in an ever-broadening array of products

EXHIBIT 9
Leading U.S.
minimill companies

Firm	Number of plants	Capacity (tons)	Products
Nucor	4	2,100,000	Bars, small structurals
North Star	4	2,050,000	Bars, rods, small structurals
Northwestern	1	1,800,000	Bars, rods, small and large structurals
Co-Steel	2	1,750,000	Bars, rods, small and large structurals
Florida Steel	5	1,560,000	Bars, small structurals

Note: The minimill segment consisted of 50 firms and 65 plants. Of total minimill production, 55 percent came from plants with less than 600,000 tons of annual capacity.

but always where their relative cost position was strongest. The largest, and generally most successful, minimill companies in 1985 are shown in Exhibit 9.

Intensified Competition

Contrary to popular impressions about imported steel, minimills' production accounted for more of the displacement of integrated companies' share than had imports. The relationship between the minimills and the integrated companies resembled a successful guerrilla war. In 1985, however, the competitive scene was changing. Having used their lower costs to force integrated companies and imports out of many markets, minimills were beginning to compete against each other. An official at an integrated company noted: "Minimills have passed the stage of taking tonnage from integrated producers. We are concentrating on more sophisticated products where they can't compete. Let them have the inefficient productions." Iverson observed: "We are now head to head against much tougher competition. It was no contest when we were up against the integrated companies. Now we are facing minimills who have the same scrap prices, the same electrical costs, and who use the same technologies."

Minimills coveted the bigger market for flat-rolled steel where profit margins were higher. But they were shut out of this segment by technological limitations. In terms of technological capabilities, productivity, workforce practices, and expanding products, Nucor was viewed as the leader among minimill producers.

VULCRAFT: THE OTHER HALF OF NUCOR

Ken Iverson said:

Most people think of us as a steel company, but we are a lot more than a steel company. The business is really composed of two different factors. One is manufacturing steel and the other is steel products. We like it if in an average year each factor contributes about 50 percent of our sales and 50 percent of our earnings. It is important for the company in the long run that we keep this balance. If one of them began to dominate the company it would cause problems we wouldn't like to see.

Products

Vulcraft was the nation's largest producer of steel joists and joist girders. Steel joists and girders served as support systems in industrial buildings, shopping centers, warehouses, high-rise buildings, and to a lesser extent in small office buildings, apartments, and single-family dwellings. Vulcraft had six joist plants, four deck plants, and three cold finish plants. Steel deck was used for floor and roof systems. In 1985 Vulcraft produced 471,000 tons of joists and girders and 169,000 tons of steel deck (Exhibit 10).

Manufacturing Process

Joists were manufactured on assembly lines. The steel moved on rolling conveyors from station to station. Teams of workers at each station cut and bent the steel to shape, welded joists together and drilled holes in them, and painted the completed product.

EXHIBIT 10
Nucor's steel joist and steel production and sales, 1975–1985

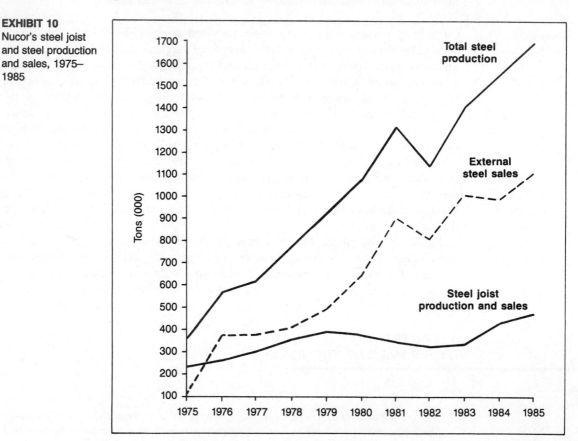

Competition Many competitors participated in the joist segment, and a large number and variety of customers bought joists. Competition centered around timely delivery and price. Joist manufacturing was not capital intensive like basic steel-making, but was more of an engineering business. Vulcraft bid on a very high percentage of all new buildings which needed joists. Sophisticated computer software was used to design the joists needed on a job and to develop bid estimates. Success also depended on marketing and advertising. Vulcraft had a 40 percent national market share in joists in 1985, making it the largest joist manufacturer in the United States. In 1985 Vulcraft manufactured joists for about 15,000 buildings. Vulcraft management pursued a strategy of being the low-cost supplier of joists.

Organization Each Vulcraft plant was managed by a general manager who reported directly to Dave Aycock, president of Nucor. Each Vulcraft general manager had spent many years in the joist business. In general, the Vulcraft division's relationships with corporate headquarters paralleled those of the steel division.

OTHER NUCOR BUSINESSES

In addition to steel and joists, Nucor operated three cold finish plants which produced steel bars used in shafting and machining precision parts; a plant which produced grinding balls used by the mining industry; and a research chemicals unit which produced rare earth oxides, metals, and salts. Exhibit 11 shows Nucor's sales by business.

KEN IVERSON AND THE NUCOR CULTURE

Iverson had consciously modeled Nucor on certain bedrock values: productivity, simplicity, thrift, and innovation.

Productivity Iverson liked to contrast Nucor with integrated companies. He recounted a field trip he took to an integrated steel plant when he was a student at Purdue: "This was the late afternoon. We were touring through the plant, and we actually had to step over workers who were sleeping there. I decided right then that I didn't ever want to work for a big steel plant." The average Nucor worker produced 700 to 800 tons of steel per year versus 350 tons per employee at integrated companies; total labor costs at Nucor averaged less than half that at integrated producers. At the production level people were arranged into groups of 25 to 35 people. Each group had a production standard to meet and a steep bonus schedule for exceeding its standard. Nucor production workers could earn $30,000 or more in a good year. Producing steel and joists entailed hard, hot, dirty, and occasionally dangerous

EXHIBIT 11
Nucor's steel deck
and cold finished
steel sales,
1977–1985

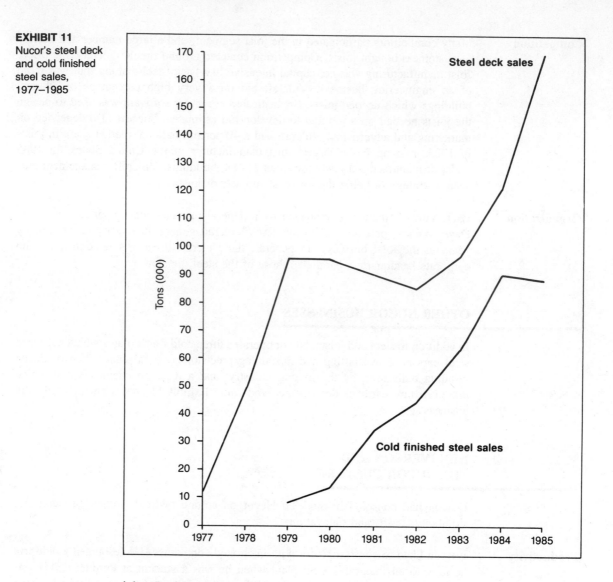

jobs. Performance at all levels of the company was rigidly tied to efficiency and profitability criteria.

Simplicity and Thrift

Iverson and other managers at Nucor had developed practices and symbols which conveyed simplicity. One of their notable achievements was a streamlined organizational structure. Only four levels separated the official hierarchy: workers, department managers, division managers, corporate. Iverson said:

> *You can tell a lot about a company by looking at its organizational charts. . . . If you see a lot of staff, you can bet that it is not a very efficient organization. . . . Secondly,*

don't have assistants. We do not have that title and prohibit it in our company. . . .
And one of the most important things is to restrict as much as possible the number of
management layers. . . . It is probably the most important single factor in business.

Iverson's pioneering approach in steel was beginning to be copied by the bigger
companies:

I spent two days as a lecturer at a business school not long ago. One of the students
heard me talk about getting rid of management layers. He spoke up and said that when
he visited U.S. Steel's new pipe mill near Birmingham, Alabama, the thing they were
most proud of wasn't the technology but that they had only 4 management layers instead
of the usual 10.

When we asked Sam Siegel about Nucor's organization, he handed us copies
of *Parkinson's Law*, a book that he keeps in ample supply for inquisitive visitors.
Parkinson's Law describes how work always expands to fit the number of workers
assigned to it.

Nucor's spartan values were most evident at its corporate headquarters. Instead
of having a handsome, expensive showcase building sited on landscaped grounds,
Nucor rented a few thousand square feet of the fourth floor of a nondescript office
building with an insurance company's name on it. The only clue that Nucor was
there was its name (listed in ordinary size letters) in the building directory. The
office decor was spartan, simple and functional. Only 16 people worked in the
headquarters — no financial analysts, no engineering staff, no marketing staff, no
research staff. The company assiduously avoided the normal paraphernalia of bureaucracy. No one had a formal job description. The company had no written mission
statement, no strategic plan, and no MBO system. There was little paperwork,
few regular reports, and fewer meetings. Iverson commented on his staff and how
it functioned:

They are all very sharp people. We don't centralize anything. We have a financial vice
president, a president, a manager of personnel, a planner, internal auditing, and account-
ing. . . . With such a small staff there are opportunities you miss and things you don't
do well because you don't have time . . . but the advantages so far outweigh the disadvan-
tages. . . . We focus on what can really benefit the business. . . . We don't have job
descriptions, we just kind of divide up the work.

Innovation   Nucor was a leading innovator among steel minimills and the joist business as
well. Plant designs, organizational structure, incentives, and workforce allocations
synchronized with cultural pressure for constant innovative advancements. Iverson
projected that minimills could eventually capture as much as 35 to 40 percent of
the steel business if they succeeded in developing technological advances which
enabled them to produce a wider variety of steel products very economically. The
breakthroughs hinged on revamping continuous casting technology. Currently, a

minimill couldn't produce certain shapes. Iverson thought the key to unlock the door was the "thin-slab caster":

> We are trying to develop a thin slab. Then we could produce plate and other flatrolled products. Right now the thinnest slab that can be produced is 6 inches thick. If we can get down to 1½ inches with the thin slab caster, then we can map out the growth for another 10 years. We could build those all over the country. We're trying to develop this new technology in our Darlington mill. The investment will probably run $10 to $20 million. Now, if we could do it, the new mills would probably cost about $150 million.

Many analysts doubted that such a breakthrough was really in the offing, but Iverson believed it would come within three years and was monitoring seven experimental programs.

**Ken Iverson:
Public Figure**

Nucor's success had made Iverson a public figure. He had been interviewed by newspapers, magazines, radio, and TV; he spoke to industry groups and business schools; and he had been called to testify before Congress. He explained why he was willing to devote his time to these extracurricular activities:

> Generally, our policy is to stay as far away as we can from government . . . except that I felt so strongly about protectionism that I thought I should make my views known — especially because our view is so different from the other steel mills. . . . Talking to investors is an important part of the company's relationship with the marketplace . . . the company gets a direct benefit and it makes good sense. . . . I do some talks at business schools just from the standpoint that I get pleasure out of that. . . . We do occasionally hire MBAs, but we haven't had such success with them.

Iverson had a casual, informal, and unaffected style. His office was neither large nor furnished with expensive decorations. For lunch he took visitors across the street to a delicatessen — their "executive dining room" — for a quick sandwich. Nucor had no executive parking spaces, no executive restrooms, no company cars. Everyone, including Iverson, flew coach class. When Iverson went to New York he rode the subway instead of taking a limousine or taxi. Other Nucor managers followed Iverson's example, shunning ostentation, luxury, and status symbols common among other successful companies.

Managers at Nucor described Iverson's management style:

> Ken is straightforward. If he says something you can pretty well count on it. He sets the tone and the direction and everybody pitches in. That's the way he acts and approaches things — directly.

> Ken is one of the greatest leaders the steel industry has ever had.

> Ken is liberal with people and conservative with money.

ORGANIZATION

Organization Structure

Following Iverson's "lean management" philosophy, only four levels of management separated Iverson from the hourly employees. At corporate headquarters they joked that with four promotions, a janitor could become CEO! Exhibit 12 depicts Nucor's organization chart. Below the corporate level the company was organized into divisions. These divisions roughly corresponded to plant locations.

Recently, under the pressure of the growing size of the company and Iverson's busy public role, the jobs of president and CEO were separated. By trying to be "everything to everyone," Iverson was spreading himself a little thin. Dave Aycock was promoted from a plant manager's job to president, responsible for day-to-day operations of Nucor; Aycock talked about his new role:

> *I worked at Vulcraft when it was acquired by Nucor in 1955. . . . I've been in this new job for about a year. . . . It's very exciting. . . . If I had actually known roughly half*

EXHIBIT 12
Nucor's organization structure

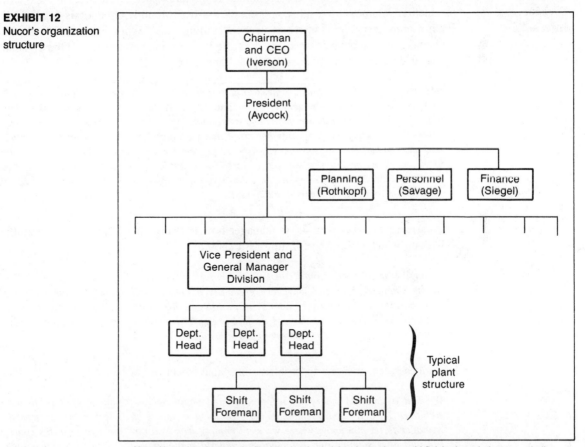

Note: Nucor has four steel mills (divisions), six joist plants, three cold finished steel plants, a grinding ball plant, and a research chemicals division — each is headed by a vice president and general manager.

of what I thought I knew, I would probably have been more valuable. . . . Most of my time has been spent learning the personalities, the reactions, and philosophies of the operating personnel. . . . Many of them were glad to see the change because they thought Ken was overworked.

Division Management

Because Nucor had no headquarters staff and because of top management's great confidence in operating personnel, division managers played a key role in decision making. Iverson said of the division managers:

They are all vice presidents, and they are behind our success. He's at that division. He's responsible for that division. They make the policies of this company. Most of them have been with Nucor at least 10 years. But his pay is based on how this company does — not on how well his division does — it's the group concept again.

Corporate-Division Interaction

Contact between divisions and corporate headquarters was limited to a report of production volume, costs, sales, and margin — the "Monthly Operations Analysis." Each month every division received the "smiling face" report, comparing all the divisions across about a dozen categories of efficiency and performance. One division manager described how Iverson delegated and supervised:

Mr. Iverson's style of management is to allow the manager all the latitude in the world. His involvement with managers is quite limited. As we have grown, he no longer has the time to visit with division managers more than once or twice a year. . . . In a way I feel like I run my own company because I don't get marching orders from Mr. Iverson. He lets you run the division the way you see fit, and the only way he will step in is if he sees something he doesn't like, particularly bad profits, high costs, or whatever. But in the four years I've worked with him I don't recall a single instance where he issued an instruction to me to do something differently.

The casewriters asked a division manager how the corporate officers would handle a division which wasn't performing as it should:

I imagine he (Aycock) would call first and come out later, but it would be appropriate to the situation. Ken and Dave are great psychologists. Right now, for instance, the steel business is showing very poor return on assets, but I don't feel any pressure on me because the market is not there. I do feel pressure to keep my costs down, and that is appropriate. If something went wrong Dave would know.

How does Nucor respond to problems in management performance?

We had a situation where we were concerned about the performance of a particular employee . . . a department manager. Ken, Dave, and I sat down with the general manager to let him know where we were coming from. So now the ball is in his court. We will offer support and help that the general manager wants. Later I spent a long evening with the general manager and the department manager. Now the department manager understands the corporate concern. Ken will allow the general manager to resolve this issue. To do otherwise would take the trust out of the system. . . . We are not going to just call someone in and say ''We're not satisfied. You're gone.'' . . . But, eventually, the string may run out. Ken will terminate people. He takes a long time to do it. I respect that. Ken would rather give people too much time than too little.

Important issues merited a phone call or perhaps a visit from a corporate officer. A division manager told the casewriters that he talked to headquarters about once a week. Divisions made their own decisions about hiring, purchasing, processes, and equipment. There was no formal limit on a division manager's spending authority. Sales policy and personnel policy were set at corporate level. Divisions didn't produce a plan, but: ''People in this company have real firm ideas about what is going on and what will be happening . . . mostly by word of mouth.''

Relationships between the divisions were close. They shared ideas and information, and sold each other significant amounts of product.

Decision Making Division managers met formally in a group with corporate management three times a year at the ''Roundtable.'' Sessions began at 7 A.M. and ended at 8 P.M. At these meetings, budgets, capital expenditures, and changes in wages or benefits were agreed on, and department managers were reviewed. Iverson waited for a consensus to emerge about an alternative before going ahead with a decision. He did not impose decisions. Corporate officers described Nucor's decision making processes:

Over a long period of time, decisions in this company have been made at the lowest level that they can — subject to staying within the philosophy of the company. We get a lot of work done without too many managers. Ken has the business courage to stay out of the small things. It takes a lot of courage for general managers to resist the temptation to control every event.

I can walk into Ken's office anytime and talk about anything I want to talk about. Agree or disagree with anything he has done. I don't agree with every decision that is made. I have the right to disagree. Sometimes I disagree strongly. Ken hears me out. Ken listens to other people. He does not feel that he is always right. Sometimes he will change his mind.

I remember when I first started to work for Nucor and I was sitting down with Ken Iverson. He told me, ''John, you are going to make at least three mistakes with this company in the first few years that you are with us. Each one of these mistakes will cost us $50,000. I want you to be aggressive, and I want you to make decisions. One word of caution. We don't mind you making the mistakes, but please don't make them all in one year.''

Ken defers a decision when the executives are strongly divided to give people a chance to consider it more. Ken is a superb negotiator. He might look at the various positions and say ''I have a compromise,'' and lay that out. Many times he can see a compromise that everyone is comfortable with.

FINANCIAL POSITION

The theme of simplicity also extended to financial matters. Sam Siegel, Nucor's vice president of finance, did not use a computer. He told the casewriters:

> *When you make too many calculations they get in the way of business. Each of the divisions uses computers for many purposes, including financial analysis. You could make an economic case for centralizing some of that here at corporate headquarters. We could save money and create all kinds of information, but then we would have to hire more people to study that information.*

Investments

No financial analysts worked at corporate headquarters. Nucor did not use sophisticated models of discounted cash flow or complicated formulas to govern capital expenditures, preferring an eclectic capital investment policy. Iverson commented: "Priority? No. We don't even do that with capital expenditures. Sometimes we'll say . . . we won't put up any buildings this year. . . . But in recent years we've been able to fund anything we felt we needed. We don't do it by priorities." Responding to a query about whether the company used an internal hurdle rate of return, Iverson said:

> *We look at it from the standpoint of whether it's replacement and if it's modernization, what the payback period is, or if it is a new facility. In many cases the payback on a new steel mill is longer than you would like, but you can't afford not to do it. I think maybe that is where other manufacturing companies go wrong — where they have these rigid ideas about investments. If you don't put some of these investments in, after four or five years you are behind. . . . You can't afford to fall behind, even if you don't get the payback. That's why the integrated steel companies didn't put in continuous casters, because they couldn't get the payback they wanted. . . . Now they have got to do it. . . . From an economics point of view they didn't do anything wrong, they didn't make a mistake.*

Financial Reporting

Each division had a controller who reported directly to the division manager and indirectly to Siegel. Siegel saw the role of his controllers as being broad: "Controllers who merely do financial work are not doing a good job. A controller should become involved with key plant operations . . . should learn the whole operation." Siegel spent only about one half of his time on strictly financial matters, contributing the other half toward "problems, issues, and projects" of importance to the company.

Financial Condition

According to Siegel, the company was in good financial condition except for having too much invested in short-term assets (Exhibits 13 and 14). Wall Street analysts had speculated about what Nucor might decide to do with its excess short-term assets.

EXHIBIT 13 Financial review, 1980–1985

	1980	1981	1982	1983	1984	1985
Net sales	$482,420,363	$544,820,621	$486,018,162	$542,531,431	$660,259,922	$758,495,374
Costs and expenses						
Cost of products sold	369,415,571	456,210,289	408,606,641	461,727,688	539,731,252	600,797,865
Marketing and administrative expenses	38,164,559	33,524,820	31,720,315	33,988,054	45,939,311	59,079,802
Interest expense (income)	(1,219,965)	10,256,546	7,899,110	(748,619)	(3,959,092)	(7,560,645)
	406,360,165	499,991,655	448,226,128	494,967,123	581,711,471	652,317,022
Earnings before taxes	76,060,198	44,828,966	37,792,034	47,564,308	78,548,451	106,178,352
Federal income taxes	31,000,000	10,100,000	15,600,000	19,700,000	34,000,000	47,700,000
Net earnings	$ 45,060,198	$ 34,728,966	$ 22,192,034	$ 27,864,308	$ 44,548,451	$ 58,478,352
Net earnings per share	$3.31	$2.51	$1.59	$1.98	$3.16	$4.11
Dividends declared per share	$.22	$.24	$.26	$.30	$.36	$.40
Percentage of earnings to sales	9.3%	6.4%	4.6%	5.1%	6.7%	7.7%
Return on average equity	29.0%	17.8%	10.0%	11.4%	16.0%	17.8%
Return on average assets	16.9%	10.3%	5.9%	7.0%	9.8%	11.2%
Capital expenditures	$ 62,440,354	$101,519,282	$ 14,783,707	$ 19,617,147	$ 26,074,653	$ 29,066,398
Depreciation	13,296,218	21,599,951	26,285,671	27,109,582	28,899,421	31,105,788
Sales per employee	150,756	155,663	133,156	148,639	176,069	197,011
Current assets	$115,365,727	$131,382,292	$132,542,648	$193,889,162	$253,453,373	$334,769,147
Current liabilities	66,493,445	73,032,313	66,102,706	88,486,795	100,533,684	121,255,828
Working capital	$ 48,872,282	$ 58,349,979	$ 66,439,942	$105,402,367	$152,919,689	$213,513,319
Property, plant and equipment	$173,074,273	$252,616,074	$239,071,390	$231,304,817	$228,102,790	$225,274,674
Total assets	$291,221,867	$384,782,127	$371,632,941	$425,567,052	$482,188,465	$560,311,188
Long-term debt	$ 39,605,169	$ 83,754,231	$ 48,229,615	$ 45,731,000	$ 43,232,384	$ 40,233,769
Percentage of debt to capital	18.2%	28.3%	17.2%	15.0%	12.6%	10.1%
Stockholders' equity	$177,603,690	$212,376,020	$232,281,057	$258,129,694	$299,602,834	$357,502,028
Per share	$12.96	$15.25	$16.60	$18.32	$21.16	$24.97
Shares outstanding	13,699,994	13,927,014	13,991,882	14,090,181	14,161,079	14,315,005
Stockholders	22,000	22,000	22,000	21,000	22,000	22,000
Employees	3,300	3,700	3,600	3,700	3,800	3,900

EXHIBIT 14
Statement of changes in financial position, 1983–1985

	1983	1984	1985
Funds provided			
Operations			
Net earnings	$27,864,308	$44,548,451	$58,478,352
Depreciation of plant and equipment	27,109,582	28,899,421	31,105,788
Deferred federal income taxes	8,200,000	5,600,000	2,500,000
Total funds provided by operations	63,173,890	79,047,872	92,084,140
Disposition of plant and equipment	274,138	377,259	788,726
Decrease in other assets	—	—	364,935
Issuance of common stock	2,201,183	2,006,460	5,387,182
Total funds provided	$65,649,211	$81,431,591	$98,624,983
Funds applied			
Purchase of property, plant and equipment	$19,617,147	$26,074,653	$29,066,398
Increase in other assets	354,170	259,229	—
Reduction in long-term debt	2,498,615	2,498,616	2,998,615
Cash dividends	4,216,854	5,081,771	5,697,290
Acquisition of treasury stock	—	—	269,050
Increase in working capital	38,962,425	47,517,322	60,593,630
Total funds applied	$65,649,211	$81,431,591	$98,624,983
Analysis of change in working capital			
Increase (decrease) in current assets			
Cash	$ (4,283,370)	$ (3,521,115)	$ 5,164,839
Short-term investments	38,445,234	37,177,195	67,269,144
Accounts receivable	16,424,874	7,297,872	1,982,204
Contracts in process	8,402,160	1,404,012	2,015,481
Inventories	7,723,168	17,242,200	4,844,503
Other current assets	(366,052)	(35,953)	39,603
Net increase (decrease)	61,346,514	59,564,211	81,315,774
Increase (decrease) in current liabilities			
Long-term debt due within one year	799,000	—	—
Accounts payable	14,186,217	(4,443,835)	2,781,762
Federal income taxes	2,278,813	8,891,286	3,892,269
Accrued expenses and other current liabilities	5,120,059	7,599,438	14,048,113
Net increase (decrease)	22,384,089	12,046,889	20,722,144
Increase in working capital	$38,962,425	$47,517,322	$60,593,630

HUMAN RESOURCES

Besides being known for its stunning success in joists and steel, Nucor was also known for its remarkable human resources practices. The casewriters visited a Vulcraft plant and talked with a department manager who had worked at Vulcraft for 16 years about what made Nucor different:

Our plants are located strategically. The company puts them in rural areas, where we can find a good supply of quality labor — people who believe in hard work. We have beaten back three unionizing campaigns in the last 10 years. These employees are very loyal. In fact, we had to hire a guard to protect the union organizers from some of our workers. We see about 3 percent turnover and very little absenteeism. They are proud of working with us. It's fun when they come to you and ask for work.

Why did Nucor do so well with employees?

Most companies want to take their profits out of their employees. We treat employees right. They are the ones who make the profits. Other companies aren't willing to offer what is needed to allow people to work. They can't see the dollar down the road for the nickel in their hand. Nucor's people make it strong.

Nucor's incentive systems had been a subject of much discussion and comment. *Fortune* estimated in 1981 that Nucor's workers earned an average of $5,000 more than union steelworkers. Moreover, Nucor workers were the highest paid manufacturing, blue-collar workforce in the United States.

Casewriter: But doesn't that prove the point — that American steelworkers earning $30,000 per year have priced the industry out of business?

Iverson: They earn every bit of it! Sure, it's generous. . . . There's a reason for it. It's hot, hard, dirty, dangerous, skilled work. We have melters who earn more than $40,000, and I'm glad they earn it. It's not what a person earned in an absolute sense, it's what he earns in relation to what he produces that matters.

The incentive system at Nucor had several key elements. John Savage, manager of personnel services, explained the company's personnel philosophy:

Our employee relations philosophy has four primary components. . . . Management's first and foremost obligation to employees is to provide them the opportunity to earn according to their productivity. . . . Next, we are obligated to manage the company in such a way that employees can feel that if they are doing their job properly, they will have a job tomorrow. . . . Third, employees must believe that they are treated fairly. . . . Lastly, employees must have an avenue of appeal if they believe they are being treated unfairly, to Mr. Iverson himself if necessary.

Everyone at Nucor participated in incentive plans. These incentives took several different forms depending on the type of work involved.

Production Incentives

Production groups of 25 to 30 employees were grouped around clearly measurable production tasks. About 3,000 Nucor employees made joists and steel under production incentives based on historical time standards. If, for example, a group produced a joist in 50 percent less than standard time, they got a 50 percent bonus. Bonuses were paid at the end of the following week. When equipment sat idle, no bonus accrued. If an employee was absent for a day, he or she lost a week's bonus — a difference amounting to as much as $7 per hour. Although workers often earned wages far above averages for manufacturing, the system was very tough:

If you work real hard and you get performance, the payment is there next week. . . . You worked like a dog and here is the money. . . . There are lots of people who don't like to work that hard, and they don't last for long. We have had groups get so mad at a guy who wasn't carrying his weight that they chased him around a joist plant with a piece of angle iron and were gonna kill him. . . . Don't get the idea that we're paternalistic. If you are late even five minutes you lose your bonus for the day. If you are late by more than 30 minutes because of sickness or anything else, you lose your bonus for the week. We do grant four "forgiveness" days a year. We have a melter, Phil Johnson, down in Darlington. One day a worker arrived at the plant and said that Phil had been in an auto accident and was sitting by his car on Route 52 holding his head. The foreman asked, "Why didn't you stop to help him?" The guy said, "And lose my bonus?"

Many Nucor workers earned between $30,000 and $40,000 per year. Nucor's monetary incentives made the company attractive to jobseekers (see Exhibit 14). Iverson told a story about hiring new workers:

We needed a couple new employees for Darlington, so we put out a sign and put a small ad in the local paper. The ads told people to show up Saturday morning at the employment office at the plant. When Saturday rolled around, the first person to arrive at the personnel office was greeted by 1,200 anxious jobseekers. There were so many of them that the size of the crowd began to interfere with access into and out of the plant. So the plant manager called the state police to send some officers over to control the crowd. But, the sergeant at the state police barracks told the plant manager that he couldn't spare any officers. You see, he was short-handed himself because three of his officers were at the plant applying for jobs!

Managerial Compensation

Department managers received a bonus based on a percentage of their division's contribution to corporate earnings. In an operating division such bonuses could run as high as 50 percent of a person's base pay. In the corporate office the bonus could reach 30 percent of base pay. Employees such as accountants, secretaries, clerks, and others who didn't work in production got a bonus based on either their division's profit contribution or corporate return on assets.

Senior officers had no employment contracts or pension plan. More than half of their compensation was based on company earnings. Their base salaries were set at about 70 percent of market rates for similar jobs. Ten percent of pretax earnings were set aside and allocated to senior officers according to their base salary. The base level was tied to a 12 percent return on shareholder's equity. Half the bonus was paid in cash, and half was deferred in the form of Nucor stock. In a profitable year officers could earn as much as 190 percent of their base salary as bonus and 115 percent on top of that in stock.

Other Compensation Incentives

Nucor also operated a profit sharing trust. The plan called for 10 percent of pretax earnings to be assigned to profit sharing each year. Of that amount, 20 percent was paid to employees in the following year, and the remainder was held to fund the worker retirement program. Vesting in the trust was 20 percent after one year and 10 percent each following year. The arrangement had the effect of making the retirement income of Nucor employees depend on the company's success. Additionally, Nucor paid 10 percent of whatever amount an employee was willing to invest in Nucor stock, gave employees five shares of stock for each five years of employment, and occasionally paid extraordinary bonuses.

Lastly, Nucor ran a scholarship program for children of full-time employees. In 1985 over 300 children were enrolled in universities, colleges, and vocational schools. Since the program's inception over 900 students had participated. One family had educated eight children on Nucor's plan.

No Layoffs

Nucor had never laid off or fired an employee for lack of work. Iverson explained how the company handled the need to make production cutbacks:

> When we have a difficult period, we don't lay anybody off. . . . We operate the plants four days a week or even three days. We call it our "share the pain program.". . . The bonus system remains in place, but it's based on four days' production instead of five. The production workers' compensation drops about 25 percent, the department managers' drops 35 to 40 percent, and the division managers' can drop as much as 60 to 80 percent. Nobody complains. They understand. And they still push to get that bonus on the days they work.

The Downside

Nucor's flat structure and steep incentives also had certain negative side effects. First, the incentive system was strictly oriented toward the short term. If a general manager was thinking about a major capital investment project, he was also thinking about reducing his short-term income. Iverson described how the ups and downs of the incentive plans affected officers: "If the company can hit about 24 percent return on equity, the officers' salary can reach 300 percent of the base amount. It maxed out in 1979 and 1980. In 1980 and 1981 total officers' compensation dropped way off. In 1980 I earned about $400,000, but in 1981 I earned $108,000. So officers have to watch their lifestyle!" Iverson's 1981 pay made him, according to *Fortune,* the lowest paid CEO in the *Fortune 500* industrial ranking. Iverson commented that it was "Something I was really a little proud of."

Second, promotions came very slowly. Many managers had occupied their current jobs for a very long time. Additionally, Nucor experienced problems in developing the skills of its first-line supervisors.

Many other companies studied Nucor's compensation plans. The casewriters asked John Savage about the visits other companies made to study Nucor's system:

> Many companies visit us. We had managers and union people from General Motors' Saturn project come in and spend a couple of days. They were oriented toward a bureaucratic style. . . . You could tell it from their questions. I was more impressed with the union people than with the management people. The union people wanted to talk dirty, nitty-gritty issues. But the management people thought it was too simple, they didn't think it would work. Maybe their business is too complex for our system. . . . We never hear from these visitors after they leave. . . . I believe it would take five to seven years of working at this system before you could detect a measurable change.

High wages and employment stability got Nucor listed in the book *The 100 Best Companies to Work for in America.* A division manager summed up the Nucor human relations philosophy this way: "It's amazing what people can do if you let them. Nucor gives people responsibility and then stands behind them." The appendix presents selected excerpts from interviews with hourly employees about their jobs at Nucor.

STRATEGIC PLANNING

Nucor followed no written strategic plan, had no written objectives (except those stated in the incentive programs), and had no mission statement. Divisions promulgated no strategic plans. We asked Sam Siegel about long range strategic planning. He confided: "You can't predict the future. . . . No matter how great you may think your decisions are, the future is unknown. You don't know what will happen. . . . Nucor concentrates on the here-and-now. We do make five-year projections, and they are good for about three months. Five to ten years out is philosophy." We also asked Bob Rothkopf (planning director) about planning at Nucor:

I work on the strategic plan with Ken twice a year. It's formulated out of the projects we are looking at. He and I talk about the direction we feel the company is going. . . . The elements of the most recent plan are that we take the basic level of the company today and project it out for five years. We look at net sales, net income, under different likely scenarios. In this last plan I looked at the potential effects of a mild recession in 1986. . . . We add new products or projects to that baseline.

Rothkopf had responsibility for generating most of the information he used in his forecasts. He often used consultants or other companies to get the information he needed. None of the other senior executives or division managers got deeply involved in this planning process.

Nucor didn't rely on its strategic planning system to make strategic decisions. Rothkopf described how strategic decisions were reached:

Projects come from all over. Some come from our general managers, or from our suppliers, our customers . . . or come walking in the door here. Iverson is like a magnet for ideas, because of who he is and what Nucor is. . . . We evaluate each project on its own, as it comes up. As each opportunity arises, we go in and investigate it. Some investigations are short; we throw out quite a few of them. We don't make any systematic search for these ideas.

Rothkopf compared Nucor's planning to formal strategic planning done by other companies:

I think there might be some advantages for us to do that sort of thing. However, our business has been pretty simple. Our businesses are all related and easy to keep track of. When a big decision comes up we discuss it. That's easy because of the simple structure of the company. . . . Planning has disadvantages . . . time-consuming . . . expensive . . . hard to get the information for it . . . tends to get bureaucratic.

Although Nucor had no formal planning system, important strategic decisions loomed on the company horizon. Exhibit 15 provides information on Nucor's strategic options.

EXHIBIT 15
Nucor's strategic
options

Strategic considerations	Option 1: Build a seamless tube mill	Option 2: Get into pre-engineered buildings
Market	About $2.5 billion Oilfield equipment companies Commodity Mature, competitive, low growth Integrated companies sell here	$350 million Small growth Numerous competitors, all sizes Regional, fragmented Not a commodity
Investment	$150–180 million	$5–7 million plant generates $15–20 million sales in four years. Want about 20 percent market share in five to six years
Time period needed	About two years	8–12 months
Fit to present activities	Could sell some product to joist division Increase efficiency	Already manufacturing parts for such buildings
Revenues/profits	Sales $240–270 million 20–25 percent profit before taxes	About same as present earning power
Support among executives	Some active support Analyses in process	Joist division favors it Corporate execs divided
Skills and resources	Know market Have most skills, others not too hard to learn	Selling to whole new market Manufacturing skills help
Downside risk	Risky, uncertain market	New market to understand Can do gradually Not very risky

Strategic considerations	Option 3: Build bar minimill	Option 4: Acquire bar minimills
Market	Same as current	Same as current
Investment	$50–75 million for a 250,000 ton mill	A six to seven year old, 175,000 ton mill costs $50 million to build Earns $10–15/ton before tax
Time period needed	18 months	±1989, 1987 earliest
Fit to present activities	Perfect fit	Obvious, yes

EXHIBIT 15
(continued)

EXHIBIT 15
(continued)

Revenues/profits	$65–75 million sales. Lose money years one and two. Over long term make $5–10 million before taxes.	$45 million sales, earns ±$1 million Under Nucor, such a mill can see sales of $60 million, earn ±$5 million
Support among executives	Quite a bit	Unknown
Skills and resources	In place, no problems	OK, in place
Downside risk	No growth in market. Must take business from entrenched competitors	Anti-trust? Company culture might not fit; exposure to union problems

Strategic considerations	Option 5: Innovative flat-rolled minimill	Option 6: Build bolt plant
Market	25–30 million tons Stable, a commodity Integrated mills dominant	$800 million Mature, stable Commodity dominated by four companies
Investment	$125–175 million for 400,000, to 600,000 ton mill	$25 million/plant
Time period needed	Could build four plants in 5–10 years	
Fit to present activities	Extends product range Sales to joist division Keeps steel/joist "balance"	Steel currently produced goes into product
Revenues/profits	Must project 25 percent profit before tax to justify Lower cost $100/ton?	$28–32 million sales per plant
Support among executives	High company support; spending $10 million to develop process at Darlington	Agreed to build one plant
Skills and resources	Don't know marketing of flat-rolled products Must learn flat-rolling of steel	Need marketing skills
Downside risk	Must invest $10–15 million in any case Hard to invest new technology Competitors leap-frog with new processes Estimate 50–75 percent chance it will work	If foreign steel is barred in United States, bolts get "dumped" here International prices of bolts unstable

EXHIBIT 15
(continued)

Strategic considerations	Option 7: Increase dividends ($.10/share now)	Option 8: Purchase Nucor stock for treasury
Market	Stockholder reaction uncertain	14,000,000 shares at $45 currently
	Number of shares × increase	Number of shares × price
Time period needed	Anytime	One to two years
Fit to present activities	Change in philosophy	Underlines management confidence
Revenues/profits	N/A	Sell shares for profit? Enrich remaining stockholders?
Support among executives	Iverson thinking about it	At the right price/earnings ratio
Skills and resources	N/A	N/A
Downside risk	If earnings slip, could pressure ability to invest	Price of stock could decline

Strategic considerations	Option 9: Diversification outside steel products or joists
Market	Faster growing markets open
Investment	Nucor has $100–150 million
	Could borrow more
Time period needed	One to two years
Fit to present activities	Depends on business
Revenues/profits	Greater profitability?
Support among executives	Very little
Skills and resources	Nucor understands heavy manufacturing
	Nucor has skills in streamlined management
	Employee-relations philosophy
Downside risk	Company has to learn new things?
	Might require different organizational set-up

NUCOR'S FUTURE: WHAT NEXT?

In spite of Nucor's remarkable successes, Iverson stated a modest, cautious view of the company's capabilities:

> *We are not great marketers or financial manipulators. . . . We do two things well. We build plants economically and we run them efficiently. We stick to those two things. . . . Basically, that's all we do. We are getting better at marketing, but I wouldn't say we are strong marketers . . . that is not the base of the company. . . . We're certainly not financial manipulators. We recognized a long time ago how important it was for us to hold down overhead and management layers.*

Iverson talked about the future of Nucor:

> *The company's position is much different than it was in past years. In the 60s we nearly went bankrupt. It was a miniconglomerate, so I got rid of half the company. We started all over again. We built steel mills. From the late 60s to the 80s our constraints were financial. We decided that we wanted debt to be less than 30 percent of capital. That restricted the number of mills we could finance. But then in the 1980s things changed. Our restraints are not financial now. We no longer see the opportunities in minimills which we saw in the 60s and 70s. So, what direction should the company go? We have about $120 million in cash and short-term securities.*
>
> *Since we don't see much opportunity for building additional minimills, we have been looking at various alternatives . . . merger or acquisition, internal growth . . . buying back our own stock . . . and other things. It goes forward by project. We looked at buying another steel company that had problems. Dave visited their plant. Bob (the planner) did some projections on what it would cost us to put that mill in shape. We also have an outside consultant working on it. That is what we have done so far (Iverson points to a report). . . . We are looking at the bolt business too. About 95 percent of bolts used in the United States are made outside of the United States. We are studying whether we should spend $25 million to build a plant. . . . Maybe we ought to buy our own stock. It reduces the number of shares and increases the per share earnings. I feel comfortable with that with the price/earnings ratio we are at.*

Was he worried about a takeover?

> *I really don't expect someone to try to take us over. We have a staggered board. So if someone tries to do it they will have to wait for quite a while to control enough directors. We have other provisions in the bylaws which would make a takeover difficult. Besides, we're in a lousy business — steel.*

What about an acquisition by Nucor?

> *We have some problems with going that route. We don't have any experience with acquisitions, all our growth has been internally generated. The second thing, we would never acquire outside our business, which is the manufacture of steel and steel products. We*

might be able to go into some nonferrous metals. But if we went into, say, textiles or something else like that . . . it's not . . . If stockholders want to invest in those businesses, let them do it themselves. Conglomeration is a lot of nonsense.

Iverson mentioned additional opportunities:

We are thinking about a seamless tube mill. That business seems to meet many of our requirements. Also, the Vulcraft people believe that we could easily enter the business of pre-engineered buildings. Although that is a new market for us, it's not very risky and it is a logical extension of the joist business.

We are also talking to the Japanese about a joint venture to produce large and medium structural steel shapes. That's a 6-million-ton market worth about $2 billion per year. It's cyclical because it's tied to the construction industry. Imports have about 32 percent of that. We might invest $200 million. We know this market but we lack some technology which the Japanese can supply. We would be 51 percent partners and run the plant.

For fifteen years, Nucor had made the right decisions. The company successfully managed the difficult balancing act of combining outstanding profitability with keeping its workforce loyal, alert, and innovative. Nucor had developed a unique corporate culture and grown rapidly. Now, the material bases for that culture and those successes were changing. The wide open opportunities in minimills had been used up. The company was getting much larger. Ken Iverson wondered where Nucor's future lay. In acquiring other minimills? Bolt plants? Repurchasing stock? Developing new technology? Diversifying? Tube mills? Pre-engineered buildings? In addition to the question of which businesses to pursue, he wondered how future growth and change would affect, and be affected by, Nucor's distinctive competence and its unique corporate culture.

REFERENCES

"Ken Iverson, Man of Steel," *Inc.*, April 1984.
Ken Iverson's speeches.
"Minimills Incentives Give Steelmaker an Edge," *Journal of Commerce*, June 3, 1982.
"Minimills, Maxiprofits," *Time*, January 24, 1983.
Nucor, Frank C. Barnes, 1984.
"Nucor Chief Executive Adds Chairman's Title," *New York Times*, June 18, 1984.
"Nucor Profits from Innovation," *Los Angeles Times*, March 6, 1984.
"Pilgrims Profits at Nucor," *Fortune*, April 6, 1981.
"Steel Man," *Inc.*, April 1986.
"Steel Minimills," *Scientific American*, May 1984.
"Steel Minimills Prosper Despite Industry Woes," *Washington Post*, August 9, 1983.
"The Going Gets Tough at the Nucor Minimill," *New York Times*, August 4, 1983.
The 100 Best Companies to Work for in America, 1984.

JIM

Jim is 32 years old, did not finish school, and has worked at Vulcraft for 10 years. He works at a job that requires heavy lifting. Last year he earned about $38,500.

This is hard physical work. Getting used to it is tough, too. After I started working as a spliceman my upper body was sore for about a month. . . . Before I came to work here I worked as a farmer and cut timber. . . . I got this job through a friend who was already working here. . . . I reckon I was very nervous when I started here, but people showed me how to work. . . . The bonuses and the benefits are mighty good here . . . and I have never been laid off. . . . I enjoy this work. . . . This company is good to you. They might let employees go if they had problems, but first they'd give him a chance to straighten out. . . . In 1981 things were slow and we only worked three or four days a week. Sometimes we would spend a day doing maintenance, painting, sweeping. . . and there wasn't no incentive. I was glad I was working. . . . I was against the union.

KERRY

Kerry is 31 years old, married, and expecting a child. He has worked on the production line for about three years.

I was laid off from my last job after working there five years. I went without work for three months. I got this job through a friend. My brother works as a supervisor for Nucor in Texas. . . . This is good, hard work. You get dirty, too hot in the summer and too cold in the winter. They should air-condition the entire plant (laughs). On this joist line we have to work fast. Right now I'm working 8½ hours a day, six days a week. . . . I get good pay and benefits. Vulcraft is one of the better companies in Florence (South Carolina). . . . Everyone does not always get along, but we work as a team. Our supervisor has his off days. . . . I want to get ahead in life, but I don't see openings for promotion here. Most of the foremen have had their jobs for a long time, and most people are senior to me in line. . . . This place is very efficient. If I see a way to improve the work, I tell somebody. They will listen to you.

OTHER COMMENTS FROM HOURLY WORKERS

I am running all day long. It gets hot and you get tired. My wife doesn't like it because sometimes I come home and fall asleep right away.

When something goes down, people ask how they can help. Nobody sits around. Every minute you are down it's like dollars out of your pocket. So everybody really hustles.

VLSI TECHNOLOGY, INC.

In February 1983, Alfred J. Stein was reviewing the position of VLSI Technology (VTI) prior to its initial public stock offering. Mr. Stein, who had been President of Arrow Electronics before joining VTI, had just completed his first year as Chairman and CEO of the new company. VTI had been formed in 1979 by Jack Balleto, Dan Floyd and Gunnar Wetlesen, all of whom had left Synertek Corporation after it was acquired by Honeywell.

VTI was formed to design and manufacture custom VLSI chips. VTI also marketed advanced circuit design tools under the name "User-Designed VLSI." These software design tools were intended to shift the function of designing complex integrated circuits from semiconductor makers to original equipment manufacturers themselves. If such a shift occurred, VTI had the potential to grow at a tremendous rate over the next few years. Al Stein's chief concerns were how to encourage the adoption of VTI's services and how to prepare for and manage the company's future growth. His most immediate concern, however, was the stock market's assessment of VTI's prospects.

VTI — THE CONCEPT

Al Stein leaned forward in his chair and spoke softly but intently:

> We have dedicated ourselves uniquely to this business; our whole strategy is based on being a fully integrated "custom" house. We are marketing our design tools and providing training programs to systems companies so they can design their own chips. Other companies in our business want to do custom designs internally. We are of the opposite opinion; we think that industry resources, that is, IC designers, are extremely limited. We want to give the design responsibility to the much larger number of systems engineers. If they design more chips than they have in the past, we hope to reap the benefits by producing those designs in our silicon foundry.

EXHIBIT 1
VTI user-designed
software and
function

Circuit design process	Corresponding software
System design	* CELL COMPILERS — Automatic implementation of system building blocks.
Logic design	* VNET — Language to describe logic method.
	* VSIM — Logic simulator to check function.
Circuit design	* SPICE — Circuit simulator to check performance.
Physical design	* STICKS — Symbolic design for unique cells.
	* GEOMETRIC EDITOR — Direct creation and modification of layout data base.
	* PLOT — Graphic output of layout data base.
Verification	* EXTRACT — Circuit extractor to regenerate logic network from implementation.
	* VSIM — Logic simulator to verify function.
	* DRC — Design rule check for compatibility with design process.

* Starred software indicates names which have been trademarked by VTI.

VTI was incorporated on August 1, 1979, in San Jose, California. The founders proposed to greatly reduce lead times for delivery of custom circuits. They planned to slash design time and costs through automation of the design process. VTI's software tools permitted an electrical engineer working at a terminal to design a circuit in graphic form using conventional electrical engineering symbols. The engineer specified the circuit elements and their relationships. The software package then verified the integrity of the circuit design and its efficiency. Once the design was complete, the software package converted the graphic representation into digital code that specified the precise layout of the semiconductor chip.

VTI licensed its design tool software to its customers under agreements which grant the customer a non-transferable, non-exclusive right to use the software for a fixed fee ranging from $58,000 to $160,000. The tools are used on the DEC VAX family of minicomputers or with Apollo Computer workstations (see Exhibit 1). A version for IBM mainframe systems was also being developed.

VTI's activities did not end with the completed design. They also planned to provide "quick turnaround" fabrication capability for prototypes and volume production of custom integrated circuits. The digital code generated by the software package would be fed into VTI's wafer fabrication facility to manufacture prototypes and later final products in volume.

ROM OPERATIONS

While anticipating growth in custom chip sales, VTI commenced production of read-only memories (ROMs) in 1982. ROMs were standard products typically manufactured in large volumes. A ROM differed from a RAM, the other primary memory product, in that the data in the ROM was permanently encoded. Data in a RAM is lost when the electric current is turned off. ROMs are typically encoded by the manufacturer. Since ROMs can be uniquely programmed (i.e., can have a unique combination of positive and negative charges within a standard grid), they have some of the characteristics of custom chips. During 1982, the company derived 76% of its revenues from ROM sales to five consumer product manufacturers. Sales to these customers were primarily for use in home video game cartridges. VTI's largest customers were Mattel, Inc. and Coleco Industries, Inc., which accounted for approximately 52% and 17% of revenues, respectively.

VTI contracted with independent companies for most of the fabrication, assembly and test of its read-only memories. These arrangements enabled the development of cash flows and important customer relationships before the opening of VTI's wafer fabrication facility in November 1982. Dan Floyd, Vice-President of Programmable Memory Operations, planned to continue using subcontractors for his orders, while VTI's fabrication facilities would be used to produce high performance custom circuits designed with the company's software tools.

CUSTOM INTEGRATED CIRCUITS

I think there are a lot of parallels in this business with the last major electronics revolution, which centered around the microprocessor. A lot of engineers felt the need to learn and use the microprocessor to avoid being pushed aside by younger engineers coming out of college. It's another opportunity/threat.

Wes Patterson, VTI Director of Systems Marketing, was discussing the complicated motivations of potential customers as they decided whether to switch from standard to custom integrated circuits. Although custom circuits had long been available, standard chips accounted for well over 95% of all semiconductor sales.

This usage pattern was due to higher design costs and longer lead times for custom products. Manufacturing realities also limited the development of custom chip usage. The key issues in semiconductor manufacturing had long been the yield of usable chips for a wafer of silicon. Semiconductor manufacturing was a delicate process that required expensive equipment operating at precise tolerances. This process did not reward adjustments of machinery to accommodate production of multiple devices. Fabrication lines usually were set up for large batches of one standard device. Producers invested in research to develop new, more complex devices suitable for wide application, and in plant and equipment designed for long production runs of standard components. These pressures have shaped competitive strategies which emphasize aggressive pricing of standardized components to maximize volume and minimize costs. These industry characteristics had proven extremely attractive to Japanese competitors, who had made major inroads into the

U.S. semiconductor market. Japanese suppliers had captured over half of the U.S. market for the latest generation of RAM products (64k units) and were expanding their activities in other high-volume, standardized product segments.

Custom chips began to have an impact in the semiconductor market only in the late 1970s. The custom chip market was stimulated by development of the microprocessor at Intel in 1970. When combined with read-only memory containing a software program, the microprocessor became a device that could be tailored to specific applications. With customized ROM, microprocessors ran products ranging from handheld toys to auto ignition systems and microcomputers. Although flexible, microprocessors themselves were still standard components; they became less effective as higher levels of performance were demanded. Dedicated devices designed for single applications proved to be far more efficient than microprocessors. Although programmable microprocessors have some of the characteristics of custom chips, primary custom products were gate arrays, standard cells, and full custom chips.

Gate arrays are preprocessed layers of silicon containing thousands of logic gates. A gate is an on/off switch in a logic circuit or a bit of information in a memory product. The bottom layers of a gate array are of standard configuration; the top one to three layers are unique for each application. The top layers specify how gates in the other layers will be interconnected to fit a customer's specific requirements. This approach offers superior performance in some applications over microprocessors; gate arrays, however, use silicon space inefficiently. Some of the gates produced in preprocessing will not be wired in the final design. One executive estimated that gate array designs typically waste at least 20% of a chip's gates in this way. Nonetheless, gate arrays have provided fast and flexible system design. IBM gave the technology instant credibility when it used gate arrays in its 4300 series computers in 1978, and more recently in its high-end 308X mainframes. Gate arrays offer quick turnaround time; makers can develop prototypes from customer specifications in twelve weeks. Systems designers in industries with extremely short product lives such as data processing or computer peripherals favor this approach; they can achieve higher density and lower cost than with standard chips. Gate array manufacturers also claim that their technology requires less design time than full custom approaches.

Standard cells can provide a more economical solution than gate arrays for users less constrained by product design deadlines. These cells are complete functional blocks drawn from a computerized "library"; they include logic functions, memories, processors and peripheral components. These cells are put into position and connected on a silicon chip in a process similar to putting standard components onto a printed circuit board. Standard cells are more efficient than gate arrays because only necessary functions are included in the design. If standard cells and gate arrays are the same size, the greater density of standard cells will allow for higher operating speed. Furthermore, because of smaller size, standard cells will realize higher yields and lower unit fabrication costs. These benefits must be weighed against the lower development costs for gate arrays; for a typical application, standard cells become more attractive at higher production volumes. (See Exhibit 2.)

	Gate array	Standard cells
Tooling costs	$10,000	$40,000
Other development costs	30,000	40,000
Total development costs	$40,000	$80,000
Chip capacity, 4-inch silicon wafer	198 chips	265 to 380 chips
Yield	5%	7–9%
Chip yield	9.9 chips	18.6 to 34.2 chips
Cost of wafer fabrication	$100	$100
Cost per chip processed	$10.10/chip	$2.92 to $5.38/chip
Breakeven requirements	5,571 to 8,475 units	

Source: *Electronics*, February 10, 1983.

The Structured Design Approach for Full Custom Chips

Developments in circuit design methodology in the late 1970s reduced the time and cost needed to design a custom VLSI circuit. A design methodology known as "Hierarchical VLSI" was developed by Professor Carver Mead of Cal Tech and Lynn Conway of the Xerox Research Center in Palo Alto. Their approach applied systems concepts to circuit design. It could be used by application engineers to lay out a simplified "floor plan" of a circuit and then to lay out individual cells in detail using design tools. Using these tools, a systems engineer could improve circuit density, put more functions on a chip, and reduce the number of components needed in a system. For example, the Apple II+ had 110 components on its printed circuit board; the next generation Apple IIE was redesigned with VLSI technology to use only thirty-one components. Custom chips become more attractive with larger unit requirements. Exhibit 3 shows an estimate of user economics for a state-of-the-art 20,000 logic gate system.

The user-designed chip had lower development costs because of the new availability of computer-aided design (CAD) tools and it made more efficient use of silicon, which cut material and overhead costs.

	Standard parts	Semi-custom (gate array)	User-designed
Number of chips	1,667	27	13
Number of circuit boards	33	2	1
Development cost	$165,000	$550,000	$395,000
Total cost for 10,000 units	$56 million	$15.2 million	$8.7 million

Source: *Dataquest*, December 1982.

Past Objections to Custom Circuits

Although the economics appeared attractive, certain risks attended the potential user of custom chips. The design process in the past had been subject to frequent errors and many manual procedures, such as verifying circuit design or the debugging of prototypes. Intricate devices such as VLSI logic circuits ran the risk of eating up man-years of design resources using traditional methods. Skilled IC design engineers available to complete these designs were scarce; there were only about 2,000 IC engineers in the United States, compared to 200,000 or more systems-level engineers. The supply situation promised to become worse in the future; the American Electronics Association projected demand for 51,300 electrical engineers in 1985. At the same time, product lives have shortened as OEMs push to use the latest chips in their systems, increasing demand.

In the past, potential users of custom chips have had three alternatives to solve these problems. To obtain chips, they could develop an internal or "captive" production capability, acquire a minority interest or complete ownership of an existing IC manufacturer, or request custom service from one of the large semiconductor manufacturers. The first option had been widely pursued; the industry had witnessed a dramatic surge of new entrants in the past twenty-five years. While some were ventures formed to exploit new technology, others were large users of chips who formed their own in-house or "captive" suppliers of semiconductors. Captive production of integrated circuits was estimated to have accounted for one third of total U.S. production in 1980 and 90% of all custom chip production. (See Exhibit 4.)

The relative advantages of vertical integration were being debated hotly in the industry. Recently, Hewlett-Packard used its captive operations to develop a 32-bit microprocessor for use in its 9000 series of minicomputers. Development took $100 million and five years; the device will be used only in HP products. In an interview with *Electronic News*, George Bodway, the general manager of HP's Computer Integrated Circuits Division, explained that HP's device would provide a substantial lead over competitors, since no equivalent product was available from merchant vendors.

Many companies have acquired semiconductor makers; major recent purchasers of chip manufacturers included GE (Intersil), Honeywell (Synertek), and IBM (30% investment in Intel). For others, the choice was to request service from the semiconductor houses like Motorola, TI, and Intel. Douglas Fairbairn, VTI Director of User-Designed VLSI software, explained that large amounts of demand were not being satisfied by such manufacturers because of economic pressures: "In the past, only customers who needed a very high volume of product could get someone to design a chip for them — say, 10,000 units and up. Below 10,000 it was not cost effective to use scarce engineering talent."

In contrast, qualified design houses were difficult to find and low volume production facilities were scarce. Moreover, timetables and performance levels for custom chips were viewed with uncertainty by most users. An effort at ITT to develop a custom chip for use in portable telecommunications gear in 1975–1976 was abandoned after two years of effort. The ITT users contracted the design process to a specialty custom producer, which was unable to design a chip that worked in the overall

EXHIBIT 4
Number of
integrated circuit
manufacturers, U.S.
market

Years	Merchant manufacturers	Captive manufacturers
1960	27	6
1965	44	11
1970	92	18
1975	108	31
1980	95	60
1983	107	65

Top 10 U.S.-based captive suppliers of integrated circuits	
Company	*Estimated 1982 production*[a]
IBM	2100
Western Electric	385
Delco (General Motors)	185
Hewlett-Packard	160
NCR	70
Honeywell	70
DEC	60
Burroughs	40
Data General	30
Tektronix	25

[a] Figures in millions of dollars.
Source: *Integrated Circuit Engineering.*

system. Although the custom chip prototypes were half the size of the chosen approach, the design process burned up almost two years before ITT cancelled the custom project; they were unwilling to delay the product's market entry to obtain a more efficient chip. Such "horror stories" had been a major barrier to user acceptance of custom. In addition, custom chips were by their nature difficult or impossible to second-source (i.e., to develop alternative supplier relationships), so that dependence on suppliers was a problem.

Potential Advantages of Full Custom

Full custom circuits were extremely efficient in their use of silicon space, yielding higher density and fewer components per application. On a systemwide basis, this advantage created an opportunity to design products with less circuit board space, fewer unique components, lower power requirements, and a smaller cooling system. In addition, fewer components meant overhead savings in packaging, testing, inventory, and documentation costs. For customers who required enough units to cover design and development costs, these advantages could provide a competitive edge over rivals using alternative technologies.

One example of full-custom's advantage in this area was the experience of Network Systems, a manufacturer of high-speed data communications equipment. The company originally approached VTI for a custom solution to cut the size of its communication hook-up for terminals, which required two printed circuit boards of 8.5 × 11 inches. These boards, which utilized a variety of standard components, cost about $250 each. A gate array manufacturer developed a solution using three large gate array circuits for a total cost of $300. VTI's approach called for one chip priced at $100. The cost of materials in the VTI chip was $25 compared to $150 for the standard component solution. Interviewed for an article on future computer technology, James Thornton, founder of Network Systems, firmly supported the trend to application-specific ICs:

> I believe the advances in semiconductors and gate densities are driving the push toward new equipment. We can now exploit the idea of really specializing. . . . Chip design is undergoing standardization in that certain cell designs are being put in a library and can be called up for use in various designs. Basically, you won't have to know how to design the circuit, only how to use the circuit or the software that is embedded in it. There will be a shift from the classic semiconductor supplier to a new silicon foundry. The ideal way is to put the design tube (CRT) in the hands of the user and let the user design the custom chip.

Decisions by users on whether to use custom chips and which type to employ would be decided by the requirements of each application. Customers in the video games market might choose ROMs with microprocessors because they were cheap, rapidly available in high volume, and the customized ROM provided some commercial security. Data processing equipment makers might choose gate arrays because of the quick turnaround time, and the higher density and lower costs relative to standard components. Military or telecommunications applications might have power and space constraints or demand unusually high performance, with a full custom chip being the appropriate technology. Users whose products had short product life cycles might require a chip with a shorter development cycle. Users desiring design security would prefer custom approaches.

Market Projections — Custom Chips

Exhibit 5 shows custom and semi-custom chips as a percent of total integrated circuit consumption. Improvements in design techniques, computer-aided engineering, support, and silicon foundry availability are expected to increase custom and semi-custom chips to 18.5% of total IC sales in 1986.

EXHIBIT 5
Custom IC consumption as a percentage of total IC consumption

	1981	1982	1983E	1986E
Full-custom	15.7	25.9	49.6	790.0
Gate arrays	36.1	45.8	59.9	530.0
Standard cells	9.5	19.0	38.8	1215.0
Total custom	61.3	90.7	148.3	2535.4
Total ICs	5140.7	5942.2	7487.2	13705.3
Custom as a percentage of ICs	1.2%	1.5%	2.0%	18.5%

Note: U.S. merchant sales only, millions of dollars.
Source: *Electronics*, January 13, 1983.

VTI — MARKETING

VTI's primary marketing effort was its six week design course. To acquaint potential customers with the design system, VTI conducted six week courses in VLSI circuit design in which students designed an actual circuit using VTI's design methodology and tools. The course fee of $6,000 included the fabrication and packaging of student prototype circuits. Companies found that tuition was often recouped by this "class project." Through the end of 1982, approximately 80 students from 35 companies had taken the course. VTI had also entered into three joint design projects where company and customer engineers worked together to meet tight design schedules. VTI planned to expand its training capacity by opening Technology Centers in Boston, Dallas, Chicago, and one European city in 1983.

According to Wes Patterson, VTI's major marketing goal for 1983 was to gain new bookings and accounts and to broaden its customer base:

> As we try to diversify our customer base and to introduce our design tools, we're in a tough spot. We can't bring on a direct sales force fast enough, and the salesmen typically aren't technical enough. We're having to create our own market through the design course. Nearly every tool sale we've made to date is directly traceable to an engineer who has been through the course. With a little pre-screening, we think we can expect 15% or more of the companies who send employees to the course to buy the tools.

Major motivations for VTI customers included security, special design requirements, and the growing need of systems designers to become intimately involved in the design process. As Patterson explained:

> A lot of our customers need proprietary protection for design ideas from imitators. The standard products look more and more the same; for example, there must be 20 producers of UNIX-driven 16-bit minicomputers; there's no product protection except for the software.

These pressures were nowhere more evident than in the viciously competitive video games market. The industry leader, Atari, had just completed layoffs of 1,700 workers and had moved assembly operations overseas in an effort to cut costs.

VTI — DESIGN OPERATIONS

The nature of the custom chip design process required a close working partnership between systems designers and their design and fabrication resources. Such a relationship could not always be provided by one of the standard components manufacturers or by vendors of semicustom approaches like gate arrays or standard cells. As Patterson explained:

> In each of these cases, he (the designer) carries his design up to a certain point, then throws it over the transom to these other companies. He doesn't know or understand them, yet he's dependent on their guarantees for delivery on time and a prototype that works.

VTI's service orientation included a willingness to produce small volume runs (e.g., 5,000 to 10,000 chips per year) unwanted by large standard components producers, and to cheaply and quickly produce prototypes. Al Stein commented:

> *If you design a chip, you want to know whether the damn thing works and you want to know in a hurry. We offer a multi-product wafer capability which consolidates a whole host of designs on one wafer for one process run. The costs of tooling for masks are $15,000 to $20,000 per mask.* By sharing the costs of that run, your costs are dramatically lowered. That service is run once a month and is an integral part of being a full-service custom house.*

VTI has been able to go from masks to prototypes in as little as two weeks, compared to fourteen weeks for large semiconductor manufacturers.

Under some customer contacts, VTI performed the entire design function. Completed design projects included a custom logic circuit for a coin operated video game, a shift register for a telecommunications application, and a RAM circuit for video arcade games. At the end of 1982, VTI was working on design contracts for six customers relating to a total of fifteen circuits. During 1982, VTI completed five custom design circuits, of which two were in production at year end. Most design contracts took sixteen to twenty-two weeks to complete.

VTI — FOUNDRY OPERATIONS

The trend to custom chips had been assisted by the evolution of the silicon foundry, a wafer processing facility emphasizing quick turnaround time (QTAT) and standardized design-manufacturing data interchange rules. VTI's fabrication facility, or "silicon foundry," was designed for quick turnaround manufacturing. For prototype and small volume runs, VTI's use of multi-project wafers (MPWs) allowed wafer fabrication costs to be shared among several designs. Compared to conventional fabrication techniques, this approach reduced mask tooling costs substantially for small production lots.

VTI also established an electronic network known as "VTINet." VTINet allowed customers to submit chip design codes from their remote locations. When fully operational, this system would permit customers to submit circuit layouts of custom chips and to use a computer terminal to determine the status of their orders in the production cycle.

VTI's fabrication facility was still under construction in early 1983, although several processing lines were in operation. Output at full capacity would be 1,000

---

* Masks are transparent glass units that contain circuitry patterns to be etched into silicon. The mask is transparent except for the circuit patterns drawn on its surface. The mask is placed over silicon coated with photo-sensitive material. When exposed to light, the silicon is "exposed," except in areas where the mask is not transparent (the circuit patterns). The resulting patterns form the basis for all silicon circuitry.

wafers per day. Current output during the startup phase in January 1983 was 100 wafers per week. Gunnar Wetlesen, director of foundry operations, estimated that an additional investment of $22 million would be required to bring the facility to full capacity.

VTI's managers believed that their long-term profitability depended on convincing users to give VTI high-volume fabrication contracts for custom chips. Wes Patterson said:

> We believe we can get the silicon business, which is the nice difference between our strategy and just being a tools company. When the guy designs a circuit that hits his own market niche and sells by the hundreds of thousands, we get to participate in that success.

To aid in securing fabrication runs, the company planned to provide a steady stream of enhancements to its proprietary design tools. As Wes explained:

> We plant a hook in these tools that brings the guy back to our foundry in the form of what we call a cell compiler library. The library contains a set of specific circuit functions. It uses parameters to provide an exact fit for the guy's requirements; nobody else can do that. The cell compiler and other enhancements can further cut design time by a factor of 3 or 4 times. To obtain a license for the enhancements, we ask for a commitment of the production from designs done with these tools, typically 80% in the first year and decreasing after that.

In 1982, ROM sales provided 76% of VTI revenues, with design tools and foundry operations making up the balance. By 1985, VTI's management hoped to reverse that ratio, so that design tools and custom foundry runs would generate 60 to 80% of sales. ROM sales were expected to continue expanding at 15% per year.

PROGRAMMABLE MEMORY OPERATIONS

"We see ROMs as our lead horse and our cash cow," commented Dan Floyd, Vice President, Programmable Memory Operations. VTI's ROM business addressed a broad segment of the market and emphasized high performance and density. The company offered five types of ROMs: standard 32K and 64K, "fast" 64K and 128K, and a 256K device. The majority of sales came from the standard 32K and 64K products. In addition, VTI designed "custom" ROMs, which incorporated random access memory and logic onto the same chip with the ROM circuitry.

The logistics of selling ROMs were relatively easy, since there were a small number of significant potential customers. According to Wes Patterson, the business was based on close relationships and assurance of delivery: "The customers knew they had our attention and that we'd jump through hoops for them. The big companies can't turn on a dime and deliver product (ROMs) inside four weeks."

VTI expanded these relationships through joint design projects for custom logic chips. The ROM strategy also meshed nicely with the tiny sales force of seven, which could cover the major customers without difficulty.

Besides generating revenues, the ROM business provided pressure to improve technological processes and reduce costs. Gunnar Wetlesen, Vice-President of Wafer Fabrication, said:

> No company has been able to develop state of the art processes for building logic unless they are also in the memory business. They need the volumes and densities to keep the technologies current. The learning curve is nothing more than continuous experimentation on a fixed data base of production runs; the more runs you have, the more opportunities to reduce costs.

VTI's manufacturing policy to date had been to subcontract ROM production in a complicated international network. After chips were designed internally, masks for the photolithography process were produced under subcontract by U.S. specialty houses. Completed masks were then flown to Japan for wafer fabrication by Ricoh and to Korea for assembly and test. At the end of the processing, completed chips were drop-shipped to customers. This strategy allowed VTI to accept ROM contracts before completing its own processing facilities and helped to fund custom chip research and development.

Now that VTI's own wafer processing facility had begun operations, Floyd expected to move the most sophisticated segment of the ROM business to it. The 128K and 256K chips would be used to drive the process technology; shared benefits would accrue in the costs, quality and capacity of custom production. A separate line within the "clean room" where the chips were fabricated would be maintained for quick turnaround of custom prototypes; this line would have only four common operations with the rest of the facility. Floyd hoped to add a packaging operation next to the wafer processing facility in 1983. The standard "jelly bean" ROMs like the 32K and the 64K would continue to be subcontracted.

COMPETITION — ROMs

Competition in the ROM market was intense because of a large number of established competitors and readily available substitutes. VTI competed with over thirty ROM suppliers, including: Synertek, a division of Honeywell founded by current members of VTI management; National Semiconductor; NEC; American Microsystems (a division of Gould); and General Instrument. Competition was based on price. Many competitors had shared costs with other product lines; entry decisions could be made on an incremental basis. Exhibit 6 shows projected prices for ROMs for the next three years.

In many low-volume applications, and in products where software revisions were required, erasable programmable memories (EPROMs) had replaced ROMs.

EXHIBIT 6
Price forecast for
ROMs

Product	1982	1983E	1984E	1985E
32K	$2.21	$ 1.53	$1.07	$0.82
64K	4.42	3.06	2.14	1.64
128K	8.86	6.12	4.28	3.28
256K	NA	12.24	8.56	6.56

EPROMs can be reprogrammed in the field using ultraviolet light to erase previous instructions. These circuits are generally more expensive than ROMs, however, and ROMs are thus more likely to be used in consumer products where the circuit features are not alterable by the user. Although price is an important competitive factor in this market, service and delivery are also important because ROMs cannot be sold from inventory; they must be manufactured to meet the customer's pattern or program.

Mask ROMs, supported by the toy and game markets, were expected to grow from $414.7 million in 1982 to 492.9 million in 1983, an increase of 19%. Sales had increased 22.6% in 1982. It was estimated that five producers (TI, Motorola, Intel, National, and Advanced Micro Devices) held 53% of the $869 million ROM and EPROM market.

COMPETITION — SEMICUSTOM

Nearly 100 companies were currently competing in the semicustom IC market. Gate array and standard cell design approaches continued to battle for market acceptance as the industry standard; as explained above, each had specific strengths and shortcomings. Six firms currently were offering cell-library design, including American Microsystems, startups International Microelectronic Products and Zymos, Synertek, NCR's Microelectronics Division, and Harris Corporation's Semiconductor Division. No Japanese suppliers had yet announced standard cell libraries in the United States. Fifty to sixty companies compete in the gate arrays market, including industry giants such as Motorola, Texas Instruments, Toshiba, and Fujitsu. Gould's American Microsystems was the largest company devoted exclusively to custom semiconductor devices and was a major participant in gate arrays.

COMPETITION — CUSTOM DESIGN TOOLS

Competition among manufacturers of integrated circuit design tools was intense. The market consisted of several large manufacturers of CAD workstations (IBM, Calma/GE, Applicon/Schlumberger, Computervision) and dozens of software suppliers who offered packages to run on these machines. Most of these companies were small startup ventures concentrating on the simulation and verification aspects of chip design. These companies included Avera, CADTEC, CAE Systems, Daisy Systems, Mentor Graphics, Metheus, and Valid Logic Systems.

The natural progression of the industry was toward further integration of the design process within one system. Although VTI's system of design tools had not yet gained significant commercial acceptance, its approach was unique in that it integrated most stages of the design process. The user could construct an electrical engineering diagram with the aid of a sophisticated graphics package and cell library. VTI's system automatically tested, optimized, and converted the electrical engineering diagram to a semiconductor circuit design. The user could then transmit the resulting data via VTINet to the fabrication facility. Although VTI's system was unique, management believed they had only a nine-month lead on the competition. New packages were being offered weekly.

In its custom design business, the company competed with many large custom circuit manufacturers, as well as the internal design centers of several original equipment manufacturers. In addition, the custom design process competed with the gate array, standard cell, and field-programmable devices (microprocessors with ROMs) just mentioned.

COMPETITION — SILICON FOUNDRIES

In the latest survey published in *VLSI Design*, a trade journal for the industry, thirty-eight companies reported that they were offering silicon foundry service, up from twenty-six the year before. Competitors included small startups like VTI, successful semicustom chip makers like American Microsystems which specialized in gate arrays and established standard components manufacturers. The commitment of these firms to the concept of the silicon foundry was unclear in January 1983. The larger houses seemed to be searching for ways to fill capacity idled by the recession, while many of the smaller firms did not yet have a complete processing facility. "The competitor that scares me to death is Intel," exclaimed Wes Patterson. "They've got the foundry, the technology and the sales force, and they still have enough entrepreneurial spirit to go after this market. Motorola and TI don't."

Intel had recently concluded an agreement with Zymos to buy a cell library for its newest high performance fabrication process. According to press reports, they hoped that the agreement would generate new business from small volume users for its silicon foundry while avoiding a company investment in design support operations.

Al Stein believed that his company's emphasis on quick turnaround time, its advanced software and design capability, and its fully integrated service-oriented approach provided it a distinct market advantage. Said Al, "There are CAD companies that sell the design tools, and companies that just do wafer processing. We're a one-stop shop."

RESEARCH AND DEVELOPMENT

VTI spent $4.2 million on research and development since its founding, including $3.3 million in 1982. Major areas of emphasis include:

Advanced software design tools for integrated circuits.

Advanced networking and communications to provide an interface between customers and the VTI silicon foundry.

Read-only memory circuits.

Semiconductor manufacturing processes.

The company's research expenditures were focused on increasing circuit density and quick turnaround time. During 1983, VTI planned to expand its VTINet capabilities to include transmission and processing of custom circuit data bases, and remote inquiry systems to allow customers to track jobs in progress.

HUMAN RESOURCES

At the end of 1982, VTI employed 193 people: 62 in research and development; 20 in manufacturing engineering; 76 in manufacturing; 18 in marketing; and 17 in general management and administration. Al Stein saw his major task as managing this group of highly talented and diverse people:

> *The success of any organization, whether it's a high technology company or a football team, is dependent on the people you have in your company. My major efforts are directed at putting together a highly talented group of people who work together well and get the job done.*

In turn, Al Stein's move to VTI as Chairman and Chief Executive Officer in February 1982 brought an important level of business and financial credibility to the company. VTI was founded by Jack Balletto, Gunnar Wetlesen, and Dan Floyd. The positions and backgrounds of company officers are shown in Exhibit 7. According to Doug Fairbairn, Vice-President of User Designed VLSI and a co-founder, Stein's strengths were his business skills and his track record:

> *He's doing here the same things that made him successful at TI and Motorola. He's concentrating on getting product out. He's burdening the company with a minimum amount of overhead for things like administration, and he's demanding absolute perfection, or as close to it as he can, from everybody in the company. Al is well respected by the financial community and his presence has focused a lot of attention on us. There's a perceived quality of assumed success rather than assumed failure.*

EXHIBIT 7
List of officers and directors

Name	Age	Position and background
Alfred J. Stein	50	Chief Executive Officer, President, and Chairman of the Board. With VTI since March 1982. Previously CEO Arrow Electronics, 1981–1982; Corporate VP of Motorola, Assistant Gen. Mgr., Semiconductor Group, Gen. Mgr., Integrated Circuits Division, 1977–1981; various positions with Texas Instruments, most recently Corporate VP, 1958–1976. Also Director of: Tandy Corporation, Applied Materials, Inc.
John G. Balletto	42	Senior Vice President and Director. President and CFO, VTI, 1979–1983; Director of Marketing, Synertek, 1973–1979; Assistant to President, Ricoh Electronics, various positions at Fairchild Camera and Instrument, 1962–1973.
Daniel W. Floyd	42	Vice President, Programmable Memory Operations and Director. With VTI since 1979. Previously Vice President of Manufacturing, Synertek, 1973–1979; Director of Wafer Fabrication, American Microsystems, and Director of Standard Products, Harris Semiconductor, 1963–1973.
Gunnar A. Wetlesen	35	Vice President, Wafer Fabrication, Technology, and Foundry Activities and Director. With VTI since 1979. Previously Director of Technology Development, 1974–1979, and Director of Memory Products, 1976–1979, Synertek; Manager of Process Technology, American Microsystems, 1968–1974.
Douglas G. Fairbairn	34	Vice President — User-Designed Technology. With VTI since December 1980. Research Staff, Xerox Corporation's Palo Alto Research Center, 1972–1980.
Kenneth A. Goldman	33	Vice President — Finance, CFO and Secretary. With VTI since 1981. Previously Group Controller, Consumer Products Group, 1979–1981, Manager of Budgeting and International Planning, 1977–1979, Memorex Corporation; Controller of MOS Division, Fairchild Camera and Instrument and other positions, 1974–1977.
Ronald C. Kasper	40	Vice-President, Sales. With VTI since 1981. Previously Managing Director, European Sales, 1978–1981, and Western Area Sales Manager, 1976–1978, Synertek; various sales positions, Electronic Memories and Magnetics, 1967–1976.

	Name	Age	Position and background
EXHIBIT 7 (continued)	David C. Evans	58	Director. President, CEO, and Chairman of the Board, Evans and Sutherland Computer Corporation, 1968–present. Previously Director of Engineering, Research and Development, Bendix Corporation.
	William R. Hambrecht	47	Director. President, CEO, and Director of Hambrecht and Quist, 1968–present. Also Director of: ADAC Laboratories, Auto-trol Technology, Computer and Communications Technology, Evans & Sutherland, Granger Associates, Magnuson Computer Systems, NBI, People Express Airlines, Silicon General, and Xidex Corporation.
	James J. Kim	47	Director. Chairman of AMKOR Electronics, Inc., and President of The Electronics Boutique, 1978–present.
	William J. Perry	55	Director. Senior Vice President of Hambrecht & Quist, 1981–present. Undersecretary of Defense for Research and Engineering, 1977–1981; President and Chief Executive Officer, ESL, Incorporated (now a division of TRW), 1964–1977. Also director of: ARGO Systems, Avantek, and Technology for Communications International.

FINANCES

VTI had grown at a rapid pace; revenues were $82,404 in 1980, $552,553 in 1981, and $21,229,251 in 1982. Net revenues in 1981 resulted primarily from course fees and rentals from the related video tape lecture series. The sharp increase in revenues realized in 1982 resulted from initial sales of ROM circuits, which accounted for 76% of revenues. VTI's management expected another sizeable increase in sales in 1983. The company's design tools were first offered to customers in 1982, and the first production runs from custom chips designed with the VTI design methods were expected at the end of 1983. These revenue gains were accompanied by heavy expenses resulting from the staffing of engineering teams, product development and marketing activities during 1981, and large capital expenditures and startup costs for the wafer processing facilities in 1982. As a result of these expenses, VTI had lost a total of $3.6 million during its first three years of operations. Exhibits 8, 9, and 10 show the income statements, balance sheets, and statement of sources and uses of VTI for the years 1980–1982.

Funds needs were expected to remain high in the foreseeable future. VTI's business strategy required a large up-front investment in equipment for the silicon foundry and in development outlays for the design tools. The company's operating plan

EXHIBIT 8
Statement of
operations

	Years ended		
	December 31, 1980	December 31, 1981	December 26, 1982
Net revenues	$ 82,404	$ 552,553	$21,229,251
Cost and expenses			
Cost of sales	73,811	139,942	14,238,656
Wafer processing start-up	—	—	2,761,547
Research and development	—	809,257	3,319,959
Marketing, general and administrative	32,453	1,229,198	3,299,819
Operating costs and expenses	106,264	2,178,397	23,619,981
Operating income (loss)	(23,860)	(1,625,844)	(2,390,730)
Interest income	2,010	151,666	831,057
Interest expense	—	(3,456)	(530,302)
Net income (loss)	$ (21,850)	$(1,477,634)	$ (2,089,975)
Income (loss) per common share	$(.01)	$(.72)	$(.53)
Weighted average common shares outstanding	1,563,000	2,054,600	3,967,507

estimated that $20 million would be required in plant and equipment investment over the next eighteen months. Rapid technological change in chip fabrication and circuit design software indicated the need for sustained development expenditures and equipment investments of this magnitude. Dataquest estimated that the industry was becoming more capital intensive each year and projected an increase in net plant over sales to 70% by 1985.

Cash flows from custom chip fabrication would increase slowly because of the long development cycle typical of VTI's OEM customers. Industry observers compared the development cycle to a "two-year wheat crop": the OEMs needed additional time for the design and development of new systems after receiving working prototypes of the custom chips; volume production runs that generated large demand for foundry services would only occur at "harvest," once the product was in the market. When volume orders for foundry business came in, VTI would have a comfortable margin; variable costs were estimated at only 20 to 30% of total costs.

For a startup venture, VTI had experienced unusual success in obtaining funds during its early years. Originally, funding was provided in December 1980 by sales of preferred stock to five venture capital firms and Evans and Sutherland Computer Corporation. The venture capitalists were among the most successful firms in the business, including Hambrecht and Quist, Rothschild, Advanced Technology Ventures and Kleiner, Perkins, Caufield & Byers. A list of major shareholders is given in Exhibit 11. William Hambrecht and William Perry of Hambrecht and Quist were directors of the company. Further funding was provided by capitalized

EXHIBIT 9
Balance sheet

	December 31, 1981	December 26, 1982
Assets		
Current assets		
Cash and cash equivalents	$ 757,928	$10,552,577
Accounts receivable, net of allowance for doubtful accounts, and customer returns of $338,000 in 1982	99,212	4,246,640
Inventories	—	1,093,304
Prepaid expenses and other current assets	49,220	58,375
Preferred stock subscriptions receivable due within 1 year	8,016,000	—
Total current assets	8,922,360	15,950,896
Plant and equipment		
Machine equipment	17,287	874,788
Leasehold improvements and equipment leased under capital leases	577,676	12,424,381
	594,963	13,299,169
Accumulated depreciation and amortization	(26,801)	(993,666)
Net plant and equipment	568,162	12,305,503
Deposits and other assets	119,220	49,286
	$9,609,742	$28,305,685
Liabilities and shareholders' equity		
Current liabilities		
Accounts payable	$ 390,925	$ 5,914,776
Accrued liabilities	197,977	1,377,640
Deferred income	147,628	761,845
Current portion of capital lease obligations	31,144	1,009,866
Total current liabilities	767,674	9,064,127
Noncurrent obligations under capital leases	318,135	10,783,129
Shareholders' equity		
Series A Preferred Stock, no par value; 6,000,000 shares authorized;		
Issued: 6,000,000 in 1982, 1,200,000 in 1981	1,973,750	9,989,750
Subscribed: 4,800,000 in 1981	8,016,000	—
Series B Preferred Stock, no par value; 2,600,000 shares authorized;		
Issued: 598,803 in 1982	1,000	1,976,102
Common Stock, no par value, 30,000,000 shares authorized;		
Issued: 4,874,464 in 1982, 2,504,000 in 1981	50,080	99,449
Retained earnings (deficit)	(1,516,897)	(3,606,872)
Total shareholders' equity	8,523,933	8,458,429
	$9,609,742	$28,305,685

EXHIBIT 10
Statement of
changes in financial
position

	Years ended		
	December 31, 1980	December 31, 1981	December 26, 1982
Working capital was applied to			
Net loss from operations	$ 21,850	$1,477,634	$ 2,089,975
Less charges to operations not involving the current use of working capital — depreciation and amortization	—	(26,801)	(966,865)
Total working capital applied to operations	21,850	1,450,833	1,123,110
Additions to plant and equipment	—	594,963	12,704,206
Increase in deposits and other assets	—	119,220	(69,934)
Total working capital applied	21,850	2,165,016	13,757,382
Working capital was provided by			
Issuance of common stock	2,500	17,580	49,369
Issuance of preferred stock	971,750	1,002,000	9,991,002
Preferred stock subscribed	9,018,000	(1,002,000)	(8,016,000)
(Increase) decrease in preferred stock subscriptions receivable due after one year	(8,016,000)	8,016,000	—
Issuance of warrant	—	1,000	100
Increases in noncurrent obligations under capital leases	—	318,135	10,464,994
Total working capital provided	1,976,250	8,352,715	12,489,465
Increase (decrease) in working capital	$1,954,400	$6,187,699	$ (1,267,917)
Increase (decrease) in working capital by component			
Cash and cash equivalents	$ 984,025	$ (238,684)	$ 9,794,649
Accounts receivable	13,203	86,009	4,147,428
Inventories	—	—	1,093,304
Prepaid expenses and other current assets	—	49,220	9,155
Preferred stock subscriptions receivable due within one year	1,002,000	7,014,000	(8,016,000)
Accounts payable	(26,328)	(364.597)	(5,523,851)
Accrued liabilities	(18,500)	(179,477)	(1,179,663)
Deferred income	—	(147,628)	(614,217)
Current portion of capital lease obligations	—	(31,144)	(978,722)
Increase (decrease) in working capital	$1,954,400	$6,187,699	$ (1,267,917)

EXHIBIT 11
Major shareholdings

	Number[a]	Percent
Evans & Sutherland Computer Corporation	1,800,000	15.7%
Advanced Technology Ventures	1,154,791	10.1
Accounts advised by Rothschild	1,154,791	10.1
The Bendix Corporation	908,267	7.9
Olivetti Realty	598,803	5.2
Kleiner, Perkins, Caufield & Byers II	577,545	5.0
Officers and directors (11 total)[b]	3,125,869	27.2
Other shares[c]	2,153,201	18.8
Total shares outstanding	11,473,267	100.0

[a] Includes all common stock and all preferred shares; preferred is convertible into common; the preferred is convertible into common at a price of $1.67 per share. Cost basis for the common is $0.025 per share.
[b] Major individual shareholders include: Alfred J. Stein, 936,889 shares; John G. Balletto, 500,000 shares; Daniel W. Floyd, 500,000 shares; and Gunnar Wetlesen, 485,000 shares.
[c] Includes shares beneficially owned and held in trust.

leases and favorable terms by customers and suppliers. With the assistance of Bendix Corporation, VTI leased the first $13.6 million of equipment and leasehold improvements associated with its facilities. Bendix also purchased Series B preferred stock from VTI. At the end of 1982, VTI's unused sources of funds consisted of $10.553 million in cash and equivalents, $3.5 million in net available capital lease financing, and $500,000 in research and development funds available from Bendix. In addition, the company possessed $2.7 million in tax carryforwards, including net operating losses, investment tax credits, and research and development credits.

PUBLIC OFFERING

VTI filed for a public offering of common stock on January 25, 1983. The preliminary prospectus estimated that three million shares would be sold at a price between $10 and $12 per share. VTI said the proceeds would be used for capital expenditures and working capital. Currently, 11.5 million shares were outstanding.

Al Stein recognized that VTI's growth potential depended on his company's access to the capital markets: "We need to raise a good amount of additional capital if we're going to grow at this rate. We think a public offering is the way to go because Wall Street is enthusiastic and our financial performance to date has been better than expected."

New registrations for initial public offerings had surged to a 1982 peak of 31 in the month of December; in the first 11 months of 1982, 186 companies had gone public, raising more than $1.1 billion. Industry participants believed that the market would continue to strengthen; for example, Morgan Stanley announced plans to manage the initial public offering for Apollo Computer in early 1983. Other new

EXHIBIT 12 Statistics on selected initial public offerings

Company	Galileo Electro-Optics	Quantum Corp	ARGO Systems, Inc.	IMAGIC	Altos Computer Systems	Systems & Computer Technology Corp.	Convergent Technologies Inc.	VTI, Inc.
Date offer filed	12/28/82	11/9/82	10/27/82	11/3/82	10/14/82	10/5/82	4/14/82	
Line of business	Manufacturer of electro-optic components	Designs and mfg. rigid disk drives	Designs and mfg. elec. reconnaissance systems	Designs and mfg. home entertainment systems	Designs and mfg. microcomputer systems	Provides application software products and services	Manufactures computer systems	Custom i/c vendor
Financial Information[a]								
Revenues	14,268	29,968	32,187	35,044	57,443	26,792	19,692	21,229
Net income	774	4,928	2,462	6,108	6,359	3,225	1,881	-2,090
Earnings per share	.57	1.13	1.08	.43	.55	.29	.15	-.53
Total assets	8,187	18,448	28,014	29,352	27,033	12,166	20,247	9,610
Shareholders' equity	1,060	13,981	9,442	8,597	14,553	8,337	13,165	-3,607
Offering data								
underwriter	L. F. Rothschild	Morgan Stanley	Hambrecht & Quist	Merrill Lynch	L. F. Rothschild	L. F. Rothschild	L. F. Rothschild	L. F. Rothschild
Securities offered	700,000 com.	2.5 million com.	606,390 com.	2.7 million com.	3.3 million com.	2.58 million com.	4 million com.	3 million com.
Price range	$8.00-$10.00	$20.50	$16.00-$18.00	$15.00-$17.00	$21.00	$16.50	$12.00-$15.00	$10.00-$12.00
Value of offering	$7 million	$51.25 million	$10.915 million	$45.9 million	$69.3 million	$42.57 million	$60 million	$36 million
P/E ratio	17.5x	18.1x	16.7x	39.5x	38.2x	56.9x	100.0x	negative
Offerings as a % of pro forma shares outstanding	38.4%	28.1%	22.2%	16.9%	23.3%	20.2%	20.8%	20.7%
Mkt. value at initial price	$18.22 million	$182.34 million	$49.272 million	$272.3 million	$297.0 million	$210.8 million	$288.7 million	$173.7 million
Aftermarket								
Bid on 1/21/83 (day before VTI filed offering)	NA	24.75	34.75	NA	26	NA	NA	
% change from initial price	NA	18.3	104.4	NA	23.8	NA	NA	

[a] Figures in thousands of dollars except per-share data.

issues rumored to be imminent included offerings for: the robotics manufacturer, Automatix; Diasonics, Inc., a supplier of ultrasound imaging systems to radiologists and cardiologists; and desktop computer maker Fortune Systems. Exhibit 12 lists selected statistics on recent public offerings.

THE FUTURE

1983 would be an important year for VTI. Stein still saw the company in its startup phase; the wafer processing facility would require several quarters to reach efficient operation and would cause continued losses. The company also needed to build acceptance for its design tools and lessen its dependence on the ROM business by adding customers for custom chips. "The thing that's holding us back is a few solid references," said Wes Patterson. "That cycle takes a couple of years. We won't have testimonials from our earliest customers until the end of 1983."

VTI needed to firmly publicize its claimed advantages in cost and performance to reach its goal of 1000 customers by 1986. As Gunnar Wetlesen explained: "The design cost, production cost, and performance are all dynamic and must achieve a new equilibrium now that CAD techniques are on the scene. It takes time to realize what's happening and switch over."

Stein was confident that VTI was in the right place at the right time:

A little semiconductor company has to find a strategy and a market niche so that it's not competing with the Motorolas, TIs and Fairchilds. There's no way from a financial or people-resources point of view that it can compete successfully with such companies. You have to have something unique. I think we do indeed have something that is different and that will, over time, change the whole semiconductor industry.

NEW HAMPSHIRE BALL BEARINGS, INC.

Theodore Kanell, president of New Hampshire Ball Bearings, sat at his desk early one July morning in 1984, studying the terms of the proposed acquisition of New Hampshire Ball Bearings (NHBB) by Minebea Co. Ltd., the Japanese electronics, controls, bearings, and machinery conglomerate. Ted thought: "It's easy to see black and white through hindsight, but there are only shades of gray in the thick of the battle."

The following paragraphs describe (1) the product and production of ball bearings; (2) the founding of NHBB by Arthur Daniels; (3) changes in the ball bearing industry, including competition in the 1970s; (4) the strategic acts of NHBB in response to these trends; (5) Minebea, the suitor; and (6) the current status of the company as Mr. Kanell considers the Minebea offer and his strategic alternatives.

THE PRODUCT

Uses

Bearings reduce friction by converting sliding friction (linear motion) to rolling friction (rotary motion). A ball bearing is a bearing that provides rolling contact and consists of hardened steel balls that roll between two hardened steel rings.

Early societies using round stone wheels to move larger stones and objects sooner or later discovered that the stone wheel rolling around an axle could be better controlled and could be made easier to operate if small sticks were placed between the axle and the bore of the wheel. Antifriction bearings were invented. The ball bearing is the most widely used antifriction bearing, although there are also needle roller bearings, tapered roller bearings, and cylindrical and spherical roller bearings.

The ball bearing has two rings, one within the other, separated by balls. A retainer may be used to hold the ball bearings in place. Ball bearings come in all sizes. The smaller bearings are referred to as precision and as miniature by convention. Miniature bearings include all ball bearings with outside diameters less than 9 millimeters (.3543 inches). Instrument or precision ball bearings are those with outer diameters

EXHIBIT 1
Sample end uses
of bearings

ABEC *quality* standard	Possible use
Miniature bearings	
(9 mm)	
1	Fishing equipment, pneumatic tools
3	Copiers, computer peripherals
5	Dental equipment, floppy disc drives
7	Flight recorders, circuit production equipment
9	Aircraft gyroscopes
Precision bearings	
(9–30 mm)	
1	Hand-held tools, flow meters
3	Photo typesetters, check-sorting systems
5	Aircraft fuel controls
7	Missile gyroscopes
9	Military aircraft gyroscopes

of 9 to 30 millimeters (.3543 to 1.1811 inches) and of ring tolerances of fifty-millionths of an inch and ball sphericity or roundness of three-millionths of an inch.

Ball bearing manufacturers recognize the Annular Bearings Engineers Committee (ABEC) quality standards. The higher the ABEC number (1 to 9), the greater the quality. These standards are primarily dimensional tolerances, although higher standards also may include dynamic characteristics such as torque and vibration limitations. The ABEC Committee is a subcommittee of the Anti-Friction Bearing Manufacturers Association (AFBMA), the industry association for ball bearing manufacturers.

Sample end uses of miniature bearings (9 millimeters of outside diameter) and precision bearings (9 to 30 millimeters outside diameters) are described in Exhibit 1.

Production

The production of the inner and outer rings and the balls that comprise the ball bearing (see Exhibit 2) can be summarized as follows (page 552):

EXHIBIT 2
Ball bearing

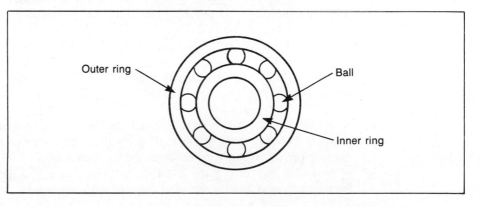

Inner and Outer Rings

1. *Cutting and boring*: Rods of stainless steel (or other material such as chrome steel or aluminum called for by the application) are cut to their approximate outside diameter and bored to their approximate inside diameter on automatic screw machines. Steel at this point is "soft" and can be notched with a file.

2. *Heat treatment*: For added strength with a resulting increased ability to be machined to fine tolerances, rings are placed in high-heat furnaces. This heat tempering makes the steel hard.

3. *Tumbling*: Rings are "tumbled" in vibrating machines with a mixture of abrasives of varying hardness and size depending on the desired finish. Tumbling removes surface imperfections and polishes.

4. *Grinding*: The outer and inner rings may have one or more tracks or races ground into their surface to accommodate the balls and/or have their inside and outside diameters sized further. Grinders can be set to produce varying levels of diameter tolerances. One ring may be processed on one or several grinders. Grinding or finishing the surfaces may be done with grinding wheels, burrs, or points. Grinding may be rough grinding (primarily concentrated on width and making the faces of the ring parallel), centerless grinding to make the outside diameter square with the face, or bore grinding to make the bore round and with the same center as the outside ring.

5. *Honing*: Rings are given a final smoothing and polishing in honing machines.

6. *Inspection*: Throughout each of the five previous steps, operators select a sample of each batch to test for ring dimensions and other characteristics.

Balls

1. *Cutting*: Wire of varying materials and widths is cut (slugged) or pressed with dies (headed) to produce the object that will become a sphere.

2. *Heat treatment*: The rough spheres may be treated in furnaces, depending on the desired characteristics.

3. *Grinding and polishing*: The cut metal is made increasingly spherical by various grinding, tumbling, and polishing steps, including simultaneous grinding of more than one surface at one time.

4. *Inspection*: The balls are sampled at each production step.

Retainers. Retainers are generally punched out of thin strips of steel by punch presses.

Assembly. The finished bearing is assembled by applying pressure to the partially positioned bearing (thus "snapping" it together), by insertion of the balls through openings or chutes in the outer rings, and by other means.

Assembly may take place in NHBB's "white room," a dustfree environment for high precision and for specified-characteristics bearings.

EXHIBIT 3
Ball bearing parts

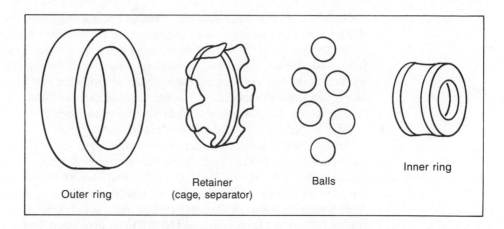

Outer ring

Retainer
(cage, separator)

Balls

Inner ring

Final Inspection and Shipping. The documentation that accompanies the order shipped to the customer may include inspection certificates and even documentation as to steel source and other product characteristics.

The parts of the ball bearing are shown in Exhibit 3.

ARTHUR DANIELS, FOUNDER OF NHBB

Arthur Daniels was born in California on October 1, 1908. Both of his parents and three of his grandparents were teachers. Daniels commented to an interviewer in 1968 that one of his grandmothers was the first white child born in Oregon, though ''her playmates were Indian children who ate worms and similar things.''

After dropping out of school to go to sea for a semester as a janitor/machinists' helper, Daniels entered the United States Naval Academy, graduating in 1931. Following graduation, Mr. Daniels was married to Dolores DePierrefeau, and spent 4 years aboard Admiral Leahy's flagship, the *USS Raleigh*. He then transferred to the Navy Reserves. Daniels received a master's degree in engineering from Harvard and joined the mechanical engineering faculty at Dartmouth College.

In 1939 Daniels invested $5,000 in the Split Ballbearing Company, which was being run by Winslow Pierce, who had patented a split ball bearing in 1921. The split bearing meant that the two ''half-moon'' segments of the bearing could be pulled apart, meaning that a failed bearing could be much more easily replaced, greatly reducing downtime for bearing failures.

Although barely afloat financially, Split Ballbearing had a resource in the tiny (one-sixteenth of an inch in diameter) miniature ball bearing capability Pierce had developed. Although Pierce, the engineering press, and the occasional engineers and researchers who wrote to Pierce or visited him in Lebanon, New Hampshire, were not particularly excited about the miniature bearing capability, Daniels was intrigued. Daniels convinced Pierce to start a separate division of Split Ballbearing, called Miniature Precision Bearings. Daniels became Miniature Precision Bearing's (MPB) part-time manager, while continuing on Dartmouth's faculty.

In the summer of 1939 MPB received an order for a dozen quarter-inch bearings from Carl Norden, who was developing a new bomb sight. This Norden order resulted in the first commercial manufacture of miniature ball bearings for the one-room, two employee company. The next months saw the Norden bomb sight orders coming in on the stationery of Sperry Gyroscope, and Split Ballbearing's MPB division began a war-related climb to profits and success.

Arthur Daniels returned to active duty after Pearl Harbor, serving 5 years. He commanded a destroyer escort in the Pacific and ended his war career against the Japanese in the Pacific on the staff of Admiral Nimitz at Pearl Harbor. After the war, Daniels decided to stick with ball bearings rather than return to Dartmouth. A disagreement between Daniels, Pierce, and Daniels's wartime "replacement," Horace Gilbert, led Daniels to found NHBB in an abandoned feed store and warehouse in Peterborough, New Hampshire, in 1946.

Some five years later Mr. Daniels described NHBB's first facility: "The warehouse was full of rats, naturally. We installed a cat, but it couldn't stand the loneliness of weekends and moved over to The Diner." It took 5½ years for NHBB to produce one million bearings but only 5 months in the spring and summer of 1953 to produce the second million. As the company grew, it was a pioneer in employee relations, offering a profit-sharing plan to its workers. By 1957 the company employed over four hundred persons.

One aspect of Mr. Daniels's personality was his sense of humor. His letter to stockholders in an early annual report ended with a sentence: "The whippoorwills have returned after an absence of about ten years, offering no explanation." A letter to stockholders and employees noted that "we'll be needing sales engineers, automatic machinists, machinists, mechanical technicians . . . any sex. . . . Come on up, we'll use you good. . . . We haven't laid off a toolmaker or die maker in 20 years. Did fire one, for punching a foreman in the nose."

The *Peterborough Transcript* (June 20, 1968) described these whimsical departures as "a sign of his dislike for the prosaic, of his feeling for the mystery, the beneficence and the enhancement of nature, and his innate conviction that it is not worthwhile to go round the world to count the cats in Zanzibar."

CHANGES IN THE
DOMESTIC BALL BEARING INDUSTRY

MPB/Pierce-Daniels began in 1939, Barden Corporation in 1942, and NHBB in 1946.

Barden Corporation was formed by the Barth family of Connecticut and Carl Norden, the bomb sight developer. Barden was active in the gyroscope, military, and precision machine tool industries and, later on, in the high-speed turbine industry. Barden was the first bearing producer to make batches of specified tolerances, as opposed to the industry practice of sorting output into varying tolerance categories or standards. An industry observer noted that "the job no one else can do, Barden does." Leaving these "high tech" applications to Barden, NHBB and MPB produced less "esoteric" miniature and precision ball bearings. Generally, MPB concentrated on the higher ABEC ratings, while NHBB was strongest in volume ABEC 1 and 3 ratings.

The three significant changes in the ball bearing industry were (1) the swings in volume and profits produced by defense orders and by technology, (2) the introduction of mass production techniques, and (3) foreign competition.

Defense and Military Orders

Volume dropped off after World War II but increased with the Korean War buildup (1950–1954). The reduced demand of the post–Korean War period led to excess capacity and a domestic price war. Competitive pressure and price cuts eased during the late 1950s.

Technology played a part in the easing of competitive pressure, as the jet aircraft industry expanded substantially. A jet plane such as the 707 might contain ten thousand miniature bearings. What technology gave to the ball bearing industry it could also take away. Shortly the strategy of smaller and smaller bearings ran into a dead end as transistors were introduced. Eventually transistors converted many bearing applications, or mechanical processes, into transistor or electronic applications. For example, the number of miniature bearings in a 707 might be reduced to two or three thousand instead of ten thousand.

During the 1960s domestic shipments increased to record levels, as competitive pressures decreased during the Vietnam buildup, most notably between 1964 and 1966. Domestic production decreased from these peak Vietnam levels during the end of the 1960s. Exhibit 4 summarizes the sales and income for the three major miniature and precision manufacturers from 1956 to 1968.

Mass Production Techniques

A second industry fact was the competitive pressure caused by the entry of such firms as General Motors (New Departure Division), Textron (Fafnir Division), and TRW (MRC Division) due to the opportunities presented by the defense buildup and, more importantly, the possibilities of mass production.

From the beginning of World War II and throughout most of the 1950s, miniature and instrument precision ball bearings required highly skilled labor with continuous and close supervision of the entire manufacturing process. True mass production and automation became possible in the late 1950s with the important step of the development of the Bryant internal grinder model C, which allowed for close tolerances of internal grinding. Bryant subsequently introduced precise yet high-volume production machines for miniature as well as instrument precision bearings. A subsidiary of the Cincinnati Milling Machine Company produced a similar internal grinder for miniature and instrument bearings (the Heald machine) and a microcentric grinder for external grinding. Flange grinders, external ball race grinders, and honing machines to further eliminate roughness after the grinding process completed the mechanical advances allowing automation in ball bearing production. One worker with

EXHIBIT 4 Sales and net income

	Barden			MPB			NHBB		
	Sales	Net income	Percentage	Sales	Net income	Percentage	Sales	Net income	Percentage
1956	$ 7.7	.7	9.1	$ 2.0	.2	10.0	$ 2.0	.1	5.0
1957	10.2	1.1	10.8	3.9	.2	5.1	3.1	.3	9.7
1958	8.6	.7	8.1	5.5	.3	5.5	3.4	.2	5.9
1959	12.1	1.3	10.7	6.8	.4	5.9	4.9	.4	8.2
1960	14.9	1.1	7.4	10.2	.8	7.8	7.1	.6	8.5
1961	14.6	1.0	6.8	10.4	.5	4.8	8.3	.7	8.4
1962	15.5	.9	5.8	9.8	.2	2.0	7.2	.5	6.9
1963	16.3	.9	5.5	10.5	.3	2.9	6.8	.4	5.9
1964	15.4	.9	5.8	9.7	.2	2.1	6.0	.2	3.3
1965	21.9	1.9	8.7	11.1	.4	3.6	7.0	.4	5.7
1966	26.9	2.9	10.8	14.1	.7	5.0	12.1	1.2	9.9
1967	30.0	2.7	9.0	19.5	1.6	8.2	17.1	2.1	12.3
1968	27.7	1.4	5.1	20.0	1.2	6.0	14.2	1.0	7.0
Index 1956 = 100	360	200		1000	600		710	1000	

Note: Figures in millions of dollars. Barden's fiscal year ends on October 31, MPB's on March 31, and NHBB's on June 30.

minimum training could adjust a group of machines to operate more or less automatically. NHBB's 1963 Annual Report noted that "automation . . . made good progress, notably in the development of machines with which one person now does the work formerly done by eight or ten." It is important to note that the improvements in machine capabilities were produced by collective efforts of the bearing manufacturers.

General Motors and others, attracted by automation and mass production possibilities, entered the miniature and precision bearing industry. Thus, the three principal U.S. manufacturers of miniature and precision bearings from World War II to 1984 — Barden Corporation, MPB, and NHBB — were joined by other domestic companies including (1) the New Departure — Hyatt Division of General Motors, (2) the Fafnir Bearing Division of Textron, and (3) the MRC Bearings Division of TRW.

Foreign Competition

The principal imports of miniature and precision ball bearings came from Europe, Canada, and, increasingly, from Japan. The industry's reaction to increased competition included turning to Washington.

The Trade Expansion Act of 1962 contained a provision (Section 232) whose purpose was "safeguarding national security." Section 232 provides that the director of the Office of Emergency Preparedness must recommend, and the president must take, action necessary to control imports "so that such imports will not so threaten to impair the national security."

Under the leadership of Mr. Daniels and others, the domestic industry trade association, the Anti-Friction Bearing Manufacturers Association (AFBMA), filed an application for an investigation with the Office of Emergency Preparedness in October 1964, concluding that "reliance upon imports for supplies of . . . miniature bearings and instrument bearings, so essential to the national defense, clearly poses a menacing threat to the national security." Two years later, after supplementary filings were submitted by both the AFBMA and by the Japanese bearing industry association, the AFBMA withdrew its application for investigation because of inadequate import data.

In January 1969 the AFBMA again submitted an application for investigation under Section 232. This 1969 *AFBMA Application for Investigation* included the following:

1. An analysis showing production, exports to the United States, and percentage of production exported to the United States by Nippon Miniature Bearing Co., Ltd. (founded in 1951 in Tokyo) and data showing Nippon's investment in fixed assets to be $4,600,000 U.S. in 1967 with planned 1968 additions of $4,200,000.

Nippon Miniature Bearings (millions of units)

Year	Production	Exports to U.S.	Production exported to U.S.
1965	3.3	.7	22%
1966	4.8	1.9	39
1967	7.4	5.1	70
1968	10.7	7.5	70

2. Data on Swiss (primarily RMB Roulements Miniatures, S.A.) and Nippon Miniature Bearings imports and domestic shipments.

Shipments (in millions of units)

Year	U.S. domestic shipments	Swiss exports to U.S.	Nippon exports to U.S.	Swiss and Nippon exports as a % of U.S. shipments
1965	13.7	2.7	.7	25
1966	20.4	2.7	1.9	23
1967	18.9	2.6	5.1	41
1968	14.5	2.3	7.5	68

3. A reminder that the U.S. government had officially recognized the strategic importance of ball bearings by banning a sale of forty-five Bryant grinders to Russia.

4. The conclusion that 65 percent to 75 percent of all U.S. consumption of miniature and instrument bearings are defense end-uses.

5. The conclusion that foreign producers had become the dominant force in the nondefense market as the domestic industry responded to urgent defense orders.

6. A request for an investigation of this "threat to national security."

The reply of the Japan industry group filed in April 1969 *(Reply of the Japan Bearing Industrial Association to the Application for Investigation)* argues in return that

1. Industry sales and profit fluctuations are caused by military procurement, not by imports.

2. Domestic capacity has been expanding even if domestic companies have been diversifying.

3. Future defense needs can be met by relatively easily accomplished domestic expansion. Thus imports from Japan do not now, and will not in the future, threaten the productive ability of the domestic bearing industry essential to national security. The Japanese reply closes with the observation that "We probably will never again experience a conventional war of global scale such as World War II where the United States was cut off from most foreign sources of supply. In any foreseeable situation other than a worldwide nuclear war, the United States could import defense-essential items from friendly nations to supplement domestic sources."

EXHIBIT 5
NHBB lost business report

Customer	End product	1966	1967
A	Motor manufacturings	$245,000	$ 600
B	Potentiometers	171,000	1,100
C	Counters	121,000	7,200
D	Motors & pots	291,000	12,400
E	Pots	164,000	0
F	Gear heads	94,000	7,600
G	Synchros & servo machinery	237,000	5,100
H	Test equipment	91,000	1,107
I	Pots	89,000	450
J	Computers	176,000	4,100
K	Gear heads	461,000	9,700
L	Clutches	62,000	450
M	Guidance & fire control systems	290,000	13,000
N	Motors	176,000	11,000
O	Motors & gear heads	144,000	7,200
P	Motors	114,000	0
Q	Atomic energy	40,000	2,100

Note: Exhibit shows business lost to Japanese imports by showing NHBB's sales to a few customers selected at random by NHBB.
Source: Company records.

In support of the AFBMA application, Mr. Daniels and his aide Theodore Kanell traveled extensively between Washington and Peterborough, submitting additional data including Exhibits 5 and 6 concerning lost business and price comparisons. MPB also participated extensively in the AFBMA application effort. Barden, however, was then involved with NMB, the Japanese manufacturer. Barden, which was withdrawing from the miniature bearing market, exchanged technology with the Japanese in exchange for an ownership position in NMB and a distribution arrangement whereby Barden distributed NMB products. This agreement was terminated after a few years.

NHBB continued to suffer earnings decline: 1968 earnings of $975,000 ($1.42 per share) fell to $149,000 ($0.22 per share) in 1969. Company officers kept up a weekly activity schedule in Washington and talked to Congressional representatives, personnel in the Office of Emergency Preparedness, and Treasury officials in their push for some kind of protection, whether it be embargoes, mandatory quotas, voluntary quotas, or tariffs. Assistant Secretary of Commerce Kenneth Davis came to Peterborough in December 1969 and noted that it is a "black and white situation

EXHIBIT 6 Price comparison, selected domestic versus Japanese prices on balls

General-Purpose Bearing Steel

	Grade 10			Grade 25		
Size	Japanese price	Domestic price	Price index[a]	Japanese price	Domestic price	Price index[a]
1/16	.98	4.63	21	.88	3.09	28
3/32	.93	3.15	30	.83	2.02	41
1/8	.78	3.38	23	.68	2.55	27
5/32	1.12	3.77	30	1.02	2.71	38
3/16	1.54	4.21	37	1.44	3.01	48

Corrosion-Resistant Steel

	Grade 10			Grade 25		
Size	Japanese price	Domestic price	Price index[a]	Japanese price	Domestic price	Price index[a]
1/32	1.55	10.75	14	—	—	—
3/64	1.70	10.48	16	—	—	—
1/16	1.76	9.18	19	1.60	8.34	19
5/64	1.64	10.23	16	—	—	—
3/32	—	—	—	1.60	7.45	21
1/8	2.18	7.00	31	2.14	5.85	37
5/32	—	—	—	3.65	7.15	51

Note: Prices in dollars per thousand balls.
[a] Price index = Japanese price as a percentage of domestic price.
Source: NHBB records.

whether or not an industry is important to defense, and I don't think there is much question that miniature and precision bearings are important.'' Davis further noted that Japan was expected to have a $1.5 billion trade surplus with the United States that year and that General Motors, Federal-Mogul, and MRC-TRW had dropped out of the bearing industry.

The AFBMA was especially encouraged by a decision (albeit after many months) by the Deputy Defense Secretary David Packard in April 1971 to order that all military purchases of ball bearings with an outside diameter of 30 millimeters or less ''must be procured from domestic or Canadian sources to the maximum extent practicable.'' At this point the AFBMA petition had been pending 26 months.

Nonetheless, in May 1971 the Office of Emergency Preparedness issued a report which, while conceding that imports were hurting the domestic bearings industry, declined to recommend any import limits. OEP Director George Lincoln stressed that the Pentagon had recently taken specific action to ''preserve the mobilization base for production of bearings.'' Lincoln concluded that, since OEP legislation restricted the OEP to consider the national security impact only, the current ''deterioration can be ascribed in some part to imports, but I consider that it has been related more directly to a sharp decline in demand.''

COMPETITION IN THE 1970s

The trends in foreign competition during the 1970s and a summary of the major players in the industry follow.

Imports and NHBB

Foreign producers included Japan's Nippon Miniature Bearing (NMB) of the Minebea group, four other Japanese companies (Koyo Seiko, NTN, NSK, and Nachi), Germany's FAG (producing bearings in Canada), RMB of Switzerland, and SKF (producing in several European countries).

Exhibit 7 shows the U.S. market for 6 post-Vietnam years. Japan represented 27 percent of the imported miniature units and 45 percent of the imported precision units in 1983, Singapore 49 percent of miniature and 37 percent of precision, and Switzerland 10 percent of miniature and 1 percent of precision in 1983. Japan's 27 percent of the 1983 miniature units was 26 percent of miniature 1983 dollar sales, Singapore's 49 percent was 41 percent of sales, and Switzerland's 10 percent was 15 percent of sales. Imports (62 percent of miniature and 65 percent of precision bearing consumption in 1983) had grown from 30 percent and 49 percent in 1973.

The Competing Companies

Barden. Barden specialized in precision grade bearings used in sophisticated aircraft and missile guidance systems and ultraprecise machine tool applications. Barden represented NMB's ABEC 1 and 3 miniature and precision bearings beginning in 1968, but this Barden-NMB agreement was terminated in 1973. Barden sold a West German manufacturer's line to replace the NMB products.

EXHIBIT 7 U.S. market data

Year	Consumption	Imports	Imports as % of consumption	Domestic production	NHBB production	NHBB % of U.S. consumption
Miniature (0–9 mm)						
1973	7.9	2.4	30.4%	6.0	2.8	35.4%
1975	7.0	2.3	32.9	5.3	2.4	34.3
1977	9.3	2.8	30.1	7.2	3.0	32.3
1979	11.5	4.1	35.7	8.0	3.6	31.3
1981	13.2	7.3	55.3	6.5	2.7	20.5
1983	14.3	8.9	62.2	5.8	3.0	21.0
Precision (9–30 mm)						
1973	108.0	53.0	49.1	56.0	4.1	3.8
1975	77.0	41.0	53.2	41.0	4.3	5.6
1977	107.0	58.0	54.2	54.0	7.4	6.9
1979	131.0	78.0	59.5	58.0	12.2	9.3
1981	121.0	80.0	66.1	45.0	12.5	10.3
1983	134.7	87.1	64.7	50.7	14.7	10.9

Note: Data in millions of units.
Source: NHBB records.

MPB. MPB expanded its miniature and precision bearings capacity at the same rate as NHBB, but concentrated on the higher ABEC grades. MPB manufactured only a limited number of high-volume ABEC 1 and 3 grades.

MPB entered into an agreement with NMB of Japan in September 1960 for joint distribution. This agreement was terminated in January 1964. Industry observers commented:

> *NMB learned a lot of technology from MPB. MPB believed it had NMB's assurance that the latter would stay out of the stainless steel bearings and would only produce chrome. Subsequent events proved that it did not have that assurance. NMB, having learned heat-treating concepts from MPB, turned to Barden for retainer technology.*

NHBB. In the late 1960s and early 1970s NHBB specialized in the high-volume, low–ABEC-class bearings. In policies it continued to follow, NHBB produced to order with only a limited inventory. Two-thirds of NHBB's manufacturing lots average 2,000 pieces with more than one-half less than 1,000 pieces. Lot sizes became smaller after the early (screw machine, heat-treating) manufacturing steps due to customized product characteristics. During this period, computer industry and military demands for higher ABEC classes were limited, although they would become most important in the 1980s. For example, in 6 to 20 millimeters, computer peripherals were expected to account for 85 percent of domestic demand for low-ABEC classes in the second half of the 1980s. Thus technological advances (such as computers and, later, videocassette recorders) continued to produce swings in demand. NHBB dealt with customers through an internal sales group with an engineering or "problem-solving" approach.

General Motors, Textron, and TRW. In 1956–1957 the Bryant Division of the Excello Corporation introduced their new series of state-of-the-art bore and race grinders. This equipment was a tremendous assistance to the industry and enabled the miniature manufacturers to significantly increase their output of small-diameter hardened and ground parts. At the same time, the machines made it easier for domestic and overseas manufacturers to move down into the miniature and instrument bearing business.

When New Departure-Hyatt Division of General Motors, Fafnir Bearing Division of Textron Corporation, and TRW Bearings Division of TRW Corporation moved into the miniature bearings market between 1956 and 1970, they were volume producers of ABEC 1 and 3 grade along with other larger size and volume series. They also manufactured these series in ABEC 5 grades on a smaller scale. Their interest in the miniature series was brought about by the increased use of miniature bearings by the military in analog computers for fire-control systems, navigation and bombing systems, and engine and flight-control units. The market decline over the 1961–1965 and 1967–1972 periods saw these manufacturers withdraw from the miniature market in order to concentrate on the more profitable volume side of their business along with their larger bearings (such as bearings for aircraft engines and precision machine tools) which carried very high unit value.

NMB. Minebea was established July 1951 as the first Japanese firm specializing in miniature bearings. NMB's managing director, Mr. Takama Takahashi, visited the United States in the fall of 1959 to explore U.S. market prospects. He also inspected MPB's facilities, and a year later MPB and NMB entered into a joint distribution effort, which lasted 3 years. In 1965 NMB entered into a technical assistance agreement with Société Nouvelle de Fabrications Aeronautiques and later into an agreement with Barden. By the late 1960s, NMB produced 70 percent of the Japanese miniature bearings exported. About 75 percent of NMB's production was exported.

NSK, Nachi, Koyo, and NTN. As bearing requirements expanded internationally because of the office automation industry and domestically within Japan because of the videocassette recorder industry, four additional major Japanese producers of larger ball bearings moved into the miniature and precision bearing marketplace. These were NSK (Japan's largest rolling-element bearing manufacturer), Nachi Fukikoshi (which was particularly strong in the precision disc drives, appliance, and automotive markets), Koyo Seiko, and NTN (Japan's second largest rolling-element bearing producer). In 1970 NTN entered into a technical agreement with Fafnir to learn the technology of quality aircraft bearings. By 1981 NTN had 60 percent of the Japanese aircraft bearing market, and it announced its intention to market aircraft bearings in Europe and America and to diversify into ultraprecision bearings. Many Japanese firms began adding subsidiary factories in Singapore and, later, Thailand, during the late 1970s and early 1980s.

FAG. FAG is Germany's largest domestic manufacturer of bearings. Their plant in Canada produces miniature and instrument bearings for sale in Canada and the United States. Production of precision instrument bearings started in 1954.

RMB. RMB of Bienne, Switzerland has been manufacturing miniature and instrument bearings since 1932. The company supplies a quality product in all precision grades throughout the world marketplace. RMB was the first producer of miniature bearings, and there are exciting stories of bearings smuggled out of Switzerland during World War II in diplomatic pouches that eventually reached the Allied war effort through Portugal.

SKF. SKF is the world's largest producer of ball bearings. Its ADR division in France started a significant push into the U.S. market in the early 1980s, aided in part by the low value of the franc relative to the dollar.

SKF Industries transferred the manufacture of 0- to 30-mm OD bearings to Europe in the midseventies and sold off much of their equipment to NHBB, where the machines were rebuilt and tooled according to NHBB methods. This gave NHBB a significant increase in capacity at the time of a major boom in the computer peripheral/office automation industry during the 1975–1980 period.

SKF had been operating in the United States under terms of a consent decree with the U.S. Department of Justice limiting imports. SKF sold its Reed Division

EXHIBIT 8
Selected data on imports

Year	Country	Units	Dollars	Dollars/unit	Percentage	
					Units	Dollars
Under 9 mm						
1979	Canada	62	126	2.03	1%	4%
	Japan	1547	1097	.71	37	35
	Singapore	1877	1173	.62	46	38
	Switzerland	676	730	1.08	16	23
	Total	4162	3126	.75	100	100
1983	Canada	114	215	1.89	2	3
	Japan	2270	2013	.89	31	31
	Singapore	4143	3191	.77	56	49
	Switzerland	827	1134	1.37	11	17
	Total	7354	6553	.89	100	100
9–30 mm						
1979	Canada	1611	1551	.96	3	4
	Japan	45,191	31,309	.69	76	74
	Singapore	10,984	7413	.67	19	18
	Switzerland	1466	1965	1.34	2	4
	Total	59,252	42,238	.71	100	100
1983	Canada	1573	1743	1.11	2	4
	Japan	38,838	24,543	.63	53	57
	Singapore	31,716	15,935	.50	44	37
	Switzerland	803	814	1.01	1	2
	Total	72,930	43,035	.59	100	100

Note: Data in thousands.
Source: NHBB records.

in Chatsworth, California, to NMB and Reed's equipment to NHBB. After the consent decree was lifted in the 1980s, SKF began to rationalize production worldwide.

Exhibit 8 summarizes imports into the United States in 1979 and 1983.

NHBB IN THE 1970s

In March 1971 Mr. Daniels reorganized the managerial group to include an enlarged "strategy board" whose stated objective was to determine "where are we and where the hell do we go from here?" The board included a half-dozen company officers "and of course Mr. Daniels." Mr. Daniel's announcement of March 25 concluded: "We will meet at noon sharp to avoid phone calls, etc., for lunch where we can have enough privacy, on call from me or any member. There will be no booze until we reach the point of just shooting the breeze.'' A letter to all employees the next day continued:

> *A lot of people here, and I get it outside too, seem to think that since I have made Cherwin president and kicked myself upstairs to chairman, I have retired. . . . As I told Cherwin and Kanell [executive vice-president] at the time, we are all going to keep doing what we've been doing, and by God, I'm still the boss, and don't you forget it.*

In January 1972 Mr. Takama Takahashi, president of Nippon Miniature Bearings, visited Peterborough, having expressed an interest in talking to NHBB principals. Although state and national flags of visitors were customarily flown from the flagstaffs outside NHBB headquarters, no Japanese flag was visible. A company official noted that ''Chairman Daniels had originally stated that in any event this foreign flag would not be flown.'' Following the visit, Mr. Daniels posted an announcement to employees: ''Japanese visitors given a quick censored plant tour to show them our horse power. I think they got the message.''

President Kanell Theodore Kanell was elected president of NHBB in March 1979. Mr. Kanell had joined NHBB in 1957 as a sales engineer whose job was to open a California sales office. He had previously been with General Electric and Bendix after serving in World War II and receiving a B.S. in mechanical engineering from the University of Connecticut. During Ted Kanell's first two weeks of NHBB employment, Mr. Daniels had traveled to California to meet with his new employee. Two anecdotes from this first meeting of an association that was to become mentor-protégé provide insight into these personalities.

Mr. Daniels and Mr. Kanell took four clients to lunch in Los Angeles. Ted Kanell, with $15 in his billfold, first tried unsuccessfully to cash a personal check, having been told to ''take care of the bill'' by Mr. Daniels. Returning to the table with the $36 lunch bill, the NHBB team was further chagrinned to find that Mr. Daniels only had $10. The client paid for the lunch and announced loudly to the client staff as the lunch group returned to the client offices: ''Quick, give these boys an order so that they will have enough money to get home to New Hampshire.''

At the conclusion of the 2-week visit, Mr. Daniels asked Ted Kanell to take him to the train station for a ride to San Francisco. Ted had never been to the Los Angeles train station, having always used airplanes for any distance traveling, but he thought he knew where the station was in downtown Los Angeles, and he did not want to seem lost or inexperienced in his new sales territory. After several moments of fast turns, peering up streets, and assuring his boss that there was no problem, Ted parked in front of a large building and walked quickly up the steps with Mr. Daniels and his baggage, as train time was rapidly approaching. Once up the marble steps, Ted realized they were in the lobby of the Los Angeles branch of the United States Post Office. Mr. Daniels looked at Ted, and asked, ''Should I go parcel post or first class?''

Anecdotes and stories such as these circulated through the company and strengthened the image of Mr. Daniels with his employees. A particular favorite in Peterborough was the response of Mr. Daniels to the critical comments by a brash, aggressive New York financial whiz about Mr. Daniel's "style of seat-of-the-pants management." "Well, at least I've been sitting in these pants for a sufficiently long period," replied Mr. Daniels.

Mr. Kanell became sales manager in 1962, vice-president for sales and a director in 1968, and executive vice-president in 1970, prior to becoming president. He received an M.B.A. from Boston University in 1974.

Post-Vietnam Strategies

MPB: Diversification. MPB's history was summarized for the casewriter by Bill Scranton, MPB's president during the period of Japanese competition. MPB joined with NHBB in attempts to get the government to act, and MPB made several attempts to diversify. In 1976 MPB was acquired by Wheelabrator-Frye. Mr. Scranton's comments are contained in Appendix A.

NHBB: Product Expansion, Automation, Engineering Service. Faced with no change in prices of low-grade miniature bearings from 1968 to 1978, NHBB tried to broaden its product line to include spherical bearings, rod ends, specially designed bearings, and bearing subassemblies to "turn a $6 sale into a $30 or $40 sale." Plant capacity was expanded 72 percent from 1976 to 1981, and a sales target of $110 to $120 million for 1985 was established in 1976.

Looking back in October 1982, Mr. Kanell told *Forbes* (October 11, 1982, page 60) that because of the Vietnam buildup:

> There was a heavy burden placed on small military suppliers like ourselves. It used to be that we would ship 4 to 6 weeks after getting an order. Well, during Vietnam our lead time went to 35 to 40 weeks. . . . It was at that time that the Japanese . . . came in and said, "We can deliver those products off the shelf overnight. Moreover, our price will be 30 percent less than you currently pay." . . . When things in Vietnam subsided, we looked around and found that Japan had cornered about 40 percent of the market . . . virtually overnight. That was 1971, the only time this company took a loss. . . . We couldn't withdraw. This was the only business we had.

Plants automated, computer-assisted design and manufacturing were used, and $8,000 worth of ball bearings per employee produced in 1971 grew to $42,000 in 1981.

Further, NHBB moved into the technical precision-engineering bearing market. Sales engineering staff was doubled. Mr. Kanell noted: "We had the reputation for being the high-volume, low-cost producer. . . . We were good if you wanted a Chevrolet, but if you wanted a Rolls-Royce, you went elsewhere."

Production

NHBB had three plant locations: (1) Peterborough; (2) Jaffrey (a few miles from Peterborough), where primary balls were produced; and (3) Laconia, which produced bearings other than ball bearings, such as torque tube, rod end, and sperical bearings. Exhibit 9 shows the original cost, cost of additions, and estimated current replacement cost for these facilities exclusive of land cost.

EXHIBIT 9
Facility costs

Plant	Date opened	Original cost	Additions	Total cost	Replacement cost
Peterborough	1956	$ 660,000	$3,840,000	$4,500,000	$13,630,000
Jaffrey	1976	380,000	620,000	1,000,000	1,520,000
Laconia	1968	910,000	2,440,000	3,350,000	5,930,000
Total		1,950,000	6,900,000	8,850,000	21,080,000

In 1984 the Peterborough facility operated at about 78 percent of capacity, with three-fourths of its business coming from custom modifications of its catalogued bearings. In the same year Jaffrey operated at 71 percent of capacity, with 90 percent of its production being standard, catalogued items and only 10 percent custom items. Laconia operated at 70 percent capacity, primarily producing spherical bearings. An automated ball bearing factory has been opened in Laconia specifically to respond to Japanese low prices, but NHBB closed this plant several years later. Peterborough and Jaffrey unit production (in thousands) is summarized in the following table (source: NHBB records).

	1979 units	%	1981 units	%	1983 units	%
ABEC 1	1,690	10.3	1,515	10.0	1,835	10.3
ABEC 3	12,300	74.6	11,050	71.9	13,365	74.7
ABEC 5	1,455	8.8	1,630	10.6	1,570	8.8
ABEC 7	1,045	6.3	1,170	7.6	1,125	6.2
ABEC 9	9	0.0	5	0.0	5	0.0
Total 0–30 mm	16,490	100.0	15,370	100.0	17,900	100.0

Production of the higher ABEC grades is more likely to be customized. The production lot size is about equally distributed among under one thousand pieces, between one and two thousand, and over two thousand pieces. NHBB's unit and dollar sales for selected ABEC classes appear in Exhibit 10.

Sales

Too much concentration on ABEC grades and sizes can be misleading, since any one customer and any one end use is likely to involve a mixture of sizes and ABEC grades. The computer disc drive, the fishing reel, and the missile gyroscope may well use larger and smaller bearings of varying ABEC quality. Another way to look at sales is to look at NHBB's top ten customers. Exhibit 11 summarizes the units shipped and dollar sales of NHBB in 1979 and 1984. Exhibit 12 reflects shifts in demand.

Economies of Scale

New Hampshire Ball Bearing estimated the consequences of economies of scale in order to measure such things as (1) the benefit of spreading fixed costs over higher

EXHIBIT 10
NHBB sales by
ABEC class

Year	Sales Units	Dollars	Average price
Miniature ABEC 1			
1979	4,687,000	2,900,000	$0.62
1983	1,778,000	2,359,000	$1.33
Change 1979–83	−62%	−19%	+115%
Miniature ABEC 3			
1979	7,507,000	6,218,000	$0.83
1983	9,020,000	10,513,000	$1.17
Change 1979–83	+20%	+69%	+41%
Miniature ABEC 5			
1979	1,172,000	2,156,000	$1.84
1983	1,162,000	3,577,000	$3.08
Change 1979–83	−1%	+66%	+67%
Miniature ABEC 7			
1979	536,000	1,582,000	$2.95
1983	507,000	1,895,000	$3.74
Change 1979–83	−5%	+20%	+27%
Precision ABEC 1			
1979	855,000	1,145,000	$1.34
1983	843,000	2,285,000	$2.71
Change 1979–83	−1%	+100%	+102%
Precision ABEC 3			
1979	1,318,000	1,484,000	$1.13
1983	2,613,000	3,777,000	$1.45
Change 1979–83	+98%	+155%	+28%
Total under 9 mm, ABEC 1, 3, 5 and 7			
1979	13,902,000	12,856,000	$0.92
1983	12,467,000	18,344,000	$1.47
Total 9–30 mm, ABEC 1 and 3			
1979	2,173,000	2,629,000	$1.21
1983	3,456,000	6,062,000	$1.75

Note: Totals do not equal total sales because of customized and other bearing sales.
Source: NHBB records.

volumes, (2) the potential percent reduction in costs that would be necessary to justify investments in capital equipment costing $100,000 per installation, and (3) the relationship between labor and materials direct costs. That company estimate is shown in Exhibit 13. The direct cost of this production is summarized in Exhibit 14.

Exhibits 15, 16, 17, and 18 present selected financial and operating data, including balance sheets and income statements for 1980 through 1984, employee, and per share data. An organization chart as of April 1984 appears in Exhibit 19.

EXHIBIT 11 Sales by top ten customers

Dollar sales rank			Unit sales		Dollar sales		Price per unit	
1979	1984	Principal end use	1979	1984	1979	1984	1979	1984
1	2	Aircraft engine fuel controls	260,000	130,000	$1,407,000	$1,765,000	$ .41	$13.58
2	a	Disc drives, pointers	1,360,000	a	1,185,000	a	.87	a
3	3	Pumps, valves for aircraft engines	95,000	80,000	835,000	1,735,000	8.79	21.69
4	6	Repair and maintenance by government agency	350,000	280,000	795,000	1,315,000	2.27	4.70
5	10	Fishing tackle	450,000	475,000	620,000	930,000	1.38	1.96
6	15	Precision blowers, fans for motors	820,000	520,000	570,000	570,000	.70	1.10
7	11	EEC distributor	255,000	75,000	565,000	845,000	2.22	11.27
8	20	Radar (and computer '79 only)	70,000	70,000	515,000	395,000	7.36	5.64
9	19	Precision motors	440,000	330,000	470,000	420,000	1.07	1.27
10	12	Distributor	250,000	480,000	385,000	780,000	1.54	1.63

[a] Market segment showed little activity in 1984 because of the decline in the computer industry.

EXHIBIT 12
New additions to the top ten customers in 1984

1984 rank in dollar sales	Sales		
	Units	Dollars	Price per unit
1. Disc drives (Singapore)	2,450,000	$1,940,000	$ .79
4. Disc drives (U.S.)	1,000,000	1,450,000	1.45
5. Disc drives (U.S.)	1,400,000	1,380,000	.99
7. Aircraft engines[a]	15,000	1,310,000	87.33
8. Stepping motors for disc drives, printers	1,365,000	1,305,000	.96
9. Blower, fans, and coolers for motors[b]	1,410,000	1,130,000	.80

[a] New customer to NHBB.
[b] 1979 orders 395,000 units, $370,000.
Source: Company records.

EXHIBIT 13
NHBB estimate of economies of scale

	Production volume in units					
	50	400	1,600	2,000	3,200	25,600
Per unit time in hours						
Set-up at 40 hours total	.800	.100	.025	.025	.013	.002
Run time[a]	.100	.072	.059	.057	.053	.038
Scrap[b]	.014	.003	.001	.001	.000	.000
Time allowed in hours	.914	.175	.085	.078	.066	.040
Cost per unit						
Labor[c]						
Set up	$ 6.40	$ .80	$ .20	$ .16	$ .11	$ .02
Run	.80	.58	.47	.46	.42	.30
Scrap	.11	.03	.01	.01	.00	.00
Total labor	$ 7.31	$1.41	$0.68	$0.63	$0.53	$0.32
Material[d]	.25	.21	.19	.19	.18	.16
Factory[e]	25.60	4.94	2.39	2.20	1.86	1.14
General administration cost[f]	9.04	1.80	.91	.84	.72	.45
Total cost/unit	$34.89	$6.95	$3.49	$3.23	$2.76	$1.75

[a] Based upon a rate of 500 per hour adjusted for 0.9 learning curve as quantity doubles.
[b] At 14% of run time adjusted for 0.95 material improvement.
[c] At $8/hr.
[d] Adjusted for 0.95 material improvement rate.
[e] 350% of total labor.
[f] At 35% of factory and material cost.

EXHIBIT 14
Direct costs and economies of scale

	Production volume in units					
	50	400	1,600	2,000	3,200	25,600
Variable cost per unit by component						
Running time	$ .80	$ .58	$.47	$.46	$.42	$.30
Setup	6.40	.80	.20	.16	.11	.02
Scrap	.11	.03	.01	.01	.00	.00
Materials	.25	.21	.19	.19	.18	.16
Total direct cost	$7.56	$1.62	$.87	$.82	$.71	$.48
Cost of component as % of direct cost						
Running	10.6	35.8	54.0	56.1	59.2	62.5
Setup	84.7	49.4	23.0	19.5	15.5	4.2
Scrap	1.4	1.8	1.2	1.2	0.0	0.0
Materials	3.3	13.0	21.8	23.2	25.3	33.3
Total	100.0%	100.0%	100.0%	100.0%	100.0%	100.0%

EXHIBIT 15
Statements of
financial position,
years ending
June 30

Assets	1984	1983	1982	1981	1980
Cash	$ 1,400	$ 9,100	$ 4,700	$ 8,100	$ 700
Accounts receivable	9,200	7,500	8,700	8,700	8,500
Prepaid expenses	800	400	500	500	500
Inventories	14,600	13,200	13,500	13,200	11,500
Total current assets	$26,000	$30,200	$27,400	$30,500	$21,200
Land and buildings	9,100	8,600	8,700	7,900	6,800
Machinery and equipment	29,500	26,300	24,900	22,400	20,300
Less depreciation	(21,500)	(19,000)	(17,200)	(15,400)	(14,000)
Other assets	2,700	600	800	800	700
Total assets	$45,800	$46,600	$44,600	$46,200	$35,000
Liabilities					
Current liabilities	$ 6,000	$ 5,800	$ 7,200	$ 8,000	$ 5,100
Long-term debt	5,000	5,500	5,700	10,800	10,700
Other liabilities	1,300	1,100	800	400	500
Total liabilities	$12,300	$12,400	$13,700	$19,200	$16,300
Common stock	11,400	11,500	10,900	10,400[b]	5,000
Retained income	24,800	22,700	20,000	16,600	13,800
Less treasury stock[a]	(2,700)				(100)
Total equity	$33,500	$34,200	$30,900	$27,000	$18,700
Total liabilities, equity	$45,800	$46,600	$44,600	$46,200	$35,000

Note: Figures in thousands of dollars.
[a] 97,200 shares were purchased in the open market during fiscal 1984 in order to clear the market of a large block of shares being offered by the estate of Mr. Daniels.
[b] Two-for-one stock split in December 1980.

EXHIBIT 16
Statement of
operations

	Years ending June 30				
	1984	1983	1982	1981	1980
Net sales	$59,000	$55,200	$60,700	$53,900	$44,400
Cost of goods sold[a]	$38,000	$33,300	$35,700	$32,500	$27,800
Engineering	2,700	2,300	2,100	1,700	1,300
Selling, general, administration[a]	11,000	10,500	11,200	9,000	7,000
Interest	600	600	600	1,200	1,200
Profit sharing	1,300	1,800	2,700	2,300	1,600
Other (net)	(700)	(800)	(500)	(100)	
Income before tax	$ 6,100	$ 7,500	$ 8,900	$ 7,300	$ 5,500
Taxes	2,700	3,400	4,200	3,400	2,500
Net income	$ 3,400	$ 4,100	$ 4,700	$ 3,900	$ 3,000
[a] Depreciation expense	2,400	2,300	2,100	2,000	1,800

Note: Figures in thousands of dollars.

EXHIBIT 17
Employee data

	1984	1982	1980	1979	1969
Total employed	1,494	1,454	1,510	1,396	1,150
Men	NA	800	815	720	521
Women	NA	654	695	676	629
Average service (years)	8	7	6	6	6
Number over 20 years	143	166	141	142	4
Over 10 years	451	436	405	412	352
Over 5 years	799	701	672	747	449
Less than 5 years	101	151	292	95	345

Note: NA = not available.

EXHIBIT 18 Selected data per share, years ending June 30

	1984	1983	1982	1981	1980
Quarterly price range in American Stock Exchange					
Qtr. 1 (July–Sept.)	40–44⅛	23¼–30	21–28	12⅞–19⅜	10½–12⅜
Qtr. 2 (Oct.–Dec.)	40⅜–44¾	28⅞–33¾	22⅞–32	17¼–29¼	8⅞–11½
Qtr. 3 (Jan.–March)	34½–46½	31½–43⅞	23¾–31¾	21⅜–33¼	9⅝–14¼
Qtr. 4 (Apr.–June)	25½–35⅞	41⅛–48	25½–29	24–32⅜	10⅞–13¾
Shareholders	1,116	1,203	1,387	1,419	NA
Shares outstanding (average)	1,658,000	1,666,000	1,652,000	1,483,000	1,372,000
Earnings per share	2.05	2.44	2.85	2.65	2.19
Dividends	.80	.80	.80	.76	.55
Book value per share	21.20	20.54	18.65	16.51	13.52

Note: NA = not available.

MINEBEA THE SUITOR

Mr. Daniels's health was fading at age seventy-three. His stock ownership of 18 percent, plus another 5 percent under his control, led to rumors of a takeover. Mr. Kanell said ''We are courted almost constantly.''

At an AFBMA meeting in 1983, Ted Kanell was talking to Mr. Takama Takahashi, the former president of Nippon Miniature Bearing who had visited Peterborough in 1972, and who was now chief executive officer of Minebea of Tokyo, the conglomerate parent of Nippon Miniature Bearing. After a few moments of cocktail-party conversation, Mr. Takahashi asked Mr. Kanell, ''Have you ever thought about how strong our two companies would be together?''

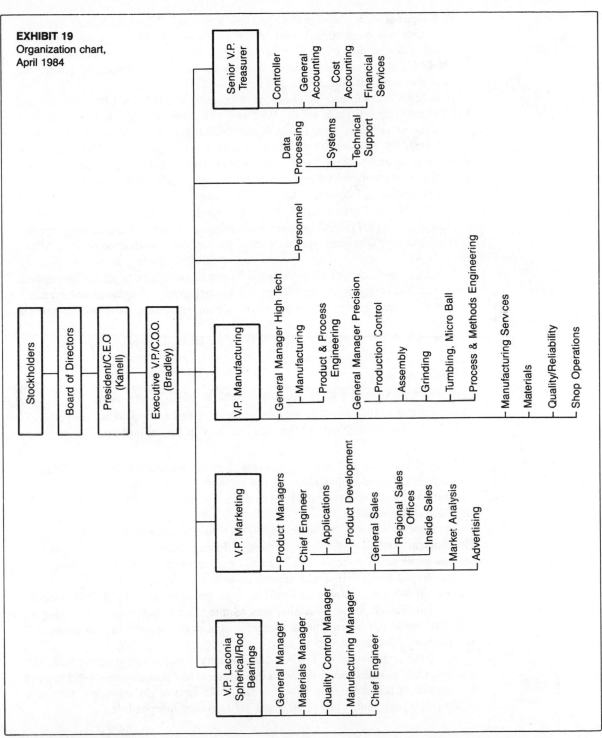

EXHIBIT 19
Organization chart,
April 1984

Source: Company records.

Although before his death in 1982 (the year before this Takahashi-Kanell meeting), Mr. Daniels had emphatically told Mr. Kanell never to bring up the subject of any kind of cooperative effort with the Japanese, Mr. Kanell felt he was responsible for NHBB's employees, customers, and stockholders. He decided to pursue the topic further with Mr. Takahashi.

Minebea Co. Ltd. had net sales of $403,000,000 and $481,000,000 for the fiscal years ending September 30, 1982 and 1983, respectively. It was estimating 1984 sales at between $580,000,000 and $620,000,000. Total assets were over $1,140,000,000 and annual capital expenditures averaged over $75,000,000. In 1983 the company became Japan's third largest loudspeaker producer by acquiring an audio components subsidiary of Sony Corporation. Minebea expanded its small precision motors and computer key boards through U.S. acquisitions in 1983 and early 1984. It was a major participant in the founding in May 1984 of NMB Semiconductor Co., Ltd. Principally, however, Minebea was the world's leading supplier of small bearings. Thailand was an increasingly important production base for Minebea.

Minebea's overseas activities included 36 plants and 66 sales offices throughout the world. The company employed over 3,500 employees in Singapore and expected to have twice that many in Thailand when its plant expansion there was completed in 1985.

Now in July 1984 Minebea's offer was on the table. This offer included:

$65 per share in cash

A commitment to invest $50 million to modernize NHBB's two plants

Assurance that NHBB would be the head of the new firm and would assume responsibility for managing Nippon Miniature Bearings' plant in California

Ted Kanell knew the feelings of his deceased friend and mentor, NHBB's founder. These feelings were well known to Ted's "boss," the board of directors. (The directors of the company in 1984, as described in the 1984 10-K Annual Report, are listed in Appendix B.)

Mr. Kanell also knew that some employees would be most opposed to the merger. The Antitrust Division of the Department of Justice might also oppose the merger because some small portions of the product market might be 60 percent controlled by the merged firms. "It would depend on how you define the relevant market," Mr. Kanell thought. "Also there could be some problem from the Defense Department." Mr. Kanell knew a decision was required, since Minebea was making an offer that could not be sweetened further. "This is the science of management," Ted thought, "judging shades of gray."

Still fresh and vibrant in Ted Kanell's memory was his last meeting with Mr. Daniels. Only minutes before his death, Mr. Daniels had said goodbye to his protégé of a quarter of a century with these words: "Take care of my company, take care of my employees, and, most of all, keep my company independent."

APPENDIX A: COMMENTS OF WILLIAM M. SCRANTON

Bill Scranton, former president of MPB, talked to the casewriter about the evolution of MPB's strategy. Mr. Scranton had joined MPB in 1950, after graduating from Princeton with a degree in mechanical engineering and Harvard Business School, plus completing military service and 6 years at Pratt & Whitney Aircraft. His comments make up the rest of this appendix.

I was newly married when I worked for Pratt & Whitney as a production foreman on the night shift. After 3 years of night shift work, I started talking to the guys at the top about a transfer. They were not totally sympathetic to me as the youngest foreman in the company, so I started looking around for a job. I had seriously considered on two previous occasions working with a small company, and I decided to go with my third chance, which I got through Harvard's placement service. The job was as production manager for Horace Gilbert at MPB. I thought I had better take the risk.

During World War II, Bud Daniels had brought in his brother-in-law, Horace Gilbert (their wives were sisters) to take his place as the operating and administration part of MPB, since the founder, Mr. Pierce, was a technical, nonmanagerial person.

After the war, Daniels and Pierce disagreed over production strategy. Pierce, who had invented the split ball bearing, had made the first miniature bearings with what was essentially watch-making technology. Daniels wanted to bring in screw machines and grinders and pursue automated production, while Pierce had become committed to the production process as opposed to the product.

Daniels left MPB and started NHBB, and, although Horace Gilbert tried to stay out of the Daniels-Pierce dispute, there was bad blood between the two brothers-in-law, aggravated by a disagreement as to whether Daniels left agreeing to stay out of the miniature ball bearing field or whether he agreed not to use Pierce's production process but was free to develop his own process.

In 1950, NHBB had the lead based upon the conventional screw machine-grinder full mechanized production system developed for miniature bearings by Daniels and Dick Cherwin. But the Korean War period was a great one to join a bearing company, because demand really was strong. Gilbert needed administrative help and I took on whatever needed doing. Everything was going straight up. MPB added people and started a night shift and we were badly back-ordered. Even elevator operators, hearing my name when I called on customers, would say, "Boy, are they looking for you!"

After the Korean War, the bad blood intensified as NHBB tried to drive MPB under by way of a price war. We all traveled with cost-volume estimates and charts, and the price cutting was extensive. There were moments when things were very tough for MPB, but we survived and caught up to NHBB's automated production lead.

Two things ended this bitter price war. One was New Departure's entry into the miniature and precision bearing business. Big companies in a market that is a sellers' market don't engage in price wars. So, a system of price leadership or administered prices evolved, aided by the other thing that made the price war end — the explosion in demand caused by the technological pull of the aircraft industry. We came into the period of major aircraft construction — the 707, DC-8, and the F101. We had lots of demand and a price umbrella, and everyone published their price lists, and things calmed down. We expanded based on forecast. We didn't know it, but we could have sold all we could make.

During this prosperous period, others entered the industry. Barden dropped down in size range into miniature bearings, and Fafnir and other larger companies started producing miniature and precision bearings. The price discipline broke, in part because of the new entrants and in part because of the swing in technology. There were no more large aircraft programs and, most importantly, the emphasis on mechanical miniaturization ended as electronics technology advanced. You miniaturize things electronically, so the mechanical technology need dropped off, the analogs were replaced by digital computers, and the days of boom demand were over.

The next big change in MPB and the industry was the Japanese competition. As executive vice-president — I did not become president until 1962 when Horace Gilbert's outside interests made it appropriate that he should become board chairman and I became president — I met Mr. Takahashi of Nippon Miniature Bearings (NMB) in 1959. Mr. Takahashi briefly toured our plant, and we began a series of negotiations with NMB.

We had earlier explored joint efforts with France's SFNA (Société Française Nationale Aeronautical) and we bought from NMB some chrome steel bearings — a small part of the market — and tried to sell them in the U.S. and in Europe, while talking about a more comprehensive arrangement. As the offers and counteroffers went back and forth, it became clear that our objectives — to have majority interest in any joint venture into which we put any technological knowledge — was not compatible with Takahashi's objective of control of the American market. Mr. Takahashi kept asking, "Don't you know how powerful our two companies could be together?" But, it wasn't possible, given each company's objective.

We broke off negotiations, and NMB finally entered into a technology agreement with Barden, which agreement gave Barden a minority interest in NMB. This agreement lasted a few years and was terminated. Barden did sell its interest back to NMB at a profit. Nonetheless, this Barden-NMB effort was a problem to the rest of us in the industry who were requesting federal assistance to limit imports in order to maintain a ball bearing industrial capacity for defense purposes.

Assessing Japanese competition during this period of predatory Japanese pricing we decided we had three courses of action: (1) to join them, (2) to turn to the government, and (3) to find a basis to compete.

We knew we couldn't join them on our terms, having already tried that option.

The government appeals took a long, long time. We eventually made a valuable convert in our congressman, Jim Cleveland, but it was a lengthy process with him and much more so with the Defense people. The process was humorous at the same time, because there I would be with representatives from our fierce competitor NHBB, each of us trying to stress the economics of the situation as plainly as possible while, at the same time, both concentrating on not revealing any costs to each other, while also straining to hear any cost data from our competitor.

Finding a basis to compete was the most difficult. Dick Cherwin, Bud Daniels, and others at NHBB talked about rolling the Japanese back into the sea. NHBB built a plant in Laconia, New Hampshire, to produce low-ABEC miniatures.

But we didn't think anyone could "roll the Japanese back into the sea," because NMB wasn't interested in short-term costs, but rather in long-term market share. We could cut back on products, but where would that leave us?

Further compounding the problem was the stock market. We were a glamor industry in the fifties, but multiples slid in the sixties and collapsed in the seventies. We couldn't raise equity without diluting earnings, and we didn't have a high multiple for acquisitions.

We made acquisitions and tried to diversify, while NHBB was trying to fine-tune. We misjudged some of our efforts to enter other markets. We opened a gyrooptic plant, which had to be closed — just as NHBB had to close their Laconia plant as the Japanese wouldn't "roll back."

We investigated an assembly plant in Mexico, having developed direct sales to the Common Market through a Holland assembly plant. We added a specialty chemical line and other diversifications, but we were sacrificing profits through these new product efforts.

A new power base was developing on the board, and Horace Gilbert's death and the sale of his stock by the estate, along with our diversification problems, meant that I lost the initiative. A banker became chairman and C.E.O., and I became chief operating officer, and the acquisition offers came in, some solicited by our banker-chairman. Although the executive team was supposed to have golden parachutes, only the pilot did, when we were sold to Wheelabrator-Frye in 1976. I left the company, but I understand Wheelabrator-Frye—which subsequently merged with Signal, and which was in turn acquired by Allied — was able to succeed at MPB by narrowing the product line and investing in equipment. It also kept and promoted the middle managers who knew the business.

Looking at MPB and the ball bearing industry from the perspective of national policies, one significant fact is the need for a large industrial market base to compete effectively. You don't have Japanese products made with other than Japanese components, if the latter exist. So when the union-pushed labor costs got high enough in critical U.S. industries such as automobiles and steel, Japan — with its U.S.-supported and -aided postwar industrial reconstruction — built an industrial base which had a snowball effect on components and related industries because they use Japanese components — bearings for example. Japan builds up its domestic demand, tools up for volume, and then eventually exports with a long-term, market-share view. Japan's efforts have been aggressive and across the board. Japanese companies, the offshore companies they control, and the limited local assembly facilities they have to go through to satisfy local requirements are part of a relentless cycle. Our experience in ball bearings is being mirrored in microchips today.

This leads to a second fact. The financial community measured us with standards that did not allow investing at the expense of current earnings whether in inventory or in future profits through capital and diversification expenditures. Since MPB was not a closely controlled ball bearing company like Timken, we had to respond to the financial community's return-on-investment and current-profit yardsticks. We all skimped on the plants, and the plants became obsolete. Conglomerates, also following national financial measuring sticks, began buying up the specialty companies, put in control systems, and brought in management that focused on profits, so the specialty divisions eventually did less well and were dumped.

These two facts were the things that killed the ball bearing industry. Except for a few specialty areas, the domestic industry is all but dead. You may never see it come back.

APPENDIX B: DIRECTORS

Nicholas Babich, fifty-four, a director since May 1984, is president, chief executive officer, and a director of Hitchiner Manufacturing Co., Inc. (investment castings and machine components manufacturing), a position he has held since November 1981.

Robert H. Bradley, fifty, a director since October 1982, is executive vice-president of the company, a position he has held since November 1981. Prior thereto, he was vice-president from April 1979. Mr. Bradley is the beneficial owner of 8,640 shares.

Theodore T. Daniels, forty-five, is a researcher and consultant in social communications and a lecturer at the University of Pennsylvania, a position he has held since September 1978. Mr. Daniels is the brother-in-law of Ernest V. Klein. He is the beneficial owner of 18,580 shares.

Michael Kaminsky, Jr., fifty-seven, a director since October 1974, is a consultant (manufacturing), a position he has held since August 1983. Prior thereto, he was vice-president of Fenwal Incorporated (manufacturer of temperature and explosion controls), a division of Kidde, Inc., from April 1982. From July 1981, Mr. Kaminsky was with A.D.E., Inc. (noncontact automatic gaging and measuring products manufacturing) as vice-president, operations. He is chairman of the Executive Compensation Committee, a member of the Audit Committee, and the beneficial owner of 3,300 shares.

Theodore Kanell, sixty-one, a director since July 1968, is president of the company, a position he has held since March 1979. He is a member of the Pension Fund Committee and the beneficial owner of 17,366 shares.

Ernest V. Klein, fifty-one, a director since January 1977, is a brother-in-law of Theodore T. Daniels and is a partner in the law firm of Gaston Snow and Ely

Bartlett (general counsel for the company), a position he has held in this and a predecessor firm since October 1966. Mr. Klein is chairman of the Audit Committee, a member of the Executive Compensation Committee, and the beneficial owner of 207,808 shares (approximately 13 percent), which includes 202,368 shares of five trusts for which he is trustee or cotrustee and shares voting and investment power. Not included in Mr. Klein's shares are 9,300 shares owned beneficially by Mrs. Klein, to which Mr. Klein disclaims any beneficial ownership.

Frederick P. Koallick, sixty, a director since September 1971, is senior vice-president (since April 1980) and treasurer (since May 1955) of the company, having served as a vice-president from May 1971 to April 1980. Mr. Koallick is a member of the Pension Fund Committee and the beneficial owner of 11,634 shares.

Henry H. Meyer, Jr., sixty-three, a director since March 1977, is vice-president of Eaton & Howard, Vance Sanders Inc. (investment counsel), a position he has held in this and a predecessor firm since June 1968. He is chairman of the Pension Fund Committee, a member of the Executive Compensation Committee, and the beneficial owner of 7,100 shares, which include 2,400 shares of two trusts for which he is cotrustee and shares voting and investment power. Not included in Mr. Meyer's shares are 2,500 shares for which Mrs. Meyer is a cotrustee and to which Mr. Meyer disclaims any beneficial ownership.

David F. Putnam, seventy, a director since October 1979, is chairman emeritus of Markem Corporation (identification and decoration machinery manufacturing), a position he assumed in May 1979. Mr. Putnam was chairman of Markem Corporation from July 1973 to May 1979 and is currently a director of that company. He is a member of the Audit and Executive Compensation Committees and the beneficial owner of 1,800 shares.

SPRINGFIELD MARINE BANK

On July 3, 1981, John Staudt, vice president–finance of Springfield Marine Bank and Marine Bancorp in Springfield, Illinois, was wondering what course to recommend on a major policy decision involving the bank's future strategy and structure. On that day the governor had signed into law, effective January 1, 1982, a bill allowing Illinois banks to merge with or acquire other banks within certain designated geographic bands through a multibank holding company structure. Staudt's job was to determine just what method the bank should adopt in expanding within the limits of the new legislation.

BACKGROUND

Illinois

Until the signing of the bill, Illinois had archaic banking laws which could be traced to before the Civil War, and it was one of the three remaining states, along with Oklahoma and West Virginia, to have no holding company or branch legislation. A number of people, both in Chicago and in downstate Illinois, had been working for nearly 30 years to alter the banking structure, first through branches but more recently through holding companies.

Until the early 1970s, the Illinois Bankers' Association (IBA) was comprised of 1,400 mostly small banks which had for years resisted any serious change in structure. In 1972, tired of the foot-dragging by the IBA, a number of the banks both in Chicago and in downstate had withdrawn from the IBA and set up a splinter trade association called the Association for Modern Banking in Illinois (AMBI).

AMBI had been working hard for the change in the legislation. There were about 250 banks in the association, but it represented well over 70 percent of all Illinois banking assets because it had for its members four of the largest Chicago banks as well as a number of other large banks around the state. AMBI's proposed

This case was prepared under the supervision of Professor Charles O. Meiburg as a basis for class discussion and not as an illustration of either effective or ineffective handling of the particular situation. Copyright © 1985 by the Colgate Darden Graduate Business School Sponsors, University of Virginia. Reprinted by permission.

legislation had been stalled in various committees for several years, but in June 1981 it passed both houses of the legislature and went to the governor for his signature. (See Appendixes A and B.)

Springfield Marine Bank

The Springfield Marine Bank was the oldest bank in the state, having been started in 1851. With assets at March 31, 1981, of over $500 million, it was the largest bank in Illinois outside of Chicago. Exhibits 1 and 2 present 1976–1980 balance sheet and income statements. It competed actively in its marketplace of Sangamon

EXHIBIT 1 Marine Bancorp, Inc., balance sheet, December 31, 1976–1980

	1976	1977	1978	1979	1980
Assets					
Cash and due from	$ 30,162	$ 29,417	$ 34,924	$ 36,015	$ 41,551
Investment securities	80,952	71,762	75,771	88,671	95,303
Federal funds sold	23,000	1,100	3,275	9,000	29,150
Loans					
Commercial	—	—	—	151,566	153,374
Real estate, construction	—	—	—	19,079	15,090
Real estate, mortgage	—	—	—	86,651	86,786
Installment	—	—	—	46,132	47,006
Total, gross	—	—	—	303,427	302,856
Unearned discount	—	—	—	(7,128)	(7,353)
Reserves for loans	—	—	—	(2,420)	(2,770)
Total, net	$198,161	$247,927	$266,648	$293,879	$292,733
Bank premises and equipment, net	3,383	7,611	9,683	11,498	12,278
Accrued interest receivables	3,105	3,535	4,486	5,913	8,265
Other assets	1,488	903	1,234	3,011	5,229
Total assets	$340,251	$362,255	$396,021	$447,987	$484,509
Liabilities					
Deposits					
Demand	$ 85,756	$ 82,556	$ 87,094	$ 86,838	$ 87,035
Savings				74,777	68,016
Time	208,531	231,541	260,725	196,225	260,846
Total	294,287	314,097	347,819	357,840	415,897
Short-term borrowings	11,908	10,325	7,644	43,691	17,604
Income taxes	1,298	1,577	923	1,348	1,395
Other liabilities	3,852	5,072	6,147	8,617	9,692
Total liabilities	$311,345	$331,071	$362,533	$411,496	$444,588
Capital					
Common stock and surplus	$ 15,000	$ 15,000	$ 15,000	$ 15,000	$ 15,000
Retained earnings	13,906	16,184	18,488	21,491	24,921
Total capital	$ 28,906	$ 31,184	$ 33,488	$ 36,491	$ 39,921

Note: Figures in thousands of dollars.

EXHIBIT 2

Marine Bancorp, Inc., income statement, 1976–1980

	1976	1977	1978	1979	1980
Interest income					
Loans	—	—	$23,768	$31,634	$37,763
Investment securities	—	—	4,204	6,015	8,432
Federal funds sold	—	—	394	225	1,898
Total	$21,246	$23,842	$28,366	$37,874	$48,093
Interest expense					
Deposits	—	—	$16,061	$20,967	$28,120
Short-term borrowing	—	—	1,053	3,746	4,374
Total	$12,262	$13,502	$17,114	$24,713	$32,494
Net interest income	$ 8,984	$10,340	$11,252	$13,161	$15,599
Provision for loan losses	$ 397	$ 485	$ 720	$ 910	$ 1,292
Net interest income after provision	$ 8,587	$ 9,855	$10,532	$12,251	$14,307
Other income					
Data processing fees	—	—	$ 1,423	$ 1,614	$ 1,790
Trust department	—	—	1,316	1,562	1,753
Other	—	—	585	784	1,012
Total	$ 2,483	$ 2,912	$ 3,324	$ 3,960	$ 4,555
Other expenses					
Salaries	—	—	$ 4,038	$ 4,661	$ 5,401
Employee benefits	—	—	625	783	858
Equipment expense	—	—	1,754	1,959	2,175
Occupying expense	—	—	774	926	1,324
Other	—	—	2,627	2,943	3,256
Total	$ 7,797	$ 8,462	$ 9,818	$11,272	$13,014
Income before taxes and security gains	$ 3,273	$ 4,305	$ 4,038	$ 4,939	$ 5,848
Provision for income taxes	560	1,228	934	1,136	1,527
Income before security gains	2,713	3,077	3,104	3,803	4,321
Security gains, net of taxes	1	1	—	—	—
Net income	$ 2,714	$ 3,078	$ 3,104	$ 3,803	$ 4,321
Income per common share	$8.48	$9.62	$9.70	$11.89	$13.51
Dividend per share	$1.50	$2.50	$2.50	$ 2.50	$ 2.50

Note: Figures in thousands of dollars.

County and had a 36 percent share of the local Springfield market, Springfield having a population of 100,000. (See Exhibit 3.)

Springfield Marine Bank also competed with local savings and loans, credit unions, finance companies, and a new local Merrill Lynch office. In Chicago, 200 miles away, two of America's largest banks, along with a 400-person Citicorp office and numerous foreign banks, were also beginning to offer local competition

EXHIBIT 3
Bank assets in
Springfield, Illinois,
December 31, 1980

Bank	Assets (in millions)	Market share
American State Bank of Springfield	$ 13	1%
Bank of Springfield	25	2
Capital Bank & Trust Company of Springfield	79	6
The First National Bank of Springfield	334	24
First State Bank of Springfield	20	1
Illinois National Bank of Springfield	264	19
Land of Lincoln Bank	68	5
Peoples National Bank of Springfield	8	1
Sangamon Bank & Trust	17	1
Springfield Marine Bank	484	36
Town & Country Bank of Springfield	48	4

in Springfield, with officers of all of those institutions and more calling regularly in Sangamon County.

On a national level, the bank competed with money market funds and all the various companies, such as American Express and Gulf & Western, that had gone into the financial services business and offered ways for the consumer dollar to be directed other than to local banks. (See Exhibit 4.)

The bank was closely held, and one result of a thin market for its stock was a deep discount in its stock price from the book value. In addition, because of a low dividend payout policy, the bank had an unusually high capital-to-asset ratio. (See Exhibit 5 for balance sheet and market price comparisons.)

The bank was familiar with the AMBI legislation, having worked closely with AMBI since its inception. Knowing the legislation would eventually pass, the bank had formed a bank holding company in 1979. During that year they had also employed a summer intern who determined that Zone 3 was the one for the bank to move into. In late 1980 a task force comprised of some of the bank's senior officers had targeted major cities in Zones 3 and 4 and had begun to pick out target banks. The bank was convinced that it would be allowed no acquisitions in Sangamon County given its predominant market share and, accordingly, had concentrated on areas outside of its traditional markets. Just about the time the legislation had passed, the bank had formulated a strategy for acquisition of banks which was basically a "town and country" approach, i.e., that the bank would acquire market positions in certain towns, normally those with populations of over 40,000, but it would acquire some country banks that were good, solid earners. The officers of the bank carried on active conversations with banks in the central band, both big and small, in an effort to explore all available options.

As the prospects for passage of the new law improved, other banks throughout Illinois began to think about how they might react to it. Appendix C is an article that appeared in the *American Banker* describing the situation.

EXHIBIT 4
Competitive financial services

	Take money/pay interest	Check-writing	Loans	Mortgages	Credit cards	Interstate branches	Money market	Securities	Insurance	Buy/plant real estate	Cash management acct	Travel agency/service	Car rental
Commercial Banks	•	•	•	•	•								
American Express	•	•	•	•	•		•	•	•	•		•	•
Merrill Lynch	•	•	•	•	•		•	•	•	•	•	•	
Prudential	•	•	•	•	•		•	•	•	•	•	•	
Sears	•	•	•	•			•		•	•	•	•	•
Transamerica	•	•	•	•			•				•		
Baldwin Piano	•	•	•	•	•		•			•	•	•	
Gulf & Western	•	•	•	•	•		•			•	•	•	
American General	•	•	•	•			•	•	•	•	•		
Beneficial	•	•	•	•	•		•			•			•
Household	•	•	•	•	•		•			•			•
Equitable Life	•	•	•	•			•	•			•		
AVCO			•	•	•		•			•	•	•	
DANA	•	•	•	•	•		•			•	•		
RCA			•	•	•		•			•			•
Control Data	•		•	•			•			•	•		
E. F. Hutton	•	•					•	•	•	•			
General Electric	•		•	•			•						
National Steel	•	•	•	•	•		•				•		

Source: Citibank, *Bank Robbers' Guide*, as reprinted in *ABA Banking Journal*, November 1981.

DECISION

The basic decision to be made was just how to get into the targeted towns. Staudt was trying to determine the direction that would be best for the bank and the bank's stockholders. He thought there were two basic ways Springfield Marine could get into new markets. One approach would be to combine with other large banks in cities such as Decatur, Champaign, and Bloomington to form a large holding company with a new name, perhaps Central Illinois Bankshares. In this case, the stockholders of each bank entering the holding company would exchange their shares for shares in the new holding company. If Marine Bank followed this strategy, it would become part of a billion-dollar operation relatively quickly, and size was an important consideration, given the size of the external environment

EXHIBIT 5 Illinois bank stocks, 1978–1981

| Other Illinois Metropolitan | Recent price | Earnings per share before security transactions | | | | 1st qtr. % Change | |
		1978	1979	1980	Trailing 12 mos.	earn. 1981	1980– 1981
1 First Bankshares (Alton)	$ 22.00	$ 2.46	$ 2.24	$ 2.37	$ 2.44	$ 0.16	+77.8%	1
2 First UTD Bancshares (Belleville)	65.00	N/A	8.55	9.27	9.05	1.91	−10.3	2
3 First Bancorp of Belleville	22.50	3.00	3.16	3.42	3.17	0.67	−27.2	3
4 Mid Continent Bancshares (Belleville)	19.00	2.17	1.82	4.93	4.76	1.07	−13.7	4
5 Corn Belt Bank (Bloomington)	250.00	41.28	47.51	57.33	62.90	21.68	+34.7	5
6 Nat'l Bank of Bloomington	39.00	4.63	4.84	2.31	2.00	0.55	−36.0	6
7 Peoples Mid Illinois Corp (Bloomington)	46.00	4.46	5.27	6.71	6.62	1.67	−5.1	7
8 1st Nat'l (Centralia)	55.00	5.91	6.78	7.70	7.63	2.17	−3.1	8
9 Champaign Nat'l	70.50	6.40	5.53	6.26	6.73	1.57	+42.7	9
10 First Nat'l in Champaign	80.00	8.42	8.07	8.79	8.43	1.07	−25.2	10
11 Palmer American Nat'l (Danville)	45.00	4.84	5.95	4.70	4.67	1.47	−2.0	11
12 Citizens Nat'l of Decatur	110.00	15.68	13.27	14.04	12.83	3.71	−24.6	12
13 First Nat'l of Decatur	80.00	12.75	13.59	12.54	12.22	3.40	−8.6	13
14 Millikin Bankshares (Decatur)	31.00	3.68	3.67	1.99	1.40	0.40	−59.6	14
15 Mid America of Edgemont	21.50	2.71	3.46	3.71	3.90	1.02	+22.9	15
16 First Freeport Corp	26.50	3.17	4.00	4.88	4.79	1.05	−7.9	16
17 Northwest Ill Bancorp (Freeport)	60.00	7.84	9.82	11.85	11.06	2.03	−28.0	17
18 First Galesburg Nat'l	100.00	7.95	8.18	8.48	7.51	1.09	−47.1	18
19 First Granite City Nat'l	39.00	5.76	6.13	6.82	6.28	1.00	−35.1	19
20 The First Nat'l of Highland	65.00	9.70	9.37	10.63	11.03	2.50	+19.0	20
21 Elliott State Bank (Jacksonville)	80.00	13.77	24.76	15.96	18.59	5.78	+83.5	21
22 City Nat'l of Kankakee	16.00	2.28	2.43	2.69	2.87	0.87	+26.1	22
23 First Trust & Savings of Kankakee	80.00	5.35	8.30	10.14	9.80	3.09	−9.9	23
24 First Nat'l of Moline	40.00	3.86	4.14	4.46	4.71	1.32	+23.4	24
25 Moline Nat'l	17.00	3.37	2.95	3.16	3.29	1.04	+14.3	25
26 First Nat'l of Morris	40.00	6.57	6.85	6.97	6.93	1.40	−14.6	26
27 Grundy County Nat'l (Morris)	28.00	3.58	3.47	2.80	2.53	0.53	−33.8	27
28 Security (Mt Vernon)	175.00	20.53	21.93	26.09	23.84	3.43	−39.6	28
29 Citizens Nat'l of Paris	150.00	16.64	17.78	20.60	14.98	2.53	−69.0	29
30 Commercial Nat'l Corp (Peoria)	28.025	5.24	5.82	5.72	5.72	1.01	+0.0	30
31 First Nat'l of Peoria	310.00	53.26	52.91	50.48	56.18	13.81	+70.3	31
32 Citizens First Nat'l of Princeton	60.00	9.50	11.33	13.80	15.20	4.71	+42.3	32
33 Mercantile Trust & Savings (Quincy)	63.00	10.79	11.95	14.11	13.37	2.85	−20.6	33
34 American Nat'l (Rockford)	325.00	73.00	85.51	90.30	75.09	14.80	−50.7	34
35 City Nat'l of Rockford	N/A	5.28	7.53	6.69	6.67	1.77	−1.1	35
36 First Nat'l of Rockford	40.00	6.41	7.19	6.53	5.61	0.48	−65.7	36
37 Illinois Nat'l of Rockford	N/A	17.45	20.86	21.84	18.92	4.56	−39.0	37
38 Finan Ser Corp (Rock Island Bank)	36.00	4.44	3.94	2.18	2.21	0.28	+12.0	38
39 First Nat'l of Rock Island	186.00	18.77	19.16	20.36	20.08	5.23	−5.1	39
40 Firstbank of Illinois (Springfield)	45.50	6.77	7.87	8.88	8.55	1.80	−15.5	40
41 Illinois Nat'l Bancorp (Springfield)	12.50	2.71	2.85	2.35	2.27	0.56	−12.5	41
42 Marine Bancorp (Springfield)	60.00	9.70	11.89	13.51	13.64	3.63	+3.7	42
43 Central Nat'l of Sterling	18.00	3.39	3.68	3.55	3.19	0.40	−47.4	43
44 First Trust & Savings of Taylorville	650.00	80.88	107.53	130.78	144.38	47.46	+40.2	44
45 Busey First Nat'l (Urbana)	600.00	84.47	106.76	114.00	110.44	32.01	−10.0	45
Other Illinois metropolitan averages					17.31		−2.1	
Combined averages					11.40		+1.4	

N/A = Not available.

EXHIBIT 5 (continued)

	Book value per share 3/31/84	Market price as a % book value	Annual growth rates, 1975–1980		Shares outstanding (000)	Assets 3/31/81 (millions)	
			Assets	EPS (BST)			
1 First Bankshares (Alton)	$ 37.49	58.7%	7.3%	5.5%	200	$101	1
2 First UTD Bancshares (Belleville)	74.50	87.2	14.7	N/A	84	113	2
3 First Bancorp of Belleville	30.99	72.6	13.4	8.2	540	280	3
4 Mid Continent Bancshares (Belleville)	41.35	45.9	8.2	12.5	320	172	4
5 Corn Belt Bank (Bloomington)	353.91	70.6	10.9	16.6	32	123	5
6 Nat'l Bank of Bloomington	36.91	105.7	5.4	−2.8	188	96	6
7 Peoples Mid Illinois Corp (Bloomington)	51.80	88.8	16.0	12.4	172	94	7
8 1st Nat'l (Centralia)	56.00	98.2	9.4	11.6	117	92	8
9 Champaign Nat'l	71.97	98.0	6.8	−5.4	164	160	9
10 First Nat'l in Champaign	92.04	86.9	7.3	7.6	96	117	10
11 Palmer American Nat'l (Danville)	46.40	97.0	13.1	10.7	184	136	11
12 Citizens Nat'l of Decatur	136.86	80.4	7.2	4.1	120	205	12
13 First Nat'l of Decatur	126.64	63.2	8.5	6.9	130	198	13
14 Millikin Bankshares (Decatur)	29.60	104.7	6.5	3.4	555	237	14
15 Mid America of Edgemont	28.45	75.6	0.7	22.0	224	78	15
16 First Freeport Corp	30.19	87.8	8.8	17.9	262	117	16
17 Northwest Ill Bancorp (Freeport)	72.90	82.3	8.9	15.8	118	125	17
18 First Galesburg Nat'l	93.56	106.9	7.0	6.4	127	128	18
19 First Granite City Nat'l	54.77	71.2	9.1	11.7	132	106	19
20 The First Nat'l of Highland	98.02	66.3	10.6	6.4	54	76	20
21 Elliott State Bank (Jacksonville)	173.24	46.2	11.3	7.0	59	124	21
22 City Nat'l of Kankakee	20.31	78.8	8.3	7.8	550	129	22
23 First Trust & Savings of Kankakee	90.42	88.5	7.0	15.4	100	135	23
24 First Nat'l of Moline	38.87	102.9	4.7	9.0	315	129	24
25 Moline Nat'l	26.55	64.0	8.5	8.2	400	135	25
26 First Nat'l of Morris	46.94	85.2	5.1	12.0	114	72	26
27 Grundy County Nat'l (Morris)	35.54	78.8	8.8	−1.0	167	65	27
28 Security (Mt Vernon)	161.24	108.5	10.9	20.5	54	93	28
29 Citizens Nat'l of Paris	142.53	105.2	5.8	15.8	45	73	29
30 Commercial Nat'l Corp (Peoria)	62.05	46.1	6.5	4.2	566	408	30
31 First Nat'l of Peoria	713.74	43.4	7.5	1.5	33	169	31
32 Citizens First Nat'l of Princeton	86.73	69.2	13.8	18.3	120	144	32
33 Mercantile Trust & Savings (Quincy)	88.91	70.9	9.0	16.4	120	108	33
34 American Nat'l (Rockford)	679.50	47.8	13.4	12.9	50	286	34
35 City Nat'l of Rockford	63.79	N/A	6.3	11.1	118	114	35
36 First Nat'l of Rockford	63.74	62.8	7.4	9.0	400	250	36
37 Illinois Nat'l of Rockford	100.13	N/A	5.2	11.6	250	244	37
38 Finan Ser Corp (Rock Island Bank)	36.85	97.7	11.1	−5.1	457	159	38
39 First Nat'l of Rock Island	203.36	91.5	7.0	8.6	100	194	39
40 Firstbank of Illinois (Springfield)	69.85	65.1	7.5	11.9	316	328	40
41 Illinois Nat'l Bancorp (Springfield)	31.44	39.8	6.6	6.5	507	265	41
42 Marine Bancorp (Springfield)	128.46	46.7	9.3	11.3	318	510	42
43 Central Nat'l of Sterling	29.75	60.5	8.3	8.7	336	119	43
44 First Trust & Savings of Taylorville	775.04	83.9	8.3	20.7	14	93	44
45 Busey First Nat'l (Urbana)	581.72	103.1	9.7	21.4	15	148	45
Other Illinois metropolitan averages		77.6	8.6	9.9			
Combined averages		77.1	8.3	10.9			

N/A = Not available.

EXHIBIT 5 (continued)

	Latest 12 months[a]		Equity as a % of assets 3/31/81	PE latest 12 months[a]	An- nual div.	Div. yield	Div. earn- ings	
	% Return on assets	% Return on equity						
1 First Bankshares (Alton)	0.50%	6.6%	7.5%	9.0	$ 1.15	5.2%	47.1	1
2 First UTD Bancshares (Belleville)	0.76	12.7	5.6	7.2	1.60	2.5	17.7	2
3 First Bancorp of Belleville	0.65	10.6	6.0	7.1	1.27	5.6	40.1	3
4 Mid Continent Bancshares (Belleville)	0.93	12.0	7.7	4.0	0.80	4.2	16.8	4
5 Corn Belt Bank (Bloomington)	1.77	19.4	9.2	4.0	4.00	1.6	6.4	5
6 Nat'l Bank of Bloomington	0.37	5.1	7.2	19.5	1.40	3.6	70.0	6
7 Peoples Mid Illinois Corp (Bloomington)	1.24	13.3	9.5	6.9	2.10	4.6	31.7	7
8 1st Nat'l (Centralia)	1.03	14.0	7.1	7.2	2.35	4.3	30.8	8
9 Champaign Nat'l	0.73	9.7	7.4	10.5	1.00	1.4	14.9	9
10 First Nat'l in Champaign	0.72	9.5	7.5	9.5	1.50	1.9	17.8	10
11 Palmer American Nat'l (Danville)	0.66	10.5	6.3	9.6	1.07	2.4	22.9	11
12 Citizens Nat'l of Decatur	0.72	9.6	8.0	8.6	4.00	3.6	31.2	12
13 First Nat'l of Decatur	0.85	10.1	8.3	6.5	2.00	2.5	16.4	13
14 Millikin Bankshares (Decatur)	0.33	4.7	6.9	22.1	1.32	4.3	94.3	14
15 Mid America of Edgemont	1.14	14.4	8.2	5.5	1.00	4.7	25.6	15
16 First Freeport Corp	1.12	16.8	6.8	5.5	1.40	5.3	29.2	16
17 Northwest Ill Bancorp (Freeport)	1.01	15.4	6.9	5.4	2.40	4.0	21.7	17
18 First Galesburg Nat'l	0.79	8.6	9.2	13.3	3.00	3.0	39.9	18
19 First Granite City Nat'l	0.82	11.9	6.8	6.2	2.40	6.2	38.2	19
20 The First Nat'l of Highland	0.83	11.8	6.9	5.9	2.35	3.6	21.3	20
21 Elliott State Bank (Jacksonville)	0.90	11.6	8.3	4.3	4.00	5.0	21.5	21
22 City Nat'l of Kankakee	1.27	15.0	8.7	5.6	0.56	3.5	19.5	22
23 First Trust & Savings of Kankakee	0.76	11.3	6.7	8.2	2.50	3.1	25.5	23
24 First Nat'l of Moline	1.16	12.6	9.4	8.5	2.20	5.5	46.7	24
25 Moline Nat'l	1.01	12.9	7.9	5.2	1.38	8.1	41.9	25
26 First Nat'l of Morris	1.11	14.9	7.4	5.9	2.52	6.3	37.4	26
27 Grundy County Nat'l (Morris)	0.64	7.4	9.1	11.1	1.00	3.6	39.5	27
28 Security (Mt Vernon)	1.45	15.9	9.3	7.3	4.00	2.3	16.8	28
29 Citizens Nat'l of Paris	0.96	10.9	8.8	10.0	6.75	4.5	45.1	29
30 Commercial Nat'l Corp (Peoria)	0.78	9.5	8.6	5.0	2.40	8.4	42.0	30
31 First Nat'l of Peoria	1.13	8.1	14.0	5.5	10.00	3.2	17.8	31
32 Citizens First Nat'l of Princeton	1.37	19.0	7.2	3.9	1.60	2.7	10.5	32
33 Mercantile Trust & Savings (Quincy)	1.53	15.9	9.9	4.7	3.40	5.4	25.4	33
34 American Nat'l (Rockford)	1.35	11.6	11.9	4.3	20.00	6.2	26.6	34
35 City Nat'l of Rockford	0.74	10.9	6.6	N/A	N/A	N/A	N/A	35
36 First Nat'l of Rockford	0.95	9.1	10.2	7.1	2.40	6.0	42.8	36
37 Illinois Nat'l of Rockford	2.06	17.9	10.3	N/A	N/A	N/A	N/A	37
38 Finan Ser Corp (Rock Island Bank)	0.62	6.0	10.6	16.3	1.60	4.4	72.4	38
39 First Nat'l of Rock Island	1.06	10.3	10.5	8.9	4.40	2.4	21.2	39
40 Firstbank of Illinois (Springfield)	0.85	12.4	6.7	5.3	2.80	6.2	32.7	40
41 Illinois Nat'l Bancorp (Springfield)	0.45	7.4	6.0	5.5	0.92	7.4	40.5	41
42 Marine Bancorp (Springfield)	0.90	11.2	8.0	4.4	3.00	5.0	22.0	42
43 Central Nat'l of Sterling	0.92	11.0	8.4	5.6	1.20	6.7	37.6	43
44 First Trust & Savings of Taylorville	2.15	21.0	11.3	4.5	28.00	4.3	19.4	44
45 Busey First Nat'l (Urbana)	1.14	20.2	5.8	5.4	50.00	8.3	45.3	45
Other Illinois metropolitan averages	0.98	12.0	8.2	7.6		4.3	33.0	
Combined averages	0.93	12.1	7.6	7.5		4.7	33.8	

[a] April, 1980–March, 1981
N/A = Not available.

threats. Nevertheless, it would probably have less than 50 percent control of the new holding company, even though it would be contributing the largest single block of equity. The present management thought they would thus lose control of the bank, since it would be operated as an affiliate of the holding company, and there was great uncertainty about what role Marine Bank's management would play in the management of the holding company. This particular approach had been followed in New England by such companies as Multi-Bank Financial Corporation and in Virginia by United Virginia Bankshares.

The other approach would be for the Marine Bank itself, with its strong capital position, to go out into the marketplace and acquire banks in the $50–70 million range. Since the bank did not want to buy banks with stock because its stock was selling at such a discount from book value, it would have to pay cash for any acquisitions. With over $40 million in capital, it figured it could borrow about $20 million. Accordingly, if it went into three markets, it could afford to pay about $7 million apiece for the banks. If, for discussion purposes, banks could command a 50 percent premium over book value, Staudt reckoned Marine would have to look at banks with about $5 million in capital, and given a typical 7 percent capital-to-asset ratio it would be looking at banks around $70 million in assets. If it took this approach, the bank might remain much smaller, because a number of smaller acquisitions would take a much longer time to build up to a billion dollars in asset size, but at least Marine Bank would have control of its own operation. Among the holding companies in other states that had adopted this strategy were the First of Cincinnati, First of Boston, Virginia National Bank, and Hawkeye (in Iowa), although these banks had at times had the option of acquiring banks by an exchange of shares.

Another factor Staudt had to consider was the imminence of interstate banking. His job was to figure out if Marine Bancorp's stockholders would be better off to join with other banks of similar size to form a large holding company in a relatively short period of time or to use its existing holding company to acquire smaller banks, grow somewhat more slowly, but retain control in one place. As he thought about these alternatives, two questions came to mind. First, if the holding company chose to retain control but grow more slowly, would it be able to reach a size sufficient for it to compete effectively with the much larger institutions that would be entering its market area? And second, which strategy would make Marine Bancorp a more attractive acquisition candidate for large banks in Chicago, New York, or other parts of the county?

Finally, Staudt had to think about the possible effect of the adoption of either strategy on the management of the bank. In Staudt's view, the Marine Bank, unlike a number of the banks he had seen active in the holding company business, had no succession problem. In fact, over the past few years, the bank had been able to attract a number of talented people to an already strong management group. Staudt himself had been recruited after 8 years at the Chemical Bank of New York. The bank also had been able to recruit personnel from nontraditional banking sources, such as Executive Vice-President Bob O'Keefe (whose entire background had been in manufacturing) and Vice-President Randy Peyser (who had been trained and worked as a professional librarian). Straudt had to consider whether such people would prefer to be a part of a larger, multibank holding company or whether they would prefer that Springfield Marine maintain its independent bank image and build itself through the addition of smaller banks. (See Appendix D.)

TIMING

It was urgent that the matter be settled soon, because of the lack of *de novo* language in the bill, meaning only the present universe of banks in any town could provide

EXHIBIT 6
Banks in selected Illinois cities

City (county)	1980 population	Bank	Assets, 12/31/80 (in millions)
Bloomington (McLean)	42,000 119,100	American State Bank of Bloomington	$ 75
		Corn Belt Bank	126
		McLean County Bank	74
		The National Bank of Bloomington	98
		Peoples Bank of Bloomington	119
		Prairie State Bank	16
Champaign (Champaign)	60,000 168,400	American National Bank of Champaign	65
		Bank of Illinois in Champaign	112
		The Champaign National Bank	154
		City Bank of Champaign	8
		The Commercial Bank of Champaign	55
		The First National Bank of Champaign	116
		Market Place National Bank	6
Danville (Vermillion)	42,500 95,200	Bank of Danville	27
		The First National Bank of Danville	128
		Lake Shore National Bank	17
		Palmer-American National Bank of Danville	133
		The Second National Bank of Danville	136
Decatur (Macon)	90,000 131,400	The Citizens National Bank of Decatur	215
		The First National Bank of Decatur	190
		The Millikin National Bank of Decatur	232
		Northtown Bank of Decatur	57
		The Pershing National Bank of Decatur	17
		South Shores National Bank of Decatur	16
		Soy Capital Bank and Trust Company	54
Quincy (Adams)	45,000 71,600	Community National Bank of Quincy	15
		First National Bank & Trust Co. of Quincy	61
		Illinois State Bank of Quincy	105
		Mercantile Trust & Savings Bank	109
		State Street Bank & Trust Company	42
		Town & County Bank of Quincy	19

Marine with an entry to the market. To get into a town, the bank would have to act fast and talk to the banks with which it wanted to be affiliated. Large Chicago banks, Staudt felt, had the luxury of a slower pace, because in their markets they had 407 banks to choose from. On the other hand, in Region 3 the markets were more discrete, with towns of up to 40,000 generally having three downtown banks and three outlying banks. (See Exhibit 6.) Staudt felt that for various reasons, they would probably be interested in only two of the three outlying banks and that other people would be looking at those banks as well.

Altogether, Staudt felt it was time to move and to make his recommendation to management quickly.

APPENDIX A: ASSOCIATION FOR MODERN BANKING IN ILLINOIS COMPROMISE LEGISLATIVE PROPOSAL

(Summary of SB578 as Amended)

Sponsors: Senators Keats-Sangmeister-Bloom (Representatives McPike-Polk)

This bill, as amended, will provide a means for banks to merge with other financial institutions and other banks, and promote convenience for bank customers by authorizing multioffice banking through multibank companies and one additional facility. (See Exhibit 7.)

HOLDING COMPANY PROVISIONS

1. Banks would be allowed to affiliate under common ownership through a multibank holding company. Illinois presently allows one-bank holding companies.
2. Five holding company regions would be established.
3. A multibank holding company could *acquire* banks only within the holding company's home region and *one* contiguous region.
4. After the date of enactment, newly chartered banks could not be acquired until they have been in existence for 10 years.

Other considerations:

1. Holding companies are regulated by the Federal Reserve under the Federal Bank Holding Company Act of 1956.
2. Federal law requires prior approval of acquisitions of both state and nationally chartered banks by both the Federal Reserve System and the Department of Justice.
3. The 1977 Community Reinvestment Act, a federal law, requires holding companies to demonstrate that they are serving the financial needs of the communities in which they are operating before additional banks may be acquired.
4. A multibank holding company could not charter any new (de novo) banks.

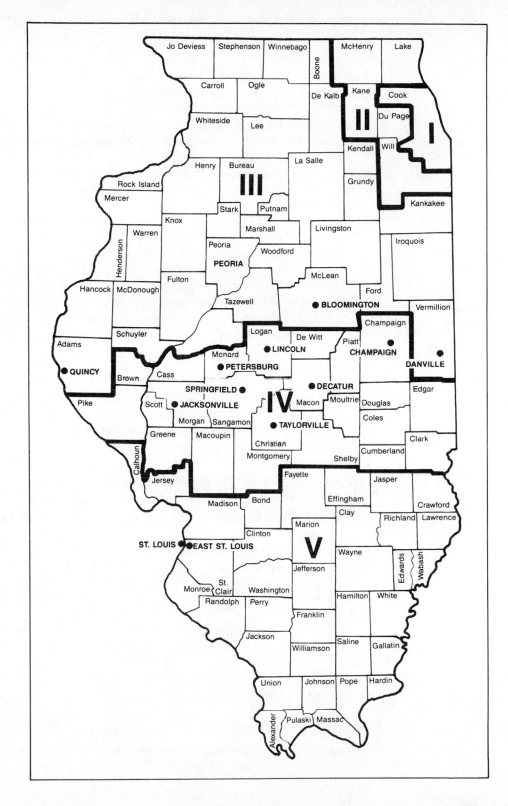

EXHIBIT 7
Proposed bank holding company regions

ADDITIONAL LIMITED
SERVICE FACILITY PROVISIONS

1. Bill allows a bank one additional facility for a total of three. Banks are presently allowed two facilities — one within 1,500 feet and another within 3,500 yards of the bank.
2. The additional one limited community service facility will be allowed only within the home office county or, if outside of the county, no further than 10 miles from the bank.
3. For the additional limited-service facility, statutory home office protection would be *one mile*. In other words, the third limited-service facility could not be established closer than one mile from the home office of another bank.
4. A bank, owned by a holding company that is based in a contiguous region, would be prohibited from establishing the facility authorized by this bill within 2 miles of a bank in any municipality of 10,000 or less population that presently has three or more banks. This "overbanked community amendment" is a further protection for existing banks. This prohibition would expire 7 years after enactment.

Other considerations:

1. The additional facility would be limited to the present powers of existing facilities including: receiving deposits; cashing and issuing checks, drafts, and money orders; changing money; and receiving payments on existing indebtedness.

APPENDIX B: ILLINOIS GOVERNOR SIGNS
LEGISLATION ALLOWING MULTIBANK FIRMS NEXT YEAR[1]

CHICAGO — The anticipated Illinois rush to form multibank holding companies has been given the final "go" sign. Gov. James R. Thompson this past weekend signed legislation allowing introduction of the multibank firms next January.

In preparation, Federal Reserve banks in St. Louis and Chicago said Monday they will begin accepting "preliminary" applications immediately.

"Applicants are welcome to come in to talk to us about their application and submit informal data," said Harold E. Uthoff, senior vice-president of the St. Louis Fed.

The St. Louis Fed will review and report initial findings to the applicants "regarding possible areas where they need to beef up."

[1] By James Rubenstein. Reprinted with permission from the *American Banker*, July 7, 1981.

ANTITRUST CONSTRAINTS

Nicholas P. Alban, assistant vice-president of the Chicago Fed, noted also that some large Loop banks "may run into anticompetitive situations" because of the language of the law that divides the state into five regions for the purpose of acquisitions.

This was a reference to Continental Illinois National Bank & Trust Co. and First National Bank of Chicago. Together they control a sizeable proportion of total state banking deposits and could be precluded from buying banks because of antitrust constraints enforced by the Fed or the antitrust division of the Justice Department.

The new law permits multibank companies to buy banks in their home regions or one contiguous region.

It also contains a provision for one additional limited-service facility, bringing to three the total allowed. These facilities are restricted to receiving deposits; cashing and issuing checks, drafts, and money orders; changing money; and receiving payments on existing indebtedness.

William C. Harris, Illinois Commission of Banks and Trust Companies, said his office on Sept. 1 will begin accepting applications to establish the third limited facility. He noted that his office has received "a good many inquiries" so far from banks as a result of the bill's passage last month by the Illinois General Assembly.

The leading supporter of the legislation, the Association for Modern Banking in Illinois, said the governor's signing of the bill "opens a new generation of progressive banking reform in Illinois."

James B. Watt, president of the group, said, "This new law will lay the cornerstone for open competition within the state's banking industry."

SURROUNDING STATES

Charles L. Daily, chairman of AMBI and of MidAmerican Bank & Trust Co. of Edgemont, East St. Louis, added in a prepared statement:

> Until now, we have been surrounded by states which already have multibank holding companies or some other form of multioffice banking — Missouri, Wisconsin, Indiana, Iowa, and Kentucky.
>
> With the advent of interstate banking just over the horizon nationally, the Illinois banking industry would have been on the brink of disaster if the General Assembly had not passed this legislation and the governor had not signed it into law.
>
> Out-of-state banks would have been able to affiliate with Illinois banks, but our own banks would not have been able to affiliate with other banks in the state.

While the association was savoring the fruits of a decades-old fight to liberalize the state's unit banking structure, the Illinois Bankers Association, a separate trade group and a loser in the battle over multibank firms, issued a new call for industry unity.

In a formal statement, James A. Fitch, president of the Illinois BA, said Illinois bankers are "battle weary" over the issue and should now "lay aside their differences and band together for the good of the people of Illinois who use banking services.

"Our customers don't want us squabbling among ourselves," he continued. "They would rather see us going to bat for them in the halls of Congress and in the recesses of regulatory agencies to bring loan rates down and interest on deposits up. Bankers fighting bankers for their own purposes does nothing to instill public confidence in the industry."

Mr. Fitch is also president of South Chicago Savings Bank.

It is unclear how AMBI will react to the Illinois BA statement.

There have been three separate trade organizations in Illinois since 1973 after AMBI, with 275 member banks, broke away from the 1,000-member Illinois BA in a dispute over branching policy. The third trade group is the Independent Community Banks in Illinois.

Mr. Watt, the AMBI president, said that organization's executive committee at a meeting in Springfield Wednesday will discuss "our future role" and Mr. Fitch's plea for reunification with the Illinois BA.

"Right at the moment we have not detected any strong movement toward our rejoining the IBA," said Mr. Watt.

Some industry observers have suggested a new trade association might be organized "combining the best elements" of both the Illinois BA and AMBI. The third group, ICBI, would be expected to remain intact because its members — mostly small downstate banks — have interests wedded more closely to a strong antibranching philosophy.

APPENDIX C: LARGE ILLINOIS BANKS START PLANNING STRATEGIES FOR NEW ERA IN STATE[1]

Multibank Holding Company Bill to Become Effective Jan. 1

CHICAGO — Banks in metropolitan Chicago and in several large downstate cities appear ready this week to lead the way in setting up multibank holding companies under an anticipated change in bank structure that would become effective next January.

In plotting acquisition strategy, large banks here and in downstate locales said

---

[1] By James Rubenstein. Reprinted with permission from the *American Banker*, June 23, 1981.

they would look first at nearby suburban areas to make initial purchases, concentrating on high-growth markets.

Despite the excitement of many bank managers who have labored long to liberalize the state's strict unit-banking laws, executives questioned about their expansion programs cautioned there could be a significant "go slow" period at first.

That would be the case, they said, if small banks ask too high a price for their stock.

In addition, high interest rates and the concern of regulators over excessive debt by some banking firms might also put a damper on the soon-to-be-born holding company movement, the executives said.

The rush to set up new bank holding companies or convert existing one-bank companies is likely to get fully underway this summer, presuming Gov. James R. Thompson signs the now-passed BHC legislation, which also gives banks an additional limited-service facility within county boundaries.

Philip W. K. Sweet, Jr., chairman of the $4.1 billion-deposit Northern Trust Co., pointed out there could be "more smoke than fire" if some outlying acquisition-minded banks jack their prices up too high.

"Some suburban banks certainly have a different philosophy on price than we do," said Mr. Sweet, noting that Northern, the city's fourth largest bank, is "examining all the acquisition possibilities in the six-county area of Chicago."

DIVIDED INTO FIVE REGIONS

As finally adopted by the Illinois House last Thursday and awaiting the governor's signature, the new bill divides the state into five regions for holding company expansion.

A multibank holding company in one region could acquire banks within its own region and one contiguous region.

Cook County (Chicago) comprises Region I, with the five collar counties of Lake, McHenry, Kane, DuPage, and Will as Region II. Three downstate areas comprise Regions III, IV, and V.

Outside of Chicago, large banks in Springfield, Rockford, Peoria, Decatur, Bloomington, and East St. Louis are also likely candidates to form holding companies, and executives of some of those banks have said that would be their intent once the law is enacted.

David E. Connor, president of the $126.6 million-deposit Commercial National Bank of Peoria and long-time downstate advocate of multibank holding companies and branching, said his institution would of course set up a holding company to acquire other banks.

"We haven't decided yet whether we want to buy banks in the Chicago collar counties (Region II) or further downstate into Region IV," said Mr. Connor, who praised the legislature for its "infinite wisdom in giving banks the option to compete."

Agreeing with the comment on inflated pricing made by Northern Trust's Mr. Sweet, the Peoria banker cautioned that some ''bank sellers might be disappointed in the eagerness of the buyers to pay the expected multiples.

''The bloom may be off the rose,'' he added, citing the less-than-optimistic outlook for earnings at many institutions.

In Chicago, Michael E. Tobin, chairman of the $1.9 billion-deposit American National Bank & Trust Co., said his bank would move as soon as feasible to establish a holding company under the Walter E. Heller International Corp. umbrella. In fact, he added, American National has already taken steps to ''reactivate'' a bank holding company.

The bank is a subsidiary of the Chicago-based Heller Corp., a commercial finance and factoring firm.

Mr. Tobin said he has also run into ''some unrealism out there'' on bank pricing.

''If the prices remain unrealistic, I can see a period of little activity'' on multibank holding companies, he said.

American National, he added, would like to expand into the collar counties, where it will seek out those banks that fit its philosophy of trying to serve small and medium-sized businesses.

Chicago's two largest banks — the $27 billion-deposit Continental Illinois National Bank & Trust Co. and the $21.4 billion-deposit First National Bank of Chicago — were generally keeping silent about their acquisition plans.

Despite the threat of antitrust rejection of prospective acquisitions, both banks are known to be scouting markets, particularly in the high-growth western suburbs of DuPage County and in Lake County, for possible partners to test ''toehold'' affiliations.

Meanwhile the estimated 55 informal banking chains spread across Regions I and II are also making plans to organize multibank holding companies in 1982. Several surveys show that out of the 1,262 Illinois banks there are 400 that could become potential affiliates of a holding company.

STILL RESTRICTIVE

Despite the general enthusiasm for the bill among many advocates of multibank holding companies, some analysts here called the proposed measure ''still fairly restrictive.''

A BHC is barred from starting de novo banks, and newly chartered institutions could not be acquired by a holding company until they had been in existence for 10 years.

Aside from BHCs, the bill also lets banks establish one additional limited-facility service for a total of three. Banks are presently allowed two facilities, one within 1,500 feet and another within 2 miles of the main office.

APPENDIX D: SENIOR MANAGEMENT PROFILES

Willard Bunn Jr., chairman of the board and chief executive officer of Marine Bancorp, Inc. and Springfield Marine Bank, was the top policy-making officer. Mr. Bunn, sixty-eight, attended Springfield Junior College and the University of Wisconsin. He joined the bank as an assistant in the Investment Department in 1935.

Willard Bunn III, president and chief operating officer of Marine Bancorp, Inc. and Springfield Marine Bank, set and monitored performance goals and provided senior supervision for both line and staff departments. He graduated from Princeton with a BA degree in 1966, and received an M.B.A. from the University of Virginia in 1968. Mr. Bunn, thirty-eight, joined the bank in 1978 as an executive vice-president.

Lee G. Gamage, executive vice-president, was in charge of the Trust Center which included the Administrative Support, Employee Benefits, Farm Management, Trust/Estate Administration, and Trust Investment Departments. Mr. Gamage, fifty-five, graduated from the University of Illinois in 1950 with a B.S. in agriculture and joined the bank in 1955 as a farm manager in the Trust Department.

Robert V. O'Keefe, executive vice-president, was head of the General Banking Services group which included the Community Services, Administrative Services, Wholesale Banking, Retail Banking, and Marketing and Product Development divisions. Mr. O'Keefe, sixty, received a B.A. degree from Dartmouth College in 1943 and joined the bank in 1980 as assistant to the chairman.

Wilbur G. Adams, senior vice-president, was head of the Administrative Services area which included the Collections Department and the Human Resources, Operations and Financial Divisions. He received a B.S. degree in commerce from the University of Kentucky in 1948. Mr. Adams, sixty, joined the bank in 1955 as an executive employee in the commercial loan area.

Donald R. Patton, senior vice-president in community services, was responsible for making the community aware of the bank and its service. Mr. Patton, fifty-nine, attended Illinois College, the University of Missouri, and the American Institute for Foreign Trade. He joined the bank in 1959 as an administrator in the Trust Department.

Stuart Brown, Jr., vice-president and cashier, headed the Retail Banking Division. He was responsible for the delivery of consumer services including retail banking, tellers, customer service, motor banks and charge cards. Mr. Brown, forty-one, received a B.A. degree from Princeton in 1962 and joined the bank in 1969 in the Operations Department.

William R. Enlow, vice-president, general counsel, and secretary of Marine Bancorp, Inc. and Springfield Marine Bank, was responsible for subsidiaries of the holding company and the management of legal affairs. A 1970 graduate of the University of Illinois, he received his Juris Doctor from the Illinois Institute of

Technology in 1979. Mr. Enlow, thirty-four, joined the bank in 1979 as a legal officer.

Ronald L. Hovermale, vice-president, was head of the Human Resources and Operations Division. He was responsible for human resource planning and development and bank operations, which included Operations, Data Processing, and Facilities Management. Mr. Hovermale, forty-two, graduated from Eastern Illinois University in 1962 and joined the bank later that year as an Assistant in the Auditing Department.

Louis Manfredo, vice-president in charge of fiscal control, was responsible for all audit and control functions. In 1950, he received a B.S. from Southern Illinois University. Mr. Manfredo, fifty-five, joined the bank in 1956 as an Executive Employee in the Auditing Department.

Don G. McNeely, vice-president, directed the correspondent banking and agribusiness departments. Mr. McNeely, forty-six, graduated with a B.S. in Animal Science from the University of Illinois in 1957. In 1963, he joined the bank as a Farm Manager in the Trust Department.

Leon J. Mizeur, vice-president of Commercial Real Estate, supervised real estate lending and loan servicing activities. Mr. Mizeur, thirty-eight, graduated from Western Illinois University in 1970 with a B.A. in Business Administration and Finance. Later that year, he joined the bank as an Administrative Assistant in the Operations Department.

J. Kent Patrick, vice-president in charge of the Data Processing Department, was Director of the Marine Bank Computer Center. Mr. Patrick, forty-four, attended Southern Illinois University in 1958 and joined the bank in 1978 as Assistant Director of the Computer Center.

J. Randall Peyser, vice-president in charge of marketing and product development, was responsible for the research and development of new bank products and services, including electronic funds transfer. Mr. Peyser, thirty-two, graduated from Duke University in 1970 with an A.B. degree and received a Master of Library Science degree from Palmer Graduate Library School in 1972. In 1981, Mr. Peyser joined the bank as a Vice President in the Trust Investments Department.

Michael J. Provines, was the manager of the Trust Center. He assisted in determining policy for the Center and its implementation. Mr. Provines, thirty-four, graduated from Eastern Illinois University in 1970. Later that year, he joined the bank as an Administrative Assistant in the Trust Investments Department.

K. M. Riley, vice-president, supervised the Asset-Based Finance Department, which included the financing of retail assets, accounts receivables, and dealer inventories. Mr. Riley, sixty-three, joined the bank in 1937 as a file clerk in the Bookkeeping Department. In 1962, he graduated from the School of Bank Administration at the University of Wisconsin.

John E. Staudt, vice-president–finance of Marine Bancorp was also vice-president and chief financial officer of Marine Bank. He was responsible for financial planning, accounting, loan review, credit analysis, and investment functions. He received a B.A. in business administration from St. Leo College in 1970 and an M.B.A. from Iona College Graduate School of Business Administration in 1977.

Mr. Staudt, thirty-three, joined the bank in 1979 as an assistant vice-president in the Correspondent Banking Department.

John M. Tallman, treasurer and comptroller of Marine Bancorp, was vice-president and comptroller of Marine Bank. He was responsible for accounting and financial controls. Mr. Tallman, fifty-five, graduated from Northwestern University in 1950 with a B.S. in accounting and joined the bank in 1955 as an executive employee in the Trust Department.

Dewey R. Yaeger, vice-president, was head of the Commercial Banking Division. He was responsible for the development of commercial banking and all commercial credit services. Mr. Yaeger, forty-one, graduated from Illinois State University with a B.S. degree in 1962 and joined the bank later that year as an administrative assistant in the Commercial Loan Department.

SPECIALTY PRODUCTS DIVISION — CONTINENTAL PACKAGING COMPANY

STRATEGY IMPLEMENTATION AT SPECIALTY PRODUCTS, 1984–1985

Continental Packaging Company's Product Line and Customers

Continental Packaging Company (CPC) was founded almost 150 years ago. After a long and successful history, Continental Packaging Company was acquired by BMF International in 1967. CPC's products include a wide variety of paper packaging materials and office products. CPC was organized into three businesses based upon types of customers. Of the three business units, Distribution Division concentrated its efforts on several thousand distributors of office and stationery products. Retail Division sold directly to certain large retail outlets. Specialty Products had a very narrowly focused business — a few very large accounts which required slightly customized products in large batches. Specialty Products was considerably smaller in sales dollars than its sister units — hence its name. Specialty Products had to take care not to intrude upon Distribution Division or Retail Division territory and customers.

In recent years, CPC had experienced some performance problems. Its leadership position eroded in some markets. Exhibit 1 shows the strategic capability profile of CPC. Some of CPC's strengths included its superior distribution channels, ability to manage financial affairs, availability of financial resources (being a division of BMF International), and its market share in college and commercial markets. On the other hand, CPC's executives believed that the company was relatively weak in product development, costs were too high, and CPC's profitability lagged behind competitors'.

The 1984 Strategic Planning Effort

When Neil Greene was appointed president of CPC in 1982, the division faced serious difficulties. Because CPC's business depends upon a derived demand, and because CPC customers are very sensitive to general economic conditions, CPC suffered during the 1981–1982 recession. Some executives felt that, prior to Greene's

Case prepared by Charles Stubbart, University of Massachusetts, © 1986. Reprinted by permission.

EXHIBIT 1
Continental
Packaging
Company's
strategic
capability
profile

	Strength rating (+3 to −3)[a]	Importance rating (0 to +3)[b]
Marketing		
Market share		
Retail Division	+1	+2
Distributor Division	+3	+2
Specialty Products Division	0	+1
Product line	+1	+2
Recognition by market	+1	+2
Market research	+2	+1
Awareness customer needs	−1	+3
Advertising	−1	+2
Sales force	−1	+3
Distribution	+2	+3
Product management	−1	+3
Product design	0	+2
Product development		
New products design	0	+2
Rate of new products introduction	−2	+1
Product development,		
Facilities and personnel	+1	+1
Manufacturing		
Costs	−2	+3
Manufacturing costs	−2	+3
Production control	+3	+2
Flexibility	0	+1
Adequate facilities	−1	⏐2
Cost of materials	−1	+1
Reliability of supplies	+1	+1
Capacity	0	+2
Financial		
Financial abilities	+1	⏐2
Management information systems	+2	+1
Financial resources	0	+2
Human resources		
Personnel policies	0	+1
Union relations	+2	+2
Turnover	+2	+1
Skill and commitment		
of work force	+1	+2
Corporate management		
Profitability	−1	+3
Senior management	−1	+3
Planning	−2	+2
Control	+1	+1
Coordination and communications	+1	+2
Organizational structure	−1	+1
Climate	−1	+2

EXHIBIT 1 (continued)

EXHIBIT 1 (continued)

Principal opportunities and threats — 1984

Opportunities
Expand market share in fast-growing wholesale segment
Expand market share in fast-growing info-processing market
Cost reduction
Develop human resources
Expand Specialty Products segment

Threats
Not positioned for new products
Changing wholesaler strategies
Undermotivated, uninspired work force
Specialty Products diverts resources better used elsewhere
Unresponsive to customer needs
Change in competitor's strategies
Commodity orientation of customers

---

[a] +3 to −3, where +3 is very strong, −3 very weak in comparison to competitors.
[b] 0 to 3, where 3 is very important.

arrival, the division had been (perhaps unconsciously) "milked." Greene concluded that many long-standing problems had progressed to a dangerous stage, that the business was unfocused, and that some type of genuine strategic planning was long overdue. Strategic planning attempts during earlier years created plans that were never adequately implemented. Executives' sentiments generally converged with Greene's thinking — something big was needed — a turnaround.

During summer of 1984, using the guidance of a consultant, fifteen top executives of CPC gathered frequently to initiate strategic planning. No fewer than 6 entire working days were spent off-site, and several series of 3 half-day, on-site sessions were held. Top executives spent hundreds of hours doing planning. Some of the planning activities included strategic capability profiles, environmental analysis, customer profiles, competitor profiles, product analysis, critical success factors, scenario generation, setting objectives, and action plans.

Initially, some executives felt skeptical about the value of this planning exercise, and some participants were reluctant to divulge everything they knew.

Comments by Executives About the 1984 Strategic Planning

During fall of 1984 (after that first year's planning sessions had concluded) CPC executives characterized the planning done that summer:

The first thing I wondered was, "How honest do they really want us to get?"

I knew it would be successful because I've seen strategic planning done elsewhere.

Greene initiated it, but he stayed in the background. He wanted to know what we thought. Greene makes me nervous when he does this.

I learned an incredible amount about our business.

When Greene came in, he realized we needed some direction. This was his way of getting it.

We did planning before, but that planning never really amounted to much. Distractions were pouring over the walls. The plans never got implemented. Those plans didn't have actions specified. These do. For example, the old plan said "de-emphasize a certain business," but nothing happened. The new plan says "stop doing a certain business by Tuesday" and it gets stopped.

It was a good idea to go off-site.

The plan gives us a common language.

The plan suits Greene's style perfectly. He is a man who wants thorough preparations and no loose ends. Greene says, "Do it right, do it once, do it now."

Given the history of the company and the style of Greene's predecessor, this is a hard religion for us to practice. But we are making strides.

Greene inherited some good programs.

When we did planning before Greene arrived, the same problems and issues came up. But the management situation couldn't resolve conflicts so nothing much was done. Fortunately, Greene doesn't have to face that.

Brother, I'm not sure we can do the things the plan calls for.

I'm not sure we understand what we're doing.

Implementing the plans is forcing some painful issues.

Planning is worthwhile. Changed our direction.

The good recent results we've had don't really come from the plan.

The plan identified goals. Easy. Now we're down to the level of people, systems, dollars, information. It's getting harder.

Greene was quite a shock to the CPC system. He's very different from his predecessor, MacDonald. Greene is aloof and reserved, MacDonald was gregarious. Greene is circumspect, while MacDonald was a "straight-ahead" fellow. Greene understands marketing and strategy, MacDonald was an operations man. . . . Strategic planning served as a way for us to get to know Greene, and vice versa.

The strategic plan stated several ambitious financial and product objectives for CPC:

$20 million after-tax profit by 1987

Increase sales 12–15 percent per year

Increase productivity 15 percent by 1987

An 8 percent return on sales after tax

Actions plans included:

Prune the product line

Reorganization

Improved service

Install an MBO system

A renewed emphasis was placed on concentrating CPC efforts on critical challenges to the firm.

MEET PAUL GOODMAN

Paul Goodman works as the operations manager for CPC. He is in his midthirties. Paul has a wife and two children. He is a jogger and an exsmoker. Paul graduated from Lowell Tech. with a bachelor of science degree in industrial management in 1971. His first job was with American Optical Company, where he held positions in distribution, warehousing, engineering, and production control. Paul came to CPC in 1977. He moved from production control manager to bindery plant manager. In 1981 corrugated products were added to his responsibilities. In July 1984 he was appointed operations manager for CPC.

His office is located in a hundred-year-old manufacturing facility beside a canal, near several sets of railroad tracks. The plant sits in an old, somewhat run-down, New England manufacturing center of intermediate size. CPC headquarters sits in a modern glass building located about 10 minutes away.

A consistent management style and philosophy shape his interactions with coworkers. Paul always notices and deals with the interpersonal elements of situations — the intentional and unintentional impacts of words and events. He demonstrates particularly good skills for giving feedback or direction in sticky situations, such as performance appraisals or when failures occur. But his style also accommodates open expressions of anger or enthusiasm. Paul constantly seeks to find the positive elements in a situation and work with them — what he calls "problem-tunities." Paul likes numbers. On the other hand, he does not have extraordinary faith in what he refers to as "bean-counting," although he usually seems to know exactly how many beans there are.

Paul is strongly committed to his marriage and his family. He will sometimes put aside work demands in favor of pressing family concerns. He worries that the work demands placed upon a company executive might erode the quality of family life. Paul leaves the plant at quitting time, usually taking some work home in his briefcase.

In the late summer and early fall of 1984 Paul Goodman was a very busy man. He had just received his promotion. At the same time, he attended an executive M.B.A. program at a well-known nearby university. Besides all that, he was a member of the strategic planning group which was meeting regularly to deal with the future strategy of CPC.

Among Paul's numerous new responsibilities in fall of 1984 was the general management of Specialty Products. Paul remarked that he found this new responsibility for Specialty Products ironic because as a factory executive, "I used to be against this business!" He explained that the special requirements and operations of Specialty Products diverted plant personnel from more important operations supporting the other two units — Distribution Division and Retail Division.

Actually, Paul welcomed the chance to take responsibility for a profit center, realizing that his upward mobility would be limited if he did not broaden his experience from manufacturing operations to include marketing, finance, and so on.

Exhibit 2 depicts CPC organization in fall 1984. Under this organization, Specialty Products reported to the manufacturing vice-president. CPC executives explained that they could not afford a traditional product-line divisional setup because of the extra costs required.

EXHIBIT 2 Continental Packaging Company's organization structure

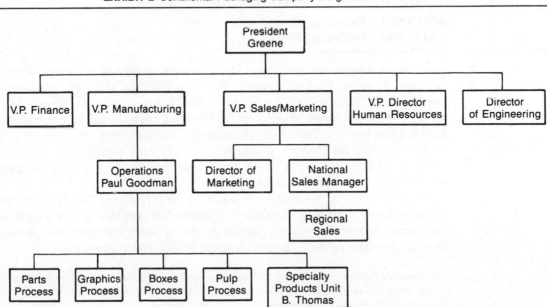

In the past, Specialty Products had never been considered an important part of CPC. In fact, during the 1984 strategic planning sessions, executives among the planning group seriously considered whether Specialty Products ought to be divested or, more likely, simply disbanded. Many executives argued that Specialty Products was a distraction and that margins would never reach satisfactory levels. CPC nearly abandoned Specialty Products. At times, however, Specialty Products looked good. When Retail Division and Distribution Division lagged, causing excess capacity in the plant to hurt profits, Specialty Products was the mechanism for soaking up that excess capacity. However, when business was good for Retail Division and Distribution Division, Specialty Products faded into a distinctly secondary role. Paul called this phenomenon "the light-switch business." Ultimately, Specialty Products survived this scrutiny — but only as a means for soaking up unused capacity — not as a genuine opportunity area. In fact, Specialty Products' mission expressly ruled out additional investment for Specialty Products except under extraordinary circumstances.

Exhibits 3 and 4 show financial data for the BMF International and the CPC. Although Specialty Products was expected to lose money in 1984, certain ambiguities remained. First, executives at Specialty Products argued that they received allocations for too much division overhead. Second, analysts could not calculate precisely how much assets were committed to Specialty Products. The reason for this confusion was that all three business units shared the same products (to a degree) and the same intermingled manufacturing equipment and processes in the plant.

SPECIALTY PRODUCTS
FALL 1984–SUMMER 1985

Bob Thomas manages the Specialty Products unit. He has been working for Continental about 20 years. Prior to managing Specialty Products, Bob held positions in manufacturing, customer service, and sales. Bob is a friendly, open person, with a smile always ready. People at CPC comment that Bob knows the products particularly well and that he loves new ideas. Occasionally, Bob has been criticized for what some people call his tendency to charge off in too many directions at once. Bob counters, "You've got to take advantage of your opportunities when you get them, not necessarily when you are ready for them."

Specialty Products concentrates its efforts in New England. The customer base includes mainly very large divisions of Fortune 500 companies with a need for customized packaging products. Special decorated boxes constitute the principal product. Specialty Products' mission is stated in the 1984 strategic plan:

> *Specialty Products is specifically authorized to pursue any customer who offers the potential for large orders of custom merchandise for resale. Specialty Products will be addressed as a growth business with the particular intent to use excess capacity. New business will be at 20 percent margin or better. Major capital investment to support this market will*

EXHIBIT 3
BMF International's
recent performance

	1980	1981	1982	1983	Projected 1984
Net sales ($000)	$899,188	$910,965	$968,491	$990,122	$1,130,000
Earnings as a percent of sales	5.6	4.7	5.3	3.6	4.5
Return on equity	17.9%	14.7%	16.5%	10.8%	15.1%

EXHIBIT 4 Operating performance and projections for Continental Packaging Company

					Projected			
	1980	1981	1982	1983	1984	1985	1986	1987
Sales	$131,682	$152,524	$151,846	$175,883	$185,477	$190,816	$220,245	$237,861
Gross profit from sales	43,191	51,400	47,831	59,624	61,763	66,976	80,389	87,532
General and administrative expenses	29,628	35,843	37,354	46,608	47,111	49,039	53,960	55,897
Selling expenses	29,628	35,843	37,354	46,608	47,111	49,039	53,960	55,897
Depreciation	3,400	3,400	2,500	5,300	3,820	4,120	4,400	4,400
Capital expenditures	8,200	9,600	5,000	2,500	2,800	6,000	6,000	6,000
Net earnings	8,296	9,304	7,896	7,563	8,160	9,350	12,554	15,461

Note: Figures in thousands of dollars.

not be made, except in unusual circumstances and after very careful examination and justification.

Recently, Specialty Products had suffered several serious reverses:

Customers, shocked by the economic contraction and high interest rates, began managing their inventories more tightly to help their cash flow.

Although Specialty Products produced custom products, customers remained sensitive to prices. Specialty Products' standard costs rose 13 percent in the most recent year in spite of continued efforts (such as installing a class-A MRP system) to drive down labor and materials costs.

Several serious quality problems upset sales efforts.

Sales force morale hit an all-time low. Without clear objectives, having little training, and believing themselves "second-class citizens" compared to salespeople in other divisions, the Specialty Products' sales effort floundered.

On the other hand, Thomas believed that Specialty Products could produce the best-made products on the market, that his in-house customer service constituted an important advantage, and that CPC's vertical integration and skillful inventory planning formed an advantage. The key problem was, according to Thomas: "How can I increase sales, increase market share, and increase margins in the face of high costs and no investment?"

Specialty Products encountered a large number and variety of competitors. Many of these companies offered only a very narrow product line from a single type of material or in just a few types of construction, choosing to compete in local or regional markets. Thus, Specialty Products faced different competitors for nearly every account. These accounts ordinarily divided their purchases among two, three, or four suppliers, preferring not to rely on a single supplier. Most supply relationships in the industry last a long time. Although binders with this type of packaging did not constitute a significant cost for most customers, nevertheless, mistakes, problems, and shortages in supply could severely disrupt a customer's operations — imposing large costs.

Specialty Products' affiliation with CPC provided an advantage insofar as customers believed that they could rely on CPC's distribution efficiency and financial health. But the image of "bigness" also carried a cost. Customers regarded Specialty Products (and CPC) as "stodgy," not dynamic. Worse, some customers (with justification) doubted CPC's long-term commitment to their particular market.

In fall of 1984, Goodman and Thomas tried to define Specialty Products' competitive situation. They called in a consultant to help them with strategic planning. Here are excerpts of an initial discussion:

Bob: As you know, Paul, Specialty Products is only a small part of the CPC pie. First, you've got Distribution Division serving the wholesalers, the contract stationers, and dealers. That's $140 million. Then there's Retail Division which takes care of another large market. Another $50 million there. Also, there was Chain, which was about $15 million — but CPC decided as a result of the 1984 planning to get out of that business. Finally, here we are at Specialty Products. We take our business from large, corporate accounts. We only take very large orders, at least $500,000 each, and we provide semicustomized products.

Paul: We get the low-margin business.

Bob: That's it.

Paul: What do we have going for us?

Bob: Well, CPC is one of the biggest, oldest, and most respected firms in the industry. The customers say that CPC can provide fast service plus a broad line of products, and we have distribution everywhere. Also, in the past, anyway, our quality has been superior in areas such as packaging, shipping, and products themselves.

Paul: But we've got high costs, right?

Bob: Yes, and that's a constant problem. Our customers will sometimes pay a little extra for quality, service, and so forth, but not much more.

Paul: That's why we've always been forced into price-cutting, and that's why margins are never good for Specialty Products.

Bob: Exactly. The sales force, whose compensation is tied to sales volume, can't resist the temptation to cut prices and promise the world. The sales force is coming off a very bad year. No bonuses. They are very demoralized.

Paul: So the problem is, how do you differentiate and innovate in a traditional, high-cost business?

Bob: Right.

Paul: According to the objectives for Specialty Products contained in the 1984 strategic plan, we need 20 percent margins and 4 percent return-after-taxes while increasing business from $8.2 million to $10.9 million.

Bob: A mighty tall order. Plus, you've got to consider that CPC won't make any capital expenditures for Specialty Products.

Paul: How do we define this market? Where do we start?

Bob: Well, one problem is that nobody keeps organized data about our business. All we have to go on are rumors, our experience, etc. We presently serve a number of very large accounts. These people always use multiple sources. For most of these accounts we are number 1 or number 2.

Paul: We've been losing ground with some of these accounts, right?

Bob: That's right. We've lost our relative share with some accounts, such as Western. Others, like Macintosh, have even displaced us to a lower slot. Most of these defeats have been caused by quality problems. There was that green gunk on some binders that we shipped to Phillips. There was that mistaken color for Becker. Altogether we've got twelve big accounts. Our competitors for this business are basically small, poorly financed outfits who serve very limited geographic areas or who go for a product niche.

Paul: We're going for customized business on basically standard products.

Bob: Yes. But I've got an idea for a four-color printing process that we could work on. For this, we would go to all kinds of corporations who publish boxes holding product information, for example. We can provide a colorful, splashy product that other suppliers can't touch. CPC even has the printing capability for this. I've already talked to advertisers about this idea.

THE COURSE OF EVENTS

This section contains a brief synopsis of important events involving implementation of CPC's plans for Specialty Products between summer of 1984 and fall of 1985.

Late Summer 1984

In July, CPC presented its strategic plan to BMF International. Executives at the parent company examined financial relationships. How much profit will CPC contribute? How much investment will be needed? They seemed to view Greene's planning efforts as slightly eccentric — "Greene's thing." Nevertheless, Greene found that the plan provided good justifications for his requests. The parent company accepted the goals outlined in the CPC plan.

The overall 1984 CPC strategic planning had finished. Executives began implementing action plans.

Serious quality problems continued to plague Specialty Products. For example, there was the infamous case of the green gunk on a product. Extensive investigation revealed that the green gunk originated in a chemical reaction brought about by exposing plated metals to moisture. Another emergency rocked the unit when a large customer received a shipment of boxes with discolored covers.

October 1984

Goodman and Thomas remained uncertain about plans to submit for their upcoming planning review meeting. They suspected that Greene harbored ideas about what Specialty Products' plans ought to entail. But Greene would not reveal his ideas. What did Greene want? Goodman took advantage of occasions when Greene was present to initiate informal discussions with Greene. The closest Greene came to evaluating Goodman's trial balloons during these asides was to remark cryptically: "You are teetering on the edge of acceptable."

Goodman and Thomas were having trouble answering basic strategy questions about Specialty Products: What was their market position? How did customers view Specialty Products/CPC? How could Goodman and Thomas discern whether a particular plan would be acceptable to Greene before having to present that plan? The most troublesome question was: "How can Specialty Products differentiate itself?" Goodman jokingly referred to one possible strategy, "We can ship you high-cost products better than anyone."

Goodman made informal contacts with quality control, accounting, marketing, and finance. How would other departments of CPC react to potential Specialty Products plans?

Thomas approached advertising agencies with his idea about a new product — the four-color lithographed cover for boxes. He claimed that nobody else had anything like it. He felt sure that CPC would manufacture this technically difficult product.

Specialty Products was experiencing paperwork snafus in October. Other departments found it hard and/or annoying to deal with the special routines needed for Specialty Products shipments, customer service, and accounting.

Goodman and Thomas tried to outline a planning document for Specialty Products. They wondered about major uncertainties. What should they include? What sequence should they follow for presenting topics? How much quantitative data? What promises are they willing to make? What kind of plan did Greene want?

Parts of that discussion follow:

Bob: Well, I've got an idea of what the plan should contain. Here it is. [shows Goodman some notes] I'd say we have 20 percent of the publisher's business. High costs hurt us. The market size is probably $400 million. Maybe the market is called "custom decorated products."

Paul: We need more information about competitors in there.

Bob: OK. I'll put in Benson, Coral, and Great Lakes.

Paul: You're kidding. Benson is in there?

Bob: Sure, they're in there. They do Washington Products.

Paul: Well, suppose the segment is $60 million, and we should say we have 10–20 percent.

Bob: I'd say $75 million.

Paul [figuring on a pad]: Let's call it 15 percent. Do we have 80 percent of our business in publishers? What do you call Honeywell? Western is different?

Bob: Call it the corporate segment.

Paul: Who else is a big competitor for the corporate business?

Bob: Nickelstone.

Paul: I never heard of Nickelstone.

Paul: Can we classify these competitors? Who is the toughest?

Bob: Probably Denton, then Creighton.

Paul: How do these competitors see us?

Bob: We're General Motors. We're an ocean liner and they are rowboats. Our size worries them. When we sneeze, they catch cold.

Paul: Let's hope we are not the *Titanic!*

Paul [reaching into his filing cabinet]: I think we should take another look at the CPC plan to get more ideas.

Bob: You know, what worries me most is that our excess capacity is in the traditional boxes. That area is not growing. That is not the best place to look for new business. I've got ideas for new materials, special printing, exciting new constructions. There are your growth areas. I personally feel we should go more for your growth areas.

Paul: We don't have the capacity. That's not our mission.

Bob: What does Greene want to see in this plan? He's a marketing man.

Paul: I'm not sure. He plays it pretty close to the vest. He'll make changes. If there are problems, he'll see them.

Bob: I feel as if we're in a defensive position.

Paul: Yeah, the squeaky wheel at CPC.

Bob: I hope the plan isn't set in concrete. Costs are the major issue.

Goodman began attacking Specialty Products' quality problems. Goodman revamped procedures for shipping Specialty Products' items, adding a final, extra quality-control inspection. He conducted meetings with manufacturing and shipping personnel in the plant to impress upon them that Specialty Products' could not afford any more quality slip-ups.

The Executive Committee (CPC's senior executives) met on October 15 to examine budgets based on functional and business unit plans derived from CPC's strategic plan. After hearing the Specialty Products plan (detailed in Exhibit 5), Greene concluded: "Sounds like the same old stuff to me. You wanted support. I'm giving it [in reference to an approval for a new job position for Specialty Products]. Now go out and get some growth."

The executive committee raised the 1985 Specialty Products sales target to $14 million from Goodman's proposal of $13 million. After the meeting, in an aside,

EXHIBIT 5
Outline of Specialty
Products' strategic
plan, October 15,
1983

1. *Charter/Mission*
   Growth business . . . unused production capacity . . . large corporate customers . . .
   custom products . . . no investment except unusual circumstances
2. *Situation*
   Concentrate in Northeast
   Few customers, mostly large divisions of Fortune 500 firms
   Binder products
   "Good" market share
3. *Problems*
   Economy hurt customers
   High costs, heavy overhead allocations
   Quality problems
   Demoralized salesforce
   Long lead-time on new product
   Regional approach limits sales
   Paperwork confusion
4. *Strengths*
   Good service due to MRP and specialized customer service
   Part of a Fortune 500 company
   Excess capacity?
   Broad line in collateral products
   Excellent distribution system
   Good product engineering
5. *Product Strategy*
   Use excess capacity
   New products
6. *Projections*

	1984	1985	1986	1987
Sales (millions)	10.0	11.3	13.5	16.5
Percent increase	0	13	20	22
Margin percent	20	23	22	21.5

Marketing Vice-President McCracken confided to Goodman, "What you have is OK, but it needs a spark." Goodman considered that meeting "a base hit, not a home run."

Here are some comments about Specialty Products from top executives after hearing Specialty Products' plans explained by Goodman.

Joe Parker, vice-president of manufacturing:

In the past, CPC has never taken Specialty Products seriously. Now that is changed. The plan Goodman and Thomas are proposing is good. Our competitors are vulnerable. Perhaps the plan is even too modest. Goodman and Thomas are too conservative. . . . Sounds like the same old stuff to me. . . . They do have organizational problems at Specialty Products, especially in the area of sales force training. Unit needs strong direction. You can achieve more sales and higher margins with better sales effort. Sure, it's unusual for a business unit to report to manufacturing, but we can't afford high-priced organizational structures. I'm thrilled about the prospects for Specialty Products. I like a challenge. In 6 or 8 months we'll know.

Frank Holden, vice-president of finance:

Specialty Products is only 5 percent of CPC's business. Some people think it could be more. I'm not sure. You could call me a borderline believer. In 1984 we missed all our targets for Specialty Products. Specialty Products has a low margin, and it's declining . . . quality problems. Specialty Products isn't even as good as it looks, because allocations of costs are dubious. It reminds me of a business we had at another company where I worked. People kept asking, "When will we crack this big market?" We never did. Getting more business and more margin will be tough. We need to see good progress in 1985. A critical year.

Dick McCracken, vice-president of marketing:

The Goodman-Thomas plan needs more work. Right now there is a widening gap between the plans and slipping results. Maybe they are now bottoming out. Specialty Products has to grow like hell. Bigger steps. Run fast. New organizational setup is real good. They need the sales manager position. . . . Problems with the customer service department. The four-color idea is interesting. Thomas knows the factory and he knows the products. Unless we come up with something new, we can't get the margins. Nasty quality problems must be solved. I think Specialty Products can meet the objectives; we just don't know all the steps yet. Plans aren't finished. We need to pin our hopes to attainable things . . . solid steps, no panaceas. Thomas shouldn't conclude that everything is okay now that they have a sales manager. My role is to help them with their marketing.

Phil Townsend, vice-president of human resources:

I don't really know much about the Specialty Products plan, except in those respects which involve personnel. My experience has been that you can't consider national accounts a real market. Customers want a broad-based supplier for these products. I don't think you can be a specialty supplier of particular products over the long run. . . . I would only intervene in their planning if they were screwing up.

Neil Greene, president:

I'm supporting Specialty Products because I think they have a market there.

November 1984   At Goodman's initiative, Specialty Products reorganized. (See Exhibit 6.) Thomas returned to an inside office (next to Goodman) from working in the field. Discussion began concerning prospects for a sales manager position. New positions were, at that time, very hard to get approved. Greene promised Goodman that the position would receive approval.

Goodman and Thomas met with their Specialty Products sales force to explain the thrust of strategic planning and the recent changes in Specialty Products' organization. Thomas was particularly enthusiastic during the sessions. A salesman remarked,

EXHIBIT 6
Specialty Products
unit reorganization

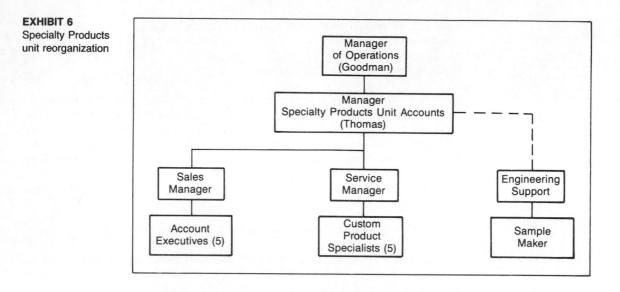

"For the first time, we have a direction." Goodman and Thomas concluded that morale had improved.

Goodman intervened to smooth ruffled feathers in disputes between Thomas and Callahan. Customer Service found Specialty Products' demands increasingly difficult to satisfy. Callahan did not like working for Thomas. Emotions ran high as Goodman spent hours with the two of them, seeking resolutions for their problems. After an extended meeting of Goodman, Thomas, and Callahan, the issue seemed ironed out.

"The spirit is here," commented Goodman. "It was a big move to get Thomas inside, instead of on the road."

Improved quality-control procedures were now firmly in place.

Goodman began working with flow charts, trying to translate the strategy he had presented to the Executive Committee into specifics. He said, "We need to know who is going to do what." He began to draft a written plan, which he said he would give to Greene. The consultant helped Goodman write the plan. Greene had not asked for a written plan.

December 1984   Goodman confided to the consultant, "I wish we were moving faster." Sales and profit figures revealed that Specialty Products fell far short of its 1984 budget requirements. (See Exhibit 7.) Goodman and Thomas could feel the psychological pressure-level rising. Specialty Products' shortcomings became a topic of frequent, sometimes bitter comment. At the December profit and loss meeting Greene commented, "Either we are going to grow this business [Specialty Products] or we are going to shut it down." Goodman and Thomas worried. Goodman remarked that the excitement had left him sleepless at night once or twice.

Discussions and feedback between Thomas and a higher-up outside the official

EXHIBIT 7
1984 actual
performance versus
budget, Specialty
Products

	1984 Budget	1984 Actual
Revenues		
Net sales	$12,309	$ 9,600
Direct costs	9,594	7,815
Gross margin	2,715	1,785
As percent of net sales	22.1%	18.6%
Variances (see Note)	374	794
Gross profit	2,341	991
As percent of net sales	19.0%	10.3%
Operating expenses		
Selling	663	666
Warehousing	1,047	850
Transportation	85	68
Total operating expense	1,795	1,584
As percent of net sales	14.6%	16.5%
Contribution	546	(593)
As percent of net sales	4.4%	(6.1)%
Overhead expenses		
Research and engineering	215	204
General and administrative	511	345
Corporate overhead	129	126
Total overhead	855	675
As percent of net sales	7.0%	7.0%
Earnings before tax	$ (309)	$(1,268)

Note: Figures in thousands of dollars. Continental Packaging Company
computed "direct costs" at a standard, then figured in any variance from
standard costs as an expense.

chain of command confused Thomas and annoyed Goodman. Angry words were exchanged between Goodman and one of his superiors.

Marketing Vice-President McCracken continued to make supportive asides to Goodman. McCracken commented that he was pleased by changes in Specialty Products.

The Thomas/Callahan dispute continued to simmer.

January 1985 The Specialty Products plan, revamped to reflect changes mandated by November's budget meeting, was formally presented to Greene. At that meeting, Goodman used transparencies to convey their plans. (See Exhibit 8.) Basically, the revised plan entailed: pushing three new product variations, continuing to investigate the new four-color process, solving quality problems, increasing penetration into existing accounts, and reorganizing. Sales volume growth targets were upped from original 12–22 percent yearly to 25 percent yearly. The Executive Committee agreed that more work on the Specialty Products plan was needed. Some executives remained

EXHIBIT 8
Specialty Products'
strategic plan

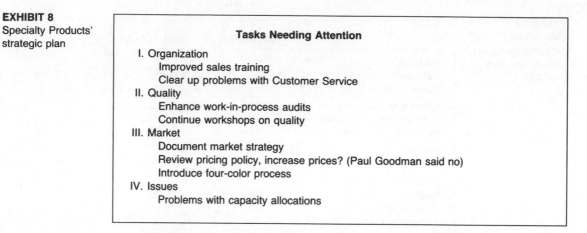

Tasks Needing Attention

I. Organization
  Improved sales training
  Clear up problems with Customer Service
II. Quality
  Enhance work-in-process audits
  Continue workshops on quality
III. Market
  Document market strategy
  Review pricing policy, increase prices? (Paul Goodman said no)
  Introduce four-color process
IV. Issues
  Problems with capacity allocations

skeptical. Greene decided that the latest month for Specialty Products was "semi-solid."

End-of-the-year work overwhelmed planning. Planning projects were all put on a back burner. Goodman's other operating responsibilities dominated his time.

CPC executives and salesmen attended their annual sales meeting in Florida. At an awards banquet (where Specialty Products received no awards) Goodman commented to Greene, "Next year we are going to win all the prizes." Greene responded, "I'd love to worry about that."

February 1985

Goodman and Thomas met with their sales force for 3 days. They discovered that the sales force was "loaded with useful competitive information." The sales force evidently appreciated the attention.

Greene remarked to Goodman (after 2 months of improving sales volume), "It's no longer a question of whether Specialty Products will succeed. It is a question of when." Goodman was pleased with the recent sales volume increases, but he still worried that the key to a successful strategy was somehow missing. He also worried that his margins were not high enough. (See Exhibit 9.)

According to Goodman, Thomas was beginning to lose sight of their strategic trajectory. Goodman constantly coaxed Thomas away from tempting new products and from under operating details. Goodman told Thomas to concentrate on the strategic aspects of the situation.

March 1985

Thomas now had his sights set on the VHS/video market, an exciting, rapidly growing business. According to Thomas, Specialty Products could manufacture and print the product packaging for video tapes. "The computer revolution will replace paper. It's so exciting! But not if you sell traditional products. If you sell traditional products, it stinks," he explained.

Specialty Products margins hovered around 16 percent. Goodman complained, "This is not good enough." A senior consultant observed that CPC remained wedded

EXHIBIT 9
1984 monthly gross margins for Specialty Products

Month	Actual margin	Budgeted margin
January	17.7	25.1
February	21.2	24.7
March	22.5	26.3
April	17.9	26.0
May	21.9	25.3
June	21.0	27.1
July	22.0	25.6
August	18.0	24.4
September	20.4	26.6
October	20.4	25.9
November	21.0	24.7
December	26.1	25.1

to sales performance rather than profitability. Improving sales volume for Specialty Products seemed to relieve some pressure from top management.

Goodman was now convinced that Specialty Products needed more business from its present customers rather than new customers. "We need to make them addicts." Until then he had been uncertain whether the strategy should concentrate on getting more business from old customers or finding new customers. Thomas was not happy with Goodman's conclusion. Thomas favored finding new products and new customers.

Goodman mentioned a recent visit of two important customers of Specialty Products, who confided that, with the improvement in Specialty Products' quality that they had experienced (and the resulting increased reliability of Specialty Products), they would give Specialty Products a greater proportion of their business.

Goodman learned about a letter from Greene to another unit, advising that unit: "You ought to copy the activities of Specialty Products. It's gaining credibility."

Goodman reflected: "Greene has given us everything we've asked for so far. He's letting us do it our way. If we don't produce, we have no rock to hide behind."

Specialty Products' new quality-control system detected a big quality problem, saving an important shipment. Goodman and Thomas were ecstatic and elated.

Problems between the Customer Service department and Specialty Products reached another boiling point. Thomas and Callahan argued vehemently. Goodman intervened.

Goodman was now working on competitive analyses. He still was not quite sure where Specialty Products had a competitive advantage or could develop one. "What is CPC? What is Specialty Products? What the hell are we? How can we make customers want us?" Paul wondered.

Martha (administrative assistant to Goodman) was busy learning to use their microcomputer. Martha's analysis of the margin shortfall helped Goodman and Thomas to stave off pressure from their superiors (and a consultant) advocating price hikes. The microcomputer provided forecasts of margins, based on different pricing structures, various mixtures of accounts, and various volumes of sales. Everyone was impressed with the new technology.

Goodman wondered if he could find a way to use MRP to achieve a competitive advantage. (MRP is an inventory management system which strives to limit work-in-process and other inventories to levels adequate to maximum efficiency. About 5,000 firms use MRP in some form.) CPC claimed that it was among the 5 percent of ''best'' users. Goodman had been a major force behind the installation of MRP at CPC.

April 1985

Goodman concluded that Specialty Products could double its business through its existing accounts. ''Do what you've got right. Get more of what you've got,'' he reasoned.

At a meeting of CPC's Executive Committee (Excom), Goodman presented Specialty Products' latest financial results and ideas. (See Exhibit 10.) Specialty Products'

EXHIBIT 10
Specialty Products' actual performance versus budget 1985

	1985 Budget	Projected 1985 actual*
Revenues		
Net sales	$10,000	$12,000
Direct costs	8,581	10,189
Gross margin	2,401	2,185
As percent of net sales	21.9%	17.7%
Variances	204	85
Gross profit	2,197	2,100
As percent of net sales	20.0%	17.0%
Operating expenses		
Selling	635	639
Warehousing	992	1,115
Transportation	88	136
Total operating expense	1,715	1,890
As percent of net sales	15.6%	15.3%
Contribution	482	210
As percent of net sales	4.4%	1.7%
Overhead expenses		
Research and engineering	210	272
General and administrative	489	516
Corporate overhead	112	113
Total overhead	811	901
As percent of net sales	7.4%	7.3%
Earnings before tax	$ (329)	$ (482)

Note: Figures in thousands of dollars.
* Based on 9 months of 1985.

continuing failure to meet margin requirements was noted by Vice-President of Finance Frank Holden. However, Greene encouraged Goodman, saying, "If you can do what you say you can do, you'll be doing fine." Some Excom members expressed concern about Thomas's performance. Goodman's reaction to the meeting was: "We're in better shape than we were. We've bought some time."

Specialty Products' tight quality-control procedures were now apparently creating more than its share of scrap and waste, thus raising costs. Goodman was concerned.

May 1985

Goodman received his personal performance appraisal covering his prior year. Goodman's appraisal of his appraisal was: "There is nothing specifically relating to Specialty Products."

Using the microcomputer to carry out "what if" scenarios regarding prices and margins, the unit forecasted 19.5 percent margin for 1985.

The 1985 strategic planning sessions began. CPC executives spent one day at a pleasant mountain resort. Topics included reviewing the 1984 plan, critiquing the 1984 planning process, stating expectations for 1985's planning process, and compiling competitor profiles. Goodman was uncertain about what should go into his 1985 plan. He observed: "No new issues seem to be coming up at the sessions. People seem to have the attitude, 'We've agreed upon what should be done. Let's get on with it.' " Sessions seemed too heavily focused on marketing issues. Greene admonished executives about "backsliding, not thinking strategically."

The surge in CPC sales during the prior 4 months now threatened maximum capacity for some types of products — especially those of Specialty Products. (See Exhibit 11.) Thomas and Goodman were increasingly worried that they would get

EXHIBIT 11
Work center capacity analysis, 1984

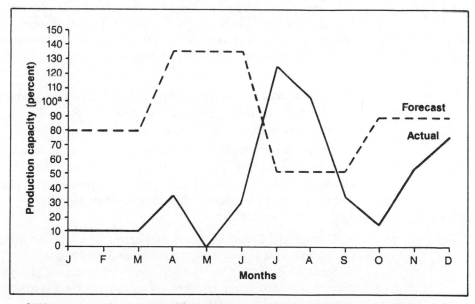

[a] 100 percent capacity means two shifts and average downtime for maintenance and breakdowns.

the "short end of the stick." The situation reminded Goodman of the "light-switch" history of Specialty Products. Goodman complained: "They're taking my capacity while asking me to grow."

An important Specialty Products customer visited the plant. According to Goodman, "They say we are outstanding. They love us." He believed that this feedback was a sign that the new strategy was working.

Goodman and a consultant worked on a written plan to encapsulate Specialty Products' strategy. While Greene had never asked for a formal, written plan, Goodman thought the plan should be written down. (See Appendix.)

Goodman invited several customers to send some of their operations personnel to Specialty Products. He offered seminars on MRP systems for them. He reasoned that Specialty Products' customers struggled under heavy pressure from their parent companies to reduce costs. If Specialty Products could persuade them to use MRP, not only would the customers feel grateful, but, more importantly, the resulting tight connection between Specialty Products' systems and customer systems would constitute a switching cost for these customers.

Although Specialty Products' mission only specified "to use excess capacity," Goodman began to consider making a capital expenditures request of $1 million for 1985. "I think we can get it," he concluded.

CPC's engineering department responds slowly to requests about product design for Specialty Products items. "They don't think we're a high-priority business. Almost all their attention is given to Retail Division and Distribution Division," observed Goodman.

June 1985

CPC executives gathered at a nearby resort for 3 more days of strategic planning. For the first time (according to Goodman), Greene discussed his objectives and expectations. Some executives said that Greene should have made his expectations clear in the beginning. Other issues were discussed:

Goodman wanted to change Specialty Products' mission to remove the "no investment criterion," but his proposal was rejected.

Some executives complained about "staff infection."

Numerous human resources difficulties had cropped up in connection with efforts to implement plans.

Goodman stated: "We have done a good job of planning, the planning is important, but enough is enough. It's time to make it all happen."

Thomas and Goodman found themselves under heavy workload pressure. "I can't afford time to hiccough," commented Bob Thomas.

Specialty Products growing sales, combined with good growth in sister divisions' sales, maintained heavy pressure on capacity. "We have diesel acceleration and disc brakes at CPC," joked Goodman.

Goodman met with Thomas to discuss Thomas's performance appraisal. Among the comments which various senior executives had written were:

The next 12 months are crucial to Specialty Products and Bob Thomas.

It's evident that BT's efforts should be directed toward general management and marketing.

Does Specialty Products really require the additional staffing that Thomas has requested?

Preliminary work on CPC's 1986 budget began.

July 1985   Goodman speculated about the sales-volume resurgence of Specialty Products.

Partly the MRP. Partly the conquest of quality problems. Our customers are doing good business, so we do good business. Where would Specialty Products be without the economic recovery? Even without the recovery, we would have done okay, maybe not as well. If the economy took another nosedive, our growth would suffer, but our base would stick. No declines from here on.

Thomas continued to talk about getting into the computer software packaging business in a bigger way. "I want to go into software packaging!" At the time, Specialty Products had a few software accounts to whom only binders were sold. Bob noted that several expanded avenues seemed open.

Specialty Products could manufacture and print materials for manuals and discs. BMF International's software development division could even provide the program product.

Specialty Products could manufacture and sell to printers.

Specialty Products could sell directly to computer firms.

Specialty Products could manufacture cases for software systems. (Specialty Products already has some accounts of this type.)

Goodman observed that this printing/packaging proposal did not fit within the Specialty Products mission. He told Thomas that it was a distraction. Thomas, unmoved by Goodman's objections, promoted the idea to Greene.

More strategic planning meetings were held. Goodman ordered T-shirts for the participants which read "S.O.B." (strategically operated businesses). Goodman, reflecting on the latest conferences, mused, "I think the fun overshadowed the planning." Goodman noticed quite a bit of "plugging one's own turf." At one point, Goodman came under some group pressure about Specialty Products during an open session, but Greene himself choked off the debate, saying: "Sure, we've got problems, but they are not strategic." Goodman said with a hint of disappointment in his voice: "Most people here still don't understand Specialty Products, and Specialty Products doesn't get much attention at these meetings. It's 99 percent everything else."

The formal Specialty Products plan remained in Goodman's desk drawer.

FALL 1985 PROBLEMS AND PROSPECTS

In early fall 1985, Thomas was preparing to meet with Greene to discuss the Specialty Products 1986 plan. At the same meeting, Thomas hoped to present his idea for software packaging to Greene. He believed that Specialty Products could double its 1985 business in 3 or 4 years, but only if new product opportunities such as software publishing were aggressively pursued. (On the other hand, Goodman felt that the same goals could be reached without the publishing software move.) In arguing for the software publishing alternative, Thomas would make the following main points:

A market is there.

There are many competitors in this business, but none who can do it all.

EXHIBIT 12

Sales performance versus budget of Continental Packaging Company's three principal business segments

1985	Sales (in 000s)	Percent sales above (+) below (−) budget	Actual margin	Budgeted margin
Distributor Division				
January	$ 8,387	+3	42.6	42.3
February	10,805	−8	42.4	42.1
March	13,003	−18	41.5	41.4
April	14,227	+1	35.9	39.1
May	9,652	−12	40.3	41.4
June	12,032	−11	39.5	41.8
July	8,753	+14	41.2	42.6
August	10,082	−5	40.9	41.8
September	12,199	+9	39.8	42.2
Retail Division				
January	$ 1,696	+0	28.9	34.5
February	1,628	+5	31.3	36.9
March	1,616	−2	25.7	36.4
April	1,694	−15	36.4	36.4
May	2,159	−4	31.6	35.3
June	4,000	+21	30.2	32.7
July	8,210	+3	32.5	32.5
August	4,968	−27	27.3	32.3
September	3,189	−4	31.8	34.3
Specialty Products				
January	$ 600	+20	18.1	24.6
February	703	+23	16.4	23.5
March	1,018	+4	15.5	23.7
April	873	+52	16.1	24.3
May	1,005	−34	22.3	24.0
June	1,208	−27	18.0	18.1
July	1,050	+22	16.0	17.5
August	750	+25	12.8	17.4
September	1,566	+18	17.4	18.6

EXHIBIT 13
Selected details of
Thomas's software
packaging proposal

This proposal involves a complete packaging operation. Specialty Products would provide printed materials, vinyl jackets, disks (from sister division of BMF International), indexing, color printing decoration, warehousing, and distribution.

Why Software Packaging?
  Fast-growing segment
  Market potential $150–$200 by 1986
  Large volume customers
  Quality image important
  Distribution important
  Fits Specialty Products' plans

Strengths of Specialty Products:
  Have full-line of products
  Warehousing
  National distribution network
  Class "A" MRP system
  Brand recognition high
  Excess capacity
  Competitors can't do *packaging*
  (Low vertical integration)

Threats:
  More competition
  Volatile market
  Credit problems of customers?

Market strategy:
  A one-step shopping center for software
    publishers with sales ≥ $5 million.

Market requires:
  Quality product
  Dependable service
  Creativity
  Competitive prices
  Prompt service

Weaknesses:
  Lack of product engineering support
  Sales and service depts. lack product
    knowledge
  High costs
  Some elements strain capacity

Forecast ($000)

	Total sales (with no new marketing personnel)	Add software specialists Additional sales	Add new sales person Additional sales
1986	$ 500	$1,000	$ 800
1987	700	2,250	950
1988	1,200	3,800	1,750

		1985	1986	1987
Total Software		2,300	4,900	8,560

CPC can make the product, including printing and decorating.

Price is important.

On-time delivery is important.

Specialty Products can sell "CPC" image.

As Neil Greene sat in his office at the executive office building awaiting Bob Thomas's arrival, he reflected upon the year's events and the future of the Specialty Products unit. Noting the difficulties Specialty Products experienced in reaching its margins, he wondered if their strategic plans were enough to reach those ambitious goals. His attention fell upon the latest projections for Specialty Products' 1985 performance (Exhibit 12). He knew that others serving on the Executive Committee still doubted Specialty Products' long-term potential. Was Specialty Products really worth the trouble? He wondered whether he should approve Thomas's software packaging idea (Exhibit 13). Looking ahead to the annual capital budgeting process, he wondered whether a request for $1 million in investment for Specialty Products ought to be granted. Was strategic planning taking hold at CPC? Greene had a lot on his mind as his secretary announced Bob Thomas's arrival. Bob Thomas walked in, carrying details of his plans and projections (Exhibit 14).

EXHIBIT 14
Selected information from Thomas's presentation of Specialty Products' strategic plan to Greene, October 11, 1985

Strengths

Outstanding service
Commitment to market
Financial strength
Vertical integration
Specialized sales force
High level of quality assurance
Using MRP system to "tie" customers

Threats

Price cutting by competitors
Increasing industry capacity
High interest rates
Don't know competitors in software

Weaknesses

Poor engineering support/product development
High prices
"Red tape" of company systems
Limited capacity
Shortage of skilled production personnel for some key areas
Seasonal capacity problem brought on by sharing facilities with other company units
Outdated equipment

1985 Market Strategy

Increase market share
Establish position in software publishing
Develop auditing, consulting, professional education markets
MRP, service, quality as main competitive weapons

Projections

	1986	1987	1988
Sales (millions)	18.5	22.5	26.6
Margin (dollar)	3.3	4.2	5.3
Margin (percent)	18	19	20

APPENDIX: SELECTED PARTS OF SPECIALTY PRODUCTS' WRITTEN PLAN, APRIL 1985

MEMO TO: Neil Greene

FROM: Bob Thomas

SUBJECT: Strategy

Introduction

For years Specialty Products has drifted. The aim of the present management of Specialty Products is to give purpose and direction to this business. This plan outlines the way we think this can be done.

Critical Issue

How can we transform a business with relatively high costs, a history of quality problems, and a near-commodity product into a strong leadership position in satisfying customer needs?

Specialty Products' Mission

Specialty Products focuses on customers having a potential for large orders of custom products using standard construction. Principal market segments presently include accountants and we plan to extend this market to high-tech industries and advertising agencies (as a conduit to new customers). While Specialty Products is seen as a growth business, the growth is limited by available capacity.

Objectives

Penetration of existing accounts (specifics)

Margin (specifics)

Sales (specifics)

New products (specifics)

Reputation (specifics)

Quality (specifics)

Personnel (specifics)

Target Markets

Present main markets
   Others

New markets
   High tech/computer
   Advertising agencies
   Others

Competitive Advantage

In order to achieve the ambitious objectives outlined above, Specialty Products must create a competitive advantage. We believe that this competitive advantage can be secured by combining some advantages Specialty Products has with some of our "hidden assets."

The advantages we plan on using are ones which create added value for customers of Specialty Products. The overall logic is to be better and different in ways that are not traditional in this business and which cannot be easily copied by our rivals.

Quality

We expect to achieve a level of quality that cannot be matched by smaller competitors. This is attainable through manufacturing, engineering.

Service

Because of our size, sophistication, and experience we can be a leader in service.

MRP

We will use the MRP system to lower our costs, to help our customers lower their inventories, and as a promotional technique.

Innovation

(Several new products mentioned)

Action Plans

We have already made a number of strides in the right direction, but much remains to be done. Here is our report of progress and our work-in-progress. (This part of the plan gave details of actions accomplished and actions remaining.)

Forecasts

The steps we have taken and those we plan to take should result in financial performance as follows:

Forecast for Specialty Products

	1984 actual	1985	1986
Sales	9,600,000	14,200,000	18,000,000
Margin percent	18.0	20.2	21.0

Conclusion

Being a high-cost competitor places a constraint on strategy. Because of our position, we need to find ways to add value to our offerings that steer us away from price competition. It is our judgment that the combinations of quality, service, reliability . . . can support the higher prices *and* higher volume we need in order to attain the objectives which have been set.

THE AMERICAN EXPRESS COMPANY

American Express company executives, meeting in their new fifty-one-story headquarters in the financial district of lower Manhattan, look to the future with a certain optimism. As the chairman and CEO, James D. Robinson, III, put it, "We are extremely active in two of the world's greatest growth industries: financial services and tourism."[1] A trusted name since 1850, AMEXCO looks to the second half of the eighties and into the nineties with a corporate philosophy and values anchored in entrepreneurship, quality, integrity, and service. A brief history of the company appears in Appendix A.

Flushed with the apparent success of its major acquisitions, AMEXCO's total assets had tripled from 1982 to nearly $62 billion by the end of 1984. This international financial supermarket (Exhibit 1) employs 77,000 people in more than 2,000 offices spread throughout 131 countries. Much of its incredible growth has occurred in only 3 years, "faster than expected because of profound changes in insurance, banking and securities wrought by the interplay of higher interest rates, technology and deregulation."[2]

During this period of expansion, AMEXCO revenues doubled to almost $13 billion with net income increasing from $466 million to $610 million (Exhibit 2). Through 1982 AMEXCO enjoyed its thirty-fifth consecutive year of increased earnings. This ended in 1983 with an 11 percent decrease in net income primarily attributed to problems at Fireman's Fund. By the end of 1984, AMEXCO showed respectable growth in net income of 18 percent.

The competition has a very healthy respect for the strength of AMEXCO. Dee Hock, former managing director and CEO of VISA International, commenting on

[1] "American Express: Financial Powerhouse," *Dun's Business Month,* December 1983, p. 39.

[2] Arlene Hershman, "The Supercompanies Emerge," *Dun's Business Month,* April 1983, p. 44.

© William D. Wilsted. Financial and organizational data are taken from *American Express Company 1984 Annual Report* unless otherwise noted. Reprinted by permission.

EXHIBIT 1 The American Express Company (December 1984)

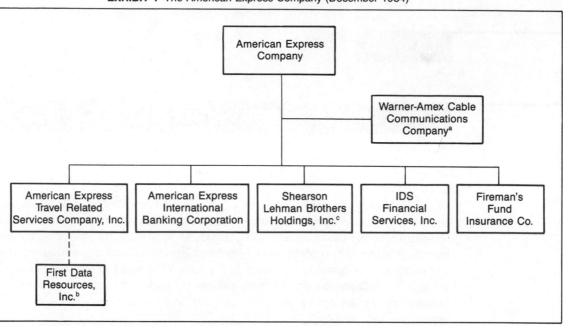

Source: Constructed from information contained in American Express Company 1984 Annual Report.
a AMEXCO owns 50 percent.
b TRS owns 75 percent of capital stock of the largest third-party data processor of debit and credit cards in the United States.
c Includes fourteen major subsidiaries of which Shearson Lehman Brothers, Inc. is the principal.

combat with AMEXCO, said:

> They [AMEX] are rough, tough, smart competitors with tons of money. There is very little they will not do to achieve their objectives. The advantage of American Express is that James Robinson can say, "To the left, march" and they do. I couldn't think of doing that. Each of our institutions [members] is totally independent.[3]

George Ball, president and CEO of Prudential-Bache Securities Inc., was quoted in April 1984 as saying, "Four years ago [AMEX] was a plastic card company, but with the addition of Lehman, AMEX is a fully fleshed-out financial services confederation of the type that will be dominant in tomorrow's marketplace."[4] Herbert E. Goodfriend, an analyst with Prudential-Bache, calls American Express "unquestionably the premier company in the financial services industry."[5]

The financial services supermarket is considered to operate in one or more of five major businesses. They include banking, credit cards, insurance, real estate,

[3] Leonard A. Schlesinger, Robert G. Eccles, John J. Gararro, *Managing Behavior in Organizations* (New York: McGraw-Hill, 1983), p. 479.

[4] "The Golden Plan of American Express," *Business Week,* April 30, 1984, p. 118.

[5] "American Express: Financial Powerhouse," p. 38.

EXHIBIT 2 Consolidated summary of selected financial data

	1984	1983	1982	1981	1980
Operating results					
Revenues	$12,895	$ 9,770	$ 8,093	$ 7,291	$ 6,426
Percent increase in revenues	*32%*	*21%*	*11%*	*13%*	*26%*
Expenses	12,159	9,253	7,339	6,586	5,830
Income taxes	126	2	173	181	130
Net income	610	515	581	524	466
Percent increase (decrease) in net income	*18%*	*(11)%*	*11%*	*12%*	*23%*
Assets and liabilities					
Time deposits	$ 5,470	$ 4,071	$ 2,127	$ 1,784	$ 1,120
Investment securities					
Carried at cost	13,449	12,766	7,163	6,446	6,026
Carried at lower of aggregate cost or market	315	211	81	148	166
Carried at market	8,566	1,709	948	917	1,235
Accounts receivable and accrued interest, net	14,802	11,497	9,204	8,191	6,825
Loans and discounts, net	7,089	6,642	4,379	3,929	3,811
Total assets	61,848	43,981	28,311	25,252	22,731
Customers' deposits and credit balances	13,262	12,511	6,810	6,218	5,818
Travelers checks outstanding	2,454	2,362	2,177	2,468	2,542
Insurance and annuity reserves	8,831	7,667	4,323	4,110	3,856
Long-term debt	3,839	2,643	1,798	1,293	1,293
Shareholders' equity	4,607	4,043	3,039	2,661	2,430
Common share statistics					
Net income per share	$ 2.79	$ 2.53	$ 3.02	$ 2.79	$ 2.59
Cash dividends declared per share	$ 1.28	$ 1.26	$ 1.125	$ 1.025	$ 1.00
Average number of shares outstanding	217	203	192	188	180
Shares outstanding at year-end	217	213	191	188	185
Number of shareholders of record	*51,211*	*45,753*	*36,580*	*36,611*	*34,735*
Other statistics					
Number of employees at year-end					
United States	*59,420*	*53,740*	*48,533*	*43,315*	*39,475*
Outside United States	*17,027*	*16,716*	*15,472*	*14,994*	*15,556*
Total	*76,447*	*70,456*	*64,005*	*58,309*	*55,031*
Number of offices at year-end					
American Express offices worldwide	*1,472*	*1,356*	*1,160*	*1,066*	*1,046*
Representative offices	*810*	*797*	*760*	*782*	*782*
Total	*2,282*	*2,153*	*1,920*	*1,848*	*1,828*

Note: Data in millions, except per share amounts and where italicized.
Note: Operating results for the year ended December 31, 1983 do not include the effect of the acquisition of Investors Diversified Services, Inc., accounted for as a purchase as of December 31, 1983. Where applicable, amounts and percentages for 1984 include the effect of the acquisition of Lehman Brothers Kuhn Loeb Holding Co., Inc., accounted for as a purchase as of May 11, 1984.
Source: American Express Co. 1984 Annual Report.

EXHIBIT 3 The six financial-services leaders

	Banking	Credit cards	Insurance	Real estate	Securities
American Express Co. Assets: $30 billion Revenue: $8.1 billion Net income: $581 million	—	(1)	(2)	(3)	(1)
BankAmerica Corp. Assets: $122.5 billion Revenue: $4 billion Net income: $451 million	(1)	(1)	(3)	(1)	(2)
Citicorp Assets: $130 billion Revenue: $5.2 billion Net income: $723 million	(1)	(1)	(3)	(1)	—
Merrill Lynch & Co. Assets: $20.7 billion Revenue: $5 billion Net income: $309 million	—	(3)	(2)	(2)	(1)
Prudential Insurance Co. of America Assets: $76.5 billion Revenue: $18.5 billion Net income: $2.13 billion	—	(3)	(1)	(2)	(1)
Sears, Roebuck & Co. Assets: $36 billion Revenue: $30 billion Net income: $861 million	(2)	(1)	(2)	(2)	(1)

(1) = Major factor in this industry.
(2) = Medium-sized factor in this industry.
(3) = Small factor in this industry.
Source: "The Supercompanies Emerge," *Dun's Business Month,* April 1983, p. 44.

and securities. AMEXCO is looking for ways to enter the domestic U.S. banking business; Citicorp wants to enter the securities business. Sears, Roebuck, and Co. and Bank America are both involved in all five major businesses. Prudential-Bache and Merrill Lynch, the other two principal financial supermarkets, like AMEXCO, lack domestic banking operations.[6] AMEXCO currently outstrips all the others in the travel-related services industry. Exhibit 3 shows six companies that have major positions in a number of critical financial-services businesses (at end of 1982).

According to a 1984 survey conducted by the *American Banker,* people rate American Express products and services higher than those of any other top financial

[6] "The Supercompanies Emerge," p. 45.

services firm in the United States. The same survey indicates that the American Express name is best known among consumers.[7]

AMEXCO'S MAJOR COMPANIES

Assembled under the American Express corporate roof are five major companies. They include American Express Travel Related Services Company, Inc. (TRS), American Express International Banking Corporation (AEIBC), Shearson Lehman Brothers, Inc. (SLAX), IDS Financial Services Inc. (IDS), and Fireman's Fund Insurance Companies (FF). Additionally, AMEXCO owns 50 percent of Warner AMEX Cable Communications. Appendix B presents 1982–1984 financial data by service category. Appendix C presents 1983–1984 financial data by subsidiary. Following is a discussion of each of these companies.

American Express Travel Related Services Company

Perhaps the oldest name in travel is TRS, the flagship organization of AMEXCO. The company was founded in 1850 and became a separate company under the AMEXCO banner in 1983. Annual growth in revenues exceeded 18 percent from 1982 to 1984. TRS is in the process of modernizing and is emerging as the most customer-responsive travel and credit card service company in the world with great profit potential.

TRS has grown and developed a great deal since its early days as a small package and funds freight company. Currently, TRS is best known for its worldwide network of travel offices, charge card, and traveler's cheques (without which you do not leave home). In addition, TRS offers direct mail merchandise services, publishing (*Travel and Leisure* and *Food and Wine*), and data processing services. TRS is also moving into communications, providing AMEX card members access to MCI. This is primarily a billing service providing MCI long-distance dialing through what AMEXCO calls "Expressphone."

In 1985, TRS launched "Project Hometown America" which raises money for local communities by contributions from American Express Card purchases, AMEX traveler's cheques, purchases of travel packages, and new card applications. TRS continues to utilize extensive advertising which, among other things, features tie-ins with major hotels, resorts, car-rental companies, and Eastern and United Airlines.

TRS operates 1,200 offices in more than 131 countries. Overseas travel has been popular due to the strength of the American dollar and TRS has capitalized on this opportunity. In 1984 and early 1985, TRS acquired new travel companies in Pittsburgh, Denver, and thirty-eight locations in the United Kingdom.

While the proliferation of plastic money and automatic teller machines (ATM) have eaten into the traveler's cheque market, AMEXCO still sold $15.1 billion in 1984, an increase of 9.1 percent over 1983. The average outstanding traveler's

---

[7] *American Express Company 1985 Annual Report*, p. 4.

cheque's volume in 1983 was $2.6 billion, up 8.3 percent. It is on these outstanding cheques, or "float," that TRS makes its profit, which in 1982 was $76 million before taxes. In 1962 the traveler's cheque float accounted for 80 percent of AMEXCO's total income. Twenty years later, it was responsible for only 11 percent of the total income. (Credit cards accounted for 24 percent of income; Fireman's Fund, 36 percent; and Shearson, 18 percent in 1982.) It is the lessons learned from managing the traveler's cheque float that make AMEXCO's management of cash balances anywhere within the corporation masterful.[8]

By the end of 1984 there were more than 20 million American Express Cards in force throughout the world, an increase of 17 percent over 1983. Credit card charge volume grew 24 percent to $47.6 billion during the same time. One out of every four cardholders lives overseas and the card is issued in twenty-eight currencies. In 1984, 125 mainland Chinese establishments accepted the card compared to 14 in 1983.

In August 1984, the platinum card ($250 fee, by invitation only) was offered in addition to the green card (offered since 1958) and the gold card (first offered in 1981). In 1984, AMEXCO added major retailers such as the May Company and the J. C. Penney Company as establishments that accept the American Express Card. TRS also acquired Health Carecard, Inc., a company whose product combines medical record keeping with payment capabilities.

The American Express Card differs from other plastic cards in distinct ways. It must be paid in full monthly (unless special arrangements have been made in advance) and the annual fee is more than other cards. (In 1985 the green card fee increased by 30 percent to $45.) These facts, coupled with economies of scale in billing and extensive experience in managing moving cash balances, make the American Express Card unique and highly profitable.

Another segment of TRS is direct marketing. When American Express began in 1974 to include product inserts in its 5 million monthly bills, it did not envision a merchandise services division of $185 million in sales just 10 years later. The growth of TRS's direct mail business is largely the result of its sophisticated use of customer segmentation based on the exact purpose for which each cardholder uses the card. Particular product mailings are targeted with precision to those customer groups with the greatest potential buying interest in that product. The merchandise services division has six target customer segments:

The frequent traveler, to whom it sells products and services to make business and travel more enjoyable

The upscale male consumer, to whom it sells state-of-the-art electronics for home entertainment and personal productivity

The upscale female consumer, to whom it sells products related to home design and household invention

---

[8] Priscilla S. Meyer, "Cheques and Balances," *Forbes*, March 14, 1983, p. 50.

Business executives of small- to medium-sized companies, to whom it sells products for the office that will increase chances for success

Portions of each of the above, to whom it offers new products on a test basis

Portions of each of the first four groups, to whom it offers various services, including magazine subscriptions at discounted prices[9]

A key to the merchandise services division's success is its strategy of offering exclusive merchandise. Whenever possible, TRS strives to be the sole source of the merchandise it offers. More than 90 percent of the noncatalog merchandise offered is exclusive. TRS seeks manufacturers who will modify certain aspects of a product just for AMEXCO. As a result, TRS sold 18,000 IBM electric typewriters in 1983 and 42,000 Gucci watches in 1982 and 1983.[10]

The strengths that TRS has identified as its basis for its marketing approach are:

The prestige attached to owning an American Express card

The excellent customer service provided by AMEXCO

A vast, affluent cardmember customer base (over 11 million in the United States)

AMEXCO's orientation toward business

AMEXCO's adeptness at packaging goods and services

A very strong overall quality image

Strong information processing skills[11]

The goals of the merchandise services division are: to continue to use the strong name recognition of American Express to generate sales to new customers; to provide the best service available in direct merchandising, with new, quality products tailored to the customers' needs; and to go outside the AMEXCO cardmember base to allow customers to pay for merchandise by Visa, MasterCard, or other credit cards.[12]

In publishing, TRS saw new highs in both ad pages and revenues in 1984. With almost a million paid subscribers, *Travel and Leisure* saw an increase of 23 percent in advertising revenues over 1983. *Food and Wine*, with 600,000 paid subscribers, saw an 18 percent increase in advertising revenues over 1983.

Since 1984, TRS has owned 75 percent of the capital stock of First Data Resources, Inc. This data processing company is the largest third-party processor of debit and credit cards in the United States. It is this acquisition that gives AMEXCO its economies of scale in processing transactions.

[9] Larry Jaffee, "AMEX Targets Mailings Precisely to List Segments," *Direct Marketing*, May 1984, p. 78.

[10] Ibid., p. 79.

[11] Ibid., p. 78.

[12] Ibid., p. 86.

Historically TRS has exhibited a great deal of support for the arts. From 1979 through 1984 TRS sponsored fifty projects, in one hundred cities, over five continents, to bring the arts closer to the people (at a cost of $20 million in 1984).[13] In AMEXCO's opinion, it has been worth the investment. AMEXCO has gained recognition within these communities and increased opportunities to attract potential customers and financial institutions. The "Project Hometown America" mentioned earlier is an extension of AMEXCO's charitable, goodwill efforts, while it offers potential tax advantages.

American Express International Banking Corporation

Growing out of a need to provide the travel-hungry American tourist financial services abroad after World War I, AEIBC was founded in 1919 as the American Express Company, Incorporated. In 1968, the name was changed to American Express International Banking Corporation.

By 1980 AMEXCO was itching to get rid of its overseas bank, AEIBC. The bank, under the direction of Richard Bliss, had been attempting to establish itself as a big investment banking concern in London. In 1981 Robert F. Smith, formerly AMEXCO's treasurer, took over as vice-chairman of the bank. Smith quickly changed the direction of the bank by slashing its operating costs and paring down its attempt to offer every service imaginable. The bank began to focus on trade finance and private banking for wealthy individual clients. AEIBC evolved into a deal-making organization with trade-related transactions involving export credit guarantees from Western governments.

The big improvement in AEIBC performance through 1983 was clearly a result of sheer cost-cutting. Total operating expenses fell from 63 percent of net financial revenue in 1981 to 52 percent in 1983. Also figuring prominently in the improvement was the acquisition of the Trade Development Bank (TDB) in Switzerland in March 1983. At $800 million in shareholders' equity, the combined bank has more than twice the equity of the old AEIBC. That, in turn, reduced AEIBC's Latin American debt from four times equity to a more manageable, yet still concerning, two times equity.[14]

To acquire the TDB, AMEXCO paid more than 50 percent over the book value of TDB stock. Many believe that AMEXCO paid the premium price to obtain the services of Edmond J. Safra, Lebanese-born banking genius and owner of TDB.[15] Safra needed U.S. government approval to become CEO of AEIBC (a condition of sale). Although the sale was made in January 1983, Safra did not set foot in AMEXCO's corporate offices in New York throughout the year. While waiting for U.S. approval, AMEXCO top executives visited and called Safra frequently (he has controlling interest in other U.S. banks) at his TDB office in Geneva to get

[13] Susan Bloom, "Beauty and the Bottom Line," *Business Quarterly,* Fall 1984, p. 86.

[14] "AMEX's Bank: A Wallflower Suddenly Blossoms," *Business Week,* January 9, 1984, p. 101.

[15] Gwen Kinkead, "The Mystery Man American Express Is Banking On," *Fortune,* December 12, 1983, p. 142.

the benefit of his advice and banking instincts.[16] Safra continued running TDB and in 1984 was elected to AMEXCO's board of directors.

As a result of these moves, the AEIBC was a welcome member of the AMEXCO family in early 1984. The former wallflower is a highly profitable bank with $13 billion in assets.[17] The AMEXCO hierarchy sees a great potential for marketing Shearson/American Express Inc. services through the AEIBC. 1984 was a year of record profits for AEIBC, even though it was a year that will be remembered as one of the most difficult in international banking. Net income in 1984 increased 15 percent to a record $156 million after a 126 percent increase to $136 million from 1982 to 1983.

Today, with 82 offices in 39 countries, AEIBC includes international private banking, trade financing operations, correspondent banking (more than 2,000 active correspondent bank relationships worldwide), treasury and foreign exchange services, equipment financing (American Express Leasing Corporation), and military banking for the U.S. Armed Forces overseas.

Citicorp has been a pioneer among the major financial supermarkets in pushing for changes in the law that would permit it, a leader in domestic banking, into the insurance field.[18] Citicorp has made inroads in this regard in South Dakota. If Citicorp is successful on a national basis, the door would be open for AMEXCO, if they so choose, to move into the domestic banking industry either as a separate AMEXCO company or as a division of AEIBC.

Fireman's Fund Insurance Company

Since 1863, when it was founded in San Francisco, Fireman's Fund Insurance Company has grown to be a leading provider of insurance protection for individuals, groups, businesses, and institutions, offering a broad range of property, liability, life, accident, and health insurance. Acquired by AMEXCO in 1968, FF products are offered through more than 10,000 independent agents and brokers throughout the United States.

In 1979 and 1980 the property and casualty industry experienced serious trouble due to price-cutting on many types of policies. In 1981, under the leadership of Fireman's Fund CEO Myron Dubain, FF cut a deal with the Insurance Company of North America to swap certain casualty policies. The swap allowed both companies to discount the loss reserves required on their newly acquired policies, without disclosing a change in accounting practices on their financial statements or to their respective boards of directors. This accounting sleight-of-hand increased FF's reported pretax profits by $66 million in 1981–1982, but resulted in a negative cash flow due to an additional $30 million tax bill[19] (Exhibit 4).

In 1982, Edwin F. Cutler became FF's CEO with guidance from AMEXCO to

[16] Ibid.

[17] "AMEX's Bank: A Wallflower Suddenly Blossoms," p. 101.

[18] Carol J. Loomis, "Fire in the Belly at American Express," *Fortune*, November 28, 1983, p. 87.

[19] Carol J. Loomis, "How Fireman's Fund Stoked Its Profits," *Fortune*, November 28, 1983, pp. 99–104.

EXHIBIT 4
Fireman's Fund net
income

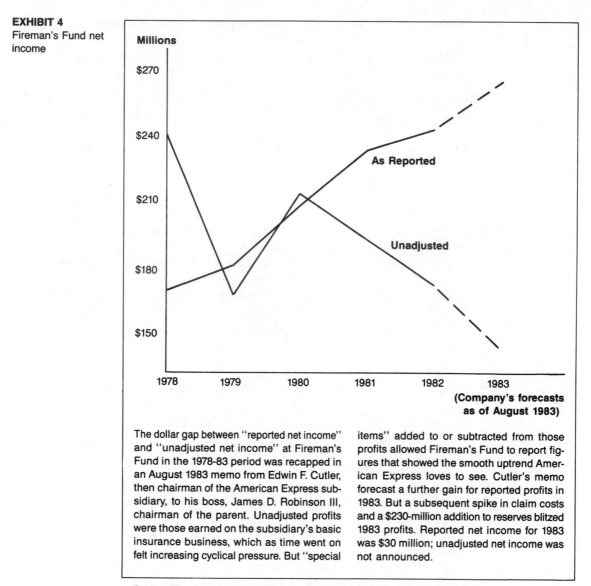

The dollar gap between "reported net income" and "unadjusted net income" at Fireman's Fund in the 1978-83 period was recapped in an August 1983 memo from Edwin F. Cutler, then chairman of the American Express subsidiary, to his boss, James D. Robinson III, chairman of the parent. Unadjusted profits were those earned on the subsidiary's basic insurance business, which as time went on felt increasing cyclical pressure. But "special items" added to or subtracted from those profits allowed Fireman's Fund to report figures that showed the smooth uptrend American Express loves to see. Cutler's memo forecast a further gain for reported profits in 1983. But a subsequent spike in claim costs and a $230-million addition to reserves blitzed 1983 profits. Reported net income for 1983 was $30 million; unadjusted net income was not announced.

Source: "The Earnings Magic at American Express," *Fortune,* June 25, 1984, p. 58.

further increase profits. From January to September 1983, FF dropped its premium prices and generated a 13 percent increase in written premiums while the insurance industry average was only about 4 percent.[20]

In the third quarter of 1983, a sharp rise in claims forced FF to add $10 million

[20] Carol J. Loomis, "How Fireman's Fund Singed American Express," *Fortune,* January 9, 1984, p. 80.

to its loss reserves, which resulted in a fourth-quarter after-tax net loss of $10 million.[21]

A *Fortune* article in November 1983 exposed the paper profits of 1981–1982 and seriously undermined the credibility of FF's and AMEXCO's financial statements.[22]

In December 1983 Cutler was removed as CEO and replaced by acquisition and financial wizard Sanford Weill, an executive with no prior insurance experience. FF simultaneously announced a reduction in its work force of 14,000 by more than 10 percent through retirement and attrition in an effort to reduce costs.

In December 1983, AMEXCO's board of directors added $230 million to FF's loss reserves which contributed to a drop in AMEXCO earnings from $700 million to $520 million for 1983. A public announcement by AMEXCO on December 12, 1983 regarding FF's financial problems caused a single-day drop in AMEXCO stock from $32 to $29 per share.[23] FF's performance, or lack thereof, was the principal reason why AMEXCO had its first downturn in earnings in 36 years.

In the first quarter of 1984, Sandy Weill cut 1,200 employees from the payroll, estimating a $40–50 million annual saving. Weill announced a three-step strategy to become the low-cost producer in the industry: lay-offs and cost cutting, combined with increased efficiencies in decision making due to more autonomy at lower levels; top management compensation tied to performance; and a revamping of FF's data processing system.[24]

The first quarter of 1984 saw a modest $10 million profit, but in the second quarter 1985 FF reported a quarterly loss of $71.7 million on revenues of $1 billion. Once again AMEXCO felt compelled to add $187 million to FF's loss reserves.[25]

By July 1985, Sandy Weill was replaced as CEO of Fireman's Fund by John J. Byrne, former CEO at Government Employees Insurance Company.[26] In December 1985, FF changed executive vice-presidents, with James Ridling, formerly of Crum and Foster, replacing Donald McComber. As the year closed, AMEXCO owned 41 percent of FF.[27]

Shearson Lehman/ American Express

Synergy — the art of making one plus one equal three — was the underlying impetus behind the broad concept of creating financial supermarkets, which, in turn, led to the stampede of acquisitions of large brokerage firms by giant outsiders in 1981. As part of the stampede, AMEXCO acquired the prestigious Wall Street brokerage

[21] Ibid.

[22] Loomis, "How Fireman's Fund Stoked Its Profits," pp. 99–104.

[23] Loomis, "How Fireman's Fund Singed American Express," p. 80.

[24] Mary Row, "Can Sandy Weill Turn Fireman's Fund Around," *Institutional Investor*, May 1984, pp. 110–112.

[25] Carol J. Loomis, "The Earnings Magic at American Express," *Fortune*, June 25, 1984, p. 60.

[26] "A New Chief for Fireman's Fund," *Business Week*, August 5, 1985, p. 38.

[27] "Who's News," *Wall Street Journal*, December 19, 1985, p. 14.

firm Shearson at a price of approximately $1 billion. The merger was, to some degree, a response to the Prudential-Bache merger. Sandy Weill, Shearson's CEO at the time, did not want to risk being left behind by the entry of the largest U.S. insurer into the securities business. The merger between AMEXCO and Shearson was brought about by the two firms' belief that the barriers of tradition and regulation separating banking, brokerage, and insurance would eventually evaporate.[28]

In 1984 Shearson, under the leadership of their new CEO, Peter Cohen, purchased the 134-year-old investment bank of Lehman Brothers Kuhn-Loeb. This acquisition provided AMEXCO with additional strength in investment banking and fixed-income trading. As a result, SLAX wields this investment banking strength with a broad-based, soundly capitalized trading capacity and a global distribution network with over 5,000 professional financial consultants in 354 offices located in forty-four states and fifteen countries. Through these consultants, SLAX offers stocks, bonds, options, futures, commercial paper, certificates of deposit, insurance, and tax-advantaged investments as well as investment banking, pension and investment management, real estate, and mortgage banking services.

Mergers such as this have had the effect of moving retail brokers closer to becoming financial consultants, although the SLAX brokers can now refer their clients with specific problems to the specialists who may reside in one of their sister companies and who also fall under the AMEXCO umbrella. This is due in large part to AMEXCO's purchase of such firms as Balcor (the nation's largest real estate syndicator) and Investors Diversified Services and Ayco (both well-known financial planning firms).[29]

Among the mergers' by-products, none seems to have benefited the brokers more than the reputation of AMEXCO. SLAX staff members acknowledge an overnight surge in client confidence. "Once Shearson teamed up with American Express, we got the credibility we needed."[30] Other beneficial side effects include the infusion of capital by AMEXCO (which has enabled many of the brokers to obtain desktop computers, which improves their service to the client); the ability to attend workshops on specific products and selling skills; and stepped-up advertising campaigns to enhance their visibility.

The effect of these advantages can be seen in the year-end summary of activities for SLAX for 1984. The company managed over 300 underwritings in U.S. and international markets. The corporate finance division represented clients in more than 70 completed mergers, acquisitions, and divestitures with an aggregate transaction value of over $12 billion. The public finance division managed tax-exempt financings of $28 billion for state and local governments in 1984. Shearson also

---

[28] Anthony Bianco, "How A Financial Supermarket Was Born," *Business Week*, December 23, 1985, p. 10.

[29] Andrew Marton, "What Have the Megamergers Meant for Brokers," *Institutional Investor*, March 1984, pp. 147–150.

[30] Ibid., p. 148.

recognized a 135 percent rise in revenues in the fixed-income sector and an 8.4 percent increase in revenues from the sale of tax-advantaged investments.

However, there have been certain drawbacks to the merger. The presence of AMEXCO has diminished the informal atmosphere that previously existed at Shearson. "A certain impersonality has emerged, it is no longer the closely knit firm it once was."[31] The bureaucratic system of the conglomerate is also frustrating to the Shearson staffers: "It takes six weeks to get some requests through."[32] Along with the abundance of products has come an abundance of paperwork. Equally as frustrating is the fact that the parent company, as of March 1984, had not yet released the names of its 9 million green-card holders to the brokerage firm. This single source of potential clients could easily double or triple Shearson's client base.[33]

Despite these drawbacks, it is the consensus of the brokerage community that the full effects of the mergers will not be felt for some time. They are convinced that these mergers will give rise to a new breed of broker, one able to deal with a larger client base by supplying a wider range of financial services.

IDS Financial Services, Inc.

IDS Financial Services, Inc. (IDS) was established in 1894 to help people and businesses manage money and achieve their financial goals. Through its sales force of more than 4,400 representatives, IDS offers sound financial plans and the products and services to fulfill those plans. Among its offerings are investment certificates, mutual funds, life insurance, annuities, unit investment trusts, IRAs, limited partnerships, and management and fiduciary services for pension and employee benefit plans. IDS has traditionally concentrated on the lower end of the investing public (incomes in the $25,000–$75,000 range).

IDS was acquired by AMEXCO in January 1984 as part of its multibrand approach to providing financial services.[34] In addition to adding the American Express name to the IDS banner, this merger has also resulted in more training opportunities for the IDS sales force and a continual flow of new and upgraded products. With AMEXCO's support, IDS has launched its most aggressive advertising campaign ever in an attempt to provide the company with further exposure.

Investors were apparently not impressed by AMEXCO's purchase of IDS. In fact, AMEXCO's stock plummeted from $45 to $28 in the year after the announcement of the merger. This was a much greater drop than that of the stock market averages during the same period. However, at the end of 1985, AMEXCO's stock was up to approximately $52.

[31] Ibid.

[32] Ibid.

[33] Ibid.

[34] "The Golden Plan of American Express," p. 119.

Warner Amex (W-A)

In the late seventies, "gripped with doubts about its competitive position in checks and cards,"[35] AMEXCO sought acquisitions in the communications arena. After trying to buy the McGraw-Hill publishing company and looking at others in the field, AMEXCO settled on 50 percent of Warner-AMEX, a cable TV company that has grown to be the sixth largest cable operator in the United States.

W-A owns 104 cable television systems in twenty-one states serving 1.2 million subscribers, but has done poorly with big-city franchises. In its first 5 years of co-ownership, AMEXCO has contributed more than $300 million to W-A's operations.[36] In 1983, AMEXCO's share of operating losses was close to $40 million. In 1984, Drew Lewis, W-A CEO, reduced pretax losses to $94 million with net losses falling from $99 million to $25 million. Looking to 1985 and beyond, W-A owns almost two-thirds of MTV Network which also includes the VH-1 and the Nickleodeon Children's channels. W-A also owns 19 percent of the Showtime Movie channel.

The Cable Company Policy Act of 1984 provided for rate deregulation after 2 years, which will allow cable operators to function in a more competitive market, which may contribute to greater economic stability in the industry. In 1984 W-A sold cable systems in Pittsburgh, Chicago, St. Louis, and twenty smaller locales as well as its regional sports programming service and its security division. Contract modifications in its urban franchises in Milwaukee, New York City, and Dallas were also a part of the cost-containment strategy launched in 1984.

According to Drew Lewis:

This year [1984] marked a turning point for Warner-Amex. The foundation for the future is now in place and Warner-Amex is moving forward toward its goal of profitability. The cable industry is entering an era of realism and its future is bright. Warner-Amex is well positioned for a key role in that future.[37]

THE FINANCIAL SUPERMARKETS

Deregulation has given rise to many investment alternatives. Americans spent $200 billion in 1982 for financial services with an estimated margin of 25 percent.[38] These facts, coupled with tax breaks for IRAs and capital gains, stimulate demand and encourage supplies of financial services to enter the market. A major barrier to expansion into the financial supermarket category has been the legal restrictions on combining banking operations with insurance or investment banking, or interstate branching by security brokers with investment banking.

As the supermarkets emerge, there is competition to become the low-cost financial service provider. ATMs and 800 telephone numbers make personal banking more efficient and easier for most types of financial transactions. Technology with its

[35] Loomis, "Fire In the Belly At American Express," p. 88.

[36] Ibid.

[37] *American Express Company 1984 Annual Report*, p. 47.

[38] Hershman, "The Supercompanies Emerge," p. 44.

inherent efficiencies makes pursuit of a low-cost strategy more feasible. Other ways to pursue a low-cost strategy include the use of service representatives (rather than more expensive account executives) to handle walk-in low-margin investment clients, selling to individuals at the workplace (corporate benefit programs), and vertical integration.[39]

The supercompanies plan to go after the middle-income families earning $20,000 to $50,000 a year. The company that can profitably serve the middle-income investor is going to make a potload of money, as this market group contains the most people. Further strategies will be to have a broad and diversified base of revenues to overcome the large cycles of financial services. Furthermore, geographic diversification will be necessary to cover costs and enjoy the economies of scale of mass marketing. One method of mass marketing is the national ad campaigns that have just begun. These mass marketing strategies will be aimed at reaching as many people as possible and trying to gain national recognition for each company as a full-service financial provider. Banks have the inside track here as cash and checks are the centerpiece of financial transactions.[40]

AMEXCO considers itself to be in the financial and travel-related service industries. While each of its corporate companies is a separate profit center, AMEXCO attempts to capitalize on its corporate synergy by using multiple distribution channels that target select market segments with strong brand-name products and services. Cross marketing, another synergy of the financial supermarket, allows an AEIBC customer in West Germany, for example, to buy securities or real estate in the United States through SLAX.

In terms of vertical-integration economies, AMEXCO owns Balcor, a firm that puts together and manages real estate syndications which can then be sold through SLAX account executives to potential investors. Another economy of scale is its low-cost, high-speed data processing capability (First Data Resources, Inc.) on which AMEXCO spends $300–400 million annually for hardware and software improvements. A clear goal is for AMEXCO to be the low-cost processor of financial transactions.[41]

As a financial supermarket, AMEXCO competes on many levels within international, national, and regional markets. In the industry, AMEXCO competes with the other financial supermarkets on a corporate basis. This competition includes Sears Roebuck, Prudential-Bache, Bank America Corporation, Citicorp, and Merrill Lynch. To a lesser degree, AMEXCO competes with potential financial supermarkets such as Travelers, Transamerica, Aetna, and Security Pacific Bank. On a regional basis, AMEXCO competes with growing financial empires such as First Interstate Bancorp.

Looking at the leaders (AMEXCO, Sears, Prudential, and Merrill Lynch), it is clear that all are spending money as never before in efforts to revamp their business

[39] Ibid., p. 49.

[40] Ibid., pp. 44–50.

[41] Ibid., p. 50.

identities. The strategy for these firms is twofold: first, to make consumers comfortable with once unheard-of combinations of merchandise the supermarkets now offer (e.g., risky tax shelters and riskless life insurance or, in Sears' case, stocks and socks) and, second, to distinguish each firm from its competitors.[42]

Achieving the first goal (one-stop shopping) will take time. A recent sampling survey revealed that most respondents did not see many benefits in one-stop financial shopping. The survey results indicated that younger adults are more receptive to the idea than older ones.[43]

In terms of differentiation, Merrill Lynch ("to be all things to some people") has said frankly that it is after affluent households with incomes over $50,000.[44] This involves courting young professionals, who may not have big incomes now, but seem likely to at some point in the future. Sears is capitalizing on its image of trustworthiness and is using a celebrity spokesman, Hal Holbrook, to convey that image in TV advertising ($3.1 million in first-quarter 1984).[45]

American Express is trying to cover all the bases. The company offers its credit card in three versions — green, gold, and the ultraexclusive platinum card — with the intent to intercept investors at three levels of wealth.

IDS Brokerage firm has always concentrated on the lower end of the investing public (incomes in the $25,000–$35,000 range). For the middle and upper range, there is Shearson. And then for the corporate client, Shearson has the investment banking firm of Lehman Brothers.[46]

American Express ads reflect its multibrand approach. There is intentionally no similarity between IDS ads and those for Shearson Lehman. It is too early to judge the effectiveness of the IDS ("IDS doesn't cater to get-rich-quick schemes") or the Shearson ads ("for the serious investor").[47]

Prudential's advertising is aimed at households with annual incomes of at least $50,000.[48]

THE OUTLOOK

Synergy was touted as the motivation behind the rash of acquisitions and mergers among the financial giants in the early 1980s, but, halfway through the decade,

[42] Geoffry Colvin, "Would You Buy Stocks Where You Buy Socks?" *Fortune*, July 9, 1984, p. 50.

[43] Ibid., p. 130.

[44] Ibid.

[45] Ibid., p. 133.

[46] Ibid., p. 131.

[47] Ibid., p. 133.

[48] Ibid., p. 131.

analysts claim that "when it comes to the financial supermarkets' synergy, one plus one well might end up equaling one."[49]

The torrid pace of AMEX's diversification drive is, however, straining its ability to control its far-flung operations. "Their management team has been assembled mostly by purchase," says Walter B. Wriston, CEO of Citicorp. "I don't think there's any question that if a team has played together for 10 years, you have a better chance on Saturday afternoon than the all-star team that was assembled that morning."[50]

Sanford Wiell, who brought Shearson into the AMEXCO family in 1981 and started to turn FF around in 1984, left AMEXCO in 1985. The leadership position at FF has been anything but stable with five CEOs in 6 years. Lewis Gerstner, Jr., CEO of the TRS, is rumored to be unhappy with decisions being made at New York corporate headquarters.[51] Weill's protégé, Peter Cohen, CEO at Shearson Lehman at thirty-six, may not sit well with some of AMEXCO's older executives. If AMEXCO has a major weakness, it may be in senior management, which is often accused of buying its talent rather than grooming it, notwithstanding the fact that such notables as Henry Kissinger and Edward Safra have recently been added to the AMEXCO board of directors. Could the problems at Fireman's Fund mean the beginning of the end of AMEXCO's involvement in insurance? Down to only 41 percent ownership, AMEXCO could be looking to cut bait altogether if and when the price is right.

Warner-Amex has yet to see black ink. How long will AMEXCO dabble in the communications/entertainment industries without a winner?

Visa, MasterCard, and others (including possibly Sears' new entry, Discover) pose a challenge to the AMEX card's dominance. They have erased all vestiges of complacency at TRS.[52]

IDS margins have been considered thin and visibly low. An announcement in December 1985 indicated that AMEXCO was pumping $65 million to expand IDS's business lines, giving IDS capital of more than $900 million.[53] In the same announcement, AMEXCO added $175 million to AEICB, which apparently is now a successful member of the AMEXCO family.

Will AMEXCO, regulations permitting, expand into domestic banking? Will AMEXCO's success in direct marketing take it into retail sales to compete with Sears through acquisition of a retailer such as J. C. Penney or Montgomery Ward? Can AMEXCO make greater use of First Data Resources to further cut internal costs or sell data processing services at a profit?

Are there economies to be gained, as well as synergistic effects, by placing IDS under SLAX management? Would such a move reduce internal competition for

[49] Bianco, "How a Financial Supermarket Was Born," p. 10.

[50] "The Golden Plan at American Express," p. 118.

[51] Ibid., p. 120.

[52] "The Golden Plan of American Express," p. 119.

[53] "Business Briefs," *Wall Street Journal*, December 20, 1985, p. 8.

investors in AMEXCO's three-tiered investment strategy (Lehman — wealthy corporate, Shearson — middle income, IDS — small investor)? Or, conversely, is this too broad a front on which to attack?

APPENDIX A: HISTORY OF GROWTH OF AMEXCO

1850: American Express evolves from the merging of three small freight companies for delivery of small packages and funds by rail and horseback. American Express agents are expected to foil the efforts of masked bandits.

1891: The first traveler's checks are introduced by American Express.

1900: American Express opens the first overseas travel office in Paris.

1919: The American Express Company, Incorporated (known as the "Inc Company") is formed to provide financial services for post–World War I American travelers.

1958: The famous green travel and entertainment charge card is introduced.

1968: The international banking operation known as the Inc Company changes its name to the American Express International Banking Corporation (AEIBC).

American Express acquires the Fireman's Fund Insurance Company.

1981: Shearson investment firm is added to the growing AMEXCO financial empire.

1983: AMEXCO buys the Geneva-based Trade Development Bank and joins it to AEIBC.

AMEXCO formally establishes the American Express Travel Related Services Company, Inc., as one of the five major entities of AMEXCO.

IDS Financial Services, Inc. (a leader in financial planning) joins the AMEXCO corporate family.

1984: Shearson/American Express acquires Lehman Brothers, Kuhn, Loeb Holding Co. Inc. to join the AMEXCO financial conglomerate as Shearson Lehman Brothers, Inc.

APPENDIX B: FINANCIAL PERFORMANCE BY SERVICE CATEGORY

The company is principally in the business of providing travel related services, international banking services, investment services, investors diversified financial services and insurance services throughout the world. Travel Related Services principally consists of the American Express Card and Travelers Cheque operations. The results of the company's 50 percent interest in Warner Amex are included in "Other and Corporate." The following tables present certain information regarding these industry segments at December 31, 1984, 1983 and 1982 and for the years then ended (millions).

TABLE 1 1984 data

	Travel Related Services	International Banking Services	Investment Services	IDS Financial Services	Insurance Services	Other and corporate	Adjustments and eliminations	Consolidated
Revenues	$ 3,620	$ 1,548	$ 2,280	$1,576	$4,025	$ 82	$ (236)	$12,895
Pretax income (loss) before general corporate expenses	$ 625	$ 193	$ 168	$ 95	$ (114)	$ 16	$ (18)	$ 965
General corporate expenses	—	—	—	—	—	(229)	—	(229)
Pretax income (loss)	$ 625	$ 193	$ 168	$ 95	$ (114)	$ (213)	$ (18)	$ 736
Net income (loss)	$ 387	$ 156	$ 103	$ 62	$ 43	$ (125)	$ (16)	$ 610
Assets	$12,542	$13,768	$22,735	$6,411	$7,735	$1,239	$(2,582)	$61,848

Insurance services comprises the following:

	Property-Liability				Life and other	Total insurance services
	Commercial lines	Personal lines	Investment income	Total		
Revenues	$ 2,017	$ 817	$ 429	$3,263	$ 762	$ 4,025
Pretax income (loss)	$ (558)	$ (40)	$ 404	$ (194)	$ 80	$ (114)

TABLE 2 1983 data

	Travel Related Services	International Banking Services	Investment Services	IDS Financial Services	Insurance Services	Other and corporate	Adjustments and eliminations	Consolidated
Revenues	$ 2,889	$ 1,437	$ 1,826	—	$3,784	$ (6)	$ (160)	$ 9,770
Pretax income (loss) before general corporate expenses	$ 445	$ 183	$ 326	—	$ (242)	$ (17)	$ (10)	$ 685
General corporate expenses	—	—	—	—	—	(168)	—	(168)
Pretax income (loss)	$ 445	$ 183	$ 326	—	$ (242)	$ (185)	—	$ 517
Net income	$ 301	$ 136	$ 175	—	$ 30	$ (117)	$ (10)	$ 515
Assets	$10,226	$13,287	$ 9,060	$5,410	$7,057	$1,095	$(2,154)	$43,981

Insurance services comprises the following:

	Property-Liability				Life and other	Total insurance services
	Commercial lines	Personal lines	Investment income	Total		
Revenues	$ 1,925	$ 783	$ 437	$3,145	$ 639	$ 3,784
Pretax income (loss)	$ (609)	$ (95)	$ 452	$ (252)	$ 10	$ (242)

TABLE 3 1982 data

	Travel Related Services	International Banking Services	Investment Services	Insurance Services	Other and corporate	Adjustments and eliminations	Consolidated
Revenues	$ 2,516	$ 1,025	$ 1,318	$3,356	$ 14	$ (136)	$ 8,093
Pretax income before general corporate expenses	$ 363	$ 101	$ 228	$ 220	$ (5)	—	$ 907
General corporate expenses	—	—	—	—	(153)	—	(153)
Pretax income	$ 363	$ 101	$ 228	$ 220	$ (158)	—	$ 754
Net income	$ 247	$ 60	$ 124	$ 244	$ (94)	—	$ 581
Assets	$ 8,445	$ 7,681	$ 6,351	$6,513	$ 784	$(1,463)	$28,311

Insurance services comprises the following:

	Property-Liability				Life and other	Total insurance services
	Commercial lines	Personal lines	Investment income	Total		
Revenues	$ 1,947	$ 640	$ 348	$2,935	$ 421	$ 3,356
Pretax income (loss)	$ (95)	$ (22)	$ 328	$ 211	$ 9	$ 220

APPENDIX C: AMERICAN EXPRESS AT-A-GLANCE

This appendix contains excerpts from the American Express 1984 Annual Report, wherein American Express explains its different activities, with accompanying data.

1. American Express: Top Rated by Independent Study. American Express products and services hold the confidence of millions of people. They look to American Express brand names for better ways to make, use and protect their money. In a survery in 1984, the *American Banker* found that people rate American Express products and services higher than those of any other top financial services firm in the United States.

	Who consumers know (%)[1]
American Express	75
Prudential Insurance	72
Bank of America	70
Merrill Lynch	66
Beneficial Finance	55
Sears Roebuck	54
Citicorp	53
Chas. Schwab	21

2. Travel Related Services. Travel Related Services began the American Express tradition of reliable service in 1850 by moving freight. Today, it moves people and their buying power around the world. People know the quality of the American Express Card, Travelers Cheque and Travel Services.

(Millions, except percentages)	1984	1983	Percent increase
Revenues	$ 3,620	$ 2,889	25%
Net income	$ 387	$ 301	29
Card charge volume	$47,638	$38,356	24
Travelers Cheque sales	$15,116	$13,862	9
Total assets	$12,542	$10,226	23
Average Travelers Cheques outstanding	$ 2,634	$ 2,437	8
Cards in force	20.2	17.3	17
Return on average shareholder's equity	25.3%	24.1%	

[1] Multiple responses permitted. Adapted from the *American Banker*.

3. International Banking Services. At American Express International Banking Corporation, the accent is on "international." The Bank helped American Express expand internationally following World War I. Today, 82 offices in 39 countries offer export financing, private banking and other select services.

(Millions, except percentages)	1984	1983	Percent increase (decrease)
Net income from International Banking Services	$ 156	$ 136	15%
Loans and discounts	$ 6,272	$ 6,290	—
Reserve for loan losses	$ 165	$ 162	2
Total assets of American Express International Banking Corporation	$13,875	$13,309	4
Customers' deposits and credit balances	$10,517	$10,328	2
Shareholder's equity of American Express International Banking Corporation	$ 897	$ 819	10
Primary capital to average assets	7.64%	7.05%	
Return on average assets	1.15%	1.04%	
Return on average shareholder's equity	17.81%	17.67%	

4. Investment Services. Shearson Lehman Brothers Inc. evolved from strategic acquisitions — most recently, Lehman Brothers. Today, Shearson Lehman melds this investment banking franchise with strong trading and distribution capabilities.[2]

(Millions)	1984	1983	Percent increase (decrease)
Revenues	$ 2,280	$ 1,826	25%
Pretax income	$ 168	$ 326	(49)
Net income	$ 103	$ 175	(41)
Total assets	$22,735	$ 9,060	151
Total capital, including subordinated debt, of Shearson Lehman Brothers Inc.	$ 1,896	$ 1,057	79
Assets managed and/or administered	$64,939	$47,144	38

5. IDS Financial Services. IDS Financial Services Inc. and its subsidiaries have earned people's trust, through outstanding financial advice and services, since 1894.

[2] Note: Investment Services 1984 amounts include the effect of the acquisition of Lehman Brothers Kuhn Loeb Holding Co., Inc., accounted for as a purchase as of May 11, 1984.

The 4,400 representatives of IDS provide financial plans and products that stand the test of time.[3]

(Millions)	1984	1983	Percent increase (decrease)
Revenues	$ 1,576	$ —	—
Pretax income	$ 95	$ —	—
Net income	$ 62	$ —	—
Individual life insurance in force	$13,818	$11,424	21%
Assets owned and/or managed:			
Assets managed for institutions	$ 3,080	$ 3,650	(16)
Assets owned and managed for individuals:			
Owned assets	$ 6,411	$ 5,410	19
Managed assets	$ 9,812	$ 9,162	7

6. Insurance Services. Fireman's Fund Insurance Companies was born in San Francisco in 1863 to provide protection against the frequent fires that ravaged the city. Today, Fireman's Fund is an industry leader in developing new products and new approaches to marketing.

(Millions, except percentages)	1984	1983	Percent increase
Fireman's Fund Insurance Companies			
Revenues	$ 4,025	$ 3,784	6%
Net income	$ 43	$ 30	42
Total assets	$ 7,735	$ 7,057	10
Shareholder's equity	$ 1,485	$ 1,304	14
Return on average shareholder's equity	3.1%	2.2%	
Property-Liability Companies			
Premiums written	$ 2,834	$ 2,781	2
Underwriting ratio	121.1%	126.0%	
Loss and loss expense ratio	86.4%	86.5%	
Expense ratio	32.2%	36.6%	
Policyholder dividend ratio	2.5%	2.9%	
Life Companies			
Premiums written	$ 655	$ 539	21
Life insurance in force	$23,133	$15,493	49

[3] Note: The acquisition of IDS Financial Services was accounted for as a purchase effective December 31, 1983. Therefore, revenues, pretax income and net income for 1983 are not presented.

CASE 25

ASHLAND OIL, INC.

EARLY HISTORY

In 1924, Swiss Oil, an oil and gas exploration and production company based in Lexington, Ky., bought a small refinery near Catlettsburg in eastern Kentucky. Twelve years later the refinery was so successful that it merged with Swiss to form Ashland Oil & Refining Company. Since then, Ashland's history has included a significant number of acquisitions. The company grew initially by acquiring refining capacity, pipelines, and crude supply. Acquisitions included Allied Oil Company and Freedom-Valvoline Oil Company. In the 1960s, the company took its first step toward diversification by entering the chemical business. In 1962, it purchased United Carbon Company. This was followed by the acquisition of other chemical-producing companies. These chemical companies and Ashland's petrochemical operations were consolidated in 1967 to form Ashland Chemical Company.

During the 1960s, the company also expanded into highway construction and construction materials supply. In 1975, the construction company, later operated through APAC (Ashland Paving and Construction), was formed to encompass all the company's construction activities.

By the 1970s, Ashland Oil, Inc., as the parent company was called, had grown into a large conglomerate. In 1985, Ashland was the 48th largest industrial corporation in the United States with operations in refining, transporting, and marketing petroleum products; chemicals; coal; oil exploration; highway construction; and engineering services.

EXPLORATION ROLLERCOASTER

During the later 1960s, under Chairman and C.E.O. Orin Atkins, the company diversified heavily into crude oil exploration and production. These activities required

This case was written by John J. Craighead, research assistant, and Robert R. Gardner, associate director of the Maguire Oil and Gas Institute, under the direction of Professor M. Edgar Barrett. It was prepared as a basis for class discussion rather than to illustrate either effective or ineffective handling of an administrative situation. Copyright © 1986 by M. Edgar Barrett. Reprinted by permission.

an initial investment of $43 million between 1966 and 1969. One of these early exploration efforts resulted in eight dry holes in the Santa Barbara channel and an $8 million write-off. Exploration success continued to elude Ashland in the 1970s, when more write-offs were taken for abandoned projects in Alaska, Iran, and the Java Sea. Although it did drill some successful wells, by 1977 the company could supply only 20 percent of the crude oil requirements for its refineries. Citing high exploration costs (Ashland spent almost $900 million on exploration between 1972 and 1978) and lack of results, the company abruptly began selling much of its oil- and gas-producing property in 1978. The company sold its interest in Ashland Oil Canada Limited for $316 million in October 1978. In March and April 1979, the company sold various producing properties and leases in the Rocky Mountains, Southeast, Southwest, Midcontinent and Gulf Coast regions of the United States for $731 million. In the same year, Ashland sold all its interest in North Sea producing properties for $94.5 million. Management decided that the more than $1 billion raised from these property sales would be used for retiring debt, repurchasing stock, paying higher dividends, and making new acquisitions. In addition, funds were used to buy higher-priced crude and to pay an additional $256 million in taxes that resulted from the sale.

Following the property sales, Ashland became even more dependent on foreign sources of crude. Foreign supplies accounted for roughly 70 percent of the firm's crude requirements, most of this coming from OPEC countries. Iran in particular supplied more than 20 percent of Ashland's crude. (Crude supply from Iran was cut off entirely on November 12, 1979, when President Carter suspended imports of Iranian oil following a well-publicized incident in which American citizens in Iran were taken hostage.) Less than 4 percent of Ashland's crude oil requirements in 1980 came from production owned by Ashland.

COMPANY OPERATIONS BY 1985

Refining

In 1985, Ashland was the nation's largest independent refiner of petroleum products. All refining operations were controlled by Ashland Petroleum Company, a subsidiary of Ashland Oil. It operated refineries in Catlettsburg, Ky.; St. Paul Park, Minn.; and Canton, Ohio, with a total daily capacity of 357,000 barrels. Ashland's refineries operated at 83 percent of capacity in 1985, running an average of 297,458 barrels per day (bpd) of crude. (By comparison, the nation as a whole had a refinery utilization of 76.0 percent in 1984.[1]) The company supplied 7.9 percent of this amount with its own crude. (Exhibit 1 shows Ashland's crude oil and gas production.) The main refinery in Catlettsburg, Ky., included a recently completed 40,000 bpd reduced crude conversion complex. This conversion process increased the yield of gasoline, diesel, and jet fuel from heavy and high-sulfur crude or allowed current

---

[1] *National Petroleum News 1985 Factbook,* p. 134.

production levels to be maintained while using 20 percent less light crude.[2] In 1985, refining, wholesale marketing, and transportation of petroleum products amounted to 48 percent of the company earnings.[3]

Marketing

Marketing was also under the control of Ashland Petroleum. The company marketed gasoline through 1,910 outlets located throughout the Midwest and Mid-Atlantic states. The company owned 520 of these outlets, including 347 SuperAmerica convenience stores. The remaining 173 of these Ashland-owned outlets were independently operated, but sold gas under the Ashland name.

SuperAmerica sold one-fourth of all Ashland's gasoline. These convenience stores, or "C-stores," were on a larger scale than most of Ashland's competitors. SuperAmerica stations often had as many as thirty-six pumps. The store operation inside was larger than most convenience stores as well and could be described as a minigrocery store. SuperAmerica stations offered a wide variety of "nongas" merchandise, which accounted for approximately half of the stores' total sales. In addition to food products, the stores carried their own brand of cigarettes and (in some outlets) liquor.[4] Outlets in the Minneapolis-St. Paul area offered fresh-baked goods under the SuperMom's brand name.

Also part of Ashland Petroleum was Valvoline Oil Company. A registered trademark since 1873, Valvoline brand motor oil was the third-largest-selling motor oil in the nation in 1985 (in a motor oil market that Ashland officials considered to be extremely competitive). Valvoline products were sold through 107,000 retail outlets (including SuperAmerica) and in more than ninety-six countries throughout the world.

Exploration and Crude Supply

The subsidiary in charge of exploration and production was Ashland Exploration, Inc. With the sale of most of its producing properties in 1978 and 1979, the company was left with only a fraction of its former production. By 1985, Ashland's domestic producing interests were concentrated in the Appalachian region and the Illinois Basin. New drilling occurred primarily in the Houston region, mostly in southern Louisiana, with offshore drilling planned for the Gulf of Mexico.

All foreign operations were located in Nigeria. Foreign reserves rose to 49.2 million barrels during 1984, up 29.5 million barrels from the previous year.[5] This increase was mostly due to development of the Akam field, offshore Nigeria. The division expected to complete a floating storage facility in early 1986 which would

[2] "Ashland Oil Begins Production at Facility for Crude Conversion," *Wall Street Journal*, April 12, 1983, p. 3.

[3] "Remarks by John R. Hall, Chairman and Chief Executive Officer Ashland Oil, Inc. at the Year-end Presentation to Security Analysts," November 6, 1985, p. 13.

[4] "Ashland Believes It Can Pump Out Earnings Despite Uncertainties Concerning Oil Refining," *Wall Street Journal*, February 26, 1985, p. 63.

[5] "Nigerian Exploration Efforts Help Boost Ashland's Proved Reserves," *The Oil Daily*, November 9, 1984, p. A2.

EXHIBIT 1
Ashland's net oil and
gas production

	1985	1984	1983	1982	1981	1980
Crude oil (bpd)						
United States	2,755	2,500	2,700	2,700	2,800	3,100
Foreign	20,781	19,100	14,000	13,900	9,500	9,600
Total crude	23,536	21,600	16,700	16,600	12,300	12,700
Natural gas (mcf/day)						
United States	32,156	29,000	27,000	27,000	28,000	26,000

Note: Figures for fiscal year ending September 30.
Source: Ashland Oil company documents.

allow production to begin from eight development wells at the offshore Adanga field in Nigeria. The company's 5-year production data is shown in Exhibit 1.

Chemicals

Ashland Chemical Company, a wholly owned subsidiary of Ashland Oil, engaged in the manufacture, distribution, and sale of a wide variety of chemical products. It was divided into several specialty divisions.

One of these specialty divisions, Industrial Chemical and Solvents, was the largest distributor of industrial chemicals in the country. It sold its own products, as well as those of many other manufacturers, through seventy-seven distribution centers located throughout North America. The division specialized in supplying mixed truckload and less-then-truckload quantities to the paint, oilfield, automotive, paper, and rubber industries. This flexibility was said to allow them to sell to small, specialized companies that purchased in smaller quantities than large firms.

Ashland manufactured and sold high-purity chemicals to the electronic and high technology industries through its Electronic & Laboratory Specialty Division. These liquid chemicals and gases were used in manufacturing silicon chips. The Petrochemicals Division marketed aromatic hydrocarbons, malic anhydride and other petroleum-based products.

Coal

The company was a major coal producer through Ashland Coal Inc., a 65-percent-owned subsidiary, and Arch Minerals Corporation, in which the company had a 50 percent interest. These firms mined coal in Alabama, Illinois, Kentucky, West Virginia, and Wyoming and sold to electric utilities and industrial users. Combined sales of these operations placed Ashland among the top coal producers in the nation.

Engineering and Construction

Ashland's Engineering and Construction unit was composed of the APAC construction subsidiaries and a group of companies known as the Engineering Services Group, which were acquired in 1981 as part of the purchase of U.S. Filter Corporation.

Ashland's APAC subsidiary manufactured construction material and performed contract construction work. This contract work included paving highways, shopping centers, and parking lots. APAC operated in 13 Sunbelt states, with its administrative offices in Atlanta. The subsidiary owned 131 asphalt plants and 18 quarries.

The Engineering Services Group included several firms that were involved in architectural design, engineering services, and project management. One of these subsidiaries, Holmes and Narver, had designed security systems for the Los Angeles Olympics. Williams Brothers Engineering Company, another firm within the Engineering Services Group, was a leader in the design of oil, gas, and water pipelines and was a leading supplier of pipeline engineering services on the Alaskan North Slope. Projects of other firms included managing airport expansion and manufacturing pollution-control equipment.

STRATEGY DECISIONS, 1980–1983

Diversification into Unrelated Businesses

In addition to retiring debt, repurchasing stock, and paying increased dividends, management targeted a major portion of the cash raised from the 1978–1979 property sales for acquisitions in areas outside Ashland's normal operations. Ashland's 1981 annual report contained the following statement:

> *Since the early 1970s, the climate for U.S. business in general and the petroleum industry in particular has been affected increasingly by events beyond the control of either individual companies or the U.S. government. To survive and prosper in such a volatile environment, companies must be willing to reappraise traditional operations and aggressively explore and develop new business opportunities.*

These words came on the heels of two major acquisitions by Ashland. In the first of these, the firm entered the insurance business on January 1, 1981, with the purchase of the Integon Corporation for $238 million. (Payment was composed of $116 million in cash and $122 million of preferred stock. The excess $88,148,000 of the cost over the fair value of the assets acquired would be amortized over a 40-year period using the straight-line method.) Integon was an insurance holding company based in Winston-Salem, North Carolina. The company's primary business was the sale of life and health insurance; home protection policies; group life, annuity and health policies; and credit life and health policies. Through its subsidiaries, Integon also conducted a multiple line property and casualty insurance business, covering such risks as auto liability, fire, and workers' compensation. Integon Mortgage Guaranty Corporation, another subsidiary, was engaged in the mortgage guaranty business in the southeastern United States. Integon Realty Corporation invested in income-producing projects such as motels and office buildings and provided mortgages in the form of construction loans for new projects. As of August 31, 1981, Integon had a total of $10.6 billion of life insurance in force.

In the second of its major acquisitions, Ashland purchased United States Filter Corporation on January 1, 1981 for $402 million. (Payment was composed of $376 million in cash and $26 million in 13.5 percent notes. Goodwill of $150,532,000 would be amortized over 40 years by the straight-line method.) U.S. Filter was the parent company of a number of foreign and domestic firms whose activities included engineering and project management services for the oil, mining, pipeline, and steam-generation industries; design and manufacture of environmental control systems; production of steel castings for use in pumps, valves, turbines, and compressors for the petroleum, chemical, and power-generation industries; production of specialty chemicals for industry and marine shipping; design and manufacture of industrial process instruments; coal mining; and cement production. In 1980, U.S. Filter earned nearly $28 million on sales of $865 million.[6]

Ashland immediately transferred the specialty chemical division (Drew Chemical) of U.S. Filter to Ashland Chemical. The remaining U.S. Filter units were placed into a new subsidiary called Ashland Technology. The catalyst and clay operations of U.S. Filter were sold for $99 million in late 1981. Ashland Technology was divided into four operating groups: (1) the Engineering Services and Power Generation Group, (2) the Process Instruments Group, (3) the Environmental Systems Group, and (4) the Metal Fabrication and Casting Group.

Ashland officials made the following comments concerning the acquisitions of Integon and U.S. Filter and their position in future strategy:

> Ashland's strategy has been to further diversify its asset base, enhance its flexibility to adapt to changes and take advantage of new opportunities as they arise. In 1981, the strategy moved forward dramatically with the two largest acquisitions in Ashland's history. Through U.S. Filter the company has expanded its chemical operations and acquired a very solid base in the fields of engineering services for energy-related projects and environmental control systems for industry. Through Integon, the company has entered the vital and rapidly expanding insurance industry. These new fields promise to enhance Ashland's financial strength and technological and engineering capability while at the same time opening doors for further growth into new areas of business.
>
> Having made these two acquisitions, the company's strategic planning will now be concentrated in the following areas: (1) further strengthening of current operations and divestiture of any operations which do not hold strong prospects for growth, (2) continued reduction in operating costs, (3) further strengthening of the balance sheet, and (4) development of the company's many promising new technologies, such as the RCC process, as sources of income. Continuing diversification efforts will be highly selective and in areas compatible with existing core operations, to stimulate growth as well as new business opportunities. With the addition of Integon and U.S. Filter, we now have strong positions in energy, chemicals, construction, engineering and technology, and insurance. These will be our primary areas for expansion in future years.[7]

Management Changes

In September 1981, Orin Atkins unexpectedly retired as Ashland's chairman and chief executive officer. He was replaced by John R. Hall, a 24-year company veteran and, most recently, vice-chairman.

The exact reasons for Atkins's retirement were not made public at the time.

[6] U.S. Filter Corporation, 1980 Form 10-K, p. F-4.

[7] Ashland Oil, Inc., 1981 Annual Report, pp. 7–8.

Several months later, however, rumors of impropriety involving Atkins began to surface.[8] In 1980, on his personal order, Ashland paid $1,350,000 to a wealthy Libyan middleman, Yehia Omar, in return for his securing a contract with the country of Oman to supply 20,000 barrels of crude a day to Ashland. Soon after, top Ashland officials met to discuss whether this payment was legal. (These concerns were raised because under the 1977 Foreign Corrupt Policies Act, corporate payments to foreign government officials were illegal.) Since Omar had at one time carried an Omani diplomatic passport, it was possible that Ashland, by making these payments, had broken the law. The company's directors commissioned an independent investigation to look into the matter. The findings of this investigation cleared Atkins and Ashland of violating any U.S. law because Omar had not been an Omani official at the time of the payment. However, even though no law had been broken, the report criticized the impropriety of such payments.[9]

In early September 1981, Atkins met privately with several of Ashland's directors. It was reported that, at the meeting, the board voiced strong concerns regarding both Ashland's diversification moves and the nature of the Omani transaction.[10] "An element of the board thought we were doing too many things too fast," recalled F. H. Ross, a director and former Ashland executive.[11] Moveover, the company had just reported a 76 percent drop in profits for the months ending June 30, 1981. In a meeting on September 17, 1981, outside directors sought and received Atkins's resignation.[12]

Changing Economic Situation

The economic conditions that existed by the early 1980s were very different from what Ashland and many other U.S. firms had forecasted. Ashland's 1977 strategic plan had anticipated U.S. energy demand to increase steadily from 38.3 million barrels a day (mmbpd) of oil equivalent in 1978 to 47 mmbpd oil equivalent by 1990. In fact, actual U.S. energy demand was falling by the early 1980s. Real GNP growth was 1.3 percent annually instead of the 3 percent to 4 percent that had been expected. Interest rates were much higher than the company had anticipated. Furthermore, the U.S. economy experienced back-to-back recessions in 1980 and 1981–1982.

World crude prices, which had increased by this time to record levels, forced Ashland to use a greater portion of its cash flow on crude supplies for its refineries. At the same time, U.S. demand for petroleum products was falling. The national recession, high inflation, increased automobile fuel efficiency, and individual conser-

---

[8] "Ashland Oil Chief's Sudden '81 Departure Is Linked by Insiders to an Oman Payment," *Wall Street Journal,* May 16, 1983, p. 4.

[9] "Dubious Deals, Ashland Oil Criticizes Its Payments to Libyan To Get Oman's Crude," *Wall Street Journal,* May 24, 1983, p. 1.

[10] It was reported, for instance, that Ashland lost $2.3 million in a venture designed to produce reusable sausage casings. ("Dubious Deals," op. cit.)

[11] Ibid.

[12] "Ashland Oil Chief's Sudden '81 Departure," op. cit.

vation were all factors that led to a 6.4 percent drop in petroleum product demand in 1980.[13] The spread between crude and product prices had become so narrow that, in some instances, the prices received for petroleum products were less than refiners' crude oil costs.[14]

Alternative Sources of Energy

The economic conditions that existed in the early 1980s led Ashland officials to make investments that would take advantage of the situation. Since low-grade crude was cheaper and more readily available than light crude, the company converted some of its refineries so they could handle lower grades. In 1981, Ashland also began building a new 40,000 bpd refinery in Catlettsburg, Ky., that utilized its RCC process. The project cost was initially estimated at $190 million (though the final cost was $295 million).[15] The company justified the investment based on an estimate that the new refinery would increase pretax earnings by $10 million a month.[16]

With crude oil so expensive and in such short supply during the early 1980s, alternative methods for producing hydrocarbons became more attractive. One process, coal liquefaction, converted coal to liquid hydrocarbons. Ashland participated with the Department of Energy and other companies in building a coal liquefaction pilot plant near its main refinery in Catlettsburg. The company also planned a joint venture to build a commercial-scale liquefaction facility. Under the proposal, Ashland and five or six other companies would each invest $100–150 million in the project. The group would then negotiate guaranteed loans with the federal Synthetic Fuels Corporation. By 1982, Ashland had spent a total of $13 million on both projects.[17]

Hall's Initial Strategy

After John R. Hall took office in late 1981, he outlined a new direction for the company, which included three major strategic goals.[18]

The first goal was to strengthen the core business — refining. He proposed doing this by reducing the cost of raw materials used, namely crude oil. This was to be accomplished by becoming less dependent on foreign suppliers, which, as in the case of Iran, tended to be less reliable and more expensive than domestic sources. Hall also proposed reducing operating costs, mainly by improving refining efficiency. He wanted to put more emphasis on the marketing of Ashland's refined products as a way to strengthen the core business. This would involve increasing sales efforts

[13] Ashland Oil, Inc., 1980 Annual Report, p. 11.

[14] Ashland Oil, Inc., 1981 Form 10-K, p. 3.

[15] Ashland Oil, Inc., 1983 Form 10-K, p. 1.

[16] "Ashland Oil Begins Production," op. cit.

[17] "Ashland to Quit Role in Project For Synfuels," *Wall Street Journal,* November 23, 1982, p. 4.

[18] "Ashland Oil: Sequel To The Asset Redeployment Program," presented by John R. Hall at the Seminar for Senior Executives in the Oil & Gas Industry, Vail, Colorado, June 25, 1985.

and improving distribution of finished products. Reducing overhead was the final area in which Hall proposed strengthening the core business.

Hall's second major goal was to strengthen the financial situation of the company. Again Hall outlined several ways to achieve this. First, the company would try to maintain an "A" bond rating with the two major bond-rating services. To do this, it was felt that they would have to reduce the ratio of debt (plus preferred stock) to total capitalization to less than 40 percent. This was to be accomplished by repurchasing preferred stock and reducing long-term debt. Second, Hall wanted to achieve an overall return on equity of 17 percent, a return on assets of 12 percent, and a return on investment of 15 percent. Third, Hall hoped to reduce the dividend payout to 30–40 percent of normalized primary earnings. Fourth, he proposed improving the company's balance sheet by achieving real earnings-per-share growth. Finally, he desired to reduce corporate overhead. This could be accomplished, he asserted, by reducing G&A expenses through layoffs or realigning the corporate organization.

Hall's third major goal was defined under the broad heading of "diversifying profitability." For Ashland, diversification involved reducing dependence on the refining end of the business for earnings and cash flow. Hall stated that effective diversification could be achieved in two ways: (1) through investment in other segments of Ashland that had potential for profitable growth and (2) by acquiring outside businesses in either related or nonrelated fields.[19]

COMPANY DEVELOPMENTS AND DECISIONS

Refinery Closings

In 1980, Ashland operated seven refineries with a total daily capacity of 457,000 bpd. Throughout that year, its refinery system operated below capacity and processed an average of 363,000 bpd. The Findley refinery in Ohio, with a capacity of 21,000 bpd, was closed in the spring of 1981. A little over a year later, operations were suspended at the Buffalo, N.Y., refinery. The company blamed an "unprecedented decline in the demand for petroleum products" and "bleak prospects for a rebound" for this latest closing.[20] A third refinery in Louisville, Ky., closed its doors in April 1983. The company planned to make up the 13,000 bpd that the Louisville refinery had been producing by increasing operations at its main refinery in Catlettsburg, which was operating at 70 percent of capacity.[21]

In April 1985, the company suspended crude oil processing operations at its 7,000-bpd Freedom, Pa., refinery. The facility continued to operate as a product terminal and motor oil blending and packaging plant. The remaining refineries at

[19] Ibid.

[20] "Ashland Oil Unit To Idle Refinery Near Buffalo, N.Y.," *Wall Street Journal,* May 11, 1982, p. 12.

[21] "Ashland Expects Loss In Fiscal 2nd Quarter, Mulls Dividend Cut," *Wall Street Journal,* March 18, 1983, p. 7.

EXHIBIT 2
Ashland Oil refinery
capacity and
utilization (barrels
per stream day)

	1985	1984	1983	1982	1981	1980
Catlettsburg, Ky.	220,000	220,000	195,000	195,000	195,000	220,000
St. Paul, Minn.	69,000	69,000	69,000	69,000	69,000	69,000
Canton, Ohio	68,000	68,000	68,000	68,000	68,000	66,000
Buffalo, N.Y.	—	—	—	—	48,000	48,000
Louisville, Ky.	—	—	—	26,000	26,000	26,000
Findlay, Ohio	—	—	—	—	—	21,000
Freedom, Pa.	—	7000	7000	7000	7000	7000
Total	357,000	364,000	339,000	365,000	413,000	457,000
Crude oil refined (bpd)	297,000	301,813	285,029	312,200	321,499	363,427
Refinery runs/ capacity	83%	83%	84%	86%	78%	80%

Source: Ashland Oil company documents.

Catlettsburg; Canton, Ohio; and St. Paul Park, Minn., were equipped to process a wider variety of crudes, including low-quality crude. (See Exhibit 2.)

Acquisitions

Late in 1982, the company bought the crude oil gathering and transportation system of Scurlock Oil of Houston for $80 million. Scurlock's system, mostly in Texas and Louisiana, included 2,300 miles of oil pipeline (capable of moving 200,000 bpd of crude) as well as 2.5 million barrels of storage capacity. This system gave the company access to a significant amount of domestic crude, kept it in contact with major domestic producers, and allowed it to make offers to purchase the oil it transported. "We believe the acquisition will prove to be one of the most beneficial ever made," said Charles J. Luellen, president of Ashland Petroleum and senior vice-president of Ashland Oil, "because it will substantially increase our supply of secure, economically priced U.S. crude oil."[22] "This was a very positive acquisition," echoed John Dansby, Ashland's vice-president of planning. "It's hard to imagine a single decision that could have had a more decisive impact on the company."[23] Overnight, the Scurlock acquisition had increased Ashland's supply of domestic crude by 60,000 to 80,000 bpd.[24] Scurlock also had the advantage of posting the price it was willing to pay for crude. This allowed Ashland to adjust its purchasing price just like other majors did.

The company also acquired Tresler Oil Company in 1982. Tresler marketed oil products in the Ohio River Valley and operated a river-front petroleum-product

[22] "A Troubled Ashland Banks On Chemicals," *Chemical Week,* June 23, 1982, p. 44.

[23] John Dansby, vice-president strategic planning, Ashland Oil, Inc. (December 3, 1985 interview, Ashland, Ky.).

[24] Ibid.

storage terminal. Ashland officials believed this acquisition would strengthen the company's marketing and distribution network for refined products in the Ohio River market.

Coal

In November 1982, Ashland pulled out of its proposed coal-liquefaction project. The company suspended participation because of uncertainty about crude prices, the massive capital investment necessary to construct the project, exposure to possible cost overruns, and tax law changes that reduced the tax benefits of the project. Ashland officials said costs of the project had been expended as incurred, so the decision would not affect the company financially.[25]

In June 1981, Ashland sold a 25 percent interest in Ashland Coal to Saarbergwerke A.G. of West Germany for $102.5 million in cash. Saarbergwerke was 74 percent owned by the West German government. Proceeds from the sale were used to retire short-term obligations of Ashland Coal. Company officials said the deal provided Ashland Coal with a new export dimension in its overall marketing activity.[26]

The company sold an additional 10 percent of Ashland Coal in June 1982 for $44.3 million to Carboex S.A., a coal supply firm owned by the Spanish government. This reduced Ashland's ownership of the coal subsidiary to 65 percent.[27]

Cost Control and Debt Reduction

In an attempt to promote efficiency and cost control in all operations, Ashland Oil, the parent company, was realigned along the lines of a holding company. A core group, made up of seven top parent-company executives, monitored and reviewed the overall performance of the divisions. However, day-to-day operational decisions were turned over to divisional managers. This management structure was expected to give the divisions something close to the autonomy of separate companies.[28] By taking on their own administrative functions, the divisions were said to avoid a good measure of bureaucracy and to respond faster to market forces.[29] Through this process of realignment, Ashland was able to trim corporate staff by one-third.

Between 1981 and 1985, Ashland reduced debt and capitalized leases by $206 million. This included exchanging $23,167,000 of capital stock for long-term debt in 1983. During the same 5-year period, the company reduced preferred stock by $109 million. In 1985 alone, the company reduced redeemable preferred stock by $54 million and long-term debt and capitalized leases by $41 million. As of September 30, 1985, long-term debt, capitalized leases, and redeemable preferred stock represented 39 percent of total capitalization, compared to 44 percent the year before.

[25] "Ashland Drops Breckenridge H-Coal Project," *Oil & Gas Journal*, November 29, 1982, p. 43.

[26] "Ashland Nears Sale of Coal Unit Stake to West Germany," *Wall Street Journal*, May 28, 1981, p. 7.

[27] Ashland Oil, Inc., 1982 Form 10-K, p. 7.

[28] "A Troubled Ashland Banks On Chemicals," op. cit.

[29] Ibid.

EXHIBIT 3
Summary of
earnings per share
and dividends per
share

	1985	1984	1983	1982	1981	1980	1979
Earnings							
From operations and investments	$4.12	$2.13	$2.23	$4.75	$2.22	$6.49	$ 5.31
From divestitures and write-offs		(9.53)		.54		.31	10.24
From extraordinary gain from exchange of common stock for long-term debt			.23				
Total earnings per share	4.12	(7.40)	2.46	5.29	2.22	6.80	15.55
Dividends per share	1.60	1.60	2.20	2.40	2.40	2.20	1.80

Source: Ashland Oil company documents.

(Appendixes B and C provide greater detail on this subject.) Exhibit 3 shows earnings per share and dividends per common share paid by the company.

Integon

To compete in the increasingly competitive deregulated insurance industry, Integon, in 1982, started selling a more flexible universal life policy offering a higher yield to policyholders. During fiscal 1983, the insurance company sold most of its group accident and health business — reportedly because of rising costs of healthcare claims.[30] Exhibit 4 shows Integon's financial results for 1981 through 1984.

For the 6 months ending February 29, 1984, Integon's profits declined 59 percent to $4.9 million (from $7.8 million in the year-earlier period).[31] At Ashland's annual meeting in January 1984, William Seaton, vice-chairman and chief financial officer, said that Integon's income had decreased because of higher losses on property and casualty insurance. Further, he said, volatile interest rates and other available investment opportunities made Integon's ordinary life insurance policies less attractive to consumers.[32] Policyholders continued to surrender ordinary life insurance policies at higher than normal rates.

Ashland Technology

By late 1983, it was becoming clear, as well, that many units within Ashland Technology were not performing up to company expectations.[33] Most of the former U.S. Filter businesses were not market leaders and company officials concluded

[30] Ashland Oil, Inc., 1983 Annual Report, p. 30.

[31] "Ashland Oil Seeks Buyer for Integon, Its Insurance Unit," *Wall Street Journal,* May 22, 1984, p. 10.

[32] Ibid.

[33] "Ashland Oil: Trying to Cope With a Diversification Hangover and a Lingering Scandal," *Business Week,* November 7, 1983, p. 134.

EXHIBIT 4
Summary of Integon
financial results (in
millions)

	1984	1983	1982	1981
Net income	$9	$13	$14	$8
Life insurance in force	14,332	12,324	9,314	10,600

Source: Ashland Oil company documents.

EXHIBIT 5
Summary of
Ashland Technology
financial results

	1984	1983	1982	1981[a]
Sales and operating revenue	$677,239	$633,123	$817,727	$588,786
Operating income	21,916	700	22,506	8,798
Funds provided from operations	34,863	18,720	20,100	22,522
Backlog of projects	614,000	527,000	666,000	784,000

Note: Figures in thousands of dollars, for fiscal year ending September 30.
[a] Includes only nine months starting January 1.
Source: Ashland Oil company documents.

that they probably paid too much for U.S. Filter.[34] Segment data for Ashland Technology appears in Exhibit 5.

BACK TO BASICS

Divestiture and Redirection

In September 1984, Ashland announced plans to sell Integon and most of the U.S. Filter units (by now part of Ashland Technology) it had acquired just 4 years earlier.[35] The decision resulted in a one-time charge against after-tax earnings of $271 million in the fourth quarter of 1984. The write-down included the difference between the book value of the units to be divested and the $300 million after-tax proceeds expected to be generated from their sale in fiscal 1985.[36] It also included the write-down of an unprofitable methanol plant in Louisiana. After taking the charge, Ashland showed a net loss of $172 million for the year.

Ashland's 1984 "Letter to the Stockholders" justified the divestment and write-downs as follows:

[34] Ibid.

[35] As part of the divestment, Ashland sold all of Ashland Technology with the exception of the engineering services group, Riley-Beaird (which was part of the metal fabrication and casting group) and the recently acquired Daniel, Munn, Johnson & Mendenhall (an architecture and civil engineering firm).

[36] "Back to the Basics, with a $270 Million Loss," *Chemical Week,* September 26, 1984, p. 9.

After careful study, we decided to reduce the scope of our activities in order to concentrate resources in growth areas which offer the greatest potential return to shareholders. We expect the divestiture to generate approximately $300 million which we plan to use to reduce outstanding preferred stock, retire debt and fund investments in growth businesses. Although the write-offs adversely affected the debt-equity ratio by reducing shareholders' equity, the balance sheet will be strengthened by our planned use of the proceeds. In addition, earnings per share will be improved as outstanding preferred stock is reduced. Despite the impact on 1984 earnings, we believe the divestiture and use of proceeds will be in the long-term best interest of shareholders.[37]

The company continued to pursue two of its three original major goals: strengthening the refining business and improving the balance sheet. However, the third goal, to diversify profitability, was altered. Ashland managers were determined that they would no longer attempt to diversify by acquiring businesses in nonrelated industries. Rather, they would attempt to reduce Ashland's reliance on refining by investing only in related nonrefining businesses. Moreover, Ashland officials planned to divest unprofitable units and concentrate on ones that had proved consistently successful.

In particular, six of Ashland's existing businesses had been identified in late 1983 as growth areas that the firm would actively pursue. Management hoped these areas would provide increased profits as well as diversification away from refining. These areas were: (1) Valvoline Motor Oil, (2) SuperAmerica convenience stores, (3) chemical distribution, (4) specialty chemicals, (5) domestic exploration and production, and (6) engineering services.

In selecting these six areas, Ashland's management had particularly emphasized their firm's competitive position in each of the various businesses. Once these businesses were selected, they were analyzed under varying scenarios in an attempt to gauge their relative contributions to corporate income. In so doing, Ashland officials determined that these six areas might well be sufficient to meet the firm's financial goals.

Valvoline

Company officials believed success for Valvoline could be achieved through innovative marketing and product flexibility. The firm, for example, sponsored auto racing teams, which allowed the Valvoline trademark to be displayed on race cars during such races as the Indianapolis 500. They were also an active sponsor of NCAA basketball games.

The Valvoline division had recently introduced several new products, including FourGard Motor Oil (an oil specifically designed for small, four-cylinder passenger cars) and Turbo V (an oil designed for turbo engine cars).

Management intended to start packaging its Valvoline products in one-quart plastic bottles in 1986, as some other motor oil companies already had. By the summer of 1986, it expected all nine U.S. packaging plants to be able to produce the plastic bottles. Valvoline targeted the do-it-yourself consumer and sold its motor oil mostly through distributors, such as K-Mart, rather than through service stations.

[37] Ashland Oil, Inc., 1984 Annual Report, pp. 2–3.

EXHIBIT 6
U.S. annual share-
of-purchases for all
motor oil

	1984	1983	1982	1981	1980
Carried out by purchaser	69%	70%	71%	70%	69%
Installed where bought	31	30	29	30	31

Source: *1985 National Petroleum News Factbook.*

EXHIBIT 7
Ashland Petroleum
Company financial
summary

	1985	1984	1983
Sales and operating revenues	$5,377	5,678	5,700
Operating income			
Refining, wholesale marketing, and transportation	$ 180	40	138
Retail marketing[a]	$ 12	13	4
Valvoline	$ 43	40	39
Other	$ (22)	27	(5)
Total	$ 213[b]	120[b]	176

Note: Figures in millions.
[a] Includes SuperAmerica.
[b] Includes $12 million in income from unusual items in 1985 and $46 million in 1984.
Source: Ashland Oil company documents.

As Exhibit 6 illustrates, do-it-yourself consumers constituted more than two-thirds of the motor oil market.

Valvoline was third in motor oil market share behind Quaker State and Pennzoil. Valvoline management foresaw growth for their product in further market share penetration and expected to be the number two motor oil marketer by 1990.[38]

The Valvoline product line was expanded in September 1985 with the purchase of IG-LO Products Corporation. IG-LO was the nation's largest packager and marketer of refrigerant for automobile air-conditioners. Operating results for Valvoline, included as a part of the entire Ashland Petroleum Company's results, are shown in Exhibit 7.

SuperAmerica

Ashland officials planned to continue the rapid expansion of SuperAmerica by adding fifty new outlets each year. Many of these were planned in Southern Florida, which was outside SuperAmerica's established retail areas of the upper Midwest (where SuperAmerica held a 20 percent share of the retail gasoline market in the Minneapolis-St. Paul area) and the central Ohio Valley.

[38] "1984 Year-End Presentation," by John F. Boehm, vice-president of Ashland Petroleum Co. and president of Valvoline Oil Co., November 7, 1984, p. 14.

EXHIBIT 8
SuperAmerica
financial and
operating data

	1985	1984
Sales and operating revenues	$902	$810
Operating income[a]	$12	$13
Merchandise sales	$241	$212
Number of stores	347	306
Average gallonage per store per month	143,000	142,000

Note: Figures in millions.
[a] Includes other retail operations.
Source: Ashland Oil company documents.

Each new store required an investment of approximately $1 million, including land. Start-up costs were expensed as they were incurred. Each SuperAmerica outlet pumped an average of 143,000 gallons of gas per month. (By comparison, the average U.S. gasoline outlet pumped 66,311 gallons per month in 1984.[39]) Super-America also averaged $700,000 of nongas sales per year per outlet. (The average C-store, meanwhile, had $460,000 of in-store annual sales in 1984.[40]) Whereas most C-stores attracted customers with lower gas prices and then took relatively high margins on food items, Ashland management stressed that SuperAmerica's food and merchandise were priced competitively with lower-margin traditional grocery stores. Operating information for SuperAmerica is shown in Exhibit 8.

Chemical Distribution

Chemical distribution was conducted in part by the Industrial Chemical and Solvents Division. Ashland management intended to increase the number of distribution centers and offer a greater variety of products. The IC&S Division added three new distribution centers in 1985. In addition, Ashland bought General Polymers National in 1983 for $10 million. General Polymers manufactured thermoplastic resins and had distribution centers in Ohio, Illinois, Minnesota, and Texas. During 1985, General Polymers added two distribution centers, in Portland, Ore., and Seattle, bringing the total number of locations to sixteen. The company's goal was to have twenty locations by 1988.[41]

Specialty Chemicals

The specialty chemicals area of Ashland Chemical was seen by management as a means of establishing a niche in the chemical business. This division produced chemicals to fill a specific demand, such as the high-purity chemicals sold to the electronics industry. During 1983 and 1984, Ashland Chemical made several acquisitions and divestitures. The specialty chemical area acquired Scientific Gas Products, which produced and marketed equipment and high-purity gas to the electronics,

[39] *National Petroleum News 1985 Factbook,* p. 116.

[40] Ibid., p. 122.

[41] Ashland Oil, Inc., 1985 Annual Report, p. 17.

EXHIBIT 9
Ashland Chemical
financial data

	1985	1984	1983
Sales and operating revenues	$1,499	$1,501	$1,208
Operating income (loss)			
Chemical Distribution	40	42	36
Specialty Chemicals	28	27	11
Commodity Chemicals	22	3	(20)
Other	(22)	(17)	(26)
Total	68	55	1

Note: Figures in millions.
Source: Ashland Oil company documents.

medical, and industrial laboratory markets. It had facilities in Colorado, California, New Jersey, and Texas.

Two other large acquisitions were made by Ashland Chemical during this time, as well. Goodyear's adhesive manufacturing facilities and technology were acquired in 1984. Goodyear officials claimed to have sold the line because it did not match its business objectives.[42] In October 1985, Ashland agreed to purchase J. T. Baker Chemical Company. Ashland officials said the acquisition would permit them to broaden the line of chemicals the company offered to the electronics, semiconductor, laboratory, and other specialty markets. Baker's worldwide operations had annual sales of $80 million. Data on Specialty Chemicals and Chemical Distribution is shown in Exhibit 9.

Domestic Exploration and Production

Though the company had moved increasingly back into exploration since the massive divestitures of the late 1970s, company officials stressed that their reasons were now entirely different. They claimed no longer to view exploration and production as a means of supplying crude to their refineries (as the major companies did). Instead, said officials, they viewed exploration and production as a source of profits. This time, said Hall and his administration, the company would limit its efforts to projects with high probability of success. In this way, the exploration segment of the firm would function much more like an independent producer.[43] The company's goal for exploration and production was simply to "create value for the shareholder."[44] In effect, said John Dansby, Ashland's vice-president of planning, the company considered exploration and production just another nonrefining segment whose profits would contribute to the diversification plan.

As part of this new effort, Ashland, in 1981, brought in the former chief geologist of Shell Oil Co. to head Ashland Exploration. Until then, E&P operations had been limited to Nigeria, the eastern United States, and the Gulf Coast area. (Only

[42] "Ashland Oil Acquisition," *Wall Street Journal*, February 2, 1984, p. 10.

[43] "Ashland Oil: Sequel To The Asset Redeployment Program," op. cit., p. 25.

[44] John Dansby interview, op. cit.

EXHIBIT 10
Engineering
Services financial
and operating data

	1985	1984	1983
Sales and operating revenue	$396	$336	$287
Operating income	14	7	4
Backlog	345	466	492

Note: Figures in millions.
Source: Ashland Oil company documents.

domestic exploration and production operations, however, were considered to be one of the six so-called growth areas.) Domestic exploratory drilling was carried out in Texas and Louisiana and, by 1985, had resulted mainly in natural gas discoveries. Additions to domestic oil reserves came primarily from developmental drilling in the eastern United States. (See Table 6 in the appendix.)

Engineering Services

The last growth area, engineering services, included the remaining units from the U.S. Filter sell-off and the Los Angeles-based Daniel, Mann, Johnson & Mendenhall (DMJM). DMJM's projects included joint management of the Los Angeles International Airport expansion and design of the Baltimore Metro System.

The combination of DMJM, Holmes & Narver, and Williams Brothers made Ashland one of the leading providers of architectural, engineering, and other technical services. Holmes & Narver ranked sixth in total billings among the top five hundred design firms ranked by *Engineering News-Record*. DMJM placed in the top ten, while Williams Brothers was in the top fifty.[45]

According to company officials, the engineering services group required only limited capital expenditures. All firms within this growth area were heavily reliant on contracts from government entities.[46] Results for engineering services are shown in Exhibit 10.

OVERALL GOALS AND OBJECTIVES

The stated overall objective of Ashland's late 1983 shift in strategy was to reduce the percentage of earnings coming from refining by substantially increasing the earnings from the six growth areas. Exhibit 11 provides data on Ashland's stated 1990 goals regarding relative contribution to earnings. It also provides information on the firm's progress toward these goals.

Management further stated that it would like the firm's nonrefining businesses to be able to support earnings of $5 per share — even if refining should earn nothing.[47]

[45] Ashland Oil, Inc., 1984 Annual Report, pp. 27–28.

[46] "Remarks by John R. Hall," op. cit., p. 12.

[47] "Ashland Oil: Sequel To The Asset Redeployment Program," op. cit.

EXHIBIT 11
Ashland's relative
contribution to
earnings

	1983	1985	Proposed 1990
Refining and wholesale marketing	51%	48%	25%
Six growth areas	37	40	60
Other businesses	12	12	15

Source: Ashland Oil company documents.

APPENDIX: ASHLAND OIL, SELECTED FINANCIAL DATA

TABLE 1 Consolidated statements of income

	Years ended September 30		
	1985	*1984*	*1983*
Revenues			
Sales and operating revenues (including excise taxes)	$8,183,733	$8,544,064	$8,108,169
Other	54,206	77,168	91,302
	8,237,939	8,621,232	8,199,471
Costs and expenses			
Cost of sales and operating expenses	6,745,700	7,214,937	6,960,088
Excise taxes on products and merchandise	292.510	291,500	255,870
Selling, general, and administrative expenses	606,808	611,338	564,574
Depreciation, depletion, and amortization (including capitalized leases)	202,174	212,547	192,006
Foreign exploration taxes	38,690	38,887	30,905
	7,885,882	8,369,209	8,003,443
Operating income	352,057	252,023	196,028
Other income (expense)			
Interest income	20,309	19,723	31,821
Interest expense	(67,413)	(80,814)	(78,501)
Equity income	10,421	20,387	27,517
Other — net (including corporate administrative)	(57,014)	(67,446)	(72,807)
Divestitures and asset write-offs	(39,652)	(286,641)	—
Income (loss) before income taxes and extraordinary gain	218,708	(142,768)	104,058
Income taxes	71,986	29,710	7,421
Income (loss) before extraordinary gain	146,722	(172,478)	96,637
Extraordinary gain from exchange of common stock for long-term debt	—	—	6,196
Net income (loss)	$ 146,722	$ (172,478)	$ 102,833
Earnings (loss) per share			
Income (loss) before extraordinary gain	$4.12	$(7.40)	$2.23
Extraordinary gain	—	—	.23
	$4.12	$(7.40)	$2.46
Average common shares and equivalents outstanding	28,227	27,783	27,011

Note: Figures in thousands (except per-share data); years ended September 30.
Source: Ashland Oil, Inc., 1985 Annual Report.

TABLE 2 Consolidated balance sheets

	Years ended September 30	
	1985	*1984*
Assets		
Current assets		
Cash and short-term securities	$ 173,391	$ 132,111
Accounts receivable (less allowances for doubtful accounts of $27,409,000 in 1985 and $29,097,000 in 1984)	923,822	939,831
Construction completed and in progress — at contract prices	70,770	67,176
Refundable income taxes	—	33,837
Inventories	306,607	393,613
Deferred income tax benefits	62,360	59,605
Other current assets	58,782	50,799
	1,595,732	1,676,972
Investments and other assets		
Noncurrent net assets of operations held for sale	157,000	262,217
Investments in and advances to unconsolidated subsidiaries and affiliates	172,492	167,020
Cost in excess of net assets of companies acquired (less accumulated amortization of $4,626,000 in 1985 and $3,176,000 in 1984	50,107	48,190
Advance coal royalties	58,366	55,157
Other noncurrent assets	77,932	80,643
	515,897	613,227
Property, plant, and equipment		
Cost		
Petroleum	1,773,309	1,711,457
Chemical	335,154	305,428
Coal	180,503	185,631
Engineering and construction	379,132	353,325
Exploration	582,194	469,581
Other	8,037	8,089
Corporate	61,269	64,641
	3,319,598	3,098,152
Accumulated depreciation, depletion, and amortization	(1,503,594)	(1,351,410)
	1,816,004	1,746,742
	$3,927,633	$4,036,941
Liabilities and stockholders' equity		
Current liabilities		
Debt due within one year (including short-term notes of $1,200,000 in 1985 and $726,000 in 1984)	$ 30,455	$ 49,644
Trade and other payables	1,314,278	1,423,721
Contract advances and progress billings in excess of costs incurred	34,577	52,566
Income taxes	47,774	89,639
	1,427,084	1,615,570

TABLE 2 (continued)

	Years ended September 30	
	1985	*1984*
Noncurrent liabilities		
Long-term debt (less current portion)	510,467	544,846
Capitalized lease obligations (less current portion)	105,519	113,204
Other long-term liabilities and deferred credits	268,675	225,980
Deferred income taxes	380,240	331,783
Minority interest in consolidated subsidiaries	57,223	56,288
	1,322,124	1,272,101
Redeemable preferred stock (1985 redemption value — $260,305,000)	249,014	303,371
Common stockholders' equity		
Common stock, par value $1.00 per share		
Authorized — 60,000,000 shares		
Issued — 28,672,000 shares in 1985 and 28,264,000 shares in 1984	28,672	28,264
Paid-in capital	229,135	217,979
Retained earnings	690,621	619,373
Deferred translation adjustments	(12,682)	(14,506)
Common shares in treasury — at cost (285,000 shares in 1985 and 252,000 shares in 1984)	(6,335)	(5,211)
	929,411	845,899
Commitments and contingencies	$3,927,633	$4,036,941

Note: Figures in thousands for years ending September 30.
Source: Ashland Oil, Inc., 1985 Annual Report.

TABLE 3 Statements of changes in consolidated financial position

	Years ended September 30		
	1985	1984	1983
Funds retained from operations			
Income (loss) before extraordinary gain	$ 146,722	$(172,478)	$ 96,637
Expense (income) not affecting funds			
Depreciation, depletion and amortization	209,102	212,547	192,006
Deferred income taxes	53,981	49,894	24,084
Equity income — net of dividends	(4,981)	(16,785)	(21,032)
Divestitures and asset write-offs — net of current income taxes	25,952	291,915	—
Other — net	16,452	12,356	1,547
Funds provided from operations	447,228	377,449	293,242
Decrease (increase) in working capital	(89,541)	(64,405)	(26,799)
Dividends	(74,142)	(76,165)	(94,449)
	303,545	236,879	171,994
Funds provided from (used for) financing			
Issuance of long-term debt and capitalized lease obligations	63,417	59,623	7,827
Issuance of common stock	11,672	9,820	34,593
Repayment of long-term debt and capitalized lease obligations	(123,706)	(57,315)	(91,633)
Purchase, conversion and exchange of capital stock	(56,813)	(36,386)	(9,543)
Increase (decrease) in short-term notes	474	(15,057)	134
	(104,956)	(39,315)	(58,622)
Funds provided from (used for) investment			
Additions to property, plant and equipment	(290,371)	(279,675)	(322,074)
Net assets of companies acquired			
Working capital (excluding cash and short-term securities)	—	(996)	(5,373)
Property, plant and equipment	—	(18,445)	(1,808)
Investments and other assets	—	(42,019)	(2,621)
Noncurrent liabilities	—	2,060	—
Proceeds from sale of operations (including working capital of $44,900,000 in 1985)	87,715	13,923	—
Net book value of property, plant and equipment disposals	23,717	51,970	55,874
Other — net	21,630	41,374	47,408
	(157,309)	(231,808)	(228,594)
Increase (decrease) in cash and short-term securities	$ 41,280	$ (34,244)	$(115,222)
Changes in components of working capital			
Decrease (increase) in current assets			
Accounts receivable	$ (18,010)	$ (13,680)	$ 78,689
Construction completed and in progress	(3,594)	(6,477)	2,644
Refundable income taxes	33,837	(8,366)	(25,471)
Inventories	56,123	(5,133)	(22,619)
Deferred income tax benefits	(10,912)	(43,949)	(4,098)
Other current assets	(9,218)	(7,829)	(2,281)
Increase (decrease) in current liabilities			
Trade and other payables	(84,068)	(24,950)	(17,068)
Contract advances and progress billings	(17,814)	(19,308)	(16,915)
Income taxes	(15,885)	65,287	(19,680)
	$ (69,541)	$ (64,405)	$ (26,799)

Note: Figures in thousands of dollars.
Source: Ashland Oil, Inc. 1985 Annual Report.

TABLE 4 Six-year selected financial information

	1985	1984	1983	1982	1981	1980
Summary of operations						
Revenues						
Sales and operating revenues (including excise taxes)	$8,184	$8,544	$8,108	$9,110	$9,506	$8,366
Other	54	77	91	94	75	64
Costs and expenses						
Cost of sales and operating expenses	(6,745)	(7,215)	(6,960)	(7,837)	(8,453)	(7,278)
Excise taxes on products and merchandise	(293)	(291)	(256)	(245)	(244)	(247)
Selling, general, and administrative expenses	(607)	(611)	(564)	(570)	(564)	(370)
Depreciation, depletion, and amortization	(202)	(213)	(192)	(171)	(153)	(131)
Foreign exploration taxes	(39)	(39)	(31)	(52)	(38)	(40)
Operating income	352	252	196	329	129	364
Other income (expense)						
Interest income	20	20	32	57	100	80
Interest expense	(67)	(81)	(79)	(79)	(98)	(89)
Equity income	11	20	28	13	23	11
Other — net (including corporate administrative)	(57)	(67)	(73)	(108)[a]	(34)[b]	(50)
Divestitures and asset write-offs	(40)	(287)	—	28	—	9
Income (loss) before income taxes and extraordinary gain	219	(143)	104	240	120	325
Income taxes	72	29	7	59	30	120
Income (loss) before extraordinary gain	147	(172)	97	181	90	205
Extraordinary gain from exchange of common stock for long-term debt	—	—	6	—	—	—
Net income (loss)[c]	$ 147	$ (172)	$ 103	$ 181	$ 90	$ 205
Balance sheet information						
Working capital						
Current assets	$1,596	$1,677	$1,630	$1,766	$1,867	$1,862
Current liabilities	(1,427)	(1,616)	(1,551)	(1,614)	(1,662)	(1,355)
	$ 169	$ 61	$ 79	$ 152	$ 205	$ 507
Total assets	$3,928	$4,037	$4,133	$4,210	$4,122	$3,358
Capitalization						
Long-term debt (less current portion)	$ 510	$ 545	$ 528	$ 585	$ 583	$ 462
Capitalized lease obligations (less current portion)	106	113	147	175	187	167
Deferred income taxes	380	332	290	252	206	123
Minority interest in consolidated subsidiaries	57	56	55	56	39	—
Redeemable preferred stock	249	303	344	353	358	245
Common stockholders' equity	929	846	1,085	1,047	972	907
	$2,231	$2,195	$2,449	$2,468	$2,345	$1,904
Cash flow information						
Funds provided from operations	$ 447	$ 377	$ 293	$ 380	$ 248	$ 339
Funds used for						
Additions to property, plant, and equipment	290	280	322	423	281	79
Dividends	74	76	94	99	94	264
Common stock information						
Earnings (loss) per share	$ 4.12	$ (7.40)	$ 2.46	$ 5.29	$ 2.22	$ 6.80
Dividends per share	1.60	1.60	2.20	2.40	2.40	2.20

Note: Data in millions except per-share data.
[a] Includes a loss of $26,000,000 from the write-off of investments in and loans to a foreign company and $22,000,000 in employee retirement, termination, and relocation costs.
[b] Includes a gain of $23,000,000 from prepayment of long-term debt.
[c] Divestitures and asset write-offs did not have a material effect on net income for 1985, but resulted in a net loss of $265,000,000 in 1984 and net income of $16,000,000 in 1982.
Source: Ashland Oil Inc., 1984 and 1985 Annual Reports.

TABLE 5 Five-year information by industry segment

	Years ended September 30				
	1985	1984	1983	1982	1981
Sales and operating revenues					
Petroleum (including excise taxes)	$5,377	$5,678	$5,700	$6,485	$7,044
Chemical	1,499	1,501	1,208	1,197	1,330
Coal	196	197	150	177	175
Engineering and construction	1,217	1,292	1,152	1,330	1,144
Exploration	287	276	226	241	190
Other	1	1	4	41	85
Intersegment sales	(393)	(401)	(332)	(361)	(462)
	$8,184	$8,544	$8,108	$9,110	$9,506
Operating income (loss)					
Petroleum	$ 213	$ 120	$ 176	$ 220	$ (6)
Chemical	68	55	1	28	41
Coal	15	19	—	16	15
Engineering and construction	54	45	2	36	38
Exploration (net of foreign exploration taxes)	5	15	20	39	42
Other	(3)	(2)	(3)	(10)	(1)
	$ 352	$ 252	$ 196	$ 329	$ 129
Identifiable assets					
Petroleum	$1,782	$1,831	$1,885	$1,775	$1,571
Chemical	496	503	423	402	463
Coal	220	226	195	244	209
Engineering and construction	433	503	602	675	672
Exploration	414	364	264	210	129
Other	7	15	8	11	117
Corporate	576	595	756	893	961
	$3,928	$4,037	$4,133	$4,210	$4,122
Funds provided from operations					
Petroleum	$ 242	$ 201	$ 224	$ 233	$ 59
Chemical	63	53	18	44	52
Coal	27	30	12	27	30
Engineering and construction	58	63	34	46	63
Exploration	67	66	49	69	40
Other	1	4	—	5	(2)
Corporate	(11)	(40)	(44)	(44)	6
	$ 447	$ 377	$ 293	$ 380	$ 248
Additions to property, plant, and equipment					
Petroleum	$ 86	$ 87	$ 186	$ 214	$ 118
Chemical	39	22	20	27	35
Coal	7	26	11	43	23
Engineering and construction	30	26	20	26	28
Exploration	120	116	74	92	35
Other	—	—	2	1	4
Corporate	8	3	9	20	38
	$ 290	$ 280	$ 322	$ 423	$ 281

TABLE 5 (continued)

TABLE 5 (continued)

	Years ended September 30				
	1985	1984	1983	1982	1981
Depreciation, depletion, and amortization					
Petroleum	$ 93	$ 92	$ 80	$ 72	$ 64
Chemical	24	23	21	19	16
Coal	11	12	14	17	16
Engineering and construction	27	36	40	38	36
Exploration	47	42	28	13	11
Other	—	—	1	4	4
Corporate	7	8	8	8	6
	$ 209	$ 213	$ 192	$ 171	$ 153

Note: Figures in millions.
Source: Ashland Oil, Inc., 1985 Annual Report.

TABLE 6 Crude oil and natural gas reserves

	1985			1984			1983		
	U.S.	Nigeria	Total	U.S.	Nigeria	Total	U.S.	Nigeria	Total
Crude oil reserves (in millions of barrels)									
Proved developed and undeveloped reserves									
Beginning of year	5.5	49.2	54.7	5.7	19.7	25.4	6.2	11.5	17.7
Revisions of previous estimates	(.1)	2.8	2.7	(.1)	—	(.1)	—	—	—
Extensions and discoveries	.6	4.3	4.9	.8	36.5	37.3	.5	13.3	13.8
Production	(1.0)	(7.6)	(8.6)	(.9)	(7.0)	(7.9)	(1.0)	(5.1)	(6.1)
End of year	5.0	48.7	53.7	5.5	49.2	54.7	5.7	19.7	25.4
Proved developed reserves									
Beginning of year	5.2	34.5	39.7	5.2	19.7	24.9	5.8	11.5	17.3
End of year	4.9	45.5	50.4	5.2	34.5	39.7	5.2	19.7	24.9
Natural gas reserves (in billions of cubic feet)									
Proved developed and undeveloped reserves									
Beginning of year	213.9			206.2			208.5		
Revisions of previous estimates	(4.6)			(.2)			4.6		
Extensions and discoveries	18.7			18.7			2.8		
Production	(11.7)			(10.8)			(9.7)		
End of year	216.3			213.9			206.2		
Proved developed reserves									
Beginning of year	161.6			155.2			151.6		
End of year	166.6			161.6			155.2		

Note: Data for years ended September 30.
Source: Ashland Oil, Inc., 1985 Annual Report.

TABLE 7 Selected operating information

	Years ended September 30				
	1984	*1983*	*1982*	*1981*	*1980*
Net proved developed and undeveloped reserves[a]					
Crude oil (millions of barrels)					
United States	5.5	5.7	6.2	6.3	6.2
Nigeria	49.2	19.7	11.5	10.8	12.7
Natural gas (billions of cubic feet)[b]	213.9	206.2	208.5	216.9	213.3
Net production					
Crude oil (barrels per day)					
United States	2,508	2,677	2,725	2,815	3,141
Foreign					
Nigeria					
Onshore	11,858	14,066	12,079	7,505	6,876
Offshore	7,222	—	—	—	—
Sharjah	—	—	1,761	1,927	2,660
Natural gas (thousands of cubic feet per day)[b]	29,483	26,715	27,360	28,359	26,321
Average sales price					
Crude oil (per barrel)					
United States	$28.84	$29.59	$32.68	$35.04	$32.90
Foreign	29.95	31.74	35.44	37.61	33.70
Natural gas (per thousand cubic feet)[b]	3.59	3.26	2.74	2.26	1.82
Net producing wells					
Crude oil					
United States	1,531	1,516	1,475	1,451	1,487
Foreign	24	16	16	11	13
Natural gas[b]	1,015	902	899	949	896
Net oil and gas acreage (thousands of acres)					
Producing					
United States	514	501	501	495	489
Foreign	174	75	98	98	98
Undeveloped					
United States	337	288	277	269	277
Foreign	—	99	99	99	99
Drilling activities					
Net productive exploratory wells drilled					
United States	20	4	8	7	—
Foreign	3	—	—	—	3
Net dry exploratory wells drilled					
United States	24	18	6	3	1
Foreign	—	3	—	—	—
Net productive development wells drilled					
United States	51	31	60	26	29
Foreign	6	7	5	2	2
Net dry development wells drilled					
United States	8	6	5	1	8
Foreign	1	1	—	—	—

[a] United States crude oil and natural gas reserves are reported net of royalties and interests owned by others. Nigeria crude oil reserves relate to reserves available to Ashland, as producer, under a long-term production-sharing contract with the Nigerian National Petroleum Corporation.
[b] Amounts relate to U.S. operations. Ashland has no material natural gas reserves outside the United States.
Source: Ashland Oil Inc., Financial & Operating Supplement 1984.

TABLE 8 Sales, production, and processing data

	Crude oil processed (in barrels)		Refined products produced (in barrels)				
Year ended September 30	Total for the period	Average per day	Gasoline jet fuel, aromatics, & naphthas	Kerosene & distillates	Heavy fuel oils	Asphalt	Other
1984	110,463,493	301,813	68,993,847	25,415,162	3,880,719	6,222,736	3,108,061
1983	104,035,875	285,029	65,221,538	23,434,424	4,381,274	5,887,099	3,248,995
1982	113,953,033	312,200	66,945,886	28,036,535	7,629,663	5,866,136	2,320,887
1981	117,346,974	321,499	69,708,758	23,780,197	10,705,817	6,647,059	1,497,295
1980	133,014,201	363,427	76,205,915	27,133,078	12,851,355	9,243,840	3,805,802
1979	134,225,778	367,742	71,039,800	31,920,124	11,785,281	10,783,068	4,988,164
1978	128,827,589	352,952	71,898,241	29,153,321	11,839,621	9,829,217	3,763,301
1977	130,752,556	358,226	70,983,767	31,155,164	12,952,142	8,232,363	5,213,858
1976	127,425,451	348,157	69,181,740	31,027,020	12,172,167	7,746,326	5,895,269

Sales (in barrels)

Year ended September 30	Gasoline jet fuel, aromatics, & naphthas	Kerosene & distillates	Heavy fuel oils	Asphalt	Other
1984	79,942,401	29,492,890	13,386,085	7,335,784	7,409,397
1983	73,732,045	25,745,913	22,369,293	6,224,221	7,192,872
1982	75,601,370	29,894,597	28,791,680	7,009,221	6,768,048
1981	76,506,260	27,681,764	40,718,069	7,130,262	7,921,595
1980	82,832,857	29,714,190	52,830,738	9,851,572	6,946,309
1979	85,170,381	34,787,595	53,264,429	11,238,881	9,184,310
1978	82,729,048	35,199,381	48,496,000	10,654,214	8,634,643
1977	82,647,976	35,762,119	52,846,571	9,376,714	8,034,905
1976	80,962,190	34,337,810	47,721,071	8,902,286	8,238,500

Source: Ashland Oil, Inc., 1984 10-K.

TABLE 9 Debenture information

Debenture	Trustee	Rating	
		Moody's	Standard & Poor's
4.725% Sinking fund debentures, due 1988	Chemical Bank	A3	BBB+
4.875% Sinking fund debentures, due 1987	Citibank, N.A.	A3	BBB+
6.15% Sinking fund debentures, due 1992	Citibank, N.A.	A3	BBB+
8.00% Guaranteed debentures, due 1987	Citibank, N.A.	—	—
8.20% Sinking fund debentures, due 2002	Citibank, N.A.	A3	BBB+
8.80% Sinking fund debentures, due 2000	Citibank, N.A.	A3	BBB+
4.75% Convertible subordinated debentures, due 1993	Chase Manhattan Bank, N.A.	Baal	BBB
11.10% Subordinated debentures, due 2004	Chase Manhattan Bank, N.A.	Baal	BBB

Source: Ashland Oil, Inc., *Financial & Operating Supplement 1984.*

THE ALCOHOLIC BEVERAGE INDUSTRY

This case describes the alcoholic beverage industry in North America. Coverage includes (1) production techniques for distilled spirits, (2) production economics, (3) distribution, (4) consumption, (5) market segments, (6) antialcohol campaigns, (7) distillers, (8) an overview of the liquor industry cases, (9) the production of beer, (10) the brewers, (11) an overview of the brewing industry cases, (12) wine markets and production, (13) the wine companies, and (14) an overview of the wine cases.

PRODUCTION TECHNIQUES FOR DISTILLED SPIRITS

At the simplest level, all distilled spirits are produced through the distilling process that capitalizes on alcohol's property of boiling at lower temperatures than water. Alcohol is produced by fermentation. The natural sugar, found in a vast range of vegetable products which includes almost every type of grain and fruit, is converted into alcohol by the action of yeasts. These yeasts break down the sugar in the fermentation process which produces alcohol. Occasionally, starch is used to produce alcohol. A starch is cooked in a mash that is converted to sugar.

Alcohol can be continuously purified to neutralize all the flavors and aromas of the original fruits or grains. These neutral spirits can be sold as soon as they are produced and can be mixed with soft drinks or juices.

Other alcoholic beverages are produced either by retaining the taste of the original grains (as, for example, bourbon, which has a base continuously distilled from either corn or rye) or by mixing additives (as in gin, flavored with juniper berries). Molasses is the base for rum, as grapes are the foundation for wine. These spirits are then aged in oak casks or barrels for varying periods of time. Blends are produced, as the name indicates, by blending natural spirits with neutralized spirits.

The alcohol contained in beverages is expressed as a percentage (e.g., sake, the Japanese rice wine, is 16 percent alcohol), or, in the United States, as proof,

Case prepared by John Barnett, University of New Hampshire. Copyright © 1987. Reprinted by permission.

determined by doubling the alcohol percentage. Thus, 100-proof whiskey is 50 percent alcohol; 80-proof is 40 percent alcohol.

PRODUCTION ECONOMICS

The production differences between "brown" straight and blended whiskies and "white" neutral spirits have obvious economic impact. These include:

raw materials costs

continuous (neutralized) versus batch ("brown goods") processing

aging, including both container (oak barrel) costs and inventory carrying charges (both interest and evaporation)

DISTRIBUTION

Distribution by the government is the norm in Canada (via provincial liquor boards) and in seventeen states in the United States. These "control" states have state monopolies on retail distribution.

The distillers or importers deal with either the control-state retailer or independent retailers through a network of wholesalers. These wholesalers are the "push-through" distribution system which is of increasing importance with advertising restrictions, including the prohibition of radio or television advertising of spirits.

Regional tastes are strong. New York is a big consumer of scotch, and California of tequila. Per capita consumption in Washington, D.C., is five times that of West Virginia. Bourbon is popular in the South and Canadian whisky in the North. (Note: Canadian and Scotch is *whisky* without an "e"; its plural is *whiskies*. Irish or American is *whiskey* with a plural of *whiskeys*.)

CONSUMPTION

International consumption of distilled spirits is shown in Exhibit 1. Exhibit 2 shows total U.S. consumption and the change in market share of various whiskeys and nonwhiskeys from 1955 to 1982. The drinking trends in the United States are shown in Exhibit 3.

Two strong trends in distilled spirits are mixability and lightness. Distilled spirits have been mixed with soft drinks (e.g., rum and coke) and fruit juices (e.g., Harvey Wallbangers). The fastest-growing segment of all alcoholic beverages in the 1980s was wine and fruit juice mixes or "wine coolers." The trend toward lightness was led by Scotch and Canadian whiskies in the 1960s. During the 1980s many consumers switched to light beer and wine.

EXHIBIT 1
Per capita
consumption by
country, 1982

	Consumption of 750 ml 80-proof bottles
East Germany	15.8
Canada	11.3
Russia	11.0
United States	9.7
West Germany	8.3
Sweden	8.1
Italy	6.3
Britain	5.3
Australia	4.0
Argentina	3.0

Source: *The Economist,* December 22, 1984.

EXHIBIT 2
U.S. consumption

	Millions of gallons consumed			Market share		
Whiskeys	1955	1964	1982	1955	1964	1982
Blends	82	75	—[a]	40%	26%	—[a]
Straight[a]	46	70	98	23	24	22
Scotch	12	28	45	6	10	10
Canadian	9	17	54	5	6	12
Bonded[b]	13	8	—[a]	6	3	—[a]
Total whiskeys	162	198	197	80%	69%	44%
Nonwhiskeys						
Gin	21	31	41	10%	11%	9%
Vodka	7	28	98	4	10	22
Rum	3	6	31	1	2	7
Brandy	5	9	22	2	3	5
Other	7	15	58	3	5	13
Total nonwhiskeys	43	89	250	20%	31%	56%
Total distilled spirits	205	287	447	100%	100%	100%

[a] Straight whiskey is one that is not blended, such as bourbon. Straight whiskey is natural, i.e., it has not been neutralized and it contains no neutral spirits. 1982 figures for straight include blends and bonded.
[b] Bonded whiskeys are straight whiskeys that are "sealed" and "bonded" to indicate that they are 100-U.S.-proof (50 percent alcohol) as opposed to the normal 86-proof in the United States and 70-proof in Canada.
Source: Heublein, Inc., Harvard Business School 373–103, *The Economist,* December 22, 1984.

EXHIBIT 3
U.S. per capita
consumption

Beverage	1968		1978		1985	
	Gallons	Market share	Gallons	Market share	Gallons	Market share
Beer	17.3	86.1%	23.1	84.9%	23.8	85.3%
Wine	1.1	5.5	2.1	7.7	2.4	8.6
Distilled spirits	1.7	8.4	2.0	7.4	1.7	6.1
Total	20.1	100.0%	27.2	100.0%	27.9	100.0%

Source: "Beverage Industry," *Advertising Age,* February 16, 1987, p. S-1.

One distiller, Seagram, possibly assuming that "lightness" meant "low alcohol," launched an advertising campaign of "equivalency" in 1985, "showing that four 1-oz. jiggers of 80-proof spirits contain no more alcohol than four 10-oz. glasses of beer or four 3-oz. glasses of wine" (*Business Week,* March 22, 1985, p. 229).

Nicholas Furlotte wrote on new styles and new tastes in drinking in *Advertising Age* (February 16, 1987):

A top executive . . . wanted to know [*if*] *I think the martini . . . would make a comeback. . . . There is no such thing as a comeback in the alcoholic beverage industry. . . . Once a brand has gone into decline it has never been successfully revived. . . . Once a category has gone into serious decline, it has never been brought back. . . .*

We are embarking on a new era of alcoholic beverage products and markets. . . .

Because taste preferences are evolutionary rather than cyclical, each generation claims a certain type of drink as its own. There was a time when the drink was bourbon. Later it was vodka, then white wine, and now, perhaps, bottled water.

But, of all the demographic groups influencing the alcoholic beverage industry today, none is having a greater effect than the generation brought up on the sweet, fizzy taste of soda pop.

Mr. Furlotte then cited the efforts of Joseph E. Seagram & Sons with its spirits-based cooler line, James Beam's Zzzingers and Schnapps-based cooler, Heublein's Tropic Freezer ("a sort of cherry slush for adults"), Schiefflin's Petite Liqueur (a wine-based cordial), and Kobrand's Alize (a passion fruit and cognac mix). "These and future new drinks may do for prepared cocktails what Lean Cuisine has done for TV dinners."

Furlotte also suggested that (1) cooler sales will now be a battle for market share and profitability, as enormous growth gains are over ("By 2000, coolers will be about as important as Boone's Farm is today") as consumers tire of the product, (2) the over-fifty age group will be more and more important, (3) the high-priced premium segments will continue their growth, (4) marketing programs, especially discounts and coupons, will cut into brand loyalty, (5) comparative brand advertising will increase, (6) imported beers will grow, and (7) U.S. wine tastes will become more sophisticated, but "the U.S. will never be a wine-drinking country."

Mr. Furlotte concluded: "In 20 years, the last of the serious martini drinkers will have vanished from the face of the earth and the drink will never be heard of again."

Patricia Winters, writing in the same special report edition of *Advertising Age,* described a whole new trend in the alcoholic beverage industry that resulted "when you mix cayenne pepper, a bottle of vodka, and a yuppie." Absolut Peppar, Stolichnaya's Zubrowka (vodka flavored with buffalo grass), Chef Paul Prudhomme's Cajun martini, Stolichnaya's pepper-flavored Pertsovka "Pepper Stoli, The Hot Vodka," and Stolichnaya Okhotnichya and Limonnaya are illustrations of this trend. Jack Shea of Heublein, marketer of Smirnoff, noted in *Advertising Age* (op. cit.) that Heublein was "not going to risk the reputation of the world's No. 1 vodka on a fad."

MARKET SEGMENTS

Price and perceived quality are factors distinguishing a premium market from the bottom-of-the-market commodity products. Seagram's Crown Royal (Canadian) and Chivas Regal (Scotch) are good examples of premium spirits, as is Heublein's Smirnoff (which leaves you breathless).

What contributes to a differentiated or quality product? The quality of materials, the aging process, and the blender's art are certainly a few of the critical factors for premium beverages. Shifting consumer tastes and product promotion help determine market success.

ANTIALCOHOL CAMPAIGNS

Environmentalists are concerned about the litter aspects of alcoholic beverages, especially beer cans. Various states are trying bottle deposits, packaging taxes, and other antilitter projects.

More importantly, the abuse of alcoholic beverages is being attacked through specific drunk-driving citizens' action and advertising campaigns. Mothers Against Drunk Driving (MADD) is especially vocal. Many states are enacting not only stiff drunk-driving laws, but also host-liability laws.

The Center for Science in the Public Interest (CSPI), a consumer-advocacy group in Washington, D.C., began a series of campaigns to restrict or eliminate alcohol advertising in the 1980s. CSPI wants product warnings on beverages and in any allowed advertising, increased excise taxes on alcohol, and elimination of alcohol company sponsorship of concerts and campus parties.

The critics of alcohol point to the 98,000 deaths related to alcohol in 1985 versus 3,600 deaths in the same period related to cocaine, heroin, and other drugs.

A spokesperson for the National Council on Alcoholism commented that it is "certainly in the alcohol industry's interest to keep [the current] debate focused on drug abuse" (*Christian Science Monitor,* September 24, 1986). A drug and alcohol abuse counselor concluded: "If alcohol were suddenly to be discovered today, it would probably be classed as a [Drug Enforcement Agency] Schedule Two drug along with cocaine and some of the barbituates" (ibid).

Bill Coors, Chairman of the Adolph Coors Company, spoke about the most critical issue facing Coors and the brewing industry:

> *Abuse of our product! Alcoholism! We can't change people's life-styles by advertising. Alcohol is a way of managing stress, just like overeating. The American Medical Association says alcoholism is a disease. How can they be so naive as to treat the product as though it is the problem?*[1]

THE COMPANIES

The five largest distillers in North America in 1964 were Seagrams Distillers Corporation (with liquor sales of $720 million in 1964), Hiram Walker ($500 million), National Distillers ($430 million), Schenley ($390 million), and Heublein ($120 million).

Seagram came to the United States in 1933 as Prohibition ended. It was the American arm of the Samuel Bronfman Canadian firm formed by the 1928 merger of Bronfman's Distillers Corporation with Joseph E. Seagram and Sons, Ltd., of Ontario. Hiram Walker of Massachusetts founded the Canadian distiller of the same name in 1858 and introduced Canadian whisky to the United States in the last half of the nineteenth century. National Distillers was formed in the 1920s out of the Midwest-U.S.-based whiskey trust. Organized in Illinois in 1887, this pooling and control device was officially known in its early years as the Distillers' Cattle Feeders' Trust. Schenley was formed in 1920 by Lewis Rosenstiel, who purchased a medicinal distillery, the Schenley Products Company, based upon his belief that the Eighteenth Amendment (Prohibition) passed that year would not last. Heublein was established in 1875 by Gilbert and Louis Heublein as an importer of foods and beverages. In 1892 the Heublein brothers produced prepared cocktails. They incorporated themselves as G. F. Heublein & Bro. in 1899.

Seagram's V.O., a Canadian whiskey, had been the number one brand in the United States since the end of Prohibition. Hiram Walker was also active in the Canadian whiskey market in the United States with its Canadian Club brand, while Heublein had the most limited product line, with one product, Smirnoff vodka, accounting for about half of its liquor sales.

Seagram's Seven Crown was surpassed as the number one brand in the United

---

[1] C. L. Hinkle and E. F. Stinemann, "Adolph Coors Company," *Cases in Marketing Management* (Englewood Cliffs, NJ: Prentice-Hall, 1984), p. 445.

EXHIBIT 4
U.S. leading brands

1983 rank	Millions of cases sold		
	1983	1978	1968
1. Bacardi	7.7	6.1	2.1
2. Smirnoff	5.7	6.2	3.2
3. Seagram's Seven Crown	4.9	6.2	7.9
4. Canadian Mist	3.4	2.3	—
5. Jim Beam	3.2	2.8	2.5
6. Seagram's V.O.	3.1	3.9	3.5

Source: *The Economist*, December 22, 1984.

States by Smirnoff and, subsequently, also by Bacardi rum in the early 1980s. Exhibit 4 summarizes U.S. sales of the leading brands.

The Canadian market is naturally smaller than the U.S. market. For example, two of the top U.S. brands in 1978, Bacardi and Smirnoff (which together sold 12,300,000 cases in the United States) sold 2,000,000 cases in Canada in the same year. Seagram's V.O. sold 3,900,000 cases in the United States in 1978 and 500,000 in Canada.

The strategies of the largest distillers often were based upon a combination of premium products and a strong distribution system. Medium-sized distillers such as James Beam might specialize in straight bourbon products, while some distillers might concentrate on one brand, lower-priced goods, or private labeling for the big liquor retailers.

With static or declining demand, liquor distillers turned to new products that are appealing in themselves (such as Bailey's Irish Cream) or are mixable (rum). General Wines' 1982 product, Dr. McGillicuddy's Mentholmint Schnapps, built on the growth pattern of peppermint schnapps.

By 1984 Seagram had the third (Seven Crown), eighth (V.O.), and tenth (Seagram's Gin) best-selling U.S. brands. Hiram Walker (Hiram Walker Resources) had the eleventh (Canadian Club) leading brand. National had the sixth (Windsor Supreme) and the thirteenth (Gibley's Gin). Schenley, now a part of Rapid-American, had the fifteenth brand, Dewar's, while Heublein, now part of R. J. Reynolds, held the second (Smirnoff) and the ninth (Popov) best-selling U.S. brands.

The number one brand in 1984 was Bacardi. Fourth was Canadian Mist, and seventh was Jack Daniel's, both part of Brown-Forman, who specialized in "brown goods," also producing Early Times and Southern Comfort. Fifth came Jim Beam, distilled by the Beam division of American Brands.

Brown-Forman is frequently cited as an example of a successful "niche" strategy, resulting in industry-leading margins through the concentration on leading brands. On the other hand, Seagram and Hiram Walker are examples of diversifying businesses. Hiram Walker Resources consists of Hiram Walker Gooderham & Wort's (distilling), Home Oil (natural resources), and Consumers' Gas (a Toronto gas utility). Seagram in the 1980s exchanged ownership in oil and gas for ownership in Du Pont.

National Distillers' brands were doing well due to aggressive pricing and advertising. National had reduced its Old Crow bourbon prices and had started advertising Windsor Supreme-versus-V.O. taste tests. National introduced its DeKuyper's Peachtree Schnapps in October 1984; during 1985 it sold over 1.5 million cases and was the 24th largest U.S. brand. 1985 sales are shown in Exhibit 5.

Industry analysts, noting the overall drop in wine, beer, and liquor industry growth rates, concluded that many large companies would be milking the cash cows that were the liquor operations. As (1) life-styles move to white liquor and fruit juice or even totally away from alcoholic beverages, (2) advertising and labeling regulations increase (such as New York City's sign, "WARNING: Drinking alcoholic beverages during pregnancy can cause birth defects"), and (3) governments use alcoholic beverages as sources of increased excise taxes to close budget deficits, companies are expected to cut advertising and to prune brands within their liquor operation.

In 1985 analysts commented on Heublein's success with Popov, as well as National's wonder product, Peachtree Schnapps, which hit 1.5 million cases in one year. Peachtree schnapps had 50 percent of the schnapps market and was included in such new drink promotions as the "Fuzzy Navel," a combination of orange juice and Peachtree Schnapps.

Other new products in the mid-1980s were (1) alcohol in a can, as in Jim Beam ZZZingers, bourbon and soda in a can, (2) "digestives" based on European after-

EXHIBIT 5
U.S. sales by brand, 1985

Rank		Brand	Company	Millions of 9-liter cases	
1985	1984			1985	% change 1984–1985
1	1	Bacardi	Bacardi	8.5	+0.5%
2	2	Smirnoff	Heublein-Reynolds	7.7	+0.1
3	3	Seven Crown	Seagram	5.1	−4.8
4	4	Canadian Mist	Brown-Forman	4.3	+3.1
5	5	Jim Beam	Beam-American Brands	4.1	+1.5
6	9	Popov	Heublein-Reynolds	4.0	+4.9
7	6	Windsor Supreme	National	3.8	—
8	7	Jack Daniel's	Brown Forman	3.6	−1.4
9	8	V.O.	Seagram	3.6	+0.6
10	10	Seagram Gin	Seagram	3.2	—

Source: John C. Maxwell, Jr., "The Liquor Industry in 1985." New York: Furman, Selz, Mager, Dietz & Birney.

dinner drinks, and (3) sparkling liqueur, such as Schiefflin's Petite Liqueur, a combination of cognac and sparkling wine.

In 1985, imported liqueurs, imported brandy, imported rum, and imported vodka were the only distilled spirits showing any growth rates over 1984. Bonded and straight whiskeys were down 4.1 percent, blended whiskeys down 6.3 percent, Canadian down 0.3 percent, Scotch down 4.0 percent, domestic vodka down 1.4 percent, and domestic gin down 4.0 percent.

LIQUOR INDUSTRY CASES

Heublein. In 1965 Heublein is trying to continue its spectacular growth in both sales and profits. A great deal of this success is due to Smirnoff, Heublein's premium vodka which capitalized on the consumer's preference for lighter tastes in alcoholic beverages. Heublein now is considering the acquisition of a brewing company, Hamm's.

Coca-Cola and The Wine Spectrum. Coke now owns Taylor wines, and wonders how to apply its marketing skills to the wine industry.

Seagram. The first Seagram case focuses on the company's early history, management, and organization for the Canadian market. Seagram products and those of its competitors are analyzed over the 1977–1980 period, with some analysis based upon product portfolio techniques. Charles Bronfman heads up this Montreal-based "collegial" management team.

The second Seagram case shifts the focus from Montreal to New York and from Charles to Edgar Bronfman. Seagram sells its oil and gas operation for $2.3 billion, and seeks to reinvest the sale proceeds. Ultimately, Seagram becomes a major owner of Du Pont.

Simultaneously (1981–1983) Seagram reviews its wine strategy. Mary Cunningham is hired to develop a focused wine strategy, and Seagram acquires Taylor and The Wine Spectrum from Coca-Cola to complement its own Paul Masson and other wines.

THE BREWING INDUSTRY

Beer Production Process

The brewing process for beer begins with a mash produced by grinding malted barley (malt). Hops and other aroma and taste determinants are added. Next, yeast is added, which ferments. Fermentation may take a week or less, and aging varies from a few days to a few months. Finally, beer is filtered, carbonated, and packaged.

The brewing industry ferments using a top-fermentation yeast to produce ale or a bottom-fermentation yeast to produce lager beer. Specialty brewing products include stout (heavier and darker than ale) and bock beer (dark brown in color because roasted malt is used).

The Brewers   The history of the brewing industry since World War II has been a history of increasing competition and concentration. The over 400 firms in 1945 shrunk to 250 in the mid-1950s, 150 in the mid-1960s, and 50 in the mid-1970s. The top ten brewers in the United States controlled 40 percent of the market in 1950, 50 percent in 1960, and 60 percent in 1965. The top twenty-five brewers had a market share of 60 percent in 1950 and 85 percent in 1965. By the mid-1970s the top four breweries' share of 20 percent in 1950 had become 60 percent.

In the mid-1960s the leading national breweries (Anheuser-Busch, Schlitz, and Pabst) competed with expanding regional breweries (Falstaff, Carling, and Hamm) and strong local breweries (National in Baltimore, Schmidt's in Philadelphia, Coors in Denver, Olympia in Washington State, Dixie in New Orleans, and Schaefer, Rheingold, and Ballantine in New York).

Industry analysts argue that there is little brand loyalty among beer drinkers. Advertising is an important part of strategy and is often tied to sports sponsorships.

Competition, especially in advertising, and industry concentration through expanding markets and acquisitions intensified in the 1970s. Industry observers attribute this intensification to Philip Morris's acquisition of Miller Brewing Company. Recognizing the significant economies of scale in the brewing industry, especially in marketing, Philip Morris applied their aggressive marketing strategies to Miller. Eventually, the other national brewers responded by increasing their marketing efforts. Exhibit 6 depicts the trend in advertising dollars per barrel among the industry leaders.

Analysts of the beer industry in the mid-1980s predicted (1) a stable cost environment, with slight but absorbable packaging and raw materials cost increases, (2) limited potential for volume improvement with domestic volume flat and a slight imported volume increase, (3) decreased capacity (1985 closings by Pabst, Stroh, and Miller reduced industry capacity by 20 million barrels or 10 percent), and (4) increased national competition as each national company sees the others as sources or opportunities for increasing the company's market shares, which should impact negatively on regional brewers. Anheuser-Busch and Coors were particularly cited as national brewers with expected strong market share gains. Anheuser moved toward its 40 percent market share objective by the end of the 1980s, and Coors grew in California, Florida, Texas, and New England, the last its primary 1985 expansion area. Coors' light beer experienced strong market growth recently, supported by aggressive marketing.

Ernest Nordtvedt described the effects of the intense marketing efforts of the large national brewers, such as Anheuser Busch and Miller, on a local brewery in his working paper "Dixie Brewing Company, Inc." (North American Case Research Association, 1986 annual meeting). Dixie was the "local beer" of New Orleans. Dixie was founded in 1907 and survived Prohibition by making ice cream, soft drinks, and "near beer." In 1969 Dixie had a market share of 29 percent and was the leading brand in New Orleans, selling 240,000 barrels of beer a year. By 1975 Dixie was producing 190,000 barrels of beer and its market share was 17 percent. By 1984 Dixie's production was under 100,000 barrels, as Dixie, like other regional

EXHIBIT 6 Top brewers' advertising, 1964–1979

	1964				1974				1977				1979			
	Barrels sold (000,000)	Advertising			Barrels sold (000,000)	Advertising			Barrels sold (000,000)	Advertising			Barrels sold (000,000)	Advertising		
		Rank	Million $	Per barrel		Rank	Million $	Per barrel		Rank	Million $	Per barrel		Rank	Million $	Per barrel
Anheuser-Busch	10	1	$33	$3.30	34	1	$12	$0.35	37	1	$45	$1.22	46	1	$87	$1.89
Schlitz	8	2	$34	$4.25	23	2	$18	$0.78	22	3	$40	$1.82	17	3	$49	$2.87
Pabst	7	3	$16	$2.29	14	3	$8	$0.57	16	4	$11	$0.69	15	4	$18	$1.22
Falstaff	6	4	$15	$2.50	—	—	—	—	—	—	—	—	—	—	—	—
Carling	5	5	$16	$3.20	—	—	—	—	—	—	—	—	—	—	—	—
Coors	—	—	—	—	12	4	$1	$0.08	13	5	$4	$0.31	13	5	$15	$1.16
Miller	—	—	—	—	9	5	$12	$1.33	24	2	$42	$1.75	36	2	$76	$2.10

Source: Advertising in *Leading National Advertisers*; barrel sales in *Advertising Age*, for selected years.

brewers, suffered the consequences of both the intense advertising campaigns and increased price competition being waged by the national brewers. Dixie was at insolvency's door when it was sold to a beer distributor who was interested in private-label beer production. Selected financial data for Dixie follow:

	1984	*1980*	*1976*
Sales	$7,300,000	$11,800,000	$9,800,000
Operating profit	(600,000)	300,000	(200,000)
Total assets	2,700,000	4,300,000	3,200,000
Shareholders' equity	($1,800,000)	$ 2,700,000	$2,800,000

The beer industry had seen, by 1985, the disappearance of major 1980 competitors as well as the elimination of regional brewers such as Dixie. Olympia, Pabst, and Schlitz were all part of larger brewers. Anheuser-Busch, which had a market share of 28 percent in 1980, had responded aggressively, if belatedly, to the Miller threat. Miller, for its part, had reached a 21 percent market share in 1985, down slightly from its 22 percent peak. Stroh, a 4 percent market share in 1980, had acquired Schlitz and a 13 percent market share by 1985. Some formerly successful brands seemed to be following a liquidation strategy.

Coors, Budweiser, and Miller were expected to continue their national strategies based upon national consumer identification similar to the soft drink industry. These national brewers, however, were faced with competition outside the industry — white wine, wine coolers, diet drinks, and fruit juices as substitutes for beer. These substitute products, the antialcohol social action programs, and the current health-and-exercise life-style all led to a sober forecast for the brewing industry.

Miller revamped its national strategy in the face of its declining sales of Miller's High Life (23.3 million barrels in 1979 — second to Budweiser's 31.4 million — versus 20.3 million in 1982 and 14.1 million in 1984). Miller changed advertising agencies and themes — from Backer & Speilvogel's "Welcome to Miller Time" to J. Walter Thompson's "Made the American Way" — and introduced a packaged draft beer (Miller Genuine Draft — "Look guys, no keg") to capitalize on continued market research that indicated consumers preferred draft beer. Although Coors is also a draft beer, a Miller spokesperson noted that Coors had not promoted that attribute, and consumers did not think of Coors as a draft beer (*Advertising Age,* February 16, 1987, p. 59).

Coors has risen from twelfth to fourth place among the nation's brewers in the second half of the 1960s, but slipped to fifth place in 1975 and sixth in 1982. William (chairman and CEO) and Joseph (president and COO) Coors wrote in their 1981 Annual Report that "we intend to move Coors back into the number one position in our sales territory." Joseph Coors' son Peter, division president, commented:

Miller changed the ball game by applying cigarette marketing concepts, and Anheuser responded with a vengeance. We were late fighting back.

Coors was perceived as America's fine light beer. Then Miller's Lite came out. In 1978 we hit with Coors Light, a move that saved our bacon.''[2]

Peter Coors noted further that "our products were so popular we didn't have to put much effort into marketing." Coors' increased advertising efforts follow:[3]

Year	Amount
1977	$15,500,000
1978	$33,500,000
1979	$46,400,000
1980	$66,800,000
1981	$84,500,000
1982 (estimated)	$80,000,000

As these national firms compete, industry analysts underline Coors' and Anheuser's gross profit advantage over competition. Marc Cohen, writing in "The Brewing Industry" for Sanford C. Bernstein & Co., New York (March 1986), estimated gross profit per barrel by brewer for 1985 as follows:

Coors	$24.35
Anheuser-Busch	23.45
Miller	19.30
Heileman	13.55
Average	$21.25

Operating profit per barrel was estimated by Goldman Sachs research for 1983 as $10.50 for Anheuser-Busch, $6.06 for Miller Brewing, $10.47 for Coors, $1.08 for Pabst, $5.94 for Heileman, and $7.96 for the industry on the average. For 1980 these same data were Anheuser-Busch, $5.73; Miller, $3.88; Schlitz/Stroh, $2.01; Coors, $6.29; Pabst, $1.42; Heileman, $4.78; and the average industry, $4.56.[4]

Exhibit 7 summarizes Bernstein's estimates of the total U.S. market by segments; Exhibit 8, shipments and shares of U.S. brewers; Exhibit 9, volume and share of premium; Exhibit 10, volume and share of light; and Exhibit 11, volume and share of popular-priced beers. Imported beer brands are covered in Exhibit 12.

[2] Hinkle and Stineman, op. cit., p. 438.

[3] Hinkle and Stineman, op. cit., p. 443.

[4] A. A. Thompson, Jr. and A. J. Strickland III, *Strategic Management* (Plano, TX: Business Publications, 1987), p. 519.

EXHIBIT 7
Brewing industry
barrelage and
market
segmentation

	1980	1984
Barrelage (millions of barrels)		
Imports	4.6	7.2
Superpremiums	10.1	8.8
Premium	96.0	83.2
Light	23.5	36.0
Popular	40.8	43.2
Malt liquor	5.2	5.7
All others	1.0	1.1
Market share		
Imports	2.5%	3.9%
Superpremiums	5.6	4.8
Premium	53.0	44.9
Light	13.0	19.4
Popular	22.5	23.3
Malt liquor	2.8	3.1
All others	0.6	0.6
Total	100.0%	100.0%

Source: R. S. Weinberg and Associates, The Beer Institute, and Bernstein estimates.

EXHIBIT 8
Shipments and
market share of U.S.
brewers

	1980	1984
Shipments (millions of barrels)		
Anheuser-Busch	50.2	64.0
Miller	37.3	37.5
Stroh	6.2	23.9
Heileman	13.3	16.8
Coors	13.8	13.2
Other	60.5	29.8
Total	181.2	185.2
Market share		
Anheuser-Busch	27.7%	34.6%
Miller	20.6	20.3
Stroh	3.4	12.9
Heileman	7.3	9.1
Coors	7.6	7.1
Other	33.4	16.1
Total	100.0%	100.0%

Source: *Beer Marketers Insights,* corporate reports, and Bernstein estimates.

EXHIBIT 9

Brewing industry segmentation for regular premium beers

	1980	1984
Volume by brand (millions of barrels)		
Budweiser	34.6	44.5
Miller High Life	23.1	13.9
Coors Premium	11.3	8.5
Stroh	5.6	5.3
Old Style	3.9	4.1
Others	17.5	6.9
Total	96.0	83.2
Share by brand		
Budweiser	36.0%	53.5%
Miller High Life	24.1	16.7
Coors Premium	11.7	10.2
Stroh	5.8	6.4
Old Style	4.1	4.9
Others	18.3	8.3
Total	100.0%	100.0%
Share by company		
Anheuser-Busch	36.0%	53.5%
Miller	24.1	16.7
Coors	11.7	10.2
Heileman	6.3	7.6
Stroh	5.8	6.4
Others	16.1	5.6
Total	100.0%	100.0%

Source: *Beer Marketers Insights,* R. S. Weinberg and Associates, corporate reports, and Bernstein estimates.

Brewer capacity and number of breweries was estimated by Goldman Sachs research department for 1983 as follows:[5]

Company	*1983 capacity (millions of barrels)*	*Number of breweries*
Anheuser-Busch	66.0	11
Miller Brewing	44.0	6
Stroh	29.0	7
Pabst Brewing	14.0	4
Adolph Coors	15.0	1
Heileman	26.0	11
Others	27.9	38
Total	220.9	78

[5] Thompson and Strickland, op. cit., p. 497.

EXHIBIT 10
Brewing industry
segmentation for
light beers

	1980	1984
Volume by brand (millions of barrels)		
Lite	13.0	17.9
Coors Light	2.5	4.6
Bud Light	—	4.3
Michelob Light	2.2	2.4
Old Milwaukee Light	0.1	1.5
Natural Light	2.2	1.1
Others	3.5	4.3
Total	23.5	36.0
Share by brand		
Lite	55.3%	49.7%
Coors Light	10.6	12.6
Bud Light	0.0	11.8
Michelob Light	9.1	6.7
Old Milwaukee Light	0.6	4.2
Natural Light	9.4	3.1
Others	14.9	11.9
Total	100.0%	100.0%
Share by company		
Miller	55.3%	49.7%
Anheuser-Busch	18.6	21.5
Coors	10.6	12.6
Stroh	2.1	6.7
Heileman	2.1	2.9
Others	11.3	6.5
Total	100.0%	100.0%

Source: *Beer Marketers Insights,* R. S. Weinberg and Associates, corporate reports, and Bernstein estimates.

Modern Brewery Age Blue Book for 1978 had estimated 1978 capacity in millions of barrels for the top five brewers as Anheuser-Busch, 44.3; Miller, 28.0; Schlitz, 32.0; Pabst, 19.0; and Coors, 15.0.

BREWING INDUSTRY CASES

Heublein-Hamm's. In 1965 Heublein is considering the acquisition of Hamm's, the number eight U.S. brewer. Heublein's current success is primarily due to Smirnoff vodka, and the company, seeking additional growth, looks at Hamm's.

Joseph Schlitz. By the end of 1980 Schlitz, once the number one brewer in the United States, had slipped to fourth place behind Anheuser-Busch, Miller, and Pabst. Plant expansion in the mid-1970s was straining resources at a time when

EXHIBIT 11
Brewing industry
segmentation of
popular-priced
beers

	1980	1984
Volume by brand (millions of barrels)		
Old Milwaukee	4.6	7.0
Busch	2.9	5.1
Schaefer	2.8	4.0
Milwaukee's Best	—	2.4
Pabst Blue Ribbon	9.6	5.4
Carling	1.0	1.8
Meister Brau	—	1.7
Others	19.9	15.8
Total	40.8	43.2
Share by brand		
Old Milwaukee	11.3%	16.2%
Busch	7.2	11.8
Schaefer	6.7	9.3
Milwaukee's Best	—	5.6
Pabst Blue Ribbon	23.5	12.5
Carling	2.5	4.2
Meister Brau	—	3.9
Others	48.8	36.6
Total	100.0%	100.0%
Share by company		
Stroh	0.5%	32.1%
Anheuser-Busch	7.2	11.8
Heileman	11.4	15.0
Miller	—	9.5
Others	80.9	31.6
Total	100.0%	100.0%

Source: *Beer Marketers Insights*, R. S. Weinberg and Associates, corporate reports, and Bernstein estimates.

Miller, backed by Philip Morris, was greatly intensifying competition in an already highly competitive industry. Further, Schlitz changed its formula and technology, with a resulting taste change in the mid-1970s. This taste change lost the company many Schlitz fans.

Finally, Schlitz faces a stockholder-management conflict, aggravated by the fact that the majority of stockholders are members of the family that owned and led the Schlitz Company for over one hundred years.

The Adolph Coors Company. Coors has pursued a single product strategy, producing Coors at a single brewery using Rocky Mountain spring water and natural ingredients. This family-run organization asks itself in 1983 if it can continue to be a regional brewer.

EXHIBIT 12
Imported beer sales
and shares

Brand	Rank		Millions of barrels		Market share	
	1984	*1980*	*1984*	*1980*	*1984*	*1980*
Heineken	1	1	2.4	1.7	33.1%	37.8%
Molson	2	2	1.0	1.0	13.4	22.4
Beck's	3	3	0.6	0.2	9.0	5.1
Moosehead	4	6	0.5	0.2	6.5	4.0
Labatt's	5	5	0.3	0.2	4.5	4.9
St. Pauli Girl	6	7	0.3	0.1	3.7	1.7
Dos Equis	7	4	0.2	0.2	2.4	4.9
Carling O'Keefe	8	—	0.2	—	2.2	—
Amstel Light	9	8	0.1	0.1	1.8	0.3
Corona Extra	10	—	0.1	—	1.7	—
Total			5.7	3.7	78.3	81.4

Source: John C. Maxwell, Jr., "Annual Brewing Survey." New York: Furman, Selz, Mager, Dietz & Birney, November 8, 1985.

Pabst Brewing Company. Between 1981 and 1983 the strategies at Pabst are distracted from the important events within the brewing industry — especially intensifying competition and concentration — by a series of hostile takeover attempts. Fleeing from the raiders sends Pabst into managerial and organizational stresses and strains and also into its own takeover attempts as Pabst makes a bid for Schlitz.

THE WINE INDUSTRY

Wine Markets and Production

The wine market may be segmented into (1) cocktail and dessert wines, such as sherries or ports, which are heavy and sweet with a high alcohol percentage (14–20 percent); (2) sparkling wines such as champagne or "pop" wines, which are given "bubbles" by putting carbon dioxide into a second fermentation process; and (3) table wines with 10–14 percent alcohol content. The higher-quality table wines use grape varietals such as burgundy, cabernet sauvignon, or pinot chardonnay.

The production economics vary according to grape costs and marketing, with production costs being relatively constant except in very low or very high quality wines. Exhibit 13 breaks down production and marketing costs for high-quality, low-volume imported wine and an above-average-quality, high-volume U.S. domestic wine.

Wine Companies

Gallo was not only the dominant U.S. producer, but was also the world's largest by the 1980s. Gallo's 50 million cases of volume early in the 1980s clearly outweighed

EXHIBIT 13
Estimated cost
breakdown

	U.S. domestic premium[a]	High-quality French import
Grapes	55%	25%
Production	20%	45%
Advertising	5%	15%
Selling	10%	5%
Other marketing, including excise taxes	10%	10%
Retail price per bottle (1980)	$2.40	$6.50

[a] Such as Gallo, Masson, or Taylor.

the other U.S. national wine companies, such as Heublein (23 million), Seagram (20 million), and Coca-Cola's Wine Spectrum (9 million). Many foreign wine producers ranging from high-quality to the "fun" wines (Riunite, with 9 million cases) entered the U.S. market in anticipation of the time when the average U.S. consumption would move from its 1980 amount of about 8 liters to California's 17 liters or, eventually, to Germany's 25 liters.

The cost structure of the U.S. wine companies varied significantly with strategy. A fully integrated company (one with in-house grapes and glass manufacturing) with modern production facilities — such as Gallo — was estimated by an industry observer to have a pretax return on sales of 15–20 percent. A lower-quality grape and minimal production costs of a Riunite might mean a 25 percent pretax return on sales, even considering marketing costs. On the other hand, a full-line national wine company that lacked vertical integration might be faced with low returns on sales (3 percent) for its generic table wines, which are often half or even more of its business.

Industry analysts, for example, noted the difference between Paul Masson's table wine margin of less than 5 percent versus Gallo's 25–30 percent profit margin. Paul Masson's champagnes and sparkling wines equaled Gallo's overall margins, but they were only 10 percent of Masson's sales. Wine prices for generic table wines could not get too high because of Gallo's dominance, which was especially noticeable in supermarkets.

Heublein, the number two U.S. producer, had Inglenook, Italian Swiss Colony, Petrie, and other brands in its United Vintners wine subsidiary. United Vintners' numerous brands and ten separate production facilities resulted in a lack of economies of scale.

The Taylor California Cellar's brands within Coca-Cola's Wine Spectrum were especially aggressive advertisers. The beverage industry publication, *Impact*, estimated that Taylor California Cellars spent $1.72 per case on advertising ($8 million in total) versus $1.64 for Paul Masson ($12 million in total) or $0.50 for Gallo ($22 million in total).

Major wine companies selling in the United States include Almaden, Brown Forman, Coca-Cola's Taylor, Gallo, Riunite, Seagram's Paul Masson, and United Vintners.

Almaden produced only about one-fifth of its wine, purchasing grapes crushed by or wines produced by others. Almaden's creativity was evidenced by its packaging, as it introduced the 1.5-liter jug wine in the 1970s and supplied at least half the boxed wine sold in the United States during the 1980s.

Brown-Forman Distillers built from an extended relationship with Korbel Champagne and duplicated its premium image (Jack Daniel's Tennessee Whiskey, Old Bushmills' Irish Whiskey, and Martel cognacs) in its wines. It acquired distribution rights to Bolla and Cella wines in 1968, Noilly Prat vermouth in 1971, and a 25-year extension of its Korbel rights in 1978. It also acquired a 40 percent interest in Bolla in 1972. Brown-Forman's premium market image is supported, then, in wine with an importation and distribution strategy.

Taylor Wines were carrying Coca-Cola's marketing strategy into quality wines. Taylor initially concentrated in the early 1980s in marketing, advertising, and distribution, innovating with comparison taste tests and aggressive couponing.

Gallo's profitability (estimated at about 10 percent return on sales and assets in the early 1980s, with both sales and assets estimated at approximately $500,000,000) was due to its economies of scale. Gallo was dominant in its production, marketing, and distribution. Production economies including crushing, bottling costs (which were perhaps one-half of its competitors' due to its speed of production), storage (Gallo had four large production facilities, which transferred technology from plant to plant), and grape costs. Its distribution economies were volume-related, as Gallo often achieved supermarket turnover double its closest competitors'. Gallo's lower-priced wine was Carlo Rossi, and it also produced dessert and sparkling wines. Gallo's market share was estimated at one-fourth nationally and over one-third in supermarkets.

Riunite's "fun" wine obviously filled a market need, as it increased by 50 percent in the 1970s based on its sweet wine that introduced non–wine drinkers to wine. Riunite was the largest Italian producer, so that its lower labor cost and concentrated (U.S. only) marketing allowed it to compete favorably with U.S. wines.

Seagram's majority of wine sales came from Paul Masson, a premium wine that competed with Gallo and the increasingly strong Taylor. Seagram also marketed imported (Barton & Gustier, Mumm) and high-quality, low-volume varietals.

United Vintners, Heublein's wine division, had a large number of brands which worked against economies of scale. An industry observer thought the company would be a successful competitor if it could upgrade its Colony label to the premium category.

Exhibit 14 suggests a way of analyzing wine products in terms of price per bottle and marketing effort per bottle.

EXHIBIT 14
Marketing effort and
price per bottle

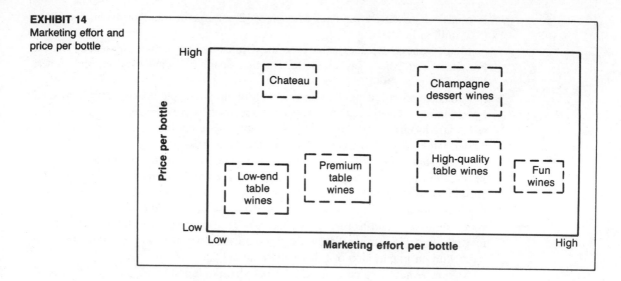

By the early 1980s U.S. wine distribution was essentially (92 percent) handled by individual wholesalers. Three-quarters of those wholesalers also handled spirits. An industry observer noted that Gallo distributed 60 percent of its product through supermarkets versus 40 percent for Seagram's Paul Masson. Seagram was 5 percent higher than Gallo in liquor chains (25 percent versus 20 percent) and liquor stores (20 percent vs. 15 percent), and 10 percent higher in on-premise outlets such as restaurants.

Other U.S. domestic wineries may utilize independent, high-quality strategies or else private labels or subcontracting excess capacity. Franzia, for example, provides a significant part of Taylor's grape supply, Taylor having none of its own grapes. Taylor California Cellars wine was bottled at Franzia's bottling facility in the late 1970s and early 1980s.

Wine industry analysts not only had to deal with mergers and changing strategies, but with new-product complexities. The central new-product question in the mid-1980s was the wine cooler. Do wine coolers compete with wine? With beer? With soft drinks?

Sutter Home Winery started a new-product trend when it sought a solution to its oversupply of zinfandel grapes. In 1979 Sutter introduced a few thousand cases of white zinfandel, which it increased to 25,000 cases in 1980. Blush wines — fruity, light pink wines offering the white wine drinker more choice and flavor — were off and booming. Sutter made 1.5 million cases of white zinfandel in 1985 and aimed at 2.25 million in 1987. By the mid 1980s over 100 wineries made blush wine.

WINE INDUSTRY CASES

Coco-Cola Wine Spectrum. Coca-Cola forms its Wine Spectrum division primarily from its 1977 acquisition of Taylor Wine Company. Coca-Cola studies growth rates and industry economies, while contemplating an aggressive marketing campaign including "head-to-head" taste tests.

Seagram. In 1983 Seagram, having hired Mary Cunningham to help formulate a wine strategy for its domestic (Paul Masson) and important foreign wineries (Sandeman, Barton & Gustier, and Mumm), acquires Coca-Cola's Wine Spectrum. The acquisition suggests Seagram can now formulate a new competitive strategy against Gallo.

The Ontario Wine Industry. The heavily regulated Ontario wineries are becoming increasingly concentrated. While the powerful grape growers resist conversion to higher-quality grapes, the trends in consumer tastes seem to mandate some major product upgrading by the Ontario companies.

Inniskillin. A new, very small Ontario winery formed in 1974 to make high-quality wine is contemplating significant expansion in 1978.

HEUBLEIN, INC.

With growth in sales and profits since 1959 far outstripping that of the liquor industry's "Big Four," by 1965 Heublein, producer of Smirnoff vodka and other liquor and food items, had become the fifth largest liquor company in the United States (see Exhibits 1, 2, and 3).

Ralph Hart, Heublein's president since 1960 and a former executive vice president of international marketing for the Colgate-Palmolive Company, commented on the company's assets:

Although liquor products account for most of our sales at the present time, we consider ourselves in the consumer goods business, not the liquor business. Liquor is a consumer good just like toothpaste and is sold the same way.

To be successful in this business, you need three things: a good product, distribution, and advertising. You must have a good product. If you don't, the consumer will find you out and you will not get any repeat purchases. You also need good distribution so the consumer will be able to get your product easily and conveniently. Finally, you

EXHIBIT 1
Five largest liquor companies, 1965

Industry rank	Company	1964 liquor sales	1965 total sales	Total sales gain, 1959–1965	Profit gain 1959–1965
1	Distillers Corporation	$718	$1,005	37%	52%
2	Hiram Walker	598	530	28	46
3	National Distillers	430	829	44	24
4	Schenley Industries[a]	390	461	0	33
5	Heublein, Inc.	123	166	89	259

Note: Figures in millions of dollars.
[a] Figures estimated.

EXHIBIT 2 Consolidated balance sheets, selected years, 1955–1965

	Years ending June 30				
	1955	1960	1963	1964	1965
Assets					
Current assets					
Cash	$2,298	$3,925	$2,744	$3,357	$3,338
Time deposits			6,000	1,750	
Marketable securities	9	4,883	1,000		4,048
Investment in whiskey certificates		593	1,069	150	
Accounts and notes receivable	5,157	12,426	17,835	18,668	19,010
Inventories	5,825	8,269	9,127	13,347	16,323
Prepaid expenses	297	382	356	325	548
Total current assets	$13,586	$30,479	$38,130	$37,597	$43,267
Long-term assets					
Property, plant and equipment — net	$3,254	$5,793	$6,363	$7,339	$7,502
Deferred charges, other assets, and goodwill	223	416	1,068	3,659	5,383
Total long-term assets	$3,477	$6,209	$7,431	$10,998	$12,885
Total assets	$17,063	$36,688	$45,561	$48,595	$56,152
Liabilities and stockholders' equity					
Current liabilities					
Notes payable to banks	$2,000				
Accounts payable	687	$1,933	$2,078	$2,417	$3,584
Federal income tax	531	2,857	3,607	4,129	4,701
Accrued liabilities	513	2,688	4,044	5,175	5,774
Cash dividends payable	98	299	733	721	986
Long-term debt due within one year	301	631	777	850	1,013
Total current liabilities	$4,129	$8,408	$11,239	$13,292	$16,059
Long-term liabilities					
Long-term debt due after one year	$4,699	$5,388	$3,239	$2,416	$1,403
Deferred federal income tax			154	248	316
Minority interest				272	
Total long-term liabilities	$4,699	$5,388	$3,393	$2,936	$1,719
Stockholders' equity	$8,235	$22,892	$30,929	$32,368	$38,374
Total liabilities and stockholders' equity	$17,063	$36,688	$45,561	$48,595	$56,152

Note: Figures in thousands of dollars.
Source: Heublein records.

must have a good, convincing story to tell the consumer about why he should buy your product, and you tell it through advertising.

In 1965 Heublein's management had three long-range goals: to make Smirnoff the number one liquor brand in the world; to continue a sales growth of 10% a year through internal growth, acquisitions, or both; and to maintain Heublein's return on equity above 15%.

EXHIBIT 3 Consolidated income statements, years ending June 30, 1955–1965

	1955	1956	1957	1958	1959	1960	1961	1962	1963	1964	1965
Net sales	$37,222	$68,543	$82,064	$87,839	$87,647	$103,169	$108,281	$116,142	$121,995	$135,848	$165,595
Cost of sales[a]	29,503	53,219	63,234	67,231	67,276	78,028	80,419	85,793	89,500	99,575	121,503
Gross profit	$7,719	$15,325	$18,830	$20,608	$20,372	$25,140	$27,862	$30,349	$32,495	$36,273	$44,092
Expenses											
Selling and advertising	$4,650	$8,013	$10,617	$12,613	$12,710	$14,276	$16,089	$16,444	$18,271	$20,477	$24,551
Administrative and general	1,479	2,288	2,699	2,822	2,561	2,783	3,205	4,111	3,710	3,485	4,257
	6,130	10,301	13,315	15,434	15,271	17,060	19,293	20,555	21,981	23,962	28,808
	1,590	5,024	5,515	5,176	5,100	8,080	8,569	9,794	10,514	12,312	15,284
Other[b]	189	316	407	519	638	293	168	199	(339)	(18)	(112)
	1,401	4,708	5,109	4,654	4,462	7,788	8,401	9,595	10,852	12,330	15,397
State and federal income taxes	733	2,531	2,697	2,524	2,399	4,232	4,587	5,188	5,830	6,516	8,021
Net income	$667	$2,177	$2,411	$2,130	$2,063	$3,556	$3,814	$4,407	$5,022	$5,814	$7,376

Note: Figures in thousands of dollars.
[a] Includes federal excise taxes on the withdrawal of distilled spirits from bond. These totaled $90 million for the fiscal year 1965.
[b] Interest income, interest expense, and miscellaneous.
Source: Heublein records.

A major acquisition opportunity was being considered in the fall of 1965 as one means of meeting these goals. The potential acquisition (Hamm Brewing Company) raised a number of short-term as well as strategic issues, however, which Hart wanted to consider carefully. Hamm was almost as large as Heublein in sales, and therefore the impact of the acquisition on Heublein was certain to be significant. The beer and liquor industries were in many respects similar, but Heublein had had no direct experience in the beer industry. Hart emphasized that the kinds of opportunities being sought were not just profitable financial deals, but rather firms whose operations Heublein's management believed it could improve. Heublein's acquisition policies had been explained more fully by Hart in a 1965 presentation before the Los Angeles Society of Security Analysts:

> *Frankly, we take a long, hard look at any potential acquisition. We ask ourselves: "Will the new product or company we acquire have a potential at least equal to existing Heublein products, in order not to dilute present equity? Will new products lend themselves to our channels of distribution and marketing techniques? Will these products have sufficient gross margin to allow for our type of distribution, advertising, and merchandising?"*

The question of the Hamm acquisition, then, had to be decided in the context of Heublein's position and strategy and the trends in its basic markets.

COMPANY BACKGROUND

Market

Between 1955 and 1964, U.S. consumption of distilled spirits increased from 199 million wine gallons to 277 million, or 39% (see Exhibit 4).[1] By the latter year some 60 million Americans — about 53% of the adult population — drank some sort of alcoholic beverage and spent about $6.5 billion for liquor, about one-third of the amount spent for public elementary and secondary school education. Excise taxes on these sales ($10.50 per proof gallon in 1965) provided the federal government with about $2.5 billion in 1964, more than the revenue from any other single source except for personal and corporate income taxes.

Rising sales of liquor could be attributed to various causes, including population growth, increased personal discretionary income contributing to a slightly higher per capita consumption, changing social mores, the declining proportion of people

---

[1] Several terms in common use in the industry require definition:

Proof is a term used to specify the proportion of alcohol in a product. The proof number is equal to twice the percentage of alcohol (by volume) in the product.

A *proof gallon* is any volume that contains the same amount of alcohol as a gallon of 100-proof spirits.

A *wine gallon* is a gallon by volume (regardless of proof). Thus a gallon (five-fifths) of 80-proof vodka would be one wine gallon but only 8/10 proof gallons.

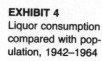

EXHIBIT 4
Liquor consumption
compared with pop-
ulation, 1942–1964

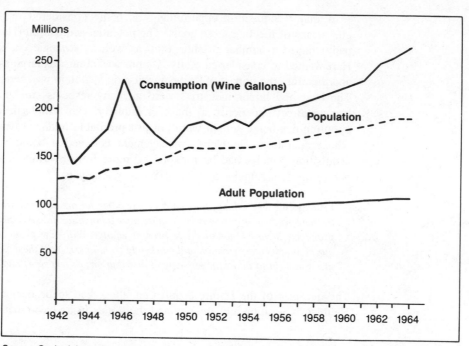

Source: Gavin Jobson Associates, Inc., *The Liquor Handbook, 1965;* cited by Glore Forgan, Wm. R. Staats Inc., in *Heublein, Inc.,* December 1965.

in "dry" states, and changes in the population makeup by age group. Edward Kelley, Heublein's executive vice president, felt the growth in liquor consumption between 1955 and 1964 was primarily the result of the increase in per capita consumption, which appeared to be related to the growth in personal discretionary income, and of the spread of drinking to more segments of the population and on more occasions.

Predicting the future in relation to income and demographic changes, industry sources looked forward to an even faster growth in consumption from 1965 to 1970 than was the case from 1955 to 1964 — 4.5% or more a year, as compared with 3.6%. Since the Bureau of the Census forecast that the 25-to-54 age group would increase an average of nearly 17% between 1970 and 1980, many industry observers felt the picture beyond 1970 looked even better than that between 1965 and 1970.

Market Changes   Demand for the various categories of liquor was changing as well as growing between 1955 and 1965 (see Exhibits 5 and 6), with a dramatic shift in consumer preference to straight whiskeys, imported whiskeys, and the nonwhiskeys and away from the blended and bonded whiskeys. While some observers felt this represented a return to the pre–World War II relationship that provided straight whiskeys with a slight

EXHIBIT 5
Whiskey consumption trends, 1955–1964

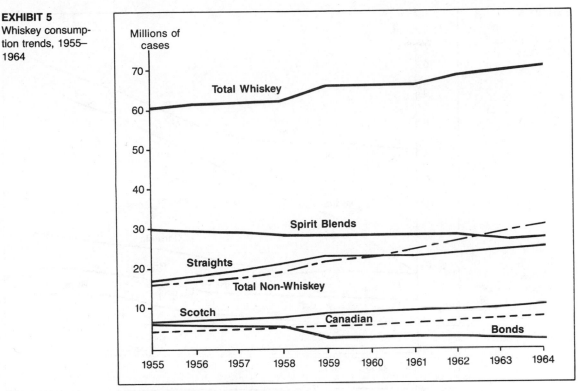

Note: Expressed as a 3-year moving average.
Source: Gavin Jobson Associates, Inc., *The Liquor Handbook, 1965;* cited by Glore Forgan, Wm. R. Staats Inc., in *Heublein, Inc.,* December 1965.

edge over blended whiskeys, most industry sources felt the shift in consumption reflected a trend toward lightness in liquor taste. According to Roger Bensen:

> *The most probable reason [for the trend toward lightness] is that people drink mainly to satisfy social and status needs and for effect, and not inherently for taste. The taste of many liquors is something which new drinkers find difficult to assimilate. Hence, they turn to various cocktails or mixed drinks to disguise the original flavor of the liquor product. And to complete the pattern, people achieve further fulfillment of social and status needs by using the newer, more current, more exotic liquors and cocktail formulations as a vehicle for their drinking.*[2]

Some of the most important of these changes are reflected in the figures for distilled spirits entering trade channels shown in Exhibit 7.

[2] Roger D. Bensen, *Heublein, Inc.,* Investment Research Department, Glore Forgan, Wm. R. Staats Inc., December 1965, p. 21.

EXHIBIT 6
Nonwhiskey consumption trends, 1955–1964

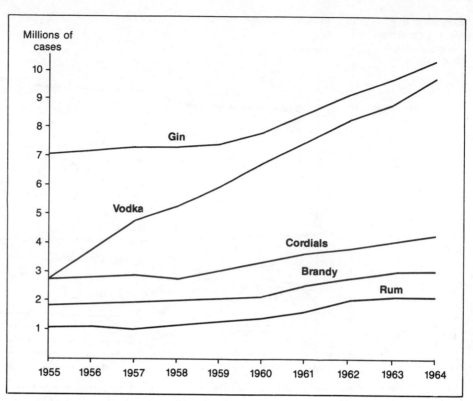

Note: Expressed as a 3-year moving average.
Source: Gavin Jobson Associates, Inc., *The Liquor Handbook, 1965;* cited by Glore Forgan, Wm. R. Staats Inc., in *Heublein, Inc.,* December 1965.

According to many industry observers, one of the more important developments in the liquor industry between 1960 and 1965 was the growth of bottled cocktails. Although they had been on the market for over 50 years, they had shown little growth until 1960. In that year, Heublein, which had almost all of the market at that time, developed a new product formulation, package, and promotional campaign for its line of bottled cocktails. By 1965 volume had increased 100% to an estimated 1.9 million wine gallons, as Distillers Corporation (Seagram), Hiram Walker, Schenley, and others entered the market. Heublein, whose volume increased 60% during the period, still had 55% of the market in 1965. The convenience, low consumer price (only a few pennies more than comparable drinks mixed at home), and the trend toward lightness caused one liquor authority to predict that bottled cocktails might represent close to 10% of the industry's volume by 1975.

Trends in Competition

Between 1955 and 1965 the majority of the companies in the liquor industry followed one of two broad strategies. Most of the medium-sized companies aggressively marketed their products in traditional ways. They did not increase, decrease, or

EXHIBIT 7
Market changes for
distilled spirits,
1955–1964

Product type	Volume (millions of wine gallons)		Market share		Change in volume 1955–1964
	1955	*1964*	*1955*	*1964*	
Whiskeys					
Bonded	12.9	7.9	6.3%	2.8%	(39)%
Straight	46.1	69.6	22.7	24.3	51
Blended	81.5	74.7	40.0	26.1	(8)
Scotch	12.3	28.3	6.0	9.9	130
Canadian	9.2	17.2	4.5	6.0	87
Total all whiskey	161.5	197.9	79.5%	69.1%	22 %
Nonwhiskeys					
Gin[a]	20.7	31.1	10.2%	10.9%	50 %
Vodka[a]	7.0	28.1	3.4	9.8	302
Rum	2.7	5.9	1.3	2.1	119
Brandy	4.6	8.7	2.3	3.0	89
Other	6.6	14.6	3.3	5.1	121
Total nonwhiskeys	41.8	88.4	20.5	30.9	111
Total distilled spirits	203.3	286.3	100.0%	100.0%	41 %

[a] Gin and vodka were unique among the distilled spirits since they required no aging. The principal distinction between gin and vodka was that the juniper berry flavor was added to grain neutral spirits to produce the former, while as many flavor-producing ingredients as possible were filtered out from grain neutral spirits to produce the latter.

change their product line, nor did they attempt to diversify out of the liquor business. None of these companies had a complete line of liquor products, and some had only one or two products. Several of these companies, however, experienced extremely rapid growth during this period. Their success could generally be attributed to having a leading product in one or two of the more rapidly growing segments of the liquor market.

The four major distillers also marketed their products in traditional ways. However, with the exception of Hiram Walker, each of these companies attempted to diversify out of the liquor industry through acquisitions, though liquor accounted for the major portion of the sales of each of these companies in 1965. Moreover, with the possible exception of National Distillers, the major distillers no longer seemed to be interested in further diversification outside of the liquor business in the mid-1960s. Rather, they began to compete more vigorously in all segments of the liquor market during 1964 and 1965, particularly the more rapidly growing segments. The increased competition, coupled with the trend toward lightness, caused John Shaw of Equity Research Associates to predict that "marketing efforts will become more consumer-oriented, stressing appetite appeal in much the same way as the food industry. Overall, advertising and promotional costs can be expected to trend higher, as brand competition remains intense."[3]

Among the companies that had grown rapidly or that competed directly with Heublein were James B. Beam Distilling, Paddington Corporation, Distillers Corporation–Seagram Co. Ltd., and Schenley.

Methods of Distribution

Distribution of liquor took two basic forms at the beginning of 1966. In 18 "control states," a state-regulated agency was responsible for the distribution and sale of distilled spirits. Generally the marketer sold the product to the state agency at the national wholesaler price and allowed the state to distribute the products as it saw fit. These states often had laws restricting the type of point-of-purchase advertising that a company could undertake. In the other 32 states, called "open states," distribution was through wholesalers who redistributed the product to the retailers, who sold the product to the ultimate consumer. From 1958 to 1964 the number of these independent wholesalers declined almost 43%, leaving only 2,305 wholesalers in 1964 who were licensed by the Federal Alcohol Administration to deal in distilled spirits. This trend, which was similar to that in other consumer-product industries, was primarily caused, according to industry observers, by a serious profit squeeze on the wholesaler, whose costs of operation increased while the retail prices of inexpensive liquors declined because of intense competition — a situation that was aggravated by the spread of private labels. While distillers had not felt the effects of this squeeze by 1964, there was a feeling among some industry observers that distillers might have to lower their prices to wholesalers or lose lower volume lines if the trend continued.

Cost Structure

The cost of producing liquor products, excluding federal and state taxes on the raw materials, was relatively low compared to the retail selling price. For example, high-quality vodka reportedly cost about 61 cents a fifth to produce and retailed at $5.75. Federal taxes on raw materials (assuming an 80-proof product) were $1.68 per fifth. In addition, the costs of production, excluding federal and state taxes on raw materials, were often not much different for high-priced and low-priced liquors, even though they were often made through different processes that were said to result in differences in taste and quality between the high-priced and low-priced liquors.

HEUBLEIN'S HISTORY

The House of Heublein was founded in 1859 in Hartford, Connecticut, by Andrew Heublein, a painter and weaver by trade. At that time, the House of Heublein was a combination restaurant, café, and small hotel. By 1875 Andrew's two sons, Gilbert

---

[3] John Shaw, *Trends in the Liquor Industry,* Equity Research Associates, August 30, 1965, p. 6.

and Lewis, were running the business. They branched out by conducting a wholesale wine business in addition to expanding the original operations. In 1892, through a combination of fortuitous circumstances, Heublein invented the bottled cocktail. From this time until the start of national Prohibition, Heublein's principal business was the production and sale of distilled spirits.

In 1907 Heublein began importing Brand's A-1 steak sauce and later, when World War I disrupted the importation, acquired the manufacturing rights to the product in the United States. When Prohibition forced Heublein to close down its liquor plant in 1920, the company transferred key personnel to food operations. Until the repeal of Prohibition in 1933, A-1 steak sauce was Heublein's principal product.

In 1939 John Martin, Heublein's president and one of the company's principal stockholders, acquired the rights to Smirnoff vodka from Rudolph Kunett. Although Heublein sold only 6,000 cases of Smirnoff that year, a carefully planned promotional campaign, which was put into operation immediately after World War II, aided in boosting the sales of Smirnoff to over one million cases per year by 1954. As the vodka market expanded, Heublein introduced Relska vodka in 1953 and Popov in 1961, so as to have entries in the middle- and low-price segments of the market. Although Smirnoff remained Heublein's principal product from 1959, when it accounted for over 67% of sales, to 1965, when it accounted for 51% of sales, Heublein began in 1959 to diversify its product line and to expand its international operations.

Heublein used both internal growth and acquisition to broaden its product line. In 1960 it began a campaign to increase the sales of its bottled cocktails by introducing new kinds of cocktails and promoting the entire line more heavily. As Heublein's sales began to increase, other distillers, principally Distillers Corporation, began to market their own cocktails. By 1965 sales of bottled cocktails exceeded 850,000 cases a year, more than double the 1960 sales, and Heublein still claimed 55% of the market.

In 1961 Heublein made two acquisitions that strengthened its specialty food line. Timely Brands, which manufactured and marketed a complete line of ready-to-use, home dessert decorating products including Cake-Mate icing and gels, was acquired in June. In July Heublein acquired Escoffier, Ltd. of London, makers of 23 famed gourmet sauces and specialties.

Heublein made two more acquisitions during this period, both of which were designed to broaden and strengthen its liquor line. In April 1964 Heublein acquired Arrow Liquors Corporation for an estimated cost of $5.7 million. Arrow's principal products were its line of cordials, including Arrow peppermint schnapps and Arrow blackberry brandy, and its domestically bottled, bulk-imported scotch, McMaster's. According to Edward Kelley, the three principal reasons for the Arrow acquisition were that Heublein expected the cordial and scotch markets to grow in the future, that Arrow had products that were among the leaders in these markets in the control states, and that Arrow had a small but extremely competent management.

In January 1965 Heublein acquired Vintage Wines for approximately $2.2 million.

Vintage, whose sales were about $4 million at the time of the acquisition, was integrated with the Heublein Liquor Division. Vintage's principal product was Lancers Vin Rosé, an imported Portuguese wine that accounted for about 50% of the company's sales.

The expansion in Heublein's international operations consisted primarily of the establishment of franchise operations in 21 additional foreign countries, which raised the number of such operations from 11 in 1959 to 32 in 1965.

COMPANY OPERATIONS

Financial Situation

During the 1965 fiscal year, Heublein earned $7.4 million on sales of $166 million, which represented roughly a 19% return on stockholders' equity. Between 1959 and 1965, Heublein's sales growth, profit growth, and return on equity far exceeded the average of the four major distillers (see Exhibit 1). In addition, even though Heublein was spending nearly twice as much (as a percentage of sales) on advertising as the average of the four major distillers and had increased the company's dividend/payout ratio to 50% of earnings, the company had a cash flow of $8.6 million in 1965, about 22% on equity, which compared favorably with the 9% average of the four major distillers.

Product Line

At the end of 1965 Heublein was marketing well over 50 products through its four divisions. While vodka was the company's principal product, accounting for 62% of 1965 sales, the company's product base had been broadened considerably since 1960 by acquisitions, internal growth, and new marketing agreements (see Exhibit 8). Heublein's product-line strategy was to market high-quality consumer products, which provided the high margins necessary to support intensive advertising. Heublein aimed its promotions of these products at the growing, prosperous, young-adult

EXHIBIT 8
Sales mix for selected years, 1950–1965

	Smirnoff Vodka	Other vodka	Total vodka	Other alcoholic beverages	Food	Total
1965	51%	11%	62%	30%	8%	100%
1964	58	12	70	21	9	100
1963	62	12	74	16	10	100
1962	63	11	74	16	10	100
1961	64	11	75	19	6	100
1960	67	9	76	18	6	100
1955	61	2	63	32	5	100
1950	27	—	27	63	10	100

Source: Heublein records.

market. The company was also interested in phasing out some of its less profitable lines whenever possible.

The liquor products division accounted for over 80% of Heublein's 1965 sales. Its principal product was Smirnoff vodka, the fourth largest selling liquor brand in the United States in 1965, with estimated annual sales of 2.3 million cases. Company officials expected that Smirnoff, with its faster rate of growth, would move ahead of the third-place brand (Canadian Club, 2.4 million cases) and the second-place brand (Seagram's VO, 2.5 million cases) within three years.

In 1965 Smirnoff had 23% of the total vodka market and outsold the second-place vodka brand by over four to one. In addition, Smirnoff was the only premium-priced vodka on the market in 1965, since the wholesale price of Wolfschmidt had been lowered in 1964 in an effort to stimulate sales. After considering this action, Hart decided the appropriate response was to raise Smirnoff's wholesale price $1 per case and to put the additional revenue into advertising. Although Wolfschmidt's sales more than doubled, this increase appeared to come from the middle-priced segment of the vodka market, since Smirnoff's sales also increased 4% over the previous year and were running over 10% ahead in 1966. Smirnoff also appeared to be immune to the spread of the hundreds of private-label vodkas, since, according to company officials, these products obtained their sales from the 15% to 30% of the vodka market that was price conscious.

As a result, many industry observers expected Smirnoff to dominate the vodka market well into the future, particularly since Smirnoff could, on the basis of its sales volume, afford to spend $7 million to $8 million on advertising, while its closest rival could afford to spend only $2 million before putting the brand into the red.[4]

Relska, a medium-priced vodka, and Popov, a low-priced vodka, were produced and sold primarily to give Heublein's distributors a full line of vodka products. They accounted for 11% of company sales in 1965. They were cheaper to produce than Smirnoff but were not as smooth to the taste, according to company officials.

Heublein bottled cocktails sold an estimated 500,000 cases in 1965, about 55% of the bottled cocktail market. Nevertheless, Heublein was beginning to receive competition from the national distilling companies, particularly Distillers Corporation, whose U.S. subsidiary, Seagram, was marketing a similar line. Hart, however, welcomed this competition. He commented to the Los Angeles Society of Security Analysts in 1965:

> We believe the idea of bottled cocktails has not been completely sold to the American public. We were therefore delighted when we learned that one of the major companies

---

[4] Roger D. Bensen, *Heublein, Inc.,* Glore Forgan, Wm. R. Staats Inc., December 1965, p. 25; in 1963, according to the *Liquor Handbook,* Heublein spent $1.4 million to advertise Smirnoff, while total advertising for all other vodka brands during the same year was $1.2 million.

in the liquor industry was introducing a new line of cocktails and that there would be heavy expenditures in advertising and merchandising to promote their usage to the public.[5]

We are of the opinion that, as the cocktail market expands, our share will decrease, but Heublein cocktails will continue to be the leader and our cases will show remarkable increases.

Hart explained that distribution was one of the principal reasons why Heublein would keep its number one position. "We secured distribution in 1960 when the other companies weren't too interested in cocktails. Since a distributor will usually carry only two or three lines, this means that he will have Heublein and Calvert or Heublein and Schenley: in other words, Heublein and somebody else. . . . In addition to being first, Heublein's wide line will also help us get and maintain distribution." In 1965 Heublein's bottled cocktail line included manhattans, vodka sours, extra dry martinis, gin sours, whiskey sours, side cars, vodka martinis, daiquiris, old-fashioneds, and stingers.

During 1964 the liquor products division reintroduced Milshire gin. For years Milshire had been a regional gin selling about 100,000 cases a year. However, in 1963 the promotional budget was deemed sufficient to devote some real attention to Milshire. To prepare for this, the old inventory was sold off, the product was reformulated, and the package was redesigned. The principal difference in the product was that its botanical and aromatic content was lowered by filtering it through activated charcoal in a process similar to that used to make Smirnoff. The net effect was to make the gin "lighter." Sales for 1964 increased to 150,000 cases, a significant jump but still very far behind the 2.1 million cases of Gordon's, the leading brand.

In 1966 Heublein reached an agreement with Tequila Cuervo S.A. to be the exclusive U.S. marketer of José Cuervo and Matador tequilas and a cordial based on the same spirit. Heublein planned to market these products on a nationwide basis through the Liquor Products Division, which also marketed Harvey's sherries, ports, and table wines; Bell's scotches; Gibley's Canadian whiskeys; Byrrh aperitif wine; and the products of Vintage Wines, Inc.

The Arrow division accounted for about 10% of Heublein's sales in 1965. The division's principal products were Arrow cordials, liqueurs, and brandies, and McMaster's scotch. Though Arrow's distribution system was particularly strong in the control states, its distribution in the open states was strengthened in 1965 when Heublein discontinued the production of its line of Heublein cordials and substituted the Arrow line.

Although the sales of the food division more than doubled between 1961 and 1965, they accounted for only 8% of the company's 1965 sales. Nevertheless, A-1 steak sauce was the company's number two profit producer in 1965, second only to Smirnoff vodka. Other food products included Cake-Mate icings and gels, Escoffier

---

[5] Heublein spent $2 million advertising its line of bottled cocktails in 1965. Seagram spent $1.5 million advertising its Calvert line the same year.

EXHIBIT 9
Advertising
expenditures of
major liquor
companies, 1965

	Advertising	Sales	Advertising as a % of sales
Distillers Corp. Seagram	$43,750	$762,520	5.7%
Schenley Industries	23,100	380,200	6.1
National Distillers & Chemical	19,668	810,900	2.4
Hiram Walker — Gooderham & Worts	17,750	498,174	3.6
Heublein	17,495	165,522	10.6

Note: Figures in millions of dollars.
Source: *Advertising Age,* January 3, 1966, p. 46.

sauces, Grey-Poupon mustard, and Maltex and Maypo cereals. In 1965 Heublein reached an agreement with the Costal Valley Canning Company of California to distribute and market Snap-E-Tom Tomato Cocktail, a tomato juice flavored with onion and chili pepper juices. It was designed for the premeal juice and the cocktail mixer markets, both of which had high profit margins.

Marketing

Heublein's unique advertising and promotion policies and campaigns set Heublein apart from the other liquor companies (see Exhibit 9). Heublein considered liquor to be a branded consumer product and viewed itself as a marketer of high-quality consumer products rather than as a liquor company. As a result, Heublein developed intensive advertising campaigns to sell its products for the growing, affluent young-adult market, since it believed it was easier to get a new customer in this market than to get a 40-year-old scotch drinker to switch to vodka. Because of the importance attached to advertising, Heublein spent 10.6% of sales for advertising in 1965, nearly double the expenditure of Distillers Corporation.

In addition, Heublein was an aggressive innovator among liquor industry advertisers. In the 1950s industry self-regulation prohibited depicting a woman in an advertisement for a liquor product. In 1958 Heublein advised the Distilled Spirits Institute that it believed this ban on the portrayal of women was "obsolete, hopelessly prudish, and downright bad business." Finally, the DSI agreed, and Heublein became the first liquor company to portray women in its ads under the new DSI self-regulation, an advertising practice later followed by nearly every major distiller. Heublein also pioneered a change in DSI regulations to permit liquor advertising in Sunday supplements. At the end of 1965, Heublein was pushing for the use of liquor advertisements on radio and TV similar to beer and wine advertisements.

Another unique feature of Heublein's marketing was its promotions, which were designed to appeal to the young-adult group and used celebrities and off-beat approaches to gain attention (see Exhibit 10). An example of this approach was the Smirnoff Mule promotion launched in May 1965. The promotion, Heublein's largest for a single drink, was designed to catch discotheque popularity on the upswing.

EXHIBIT 10
Smirnoff Mule advertisement

THE SMIRNOFF MULL—SKITCH HENDERSON MADE IT A SONG. 'KILLER JOE' PIRO MADE IT A DANCE

NEW DRINK...SMIRNOFF® MULE
It swings!

Taste the new party favorite that's sweeping the country, the swingingest drink since Smirnoff invented vodka. It's the Smirnoff Mule, made with Smirnoff and 7-Up®. Just pour a jigger of Smirnoff over ice. Add juice of ¼ lime. Fill Mule mug or glass with 7-Up to your taste. *Delicious!* Only smooth, flawless Smirnoff, filtered through 14,000 pounds of activated charcoal, blends so perfectly with 7-Up. That's why the fuel for your Mule must be Smirnoff! *It leaves you breathless®*

SMIRNOFF VODKA 80 AND 100 PROOF DISTILLED FROM GRAIN STE P·ERRE SMIRNOFF FLS. (DIVISION OF HEUBLEIN). HARTFORD. CONN.

The total investment was about $2 million for advertising, merchandising, and sales promotion. The *New York Times* commented:

> *Included in the Smirnoff advertising mix are a drink, called the Smirnoff Mule; a song and dance, called simply The Mule; a recording called Skitch Plays "The Mule"; a copper-colored metal mug in which to drink the Smirnoff Mule, and a recent phenomenon called the discotheque. . . . [Heublein's advertising agency] the Gumbinner-North Company has recruited such vodka salesmen as Skitch Henderson, Carmen McRae, and Killer Joe Piro to put it over. . . . In addition to Smirnoff ads, The Mule will be featured in local advertising by the 7-Up people.*[6]

Distribution

Heublein sold its products directly to state liquor control boards in the 18 control states and to approximately 235 wholesale distributors in the 32 open states and the District of Columbia. Food products were sold through food brokers and wholesalers. It was Heublein's policy to strive to create mutually profitable relationships with its distributors. For example, one of the reasons for the creation of Popov vodka was to give Heublein's distributors a low-priced vodka brand to sell.

International Operations

At the end of 1965 Heublein was involved in three types of overseas activities. The largest and most important was its licensing operation. Distillers in 32 foreign countries, including Austria, Denmark, Greece, Ireland, New Zealand, South Africa, and Spain, were licensed to manufacture and market Smirnoff vodka. When selecting a franchise holder, Heublein looked for a local distiller who had good production facilities and who was a good marketer in his country, believing that this policy allowed Heublein to get established faster than if it tried to set up its own plant and also that it improved relations with the local government.

Under these franchise agreements, the distiller produced the neutral spirits in the best way possible in his country. To maintain quality control, however, Heublein installed and owned the copper filtration units and shipped the charcoal to these locations from Hartford. This was done at cost. The contracts called for a license fee (about 10% of sales) and also stipulated that certain amounts be spent by the franchisee for advertising. Usually, during the first three or four years, Heublein would add its 10% license fee to these advertising funds in order to help build up the business. Plans were under way at the end of 1965 to begin operations in six more countries, including Ecuador, India, and Nigeria.

Heublein also exported Smirnoff, primarily to U.S. military bases overseas. In addition, in 1965 Heublein opened an operation in Freeport, Jamaica, to produce Smirnoff and other Heublein liquor products and to market these products to customers, such as ship's chandlers and diplomatic agencies, who could purchase tax-free liquor.

Between 1961 and 1965 Heublein's export sales increased 99%, royalties from licenses 145%, and profits from international operations 458%. In 1965 net export

[6] Walter Carlson, "Advertising: Smirnoff Harnesses the Mule," The *New York Times*, June 27, 1965.

sales stood at $1.2 million and profits before taxes from international operations, including license fees, were $880,000.

Production

At the end of 1965 Heublein owned and operated three plants throughout the United States, with an annual capacity of 20 million wine gallons for all product lines, and was building a plant in Detroit to replace the old Arrow plant. The plant was to cost $4.5 million and to have an annual capacity of 5.5 million wine gallons. When completed, it would give Heublein a total annual capacity of 25.5 million wine gallons. All of Heublein's plants were highly automated. (Heublein had about 975 employees in 1965, of whom slightly less than half were hourly employees. In 1965 labor costs were only 3% of the total cost of sales.)

Heublein did not produce the grain neutral spirits for its gin and vodka production but rather purchased these requirements on contract and the open market from four distillers. The company maintained facilities in the Midwest for the storage of 8 million proof gallons, however, in case none of these suppliers could meet Heublein's stringent quality requirements. At 1965 consumption rates, this represented about a year's supply.

According to Heublein, even the high-quality grain neutral spirits it received from its suppliers contained too many impurities for direct use in Smirnoff. The first step in Smirnoff production was, therefore, to redistill these grain neutral spirits. At the end of the redistillation, the alcohol was 192 proof. It was then blended with distilled water to reduce the mixture to 80 proof. The mixture was then filtered slowly through 10 copper tanks containing over 14,000 pounds of activated charcoal. The filtering process required eight hours. According to company officials, it was during this process that the vodka became smooth and mellow and acquired its mild but distinctive taste. The only remaining step was to bottle the finished product, since vodka requires no aging.

Heublein also redistilled the grain neutral spirits used in the production of its charcoal-filtered Milshire gin. However, the company did not redistill the liquors (purchased on the open market) used in the production of Heublein cocktails.

Most of the food products were manufactured at Hartford or at the plant in Burlington, Vermont. Heublein insisted on the same high-quality standards in the purchase of raw materials and the production of its food products that it required in its liquor production

PROPOSED HAMM ACQUISITION

Early in the fall of 1965, Heublein's top management was seriously considering the possible acquisition of the Theo. Hamm Brewing Company. They were particularly interested because they felt Hamm could profit immensely from what they felt was Heublein's major strength — the ability to market a consumer product extremely well. If the acquisition were consummated, Heublein would become the first company to engage in the production and sale of both beer and liquor.

Under the proposed agreement Heublein would acquire all of the outstanding shares of Hamm's common in exchange for 420,032 shares of Heublein's 5% preferred and 200,031 shares of Heublein's 5% convertible preferred. Both preferreds had a par value of $100; the latter was convertible into three shares of Heublein common, subject to certain provisions against dilution of earnings. Although Hamm's stock was held by a family group and did not have a market price, Heublein's board estimated that the aggregate fair value was in excess of $62 million, or book value (see Exhibit 11). The proposed agreement stipulated that each class of preferred would have the right to elect one person to Heublein's board. In addition, it was

EXHIBIT 11
Hamm Brewing Company consolidated balance sheet

	Nov. 30, 1964	Sept. 30, 1965
Current assets		
Cash	$3,475	$3,153
Certificates of deposit	2,000	500
Commercial paper and marketable securities (at cost)[a]	26,560	24,044
Accounts receivable (net)	5,452	7,959
Inventories	5,352	6,479
Prepaid expenses	898	891
Total current assets	$43,737	$43,027
Investments and other assets	6,467	6,536
Property, plant, and equipment (net)	26,381	26,930
	$76,585	$76,493
Current liabilities		
Trade accounts payable	$2,639	$2,926
Salaries and wages	1,207	1,304
Customers' deposits	932	1,151
Miscellaneous accounts payable and accrued expenses	470	1,301
Taxes other than taxes on income	2,038	2,299
Federal and state taxes on income	2,657	2,559
Dividends payable	1,538	660
Sinking fund deposits due in one year	100	100
Total current liabilities	$11,580	$12,302
8% debenture bonds	1,400	1,400
Stockholders' equity		
Capital stock	55,083	26,432
Capital surplus		26,273
Earned surplus	8,521	10,086
	$76,585	$76,493

Note: Figures in thousands of dollars.
[a] The market value of these securities was $28.1 million in 1964 and $25.7 million in 1965.
Source: Heublein acquisition study.

provided that the $25 million of securities indicated on the Theo. Hamm Brewing Company consolidated balance sheet as of September 30, 1965, would be liquidated and used to buy out dissident Hamm stockholders prior to the acquisition by Heublein. This would have the effect of reducing Hamm's working capital and stockholder equity by about $25 million before the purchase.

Hamm's History and Competitive Position

Hamm was a family-owned brewing company. During the five years preceding the proposed acquisition, sales and profits had remained relatively stable (see Exhibits 12 and 13). However, since industry sales had increased slightly more than 11% during this period, Hamm's market share had declined from 4.5% to 3.7%. In addition, Hamm's return on sales had lagged behind that of the industry leaders (see Exhibit 14 and the appendix).

Hamm sold three brands of beer at the end of 1965: Waldech (premium price), Hamm's (premium and popular price), and Buckhorn (lower price). The 1964 sales breakdown among these brands had been 17,800 barrels for Waldech, 3,624,700 barrels for Hamm's, and 57,800 barrels for Buckhorn. (A barrel is equivalent to 31 U.S. gallons.) In addition, in 1964 Hamm had produced some beer for sale to the Schaefer Brewing Company under the Gunther brand.

In 1965 Hamm's beer was sold in 31 states and the District of Columbia, with most sales concentrated in the Midwest, West, and Southwest. Hamm relied exclusively for its distribution on 479 independent wholesalers, most of whom carried other brands of beer. Although these wholesalers could terminate their relationship with Hamm at will, none of them accounted for more than 2.5% of Hamm's 1964 sales.

According to some industry observers, Hamm's four breweries were among its principal assets. Three of these were owned outright, while the fourth was leased. The location and annual productive capacity of each of these plants was as follows:

Location	Barrels per year
St. Paul, Minn.	2,550,000
San Francisco, Calif.	1,000,000
Los Angeles, Calif.	500,000
Houston, Tex. (leased)	450,000
	4,500,000

According to industry estimates, the cost of replacing Hamm's 1965 capacity would be about $135 million, or more than double the proposed purchase price. This estimate was based on an industry rule of thumb, which set the cost of new plant construction at $30 to $35 per barrel at the end of 1965.

Like Heublein, Hamm purchased most of the raw materials needed for its production — malt, barley, hops, and corn grits — from various independent suppliers. About one-fourth of its malt and hops requirements were met by wholly owned subsidiaries.

EXHIBIT 12 Hamm Brewing Company consolidated income statements

			Years ending November 30			10 months ended September 30 (unaudited)	
	1960	1961	1962	1963	1964	1964	1965[d]
Revenues							
Sales less allowances	$119,881	$115,874	$114,885	$119,584	$124,233	$106,109	$109,449
Interest	161	240	270	575	958	748	941
Dividends	81	62	50	51	61	58	42
Other	283	95	175	196	351	301	359
	$120,407	$116,272	$115,380	$120,405	$125,602	$107,217	$110,791
Costs and expenses							
Cost of goods sold[a]	$89,843	$86,314	$86,595	$90,878	$95,388	$81,004	$84,597
Selling, delivery, advertising, general, and administrative expenses	16,263	17,065	16,200	18,534	21,423	18,196	19,026
Interest							
Long-term debt	235	164	120	120	120	100	100
Other	8	159	2	16	13	12	—
	$106,349	$103,702	$102,918	$109,548	$116,945	$99,312	$103,723
Earnings before taxes on income	$14,057	$12,570	$12,462	$10,857	$8,657	$7,905	$7,068
Taxes on income							
Federal	$6,750	$6,150	$6,100	$5,100	$3,900	$3,550	$3,000
State	450	400	400	275	300	275	225
	$7,200	$6,550	$6,500	$5,375	$4,200	$3,825	$3,225
Net earnings (excluding the operations of the eastern division and related distributing subsidiaries)	$6,857	$6,020	$5,962	$5,482	$4,457	$4,080	$3,843
Loss on operations of eastern division and related distributing subsidiaries less applicable income tax benefits[b]	1,092	1,717	2,124	1,408	—	—	—
Net earnings	$5,765	$4,303	$3,838	$4,074	$4,457	$4,080	$3,843
Preferred stock dividend requirements	210	210	210	210	210	175	142
Earnings applicable to common stock	$5,555	$4,093	$3,628	$3,864	$4,247	$3,905	$3,701
Per common share data (dollars)							
Earnings applicable to common stock[c]	$2.14	$1.57	$1.40	$1.49	$1.63	$1.50	$1.40
Cash dividends declared			.40	.95	1.25	.50	.75

Note: Figures in thousands of dollars except per share data.
[a] Includes federal and state excise taxes of between $32 and $38 million for each period.
[b] In 1960, the company acquired brewing facilities in Baltimore, Maryland, which were sold in 1963 for $6 million, the approximate net carrying amount of the facilities. Applicable income tax benefits ranging between $1.2 and $2.1 million have been netted against loss on operations of eastern division and related distributing subsidiaries for the years 1960–1963 inclusive.
[c] Based on the number of shares outstanding at the end of each period as adjusted for the recapitalization during the year ending November 30, 1961.
[d] Earnings for the 10 months ending September 30, 1965 were adversely affected by nonrecurring legal and centennial expenses aggregating to approximately $400,000.
Source: Heublein acquisition study.

EXHIBIT 13 Heublein and Hamm pro forma combined income statements

Years ending Heublein, June 30 Hamm, November 30	1960	1961	1962	1963	1964	10 months to Sept. 30, 1965
Net sales	$223,050	$224,156	$231,027	$241,579	$260,082	$249,056
Cost of sales	167,872	166,732	172,389	180,378	194,963	187,059
Selling, general, and administrative expenses	33,323	36,359	36,755	40,515	45,385	43,164
Other income (deductions)						
Interest and dividend income	352	417	444	865	1,287	1,217
Interest expense	(560)	(595)	(363)	(344)	(342)	(215)
Miscellaneous — net	198	85	93	503	308	320
	(10)	(93)	174	1,024	1,253	1,322
Income before income taxes	21,845	20,972	22,057	21,710	20,987	20,155
Provision for income taxes	11,432	11,137	11,688	11,205	10,716	9,966
Net income before loss on discontinued operations of Hamm	10,413	9,835	10,369	10,505	10,271	10,189
Loss on discontinued operations of Hamm, less applicable income tax benefits	1,092	1,717	2,124	1,408	—	—
Net income	9,321	8,118	8,245	9,097	10,271	10,189
Deduct pro forma adjustments						
Interest and dividend income	219	275	290	591	981	950
Interest expense	1,209	983	975	501	122	85
Income taxes	(738)	(638)	(652)	(549)	(496)	(418)
	690	620	613	543	607	617
Pro forma net income	8,631	7,498	7,632	8,554	9,664	9,572
Preferred dividend requirements Heublein:						
5% preferred stock	2,100	2,100	2,100	2,100	2,100	1,750
5% convertible preferred stock	1,000	1,000	1,000	1,000	1,000	833
	3,100	3,100	3,100	3,100	3,100	2,583
Pro forma earnings applicable to common stock	5,531	$4,398	$4,532	$5,454	$6,564	$6,989
Pro forma earnings per share (dollars)						
Assuming no conversion of convertible preferred stock	$1.15	$.91	$.93	$1.12	$1.37	$1.43
Assuming full conversion of convertible preferred stock	1.21	1.00	1.01	1.18	1.40	1.43
Actual Heublein earnings per share[a]	.74	.79	.91	1.03	1.21	1.30

Note: Figures in thousands of dollars except per share data.
[a] Heublein shares outstanding in June of 1965, 4.9 million; approximate market price/share in 1965 (to September) $26–27.
Source: Heublein acquisition study.

The Brewing Industry

At the end of 1964 the beer market was approximately the same size as the distilled spirits market, about $6.4 billion a year (see Exhibit 15). In addition, from 1960 to 1964 the beer market had grown at approximately the same annual rate as the liquor market, about 2.5%. Per capita beer consumption had increased moderately during the period.

Since people began consuming beer at a younger age than they did liquor, industry

EXHIBIT 14 Leading brewers' returns on 1964 sales

	Total revenues ($000)	Pretax net ($000)	Profit margin	Barrels sold (000)	Pretax returns/ barrel
Anheuser-Busch	$491,384	$39,312	8.00%	10,235	$3.84
Schlitz	311,394	28,277	9.08	8,266	3.42
Pabst	227,610	20,421	8.97	7,444	2.74
Falstaff	211,943	13,604	6.42	5,815	2.33
Hamm	125,602	8,657	6.89	3,719	2.33

Source: Company annual reports.

observers expected beer consumption to increase as much as, if not more than, liquor consumption through 1970. Most of this increase was expected to be in the sale of packaged beer, since the sale of draft beer had decreased from 22% of total beer sales in 1955 to 19% in 1964.

The same observers felt that brand loyalty was not as strong for beer as for liquor. Nevertheless, the economies of high-volume production and the use of costly advertising (see Exhibit 16) seemed to be causing a gradual concentration of the beer industry; the number of breweries operated in the United States decreased from 329 to 211 between 1953 and 1963. Moreover, the percentage of sales accounted for by the largest brewing companies had been on the increase (see Exhibit 17).

EXHIBIT 15
Consumer expenditures on alcoholic beverages, 1942–1964

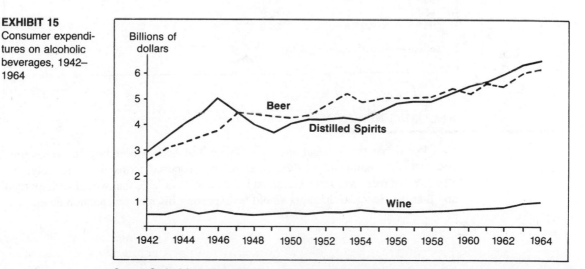

Source: Gavin Jobson Associates, Inc., *The Liquor Handbook, 1965;* cited by Glore Forgan, Wm. R. Staats Inc., in *Heublein, Inc.,* December 1965.

EXHIBIT 16
Advertising
expenditures of
major brewers, 1965

	Advertising ($000)	Sales ($000)	Advertising as a % of sales
Joseph Schlitz Brewing	$34,200	$311,375	11.0%
Anheuser-Busch	32,500	491,384	6.6
Pabst Brewing	15,900	227,610	7.0
Carling Brewing	15,500	412,306	3.8
Falstaff Brewing	15,000	211,943	7.0

Source: *Advertising Age,* January 3, 1966, p. 46.

EXHIBIT 17
Market share of
major brewers

	Top 25	Top 10
1964	83.7%	57.7%
1963	82.2	56.8
1962	79.9	55.0
1961	77.4	52.8
1960	75.1	51.4
1959	73.8	50.0
1958	70.5	45.9
1957	69.2	45.2
1956	67.5	44.4
1955	64.3	42.7
1954	62.1	40.8
1953	61.3	40.1
1952	60.2	40.8
1951	57.5	39.2

Source: Research Company of America.

RECOMMENDATION

Hart knew that the negotiations with Hamm had been proceeding for some time
and that any significant modifications in the proposed terms were unlikely. He
also felt that there was little additional information available that would be important
and that the Heublein directors would be expecting his recommendation soon.

APPENDIX: BEER — LARGER MARKETS, TOUGHER COMPETITION

The bigger it gets, the rougher it gets. That sums up the brewing industry, which has just had its best year ever. But no one brewer had an easy time of it, and the competition will get even stiffer in the years ahead.

Kenneth Ford, managing editor

No one in the brewing industry had anything but kind words last week for the nation's growing number of young adults.

Not only were they quaffing their share of brew and more besides, but even more significant, they appeared willing to cast aside some old-fashioned concepts about beer being a "blue-collar" drink.

For the nation's 190 brewers (four fewer than the year before) the moral was that patience pays off. All during the long, dry decade of the fifties, the industry watched total consumption lag behind population growth and per capita consumption remain static at a low level. Brewers pinned their hopes on the vast crop of war babies of the forties, hoping that when they reached drinking age they would set off a beer boom, but also fearing they might move from the innocence of Coke to the decadence of martinis in one easy step.

They didn't. When the 1963 figures were totaled up at this time last year, there were clear signs that the brewing industry was on the move at last. No one outside the industry realized how fast it was moving until the 1964 totals came in last month.

The results: total sales (consumption) climbed to 98.5 million barrels, up 5% from 1963's 93.8 million barrels. Per capita consumption, the more meaningful measure of marketing effectiveness, jumped to 15.7 gallons, up 2.6% from 1963's 15.3 gallons. Both gains were the best year-to-year increase posted by the industry since 1947.

It is a certainty that the industry will cross the 100-million barrel barrier in 1965. The only question is whether it will reach 101 million or 102 million barrels. No one will be unhappy if it doesn't go that high — the industry's most optimistic forecasters hadn't expected it to reach the 100-million barrel level until 1967.

But though the overall industry outlook is sudsy, neither leaders nor laggards are finding it easy selling.

Competition has never been fiercer. The nation's top ten brewers have staked out 57.7% share of the total market, selling 56.6 million barrels of that 98.5 million total. The next 14 ranking brewers take 25.4% of the total, or 25 million barrels. All together, the top 24 brewers, each doing better than one million barrels apiece, account for 82.9% of total sales, some 81.6 million barrels.

But even what would be a normally respectable gain was not enough to hold the previous year's position, much less advance, in the top 24 standings.

LOSSES AND GAINS

Carling dropped in 1964 from 4th to 5th; Hamm from 7th to 8th; Rheingold from 10th to 11th; Lucky Lager from 13th to 16th; Pearl from 17th to 18th; Narragansett from 19th to 21st; and Jackson from 23rd to 24th. Yet five had made sales gains — Carling's posted a 1.7% increase; Rheingold a 3.1% increase; Pearl a 5.4% increase; Narragansett a 2.8% increase; and Jackson a 2.2% increase.

The leading brewers had set such a blistering pace that merely running to keep up just wasn't fast enough.

First-place Anheuser-Busch (Budweiser–Busch Bavarian–Michelob) achieved a 10.1% gain that carried it across the 10-million barrel level, an industry record, and gave it a 10.5% share of the total market. Anheuser-Busch's (A-B) phenomenal performance was the culmination of marketing programs set in motion as long as a decade ago. Basically, these concentrated on development of marketing executives, achieving the best possible communication with its 900 wholesalers throughout the country and expanding plants into growing markets. (Its new Houston brewery will be ready next year.)

Though A-B is one of the heaviest advertisers in the industry, it makes only evolutionary changes in its advertising program from year to year. "''Where There's Life There's Bud'' (1963) became ''That Bud, That's Beer'' (1964) and now becomes ''It's Worth It, It's Budweiser'' (1965).

Expansion-minded Schlitz, eyeing the heavier-beer-drinking Canadian market (per capita consumption 16.4 gallons) tried to migrate north by buying control of Canada's Labatt Brewing, but found itself ensnarled in antitrust actions and other legal complications. The time and attention it had to devote to these were reflected in only a 5.3% gain, in contrast to 1963's 13% gain.

Another 11.6% gain like the one Pabst made last year might well knock Schlitz out of second place. And fast-rising Falstaff is a factor that Schlitz and Pabst marketing executives both must reckon with in the year ahead.

Falstaff surprised everyone by clipping Carling out of fourth place in the brewing industry. Carling had made sixteen consecutive sales gains that brought it up from 19th in the industry and was generally conceded to be the brewer to watch. Controlled by Canadian entrepreneur E. P. Taylor, its marketing strategy is based on two rules: build plants where the markets are growing (it now has nine in the U.S.) and advertise heavily.

But it was Falstaff's ambition and innovation that carried it ahead. It markets only one brand of beer, Falstaff, in 32 states westward from Indiana. These states have 45% of the nation's population but consume less than 45% of total beer production.

A COMPETITOR TO RESPECT

"If we were in the other 18 states, we'd be selling 10.5 million barrels instead of 5.8 million," says George Holtman, vice president, advertising. Holtman's boast is not idle. That Falstaff is a competitor to respect is attested to by Hamm's decline of 2.5%. Both collided competitively in the Midwest generally and the Chicago market in particular. Falstaff began moving into Chicago three years ago and the 1964 figures reflect its arrival. Similarly, it began moving into the West Coast in recent years where traditional beer sales patterns are changing, too. Lucky Lager, long the leading West Coast brand, slumped 15.1%, dropping below the two-million barrel level under the impact of competition from Falstaff and other interloping brewers. Among them: the Schlitz-Burgemeister brand team, Falstaff, Budweiser, and Carling. The latter is going to build its own brewery in the San Francisco area, which should make conditions in the important California market (it accounts for about 7.5% of total consumption alone) even more competitive.

But the moral is not that the big, bad national brands come in and knock off the poor little locals. Washington-based Olympia, strong in the Northwest, and Denver-based Coors both are making significant progress on the West Coast. Olympia scored a 22.1% increase, and Coors, long the strong man of the Rocky Mountain empire, boosted advertising budgets by 11% and barged into California. Results: a 12% sales increase.

In the big New York market, it was a locally based brewer that led the pack — Brooklyn's Schaefer Brewing. Schaefer soared to 4,250,000 barrels — up 10.1%, while Newark-based Ballantine dropped 3.9% and Rheingold, up 3.1%, slipped out of the top 10 and found its claim to being top brand in the New York metropolitan area under severe pressure.

Ballantine, long handled by the Wm. Esty Co., is now looking for a new advertising agency. Rheingold, sold by the Liebmann family to Pepsi-Cola United Bottlers, switched agencies again. In recent years it has gone from Foote Cone & Belding to J. Walter Thompson, back to FCB, and is now at Doyle Dane Bernbach. Rheingold, under the aegis of its new management, reportedly was moving ahead at year's end behind a barrage of television and radio spots.

COMPETITION KEEN IN EAST, TOO

Throughout the East, competition was similarly strong. Philadelphia-based Schmidt (Schmidt–Prior–Valley Forge) gained 13.3%, Baltimore-based National climbed 21.5%, and Manhattan-based Ruppert, strong in New England, moved ahead 22.5%. Rochester-based Genesee (up 20.2%) cemented its already strong position in upstate New York.

One result of this fierce competition was increased ad budgets. With most brewers offering what economists call "poorly differentiated products," i.e., sameness —

images were the most important function in marketing. Most brewers, in *Printers' Ink*'s annual marketing survey, of course declined to give data on ad expenditures, though a few admitted increases ranging from four to six percent. However, the industry operates on a so-much-per-barrel basis in its ad budgeting. *Printers' Ink*'s study of beer advertising expenditures (October 2, 1964, page 25) found the industry average was 96 cents a barrel for the four measured media. This would put total spending in a 98.5-million-barrel year at $94.4 million in those media. This, however, is only about one-third of total expenditures. Big chunks of money go for "rights" to broadcast sports events, a staple of beer marketing. For instance, Schlitz, now building a new brewery in Texas, paid out $5.3 million for rights to the Houston Colts games.

"It's all part of becoming a new resident of the area," a Schlitz spokesman explained. "We want to get known fast and this is how you do it."

So important are sports sponsorships that they significantly influence marketing strategy. For example, Schmidt's bought the old Standard Beverage plant in Cleveland from Schaefer (which then bought the old Gunther plant in Baltimore from Hamm). Schmidt originally intended to use the Cleveland brewery to supply its markets in western Pennsylvania and western New York state and had no immediate intention of entering the northeastern Ohio market. But the opportunity arose to buy a participation in radio-sponsorship of the Cleveland Browns games. Schmidt's bought it and entered the market immediately.

CAN U.S. COMPETE ABROAD?

For the past few years, American brewers have enviously watched the success of imported European beers in the U.S. The European imports sell less than one percent of the total sold in the U.S. but their profit margins are far better than the domestic brewers achieve on a unit basis. Would the same not hold true for U.S. and Canadian beers overseas? It is also a way to rise above the cannibalistic competition in the U.S. The other way is to increase the beer consumption of the American drinker. Though 1964's 3.3% increase in per capita consumption was the best in recent years, the industry lags far behind the high of 18.7 gallons set in 1945 or even the postwar 18.4 gallons quaffed in 1947.

New products may help. Schlitz, Pabst, and National are now strongly promoting malt liquor brands. A-B's Michelob and Hamm's Waldech in the super-premium class are upgrading beer's image and adding a new group of customers.

But it is a packaging development that may be of the most far-reaching significance. This is the home keg of draft beer that fits neatly into the family refrigerator. In the consumption battle, beer's increase in share must come from soft drinks, coffee, tea, and such — not merely from population growth or competitors' customers.

In the decade ending in 1963, beer consumption increased only 12% while the population grew 19%. Soft drinks shot up 48%, soluble coffee 158%, and tea 20%.

The confirmed beer drinker guzzles about six quarts a week on a yearly averaged-out basis. That's about two and a half 12-ounce cans at a time.

What the industry must attract is the glass-at-a-time sipper. That's not much at a time, but there are an awful lot of them and enough sips by enough people can boost beer back near the 20-gallons-per-capita consumption level of pre–World War I days.

It will take a revolution in American beer-drinking patterns to do it, but it could happen.

Source: *Printers' Ink,* Feb. 12, 1965. Reproduced by permission.

THE ONTARIO WINE INDUSTRY

Winemaking began in Canada in 1636. The first vintners were Jesuit missionaries who made sacramental wine (it is said) from native grapes growing along the St. Lawrence River. The first commercial enterprise of record, however, was Clair House, established near Toronto in 1811 by Corporal Johann Schiller. The oldest continuing winery was founded by George Barnes in Toronto in 1873.

The cultivation of domestic grapes was developed in Southern Ontario coincident with the opening of the commercial wineries. By the turn of the century over 4,000 acres were in production and by 1916 Canada had ten wine companies. After the first World War, production and the number of companies grew at an even faster rate, swept along by the contrary political currents of the prohibition movement. Due to pressure from grape growers, wine escaped the clutches of the Ontario Temperance Act and became the only alcoholic beverage legally sold in Ontario. By 1926 there were forty-five companies and by 1927, fifty-seven.

As the only legal supplier of alcohol in Ontario with a large, if illegal, export market in the United States, the industry had to struggle hard to meet demand. With considerable effort and by adding formaldehyde, coal tar, and dyes to provide flavor, body, and color to the wines, some companies managed to "stretch" a ton of grapes from a normal yield of 700 l of wine to as much as 2,700 l.

Unfortunately, what the government gave, it could also take away. In 1927 the Ontario Temperance Act was repealed. The Liquor Control Board of Ontario (LCBO) was set up to control the sale of alcohol. The LCBO established quality standards for wine and tested to ensure that they were met. By 1930 there were only about twenty-seven Ontario wine companies and by 1943 only eight remained. Between 1927 and 1973 no new wineries were licenced in Ontario.

THE CANADIAN AND ONTARIO WINE MARKET

Between 1964 and 1976 per capita wine consumption in Canada increased spectacularly at an 11 percent compounded rate. This growth was paralleled in other historically

Case prepared by Joseph N. Fry with Christopher J. Bart and Paul W. Beamish. © The University of Western Ontario. Reprinted by permission.

EXHIBIT 1
Consumption of wine in liters per capita in selected countries

	1964	1976	Compound growth rate
France	124.0	101.30	(1.6%)
Italy	106.0	99.70	(0.5)
Portugal	83.0	97.80	1.3
Spain	65.0	71.00	0.7
Switzerland	41.0	43.50	0.5
Hungary	31.0	34.00	0.7
West Germany	13.0	23.60	5.1
Czechoslovakia	4.0	16.50	12.5
Belgium	8.0	15.70	5.7
U.S.S.R.	4.0	13.40	10.6
Denmark	3.0	12.53	12.6
The Netherlands	3.0	11.34	11.7
Australia	6.0	11.20	5.3
Sweden	4.0	8.47	6.4
Canada	2.0	7.00	11.0
United States	4.0	6.64	4.3
United Kingdom	2.0	5.64	9.0

Source: GATT statistics.

low-use countries such as Czechoslovakia, Denmark, and the Netherlands (Exhibit 1). In contrast, per capita consumption in the traditionally "heavy-consumption" countries, such as France, Italy, Portugal, and Spain, exhibited the marginal growth pattern of a mature commodity.

In terms of growth, wine consumption in Canada also outpaced consumption of other alcoholic beverage categories. The Canadian annual growth rates for wine, spirits, and beer in the 1964–1976 period were 11, 3, and less than 1 percent, respectively, on a per capita basis.

The increasing popularity of wine in Canada was attributed to a number of forces including increased affluence and sophistication, lower drinking ages, and persuasive marketing programs. Regardless of their particular influences on overall consumption, these same forces also fundamentally changed the wine-type preferences in the market.

Traditionally, Canadians favored the high-alcohol, fortified dessert, or appetizer wines — those with 14–20 percent alcohol and particularly those that cost less than $2.50 for a 750 ml bottle. As one industry wag put it some time ago, "Canadians make their wine purchases on the basis of the biggest bang for the buck." More recently, however, reflecting the impact of the not necessarily consistent phenomena of increased sophistication and mass merchandising, there has been a pronounced shift in consumption to the low-alcohol table and sparkling wines. (See Exhibit 2.)

EXHIBIT 2
Trends in con-
sumption of wine
in Canada

	12 months ended March 31					
	1972	*1973*	*1974*	*1975*	*1976*	*1977*
Not exceeding 14% alcohol by volume	51,400	64,400	70,300	78,200	86,700	101,600
% of total	49.7%	56.5%	60.2%	63.7%	65.6%	70.8%
14–20% alcohol by volume	52,100	49,600	46,500	44,500	45,400	42,000
% of total	50.3%	43.5%	39.8%	36.3%	34.4%	29.2%
Totals	103,500	114,000	116,800	122,700	132,100	143,600

Note: Measures in thousands of liters.
Source: Wine Council of Canada (originally calculated in imperial gallons).

Domestic Versus Import Supply

Coincident with growing consumption and shifting tastes, the share of the Canadian market held by domestic producers declined steadily, and by 1977 imports had captured over half the market. (See Exhibit 3.)

The Ontario Market

Trends in the Ontario market paralleled the national experience. Table wines increased dramatically in popularity (Exhibit 4). Imports steadily increased their share, and, of particular importance to Ontario producers, Ontario wine production, as a share of national wine production, dropped from 76 percent in 1967 to 62 percent in 1974.

The shift in market preference to table wines caught the Ontario wine industry unprepared. They were poorly armed in reputation, skills, grape supply, or flexibility of structure to do battle with imports.

Traditionally, Ontario wines were made from the native northeastern American labrusca grape — grapes hardy enough to survive the Canadian winter, but possessing a distinctively sharp "foxy" taste. This taste could be disguised in fortified wines

EXHIBIT 3
Wine sold in Canada

	12 months ended March 31					
	1972	*1973*	*1974*	*1975*	*1976*	*1977*
Canadian-produced wine sales	67,700	72,200	71,200	69,300	69,300	69,900
% share	65.4%	63.3%	61.0%	56.5%	52.5%	48.7%
Foreign wine sales	35,800	41,800	45,700	53,400	62,700	73,800
% share	34.6%	36.7%	39.0%	43.5%	47.5%	51.3%
Totals	103,500	114,000	116,900	122,700	132,000	143,700

Note: Measures in thousands of liters.
Source: Canadian Wine Institute Report (originally calculated in imperial gallons).

EXHIBIT 4

Wine consumption in Ontario in (000) liters by type and origin

Class	1972–1973	1973–1974	1974–1975	1975–1976	1976–1977
Ports, sherries, and other dessert wines	12,400	12,400	12,000	11,900	11,700
% Canadian	69	66	61	58	56
Full sparkling, champagne, etc.	1,300	1,900	1,400	1,600	1,900
% Canadian	69	77	61	56	55
Table wines					
Crackling	2,500	2,100	2,000	2,000	2,400
% Canadian	67	56	51	47	45
Rosé	3,200	3,300	3,600	3,700	3,900
% Canadian	49	43	39	39	41
Red	6,700	7,500	8,900	10,700	12,800
% Canadian	39	38	34	33	34
White	4,300	4,800	5,400	7,100	9,600
% Canadian	41	38	33	28	27
Total table	16,700	17,800	19,900	23,600	28,600
% Canadian	46	41	37	34	33
7% Sparkling	2,300	2,900	3,500	4,200	4,700
% Canadian	100	100	100	100	100
Cider	400	500	700	1,000	900
% Canadian	91	90	87	89	84
Grand total	33,100	35,400	37,500	42,200	47,900
% Canadian	60	57	53	49	47

Note: Percentages are percentage of class by volume by year. Quantities were originally estimated in imperial gallons.

or ameliorated sparkling wines but made the labrusca grape quite unsuitable for the production of table wine. While market tastes centered on fortified wines, no serious problem was apparent. As tastes changed, however, the industry shifted very slowly to using a series of hybrid grapes (a cross between the European vitis vinifera grape and the vitis riparia or vitis rupestris) suitable for quality table wines. The hybrids, in fact, did not become available in commercial quantities until the mid-1970s.

By the mid-1970s, imports dominated the Ontario table wine market, particularly in the medium- and premium-priced segments (Exhibit 5). Canadian table wines, regardless of origin, were confined to the low-price segment and had, through years of marked indifference or uncertainty, acquired a less than impeccable reputation.

This phenomenon raised the question of whether the rising market share of imported wines was the result of a perceived higher quality or whether consumers simply associated higher quality with higher price. U.S. studies found that price and perceived quality were closely correlated. Despite this correlation, low-priced imported table

	Low price (less than $2.50)		Medium price ($2.50 to $4.00)		Premium price (greater than $4.00)		Total %
	C	I	C	I	C	I	
Table wines							
Red	33.6	20.9	—	36.3	—	9.2	100.0
White	26.2	9.3	—	57.3	—	7.2	100.0
Rosé	41.6	1.7	—	56.5	—	0.1	100.0

Low-price segment
— Less than $2.50/750 ml
— Less than $3.33/l (1,000 ml)
Medium-price segment
— $2.50–$4.00 for 750 ml
— $3.33–$5.33 for 1,000 ml
C — Canadian.
I — Imported.

High-price segment
— Greater than $4.00/750 ml
— Greater than $5.33/l

Source: LCBO price list, LCBO statistics.

wines were consumed at a high enough rate in Ontario to indicate that European table wines were perceived as innately superior to the domestic products.

The problem for Ontario wineries was even more complex, however, for they were forced, by regulation, to use Ontario-grown grapes almost exclusively and the new hybrids were widely regarded as the highest-priced in the world.

For example, wineries in British Columbia could import bulk wine for bottling from California for as little as 22 cents per liter before transportation costs. The same product, made either in British Columbia or Ontario from locally grown grapes, was estimated to cost between 80 and 85 cents per liter; 50 cents per liter for the raw grape juice alone and 30–35 cents per liter for processing. In addition, wine was conventionally shipped by rail. The cost of rail transportation from Kelowna, British Columbia, to Toronto, Ontario, was approximately 12.5 cents per 750 ml bottle. Consequently, the ability of Ontario wineries to compete in terms of cost and, in some instances, quality with other Canadian wine manufacturers (who could import substantial quantities of grape juices or concentrates) deteriorated.

Over the years, provincial liquor control boards had developed ways of offering preferential treatment (for example, in price and display) to locally produced wines. In 1978 Ontario provincial table wines and champagne were subject to a 47 percent markup from the producer's selling price, while "out-of-province" wines and imported wines were marked up 105 percent and 123 percent, respectively. Other provinces had their own but similar schemes as shown in Exhibit 6. A small annual drop in sales of Ontario wines to other provinces was experienced after 1972, partly as a result of this form of provincial protectionism.

EXHIBIT 6

Selected provincial liquor commission markups for 1977

Ontario	
Ontario table wines and champagne	37%
Ontario fortified, dessert, and 7% sparkling	60
All out-of-province wines	95
Imported wines	117
Quebec	
All Quebec-made wines	85
All out-of-province wines	95
No information on imported wines	
British Columbia	
B.C. table, sparkling, and crackling wines and champagne	45
B.C. fortified and dessert wines	78
All other Canadian wines and imported table, sparkling, and crackling wines and champagne	100
Imported fortified and dessert wines (uncertain)	113–122
New Brunswick	
Canadian and imported dessert wines	132
Canadian and imported table wines and sparkling wines	105

Note: Ontario markups increased in 1978.
Source: Canadian Wine Institute.

Wine Types and the Wine Drinker

In Ontario the wine market was conventionally segmented into three major classes: (1) appetizers and desserts, (2) table wines, and (3) crackling and sparkling wines. The first category represented heavy and sweet wines, such as ports and sherries, with a high alcohol content (14 percent to 20 percent by volume). They required aging for at least 3 years. Table wines, the second class, included reds, whites, and rosés, usually with 10 percent to 14 percent alcohol content by volume. Some crackling and full-strength sparkling wines were also grouped into this category. The third classification differentiated between crackling and sparkling wines on the basis of effervescence. This bubbly effect was caused by introducing carbon dioxide during a secondary fermentation process. Also included in this third group were the 14 percent alcohol champagnes and the 7 percent alcohol "pop wines" such as Baby Duck and Baby Bear. Consumers believed these 7 percent alcohol wines resembled "soda pop" — hence the name "pop wines."

Exhibit 7 presents a forecast, prepared by the LCBO, of wine consumption by class through 1984.

The wine consumer in the mid-1970s, ignored for some time, became the subject of a number of market studies sponsored by such groups as the Canadian Wine Institute[1] and the Ontario Wine Council.[2] These studies found that:

[1] Canadian Wine Institute, "A History" (August 1977) and "Statistical Tables and Wine Information Materials" (August 1977).

[2] Currie Lehman Ltd., "Report to the Wine Council of Ontario" (1976).

1. Growth of the total wine consumption was related to growth of the total adult population, but more particularly, growth in per capita consumption was highly related to growth in disposable income.

2. Wine tended to be used as a substitute for beer, but as a complement for spirits and was more income-sensitive (in demand) than either.

3. Wine was a lightly used beverage. Only 40 percent of Ontario adults had used wine as compared to 52 percent who used beer, 69 percent who used liquor, and 75 percent who used soft drinks. Even among wine users, consumption was low, averaging 3 ounces per week compared to corresponding figures of 70 ounces of beer and 7 ounces of liquor.

4. Wine consumption was associated with particular occasions — while entertaining guests, during the evening meal, or during the Christmas/New Year season.

5. Age, education, and sex all influenced wine consumption. As with soft drinks and beer, per capita consumption was highest in the eighteen- to twenty-four-year-old age group. The high-school educated accounted for 55 percent of the adult population and 65 percent of wine consumption. There was a distinct preference for table wines among the university educated. Women preferred sparkling, rosé, and white wine; men, red table wine. Finally, although female consumption of wine was less than that of men, a higher proportion of women drank wine.

6. Among all users, European imports were preferred to domestic wines. University educated users were far more likely to try new wines, with 60 percent of this

EXHIBIT 7 LCBO forecasts of Ontario wine market in (000) liters

	1977	1978	1979	1980	1981	1982	1983	1984
Total wine	46,400	51,100	56,200	60,700	65,500	70,800	75,700	81,000
% Growth		10.0	10.0	8.0	8.0	8.0	7.0	7.0
Adult population (M)	5,300	5,500	5,600	5,700	5,800	5,900	6,000	6,100
% Growth		3.8	1.8	1.8	1.8	1.7	1.7	1.7
Per capita consumption	8.8	9.3	10.0	10.6	11.3	12.0	12.6	13.3
% Growth		5.7	7.5	6.0	6.6	6.2	5.0	5.6
Total table	26,500	30,600	35,100	39,400	43,900	48,800	53,800	59,100
% Growth		15.5	14.7	12.3	11.4	11.2	10.2	10.0
Total full sparkling and crackling	3,900	4,100	4,200	4,200	4,100	4,000	4,000	3,900
% Growth		5.1	2.4	0.0	(2.4)	(2.4)	0.0	(2.5)
Total 7% sparkling	4,800	5,300	5,600	5,900	6,200	6,500	6,800	7,200
% Growth		10.4	5.7	5.4	5.1	5.0	4.6	5.9
Total sherry and port	7,100	6,700	6,400	6,300	6,100	6,100	6,100	6,100
% Growth		(5.6)	(4.5)	(1.2)	(3.2)	0.0	0.0	0.0
Remainder	4,100	4,500	4,800	5,000	5,200	5,300	5,100	4,800
% Growth		10.0	6.7	4.2	4.0	2.0	(3.8)	(5.9)

Note: LCBO shipments only.
Source: Currie Lehman Report (Originally calculated in imperial gallons)

group having tried Ontario varietals.[3] A majority of university educated users who had tried Ontario varietals, however, did not continue to use them. In contrast, while only 31 percent of high-school and primary-school educated users had tried Ontario varietals, they usually continued to use them. Their preference for them appeared to be rooted in the fact that these wines were either "Canadian," low-priced, or both.

7. Users tended to switch from sweet to dry wine as they gained experience. Entry patterns into wine consumption shifted through time. In the 1950s the novice began with dessert wines, in the 1960s with sparkling wines, and in the 1970s with sparkling, dessert, and low-priced table wines.

8. The table wine market appeared to be going through a complete "Europeanization cycle" with vintaging (i.e., designating the year in which the grapes were grown) and varietal labeling (i.e., designating the type of grapes used in the production of wine such as Marechal Foch, Pinot Chardonnay, and Chelois) becoming increasingly popular.

A recurring fact of market studies relating to alcoholic beverages is that individuals tend to understate their consumption. Point 3 indicates total wine consumption in Ontario at only about one-fifth the true consumption figure.

INDUSTRY STRUCTURE

In Ontario and the rest of Canada, the participants in the wine industry could be classified into four distinct sectors: the provincial regulatory bodies, the retail outlets, the grape growers, and the wine companies. The activities and interrelationships of the sectors were quite complex. A capsule summary is available in Exhibit 8.

The Regulatory Agencies

The aims of relevant government policy in Ontario were to control the use of alcohol for health reasons, to generate revenue, to ensure a satisfactory distribution of products in order to meet consumer demand, to provide enjoyment, and to encourage commercial enterprise within the province.

To accomplish these objectives there were three agencies designed to regulate the production and distribution of alcoholic beverages. These were the Ontario Grape Growers' Marketing Board (OGGMB), the Liquor Control Board of Ontario (LCBO), and the Liquor Licensing Board of Ontario (LLBO).

The OGGMB was created by the Ontario Farm Products Marketing Board to represent all Ontario grape growers in their dealings with grape processors — wineries and the grape jam and juice manufacturers. In 1978, twenty members, elected by the registered grape growers at their annual meeting, comprised the OGGMB. The OGGMB's principal power rested in its authority to license both the grape growers and the processors, thereby regulating supply.

---

[3] A varietal is a wine made from at least 80 percent of one type of grape, e.g., Chelois or Marechal Foch.

EXHIBIT 8 Industry structure

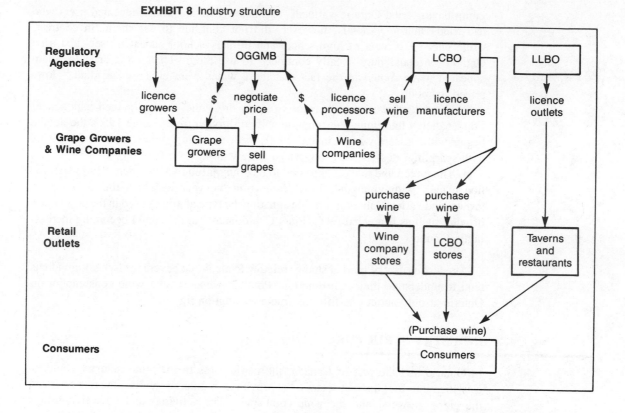

Unlike other provincial marketing boards, this agency did not, as a rule, take physical possession or ownership of the grapes grown by its members. The growers dealt directly with the wineries when purchasing or selling grapes. The OGGMB, however, negotiated the price structure for all Ontario grapes and acted as a collection clearing house. As a result of its functions, this agency provided stability to the marketplace and to the price of grapes.

The LCBO was the provincial government agency responsible for controlling the distribution of all alcoholic beverages in Ontario through its own LCBO retail stores as well as the wine companies' outlets. All wineries, both domestic and foreign, had to apply to the LCBO to have their products listed for sale in Ontario. Canadian and imported listings in Ontario as of early 1977 are summarized in Exhibit 9. This agency regulated the production of wine by licencing manufacturers and by setting standards for hygiene and the amount of sugar and chemicals that could be added. The LCBO limited the amount of wine that could be made from one ton of grapes (i.e., the stretch) to 1,140 l.

For restaurants and taverns wishing to sell spirits, wine, and beer to their patrons, it was necessary to obtain a permit or licence from the third regulatory agency in Ontario — the LLBO.

EXHIBIT 9 Canadian and imported listings

Canadian	Andres			Brights			Jordan			Chateau-Gai		
	Jul. 76	Apr. 77	Nov. 77	Jul. 76	Apr. 77	Nov. 77	Jul. 76	Apr. 77	Nov. 77	Jul. 76	Apr. 77	Nov. 77
Dry White	1.85	1.45	1.75	2.15	1.80	1.90	1.95	1.60	1.85	2.20	1.80	1.95
Marechal Foch[a] red	2.40	1.95	2.20	2.70	2.20	2.20	2.95	2.45	2.25	2.85	2.00	2.25
de Chaunac[a] red	2.40	1.95	2.35	2.50	2.00	2.00	—	—	—	—	1.85	2.00
Still rosé	1.70	1.40	1.60	1.90	1.50	1.60	1.85	1.50	1.85	1.90	1.50	1.80
Champagne	4.55	3.85	4.95	4.95	4.20	4.95	4.95	4.20	5.00	4.85	4.00	4.95
Sparkling	3.40	2.80	2.95	4.15	3.40	3.40	—	—	—	3.70	3.00	3.30
7%	2.45	2.40	2.50	2.35	2.30	2.50	2.35	2.30	2.50	2.45	2.65	2.50

Imported	Jul. 1976	Apr. 1977	Nov. 1977
Lion d'Or	2.56	2.71	2.75
Prix Blanc	2.60	2.50	3.43
Selection (Kressman) White	2.38	2.30	2.49
Colli Albani White	2.15	1.97	1.97
Jaszberenyi Rizling	1.97	2.08	1.97
Mommessin Export Red	3.00	3.25	3.35
Selection (Kressman) Red	2.45	2.38	2.71
Valpolicella (Bosca)	2.65	2.65	2.65
Yago	2.55	2.65	2.50
Szekszardi Red	1.97	1.97	1.97

Note: Many of the imported brands are sold in volumes ranging from 25 to 35 ounces. All prices shown have been calculated (where necessary) for 26 ounce (750 ml) equivalents.

[a] The price of Inniskillin's Marechal Foch was $2.90 in April 1977 and $3.30 in November 1977. De Chaunac was $2.70 in April 1977 and $2.90 in November.

Sources: Ontario Liquor Store Price Lists #50 (July 1976) #51 (April 1977) and #52 (November 1977).

Retail Outlets

As a result of this government structure, wine could be purchased only in LCBO retail outlets, individual wine company stores licensed by the LCBO, and restaurants or taverns licensed by the LLBO.

Approximately 80 percent of consumer purchases were made at the 560 LCBO stores with 47 percent of these purchases in the self-serve outlets. In comparison, only about 10 percent of consumer purchases were made in restaurants and taverns. These latter outlets tended to promote imported wines since they offered a better gross margin to the restaurant owners.

Although there were fifty-two winery-operated outlets located on site at the wineries and in major population centers, their sales as a percentage of total wine sales declined from 31.9 percent in 1972 to 19.3 percent in 1977. There was little enthusiasm within the industry for increasing the number of these outlets, since they tended not to be profitable.

Distribution through food stores represented an area of potential growth for the wineries. Existing legislation limited this to wine company–operated boutiques; Jordans had opened five of these in Towers department stores and Brights was actively considering supermarket outlets. Quebec had recently permitted general distribution of wine through food stores with dramatic effects on sales. And in the United States there were examples of a doubling of per capita wine consumption after the extension of distribution to food stores. Such a change in policy in Ontario, however, was a complicated political decision (and economic decision too because of LCBO revenues). There was some sentiment in this direction, but few observers predicted early action.

The Grape Growers

In Europe, the farmers who grew the grapes were involved in making wine directly or through a local cooperative. In Ontario, the growing of grapes and the production of wine were performed by two separate groups, the growers and the wineries. In Ontario, in 1977, there were some 836 grape growers, concentrated in the Niagara belt region of southwestern Ontario. Production levels of Ontario-grown grapes used by Canadian wineries, by grape type, are shown in Exhibit 10. There were several other uses for Ontario-grown grapes. Besides those grapes used by other

EXHIBIT 10
Ontario grape production used by Canadian wineries

Year	Labrusca		Hybrids & viniferas		Total tons
	Tons	%	Tons	%	
1972	32,233	81.2	7,468	18.8	39,701
1973	38,222	82.7	7,980	17.3	46,202
1974	32,444	70.2	13,786	29.8	46,230
1975	31,312	67.8	14,871	32.2	46,183
1976	27,280	62.4	16,447	37.6	43,727

Source: Ontario Wine Council.

processors, there were fresh market sales and exports. In some years there was a surplus of Ontario-grown grapes.

The average yield was estimated to be 5 tons per acre of the hybrids, 4 tons of the labrusca, and 3 tons of the vinifera. These yields, of course, were subject to considerable fluctuation depending upon the type of grape grown, seasonal conditions, and grower care.

In the midst of a shift from labrusca to varietals, the growers, according to the OGGMB, lost money in grape production. A 1976 study estimated this loss to be $56 per acre in 1975 and $149 per acre in 1976 — both years in which there was a surplus of the labrusca types. Another study by a private winery, of a 100-acre farm, implied, however, that losses, if any, were due to dependence on the labrusca types. The study claimed that, despite greater care and higher costs, hybrid and vinifera varieties were capable of yielding substantial profits per acre. Unfortunately, the report did not include charges for growers' wages nor did it consider the return on investment in vines and land. Land costs alone were considered high, ranging between $5,000 and $7,000 per acre for a producing farm, and $3,000 for raw land in the Niagara Peninsula.

Under some pressure for years, the grape growers developed a close relationship with the government, particularly through the medium of the OGGMB. Through time, the growers were never reticent to use their political ties to the extent they could to serve their purpose.

The Wine Companies

By 1977 only nine of the thirty-one Canadian wine manufacturing facilities were located in Ontario because of a movement during the 1960s to locate their plants near to markets rather than to sources of grapes. One reason for this relocation lay in the preferential treatment given to local wineries by the various provinces. The major impetus to move, however, was that in Ontario the wine companies' purchases of grapes were restricted to those available through OGGMB. Outside Ontario, wine companies could consider other less expensive sources of supply, such as bulk wine and grape concentrate from Europe, the northeastern United States, and California.

COOPERATION AND CONFLICT IN THE INDUSTRY

In the early and mid-1970s the Ontario wine industry experienced substantial difficulties. One of the most critical problems was a shortage of hybrid grapes. Although Brights Wines had been experimenting with the production of nonlabrusca varieties since the early 1930s, by 1964 the hybrid constituted only 16 percent of the total grapes used in Ontario for winemaking. Even when a government-sponsored wine conversion program was implemented in 1975, only 40 percent of its target was achieved by 1977. As a result preliminary figures for 1977 indicated that hybrids and vinifera grapes were still just a little more than 50 percent of all the grapes delivered to wineries.

Many charges were laid by the growers and the wine companies against each other for the slow changeover to new varieties. The grape growers complained that, because of the wine industry's slowness to shift to nonlabrusca table wines, they did not have the confidence to invest in the new varieties that required 5 years to mature. The wineries, on the other hand, rebutted that their ability to innovate was hampered because of the growers' resistance to hybrids. The wineries also argued that, without a free market for grapes (as there was in the United States), they were continuing to subsidize the purchasing of unwanted labrusca varieties.

Whatever the reason, growers' resistance to change was strong, and formal cooperation between the two groups was, at best, tenuous. Although there were long-term contracts between the growers and the wineries, many industry observers agreed that these contracts fell far short of a guarantee to purchase agreed quantities of grapes at agreed prices.

The Ontario Wine Industry Assistance Programme

In 1975 the wine companies, the growers, and the government briefly joined forces to help implement the Ontario Wine Industry Assistance Programme. The OWIAP directed LCBO stores in major centers to carry all Ontario wines regardless of sales volume and to create room for these wines by delisting poor-selling imports. The program permitted point-of-purchase wine displays, liberalized the regulations governing "life-style wine advertising," and allowed for the expansion of winery-operated stores.

Prior to the program, prices of Canadian table wines were generally kept low by competing imports. Because the managers of LCBO retail outlets were assessed on the basis of the gross revenues of their stores, they naturally preferred to restrict the shelf space given to domestic wines since liquor and the higher-priced imports provided greater contributions to revenue. Since the program began in 1975, Ontario wineries had increased prices somewhat but had not been able to recapture lost market share.

OGGMB and LCBO Policies

The OGGMB and LCBO were sources of both help and hindrance to the wine producers. For the most part the regulatory bodies tended to help preserve the grape growers' position. For instance:

1. The OGGMB persistently resisted wine industry proposals to alter the rigid classification of grapes without regard to quality — although this position was modified in 1978.

2. In 1975 and 1976, when 16 percent and 19 percent respectively of the labrusca grapes produced went unharvested, the OGGMB obtained low-interest loans from the federal and provincial governments to purchase the surplus. These governments later forced the wine companies to purchase the grapes from the OGGMB.

3. The OGGMB also regulated the supply of imported grapes and concentrates used for blending or bottling. Yet when this agency decided to allow bulk wine imports of up to 15 percent of a winery's annual domestic production volume, the growers rendered this proposal ineffective by obtaining restrictions from the LCBO regarding the wineries' ability to add water and other additives to the output of one ton of grapes.

4. The wine producers' plans for a major advertising campaign were cut short when a LCBO markup reduction was passed on to the consumer rather than to the wineries.

Government Policies

Because of the actions and policies of the regulatory agencies, many people believed that the government's attitude toward the wine industry was becoming increasingly dispassionate. Even the province's price structure of reduced markups for domestic Ontario wines was no longer regarded as sacrosanct. In fact, in a March 1978 budget speech, the treasurer of Ontario hinted at the possible unconstitutionality of the discriminatory markups on out-of-province Canadian wines and suggested that such protection might be discontinued in the near future.

The federal government seemed equally unconcerned about the future of the Canadian wine industry. During the 1960s and early 1970s, for example, Canadian manufactured goods were traded for wine from Spain and some Eastern Bloc countries.

COMPETITION IN ONTARIO

Four companies, Jordan, Andres, Brights, and Chateau-Gai, dominated the domestic sector of the wine market in Ontario, accounting, in 1976–1977, for some 82 percent of domestic sales. With the exception of the 7 percent alcohol sparkling and dessert wines, where there were segment leaders, the domestic sector was fragmented among the leading companies and other smaller entrants. In the table wine sector, in particular, there was no Ontario producer in a strong market share position. A price comparison of selected Ontario and imported wines for the 1976–1977 period is given in Exhibit 11.

Andres Wines Ltd.

Andres was founded in 1961 in Port Moody, B.C., by the Pellar family and became an Ontario producer in 1970. Its expansion from sales of under $1 million in 1967 to over $21 million in 1977 was the result of innovative promotion, marketing, and financial strategies. Anticipating that Canada would follow U.S. trends, the company concentrated its major effort in 7 percent alcohol sparkling wines and reaped the benefits, through economies of scale in advertising and production, of a dominant market share in the most rapidly growing sector. In creating its major brand, Baby Duck, Andres had broken with wine-marketing tradition. Although other wineries had similar 7 percent products, none had adopted the attitudes and spending levels essential to match Andres' proprietary brand/consumer packaged goods approach. One industry source estimated that Andres, for example, spent as much on promotion as the rest of the industry combined.

Andres was also one of the first companies to adopt a strategy of locating wineries by market rather than raw material source. By 1975 Andres operated six wineries from Nova Scotia to British Columbia. Finally, the company backed its expansion

EXHIBIT 11
Canadian and
imported listings
compiled from
provincial liquor
authorities' price
lists, 1977

Category	Canadian	Imported
Sherry	53	34
Port	22	15
Apertif wine	3	10
Vermouths	11	19
White table wine	56	200
Red table wine	90	250
Rosé table wine	31	25
Crackling wine	21	16
Champagne	23	21
12% sparkling wine	6	24
7% sparkling wine	59	—
Cider	11	6
Other	21	27
Total	407	647
% share	39%	61%

Source: LCBO listings, March 31, 1977.

strategy with an aggressive financial policy, mortgaging all assets as soon as they were acquired and accepting a debt/equity ratio considerably above that of the other major wineries.

More recently, with the decline in growth rate of the pop wine sector in the mid-1970s, Andres began to explore the possibility of licencing its products overseas. It also purchased Chateau-Richelieu, and started to sell table wines with labels featuring both the Andres and the Richelieu names. The emerging branding strategy focused the Andres label on the 7 percent alcohol sparkling wines and introduced the Richelieu name for varietal table wines. Also, in the belief that the current generation of pop wine drinkers were the greatest potential market for its leading brand, Andres attempted to "age" the image of Baby Duck to retain consumer loyalty.

Chateau-Gai Wines Ltd.

Chateau-Gai was founded in 1928 and became a wholly owned subsidiary of John Labatts in 1973. Chateau-Gai was a full-line producer and had well-equipped research facilities for developing new types of wine. After acquiring Chateau-Cartier in 1976, the company attempted to create two different images. Low-priced products were associated with Chateau-Cartier, while higher-priced products were linked to Chateau-Gai. In an attempt to turn the company around, Labatts introduced a new top management team with considerable experience in consumer marketing and cost control. The company operated production facilities in Ontario, British Columbia, and New Brunswick.

Jordan & Ste-Michelle Cellars Ltd.

Jordan was founded in Niagara Falls in 1920, and in 1972 became a subsidiary of Carling O'Keefe, the brewing company, which in turn was controlled by Rothmans, the international cigarette manufacturer. Jordan was also a full-line producer, but its marketing emphasis had been on the low-priced pop wines sector. The company was known to be interested in increasing its position in the table wines sector and to be considering acquisitions as a means of gaining faster access to this market. In 1977 Jordan was the largest Canadian winery with national sales of nearly $30 million. The company had wineries in Ontario and each of the western provinces.

T. G. Brights & Co. Ltd.

Brights was founded in Toronto in 1874. In 1933 control passed to the late Harry C. Hatch, head of the Windsor-based distillery, Hiram Walker and Sons Ltd., and a group of associates. Although the company is no longer the largest producer, it dominated the Ontario wine industry for many years. The company enjoyed excellent relations with the growers and pioneered research into the growing of vinifera and hybrid grapes in its own vineyards in Ontario. Brights operated a large winery in Niagara Falls, Ontario, and two smaller wineries in Quebec. Between June 1977 and June 1978, all the senior executives of Brights, except the director of viticulture, changed.

Brights' marketing strategy was traditionally split between the champagne and the dessert wine segments. The general decline in the dessert segment resulted in considerable excess of inventory and serious overcapacity. Brights did not try to go after the growth in the pop wine segment. In spite of prolonged experimentation with table wines, the company had not succeeded in capturing a major portion of that segment either. The recent changes in the senior management were believed, by industry observers, to indicate a further effort to change from the dessert wine emphasis.

PROFITABILITY AND INVESTMENT

The domestic wine industry operated at profit rates substantially below those of the brewing or distilling industries (Exhibit 12). Comparatively, the wine industry was marked by a high investment level per production employee and a low rate relative to investment. These characteristics, combined with the market shift to table wines, created serious profit difficulties.

Historically, most wineries were set up to produce and market either dessert or pop wines. These facilities were not easily convertible to table wine production, and thus, as the market changed, the traditional facilities operated under capacity. Andres and Brights, for example, with Ontario wineries of 3.2 and 7 million gallon capacities, operated in 1976 at 60 percent and less than 50 percent capacity, respectively. Furthermore, a shift in production to table wines required new investment in plant and machinery.

These inflexible investment problems were compounded by the fact that product line profit margins were much lower for table wines than for dessert and pop wines.

EXHIBIT 12
Capital investment
comparison of
Canadian wineries
with breweries and
distilleries, 1974

	Wineries	Breweries	Distilleries
Sales to tangible net worth	1.20	1.52	2.29
Value of shipments ($ million)	79.8	612.9	488.4
Tangible net worth ($ million)	66.5	403.2	213.3
Fixed assets to tangible net worth (%)	49.9	51.9	95.0
Fixed assets ($ million)	33.2	209.3	202.6
Number of production-related workers	606	6,709	3,424
Plant investment/production employee	$55,000	$31,000	$59,000
Profit on sales (%)	6.3	6.6	13.9
Profits on tangible net worth (%)	8.2	15.1	20.6

Source: Dun & Bradstreet.

In fact, the industry estimated the average net profit on table wine production in 1976 to be 3.8 percent of sales as compared to 19 percent for sales of dessert wines and 30 percent for pop wines.[4]

Finally, the pricing policies of the cheaper imports placed constraints on the ability of Ontario producers to raise prices. As a result, industry selling prices increased at a compound rate of only 6 percent during the period 1973–1976, while costs increased at the rate of 9 percent annually.

PROBLEMS FACING NEW ENTRANTS

Perhaps the major barrier to entry in the mid-1970s was the industry's disappointing recent performance. New investment capital was simply not attracted. Given the overcapacity in the industry and the declining market share of Ontario wines, it would seem that acquiring large and established wineries at depressed prices would have been the best way for a potential entrant to enter the market. Significantly, however, no one stepped forward to purchase Turners, which closed in 1977.

It is also conceivable that a new entrant might have followed Andres' example of selecting the right market segment and then expanding production. Initial entry to the 14 percent-plus alcohol-content segment, however, was almost impossible. This segment of the market had been declining steadily, giving rise to surplus capacity. Since dessert wines were aged for several years, working capital requirements were high. Furthermore, the dessert wine producers had accumulated very high inventories as a result of "forced purchases" of surplus grapes in the early 1970s. Thus, the existing producers had considerable power to prevent a potential entrant from establishing a foothold in this segment.

Although the minus-percent alcohol-content sector experienced better growth, it was dominated by Andres which was prepared to react aggressively to any attempt

[4] Wine Council of Ontario, "Ontario Industry Profit Structure," 1976.

at encroachment on its markets. Morever, the growth rate in this segment was slowing and, if U.S. experience was a reliable guide, would stagnate in another 3 or 4 years.

The table wine market, on the other hand, was growing rapidly and was expected to constitute about 75 percent of all wine sales by volume within 8 years. The opportunity for new entrants here was that by operating on a small scale, they could specialize in a market segment with a potentially large volume of sales.

Since 1975 two of the three new entrants have begun producing table wines. Yet, it is too early to judge the success of this strategy. Given high variable costs (about 63 percent of net sales) and relatively high capital investment per gallon, small producers face a formidable challenge, particularly if they compete in the low-priced segment. A break-even analysis for a new winery entering the table wine sector is presented in Exhibit 13, and suggests that the best opportunity, from a financial standpoint, is in the above-average-quality segment. Exhibit 14 summarizes the cost components of an imported wine and a domestic wine to the Ontario consumer.

EXHIBIT 13

Typical break-even volume for an average- and above-average-quality winery with 1,140,000 ℓ capacity, 1977

	Average quality[a]	Above-average quality[a]
Shelf price ($/liter)	2.90	4.65
Revenue from LCBO ($/liter)	1.61	2.64
Variable costs ($/liter)	1.13	1.67
Contribution margin ($/liter)	0.48	0.97
Fixed costs		
Depreciation[b]	$ 65,000	$ 65,000
Interest[c]	57,000	98,500
Administrative and selling	210,000	210,000
Total fixed costs	$332,000	$373,500
Break-even sales volume (liters)	691,667	385,052

[a] *Average quality* and *above-average quality* are subjective terms used to arbitrarily define the taste characteristics of table wines in the "low-price" (less than $3.33/ℓ) and "medium-price" wine categories, respectively. "High-price" corresponds to "superior-quality." See Exhibit 5.

[b] Based on an estimated cost of $1.6 million for a 1,140,000-ℓ winery, with $1.3 million being amortized over 20 years.

Land	$ 300,000
Building	600,000
Equipment	500,000
Storage tank and oak casks	200,000
	$1,600,000

[c] Interest charge at 9 percent based on a working capital requirement for 9 months of $1,460,000 for an above-average-quality winery and $1,270,000 for 6 months for an average-quality winery operating at full capacity. However, working capital requirements will vary with production. For example, when production equals 334,000 liters in an above-average-quality winery, working capital requirements are only $0.814/ℓ. At full capacity, the working capital requirement increases to $1.28/ℓ for the entire output.

Source: Author's estimates.

EXHIBIT 14 Cost comparison

Derivation of cost of 26.4-ounce (750-ml) bottle of imported wine (1977) to consumer		Derivation of cost of 26.4-ounce (750-ml) bottle of Ontario wine (1977) to consumer	
Selling price from producer	$2.00	$2.00	Selling price from producer
Freight	.19	—	Freight (included in selling price)
Federal customs ($0.20/Imperial gallon)	.03	—	Federal customs
Federal excise tax ($0.50/Imperial gallon)	.08	.08	Federal excise tax ($0.50/Imperial gallon)
Federal glass tax $\dfrac{26.4}{160} \times 15\%$	.02	—	Federal glass tax
Subtotal	2.32	2.08	Subtotal
Federal sales tax (12%)	.24	.24	Federal sales tax (12%)
Subtotal	2.56	2.32	Subtotal
LCBO markup (115%)	2.94	.86	LCBO markup (37%)
Subtotal	5.50	3.18	Subtotal
Ontario retail sales tax (10%)	.55	.32	Ontario retail sales tax (10%)
Price to consumer	$6.05	$3.50	Price to consumer

Note: A 7–14 percent alcohol content assumed for both the imported and domestic wines. Note the leverage effect of a $0.05 increase in selling price from producer. With imported wine, cost to consumer increases $0.15 and, with domestic wine, $0.10. (LCBO rounds to the nearest $0.05.)

INNISKILLIN WINES INCORPORATED

In 1971, Hugh Johnson, the noted British wine authority, completely omitted Canadian wines from his famous *Wine Atlas*, explaining later that: "The foulness of taste is what I remember best — an artificially scented, soapy flavour." The criticism incensed Canadian vintners, especially from Ontario, who challenged Johnson to take part in blind taste tests. But the doyen of Canadian wine detractors left these challenges unanswered. Then, in a 1975 tasting session, organized in London, England, the same Hugh Johnson confessed to surprise with the Canadian wines which, he said, "bore no resemblance whatsoever to wines I tasted several years ago. My favourite without doubt was the Inniskillin 1974 Marechal Foch."

Obviously a lot of wine, Canadian wine, had passed under the bridge since 1971. The praise was particularly significant to Inniskillin because the Marechal Foch was one of only three table wines made by the company during its first fiscal year. Subsequently, the company's growth accelerated from the 23,000 liters of table wine made from the 1974 harvest crush (1974–1975 fiscal period) to 334,000 liters from the 1977 crush (1977–1978 fiscal period). So successful was the winery's product that the entire output had sold each year within several months of availability.

Industry observers agreed that Donald Ziraldo, the twenty-nine-year-old president of Inniskillin, and his partner-winemaker Karl Kaiser, had taken a huge gamble with Inniskillin. With the company showing its first profit in fiscal 1977, the partners were beginning to feel the gamble was paying off.

DONALD ZIRALDO

Donald Ziraldo was a confident, good-looking, Canadian-born individual of Italian descent. He had gained early experience in agriculture working while a boy on his family's farm near St. Catharines, Ontario. Later, while he was a student at Denis Morris High School, his father died and Donald assumed responsibility for the business aspects of the farm operation.

Case prepared by Joseph N. Fry with Christopher J. Bart and Paul W. Beamish. © The University of Western Ontario. Reprinted by permission.

When he graduated from the Ontario College of Agriculture in Guelph in 1971, Ziraldo converted the family property into a housing development, Ziraldo Estates, and purchased a new location for the farm and nursery just west of the town of Niagara-on-the-Lake, Ontario. The 100-acre farm was situated on the scenic Niagara Parkway and was considered part of Ontario history because a colonel in the Inniskillin regiment stationed at Niagara-on-the-Lake during the War of 1812 had formerly made his home on the farm. The main business of the farm was growing grape vines, especially the European vitis vinifera and the new hybrids which were steadily replacing native North American varieties, such as the Concord and Niagara labrusca vines, in Ontario vineyards.

Starting Up

Sitting in his office, in the midst of bottles of the latest vintage Marechal Foch, Vin Nouveau, and Chelois, Ziraldo, dressed in an immaculate suit, leaned back in his chair and recounted the early beginnings of Inniskillin Wines:

> One day, in 1972, Karl Kaiser came in asking for grapes to make wine. He had heard we were growing hybrids. Like a lot of Europeans, he made wine in his basement. He was persistent, but we were sold out.
>
> Later I had a chance to taste a bottle of Karl's wine. It was terrific! I couldn't believe he had made it from local grapes. I drank a lot of wine and beer with Karl over his kitchen table during the next few weeks and we got to thinking. Why not start a "boutique" winery that would produce good table wines in small quantities? So a few weeks later, I set up a meeting with a Mr. Harris, the deputy commissioner of the LCBO [Liquor Control Board of Ontario]. Harris said that no licence to manufacture wine had been granted since 1929. Even Andrew Peller, the founder of Andres wines, couldn't get one in 1956 and was forced to start up in British Columbia.
>
> I returned and told Karl that there was not much point in pursuing the idea. However, several months later, Major General Kitching, the board's chairman, heard about our inquiry and seemed keen about it. I had a meeting with the general and he suggested we prepare a sample batch for examination by the board's tasters.
>
> Karl prepared a few barrels of wine in my home in St. Catharines, and we wrote a brief outlining the type of wine we envisaged. By fall 1974, we were ready. The LCBO examiners conducted chemical and blind taste tests and gave a score of 59, one point below the minimum passing standard. They were willing, however, to take into consideration the limited facilities and difficult preparation conditions. So we got our manufacturer's permit to produce up to 45,500 liters of table wine of 1974 vintage. Then, in June 1975, we were granted our Ontario winery licence. We could hardly believe it.

During the fall of 1974, Ziraldo moved to strengthen the company, bringing in three new shareholders — Peter Sullivan, Ted Ralfe, and Alain Regaud. Sullivan, a grape grower, was to provide Inniskillin with a secure supply of quality hybrid grapes, which were still in short supply. Ralfe, a lawyer and Sullivan's brother-in-law, was to represent the company in all legal matters. Rigaud, Sullivan's partner, had worked as a winemaker for Chateau-Gai wines, studied 2 years at the Institute of Oenology in Dijon, France, and spent 3 years as a lab technician at the French

Institute Cooperatif de Vin. It was felt that he would supply the commercial experience that Kaiser lacked.

Thus Inniskillin began its first season in 1974 with Rigaud as oenologist and Kaiser as cellar master. Capital was supplied primarily through shareholder's loans with Ziraldo as the major source of shareholder capital and guarantor of the company's loans. Ziraldo, Sullivan, Kaiser, Ralfe, and Rigaud held 30 percent, 15 percent, 20 percent, 15 percent, and 20 percent, respectively, of the common shares. Trade suppliers and the banks were skeptical of the new venture and demanded personal guarantees for all debts. "Everybody who looked at the project told us it was one of the riskiest ventures they had ever seen," said Ziraldo. "Today they look at us and say 'What a great company' but they had no idea what was going on behind the scenes."

To be sure, the new management team experienced difficulties from the beginning. Rigaud and Ziraldo disagreed over equipment purchases. Rigaud demanded the most modern equipment available while Ziraldo, conscious of the difficulty of financing, was content to purchase secondhand equipment at bargain prices. There were also constant clashes of personality and philosophy between Rigaud and Kaiser. Matters finally came to a head in the fall of 1975 during the grape-crushing season. Differences over production and types of wine forced Ziraldo to buy out Rigaud and Sullivan and to reorganize the company with Ziraldo, Kaiser, and Ralfe holding 55 percent, 30 percent, and 15 percent of the outstanding shares, respectively.

Building Sales

Promotion was Ziraldo's most conspicuous flair. He was sometimes called a wine "evangelist," but his manner was one of relaxed warmth and enthusiasm. "He gets more publicity per gallon than the rest of the industry put together," one competitor complained.

From the start, Ziraldo committed himself to creating a following for his wines. He set out to convert opinion leaders in the industry and the media. His first step was a personal selling effort to get Inniskillin on the wine lists of prestigious restaurants and wine bars in Toronto, Ontario.

> To sell a proprietor or manager, I'd offer to give him and his staff a tasting session. A number of times, however, I was asked to leave the restaurant before they had even tasted the wine. I remember one European restauranteur who told me that he had tried a Canadian wine 10 years ago and that he "wouldn't wash his feet in it." Boy, old myths die hard. But, if I got in the door, I'd personally see that the waiters, who serve the wine, and might persuade customers to order it, knew the story behind it.

His efforts succeeded in getting Inniskillin wines listed in some choice locations: Three Small Rooms, Fingers, Valhallah Inn, the Royal York Hotel, and the Ontario Art Gallery.

At the same time, Ziraldo pressed to enter Inniskillin wines in public tasting competitions. He achieved early success. A 1974 vintage Marechal Foch entered in the 1976 *Toronto Globe and Mail* competition and placed first against many European wines including a Chateau de la Perriere, Brouilly (one of the nine first growths of Beaujolais), much to the French judges' amazement. "And then there's the Hugh Johnson story," says Ziraldo with a smile. "I tell you, every journalist who writes about us uses it."

Inniskillin and Ziraldo, however, became news. Numerous stories appeared on Donald Ziraldo's gamble and how he was heading the quiet revolution in the Ontario wine industry. The C.B.C. filmed a documentary on the company during the 1977 crush. Ziraldo was elected chairman of the Niagara-on-the-Lake Industrial Development Commission. Inniskillin wines were served at Ontario government functions and at the 1977 Commonwealth Conference in Toronto. The winery buzzed with visitors from the business world, wine societies, and universities.

With growing public awareness, there also came increased commercial recognition. A major commercial food chain proposed distribution of Inniskillin wines through a series of wine "boutiques" in their food stores — an offer rejected by Ziraldo because Inniskillin did not have sufficient production volume and because he felt the promotion was not in keeping with the Inniskillin image. And, of course, there was the signal rite of passage for a young company, an offer to buy from a major Canadian firm. Ziraldo recounted the decision not to sell:

> After meeting with the president, Karl and I stood out in the parking lot talking about their offer. We knew it wasn't for us. The buyer was too big and we'd lose control of our operations. You see, we have a big advantage over most wineries. With the size of our operations, its almost like making wine in a basement.

Looking Ahead   Continuing, Ziraldo said:

> Basically, we're a small company making very good wines. There're only four of us full-time right now. Karl makes it — he's a genius. He has a real talent to judge grapes and get the best out of them. I sell it. Marion is our secretary and bookkeeper and also helps me with the promo. And J. R. helps Karl out. Our biggest problem now is filling the demand for our wines.
>
> For me, the zest of this business has come from the challenges, the day-to-day crises. I guess when the challenges stop, that's when I'll think about moving on. I'd like to change the image of Canadian table wine and get the people's support so we can continue to do what we're doing. And it's Canadian. That's very important to me because we've got a long way to go in the table wine business. We are way, way behind. But right now it's a challenge. You know, when we take a break and sit down over a glass of wine, it sort of makes up for all the problems.

KARL KAISER

About 300 yards from the administrative offices on the farm property stands a converted barn which houses the fermentation tanks, wine press, storage tanks, and rows of Portuguese white oak casks of the winery. From the outside, it looks like a milking shed at any dairy farm. Inside, Karl Kaiser, age thirty-five, the stocky Austrian-born winemaker, works in a cramped corner office behind a door with a sign that says, "Employees will please wash their feet before returning to work." Raised in a monastery, Kaiser was introduced to fine wines when he was nine years old. He came to Canada in 1969 with his Canadian wife and children and recalls his first exposure to Canadian wine with a grimace: "It was a dry red and it was horrible . . . harsh and bitter. I decided right there that I would have to make my own wine."

Kaiser enrolled at Brock University, where he earned his Honours B.Sc. in chemistry and was continuing work on a master's degree. Although he had learned wine making from his grandfather in Austria, he felt that a chemist's degree would give him the background to really combine the science and art of wine making. For one of his first class experiments, he made some champagne. He recalled:

> *Everybody at Brock knew that I was interested in wine. But getting the right kind of grapes was difficult then. Not only were the new hybrids in short supply, but no one wanted to sell them to a home winemaker like me. There was no money in it for them. I met Don when I heard that he was growing hybrids. When he tasted my wine, he couldn't believe I made it from local grapes. When I said to him half-jokingly, "I'll make the wine and you sell it," I didn't think Don was going to do anything about it. But he had the courage to act on it.*

Making Wine   Kaiser went on to explain the company's production process:

> *One doesn't have to be a wizard to make a good wine. There are no secrets, no magic recipes. I don't go around with little salt shakers putting stuff in here and there.*
>
> *We're small and so we're flexible. In California the best wines are always made by the smaller producers. Good judgment and instinct are important. You need a feel for the grapes. Each variety requires different care and everything really happens in about 2 months — September and October.*
>
> *Don's vineyard only supplies about 40 percent of our current needs. The rest of the grapes have to be purchased from outside sources. In the beginning, nobody wanted to deal with us, but now we have a bit of a reputation. More and more wineries are after the hybrids, however, so they are still pretty short in supply. The harvest itself lasts maybe 4 to 5 weeks and the grapes ripen on the vines very rapidly. Different varieties mature at different times, making our manpower-scheduling problems very difficult. Don's vineyard is harvested by hand which is quite costly. Most other farms do it by machine. Mechanical harvesting also pierces the grape and leaves it open to attack by wild yeasts and bacteria, so we have to crush the grapes as soon as possible. We try to minimize these problems by maintaining a close contact with the growers.*
>
> *The grapes usually arrive in standard one-ton bins. I inspect each load for defects and determine sugar content and acidity.*
>
> *While the grapes are being crushed, I add a small amount of sulphur dioxide to control fermentation and prevent spoilage by wild yeasts and bacteria. After the crush, the free-run juice is collected in a pan and pumped to one of our stainless steel fermentation/storage tanks.*

Once the juice is in the tanks, I assist to create the necessary conditions for fermentation. This primary alcoholic fermentation lasts 5 to 6 days on a red wine and ends when the sugar content is fermented.

The reds also require separate fermentation to extract the right color from the grape skins. I also encourage our reds to go through a malo-lactic fermentation lasting 4 to 6 weeks to reduce acidity and give a smoother tasting wine. The process is not well understood, and we received a PAIT grant from the Federal Department of Industry, Trade and Commerce to investigate it. Currently, we're one of the few who use malo-lactic fermentation.

After fermentation, the wine is very cloudy and the suspended particles have to be removed, so we clarify it by means of a centrifuge. Then comes perhaps the most critical part. Fining agents such as bentonite and gelatin have to be added to remove extraneous matter which might spoil the wine and impair its smell and taste. Too much and you strip the wine of its color and taste. Too little and harmful matter is left in the wine. You have to know what you're doing.

There is no guarantee against a bad batch. I worry about bacteria invading and destroying the wine, which could easily happen, since we don't pasteurize and since we don't have the most modern equipment.

Anyway, the wine is then further clarified by filtering through a cellulose filter press. It's then ready for aging. Here the wine simply sits in a tank while its color stabilizes and its bouquet develops. The reds are aged in oak cooperage for 3 to 6 months. The earliest the wine can be bottled is 6 to 8 months after the grapes have been crushed. Then it's loaded into a tanker truck and shipped for custom bottling, corking, and labeling.

From a maintenance standpoint, there are not too many problems with our machines because we keep them in good operating condition with regular cleanings, and careful storage during the rest of the year. Sure, some pumps break down, but our emergency repairs have always worked so far.

This year [1977 vintage], our production reached about 334,000 liters. The crusher and the wine press handled this quantity only because we worked 24 hours a day. In addition, this building we're in has no more room and the receiving facilities are inadequate. I also won't store wine in tanks outside because I'm not sure what effect the varying temperatures would have on it.

Right now I have one full-time assistant, J. R., who helps me in analyzing the wines. There're only the two of us full-time in production, so we both have to get involved in the messy jobs like cleaning out the tanks.

The Future

Kaiser outlined his ambitions for the future:

I want to make an outstanding Canadian wine which has been vinified in the old world tradition. I get a great deal of pleasure from my job because I enjoy total freedom to make production decisions. I wouldn't want to lose the personal control I have over the wines we make. We had a problem like this with Alain Rigaud. Don made him the winemaker here and Alain and I never got along . . . the whole thing pushed Don and me apart. Things are okay today though. We have a good business relationship and work well as partners.

We don't want to become too big, ever. You get too big and you lose control. Our wines are good because they have qualities that only we can deliver. Like all good wines, they are unique in that they reflect the skills and care of the particular wine maker.

POLICIES AND PROGRESS

Production

In fiscal year 1977–1978 (the 1977 crushing season), Inniskillin continued its line of vintage wines produced in the previous year — a Marechal Foch (red), a Rosé, a Seyval Blanc (white), a Chelois (red), and a blended wine called Vin Nouveau. This line was in keeping with the original strategy of developing entirely on varietals.[1] Inniskillin also began producing limited editions of Gamay and Chardonnay — small quantities of estate bottled wines (i.e., the grapes came from vineyards under the control of the winery) based on pure vitis vinifera grapes. These limited editions were sold exclusively through chosen outlets such as the LCBO Rare Wines store and the Prince of Wales restaurant in Niagara-on-the-Lake.

Both Kaiser and Ziraldo had originally hoped to age their wines. Cash shortages and the sheer demand for Inniskillin's wines had prevented them from so doing. Both hoped that if capacity was increased, this policy could be implemented. In the meantime, they had vintaged (i.e., at least 85 percent of the wine originated in the designated year) all their wines so that their customers might, if they wished, lay them down in their own cellars.

Pricing

Inniskillin wines were presented to the public as a Canadian wine of a quality comparable to that of the medium-priced European imports. A 1976 vintaged Marechal Foch, for example, retailed for $3.30 (750 ml) while the varietal wine of the same name marketed by Andres (not vintaged) or Brights (vintaged) sold for $2.20. In general, though, Inniskillin's prices were lower than those of French "appelation controlée" wines but about the same as those of the lower-priced French blended imports such as Momessin Export ($3.40) and Calvert Lion Rouge ($3.70). The popular Hungarian Szeksardi was available for only $2.65.

Distribution

Inniskillin had benefited from the LCBO's near monopoly on distribution. Government regulations required that any Ontario wine be listed in all high-volume A-designated stores and in a specified number of medium-volume B-designated stores. This assured Inniskillin access to a distribution network at a very low cost. Inniskillin also obtained a license to sell wine from its winery on the Niagara Parkway — a lucrative tourist attraction. By having its own retail outlet, Inniskillin was able to keep for itself the 47 percent LCBO markup on selling price.

[1] A varietal is a wine made at least 80 percent from one type of grape, e.g., Chelois or Marechal Foch.

Accounting   Inniskillin employed a simple actual full-process cost accounting system. The system, at the end of the fiscal year, provided an average product cost which could then be used to relieve the work-in-process account and to determine the cost of goods sold.

At the end of the fiscal year, July 31, a physical count was made of the raw material inventory which was then valued using the latest cost price. By this time, Inniskillin had bottled most of its wine, except for a small quantity set aside for aging in oak casks.

Because the company's cash requirements were highly seasonal with peaks in November, when the growers were paid, and in May, when the bottling expense was met, these needs had to be covered by working capital bank loans.

Cost control was done on an informal basis. Daily records for posting to the ledger were kept by Ziraldo's secretary, Marion. The general ledger and the financial statements were prepared by Ziraldo's sister-in-law, Judy. Ziraldo, however, was beginning to feel the need for some data that tied costs to particular wine types so that he could make decisions about which wines to make and what prices to charge. Several attempts were also made to get Kaiser to keep costs records, which he had so far successfully resisted. In addition, no formal track was kept of yields per ton of grapes, spillage, labor productivity, or machine performance. Company financial statements are presented in Exhibits 1, 2, and 3.

Future Plans   After the 1977 crush, Inniskillin bought out Ralfe because the latter was exhibiting less interest in the operations of the winery. Both Ziraldo and Kaiser were unsure, however, about the steps Inniskillin should take for the future.

The company had just made its first profit in fiscal 1977. The demand for Inniskillin's wines appeared to be stronger than ever. Although it was still not regarded by industry observers as an established winery, the company had enjoyed generous publicity from its inception and Inniskillin now had a good reputation. Both Ziraldo and Kaiser wanted to see the operations grow. The two men were well aware of problems and frustrations associated with a small cottage winery in an industry rushing to adapt to a changing environment.

Ziraldo and Kaiser pondered the alternatives available to them. There seemed three choices or strategies which could be pursued. These were: to sell out to a willing buyer, to continue operations with the present production capacity of 334,000 liters, or to expand the winery's production facilities, probably to about 1,140,000 liters.

If they were to go ahead with the last alternative, they knew the decision would have to be made quickly in order to have the facilities for the 1978 vintage season. Otherwise, they would be delayed at least another year. The partners now felt that they were on the verge of another gamble but this time the stakes were even higher!

EXHIBIT 1
Balance sheet as of
July 31, 1977

	1977	1976
Production (in liters)	159,000	54,500
Assets		
Current		
Cash	$ —	$ 3,052
Accounts receivable	144,103	26,438
Inventory, at cost	104,151	85,190
Prepaid expenses	934	780
	249,188	115,460
Fixed (net)		
Leasehold improvements	10,053	3,134
Equipment	58,958	53,075
Vehicle	1,120	1,540
	70,131	57,749
Other		
Deferred development costs	—	11,608
Total assets	$319,319	$184,817
Liabilities		
Current		
Bank overdraft	$ 26,361	$ —
Bank loan	60,000	89,000
Accounts payable and accrued liabilities	72,444	20,582
Current portion of long-term	5,000	8,553
	163,805	118,133
Long-term		
Ontario Development Corporation	47,242	49,317
Shareholders' loans, postponed	97,075	61,838
	144,317	111,155
Current portion	5,000	8,551
	139,317	102,604
Deferred income taxes	3,200	—
Shareholders' equity		
Share capital		
Authorized		
40,000 common shares of no par value issued and fully		
paid 20 common shares	20	20
Retained earnings (deficit)[a]	12,977	(35,940)
	12,997	(35,920)
	$319,319	$184,817

Note: No sales in fiscal year 1975.
[a] Incorporation costs of $625 were written off in fiscal year 1975.

EXHIBIT 2
Statement of earnings for the year ended July 31, 1977

	1977	1976
Sales[a]	$300,859	$ 54,196
Cost of goods sold	200,857	60,149
Gross margin (loss)	100,002	(5,953)
Expenses		
Market, development, travel & promotion	7,539	5,740
Amortization of development costs	11,608	5,571
Administrative & general[b]	7,525	5,526
Interest & service charges	14,352	10,459
Professional fees	5,419	1,561
Vehicle operation	1,442	668
	47,885	29,525
Net earnings (loss) from operations	52,117	(35,478)
Other income	—	163
Net earnings (loss) before income taxes	52,117	(35,478)
Income taxes, deferred	3,200	—
Net earnings (loss) for the year	$ 48,917	$(35,315)

[a] No sales in fiscal year 1975.
[b] The president has taken no salary since the company's incorporation. The secretary-bookkeeper's salary is shared between Inniskillin and Ziraldo Nursery Farms Ltd.

EXHIBIT 3
Statement of cost of goods sold for the year ended July 31, 1977 (with comparative figures for 1976)

	1977	1976
Work in progress, beginning of year	$ —	$ 34,767
Raw materials		
Inventory, beginning of year	891	7,138
Purchases[a]	232,572	56,305
Freight, duty & storage	11,131	3,238
Less inventory, end of year	(6,647)	(891)
	237,947	100,557
Direct labor	32,713	21,752
	270,660	122,309
Factory overhead		
Laboratory, insurance, maintenance & utilities	17,540	14,558
Amortization of leasehold & depreciation	10,161	7,581
	27,701	22,139
	298,361	144,448
Work in progress, end of year	—	—
Finished goods inventory, end of year[b]	97,504	84,299
Cost of goods sold	$200,857	$ 60,149

[a] Purchases account in 1977 includes the opening finished goods inventory from 1976.
[b] There was no finished goods inventory in 1975.

COCA-COLA WINE SPECTRUM

Albert Killeen, general manager of Coca-Cola's newly formed Wine Spectrum division, was concerned about mounting delays in a "revolutionary" comparative advertising campaign for Taylor California Cellars wines. Not only was this the first major campaign of the Wine Spectrum division involving the California Cellars winery, the Taylor name, and bottling by Coca-Cola of New York's Franzia subsidiary, but issues had also arisen over the legality of comparative taste tests for wines. After three months of discussions with lawyers and federal officials, Killeen had still been unable to get a ruling; basically, it all boiled down to: "Do we wait for, probably, another year or go ahead and risk legal actions?"

Prior to the 1977 acquisition of Taylor Wine Company by Coca-Cola Inc., Taylor management had promoted the concept that wine was right for any time and any place in "Taylor territory." They had also worked to educate consumers to appreciate New York wines by using the "answer grape." Since California wines were blended into Taylor products, a later campaign used the term "Californewyork" to try to broaden the appeal of Taylor wines. However, Taylor's marketing organization had never seen wine commercials quite like the introductory campaign proposed by its new advertising agency (see Exhibit 1). The new ads were based on a comparative taste test that not only named Taylor California Cellars as the best, but named the competing wines.

The problem with the new ad campaign was that of determining whether comparative advertising of wine was allowed under federal regulations. The Federal Bureau of Alcohol, Tobacco, and Firearms (BATF) had regulatory powers over the industry's advertising, but officials had refused to give any determination. The courts had also refused to hear the case prior to action being taken by Taylor. BATF was reviewing its regulations on the wine industry but contended that only after running the ads would competitors bring forward the evidence necessary for them to make their judgment. BATF would not protect Coca-Cola or Taylor from legal consequences should they be found in noncompliance with regulations. While it was generally

Prepared by William R. Boulton and Phyllis G. Holland. Copyright © 1979 by University of Georgia. Reprinted by permission.

EXHIBIT 1 Comparative taste test advertisement script

Program: "San Francisco Wine Test"	Client: Taylor Wine Company
VIDEO	*AUDIO*
Open on: Taster (male) inspecting glass and sniffing	*Announcer v/o:* a new California Rhine wine is judged against its competitors. Twenty-seven wine experts gather in San Francisco
Cut to: MASTER SHOT	
Title: JULY 22, 1978	
Cut to: Taster (male) sniffing	to compare four
Titles: A-C. K. Mondavi Rhine	
B-Taylor California Cellars Rhine	
C-Almaden Mountain Rhine	
D-Inglenook Navalle Rhine	
Cut to: Taster (male) sniffing	California Rhine wines.
Cut to: Four glasses and hand writing	Which was judged best?
Cut to: Tasters in foreground, Judge and Nationwide Consumer Testing Institute Representatives in background	"Ladies and gentlemen, the wine you have judged best is
Titles: A, C, and D OUT	Wine B."
REMAINING:	
B. Taylor California Cellars Rhine	
Cut to: Four glasses. Hand places Taylor bottle in front	*Ann'r v/o:* Wine B. New Taylor California Cellars Rhine
Title: OUT	Taylor California Cellars
Title: Taylor Label	
Cut to: Glass A	
Title: C. K. Mondavi Rhine	*Ann'r v/o:* Judged better than C. K. Mondavi
Pan to: Glass C	
Title: Almaden Mountain Rhine	Better than Almaden
Pan to: Glass D	
Title: Inglenook Navalle Rhine	Better than Inglenook
Cut to: Taylor Label	*Taster* (*male*) v/o: "An interesting wine."
Title:	*Ann'r v/o:* But when you cost a little more, you better be better.

© 1978 The Taylor Wine Company, Inc., Hammondsport, N.Y. 14840.

known that misleading or disparaging ads were not permitted, specific guidelines on comparative taste tests in wines were not expected for another year.

THE WINE INDUSTRY IN THE UNITED STATES

In 1972, wine prices were rising dramatically and there was great interest in entering the industry. New wine grape acreage soared, with more acreage planted in 1971,

1972, and 1973 than the total of all previous plantings. In addition, speculators observed that foreign wines selling for $25 per case in the 1950s were selling for $500 to $1,000 per case and began to put bottles in storage. The 1972 vintage was bad and did not sell well, and the 1973 harvest was the largest in history. The increased supply led to a decline in prices that accelerated when the speculators put the hoarded wine on the market. By the time the first wine from the new plantings hit the market in 1974, inventories were at an all-time high and the oversupply was further increased by another large harvest in 1975. In 1972, the average return to a California grower per ton of grapes crushed was $217. In 1974 the return dropped to $131 and to $100 in 1975.[1]

By 1976 conditions were improving. Inventories were slowly being worked off and more grape vines were taken up than planted. Even though prices began to rise, producers were still cautious. In describing the future direction of the market, Taylor management indicated in 1976:

In general, 1974 and 1975 were characterized by large grape harvests throughout the United States. It is believed that adverse weather conditions caused a smaller crop in 1976. However, increased grape harvests in the future may be anticipated as a result of substantial grape acreage which was planted in 1971 through 1974 and should mature approximately four years after planting. Grapes are a commodity which will continue to be affected by weather conditions, diseases and grower practices, which cause uncertainty for the crop until each annual harvest is near. Despite increases in many production costs, the abundance of grapes and large wine inventories have generally restricted wine price increases on an industry-wide basis. Furthermore, as discretionary income is believed to impact directly on wine consumption, recent economic conditions have contributed to relatively level industry sales.

Wine Consumption in the United States

Wine consumption in the United States was increasing both in absolute amounts and per capita. In 1977, 6 percent more wine entered distribution channels than in 1976 and the same advance was predicted for 1978. Wine consumption was 400 million gallons in 1977 or 1.85 gallons per capita, as compared to 1.7 gallons in 1976: "Wine sales in the foreseeable future should grow 8% a year, versus less than 3% for distilled spirits, according to Marvin Shanken, editor of *Impact,* a widely respected liquor industry newsletter (soft drink sales are growing 7% annually). By 1980, says Shanken, wines will overtake distilled spirits in gallons."[2]

Per capita consumption in the United States varied geographically, with the highest consuming states being on the east and west coasts. Highest per capita consumption was 5.41 gallons in Washington, D.C. — a far cry, though, from the Italian average of 26 gallons or the French average of 24. Twenty-two percent of the wine sold in the United States was sold in California, 10.6 percent in New York, 5.1 percent in Illinois, followed by New Jersey with 4.5 percent and Florida with 4.3 percent.

[1] Gigi Mahon, "Everything's Coming Up Roses," *Barron's* 56, June 7, 1976, pp. 11–16.

[2] "Beverages: Basic Analysis," *Standards and Poors Industry Surveys*, October 19, 1978, p. B-71.

Wine consumption was greatest in the 21–40 age group (which was growing as a percentage of the population) and was also greater among the more affluent income groups. Factors underlying increased wine consumption were said to be a growing preference for lighter, drier beverages, the availability of broadcast media to efficiently create a nationwide market, and growing purchases by women. A *Forbes* article stated that wine is "increasingly purchased by women right along with groceries. According to *Progressive Grocer,* the trade publication, 35% of all wine is sold in supermarkets. In addition more wine (particularly dry white wine) is now being sipped before dinner — as a fashionable substitute for the Martini and Bloody Mary."[3]

Wine Production in the United States

In 1976 Taylor management noted several facts about U.S. wine production:

California is the largest wine producing area in the United States, with New York State being the second largest producing area. Based upon the latest available industry estimates, California production increased 47 percent from 239.6 million gallons in 1969 to 351.9 million gallons in 1975. During this same period, wine production in New York increased approximately 32 percent from 26.3 million gallons to 34.7 million gallons. Based upon the most recent industry estimates, during 1975, 84 percent of U.S. wine produced (but not necessarily sold) was produced in California and 8 percent in New York. Taylor and many other non-California wine producers use California wines for blending purposes to achieve certain flavor characteristics.

In 1977 there were 615 wineries in 30 states, an increase of 41 percent from 435 in 1970. California had the largest number with 353, followed by New York with 39. Ohio, Oregon, Michigan, and Pennsylvania each had 16. Average production was 20,000 gallons per year as compared to Gallo's production of 100 million gallons annually. Many of the smaller wineries were still waiting for their first vintage. Exhibit 2 shows the ownership of major brands in the wine industry.

Independent wineries are seldom publicly held and are rapidly being acquired by large firms who are increasingly aggressive marketers. Profiles of major competitors are included in Exhibit 3. At the same time, small "mom and pop" wineries have proliferated in the premium wine segment with sales going to local communities. There is little chance that they can expand beyond restricted market areas because of their small size, legal restrictions of interstate wine sales, and the wide variations in their product quality.

Most wine sold in the United States is produced in California. Exhibit 4 shows market share by origin of wine. Import prices have generally increased more than domestic prices because of inflation and the devaluation of the dollar. The packaging of some French wine in flexible plastic film pouches is one effort to maintain competitive costs.

Some wineries own grapevines while others buy from independent growers. For those depending on outside growers (Almaden uses 85–90 percent outside grapes and Taylor 90 percent), relationships with growers are very important. In hard

---

[3] "Coke Takes a Champagne Chaser," *Forbes,* 118: October 15, 1976, p. 66.

EXHIBIT 2 Major U.S. wineries

Company	Brands	Ownership (date of acquisition)	1977 wine sales[b]
E&J Gallo	Gallo	Private	$370,000,000
United Vintners	Colony Italian Swiss Colony Inglenook	Heublein (1969)	$201,751,000
Franzia-Mogen David	Franzia Mogen David	Coca-Cola Bottling (N.Y.) (1970, 1973)	$ 59,900,000
Almaden Vineyards	Almaden	National Distillers (1967)	$ 88,023,000
Canadaigua Wine Co.	Richard's Wild Irish Rose	Public	$ 35,605,000
The Taylor Wine Co.	Taylor Great Western	The Coca-Cola Co. (1976)	$ 59,600,000
Paul Masson Vineyards	Paul Masson	Seagram (1945)	$ 70,000,000[a]
Mont La Salle	Christian Brothers	Private	$ 50,000,000[a]

[a] Casewriter's estimate.
[b] Where companies are owned, sales figure is that of owner.

times, the vintner buys grapes to subsidize the growers in order not to jeopardize future supplies. This practice can lead to large inventories and make storage capacity an important factor. Aging requirements for premium and sparkling wines also add to storage requirements. White wines require significantly less aging than red wines of comparable quality. Exhibit 5 shows storage capacities of twelve U.S. wineries, which account for 73 percent of the storage capacities of the 100 largest wineries. All except Taylor are in California.

Advertising

The entry of large companies into the wine industry has been accompanied by an increase in advertising budgets and the advent of mass marketing techniques. Almaden has increased advertising by 100 percent since 1974 while Taylor's advertising has increased 33 percent. The largest advertiser, Gallo, on the other hand, has increased its ad budget only about 9 percent. In 1977, however, Gallo spent over $12 million on advertising while Taylor and Almaden spent about $2 million. Since all segments of the alcoholic beverage industry compete to some extent, the level of wine advertising is partly affected by promoting of beer and spirits.

Regulation

Wine is subject to regulation from all levels of government. State and local governments regulate the sales of alcoholic beverages and in some states legislation has been proposed to regulate packaging. At the federal level, the Treasury Department's Bureau of Alcohol, Firearms, and Tobacco (BATF) regulates advertising and labeling. New advertising guidelines were expected late in 1979, and new labeling requirements

EXHIBIT 3
Profiles of major
competitors in the
wine industry

E & J Gallo

With a sales volume nearly double its closest competitor, Gallo has more influence in the wine industry than any other U.S. company. Because Gallo purchases 40 percent of the California grape harvest, the company is in the position of impacting grape prices throughout California. In addition to the winery, Gallo operations include vineyards, apple orchards, one of the West's biggest bottling plants, one of California's largest trucking companies, and several big wine distributors. The founders of the winery, Ernest and Julio Gallo, are active in the firm; Julio oversees the wine making and Ernest looks after everything else.

Gallo is the only large winery that doesn't offer tours and Ernest is noted for his secrecy about operations. At the same time, Gallo has served as a training ground for many vintners who have gone on to other companies.

In recent years, Gallo has upgraded its product line and its prices. Once known for pop wines like Thunderbird, Ripple, and Boone's Farm, the company stopped advertising these wines and began to emphasize the higher priced varietal and proprietary wines. Although sales and market share temporarily suffered, profits increased steadily.

Gallo is noted for producing a quality wine at a low price. Hearty Burgundy had been called the best wine ever made for the money and because of the cost advantage of the bottling plant, Gallo has sometimes been in the position of selling wine below cost while making a profit on the bottles.

United Vintners

United Vintners is 82 percent owned by Heublein, Inc., the major U.S. producer of vodka (Smirnoff) and the owner of Kentucky Fried Chicken. The range of products of UV included pop wines (Annie Green Springs, T. J. Swann), Colony, Italian Swiss Colony, Inglenook table and dessert wines, and high-quality wines from Beaulieu Vineyards. The company also distributed Lancer's wine from Portugal.

United Vintners has been in the wine industry since the late '60s and is the second largest seller of wines; sales totaled $226.1 million in 1976, but fell to $201.8 million in 1977. Recent advertising campaigns have emphasized the personality of the drinker rather than attributes of its wines.

Franzia-Mogen David

Coca-Cola Bottling Company of New York purchased Mogen David in 1970 and Franzia Brothers in 1973. The former is known for sweet table, fruit, and specialty wines whereas the latter produces a range of California dry red and white wines; table wines; rosé, sparkling, and dessert wines; and brandy. In addition to bottling and distributing soft drinks (Dr. Pepper and Seven-Up besides the Coca-Cola line), the company's subsidiaries produce Igloo plastic coolers and other plastic products. The company owns two steamboats, the *Mississippi Queen* and the *Delta Queen*, and a TV station. It is one of the largest independent soft drink franchises in the world.

In 1977 wine sales of Mogen David and Franzia brands totaled almost $60 million, down slightly from $60.8 million in 1976; the operations of the Franzia unit were not profitable in 1977. Recent Mogen David commercials urged consumers to drink Mogen David because of its taste — even though it lacked "snob appeal."

EXHIBIT 3
(continued)

Almaden

National Distillers and Chemical Corporation acquired full ownership of Almaden in 1977. One of the four largest distillers in the United States, National Distillers was also active in chemicals, petrochemicals, brass mill products, and textiles.

Almaden had sales of $88 million and an operating profit of $14 million in 1977; in 1978 sales increased to $117.5 million and operating profits rose to $17.2 million.

Canandaigua Wine Co.

Canandaigua sold primarily dessert wines, and one product, Richard's Wild Irish Rose, accounted for over two thirds of its sales. The company owned wineries in New York, California, South Carolina, and Virginia and its 1977 sales were in the $35 million range.

Paul Masson Vineyards

Seagram Company Ltd., of which Paul Masson is a division, was in 1977 the world's largest producer and marketer of distilled spirits and wines. Case volume of Paul Masson wines was reported to be growing about 15 percent annually. The Paul Masson brand enjoyed a good reputation in the industry and was one of the better known brands among consumers.

were to take effect in January 1983. These requirements state that if place of origin (e.g., California) is identified on the bottle, 75 percent of the grapes must be from that place and if a viticultural area is identified (e.g., Napa Valley), 85 percent of the grapes must be from there. These standards match those prevailing in the European Common Market.

EXHIBIT 4
Market share by
origin of wine (1977)

Origin		Share	Volume increase (decrease) from '76
Domestic		82.8%	
California	86.1%		6.0%
Others	13.9%		(4.1)
	100.0%		
Imports		17.2%	
Italy	43.0%		29.1%
France	19.4		12.2
Germany	15.3		18.5
Spain	9.4		(6.1)
Portugal	8.6		3.0
Other	5.0		
	100.0%		

EXHIBIT 5
Storage capacities
of 12 U.S. wineries

Winery	Storage capacity (millions of gallons)
E&J Gallo	226
United Vintners (Heublein)	110
Guild Wineries	57
Vie Del Co.	37.1
Bear Mountain	36
Taylor (Coca-Cola)	31.3
Sierra Wine Corp.	30
Almaden (National Distillers and Chemicals)	29.4
Franzia Bros. (Coca-Cola, N.Y.)	28.3
Paul Masson (Seagram)	28
The Christian Brothers	27.5
A. Perelli-Minette & Sons	20

In addition to regulation, wine is subject to taxation from all levels of government. Federal excise tax is $.17 per gallon on table wines, $.67 per gallon on dessert wines, and $3.40 per gallon on sparkling wines.

THE TAYLOR WINE COMPANY

The Taylor Wine Company, at the time of acquisition by Coca-Cola, was a leading domestic producer of premium still and sparkling wines, marketed under the "Taylor" and "Great Western" labels; it was also the largest producer of premium domestic champagnes. The record of Taylor Wine Company from 1972 to 1976 reflected the cyclical swings in the industry during that period. In 1973, record sales of $51 million registered an 18 percent increase over 1972, with profits up 25 percent to $6.8 million or $1.57 per share. In 1974, sales increased to $56 million while profits increased to $6.9 million or $1.58 per share. Results worsened as Taylor reported sales and profits of $57.6 million and $5.4 million, or $1.24 per share, in 1975 and $59.6 million and $5.6 million, or $1.30 per share, in 1976. In explaining these results, Taylor's management said:

> During the four years 1969–1972, the volume of wine entering U.S. marketing channels increased 10–14% per year. As a result of this growth and anticipated continued growth, substantial vine plantings and wine production occurred during the period 1971–1974. However, due to economic conditions in 1973 through 1975 the expected rate of growth in wine sales was not realized, and the industry faced a period of surplus wine inventories and grape crops. Taylor believes that its sales for the fiscal years 1975 and 1976 were adversely affected by competitive pricing conditions attributable to the foregoing factors. In its effort to maintain profit margins, Taylor has generally held or slightly increased

its prices to distributors during this period, even though, based upon retail prices, it is believed that a number of wine producers have reduced prices. However, inflationary pressures, which increased costs, resulted in reduced profit margin percentages in fiscal 1974 and 1975. A decrease in some material costs and improved cost controls resulted in a modest improvement in profit margins for 1976, although gallons sold declined slightly.

Taylor's *1976 Annual Report* stated that the company had "successfully weathered the recession of the past two years and is in a strong position to take advantage of the recovery the wine industry appears to be experiencing." In addition to the recovery, 1976 also marked the end of the Taylor family's participation in the company's management and its merger with the Coca-Cola Company.

Merger with Coca-Cola

On August 6, 1976, Lincoln First Bank of Rochester, New York, put out a preliminary prospectus for sale of 603,000 of the 900,000 shares of Taylor stock it held for trust customers. The motive for the sale was to raise cash for the trusts involved and Taylor was informed of the proceedings because 10 percent of the outstanding stock was involved. Several companies responded to the prospectus including Coca-Cola, PepsiCo, Beatrice Foods, Norton-Simon, and five private investors headed by Marne Obernauer (a former Taylor director and owner of Great Western before it was purchased by Taylor). Coca-Cola was interested in more than the 603,000 shares so when Coca-Cola and the Bank reached an agreement, the secondary offer was withdrawn and Coca-Cola entered into merger talks directly with Taylor.

After Taylor's board's approval of the proposed merger, Taylor's president, Joseph Swarthout, explained to the shareholders in the December 2, 1976, prospectus:

The U.S. wine market has never been more competitive. As I stated at our Annual Shareholders' Meeting in September, our major competitors are stronger than ever. In several cases they have significantly stronger financial backing than we have. Under these conditions, it becomes increasingly difficult to improve, or even maintain, our share-of-market.

I have had the pleasure of being an employee of this company for more than thirty years. I have been a corporate officer since 1955. They have been interesting years of growth and opportunity. It is now my firm belief that The Taylor Wine Company would enjoy substantially greater opportunities for success in the future through the financial strength and diversity of the Coca-Cola Company.

Industry observers speculated that Taylor management was frightened by several of the "unfamiliar" companies showing interest in the 603,000 shares of Taylor's stock and looked at the Coca-Cola merger as a way of preventing a greater evil. There did, however, appear to be possibilities for strategic fit with Coca-Cola, as indicated in Coca-Cola's description of its business:

The Coca-Cola Company is the largest manufacturer and distributor of soft drink concentrates and syrups in the world. Its product, "Coca-Cola," has been sold in the United States since 1886, is now sold in over 135 countries as well and is the leading soft drink product in most of these countries.

In 1978, soft drink products accounted for 76 percent of total sales and 87 percent of total operating income from industry segments. Soft drink products include Coca-Cola, Fanta, Sprite, TAB, Fresca, Mr. PiBB and Hi-C Brand. Coca-Cola accounts for over 70 percent of all Company soft drink unit sales, both in the United States and overseas.

The worldwide soft drink operations of the Coca-Cola Company are organized into three operating groups: the Americas Group, the Pacific Group and the Europe and Africa Group. The Company's largest markets within its Americas Group are the United States, Mexico, and Brazil. The largest markets within the Pacific Group are Japan and Canada. The largest market in the Europe and Africa Group is Germany. In 1978, overseas markets accounted for some 62 percent of total soft drink unit sales.

In the United States, 67 percent of soft drink syrup and concentrate is sold to more than 550 bottlers who prepare and sell the products for the food store, vending and other markets for home and on-premise consumption. The remaining 33 percent is sold to approximately 4,000 authorized wholesalers who in turn sell the syrup to restaurants and other retailers. Overseas, all soft drink concentrate is sold to more than 900 bottlers. Approximately 90 percent of the syrup and concentrate is sold for further processing outside the Company before sale to the ultimate consumer, both in the United States and overseas. The remaining 10 percent is converted into consumable soft drinks before being sold by the Company.

Through the Foods Division, the Company manufactures and markets Minute Maid and Snow Crop frozen concentrated citrus juices, Minute Maid chilled juices and related citrus products, and Hi-C ready-to-serve fruit drinks and powdered drink mixes. The Foods Division also markets coffee and tea under the ''Maryland Club,'' ''Butter-nut,'' and other brands, as well as to private label and institutional accounts.

Exhibits 6, 7, and 8 show the combined pro forma summaries of operations, net profits, and balance sheet statements for the merged companies.

Under the terms of the merger agreement approved by stockholders of both companies in January 1977, all outstanding shares of Taylor stock were converted into shares of common stock of Coca-Cola at the rate of one share of Coca-Cola stock for each 3.75 shares of Taylor stock. No changes in Taylor management were planned and the company was to operate as a wholly owned subsidiary of Coca-Cola with Coca-Cola officials on its Board of Directors. Exhibit 9 shows the stock price movements for Coca-Cola and Taylor.

Taylor Wine Company Operations

At the time of the merger proposal, Taylor described its operations as follows:

Taylor is a leading domestic producer of premium still wines. It is also the largest domestic producer of sparkling wines using the traditional French method of fermentation in the bottle, as contrasted with the bulk process in which the wine is fermented in large volume.

Taylor's 63 types of sparkling and still wines are produced and marketed exclusively under two trade names representing its two wine divisions. The Pleasant Valley division, the successor to the Pleasant Valley Wine Company, acquired by Taylor in 1961, produces and markets its wines under the Great Western name. Historically, these divisions have utilized separate production and marketing techniques, and the wines produced by each division traditionally have had different characteristics and consumer brand loyalties. As a result, they have continued as separate divisions since 1961 and presently maintain

EXHIBIT 6 The Coca-Cola Company and subsidiaries and the Taylor Wine Company, Inc., pro forma combined summary of operations (unaudited)

| | 1971 | 1972 | 1973 | 1974 | 1975 | Six months ended June 30 | |
						1975	1976
Net sales	$1,772,029	$1,927,242	$2,201,410	$2,579,754	$2,932,457	$1,476,764	$1,508,416
Cost of goods sold	$ 949,124	$1,021,889	$1,179,168	$1,576,068	$1,745,238	$ 904,183	$ 835,472
Taxes on income	$ 165,270	$ 179,661	$ 194,007	$ 173,899	$ 226,750	$ 106,372	$ 129,008
Net profit[a]	$ 173,238	$ 197,004	$ 221,862	$ 201,356	$ 224,951	$ 122,344	$ 144,483
Per share:							
Net profit[a]	$2.85	$3.24	$3.64	$3.30	$4.01	$2.00	$2.37
Cash dividends declared	$1.58	$1.64	$1.80	$2.08	$2.30	$1.15	$1.32
Average number of shares outstanding[b]	60,730	60,860	60,937	60,996	61,050	61,049	61,078

Note: Figures in thousands except per share amounts. Estimated expenses of this proposed merger will be approximately $700,000. These expenses, which have not been included in the above pro forma presentation, will be deducted from operations of the resulting combined company for the period in which they are incurred.

[a] In 1974 the Coca-Cola Company adopted the last-in, first-out accounting method for certain major classes of inventories as explained in the financial statements of the Coca-Cola Company and subsidiaries. For the year ended June 30, 1975, Taylor also adopted the last-in, first-out method of valuation for all its inventories as explained the Taylor statement of income. These accounting changes had the effect of reducing pro forma net profit for 1974 by $32,329,548 ($.53 a share).

[b] The pro forma average number of shares outstanding represents the average number of shares of the Coca-Cola Company outstanding during each period after giving retroactive effect to the average number of Taylor shares outstanding during each period converted into shares of the Coca-Cola Company on a .267 for 1 basis.

EXHIBIT 7 The Coca-Cola Company and subsidiaries and the Taylor Wine Company, Inc., pro forma combined net profit and per share data (unaudited)

	1971	1972	1973	1974	1975	Six months ended June 30	
						1975	1976
Net profit (in thousands)							
The Coca-Cola Company, historical	$167,815	$190,157	$214,981	$195,972	$239,305	$119,762	$141,763
The Taylor Wine Company, Inc., historical	5,471	6,847	6,881	5,939	5,646	2,582	2,720
Pro forma combined	$173,286	$197,004	$221,862	$201,365	$244,951	$122,344	$144,483
Net profit per common share							
The Coca-Cola Company:							
Historical	$2.82	$3.19	$3.60	$3.28	$4.00	$2.00	$ 2.37
Pro forma combined[a]	2.85	3.24	3.64	3.30	4.01	2.00	2.37
The Taylor Wine Company, Inc.:							
Historical	1.29	1.57	1.58	1.24	1.30	.59	.63
Pro forma combined[b]	.76	.86	.97	.88	1.07	.53	.63
Cash dividends declared per common share							
The Coca-Cola Company, historical	1.58	1.64	1.80	2.08	2.30	1.15	1.32
The Taylor Wine Company, Inc.:							
Historical	.48	.50	.56	.60	.62	.30	.31
Pro forma combined[b]	.42	.44	.48	.56	.61	.31	.35
Book value per common share							
The Coca-Cola Company:							
Historical							21.57
Pro forma combined[a]							22.13
The Taylor Wine Company, Inc.:							
Historical							13.67
Pro forma combined[b]							5.90

[a] Pro forma combined amounts per share for the Coca-Cola Company are based on average number of shares outstanding during each period and as of June 30, 1976, after giving retroactive effect to the conversion of Taylor shares into shares of the Coca-Cola Company on the basis of the exchange ratio for the merger, at .267 shares of the Coca-Cola Company for each share of Taylor.

[b] Pro forma combined amounts are based on .267 shares the Coca-Cola Company exchanged for each share of Taylor.

Source: Prospectus.

EXHIBIT 8 The Coca-Cola Company and subsidiaries and the Taylor Wine Company, Inc., pro forma combined condensed balance sheet as of June 30, 1976 (unaudited)

	Coca-Cola	Taylor	Adjustment[a]	Pro forma combined
Assets				
Current Assets:				
Cash	$ 78,571	$ 1,173		$ 79,744
Marketable securities	229,793			229,793
Trade accounts receivable — net	250,947	4,356		255,303
Inventories	374,920	41,766		416,686
Prepaid expenses	28,467	180		28,647
Total current assets	962,698	47,475		1,010,173
Property, Plant and Equipment — net	647,684	26,462		674,146
Other Assets	209,641	902		210,543
Total	$1,820,023	$74,839		$1,894,862
Liabilities and stockholders' equity				
Current Liabilities:				
Notes payable including current maturities of long-term debt	$ 24,891	$ 3,037		$ 27,928
Accounts payable and accrued accounts	337,129	3,656		340,785
Accrued taxes including taxes on income	121,763	1,729		123,492
Total current liabilities	483,783	8,422		492,205
Long-Term Liabilities and Deferred Taxes	44,092	6,904		50,996
Total liabilities	527,875	15,326		543,201
Stockholders' Equity:				
Common stock — no par value — The Coca-Cola Company	60,485		$ 1,173	
Common stock — $2 par value — The Taylor Wine Company, Inc.		8,707	(8,707)	
Capital surplus	87,938	9,930	7,534	105,402
Earned surplus	1,159,090	40,876		1,199,966
Treasury shares	(15,365)			(15,365)
Total stockholders' equity	1,292,148	59,513		1,351,661
Total	$1,820,023	$74,839		$1,894,862

Note: Figures in thousands of dollars.
[a] The pro forma adjustment reflects the issuance of 1,161,000 common shares of the Coca-Cola Company upon conversion of each of the presently issued common shares of Taylor for .267 common shares of the Coca-Cola Company pursuant to the terms of the merger.

EXHIBIT 9 Comparative stock prices

	Taylor common stock		Coca-Cola common stock	
	High bid price	*Low bid price*	*High sale price*	*Low sale price*
1974				
First Quarter	$38.25	$23.75	$127.75	$109.50
Second Quarter	24.25	16.50	118.375	98.375
Third Quarter	17.75	12.25	109.00	48.00
Fourth Quarter	13.75	9.25	68.75	44.625
1975				
First Quarter	20.875	10.125	81.50	53.25
Second Quarter	19.50	16.00	93.50	72.75
Third Quarter	18.375	11.00	92.00	69.625
Fourth Quarter	15.375	10.75	89.75	69.875
1976				
First Quarter	17.50	13.50	94.25	82.00
Second Quarter	15.50	12.25	89.00	77.625
Third Quarter	19.375	12.875	89.625	82.875
Fourth Quarter, November 20, 1976	20.25	16.875	86.25	76.25

The Coca-Cola Company announced that it had entered into merger negotiations with Taylor on September 8, 1976, and preliminary agreement on the exchange rate was announced on October 14, 1976.

their own advertising, marketing, production and storage capacity and operational staffs, although legal, financial, accounting, personnel and other functions are performed at the corporate level.

Wines are classified as either "still" or "sparkling." Still wines containing 14 percent or less alcohol are generally referred to as "table" wines and those containing 14–21 percent alcohol are generally referred to as "dessert" wines. Sparkling wines are those which are effervescent and contain not more than 14 percent alcohol.

Employees

Taylor employed approximately 670 full-time employees. Because of the increased use of mechanized harvesting equipment, the number of seasonal workers hired by Taylor had declined in recent years. Approximately 15 seasonal workers were employed during the 1976 grape harvest as compared with approximately 200 such workers employed during the 1967 harvest. A few additional seasonal workers were sometimes employed at the winery for the grape pressing operations. Taylor maintained a pension plan to which it made annual contributions and which allowed employees to make voluntary contributions; it also provided group life and medical benefits for its regular full-time employees. The employees of Taylor were not represented by any unions, and Taylor believed that its employee relations were satisfactory.

Marketing   Taylor's wines were sold throughout the United States. Both Taylor and Pleasant Valley advertised through television, magazines, and newspapers. In addition, each division provided promotional materials to its customers for eventual use by retailers. In recent years, advertising, sales promotion, and selling expenditures by Taylor approximated 17 percent of net sales.

In 1976, the Taylor and Great Western product lines were marketed by 64 and 34 salesmen, respectively. Taylor's products were sold primarily to 490 wholesale distributors and through 27 brokers. With few exceptions, Taylor and Great Western wines were handled by different distributors in the respective geographic locations. Brokers were primarily used by Taylor to sell its products in states where no distribution agreements existed and in some of the 15 so-called "control" states where Taylor's customer was the local or state agency that controlled the purchase and distribution of alcoholic beverages. In some control states, such as Pennsylvania, sales were made directly by Taylor to the appropriate governmental agency. (A distributor purchases Taylor's products for resale to retailers, whereas brokers act on behalf of Taylor on a commission basis.) Taylor maintained one price list for all purchases (F.O.B. the winery) and did not engage in selective discounting.

In 1976, no distributor accounted for more than 7 percent of Taylor's net sales, and no state control agency accounted for more than 10 percent of Taylor's net sales except Pennsylvania which accounted for 11 percent. The largest markets, by state, for Taylor's products were New York, Pennsylvania, New Jersey, and Illinois. In addition to the wine sold through distribution channels outlined above, a small volume of wine was sold by Taylor directly to airlines and exported to United States armed forces, embassies and consulates abroad, and some foreign countries.

Taylor's sales volume was seasonal and was affected by price adjustments and the introduction of new products. Normally, sales volume was greatest in the last calendar quarter and smallest in the third calendar quarter. Sales volume for the first and second quarters was normally about the same. Preannounced price increases and new product introductions typically resulted in anticipatory buying by Taylor's customers.

In addition to normal and continuous product advertising, it was Taylor's practice to conduct individual promotional programs at various times during the year for certain of its wines and brands.

The vast majority of Taylor's products were bottled in one-fifth gallon (25.6 oz.) and 1.5 liter (50.7 oz.) sizes. Metric conversion was legally required as of January 1, 1979, and, at that time, the one-fifth gallon size was expected to be converted to a .75 liter (25.4 oz.) size. In early 1976, Taylor converted the half-gallon (64 oz.) size to 1.5 liter size. Taylor did not produce wine for bulk sale to other wineries. Exhibit 10 shows the market sizes and Taylor's position in the table, dessert, and sparkling wine segments.

Wine   During the last five years, vineyards owned and operated by Taylor supplied approxi-
Production   mately 10 percent of its annual grape requirements. Taylor had over 850 acres of

EXHIBIT 10

Marketing of wines in the United States

	1971	1972	1973	1974	1975
Table wines[a]					
U.S. produced	159,510	182,640	190,469	201,634	219,171
Foreign produced	26,356	37,741	45,658	42,153	40,524
Total	185,766	220,381	236,127	243,787	259,695
Taylor	2,840	3,504	4,574	5,123	5,264
Taylor market share[b]	1.5%	1.6%	1.9%	2.1%	2.0%
Dessert wines[a]					
U.S. produced	87,551	86,976	82,637	78,447	80,659
Foreign produced	8,023	7,325	7,487	7,437	6,867
Total	95,574	94,301	90,124	85,884	87,526
Taylor	4,420	4,465	4,577	4,752	4,683
Taylor market share[b]	4.6%	4.7%	5.1%	5.5%	5.4%
Sparkling wines					
U.S. produced	22,005	20,323	18,935	18,008	18,424
Foreign produced	1,877	1,976	2,081	1,804	1,928
Total	23,882	22,299	21,016	19,812	20,352
Taylor	1,697	1,738	1,763	1,688	1,605
Taylor market share[b]	7.1%	7.8%	8.4%	8.5%	7.9%
Total of all categories					
U.S. produced	269,066	289,939	292,041	298,089	318,254
Foreign produced	36,156	47,042	55,226	51,394	49,319
Total	305,222	336,981	347,267	349,483	367,573
Taylor	8,957	9,707	10,914	11,563	11,552
Taylor market share[b]	2.9%	2.9%	3.1%	3.3%	3.1%

Note: Figures in thousands of gallons.
[a] Still wines with less than 14 percent alcohol have been included in table wines and those with greater than 15 percent alcohol have been included in dessert wines.
[b] Taylor as a percentage of total.
Source: Wine Institute Statistical Reports for other than Taylor statistics.

vineyards in production, with an additional 450 acres of such plantings not yet in full bearing. Of the 450 acres, 420 acres overlooking Seneca Lake, the largest of the Finger Lakes, were recently purchased and planted and were expected to be in full bearing by 1980. The balance of Taylor's annual grape requirements was supplied by more than 450 independent growers from approximately 11,500 acres, located principally in the Finger Lakes region of New York State. A portion of Taylor's grape requirements was purchased from counties in the far western part of New York State.

Taylor had contracts with all independent growers from whom it purchased grapes, and a large number of these growers had been supplying Taylor for many years. These contracts required Taylor, on or before August 1 of each year, to announce the prices it would pay for grapes to be purchased in the fall harvest as well as the quantities it would purchase. Taylor financed its grape purchases through short-term financing. Harvesting generally occurred for approximately eight weeks in September and October. Growers had the right to cancel their contracts during the first two weeks of August; and during November of each year, either the grower or Taylor could cancel the contract. In the past five years, four growers exercised their cancellation rights. On July 30, 1976, Taylor announced it would purchase approximately 70 percent of the grape tonnage purchased in 1975; this was the first time that the announced quantities did not constitute substantially the entire crop of its growers under contract. The average per-ton price paid to growers for grapes for the 1976 harvest was approximately 86 percent of that paid in the 1975 harvest. The company maintained an advisory service program for its independent grape growers, providing them with information with respect to fertilization, cultivation, soil analysis, disease control, and planting. In addition, it conducted experimental work in its own vineyards and in conjunction with the New York State Agricultural Experiment Station located in nearby Geneva, New York.

Taylor purchased about 25 percent of its wine needs from several California suppliers for blending purposes and also bought ingredients for certain wines the flavor characteristics of which were derived from grapes not grown in the eastern United States. In addition, wine spirits, sugar and other ingredients, and packaging materials were obtained from several sources. The company believed its sources of supply were adequate and anticipated no shortage in the foreseeable future of grapes supplied by independent growers or of land suitable for growing the varieties and quality of grapes required for its wines.

Taylor's current manufacturing facilities had a total bottling capacity of approximately 4,070 cases per hour. Aging of Taylor's sparkling and still wines normally took up to two years, although wines could be stored for substantially longer periods. As a result of this aging process, and to guard against crop shortages, Taylor, like many companies in the wine industry, maintained inventories that were large in relation to sales and total assets. The company's inventories usually peaked in late October shortly after the grape harvest. In October 1975, Taylor's wine inventories totaled 25.2 million gallons. This figure declined to 20.7 million gallons in July 1976 and then rose again to 25.5 million gallons in October 1976. Taylor had approximately 31.1 million gallons of wine storage capacity, of which 24.7 million gallons was tank storage and 6.4 million gallons was bottled storage. Because of operating limitations, the effective tank storage capacity was limited to approximately 85 percent or 21 million gallons. On June 30, 1976, the cost (LIFO basis) of Taylor's inventory of still wines in bulk and sparkling wines in process was approximately $30.8 million.

Acquisition by Coca-Cola

Analysts on Wall Street identified several factors that seemed to make the Taylor acquisition a bargain for Coca-Cola. By maintaining premium prices while others were cutting prices, Taylor had maintained its profitability and its record of increasing dividends. Although not investing heavily in such capital projects as a bottle factory, the company had kept its facilities up to date and in good shape. The slipping market share and lack of national image for Taylor were the kinds of problems that Coca-Cola's $387 million in cash could solve. Taylor was not deep in debt, was profitable, and was in a position to capitalize on what Coca-Cola saw as another wine boom.

Coca-Cola's decision to enter the wine industry was discussed in its publication, *Refresher USA*:

> Our Company's figurative foray into the vineyards came only after a very careful study of the market, a study which revealed some extremely positive indication of growth potential for wine in this country.
>
> The study's major conclusion was that the wine boom that began in the United States in the 1960s will continue through the 1970s and beyond. In other words, the popularity of wine is here to stay.
>
> "More than 60 percent of the adult U.S. population now consumes wine, which has become an everyday dinner beverage in many households," says Thomas Muller, manager of administration and development for the Wine Group (changed to Wine Spectrum in 1978). "And as distribution expands from specialty stores to supermarkets, women are becoming an increasingly important group of purchasers as well as consumers of wine."
>
> Another major factor favorably affecting sales, says [Albert] Killeen [president of the Wine Spectrum] "is an accelerating general cultural interest in wine. There's almost an art form to it that could be called 'winesmanship' as people gain more knowledge about wine.
>
> There's a great interest in such activities as wine tasting, vineyard tours, and wine with food. Many people are studying how to develop a wine cellar, the ritual of chilling, decorking, decanting, and serving wine."
>
> "Among college students there is a decided preference for wine over other alcoholic beverages," observes Grant Curtis, vice-president and marketing services manager for Taylor Wine. "To give you an idea of what an important growth factor that is, there are 28 million college graduates in the United States today; by 1985, there will be nearly double that number — 45 million. And these young adults are carrying their preference for wine into their post-college lives."

BUILDING THE WINE SPECTRUM DIVISION

After the Taylor acquisition, Coca-Cola purchased two California vineyards. Sterling Vineyards was the 100th largest winery in the United States with a capacity of sixty-thousand cases per year. Sterling president Michael P. W. Stone described his product:

> We are one of the half-dozen or so of the smaller California wineries which seek to position their products at the extreme upper spectrum of the premium line of wines. Wines generally are classed as standard, medium-range, and premium: we are aiming to what you might call "superpremium."

The winery's four red and four white wines were grown and bottled on premises and were classified as estate-bottled, vintage wines. Killeen commented on plans for Sterling:

Sterling Vineyards' development as a wine-growing and -producing enterprise will remain unchanged. It will continue to have as its objective the production of the finest Napa Valley premium estate bottled wines in the U.S. Production will continue to be restricted and the uncompromising practices that have made Sterling Wines highly respected will be continued by the existing staff at Calistoga.[4]

The purchase of the Monterey Vineyards near Gonzales, California, was announced by Coca-Cola in November 1977. Monterey County was one of the last regions in California to be planted in wine grapes and its wines have been characterized as having "an intense varietal flavor, thinner body, and more fruitiness and crispness." Monterey was completed in 1975 and much of the production equipment was designed by its president, Richard Peterson, a Ph.D. in agricultural chemistry and former employee of Gallo and Beaulieu. The construction of the winery was somewhat unorthodox — the foundation was laid, then the production equipment was installed, and finally the walls and roof were put up. Monterey owned no vineyards and produced eight varietals and one blend. Production capacity was 7 million cases and storage capacity was 2.2 million gallons.

Taylor, Great Western [Pleasant Valley], Sterling, and Monterey became the components of the Wine Spectrum Division of the Coca-Cola Company; together, these wine operations made Coca-Cola the fifth largest factor in the U.S. wine industry. Albert E. Killeen served both as executive vice-president of Coca-Cola and president of the Wine Spectrum. He had responsibility for directing and coordinating the company's wine interests and served as chairman of the board of directors of each winery. He had previously served as corporate marketing director and executive vice-president for marketing at Coca-Cola.

Killeen assessed the strengths of the components of the Wine Spectrum as follows:

Taylor is the keystone of the Company's wine business because of its reputation for quality, its strong distribution system, and its fine sales organization. The Sterling and Monterey wineries add geographic balance as well as new brands of varietal wines to our product mix. We now have really the best of both worlds — the distinguished tradition of wine-making from the Finger Lakes region of New York State known for its fine champagne and sherries, and the fresh and exuberant ambience of the California growing regions, known for their table wines. Even the two California wineries were carefully chosen to balance one another. One is in a region that produces a very fine Cabernet Sauvignon grape, for example; the other in a much cooler region, fosters some of the best Johannisberg, Riesling and Gruner Sylvaner grapes available anywhere. So our combination of vineyards puts us in a prime position for taking advantage of opportunities to produce a wide variety of high-quality American-grown wines for optimum acceptance among American consumers and consumers around the world.[5]

---

[4] "The Coca-Cola Company Acquires Sterling Vineyards," Coca-Cola press release, August 8, 1977.

[5] *Refresher, USA,* 4 (1977), p. 15.

The importance of the Taylor name to Coca-Cola was illustrated in the following news item:

> Walter S. Taylor, a grandson of the founder of the giant Taylor Wine Company, must take his last name off the labels of bottles containing wine produced by his own company, Bully Hill.
>
> So said Federal Judge Harold Burke in the United States District Court in Hammondsport, N.Y., yesterday. The judge upheld a request by the Coca-Cola Company, of Atlanta, for an injunction forbidding Mr. Taylor to use the name because of confusion over the wine made by Taylor Wine Company, which Coca-Cola had purchased last year. Mr. Taylor had been a vice-president of Taylor Wine, but left some years before Coca-Cola acquired control.
>
> Mr. Taylor said he planned to appeal the ruling. However, he added, the family name will be scratched out by hand on the Bully Hill bottles, pending resolution of the case. The "Walter S." will stay.[6]

National Status Sought for Taylor

The immediate result of Coca-Cola's acquisition was the introduction of a new line, Taylor California Cellars. The line was composed of four generic wines — chablis, rhine, rose, and burgundy — which were developed and blended by Dr. Peterson of Monterey Vineyards. The wines were bottled at Franzia Brothers, a subsidiary of Coca-Cola of New York. Taylor provided the label name and the distribution system. Prices for California Cellars were set slightly higher than other premium generic wines. The introductory ad campaign for California Cellars became the reason for the BATF dispute.

Taylor's advertising agency had commissioned a national consumer group to conduct a series of taste tests to compare the new wines with more established names in California premium wines. The results of the tests placed three California Cellars wines in first place in generic categories and one in second place. (See the appendix.) Their results were used as a basis for the introductory ad campaign for the fall of 1978 in the East and in Southern California.

Comparative advertising was a break with traditional wine advertising and there was some question also about whether it was allowed under federal regulations. Taylor sought clearance to use the ads from the Bureau of Alcohol, Tobacco, and Firearms, but was refused. The BATF also refused to prohibit the ads. Taylor then sought court action to gain approval for its commercials but the court ruled that there were no grounds for suit because the ad had not been ordered stopped. Part of the problem resulted from the fact that the Bureau was about to review advertising regulations and new guidelines were not expected for a year after the California Cellars campaign was scheduled to begin. The Bureau was unwilling to pre-clear taste test advertising until it had held hearings and developed standards for review. Prohibitions against taste test ads were based on a 1954 ruling dealing with beer. One BATF official stated: "It is not the Bureau's position that all comparative taste test advertising is misleading and therefore prohibited. It is the Bureau's

---

[6] "People and Business," *New York Times*, August 16, 1977, p. 58.

position that misleading advertising of wine be prohibited.''[7] The decision as to whether or not Taylor's ads were misleading was to be left until the ads were aired and complaints were filed. In view of the uncertainty surrounding the campaign, an alternative series of introductory ads was prepared which did not use taste test information.

Penalties for improper advertising ranged from a "letter of admonition" to suspension of vintners' license to criminal prosecution. The possibility of suits from competitors was also present.

Strategies and Future Outlook

Regarding the prospects for the Wine Spectrum division, Coca-Cola stated the following in its *1978* Annual Report:

> *The United States wine market is expected to grow at a healthy rate in the years ahead; annual growth in table wines alone may surpass 10%. United States wine consumption today is at only 5% to 10% of the per capita levels of many European markets. Production, packaging, marketing, merchandising, advertising and promotional programs are now being developed to take advantage of this unique growth opportunity.*
>
> *The Wine Spectrum units are attempting to exceed industry growth by following these strategies: (1) establish strong production and distribution bases; (2) develop a balanced industry position with quality products from both coasts of the United States; and (3) employ strong and innovative marketing, merchandising, and advertising programs targeted at both the trade and the consumer.*

APPENDIX: BACKGROUND INFORMATION ON THE ADVERTISING CAMPAIGN FOR TAYLOR CALIFORNIA CELLARS

WINE TASTING TEST

The advertising for the introduction of Taylor California Cellars is based on a scientifically structured and carefully monitored wine tasting test, a study that relied on the objective ratings of a panel of twenty-seven recognized wine experts and which clearly establishes this new brand of premium generic wine as one of the finest of its genre.

To ensure the validity and accuracy of the competition, Kenyon & Eckhardt, agency of record for Taylor California Cellars, commissioned the Nationwide Consumer Testing Institute, Inc. (NCTI) to design and implement the tasting test.

The NCTI project sought to determine the rank preference of four brands of California wine in four different categories.

Specifically, the wine tasting competition included the following four tasting tests:

[7] Richard C. Gordon, "Try Taste Test Ads, Taylor Told, But U.S. Won't Give Prior OK," *Advertising Age*, 49 (August 21, 1978), pp. 1, 70.

1. *Chablis Tasting*
    (a) Almaden Mountain White Chablis
    (b) Inglenook Navalle Chablis
    (c) Sebastiani Mountain Chablis
    (d) Taylor California Cellars Chablis
2. *Rosé Tasting*
    (a) Almaden Mountain Nectar Vin Rosé
    (b) Inglenook Navalle Vin Rosé
    (c) Sebastiani Mountain Vin Rosé
    (d) Taylor California Cellars Rosé
3. *Rhine Tasting*
    (a) Almaden Mountain Rhine
    (b) Inglenook Navalle Rhine
    (c) C. K. Mondavi Rhine
    (d) Taylor California Cellars Rhine
4. *Burgundy Tasting*
    (a) Almaden Mountain Red Burgundy
    (b) Inglenook Navalle Burgundy
    (c) Sebastiani Mountain Burgundy
    (d) Taylor California Cellars Burgundy

PANEL OF EXPERTS

To reach the highest standards of integrity, the tasting tests required a panel of qualified and unbiased wine tasters, in a blind study, to rank each wine according to preference.

Careful and detailed screening procedures governed the search for the wine tasters to participate in the test. NCTI specified, for instance, that no taster could have any financial interest in or affiliation with: a wine producer, wholesaler or retailer; any publication dealing with wine or reviewing the quality of wine; or a restaurant. Nor could any participant be associated with an advertising agency or market research firm.

As a further requirement, each participant had to have a minimum of five years tasting experience and was required to average at least twelve tastings per year.

NCTI chose the San Francisco Vintners Club, a nonprofit private wine tasting group, as a starting point for recruitment because of its reputation within California wine tasting circles. The club also is not affiliated with any wine producer and its members routinely participate in weekly wine tastings, generally organized according to the identical principles and twenty-point Davis rating system the NCTI intended to use in its own study.

Sixty-four percent of the twenty-seven-member panel was chosen from this group. The remainder was composed of other serious wine tasters who were members of such other respected wine tasting societies as Les Amis du Vin, Knights of the

Vine, and Berkeley Food and Wine Society. Like the tasters from Vintners Club, each participant was chosen for his or her experience and familiarity with tasting protocol.

The resulting line-up of participating tasters far exceeded those initial qualifications. Most of the respondents had well over five years of tasting experience and several had 20 years or more. In fact the 27 panel members averaged 12.3 years of wine tasting experience.

Likewise, the frequency with which each panel member participated in wine tasting tests averaged fifty per year, far exceeding the minimum standards established by NCTI.

TEST PROCEDURE

The details of the testing procedure itself were no less demanding than those governing the selection of the panelists. The wine tasting format of the Vintners Club was chosen as the model to be followed by NCTI, specifically because of the club's meticulous and established protocol, including the use of the twenty-point Davis rating system.

The tastings were conducted on July 22, 1978, in San Francisco at the Stanford Court Hotel.

Identical settings and procedures were replicated for each of the four wine tastings. All wine was served in odorless glasses marked only by A, B, C, or D.

In accordance with standard tasting procedures, the panelists moved from tasting the drier wines first to the sweeter wines. Within this order — chablis, rosé, rhine, burgundy — the individual wines were also rotated so that, for example, Glass A contained a different brand of wine in each test.

Great care was also taken in the purchase of the competitive wines to ensure that the competitive wines in the tasting were also recently bottled. Naturally, each of the wines was served at the appropriate temperature.

THE RESULTS

Using the twenty-point Davis rating system, the tasters evaluated ten different properties of each wine and ranked the four wines in each test in order of preference.

When the results were tabulated, Taylor California Cellars was judged superior in the rosé, burgundy, and rhine tastings and a very close second in the chablis testing.

JOSEPH E. SEAGRAM & SONS, LIMITED

Charles Bronfman, as part of his duties as chairman of Joseph E. Seagram & Sons, Limited, was reviewing the company's products and brands for the 1980 planning cycle. Seagram's Crown Royal continued its domination of the market for higher-priced Canadian whisky, but there had been, from 1977 to 1980, a significant increase in both the volume and share of lower-priced Canadian whiskies, an area in which Seagram was not particularly active. Further, Seagram's dominance in the U.S. market through Canadian exportation of Seagram's Seven Crown, a dominance that began in 1934, had come to an end in 1978. The success of lighter spirits in general, and Smirnoff vodka in particular, had not been anticipated by Seagram.

In addition, historical expansion through acquisition and the introduction of new brands to either meet competitive threats or capitalize on regional tastes had resulted in a proliferation of Seagram products in certain market categories. Seagram managers were beginning to question the absolute and relative profitability of some of these brands.

Finally, any product and brand management decisions would have to include the variables of the roles of company tradition and of the government. Joseph E. Seagram & Sons, Limited, and the parent Seagram Company in New York were managed by Charles Bronfman and Edgar Bronfman, whose father had been the dominant influence not only in the creation of the modern Seagram company and in the establishment of its values, but also in the creation of the world whisky business. On the government side, the Canadian government and its provincial counterparts were not only regulators of the company's production, advertising, and distribution, but were, simultaneously, competitors and customers of Joseph E. Seagram & Sons, Limited.

The following pages describe the company and the legacy of Mr. Samuel Bronfman, the distilling industry in Canada, and the status of Seagram's products and marketing strategy in 1980.

COMPANY BACKGROUND AND ORGANIZATION

In 1980, the Seagram Company was the largest distiller in the world. Within the Seagram Company, Mr. Charles Bronfman was charged with both worldwide and Canadian responsibilities. Worldwide responsibilities were part of Mr. Bronfman's duties as chairman of the Executive Committee of the parent Seagram Company. Canadian responsibilities stemmed from Mr. Bronfman's role as chairman of Joseph E. Seagram & Sons, Limited, the Canadian whisky distilling and distribution subsidiary of the Seagram Company.[1]

The organization of the Seagram Company and Joseph E. Seagram & Sons, Limited, is summarized in Exhibit 1.

The parent company, the Seagram Company, had Mr. Edgar M. Bronfman (Charles's older brother) as chairman, Mr. Charles Bronfman as chairman of the Executive Committee, and Mr. Philip Beekman (formerly president of Colgate-Palmolive International) as president. While financial and accounting policies including transfer prices were decided by the parent company, the Joseph E. Seagram & Sons, Limited, executives were responsible for: marketing of all Seagram's products in Canada; all production and distilling within Canada, based upon sales forecasts for U.S. markets developed by the parent company; Jamaican and Israeli international operations; and the implementation of any parent-company policies that pertained to the Canadian subsidiary, Joseph E. Seagram & Sons, Limited. Eighty percent of the parent company's stockholders were Canadian, and annual meetings were held in Montreal. The company's stock was traded on the major American and Canadian stock exchanges. About 30 percent of Seagram stock was controlled by the Bronfman family.

Outside directors of the Seagram Company shown in the 1979 Annual Report included the chairmen of Power Corporation of Canada, Bell Canada, Bank of Montreal, Wood Gundy, and Canadian Pacific Limited, plus the senior partner of Goldman, Sachs and the president of Cemp Investments Ltd.

Reporting to Mr. Griffin as president of Joseph E. Seagram & Sons, Limited, were executive vice-presidents for finance and administration (Mr. Babich), marketing (Mr. Roche), and production (Mr. Jellinek). The atmosphere at the Peel Street Seagram building was informal and collegial. The top executives often dropped into each others' offices to discuss problems in an operating manner that did not suggest rigid, formal chains of command.

In describing his personal views of career planning and employee selection to the casewriter, Mr. Bronfman discussed the importance of compatibility of personal goals, corporate objectives, and the goals of other managers. He commented, "Make sure that your fellow managers walk down the same side of the street with you. If you are interested in quality, don't associate yourself with the high-volume, mass merchandiser."

---

[1] *Whisky*, when Canadian or Scotch, is spelled without an "e"; its plural is *whiskies*. *Whiskey*, when American or Irish, is spelled with the "e"; its plural is *whiskeys*.

EXHIBIT 1
Seagram organiza-
tion chart

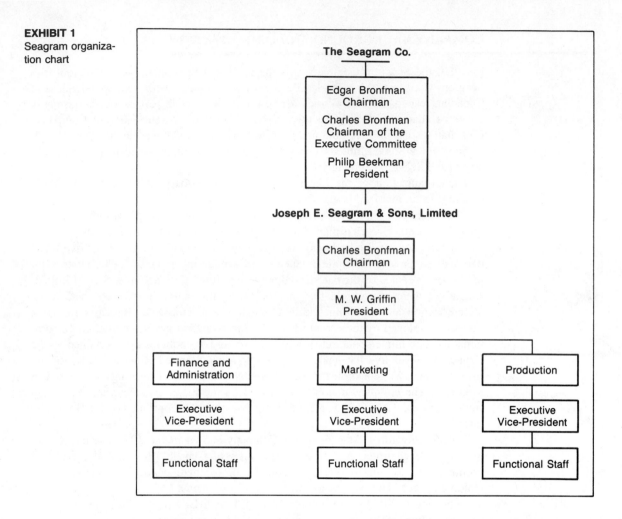

Charles Bronfman impressed the casewriter as a sensitive and thoughtful person, gracious if somewhat shy. The reserved manner was obviously only an occasional behavior pattern, as evidenced by the personal stories of his emotional opposition to the Quebec separatist movement and especially his quick and positive response to the opportunity to own the Montreal Expos. The Expos, a personal investment by Charles, was a source of satisfaction and interest to company personnel as well as to Charles, and indeed the whole nation rallied behind the Expos during their National League playoff efforts.

The Beginning   Mr. Samuel Bronfman, Charles's father, operated a liquor mail-order business with his brother prior to World War I. Operating initially in the Prairie provinces, the firm soon had warehouses and mail-order outlets throughout Canada. During the

1920s, however, the governments of each province took over the control and sale of liquor.

Mr. Samuel Bronfman then founded Distillers Corporation Ltd. and built a distillery in the LaSalle suburb of Montreal to supply the new provincial liquor boards and commissions. In 1926 Distillers acquired the shares of Joseph E. Seagram & Sons, Limited, of Waterloo, a distillery founded in 1857. Also in 1926 the company entered into an agreement with The Distillers Company Limited of Great Britain, then the world's largest distilling firm. The initial arrangement, the company's first international venture, gave Seagram's rights to well-known brands of scotch whisky. Sales of scotch exceeded Canadian whisky in the early 1920s, since Canadian distilleries had been shut down by government edict during World War I.

One of the most significant events in Seagram's history was Prohibition in the United States. Mr. Samuel Bronfman became convinced in the late 1920s that Prohibition was a failure and would be repealed. Seagram expanded production at LaSalle and Waterloo and began to mature whiskies in expanded warehouse facilities. Having acquired some distilleries in the United States upon the repeal of Prohibition, Seagram postponed the immediate profits American distillers were making. Instead Seagram shipped its 4-, 5-, and 6-year-old whiskies from Canada, blended them with neutral distilled spirits, and produced aged spirits. The company introduced Seagram's Five Crown and Seagram's Seven Crown in August 1934. In 60 days their whiskies were outselling all others throughout the United States. Seagram's Seven Crown held the number one brand position exclusively in the United States until 1978, when Bacardi's white rum sales equalled Seven Crown.

The Distilling Process

Canadian whisky is produced by Seagram in six steps.

1. Ripe grain, primarily corn, but also rye for Canadian whisky's distinctive taste, is delivered to the distillery by farmers who often have long-term contracts to supply Seagram.

2. After testing and analysis, grain is milled to a coarse meal, mixed with malt and water, and cooked to a mash. During this time, the added malt enzymes break down the starch molecules in the grain and the mash becomes maltose.

3. The maltose mash is pumped into fermentation tanks or vats where yeast is added as a fermenting agent. The yeast absorbs the maltose and this creates alcohol in this fermentation process. Yeast also adds flavor during fermentation, but principally yeast is multiplying rapidly through the absorption of the maltose molecules. This rapid multiplication is evidenced by bubbling at the surface of the fermentation vats.

4. After 3 to 4 days when the fermentation is complete, the result, about 7–8 percent alcohol, called distiller's beer, is now heated. This heating causes the alcohol to evaporate; alcohol vapors concentrate on the top of the distilling "tower" or vertical tubing. These distilled alcohol vapors run off from the top into cooling condensers. The condensed alcohol may go through a series of redistillation processes in the distilling tower or column still.

5. The distilled alcohol is next aged in 45-gallon, kiln-dried white oak barrels which have been fired so that there is a one-eighth-inch lining of charcoal in the barrel. The charcoal and wood of the barrel interact with the 45 gallons of spirits during this aging process, as the spirits filter through the charcoal to the wood, producing color, flavor, and aroma in the spirits.

6. The spirits, aged for varying periods of time, are blended. As many as eighty different individual whiskies may make up the blended product which combines the characteristics of each individual whisky through the blender's art.

The skills of the Seagram blender are a critical resource. Seagram's blenders are active throughout the production cycle, especially in sampling and testing the aged whiskies.

International Operations

The company continued to grow internationally after World War II. Early postwar expansion was directed at Mexico and Central and South America. Expansions were typically made in areas where company executives had some personal relationships. By mid-1972, an overseas subsidiary was active in Mexico, Costa Rica, Venezuela, Brazil, Argentina, France, Italy, and Germany. Operating plants of Seagram are now found in twenty-four countries. Seagram's products are sold in over 100 countries through 475 distributors.

The basis of the company's international sales is the "two-way-street" concept. For example, Canadian, American, and Scotch whiskies are shipped to France and Italy; French and Italian products are shipped to Canada, the United States, and Great Britain. This two-way-street premise extends to all countries where Seagram facilities are located. Mr. Samuel Bronfman referred to this policy as "the spine of our business. It brings and holds together our worldwide operation."

In 1965, the Seagram Overseas Sales Company was formed. In each country where production facilities are located, the company maintains a marketing organization to sell locally produced products as well as imported products from other Seagram companies.

The Company in the Seventies

The Seagram Company has enjoyed constant growth throughout its history with sales and assets passing $1 billion (U.S.) in 1968 and $2 billion (U.S.) in 1978. Exhibit 2 presents selected financial highlights of the parent company from the company's 1978 and 1979 Annual Reports.

The common stock of Seagram has traded between $19 and $59 in the 1975–1980 period, as shown in Exhibit 3.

Seagram's brands include Seagram's Seven Crown (the largest selling brand in the United States for over 30 years), V.O., Crown Royal, Chivas Regal, Glenlivet, Barton and Guestier Wines (B & G), G. H. Mumm Champagne, Myers's Rum, Leroux liqueurs, and many others. The United States market had historically represented 75–85 percent of total Seagram sales.

EXHIBIT 2 Financial summary

Fiscal year	1979	1978	1977	1976	1975	1974
Sales and other income	$2,554,096	$2,272,584	$2,184,263	$2,057,426	$1,936,795	$1,846,347
Operating income	277,971	235,383	215,170	189,216	183,164	173,438
Income before foreign exchange fluctuations and extraordinary items	199,622	93,029	85,540	80,523	74,120	81,575
Foreign exchange gains (losses)[a]	(19,322)	(2,465)	1,533	—	—	—
Net income	168,159	90,564	87,073	80,523	74,120	81,575
Net income per share	4.79	2.58	2.48	2.30	2.11	2.33
Dividends	31,883	28,566	28,917	27,970	27,970	27,096
Dividends per share (Canadian currency)	1.07	.906	.848	.80	.80	.775
Working capital provided from operations	220,127	214,184	203,278	183,074	155,481	138,648
Capital expenditures						
Spirits and wine	44,167	43,551[b]	33,034	59,535	77,362	45,287
Oil and gas	138,795	111,973	73,575	83,671	54,546	59,916
Total	182,962	155,524	106,609	143,206	131,908	105,203
At fiscal year-end						
Total assets	2,437,076	2,297,666	2,048,767	2,161,193	1,991,314	1,766,058
Shareholders' equity	1,221,636	1,085,560	1,023,562	965,406	912,853	866,703
Shareholders' equity per share[c]	34.83	30.95	29.18	27.52	26.02	24.71
Inventories	1,047,186	962,628	831,214	841,295	807,098	684,064
Property, plant, and equipment — spirits and wine (net)	376,225	390,565	361,184	361,976	332,118	278,668
Oil and gas properties (net)	463,574	376,446	312,629	298,295	277,228	264,238
Short-term investments	6,683	30,438	33,077	90,651	11,404	8,871
Short-term debt	285,543	190,149	92,657	188,430	277,164	299,424
Long-term indebtedness	421,098	512,064	515,798	595,591	471,900	291,747
Stock price (Canadian currency)	34.25	28.63	22.50	23.38	32.00	32.00

Note: U.S. dollars in thousands, except per share amounts.
[a] Includes related tax effects.
[b] Includes capital assets of $19,431,000 arising from the acquisition of The Glenlivet Distillers Ltd.
[c] The number of shares outstanding during the period had been 35,077,400.

EXHIBIT 3
Selected financial
statistics

Year	Earnings per share[a]	Dividends per share[a]	Dividend pay out	Price range
1975	2.11	.80	38%	37–25
1976	2.30	.82	36	31 5/8–19 3/8
1977	2.48	.88	35	24–19 1/4
1978	2.58	.97	38	29–20 3/8
1979	4.79[b]	1.12	23	42 1/4–27 1/4
1980				59–33

Note: Figures in U.S. currency except dividends.
[a] 35,077,400 shares.
[b] Includes $2.15/share gain on change in British tax laws.
Source: *Moody's Handbook of Common Stocks: Summer 1980.*

The Legacy of "Mr. Sam"

Joseph E. Seagram & Sons, Limited's first president was Charles's father, Samuel Bronfman, who built Seagram into the largest liquor company in the world through the growth and development of his North American operations. As well Mr. Bronfman initiated the first international operations and developed the "two-way-street" philosophy of the firm in the international environment. Mr. Samuel Bronfman also introduced the first campaign to drink moderately in 1934. The first advertisement opened with the line "We who make whisky say: 'Drink Moderately'." Seagram received 150,000 complimentary letters including praise from clergymen. Mr. Samuel Bronfman died in 1971. Brian Murphy called Mr. Bronfman "the man who had done more than anyone else to shape the world whisky business in modern times."[2]

In a supplement to the 1970 Annual Report, "Mr. Sam" commented upon his 60 years of association with the company:

It has been written of me that I have an instinct for dynasty. Be that as it may. I have been privileged to play a forceful part in the development of a great industry, and I have done so with the constant support of family, friends, and often the sons of friends. To me these generations of fond memories and loyal companionship are not the least part of the achievement.[3]

Mr. Bronfman described the early involvement of his sons in the firm:

When my sons Edgar and Charles were in their "teens," they began to spend their weekends and college summers in our LaSalle plant. Under the capable guidance of our production experts, they acquired a great store of knowledge about our Industry in general and our business in particular.

Following production experience, they gained a thorough foundation in administration and later in sales. Edgar, who is the older, at one time moved a desk into my office and

[2] B. Murphy, *The World Book of Whiskey.* Glasgow and London: Collins, 1978.

[3] Samuel Bronfman, *From Little Acorns*, Montreal, 1970, p. 15.

was at my side daily observing, listening, asking questions, and gaining invaluable experience.[4]

Mr. Samuel Bronfman also described the development of Seagram's overseas business:

Scotland

Following Repeal [of Prohibition] in the United States, it was clear to me that if we were to become a truly great international distilling company, we must enter the Scotch whisky business.

With this thought in mind, I travelled to Scotland in 1935, called on my friend James Barclay and, through him, acquired the Robert Brown Company which had been established in 1861. With this company as our base, we began immediately to lay down stocks of select Scotch whiskies for maturing.[5]

France

. . . Our first business connection with France was made by the great Canadian ambassador — Seagram's V.O. Our next connection was made from the United States. There I brought in Oscar Wile to head our Browne Vintners Company. . . . Oscar had been in the importing business in America long before Prohibition and had many friends in the Wine Industry in Europe.

On one of his many visits to France, he became friendly with Réné Lalou, president of G. H. Mumm & Co. My son-in-law, Baron Alain de Gunzburg, who resides in Paris, was also a friend of Mr. Lalou. This tri-partite friendship eventually led to our Company taking a major position in Mumm, which was and is a public company.[6]

Israel

In 1962, Charles was in Israel and became intrigued with the possibilities of developing a new liqueur which would be exclusive to Israel. . . . Using Jaffa oranges as the base, with time-consuming patience, so necessary in creating a new liqueur, Charles and our experts eventually solved the problem. . . . Appropriately, Charles named the new liqueur Sabra, a word to designate native-born Israelis. He went on to work closely with our packaging design people and together they created a most distinctive package which reflects both the ancient and the modern.[7]

Mexico

Several years ago my wife and I spent a holiday in Mexico. We weren't there very long before I was looking into possibilities for our business. I was greatly impressed with the progress Mexico was making toward becoming an industrialized nation and decided that we should build a plant there. . . . We have a very happy relationship with the Saenz family, who have the largest sugar business in the country and an interest in our Company. Aaron Saenz is chairman and Aaron Jr., affectionately known as "Chato," is president and takes a very active interest in our welfare.[8]

[4] Ibid., p. 26.

[5] Ibid., p. 34.

[6] Ibid., p. 38.

[7] Ibid., p. 45.

[8] Ibid., p. 47.

Venezuela

For many years in Venezuela the Curiel Company were our agents and Benjamin Chuma-
ceiro was associated with that firm. One day Benny came to me and explained that he
had two sons and would like to go into business for himself to build an organization
which later his sons would carry on.

I was very much impressed with Benny Chumaceiro and agreed on the spot to join
with him.[9]

Mr. Bronfman had strong ideas about the role of business in society. He noted:
"The horizon of industry, surely, does not terminate at the boundary-line of its
plants; it has a broader horizon, a farther view, and that view embraces the entire
Nation."

Mr. Charles Bronfman discontinued his university studies to work full-time in
the company. After his father's death, Mr. Charles Bronfman succeeded him as
president of the company. Exhibit 4 illustrates today's moderation advertising, one
of many concepts of his father that Charles Bronfman continued.

PRODUCTION

The principal difference between Seagram and its main competition, Hiram Walker,
Inc., was that Seagram aged the whiskies in casks (always of oak) instead of blending
the whiskies first and then aging the blend. Seagram felt that this procedure gave
them much greater control of the variables of the distilling business and thus greater
flexibility, both of which led, it was felt, to a finer product. (The exterior of the
Montreal headquarters building was emblazoned with Seagram's motto of "Integrity,
Craftsmanship, Tradition.")

The distilling process results in large inventory investments and a long inventory
planning cycle. Firms doing any significant maturing of whiskies have a high percentage of assets invested in inventories. Since alcohol evaporates, Seagram allows for
a 3 percent annual loss. The loss is automatically programmed into its production-
planning/inventory-control procedures.

The planning cycle encompasses the ages of fine whiskies. For example, Crown
Royal is a 10-year-old whisky. Joseph E. Seagram & Sons, Limited, has a Crown
Royal production-control system that in 1979 includes the period 1969–1989, as
1969 whiskies are being bottled and 1979 whiskies are being laid down for blending
and bottling in 1989.

The production-cost-control system at Seagram is one of standard direct cost.
The administrative control of Canadian production is based on measures of efficiency
and on a standard direct-cost system. Operations are judged based on manhours of
labor and various measures of costs, quality, and yields.

As Mr. Babich, the executive vice-president for finance and administration, put
it:

[9] Ibid., p. 49.

EXHIBIT 4
Moderation adver-
tising example

There'll never be another Vice President like Richard.

Never.

The President made that promise to himself last Thursday afternoon, after Richard blew an important new-business presentation.

Richard isn't incompetent. The villain is his lunches, or rather the too-many drinks he often has at lunch. Come afternoon, he's just not as sharp as he was in the morning.

Richard is playing dice with his health. His old-fashioned business style is also sabotaging his career. Today, with competition so rough and stakes so high, even the most generous company can't be patient for long with an employee whose effectiveness ends at noon.

If you're a friend, do Richard a favour by reminding him of the good sense of moderation.

You can bet the man eyeing his job won't help him.

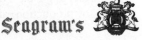
Seagram's

Under the old 1958 system, absorption costing did not permit the accurate evaluation of the individual production elements. To correct this situation, outside consultants and plant operating managers developed a system of standard direct costing. . . .

The system required a six-month's conversion period, and no one understood it. Some standards were wrong, but the system was implemented. After periods of monthly visits to question variances and to review standards, we finally developed a management tool that works.

This conversion process allowed for participation at all production levels in the development of the new cost system.

Initially, the Montreal executives set general objectives of yields and costs. Next, the plant production manager and his staff set detailed standards for the next year, which must be approved by Montreal, during the January–April planning cycle. (The fiscal year ends July 31.) The plant manager's performance is evaluated based on his costs, quality, and yield.

The Canadian production process is almost entirely self-sufficient, as the firm imports only minimal quantities (5 percent of its glass and 8 percent of its corn) from the United States. There are six production centers in Canada:

Location	Number of employees	Function
LaSalle (Quebec)	400	Production, bottling (rum, grain)
Amherstburg (Ontario)	300	Production, bottling (grain)
Waterloo (Ontario)	250	Production, bottling (grain)
Gimli (Manitoba)	160	Production, bottling (grain)
Beaupre (Quebec)	60	Production (grain)
Richibucto (New Brunswick)	60	Production, bottling (rum)

While LaSalle, Beaupre, Waterloo, Gimli, and Richibucto serve primarily Canadian markets, the Amherstburg center serves U.S. markets. The general distribution of cost and production is approximately: materials, 55 percent (grain, 38 percent; bottling, 17 percent); labor, 20–25 percent; overhead and profit, 20–25 percent. The selling price of whisky is illustrated in Exhibit 5.

Finance and Administration

Since New York headquarters established the transfer prices of Canadian production exports to the United States, Canadian administrative attention was focused on (1) meeting New York estimated production requirements, (2) cost control and efficiency of production, and (3) Canadian marketing.

Production efficiency and control were based on standards of yields and efficiencies. Marketing control and evaluation were based on market-share and product-contribution reports, including actual versus planned results. Appendix A presents excerpts from the monthly "Analysis of Operations" submitted to the top executives in Montreal. The financial and accounting reporting system produces market-share

EXHIBIT 5
Sample retail price
(1980), B category
(Ontario)

	Case of 12 bottles	Per bottle
Factory selling price		
F.O.B. plant	$ 23.00	$1.92
Add: federal excise duty based on proof gallons	22.45	1.88
Subtotal	45.45	3.80
Add: 12% federal sales tax	5.45	.45
Subtotal	50.90	4.25
Add: provincial liquor board markup	50.90	4.25
Subtotal	101.80	8.50
Add: provincial tax of 10%	10.20	.85
Retail price	$112.00	$9.35

data one day, cost-control and product-contribution data 5 days, and plant-operations data 11 business days after the end of the month.

Incentive Compensation

Top managers and executives in 1979 were undergoing a change in their evaluation and incentive programs. Where previously bonuses had been based on variance control for production executives and market shares for sales executives, incentives and evaluation began to include specific objectives and special projects. Appendix B describes this new plan.

Marketing

Seagram's marketing organization and strategy are discussed, along with a description of Seagram's products, later in the case. In general, marketing decisions of a strategic nature were made in Montreal and were communicated to regional operating marketing companies.

THE DISTILLING INDUSTRY IN CANADA

Distilled spirits are made in Canada by fourteen distillers operating thirty-seven distilleries. These fourteen private companies sell their product within Canada to the ten provincial and two territorial governments, their sole Canadian customers.

Government regulation and control of the distilling industry include regulations of distilling, aging, labeling, warehousing, and shipping based on the Food and Drug Act and the Excise Act. Further, the provincial and territorial liquor boards retain all right to retail spirits to the public. The provincial and territorial liquor boards choose the brands they will list, display, and sell. With limited shelf space, distillers' salespeople are often asked, "What brand will you delist if we agree to add your new brands?" These boards also grant licences to bars, restaurants, and pubs. Finally, each liquor board regulates advertising and sales activities, ranging from no advertising (New Brunswick, Prince Edward Island, and Saskatchewan) to various allowances for newspaper, magazines, and displays.

The provincial liquor control boards report to various departments as follows: Alberta, Solicitor General; British Columbia, Consumer and Corporate Affairs; Manitoba, Tourism; New Brunswick and Newfoundland, Finance; Northwest Territories, Commissioner's Office; Nova Scotia, Highways; Ontario, Consumer and Commercial Relations; Prince Edward Island, Premier's Office; Quebec, Trade and Commerce; Saskatchewan, Environment; and Yukon, Commissioner's Office.

Monies from the provincial markup on liquor sales for provincial financing, and from federal taxes on spirits for federal financing, are very significant. For example, federal excise taxes and duties on spirits and beer exceeded $500,000,000 annually in the late 1970s.

As shown in the sample retail price figures in Exhibit 5, to the distillers' price of every case of spirits is added the federal excise duty and federal sales tax. The provincial liquor boards then add the freight charges, exchange rate, and differentials in the case of imported products to arrive at their cost. Thus, liquor boards, in effect, double their landed cost by adding provincial markup and on top of this add the provincial sales tax to arrive at the final retail price for each bottle. One government official commented: "What would you rather have us do, tax bread or booze?"

Across Canada in general, about 50 percent of the population do not drink; of the 50 percent that do drink, approximately 30 percent would be classified as light drinkers and 20 percent as heavy drinkers. One interesting result of the range of drinking habits is the difficulty of market research, since respondents' replies on their drinking habits are suspect at best.

One industry spokesman noted that it was unlikely that any of the provincial liquor boards would allow dual distribution (e.g., additional private distribution of alcoholic beverages) because of the tax revenue consequences. All provincial liquor boards across Canada have taken a serious look at the Quebec experience of distributing wine in grocery stores. Although beer had been distributed in the "mom-and-pop" stores for a number of years in Quebec, this policy was recently liberalized to extend to twenty brands of the inexpensive wines, ten of which were the QLB-owned brands and the remaining ten were all bottled in Quebec. These brands were among the least expensive on the QLB's wine list and carried a 20–25 cent premium in the grocery stores compared to the Quebec Liquor Board (QLB) price. The QLB forecasts about $6 million in sales of these inexpensive wines in private outlets. Nonetheless, the private distribution produced $50 million in sales and seriously affected the position of the liquor board's distribution outlet. The Quebec Liquor Board has attempted to draw customers back into their outlets by introducing an advertising campaign. The revenue effects are especially detrimental to the Quebec Liquor Board because consumers have traded down to buy the less expensive wines and avoid going to the QLB outlets. Thus other wines that are distributed only through QLB outlets have suffered. The Quebec Liquor Board's absolute margins on these inexpensive wines are of course much less because they are lower-priced wines, notwithstanding the 100 percent markup. It is not clear what effect if any the QLB advertising strategy will have on reversing this adverse (from the QLB point of view) distribution trend.

AM and FM radio and TV regulations prohibit the advertising of spiritous liquors. They do permit the advertising of beer and wine. Although advertising on broadcasting stations comes under federal jurisdiction, the provinces also exercise authority over the distribution and sale of alcoholic beverages, including their advertising and promotion. This is the reason why in certain provinces it is necessary to obtain clearance through their liquor-control boards or commissions as well as from the Canadian Radio-Television and Telecommunications Commission (CRTC) for beer and wine advertisements. At the present time, Ontario, Quebec, Nova Scotia, Manitoba, and Alberta have this requirement. In Newfoundland, only CRTC clearance is required.

The main criterion in the approval of scripts is adherence to standards of good taste. In a time of quickly changing standards, perception of what is in good taste has become highly individualistic.

Other standards applied by the committee are that advertising should not attempt to influence nondrinkers to drink or be associated with youth or youth symbols. It should not attempt to establish a certain product as a status symbol, a necessity for the enjoyment of life, or an escape from life's problems. Finally, it should not show persons engaged in activity in which the consumption of alcohol is prohibited.

Commenting upon the regulation of advertising by federal and provincial bodies, Mr. Ed Nodwell, executive vice-president and manager of the Montreal office of McConnell advertising, said:

> *Regulations governing the sale and promotion of alcoholic beverages have been with us for a long time and I suppose those of us who work or have worked in that industry have simply adjusted to them to the point where we don't challenge their rationality.*
>
> *In Quebec, a liquor ad running in a newspaper can have a maximum size of 1,200 agate lines and two ads of that size may appear in any newspaper.*
>
> *In Manitoba, the ad size can be 1,250 lines but only one advertisement per company per issue. I wonder what momentous events swing on that 50-line difference between Manitoba and Quebec.*
>
> *That is only one of the old and small irritants we have come to accept. A few years ago British Columbia unilaterally decided that there would be no advertising in B.C. for any tobacco or alcoholic beverage product, creating confusion, cost, and inconvenience among advertisers, agencies, publishers, and everyone else involved in the challenged industries.*

Exhibit 6 presents the Association of Canadian Distillers sales figures based on data supplied by the provincial liquor boards, data which provide an extensive data bank for industry research.

Tastes varied substantially by province, as Exhibit 7 shows.

EXHIBIT 6
Total sales of cases
of twelve 25-oz.
bottles

	1974	1975	1976	1977	1978
Total spirits	*20,326*	*20,799*	*21,710*	*22,270*	*22,845*
Index 1974 = 100	100	102	107	110	112
Canadian whisky	*8,485*	*8,459*	*8,799*	*8,912*	*9,100*
Index 1974 = 100	100	100	104	105	107
Percent of total	41.7	40.7	40.5	40.0	39.8
Domestic rum	*2,805*	*2,842*	*3,014*	*3,091*	*3,267*
Index 1974 = 100	100	101	107	110	116
Percent of total	13.8	13.7	13.9	13.9	14.3
Domestic vodka	*1,847*	*2,040*	*2,189*	*2,358*	*2,518*
Index 1974 = 100	100	110	119	128	136
Percent of total	9.1	9.8	10.1	10.6	11.0
Scotch whisky	*1,424*	*1,466*	*1,535*	*1,575*	*1,554*
Index 1974 = 100	100	103	108	111	109
Percent of total	7.0	7.0	7.1	7.1	6.8
Gin (domestic and imported)	*1,951*	*1,914*	*1,889*	*1,848*	*1,828*
Index 1974 = 100	100	98	97	95	94
Percent of total	9.6	9.2	8.7	8.3	8.0

Note: Data in thousands.

EXHIBIT 7
1978 usage by
volume by spirit
class

Spirit	National percentage	Provincial percentage			
		Low		*High*	
Canadian whisky	39.8%	9.2%	Quebec	61.9%	Saskatchewan
Domestic rum	14.3	12.2	Quebec	47.1	Nova Scotia
Domestic vodka	11.0	4.8	Newfoundland	17.5	Yukon
Scotch	6.8	3.7	Prince Edward Island	9.3	British Columbia
Gin	8.0	3.6	Saskatchewan	32.6	Quebec

SEAGRAM'S PRODUCTS AND MARKETING STRATEGY

Seagram's marketing strategy can perhaps be best summed up by the three words
that appear on the House of Seagram crest: "Integrity, Craftsmanship, Tradition."
The legacy of the late Mr. Bronfman, Mr. Sam as he was affectionately called by
his managers, was quality blended whiskies. This tradition accounts for the bulk
of Seagram's sales due to Five Star, V.O., and Chivas Regal. Mr. Sam's only
admitted mistake was late entry into the vodka market, which grew rapidly without
any significant Seagram entry in the field. Although Seagram has some late entries

in the vodka market, one market manager of a competitor in vodka explained that "They [Seagram] were convinced that light drinks would never become a major factor in the liquor business even when it was changing right before their eyes. They were just complacent and arrogant." Seagram's senior management, however, commented that their interest was in quality and craftsmanship, attributes of blended whisky more than vodka.

Organization

After World War II, Seagram was organized on a regional sales basis. Each regional sales company dealt with a few brands in each province; very little advertising was done and, although all brands were available to each regional sales company, in general the larger brands grew. The sales company carried the little brands because they had no choice. Each regional sales company only dealt with a few or perhaps one province. Fourteen years ago the company was reorganized into a national marketing organization. In this context, there were four national marketing companies within the House of Seagram: Joseph E. Seagram & Sons, Limited; Thomas Adams Distillers Ltd.; Canadian Distillers Ltd.; and International Wines and Spirits. Each manages its own brands, although Seagram now has a centralized staff organization which provides research and planning.

These national companies have regional marketing branches. For example, in 1972–1973, Seagram formed a series of regional marketing companies selling regional brands such as B. C. Special (British Columbia), Lord Selkirk rum and Pickwick gin (Manitoba), Montmorency (Quebec), and Flagship rum, Whitehall gin, and Atlantic whiskies (Nova Scotia).

These regional marketing companies served several important functions, including executive development. Several M.B.A.s were given assignments as directors of these regional companies. In directing the regional companies, their managers gained experience early in their careers in price competition and liquor board relations. The period was almost a "constant price war," as an industry observer noted.

Seagram's Advertising

Advertising is primarily newspaper and magazine advertisements showing the product, along with moderation advertising previously mentioned. That Seagram's promotional strategy revolves almost exclusively around the use of print within paid media is due in part to the provincial and federal restrictions on liquor advertising in broadcast media. The Broadcasting Act and various provincial trade legislations have impinged upon the appearance of liquor advertising in broadcast media. British Columbia's former NDP (New Democratic Party) government enacted an outright prohibition of all liquor and tobacco advertising. One prairie province has also restricted liquor life-style ads, defining life-style advertising as any ad with people in it. To contend with this patchwork of overlapping piecemeal regulation across Canada, Seagram has restricted itself principally to print media and has largely restricted its creative strategies to "bottle and glass." In this manner, separate advertisements do not have to be prepared to correspond to each individual provincial regulation: instead, the ad conforms to the strictest of any province's regulations.

Pricing

Following its "craftsmanship" strategy, Seagram has concentrated on the higher-price market segments. In absolute dollars, Crown Royal and V.O. were and are the most profitable brands. During the early 1970s, however, price competition became stronger within the industry. Canadian whisky, which was classified by price categories ("A" being the highest), saw a shift to the lower-price categories.

The Canadian market had an average growth rate of approximately 10 percent per year during the 1970–1973 period. As one industry observer noted: "This was perceived by the smaller distillers as offering an opportunity for growth. The small distillers introduced new products below existing floor pricing, most notably in the 'F' category."

Seagram believed the profit margin in the F category was insufficient, and they did not enter this category until the mid-seventies. Some of the entries have been repositioned from the E category and some are new entries. Two "fading" brands, Four Roses and (more recently) Lord Calvert, were repositioned in the F category. Neither brand bears the Seagram's name, because of a cannibalization risk against Seagram's best-selling brand Five Star in the E category.

Seagram aggressively markets V.O. and Crown Royal and these brands contribute the most significant amount of gross margin dollars. Captain Morgan has been a successful brand in all three of the rum categories (white, light, and dark), although Bacardi's lead in the former two categories is substantial. Certainly, Mr. Bronfman's marketing decision must encompass pricing, including tactics appropriate for the leader in an increasingly price-competitive industry.

Brand Proliferation

Recently the Seagram's management listed all of their brands ranked from top to bottom in terms of gross contribution. Upon reviewing the brands on the second of two pages of this memo, management inquired whether or not these "page two brands" were in fact providing any net contribution. At that time, Seagram marketed over eighty-two different brands of distilled products across Canada. The answer given was that not all of these brands provided a profitable net margin to Seagram. Some of these unprofitable brands were carryovers from previous organizational structures. Some brands were marketed exclusively in one province. There were other brands marketed in only a few provinces.

In addition to pricing plans, then, Mr. Bronfman had brand management decisions to make. Fortunately, the industry had a wealth of market data.

Market Data

Appendix C presents Canadian whisky market share data by manufacturer. Category rank indicates which price category (A = highest, F = lowest price) the brand is in and what rank it is within that category. Thus, Hiram Walker's Canadian Club is the largest seller overall and is first in the B category. Similarly, Seagram's V.O. is fourth overall in Canada whisky and second within the B price category. At one time Seagram's boasted Canada's largest-selling Canadian whisky, Five Star; however, as this product category (E) has declined, Five Star has declined with it. Recently Five Star's sales have leveled off and share has increased in the face of a declining category. This decline is due to an increase in both volume and share of the F (lower than Five Star) price category. The top four Canadian whiskies consist of two Hiram Walker brands (Canadian Club and Walker's Special Old) and two Seagram's brands (Five Star and V.O.). These are number 1 and 2 brands in the two largest categories. The more rapidly growing category is F, the low-priced whiskies introduced in 1971 in the western provinces. Ontario, Canada's largest Canadian-whisky-drinking province, has a price floor and the F category whiskies fall below this. Their success has come largely in the West where ''age claims'' predominate the promotional strategies. For example, Carrington advertises a 5-year-old whisky at a 3-year-old price. Because of their lower price, the margin contribution in the F category is significantly lower. The C category whiskies are an odd in-between. In category D, the 5- to 6-year-old age whiskies (Seagram's 83 and Gilbey's Black Velvet) predominate. Crown Royal stands alone on top of the A category, 10-year-old aged whiskies.

Appendix C also includes an analysis of all Seagram's products (listed first) and also the most popular brands, regardless of manufacturer, in each of the price categories A through F. The brands' position within that category as of 1980 is indicated to the left of the brand name.

Appendix C also presents data on scotch, vodka, gin, and rum sales in cases. Again, all of Seagram's and also the most popular brands regardless of manufacturer are shown, with category ranking indicated to the left of the brand name. Distillers' Johnnie Walker Red is Canada's leading selling scotch, followed by Walker Gooderham's Ballantines. Hobb's Cutty Sark ranks fourth, following Gilbey's J & B. Seagram's Chivas Regal has a 3.5 percent market share on a case basis, but due to its price accounts for a larger market share on a dollar basis. Smirnoff brand vodka accounts for almost half the vodka sales in Canada. Gordon's (distributed by Seagram) is Canada's largest-selling domestic gin, followed by Gilbey's, while Meaghers' imported Beefeater is the single best-selling Canadian brand. The sale of each of these brands varies considerably on a province-by-province basis.

The casewriter prepared the enclosed graphic analyses of Seagram and Walker products. These analyses are based upon product portfolio management concepts, which are described in Appendix D.

The first analysis, Exhibit 8, shows total industry growth rates and market share based on 1977–1980 data. Thus, the highest-growth product was vodka — with a 36 percent growth — while the highest-growth product in terms of market share was Canadian whisky — 40 percent. Exhibit 9 covers the B category of higher-priced Canadian whisky. Exhibit 10 shows the lower-priced E whisky; and Exhibit 11, gin.

Other product portfolio observations of the casewriter follow:

Category A: Seagram's star, Crown Royal, enjoys 65 percent of the market and has a 16 percent growth in a category that is growing at 5 percent.

Category D: Walker Imperial, with 11 percent market share in category D, was repositioned down from category C. Some of its share may have been at the expense of Walker Gold Crest, which dropped from almost 300,000 cases to 40,000

EXHIBIT 8 Canadian total spirits (by volume)

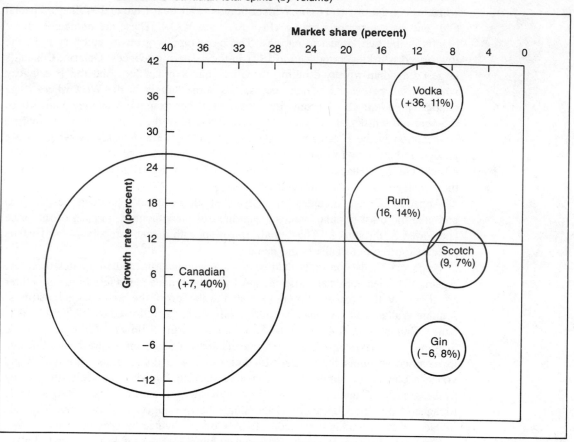

Circle radius scale: 1 cm = 1 million cases, 1980 volume.

cases following Imperial's introduction. At the same time, Gilbey took Black Velvet (300,000 cases in 1977) up to category B (150,000 cases in 1980).

Category F: Seagram's F category products ranged from a 1977–1980 growth of 870 percent (Lord Calvert) to 0 percent growth (Three Star) while Walker went from 480 percent (G & W) to 42 percent (58).

Scotch: Walker's Ballantine grew at 3 percent to an 11 percent market share versus Chivas Regal's minus-14 percent growth with 3 percent market share.

Vodka: Seagram discontinued several brands, but no brand challenged Smirnoff.

Rum: Seagram's several brands had insignificant market share, except Morgan's 12 percent (versus 42 percent for Bacardi). Morgan's growth was 16 percent versus Bacardi's 6 percent.

EXHIBIT 9
Category "B" Canadian (by volume)

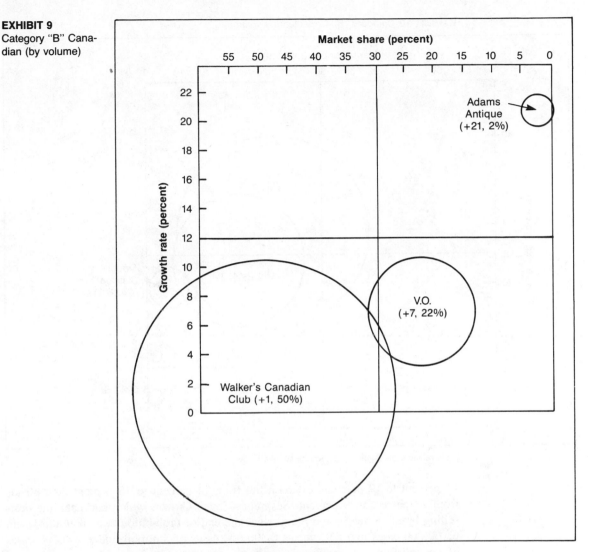

Circle radius scale: 1 cm = 100,000 cases, 1980 volume.

Exhibit 12 presents data on the performance of selected Canadian distillers.

The American Market and Long-Term Trends

As Mr. Bronfman turned to the Canadian marketing plan, he kept in mind certain facts about trends in the United States:

1. While Canadian whisky had increased from 9 percent to 12 percent of total spirits consumed in the past decade in the United States, vodka had grown from

EXHIBIT 10 Category "E" Canadian (by volume)

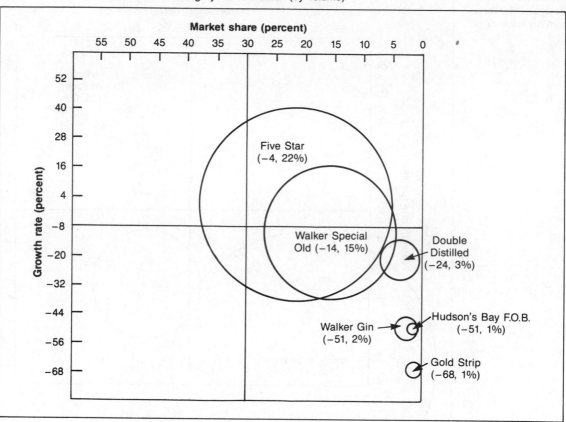

Circle radius scale: 1 cm = 100,000 cases, 1980 volume.

11 percent to 19 percent. Bourbon fell from 24 percent to 15 percent, and blends from 21 percent to 9 percent. Seagram's Seven Crown, which had been the best-selling brand in the United States since the end of Prohibition, was now third with 6,100,000 cases in 1979, versus 6,300,000 cases of Smirnoff and 7,200,000 cases of Bacardi Rum.

2. Americans could no longer be categorized as single-product (bourbon, gin, or scotch) drinkers, as the past decade saw the spread of exotic drinks, cordials, and wines.

3. While the adult population was increasing and drinking ages were being lowered, consumption increased at an annual rate of less than 2 percent in the American market.

Mr. Bronfman knew it was important to consider the possibility of similar trends in Canadian consumption, as he reached decisions on product pricing, promotion, and brand management.

EXHIBIT 11
Gin (by volume)

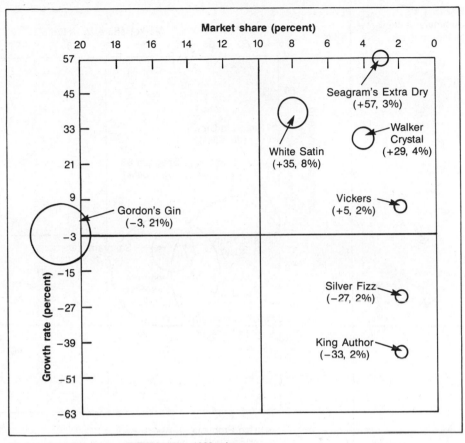

Market share (percent)

Growth rate (percent)

Seagram's Extra Dry
(+57, 3%)

Walker
Crystal
(+29, 4%)

White Satin
(+35, 8%)

Gordon's Gin
(−3, 21%)

Vickers
(+5, 2%)

Silver Fizz
(−27, 2%)

King Author
(−33, 2%)

Circle radius scale: 1 cm = 100,000 cases, 1980 volume.

EXHIBIT 12
Summary of selected products

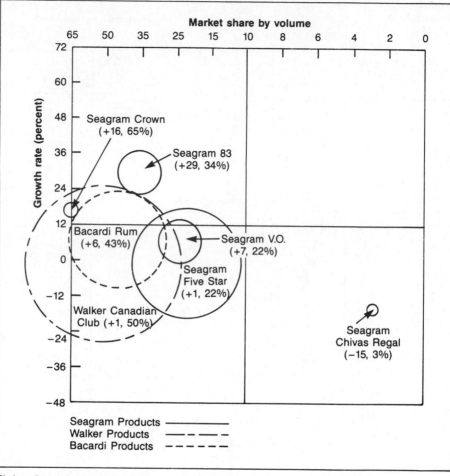

Circle radius scale: 1 cm = 200,000 cases, 1980 volume.
Seagram Products ————
Walker Products —·—·—
Bacardi Products — — —

Brand	1980 volume (thousands of cases)	1977–1980 growth rate	Category market share
Walker's Canadian Club	1,098	1%	50
Smirnoff (Gilbey)	993	−12	37
Bacardi (FBM)	903	6	43
Seagram Five Star	818	−4	22
Seagram V.O.	492	7	22
Seagram 83	374	29	34
Seagram Crown Royal	107	16	65
Seagram Chivas Regal	48	−15	3

APPENDIX A: EXCERPTED ANALYSIS OF OPERATIONS (CONFIDENTIAL AMOUNTS OMITTED)

INTEREST — LONG-TERM

The latest outlook of XXX is XXX worse than the original plan because the devaluation of the Canadian dollar has added to the Eurobond interest cost which is payable in U.S. currency.

FOREIGN EXCHANGE GAIN

The latest outlook of XXX is XXX better than originally forecasted due to the devaluation of the Canadian dollar. The original plan was based on an exchange rate of XXX while the rate used for the outlook is XXX.

DOMESTIC MARKETING CONTRIBUTION

Net contribution is now expected to reach XXX or XXX below original plan.

A shortfall in volume and higher planned advertising and research expenditures are expected to be largely offset by some XXX extra due to the April 1 price increases:

Due to volume (down XXX c/s)	XXX
Due to price increase	XXX
Change in imputed cost of wines	XXX
Increase in brand advertising	XXX
Increase in other expenses	XXX
	XXX

U.S.A. MARKETING CONTRIBUTION

Changes in volume account for improved contribution for both the 7 months actual and the latest outlook for the year.

EXPORT MARKETING CONTRIBUTION

Contribution is better than plan after 7 months due to a prior-year adjustment of marketing expenses. This adjustment also accounts for the variance between the original plan and latest.

SHIPMENT VOLUME ANALYSIS

Seagram

Total shipments are expected to be XXX cases below original plan for the year. To the end of February, shipments are XXX cases below plan which would indicate volumes would firm up during the past 5 months.

V.O. shipments are projected to be XXX cases below plan at XXX cases, compared to XXX cases last year. After the first 7 months, shipments are XXX cases under plan, with shortfalls of XXX cases in Ontario, XXX in Quebec, XXX in B.C., and XXX in Alberta.

Five Star is expected to be XXX cases below plan at XXX cases, compared to XXX last year. For the 7-month period, actual shipments are XXX below plan with shortfalls of XXX cases in Ontario, XXX in B.C., XXX in Saskatchewan, and XXX in Manitoba.

U.S.A. Market

Total shipments to date are XXX cases above plan and are expected to be XXX cases above plan for the year. This expected improvement is primarily due to higher inventories in Detroit and Champlain. The latest outlook for year-end inventory levels at these warehouses is XXX cases higher than originally forecasted, of which XXX cases are V.O. and XXX are Crown Royal. To the end of February, actual shipments of V.O. are XXX cases above plan and in the latest outlook V.O. is XXX cases above. Crown Royal shipments are XXX cases higher than plan to date and are expected to be XXX cases higher by year-end.

ADMINISTRATION

Total year expenditures are now projected at XXX, XXX higher than original forecast. After the first 7 months, administration is XXX over forecast.

PRODUCTION OVERHEAD

The latest projection for the year is XXX, 2 percent lower than original forecast.

While labor and expense variances are XXX better than the original plan to date, they are expected to be only XXX better by year-end, principally due to the effect of the new contracts.

Unfavorable grain purchase price variances originally forecast as nil, are XXX to date and the latest outlook for the year projects this to grow to XXX. Other purchase price variances originally forecasted at nil are now expected to be XXX for bottling materials, XXX for molasses, and XXX for fuel and electricity.

APPENDIX B: CORPORATE INCENTIVE BONUS PLAN B

This plan is based on the attainment of approved goals and objectives. It is applicable to designated executives and managers in administration, marketing, and production divisions.

In each fiscal year, the president will allocate an amount of money that can be used in each division for distribution to eligible participants.

A. ESTABLISHING GOALS

1. It is the responsibility of each participant to set goals for each fiscal year and to have these accepted by his or her manager.
2. One or two goals related to each major job responsibility should be formulated and reviewed with the manager.

A list of the agreed goals will be established in writing.

B. DEFINING GOALS

1. Goals are the end results to be achieved within a stated period of time, usually one year.
2. Goals should be stated in terms of the results to be accomplished — not as activities or tasks of the individual.
3. Goals must be expressed precisely in measurable terms, not as generalized statements about improvements.

C. TYPES OF GOALS

Each goal shall be categorized in one of the following types:

1. *Normal Activity Goals*: These pertain to the regular requirements and responsibilities of the individual's job. They should involve improvement of existing performance levels and/or maintenance of established standards.
2. *Extraordinary Activity Goals*: These are goals of an innovative nature over and beyond the usual responsibilities. They involve some original, new, or different way to produce desirable results.
3. *Long-Term Project Goals*: These involve projects that have potential for improving corporate profitability or position but which may not be completed within the current year.

To have a balanced set of objectives, each participant's goals should include some of each type.

D. REVIEWING PROGRESS

1. At four-month intervals, the subordinate and his or her manager will discuss progress toward achievement of each goal and revise goals that are found to be unrealistic.
2. At the end of the year, the subordinate will prepare a written statement of his or her achievement.
3. The subordinate and his or her manager will discuss this statement, their objectives being (1) to agree, as completely as possible, on what has and has not been accomplished; (2) to determine causes for any lack of achievement; and (3) to make plans, as needed, for improved future performance.
4. The subordinate will prepare a written summary of the agreement and conclusions reached in (3).

E. EVALUATION OF ACCOMPLISHMENT

The extent of achievement will be determined as follows:

1. *Determine general performance level*
   For each goal, select which of the five column headings best describes the employee's accomplishment, that is, "Major Goal OverAchievement," "Definitely Exceeded Goal," "Substantially Achieved Goal," and so on.

Major goal overachievement	Definitely exceeded goal	Substantially achieved goal	Definite goal shortfall	Major goal shortfall
80–100 points	60–80 points	40–60 points	20–40 points	0–20 points

TABLE 1 Top brands of Canadian whisky, total — all categories, 1977–1980

Brand (distiller)	1978–1980 category rank	1977		1978		1979		1980	
		Sales volume (index)[a]	Category market share	Sales volume (index)[a]	Category market share	Sales volume (index)[a]	Category market share	Sales volume (index)[a]	Category market share
Canadian Club (Walker)	B_1	1,084,403 (100)	55.3%	1,053,451 (97)	53.4%	1,095,569 (101)	53.9%	1,097,686 (101)	49.9%
Five Star (Seagram)	E_1	849,106 (100)	21.1	846,912 (100)	22.3	830,286 (98)	22.8	817,692 (96)	22.1
Walker Spec. Old (Walker)	E_2	653,463 (100)	16.3	571,444 (87)	15.1	556,535 (85)	15.3	563,034 (86)	15.2
Seagrams V.O. (Seagram)	B_2	457,638 (100)	23.3	503,529 (110)	25.5	489,634 (107)	24.1	491,933 (107)	22.3
Silk Tassel (McGuinness)	E_3	341,976 (100)	8.5	356,441 (104)	9.4	358,814 (105)	9.9	385,122 (113)	10.4
Gilbey Black Velvet (Gilbey)	D_1/B_4	332,449 (100)	26.2	325,584 (98)	25.1	15,309 (5)	.8	149,400 (45)	6.8
Seagrams 83 (Seagram)	D_2/D_1	291,237 (100)	23.0	318,019 (109)	24.6	337,321 (116)	26.0	374,313 (129)	33.8
Royal Reserve (Corby)	E_4	266,448 (100)	6.6	264,089 (99)	7.0	269,929 (101)	7.4	294,936 (111)	8.0
Schenley Gold Wedding (Schenley)	D_4/E_5	103,373 (100)	8.1	107,405 (104)	8.3	183,541 (178)	5.0	243,517 (236)	6.6
Alberta Premium (Alberta)	E_6	196,206 (100)	4.9	201,119 (103)	5.3	200,042 (102)	5.5	222,892 (114)	6.0
Alberta Windsor DeLuxe (Alberta)	F_1	127,660 (100)	10.2	164,356 (129)	10.5	185,801 (146)	11.1	213,404 (167)	12.1
Gilbey Triple Crown (Gilbey)	E_6/E_7	270,263 (100)	6.7	248,005 (92)	6.5	221,853 (82)	6.1	209,830 (78)	5.7

Note: Figures are for 25-oz. cases.
[a] Index 1977 = 100.

TABLE 2 Canadian whisky

Brand (distiller)	1977 Sales volume	1977 Market share	1978 Sales volume	1978 Market share	1979 Sales volume	1979 Market share	1980 Sales volume	1980 Market share
"A"								
1 Crown Royal (Seagram)	92,215	58.4%	102,717	61.9%	106,153	62.4%	106,892	64.7%
2 Alberta Springs (Alberta)	12,420	7.8	15,145	9.1	16,488	9.7	16,352	9.9
3 Captains Table (McGuinness)	11,648	7.4	11,631	7.0	12,034	7.1	11,262	6.8
4 Very Special Package (Corby)	9,179	5.8	8,075	4.9	8,709	5.1	9,232	5.59
5 Carleton Tower (Walker)	11,628	7.4	11,055	6.7	9,767	5.7	7,234	4.4
Total "A"	157,865	1.8	165,840	1.8	170,048	1.9	165,289	1.8
Total index, 1977 = 100	100		105		108		105	
"B"								
2 Seagram V.O. (Seagram)	457,638	23.3	503,529	25.5	489,634	24.1	491,933	22.3
7 Adams Antique (Seagram)	42,572	2.2	46,316	2.4	48,874	2.4	51,457	2.3
1 Canadian Club (Walker)	1,084,403	55.3	1,053,451	53.4	1,095,569	53.9	1,097,686	49.9
3 Wiser's DeLuxe (Corby)	138,780	7.1	152,015	7.7	174,463	8.6	205,202	9.3
4 Black Velvet (Gilbey), see "D"					15,309	.9	149,400	6.8
Total "B"	1,960,431	22.0	1,971,920	21.7	2,032,466	22.4	2,202,079	24.0
Total index, 1977 = 100	100		101		104		112	
"C"								
1 Schenley O. F. C. (Schenley)	42,497	16.6	130,200	42.6	136,591	51.0	149,918	60.3
2 Walker Imperial (Walker), see "D"	92,737	36.3	84,152	27.6	43,328	16.1	2	0.0
Total "C"	255,327	2.9	305,491	3.4	269,549	3.0	248,512	2.7
Total index, 1977 = 100	100		120		106		97	
"D"								
1 Seagram 83 (Seagram)	291,237	23.0	318,019	24.6	337,312	26.0	374,313	33.8
2 Adams Private Stock (Seagram)	160,504	12.7	164,158	12.7	173,852	13.4	176,947	16.0
14 H. Bay Fine Old (Seagram)	18,213	1.4	18,445	1.4	17,584	1.3	15,246	1.4
15 Canada House (Seagram)	17,403	1.4	15,642	1.2	14,697	1.1	11,892	1.1
1 Black Velvet (Gilbey)	332,449	26.2	325,584	25.1				
3 Walker Imperial (Walker)					43,824	3.3	128,164	11.6
4 McGuinness Gold Tassel (McGuinness)	88,852	7.0	94,155	7.3	93,988	7.3	94,541	8.5
6 Walker Gold Crest (Walker)	50,979	4.0	42,556	3.3	285,383	22.0	42,151	3.8
Total "D"	1,267,916	14.2	1,294,270	14.2	1,295,792	14.3	1,109,134	12.1
Total index, 1977 = 100	100		102		102		87	

Note: Figures are for 25-oz. cases.
[a] Index 1977 = 100.

TABLE 2 (continued)

Brand (distiller)	1977 Sales volume	1977 Market share	1978 Sales volume	1978 Market share	1979 Sales volume	1979 Market share	1980 Sales volume	1980 Market share
"E"								
1 Five Star (Seagram)	849,106	21.1%	846,912	22.3%	830,286	22.8%	817,692	22.1%
11 Double Distilled (Seagram)	128,538	3.2	113,175	3.0	108,480	3.0	98,130	2.7
14 Gold Stripe (Seagram)	125,679	3.1	91,991	2.4	56,422	1.6	40,904	1.1
18 H. Bay F. O. B. (Seagram)	51,284	1.3	43,630	1.2	32,760	.9	25,359	.7
2 Walker Spec. Old (Walker)	653,463	16.3	571,444	15.1	556,535	15.3	563,034	15.3
3 McGuinness Silk Tassel (McGuinness)	341,976	8.5	356,441	9.4	358,814	9.9	385,122	10.4
4 Corby Royal Reserve (Corby)	266,448	6.6	264,089	7.0	269,929	7.4	294,936	8.0
12 G & W Bonded Stock (Walker)	154,263	3.8	113,770	3.0	88,740	2.4	75,186	2.0
Total "E"	4,018,264	45.1	3,794,313	41.7	3,639,196	40.1	3,693,506	40.2
Total index	100		94		91		92	
"F"								
6 H. Bay Special (Seagram)	44,384	3.5	63,636	4.4	78,724	4.7	89,638	5.1
7 Four Roses (Seagram)	30,296	2.4	62,793	4.0	73,605	4.4	84,304	4.8
20 Three Star (Seagram)	26,384	2.1	25,313	1.7	20,535	1.2	26,253	1.5
17 Lord Calvert (Seagram)	3,669	.3	21,110	1.3	28,132	1.7	35,583	2.0
36 Atlantic Special (Seagram)	6,279	.5	5,804	.4				
42 Homestead (Seagram)	4,912	.4	1,825	.1				
1 Alberta Windsor DeLuxe (Alberta)	127,660	10.2	164,356	10.5	185,801	11.1	213,404	12.1
2 Carrington Can. Spirit (Alberta)	140,851	11.3	155,486	10.0	160,080	9.6	169,059	9.6
3 G & W Bonded Stock (Walker)	27,780	2.2	73,401	4.7	109,455	6.5	160,268	9.1
4 Silver Tassel (McGuinness)	42,065	3.4	87,756	5.6	117,935	7.0	137,078	7.4
15 Walker's 58 (Walker)	35,228	2.8	31,362	2.0	46,564	2.8	49,885	2.8
Total "F"	1,252,113	14.0	1,568,695	17.2	1,676,893	18.5	1,768,882	19.3
Total Canadian whisky	8,911,915		9,100,528		9,083,934		9,187,402	
Total index	100		125		134		141	
Total whisky index	100		102		102		103	

Note: Figures are for 25-oz. cases.
[a] Index 1977 = 100.
Source: Association of Canadian Distillers, *Consolidated Brand Report* (Ottawa: 1978, 1980).

TABLE 3 Top brands — total all categories

Brand (distiller)	1977		1978		1979		1980	
	Sales volume	Market share	Sales volume	Market share	Sales volume	Market share	Sales volume	Market share
Scotch whisky (25-oz. cases)								
10 Chivas Regal (Seagram)	55,603	3.5%	58,427	3.8%	54,969	3.6%	47,923	3.2%
12 St. Leger (Seagram)							39,409	2.6
15 Queen Anne (Seagram)							30,128	2.0
100 Pipers (Seagram)	16,859	1.1	11,872	.8				
Black Watch (Seagram)	4,262	.3	5,857	.4				
20 Hudson's Bay Best Procurable (Seagram)	5,526	.4	5,572	.4			18,684	1.2
Passport (Seagram)	4,313	.3	3,641	.2	11,865	.8		
1 J. Walker Red (Distillers)	215,612	13.7	222,456	14.3	202,484	13.4	210,229	13.8
2 Ballantines (Walker)	155,264	9.9	158,707	10.2	157,968	10.5	159,746	10.5
3 J & B (Gilbey)	99,121	6.3	99,476	6.4	101,649	6.7	105,295	6.9
4 Cutty Sark (Hobbs)	112,810	7.2	106,400	6.8	93,254	6.2	84,167	5.5
Total	1,575,487		1,554,432		1,511,350		1,519,197	
Total index, 1977 = 100	100		99		96		96	
Vodka (25-oz. cases)								
13 Bolshoi (Seagram)	60,085	2.6%	54,529	2.2%	49,564	1.9%	41,803	1.6%
16 Prince Igor (Seagram)	47,504	2.0	40,260	1.6	37,586	1.5	38,778	1.4
18 Hudson's Bay (Seagram)	10,655	.5	23,246	.9	22,374	.9	28,517	1.1
Gordon's (Seagram)	19,846	.8	20,322	.8				
Nikolai (Seagram)	20,665	.9	17,462	.8				
Natasha (Seagram)	6,636	.3	6,969	.3				
Moichev (Seagram)	6,149	.3	6,527	.3				
Kolomyka (Seagram)	1,205	.1	4,073	.2				
1 Smirnoff (Gilbey)	1,125,235	47.7	1,131,132	44.9	1,008,055	39.5	993,277	36.7
2 Alberta (Alberta)	158,782	6.7	170,986	6.8	185,501	7.3	198,259	7.3
3 McGuinness Red Tassel (McGuinness)	138,443	5.9	171,968	6.8	150,836	5.9	165,485	6.1
10 Crystal (Walker)	26,758	1.1	27,742	1.1	42,427	1.7	50,397	1.9
11 G & W Skol (Walker)	33,593	1.4	30,717	1.2	41,911	1.7	50,152	1.9
Total vodka domestic	2,358,331		2,517,584		2,552,013		2,705,281	
Total index 1977 = 100	100		107		108		115	

TABLE 3 (continued)

Brand (distiller)	1977 Sales volume	1977 Market share	1978 Sales volume	1978 Market share	1979 Sales volume	1979 Market share	1980 Sales volume	1980 Market share
Dry gin (25-oz. cases)								
1 Gordon's (Seagram)	250,044	20.4%	251,313	20.5%	247,276	20.9%	243,510	20.5%
4 White Satin (Seagram)	69,970	5.7	71,414	5.8	84,143	7.1	94,272	7.9
10 Seagram Ex. Dry (Seagram)	20,339	1.7	27,572	2.2	30,989	2.6	31,840	2.7
12 King Arthur (Seagram)	41,601	3.4	38,921	3.2	29,588	2.5	27,920	2.4
15 Silver Fizz (Seagram)	29,315	2.4	24,470	2.0	24,141	2.0	21,561	1.8
16 Vickers (Seagram)	17,593	1.4	21,407	1.7	16,595	1.4	18,392	1.6
23 Hudson's Bay London Dry (Seagram)	12,961	1.1	11,910	1.0				
2 Gilbey's (Gilbey)	234,213	19.1	221,034	18.0	204,869	17.3	182,066	15.3
3 Schenley London Dry (Schenley)	62,295	5.1	77,397	6.3	83,450	7.0	98,713	8.3
7 Walker's Crystal (Walker)	33,337	2.7	29,210	2.4	36,918	3.1	42,910	3.6
Total domestic dry gin	1,223,907		1,228,093		1,184,751		1,189,301	
Index	100		100		97		97	
White rum (25-oz. cases)								
2 Captain Morgan (Seagram)	218,846	11.4%	230,456	11.4%	243,529	12.1%	255,012	11.9%
7 Myers's White (Seagram)	22,063	1.2	23,769	1.2	46,329	2.3	52,735	2.5
9 Wood's White Sail (Seagram)	56,065	2.9	54,304	2.7	49,861	2.5	49,726	2.3
21 Tropicana (Seagram)	13,452	.7	12,610	.6				
15 Hudson's Bay (Seagram)	8,103	.4	10,697	.5	16,622	.8	18,364	.9
26 Atlantic Flagship (Seagram)	6,621	.3	8,422	.4				
34 Whistler (Seagram)	848		2,715	.1				
40 Trelawny (Seagram)	678		1,748	.1				
1 Bacardi Carta Blanca (FBM)	851,823	44.3	889,322	44.1	872,689	43.2	902,732	42.5
3 Ron Carioca (Schenley)	143,128	7.4	147,125	7.3	141,015	7.0	165,738	7.8
11 Maraca Deluxe (Walker)	49,409	2.6	46,784	2.3	43,077	2.1	40,803	1.9
12 Gov'ment House (Walker)	10,926	.6	20,214	1.0	30,244	1.5	38,336	1.8
Total white, domestic	1,924,082		2,016,616		2,018,272		2,135,608	
Total index	100		105		105		111	

TABLE 3 (continued)

TABLE 3 (continued)

Brand (distiller)	1977 Sales volume	1977 Market share	1978 Sales volume	1978 Market share	1979 Sales volume	1979 Market share	1980 Sales volume	1980 Market share
Light rum (25-oz. cases)								
4 Captain Morgan Gold (Seagram)	52,244	8.4%	51,796	7.9%	50,744	7.6%	51,694	7.6%
1 Bacardi Carta de Oro (FBM)	180,164	29.0	185,437	28.3	185,740	27.9	193,048	28.5
2 Lamb's Palm Breeze (Corby)	119,669	19.3	118,326	18.1	116,648	17.5	113,178	16.7
3 Gov. Gen. Light (Gilbey)	101,030	16.3	96,073	14.7	88,825	13.3	78,235	11.6
Total light, domestic	620,517		654,269		666,251		676,388	
Total index	100		106		106		111	
Dark rum (25-oz. cases)								
2 Captain Morgan Black (Seagram)	139,666	25.5	139,151	23.3	136,031	22.6	137,331	22.1
4 Wood's Old Navy (Seagram)	28,774	5.3	34,089	5.7	34,311	5.7	37,295	6.0
1 Lamb's Old Navy (Corby)	160,562	29.4	142,545	23.9	147,276	24.5	149,924	24.2
3 Screech (NLC)	10,318	1.9	51,840	8.7	50,084	8.3	51,739	8.3
Total dark, domestic	545,989		596,475		601,638		620,455	
Total domestic rum	3,090,588		3,267,361		3,286,161		3,432,451	
Total index	100		106		106		111	

Note: Summing the volume for brands identified and their respective market shares will not equal industry volume. To illustrate, the total scotch whisky figure, 1,575,487, is for all total sales in the industry by all brands of scotch whisky, not just the nine brands identified. Also, the market share percentages are for the identified brands only, which represent only their respective part of the total market.
Source: Association of Canadian Distillers, *Consolidated Brand Report* (Ottawa: 1978, 1980).

Product portfolio management as developed by the Boston Consulting Group emphasizes the assumed relationship between market share and per unit profitability. As market share increases, and as the total industry growth increases, the experience curve effect on production costs makes market share in a growth industry attractive through its relative profits. Product portfolio managers, then, should analyze products by means of a product-growth–market-share matrix, using a circle of proportional size for each single product's sales. As growth slows or market share declines, proceeds from declining products should be invested in ones with increasing market shares or relative growth, unless reinvestment in slow growth and declining share is the only alternative. Underlying the movement of products over the matrix are the industry's and company's decisions and the product life cycle itself.

The growth–market-share matrix is summarized in Figure 1.

The best portfolio strategy is utilizing funds from cash cows to make star products from question marks.

After a product portfolio analysis is completed for the firm and its competitor, the marketing strategist then assesses one's own position versus the industry in general and competitors in particular, funds balance and the distribution of products, and the movement or trend of products over a period of several years.

FIGURE 1
Growth–market-share matrix

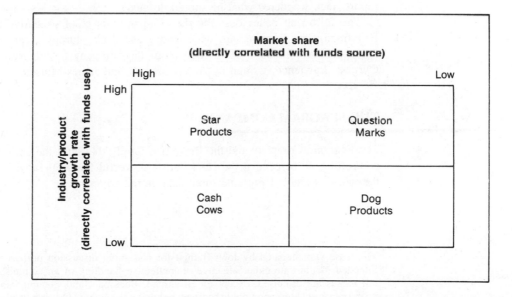

CASE 32

THE SEAGRAM COMPANY LTD.

In the fall of 1983 Jack Murphy wondered what personal strategy he should pursue regarding his future with the Seagram Company, the world's largest wine and spirits company. Jack's current position was manager in the new products department at corporate headquarters in New York, but he had spent several years in marketing management of Seagram's wine products. His wine experience at Seagram had been exciting, as the 4 years included a major strategic study under Mary Cunningham and a major acquisition of Coca-Cola's Wine Spectrum by Seagram. Jack saw opportunities within Seagram's wine expansion program and within Seagram's corporate staff as a strategic planner.

It had been 10 weeks since he had completed and distributed a strategic planning report. Jack wondered what he should do next.

The following pages describe the company, its chief executive officer (Edgar Bronfman), the Cunningham wine study, and Jack Murphy's career at Seagram. An appendix contains a 1984 analysis of the company by the New York firm of Cyrus J. Lawrence, written by Anton Brenner and James Murren.

THE SEAGRAM COMPANY

The Seagram Company and the Bronfman family that built the company (currently controlling 40 percent of the stock) are a powerful financial force in America and the world. Exhibit 1 presents some data on the company.

EXHIBIT 1
Company finances

	1983	1982	1981	1975
Spirit and wine revenues	$2,647.6	$2,826.2	$2,772.7	$1,818.1
Income after taxes				
Spirits and wine	231.0	291.3	273.6	141.2
Dividend and investment				
income	117.1	110.3	180.2	—
Equity in Du Pont unremitted				
earnings	96.9	75.8	—	—
U.S. oil and gas			6.8	38.5
Total after-tax income	333.4	297.4	285.6	82.6
Total assets	5,304.7	5,041.0	5,833.6	2,023.0
Income per share	3.53	2.95	2.86	.79
Year-end stock price	35.00	15.46	17.54	10.25

Note: In thousands of dollars except per share data.

Seagram's strategy has emphasized the marketing of quality premium brands. Five brands — Chivas Regal, Crown Royal, 7 Crown, V.O., and Seagram's Gin — account for about 50 percent of its profits. It is active in the rum segment (Myers's) and in both the imported wine (Mumm, B&G) and domestic wine (Paul Masson, Gold Seal) markets.

The American market accounts for about 70 percent of Seagram's sales. Exhibit 2 shows selected U.S. brands over a 15-year period as reported by *The Economist*. An organization chart for Seagram's U.S. operations appears in Exhibit 3.

EXHIBIT 2
U.S. sales

1983 rank	Brand	1983	1978	1968
1	Bacardi	7,670	6,200	2,100
2	Smirnoff	5,700	6,150	3,200
3	Seagram's 7 Crown	4,900	6,200	7,850
4	Canadian Mist	3,350	2,300	—
5	Jim Beam	3,200	2,750	2,520
6	Seagram's V.O.	3,050	3,875	3,475
10	Seagram's Gin	2,525	2,350	1,050

Note: Figures in thousands of cases.
Source: *The Economist*, December 22, 1984, p. 9.

EXHIBIT 3
Seagram's U.S.
operations

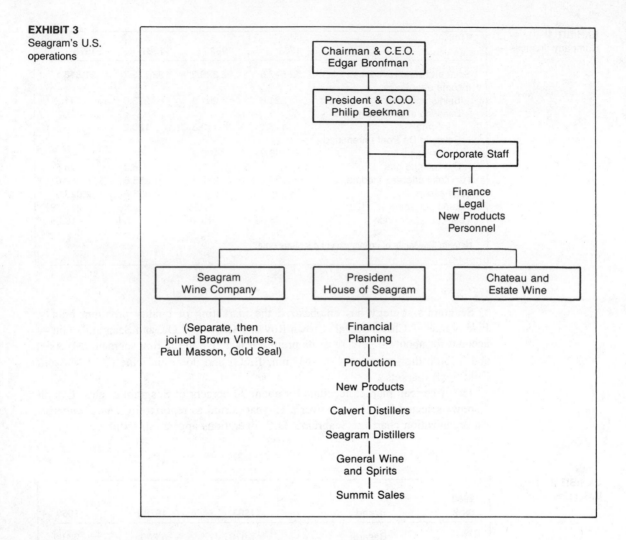

THE CHAIRMAN AND CHIEF
EXECUTIVE OF SEAGRAM CO. LTD.

Edgar Bronfman joined his father's business soon after graduation from McGill University in Montreal, became head of the U.S. subsidiary at twenty-nine, and was long tainted by his reputation as a jet-set playboy. "It was not the best way to do it," says Bronfman, assessing his own ascent to corporate power. "But there was no other way, considering my father and his personal philosophy and drive."

Recalls a retired Seagram executive: "Edgar was always bright. But he was flippant and sometimes prone to shoot from the hip." During the early 1970s, he was preoccupied with personal matters — a foray into the movie business, a divorce and an annulment, and the kidnapping of his oldest son. Bronfman was away from the company for much of that time, and Jack Yogman, a protégé of Bronfman's father, ran its day-to-day affairs. Yogman, an executive vice-president, was largely responsible for expanding Seagram's wine operations.

By late 1975, with Seagram's earnings declining steadily in the wake of the recession, Bronfman began to devote more attention to the company. He turned the executive suite of the sale subsidiary that handles the flagship liquor brands into a revolving door; in 6 years there were about five presidents. To Seagram's board of directors, traditionally made up of insiders, he added Canadian business luminaries: the heads of the Bank of Montreal, Canadian Pacific, and Power Corp. of Canada. And he ousted Yogman, whom he feared was wresting managerial control of the company away from him.

Bronfman is a tall, dapper, handsome man with a fastidious manner. Suave and often charming, he possesses traces of the boiling temper for which his father was famous. Even though he ousted Yogman 5 years ago, former aides say that any favorable mention of Yogman is sure to produce an explosion of that temper.

Bronfman lives in a Fifth Avenue penthouse apartment with his third wife — an Englishwoman about 20 years his junior — and their two small children. He has four sons and a daughter from his first marriage. His oldest son, Sam Bronfman II, now twenty-eight, is a brand manager for Seagram's Paul Masson Vineyards in California. "The decision [to take the job] was his, not mine," says Bronfman. "I have no heir apparent at this time." Another son, Edgar, Jr., twenty-six, was an independent movie producer in California.

When he is in New York, Bronfman jogs twenty-five blocks each morning to his office, which is decorated with Rodin statuary and Miro tapestries. Weekends he flies in a personal jet with his family to a recently acquired estate in the Virginia hunt country. Bronfman is involved in twenty-one philanthropic entities and maintains a computer to track his contributions. One beneficiary is a medical foundation that supports research on alcohol-related disease.

As he embarks on his new acquisition adventures, Bronfman is at ease with himself. "I'm having a very happy, constructive, and challenging business career," he says. The biggest challenge is yet to come: acquiring companies and integrating them into Seagram so that he can, as he puts it, "build on what my father accomplished."

Bronfman has also put his stamp on his father's company with a major revamping in marketing. It began about 5 years ago, when Bronfman says he "perceived that we didn't have a strong marketing thrust." At the time, that assessment applied to the whole liquor industry, which concentrated simply on pushing unit sales, not on the more sophisticated marketing approach of other packaged goods industries. Says Marvin R. Shanken, publisher of *Impact,* an influential wine and spirits trade publication: "The industry was one of the slower Goliaths to change into the twentieth century era of marketing."

Seagram was a pioneer in making that change. Bronfman, who has an obsession about improving the company's marketing stature, has told subordinates that "when they talk about marketing at the Harvard Business School, I want them to mention Seagram first." To achieve that eminence, he hired Beekman as president (after reportedly failing to recruit Anthony J. F. O'Reilly, now head of H. J. Heinz Co.), brought in a band of other high-powered consumer marketers, doubled Seagram's advertising budget, and began to take more seriously such practices as market research and strategic planning.

Just as important, Bronfman increased prices aggressively to strengthen Seagram's sagging profit margins — and the competition eagerly followed. Until then, the liquor industry has used price cutting to build volume, so that in a period of severe inflation, the industry raised its prices only minimally. Seagram and the industry also shifted their basic marketing strategy from what Shanken calls the "push approach" — forcing volume up through the distributor — to the "pull approach" — reaching the consumer directly through increased advertising to stimulate demand.

"You can get just as drunk drinking cheap stuff as expensive stuff," says Bronfman. "So what you're really selling is glamour and an impression."[1]

Shortly before the Sun deal, Bronfman increased Seagram's cash hoard by selling the company's 38-story office building on Manhattan's Park Avenue. An elegant bronze and glass structure built in 1957 at a cost of $41 million, the building has been a much admired symbol of the Bronfman business empire. But Edgar Bronfman shows little sentimental concern for symbols. "The building had been depreciated to such an extent that it was not particularly profitable or wise to keep it," he says. "We thought we had better use for the money." The company sold the building for $85.5 million to a pension fund and will retain its U.S. headquarters there on a 15-year lease with options to renew for an additional 30 years.

Central to the Seagram Company is the personal managerial style of Edgar Bronfman. One ex-Seagram officer commented:

> *I have a 5-year theory about Edgar Bronfman. From the time you meet Edgar you have a maximum of 5 years of life within the company. Within 5 years Edgar will find something to hate, and you'll be dead. Edgar has a history of incredible love affairs with new executives, and of course the kind of guy Edgar likes is the brash, aggressive type, but you can't continually be aggressive in front of Edgar.*
>
> *People who survive at Seagram do so because they spend a lot of time thinking about what Edgar wants, and it's very hard to do, because he can change. He's very mercurial.*
>
> *So there's an organizational paranoia, and that slows everything down, but still things get done.*

STRATEGIC PLANNING AT SEAGRAM

Seagram made major strategic decisions during the 1980s, decisions centering around (1) the sale of oil and gas properties, (2) the reinvestment of the oil and gas proceeds,

---

[1] "What Edgar Bronfman Wants at Seagram," *Business Week*, April 27, 1981.

and (3) the expansion of its wine activities in North America. These strategic decisions involved, among others, Mr. Charles Bronfman (chairman of the Executive Committee of the Seagram Company), his older brother Edgar Bronfman (chairman of the Seagram Company), and Mr. Philip Beekman (president of the Seagram Company). Their decision-making style can be seen in these three major decisions.

Texas Pacific Sale

Mr. Samuel Bronfman wrote in 1970:

> *Foreseeing the requirements for energy in the 1950's and the 60's, and the almost unbelievable demand of the 70's, I was motivated in 1953 to cause Joseph E. Seagram & Sons, Inc. to begin investing in the petroleum industry — the energy business. As our first venture we organized the Frankfurt Oil Company with headquarters in Bartlesville, Oklahoma. . . . A reorganization followed and in due course the Frankfurt headquarters was moved to Dallas, Texas. . . . At this [1963] point, we ventured further to purchase the venerable Texas Pacific Coal and Oil Company. . . . Frankfurt adopted the name Texas Pacific Oil after the acquisition.*
>
> *Today, we at Seagram have every reason to be proud of our venture into the energy business. We have made possible the building of an oil company which has brought a new dimension to our corporate organization.*[2]

The 1979 Annual Report contained the following industry segment information:

	1979	1978	1977	1976	1975
Revenues					
Spirits and wine	$2,363,218	$2,103,809	$2,017,867	$1,900,939	$1,813,717
Oil and gas	190,878	168,775	166,896	156,487	123,078
	$2,554,096	$2,272,584	$2,184,263	$2,057,426	$1,936,796
Operating income					
Spirits and wine	$ 228,697	$ 189,985	$ 167,687	$ 156,862	$ 151,125
Oil and gas	62,933	55,908	56,755	40,452	39,358
Corporate expense	(13,659)	(10,510)	(9,272)	(8,088)	(7,319)
	$ 277,971	$ 235,383	$ 215,170	$ 189,216	$ 183,164
Identifiable assets					
Spirits and wine	$1,938,916	$1,901,812	$1,711,290	$1,818,047	$1,657,974
Oil and gas	498,160	896,854	337,477	343,146	333,340
	$2,437,076	$2,297,666	$2,048,767	$2,161,193	$1,991,314

On April 11, 1980, the Sun Co. made an offer for Seagram's subsidiary, Texas Pacific Co. Sun Co.'s offer was $2.3 billion in cash, although Seagram "keeps all

[2] From Supplement to 1969–1970 Annual Report of Distillers Corporation — Seagram Limited, issued October 1970, Montreal, Canada, pp. 68–69.

of Texas Pacific's international oil and gas properties, and after certain criteria are met, retains a 49 percent interest in nonproducing properties and a 25 percent interest in producing properties."[3] Mr. Philip Beekman commented:

"I don't think we are going to be in a hurry to do anything with all that money. We will move carefully, very cautiously. We may look around in industries related to what we have here, and see what will give us the best possibility of growth."

But he stresses that he is ruling no industry out, not even the energy industry, despite the Sun deal.

Whatever the company decides to do with the money, Beekman will have a major role in making that decision, says a fellow Seagram executive.

Beekman's office sits between, and is connected to those of Edgar Bronfman, Seagram chairman of the board, on the right and Charles Bronfman, chairman of the executive board on the left.

"We form a three-headed hydra," says Beekman. "I think that more and more companies in this country which have to deal with worldwide marketing and sales decisions will have something like our setup here. Sort of an 'office of the president.'"

Responsibilities overlap, says Beekman, but generally "Edgar and I will oversee Europe and Latin America and Charles and I will oversee the Far East and Canada."[4]

As Sun's cash payment was received in September 1980, a long line of investment advisers and myriad investment proposals confronted the top executives of the firm.

In the company's first interview since the sale of its U.S. oil and gas properties to Sun Co. for $2.3 billion, Seagram chairman Edgar Bronfman said on September 17, 1980, that the firm is considering a maximum of three acquisitions.

But Mr. Bronfman said Seagram will do nothing before next year. He stressed that Seagram is keeping its options open "until we can assess this mammoth opportunity."

The officials emphasized that Seagram is not focusing on the consumer goods area for acquisitions possibilities, despite Wall Street's expectations. Analysts have speculated that Seagram would use the Sun proceeds to buy a consumer goods concern with promising products that could benefit from Seagram's marketing expertise in wine and spirits. Colgate Palmolive, Norton Simon, Standard Brands and Gillette have been mentioned as candidates.

But Mr. Bronfman said that the company is prepared to consider just about anything except atomic energy and the steel business.

Seagram has hired Arthur D. Little to help plan for use of the proceeds. The Little organization, Mr. Bronfman said, will prepare a macro-study of the world business environment for the 1980's and 1990's and Seagram's place in it. "This study, which is under way, will be completed in about three months, and Seagram will then go to a micro-study to narrow down the fields we're interested in," Mr. Bronfman said.

An action program will be ready for Seagram's board before next July 31, he said.[5]

[3] "Liquor Industry Hurting But Cash Eases Seagram's Pain," *Los Angeles Times*, August 12, 1980, part IV, p. 1.

[4] "Seagram Considers Acquisitions Policy," *International Herald Tribune*, September 17, 1980, p. 9.

[5] *Los Angeles Times*, op. cit.

Reinvesting the Sun Oil Proceeds

Seagram pursued St. Joe Minerals in March 1981 and Conoco, Inc. in June 1981. Seagram offered to pay about $2.1 billion for St. Joe Minerals, the top U.S. producer of lead and zinc and a major miner of coal. "If our offer is successful, we are most desirous that St. Joe's management team stay with the company and continue building it," Mr. Bronfman said. Senior officials for St. Joe, calling the bid grossly inadequate, recommended that their board reject the offer.

> In addition to St. Joe, Lazard Freres & Co., dealer manager for the offer, was studying several other companies as possible Seagram acquisition targets. But the spotlight narrowed on St. Joe, and a special meeting of Seagram's board was called for last Tuesday night in Montreal. The directors and a team from Lazard Freres, led by senior partner Felix Rohatyn, sat down at 7 P.M. in the second-floor boardroom in Seagram's squat, castlelike headquarters building on Peel Street in Montreal. Mr. Bronfman spoke for about 10 minutes, providing background information on Seagram's months-long acquisition planning and management's recommendation to offer for St. Joe.
>
> Mr. Rohatyn and other Lazard Freres officials then made their presentation, which lasted almost two hours. They were interrupted frequently by questions from the directors.
>
> Seagram's board took its customary break and adjourned to a nearby room to dine on smoked meat and lobster sandwiches, washed down with some of the distiller's products.
>
> St. Joe Minerals Corp., fighting a $2 billion takeover bid by Montreal's Seagram liquor empire, got a U.S. federal judge's approval yesterday to sell off its Canadian subsidiary and seek a merger with Fluor, a big engineering firm.[6]

Joseph E. Seagram & Sons on April 9, 1981, withdrew its $45-a-share offer to buy St. Joe Minerals Corp., making Fluor Corp. the apparent winner in the bidding contest.

A federal judge blasted St. Joe Minerals, accusing its management of following a "scorched earth" policy for vowing to liquidate before accepting a takeover bid from Joseph E. Seagram & Sons. Judge Milton Pollack of the U.S. District Court in New York said St. Joe's actions were motivated solely by a fear that a Seagram's takeover "may end the tenure of the present directors and key officers" and was "not defensible as good corporate business."

"Bronfman's ego may have been bruised in the St. Joe imbroglio, but Seagram came out with a profit of at least $10 million on the 466,000 shares of St. Joe purchased before the tender offer and sold after its withdrawal."[7]

On June 23, 1981, Seagram said it "intends, depending on future developments, to acquire a number of" Conoco common shares, although it did not specify how many. A Seagram spokesman said his company already owns some Conoco stock, but he declined to say how many shares:

[6] "St. Joe Minerals Directors Spurn Offer by Seagram, Plan an Innovative Defense," *Wall Street Journal*, March 13, 1981, p. 4.

[7] "What Edgar Bronfman Wants at Seagram," *Business Week*, April 27, 1981, pp. 135–142.

To Edgar Bronfman, who became the chief executive officer of Seagram after his father died in 1971 at the age of eighty, Conoco offers a chance to outdo the legendary patriarch who built Seagram into the world's largest distillery operation and then left a 34 percent interest to his two sons and two daughters. Edgar Bronfman became a U.S. citizen in 1955. His brother, Charles, fifty, lives in Montreal and, although he is deputy chairman of Seagram, does not participate in day-to-day operations of the company, according to a Seagram spokesman.[8]

The 40.7 percent bid for Conoco might not have happened if it were not for a rebuff from Conoco, impeccable timing by Mr. Bronfman, and the help of Mark Millard, a seventy-three-year-old Russian emigre who is senior managing director of Shearson Loeb Rhoades. It was in fact Mr. Bronfman's third proposal to Conoco. The first was made privately on May 29 when Conoco was still embroiled in a takeover battle with another Canadian company, Dome Petroleum.

When Conoco's shareholders tendered an overwhelming 54.8 million shares in response to Dome's offer for 22 million shares, there appeared to be enough left over for another suitor, and Mr. Millard, according to associates, turned to Mr. Bronfman. The Seagram directors offered to buy 35 percent of Conoco but assured Conoco Chairman Ralph E. Bailey that they were willing to work out a friendly compromise.

The day after Conoco agreed to sell Dome its Hudson Bay interests for $1.68 billion in cash and stock, a team from Conoco began to work with Seagram to sell another chunk of its stock. "Mr. Bailey felt more comfortable with an offer for 25 percent, so we went with that," said a source at Seagram.[9]

The formal offer to buy 25 percent of the company for $2 billion included a promise from Mr. Bronfman to leave Conoco's management alone for 15 years. To his surprise, the offer was rejected unanimously by Conoco's board on June 17. "We only agreed to proceed on a friendly basis while Conoco was still involved with Dome," said a Seagram source, "but once that agreement was reached, we did not feel obliged to continue on a friendly basis. But we did, and Mr. Bronfman was very disappointed by the board's decision."[10]

The Seagram foray into the oil and gas business has been guided by Mr. Millard, a former economics professor at the University of Heidelberg. He first advised Edgar Bronfman's father to buy the Texas Pacific Co. in 1963 for a mere $50 million in cash and a $216 million payment for future production. Seagram hired Howard Hinson, then a Conoco director, to head the new acquisition. At one time Mr. Hinson had a reputation in the oil industry of having discovered 2 percent of the oil reserves in the noncommunist world.

After Mr. Hinson had expanded Texas Pacific's 350,000 undeveloped acres to

---

[8] Ibid.

[9] "After First Rebuff, Seagram Now Goes After Control of Conoco," *International Herald Tribune*, June 30, 1981, p. 9.

[10] Ibid.

4 million acres, Mr. Millard stepped in once again. He negotiated the sale of Texas Pacific's domestic oil and gas property to Sun Co., which not only gave Seagram $2.3 billion but also assured it of keeping an interest in the property if it turns out to be worth more. "That's Millard's style," said John G. McMillian, chairman of the Northwest Energy Co., the operating partner for the $25 billion Alaskan natural gas pipeline. "He always gets in on the future, and it never looks like anything to everyone else, but it always works out to be a hell of a deal." [11]

Following Seagram's offer, Mobil and Du Pont entered into the biggest takeover battle in U.S. history. Conoco, after warning that the Seagram offer "escalates the continued Canadianization of American natural resources to a new and more dangerous level" and that "Mobil's proposed acquisition poses the most important public policy questions," recommended to shareholders that the Du Pont merger offer be accepted. Seagram acquired 27 percent of Conoco, which was then merged into Du Pont.

Making such a colossal investment in a shaky economy would have daunted many industrialists, but Edgar Bronfman found the challenge, well, intoxicating. "Business is like a game," says Bronfman, 52, who personifies more than any other figure the merger mania of 1981. "And winning is fun." [12]

Seagram now owns 20 percent of Du Pont, more than any single member of the Du Pont family. To ease fears that Seagram might move to take over the company, Bronfman agreed not to buy more than another 5 percent of Du Pont's outstanding stock during the next 15 years. In return, Edgar and his brother, Charles, were added to the Du Pont board.

When Edgar had all that money to spend, he asked himself, "What would Father do?" "I realized, hell, he never had $3.7 billion." [13]

Sun, Du Pont, and the Wine Spectrum

In summary, in 1980 the Seagram Company sold its Texas Pacific oil and gas properties for $2.3 billion to Sun Company. Seagram's chairman, Edgar Bronfman, wrote in the 1980 Annual Report:

> *Redeploying such a massive pool of capital is a most serious undertaking, one that we believe should be pursued in a prudent, orderly and highly analytical manner. . . . Rarely does a company of Seagram's size have an opportunity to examine the world and then, with virtually unfettered freedom of choice, position itself to take full advantage of the conditions that will prevail in the last two decades of this century and into the next.*

In 1981 the oil and gas properties proceeds were used to acquire a 20 percent interest in E. I. du Pont de Nemours & Company, the seventh largest industrial corporation in North America. Seagram and Du Pont entered into a standstill agree-

[11] Ibid.

[12] Quoted in "A Liquor Baron Enlivens a Year of Corporate Merger Mania," *People*, December 1981, pp. 62–63.

[13] Ibid.

ment wherein Seagram agreed not to buy more than 25 percent of Du Pont's voting stock, and Du Pont received a right of first refusal in the event Seagram offered its Du Pont stock for sale.

Forbes (January 21, 1982, page 50) quoted Edgar Bronfman on Du Pont and Seagram:

> *Some Du Pont directors are more equal than others. Du Pont is doing what we would want but it's much slower than Seagram would be. . . . I'd like to buy a drug company. I'm excited about pharmaceuticals, and I expect the multiples to go higher.*

Finally, in November 1983 Seagram acquired the Wine Spectrum from the Coca-Cola Company. The Wine Spectrum brands included Taylor California Cellars and Great Western Champagne. Edgar Bronfman wrote in the 1983 Annual Report that the purchase

> *involved all properties of The Wine Spectrum, including Sterling Vineyards, the Monterey Vineyard, and the Taylor Wine Company. The Wine Spectrum has enjoyed extraordinary growth. The combination of it and Paul Masson firmly establishes the Company as the second largest domestic wine producer in the United States. We believe that the U.S. wine market will experience solid growth in the years to come, and Seagram will be a major force in that growth.*

R. C. Goizueta, chairman and CEO of Coca-Cola, said in a September 1983 press release:

> *In line with our corporate strategy, we are constantly striving to concentrate our resources in the areas of our business where the returns on assets are highest . . . we believe this is an appropriate time to realize the value of [the Wine Spectrum] . . . [and] we will fully recapture our investment in the wine business.*

MARY CUNNINGHAM

In 1981, Mary Cunningham began a strategic planning assignment at Seagrams concerning the worldwide wine business. Mary had come from a controversial position at Bendix. She entered a fluid organization at Seagram as Seagram moved executives in and out of the wine companies and realigned wine companies. Jack Murphy commented on Mary Cunningham and Seagram:

> *Mary Cunningham came to Seagram on the recommendation of Phil Beekman. Nobody really knew in the beginning what Mary was going to be doing. But it soon became known that she was to do a worldwide study of Seagram's wine business. The reaction at Brown Vintners, the group handling imported wine, was anger because we had a lot of people who had been in the wine business a long time who certainly had a better background to make such a study.*
> *But Cunningham comes into the corporate scene just as Gene Barrett comes into*

Brown Vintners to supervise the combination of Brown Vintners and Paul Masson. Previously Phil Beekman had brought in Ken Sears to take over the House of Seagram.

Mary was totally on her own at the corporate level and communicated only with Phil and Edgar. She hires Strategic Planning Associates to do the wine study. And everyone in Brown Vintners is asking "why can't I do that," especially since Mary is paying them a generous six-figure retainer.

Gene Barrett realized that Mary's in, so he knows to join her, not fight her. Barrett got along very well with Mary. But the whole atmosphere was secretive. We weren't allowed to see the Cunningham report.

I thought Mary was totally socially unstable. Talking to Mary was like talking to a computer. She spoke as if she were a tape recorder. But everyone was afraid of her.

An executive who had spent 20 years at Seagram described Mary as "the most arrogant person I had met in my business career. She was more arrogant than Edgar and with much less reason."

And an ex-Seagram senior executive remarked that

While most were willing to give Mary the benefit of the doubt, by the end of her study, she had managed to alienate about everyone in the company. Once the strategic study was complete, it was suggested that she seek other opportunities since the decision had been made to exclude her from the implementation of the study's recommendations.

Following her departure from Seagram, Mary Cunningham wrote a book which *Vogue* described as an autobiography in which

the business world's scarlet woman tells her side of the "Bill and Mary Show.". . . It's been almost four years now since Mary Cunningham's life became a major media event. Then twenty-nine, she was forced to resign her post as Vice President for strategic planning at the Bendix Corporation because of rumors that her meteoric rise there was not due to her superior abilities but to her sleeping with her boss, Bendix chief Bill Agee. Cunningham and Agee always denied those rumors; but rumors were fueled anew when, twenty months after she left Bendix, she and Agee married.

THE CUNNINGHAM WINE STUDY

The comprehensive wine study presented to management in January 1982 contained many conclusions and recommendations centering around economies of scale and the U.S. market, including

1. Small, subscale wineries, whose production capacities had driven marketing strategies, should be divested.
2. Major economies of scale are not now possible with Seagram's very broad brand portfolio, which means that its overall rank of sixth by volume still means low market shares in individual segments.
3. The U.S. market is the critical market.

4. The U.S. market is changing toward (1) sophisticated high-turnover supermarkets and liquor chains, (2) greater price sensitivity in the quality (but not premium) high-volume market, and (3) increased concentration.
5. Higher advertising and marketing expenses must be incurred to protect and build market share.
6. Production costs must be lowered through economies of scale to pay for marketing costs.
7. The high-volume, quality segment has relatively more important production and marketing costs than grape costs, which are determined by Gallo to a large extent.
8. Seagram's major competitors (Gallo, Taylor, and Banfi-Riunite) have greater scale, lower costs, and more focus.
9. "Quality" acceptability has a fairly broad range.
10. The short-term strategy should be a controlled expansion of Paul Masson through price appeals, focused advertising, and a consolidated (Masson, Gold Seal, Brown Vintners) sales force.
11. The long-term strategy should change the rules of the game through the construction of an East Coast facility using frozen-concentrate technology and overseas sources to make the "fun" and "light" wines.

The study asserted that the long-term outlook for wine was good. There was a dramatic, clear correlation between low prices and per capita consumption across all countries. Looking at the current U.S. base of a total of about 200 million cases a year sold by Gallo (51 million), Heublein-United-Vintner-Inglenook-Swiss Colony (23 million), Seagram (20 million), National Distilleries-Almaden (14 million), the Wine Spectrum (9 million), and Riunite (9 million), there would be an increase of 410 million cases if the U.S. market grew to Germany's level of per capita consumption. There would be an increase of 225 million cases if U.S. consumption reached California levels. There would be an increase of 15 million cases if all of the open (non–state store) states allowed wine to be sold in groceries and of 10 million cases if all of the control states allowed wine to be sold in groceries. (Open states without grocery sales of wine are Colorado, Kansas, Oklahoma, North Dakota, Tennessee, Kentucky, and New York. Control states without grocery sales include Utah and Pennsylvania.)

Seagram expected the U.S. market to reach 340 million cases by 1985. This wine was distributed primarily by individual wholesale distributors, who handled more than 90 percent of the wine sold. Retail sales were primarily through supermarkets and chains (45 percent), restaurants (35 percent), individual markets or liquor stores (15 percent) and control states (5 percent).

Overall, the wine study predicted a growth of 8 percent over the next 10 years in table wine sales. The long-term objective would be to improve profit margins on table wines, which were the majority of Paul Masson's sales.

The study also considered the many dimensions of the wine segmentation issue, including product, region (emerging versus mature markets), economic base (price, grapes, distribution), consumer, occasion (dinner, "fun" celebration), taste/color, and packaging.

In summary, the essence of the wine report was "go for it or get out." "Go for it" meant action now to defend against Gallo and Taylor. The report recommended major capital investment in Paul Masson's expansion. Seagram had over $600 million invested in wine worldwide, with 25 percent of that investment in Paul Masson assets. The report recommended long-term investment of almost three times current Masson assets.

In the October 15, 1983 issue of *Impact* (a wine and spirits executive publication), the editor interviewed Edgar Bronfman about Seagram and the Wine Spectrum, the acquisition that brought Seagram from a 6 percent to an 11 percent market share.

Mr. Bronfman: "We have always known that Paul Masson was too small, and had to grow rapidly. . . . It seemed to us that by acquiring the Wine Spectrum we could have a short cut to profitability simply by economies of scales. . . . We will obviously have to emerge out of all this with a marketing plan that makes sense. But to say that we have given a lot of thought to brand positioning after the merger takes place would be incorrect; we have not. . . .

"The Wine Spectrum and the Seagram Wine Division are losing money. . . . My brother asked me, 'How do the numbers look?' and I said: 'Charles, I can give you any scenario you want. I can give you a scenario that says the numbers are terrible. I can give you a scenario that says the numbers are good. I can give you a scenario that says the numbers are terrific.' "

The editor: "So the statement in the *New York Times* that Mary Cunningham engineered the deal — I think they call it her 'brain child' — is not true?"

Mr. Bronfman: "That is correct. . . . And when this idea occurred to me — in fact, I may be so bold as to say it was my idea — the only person I consulted with, aside from my brother, was Phil Beekman."

The editor: "Why has Coke decided to unload their wine operation?"

Mr. Bronfman: "If I were Coca-Cola, I would resent the word *unload*."

The editor: "I choose my words very carefully."

As the Wine Spectrum deal was implemented, Gold Seal plants were closed and processing consolidated into Taylor–New York. Similarly, Paul Masson's production was folded into the much more extensive Taylor California facilities. Taylor California, for example, had a glass manufacturing plant while Paul Masson did not. Jack commented: "The overriding interest, which was initiated by Mary Cunningham, was to get big or to get out. Fifty times a day the words *economies of scale* were thrown around Seagram."

The vast majority of the Taylor marketing people (including three Taylor managers who were offered the Seagram Wine Company presidency) would not accept the

Seagram offer to relocate to New York. The exception was the original manager who took Taylor into the national market, but this Taylor "hero" quit after 6 weeks and went over to a Seagram competitor.

An ex-Seagram manager commented on the Wine Spectrum acquisition:

> What's $200 million to Edgar Bronfman? It's less than 10 percent of the Texas Pacific price. The Wine Spectrum purchase is a big-picture move that protects Paul Masson, which was getting hammered by Taylor just as Almaden and others were hammered, and when the Gallo brothers die maybe profits will be possible in what is now a low-margin business, made worse by the high dollar which makes the imports less expensive.
>
> Edgar can make this kind of bold stroke because he doesn't have to worry about the money and he doesn't have to answer to anybody. Edgar will do what he wants to do, or sometimes it's Edgar and his brother Charles, and that's it.

JACK MURPHY AT SEAGRAM

Jack came to Seagram from Heublein in California in 1978, where he had spent 2 years in marketing management. Prior to Heublein, Jack had spent 6 years at Colgate-Palmolive, also in marketing management. Seagram is known for paying its executives well, and Jack was no exception. He commented:

> There was at that time a division of Seagram called Paul Masson Vineyards, which included all of Paul Masson and most imports (G. H. Mumm & Co., Barton & Guestier, Kayser Wines, Cherry Kijafa, Ricasoli, and Black Tower). The small California vineyards and premium imports were in a separate Seagram's division called Chateaux and Estates. Chateaux and Estates was principally a marketing and distribution division.
>
> Seagram decided in 1978 to split the imports off by themselves, the motivation being that imports were growing like crazy and domestics were pretty stagnant. Seagram owned 70–80 percent of these import properties, but they were running at one-half of capacity. For example, in Italy there were three wineries, running at 40–50 percent capacity, with an additional winery that had been built but never used. But under Italian laws you had to pay for full staff at full capacity, regardless of operating levels.
>
> So I was hired at a very nice salary to work in this new company, then called Brown Vintners, charged with marketing responsibility for the imported wines. Paul Masson had now only domestic wines and Brown Vintners only imports, and this was the beginning of incredible things.
>
> The executive vice-president of marketing for Brown Vintners was an ex-Colgate guy, Clark Johnson, who's now president of Fleischmann's. He hired me. So this was kind of Phil Beekman's marketing company as opposed to Edgar's, since Phil had been president of Colgate International. Irving Black, who had been national sales manager of Paul Masson, was made president of Brown Vintners.
>
> I was initially responsible for the national introduction of Black Tower, and they gave us a lot of money to play with. We test-marketed for 18 months and we had an $8 million budget, including $2 million for the test market.
>
> We were the showcase for the marketing presentations. We would come in and do it the Colgate way.

Our biggest dread was to have to make a marketing presentation to Edgar. He had a tendency to get into side conversations or appear to be preoccupied; when his attention came back to the meeting he'd ask questions about a brand that had been discussed 20 minutes earlier. And we'd have to reconstruct the meeting and start again.

During these years Paul Masson began to get into trouble, as Taylor under Coca-Cola stepped up its marketing efforts. Taylor was now marketing people, and they did a great job.

After 8 months as head of Brown Vintners, Irving Black, who was not satisfactory as president, went back to Paul Masson. He was a great salesman, but not a good president. But Edgar loved him, and the salesman type, so he went back to Paul Masson. That's the way you got to the top. Certain people were Edgar's people, and they were sales people. Paul Masson under Irving Black was being mismanaged, while Taylor was wheeling and dealing with coupons and breaking unwritten rules of the game with head-to-head taste-tests with competitor's brands. But Seagram and Heublein and others just sat back and watched it all happen. Paul Masson management just shook its head and said, "Wow, Taylor is really gaining a lot of market share," and took no defensive actions.

So Paul Masson was going down the tubes and Brown Vintners was going great. So Edgar and Phil decided they had better bring these two companies together, motivated in part by the Cunningham study.

One of the things Phil had done was to bring in Ken Sears as head of the House of Seagram, the organization under which the wine companies fell. Ken was a marketer like Phil, but of course all the old-time Seagram sales types — as opposed to marketers — distrusted him. The spirits sales mentality was to be buddies with the distributors, while the marketing guys were oriented toward new products and market research. The heads of all the spirits companies were Edgar's boys, not Phil's and so the wars started — several levels above me. But the sales people knew that Phil lent a lot of legitimacy to a basically dirty business.

Meanwhile, within Brown Vintners, they brought in a guy from the spirits business to replace Black as Brown Vintners' president, Ray Stewart. He was also unsatisfactory and was fired after a year and a half. So in came Gene Barrett, to head up Brown Vintners as it is being tied to Paul Masson.

Gene Barrett was a lawyer with 10 years government experience, an unbelievably bright guy. He had represented Seagram in the Japanese joint venture with Kirin.

Jack's work environment changed in an important way at this time. Clark Johnson, his Colgate colleague and boss, left Seagram and was replaced by Greg Netherton, a "do-as-you're-told" manager.

So Barrett was fabulous but extremely political, and was hooked into Edgar by the family ties. He realized we had no big winners in the wine business to get us in tight with the distributors, so he decided to get a loss leader to strengthen distributor relationships. We had to get the distributors' attention. Black Tower and Partager, a French table wine, became those leaders to make some money for our distributors so they would push our other lines. Partager sold at $1.99 and while we didn't make much money, we sold a lot of cases. And the distributors make you.

As Paul Masson was pulled in, we also pulled in Gold Seal, the New York State wines. Then came the Delta project, which was a test program designed to validate the Cunningham "get big" strategy.

So I was given the assignment to make some of the high-price, low-price, high-spending, less-spending market tests as a result of the Delta project. I became the Delta project manager, and spent $4 million on testing these price-promotion variables, as Barrett oversees the implementation of the Cunningham project.

Just as the testing is going on, Barrett leaves for another Seagram position and they bring in Lionel James from Gold Seal. Lionel was an English master of wines, and came in as president of what was now called the Seagram Wine Company, which had in it Brown Vintners, Paul Masson, and Gold Seal.

I was a vice-president as Lionel James came in, and I was testing price-promotion sensitivities. Unfortunately, the bottom was falling out of the wine market and all the competition was cutting their prices. And so the results of the tests were invalid, and corporate decided to fight back with price and to cut way back on advertising and to stop the Delta tests. So I was out of a job in the sense that I was vice-president running the Delta project and there's no Delta project. And my immediate boss, Greg Netherton, doesn't understand marketing and doesn't like me telling him so.

I suppose if I had had a wife, kids, and a mortgage, I might have played a totally different game. But I was too honest. And Seagram executives are used to making decisions not on the basis of the facts in front of them, but rather on the basis of what their boss wanted. They totally played the game. This stemmed from the top. Edgar wanted you to do what he told you, and this concept permeated the company. "Do what you're told." And this fostered weak leadership.

My assignment also included a big segmentation study. That study was excellent in my opinion, but it was very poorly received within the company, since we placed Masson and Taylor in the same segment. People within Seagram had convinced themselves that Masson and Taylor were not in the same market segment, because if they were, it meant we were competing with ourselves.

People at Seagram play with information and fool themselves. I had all the proof in the world, including price, quality, and consumer expectations, that Taylor and Masson were competing with each other.

At this point Jack turned to Phil Beekman. Phil got Jack transferred to manager of new products at the corporate level again at a very competitive salary. As Jack became the new-products corporate manager, Seagram bought the Wine Spectrum.

I reported to Harvey Gold, who had been brought in by Ken Sears. Just before I took the new-products job I had been offered the job of vice-president–marketing for Fromm & Sichel, the distribution operation for Christian Brothers. I turned that down because I knew that Seagram was going to sell Fromm & Sichel, which they did 2 months later, even though the job was based in San Francisco.

Lionel James now gets sent to the international area, and Gene Barrett comes back into Seagram Wine Company as acting president to oversee the merger with the Wine Spectrum. Ken Sears, who had opposed the Wine Spectrum acquisition from the beginning and who was subsequently left out of all further Wine Spectrum discussions, also resigns at this time.

My next project was a strategic planning report I decided to write on my own initiative, based on my experience in the spirits companies.

Corporate new products was in charge of both spirits and new wine products although the spirits and wine companies had their own new-products groups. I wanted spirits experience, so I visited all the spirits sales companies. Then I discovered that nobody talked to each other. For example, both the Calvert Distillers and the Seagram Distillers were working on a light whiskey, but neither would tell the other anything.

This total independence and lack of communication led me to write the Strategic Planning Report. I wrote that the corporation in strategic planning should set up an interdivisional planning committee to coordinate all the market research and new-product planning, and should periodically report to Edgar and Phil. I also included specific recommendations about product policy, especially a premium vodka, capitalizing on our winners like Chivas, and getting into new product areas.

I sent my report to Harvey Gold with a copy to Phil. I never heard anything from either Phil or Harvey. So after a few weeks I sent copies to everybody.

ALTERNATIVES

As Jack reviewed his options within Seagram, they seemed to include staying in new products, trying to build a corporate strategy group, or returning to the wine companies.

First, Jack knew he could stay indefinitely in new products, especially with Phil Beekman's support. The job was becoming boring, though, as spirits was experiencing little growth. Jack thought Seagram had to develop an outstanding vodka to get life back into the spirits business. But he was unsure where within the spirits companies vodka might be developed. Further, he had no direct tie to Edgar and little if any contact with Edgar or the spirits top executives.

New products in wine, Jack felt, was essentially a question of marketing "sizzle." Taste was very much secondary, as Riunite had proved. The consumer knows very little about wine. For example, Black Tower was a decidedly sweet Liebfraumilch, yet in market test after market test, consumers would praise its dryness.

And further, there was the question of the role of a corporate new-products effort, given the political corporate culture of Seagram and the individual new product groups.

As for the second option (trying to build a platform for his efforts and for the strategic planning process at Seagram through the formal assignment of strategic planning responsibilities to a corporate group), Jack was unsure what this group's mandate should be or how he should try to get it organized, given the lack of response to his earlier strategic planning memorandum.

A third option was to return to the wine companies. A massive effort would be needed to coordinate the Taylor-Masson marketing program spanning product selection, distribution, testing, and promotion. On the other hand, perhaps a less risky if less challenging position might be available in the small, high-quality wine companies.

Any move into wine should be based upon the probable success of Masson, Masson-Taylor, Taylor, or the quality small wines, Jack believed. "The bearers of bad news never seem to last long at Seagram," Jack thought.

Another dimension to the three options was the question of allies. Should Jack impose on Phil Beekman again or should he seek new allies such as the "heir apparents"?

It was clear to Jack that the Bronfman sons (Edgar Jr. and, to a lesser extent, Sam) would hold high executive posts in the company. Jack expected the younger, but more aggressive, Edgar Jr. might lead the House of Seagram after his current tour as managing director of Seagram-Europe. Edgar's distaste for failure and his determination not to fail were known within the company.

Sam might take a role in the wine companies, Jack thought. Sam was well liked by the distributors and by others in the company, but was not expected to equal his younger brother in responsibility or authority.

Based upon the high probability of Edgar Sr.'s succession by Edgar Jr. and the attendant rise of Sam, Jack Murphy might pursue a tactic of seeking out either son as an ally-sponsor-patron.

Though he was unsure of Sam's marketing ideas, Jack had heard that Edgar Jr. was anxious to revise the "moderation" advertising done by the firm since the end of Prohibition. Falling sales, rising government taxes on alcohol, and regulatory restrictions including advertising constraints were unfair in Edgar Jr's opinion, according to company rumors. It was said that Edgar Jr. wanted to open a national campaign to advertise the equivalency of a 12-ounce can of beer, a 5-ounce glass of wine, and a 1¼-ounce shot of 80-proof whiskey. Such a campaign should provide executive opportunities, Jack believed. Nonetheless, he knew that large public interest national organizations were currently petitioning the Federal Trade Commission to impose severe restrictions on alcohol advertising plus mandatory warnings in ads and on the products themselves.

As Jack began his decision making, he prepared the diagram of Seagram shown in Exhibit 4.

APPENDIX: OUTSIDE ANALYSIS

Investment researchers for the New York firm, Cyrus J. Lawrence, Anton Brenner and James Murren, wrote the analysis in this appendix in their April 1984 comment on Seagram (Cyrus J. Lawrence beverage follow-up, New York).

CYRUS J. LAWRENCE ANALYSIS

The Seagram Company Ltd. is the leading producer and marketer of distilled spirits and wine. Although Seagram's products are sold in over 200 countries, North America is the Company's largest single market, accounting for 69% of total sales.

During the past few years, preferences for spirits and wine have diversified and overall demand for spirits has declined. Virtually every major spirit category has suffered declining consumption. Hit the hardest were the whiskey brands, which

EXHIBIT 4
Company structure

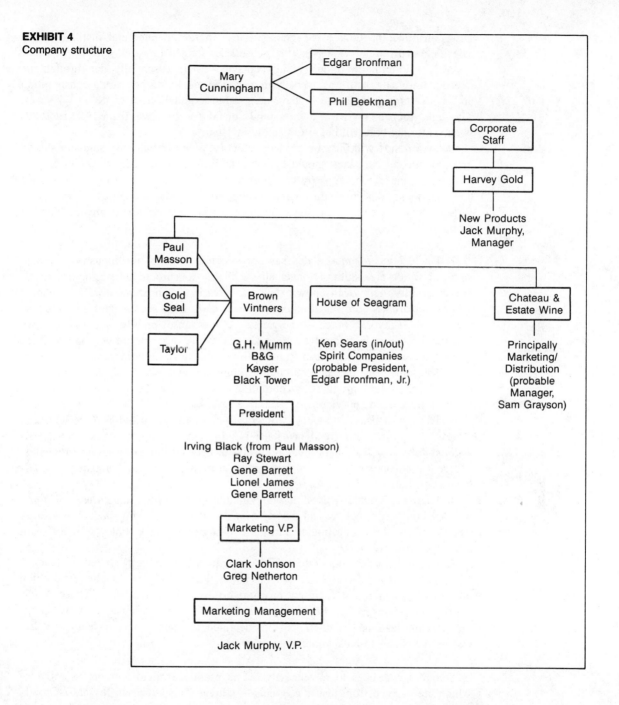

now constitute the bulk of Seagram's sales. In fact, while total distilled spirits sales declined roughly 1.4% in 1983, case sales of whiskeys fell 4%.

We are looking for industry shipments to remain essentially flat through the decade. Case sales will be adversely impacted by declining per capita consumption and a receding growth rate in the young adult population, ages 18 to 34 years. This age group increased at a compound annual rate of 2.7% from 1972 to 1982, is currently flat and will begin to decline in 1986.

Growth trends will vary by product category. The non-whiskey segment should grow, while the whiskies should continue their long-term slide. Seagram has responded to these conditions by reducing the production capacity of its distilleries and introducing and marketing brands in the more popular categories.

Some of the trends in existence during the past few years still prevail. Among them:

1. The decline in liquor sales has not affected many of the industry's brands, some of which are getting stronger all the time. Consumers have remained loyal, but apparently their loyalty now extends to a variety of brands. More and more it seems that drinkers are not drinking as much Canadian, scotch, bourbon, etc., as they are their favorite brand in the category. In a sense, brands as a concept have become a category in themselves. For example, while case sales of bourbon declined approximately 4.3%, American Brands' Jim Beam showed an increase of 3%.

2. The same principle applies to most premium brands in the industry. Consumers have supported these products by continuing to seek the image of status and prestige the premium brands provide.

3. The non-whiskey, "white," category has continued to outpace the whiskey, "brown," group. This trend has been building in the eighties and whites now account for over 50% of the market. While largely attributed to strong rum sales, in recent years other categories such as vodka, cordials, brandy and prepared cocktails have contributed to this trend.

4. There is particularly good growth potential in the cordial/liqueur area. Companies are constantly seeking and finding new product niches with successful results. "Knockoffs" of existing brands such as Paddington Corp.'s Bailey's Irish Cream have been lucrative also.

5. The only brown liquor to exhibit growth (albeit modest) in recent years is Canadian whisky. Most of the growth has taken place among the bulk brands (bottled in the U.S.), which now represent nearly two-thirds of its U.S. sales. These brands convey the prestige of an imported label, but at moderate prices. Seagram's V.O. brand is the leading Canadian, but has declined in sales in recent years as it has lost market share to bulk imports.

Seagram continues to rely heavily on its premium brands for profits, 50% of which are derived from just five brands — Chivas Regal, Crown Royal, 7-Crown, V.O., and Seagram's Gin. These brands command a high price, return high margins and therefore the Company can accept lower volume as consumption declines. Seagram had adopted a very aggressive pricing policy in the past and has probably priced up its products too quickly. This should about eliminate the ability to raise prices in the near term, particularly as sales volume remains soft. However, margins are expected to remain stable as a result of the economic recovery's generated relief on the cost front, i.e., fuel costs, cost of dry goods, gas prices, etc. In addition, since the recession is finally behind us, consumers are now expected to trade back up to the premium-priced brands.

Seagram has not been overly successful in introducing new products into the market and in response, the Company has moved to develop proprietary products in proven areas of strength. As a result, the Company has reaped additional benefits from its popular Myers's Rum by successfully introducing Myers's Original Rum Cream and Captain Morgan Spiced Rum. These products experienced a 5–6% increase in sales this past year. In other areas, the recent introduction of Seagram's Imported Vodka illustrates a renewed effort by the Company to compete directly against the leading vodka brand, Smirnoff. In addition, V.O. has beefed up marketing for its cordial line, Leroux, and is planning a number of product introductions in this area. Considering the scenario for the liquor industry, Seagram's effectiveness in the non-whiskey category is integral to the Company's overall performance in distilled spirits.

In 1982 Seagram entered into a venture with Coca-Cola Bottling Co. of New York to market a quality line of mixers. Under the agreement, Coke NY formulates, bottles and markets the mixers while Seagram is required only to license its name. In return for the use of the Seagram name, V.O. receives fixed-per-case royalties. The line has already captured 20% of the NYC market, the world's largest market for mixers, and is cited for distribution in selected cities throughout the country. While Seagram will not experience significant earnings from this venture in the near term, revenues will be generated, and at no risk to the firm. A rather nice by-product of this venture is that the brand-name "Seagram" can once again be seen in television commercials, for the first time since liquor ads were banned.

On the other hand, while the wine market has also slowed perceptibly in recent years, this industry enjoys rather promising growth prospects and is expected to grow by 4–5% in units over the remainder of the 1980s. Seagram intends to participate in and contribute to this growth. Last November, the Company acquired The Wine Spectrum from the Coca-Cola Company for $200 million. The Wine Spectrum includes the Taylor Wine Company, maker of Taylor California Cellars and Great Western Champagne. Coke bailed out of the wine business because it was not satisfied with the return on assets it received from The Wine Spectrum. Seagram will similarly experience a nominal return on its investment in the near term; however, we are under the impression that the Company has anticipated and accepted this scenario and is more interested in gaining market share. By acquiring The Wine Spectrum, V.O. immediately went from #6 in the wine industry to a strong second place with 11.7% of the market. Therefore, the acquisition is a reasonable long-term investment which should eventually reduce costs through economies of scale and provide a suitable return to V.O.'s stockholders.

However, the outlook for U.S. producers is not entirely sanguine, at least for the near term. Profitability will be under pressure from rising imports and excessive supplies and competition will be intense, both domestically and abroad. While wine consumption increased approximately 2–3% in 1983, domestic consumption rose only about 0.2% as opposed to a 6.4% rise in imports. Imports have accounted for an increasing share of the wine market in recent years. In fact, over the last ten years, market share for imports has soared to 24% from 16%, mostly through growth in Italian wines. Import growth reflects the effects of increased marketing efforts and, more recently, the strong U.S. dollar, which allows prices of imports to be very competitive with domestic wine prices.

The promise of strong growth has resulted in an expansion rate of producing facilities that has exceeded the growth of the market. This has created an imbalance between wine supplies and demand which will persist during the next couple of years.

In this period of relatively flat growth, Seagram's Paul Masson vineyards experienced some strength by holding its position when many consumers sought lower-priced products. Seagram benefited from the growth of the imports through Partager and Black Tower, gaining market share in the French and German wine categories, respectively. Barton & Guestier French wines have fared well and Sandeman Sherry and Port have made solid gains.

By selling out for only marginally more than it has invested since the acquisition in 1977, Coke joins Pillsbury, Beatrice Foods and Stroh Brewery — all of which have tried the wine business, soured on it, and dropped out. Coke bailed out because it was not satisfied with return on assets (ROA) of only 2.7 percent it received from The Wine Spectrum. We do not expect Seagram's ROA from The Wine Spectrum to improve substantially on Coke's return. However, V.O. is more interested in market share in the wine business at this time than in maximizing profits. Purchased for $200 million, The Wine Spectrum moves V.O. from #6 in the industry to a strong second place with 11.7% of the market. While we do not feel V.O. will receive a good return on its investment in the near term, Seagram has achieved the critical mass it has been looking for and will benefit in the long term through economies of scale.

While we are reasonably certain that V.O. will continue to cover costs in its spirits and wine operations, we expect modest earnings growth in this area, perhaps 2–3%. However, the company's Du Pont holdings should continue to generate substantial earnings power and provide a strong catalyst for future growth.

JOSEPH SCHLITZ BREWING COMPANY

In early May, 1981, Frank Sellinger, Vice Chairman and Chief Executive Officer of Joseph Schlitz Brewing Company, headed the management team of a struggling company in a highly competitive industry. Schlitz, once the number one brewer in the United States, had slipped to fourth place at the end of 1980, behind Anheuser-Busch, Miller and Pabst. Furthermore, massive advertising expenditures, technological changes, strengthened quality controls, and fiscal belt-tightening had not yet resulted in the turnaround which will return the company to its once proud position.

THE BREWING INDUSTRY IN 1981

Economic and Demographic Trends and Conditions

The United States economic recession of the 1980s, characterized by high price inflation and interest rates, had a noticeable impact on the brewing industry. The following problems were indicative of the economic dilemma of the 1970s:[1]

1. Declining real discretionary income and consumers' inclination to purchase high-priced goods in expectation of further price increases slowed sales increases of inexpensive consumer products. (See Exhibit 1.)
2. High interest rates discouraged wholesalers from building inventories too far in advance of anticipated sales.
3. Increasing costs of advertising, materials, fuel, labor, packaging, and equipment could not easily be passed on to the consumer, due to a highly competitive con-

---

[1] "Beverages and Tobacco: The Outlook," *Standard and Poor's Industry Surveys*, March 2, 1980, p. B-80–81; and "Beverages and Tobacco Current Analysis," *Standard and Poor's Industry Surveys*, November 6, 1980, p. B-54.

This case was prepared by M. Fenton, S. Taudman, R. Neiman, T. Merriman, and P. Norton under the supervision of Professor Sexton Adams (North Texas State University) and Professor Adelaide Griffin (Texas Woman's University). Copyright © 1981 by Sexton Adams. Reprinted by permission.

EXHIBIT 1
Selected U.S.
economic data

	Gross National Product	Disposable personal income[a]	Personal consumption expenditures				Consumer Price Index	
			Total	Durables	Non-durables	Alcoholic beverages	All items	Beer
1973	1235.0	854.7	767.7	121.8	309.3	9.4	133.1	115.6
1975	1202.3	859.7	774.6	112.7	306.6	—	161.2	140.3
1977	1340.5	929.5	861.7	138.2	332.7	—	181.5	145.9
1978	1436.9	981.6	904.8	146.3	347.7	—	195.4	154.0
1979	1483.0	1011.5	930.8	146.6	354.6	—	217.4	170.0
1980P	1481.8	1018.6	934.1	135.6	357.6	11.3	246.8	192.0
1985E	1803.3	—	1184.4	207.3	436.1	13.4	—	—
1990E	2112.8	—	1428.7	262.7	505.5	15.4	—	—

P = Preliminary figures.
E = Estimated by Bureau of Labor Statistics.
[a] Billions of 1972 dollars.
Sources: Department of Commerce's Bureau of Economic Analysis and Department of Labor's Bureau of Labor Statistics.

sumer beer market which made price competition and price promotion especially risky since beer consumers are largely price-sensitive, impulse buyers.

Standard and Poor's forecasted continuing inflation in a slowing economy for the 1980s, so expectations for stronger industrial performance were conservative.

Schlitz had concentrated on controlling internal costs, but according to Board Chairman Daniel McKeithan, "The ultimate resolution must come through a more moderate federal spending policy." He further stated in Schlitz's 1979 Annual Report that:

> Warnings that a recession is under way are of some concern to us, but ours is a product that is part of the fabric of American life and for which there is historically a moderately growing demand. In times of more moderate consumer spending, the true value of fine malt beverages becomes more apparent in the marketplace.

Volume growth in the beer industry had been a function of the development of new markets and demographic factors. Demographic factors had been significant due to the "Baby Boom" after World War II. As a result, the eighteen to forty-four year-old primary beer-drinking group had grown much faster than other population segments. That growth, however, will begin to diminish as the end of the 1980s approaches (see Exhibit 2). To compensate for a smaller population of the beer-drinking age group, per capita consumption must increase to sustain growth. Thus far there is a definite trend of increasing per capita consumption (see Exhibit 3). Industry expectations were for continued growth in per capita consumption through broadening of product lines and successful marketing efforts. Some industry

EXHIBIT 2
U.S. population
projections

Age group	1980		1985		1990	
	Population (millions)	Percentage of total	Population (millions)	Percentage of total	Population (millions)	Percentage of total
Under 5 years	16.0	7.2%	18.8	8.1%	19.4	8.0%
6–17 years	46.0	20.7	43.5	18.7	45.3	18.6
18–24 years	29.5	13.3	27.9	12.0	25.1	10.3
25–29 years	18.9	8.5	20.6	8.8	20.2	8.4
30–34 years	17.2	7.8	19.3	8.3	20.9	8.6
35–39 years	14.0	6.3	17.3	7.4	19.3	7.9
40–44 years	11.7	5.3	14.1	6.1	17.3	7.1
45–54 years	22.7	10.2	22.4	9.6	25.3	10.4
55–65 years	21.2	9.5	21.7	9.3	20.8	8.5
65+ years	24.9	11.2	27.3	11.7	29.8	12.2
All ages	222.2	100.0	232.9	100.0	243.5	100.0

Note: Includes Armed Forces abroad.
Source: U.S. Department of Commerce, Population Series P-25.

forecasters estimated annual per capita beer consumption of 27.6 gallons by 1990, an increase of 48 percent over twenty years.

Competing with malt beverages for consumer preference were distilled spirits, wines, and soft drinks (see Exhibit 3). All had experienced per capita consumption increases, but the most dramatic had been wine consumption. A significant change

EXHIBIT 3
U.S. per capita
consumption
of beverages
(in gallons)

	Wines	Beer	Distilled spirits	Total alcoholic	Soft drinks
1970	1.26	18.7	1.83	21.79	27.0
1971	1.43	18.6	1.85	21.88	28.7
1972	1.62	19.4	1.89	22.91	30.3
1973	1.66	20.2	1.93	23.79	31.9
1974	1.62	21.1	1.97	24.69	31.6
1975	1.70	21.6	1.98	25.28	31.4
1976	1.75	21.8	1.98	25.53	34.2
1977	1.80	22.7	2.00	26.50	36.3
1978	1.98	23.5	2.04	27.52	37.6
1979	2.02	24.3	2.04	28.36	38.9
1980 E	2.16	24.5	2.02	28.68	NA

E = Estimated.
NA = Not available.
Sources: Wine Institute, U.S. Brewers Association, Distilled Spirits Council of the U.S., *Beverage Industry*, and U.S. Department of Commerce.

EXHIBIT 4
Top ten beer brands

Rank	1980 market share	Brand	1980 production
1	19.4%	Budweiser	33.9%
2	13.6%	Miller High Life	23.8%
3	7.5%	Miller Lite	13.2%
4	6.5%	Coors	11.4%
5	6.4%	Pabst Blue Ribbon	11.2%
6	4.9%	Michelob	8.5%
7	4.3%	Schlitz	7.5%
8	2.3%	Old Milwaukee	4.0%
9	1.6%	Busch	2.8%
10	1.5%	Michelob Light	2.6%

Source: *Beverage Industry*, February 13, 1981.

in American drinking habits occurred in 1980 as wine displaced distilled spirits in consumption. Some analysts saw this as a trend toward lower-alcohol-content drinks. Others pointed to a growing preference for wine as an accompaniment to meals, and the availability of wines in food stores to account for increased consumption. Industry projections looked for a per capita consumption of 4.3 gallons by 1990, an increase of 250 percent over twenty years!

Standard and Poor's noted a shift in consumer preference toward domestic (as opposed to imported) wines. Imports were off 3.5 percent through the first eleven months of 1979, while data for the first three quarters of 1979 indicated California wines grew 5 percent. California is the dominant state supplying American wines: 68.5 percent of all wines in the U.S. market, 88 percent of all domestic wines in 1978, with white table wines predominant.

Industry Analysis

The brewing industry, characterized by an annual volume gain of 2.7 percent in 1980, was fiercely competitive. The industry leaders, Anheuser-Busch and Miller Brewing (owned by Philip Morris), dominated the market, as reflected in Exhibits 4 through 7. Their combined 1980 production was 50 percent of the entire industry.

EXHIBIT 5
Beer production
by brand

Brewer	1978	1979	1980	Change '79–'80
Anheuser-Busch				
Budweiser	27.0	30.0	33.9	13.0%
Michelob	7.5	8.0	8.5	6.3
Busch	3.6	3.2	2.8	(12.5)
Michelob Light	1.0	2.0	2.6	30.0
Natural Light	2.5	3.0	2.5	(16.7)
Total	41.6	46.2	50.3	8.9
Miller				
High Life	20.8	23.6	23.8	.8
Lite	9.5	11.2	13.2	17.9
Lowenbrau	1.0	0.9	1.2	33.3
Other	—	0.1	0.1	0
Total	31.3	35.8	38.3	7.0
Pabst				
Pabst	12.7	12.3	11.2	(8.9)
Old English (Malt)	0.5	0.7	1.0	42.9
Red, White & Blue	0.5	0.9	1.2	33.3
Blitz	0.3	0.5	0.8	60.0
Pabst Light	0.6	0.7	0.6	(14.3)
Other	0.8	—	0.2	—
Total	15.4	15.1	15.0	.7
Schlitz				
Schlitz	13.0	10.5	7.5	(28.6)
Old Milwaukee	3.6	3.7	4.0	8.1
Schlitz Malt	1.8	1.9	2.2	15.8
Schlitz Light	0.8	0.6	0.4	(33.3)
Erlanger	—	—	0.4	—
Other	0.4	0.1	0.2	100
Total	19.6	16.8	14.7	(12.5)
Coors				
Coors	12.4	11.3	11.4	.9
Coors Light	0.5	1.6	2.3	43.8
Total	12.6	12.9	13.7	6.2

Note: Figures in millions of barrels.
E = Estimate.
Source: *Beverage Industry*, February 13, 1981.

Indeed, trends toward greater concentration were evident. For example, production by the top six brewers in 1980 accounted for 82 percent of the industry total compared with 73 percent in 1975 and 59 percent in 1971.

The performance of the two industry leaders was quite different from that of the remaining competitors. Anheuser-Busch and Miller faced a problem meeting demand for their products due to a lack of capacity. Thus, Anheuser-Busch acquired Schlitz's 5.4 million-barrel Syracuse, New York, brewery in 1980, in an attempt

EXHIBIT 6 Brewers' production and estimated year-end 1980 capacity

Brewer	1971	1972	1973	1974	1975	1976	1977	1978	1979	1980	Change 1979–1980	Year-end capacity 1980E
Anheuser-Busch	24.3	26.6	29.9	34.1	35.2	29.1	36.6	41.6	46.2	50.3	8.9%	53.5
Miller	5.1	5.4	6.9	9.1	12.9	18.4	24.2	31.3	35.8	38.3	7.0	45.0
Pabst	11.8	12.5	13.1	4.3	15.7	17.0	16.0	15.4	15.1	15.0	(.6)	17.5
Schlitz	16.7	18.9	21.3	22.7	23.3	24.2	22.1	19.6	16.8	14.7	(12.5)	25.0
Coors	8.5	9.8	10.9	12.3	11.9	13.5	12.8	12.6	12.9	13.7	6.2	15.0
Heileman	9.4	9.9	10.5	9.5	10.0	9.6	10.6	10.5	11.3	13.3	17.7	14.5
Stroh	3.7	4.2	4.6	4.4	5.1	5.7	6.1	6.3	6.1	6.2	1.6	7.3
Olympia	4.2	4.4	4.7	5.3	6.6	7.3	6.8	6.7	6.1	6.1	0.0	9.0
Schaefer	5.6	5.5	5.6	5.7	5.9	5.2	4.7	3.9	3.5	3.6	2.9	5.0
Genesee	1.6	1.7	1.9	2.1	2.4	2.5	2.8	3.0	3.4	3.6	5.9	4.0
Schmidt	3.2	3.2	3.5	3.5	3.3	3.5	3.5	3.8	3.8	3.5	(7.9)	4.3
General	5.1	6.2	6.0	5.8	6.1	4.2	4.0	3.5	3.0	2.6	(13.3)	8.8
Pittsburgh	1.2	0.9	0.9	1.0	1.0	0.9	0.7	0.6	0.7	1.0	42.9	1.5
All others	29.2	24.2	20.5	17.6	10.9	11.2	8.2	6.0	6.0	3.2	(46.7)	3.5
Total	129.6	133.4	140.3	147.4	150.3	152.3	159.1	164.8	170.7	175.1	2.6	213.9
Less tax-free exports and military	2.2	1.6	1.8	1.9	1.7	1.9	2.2	2.6	2.6	2.6	0.0	
Total	127.4	131.8	138.5	145.5	148.6	150.4	156.9	162.2	168.1	172.5	2.6	
Imports	0.9	0.9	1.1	1.4	1.7	2.4	2.5	3.5	4.4	4.6	4.5	
Total U.S. consumption	128.3	132.7	139.6	146.9	150.3	152.8	159.4	165.7	172.5	177.1	2.7	

Note: Figures in millions of barrels.
Source: *Beverage Industry*, February 13, 1981.

to gain additional capacity. Other principal additions to Anheuser-Busch's capacity included a 4.4 million-barrel expansion of its Williamsburg, Virginia, plant in 1980 and 6.2 million-barrel expansion in Los Angeles in 1981.

Miller, the nation's second-largest brewer, had opened breweries in California and Georgia in 1980 which increased its capacity another 15 million barrels. Miller also planned to open a 10-million-barrel brewery in Trenton, Ohio, in 1982, which would bring its capacity even with that of Anheuser-Busch.

Assuming Anheuser-Busch and Miller were able to sell the additional production of the expansion, Standard and Poor's believed their combined market share could be 60 percent by 1983. Anheuser-Busch's stated goal was 40 percent market share by the end of the 1980s, while Miller's was, of course, to overtake Anheuser-Busch.

The second-tier brewers faced a stiff uphill climb against Anheuser-Busch and

EXHIBIT 7 Estimated market share by region for the top six brewers, full year 1979

	Anheuser-Busch	Miller	Schlitz	Pabst	Coors	Heileman	Total top 6	All other	Total industry
New England	33%	33%	9%	4%	—%	2%	81%	19%	100%
Mid-Atlantic	25	18	4	7	—	3	57	43	100
Total Northeast	27%	22%	5%	6%	—%	3%	63%	37%	100%
East North Central	16%	20%	5%	18%	—%	17%	76%	24%	100%
West North Central	23	19	9	15	12	13	91	9	100
Total North Central	18%	19%	6%	17%	3%	16%	80%	20%	100%
South Atlantic	35%	26%	16%	10%	—%	2%	88%	12%	100%
East South Central	28	41	12	7	—	5	92	8	100
West South Central	21	23	23	2	21	1	89	11	100
Total South	29%	27%	18%	7%	7%	2%	89%	11%	100%
Mountain	32%	13%	8%	3%	29%	4%	89%	11%	100%
Pacific	36	11	7	4	18	6	81	19	100
Total West	35%	12%	7%	3%	21%	5%	83%	17%	100%
Total all regions	27%	21%	10%	9%	8%	7%	81%	19%	100%

Note: Discrepancies due to rounding. 1980 data not available.
Source: U.S. Brewers Association, Beer Marketer's Insights, Inc., and Sanford C. Bernstein & Co.

Miller. Schlitz and Pabst had dropped volume in 1980, Stroh and Olympia held ground, and Coors and Heileman posted above-average gains. Stroh announced merger plans with F. M. Schaefer (ninth ranked) to be complete by 1985. Olympia, although holding volume steady, experienced a 59 percent earnings drop in 1980.

In 1981, Coors planned to expand into three more states (Arkansas, Louisiana, and Tennessee, which would bring its total to twenty), but also was diversifying into non-brewing business such as coal mining, and gas and oil exploration. Also, the successful 1980 marketing strategies of Coors *Light* helped boost its volume 6.2 percent, which, in turn, led to industry speculations that an East Coast brewery might be forthcoming.

Heileman was the fastest growing brewer in 1980 with a volume increase of 17.7 percent over 1979. During the 1970s, Heileman developed a strategy of acquiring a large number of troubled brewers at very low cost and turning them around quickly, as it did with Carling and Rainier, bought in 1979 and 1977, respectively. With more than forty labels, Heileman used many strategies to promote its beer. Six brands were sold nationally and the remainder, regionally, as Heileman capitalized on the regional demand for acquired brands, its excess capacity, and its wholesaler relationships.

Industry analysts predicted a shift away from an emphasis on volume growth to

EXHIBIT 8 Percentage distribution of barrelage by region for the top six brewers (full-year 1979)

	Anheuser-Busch	Miller	Schlitz	Pabst	Coors	Heileman	Total top 6	All other	Total industry
New England	7%	9%	5%	3%	—%	2%	6%	6%	6%
Mid-Atlantic	15	13	6	12	—%	8	11	34	16
Total Northeast	22%	22%	11%	15%	—%	10%	17%	40%	21%
East North Central	12%	18%	10%	40%	—%	49%	18%	23%	19%
West North Central	6	7	7	13	12	15	9	3	8
Total North Central	18%	25%	17%	54%	12%	64%	27%	26%	27%
South Atlantic	20%	19%	25%	18%	—%	4%	17%	10%	15%
East South Central	5	10	6	4	—	4	6	2	5
West South Central	8	12	26	2	30	2	12	6	11
Total South	34%	41%	57%	24%	30%	10%	35%	17%	31%
Mountain	7%	4%	5%	2%	22%	4%	6%	3%	6%
Pacific	20	8	10	6	36	13	15	14	15
Total West	26%	11%	15%	8%	57%	16%	21%	17%	20%
Total all regions	100%	100%	100%	100%	100%	100%	100%	100%	100%

Note: Discrepancies due to rounding. 1980 data not available.
Source: U.S. Brewers Association, Beer Marketer's Insights, Inc., and Sanford C. Bernstein & Co.

profitability improvement by Anheuser-Busch and Miller even though price-sensitive consumers were expected to make price escalation risky.

Overall, then, the pricing outlook for 1981 was uncertain. Higher costs for malt, barley, advertising, and packaging had to be offset by an 8 to 9 percent price increase according to Joseph Doyle of Smith Barney Harris Upham and Company, Inc. On the other hand, since 1975, beer prices had risen at only two-thirds the rate of increase for the Consumer Price Index (CPI), and analysts expected the 1981 rate of increase in beer prices to be less than the CPI.

Industry experts agreed with analyst Harold Davidson that: "the dominant parameter in marketing scale economy is not the total number of different markets a brewer is in, nor even his total volume. It is the share of the market he holds in his areas. Thus, it is possible for a strong regional to have more favorable marketing scale economies than a weak national."[2]

As Exhibits 7 and 8 indicate, all brewers except Anheuser-Busch and Miller showed a highly regional sales pattern which made them quite vulnerable to concen-

[2] Harold Davidson, "The Bell Doesn't Toll for All Small Brewers," *Beverage World*, March, 1981, p. 31.

trated assaults by the top two. A particularly competitive area was the West South Central region (see Exhibit 9). Texas was the largest market in this region with the top four competitors holding the following market shares in 1979:

Brand	Share
Schlitz	25%
Coors	23
Anheuser-Busch	20
Miller	18

The significance of Texas sales to Coors and Schlitz is easily understood by the fact that 23 percent of Coors' 1979 total sales volume and 20 percent of Schlitz's were from Texas.

Market Expansion

In an effort to compete successfully in the malt beverage market, domestic brewing companies had tried during the preceding two decades to grow through acquisitions, introduction of new products, and increased advertising. Growth into non-malt beverage production had also been seen as brewers entered container manufacturing, other alcoholic and non-alcoholic beverage industries, snack food sales, and even the energy field.

As a result of acquiring smaller, regional breweries and maintaining the local brands, the number of brewing companies continue to fall. Thus, in 1979 the total was forty-two, just half of the 1969 total. The number of breweries has also continued to decline as well, as shown in Exhibit 10.

Product line expansion had been characterized by the introduction of low-calorie, super-premium, and imported beers, plus cream ale, malt liquor, and "dark" beer. With the introduction of Miller's *Lite* into the beer market in 1975, the low-calorie beer segment increased drastically in popularity. This product was less costly to produce and yet could be sold at a premium price. Consequently, all of the major brewers competed in this segment by 1981.

Super-premium products were led by Anheuser-Busch's *Michelob*. However, entries were also made by Schlitz (*Erlanger*), Pabst (*Andeker*), Heileman (*Special Export*), and Coors (*Herman Joseph's*). Industry sources predicted that Miller would introduce a super-premium (probably named *Frederic Miller*) in 1981.

In 1979, the imported beer market grew 25 percent (400 percent since 1970), but continued to amount to only 2 to 3 percent of the total U.S. market. This market was shared by over one hundred brands and dominated by few. The growth rate in the imported beer market had not gone unnoticed by the domestic brewers, though. Most domestic brewers competed with imports using their super-premium product, but recognized the appeal in foreign beers. Consequently, some brewers had obtained the rights to produce and market foreign-brand beers domestically (as Miller had with *Lowenbrau*), while others simply distributed foreign beers for foreign

EXHIBIT 9 West South Central region barrelage and market share by major brewer

	1974	1975	1976	1977	1978	1979	1980E	1984E	
Barrels shipped (millions)									
Anheuser-Busch	3.0	3.0	2.3	3.0	3.5	3.9	4.4	4.9	6.5
Miller	0.8	1.6	2.0	2.7	3.5	4.4	5.0	5.5	7.0
Schlitz	4.8	.5.0	4.8	5.1	4.7	4.3	3.9	3.5	2.8
Pabst	0.2	0.2	0.2	0.3	0.3	0.3	0.3	0.3	0.4
Coors	2.4	2.6	3.7	3.7	3.7	3.9	4.6	4.6	5.3
Heilemen	0.2	0.2	0.2	0.2	0.2	0.2	0.2	0.2	0.2
Total top 6	11.4	12.6	13.2	15.0	15.9	17.0	18.0	19.0	22.2
All others	3.4	2.9	2.7	2.2	2.2	2.0	1.9	1.8	1.5
Total all brewers	14.8	15.5	15.9	17.2	18.1	19.0	19.9	20.8	23.7
Market share									
Anheuser-Busch	20%	19%	15%	17%	19%	21%	22%	24%	29%
Miller	5	10	13	16	19	23	25	26	32
Schlitz	32	32	30	30	26	23	20	17	11
Pabst	1	1	1	2	2	2	2	1	2
Coors	16	17	23	22	20	21	21	22	20
Heileman	1	1	1	1	1	1	1	1	1
Total top 6	77%	81%	83%	87%	88%	90%	90%	91%	95%
All others	23	19	17	13	12	10	10	9	5
Total all brewers	100%	100%	100%	100%	100%	100%	100%	100%	100%
Barrelage growth (annualized compounded growth rate)									
Anheuser-Busch		0 %	(23)%	30 %	17 %	11 %	13 %	11 %	10 %
Miller		100	25	35	30	26	14	10	8
Schlitz		4	(4)	6	(8)	(9)	(9)	(10)	(7)
Pabst		n/m	n/m	n/m	n/m	n/m	n/m	n/m	10
Coors		8	42	0	0	5	8	10	5
Heileman		n/m	n/m	n/m	n/m	n/m	n/m	n/m	n/m
Total top 6		11 %	5 %	14 %	6 %	7 %	6 %	6 %	5 %
All others		(15)	(7)	(19)	0	(9)	(5)	(5)	(6)
Total all brewers		5 %	3 %	8 %	8 %	5 %	5 %	5 %	5 %

Note: Discrepancies due to rounding.
n/m = not meaningful.
Pabst barrelage includes Blitz-Weinhard brands beginning April 1, 1979. Heileman barrelage includes Falls City and Carling-National Brands beginning January 1, 1979 and April 1, 1979, respectively.
Source: U.S. Brewers Association, Beer Marketer's Insights, Inc., and Sanford C. Bernstein & Co.

EXHIBIT 10
Number
of breweries
authorized
to operate
in the United States

Year	Number of breweries
1968	163
1969	158
1970	154
1971	148
1972	147
1973	122
1974	111
1975	102
1976	97
1977	94
1978	89
1979	90
1980	88

Source: U.S. Department of the Treasury,
Bureau of Alcohol, Tobacco, and Firearms.

firms. Thus, Anheuser-Busch marketed a German beer, importing *Wurzburger Hofbrau* in bulk and bottling it in the United States.

In the battle for market share, advertising expenditures had risen dramatically over the past decade, as shown in Exhibits 11 and 12. Rates for advertising in the broadcast and print media had escalated along with inflation, forcing brewers to re-examine these marketing expenditures in light of profitability. Industry analysts predicted a peaking of these costs in relation to revenues in 1981 and an emphasis toward non-media marketing programs designed to improve sales in specific, targeted markets.

Non-brewing endeavors like container manufacturing had grown as a result of rising packaging costs. Self-manufacturing of cans by brewers had shown an increasing trend with Anheuser-Busch participating not only in the production of cans for its own needs, but also in the development of advanced aluminum technology with Alusuisse, a Swiss aluminum company. Several brewers were also involved in recycling efforts as well. Glass containers were becoming more popular too. Cans

EXHIBIT 11
Media advertising
expenditures
for brewers

Company	1976	1977	1978	1979
Anheuser-Busch	$25.2	$45.0	$63.1	$87.1
Miller	29.0	42.1	64.0	75.0
Pabst	9.1	10.8	18.0	18.3
Schlitz	33.4	40.7	40.6	48.2

Note: Figures in millions of dollars.
Source: Leading National Advertisers, Inc. and Sanford C. Bernstein & Co., Inc.

EXHIBIT 12
Brewer's
expenditures
per barrel

Company	1976	1977	1978	1979
Anheuser-Busch	$0.89	$1.24	$1.52	$1.89
Coors	0.11	0.31	0.65	1.16
Miller	1.58	1.74	2.06	2.10
Pabst	0.54	0.68	1.17	1.22
Schlitz	1.38	1.85	2.08	2.87
Industry average[a]	0.97	1.28	1.61	1.92

[a] Weighted by estimated sales volume
Source: Goldman Sachs Research based on Leading National
Advertisers, "Ad $ Summary" (six measured media).

represented 64 percent of beer packaging in 1978 (latest available data), with that percentage expected to decrease as the costs for glass bottles continued to become more favorable.

Expansion into soft drinks by Anheuser-Busch (*Root 66* root beer), wine by Schlitz (Geyser Peak Winery), snack foods by Anheuser-Busch (*Eagle* snack line), and energy exploration by Coors (gas and coal) further indicated diversification opportunities for brewers. Philip Morris, of course, added to its diverse holdings with its acquisition of Miller Brewing Company in 1970.

Industry Financing

The maturity of the beer market had created intense competition which was also the position of the overall beverage industry. Exhibit 13 shows performance indicators for the overall beverage industry. Earnings predictions for the top five brewers by industry analyst Andrew J. Melnick appear in Exhibit 14.

The brewing industry was a capital-intensive business with a high percentage of fixed costs. As indicated in the composite statistics of the brewing industry in Exhibit 15, the average operating margin was 10.5 percent, with an average net profit margin of 4.1 percent. The *Value Line* projections for 1982–85 (shown in Exhibit 15) indicated a rise in the industry operating margin to 11 percent and a rise in the net profit margin to 4.5 percent.

Labor

The labor force in the brewing industry was largely unionized. Consequently, strikes in the industry could seriously hamper competitive strategies. For example, a 100-day strike of Anheuser-Busch production workers in 1976 resulted in a 17 percent loss of volume. At the same time, Miller gained 43 percent.

The average salary of production workers employed in the industry jumped 88.1 percent between 1970 and 1977, making brewing workers the highest paid employees in the beverage business with an average annual wage of $18,942 according to the U.S. Department of Commerce. Nonproduction employees' wages rose 72 percent for a 1977 average of $20,806. Government figures placed the average annual salary for *all* beer industry employees for 1979 at $19,493.

EXHIBIT 13 Beverage industry yardsticks of management performance

	Profitability								Growth			
	Return on equity				Return on total capital				Sales		Earnings per share	
	5-year average	5-year rank	Latest 12 months	Debt/ equity ratio	Latest 12 months	5-year rank	5-year average	Net profit margin	5-year average	5-year rank	5-year average	5-year rank
G. Heileman Brewing	30.2%	1	33.7%	0.3	23.9%	2	22.3%	4.8%	26.2%	1	30.3%	1
Coca-Cola	23.6	2	21.6	0.0	20.2	1	22.3	7.4	14.1	4	11.9	4
Pepsi	21.9	3	22.1	0.5	15.3	3	16.0	4.9	19.6	2	16.5	2
Brown-Forman Dist.	16.8	4	23.9	0.4	17.1	5	13.0	8.2	11.7	7	16.2	3
Heublein	16.2	5	16.8	0.5	12.0	7	11.7	4.1	9.7	9	9.3	9
Anheuser-Busch	15.6	6	18.1	0.5	11.5	9	10.0	5.2	13.7	5	9.3	8
Royal Crown	15.0	7	12.5	0.6	9.3	4	13.0	2.9	13.6	6	3.4	11
National Distillers	12.9	8	10.5	0.3	8.4	8	10.2	5.0	8.2	11	10.8	5
Adolph Coors	12.8	9	10.8	0.0	10.0	6	12.1	8.2	11.5	8	7.9	10
Seagram	10.8	10	11.8	0.4	9.8	10	8.4	5.7	6.3	12	10.3	6
Olympia Brewing	8.5	11	4.3	0.2	4.1	11	7.4	0.8	17.1	3	10.1	7
Pabst Brewing	6.8	12	4.1	0.1	3.7	12	6.2	1.3	8.4	10	-4.3	12
Schlitz	0.7	13	def	0.3	def	13	1.4	def	5.4	13	-44.4	13
Industry medians	15.0		12.5	0.3	10.0		11.7	4.9	11.7		10.1	
All industry medians	15.8		16.1	0.4	11.0		11.1	5.0	14.3		13.9	

Source: *Forbes*, January 5, 1981, p. 216.

EXHIBIT 14
Brewers' earnings projections

	Earnings per share			P/E ratio	
	1980	1981E	1982E	1981E	1982E
Anheuser-Busch	$3.80	$4.50	$5.00	7.9	7.1
Coors	1.86	2.20	2.70	6.6	5.4
Heileman	3.98	4.70	5.40	7.1	6.1
Pabst	1.55	1.30	1.65	13.1	10.3
Schlitz	0.93	0.90	0.90	11.3	11.3

Note: E = Estimate.
Source: Andrew J. Melnick, "Brewing Industry Review," for Drexel Burnham Lambert, Inc., March 17, 1981, p. 819.

While wages have increased between 1970 and 1977, the number of employees has dropped by 23.2 percent during the same period. This includes an 18.2 percent drop among production workers and a 33.2 percent drop among nonproduction workers. Cost-cutting efforts, production slumps, technological improvements, and industry consolidation were cited as the principal reasons for the drop, which has resulted in average annual percentage increases in output per employee hour and output per employee of between 6.3 and 8.8 for the 1973–1978 period.

The Brewing Process

In the 1970s and early 1980s the actual brewing process involved the production of beer from malted barley, hops, and water, with or without the addition of other carbohydrate materials. Malted barley or malt was the principal brewing ingredient. The brewing functions outlined in Exhibit 16 were typical of the basic brewing process. The following is a brief description of that process:

Production stage	Description
Mashing	The brewer grinds the malt, producing a liquid grain residue.
Lautering	The grain is passed through a straining device which removes insolubles, creating a clear liquid called wort.
Kettle boil	Hops or extracts are added to give aroma and taste.
Wort cooling	The wort is sent through a hop strainer to remove protein-like semisolids by settling, filtration, and centrifugation.
Yeast pitching	Yeast is added to the wort and it is allowed to grow and ferment. (Active growth of the yeast takes forty-eight hours.)
Lagering	At the end of primary fermentation, lasting four to seven days, the yeast settles to the bottom of the fermenter. (Note: brewers vary the length of time they age beer, varying from a few days to a few months. Lagering is done in an environment of 0–10 degrees Centigrade.)
Finishing and packaging	The new beer is given a brief, chill-proofing treatment, filtered, carbonated, and packaged. (Note: In the 1980s, over 80 percent of packaged beer was put into cans or bottles, which were then pasteurized.)

EXHIBIT 15 Beer industry composite statistics

	1976	1977	1978	1979	1980E	1981E	1983–1985E
Sales ($mil)	6,327.8	6,437.4	7,235.8	8,412.7	9,700	11,200	16,300
Operating margin	12.9%	12.3%	11.1%	10.6%	10.5%	10.6%	11.0%
Depreciation ($mil)	205.6	230.2	254.8	273.8	305	340	475
Net profit ($mil)	292.2	281.5	265.1	290.5	400	370	740
Income tax rate	46.3%	43.3%	44.8%	36.6%	40.0%	41.5%	43.5%
Net profit margin	4.6%	4.3%	3.7%	3.5%	4.1%	4.2%	4.5%
Working capital ($mil)	666.6	736.6	739.3	692.2	800	880	1,650
Long-term debt ($mil)	938.7	906.0	965.9	1,064.6	1,325	1,525	1,400
Net worth ($mil)	2,424.3	2,556.9	2,659.9	2,887.2	3,260	3,660	5,400
% earned total capital	9.8%	9.1%	8.4%	8.4%	10.0%	10.5%	12.0%
% earned net worth	12.1%	11.0%	10.0%	10.1%	12.5%	13.0%	14.0%
% retained to common eq.	8.4%	7.3%	6.1%	6.8%	9.5%	10.0%	10.5%
% all divds. to net profit	32%	35%	40%	34%	25%	25%	25%
Avg. annual P/E ratio	12.4	10.3	10.6	9.9	—	—	14.0
Avg. annual divd. yield	2.5%	3.3%	3.7%	3.4%	—	—	1.8%

Note: E = estimate.
Source: *Value Line*, March 6, 1981, p. 1553. Reprinted by permission of the publisher. Copyright 1981, Value Line, Inc.

EXHIBIT 16
Schematic of the
brewing process

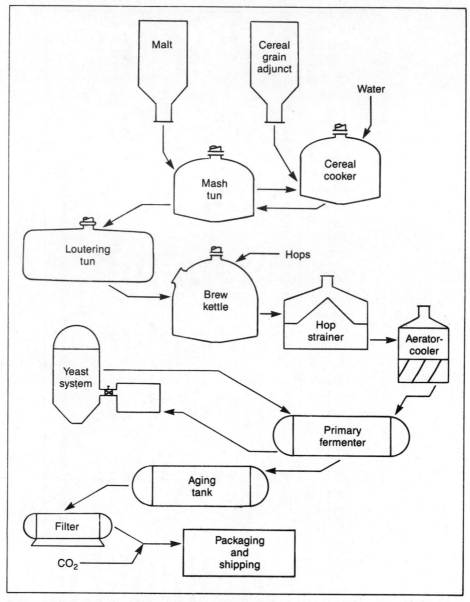

Source: Clifford F. Gastineau, William J. Darby, and Thomas B. Turner, eds., *Fermented Food Beverages in Nutrition* (New York: Academic Press, 1979), p. 247.

At the brewery, all product was shipped within twenty days of production, with the average time in inventory of two to three days. Only full truck, railcar, or container loads were shipped from the brewery. Thus, wholesalers were required to order sufficient product to fill a vehicle. However, if packaged beer is not consumed within ninety to one hundred days after packaging, a noticeable degradation in quality takes place.

Technology

In 1981, the latest development in achieving a nitrosamine- (known carcinogen) free beer consisted of the removal of most organic compounds, color, and heavy metals through the use of ozone, which replaced the chemical treatment of water, which was considered the source of the nitrosamine problem. Some advantages of ozonation over chemically treated water included: bacterial disinfection, color removal, odor removal, viral inactivation, taste removal, and algae removal. The largest application for ozone was the cooling water and boiling water, since algae growth and scaling were the largest problems in the industry. Recent studies of ozone treatment by the Jet Propulsion Laboratory indicated savings of 55 percent on operating costs, via savings on water and chemicals.

Government Controls and Litigation

Federal, state, and local governmental actions have also provided opportunities and threats to the brewing industry. Restrictions, implemented from 1980 until May 1981, on grain sales to the Soviet Union had a leveling effect on grain costs. With the discovery that many beers contained traces of nitosamines, a potent carcinogen, the Food and Drug Administration (FDA) ordered brewers to adjust production methods to reduce the level of nitrosamines to less than five parts per billion by the beginning of 1980. Schlitz made the necessary adjustments and according to Chairman McKeithan's comments at Schlitz's 1980 Annual Stockholder's Meeting: "All of our beer products are within the FDA guidelines . . . in short, nitrosamines are not a problem with any Schlitz malt beverage."

The federal Bureau of Alcohol, Tobacco, and Firearms (ATF) continued to consider and reconsider regulatory requirements regarding alcoholic beverage advertising, trade practice regulations, and ingredient labelling requirements. Topics covered in proposed regulations in 1981 included delineation of the use of the terms "light" and "natural," definitions of false and disparaging advertising covering rules for comparative taste tests, and bans on the use of "active" athletes or athletic events where participants consume alcoholic beverages before or during the event.

Statistics indicated an increase in alcohol abuse and the dangerous characteristics of alcohol (e.g., for pregnant women, highway safety, teenager abuse, etc.) prompted the federal government to begin efforts to curb alcohol abuse. Although warning labels were discussed, no statutory or regulatory action was initiated by 1982. Public awareness and education efforts were under way via television and radio media, schools, and social agencies, however. Also, some local jurisdictions began taking action to ban alcohol consumption on public property in order to combat crime and civil disturbances, and to promote highway safety.

Related to the above has been a slowly developing, yet accelerating emphasis on changes in state laws raising the minimum drinking age. During the turbulent sixties when eighteen-year-olds were drafted into military service for Vietnam, many states lowered the age of majority (drinking, voting, etc.) to eighteen. Since then, however, alcohol abuse by teenagers has prompted several states to initiate and/or finalize legislation to raise the legal drinking age to nineteen, twenty, or twenty-one.

Several states and local jurisdictions also enacted legislation concerning beverage containers and packaging. Included were bans on pull-tabs, nonbiodegradable plastic connecting devices, and nonreturnable bottles, and mandatory deposits on beer and soft drink beverage containers. Another approach known as a "litter tax" imposed a percentage tax on gross sales for all industries in which products contributed to litter (newspapers, bottlers, canners, supermarkets, brewers, etc.). A summary of such legislation and pending legislation is contained in Exhibit 17.

Although Schlitz opposed all attempts to restrict packaging and to require deposits, management supported the "litter tax" because it was a broad-based tax on all components of the solid waste stream. Thus, according to Schlitz's 1977 Annual Report: "Such a tax would finance resource recovery and community-wide litter programs which deal more completely with the problem. . . ." Schlitz's management also believed that further enactment of deposit bills and packaging restrictions laws would not materially affect its relative position in the brewing industry "since the impact will fall on all members of the industry" (1977 Annual Report).

At a time when most American industries were actively advocating reducing governmental influence in their affairs, brewers were actually inviting governmental inquiries in efforts to seek competitive advantages.

Some examples of such strategies included:[3]

The Miller Brewing Company's request to the Federal Trade Commission (FTC) to prohibit Anheuser-Busch from using the word "natural" in reference to its products

The Miller Brewing Company's challenge of Anheuser-Busch's promotion of *Michelob Light* as a light beer because it contained more calories than certain other light beers

Miller also contested as a trademark infringement several brewers' (including Schlitz's) use of the term "light" and "lite" in marketing low-calorie beer

Miller's dispute of Anheuser-Busch's advertising claim that dark bottles were better than clear ones

Miller, in turn, was questioned for marketing its domestic product as *Lowenbrau*, a foreign beer name

The Justice Department and FTC were also carefully monitoring the industry trend toward greater concentration and consolidation. Some greater leniency has

---

[3] "Beverages and Tobacco: The Outlook," p. B-71.

EXHIBIT 17
Litter control
legislation at the
state level

	Mandatory deposits	Litter/ recycling laws	Bans metal pull tab tops	Bills pending	
				Restrictive container	Litter/ recycling
Alaska					●
California		●	●		
Colorado		●			
Connecticut	●	●	●		
Delaware	●a		●		
Georgia		●c			
Hawaii			●		
Iowa	●				
Kentucky		●			
Louisiana				●	●
Maine	●		●		
Massachusetts			●	●	
Michigan	●b		●		
Minnesota			●		
Montana				●	
Nebraska		●			
New Jersey				●	
New York				●	
Ohio					●
Oregon	●b		●		
Pennsylvania				●	
South Carolina		●	●		
Vermont	●		●		
Virginia		●	●		
Washington		●			

Note: Table shows laws either enacted or passed, but not effective as of June 1980.
a Laws contingent upon enactment by Md. and Pa.
b Two-tier deposits.
c Voluntary program.
Sources: Can Manufacturers Institute, Glass Packaging Institute, and National Can Corp.

been seen in the approval of mergers, as evidenced by the approval of Heileman's acquisition of Carling in 1979, since the same acquisition by Pabst had earlier been discouraged.

SCHLITZ'S BACKGROUND AND HISTORY

The Joseph Schlitz Brewing Company was incorporated in Wisconsin in 1920, growing out of a company established in Milwaukee in 1849 by August Krug. Joseph Schlitz took over at Krug's death in 1856. At Schlitz's death in 1875, the company was willed to August Krug's four nephews, the Uihleins, with the stipulation that the name remain unchanged. At the end of 1980, the Uihlein family retained an estimated 60 to 75 percent of the stock of the company. Until 1976, the Joseph Schlitz Breweries had been headed by a Uihlein for four generations, when Chairman Robert Uihlein died of leukemia at the age of sixty. Daniel McKeithan, the present Chairman, was previously married to a Uihlein and had served as a director of the company. The family had such respect for his abilities that they made him Chairman after Robert Uihlein's death, despite the fact he was divorced and there were other Uihleins available to take over the position. In 1981 Schlitz was one of the largest U.S. corporations still under family control.

The Joseph Schlitz Brewing Company had grown from a one-brand, single-plant brewery to a six-brand, multi-plant company. Its product line included *Schlitz* (a premium beer), *Schlitz Light, Old Milwaukee* (popularly priced), *Old Milwaukee Light, Schlitz Malt Liquor,* and *Erlanger* (a super-premium beer). In addition to its six brands, Schlitz operated five aluminum can manufacturing plants through its container division. Other subsidiaries of the company included Geyser Peak Winery, a wholly owned subsidiary in Geyserville, California, acquired in 1972, which produced and sold twelve different wines under the brand labels *Voltaire* and *Summit*; and Murphy Products Company in Burlington, Wisconsin, a wholly owned subsidiary acquired in 1971, which processed and marketed animal feeds and feed concentrates from by-products of brewery grains. C & D Foods, a subsidiary of Murphy Products Company, grew and processed ducklings, which were sold to food wholesalers and major food chains. Schlitz also had investments in two Spanish breweries (La Cruz del Campo and Henninger Espanola) which did not contribute significantly to Schlitz's operations.

SCHLITZ'S CURRENT OPERATIONS

Organization and Management

Schlitz's organization structure as of May 1, 1981, is shown in Exhibit 18, with further detail on the organization of its marketing and operations departments shown in Exhibit 19. The container division, as well as the wholly owned subsidiaries reported directly to the president, as did the areas of finance, sales, government and legal, purchasing and materials services, and general counsel. The average age of all Schlitz officers on March 1, 1980, was fifty. Over the past several years, Schlitz had attempted to strengthen its management by recruiting marketing executives from the beverage industry. As noted, the Uihlein family owned a significant portion of the stock in Schlitz and the family continued to be involved in the operations of the company. Thus, a former president of Schlitz, Roy C. Satchell, said he left the company because he would never feel free to run it. "There were not many family members in management, but the family did influence the company behind the scenes."[4]

---

[4] Charles G. Burck, "Putting Schlitz Back on the Track," *Fortune*, April 24, 1978, p. 46.

EXHIBIT 18 Schlitz's 1977–1980 organization chart

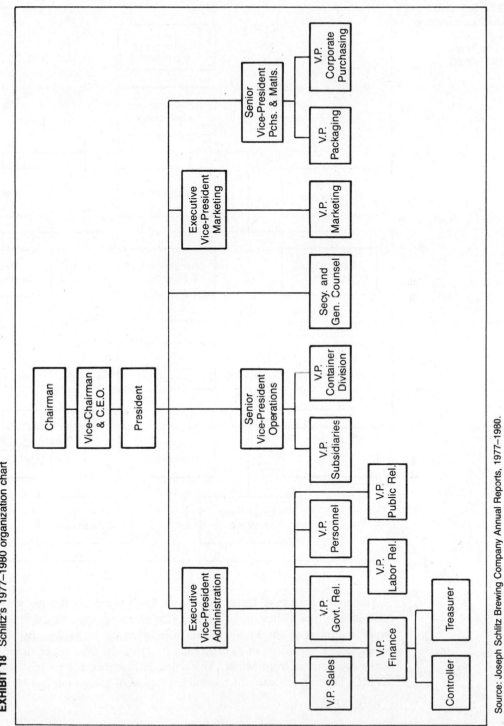

EXHIBIT 19
Schlitz's marketing
and operations
departments,
1977–1980

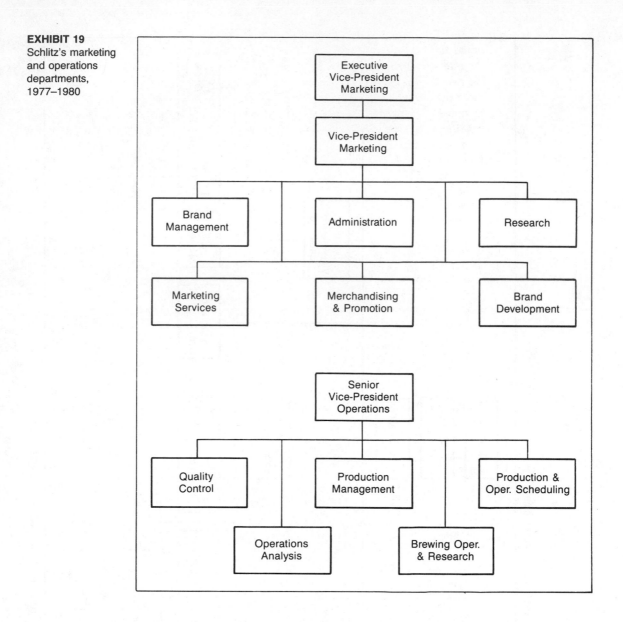

The major problems facing Schlitz in 1981 began in the early 1970s, when competition from Miller began affecting the entire brewing industry because of the large amount of funds Philip Morris was investing in Miller. By 1976, Schlitz completed the expansion of its plant capacity just as its sales began dropping because of the competition from Miller. This sales decline was aggravated by a change in Schlitz's brewing process which resulted in a loss of a large number of loyal Schlitz-brand drinkers. In addition, management at this time was faced with a cloud of indictments alleging improper payments to distributors, while constant feuding among the two-hundred-plus descendents of Uihleins perpetually diverted management from more important things. After Frank J. Sellinger joined the company in 1977, Schlitz mounted an aggressive internal campaign to increase efficiency and spur new product development. The end result was an increase in 1980's profits and vigorous activity with new products such as *Erlanger*, an all-barley malt beer, and *Old Milwaukee Light* beer. Publicity releases from Schlitz in 1981 characterized Sellinger as follows:

> *In his forty-four years in the brewing industry, Frank J. Sellinger has become one of the most knowledgeable figures in the industry. There is no major part of the beer business with which he is not personally familiar.*
>
> *Today, at age sixty-six, Frank J. Sellinger could be in sunny retirement. Instead, he's battling with gusto in the much publicized beer wars and, as Chief Executive Officer of Joseph Schlitz Brewing Company, is a pivotal member of the new management team that is leading the firm out of the trenches and into the attack.*

Operations

As of May 1981, Schlitz maintained five breweries and five canning facilities in the United States. Prior to 1981, Schlitz had also operated a brewery in Syracuse, New York and a brewery in Honolulu, Hawaii. However, the sale of these breweries was necessary according to management, because the company was operating at only 54 percent of its capacity in 1979. This divestiture left Schlitz with a brewing capacity of 25.6 million barrels (see Exhibit 20 for a breakdown by brewery). Thus, in 1980, the five remaining breweries operated at a capacity of 58 percent, compared to Schlitz's prior capacity utilization of 54 percent in 1979, 62 percent in 1978, and 75 percent in 1977. This decline in capacity utilization occurred because Schlitz's volume had dropped from a high of 24.2 million barrels in 1977 to 15.7 million barrels in 1980, an overall decline of 35 percent.

EXHIBIT 20
Schlitz brewery capacities

Location	1977	1978	1979	1980
Milwaukee	6.8	6.8	6.8	6.8
Memphis	5.5	5.5	5.5	5.5
Syracuse	2.0	5.4	5.4	—
Winston-Salem	5.0	5.0	5.0	5.0
Longview	3.8	3.8	3.8	3.8
Los Angeles	3.0	3.0	3.0	3.0
Tampa	1.5	1.5	1.5	1.5
Honolulu	0.4	0.4	—	—
Total	28.0	31.4	31.0	25.6

Note: Data in millions of barrels.
Source: Schlitz Annual Reports.

In 1978, *Fortune* observed that: "[Schlitz's] breweries as a group are still the most efficient in the industry."[5] Schlitz continually studied methods to improve the efficiency of its breweries. One typical study involved Johns-Manville, its filter aid supplier. Jointly Schlitz and Manville studied filtration at Schlitz breweries, with the result that Schlitz instituted standardized filtration procedures at all breweries which increased filter run times 20–25 percent and simplified maintenance schedules. Hours of labor per barrel filtered were also reduced, and purchasing and invoicing were simplified.

In 1970, Schlitz entered the container industry by constructing a can manufacturing plant in Oak Creek, Wisconsin, with a capacity of two billion cans per year. By 1980, Schlitz had constructed four more canning plants located in Winston-Salem, North Carolina; Longview, Texas; Tampa, Florida; and Los Angeles, California, with a total capacity of over three billion cans and lids per year. Production in 1980 amounted to 4.6 billion cans, utilizing approximately 92 percent of Schlitz's capacity and 3 percent of the total aluminum used in the United States. In addition, the self-manufacture of cans and lids provided approximately 90 percent of the company's requirements in 1980.

In the mid-1970s, Schlitz also phased in a more efficient brewing process which saved money, but as noted, customers did not like the new beer. Schlitz completed this conversion after eight years of research and a large capital investment. The change, known as "Accurate Balanced Fermentation," kept the yeast in active suspension for the exact time necessary to complete fermentation. In a further effort to cut costs, Schlitz also put in more corn syrup and less barley malt, the relatively expensive ingredient commonly used to give beer its flavor and body. To address this problem and get uniform quality and taste from each brewery, Sellinger imposed strong central controls on all plants shortly after he joined the company in 1977. Among other things, he required that Schlitz's tasting department get daily samples from each plant. Quality control was also improved by having test control personnel report directly to Milwaukee and by giving them final say over what left each plant.

Marketing

In 1977, Schlitz marketed four of the nine American beers in national distribution, more than any other brewer. Since that time, Schlitz's two major brands, premium-priced *Schlitz* and popular-priced *Old Milwaukee*, have both lost market share. (Market share in Texas dropped 4 percent in 1979, with the gain to Anheuser-Busch and Miller.) In addition, *Schlitz Light*, introduced in 1975, has continually fallen below sales expectations, despite reformulations and repackaging to improve its image. Also, in 1979 Schlitz entered the fast growing and highly profitable super-premium category with *Erlanger* to compete with earlier introductions by Anheuser-Busch (*Michelob*) and by Miller (*Lowenbrau*). Only one year later it was expanded nationally. This is an impressive statistic for any product, but *Erlanger*

[5] Charles G. Burck, p. 50.

still had a long way to go to catch up. Schlitz also test marketed another light beer in 1979, *Tribute*, later renamed *Old Milwaukee Light*, and its expansion to full nationwide distribution was planned for the summer of 1981.

The one area where Schlitz led the industry was with malt liquor, specifically the *Schlitz Bull* brand. Sales of this malt liquor represented about 3 percent of the total beer market and, according to company executives, aggressive advertising had been responsible for its success. Schlitz's strength in each region of the United States is indicated in Exhibit 21.

According to Schlitz representatives, Schlitz conducted major segmentation studies on a periodic basis to determine how to properly position its brands in the marketplace. These studies identified need segments of beer drinkers, including both those with physiological needs and those with psychological needs. Schlitz also conducted a major consumer tracing study each year to determine to whom commercials should be targeted from a media standpoint. These studies aided Schlitz in developing demographic profiles of its target drinkers as well as brands that were bought by different demographic groups. It also allowed Schlitz to determine the target groups it should attempt to reach via different media, such as television, radio, print, and outdoor advertising.

In 1981, advertising agencies which handled the Schlitz account included: J. Walter Thompson (Chicago) for the *Schlitz* and *Erlanger* brands; Della Fermina, Travisano, and Partners (New York) for *Schlitz Light*; Benton and Bowles (New York) for *Schlitz Malt Liquor*; and B.B.D. & O. International (New York) for *Old Milwaukee*.

For most of the 1970s, the *Schlitz* (premium beer) brand accounted for over 60 percent of Schlitz's sales. Schlitz's famous advertising campaign for its premium, "Go for the Gusto," had been very successful for many years. By 1977, however, *Schlitz's* advertising began to lose its edge. To revive itself, Schlitz introduced a series of formidable beer drinkers who responded to a suggestion that they abandon *Schlitz* for another beer. The beer drinker would glower into the camera and demand, "You want to take away my gusto?" The commercials did not receive a good reception from most viewers, though, and were dropped in the fall of 1977 and replaced by the traditional "gusto" commercials.

In January 1978, Schlitz invited a select group of advertising agencies to prepare bids for acquisition of the Schlitz account since it was dissatisfied with the directions of advertising strategy being pursued by Burnett, Ted Bates, and Company. Even so, many in the advertising industry felt Schlitz had created the advertising problem itself by pressuring Burnett to drop the "gusto" campaign. Eventually, Schlitz selected the J. Walter Thompson Agency to coordinate the Schlitz premium account. Thompson had been the agency which handled the Schlitz account previously (1956–61).

In August 1979, J. Walter Thompson initiated a *Schlitz* premium marketing program featuring strenuous activities and people who reached for the gusto. This was the so-called "Go for it" campaign. Packaging for *Schlitz* premium was also changed at this time to a tapered "classic" bottle, with slim lines and a gold foil

EXHIBIT 21 Schlitz barrelage by region (millions)

	1974	1975	1976	1977	1978	1979	1980	1981E	1984E
New England	2.3	2.2	2.1	1.7	1.2	0.9	0.7	0.6	0.3
Mid-Atlantic	1.3	1.2	1.7	1.7	1.5	1.0	0.8	0.7	0.4
Total Northeast	3.6	3.4	3.8	3.4	2.7	1.9	1.5	1.3	0.7
East North Central	3.2	3.1	2.9	2.5	2.1	1.7	1.4	1.2	0.9
West North Central	1.9	2.0	2.0	1.7	1.4	1.2	1.0	0.8	0.5
Total North Central	5.1	5.1	4.9	4.2	3.4	2.9	2.4	2.0	1.4
South Atlantic	5.0	5.1	5.5	4.8	4.7	4.2	3.9	3.6	2.7
East South Central	2.3	2.3	2.3	1.9	1.4	1.0	0.9	0.8	0.6
West South Central	4.8	5.0	4.8	5.1	4.7	4.3	3.9	3.5	2.8
Total South	12.1	12.4	12.6	11.8	10.8	9.5	8.7	7.9	6.1
Mountain	0.7	0.8	0.9	0.9	0.9	0.8	0.7	0.6	0.5
Pacific	1.2	1.6	2.0	1.8	1.8	1.7	1.6	1.5	1.2
Total West	1.9	2.4	2.9	2.7	2.7	2.5	2.3	2.1	1.7
Total all regions	22.7	23.3	24.2	22.1	19.6	16.8	14.9	13.3	9.9

Note: Discrepancies due to rounding.
E = estimate.
Source: U.S. Brewer's Association, Beer Marketer's Insights, Inc., and Sanford C. Bernstein & Company.

label, and distribution to bars and restaurants was given major importance in the overall effort.

In 1980, Thompson shifted the Schlitz advertising from the revised "Gusto" campaign to one involving the use of Schlitz's president Frank Sellinger. This type of advertising was begun in the beer industry in March 1979 when Pittsburgh Brewing introduced the first such ad. They were followed shortly thereafter by the F. X. Matt Brewing Company, and then by Schlitz. Both Pittsburgh and Matt were regional brewers and the president concept was highly successful for them. Schlitz also felt the president concept had improved sales, but no conclusive figures were available by early 1981. These campaigns received positive responses from beer wholesalers, however, a very important group in the industry. In 1981 Schlitz planned to film yet another commercial with Frank Sellinger, who had appeared in its two previous presidential commercials.

During 1980, Schlitz also initiated a taste test during National Football League playoff games. In this context, the 1980 *Schlitz Annual Report* stated: "More than one hundred million Americans watched the Super Bowl (1981) which included the fifth of Schlitz beer's Great American Beer Tests. In these unique live television commercials, beer drinkers compared the taste of Schlitz and their regular brand of beer — with impressive results for Schlitz." During these taste tests, the participants identified themselves as drinkers of a competing beer brand. The highest percentage of drinkers selecting their regular beer brand in preference to Schlitz in these taste tests was 54 percent for Budweiser. Schlitz also placed among the top three brands in several regional taste tests conducted by various news media during this period. Some industry observers expressed skepticism about the results and effectiveness of these tests, however. They noted that most American beers, unlike most European brands, were subtly flavored and that a trained palate was required to distinguish among such beers. They also noted that probably no more than one person in one hundred had such a palate so that the test was really like a coin flipping contest which should produce 50/50 results over the long run. In addition, one former Schlitz marketing executive expressed doubts that the tests would prompt anyone to try Schlitz. Schlitz beer's reputation was so bad, he contended, that many people were actually ashamed to be seen drinking it. He suggested that no matter how favorable the results may seem, television viewers would automatically reject them.

Despite those reservations, the Great American Beer Tests represented a major part of Schlitz's strategy of heavy television advertising for sports events. Thus, in 1980, Schlitz estimated that its commercials run during network sporting events were seen seven times per month in 91 percent of American households.

The remaining brands brewed by Schlitz each had its own advertising campaign and packaging strategy tailored to reflect its particular advantages. Among these brands, *Old Milwaukee* beer was second in sales volume for Schlitz. Its advertising strategy included point of sale advertising and radio and television commercials that reenforced its name with the following jingle: "Whenever you think of the town of Milwaukee, you think of beer — and *Old Milwaukee* tastes as great as its name.''

Schlitz Malt Liquor, the largest selling malt liquor in the U.S. and third largest volume seller for Schlitz, utilized an advertising campaign centered around the famous *Schlitz Malt Liquor* bull. *Erlanger*, Schlitz's new super-premium beer which went national in April 1980, featured advertisements emphasizing its unique bottle and the slogan, ''Taste the Moment.''

Old Milwaukee Light, introduced in August 1980, debuted with the slogan: ''We got the taste of light right.'' The *Old Milwaukee Light* advertising campaign for the first quarter of 1981 featured a discount in price of *Old Milwaukee Light* and *Old Milwaukee*, accompanied by the slogans ''The price of great taste just went down'' and ''It doesn't get any better than this.''

Since the mid-1970s Schlitz had not been able to match Anheuser-Busch and Miller in total advertising dollars; on a per barrel basis, however, Schlitz led the industry (see Exhibit 12). Furthermore, in 1977 Schlitz executives in their Annual Report announced that ''[We will be] striving to develop advertising that is more cost effective than that of our competition.'' Frank Sellinger summarized Schlitz's advertising opportunities for the future as follows:[6]

> *The brewing industry has become a marketing battleground with the continuing barrage of advertising. It must confuse the consumer. Sometimes I'm not sure if people know whether they're buying a good beer or clever advertisement. We're trying to cut through that confusion with a simple message: we brew superior beer; try it and judge for yourself.*

Litigation

Legal battles have continually plagued Schlitz. A six-year-old antitrust lawsuit filed by the Pearl Brewing Company of San Antonio, Texas, and seven of its independent wholesalers was finally settled in 1977 with Schlitz agreeing to pay Pearl $2.6 million.

The same year, a Securities and Exchange Commission (SEC) civil suit was filed which alleged violations of the antifraud, proxy, and reporting provisions of federal securities law, particularly in regard to the company's domestic marketing practices and relationship with Spanish brewing investments designed to evade Spanish tax and exchange control laws. The suit was settled in 1978. Schlitz, without admitting or denying any of the allegations, consented to:

1. A permanent injunction prohibiting future violations
2. The appointment of a Special Review Person by the SEC to review Schlitz's procedures followed in its internal investigation, accounting, and bookkeeping practices in the Export Marketing Division, disclosures, and to make recommendations regarding past and future disclosures

[6] Brooker, p. 3.

3. The establishment of an Audit Committee of the Board of Directors, comprised of three outside directors, to review the company's financial controls and accounting procedures

In 1978, Schlitz was also indicted (on March 15) on three counts of felony tax fraud, one misdemeanor charge of conspiracy, and seven hundred individual misdemeanor counts allegedly in violation of the Federal Alcohol Administration Act (FAAA) following a three-year federal grand jury investigation assisted by the Treasury Department's Alcohol, Tobacco, and Firearms (ATF) division and the Internal Revenue Service (IRS). These charges stemmed from questionable marketing practices including the furnishing of products, equipment, services, and possible cash payments by Schlitz to retail accounts to induce the purchase of Schlitz company products. Settlement was reached in November 1978, with all but one count dismissed, including the felony tax fraud counts. Schlitz, although again not admitting any wrongdoing, agreed to pay $761,000 and to refrain from any questionable marketing practices in the future.

In 1979, the United States Court of Appeals Seventh Circuit upheld the dismissal of claims filed by the Miller Brewing Company against Schlitz in 1975. Miller had alleged trademark infringement in the way Schlitz used the term "light" in distributing *Schlitz Light* beer. The court reaffirmed an earlier determination that the word "light" and "lite" may not be exclusively appropriated by Miller as a trademark. The appeals court remanded for trial Miller's claim against Schlitz for unfair competition.

During this same period, Schlitz faced various other allegations and suits (both criminal and civil) in the antitrust areas of price fixing, monopolization, and illegal trade promotions. These allegations were all resolved by 1980 with no material erosion of Schlitz's position.

Finance

After nearly three decades of growth, Schlitz's sales began falling in the late seventies. Consequently, the company logged five straight quarters of red ink beginning with the fourth quarter of fiscal 1978. However, as of December 31, 1980, four straight quarters of profits had been reported, even though barrel shipments continued to decline. Despite these reported profits, Schlitz clearly faced a challenge in turning around the sales of its *Schlitz* brand (see Exhibits 22–25). Stock prices declined with sales (see Exhibit 26).

In 1980, Schlitz's earnings from operations were $30.1 million compared to a $77 million loss in 1979 and earnings of $36.0 million in 1978. In 1980, sales increased slightly to $897 million from $894 million in 1979. Sales of cans and lids to outside parties amounted to $78.9 million in 1980, $76.5 million in 1979, and $36.9 million in 1978. The key factors in the company's 1980 earnings performance included higher beer selling prices, lower production costs, and higher interest income. Thus, beer selling prices increased approximately 10 percent in 1980, while lower production costs and higher interest income were related to the closing of

EXHIBIT 22
Schlitz's
consolidated
balance sheets
for years ended
December 31

Assets	1979	1980
Current assets		
Cash	$ 10,661	$ 8,097
Marketable securities, at lower of cost or market	30,525	134,525
Accounts receivable, less reserves of $913 in 1980 and $891 in 1979	25,011	31,049
Receivable from sale of assets	30,000	30,000
Refundable income taxes	24,292	—
Inventories, at lower of cost or market	55,491	54,571
Prepaid expenses	5,501	3,756
Total current assets	181,481	261,998
Investments and other assets		
Notes receivable and other noncurrent assets	63,028	38,621
Investments	16,407	14,514
Land and equipment held for sale	6,711	6,710
	86,146	59,845
Plant and equipment at cost	661,305	663,176
Less accumulated depreciation and unamortized investment tax credit	319,783	346,056
	341,522	317,120
	$609,149	$638,963

Liabilities		
Current liabilities		
Notes payable	$ 2,084	$ 920
Accounts payable	47,393	49,833
Accrued liabilities	44,495	39,790
Federal and state income taxes	157	10,284
Total current liabilities	94,129	100,827
Long-term debt	131,032	119,767
Deferred income taxes	85,439	92,834
Shareholders' investment		
Common stock, par value $2.50 per share, authorized 30,000,000 shares, issued 29,373,654 shares	73,434	73,434
Capital in excess of par value	2,921	2,921
Retained earnings	228,822	255,808
	305,177	
Less cost of 310,672 shares of treasury stock	6,628	6,628
Total shareholder's investment	298,549	325,535
	$609,149	$638,963

Note: Dollars in thousands except per share data.

EXHIBIT 23
Schlitz's statements of consolidated earnings (loss) for years ended December 31

	1978	1979	1980
Sales	$1,083,272	$1,042,583	$1,027,743
Less excise taxes	172,431	148,427	131,076
Net sales	910,841	894,156	896,667
Cost and expenses			
Cost of goods sold	729,854	746,415	721,278
Marketing, administrative, and general expenses	144,939	155,439	145,304
	874,793	901,854	866,582
Earnings (loss) from operations	36,048	(7,698)	30,085
Other income (expense)			
Interest and dividend income	3,311	4,485	21,796
Interest expense	(15,359)	(12,784)	(11,508)
Gain on repurchase of debentures	114	1,175	4,153
Gain (loss) on disposal of assets	(3,045)	(86,076)	596
Miscellaneous, net	(299)	54	734
	(15,278)	(93,146)	15,771
Earnings (loss) before income taxes	20,770	(100,844)	45,856
Provision for income taxes	8,809	(50,199)	18,870
Net earnings (loss)	$ 11,961	$ (50,645)	$ 26,986
Net earnings (loss) per share	$.41	$(1.74)	$.93

Note: Dollars in thousands except per share data.

EXHIBIT 24
Schlitz's statements of consolidated retained earnings and capital in excess of par value for years ended December 31

	Retained earnings	Capital in excess of par value
Balance, December 31, 1977	$286,978	$2,921
Net earnings, 1978	11,961	—
Cash dividends declared, $.47 per share	(13,660)	—
Balance, December 31, 1978	285,279	2,921
Net loss, 1979	(50,645)	—
Cash dividends declared, $.20 per share	(5,812)	—
Balance, December 31, 1979	228,822	2,921
Net earnings, 1980	26,986	—
Balance, December 31, 1980	$255,808	$2,921

Note: Dollars in thousands except per share data. The statement of accounting policies and accompanying notes to consolidated financial statements are an integral part of these statements.

EXHIBIT 25 Schlitz's five-year financial summary

	1976	1977	1978	1979	1980
Sales including excise taxes	$1,214,662	$1,134,079	$1,083,272	$1,042,583	$1,027,743
Net sales	999,996	937,424	910,841	894,156	896,667
Earnings (loss) from operations	112,645	60,855	36,048	(7,698)	30,085
Net earnings (loss)	49,947	19,765	11,961	(50,645)	26,986
Depreciation of plant and equipment	35,685	41,127	45,946	44,516	34,445
Working capital provided from operations	101,178	85,423	68,179	41,638	63,307
Capital expenditures	111,234	35,670	14,461	11,426	9,778
Total assets	737,843	726,762	691,935	609,149	638,963
Net working capital	36,070	47,694	40,254	87,352	161,171
Current ratio	1.4 to 1	1.6 to 1	1.4 to 1	1.9 to 1	2.6 to 1
Plant and equipment, net	585,785	564,620	526,596	341,522	317,120
Long-term debt	223,195	196,506	140,362	131,032	119,767
Long-term debt to total capital ratio	38.5%	35.5%	28.3%	30.5%	26.9%
Average number of shares outstanding	29,063	29,063	29,063	29,063	29,063
Per-share data:					
Net earnings (loss)	$1.72	$.68	$.41	$(1.74)	$.93
Dividends	.68	.68	.47	.20	—
Shareholders' investment	12.27	12.27	12.22	10.27	11.20
Barrels of beer sold	24,162	22,130	19,580	16,804	14,954
Brewery capacity in barrels	27,000	29,500	31,400	31,000	25,600

Note: Amounts in thousands except per share data.

EXHIBIT 26
Price range
of Schlitz's
common stock

	1979		1980	
	High	*Low*	*High*	*Low*
First quarter	12⅜	9⅞	9¼	5
Second quarter	13⅜	9	8¼	6¼
Third quarter	12⅛	9⅛	9⅛	7
Fourth quarter	13⅜	7⅞	9⅞	7¼

Stock listed — New York Stock Exchange.
As of February 13, 1981, there were 17,622 holders of record of Schlitz
common shares.

the Syracuse brewery, sold in February 1980. Also, the success of Schlitz's cost-cutting efforts, evident in Exhibits 27 and 28, were due to cutbacks of personnel over the previous four years, a gradual decrease in expenditures in Schlitz's capital improvements program, and discontinuation of quarterly dividends since the third quarter of 1979. Specifically, during the period 1977–81, Schlitz's staff was cut by 20 percent.

At the time of the sale of the Syracuse brewery, Anheuser-Busch agreed to a purchase price of $100 million, payable in three installments over a two-year period. The $30 million payable in January 1981 was received and the last payment of $35,714,000 plus interest, was due in January 1982.

Plant and equipment was carried at cost and included expenditures for improvements to existing facilities as well as expenditures for new facilities. Plant and equipment totals as of December 31, 1980 and 1979, are shown in Exhibit 27. Operating and per barrel results are shown in Exhibit 29.

EXHIBIT 27
Schlitz's plant and
equipment analysis

Plant and equipment	1979	1980
Land	$ 9,007	$ 8,754
Building	114,177	114,782
Machinery and equipment	459,032	463,516
Cooperage and pallets	44,932	42,977
Construction in progress	4,157	3,147
	661,305	663,176
Accumulated depreciation	(305,420)	(334,431)
Unamortized investment tax credit	(14,363)	(11,625)
Total	$341,522	$317,120

Provision for depreciation was calculated using the "Straight-line
Method."
Source: Joseph Schlitz Brewing Company, *1980 Annual Report*,
p. 14.

EXHIBIT 28 Schlitz's cash flow, 1976–1981 (millions)

	1976	1977	1978	1979	1980	1981 est.
Internal sources						
Net income	$ 49.9	$19.8	$ 12.0	$(50.6)	$ 30.0	$ 30.0
Depreciation	31.9	36.4	41.1	39.5	33.0	30.0
Deferred tax	19.1	20.9	14.1	(23.4)	3.0	5.0
Other (mostly ITC)	15.8	3.5	—	—	—	—
Total	$116.7	$80.6	$ 67.2	$ 34.5	$ 66.0	$ 65.0
Internal uses						
Dividends	$ 19.8	$19.8	$ 13.7	$ 5.8	—	—
Capital expenditures, net	110.1	24.5	9.5	(95.2)[b]	11.0	12.0
Debt repayment	34.5	26.7	70.8	9.3	12.0	10.0
Other	(5.8)	(2.0)	(4.7)	(1.6)	—	—
Increase in working capital[a]	(2.4)	19.1	(12.0)	32.6	10.0	5.0
Total	$156.2	$88.1	$ 77.3	$ 49.1	$ 33.0	$ 27.0
Net internal cash	$ (39.5)	$ (7.5)	$(10.1)	$ 14.6	$ 33.0	$ 38.0
External sources						
Equity, net	—	—	—	—	—	—
Debt	$ 45.0	—	$ 14.6	—	—	—
Other[c]	—	—	—	—	$ 40.0	$ 30.0
Total	$ 45.0	—	$ 14.6	—	$ 40.0	$ 30.0
Net change in cash	$ 5.5	—	$ 4.5	$ 14.5	$ 73.0	$ 68.0
Year-end cash	29.5	22.1	26.6	41.2	114.2	182.0

[a] Excludes cash and equivalents.
[b] Largely the disposal of the Syracuse Brewery.
[c] Receivable from sale of brewery.
Source: Emanuel Goldman, "The Brewing Industry," *Bernstein Research*, 1980.

THE FUTURE

In 1981, Schlitz's top management felt that they were operating in a capital-intensive business where inflation and price changes could hit particularly hard. Nonetheless, Schlitz had identified two keys to its planned future growth: demographic factors and the ability to develop new markets. Specifically, the company felt that with the right combination of marketing strategies and new products, per capita beer consumption should increase. Consequently Schlitz planned to continue to make major commitments in all areas of marketing support, especially to advertising designed to generate positive images for new and established brands. In this context, Frank Sellinger stated in 1980: "I think that this opportunity to run Schlitz is probably the biggest thing I've ever done. I knew the problems when I came here three years ago. I felt then . . . and I continue to feel — that I can help correct them."[7]

[7] "Is the Gusto Forever Gone?" *Forbes* (126:12) 34.

EXHIBIT 29 Selected Schlitz operating results, 1976–1981 (millions)

	1976	1977	1978	1979	1980	1981 est.
Barrels sold	24.16	22.13	19.58	16.80	14.70	13.20
Sales	$1,214.7	$1,134.1	$1,083.3	$1,042.6	$1,040.0	$1,030.0
Net sales	$1,000.0	$ 937.4	$ 910.8	$ 894.2	$ 910.0	$ 910.0
Cost of goods sold	755.7	726.4	723.2	740.2	740.0	730.0
Marketing, general, and administrative expenses	131.6	150.1	151.6	161.6	135.0	150.0
Earnings from operations	$ 112.7	$ 60.9	$ 36.0	$ (7.7)	$ 35.0	$ 30.0
Interest and other expense, net	16.0	25.8	15.3	93.1[a]	(15.0)	22.0
Pretax income	$ 96.7	$ 35.0	$ 20.8	$ (100.8)	$ 53.0	$ 52.0
Tax rate	48.4%	43.6%	42.4%	—	42.0%	43.0%
Net income	$ 49.9	$ 19.8	$ 12.0	$ (50.6)	$ 30.7	$ 29.6
Net per share	$ 1.72	$ 0.68	$ 0.41	$ (1.74)	$ 1.05	$ 1.00
Per barrel						
Sales	$ 50.27	$ 51.25	$ 55.33	$ 62.04	$ 70.74	$ 78.03
Net sales	$ 41.39	$ 42.36	$ 46.52	$ 53.21	$ 61.90	$ 68.94
Cost of goods sold	31.28	32.82	36.94	44.05	50.34	55.30
Marketing, general, and administrative expense	5.45	6.78	7.74	9.62	9.18	11.36
Earnings from operations	$ 4.66	$ 2.75	$ 1.84	$ (0.46)	$ 2.38	$ 2.27
Interest and other expense	0.66	1.17	0.78	5.54	(1.02)	(1.67)
Pretax income	$ 4.00	$ 1.58	$ 1.06	$ (6.00)	$ 3.60	$ 3.94
Net income	$ 2.06	$ 0.89	$ 0.61	$ (3.01)	$ 2.09	$ 2.24

[a] Loss on sale of Syracuse Brewery.
Source: Emanuel Goldman, "The Brewing Industry," *Bernstein Research*, 1980.

THE ADOLPH COORS COMPANY

Coors had been very profitable and grew by emphasizing a single, premium brand of beer. It was the only major brewer located in the Rocky Mountains, with one large production facility in Golden, Colorado. While it had expanded into other states and was the sixth largest brewer in 1982, it was still a regional brewer.

In the 1980s, Coors faced increasingly stronger competition from two national brewers, Anheuser-Busch and Miller. Given the slow industry growth rate for beer sales in recent years, some industry analysts felt that an industry shake-out would occur. Regional brewers would be the most susceptible to going bankrupt or being acquired during such a consolidation. While Coors had been strong up through the 1970s, could it remain successful as just a regional brewer in the 1980s? Thus, two distinct strategic alternatives presented themselves to the Coors family who held tight control of the firm. Should the firm remain a regional brewer or go nationwide in the production and marketing of beer?

HISTORY

Adolph Herman Joseph Coors, a German immigrant, and Jacob Schueler, a Denver businessman, began brewing in an old tannery in the Clear Creek Valley of Golden, Colorado, in 1873. They called it the Golden Brewery. Coors was attracted to the area because of the numerous springs flowing from the Rocky Mountains. He realized the importance of water in the brewing process. In 1880, Coors bought out Schueler and renamed the successful venture Coors Golden Brewery.

The company thrived until Prohibition, but managed to survive through it by selling near beer and malted milk. It also developed several manufacturing operations for producing cement and porcelain during that same period. While Coors did well, such was not the case for breweries in general. From 1910 to 1933, the number of breweries was cut in half from 1,568 to 750.

This case was prepared by Jeffrey M. Miner (M.B.A. in finance) and Larry D. Alexander (assistant professor of strategic management), Department of Management, College of Business, Virginia Polytechnic Institute and State University. Copyright © 1985 by Jeffrey M. Miner and Larry D. Alexander. Reprinted by permission.

After Prohibition, Coors Company experienced phenomenal growth. Still, it remained a regional brewery which produced only one type of beer from a single brewery. Its beer was sold in eleven western states in 1970, with California being its largest market. By that same year, this regional brewer also became the nation's fourth largest brewer.

Coors beer began to develop a mystique in the early 1970s, perhaps because it was the only beer brewed with pure Rocky Mountain spring water. Many people thought it was of higher quality than other beers. Coors conveyed environmental purity and a western image, which were important at that time. Also, Easterners could not get the beer except at very high prices, which added to its mystique. The movie *Smokey and the Bandit* had as a plot the degree to which some people would go to get Coors beer. Celebrities such as Paul Newman and Clint Eastwood regularly drank Coors beer on movie sets. Even President Ford carried the beer on board Air Force One.

Coors, the market leader in nine of the eleven states it served including California, then turned to geographic expansion. The company began selling beer in Texas and other nearby states where it quickly gained market share. Its 1975 sales of $520 million represented a $270 million increase over 1971. Operating margin was 28 percent in 1975, the highest in the industry, and profit per barrel averaged almost $9, almost twice that of the industry leader, Anheuser-Busch. As a Coors marketing vice-president put it at that time, "You could have sold Coors beer in Glad bags."[1]

Coors' tremendous success, however, did not last. The company began to lose market share in many of its sales territories. There were several reasons why this occurred. First, Coors suffered from a negative public image. A brewery workers' union strike in 1977 led to a boycott of Coors beer by numerous AFL-CIO unions. Second, Joe Coors' ultraconservative philosophy alienated a number of groups, including women, Blacks, Hispanics, and gays. Third and most important, Coors failed to realize that the industry was changing. Miller Brewing, which was acquired by Philip Morris in 1970, was the first to recognize that beer drinkers were not a single market, but rather a number of differentiated segments. Whereas Anheuser-Busch used price and lower costs to compete with Schlitz in the 1960s, Miller shifted that emphasis toward heavy advertising and promotion and development of new products to appeal to specific segments in the 1970s. This new strategy helped Miller jump from eighth at the start of the decade to second by 1977.

Unfortunately, Coors ignored the signs for quite a while, continued with its production orientation, and brewed only one beer, Coors Premium. Coors' advertising expenditures were the lowest in the industry. In 1977, they were only about $.25 per barrel compared to an industry average of over one dollar. A marketing battle ensued as Miller attempted to unseat Anheuser-Busch from the number one spot, and Coors suffered from it.

Coors' loss in market share was most dramatic in California, its traditional stronghold. Share dropped from 40 percent in the mid-1970s to under 20 percent by 1982. The loss for Coors was a gain for Anheuser-Busch which then controlled about 47 percent of that market. Coors also lost share to Miller in Texas, another former stronghold. Overall, Coors dropped from being fourth-place brewer in the early 1970s to sixth place in 1982. Volume was 13.5 million barrels in 1976, a 9.1 percent market share, and earnings were $76 million on sales of $594 million. In 1982, however, volume dropped to 11.9 million barrels, which represented only a 6.6 percent share, while earnings were only $40 million on sales of $915 million.

MANAGEMENT

Adolph Coors Company had sustained itself for over one hundred years as a family-owned and -managed business. The Coors family had a pervasive influence over all aspects of company operations. Since 1970 the top spot had actually been shared by two brothers, William and Joseph Coors. Their late brother, Adolph Coors III, would have been chief executive had he not been killed in 1960. Adolph Coors II retained control of the company until he died in 1970, when control was passed on to Bill and Joe. In the early 1980s, Joe's two oldest sons, Jeff and Peter, were added to the management team, supposedly to provide a transition between the two generations of management.

Bill Coors, age sixty-six, was the elder of the two. His official position was chairman and chief executive officer. He handled the technical side of the business and had a reputation for being a genius in the brewing industry. Joe Coors, age sixty-five, was the president and chief operating officer and oversaw the financial and administrative functions. In reality, each brother acted in any capacity he wanted and there were no formal lines of authority. Their apparent lack of rivalry amazed outsiders. Both men were lean, tall, rugged Westerners who were very open and personal with employees. In fact, each was referred to as Bill and Joe by all employees, rather than by their famous last name.

The brothers devoted themselves to brewing the finest-quality beer that they could. Bill and Joe did not put much faith in that mystique bit. They genuinely believed they simply made a better product and that was why it sold so well. Bill was well respected for his technical know-how and was chairman of the United States Brewers Association. The brothers had shunned the public eye in the past; however, the company's more recent unfavorable public image had forced them to be more open with the public. Joe, a longtime conservative, was very outspoken and his views tended to alienate a number of minority groups.

The brothers realized that in the new competitive brewing industry of the 1980s, maintaining market share and survival were key goals. This was one reason that they decided to infuse fresh thinking in the management team when they brought Jeff and Peter into top management in 1982.

Peter Coors, age thirty-six, and Jeff, age thirty-eight, were named division presidents in 1982 when an expanded four-man office of the presidency was created. They both had engineering degrees from Cornell. Peter also had an M.B.A. degree and was involved in the sales and marketing aspect of the company. He initiated the company's first market research in the early 1970s, which his father disapproved of at the time. However, since he realized that the low-calorie beer market segment was growing rapidly, he proved instrumental in developing Coors Light. Both Joe and Bill opposed this move at first. Peter was heir apparent to the presidency and more easily handled the pressures of being a public figure. Jeff oversaw research and development operations and was a one-man research team in the early 1970s. By the early 1980s, that department had grown significantly in size and importance. Jeff also headed up all new product development efforts at Coors in the 1980s.

Both were responsible for shifting the emphasis toward advertising, price competition, and new product introduction. These actions probably helped the company to survive. The pair disagreed with each other and also with Bill and Joe, but the differences tended to be constructive.

PRODUCTION

Coors was considered a maverick among brewers because its brewing process defied industry norms. However, the company was very highly regarded in the industry as a quality and technologically superior brewer. With Coors' single brewery, which had a 20 million barrel capacity, uniformity and quality were easier to maintain. The drawback, however, was that transportation costs were quite high and there were significant logistics problems in producing and packaging different kinds of beer in the same brewery.

All raw materials and finished products were constantly monitored for uniformity and quality. Coors used the highest-quality ingredients possible. The water was pure Rocky Mountain spring water from over forty springs located on the brewery grounds. Rarely was water in its pure form suitable for brewing, but no chemical alterations of this water were necessary. Coors supplied its own special barley seed, Moravian III, to contract farmers in the West. Coors bought hops from growers in Washington and Idaho and imported two types from Germany. Coors also had its own malt house to ensure that proper aging of the barley was adhered to. Rice, grown for Coors in California and Arkansas, was used to give the beer its light body. A computer was used extensively to monitor many steps in the brewing operation, and flavor checks were performed regularly at each step. In addition, trained personnel routinely evaluated the quality of all ingredients and the final product.

Coors' brewing process was unique because it was entirely natural. No artificial ingredients were used. Since all biochemical processes were allowed to occur naturally, Coors had one of the longest brewing processes in the industry. It took an average of 68 days to brew and package the beer. Coors Light took even longer to produce because extra time had to be allowed for enzymes to dissolve the sugars.

In keeping with its natural brewing philosophy, Coors approached the problem of germ control in a unique way — the beer was not pasteurized. In 1959, company scientists discovered a better way which involved a series of filters combined with controlled conditions. The filling process was so germ-free that it was likened to a sterile operating room.

Coors' filling process was designed to keep the beer cold at all times. This was supposed to enhance the flavor since heat was thought to take away some of the beer's body and flavor. Packaging was a completely computerized operation to maintain Coors' goals of uniformity and quality. The computer told the forklift drivers which pallets to pick up and where to put them. Because of this system, Coors did not require a warehouse. Beer that came off the line was sent almost immediately to trucks and railcars for distribution.

Coors was trying to minimize pollution caused by its packaging materials. The company was the founder and leader of used aluminum can recycling. In 1979, 80 percent of its aluminum cans used in packaging were recycled. Coors paid out over $33 million for them. The major source for these cans were the recycling centers located at Coors' distributorships. Also, fifty can banks, which were reverse vending machines for aluminum cans, were being test marketed. This approach helped to make recycling more convenient for consumers. This program also enabled the company to be less dependent on the aluminum market. Recycling was not only cost-effective for the company, it also provided consumers with supplemental income.

Brewery wastes were always a problem, but Coors had developed a method to transform much of this waste into animal feed. An average of 4 million gallons of industrial wastes were processed daily at Coors. The company was a leader in the efficient use of waste water, yielding only 3.5 barrels of it per barrel of beer, compared to 8 for most brewers.

Coors was also committed to energy conservation. The company began converting to coal in 1976 and by 1980 was virtually 100 percent coal-dependent. This move was relatively risk-free since Coors sat in the middle of America's most plentiful coal supply. Also, recycling saved about 95 percent of the energy required to produce new aluminum from bauxite.

Clearly, Coors was the most energy-efficient brewer in America, with the lowest B.T.U. per barrel ratio in the industry. Its engineering capabilities enabled the company to become nearly energy self-sufficient while maintaining rigid pollution-control standards. For example, Coors had been able to remove 99.5 percent of the pollutants caused by burning coal.

MARKETING

In the 1980s, Coors' marketing capabilities were improving, but still did not compare to many of its major competitors'. However, it had come a long way since the midseventies when the company brewed only one product, did no market research, and spent next to nothing on advertising. By the early 1980s, Coors was trying to remedy this through extensive advertising, promotion, and development of new products to cater to different segments of the beer-drinking population.

Coors switched its emphasis from producing one beer of superior quality to producing assorted products of superior quality. Until 1978, Coors Premium was the only beer that the company produced. Management felt that this was a superior beer and they simply did not need another brand. Coors Premium was considered to be a rich and light-bodied beer and contained 138 calories per 12 ounces. This beer was still the staple for the company and the fourth best selling brand of beer in the nation. The company sold 8.4 million barrels of Premium in 1982, but this was down some 19 percent from 1981, mainly due to increased competition and the recession. By 1983, however, Coors also marketed other brands of beer to different market segments.

Coors Light was introduced in 1978 in response to the fast-growing light beer segment. The company had earlier insisted that Coors Premium was light enough, but later realized the importance of developing a new product for this important growth segment. Coors Light contained 105 calories per 12 ounces. In an effort to provide a light beer with quality taste, Coors spent a great deal of time developing this product. Not surprisingly, it also used all natural ingredients. The brand grew substantially since its introduction, but remained far behind the leader, Lite beer from Miller. The company sold 3.2 million barrels of Coors Light in 1982, an increase of 2.1 million over 1980. However, many analysts felt that this growth had been at the expense of Coors Premium, which was another reason for Premium's sales decline.

In 1983, Coors started test marketing a new premium brew called Golden Lager 1873 because the company recognized that both Coors Premium and Light appealed to basically the same type of beer drinkers. Company research showed that many drinkers wanted a heartier-tasting beer. Coors hoped that Golden Lager would compete effectively with the national leaders in this category, Anheuser-Busch's Budweiser and Miller's High Life. The company tried to add credibility to the brand by linking it with its Rocky Mountain heritage. Initially, it was tested in selected cities in the South and West. Coors also hoped that the new beer would help fill the brewery's excess capacity.

Coors had also tried to appeal to the growing import and superpremium beer market segment. George Killian's Irish Red Ale from France had been sold to Coors, which began testing the product in 1980. Successful results prompted a marketwide rollout in 1982. The company claimed that high initial sales indicated that the product had already developed a strong following.

Earlier in 1980, Coors began testing its first superpremium brand, Herman Joseph's 1868. It was very rich and full-bodied, which was achieved through a longer brewing and aging cycle. Coors hoped that the beer would be able to compete with Anheuser-Busch's Michelob, the leader in that segment. In 1982, the beer was still being tested in six states, but it had not yet been very successful. As a result, Herman Joseph's was periodically reformulated, repackaged, and readvertised, but it had never topped 100,000 barrels.

In an industry as competitive as brewing, it was important for Coors to generate a strong following for its products. Advertising and promotional skills were a great concern, probably because the firm had grown complacent in its century of operation. Fortunately, Coors management realized that it could no longer rely on its product's mystique to cure marketing problems. Since 1975, advertising expenditures increased dramatically as shown in Exhibit 1. However, Coors made frequent ad theme changes over the past few years, which gave the company a branding identity problem.

To complement its own marketing department, Coors also enlisted the aid of two top advertising agencies. Advertising for Coors Premium emphasized its purity, freshness, and superiority. The campaign was supported by in-store point-of-purchase displays which cost much less than television and were probably fairly effective. On television, Coors depicted its beer being drunk in traditional beer-drinking settings, such as bars and parties; ads were targeted at those who drank three or four beers at a time. Coors Light had an energetic new campaign to attract more consumers in the low-calorie segment. It focused on the unsurpassed taste in informal active settings.

Coors used outdoor billboards as a secondary medium, which was not standard for the industry. Billboards were used to depict the image of the snow-covered Rockies. This medium was used mainly for Coors Premium. While Coors previously used radio advertising to a rather limited extent, it was used more extensively in the 1980s for Coors Light.

Advertising and promotional efforts were increased in 1982 to the young-adult segment which, while declining in absolute numbers, was usually where brand loyalty was established. Campaigns to improve Coors product awareness among Blacks and Hispanics, who accounted for a significant proportion of the target market, had been initiated. Corporate messages aimed at these groups tried to persuade

EXHIBIT 1
Coors advertising
expenditures,
1975–1983

Year	Expenditure (in millions)
1975	$ 1.2
1976	2.0
1977	15.5
1978	33.5
1979	46.4
1980	66.8
1981	85.8
1982	88.1
1983	over 88.1

Source: *Adolph Coors Company: 1980 Annual Report* and *Adolph Coors Company: 1982 Annual Report*. Also see Robert F. Hartley's "Coors — We Are Immune to Competition," in his *Management Mistakes* (Columbus, Ohio: Grid, 1983), pp. 139–53.

them to give the company a chance and dispel Coors' negative image, which still lingered on. Coors felt, however, that its new, open, straightforward public relations efforts would help win these consumers over to its side.

Perhaps the most important way in which brewers advertised their products was through sports promotions, especially on television. Coors focused on both participative and spectator sports events, selecting these events based on a sports activity study performed by the company. Its recent sports emphasis had been on motor sports and cycling. In 1980, many Coors distributors registered sizeable sales increases before, during, and after various Coors-sponsored sporting events. Sports promotion also helped Coors gain valuable national exposure. However, it should be pointed out that Coors and other smaller brewers had some difficulty finding available spots on nationally televised sports due to exclusive arrangements that Anheuser-Busch and Miller had established with the networks.

Coors had over 350 distributors in its marketing territory. These distributors usually had to be large because Coors insisted that its products be refrigerated during distribution. This required both the company and its distributors to undertake added expenses and pains to keep the beer cold so that the flavor of the beer was preserved until it got to retailers. All beer was shipped from Coors in insulated railcars or refrigerated trucks. Distributors in turn were required to keep the beer refrigerated in their warehouses. Coors thus usually only took on veteran wholesalers who could make the necessary investments in refrigeration and insulation. The beer was placed in special vaults and kept at a constant 35 degrees. Because of this requirement, distributors had to pay an additional $100,000 or more each year just to keep Coors beer cold.

Retailers were encouraged to keep Coors beer refrigerated at all times, but because of increased promotions, there were often floor displays at room temperature. The company claimed that it would not harm Coors beer or cause it to lose its flavor any faster than any other beer on the market. To further ensure that flavor was preserved, the distributors were required to rotate retailer stocks every 60 days. This 60-day rotation rule was the strictest in the industry.

The distributors also played a vital role in marketing the product. They set up point-of-purchase displays in retail outlets, prepared local advertising, and developed customer relations. In order to maintain better relations with its distributors, Coors established its own television network, Second Century, in 1980. Stories were periodically done on different wholesalers. Distributors had to purchase the equipment to view the films, but over 90 percent had already done so. Brewery employees also viewed what the distributors were doing on this network.

The company also owned six of its own distributorships, not to compete with the independent wholesalers, but to give Coors' management firsthand knowledge of actual conditions in the field. It also enabled the company to analyze local and regional consumer patterns, train management in marketing and sales, and test new programs before they were introduced everywhere.

Approximately 78 percent of Coors' products were shipped by rail. The remaining 22 percent were shipped by truck. Of this, 14 percent went by common carrier or trucks owned by Coors distributors, and 8 percent went by the Coors Transportation

Company. This wholly owned subsidiary had grown in the past couple of years since only 3 percent of Coors' products used it in 1980. The company was formed in 1971 to provide hauling flexibility. It operated 132 temperature-controlled trailers and 52 tractors. Each truck traveled about 215,000 miles a year. The purpose was to reach distributors who did not have rail service, to handle emergency loads, and to haul to areas where profitable backhauls were available. Backhauls usually brought food products into the Denver area. The company was also formed as a reaction to rising railroad rates.

The advantage of having this flexibility was exemplified in 1980, when Coors was entering Arkansas. Thousands of extra cases were needed because demand had been underestimated. It could have turned into embarrassing shortages just when the company was trying to establish itself in a new territory. Fortunately, it turned into extra sales because of quick, back-up trucking by Coors' trucks.

Coors had recently begun a two-pronged approach to gain market share. One way was to expand further into the East, and the other was to reverse share losses in its traditional twenty-state territory, most notably in California and Texas. Neither way promised to be an easy task. The effort would mean head to head competition with leaders Anheuser-Busch and Miller and would require huge marketing expenditures. Coors had been trying to meet advertising expenditures, but aggressive marketing was still a relatively new experience for Coors.

In 1983, Coors' biggest expansion campaign yet was undertaken to enter the Southeast market. This region was considered to be a growth area by many brewers. It appeared that the mystique was still alive in the Southeast, where there had been strong initial customer acceptance of Coors Premium and Light. Initital sales were going well in 1983 for both brands in this region. While competition in this area was intense, Coors had selected large distributors who were well established in their markets to help implement this effort.

This expansion was also supported by heavy advertising on radio and television which stressed the fact that Coors could finally be purchased in the region. With that expansion, Coors marketed its products in twenty-six states and the District of Columbia. However, the good news was tempered by two points. First, some analysts feared that perhaps the sales in the Southeast increased so very rapidly because of the novelty factor. Thus, they suggested that more time would be needed to determine if Coors' success would be maintained. Second, Coors' transportation costs to the Southeast were very high. One estimate was that the cost of shipping from Golden, Colorado, to the Southeast was $7–8 per barrel, compared to an industry average of $3 per barrel.

Coors had purchased land options for the possible erection of another brewery in Virginia or Tennessee. However, there were no plans to begin building any time soon. If the company were to acquire or build another plant, a marketing problem could arise, since Coors' identity was associated with pure Rocky Mountain spring water. Jeff Coors remarked, ''Now, you can make good water out of anything. We haven't crossed the hurdle of what impact we'd suffer if we dropped the Rocky Mountain water theme. But you never know. We might produce an entirely different beer for the East.''[2] However, one analyst suggested that the delaying of the plant would only allow the competition time to solidify their hold even further on eastern and southeastern markets.

FINANCE

Coors had always been strong financially. Exhibits 2 and 3 show the consolidated balance sheets and consolidated income statements for the years 1980–1982. The

EXHIBIT 2
Adolph Coors Company consolidated balance sheets

	December 28, 1980	December 27, 1981	December 26, 1982
Assets			
Cash	$ 87,883	$ 76,614	$ 71,251
Accounts and notes receivable	57,930	66,667	64,909
Inventories	149,504	115,677	118,658
Prepaid expenses	28,856	34,282	34,614
Income tax prepayments	6,036	2,215	4,236
Total current assets	330,209	295,455	293,668
Properties, net	556,419	652,090	702,769
Excess of cost over net	2,649	2,567	3,029
Other assets	5,108	6,272	8,448
Total assets	$894,385	$956,384	$1,007,914
Liabilities and equity			
Accounts payable	$ 48,923	$ 40,033	$ 45,601
Salaries, vacation	25,677	27,488	25,543
Taxes (not income)	19,872	18,494	17,252
Income taxes	3,427	9,922	2,789
Accrued expenses	18,195	21,577	28,820
Total current liabilities	116,094	117,514	120,005
Deferred income taxes	60,149	75,968	95,097
Other long-term liabilities	6,042	9,335	9,600
Capital stock:			
Class A common, voting	1,260	1,260	1,260
Class B common, nonvoting	11,000	11,000	11,000
Total	12,260	12,260	12,260
Paid-in capital	2,011	2,011	2,011
Retained earnings	724,284	765,751	795,396
Total	738,555	780,022	809,667
Less treasury shares	26,455	26,455	26,455
Total equity	712,100	753,567	783,212
Total liabilities and equity	$894,385	$956,384	$1,007,914

Note: Dollar amounts in thousands.
Source: *Adolph Coors Company: 1982 Annual Report*, pp. 12–13.

EXHIBIT 3
Adolph Coors
Company
consolidated income
statements

	December 26, 1980	December 27, 1981	December 26, 1982
Sales	$1,012,198	$1,060,345	$1,032,297
Less excise taxes	133,301	130,429	117,039
Net sales	887,897	929,916	915,258
Costs and expenses			
Cost of goods sold	629,758	659,623	659,033
Marketing, general, and administrative	146,293	181,348	185,076
Research and development	14,256	16,848	15,230
Total	790,307	857,819	859,339
Operating income	97,590	72,097	55,919
Other			
Interest income	(16,514)	(13,788)	(10,411)
Interest expense	1,563	1,601	2,480
Miscellaneous	6,764	4,651	(1,298)
Total	(8,187)	(7,536)	(9,229)
Income before taxes	105,777	79,633	65,148
Income taxes	40,800	27,663	25,000
Net income	64,977	51,970	40,148
Beginning retained earnings	668,939	724,284	765,751
	733,916	776,254	805,899
Cash dividends	9,632	10,503	10,503
Ending retained earnings	$ 724,284	$ 765,751	$ 795,396

Note: Dollar amounts in thousands.
Source: *Adolph Coors Company: 1982 Annual Report*, p. 10.

company went public in 1975, only because it needed to raise money to pay inheritance taxes on the estate of Adolph Coors II. These public shares were traded over the counter and there were some 9,000 shareholders in 1983. However, this public stock was class B nonvoting, so outsiders did not have a say in management decisions. The Coors family owned 35 percent of the class B shares and 100 percent of the 1.26 million shares of class A voting stock. Thus, the Coors family controlled their stock so much so that no other firm would be able to acquire it unless management allowed it. That did not appear very likely given the history of this maverick brewery.

Another aspect of Coors' financial approach was the company's refusal to borrow money. This was a family tradition which dated back to the company's beginnings. Coors' capital structure consisted almost entirely of common stock. Also, since the company did not plan to issue any more stock, all future expansion would have to be financed through internally generated cash. Its normal cash balance was around $70 million, but Coors planned to increase this. Although lack of debt was a sign of financial strength, this avoidance of debt financing altogether sometimes caused the company to bypass attractive opportunities. One was the addition of an eastern plant, which the company agreed was necessary to offset huge transportation costs of shipping to eastern markets. Another example related to Coors' can-manufacturing facility, which developed the technical process for making the two-piece aluminum can. However, the company sold the process to Continental Can Company and American Can Company because Coors would have had to borrow money to begin production.

RESEARCH AND DEVELOPMENT

Coors was often considered to be the most technically advanced brewery in the world. The company had Colorado's single largest engineering crew for any private-sector firm. R&D was concerned with developing new products, brewing techniques, and packaging techniques. Coors had developed technical superiority in ceramics and aluminum cans. There was an extensive barley R&D program, which had genetically developed Coors' own special variety called Moravian III. Yeast cells, used in the brewing process, were specifically selected for testing to develop new and better strains to upgrade the quality of its beer. Farmers wanted a higher yield for their crops and Coors wanted reliable sources of supply, so much of the company's research dealt with counseling farmers on how to get higher yields while maintaining Coors' standards. The company also did research on how to get more out of the grain in the production process. They were now reusing many things that used to be thrown away.

Not all R&D efforts had been successful, however. The press-tab can was developed to stop pollution from ring-pull tabs. The idea was good, but it failed because the can was hard to open and consumers often cut their fingers in the process.

Jeff Coors, who was responsible for R&D, became the first American in a quarter-century to present a technical paper at the European Brewing Convention in 1979. R&D was a relatively minor part of the company's operations before Jeff became involved in the early 1970s. While many advancements in the industry occurred in the 1960s and 1970s, Jeff did not see any major technical breakthroughs on the horizon in the 1980s. Research appeared to have taken a distant back seat to marketing; however, Coors remained committed to R&D. Bill Coors' credo was, "If technology exists, use it. If it doesn't, develop it."[3]

HUMAN RESOURCES

Coors employed about 8,600 people in 1983, down some 850 from 1981. Company officials blamed the layoffs on the recession, which reduced industry demand. Coors tried to develop its own personnel so they could later be promoted from within. This required extensive education and training programs. The company's television network, Second Century, had also been used to produce in-house training programs.

Coors was committed to equal employment opportunity and supported an active affirmative action program. Minority employment agencies were used to recruit minorities, which represented 13.4 percent of the work force in 1979. Coors also had an employee opportunity training program which hired exconvicts, disabled veterans, and the disadvantaged and trained them for responsible positions within the firm.

An average salary for a Coors production worker was $20,000 a year and Coors offered fringe benefits totaling an additional $5,800 per employee per year. Clearly, these wages and benefits were considered higher than the average for Golden, Colorado, a city of approximately 11,000 people.

Coors' management maintained that business should operate as a free enterprise; thus, the company was philosophically opposed to unions. Unfortunately, Coors' brewery workers were unionized and represented a large proportion of the work force. They went out on strike in 1977. The issue was not money but rather that the company was forcing employees to take lie detector tests. A boycott of the company's products ensued, but Coors management stood its ground, replaced many of the striking workers, and rehired those who wanted to return.

In 1978, Coors' brewery workers voted out the union and the boycott's effect diminished. In 1982, the "60 Minutes" television show did a story on Coors to try to uncover human rights violations. The show, often noted for its revealing stories, found no such violations, which somewhat helped to ease Coors' negative image. As of 1983, Coors was still operating without a union.

Coors was very concerned about employee health and well-being. The American Center for Occupational Health, a Coors subsidiary, was committed to safer working conditions. The company provided healthcare tests and services to Coors' employees and other businesses, and in 1982 was completing the development of a light-weight, compact health-testing machine.

Coors opened a wellness center on its brewery property in 1981. All employees, retirees, spouses, and dependents were allowed to use the facility, which contained a track, trampolines, weight sets, stationary bicycles, and other equipment. The center also sponsored programs in physical fitness, nutrition, stress management, weight control, stopping smoking, and alcohol education. The staff was comprised of experts in each field. Thus far, it had been very successful. Bill Coors was not worried whether the center could be cost-justified; he simply wanted it to promote health and happiness. Coors also funded participation in various sports for a number of employees and many were sent to survival training courses. In sum, management regarded physical fitness as very important.

COORS' VERTICAL INTEGRATION AND DIVERSIFICATION EFFORTS

In keeping with Coors' philosophy of independence in all aspects of operations, it became the most vertically integrated firm in the industry. Exhibit 4 shows Coors'

EXHIBIT 4
Coors operations

Ceramic Manufacturing Plants
Benton, Arkansas
El Cajon, California
Golden, Colorado
Grand Junction, Colorado
Hillsboro, Oregon
Norman, Oklahoma

Foreign Operations Not Shown
Singapore
Glenrothes, Scotland
Rio Claro, Brazil

Rice Mill
Weiner, Arkansas

1983 Expansion
Alabama
Florida
Georgia
North Carolina
South Carolina
Eastern Tennessee
Virginia
District of Columbia

Grain Elevators
Burley, Idaho
Delta, Colorado
Huntley, Montana
Longmont, Colorado
Monte Vista, Colorado
Worland, Wyoming

Paper Converting Plants
Boulder, Colorado
Lawrenceburg, Tennessee

Main Offices
Golden, Colorado (largest single brewery
    and aluminum can manufacturing plant
    in the United States)

Company-Owned Distributorships
Boise, Idaho
Denver, Colorado
Omaha, Nebraska
Spokane, Washington
St. Louis, Missouri
Tustin, California

Glass Bottle Manufacturing Plant
Wheat Ridge, Colorado

Source: *Adolph Coors Company: 1982 Annual Report*, p. 26.

operations throughout the United States. Coors had attempted to control its raw materials supply by having contract farmers grow its barley and rice and by maintaining its own malt house. Coors also had its own supply of packaging materials. It owned a can-manufacturing plant (the largest single such plant in the industry), a glass-manufacturing plant, and a paper mill. Coors Energy Company owned a coal mine and 249 natural gas and oil wells; it also leased rights to 330,000 acres. Coors owned its own truck fleet and waste-treatment facility, and company engineers designed and constructed most of its own machinery and equipment. This was all very important for cost control, stability, and independence from supplier price hikes and shortages. Clearly, Coors believed in vertical integration, both forward and backward.

Coors had also diversified into companies not directly related to brewing, though they complemented the primary product. Coors Porcelain Company was one of the world's foremost suppliers of technical ceramics, mainly for the computer industry and energy firms. The company was trying to decide whether to compete in the $1 billion a year dental restoration industry. Coors Food Products Company did well in 1982, acquiring a snack food company which made potato chips. The Coors subsidiary also packaged rice and competed in the rice flour and cereal markets. They were experimenting with bread products made from brewers grain 28, a high-protein by-product of the brewing process. Variety breads were growing by 15 percent yearly. They also made cocomost, a cocoa substitute derived from brewer's yeast.

COORS' COMPETITION

Since Miller Brewing's effect on the industry was discussed earlier, only Anheuser-Busch, Stroh, and Heileman are profiled here. While Anheuser-Busch was the industry's giant, the two second-tier brewers were similar to Coors in size but followed different strategies. Exhibit 5 contains a list of the top six brewers and their major products in order of volume sold. Exhibits 6 and 7 show market share by company and brand.

Anheuser-Busch   Anheuser-Busch was the number one brewer in the United States ever since it took over that spot from Schlitz in the late 1950s. The giant lumbered along until the 1970s, when an onslaught by Miller to knock it out of its top position caused August Busch III, the company's chief strategist, to rethink his game plan. In large part, he began to copy Miller's methods. He determined that Miller's success was a direct function of heavy advertising in sports media, product diversification, and a switch in emphasis to the beer-drinking young adult segment. This strategy change occurred in 1977 and has often been seen as the turning point in the industry. From then on, Anheuser-Busch steadily pulled away from Miller. It was the best-performing brewer in 1982, with a market share of 32.7 percent. Its 59.1 million barrels sold topped Miller's by almost 20 million.

By 1983, the firm was pursuing a total marketing effort, continuing to focus on the young adult segment with a well-balanced line of quality beers. The Budweiser brand, by far the nation's best-selling beer and leader in the premium segment, represented an amazing 40.7 million of total barrels sold. Michelob was the leader in the superpremium segment. While Miller controlled 60 percent of the light-beer segment with its best-selling Lite, Anheuser-Busch had set its sights on taking over that market. It marketed three light beers with different tastes, prices, and images, and controlled 28 percent of the segment. Budweiser Light, introduced in 1982, had become the second best-selling light beer already. This brewing giant also had its sights on international expansion. Budweiser was already the best-selling import in Japan, and it was also strong in Canada.

The firm was the nation's biggest sponsor of sporting events. It had the twenty-second largest advertising budget among all U.S. firms, and it far outdistanced all competitors in television advertising. Furthermore, Anheuser-Busch was locked into many exclusive contracts as was Miller. The company's operating efficiency was outstanding, and it boasted the highest profit per barrel in the industry. It had the best distribution system in the industry and its plants were located strategically throughout the United States. It was committed to new capacity increases, especially in Los Angeles. Like Coors, the company had vertically integrated to better control

EXHIBIT 5
Top six brewers
and their major
brands, 1982

1. Anheuser-Busch
   Budweiser
   Michelob
   Busch
   Michelob Light
   Bud Light
   Natural Light

2. Miller
   High Life
   Lite
   Lowenbrau

3. Stroh/Schlitz
   Old Milwaukee
   Stroh's
   Schlitz
   Schaefer
   Schlitz Malt Liquor
   Old Milwaukee Light
   Stroh Light
   Goebel
   Schlitz Light
   Erlanger

4. Heileman
   Old Style
   Schmidt's
   Blatz
   Black Label
   Colt 45 Malt Liquor
   Old Style Light
   Blatz Light
   Black Label Light

5. Pabst
   Pabst
   Red, White & Blue
   Olde English Malt
   Blitz
   Pabst Light
   Jacob Best
   Andeker

6. Coors
   Coors Premium
   Coors Light
   George Killian's Ale
   Herman Joseph's 1868

Source: Paul Mullins. "Brewing Industry Has Flat Growth in '82," *Beverage Industry*, January 28, 1983, p. 31.

EXHIBIT 6
Brewers' estimated
market shares

	1979	1980	1981	1982E
Anheuser-Busch	26.8%	28.2%	30.0%	32.3%
Miller	20.8	20.9	22.2	21.8
Stroh/Schlitz	15.3	13.9	12.9	12.8
Heileman	6.6	7.5	7.7	7.9
Pabst	8.8	8.5	7.4	6.8
Coors	7.5	7.8	7.3	6.6
Olympia	3.5	3.4	3.1	2.8
Genesee	2.0	2.0	2.0	1.9
Schmidt	2.2	2.0	1.6	1.8
General	1.7	1.4	1.2	1.0
Pittsburgh	0.4	0.6	0.5	0.5
Others	4.4	3.8	4.1	3.8

Source: Paul Mullins. "Brewing Industry Has Flat Growth in '82," *Beverage Industry*, January 28, 1983, p. 34.

EXHIBIT 7
Top ten beer brands
in 1982

	Market share	Volume (millions of barrels)
Budweiser	22.0%	40.0
Miller High Life	11.0	20.0
Miller Lite	9.6	17.5
Coors Premium	4.6	8.4
Michelob	4.6	8.3
Pabst	4.5	8.1
Old Milwaukee	3.1	5.7
Stroh's	3.0	5.6
Old Style	3.0	5.5
Schlitz	2.6	4.7

Source: "Many Top Brews Give Ground to Other Brands," *Beverage World*, April 1983, p. 33.

raw material supplies and costs. The firm's growth was expected to continue and recent capacity expansions would increase pressure to capture more market share. Some industry observers felt that Anheuser-Busch might control 40 percent of the market by 1990.

Stroh Brewing Company

Stroh saw merger as the only way to survive against the two industry giants. The company acquired Schlitz in 1982, which had been suffering vast market declines. The merger put Stroh in the third spot in the brewing industry. Management was quite strong and had done a good job with its Stroh brand. However, the company had put itself at a disadvantage because it had leveraged itself so heavily with debt. Key problems for Stroh were how to successfully integrate its acquisitions into the company and how to reverse the sales decline of its Schlitz brand.

Stroh was not advertising the Schlitz brand very much in 1983, although there were plans to step it up in the near future. The company appeared to be using cash flow from the brand to finance marketing expenditures for its best-selling brand, Old Milwaukee. It was being promoted with heavy television advertising and cents-off coupons, which were fairly new to this industry. Many analysts attributed the success of Old Milwaukee, a popular-priced brand, to the 1981–1983 recession.

G. Heileman Brewing Company

Heileman, like Coors, had been very successful as a regional brewer. It was targeted for markets in the Midwest and Northwest, but was presently the fourth largest brewer in the United States. The company had increased barrelage dramatically over the past few years, from 4.5 million barrels in 1975 to 14.9 million in 1982. It was the only major brewer besides Anheuser-Busch to register a sales gain in 1982.

In 1982, Heileman took a big step toward long-term viability by acquiring Pabst and its 49 percent share of Olympia. However, due to objections raised by the Department of Justice, a new Pabst entity was spun off to the remaining Olympia shareholders. Heileman strongly believed that continued consolidation of second-tier and small brewers was needed to more effectively compete. (As a side note, seven of the top eleven brewers were involved in acquisitions or attempted acquisitions in 1982.)

Heileman also had very good management. The company was unusually adept at being able to market more than three dozen regional beers, of which Old Style was the best-selling. It also had a very good cost structure which was quite competitive with that of Anheuser-Busch. To remain competitive, Heileman knew it had to expand into new markets. But having regional products might have helped the company to target some of its products to local market conditions.

There were two potential problems for Heileman. First, it served only the popular-priced market segment. This was one of the reasons that the company did so well in the face of a recession. Lack of brand loyalty may be in Heileman's favor, however, if people continued to trade down from higher-priced brands. Second, Heileman tried to remain well under Anheuser-Busch's prices; unfortunately, the industry giant had not raised prices in Heileman's market for about 2 years. If an increase did not come shortly, profit margin pressures might reduce Heileman's profitability.

LEGAL AND POLITICAL ISSUES

A number of legal and political issues were becoming more prevalent in the brewing industry. First, the vast number of traffic deaths related to alcohol had increased dramatically. There had been numerous bills introduced in the U.S. Congress to raise the legal drinking age nationally to twenty-one, and such bills were gaining increasing support. Raising the age would cause a decrease in beer sales. Perhaps substitutes, such as near beer, would crop up. Also, a number of consumer groups were asking the Consumer Protection Agency to look into the advertising practices of brewers. They claimed that brewers were encouraging the consumption of alcohol by highly vulnerable younger groups, which brought about heavy drinkers.

The company was now distributing counter cards and posters to bars throughout its marketing area with a message from E.T., the extraterrestrial. E.T. advised, "If you go beyond your limit, please don't drive. Phone home."[4] Coors had a long-standing policy against alcohol abuse. It sponsored alcohol awareness classes at its wellness center and supported many organizations that dealt with alcohol abuse.

Another major issue was the threat of mandatory deposits for bottles and cans. This would increase the price of beer and decrease customer convenience, possibly affecting demand. The difficulties in handling, shipping, and selling beer under this law were well known, as 18 percent of the beer sold in the United States in the early 1980s was covered by such laws. The law's rationale was to cut down on litter along the roadside, in the city, or out in the country. However, recycling might be an alternative means to accomplish this. Coors had a vigorous program for recycling both bottles and cans.

A third issue was excise taxes. Various state legislatures currently had bills to raise the excise tax on beer. There had also been some activity at the federal level. A number of groups had advocated taxing all alcoholic beverages by their alcohol content, which would result in drastically higher taxes on malt beverages. This, too, would result in increased prices for the consumer.

PRODUCT/MARKET OPPORTUNITIES

Under market penetration, Coors could more heavily advertise its products on television. Radio might also be a promising medium for beer advertising. One survey revealed that beer drinkers spent only about 33 percent of their media time watching television, while 47 percent of their time was spent listening to radio, which was less expensive for advertisers.[5] Another method could be increased price competition through such means as price cuts, cents-off coupons, and rebates. Coupons might attract more women who then did not buy much beer. Finally, Coors could merge with other brewers, which could help it penetrate existing markets with a wider selection of products.

Under market development, Coors could continue to expand nationally. This could be done by expanding its own facilities or by acquiring another brewery to give it additional capacity. A list of the top forty breweries in the United States is shown in Exhibit 8. Expansion abroad might also be a viable alternative, especially since Anheuser-Busch was doing well in Japan. Clearly, this latter option would require additional plants to make it feasible.

Under product development, Coors could develop near beer or other nonalcoholic beverages in response to a raising of the mandatory drinking age. Near beer was one product that helped Coors survive during Prohibition. It could also sell bottled spring water. Coors could also develop plastic containers for beer products, which would be a response to the threat of mandatory deposits and a way to lower transportation costs with lighter plastic containers. Another alternative would be to develop a beer product for the popular-priced segment for a more complete line of products. Coors could also import a name brand to compete more effectively in that segment. Coors' engineers could do consulting jobs for area firms. Finally, Coors Porcelain Company could accelerate its plans to get into the lucrative billion dollar a year dental restoration market.

Finally, under diversification, Coors could consider other glass products, such as test tubes. Also, the company could get into areas related to the beverage industry, such as soft drinks and distilled spirits.

EXHIBIT 8 Top forty U.S. commercial brewers

	1983 sales (31-gallon barrels)	Percent gain or loss over 1982	Headquarters
1. Anheuser-Busch, Inc.	60,500,000	2.4%	St. Louis, MO
2. Miller Brewing Co.	37,500,000	−4.6	Milwaukee, WI
3. The Stroh Brewery Co.	24,300,000	6.1	Detroit, MI
4. G. Heileman Brewing Co.	17,549,000	20.9	LaCrosse, WI
5. Adolph Coors Co.	13,719,000	15.1	Golden, CO
6. Pabst Brewing Co.	12,804,000	—[c]	Milwaukee, WI
7. Genesee Brewing Co.	3,200,000	−5.9	Rochester, NY
8. Christian Schmidt & Sons	3,150,000	0.0	Philadelphia, PA
9. Falstaff Brewing Co.	2,704,884	−15.1	Vancouver, WA
10. Pittsburgh Brewing Co.	1,000,000[a]	1.0	Pittsburgh, PA
11. Latrobe Brewing Co.	700,000[a]	0.0	Latrobe, PA
12. Champale Products Corp.	450,000[a]	4.7	Trenton, NJ
13. Hudepohl Brewing Co.	400,000[a]	0.0	Cincinnati, OH
14. The F. X. Matt Brewing Co.	400,000[a]	0.0	Utica, NY
15. Eastern Brewing Co.	350,000[a]	0.0	Hammonton, NJ
16. The Schoenling Brewing Co.	315,000[a]	5.0	Cincinnati, OH
17. Joseph Huber Brewing Co.	272,000	−1.1	Monroe, WI
18. The Lion Inc. — Gibbons	230,000	0.0	Wilkes-Barre, PA
19. D. G. Yuengling & Son	143,000	0.0	Pittsburgh, PA
20. Jones Brewing Co.	122,000	−2.9	Smithton, PA
21. Dixie Brewing Co., Inc.	113,000	−24.7	New Orleans, LA
22. Jacob Leinenkugel Brewing	67,000	−1.5	Chippewa Falls, WI
23. Fred Koch Brewery	60,000	−7.7	Dunkirk, NY
24. Stevens Point Brewery	48,900	0.8	Stevens Point, WI
25. Cold Spring Brewing Co.	40,000[a]	0.0	Cold Spring, MN
26. Spoetzl Brewery, Inc.	36,000	−3.0	Shiner, TX
27. August Schell Brewing Co.	35,000	0.0	New Vim, MN
28. Straub Brewery, Inc.	35,000	0.0	St. Mary's, PA
29. Anchor Steam Brewery Co.	33,500	16.6	San Francisco, CA
30. Walter Brewing Co.	26,800	−3.9	Eau Claire, WI
31. Dubuque Star Brewing	5,400[b]	−75.3	Dubuque, IA
32. Old New York Beer Co.	3,629[a]	—	New York, NY
33. Geyer Brothers	3,500	−12.5	Frankenmuth, MI
34. Redhook Ale Co.	3,000	—	Seattle, WA
35. William S. Newman Brewing	2,800	12.0	Albany, NY
36. River City Brewing Co.	2,500	108.3	Sacramento, CA
37. Sierra Nevada	2,200	25.7	Chico, CA
38. Yakima Brewing	1,400	—	Yakima, WA
39. Boulder Brewing Co.	500	25.0	Longmont, CO
40. Thousand Oaks Brewing	232[a]	—	Berkerly, AZ

[a] Estimate.
[b] Less than a full year's production.
[c] Due to Pabst-Olympia merger, 1983 figures are not comparable to 1982.
Source: *Modern Brewery Age Blue Book, 1984* (Stamford, Conn.), pp. 6, 8, 10, 168.

THE FUTURE

The Coors family remained confident of their firm's success in the future. Bill and Joe Coors felt their firm had survived because of the superior quality of its product. But, would quality and its Rocky Mountain mystique be enough to survive a changing industrial structure?

It appeared that slow growth would continue to plague the U.S. brewing industry. This meant that any significant increase in sales by one brewer would be at the expense of other competitors. In addition, increased concentration among brewers — via acquisitions, mergers, and bankruptcies — would continue and it was predicted that the top three firms could have up to 80 percent of the market by 1990.[6] As a result, a major strategic decision faced Coors management in the mid-1980s. Could Coors remain a regional brewer and be successful? If so, what would it need to do differently as a regional brewer to compete against the national breweries and other regional firms. Conversely, should Coors go into nationwide production and distribution? These two clear strategic alternatives presented themselves to the Coors family members in top management.

Over the years, Coors had increased its territory to twenty-six states and Washington, D.C. It had announced that it would add Alaska and Hawaii by the end of 1983, and move into Maryland in early 1984. But would this be enough to compete against the two national giants, Anheuser-Busch and Miller? Could one production facility serve a nationwide distribution or would Coors have to operate additional breweries? The alternative — remain regional or go nationwide — that Coors management would select remained undetermined as 1983 came to a close.

REFERENCES

1. "A Test for the Coors Dynasty," *Business Week*, May 8, 1978, p. 69.
2. Bob Lederer. "Can Coors Survive its Image?" *Beverage World*, April 1979, p. 49.
3. Bob Lederer. "Coal Power," *Beverage World*, September 1978, p. 58.
4. *Ibid.*, p. 47.
5. "Industry News," *Beverage Industry*, April 10, 1983, p. 58.
6. Michael C. Bellas. "Beer Wholesaler Sales Concentration: Implications for the 80s and Beyond," *Beverage Industry*, January 28, 1983, p. 30.

PABST BREWING COMPANY

This case focuses on the battle for Pabst that occurred during the early 1980s. This battle allows one to assess the motives of the various combatants. The reader should answer such questions as: What did each combatant want? What did each get? What should the survivor do now?

COMPANY HISTORY

The Pabst Brewing Company was founded in Milwaukee in 1844, 4 years before Wisconsin became a state. In 1893, at the Columbian Exposition in Chicago, Pabst won the highest award in competition with beers from all over the world. In that same year, sales topped one million barrels, making Pabst the largest brewer in the United States.

During Prohibition in the 1920s and early 1930s, Pabst, like other brewers, manufactured nonalcoholic products such as Pabst cheese, "near beer," tonic, malt syrup, and soft drinks. As Prohibition drew to a close, Pabst completed a merger with the Premier Malt Products Company of Peoria, Illinois. When the brewery resumed beer production at its original location and at its new Peoria plant, Pabst became a pioneer in the brewing of the same beer in separate geographic locations. The company opened its Newark, New Jersey, plant in 1945 and bought its Los Angeles Brewery in 1948, which made Pabst the first American brewer with plants from coast to coast.

In 1958, Pabst purchased another Milwaukee brewery, the Blatz Brewing Company. James C. Windham, president of Blatz at the time, was made president and chief executive officer of Pabst. In 1972 Windham was also elected chairman of the board.

At the time Windham assumed leadership of the company, Pabst's sales had been declining; the company ranked thirteenth in brewing industry sales. Under Windham's administration, however, Pabst was restored to prominence, becoming

Case prepared by Mark Kroll, University of Texas at Tyler, and John Hogan, Sam Houston State University. Reprinted by permission.

the third largest brewer in the nation. Production and sales of Pabst beer jumped from 1.9 million barrels in 1960 to 13.1 million barrels in 1973.

THE BEER PRODUCT

Beer is a food product made from barley malt, hops, grain adjuncts, yeast, and water. The relatively small amount of alcohol in most beers results from the fermentation of barley malt and other cereal grains by yeast. Seven major categories of beer are marketed by the major brewers.

Premium or Regular Beer

Sales in this category represent about 45.6 percent of total U.S. beer sales. This category includes Budweiser, Miller High Life, Coors, Stroh's, Old Style, Ranier, and Schlitz. In 1970 popular beer was the dominant segment of the beer market. However, by 1975 premium beer outsold popular brands by nearly 6 million barrels. Until 1983 premium beer sales continued to gain popularity while popular price brands lost market share. However, during 1983 and 1984 that trend appears to have been reversed as premium beer sales declined and popular beer sales increased.

Low-Calorie, Light Beer

The introduction of Miller Lite in 1975 created this segment, which now accounts for about 19.1 percent of total beer sales in the United States. This category includes Miller Lite, Coors Light, Bud Light, and Michelob Light. Light beer sales grew at an annual rate of 43 percent from the end of 1975 through 1982 compared to total industry growth of only 2.8 percent per year for the same period. However, light beer sales growth slowed dramatically during 1983–1984 to an annual rate of less than 6 percent.

Superpremium Beer

This segment comprises approximately 4.9 percent of the total sales volume of the U.S. beer industry. The growth rate of the superpremium category averaged 11.2 percent from 1975 to 1982. However, sales volume declined 2.0 and 4.6 percent during 1983 and 1984, respectively. The price of domestic superpremiums is generally 20 to 40 cents per six-pack greater than premiums. Brands in this category include Michelob, Lowenbrau, Herman Joseph's, and Henry Weinhard's.

Popular-Priced Beer

Beers in this category are priced lower than premium brand beers. Products in this segment include Old Milwaukee, Busch, Schaefer, Carling, Meister Brau, Milwaukee's Best, and generic beers. More than half of Pabst Blue Ribbon is sold at popular prices. Popular-priced beer accounts for 22 percent of total beer sales in the United States. Sales volumes of this category of beer declined at an annual rate of 7.5 percent between the end of 1975 and 1982 as brand segmentation flourished. In 1983 and 1984 that trend was reversed and sales grew 2.9 and 3.3 percent, respectively.

Malt Liquor

Malt liquor sales accounted for 4.3 percent of domestic sales during 1984. The leading brands include Schlitz, Colt 45, Olde English, Champale, and Mickey's.

Sales grew from 3.8 million barrels in 1975 to a peak of 6.5 million barrels in 1983 and then declined in 1984 to 5.8 million barrels.

Imported Beer   Imported beer sales represented about 3.9 percent of total beer sales in the United States during 1984. Between the end of 1975 and 1982 imported beer sales grew at an annual rate of 19.2 percent. During 1983 and 1984, sales grew 8.6 and 1.3 percent, respectively. The dominant brands in this category are Heineken, Molson, Beck's, Moosehead, and Labatt's.

Low-Alcohol Beer   Several major brewers have introduced a low-alcohol beer product in an attempt to capitalize on changing social attitudes that are more critical toward alcoholic beverages. However, only Anheuser-Busch's LA brand had achieved a measurable market share of 400,000 barrels for 1984. The future growth potential of this minor market segment is unclear.

THE BEER INDUSTRY — 1985 STATUS

There are fewer than forty companies currently brewing beer in the United States, and the industry today is highly competitive. The flurry of mergers, acquisitions, and reorganizations that beset this industry over the past few years has subsided — at least for the moment. Now the question is, amidst all the maneuvering, who gained and who lost? The jury is still out on that one, but it seems safe to say that there are now just six serious contenders in the United States brewing industry: Anheuser-Busch, Miller (a subsidiary of Philip Morris), Heileman, Coors, and privately held Pabst and Stroh.

The "big six" beer producers are off and running in a race for market share that could determine who survives through the eighties in an industry that is growing little, if at all. The basic problem is that the beer industry is mature, and demographic trends are working against all brewers. For the first time in years, the number of eighteen- to twenty-four-year-olds — who drink the most beer — declined in 1982. As the population continues to age in the decade ahead, the challenge for beer companies will be to attract new drinkers, while maintaining the loyalty of adults in the twenty-five to forty-nine age group.

In addition to changing demographics, changing social values are also negatively impacting the beer industry. Increased concerns for physical fitness, growing institutional sanctions against alcoholic beverage consumption, and rising popularity of nonalcoholic beverages have all hurt beer consumption. Whether or not these trends will continue is a critical question facing the brewing industry.

The brewing industry grew at a compounded annual rate of about 3.2 percent from 1978 through 1981, but in 1982 and 1983 the growth rate dropped dramatically. In 1984 beer consumption failed to grow for the first time in 27 years. However, some of the larger brewers have successfully developed licenced brewing contracts with various foreign brewers, and it appears that there may very well be a thirsty world out there waiting for American beer. Many, however, including industry

EXHIBIT 1 U.S. brewing industry sales volume and share by firm (millions of barrels)

Brewer	1984 Volume	1984 Share	1983 Volume	1983 Share	1982 Volume	1982 Share	1981 Volume	1981 Share	1981–1984 change Volume	1981–1984 change Share
Anheuser-Busch	64.0	35.0%	60.5	32.9%	59.1	32.4%	54.5	30.0%	9.5	5.0%
Miller	37.5	20.5	37.4	20.3	39.3	21.5	40.3	22.2	−2.8	−1.6
Stroh's	23.9	13.1	24.3	13.2	22.9	12.6	23.4	12.9	0.5	0.2
G. Heileman	16.8	9.2	17.5	9.5	14.5	7.9	14.0	7.7	2.8	1.5
Coors	13.2	7.2	13.7	7.5	11.9	6.5	13.3	7.3	−0.1	−0.1
Pabst[a]	11.6	6.3	12.8	7.0	17.5	9.6	19.2	10.6	−7.6	−4.2
Top six U.S. brewers	167.0	91.4	166.2	90.4	165.2	90.6	164.7	90.5	2.3	0.8
Others[b]	15.8	8.6	17.6	9.6	17.2	9.4	17.2	9.5	−1.4	−0.8
Total U.S. industry	182.8	100.0	183.8	100.0	182.4	100.0	181.9	100.0	0.9	0.0

[a] Reflects combination of Pabst and Olympia.
[b] Includes imports but excludes tax-free exports and military sales.
Source: *Beverage Industry 1986 Annual Manual.*

leader Anheuser-Busch, have forecast a ''no-growth'' environment for the remainder of the decade.

In terms of distribution, supermarkets and convenience stores hold 16 percent of all beer licences, but sell 66 percent of all beer consumed; therefore, two-thirds of all beer sold in the United States is consumed in homes, not bars. Further, it is estimated that 20 percent of American beer drinkers, white- and blue-collar working men, consume 80 percent of all beer sold in the United States.

Exhibits 1, 2, and 3 present U.S. beer sales volumes by brewer, market segment,

EXHIBIT 2 U.S. sales volume and market share by market segment (millions of barrels)

	1984 Volume	1984 Market share	1983 Volume	1983 Market share	1982 Volume	1982 Market share	1981 Volume	1981 Market share	1981–1984 change Volume	1981–1984 change Market share
Premium	83.2	45.6%	87.2	47.5%	89.0	48.8%	107.6	59.2%	−24.4	−13.6%
Popular	40.3	22.0	39.1	21.3	37.8	20.7	26.9	14.8	13.4	7.3
Light	34.9	19.1	33.7	18.3	31.5	17.3	25.1	13.8	9.8	5.3
Superpremium	8.9	4.9	9.7	5.3	10.5	5.8	11.2	6.2	−2.3	−1.3
Imports	7.2	3.9	6.3	3.4	5.8	3.2	5.2	2.9	2.0	1.1
Malt liquor	7.9	4.3	7.8	4.2	7.8	4.3	5.9	3.2	2.0	1.1
Low alcohol	0.4	0.2	0.0	0.0	0.0	0.0	0.0	0.0	0.4	0.2
Total consumption	182.8	100.0%	183.8	100.0%	182.4	100.0%	181.9	100.0%	0.9	

Source: R. S. Weinberg & Associates, Beer Marketer Insights, Inc., and *Beverage Marketing.*

EXHIBIT 3 Major U.S. brewers' best-selling brands by market segment (millions of barrels)

Brewer		1984 Volume	1984 Market share	1983 Volume	1983 Market share	1982 Volume	1982 Market share	1981 Volume	1981 Market share	1981–1984 change Volume	1981–1984 change Market share
Premium beer											
Budweiser	Anheuser	44.3	24.2%	42.7	23.2%	40.6	22.3%	39.1	21.5%	5.2	2.7%
Miller High Life	Miller	14.5	7.9	17.0	9.2	20.4	11.2	22.3	12.3	−7.8	−4.3
Coors	Coors	8.7	4.8	9.7	5.3	8.5	4.7	10.1	5.6	−1.4	−0.8
Stroh	Stroh's	5.3	2.9	5.5	3.0	5.4	3.0	5.5	3.0	−0.2	−0.1
Old Style	Heileman	5.1	2.8	5.8	3.2	5.6	3.1	5.4	3.0	−0.3	−0.2
Schmidt/Ranier	Heileman	2.4	1.3	2.3	1.3	2.0	1.1	1.7	0.9	0.7	0.4
Schlitz	Stroh's	1.7	0.9	3.2	1.7	4.1	2.2	5.7	3.1	−4.0	−2.2
		82.0	44.9	86.2	46.9	86.6	47.5	89.8	49.4	−7.8	−4.5
Popular beer											
Old Milwaukee	Stroh's	7.1	3.9	7.6	4.1	6.0	3.3	5.1	2.8	2.0	1.1
Pabst Blue Ribbon	Pabst	6.5	3.6	7.4	4.0	8.6	4.7	9.6	5.3	−3.1	−1.7
Busch	Anheuser	4.3	2.4	3.4	1.8	3.4	1.9	3.1	1.7	1.2	0.6
Schaefer	Stroh's	4.0	2.2	3.0	1.6	2.5	1.4	3.0	1.6	1.0	0.5
Carling Black Label	Heileman	2.1	1.1	1.9	1.0	1.6	0.9	1.0	0.5	1.1	0.6
Meister Brau	Miller	2.0	1.1	0.6	0.3	—	0.0	—	0.0	2.0	1.1
Milwaukee's Best	Miller	2.0	1.1	—	0.0	—	0.0	—	0.0	2.0	1.1
		28.0	15.3	23.9	13.0	22.1	12.1	21.8	12.0	6.2	3.3
Light beer											
Miller Lite	Miller	18.0	9.8	17.9	9.7	17.2	9.4	16.3	9.0	1.7	0.9
Coors Light	Coors	4.5	2.5	3.8	2.1	3.2	1.8	3.1	1.7	1.4	0.8
Bud Lite	Anheuser	4.0	2.2	3.7	2.0	3.3	1.8	—	0.0	4.0	2.2
Michelob Light	Anheuser	2.8	1.5	2.7	1.5	2.9	1.6	2.7	1.5	0.1	0.0
		29.3	16.0	28.1	15.3	26.6	14.6	22.1	12.2	7.2	3.9
Superpremium											
Michelob	Anheuser	6.7	3.7	7.0	3.8	7.4	4.1	7.7	4.2	−1.0	−0.6
Malt liquor											
Schlitz Malt	Stroh's	2.1	1.1	2.6	1.4	2.6	1.4	2.5	1.4	−0.4	−0.2
All other brands including imports		34.7	19.0	36.0	19.6	37.1	20.3	38.0	20.9	−3.3	−1.9
Total sales		182.8	100.0%	183.8	100.0%	182.4	100.0%	181.9	100.0%	0.9	

Source: *Beverage Industry 1986 Annual Manual.*

EXHIBIT 4 U.S. brewing industry selected financial data, 1984

	Anheuser-Busch	Miller	Stroh's	G. Heileman	Coors	Pabst
Operations (in millions)						
Net sales billed	$6,501.2	$10,138.0	N/A	$1,171.4	$1,132.6	$650.0
Gross margin	2,087.0	4,621.2	N/A	319.8	327.8	118.4
Sales, general, and administrative expenses	1,332.3	2,329.3	N/A	234.3	258.6	103.8
Operating margin	754.7	2,345.6	N/A	110.0	128.0	14.6
Net income	391.5	888.5	N/A	45.8	44.7	1.6
Balance sheet (in millions)						
Inventories	315.9	2,653.5	N/A	97.7	129.6	53.3
Current assets	776.3	3,640.1	N/A	164.7	365.3	84.3
Plant, equipment, and other assets, net	3,748.7	5,699.1	N/A	356.3	849.7	131.6
Total assets	4,525.0	9,339.2	N/A	521.0	1,215.0	215.9
Current liabilities	696.0	2,351.5	N/A	115.0	172.4	83.9
Long-term debt	836.0	2,059.5	N/A	59.1	0.0	61.8
Shareholders' equity	2,237.9	4,092.9	N/A	268.5	890.9	40.0
Capital expenditures	519.2	298.1	N/A	41.4	139.0	9.7
Working capital	80.3	1,288.6	N/A	49.7	192.9	0.4
Interest expense	103.0	299.1	N/A	9.1	1.4	12.7
Common shares outstanding	52.9	121.4	N/A	26.3	35.0	6.3
Market price per share	72.5	80.6	N/A	17.1	16.1	10.0
Cash dividends on common	89.7	420.0	N/A	12.6	14.0	0.0
Key financial ratios						
Gross margin to sales	32.1%	45.6%	N/A	27.3%	28.9%	18.2%
Operating margin to sales	11.6%	23.1%	N/A	9.4%	11.3%	2.2%
Return on sales	6.0%	8.8%	N/A	3.9%	3.9%	0.3%
Return on total assets	8.7%	9.5%	N/A	8.8%	3.7%	0.8%
Return on shareholders' equity	17.5%	21.7%	N/A	17.1%	5.0%	4.1%
Earnings per share	$7.40	$7.24	N/A	$1.73	$1.28	$0.08
Current ratio	1.1	1.5	N/A	1.4	2.1	1.0
Quick ratio	0.7	0.4	N/A	0.6	1.4	0.4
Debt/equity ratio	0.4	0.5	N/A	0.2	0.0	1.5
Times interest earned	7.3	7.8	N/A	12.1	90.8	1.2
Total assets turnover	1.4	1.1	N/A	2.2	0.9	3.0
Price/earnings ratio	9.8	11.1	N/A	9.9	12.6	125.0
Book value per share	$41.44	$33.72	N/A	$10.21	$25.34	$6.39
Cash dividend per share	$1.88	$3.40	N/A	$0.48	$0.40	$0.00
Sales per share	$122.90	$83.51	N/A	$44.54	$32.35	$103.99

and brand for the years 1981–1984. Exhibit 4 provides selected financial data and ratios for the six largest brewers as of 1984. Exhibits 5 through 7 provide more specific financial and operating performance data for Pabst Brewing Company. Exhibit 5 reveals that Pabst lost $23,536,000 in 1981 and has experienced turbulent times since that year.

EXHIBIT 5
Pabst Brewing
Company's four-
year financial
summary
of operations

	1984	1983	1982	1981
	After reorganization		Before reorganization	
Barrels sold	11,562	12,804	12,306	13,465
Sales, net of excise taxes	$650,038	$687,035	$649,166	$691,864
Cost of goods sold	531,610	543,552	531,608	599,324
Marketing, general, and administrative expenses	103,819	129,743	105,610	105,746
Operating income (loss)	14,609	13,740	11,948	(13,206)
Interest income	1,034	975	2,756	4,108
Interest expense	(12,662)	(9,950)	(3,567)	(1,965)
Plant closings and other dispositions	412	3,317	(3,241)	(39,791)
Miscellaneous — net	(641)	(612)	(3,600)	293
Income (loss) before income taxes and equity in net loss of Olympia Brewing Company	2,752	7,470	4,296	(50,561)
Provision (benefit) for income taxes	1,122	3,100	1,125	(27,025)
Income (loss) before equity in net loss of Olympia Brewing Company	1,630	4,370	3,171	(23,536)
Equity in net loss of Olympia Brewing Company	—	(765)	(478)	—
Net income (loss)	$1,630	$3,605	$2,693	($23,536)
Net income (loss) per share	$0.26	$0.31	$0.08	($0.72)

Note: Data in thousands except per share amounts.

BATTLE FOR PABST

During the second half of 1980, Irwin Jacobs set in motion a takeover battle for Pabst that would ultimately prove to be one of the most dramatic in recent years. Before the battle concluded, several major brewing companies were drawn into the fray.

The Combatants   *Irwin L. Jacobs.* Mr. Jacobs is a Minneapolis entrepreneur known as "Irv the liquidator." Mr. Jacobs is no stranger to the brewing business. In 1975 he paid $4.1 million for Minneapolis's Grain Belt Breweries. His attempt to manage the company was a dismal failure. While under his guidance, Grain Belt lost over $200,000 a month, and after 10 months he liquidated the company at a $4.0 million profit. About $3.3 million of that profit was attributable to his having sold the rights of Grain Belt to G. Heileman Brewing Company of La Crosse, Wisconsin.

EXHIBIT 6
Pabst Brewing
Company's
condensed
consolidated
balance sheets

	1984	1983	1982	1981
	After reorganization		Before reorganization	
Assets				
Current assets	$84,253	$96,849	$113,321	$128,143
Investment in Olympia Brewing Company	—	—	36,778	—
Properties held for sale	—	—	10,938	12,120
Intangible assets, net	—	—	15,814	14,885
Notes receivable	6,906	7,388	2,134	—
Plant and equipment, net	121,333	136,743	228,748	248,897
Other assets	3,373	2,935	1,206	—
	$215,865	$243,915	$408,939	$404,045
Liabilities and stockholders' equity				
Current liabilities	$91,437	$104,485	$90,366	$110,879
Long-term liabilities, net	61,826	84,976	38,843	13,281
Deferred income taxes	22,643	17,451	25,475	25,050
Stockholders' equity	39,959	37,003	254,255	254,835
	$215,865	$243,915	$408,939	$404,045

Note: Dollars in thousands.

Paul Kalmanovitz. Mr. Kalmanovitz is a seventy-nine-year-old immigrant who arrived from Poland in 1926, lacking funds and formal schooling. He has built a brewing empire largely on once-popular regional beers — Falstaff, Ballantine, Narragansett, Lucky Lager, Regal, Jax, Pearl, and others — acquired and then tightly managed by Mr. Kalmanovitz himself. He slashes advertising budgets, breaking the cardinal rule within the industry of promoting heavily, and he then cuts prices to reflect the lower overhead, bidding for a constituency of price-conscious beer drinkers and old-time brand loyalists. Mr. Kalmanovitz has become known in the industry as its most prolific litigant, filing suits almost routinely when the acquisition road is rocky or when other problems crop up.

William F. Smith. Mr. Smith, who in October 1982 became Pabst's fourth chief executive in 13 months, came over to Pabst from the Pittsburgh Brewing Company, producer of Iron City Beer. Mr. Smith is credited with saving the Pittsburgh brewery through his personal effort in taking strikers back to work after a 17-day walkout in 1978 and subsequently engineering a turnaround in circumstances similar to Pabst's. He is known as an aggressive executive with a strong sense of urgency, who is outwardly self-confident, a strong cost-control manager, and a capable marketer.

Mr. Smith, who earned $70,000 a year as head of the Pittsburgh Brewing Company,

EXHIBIT 7

Pabst Brewing Company beer sales by brand (millions of barrels)

	1984	1983	1982	1981	1980	1979	1978
Pabst Blue Ribbon	6.5	7.4	8.6	9.6	11.2	12.3	12.7
Hamm's & Hamm's Light	2.0	2.0	—	—	—	—	—
Olympia	1.0	1.0	—	—	—	—	—
Olde English Malt	0.9	1.0	0.9	1.1	1.0	0.7	0.5
Pabst Extra Light	0.3	0.3	0.5	0.5	0.6	0.7	0.6
Olympia Gold	0.3	0.2	—	—	—	—	—
Pabst Light	0.3	—	—	—	—	—	—
Jacob Best	0.2	0.3	0.4	—	—	—	—
Andeker	0.1	0.1	0.1	0.1	—	—	—
Olympia Light	0.1	—	—	—	—	—	—
Maxx	0.1	—	—	—	—	—	—
Lone Star	—	0.3	—	—	—	—	—
Red, White and Blue	—	0.2	1.0	1.3	1.2	0.9	0.5
Blatz	—	—	0.6	0.5	0.8	0.5	0.3
Other	—	—	0.2	0.4	0.3	—	0.8
	11.8	12.8	12.3	13.5	15.1	15.1	15.4
Sales of Olympia Brewing prior to acquisition by Pabst	0.0	0.0	5.2	5.7	6.1	6.0	6.7
Total barrels sold	11.8	12.8	17.5	19.2	21.2	21.1	22.1

Source: *Brewing Industry 1986 Annual Manual.*

stood to earn three times that amount in direct compensation from Pabst. The Pabst assignment represented a return to the Milwaukee beer scene for Mr. Smith, who was a packaging executive at the Miller Brewing Company headquarters from 1973 to 1975. While in Pittsburgh he would often visit local bars and buy beer for the customers. In Milwaukee, where Pabst was very popular, on weekends he would load a van with beer and distribute samples to tailgaters at local football games.

The motto that adorns the wall behind Smith's desk in his office at Pabst reads "Show me a good loser and I'll show you a loser." Since coming to Pabst, Mr. Smith has closed the Peoria Heights, Illinois, brewery, idling some six hundred workers, as well as winning concessions from brewery workers at the Newark plant, a move that purportedly cut operating costs by about $4 million a year. In addition, he dismissed the company's top marketing officer, the vice-president in charge of sales, and Pabst's corporate secretary.

G. Heileman Brewing Company. Heileman's forty-nine-year-old chairman, Russell G. Cleary, has been ungraciously referred to as the "guerilla fighter" of the brewing industry. He has been described as a pricing and marketing wizard. The brewing industry's major thrust in the past decade has been elimination of the nation's small and medium brewers and a concentration of over half of the country's total beer market in the hands of just two companies, Anheuser-Busch and Miller. While other local and regional brewers have failed, Heileman's industry position has advanced from 31st in 1960, with revenues of $18.8 million, to fourth in 1984, with revenues of $1.2 billion — quite an accomplishment in just 24 years.

G. Heileman is the fastest-growing beer company in the country, with a return on equity averaging 25.8 percent over the past 5 years — a rate significantly higher than the industry average. Mr. Cleary has achieved that record by acquiring at steep discounts the small regional plants the big companies had no use for, gradually building up enough capacity to achieve economies of scale in materials purchasing and administration. Furthermore, he did it mainly out of cash flow, while lowering debt gradually over the decade to a 22 percent debt-to-equity ratio, roughly the industry norm.

Mr. Cleary believes that the beer business is really a regional business. After acquiring Blatz Brewing Co., Jacob Schmidt Brewing Co., Rainier Brewing Co., and Drewery's Ltd. U.S.A., Heileman did not move in its existing brands. Instead, it continued to sell the products of those regional brewers. "If you look at the brewers below number two, you will see that they do not have uniform sales across the nation," says Cleary. "Each brand sells well in a particular area. If we were to buy Pabst or Schlitz or whoever, there would be no reason to try to sell the brands nationally. You just want to fish where the fish are."

C. Schmidt and Sons, Inc. Schmidt is a 122-year-old privately held brewing company located in Philadelphia. Schmidt, which produces Rheingold, Knickerbocker, and Schmidt's beer, is the nation's tenth-largest brewer. Schmidt made an unsolicited bid to take control of the New York brewer, F. & M. Schaefer Corporation in 1978, but was foiled when Schaefer won an injunction barring the merger on antitrust grounds.

Gauging Schmidt's size and strength is difficult, but analysts put its annual revenue at about $192 million in 1982. Schmidt has a superimage as a "popular-priced" brew and has sought to shore up its market share with purchases of smaller brewers, most recently Philadelphia-based Ortlieb Brewing Company. Schmidt has concentrated its purchases and marketing efforts close to home and has established a very strong franchise in the Philadelphia area, with extremely high penetration in the on-premises (restaurant and bar taps) market.

The Assault

In 1980, when Irwin Jacobs acquired 9.6 percent of Pabst common, he characterized his purchase to the skeptics as an investment in a well-managed company whose assets were undervalued by the market. Mr. Jacobs purchased his stake in Pabst for about $14 a share while the stock's book value at the time was approximately $33 a share, which would seem to indicate that "Irv" certainly had an eye for opportunity. When he acquired the approximately 800,000 shares of Pabst common and became the largest Pabst shareholder, Mr. Jacobs praised Pabst's management for their past exemplary performance in the face of unrelenting pressure from both the economy and the competition.

On July 2, 1981, Pabst's chairman and chief executive, Frank C. DeGuire, resigned under pressure. Mr. Jacobs demanded that he be elected chairman or vowed he would take the fight for control of the company to the shareholders. He also sought the resignation of four board members to make room for his own people. Mr. Jacobs felt the board did not own enough of the company's stock to make the kinds of tough decisions required for continued success in the highly competitive and quickly consolidating beer industry. However, Mr. Jacobs settled for a seat on the board, and the following week Pabst made a $588 million takeover bid for the ailing Joseph Schlitz Brewing Company, topping an earlier offer by G. Heileman Brewing Company of $494 million. Analysts speculated that Mr. Jacobs was going to attempt a simultaneous liquidation of both companies.

Ultimately, both Pabst and Heileman lost Schlitz to Stroh's. The Department of Justice barred Heileman from acquiring Schlitz on the grounds that the combination would produce too heavy a concentration in the Midwest and therefore substantially lessen competition. Pabst gave up when Stroh's offered to acquire 67 percent of Schlitz for $17 a share, considerably bettering Pabst's offer.

Following Pabst's failure to acquire Schlitz, director Jacobs resigned, but vowed to continue his campaign to gain control of Pabst. William F. Smith, Jr., was appointed president and chief executive officer at Pabst in October 1981.

That same year Mr. Jacobs teamed up with six associates, one of whom was Paul Kalmanovitz. This investor group controlled about 15 percent of Pabst. Mr. Jacobs declared that he had no plans to liquidate Pabst, and Mr. Smith was indisposed to let him try. Mr. Smith said that he owed his allegiance to the board that hired him and he intended to fight for the Pabst Brewing Company. Further, Mr. Smith said of Mr. Jacobs, "He't taking a lot of my time. I just wish I could get down to the job of selling beer." However, it was obvious what was driving Mr. Jacobs, as his investment in Pabst had cost him $20 million, and he had watched its value erode as Pabst's losses mounted.

On February 2, 1982, Pabst announced that it had reached an agreement in principle to acquire the Pittsburgh Brewing Company, a small but profitable regional brewer that produced Iron City and Iron City Light beers. Under the agreement, which was subject to the approval of Pittsburgh's shareholders, Pabst agreed to pay, with its common stock, the equivalent of $7 a share for the 1.1 million shares outstanding.

On February 22, 1982, Pabst received an unsolicited cash merger proposal from C. Schmidt & Sons, Inc. Pabst said Schmidt proposed to buy its 8.18 million outstanding shares for $16 a share or a total of $141 million. Schmidt's offer was only slightly above the stock's then current trading level. Pabst shares, which were sold over-the-counter, had closed the previous day at 14.25, up 1.124. On March 25, 1982, in their continued effort to merge with Pabst, C. Schmidt and Sons, Inc., increased their earlier offer of $16 a share to $20.50 a share or a total of $168 million for all of Pabst's outstanding shares. In May 1982, C. Schmidt & Sons, Inc., sweetened its offer for Pabst to $25.50 per share or a total of $208.7 million. The offer took the form of $20.50 per share in cash and $5 per share in debentures. In rejecting Schmidt's previous offers, Pabst had indicated that $25 a share in cash would be a fair price.

On December 10, 1982, the battle for Pabst escalated when Paul Kalmanovitz sued Pabst and Heileman for conspiracy. The suit charged that the defendants conspired to defraud Pabst shareholders, to injure Mr. Kalmanovitz's business, and to rig the offers in the bidding for Pabst control. The bidding was escalated when Mr. Kalmanovitz made a $32 per share offer for Pabst, which followed a new bid by Heileman at $29 a share.

Mr. Kalmanovitz denounced Heileman's alleged offer to him of $5 million if he agreed to drop his effort to acquire Pabst. At that time he was engaged in a partnership with Mr. Jacobs's investor group in an attempt to acquire Pabst. Subsequently, Mr. Jacobs's group pulled out of its agreement with Mr. Kalmanovitz to support Heileman's offer. Mr. Kalmanovitz stated that Mr. Jacobs "defected" to Heileman because Heileman paid Mr. Jacobs and his associates $7.5 million. He called the payment a "discriminatory premium over other Pabst shareholders." According to the suit, the Heileman bid violated federal law because the $5 million offer was not disclosed and the payment to Mr. Jacobs was "disguised" as a "litigation settlement." Mr. Kalmanovitz stated that the defendant's conduct was "a classic case of how insiders connive with covetous outsiders to frustrate competitive bidding and to fleece ordinary shareholders."

Pabst said that its board had noted that the Heileman offer would deliver more cash than the Kalmanovitz bid, $162.4 million compared with $132.8 million, even though Mr. Kalmanovitz's per-share offer was higher, $32 compared to $29. That was because Heileman had raised its target to 5.6 million shares and Mr. Kalmanovitz only wanted 4.2 million under the terms of his offer. However, both bidders were to complete their proposed mergers by swapping notes for the remaining Pabst shares outstanding. Heileman was to swap 10-year notes with a face value of $24 per share. Mr. Kalmanovitz was to swap 3-year subordinated notes with a face value of $26 per share.

By December 23, 1982, Kalmanovitz raised his offer for 4.2 million shares of Pabst common from $32 each to $40. Mr. Kalmanovitz's opponent in the takeover fight, Heileman, had earlier increased its offer for Pabst to $32 a share to match Mr. Kalmanovitz's previous offer. Kalmanovitz increased to 18 percent from 15 percent the interest rate on subordinate notes that were to be swapped for all remaining shares if the merger was completed.

The Vote

G. Heileman Brewing Company eventually won the long battle for control of Pabst Brewing Company, despite an apparent higher offer from Paul Kalmanovitz. Heileman received 6,730,000 of Pabst's 8.2 million shares outstanding. Heileman accepted for payment 68 percent or 5.6 million shares as of Wednesday, midnight, December 22, 1982. Heileman's bid evidently won because investors feared that Kalmanovitz would be unable to accumulate the 4.15 million shares his offer required. If Heileman was able to secure the 5.6 million shares it sought, there would not be enough remaining outstanding Pabst stock to meet Mr. Kalmanovitz's minimum. But if the offer from Kalmanovitz was higher, as it apparently was, why shareholders feared Kalmanovitz could not meet his minimum remains a mystery.

The New Pabst   The new management team at Pabst, led by William Smith, had spent the past 20 months beating back no fewer than seven takeover attempts — including multiple forays by Irwin Jacobs, Paul Kalmanovitz, and G. Heileman Brewing — and had completed a takeover of Olympia Brewing. But it was not accomplished without a cost. Pabst had to sell three of its seven breweries to Heileman (including one it acquired from Olympia) and had witnessed its planned acquisitions of Schlitz Brewing and Pittsburgh Brewing fall apart.

The transactions that eventually allowed Pabst to retain its independence were so varied and tangled that to this day misconception persists. As best as can be determined, Heileman essentially was after Pabst's brewing capacity and some of its regional brands, such as Olympia and Lone Star. In order to retain its independence, Pabst had to give Heileman three of its breweries and some of its brands. The two most important breweries surrendered were in Texas and Washington State. Heileman wanted these two particular plants due to their locations. Heileman was very much an upper Midwest brewer originally and wanted a national network of breweries. The old Olympia plant in Tumwater, Washington, gave them a Pacific Northwest entry. The Texas plant allowed them to move into a state with one of the fastest-growing populations (not to mention one of the fastest-growing demands for beer). The Pabst label and its traditional market in the upper Midwest would not be of great value to Heileman as it already had a strong entry in this market and really did not need the Pabst label.

The deal was in effect a leveraged buyout. Heileman put a great deal of debt on Pabst's balance sheet (note the changes in the balance sheet before and after reorganization) and then retired a lot of the outstanding stock. The stock they controlled they traded back to Pabst for the three breweries. The net effect was that Pabst "bought back" much of its stock through leverage and surrendering brewing capacity.

Heileman had acquired much of what it desired and left Pabst as an empty shell. Yet that fact eluded most observers because of the complexity of the transactions involved. In fact, stock market investors had, at least initially, cast their vote for Pabst's management. Pabst's common shares, valued at $26 each for purposes of the March 18, 1983 merger with Olympia, had traded shortly after the merger for as high as $66.50. Initial buyers included a majority of Pabst's twenty-three officers and directors who had, at least at last count, purchased a total of 40,000 shares.

Unfortunately, while 1983 earnings per share of $.31 were a significant improvement over 1982 results, they were well below earnings forecasted. Throughout 1983, Pabst, structurally and financially drained from the takeover struggles, continued to lose market share to the larger brewers. While barrels sold rose slightly in 1983, the losses of plants to Heileman and the overwhelming advertising budgets of larger brewers resulted in Pabst's poor market share position in all of its markets, especially in the Sun Belt.

In late 1983, August U. Pabst, the great-grandson of the founder of the firm, resigned as executive vice-president. It was his conclusion that the only hope for Pabst was to acquire another large brewer (in order to build market share instantly) or to be acquired by another brewer. However, the extremely weak financial condition of Pabst precluded any acquisitions, and the poor market share performance of Pabst's brands made the firm's acquisition at a price anything above its break-up value very doubtful.

William Smith was only a bit more optimistic at the beginning of 1984. While admitting that the firm was under extreme competitive pressures, he pointed to some bright spots. Barrelage had indeed risen in 1983 for the first time in several years. They still had four large, efficient plants located in the key Southeast, West Coast, and Midwest markets. Pabst had managed to improve production efficiency slightly. However, Smith had no illusions about the difficulties Pabst faced in the future. In 1984 earnings per share declined to $.26. Beer sales declined by 1.2 million barrels and Pabst's market share declined to 6.3 percent from 7.0 percent for the previous year despite over $100 million in advertising expenditures during 1983 and 1984.

The Final Skirmish

In early November 1984, amid speculation that Pabst was terminally ill, Pabst's common stock was trading around $6.75 a share. On November 12, based upon discussions with Pabst's financial advisor, Paul Kalmanovitz announced that he had obtained an agreement with Pabst management to support a $10 per share tender offer for all of Pabst's outstanding shares. Pabst immediately denied having such an agreement. The next day Heileman submitted a bid of $10 per share and Pabst's board announced that it would consider both proposals.

Heileman recognized that it could acquire four fairly modern breweries relatively inexpensively. At the end of 1983 Pabst had about 5,800,000 shares outstanding. At $10 a share, Heileman would be acquiring the four remaining breweries and all of Pabst's labels for $58,000,000 plus the assumption of all of Pabst's debt. Pabst's total debt was about $207,000,000. Combining these two figures, the total acquisition price would be $265,000,000. The four breweries had a combined capacity of 14,700,000 barrels. That means that Heileman would be acquiring this capacity for about $18 a barrel. (In 1982 new brewing capacity cost about $25 to $45 a barrel to build.) Heileman would also acquire the Hamm's label, a fairly successful popularly priced label.

On November 19, Kalmanovitz formally launched his $10 per share tender offer without waiting for a response from Pabst's board. Pabst responded by saying it would not support or resist Kalmanovitz's formal offer and that it would continue to discuss alternatives with Heileman.

On December 6, Pabst said it would accept, subject to shareholder approval, a sweetened $11 per share offer from Heileman. Two days later Stroh's and Schmidt filed antitrust suits to block Heileman's offer. On December 28 a federal district court granted a preliminary injunction preventing Heileman from purchasing additional Pabst shares. On January 18 a federal appeals court upheld the injunction despite Heileman pleadings that its acquisition of Pabst would not affect Stroh's ability to market beer in the Midwest.

On February 8 Heileman let its $11 per share offer expire. Four days later Pabst's board announced it would strongly support Kalmanovitz's $10 per share offer. By February 27, S & P Company, a concern controlled by Kalmanovitz, had acquired 81.3 percent of Pabst's outstanding common stock and won the remains of Pabst. By March all the Pabst officers and directors, save one vice-president, had resigned and relinquished total control to Kalmanovitz's company. In May trading of Pabst shares was formally suspended. The company was removed from Standard and Poor's index of 500 stocks and was replaced by Luby's Cafeterias.

After all the dust had settled, it was clear that Paul Kalmanovitz had acquired a company that had been severely wounded in its competition with the other major brewers. As shown by Exhibit 3, Pabst was rapidly losing market share in the popular-price market segment. With no promising Pabst entries in other market segments, Kalmanovitz's investment in Pabst did not appear to be especially promising.

REFERENCES

Beverage Industry 1986 Annual Manual.
"Heileman Wins Pabst." *Business Week* (January 10, 1983): 40.
Nelson-Horchler, Joani. "Showdown in the Sunbelt." *Industry Week* (June 13, 1983): 69–72.

PATRICK THE PORTER

THE HOTEL IN THE HILLS

The Evergreen Inn, located in northern New England, is a fashionable 250-room American-plan hotel which charges rates upward of $150 per day per guest. In this remote, exclusive summer vacation area the guests' activities center around the hotel's swimming pool, golf course, tennis courts, sauna, and two large bars and lounges. The bars are very popular and often guests relax with heavy drinking. The Evergreen Inn has achieved a superior reputation for good food, outstanding recreation facilities, and excellent service. Most of the guests return and conventions always rebook a year in advance.

Management fosters a homey, down-to-earth atmosphere. Many returning guests are known on a first-name basis.

The hotel staff is predominantly young adults, either in college or recently graduated. A staff dormitory on the grounds provides living quarters, assuring easy access for the staff and remedying the lack of alternative local accommodations.

Each autumn the Evergreen's owner and managers go south to run another luxury hotel. Typically, the few older, experienced employees take similar jobs in the southern resort areas.

PATRICK THE PRO

Patrick was one of those migrant employees. At fifty-two, he was charming. His clean, well-pressed uniform and polished shoes set off his jaunty 5-foot 5-inch frame. With merry blue eyes and a ruddy smiling face he greeted each guest, often by first name — a practice encouraged by the management. His 7 years at the inn made him the senior of the eight porters.

Pat was a favorite of the guests and regarded with affection and respect by the younger porters. Although he had no authority over his coworkers, they liked and respected him and his professional performance of the porter's duties; his snappy appearance set a standard that clearly paid off in the tips he earned. His daily rate averaged 50 percent more than his less-experienced colleagues. He would greet each guest, manage their luggage, handle their requests with just the right humor and deference. Never was he accused of "hustling tips" — a practice management explicitly discouraged.

Each porter and the door attendants were paid the minimum legal wage and had to rely on tips to earn a reasonable living. On a reasonably busy day, $100 in tips was not unusual; hence, these jobs were aspired to by other employees. In addition, the porters and door attendants were the only employees allowed to socialize with the guests in the bars and the other facilities. Patrick was a favorite when it came to entertaining the guests and staff members. His cigarette lighter with the Canadian Club insignia was at ready service for all. His favorite expression, "Faith in all the saints in heaven," was soon part of the guests' and staff's repertoire of expressions.

Several years ago Pat had been divorced amicably. His wife dropped by to see him occasionally. There were no children. Those who had known Pat over the years felt his marriage had failed because of his drinking; he had been an alcoholic for about 20 years. This, however, did not seem to interfere with his reputation as the best porter — a favorite of management, staff, and guests young and old. Although he drank, often while on the job, mints controlled traces of alcohol on his breath, and his drinking apparently did not interfere with his job performance.

Pat's social life was his drinking. He would drink alone in his room or with the guests in the lounges or entertain the staff at the employees' canteen. There was a rule against drinking in the dorm, but management made little effort to enforce it, so long as work was not affected. Pat's friends were his fellow porters and anyone who would drink with him.

Until the previous summer, Frank, a fifty-six-year-old porter, had been his closest companion, but management had reluctantly fired Frank the past Labor Day for his drinking practices. Frank's competence had been surpassed only by Patrick's. Management had found Frank to be a valuable employee who could make any guest feel at home, but his drinking had increasingly made him incapable of performing his duties, and the decision to fire him seemed the only solution.

Although most staff vacancies could be quickly filled from the local labor supply, it took longer to find personable and attractive porters and door attendants. The loss of Frank was remarked on by the guests.

SUPERVISION

Warren Watkins, the head manager at the Evergreen Inn, had a good relationship with employees and guests. He comfortably delegated authority and would involve himself only when major problems arose. Sanford Griffith was the service manager, responsible for the hiring, supervision, and firing of the kitchen staff, door attendants, porters, waiters, and waitresses. He too had an excellent relationship with guests and staff; he was neither harsh and overbearing nor too lenient. He would act on problem areas when they began to affect the reputation or service of the hotel. Griffith arranged the shift schedules for the eight porters and three door attendants. Each employee had 2 days off each week but seldom in succession. Schedules varied with the number of guests arriving and leaving. Because the labor was available to fill quickly most of the hotel's jobs, many employees were fired at the first instance of lateness or poor performance; full warning was given at the time of hiring.

Neither Watkins nor Griffith drank; both, however, recognized the high incidence of alcoholism among restaurant and hotel employees generally and among kitchen staff in particular. They knew, as did other staff, of Pat's drinking but remained uninvolved until service standards were compromised.

THIS SUMMER'S PROBLEMS

Before the July 4th weekend, Griffith fired Pat twice for late arrival and for questionable performance caused, Griffith knew, by Pat's drinking. On both occasions Patrick went to Mr. Watkins and pleaded for his job. On each occasion, Watkins overrode Griffith's decision and rehired Pat.

Among the staff who knew of the incidents, it was suspected that both Griffith and Watkins had concurred: firing Pat for his drinking served as a strong warning; rehiring was a recognition of his worth.

Griffith had become more concerned with Patrick after the second firing. He felt it was hurting his credibility with the employees, and he knew that Pat's problem was not one that would go away. After the experiences with Frank, he feared being faced with that situation again.

As the summer progressed, the firing incidents seemed to have been forgotten. Pat was doing his job, but his drinking was still heavy. Early in August Griffith expressed his concern about the problem to Watkins.

Griffith: Warren, I'm getting kind of concerned about all this drinking around here. From my porch I saw Pat and a few of the younger boys come back to their rooms staggering drunk last night, and they didn't make any secret of it either. The kids hardly drank at all in the beginning of the summer.

Watkins: This place is so isolated — they need something to do. As long as they do their work, it isn't hurting anybody. I've been told that Patrick has even sworn off occasionally for a day.

Griffith: I hope you're right.

Watkins: Me too.

AUGUST 15

One week later Patrick was late for work and had a visible hangover. It was the first time since early July. Neither Watkins nor Griffith found out about it and the other workers covered for him. Two days later he was late again. Griffith noticed and asked him what had happened. Pat said he had overslept and Griffith let it go. The next day he was late again and this time he was drunk. None of the other workers had seen him drunk on the job before. One of the bellmen voiced his irritation; it was very busy that morning with a convention checking out. An hour after Pat's arrival on the job his former wife showed up and asked him to show her around the new patio garden. He asked the other workers to cover for him while he was gone. Two hours later he returned staggering drunk. The porters and door attendants were shocked because Patrick could not perform his job.

Griffith entered the lobby to see Pat stumble and drop two bags just as a guest was emerging from the awning-covered red-carpeted entrance.

Bill B., an alcoholic, was elected a group service representative (GSR) in spring 1984 to represent the Tuesday night ''12 & 12'' discussion group of Portsmouth, New Hampshire, Alcoholics Anonymous (A.A.) group. This GSR representation meant that Bill would be expressing his group's views on issues of major importance to A.A., including (1) interaction with professional treatment centers, (2) changing group memberships such as A.A. special-interest or special-problem members (nonsmoking, dual addiction, and others), and (3) A.A. growth, flexibility, and success.

Bill reviewed his own experience with treatment centers and the new A.A. members as well as his knowledge of A.A. history and growth in preparation for discussing these issues with his group. The following paragraphs summarize the problems alcoholism creates, A.A.'s historical development, and Bill's experiences with A.A.

ALCOHOLISM

The Comprehensive Care Corporation, a social services organization, estimated that alcoholism cost industry $25 billion in lost production in 1978, while society paid $30 billion for costs of vehicle accidents, welfare, violent crime, and health and medical services. The National Institute on Alcohol Abuse and Alcoholism noted that:

Fewer than 5 percent of the country's 12–15 million alcoholics are on skid row.

50 percent of all fatal road accidents involve alcohol, and half of these are caused by alcoholism.

The suicide rate among alcoholics is fifty-eight times greater than that of the general population.

80 percent of all family violence is alcohol-related.

Children of alcoholics are 50 percent more likely than others to marry an alcoholic.

ALCOHOLICS ANONYMOUS

On May 11, 1935, a minister in Akron, Ohio, received a telephone call. The caller identified himself as Bill W. and said, "I'm a rum hound from New York." Bill W., alone in a strange town, was terrified he would forget his spiritual experience and his resulting newly found sobriety, and would begin to drink again. He started calling ministers listed in the phone book. The minister immediately thought of a friend, Dr. Bob, who was an alcoholic. Would Bill talk to the friend? Bill W., thirty-nine, a New York stockbroker, and Dr. Bob, fifty-five, an Ohio surgeon, the founders of A.A., met the next evening.

Dr. Bob told his wife he would talk to Bill W. for only 15 minutes, but the two went into a room alone and spent 6 hours. Bill W. later described the talk as "a completely mutual thing. I had quit preaching. I knew that I needed this alcoholic as much as he needed me."

Dr. Bob recalled that Bill W. "was the first living human with whom I have ever talked who knew what he was talking about in regard to alcoholism from actual experience. In other words, he talked my language."[1]

Bill W. (who had become a sober alcoholic through a spiritual experience) and Dr. Bob spent the next 2 weeks gathering together "a group of drunks, . . . talking and drinking coffee. . . . We were under awful compulsion. And we found that we had to do something for somebody or actually perish ourselves."[2]

A few days later Bill W. had to help Dr. Bob recover from a new binge by a combination of talk, tomato juice, sauerkraut, and corn syrup. Bill even gave Dr. Bob a beer just before an operation Dr. Bob had to perform. It was Dr. Bob's last drink.

Bill W. and Dr. Bob worked with fellow alcoholics in Akron until fall 1935, when Bill W. went back to New York, leaving Dr. Bob with five members. For the next 2 years they worked individually and together, as Bill W. frequently returned to Akron. The early very rigid procedures, most notably the emphasis on a personal spiritual experience, became more and more flexible.

In November 1937 Dr. Bob and Bill W. counted up the forty alcoholics they had worked with who were staying bone dry, and they were convinced they had "started a chain reaction . . . conceivably it could one day circle the whole world . . . we actually wept for joy, and Bob and [his wife] and I bowed our heads in silent thanks."[3]

Bill's vision of the future included a chain of profit-making hospitals, fund raising, paid missionaries, and a book to carry the message. Somewhat reluctantly, Dr. Bob and a bare majority of eighteen alcoholics agreed to Bill W.'s plan, most reservations being based on a fear that "going into big business and hiring paid

---

[1] *Dr. Bob and the Good Oldtimers.* New York: Alcoholics Anonymous World Services, Inc., 1980, p. 68.

[2] Ibid.

[3] Ibid.

missionaries would destroy us.'' There was a strong minority view that the program should be a free service and that A.A. should shun publicity. The biography, *Dr. Bob and the Good Oldtimers*, notes:

> *Bill eventually saw that this meeting in Akron had resulted in the first real expression of A.A.'s group conscience — instrument of the ultimate authority. . . . He cited the incident to illustrate why a strong minority should always be heeded, and concluded that the answer would usually be found in the middle — between the promoters and the conservatives.*

Bill W. left for New York to try to raise the monies required for the expansion, since the cofounders' personal finances were nonexistent, having been wiped out, first, by excessive drinking and, second, by giving vast amounts of time to the free service of alcoholics.

Bill W. approached John D. Rockefeller, Jr. After an investigation, Rockefeller gave $5,000 instead of the $50,000 requested, having concluded that money, property, and professionalism might ''spoil this thing.'' Bill W. later credited this rebuff by Rockefeller as saving the A.A. ''Fellowship,'' as the members referred to it.

In 1939 Bill W. wrote *Alcoholics Anonymous*, the A.A. message, ''the story of how men and women have recovered from alcoholism.'' The foreword stated:

> *We, of Alcoholics Anonymous, are more than one hundred men and women who have recovered from a seemingly hopeless state of mind and body. To show other alcoholics precisely how we have recovered is the main purpose of this book. For them, we hope these pages will prove so convincing that no further authentication will be necessary. We think this account of our experiences will help everyone to better understand the alcoholic. Many do not comprehend that the alcoholic is a very sick person. And besides, we are sure that our way of living has its advantages for all.*

The publication of ''The Big Book,'' a feature article in the *Saturday Evening Post* in March 1941, A.A.'s independence from an evangelical organization (the Oxford Group), and the continued Fellowship effort in New York and Ohio led to continued growth. By the start of World War II A.A. had over eight thousand members. (Six thousand appeal letters from alcoholics or their families were received in the New York office after the *Post* article.)

Dr. Bob was diagnosed as being terminally ill with cancer in the late 1940s. Before he died in 1950, he and Bill W. devised an organizational framework to carry on the business of the Fellowship. This plan, essentially unchanged today, consists of (1) the Twelve Steps and the Twelve Traditions, (2) the autonomy of the local group, (3) the independence of A.A., and (4) the local meeting.

The Twelve Steps and the Twelve Traditions

Together, the Twelve Steps outline the process of individual recovery in the A.A. Fellowship and the Twelve Traditions guide the organization's integrity, support, and growth.

The Twelve Steps, the ''recovery program upon which the Fellowship of Alcoholics Anonymous is founded,'' are:

1. We admitted we were powerless over alcohol — that our lives had become unmanageable.
2. Came to believe that a Power greater than ourselves could restore us to sanity.
3. Made a decision to turn our will and our lives over to the care of God *as we understood Him*.
4. Made a searching and fearless moral inventory of ourselves.
5. Admitted to God, to ourselves, and to another human being the exact nature of our wrongs.
6. Were entirely ready to have God remove all these defects of character.
7. Humbly asked Him to remove our shortcomings.
8. Made a list of all persons we had harmed and became willing to make amends to them all.
9. Made direct amends to such people wherever possible, except when to do so would injure them or others.
10. Continued to take personal inventory and when we were wrong promptly admitted it.
11. Sought through prayer and meditation to improve our conscious contact with God *as we understood Him*, praying only for knowledge of His will for us and the power to carry that out.
12. Having had a spiritual awakening as the result of these Steps, we tried to carry this message to alcoholics and to practice these principles in all our affairs.

This final Twelfth Step means the A.A. member introduces a person to A.A., and this "Twelfth Stepping" is the sober alcoholic's path of service.

Organizationally, the autonomous local groups are to be served by their district, their state or area, and by the General Services Board, who are "to preserve and maintain the Twelve Steps except for modification by the Fellowship," and to support the local group as it carries the message to the alcoholic. The General Services Board and the A.A. Fellowship as a whole are to be guided by the Twelve Traditions, which are:

1. Our common welfare should come first; personal recovery depends upon A.A. unity.
2. For our group purpose there is but one ultimate authority — a loving God as He may express Himself in our group conscience. Our leaders are but trusted servants; they do not govern.
3. The only requirement for A.A. membership is a desire to stop drinking.
4. Each group should be autonomous except in matters affecting other groups or A.A. as a whole.
5. Each group has but one primary purpose — to carry its message to the alcoholic who still suffers.
6. An A.A. group ought never endorse, finance, or lend the A.A. name to any related facility or outside enterprise, lest problems of money, property, and prestige divert us from our primary purpose.

7. Every A.A. group ought to be fully self-supporting, declining outside contributions.
8. Alcoholics Anonymous should remain forever nonprofessional, but our service centers may employ special workers.
9. A.A., as such, ought never be organized; but we may create service boards or committees directly responsible to those they serve.
10. Alcoholics Anonymous has no opinion on outside issues; hence the A.A. name ought never be drawn into public controversy.
11. Our public relations policy is based on attraction rather than promotion; we need always maintain personal anonymity at the level of press, radio, and films.
12. Anonymity is the spiritual foundation of all our Traditions, ever reminding us to place principles before personalities.

These steps and traditions express the "legacies" of Dr. Bob and Bill W., summarized by A.A. as "Recovery, Unity, and Service."

Local Autonomy   The authority in A.A., as the Second Tradition says, is the group conscience. A.A. is to be nonprofessional (Tradition Eight) and ought never to be organized (Tradition Nine). As A.A.'s "official" organization chart in the *A.A. Service Manual* shows, the local groups head A.A. (See Exhibit 1.) The groups are supported by district committees (state or area), by the annual General Service Conference, and by a General Service Board which handles publications (the monthly "Grapevine," the "Big Book," and others). Exhibit 2 shows the service board/group ratio between 1945 and 1983.

At the annual conference, area delegates outnumber General Service people by two to one. A.A.'s board consists of seven nonalcoholics and fourteen A.A.'s. Terms are staggered and, as in all A.A. positions, rotation and limited terms of office are mandatory. Bill W. outlined permanently important concepts or warranties about the General Service Conference and A.A. in *Twelve Concepts For World Service*:

> *General Warranties of the Conference: In all its proceedings, the General Service Conference shall observe the spirit of the A.A. Tradition, taking great care that the Conference never becomes the seat of perilous wealth or power; that sufficient operating funds, plus an ample reserve, be its prudent financial principle; that none of the Conference members shall ever be placed in a position of unqualified authority over any of the others; that all important decisions be reached by discussion, vote, and, whenever possible, by substantial unanimity; that no Conference action ever be personally punitive or an incitement to public controversy; that, though the Conference may act for the service of Alcoholics Anonymous, it shall never perform any acts of government; and that, like the Society of Alcoholics Anonymous which it serves, the Conference itself will always remain democratic in thought and action.*

Independence   Tradition Seven says that every A.A. group is to be fully self-supporting. A.A. will accept a maximum of $300 a year from any one individual. Members make

EXHIBIT 1 Structure of the Fellowship

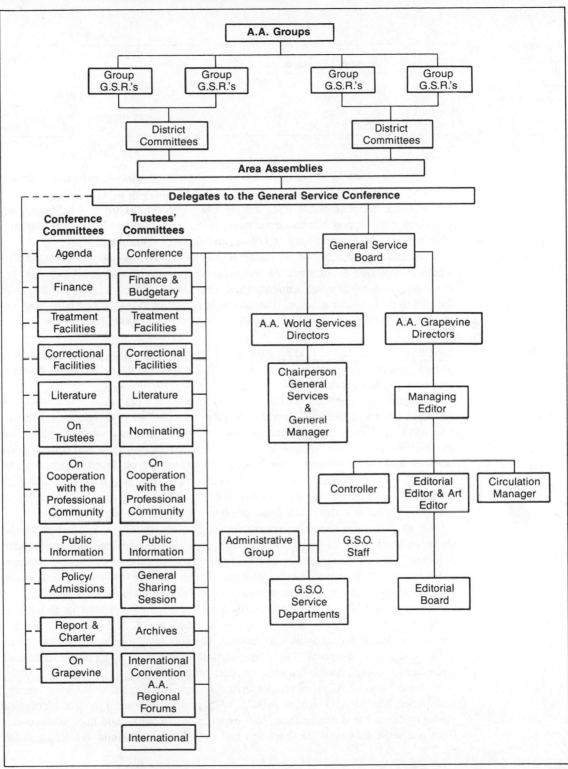

EXHIBIT 2
Alcoholics
Anonymous:
number of groups
per paid worker

Year	Number of groups
1945	98
1955	230
1983	595

contributions to the local groups. Each local group pays its own expenses (meeting room rent, refreshments, literature) and generally follows a 60–30–10 procedure for dividing the remaining funds among the local central office (the intergroup local office to support telephone services, often including hot lines, and literature distribution), the General Service Office, and the area committee.

Currently, the income of the General Services Office is about $5,000,000, of which $1,000,000 is contributions from members and others. Annual expenses are about $2,000,000 for office administration, rent, and royalties plus $1,000,000 each for printing costs and salaries. The financial health of A.A. is excellent, and the investment portfolio of bonds and equities totals about $1,000,000.

The Meeting   In 1985 A.A. had over 22,000 regular groups in North America and 7,500 overseas groups in about 100 countries. Treatment facilities and correctional institutions sponsored over 1,500 groups.

Generally, these groups held at least one meeting a week. A.A. members often attend two or more meetings, traveling to other groups if their group is not meeting. The meetings would be a mixture of newcomers and members at various steps of the twelve-step process. Members would encourage newcomers to find some regular member to be their sponsor. This sponsorship follows up on Twelfth Stepping and is the one-on-one procedure at the heart of the A.A. process. It began when Bill W. talked to Dr. Bob. As Bill B. described it, sponsorship can "take from one minute to 24 hours a day. You deal completely with the whole person."

The meetings are generally speaker or discussion meetings. Speaker meetings are those in which A.A. members tell their stories. Discussion meetings are broader in format, with a member briefly describing the drinking experience and then leading a discussion on drinking-related problems. These meetings may be closed in the sense that only alcoholics and prospective A.A. members are invited.

The typical A.A. member is described in a pamphlet reprinted in Exhibit 3. Another A.A. publication listed things A.A. does not do, including (1) furnish initial motivation for alcoholics to recover, (2) solicit members, (3) follow up or try to control its members, (4) offer religious services, or (5) provide letters of reference to parole boards, lawyers, or court officials.

In New York, A.A. members prepared a special supplement to the local weekly newspaper, *The Village Voice*, on July 23, 1985, to celebrate the 50 years of Alcoholics Anonymous and to communicate "our experience, strength, and hope of recovery from a disease that until 50 years ago had only two conclusions: the living death

EXHIBIT 3
The A.A. member

Latest survey shows accelerating increase of women and young people in A.A.[a] (One out of three is a woman; memberships of those aged thirty and under increased in the past 3 years.) Other findings reveal:

They reached A.A. by different routes (many of those surveyed gave two responses):

42 percent credit another A.A. member.
27 percent came "on my own."
21 percent credit family member.
26 percent came through counseling and therapy.
 9 percent came through family doctor.

At a typical A.A. meeting:

35–40 percent have been sober less than 1 year.
35–40 percent have been sober 1–5 years.
30–40 percent have been sober over 5 years.

The largest age group is ages thirty-one to fifty:

30 and under: 14.7%
31–50: 51.0%
50 and over: 31.8%
(2.5% did not indicate their age.)

Respondents fell into the following general categories:

	Sales & business	Homemaker	Professional	Labor
Men	19%	0.1%	17%	30%
Women	11%	25%	18%	7%

	Office & clerical	Unemployed	Retired	Other
Men	3%	7%	12%	12%
Women	15%	9%	5%	10%

[a] Almost 25,000 A.A. members participated in the largest and most comprehensive study of its kind.

of a wet-brain drunk or death itself." This supplement contained "the story of the founding of our unique fellowship, the steps that guide our recovery (now shared by some 30 other help groups), and the traditions that keep us straight. . . . Nothing better illustrates the success of A.A. than these stories of better living without chemicals." The supplement included some comments by Dr. Joseph Pursch, who gained prominence as director of the Navy alcohol rehabilitation center in Long Beach where First Lady Betty Ford first began treatments for her alcoholism and Valium addiction. Based upon "thousands of living examples," Dr. Pursch asserts that alcoholics

can be their own best therapists for the most part. . . . You and I . . . are the addicts' biggest problem . . . in spite of our intentions. . . . Recovery means switching from pills and booze to people and feelings. . . . The recovering alcoholic . . . becomes honest with himself and changes his lifestyle which . . . reduces living stress.

The supplement described A.A.'s structure as "organized anarchy," said that there are probably tens of thousands of unknown A.A. groups since no group need register anywhere, and advised that "if you are addicted to drugs only, than you can be better served by other twelve-step programs, such as Pills Anonymous. All alcoholics who also have problems with other drugs can be helped in A.A."

One of the personal stories, written by Eric P., was titled "A Gay Man's Story." Eric P. wrote: "The first A.A. meeting I went to was a gay group. . . . As I listened to [a man tell] his story, I identified. He was not only telling his story, he was telling mine. . . . What I discovered changed my life. I had to get over my own self-hatred before I could possibly contribute anything of value."

In 1981 Bill W. wrote to Dr. Carl G. Jung, recalling Dr. Jung's advice to a very early A.A. member that further medical and psychiatric treatment was useless, since the member had been an alcoholic all his life and had twice been to Dr. Jung for treatment. Bill W. told Dr. Jung that Jung's conclusion that the alcoholic's only hope lay in a spiritual or religious experience was a cornerstone of A.A. beliefs, and Bill thanked Jung.

Jung's reply from Zurich, dated January 30, 1961, included the following:

His craving for alcohol was the equivalent on a low level of the spiritual thirst of our being for wholeness, expressed in medieval language: the union with God. "As the hart panteth after the water brook, so panteth my soul after thee, O God" (Psalm 42, 1). The only right and legitimate way to such a [spiritual] experience is that it happens to you in reality, and it can only happen to you when you are on a path which leads you to higher understanding. . . . Alcohol in Latin is spiritus, *and you use the same word for the highest religious experience as well as for the most depraving poison. The helpful formula therefore is:* spiritus contra spiritum.

BILL B.

Bill B. came to A.A. in 1982, Twelfth-stepped by a friend whose improved physical appearance and mental attitude had surprised him.

She told me she had something good for me, and would I like to go to a meeting. I was in a period of heavy drinking and had had one major and a few minor automobile accidents I knew drinking was a part of. Months later, of course, I realized that drinking and the resulting noncommunication was the cause of many difficulties including my divorce. But I was fed up and went to the meeting.

Bill had grown up in New York and New England, attended college, and had a career in data processing. Early in his sobriety efforts, Bill B. chose an outspoken sponsor who would repeatedly get at the heart of any issue. For example, Bill once remarked on the ''death warmed over'' appearance of a struggling newcomer who had recently gone into and out of sobriety frequently. ''How many times do we have to put up with her coming back like this?'' Bill mused out loud. ''As many times as it takes,'' his sponsor replied.

THE TREATMENT CENTER

More and more newcomers were coming to A.A. from professional treatment centers. These centers are a fact of life and have sprung up like mushrooms as insurance plans provided more and more coverage. Bill B. commented:

A.A.'s got competition it can't ignore. Some oldtimers may not understand or deal well with the newcomers' treatment experience. Now institutional profits and professional reputations are in the balance dependent on successful rehabilitation. A.A. may risk its independence if it gets too close to these institutions.

For instance, we were offered the opportunity to Twelfth Step patients in a detoxification ward at specified hours during the week. The opportunity to carry the message was there, but at the convenience of the institution. What should we do?

What if a small meeting was suddenly outnumbered by a busload of treatment center patients coming in the door?

The influx of alcoholics and problem drinkers that have arrived under legal, social, and institutional pressure is a problem. These people arrive with their decision having been made for them in a way that assaults the very humanity A.A. is calling them back to.

One center put a permanent sign in front of a clinic proclaiming ''A.A. Meeting Inside'' while in fact there were two hour-long meetings there in one week. Under Tradition Six, has there been a violation of A.A. intent not to endorse or lend its name to an outside enterprise? Who and how should this be dealt with?

Our Eleventh Tradition implies we do no promoting. On the other hand, the treatment centers have radio spots and aggressive promotion. Should we consider some kind of marketing?

At the 35th General Service Conference in April, we talked about some treatment centers in Louisiana giving sobriety chips with A.A. on one side and the treatment center name on the other. The view then was that our name was being used improperly.

We are trying to work out coexistence in a way that best uses the particular resources of the rehab and of A.A. The rehab experience detoxifies and breaks the cycle of dependence. It introduces the patient to A.A. and the importance of a follow-up program. Without personal, social, and environmental change, the rehab patient is almost certainly going to revert to his dependence.

The most successful rehabs work closely with A.A. because A.A. has the people, the quality of energy, and the experience to provide continuing support. The patient discovers in A.A.'s Fellowship that he can reenter society with choices that are his from as supportive an environment as he may need.

The last thing a rehab wants its patients (or its backers) to see is a readmit. A.A., on the other hand, welcomes back its ''slippees.'' They are appreciated for their willingness to try again and their experience is integrated as further evidence of the plight that is

EXHIBIT 4
Number of A.A.
group meetings

Day	Daytime	Evening	Total	Comment
Sunday	3	1	4	1 day meeting closed
Monday	3	3	6	1 evening meeting closed
Tuesday	2	2	4	1 day, 1 evening meeting closed
Wednesday	2	4	6	1 day, 1 evening meeting closed
Thursday	2	4	6	
Friday	2	4	6	1 evening meeting gay
Saturday	2	3	5	

but one drink away from any member. As my sponsor once said, "As many times as it takes."

When asked how A.A. works, oldtimers most commonly respond that "It works just fine if you don't drink, go to meetings, and ask for help."

Exhibit 4 summarizes the number of A.A. local group meetings within a 15-mile radius of Portsmouth, the area for which Bill B. was a group service representative.

SPECIAL INTEREST

Bill B. commented on A.A. special-interest groups:

Policy seems to evolve from the primary thesis of carrying the message. If alcoholics in a minority or special-interest group (i.e., gays, doctors, men, women, nonsmokers) felt that what was offered was insufficient shelter for their concerns, special restricted groups have been formed for their support.

I have personal reservations about this. I've attended a gay meeting (I wasn't carded at the door) and found gay alcoholics are much like other alcoholics. I used to frequently attend a men's group. Neither did I notice that they were any different with regard to my personal experience of alcoholism.

For me, I see no reason why a part of the fellowship should set itself apart from the rest, so I've withdrawn from restricted meetings.

Increasingly we have the appearance of the dually addicted. Should we have separate procedures for booze and drug users? Some oldtimers say, "If you have a drug problem, we don't want to hear about it. Go to N.A."

But I hear A.A. saying, "I am responsible when anyone anywhere reaches out for help. I want the hand of A.A. always to be there, and for that I am responsible."

If there are instances of exclusive drug dependency, I have yet to see one.

GROWTH, FLEXIBILITY, AND SUCCESS

Bill B. commented further:

At the 35th General Service Conference they noted that our survey showed that almost half of those coming to A.A. leave before 3 months. We encourage attending 90 meetings the first 90 days. Now we usually encourage newcomers to pick their own sponsor, but maybe we need temporary sponsors.

How should we measure success? We have a procedure for taking a group inventory to counteract complacency when obvious things like a decline in membership, a breakdown in unity, or a dominant personality occurs, but how do you know when you're doing well? How do you tap into the group conscience?

Whenever we have a controversial issue, we discuss it in depth, take a moment for meditation or silence, and then call for a group conscience vote. Would this work as an evaluation tool? How do we know we're doing our best?

TWELFTH-STEPPING AND SPONSORSHIP

Bill B. talked about the extreme intimacy of sponsorships and noted that A.A. advised against sponsorship by someone of the other gender. "It just makes sense. You can be with the new member 24 hours a day, and it gets to be an amazing experience."

As regards Twelfth Stepping, Bill noted that if someone calls for help, you try to go.

Once the answering service got a call, and forwarded it to me. The next thing I knew I'm outside this guy's house, as he'd left his address, with a cop and the guy's father, who had seen the guy drunk with a gun. I called from a neighbor's phone, and the guy finally responds, since he had passed out, and I told him I was from A.A., I was there to help if desired, and did he want me to come in. Fortunately, he said yes, and I got the gun and took him to a detox and followed up.

But you have to want to come. Once I got a call from a mother who said "You've got to take my son." "No," I replied. "He's got to bring himself. Any other way would likely misfire and set the process back for years."

A.A. MEETINGS

The casewriters attended a beginners' and a regular open meeting in June. About twenty-five people attended the beginners' meeting, ten of whom spoke. A few commented on the pressure they felt to drink that day, including one who had been torn between "buying booze" and attending the meeting up until the last minute. Bill B. spoke about his recent experience in a relationship, noting that "relationships are to alcoholics as razor blades are to hemophiliacs." He jokingly warned the group that it was his turn for group support. Another spoke of a dual-addiction problem, while the last speakers recommended that newcomers get a sponsor early.

The one-hour beginners' meeting was followed by a regular open meeting with speakers from an A.A. group in Massachusetts. The three male speakers all were over fifty, in contrast to the age of the audience. There were over one hundred at this meeting, and the majority seemed to be in their late twenties, equally divided between men and women.

The speakers introduced themselves, as at the beginners' meeting, with the phrase, "I'm an alcoholic." They told of many years of drinking and of eventually facing a crisis such as being locked out of their home or going into a rehabilitation or detoxification center. This "rehab" or "detox" experience seemed different from the younger members' comments about their counselor, therapist, or legal authority making the A.A. suggestion.

The availability of group support was evident, especially in the applause that accompanied individuals receiving a first-meeting or first-, second-, third-, sixth-, or ninth-month sobriety "chip" or token.

The last speaker ended by stressing the importance of the First Step's admission of powerlessness before alcohol. This admission, the speaker advised, led to humility, which led to acceptance and finally to faith. "You can have faith," he concluded, "because this program works. This is not an experiment, this is not a religion, this is a program of recovery."

A newcomer who was well known to Bill B. came over to speak to him after the meeting. Bill allowed that he had been "curious about when this old friend would make it" to A.A. The friend asked if Bill had noticed the last speaker. Bill certainly had. His friend said simply, "That's my father."

Each meeting ended with the members commenting to each other and to themselves, "Keep coming back."

SUMMARY

Bill B. reviewed some of the issues he would have to, first, discuss with his group and, second, take any appropriate action about at the district, state, or General Service Board meetings. A.A.'s strong tradition and the critical sponsor role were being challenged by the professional treatment centers, by special interest groups within A.A., and by dual-addiction newcomers. Further, there was the ongoing problem of "success," i.e., of the sobriety rate among newcomers and members. Was it time for changes? If so, what changes should be made? How should they be made?

INDEX

Aaker, D. A., 89
Abbanat, R. F., 167, 170
Abell, D. F., 122, 170
Abernathy, W. J., 121, 122, 124
Ackoff, R., 170
Acquisition strategy,
  see situational strategies
Administrative systems, 176–177
Aguilar, F. J., 118–122
Aharoni, Y., 120–122
Alexander, L. D., 191, 194
Anderson, C., 89
Andrews, K. R., 14, 17, 67, 89, 170
Ansoff, H. I., 14, 17, 86, 89, 170
Argenti, J., 27, 29, 166, 170
Argyris, C., 191, 194
Astely, W. G., 170
Athos, A. G., 196
Austin, N., 172

Baliga, B. R., 192, 195
Bariff, M. L., 194
Barnett, J. H., 67
Barney, J., 124
Becker, L. C., 122
Bell, D., 67
Berg, N. A., 170
Bettis, R., 194
Bitondo, D., 171
Blackburn, R. S., 194
Bloom, P., 170
Boston Consulting Group
  and product portfolios, 142
Boulton, W., 122
Bourgeois, L. J., 194
Bower, J. L., 17, 170, 194
Branch, B., 194
Bright, J. R., 122
Brooks, H., 109, 122
Bruno, A. V., 90, 121, 123
Brunswik, E., 25–26, 29, 194
Brunswik, lens
  and managerial perceptions (working concept 7),
    25–26
Buchele, R. B., 89
Burgelman, R. A., 170
Burns, T., 191, 194
Burstein, M. C., 195
Business history, 14–16
Business policy, 8
Buzzell, R. D., 172

Cameron, K., 194
Carper, W. B., 67
Carroll, A. B., 65, 67
Capon, N., 67
Case method, 47
Case preparation, 47–52
Caves, R. E., 194
Chaffee, E. E., 28, 30, 167, 170
Chakravorthy, B., 194
Chamberlain, N. W., 17, 27, 30, 166, 170
Chandler, A. D., Jr., 4, 14, 17, 118, 122, 170,
    195
  see also stages of corporate development
Channon, D. F., 170
Chile and international copper, 126–133
Christensen, C. R., 17, 170, 195
Christopher, W., 170, 195
Clark, K., 122
Collier, D., 191, 195
Compensation and measurement systems, 179–185
Competence, distinctive,
  see distinctive competence
Competition,
  defined, 96
  Porter's model of (working concept 12), 106–
    108
  strategic signals of, 106
Competitive response analysis, 160–162
Congruence, 185–187
Consistency and evaluating strategy, 164
Contingency planning, 183
Cook, V. J., 90
Cooper, A. C., 120, 122, 170, 173
Coplin, W., 120, 123
Copper industry in Chile, 126–133
Corporate culture, 58–59, 180
Corporate development, stages of,
  see stages of corporate development
Customer needs analysis (working concept 11),
    103–106
Cyert, R. M., 17, 28, 30, 166, 170

Daniels, J., 195
David, F. R., 156–160, 170
David, S. H., 68
Davis, P. S., 120, 123
Davis, R. M., 68
Davis, S. M., 195
Day, G. S., 143, 170
Decentralization at General Electric, 12–13
  see also decentralized

Decentralized,
  stage three of corporate development, 4–7
DeMuzzio, E., 120, 122
Dess, G. G., 120, 123
Determining distinctive competence,
  see distinctive competence
DeVanna, M. A., 197
Development, stages of corporate,
  see stages of corporate development
Dhalla, N. K., 89
Dickel, K., 146, 172
Diffenbach, J., 120, 123
Differentiation strategy,
  see generic strategies
Directional policy matrix, 144–146
Distinctive competence, 83–86
  and comparative advantage, 83–84
  defined, 83
  in implementation selection, 185–187
  and levels of strategy, 85–86
  and market needs, 83
  and product life cycle, 83
Diversification,
  see growth matrix
  see situational strategies
Divesting,
  see exit strategies
Divisional management
  as decentralized stage two organization, 5
Donovan, N. B., 172
Doz, Y. L., 67
Drucker, P. F., 3, 17, 89, 92, 103, 123, 195
Dutton, V. E., 167, 170, 195

Edmunds, S., 123
Emery, F., 119, 123
Entrepreneur
  and stages of development, 4
Entrepreneurial,
  stage one of corporate development, 4–7
  see also stages of corporate development
Environment dependence spectrum, 116–117
Ethical values,
  see personal values,
  see also executive householder
Evaluating strategy, 160–164
Evered, R., 17, 20, 30
Executive comments, 16–17, 29, 66, 88, 122, 169, 193–194
Executive householder, 22
Exit strategies, 154–155, 159–160
Experience curve,
  see product portfolios
External environment, 93
  changes in, 99–100

Fahey, L., 120, 123, 167, 170, 195
Farley, J., 67
Farmer, R. N., 133, 135

Ferguson, M., 123
Firstenberg, P. B., 67
Fitzpatrick, M., 67
Focus (or niche) strategy,
  see generic strategies
Fombrum, C. J., 197
Formulating strategy,
  defined, 136
  generic strategies, 151–152
  and levels of strategy (working concept 17), 139–140
  as part of strategic decision process (working concept 16), 137
  situational strategies, 152–160
Frederickson, J. W., 170
Freeman, R., 17
Frohman, A. L., 171
Functional,
  level of strategy,
    see levels of strategy,
  stage two of corporate development, 4–7
    see also stages of corporate development

Galbraith, J. K., 65, 67, 123
Galbraith, J. R., 7, 186–187, 194, 195
Gale, B., 194
Garland, J., 133, 135
General Electric
  and decentralization, 12–13
  and strategic business units, 12–14
Generic strategies, 151–152
Ginter, P. M., 28, 30, 171
Global markets, 135, 137
Glueck, W. F., 167, 171
Gold, B., 121, 123
Government, 97–98, 109–112
  defined, 97
  process of, 111–112
  strategic signals of, 109–111
Govindarajan, V., 171
Grant, J. H., 68
growth matrix (Ansoff's growth vector), 146–147
Gupta, A. K., 67, 171
Guth, W. D., 17
Gutmann, P. M., 168, 171

Hall, W. K., 171, 195
Halle, D., 97, 123
Hambrick, D., 89
Hanna, R. G. C., 30, 168, 171
Harrell, G. D., 155, 171
Harrigan, K. R., 21, 30, 154, 171
Haspleslagh, P., 143, 171
Hatten, K., 120, 122
Hatten, M. L., 67
Hayes, R. H., 90
Heany, D. F., 172, 195
Hedley, B., 171
Heibroner, R., 123

Henderson, B., 171
Henry, H. W., 89
Herbert, T., 195
Hicks, E. J., 120, 122
Hirschleim, R. A., 192, 195
Hise, R., 17
Hitchens, R. E., 172
Hobbs, J., 195
Hofer, C. W., 89, 144, 168, 171
Holistic executive householder, 22
Hopkins, T. J., 22, 30
Horovitz, J., 192, 195
Hout, T., 67
Hoy, F., 65, 67
Hrebiniak, L. G., 195, 197
Huber, G. P., 192, 195
Hussey, D. E., 89, 171
Hulbert, J., 67

Iacocca, L., 53–55, 67
Identifying opportunities and threats,
    see opportunities and threats
Implementation selection model (working concept
    23), 186–187
Implementing strategy,
    administrative systems, 176–177
    compensation and measurement systems, 179–
    185
    components of, 176–185
    defined, 175
    information systems, 177–179
    selection criteria, 185–187
Industry analysis (working concept 21), 148–150
Information systems, 177–179
Integration, vertical,
    see vertical integration
International business, 124–135
    complexities, 124–125
    host country power, 125–126
    life cycle, 133–135

Jaeger, A. M., 192, 195
Jelinek, M., 195
Jelinek, M., 195
Joint venture strategy, 159
Jones, P. E., 123, 196
Joyce, W. F., 195
Jung, C. G., 24, 30

Kantrow, A. W., 122, 123, 192, 195
Karger, D. W., 30
Kast, F., 195
Katz, R. L., 171
Kazanjian, R. K., 7
Kefalas, A., 196
Kennell, J. D., 172
Kiefer, R. O., 155, 171
Kierulff, H. W., 172
Kilmann, R., 192, 196

Kimberly, J. R., 67
King, W. R., 168, 172, 195
Kirton, M. J., 67
Kitching, J., 168, 172
Klein, H. E., 119, 123
Knight, K., 195
Kotler, P., 93, 123, 135, 170
Kotter, J. P., 18, 30
Kramer, R., 68
Krasler, O. J., 123

Lawrence, P. R., 191, 195, 196
Learned, E., 17
Lebell, D., 123
Lei, D., 89
Leibenstein, H., 67
Leidecker, J. K., 121, 123
Leontiades, M., 196
Levels of strategy,
    business, 9, 11
    corporate, 9
    defined, 9
    departmental (see functional)
    functional, 12
    purpose or mission, and, 62–65
    strategy formulation, and (working concept 17),
        139–140
    strategy implementation, and, 188
    working concept 2, 9, 11–12
Levitt, T., 89
Lindblom, C. E., 24, 28, 30, 166, 172
Linneman, R. E., 123, 172
Litschert, R. J., 67
Lorange, P., 18, 89, 196
Lorsch, J. W., 191, 196
low-cost producer strategy,
    see generic strategies
Lucas, H. C., Jr., 89

MacMillan, I. C., 123, 172, 192, 196
Makrodakis, S., 124
Malik, Z. A., 30
Managerial perceptions, 25–26
Managerial roles, 23–24
March, J. G., 17, 28, 30, 166, 170
Market competition matrix, 146
Markets, 93–96, 101–106
    borderless, 94
    customer needs analysis of, 103–106
    defined, 96
    global, 135, 137
    strategic signals of, 102
Mascarenhas, B., 89
Mason, R., 68, 146, 172
Matrix analysis,
    directional policy matrix, 144–146
    growth matrix, 146–147
    market-competition matrix, 146

product life cycle–competition matrix, 144–145
product portfolios, 142
space matrix, 146
Matrix organization, 176–177
McCormick, R. E., 123
McDaniel, S., 17
McGinnis, M. A., 28, 30
McGowan, R. P., 68
McIntyre, S. M., 90
McKie, J. W., 67
McNamee, P., 121, 123
Meadows, D. H., 123
Merchant, K. A., 196
Miles, R., 123, 196
Military strategic manager, 20–22
Mintzberg, H., 18, 23–24, 30, 56–58, 68, 172,
    196
    and managerial roles, 23–24
    and organizational power, 56–58
Mission,
    see purpose
Mitchell, T. R., 170
Mitroff, I., 68, 192, 196
Moore, W. L., 123
Moran, T., 128–129, 135
Murphy, D. C., 89

Narayanan, V. K., 120, 123, 167, 170, 195
Naylor, M. E., 18, 28, 30, 196
New business strategy, 152
Newman, W. H., 68
Niche (or focus) strategy,
    see generic strategies
Nonprofit agencies, 68–70
Nutt, P. C., 68, 196

O'Connell, J. J., 18
O'Leary, M., 120, 123
Opportunities and threats,
    competition signals of, 106
    government signals of, 109–111
    market signals of, 102
    social signals of, 114–116
    strategic signals of, 101–102, 106, 109–111,
        114–116
    technology signals of, 108
Organ, T. W., 30
Organizational power, 56–58
    configurations, 57–58
Organizational priorities, 56–59
    determination by power,
        configuration, 56–58
        working concept 8, 56
Ouchi, W. G., 68, 196

Pascale, R. T., 196
Patten, R., 168, 172
Paul, R. N., 172
Pearce, J. A., III, 172, 196

Penrose, E., 119, 124
Performance evaluation,
    see compensation and measurement systems
Performance measurement,
    see compensation and measurement systems
Personal values of managers, 54–56
Peters, T. J., 6, 16, 18, 89, 172, 196
PIMS (Profit Impact of Market Strategies), 86, 143
Pitts, B., 195
Planning and control systems,
    see information systems
Polli, E., 90
Porter, M. E., 67, 119, 124, 151–152, 171, 172
    model of competition determinants, 106–108
Power, D. J., 192, 195
Power, organizational,
    see organizational power
Prahalad, C. K., 67, 194
Precursor (working concept 15), 115–116
Product life cycle (working concept 10), 78–82
Product life cycle–competition matrix (working
        concept 19), 144–145
Product portfolio (working concept 18), 142–144
Profitability signals, 32–33
Profit Impact of Market Strategies,
    see PIMS
Purpose,
    defining, 61
    levels of strategy and, 62–65

Quinn, J. B., 172

Relative Earnings Multiple, 181–182
REM,
    see Relative Earnings Multiple
Resources, 71–73
Retrenchment, 159
    see also turnaround strategies
Riggs, J., 168, 172
Risk and evaluating strategy, 162–163
Robinson, R. B., Jr., 30, 172
Robinson, S. J. Q., 172
Rockart, J. F., 193, 196
Ronstadt, R., 68
Rosenzweig, J., 195
Rothschild, W. E., 90, 196
Rowe, H., 146, 172
Rucks, A. C., 28, 30, 171
Rudden, E., 67
Rumelt, R., 168, 172

Salter, M. S., 7, 90, 170
Sampson, A., 135
SBU,
    see strategic business unit
Schecter, S., 89
Schendel, D. E., 168, 172
Schenkel, S., 18, 30
Schoeffler, S., 90, 172

Schoderbek, C., 196
Schoderbek, D., 196
Schwartz, H., 68
Scott, B. R., 172
Scott-Morton, M. S., 193, 196
Seeger, J. A., 173
Shanks, D. C., 68
Shrivastava, P., 68
Sihler, W., 197
Simon, H., 30, 68, 166, 173
Single business strategy, 152
Situational strategies, 152–168
Sloan, A. P., Jr., 30, 197
Snow, C. C., 196, 197
Social goals,
    see societal goals
Societal goals, 59–61
Social responsibility, 60–64
    see also societal goals
Society,
    defined, 97
    precursor, 115–116
    strategic signals of, 113–116
Soleri, P., 108, 114, 124
South, S. E., 90
Space matrix, 146
Stages of corporate development,
    and evolution of strategic management, 8
    working concept 1, 4–7
Stakeholder analysis (working concept 14), 112–113
Stalker, G. M., 191, 194
Steele, L., 121, 124
Steiner, G., 30, 166–167, 173
Stevens, J. M., 68
Stevenson, R. H., 90
Stopford, J., 28, 197
Strategic analysis (working concept 9), 61
Strategic business unit (SBU),
    defined, 12
    illustrated at General Electric, 12–14
    implementation alternative, 177
    working concept 3, 12–14
Strategic financial analysis, 32–34
Strategic issue analysis (working concept 22),
    150
Strategic management,
    defined, 8
    evolution of, 8–9
Strategic manager,
    defined, 19
    holistic executive householder, 22
    military general, 20–22
    performance modes, 24–25
    roles, 23–24
    working concept 4, 19–20
Strategic mapping, 149–150
Strategic planning,
    defined, 8

Strategic process,
    defined, 10
    summarized, Figure 1.3, 10
Strategy evaluation,
    see evaluating strategy
Strategy, formulating,
    see formulating strategy
Strategy formulation,
    see formulating strategy
Strategy implementation,
    see implementing strategy
Strategy, implementing,
    see implementing strategy
Strategy, levels of,
    see levels of strategy
Strategy research, 14, 27–29, 65, 86–88, 118–121,
    166–169, 190–193
Strengths and weaknesses, 73–78
Strickland, A. J., III, 71, 90
Stubbart, C., 121, 124
Summer, C. E., 18
Susbauer, J. C., 92
Sutton, C. J., 18
SWOT,
    see opportunities and threats
    see strengths and weaknesses
Synergy, 73, 163–164

Taylor, B., 173
Taylor, J. W., 172
Technological innovation,
    phases of (working concept 13), 109
Technology, 96–97
    innovation phases, 109
    strategic signals of, 108
Thain, D. H., 7
Thompson, A. A., Jr., 71, 90
Thompson, J. D., 173
Threats,
    see opportunities and threats
Tichy, N. M., 197
Tilles, S., 197
Tock, D., 120, 122
Tollison, R. D., 123
Treacy, M. E., 193
Tretter, M., 195
Trist, E., 119, 123
Turnaround strategies, 153–154
Turner, J. A., 89
Tushman, M. L., 123
Tyebjee, T. T., 90

Ulrich, D., 124
Unterman, I., 68
Utterback, J. M., 121, 124

Values,
    see personal values
Vancil, R. F., 18, 197

Veblen, T., 124
Vertical integration, 152–153, 156–157
Vesper, K. H., 92
Viability signals, 32–34
Vinson, W. O., 192, 195

Wade, D. P., 172
Wallender, H. W., III, 68
Wasson, C. R., 90
Waterman, R. M., Jr., 6, 16, 18, 89, 196
Waters, J. A., 172
Weaknesses, strengths and,
  see strengths and weaknesses
Weber, C. E., 30, 168, 173
Wells, L., 28, 197
Wheelwright, S. C., 90, 124, 173
Whetten, D., 194
Williams, J. R., 90, 173
Woo, C. Y., 173
Wood, A., 65, 68
Workability and evaluating strategy, 164
Working concept, for numbers 1 through 23 see
  below:
  Brunswik lens and perception, (7), 25–26
  customer needs analysis, (11), 103
  defined, 3–4
  directional policy matrix, (20), 144–148

implementation selection model, (23), 186
industry analysis, (21), 148–150
levels of strategy, (2), 9, 11
levels of strategy and strategic decision process,
  (17), 140
military and holistic strategic managers, (5), 20–
  22
Mintzberg's organizational power, (8), 56–57
Mintzberg's roles and styles, (6), 23–24
Porter's determinants of competition, (12), 106
precursor, the (15), 115
product life cycle, (10), 78–80
product life cycle–competition matrix, (19), 144
product portfolios, (18), 142–144
stages of corporate development, (1), 4–7
stakeholder analysis, (14), 112–113
strategic analysis, (9), 61
strategic business units, (3), 11–14
strategic decision process, (16), 137–139
strategic issue analysis (22), 150
strategic manager, (4), 19–20
technological innovation, (13), 109

Yuspeh, S., 89

Zeithaml, C., 89
Zentner, R., 124

PLU 114 6

BK361

18/08/95